THE LAW OF TRUSTS AND EQUITABLE OBLIGATIONS

THE LAW OF TRUSTS AND EQUITABLE OBLIGATIONS

Fifth Edition

PROFESSOR ROBERT PEARCE, BCL, MA, Hon LLD, FRSA

Formerly Vice-Chancellor of the University of Wales, Lampeter, and Professor of the Law of Property and Equity at the University of Buckingham

JOHN STEVENS, BCL, MA

Formerly Senior Lecturer and Deputy Head of School, School of Law, University of Birmingham, National Director of the Fellowship of Independent Evangelical Churches, and Senior Honorary Research Fellow, University of Birmingham

WARREN BARR, LLB, LLM (Th)

Senior Lecturer, University of Liverpool

OXFORD
UNIVERSITY PRESS

OXFORD
UNIVERSITY PRESS

Great Clarendon Street, Oxford OX2 6DP

Oxford University Press is a department of the University of Oxford.
It furthers the University's objective of excellence in research, scholarship,
and education by publishing worldwide in

Oxford New York

Auckland Cape Town Dar es Salaam Hong Kong Karachi
Kuala Lumpur Madrid Melbourne Mexico City Nairobi
New Delhi Shanghai Taipei Toronto

With offices in

Argentina Austria Brazil Chile Czech Republic France Greece
Guatemala Hungary Italy Japan Poland Portugal Singapore
South Korea Switzerland Thailand Turkey Ukraine Vietnam

Oxford is a registered trade mark of Oxford University Press
in the UK and in certain other countries

Published in the United States
by Oxford University Press Inc., New York

First published 1995
This edition 2010

British Library Cataloguing in Publication Data
Data available

Library of Congress Cataloging in Publication Data
Data available

Typeset by Newgen Imaging Systems (P) Ltd., Chennai, India
Printed in Great Britain
on acid-free paper by
Ashford Colour Press Ltd, Gosport, Hampshire

ISBN 978-0-19-957063-8

1 3 5 7 9 10 8 6 4 2

This edition is dedicated to our wives in gratitude for their
forbearance, understanding, and support

Chris Pearce
Ursula Stevens
Occilia Darr

Preface to the fifth edition

Equity and trusts is often (but incorrectly) seen as a dry and remote subject, divorced from everyday life. The aim of this book from its outset has been to present the subject in an accessible way, but without compromising in identifying and discussing areas of difficulty or debate. This book also endeavours to make clear the relevance of the subject in areas such as the protection of privacy, investment, pension funds, and testamentary arrangements. The reality is that everyday life is underpinned by equitable mechanisms such as the trust to a much greater extent than is immediately apparent. The way in which equity has developed its mechanisms to deal with disputes concerning ownership of the family home is undoubtedly the single most prominent area in the domestic context, and this edition of the book has been restructured to allow this area to be considered in a single chapter. Of equal significance in the commercial context is the developing jurisprudence on the liability of fiduciaries and of third parties receiving trust property or assisting in a breach of trust. There have been important new cases in both of these areas which are explored in this edition. Both areas have also been subject to continuing debate and controversy. We have sought to explain the competing arguments so that readers can make their own judgements.

When *The Law of Trusts and Equitable Obligations* was first published in 1995 it was shortlisted for the *Butterworths Prize*. The book broke new ground in its approach. Expositions of the subject in the nineteenth century and before had been characterized by an emphasis on leading cases, rather than a structured analytical approach. Most books in the twentieth century adopted a structure which lent heavily upon some traditional categorisations which underplayed the flexibility that is the genius of equity. *The Law of Trusts and Equitable Obligations* recognized that the traditional distinction between trusts and powers provides but two examples of equitable obligations on a spectrum which, like the rainbow depicted on the cover of this book, contains an almost infinite range of possibilities. Similarly, the traditional analysis of the powers of trustees under a single rubric overlooks the significance of trustees' powers serving different functions. Some powers held by trustees, but also capable of being exercised independently of a trusteeship, relate to the allocation of benefits. Others are concerned with managing the investments comprising the body of assets held on trust. By considering distributive and management powers separately, as this book does, the different functions become clearer.

For this edition of the book, Robert Pearce and John Stevens are delighted to be joined by Warren Barr as a member of the authorial team. Warren is a member and former Director of the Charity Law Unit at the University of Liverpool and was the ALT Law Teacher of the Year in 2006. He has played an invaluable part in the development of this new edition and in the introduction of new features. We have included a new chapter at the start of the book containing illustrations of the way in which equity contributes to the law of property and to other areas of personal and commercial activity. We have increased the number of figures and also provided a glossary of frequently used terms. As has already been noted, we have also introduced a chapter dedicated to the family home. Another innovation is that we shall be populating an Online Resource Centre with materials supporting the text, including a test bank of multiple choice questions, PowerPoint slides, and an interactive glossary, which we hope will prove useful to both students and to law teachers. We have endeavoured to state the law as at St Patrick's Day, 17 March 2010, indicating in the text where we expect further developments to take place. It is unsurprising that the areas in which there has been the most turbulence have been those—such as the use of constructive trusts and proprietary estoppel in relation to the family home—which were flagged in the fourth edition. It is safe to predict, in relation to the family home, that there will continue to be further turbulence in the aftermath of *Stack v Dowden*.

The way in which the tenor of the voices emerging from the senior courts changes over time to reflect the individuals in office has been particularly evident in preparing this new edition. Lord Denning's emphasis on the flexibility and discretion of equity gave way after his retirement in 1982 to the new theme, expounded by Lord Goff, and supported by the extra-judicial influence of Professor Peter Birks, that much of equity could be reinterpreted using the language of restitution. That, in turn, has been replaced by what could be described as the pragmatic contextual approach demonstrated in cases such as the majority view in *Stack v Dowden,* by the sometimes lonely voice of Lord Scott seeking to realign the doctrines of proprietary estoppel and constructive trusts, and by the extensions to privacy law fuelled by the incorporation of the European Charter on Human Rights into British law, as interpreted by Eady J and other judges. The dominant theme may now be about to move in a new direction again with the appointment of Lord Neuberger, the dissenting judge in *Stack v Dowden*, to the highly influential office of Master of the Rolls. The extent to which the creation of the Supreme Court will influence developments in equity, perhaps because the new title and constitutional position of the court emboldens its members to create and change the law, is something which can only be judged over time.

We are grateful to the members of the editorial team at Oxford University Press who have given us support and advice throughout the gestation of this edition. We would particularly like to thank them for their help in accommodating the increased number of figures and in improving the formatting of the text. We would also like to thank the many law teachers and students who have used our book over the years. Most especially, we owe a debt of gratitude to our families, who have put up with taking second place whilst the midnight oil has been burned and weekends consumed in revisions to the text.

Robert Pearce
John Stevens
Warren Barr
March 2010

Contents

(handwritten annotations: "Tues – fri 13th" next to chapter 2; "Sat 7th + Sun 8th" next to chapter 3)

PART III   ALLOCATION OF BENEFIT

List of figures

Table of statutes

Page references in **bold** indicate where a statute has been set out in part or in full

Australia

Commonwealth

New South Wales

Northern Territory

Victoria

Canada

Cayman Islands

United States

International

Table of cases

Glossary of common terms

Acquiescence assent to a set of events that can be express, or inferred from the conduct of a party.

Ad valorem proportionate to the value of the property.

Administrator a person appointed by the court to deal with the estate of a deceased person (a female administrator is known as an 'administratrix'); an administrator can also be appointed to wind up an insolvent company.

Advancement, power of enables the trustees to advance (make an immediate payment of) part of the capital to beneficiaries who are contingently interested in the trust fund, but who have not yet satisfied all the conditions for immediate payment.

After-acquired property property acquired after a trust or settlement is created. To be distinguished from future property.

Agency an arrangement where one person (the agent) acts for another (the principal), and where the acts of the agent can bind the principal.

Annuity an annual payment made in return for the payment of a lump sum (unless the contract otherwise specifies, there is no right to the repayment of all or any part of the capital).

Assignment where one person transfers the whole of his/her entitlement to property to another, so that he/she retains no rights in the property whatsoever.

Attorney, power of a form of agency under which one person (the attorney) is empowered to act for another (the principal) in executing deeds or (in the case of a lasting power of attorney) making defined decisions on behalf of the principal; also the instrument conferring this authority.

Bankruptcy a legal process started by or against an individual (a 'bankrupt') who is no longer able to meet outstanding debts owed to creditors.

Bare trust a trust in which the trustees are only effectively nominees and must act according to the beneficiaries' instructions.

Beneficiary a person entitled to the benefit or enjoyment of the trust property held by the trustees.

Beneficial interest the nature of the equitable interest the beneficiary has in a trust.

Bequest a gift of personal property made under a will.

Bona fide in good faith.

Bona vacantia property which vests in the Crown, because no other owner can be established.

Capacity to be of the age of legal majority (18) and not to be suffering from a disability that prevents the person from understanding the transaction in question. Capacity is required for making binding legal arrangements such as entering into legally binding agreements or making a will. Also known as being 'sui juris' (in charge of one's own affairs).

Capital the property (or fund) held under a trust.

Cestui que trust a beneficiary under a trust.

Charge a security for the payment of a debt or the fulfilment of an obligation that operates over identified property (*see* **mortgage**).

Charity an organization or purpose which is recognized by law as being of such public benefit as to merit special treatment.

Chattel an item of personal property (*see* **personal property**).

Chose in action property (such as copyright or the right to payment of a debt) which has no physical existence but is enforceable through legal proceedings.

Civil partners partners in a registered same-sex relationship, which gives similar property entitlements as conferred on married couples.

Claimant a person initiating an action in court (formerly known as a 'plaintiff').

Cohabitant a person living with another, in a close personal relationship, who is neither a registered civil partner nor a spouse. A cohabitant is sometimes referred to as a 'cohabitee'.

Consideration the concept of value given in return for a promise or the transfer of property, which is a prerequisite to transform a promise into a binding contractual obligation at law. In equity, consideration has a slightly wider meaning and can include the reason why a transfer is made (such as love and affection), even if no value is provided.

Constructive trust a trust that is implied or imposed by operation of law, in defined circumstances relating to unconscionable conduct by the parties.

Contempt of court   conduct which impedes the court process. In the context of equity, this would usually consist of a failure to follow an order of the court, which may lead to a fine or a custodial sentence.

Conveyance   the transfer and vesting of title to, or the creation of an interest in, property (usually land).

Conditional gift   a gift which is dependent on a specified event occurring or thing being done (eg, a gift to Charlie if she graduates with a degree in law).

Contingent interest   a right which is provisional because it is dependent on the happening of an event which has not yet taken place (eg, a gift to Clarissa if she survives her mother who is still alive).

Covenant   a contractual promise contained in a deed.

Debt   a sum of money due from one person (the debtor) to another (the creditor).

Deed   a specialized form of document, which must declare on its face that it is a deed and must be signed by the parties in the presence of a witness.

Dehors the will   literally, outside the will.

Devise   a gift of real property made under a will.

Determinable interest   an interest that ends on the happening of an event, although the event may never occur (eg, a gift of an annual sum to Davina until she qualifies as a solicitor).

Discretionary trust   a trust in which the trustees elect how to distribute property among a class of potential beneficiaries (the objects of the discretionary trust), as they in their discretion think fit.

Disclaimer   a refusal to accept either an office (such as the office of trustee) or a gift.

Disposition   a transfer of title to property.

Distributive power   power to allocate property either generally or to the members of a defined class (objects).

Donee   a person who receives either property or a distributive power.

Donor   a person who gives property by way of a gift or creates a distributive power in favour of the donee.

Election   a choice, eg, to rescind a contract or keep it in existence, or to choose a particular remedy.

Endowment   where property is given to provide a permanent fund or source of income.

Equitable title   title to property that is only enforceable in equity, and is vested in the beneficiaries under a trust.

Equitable interest   an interest that can only be enforced in equity.

Estate   either describes the property assets of a deceased person, or describes the ownership rights a person enjoys over land.

Executor   a person who acts as personal representative of a deceased person in carrying out the terms of a will and who was named in the will. (A person acting as a personal representative who is not named in the will is known as an administrator.)

Exemption clause   a contractual term designed to exclude or reduce the liability of one or other parties.

Express trust   a trust that is intentionally created.

Fiduciary   a person who has undertaken an obligation of loyalty to another and is compelled to put that other person's interests before his/her own (eg, director of a company is a fiduciary for the company shareholders).

Fiduciary obligations   the duties imposed by equity on a fiduciary to make sure that they act in the best interests of the person to whom they stand as a fiduciary.

Future property   rights to property that have not yet been acquired, but may be acquired in the future.

Gift   a gratuitous transfer of all title in property.

Gratuitous   without receiving a legally recognized benefit in return.

Holding trust   specific type of trust in which the trustees simply obey the orders of the principal, often used to conceal the true identity of the principal.

Implied trust   the label given to a trust that has not been formally declared by the parties, but is found to exist by the courts because the evidence indicates that the parties meant to create this kind of obligation (either through a resulting or constructive trust).

Inalienable   unable to transfer eg, inalienable property is property that may not be transferred.

Intangible   without physical form, eg, intangible property, such as shares in a company.

Inter alia   among other things.

Inter vivos   during one's lifetime.

Intestacy   the process relating to the distribution of an individual's property after death where an individual dies without leaving a will.

Insolvency   a legal process started by or against a company that is no longer able to meet outstanding debts owed to creditors.

Instrument the legal document that creates an obligation or transfers an interest (eg, a trust instrument is the document creating a trust).

Judicial trustee a person appointed by the court to replace a trustee or fiduciary who has acted improperly (eg, personal representatives under a will).

Knowledge the state of mind or awareness of facts necessary to the imposition of liability.

Lease an estate in land of limited duration (held by a tenant), which is created out of a large estate of another (the landlord).

Lien a right to claim or hold another's property as security for a debt.

Life interest an interest in property that lasts for the duration of the holder's life.

Maintenance, power of enables the trustees to apply the income generated by a trust fund for the maintenance of the beneficiaries, even where they are not as yet entitled to the capital of the fund.

Mortgage the creation of a specific form of charge (usually of land) to provide security for a loan.

Mortgagee the person or company that advances the loan, and receives the mortgage charge as security.

Mortgagor the person or company that receives the loan, and creates the mortgage charge over their property in favour of the mortgagee.

Nominee a person or company who holds the legal title to property and ostensibly the control of the property, but who must exercise it in accordance with the directions of their principal (person who appointed the nominee or persons to whom the nominees owe their duty).

Notice, doctrine of an equitable doctrine that affects the durability of equitable property rights. Notice can be either actual (being aware of rights) or constructive (the rights would have been revealed if reasonable enquiries had been made).

Objects the persons who may benefit from property on the exercise of a distributive power or discretionary trust.

Option a right to elect to create a binding contract to purchase property, when exercised.

Overreaching a process by which the asset value of beneficial interests in land is transferred to the proceeds of sale, so that a purchaser takes free from the beneficial interests.

Pari passu a right to share in property equally and without preference.

Parol oral (eg, a parol evidence lease is one created without writing).

Personal property rights or interests relating to property other than land.

Personal rights *see* Rights in personam.

Possession, interest in an immediate entitlement to rights or income in property (compare with an interest in remainder).

Power an authority to do something (eg, allocate property to beneficiaries).

Principal person to whom obligations are owed under a relationship (eg, agency) or fiduciary)

Priority to enforce a claim to property in preference to others.

Privity a rule of common law that provides that obligations can only be enforced by and against the parties to a transaction.

Probate court authority approving a will given to an executor to begin the administration of a deceased person's estate.

Proprietary rights *see* Rights in rem.

Protective trust a specialized form of trust, which allows beneficiaries to receive income on the property, but preventing them from transferring the right to income to someone else (sometimes called a 'spendthrift trust').

Real property rights or interests relating to land.

Receiver a person appointed (usually by court order) to receive income payments from property (eg, on the bankruptcy of an individual).

Remainder, interest in an interest granted to take effect on the expiry of an interest in possession (eg, to Lucy for life, remainder to Raoul). The person entitled to a remainder is known as a remainderman.

Residuary estate the final property of a deceased person, once all debts have been paid and any specific gifts by will have been made.

Restitution the body of law designed to prevent unjust enrichment of the defendant by the claimant.

Resulting trust an implied trust in which the beneficial interest in property results (comes back) to the person who transferred the property.

Rights in personam rights that are enforceable only against the person granting them (also known as personal rights).

Rights in rem rights that are enforceable against the whole world, not just the person granting them (also known as proprietary rights).

Secret trust a specialized form of trust used to provide for someone on death, which is secret because it does not appear in the will (fully secret) or does not disclose the beneficiaries (half-secret).

Senior courts   the new title of the High Court and Court of Appeal. Until the creation of the United Kingdom Supreme Court, these courts were known as the Supreme Court of Judicature.

Settlor   the person who creates a trust by putting (settling) his property on trust.

Spouse   a married partner.

Stranger to a trust   a third party who is neither the trustee nor beneficiary under a trust, but who deals with trust property (eg, a bank facilitating the deposit of trust funds in a trust account).

Sui juris   to be of full legal capacity. *See* **Capacity**.

Supreme Court   the court which in October 2009 replaced the House of Lords as the highest court in the United Kingdom.

Testamentary   property transfers on death made by will (wills are also known as testaments).

Testator   a male person who executes (creates) a will (a female person is known as a 'testatrix').

Title   a right to ownership of property.

Transferee   person who receives a transfer of property.

Transferor   person who transfers property to another.

Trust   although impossible to define accurately, it describes a form of property ownership in which the control and benefit to property are separated, with legal title and control vested in trustees who are compelled by equity to exercise such control for the benefit of the beneficiaries, who hold the equitable title.

Ultra vires   in excess of authority (beyond the powers of a body or person with limited authority).

Value   payment, usually in money or money's worth.

Vesting   the satisfaction of all the requirements necessary for a right to property to become unconditional; the completion of the transfer of property to a person, so that they can begin to enjoy the rights in that property.

Void (ab initio)   of no legal effect (from the outset).

Voidable   a transaction which can be set aside at the election of one party, but which is otherwise effective until set aside.

Volunteer   a person who has not given consideration for a promise to have property settled on them on trust.

Will   the instrument by which a person declares what their wishes are concerning their property after their death. The terms of the will do not take effect automatically, but have to be implemented by an executor or administrator.

PART I

INTRODUCTORY

1

Equity today

This chapter seeks to demystify the study of equity and to demonstrate the relevance of trusts and equitable obligations in everyday life. Far from a remote, difficult, or uninteresting subject, equity is a living and dynamic area of law which plays an important role in everyday life and in advancing concepts of fairness and justice within the legal system. The structure of the rest of the book is also considered at the end of this chapter.

1 Introduction

It is true that, to the student, the law of trusts and equitable obligations can seem intimidating at first, not least because it can be difficult to relate to its abstract concepts and cope with the unfamiliar and technical terminology that seems to proliferate within it. Concepts such as 'negligence' in tort, for example, are just as complex, but seem more immediate and easily accessible—it is easy to empathize with someone who has suffered physical harm through the negligent actions of another and to understand what a 'duty of care' might be; it is less easy to comprehend the importance of whether someone called a beneficiary should have a right of action against some person called a trustee for the trustee's failure to invest properly something called trust property.

It can seem an alien and alienating experience to embark on reading a text such as this. Nevertheless, equity is a subject that lies at the heart of the common law of property, and underpins a wide variety of personal and commercial arrangements. Happily, the myth that equity is either impossibly difficult or tedious is precisely that—a myth—and stems from the fact that it is undoubtedly different from many other subjects. The mystery of terminology disappears when explained, and study of this subject reveals it to be as challenging and rewarding as any other. It is also true that many equitable principles have their root in history, and that equity has been inventive over its few hundred years of existence. Indeed, such has been the contribution of equitable principles to both life and law, that it has led some people to regard equity as the equivalent of a fading film star in the twilight of his or her career; a subject whose best days are behind it.

The intention of this chapter is to explain the relevance of equity in everyday life, without distracting the reader with primary or secondary sources of law, to demonstrate that it is not a faded, historical subject, but is as contemporary and vital as any other. The purpose of the rest of this book is to dispel any remaining fears and to explain the law relating to trusts and equitable obligations in a clear and comprehensible manner, seeking to bring the subject alive by placing the law in context. It will necessarily cover all the concepts considered here, but in considerably more detail.

2 Equity and the trust

It would be impossible to embark on any meaningful discussion of the contribution of equity and the law of trusts without at least a brief word about what both these concepts are. These are, of course, explored in detail in the following chapters of this book, but equity is understood as at one and the same time both a different system of law which recognizes rights and obligations that the common law of England and Wales does not, and a system which seeks to address the inherent unfairness which can exist in following any set of rules. This rather strange set of affairs arose through historical accident, as the head clergyman, the Lord Chancellor, found himself hearing petitions for justice with which the reigning monarch was unable to find time to deal with and which could not be dealt with by the common law courts. The fact that the Lord Chancellor, as a holy man, based his decisions on concepts of fairness and good conscience created a different set of rights and obligations from those recognized at common law, and over time these principles become subject to the same doctrines of binding precedent as the common law, though they retained their different character. Nevertheless, the courts of today administer common law principles and equitable principles together, though we clearly still talk of equitable and common law rights as separate things. People will therefore be subject to equitable and common law obligations and rules, without necessarily knowing their source. Perhaps most importantly, where rules of equity and rules of common law vary on the same matter, it is always the equitable rule which prevails; it is this fact which gives equity the opportunity to continue to be relevant in modern times, as we shall see.

The trust is the most important creation of equity, and is a form of ownership of things (property) which allows someone (called a 'trustee') to manage property for someone else's benefit (called a 'beneficiary'). The trust is more than a moral obligation, as equity has imposed duties to make sure that the person managing the property does in fact make the best use of it purely in the interests of the persons named as beneficiaries. In separating the control and entitlement to things, this clever device has been used by equity in many everyday situations.

3 The role of equity and trusts in financial planning

It is often said that only three things are certain in life—birth, death, and taxes. If so, it is comforting to know that equity can allow individuals to be looked after not only for the duration of their life, but also before birth and after death. Equity, and in particular the equitable device of the 'trust', can also allow liability to tax to be minimized through lawful tax avoidance, rather than unlawful tax evasion. A young couple, planning for a family, can set up a protected fund under a trust, in which someone else will manage and invest the fund, so that any child can, say on wishing to go to University, be provided for. Three examples illustrate the value of the trust concept.

(1) Providing for retirement

Providing for oneself in old age, when one's working life is over, is an increasingly important consideration for anyone in the workplace today. The rising costs of living and quality of life that a working life can provide mean that it is more important than ever to plan properly to provide for a comfortable and happy retirement. Employers are now under legal duties to provide pension schemes for some of their employees, and will provide personal pension schemes for others. The equitable device of the trust provides an excellent means to facilitate pensions. Where a trust is used, people can pay into a trust scheme, where people with expertise manage a complicated scheme of investments, so that when scheme members retire, they are entitled to a greater sum than they paid into the scheme. In giving control to experts, whose job it is to manage the funds to increase the common pot of investment, and by placing duties upon them, the trust permits the successful operation of these schemes. The use of the trust also keeps the pension funds separate from the assets of an employer. Moreover, the use of discretions within the trust can mean that, on the death of a contributor, the benefits that have been accumulated can be used for the benefit of dependants without forming part of the deceased's estate, and so avoid inheritance tax. It is possible to create pension schemes purely on contractual rules, particularly given the reforms to privity of contract in recent years, but the trust is still widely used.

Perhaps more importantly, since a pension fund manager is managing funds which are not his own, there are very real obligations imposed on the managers (who are trustees of the pension trust for the members as beneficiaries). It is these obligations, which help make sure investments are properly entered into to both protect and enhance the pension fund, and make sure that at all times the persons are acting in good faith and not allowing themselves or others to profit from their work at the expense of the scheme members. These obligations are enforceable by the scheme members against the pension managers, so that any wrongs can be compensated.

However, even the provision of duties and sanctions for non-performance of those duties cannot always protect scheme members. The high-profile Maxwell pensions scandal of the late 1980s and early 1990s, in which thousands of innocent employees lost their pension entitlements due to a major worldwide fraud perpetrated with illegal use of pension funds, led to significant changes in pension regulation. In investigations into improving the legal framework in the wake of the scandal, the trust device was found to be a broadly satisfactory method of managing pensions, as it allowed recovery of at least some funds by some pension scheme members of the Maxwell group, as the trust provided a means to keep the funds separate from any other claims on company funds by hungry creditors.

(2) Allowing mutual provision for friends and family after death

Without meaning to seem morbid, planning what happens to one's assets after death can be just as important as planning for an enjoyable retirement. Knowing that friends and family will be financially provided for after death can be a comforting prospect, particularly as it is, sadly, impossible for anyone to take wealth with them when they die. Provision for others is normally achieved through making direct gifts of one's property in a will. It is possible, however, to set up trusts for the benefit of friends and family under a will. One advantage might be to make sure that someone is provided with a reasonable income throughout their life under a trust, rather than becoming rich overnight with a gift of money and poor by the end of the same calendar year, having spent it all on high living.

The utility of equity extends, in addition, to the situation where a couple want to make binding wishes as to how their collective property should be distributed on their death. It is a key feature of a will that it can be revoked at any time before death, so that if two people enter into identical wills to distribute their property, unless they both died at the same time, there would be nothing to stop the survivor changing his will on the death of the other. To meet this difficulty, equity evolved a doctrine called 'mutual wills', which permits joint wishes to be honoured, as where a mutual will is created, equity will prevent the survivor dealing with property against the wishes of the deceased, so that any dealing outside the terms of the will is prohibited.

(3) Secretly providing for persons after death

In life, most people do things they are not necessarily proud of. Human weakness is something that equity recognizes, and this is no more evident than in the fact that it allows someone to avoid embarrassment in death through the creation of something called 'secret trusts'. This allows for property to pass to someone, without their identity being known. When the will is read, the recipient of property left under a secret trust will not be revealed. Such devices were used by persons wishing to conceal infidelity in relationships, to spare all concerned, so that a mistress or illegitimate child of a relationship could be provided for. Under this device, property was left to a nominated person, who was in fact secretly required to act as trustee for someone else. While secret trusts may still be used for such purposes today, they can also be used simply to provide for persons who may otherwise have been forgotten, as, for example, where the circle of friends and family of the will maker has become so large and disparate that he cannot be sure that everyone is included in named provision within the will.

4 The role of equity in providing remedies

Perhaps one of the singularly most useful contributions of equity to the modern legal system, and certainly one of the most often used, is the range of remedies it has created. The common law's response to wrongdoing was traditionally to award damages. Damages are always monetary, whether the purpose is to provide compensation for a lost limb as a result of an accident, allow substitute performance to be sought following a breach of contract, or to punish someone for wrongdoing through the award of punitive damages. From its inception, equity was different. It could not originally offer damages, as damages were a remedy administered by the courts of common law, so instead grew other remedies, based on fairness and good conscience. Hence, the ability to restrain someone from acting to invade rights to privacy under the European Convention on Human Rights, a court order to stop someone from destroying pirated DVDs before a criminal trial, or to compel someone to deliver that one-of-a-kind designer outfit under a contract are just three examples of the remedies equity has made possible.

(1) Equity and the emerging right of privacy

An injunction is an equitable remedy, which is a court order to stop someone doing something, or, in more limited cases, compelling them to do something. In a number of cases the remedy has been used to protect the privacy of someone in the public eye. Prince Albert, in Victorian times, was able to prevent the unauthorized publication of private drawings. Naomi Campbell, more recently, sought to have publication of photographs of her attendance at a Narcotics Anonymous meeting stopped by means of an injunction, on the basis that it infringed her right to privacy. Ultimately, she was successful and equity came to her aid, but only on the basis that she managed to convince the majority of the House of Lords that her successful treatment depended on her right to conduct the treatment in private. The decision was not clear-cut, however, as a minority of the House of Lords felt that freedom of expression was best served by publication of the photographs, as it revealed that Miss Campbell had been less than truthful in denying allegations of drug use in the press, and that should override the right to privacy. There is thus a conflict between a right to freedom of expression of the press and a right to privacy. This conflict is currently being played out in the courts, as the boundaries of a law of privacy are being defined.

(2) Search orders

Piracy is a crime, and is nowadays more likely to be carried out in the confines of someone's spare room or, on a bigger scale, in a warehouse, than on the high seas. The illegal copying and trading of copyright material such as DVD or Blu-ray films, is a lucrative and easily facilitated crime, and it can be difficult to secure the necessary evidence to secure a conviction of perpetrators. Here again, equity has come to the rescue through the development from the 1970s onwards of what is now known as a 'search order'. This specialized form of injunction is used where there is a real possibility that necessary evidence may be destroyed or disposed of before trial if the defendant is forewarned that an action is coming. The order is granted without notice, so that the first time pirates know of the order is when it is served upon them and the illegal goods are seized. There is clear potential for abuse in such a procedure, so equity developed some procedural safeguards to try to prevent abuse (such as a business using the search order to disrupt the entirely legitimate business of a rival) and these have now become enshrined in a series of practice rules. So, for example, while the order is termed a search order, it allows for the search and removal of designated property, and cannot be used as a fishing device to remove property that was not specified or suggested in the order.

(3) Specific performance of contractual obligations

The availability of damages for breach of contract means, in effect, that there is no compulsion in contract law for anyone to actually perform a contract. Provided defaulting parties are willing to pay damages for failure to meet their contractual obligations, they can walk away from their contractual obligations. While this makes sense for everyday items, which can be purchased on the open market somewhere else if adequate damages are provided to allow this, the same cannot be said of unique or special items. Hence, if Dame Vivienne Westwood designs a dress for a fashion show, and only one is produced, it would be of little comfort to someone who enters into a contract to purchase the dress to be awarded damages if the vendor chose not to sell. In fact, such contracts arise more frequently than this example suggests, as any contract to purchase land (such as the purchase of a home) is unique, as no two pieces of land are the same. In such circumstances, equity developed the remedy of specific performance, which, as its name suggests, compels the defendant to carry out his contractual obligations. Again, ever mindful of the needs of justice and fairness, equity will not order specific performance if damages will, in fact, provide an objectively adequate remedy. Like all equitable remedies, including the injunctions discussed above, specific performance is not available 'as of right', which means that even if the requirements to receive the order are met, the courts reserve a discretion not to grant the remedy. This might be exercised, for example, where there is something in the circumstances of the case that suggests to award specific performance would cause hardship or unfairness to the defendant.

5 The flexibility of equity and the trust to respond to social needs

Quite apart from equitable remedies, equity and the trust have been used to respond to changing social needs. Two such areas are the assistance equity has given to couples that share property as their family home, and to facilitate charitable activity.

(1) Family homes

Before the mid-twentieth century, to own land was considered the privilege of the rich. Most ordinary couples rented the homes in which they lived, either from private landlords, local councils, or their employers. The rise of owner-occupation after the Second World War and mortgage finance to purchase land led to the situation which persists today that most people own, or expect to own, their own home. It is also a matter of fact that the purchase of the family home is the biggest purchase most people are likely to make in their lifetime, and will represent the greatest asset they will wish to leave to others on their death. Despite this, it is common for very little thought to be given to how the home is owned, doubtless because at the time of purchase no one wants to think of what will happen if the relationship breaks down or their partner dies. Moreover, a continuing myth that there is such a concept as 'common law marriage', which will give people rights if they have lived together for a period of time, may prevent people from thinking about such matters when they should. The result is that many homes were, and still are, bought in one person's name only, meaning that, at common law, that person is the owner of the property.

The major issue that arises on the death of either the relationship or one of the couple in such situations is about the other person's entitlement to the home. That person may have lived there for a long period of time, helped to meet the mortgage repayments, paid for household expenses, paid for redecoration and improvements to the home, looked after any children of the relationship emotionally and/or financially, and yet, at common law they would have no rights in the property. Where the couple are married (or civil partners for same-sex couples), nowadays legislation will help to determine rights to the property on divorce or death, but such legislation is not always comprehensive and was not always in force. Unmarried couples are not covered by similar legislation, in part because of the difficulty of defining the circumstances under which it should apply. Equity has, however, come to the assistance of these people, by adapting established trust law principles and equitable remedies to allow non-legal owners to acquire an interest in the home where they have acted to their detriment to do so. As will be seen, the methods used are not entirely satisfactory, either in terms of the result they attain for some persons, or in straining equitable concepts to their limits. Nevertheless, without this important contribution, these non-legal owners would have no rights whatsoever, as there have been several attempts by the Law Commission to provide a statutory solution to the problem, none of which have resulted in legislative change.

(2) Charities

Everyone is aware of the concept of charity. So ubiquitous are the brands of popular charities such as Oxfam, and TV-based charity appeals such as the BBC's annual Children in Need appeal that most people will at some time either donate to, or come into contact with, charities and charitable activity. What is less well known is that charity has a legal definition, provided by equity, and many charities are set up and operated under the trust device. The legal definition of charity seeks to regulate activity that might be regarded as charitable, so that public trust and confidence is maintained in charities. Hence, it is a requirement of any charity that the purpose that they pursue is not only one recognized as being charitable by equity, but also that the purpose is carried out in a way which is of clear benefit to the public at large. Charitable status also provides financial benefits to charities through tax savings on operating costs or donations to charitable organizations, which makes the regulation of charities and the protection of the charity brand even more important, if public trust and the public money used to pay for the tax exemptions is to be justified. The success of equity's role in this area can be seen in the diversity of activities that modern charities undertake, from providing specialized care to the infirm and to people with learning difficulties to funding important medical research into diseases such as cancer.

6 The commercial relevance of equity and the trust

The contribution of equity can also been seen in the commercial world, in innovative forms of investment management such as the so-called unit trust, and in imposing important duties and obligations on business people such as company directors to carry out tasks properly (called 'fiduciary duties'), and in providing mechanisms to deprive wrongdoers of ill-gotten gains through breach of such duties. For the moment, one example will suffice. Equity provides a method, called tracing, to allow someone entitled to property to follow that property into the hands of other persons who may have come into possession of the property, or where the original property is sold, to the proceeds of sale or any substitute property bought with those proceeds. In the commercial context, a person in a position of trust (such as an agent appointed to secure a tender for his company's building contract) is not allowed to benefit from his position by abusing his duty of loyalty. So, if the agent abused his position by taking a bribe and purchased houses with the proceeds, the company would be able to trace a right of property into the houses and seek a remedy to have the value of the houses realized for the trust.

7 Property ownership

Last but by no means least, equity has also added significant depth and sophistication to the legal conception of property ownership, which facilitates many commercial and other dealings with all types of property. Our legal conception of 'property' is based on regulating peoples' rights and entitlements over things. The common law recognizes and protects ownership. However, the idea that someone might own property, and yet be required to manage it for the benefit of some other person or persons who also have ownership rights to enjoy the benefits or fruits of the property is entirely alien to the common law. The common law concept of agency (permitting a person to make contracts on behalf of the owner) goes nowhere near as far as the equitable device of the trust; the trustee has legal ownership, but is compelled by equity to use the benefits of that legal ownership for the beneficiaries, who have the equitable ownership of property. The beneficiaries' right of equitable ownership is therefore valuable, and can be bought and sold. This helps to explain the success of equity in granting an interest to someone in the family home (discussed above), as it gives the non-legal owner a right in property that is also a valuable, financial asset. The normal advantages of the trust also mean that it is possible to have different persons entitled to different rights in the same property, such as allowing someone to live in a home limited to the duration of that person's life, and allowing others to own the home after that person's death.

Ownership is not the only property right recognized in our legal conception of property. Rights less than ownership may qualify or limit an owner's entitlement to use property, so that, for example, someone might be able to enforce a right to walk across someone else's land. While this kind of right was recognized at common law, there were strict formalities which had to be observed. Equity has been instrumental here in recognizing and allowing for the enforcement of numerous informally created rights by and against people, so that many different people can have property rights in the same item, even though perhaps only one person is the owner of the property.

8 Structure of the book

The rest of this book seeks to explore the law of trusts and equitable obligations in a complete, but accessible manner. No attempt is made to minimize any complexities in the subject; instead, the text is written to provide a picture that is both detailed and comprehensible, so that such issues are engaged with in a manner that both explains fully and elucidates the law. Similarly, academic depth is not sacrificed for the sake of simplicity, and attention will be drawn throughout the book to all significant areas of academic controversy.

The arrangement of the book adopts an analytical structure that recognizes the important distinction between the distributive and asset management function of trusts and which deals separately with the creation of equitable obligations and the checks and controls used to enforce them. The book also employs chapter headings which introduce the salient concepts of a chapter. In terms of written style, the authors have endeavoured to use accessible language, to explain core concepts before building upon them, and to provide examples and diagrams by way of illustration. A glossary of common terms is also provided to assist in understanding terminology.

The text of this book is supplemented by materials available from the online companion website. These seek to highlight significant changes that have occurred in the law since publication of this book, and to provide some interactive resources to help students engage with and test their understanding of some of the more difficult concepts explored in this book. The book is designed to be entirely self-contained, so that there is no compulsion to look at the online materials, but these provide an additional resource that can be drawn upon in building understanding of the concepts identified in the text.

2

Historical introduction

One of the peculiarities of English law is that its rules have developed from two separate court systems. Although those two systems have been merged for more than a century, it is only by looking at the history of English law that it is possible to understand what is meant by 'equity' and how it operates.

1 What is equity?

(1) A layperson's understanding

To the layperson the term 'equity' connotes justice and fairness, so that to act 'equitably' is synonymous with acting 'fairly'. For example, Psalm 96 speaks of God's justice in such terms:

> The LORD reigns.
> The world is firmly established, it
> cannot be moved;
> he will judge the peoples with equity.[1]

The idea of 'equity' has always been particularly associated with judicial decisions, and emphasizes that cases should be decided in a way which is fair and right, so that justice is achieved between the parties. However, although the branch of English law known as 'equity' may have its origins in such concepts of fairness and justice, it carries a specific and technical meaning.

(2) A legal definition

Rather than referring to an abstract concept of justice or fairness, in English law the term 'equity' describes a particular body of law, consisting of rights and remedies, which evolved historically through the Courts of Chancery. Until the late nineteenth century there were two parallel systems of law operating in England, each recognizing,

---

[1] Psalm 96 v 10: New International Version.

upholding, and applying its own distinct rights and remedies. The common law courts applied the common law and the Courts of Chancery applied equity. Although this division between courts was removed by the Judicature Acts of 1873 and 1875,[2] those rights and remedies which are today described as 'equitable' were either originally developed by and enforced through the Chancery courts, or have evolved by extension from such rights and remedies.

2 The historical development of equity[3]

(1) The common law

(a) History and emergence

Prior to the Norman Conquest of 1066 there was no developed legislature or judicature operating throughout England. Instead, a system of 'custom' was applied by a variety of decision-making bodies, ranging from the King's Council to village meetings. Custom inevitably varied with geographical location. However, the notion had already begun to evolve that justice was the prerogative of the Crown. This laid the jurisprudential foundation for the emergence of the common law in the twelfth century. The focus of the common law was the *Curia Regis*, the King's Court. During the 1180s Sir Ranulf de Glanvill wrote a treatise on 'the laws and customs of England' based on the workings of the King's Court, and produced 'a coherent system of English law deriving ultimate authority from the King'.[4] By 1234 the two common law courts, the Court of Common Pleas and the King's Bench, had developed.

(b) Writs, actions, and remedies

A plaintiff who wished to start an action in the Court of Common Pleas or the King's Bench needed to obtain a royal writ authorizing the commencement of proceedings. These writs were purchased from the King's Chancery. As plaintiffs sought redress for novel legal problems new writs were developed to meet their needs until the Provisions of Oxford in 1258 prevented the issue of new writs without the permission of the King's Council. This closed the categories of writ which were available, confining plaintiffs to bringing cases within the terms of the recognized writs, thus severely limiting the ability of the common law to develop effective redress for new types of case. The common law therefore became stultified and inflexible. Furthermore, the common law also offered only a limited range of remedies, predominantly monetary damages, to redress the wrong suffered by a successful plaintiff. This straitjacketing of the common

---

[2] See below, p 19.

[3] See Holdsworth, *A History of English Law* (7th edn, 1956), Vol 1, Ch V; Baker, *An Introduction to English Legal History* (2nd edn, 1979), Ch 6.

[4] Baker, *An Introduction to English Legal History* (2nd edn, 1979), p 12.

law was the predominant motive for the emergence of 'equity' as administered by the Courts of Chancery.

(2) The Courts of Chancery

(a) The Chancery and the Chancellor

The Chancery was essentially a department of State. The Chancellor was the Keeper of the Great Seal, a Minister of the Crown who sometimes acted in a Prime Ministerial capacity to the King.

(b) Emergence of the judicial role of the Chancellor

Despite the development of the common law, justice remained a royal prerogative, and therefore the King retained a residuum of justice which enabled aggrieved parties to appeal directly to him for redress. These appeals were initially heard by the King in Council, but by the fourteenth century they were delegated to the Chancellor, who acted on behalf of the King. By 1473 the Chancellor had begun to issue decrees by his own authority in his own name.

(c) Motivation for the emergence of the Courts of Chancery

The Chancery courts and their equity jurisdiction emerged because of the defects and rigidity of the common law, typified by the limited range of writs and the tendency to apply the strict rules of the common law even when this caused hardship, or seemed to do injustice, on the particular facts. For example, a debtor who had paid his debt but who had not ensured that his sealed bond was cancelled could be compelled by the common law to pay his creditor a second time because the bond was incontrovertible evidence of the debt. Again, the common law courts would not enforce an oral contract where the law required formalities such as proof in writing or a deed. Baker concludes that:

It was not that the common law held that a debt was due twice, or that a promise of trust could be broken; such propositions would have been as absurd then as now. It was a matter of observing strict rules of evidence, rules which might exclude the merits of the case from consideration but which could not be relaxed without destroying certainty and condoning carelessness.[5]

In contrast, the Court of Chancery developed as a court of 'conscience' to remedy these defects of the common law system. In the *Earl of Oxford's Case*,[6] heard in 1615, Lord Ellesmere explained why there was a Chancery:

[M]en's actions are so diverse and infinite that it is impossible to make any general law which may aptly meet with every particular and not fail in some circumstances. The office of the Chancellor is to correct men's consciences for frauds, breaches of trust, wrongs and oppression of what nature so ever they be, and to soften and mollify the extremity of the law.

---

[5] Ibid., p 88.   [6] (1615) 1 Rep Ch 1, at 6.

This corresponds with the conception of equity in classical writings, where Aristotle had defined 'equity' as 'a correction of law where it is defective owing to its universality'.

(d) Commencing an action in the Chancery Court

Unlike the Common Law Courts, where an action could only be commenced by means of a writ, actions in the Chancery Court were commenced by an informal bill of complaint, and the process was begun by means of a *subpoena*. Proceedings were characterized by informality, and the court could sit outside of the legal terms which determined when the Common Law Courts sat. It could sit anywhere, including the Chancellor's house.

(3) **Character of the equity jurisdiction**

(a) A court of conscience

The Chancery Courts initially functioned as courts of conscience. In 1452 Fortescue CJ responded to a legal argument presented in the Court of Chancery: 'We are to argue conscience here, not the law.'[7] The Chancellor decided cases on the basis of his own sense of justice. Inevitably, different Chancellors had different conceptions of justice so that, in Selden's well-known phrase, equity varied with the length of the Chancellor's foot.[8] In the sixteenth century Cardinal Wolsey, who was Chancellor between 1515 and 1529 despite his lack of academic training, was the cause of particular complaint because of the arbitrary nature of the justice he dispensed. Blackstone summarized the condition of the equitable jurisdiction of the Court of Chancery at the end of the fifteenth century:

No regular judicial system at that time prevailed in the court; but the suitor when he thought himself aggrieved found a desultory and uncertain remedy, according to the private opinion of the Chancellor.[9]

(b) Court of Equity

By the seventeenth century the Chancellor[10] tended to be a lawyer rather than a churchman. Decisions were reported, leading to a system of precedent and the development of a settled body of law, with distinct rights and remedies, that was almost as rigid as the common law. The Court of Chancery was no longer a simple court of conscience, but a court of 'equity' in the technical sense. For example, in *Honywood v Bennett*[11] in 1675 it was said that a contract without consideration was binding in conscience but not in equity. At the beginning of the nineteenth century the process

---

[7] Mich 31 Hen VI, Fitz Abr Subpoena, pl 23.
[8] *Table Talk of John Selden* (F Pollock edn, 1927), p 43.
[9] *Comm* iii 53.
[10] The last non-legal chancellor was Lord Shaftesbury (1673–82).
[11] (1675) Nottingham Rep (73 ss) 214.

was complete. Lord Eldon, Chancellor (1801–06 and 1807–27), reflected in *Gee v Pritchard* that:

The doctrines of [the Court of Chancery] ought to be well settled, and made as uniform, almost, as those of the common law, laying down fixed principles, but taking care that they are to be applied according to the circumstances of each case. I cannot agree that the doctrines of this court are to be changed by every succeeding judge. Nothing would inflict on me greater pain in quitting this place than the recollection that I had done anything to justify the reproach that the equity of this court varies like the Chancellor's foot.[12]

In 1878 Jessel MR stated in *Re National Funds Assurance Co*[13] that the Chancery Division of the High Court 'is not, as I have often said, a Court of Conscience, but a Court of Law'. The process of an evolutionary development of settled principle was more recently recognized by the House of Lords in *Co-operative Insurance Society Ltd v Argyll Stores (Holdings) Ltd*,[14] which concerned the availability of the equitable remedy of specific performance. Lord Hoffmann stated:

Of course the grant or refusal of specific performance remains a matter for the judge's discretion. There are no binding rules, but this does not mean that there cannot be settled principles, founded on practical considerations...which do not have to be re-examined in every case, but which the courts will apply in all but exceptional circumstances.[15]

(4) The relationship between equity and the common law

(a) Equity not in conflict with the law

Initially equity avoided conflict with the common law and the common law courts. One fundamental maxim of equity is that it acts in personam,[16] so that it does not overturn the common law. For example, if the common law considers that Theo is the owner of land, whereas equity considers Bertram to be the owner, equity does not say that the common law is wrong. Rather, it orders Theo, as legal owner, to deal with the land in a way which recognizes that Bertram is the true owner. If the defendant fails to obey such an order, he will be in contempt of court and subject to the appropriate penalties, including imprisonment.

(b) The common injunctions

With two parallel systems of law administered by separate courts it was inevitable that there would be conflict as each struggled for dominance over the other. This struggle came to a head in the early seventeenth century during the reign of James I, when the primacy of equity was finally established. It had become frequent practice for the Court of Chancery to issue so-called 'common injunctions', either ordering a party to a dispute to restrain his action at common law, or, if judgment had already been given in his favour by the common law court, to prevent him enforcing

---

12 (1818) 2 Swan 402 at 414.
13 (1878) 10 Ch D 118; see also *Re Telescriptor Syndicate Ltd* [1903] 2 Ch 174 at 196, per Buckley J.
14 [1997] 3 All ER 297.   15 Ibid., 305.   16 See below, p 34.

it. Refusal to obey these injunctions would be a contempt of court, deterred by the threat of imprisonment. These 'common injunctions' were a direct threat to the jurisdiction of the common law courts, which saw their supremacy being at stake. Sir Edward Coke, the Chief Justice of the King's Bench, held that imprisonment for disobedience of the Chancery injunctions was unlawful, and ordered the release of those affected under the writ of *habeas corpus*.[17] The Chancery Court argued that the injunctions did not interfere with the common law, as any judgment still stood, but rather concerned only the conduct of the parties. This jurisdictional civil war was finally ended in 1616, when James I issued an order in favour of the Chancery Court and the common injunctions. Despite some subsequent attempts to reverse this resolution,[18] the primacy of the Chancery Courts was well established by the end of the century. The primacy of equity has been preserved and was reaffirmed by statute in the Supreme Court of Judicature Act 1873, s 25.[19]

(5) Equity in the eighteenth and nineteenth centuries

(a) Defects

Although the supremacy of equity was firmly established by the end of the seventeenth century, its administration was affected by severe procedural defects causing extreme delay. The Chancellor was the sole judge and the court officers abused their positions. The Chancery offices, in particular that of the Master, were lucrative for the holders. The offices were sold and the purchasers appointed by the Chancellor.[20] A fee system operated for tasks performed by the officers, leading to inefficiency. For example, clerks paid by the page to produce copies of documents required by litigants developed large handwriting and made use of wide margins to maximize their income. The Masters' reports were lengthened by reciting the whole of previous proceedings verbatim. In 1824 these difficulties led to the establishment of a Commission headed by Lord Eldon, who was himself notorious for delay. At that time some £39 million derived from cases awaiting decision was held by the court.

(b) Reforms

In order to improve the administration of the equity jurisdiction a number of reforms were introduced.

(i) Reform of the personnel of the Chancery Courts

The number of persons competent to exercise the equity jurisdiction was increased. In 1813, a Vice Chancellor was appointed to assist the Chancellor, followed by a further

---

[17] See *Heath v Rydley* (1614) Cro Jac 335.

[18] For example, in 1690 a bill was introduced in the House of Lords enacting that no Court of Equity should entertain any suit for which the proper remedy was at common law. However, the bill was dropped when it was shown that it would make equity unworkable, which would lead to injustice.

[19] See below, p 20.

[20] For up to £5,000 each; roughly equivalent to £350,000 in contemporary currency.

two in 1843. In 1833, the Master of the Rolls was granted jurisdiction to sit concurrently with the Chancellor. In 1851, a Court of Appeals in Chancery was created. The other court offices were also reformed. In 1833, the office of Master became a Crown appointment with a fixed salary. In 1842, the six Clerks were abolished, as were the Masters in 1852.

(ii) Limited reform of the jurisdiction of the Chancery Courts

The Common Law Procedure Act 1854 introduced changes marking a step towards the fusion of the common law and equity jurisdictions. The effect of this Act was summarized in the report of the Judicature Commission:

> The Court of Chancery is now not only empowered, but bound to decide for itself all questions of common law without having recourse as formerly to the aid of a Common Law Court... The Court is further empowered to take evidence orally in open court, and in certain cases to award damages for breaches of contract, or wrongs, as at common law; and trial by jury, the great distinguishing feature of the common law, has recently been introduced into the Court of Chancery. On the other hand, the Courts of Common Law are now authorised to compel discovery in all cases in which a court of Equity would have enforced it in a suit instituted for that purpose. A limited power has been conferred on Courts of Common Law to grant injunctions, and to allow equitable defences to be pleaded, and in certain cases to grant relief from forfeitures.

However, the progress towards fusion was slight as the Act only applied where a Court of Equity would have granted an absolute and perpetual injunction. True fusion was only effected by the dramatic reform of the English legal system through the Judicature Acts of 1873 and 1875.

3 The Judicature Acts 1873 and 1875

(1) Restructuring the system of courts

The Judicature Acts effected a radical restructuring of the English court system. The Courts of Chancery, King's Bench, Common Pleas, Exchequer, Admiralty, Probate, and the London Court of Bankruptcy were consolidated and merged to form a single Supreme Court of Judicature,[21] now known as the Senior Courts of England and Wales,[22] divided into the High Court and the Court of Appeal. As a matter of convenience, rather than of jurisdiction, the High Court was organized into divisions, comprising the Chancery Division; King's Bench Division; Common Pleas Division; Exchequer Division; and the Probate, Divorce, and Admiralty Division.

---

[21] To be distinguished from the Supreme Court of the United Kingdom, established by the Constitutional Reform Act 2005, s 23, to replace the Judicial Committee of the House of Lords as the highest appellate court in the UK.

[22] Constitutional Reform Act 2005, s 59.

(2) Uniform jurisdiction given to judges of the Senior Courts

Although the High Court divisions reflected the former distinction between the common law and Chancery courts, the central feature of the reform was that all the judges of the Supreme Court of Judicature (now the Senior Courts)[23] irrespective of the division in which they sat, were to have both common law and equitable jurisdiction. This was achieved by the 1873 Act, s 24, which provided that all judges were to give effect to such equitable estates, rights, relief, defences, duties, and liabilities as would have been given effect by the Court of Chancery, and also to recognize and give effect to all estates, titles, rights, duties, obligations, and liabilities existing by the common law.[24] This combined jurisdiction was more recently re-enacted in the Supreme Court Act 1981, s 49(1), which provides:

every court exercising jurisdiction in England and Wales in any civil cause or matter shall continue to administer law and equity...

(3) Procedural implications of the reforms

The concurrent common law and equity jurisdiction conferred on the Senior Courts by the Judicature Acts revolutionized the process of litigation. It was no longer necessary to commence a separate action in the Chancery Court to gain recognition of an equitable right or to obtain an equitable remedy.

(4) Supremacy of equity enshrined

(a) Supreme Court of Judicature Act 1873, s 25

It has been seen that historically the supremacy of equity was maintained by the power of the Chancery Court to grant common injunctions. These were abolished by the Supreme Court of Judicature Act 1873, s 24(5), since the concurrent jurisdiction granted to judges under s 24 rendered them unnecessary. The supremacy of equity was itself placed on a statutory footing by s 25, which provided that in a number of specific instances[25] the existing equitable rule was to supersede the common law rule. Section 25(11) provided somewhat more generally that:

in all matters not herein-before particularly mentioned, in which there is any conflict, or variance, between the Rules of Equity and the Rules of the Common Law with reference to the same matter, the Rules of Equity will apply.[26]

(b) Operation of s 25(11)

Section 25(11) only operates if there is a genuine conflict between the rules of equity and the rules of common law. It was applied in the leading case *Walsh v*

---

[23] Ibid.   [24] Judicature Act 1925, ss 36–44; Supreme Court Act 1981, s 49.

[25] S 25(1)–(10).

[26] This provision is retained by the Supreme Court Act 1981, s 49(1), which provides that: 'wherever there is any conflict or variance between the rule of equity and the rules of the common law with reference to the same matter, the rules of equity shall prevail'.

Lonsdale,[27] where the defendant had agreed to grant the plaintiff a lease of a weaving mill. The rent[28] was payable yearly in advance. No legal lease was ever executed[29] but the plaintiff was allowed into possession of the mill and paid rent quarterly in arrears to the defendant. Under the common law the plaintiff had thereby become a periodic tenant of the mill. Under the terms of this periodic tenancy the rent was payable in arrears. In equity, however, the contract between the defendant and plaintiff gave rise to an equitable lease,[30] under the terms of which the rent was payable in advance, as agreed in the contract. The defendant demanded payment of rent in advance and exercised the remedy of distress to secure payment.[31] The plaintiff claimed that this distress was improper. Whether the defendant's exercise of distress was lawful or improper depended on whether the parties' relationship as landlord and tenant was governed by the legal or equitable rule. If there was a legal periodic tenancy the distress was improper as the rent was not due, whereas under an equitable lease the rent was in arrears and the defendant was entitled to exercise his right to recover it. The Court of Appeal held that as there was a conflict between the respective legal and equitable rules, s 25(11) of the Judicature Act applied and the equitable rule prevailed. The defendant's exercise of distress was therefore proper on the facts.

A further situation in which the equitable rule has been held to prevail over the legal equivalent is in the context of contractual terms as to the time when performance is expected. Whereas at common law requirements as to time were regarded as of the essence of the contract, in equity they were not, so that a party in breach of a requirement of time was not entitled to repudiate the contract for breach. Outside of commercial contracts, where stipulations as to time are regarded as crucial, the equitable rule has been held to prevail over the common law rule where there is no express agreement that time is to be of the essence.[32]

4 The fusion of law and equity

(1) The effect of the Judicature Acts

One question arising from the reforms instituted by the Judicature Acts is whether there has been a 'fusion' of law and equity. Jurisprudential debate has questioned whether there is now one single body of 'English law', which has its heritage in the

---

[27] (1882) 21 Ch D 9; see also *Job v Job* (1877) 6 Ch D 562; *Lowe & Sons v Dixon & Sons* (1885–86) 16 QBD 455.

[28] Of 30 shillings per loom per annum, with the plaintiffs agreeing to run not less than 540 looms.

[29] A legal lease would only have been created if the defendant had executed a deed—see now Law of Property Act 1925, s 52(b).

[30] This is because the defendant's contract to grant the lease was specifically performable. The equitable lease arises as a consequence of the maxim that 'equity treats as done that which ought to be done'. See Chapter 6, p 117.

[31] Distress is a common law remedy which entitles the landlord to seize goods on the rented land and sell them to recoup any arrears of rent owed by the tenant.

[32] *United Scientific Holdings Ltd v Burnley Borough Council* [1978] AC 904.

rules, rights and remedies of the previously distinct bodies of 'common law' and 'equity', or whether there has been a mere fusion of the administration of these two distinct bodies of law so that 'common law' and 'equity' are now administered by a single court replacing the pre-existing duality of courts. The traditional view is that the Judicature Acts effected only a fusion of administration, though more recent judicial sentiments seem to favour the view that there has been a substantive fusion in some sense. As this issue is examined it will become apparent that the central differences of opinion revolve around the meaning attributed to the concept of 'fusion'.

(2) Fusion of administration[33]

Traditionalists hold that the Judicature Acts merely fused the administration of equity and the common law (see Figure 2.1). In the famous words of Ashburner the result is that:

the two streams of jurisprudence, though they run in the same channel, run side by side, and do not mingle their waters.[34]

This view enjoys the support of judicial dicta contemporaneous with the passing of the Acts. For example, in *Salt v Cooper* Jessel MR commented:

the main object of the Act was to assimilate the transaction of Equity business and Common Law business by different Courts of Judicature. It has been sometimes inaccurately called 'the fusion of Law and Equity'; but it was not any fusion, or anything of the kind; it was the vesting in one tribunal of the administration of Law and Equity in every cause, action or dispute which should come before that tribunal.[35]

The Attorney-General at the time that the Acts were passed disavowed the object of fusion when explaining their effect to the House of Commons during the second reading of the Judicature Bill:

Law and Equity therefore, would remain if the Bill passed, but they would be administered concurrently, and no one would be sent to get in one court the relief which another court had refused to give...[36]

More recent statutory language also implies that law and equity remain distinct bodies of law. Section 49(1) of the Supreme Court Act 1981, which re-enacts many of the central provisions of the Judicature Acts regarding the place of equity and the common law, speaks of the 'rules of equity and the rules of the common law'.

(3) Fusion in substance

Although contemporaneous opinion may have favoured the view that the Judicature Acts had not led to the fusion of law and equity, more recent dicta have expressed the view that there has been a substantive fusion of equity and the common law, producing

---

[33] See (1954) 70 LQR 326 (Lord Evershed); (1961) 24 MLR 116 (V T H Delaney); (1977) 93 LQR 529 (P V Baker); (1977) 6 AALR 119 (T G Watkin); (1994) 14 LS 313 (David Capper), pp 315–317.

[34] Snell, *Principles of Equity* (2nd edn), p 18. See Figure 2.1.

[35] (1880–81) 16 Ch D 544, at 549.   [36] Hansard 3rd Series, Vol 216, pp 644–645.

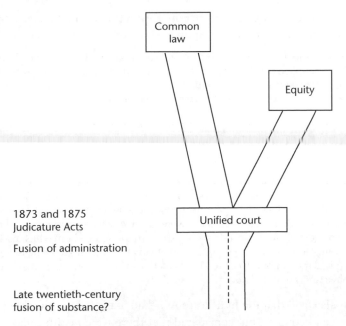

Figure 2.1 Court system

a single body of legal rules, not a mere fusion of their administration. This has been particularly evident in Commonwealth jurisdictions.

(a) Early dicta

Even some early dicta suggested that something beyond a simple fusion of the administration of law and equity had taken place. For example, in *Walsh v Lonsdale*,[37] which was considered above, Jessel MR stated:

There are not two estates as there were formerly, one estate at common law by reason of the payment of the rent from year to year, and an estate in equity under the agreement. There is only one Court and the equity rule prevails in it.

(b) More recent cases

As time passed and the separate administration of law and equity became little more than a distant memory, an increasing number of judges advocated practical realism and declared that law and equity had been fused. In the middle years of the twentieth century Lord Denning regarded law and equity as unified, and manipulated this as a justification for law reform. In *Errington v Errington and Woods*[38] he stated that 'law and equity have been fused for nearly eighty years'. In *Boyer v Warbey*[39] he argued that such fusion demanded that the common law principle of privity of estate, which allows leasehold covenants to be enforced between successors in title to an original landlord

---

[37] (1882) 21 Ch D 9.   [38] [1952] 1 KB 290, at 298.   [39] [1953] 1 QB 234.

and tenant despite the fact that they are not privy to the contractual terms of the lease, should be extended so as to apply to equitable leases:[40]

I know that before the Judicature Act 1873 it was said that the doctrine of covenants running with the land only applied to covenants under seal[41] and not to agreements under hand[42]...But since the fusion of law and equity the position is different. The distinction between agreements under hand and covenants under seal has largely been obliterated.[43]

Some twenty years later, members of the House of Lords expressed similar sentiments in *United Scientific Holdings Ltd v Burnley Borough Council*.[44] Lord Diplock specifically commented on Ashburner's metaphor:

by 1977 this metaphor has in my view become both mischievous and deceptive. The innate conservatism of English lawyers made them slow to recognise that by the Supreme Court of Judicature Act 1873 the two systems of substantive and adjectival law formerly administered by the Courts of Law and Courts of Chancery...were fused. As at the confluence of the Rhone and Saone, it may be possible for a short distance to discern the source from which each part of the combined stream came, but there comes a point at which this ceases to be possible. If Professor Ashburner's fluvial metaphor is to be retained at all, the waters of the confluent streams of law and equity have surely mingled now.

Lord Simon also held that the Judicature Acts had 'truly...brought about a fusion of common law and equity'[45] but considered that there were institutional reasons why English lawyers had been slow to accept this conclusion. First, there had been some dovetailing of the systems before the Acts themselves.[46] Second, the High Court had continued to sit in administrative divisions. Third, the conservatism of lawyers and their training tended to minimize the change that had been made.

(c) Commonwealth approaches

The courts in some Commonwealth jurisdictions have been far more strident in declaring the practical fusion of equity and the common law. For example, in *Aquaculture Corpn v New Zealand Green Mussel Co Ltd*,[47] the New Zealand Court of Appeal addressed the question whether damages, historically a common law remedy, should be available as a remedy for breach of an equitable duty of confidence. Cooke P stated:

For all purposes now material, equity and common law are mingled or merged. The practicality of the matter is that in the circumstances of the dealings between the parties the law imposes a duty of confidence. For its breach a full range of remedies should be available as appropriate, no matter whether they originated in common law, equity or statute.[48]

---

[40]   Ibid., at 245–246.

[41]   In other words, to covenants made by deed, and therefore enforceable at common law. A seal was one of the formal requirements for a deed before the Law of Property (Miscellaneous Provisions) Act 1989.

[42]   In other words, a covenant enforceable only in equity on the basis of a written agreement not made by deed.

[43]   See also Smith 'The Running of Covenants in Equitable Leases and Equitable Assignments of Legal Leases' [1978] CLJ 98.

[44]   [1978] AC 904.   [45]   Ibid., at 944.

[46]   See above, at p 17.   [47]   [1990] 3 NZLR 299.

[48]   [1990] 3 NZLR 299, at 301. See also *Catt v Marac Australia Ltd* (1986) 9 NSWLR 639 (NSW); *LAC Minerals v International Corona Resources Ltd* (1989) 61 DLR (4th) 14 (Canada). See: Capper 'Damages for Breach of the Equitable Duty of Confidence' (1994) 14 LS 313.

The New Zealand courts have similarly held that breach of an equitable duty can lead to exemplary damages or damages for mental distress,[49] which were historically only available at common law, and that an award of equitable compensation may be subject to reduction by application of the common law principles of contributory negligence.[50] This contrasts with the more conservative approach taken in England, where the award of damages for breach of an equitable duty of confidence has been justified under the Chancery Amendment Act 1858 in lieu of an injunction,[51] without the need to find an autonomous right to equitable compensation paralleling the common law right to compensatory damages for breach of duty or obligation.

The approach advocated by Lord Diplock in *United Scientific Holdings Ltd v Burnley Borough Council*[52] was also adopted by the Canadian courts in *Le Mesurier v Andrus*[53] and *Canson Enterprises Ltd v Broughton & Co*,[54] where the common law principle of remoteness of damage was held applicable to an equitable claim for damages for breach of fiduciary duty.[55] La Forest J, however, recognized that in some circumstances it is still necessary to differentiate between equitable rights and remedies and those which historically originated at common law:

There might be room for concern if one were indiscriminately attempting to meld the whole of the two systems. Equitable concepts like trusts, equitable estates and consequent equitable remedies must continue to exist apart, if not in isolation, from common law rules.[56]

(4) A single coherent body of law[57]

While the debate has not been settled clearly in favour of either view, it seems that the central problem is often the meaning invested in the term 'fusion'. If 'fusion' means that any distinction between equity and common law, and especially between equitable and legal rights and remedies, has been completely removed so that adjectivally the term 'equitable' has no continuing relevance, then it has not occurred. The law still distinguishes between legal and equitable ownership, the foundation of the trust concept which is the main subject of this book. However, it is also clear that English law no longer preserves the strict distinction between equitable and legal rules that was maintained before the Judicature Acts. The law has developed as a whole, so that there has been some synthesis of legal and equitable rights and remedies and cross-fertilization between them, and some of the old distinctions between rights and remedies historically equitable in origin and those historically of common law origin have ceased to be significant. The adjectives 'equitable' and 'common law' are useful to distinguish the different rights and remedies that make up English law but it is

---

[49] *Mouat v Clark Boyce* [1992] 2 NZLR 559.   [50] Ibid.

[51] *Saltman Engineering Co Ltd v Campbell Engineering Co Ltd* (1948) 65 RPC 203; *Seager v Copydex Ltd* [1967] 2 All ER 415; *A-G v Observer Ltd* [1990] AC 109.

[52] [1978] AC 904.   [53] (1986) 54 OR (2d) 1.

[54] (1991) 85 DLR (4th) 129.

[55] See also *Bristol and West Building Society v Mothew* [1996] 4 All ER 698, at 711.

[56] (1991) 85 DLR (4th) 129, at 152.

[57] See also Duggan, 'Is Equity Efficient?' (1997) 113 LQR 601.

submitted that Lord Diplock was correct to observe in *United Scientific Holdings Ltd v Burnley Borough Council* that:

if, by 'rules of equity' is meant that body of substantive and adjectival law that prior to 1875, was administered by the Court of Chancery but not by courts of common law, to speak of the rules of equity as being part of the law of England in 1977 is about as meaningful as to speak similarly of the Statute of Uses or of Quia Emptores. Historically, all three have in their time played an important part in the development of the corpus juris into what it is today; but to perpetuate a dichotomy between rules of equity and rules of common law which it was a major purpose of the Supreme Court of Judicature Act 1873 to do away with, is, in my view, conducive to erroneous conclusions as to the ways in which the law of England has developed in the last hundred years.[58]

The approach which best represents the prevailing judicial attitude is that the long fusion of the administration of law and equity has produced a single, coherent, body of rules which operate harmoniously together, even though some historically have their origin in equity and others in the common law. Those historical roots can often still be discerned, and in some cases may still remain significant. In other cases it may indeed be accurate to describe the rules as having merged or melded. This middle approach was articulated by the House of Lords in *Tinsley v Milligan*,[59] which concerned the question whether a plaintiff could assert a claim to an equitable interest in land by way of a resulting trust where she had acted illegally.[60] It was argued that the traditional equitable maxim that a person seeking to assert an equitable entitlement must come with 'clean hands' prevented the plaintiff asserting her right.[61] In contrast, the common law had concluded that a person whose acquisition of property was tainted by illegal conduct was entitled to assert his common law right to ownership provided that he did not need to rely on his illegal conduct to establish his title.[62] Lord Browne-Wilkinson[63] considered that such a distinction was inappropriate in the modern law:

to draw such distinctions between property rights enforceable at law and those which require the intervention of equity would be surprising. More than 100 years has elapsed since the fusion of the administration of law and equity. The reality of the matter is that, in 1993, English law has one single law of property made up of legal and equitable interests. Although for historical reasons legal estates and equitable estates have differing incidents, the person owning either type of estate has a right of property, a right in rem not merely a right in personam. If the law is that a party is entitled to enforce a proprietary right acquired under an illegal transaction, in my judgement the same rule ought to apply to any property right so acquired, whether such right is legal or equitable.[64]

Although he referred to the 'fusion of the administration of law and equity', which could be taken as supporting the orthodox position, his analysis that English law has 'one single law of property made up of legal and equitable interests' is of greater significance. This presupposes that there has been a degree of fusion in substance, but not

---

[58] [1978] AC 904, at 924.
[59] [1993] 3 All ER 65.   [60] The facts are set out below at p 30.
[61] The nature of the equitable maxims is explored at p 28.
[62] *Bowmakers Ltd v Barnet Instruments Ltd* [1945] KB 65.
[63] With whom Lord Jauncey and Lord Lowry concurred.
[64] [1993] 3 All ER 65, at 86.

so as to completely eradicate all distinctions. There are different types of ownership, different rights and remedies in English law which by historical origin are equitable and legal, and although they form one coherent body of law they must still be distinguished or identified as such because of the different 'incidents' that accompany them. A similar approach was also taken by the House of Lords in *Lord Napier and Ettrick v Hunter*, where Lord Goff considered the relationship between equitable proprietary rights and personal rights and obligations deriving from a contract of insurance:

No doubt our task nowadays is to see the two strands of authority, at law and in equity, moulded into a coherent whole; but for my part I cannot see why this amalgamation should lead to the rejection of the equitable proprietary right...[65]

Examples of situations where there is a need to draw a distinction between legal and equitable rights and remedies are abundant in English law. In relation to land, the entire scheme of the Law of Property Act 1925 is predicated upon the distinction between legal and equitable estates and interests in land,[66] and the character of an interest determines its ability to endure through transfers of the legal title. Specific performance, an equitable remedy, is only available where a contract has been entered in return for valuable consideration and not of a promise made by deed, which would be enforced by the common law.[67] A promise to create a trust will not therefore be enforced by equity in favour of a volunteer,[68] although such a promise contained in a deed, to which the intended beneficiary was a party, will entitle the beneficiary to an award of common law damages if the covenantor fails to create the promised trust.[69] The rules governing the passing of the benefit and burden of a covenant affecting freehold land are different in law and in equity, so that at law the burden of a covenant is incapable of passing to a successor in title to the original covenantor, whereas in equity the burden of a restrictive covenant is capable of passing with the land.[70] It is impossible to combine the legal and equitable rules governing the passing of the benefit and burden of such covenants, so that a covenant will not be enforceable between successors in title to the land of the original covenantor and covenantee if the benefit of the covenant has passed at law but not in equity, and the burden has passed in equity but not at law. The rules which enable a person to trace property which has been misappropriated from them are also different at law and in equity. Whereas at common law it is impossible to trace money once it has become mixed with other money,[71] equity allows tracing through a mixed fund provided that a sufficient fiduciary relationship to justify the intervention of equity can be shown.[72] In the very significant

---

[65] Ibid., at 401.
[66] Law of Property Act 1925, s 1.
[67] Equitable remedies are considered in detail in Chapter 6.
[68] *Donaldson v Donaldson* (1854) Kay 711; *Re Plumptre's Marriage Settlement* [1901] 1 Ch 609; *Re Cooks' Settlement* [1965] Ch 902.
[69] *Cannon v Hartley* [1949] Ch 213.
[70] See Jackson, Stevens, and Pearce, *Land Law* (4th edn, 2008), Ch 16.
[71] *Taylor v Plumer* (1815) 3 M & S 562; *Agip (Africa) Ltd v Jackson* [1990] Ch 265; *Bank Tejarat v Hong Kong and Shanghai Banking Corpn (CI) Ltd* [1995] 1 Lloyd's Rep 239.
[72] *Re Diplock* [1948] Ch 465.

case *Westdeutsche Landesbank Girozentrale v Islington London Borough Council*[73] the majority of the House of Lords held that whereas equity enjoys a limited jurisdiction to award compound interest when a remedy is granted,[74] the common law has no such jurisdiction and is only capable of awarding simple interest.[75] Therefore, a plaintiff seeking restitution was held not to be entitled to compound interest because his cause of action in unjust enrichment arose at common law and not in equity. This reinforces the view that it is not irrelevant where a cause of action originates. As has already been noted above, the trust emerged because, through the parallel systems of law and equity, English law developed the abstract concept of the double-ownership of property. Thus, legal and equitable title can exist simultaneously in the same item of property, enjoyed by different persons as owners.

5 The maxims of equity[76]

The maxims of equity are an attempt to formulate in short, pithy phrases the key principles which underlie the exercise of the equitable jurisdiction. They are not binding rules, nor do they provide guidance for every situation in which equity operates. Nevertheless, they provide useful illustrations of some of the principal recurrent themes which can be identified within the corpus of the rules of equity.

(1) Equity will not suffer a wrong to be without a remedy

This maxim provides the philosophical foundation of equity, namely that wrongs should be redressed by the courts if possible. Equity developed as a response to defects of the common law to provide relief where none was available. For example, equity intervened to allow a person to escape from a contract which they had entered having been misled by a mistake of fact, even though the contract was enforceable at common law.[77] Similarly, through a trust equity enabled a beneficiary to enforce an obligation to use property in a particular way where there was no remedy at common law.

(2) Equity follows the law[78]

This is arguably the most important maxim, as it underpins the operation of the equitable jurisdiction. The Court of Chancery did not override the courts of common law

---

[73] [1996] 2 All ER 961. See also [1996] RLR 3 (Birks); [1996] LMCLQ 441 (Stevens).

[74] *President of India v La Pintada Compania Navegacion SA (La Pintada)* [1985] AC 104.

[75] The Law Reform (Miscellaneous Provisions) Act 1934, s 3(1) and Supreme Court Act 1981, s 35A expressly enable the award of simple interest on claims at common law, where historically the common law had no general power to award interest at all: *London, Chatham and Dover Rly Co v South Eastern Rly Co* [1893] AC 429.

[76] See Snell's *Principles of Equity* (30th edn, 2000), pp 27–44.

[77] See eg *Cooper v Joel* (1859) 1 De G F & J 240; *Torrance v Bolton* (1872) 8 Ch App 118.

[78] See Gardner 'Two Maxims of Equity' [1995] CLJ 60.

except to remedy an injustice, and could not depart from statute. Equity does not unnecessarily depart from legal principles.[79] The fact that equity follows the law is well illustrated in the context of land[80] by the fact that the equitable estates and interests largely correspond to those at law.[81]

(3) Where the equities are equal the law prevails

This maxim means that where there are two persons with competing rights to the same item of property, one with a legal right and the other an equitable right, the legal right will take priority over the equitable right, even if the equitable right had pre-existed it. In *Wortley v Birkhead*,[82] Lord Hardwicke LC explained that this was 'by reason of that force [the Court of Chancery] necessarily and rightly gives to the legal title'.[83] In the context of land, issues of priority between competing rights, whether legal or equitable, are governed by statutory rules which have displaced the operation of this maxim and the next.[84]

(4) Where the equities are equal the first in time prevails

This maxim means that if two parties have competing equitable rights in the same item of property, and neither has the legal estate, the right which was created first enjoys priority.[85] This maxim mirrors the common law rule as to priority between competing legal rights.

(5) He who seeks equity must do equity

This maxim looks to a claimant's future conduct. If a claimant seeks equitable relief, he must be prepared to act fairly towards the person against whom it is sought.[86] For example, if a purchase is set aside in equity, the purchase money must be repaid with interest.[87]

---

[79] *Burgess v Wheate* (1759) 1 Eden 177, at 195, per Clarke MR; *Sinclair v Brougham* [1914] AC 398, at 414–415, per Lord Haldane LC.

[80] See Jackson, Stevens, and Pearce, *Land Law* (4th edn, 2008) pp 33–34.

[81] However, equity recognized a range of future interests in land not recognized at law: see Megarry and Wade, *The Law of Real Property* (6th edn, 2000), pp 104–107.

[82] (1754) 2 Ves Sen 571, at 574.

[83] Compare also *Marsh v Lee* (1670) 2 Vent 337; *E Pfeiffer Weinkellerei-Weineinkauf GmbH & Co v Arbothnot Factors Ltd* [1988] 1 WLR 150.

[84] See Chapter 3.

[85] *Willoughby v Willoughby* (1756) 1 Term Rep 763; *Brace v Duchess of Marlborough* (1728) 2 P Wms 491; *Rice v Rice* (1854) 2 Drew 73; *Phillips v Phillips* (1861) 4 De GF & J 208.

[86] See eg *Lodge v National Union Investment Co Ltd* [1907] 1 Ch 300; *Solle v Butcher* [1950] 1 KB 671; *Chappell v Times Newspapers Ltd* [1975] 1 WLR 482.

[87] *Peacock v Evans* (1809–10) 16 Ves 512.

(6) **He who comes to equity must come with clean hands**

In contrast, this maxim looks to the past conduct of the claimant. If the claimant's conduct is tainted by illegal or inequitable conduct, he may be denied the relief to which he would otherwise be entitled. For example, a tenant will not be granted specific performance of an agreement for a lease if he is in breach of the covenants it contains.[88] The maxim does not apply to conduct in general, but only that which has 'an immediate and necessary relation to the equity sued for'.[89] Therefore in *Argyll (Duchess) v Argyll (Duke)*[90] the plaintiff's adultery, which caused a divorce, was no bar to her claim for an injunction to restrain the defendant from publishing confidential material. The rationale for this maxim, as for the parallel common law rule against illegality, is to deter persons from entering into transactions which involve a dimension of illegality. However, since these rules may in practice allow one person who was party to an illegal purpose arbitrarily to retain the entire benefit of property transferred to him, because another equally guilty party is prevented from asserting any entitlement to it, the courts have systematically ameliorated their strictness through exceptions.

The operation of the equitable maxim was considered by the House of Lords in *Tinsley v Milligan*,[91] where a house was purchased jointly by a lesbian couple. Only one of them was registered as the legal proprietor to enable the other to claim dishonestly social security benefits by appearing to be a mere lodger. After the breakdown of the relationship, the partner who did not enjoy a share of the legal title claimed that she was entitled to a half-share of the house in equity arising by way of a resulting trust implied from her contribution to the purchase price.[92] The registered proprietor argued that she was prevented from asserting her equitable right because she was tainted by their illegal purpose, so that she did not come to equity with 'clean hands'. The House of Lords held by a bare majority that she was entitled to succeed in her claim. The essential disagreement between the majority and minority was not as to the existence of the maxim 'he who comes to equity must come with clean hands', but how it should be applied in circumstances where a plaintiff's claim is not itself founded on the alleged illegality. Lord Goff, who dissented,[93] took the view that the maxim should apply in its full force, since it was well established by authority and there was no justification for introducing a change,[94] even though it produced an admittedly harsh result for the plaintiff.[95] Lord Browne-Wilkinson, with whom Lord Jauncey and Lord Lowry concurred, held that the maxim should prevent a plaintiff asserting equitable title to property only if he had to rely on his illegal conduct to establish the entitlement,

---

[88] *Coatsworth v Johnson* (1886) 54 LT 520.
[89] *Dering v Earl of Winchelsea* (1787) 2 White & Tud LC 488, at 489.
[90] [1967] Ch 302.   [91] [1994] 1 AC 340.
[92] See Chapter 9 and pp 347 *et seq.*   [93] With whom Lord Keith concurred.
[94] *Curtis v Perry* (1802) 6 Ves 739; *Groves v Groves* (1828) 3 Y & J 163; *Childers v Childers* (1857) 3 K & J 310; *Tinker v Tinker* [1970] P 136; *Cantor v Cox* (1976) 239 Estates Gazette 121.
[95] Which Lord Goff recognized: [1993] 3 All ER 65, at 80.

thus ensuring uniformity with the common law rule against illegality as interpreted in *Bowmakers Ltd v Barnet Instruments Ltd*.[96] He concluded that:

although there is no case for overruling the wide principle…as the law has developed the equitable principle has become elided into the common law rule. In my judgement the time has come to decide clearly that the rule is the same whether a plaintiff founds himself on a legal or equitable title: he is entitled to recover if he is not forced to plead or rely on the illegality, even if it emerges that the title on which he relied was acquired in the course of carrying through an illegal transaction.[97]

With the operation of the maxim circumscribed in this way, the plaintiff was held entitled to succeed, since she could establish her entitlement to an equitable interest by way of a resulting trust merely by showing that she had contributed to the purchase price of the property. She did not need to rely on her illegal conduct because the underlying purpose of the purchase was irrelevant to her claim against the registered proprietor. Despite the differing approaches adopted, the House of Lords rejected any wholesale change to a general 'public conscience' test as had been proposed by the Court of Appeal,[98] as this would have required the court to weigh the adverse consequences of granting relief against those of refusing relief.

The application of the maxim was further weakened in *Tribe v Tribe*,[99] where the Court of Appeal held a father entitled to assert an equitable entitlement to shares, the legal title to which he had transferred to his son as part of a scheme to defraud his creditors. Because the shares had been transferred by a father to his son there was a presumption that the father had intended to make a gift,[100] thereby disposing of his entire interest in them. He could only demonstrate that he had retained the equitable ownership of the shares through a resulting trust if this presumption of gift was rebutted. The underlying purpose of the transaction was clearly sufficient to rebut the presumption because there was no intention that the son should own the shares for himself, but to so rebut it would require the father to rely on the illegal purpose behind the transfer. The equitable maxim would therefore apply, preventing him from claiming any equitable entitlement. In the event, the feared creditors never materialized to be defrauded and the father demanded the retransfer of the shares. The Court of Appeal surprisingly held that the father was not prevented from asserting a resulting trust of the shares, on the ground that the illegal purpose had not been carried out. This was a somewhat generous finding, since as Nourse LJ stated, this exception to the full rigour of the maxim only applies if 'the illegal purpose has not been carried into effect in any way', and the central act required to defraud the creditors, namely transferring the legal title of the shares to the son, had undeniably occurred. The conclusion that the illegal purpose had not been carried into effect was therefore artificial. It was merely fortuitous for the father that the perceived threat against which he had taken pre-emptive action was illusory.

96 [1945] KB 65.   97 Ibid., at 91.
98 [1992] 2 All ER 391.   99 [1996] Ch 107; [1995] 4 All ER 236.
100 Technically, their relationship gave rise to a presumption of advancement.

(7) Delay defeats equity

Equity will not assist a plaintiff who has failed to assert his rights within a reasonable time. As Lord Camden LC said in *Smith v Clay*:

[equity] has always refused its aid to stale demands, where a party has slept upon his right and acquiesced for a great length of time. Nothing can call forth this court into activity, but conscience, good faith, and reasonable diligence; where these are wanting, the Court is passive and does nothing.[101]

This is the foundation of the equitable defence of laches, which was applied in *Nelson v Rye*,[102] where it was held that a musician could not claim an account of earnings wrongfully retained by his manager in breach of fiduciary duty because he had waited for more than six years before commencing an action. The operation of this defence must today be considered in conjunction with the statutory rules concerning limitation of actions under the Limitation Act 1980.[103]

(8) Equality is equity

Where persons enjoy concurrent entitlement to identical interests in property, and there is no express provision, agreement or other basis as to how it should be divided among them, equity prescribes that equal division should occur, so that each receives an equal share in the property.[104] This maxim is reflected in the preference of equity for a tenancy in common, which will sometimes be implied in equity even where the common law holds that there is a joint tenancy,[105] namely[106] where joint purchasers contribute to the purchase in equal shares and there is no express allocation of the equitable interest; where persons have jointly lent money on mortgage;[107] and where property is acquired as part of a joint business venture.[108]

(9) Equity looks to the intent rather than the form

The principle behind this maxim was well stated by Romilly MR in *Parkin v Thorold*:

Courts of equity make a distinction between that which is matter of substance and that which is matter of form; and if it finds that by insisting on the form, the substance will be defeated,

---

[101] (1767) 3 Bro CC 639n, at 640.
[102] [1996] 2 All ER 186; Stevens 'Too Late to Face the Music? Limitation and Laches as Defences to an Action for Breach of Fiduciary Duty' [1997] Conv 225.
[103] See Chapter 29.
[104] *Petit v Smith* (1695) 1 P Wms 7; *Re Dickens* [1935] Ch 267; *Re Bradberry* [1943] Ch 35; *Hampton & Sons v Garrard Smith (Estate Agents) Ltd* [1985] 1 EGLR 23; see also *McPhail v Doulton* [1971] AC 424, discussed in Chapter 17.
[105] See Jackson, Stevens, and Pearce, *Land Law* (4th edn 2008), pp 370–371.
[106] See *Malayan Credit Ltd v Jack Chia-MPH Ltd* [1986] AC 549.
[107] *Morley v Bird* (1798) 3 Ves 628. This applies only to where there are joint lenders, not to the more common situation of joint borrowers.
[108] *Lake v Craddock* (1732) 2 White & Tud LC 876.

it holds it to be inequitable to allow a person to insist on such form, and thereby defeat the substance.[109]

More recently, in *Foskett v McKeown* Sir Richard Scott V-C stated that:

The availability of equitable remedies ought...to depend upon the substance of the transaction in question.[110]

Therefore, equity categorizes a covenant affecting freehold land as 'restrictive', even though worded in a positive way, if in substance it is negative.[111] Similarly, equity will not grant an injunction to enforce a negative covenant entered by an employee agreeing not to work for others if in substance this would amount to an order of specific performance of their contract of employment,[112] since equity will not enforce contracts of personal service.[113] It is not necessary to use the precise word 'trust' to create a trust, provided that in substance the settlor intended to subject the legal owner of the property to a mandatory obligation regarding its use.[114] Similarly, equity will look to the substance, and not the wording used, to determine if a clause in a contract providing for the payment of a specific sum in the event of breach is a penalty or a genuine pre-estimate of damages.[115]

(10) Equity regards as done that which ought to be done[116]

Where a contract is specifically enforceable,[117] equity regards the promisor as having already done what he has promised to do, because he can be compelled to do it. Therefore, as was seen in *Walsh v Lonsdale*,[118] a contract to grant a lease is treated as creating an equitable lease on the same terms. Similarly, because of the availability of specific performance, a contract for the purchase of land,[119] or of unique personal property,[120] will give rise to an immediate constructive trust vesting the equitable ownership in the purchaser by way of a constructive trust at the very moment that the contract is entered. The maxim also underlies the general doctrine of conversion, and the rule in *Howe v Earl Dartmouth*,[121] which requires that a trustee convert unauthorized investments into authorized investments.[122] In *A-G for Hong Kong v Reid*[123] the maxim has been held to have the implication that a fiduciary who receives

---

[109] (1852) 16 Beav 59, at 66.   [110] [1997] 3 All ER 392, at 399.

[111] *Tulk v Moxhay* (1848) 18 LJ Ch 83; *Rhone v Stephens* [1994] 2 AC 310.

[112] *Page One Records Ltd v Britton* [1967] 3 All ER 822.

[113] *Lumley v Wagner* (1852) 1 De GM & G 604.

[114] *Re Kayford Ltd* [1975] 1 WLR 279; see Chapter 11.

[115] *Kembel v Farren* (1829) 6 Bing 141; *Pye v British Automobile Commercial Syndicate* [1906] 1 KB 425; *Diestal v Stevenson* [1906] 2 KB 345; *Cellulose Acetate Silk Co Ltd v Widnes Foundry (1925) Ltd* [1933] AC 20; *Robert Stewart & Sons Ltd v Carapanayoti & Co Ltd* [1962] 1 WLR 34.

[116] See Gardner 'Two Maxims of Equity' [1995] CLJ 60.

[117] See pp 115–128.   [118] (1882) 21 Ch D 9. See above, pp 20–21.

[119] *Lloyds Bank plc v Carrick* [1996] 4 All ER 630.

[120] Eg in *Oughtred v IRC* [1960] AC 206, where there was a contract for the purchase of a beneficiary's equitable interest in shares in a private company.

[121] (1802) 7 Ves 137.   [122] See Chapter 13.   [123] [1994] 1 AC 324.

an unauthorized profit in breach of his duty of loyalty will hold the profit on constructive trust for his principal because he is subject to an equitable duty to account for the profit he received.

(11) Equity imputes an intention to fulfil an obligation

Equity places the most favourable construction on a man's acts, so that if he does something which could be construed as fulfilling an obligation he owes, equity will regard it as having this effect. For example, if a debtor leaves a legacy to his creditor, this is presumed to be a repayment of the debt.[124] The doctrines of performance and satisfaction are founded on this maxim.

(12) Equity acts in personam

This maxim refers to the fact that, as has been noted above, equity enforces its decisions by means of a personal order against the defendant, for example by an order to perform a contract, observe a trust, or refrain from some behaviour by means of an injunction. If the defendant breaches the order, he will be in contempt of court.[125] The court may exercise jurisdiction over any person within the power of the court,[126] even though the order may relate to property which is situated abroad.[127] The potential extraterritoriality of the equity jurisdiction has been recognized by the Court of Justice of the European Community (ECJ). In *Webb v Webb*[128] a father bought a flat in Antibes in his son's name, intending to retain the ownership. The ECJ held that even though the usual rule was that matters of title to immovable property, such as buildings, had to be settled in accordance with the law of the country in which it was situated, the father was entitled to pursue his claim to a share in the property under a resulting trust[129] through the English courts because it was a personal claim. It therefore upheld the decision, on the merits, of the English High Court,[130] that the son held the flat on a resulting trust for his father. In *Re Hayward*[131] it was said that it was significant that the plaintiff in *Webb v Webb* was not making any claim based on legal ownership of the property concerned. In *Re Hayward* a trustee in bankruptcy claimed to be entitled to a half share in a villa in Spain which had belonged to the bankrupt and his wife in indivisible halves,[132] but which had subsequently been transferred to the defendant by the bankrupt's widow, who claimed to be entitled to do so in her own

---

[124] *Thynne v Glengall* (1848) 2 HL Cas 131; *Chichester v Coventry* (1867) LR 2 HL 71; *Re Horlock* [1895] 1 Ch 516.

[125] See *Co-operative Insurance v Argyll Stores* [1997] 3 All ER 297 at 302–303.

[126] Namely, someone who is within the jurisdiction or on whom the court order can be served outside of it.

[127] *Penn v Lord Baltimore* (1750) 1 Ves Sen 444; *Ewing v Orr Ewing* (1883–84) 9 App Cas 34, HL; *Richard West & Partners (Inverness) Ltd v Dick* [1969] 1 All ER 289; affd [1969] 2 Ch 424, CA.

[128] [1994] QB 696.   [129] See Chapters 9 and 11.

[130] [1992] 1 All ER 17.   [131] [1997] 1 All ER 32.

[132] The Spanish equivalent of a legal tenancy in common.

right and as intestate successor to her husband's share. The property had then been registered in the name of the defendant in the property register in Minorca. The basis of the trustee in bankruptcy's claim was that the bankrupt's rights had vested in him so that there was nothing which should have passed to the bankrupt's wife and thence to the defendant. The trustee in bankruptcy was therefore seeking to have the Minorcan property register rectified to show him as half owner. Rattee J held that, under Article 16 of the 1968 Convention on Jurisdiction and the Enforcement of Judgments in Civil and Commercial Matters (adopted as law by the Civil Jurisdiction and Judgments Act 1982), the Spanish courts had exclusive jurisdiction over the matter since the proceedings had as their object 'rights in rem in immovable property'. Rattee J rejected the argument that a claim for an order to reverse the registration could be treated as a claim in personam. In his view, although English law did not recognize as sharply as some other jurisdictions the distinction between rights in rem and rights in personam, 'it is difficult to contemplate any right more clearly a right in rem than a right to legal ownership such as is claimed by the trustee [in bankruptcy] in the present case'.[133] The relationship of this case with *Webb v Webb* raises interesting questions. Since one of the rights of the beneficiaries under a trust is a right to call for a vesting in them of the legal estate, it is difficult to see why the claim of a beneficiary under a resulting or constructive trust (as in *Webb v Webb*) should not be seen as a right in rem, just like the claim in *Re Hayward*. On the other hand, the two cases differed in the way in which they were pleaded, and it may be that this is a sufficient (although unsatisfactory) distinction between them.

6 The creativity of equity

(1) Equity and the creation of rights and remedies

From a historical perspective one of the outstanding characteristics of equity has been its capacity to develop new rights and remedies for the benefit of plaintiffs. The need for such creativity within English law was the very reason for equity's genesis, and it led in particular to the evolution of the trust. Today, despite its undisputed and revered pedigree, the question has arisen whether equity retains such dynamic creative capacity. The need for ongoing creativity by equity was recognized by Jessel MR in *Re Hallet's Estate*:

It must not be forgotten that the rules of equity are not, like the rules of the common law, supposed to have been established from time immemorial. It is perfectly well known that they have been established from time to time—altered, improved, and refined from time to time. In many cases we know the name of the Chancellor who invented them...Take such things as these: the separate use of a married woman, the restraint on alienation, the modern rule

---

[133] [1997] 1 All ER 32, at 43.

against perpetuities, and the rules of equitable waste. We can name the Chancellors who first invented them, and state the date when they were first introduced into equity jurisprudence; and therefore, in cases of this kind, the older precedents in equity are of very little value. The doctrines are progressive, refined and improved; and if we want to know what the rules of equity are, we must look, of course, rather to the more modern than the more ancient cases.[134]

However, these remarks are more than a hundred years old and reflect the immediate aftermath of the Judicature Acts, and in more recent times it has been questioned whether equity retains the capacity to 'invent' new rights and remedies which seem appropriate to meet the justice of a plaintiff's case. To borrow a favourite metaphor of Lord Denning, is equity 'past the age of childbearing'?

(2) 'Equity is not past the age of childbearing'

Through the third quarter of the twentieth century Lord Denning was the strongest judicial exponent of the creativity of equity and he utilized this capacity to justify new rights and remedies to meet social needs and perceived injustices. In the context of matrimonial property, he attempted to introduce a 'deserted wife's equity' entitling a woman deserted by her husband to remain in occupation of their matrimonial home, a right which would be enforceable against strangers who acquired the property, or a mortgage over it, from the husband. This equitable right was emphatically rejected by the House of Lords, which held that the right of a wife to be provided with accommodation by her husband lacked the characteristics of identifiability, stability and permanence which would enable it to be enforced against third parties.[135] However, in a matter of years they had taken note of the need for a means by which women and cohabitants could gain proprietary entitlements to property shared with their spouses or partners by a widening of the doctrines of resulting and constructive trusts, and Parliament enacted a statutory right entitling spouses to occupy their matrimonial home. With the introduction of a wider jurisdiction to establish resulting and constructive trusts, Lord Denning went a step further and sought to establish a whole new type of constructive trust, which he described as the 'new model constructive trust', based on American restitutionary principles. The essence of this 'new model' constructive trust was that equity could impose a trust 'whenever justice and good conscience' demanded it.[136] The proposed operation of this trust is considered later in this book, but it is referred to here because it shows that Lord Denning felt it proper for judges to create such new rights where required to meet the needs of justice. In *Eves v Eves*, which concerned a woman cohabiting with her partner, he summarized how he considered equity had been responsive to the needs of practical justice:

---

[134] (1880) 13 Ch D 696, at 710.
[135] *National Provincial Bank v Ainsworth* [1965] AC 1175.
[136] *Hussey v Palmer* [1972] 1 WLR 1286.

a few years ago even equity would not have helped her. But things have altered now. Equity is not past the age of child bearing. One of her latest progeny is a constructive trust of a new model. Lord Diplock brought it into the world[137] and we have nourished it...[138]

(3) **The creativity of equity circumscribed**

Although Lord Denning championed the creativity of equity by developing the 'new model constructive trust', other judges expressed a more cautious and restrictive approach. Some judges have stated extra-judicially their feeling that equity has lost its creative power altogether. For example, in 1953 Lord Evershed expressed his opinion that:

the passing of the Judicature Act, and section 25(11) in particular, put a stop to, or at least a very severe limitation on, the inventive faculties of future Chancery judges.[139]

In 1952 Lord Denning himself expressed his concern, which he later strove to overcome, that:

The Courts of Chancery are no longer courts of equity...They are as fixed and immutable as the courts of law ever were.[140]

Two main fears seem to have influenced the courts against a creative role for equity.

(a) Reluctance to countenance judicial law making

First, some judges fear that a willingness to create new equitable rights and remedies threatens the delicate constitutional balance between the legislative and judicial arms of government because it usurps the proper function of Parliament. This fear is not unique to equity, but affects English law as a whole. This fear was expressed by Megaw LJ in *Western Fish Products v Penwith District Council*:

As Harman LJ pointed out in *Campbell Discount Co Ltd v Bridge*[141] the system of equity has become a very precise one. The creation of new rights and remedies is a matter for Parliament, not the judges.[142]

This reluctance to undermine Parliament was evident in *Westdeutsche Landesbank Girozentrale v Islington London Borough Council*.[143] The unwillingness of the majority to extend the jurisdiction of equity to award compound damages was grounded in the concern that such an extension would be an unjustifiable usurpation of the functions properly belonging to Parliament, because Parliament had twice legislated to grant the common law the power to award simple interest but had not felt it necessary to go further. As Lord Lloyd explained:

To extend the equitable jurisdiction for the first time to cover a residual injustice at common law, which Parliament chose not to remedy, would, I think, be as great a usurpation of the role of the legislature, and as clear an example of judicial lawmaking as it would have been

---

[137] In *Gissing v Gissing* [1971] AC 886. [138] [1975] 1 WLR 1338.
[139] (1953) 6 CLP 1, at 12. [140] (1952) 5 CLP 8.
[141] [1961] 1 QB 445, at 459. [142] [1981] 2 All ER 204.
[143] [1996] 2 All ER 961. See also [1996] RLR 3 (Birks); [1996] LMCLQ 441 (Stevens).

in *President of India*.[144] If it is thought desirable that the courts should have a power to award compound interest in common law claims for actions for money had and received, then such a result can now only be brought about by Parliament.[145]

In the subsequent case of *Great Peace Shipping Ltd v Tsavliris Salvage (International) Ltd*,[146] the Court of Appeal similarly stated that the introduction of a wider jurisdiction to set contracts aside on the grounds of common mistake than that available at common law[147] would require legislation, and could not be achieved through the development of an equitable jurisdiction.

(b) Danger of uncertainty

Some judges have equally expressed their concern that radical creativity by equity, generating new rights and remedies to do justice in individual cases, would result in uncertainty. The courts are reluctant to allow the situation to develop where equity could again appear subjective and attract the criticism of varying with the length of the Chancellor's foot. This concern to avoid uncertainty was particularly apposite in the context of the new model constructive trust, as the concept of a powerful proprietary remedy to be awarded on the basis of what the judge felt was 'just', without reference to clear guiding principles, was inherently uncertain. As Bagnall J stated in *Cowcher v Cowcher*:

I am convinced that in determining rights, particularly property rights, the only justice that can be attained by mortals, who are fallible and are not omniscient, is justice according to law; the justice that flows from the application of sure and settled principles to proved or admitted facts. So in the field of equity the length of the Chancellor's foot has been measured or is capable of measurement...[148]

He observed that the practical difficulty of allowing equity do justice on a case-by-case basis was that in the realm of property 'no lawyer could safely advise on his client's title'. In *Westdeutsche v Islington London Borough Council*, Lord Browne-Wilkinson refused to countenance the extension of equitable resulting trust principles to provide proprietary restitution where a payment had been made under a contract that was *ultra vires* and void because of the dangers of uncertainty:

I do not think it right to make an unprincipled alteration to the law of property (i.e. the law of trusts) so as to produce in the law of unjust enrichment the injustices to third parties... and the consequential commercial uncertainty which any extension of proprietary interests in personal property is bound to produce.[149]

In *Taylor v Dickens* Judge Weeks, QC, somewhat intemperately, vented his fear of uncertainty when he suggested that the evolution of a broad doctrine of proprietary estoppel founded on the notion of 'unconscionability' would have the effect that:

one might as well forget the law of contract and issue every judge with a portable palm tree. The days of justice varying with the size of the Chancellor's foot would have returned.[150]

---

144 *President of India v La Pintada Cia Navigacion SA* [1985] AC 104.
145 [1996] 2 All ER 961, at 1021.   146 [2004] 4 All ER 689.
147 *Bell v Lever Bros Ltd* [1932] AC 161.   148 [1972] 1 WLR 425, at 430.
149 [1996] 2 All ER 961, at 992.
150 [1998] 1 FLR 806, Thompson 'Emasculating Estoppel' [1998] Conv 210.

(4) Evolution of new rights and remedies from existing principles

Despite the reluctance of the court to 'invent' new rights and remedies, this does not mean that equity is stagnant and incapable of flexible development to meet new circumstances. The inevitability of the development of existing law was recognized by Glass JA in the Australian case *Allen v Snyder*, together with the necessary limitations on such development:

It is inevitable that judge made law will alter to meet the changing conditions of society. That is the way it has always evolved. But it is essential that new rules should be related to fundamental doctrine. If the foundations of accepted doctrine be submerged under new principles, without regard to the interaction between the two, there will be high uncertainty as to the state of the law, both old and new.[151]

The law is a coherent and dynamic whole, subject to constant re-evaluation and adjustment, sometimes culminating in the birth of new principles and doctrines. Equity has made a tremendous contribution to this whole and the continuous process of remoulding equitable rights and remedies should be seen as an essential part of this overall process of legal development. Rights and remedies which are in practice 'new' can be developed from existing principles and precedents. In *Re Diplock* the Court of Appeal said that an equitable claim:

must be shown to have an ancestry founded in the practice and precedents of the courts administering equity jurisdiction. It is not sufficient that because we think that the justice of the present case requires it, we should invent such a jurisdiction for the first time.[152]

In *Cowcher v Cowcher*[153] Bagnall J affirmed that equity was not past the age of childbearing, remaining fertile and capable of developing new rights and remedies. However, he considered that its reproductive capacity should be circumscribed so that 'its progeny must be legitimate—by precedent out of principle'. Ultimately, the 'new model' constructive trust in its broadest form was rejected by the Court of Appeal on the grounds that it did not have sufficient ancestry in the principles and precedents of equity, and was 'at variance with the principles stated in *Gissing v Gissing*'.[154]

The emergence of new rights and remedies labelled 'equitable' must be viewed within the framework of judicial development of the law as a whole. Equity does not enjoy any special ability to be more creative than other branches of law, and in recent years one of the most radical developments has occurred within what was historically the province of the common law through the recognition by the House of Lords of the right to restitution founded upon an autonomous cause of action in unjust enrichment.[155] This development parallels past common law achievements, such as the acceptance of a general law of negligence in *Donoghue v Stevenson*.[156]

---

[151] [1977] 2 NSWLR 685, at 689.   [152] [1948] Ch 465.
[153] [1972] 1 WLR 425, at 430.   [154] *Grant v Edwards* [1986] Ch 638, per Nourse LJ.
[155] *Lipkin Gorman v Karpnale Ltd* [1991] 2 AC 548; *Woolwich Equitable Building Society v IRC* [1993] AC 70; *Westdeutsche Bank v Islington London Borough Council* [1996] AC 669.
[156] [1932] AC 562.

The fears which have been expressed in relation to the ability of equity to create new rights and remedies have also curtailed the willingness of the court to introduce changes to traditional common law doctrines. For example, in *Prudential Assurance Co Ltd v London Residuary Body*[157] the House of Lords refused to overrule the ancient common law rule that a lease is void if it is not created with an ascertainable maximum duration, despite the fact that it served no useful purpose and they could find no satisfactory rationale for its existence, because of fear that so doing might 'upset long-established titles'.

(5) Examples of the creativity of equity

Despite the caution that has often been expressed about the development of new law, there have been a number of significant developments in the past half-century where judges have created new 'equitable' rights or remedies, or expanded existing principles to such a degree that a virtually new right has emerged. The majority of new developments have occurred incrementally, by progressive evolution from existing doctrines and principles. This has sometimes happened to enable old principles to apply to modern situations. For instance, the principles of resulting and constructive trusts have been reworked, so that they are unrecognizable from the concepts known by those names at the time of the Judicature Acts or the Law of Property Act 1925, to determine property rights between unmarried cohabiting partners who have acquired a home by their joint effort, without any formal legal agreement as to how the ownership should be shared. In some cases, notably in relation to Mareva and Anton Piller orders considered below, the development has been much more rapid in response to an urgent and important problem. Even in these cases, however, the courts have sought to proceed cautiously and carefully on the basis of clear criteria, to minimize the risk of uncertainty.

(a) Creation of new rights and remedies

Two examples of remedies which have been developed by equity in the past quarter century are the Mareva injunction (Freezing Order) and the Anton Piller order (Search Order).[158] These are specialized injunctions which respectively prevent a defendant from disposing of his assets to avoid meeting a possible judgment against him, or destroying material evidence. Although unknown prior to their creation in two Court of Appeal decisions, they have come to be essential elements of civil procedure and litigation, and have been described by Donaldson LJ as the 'law's two "nuclear" weapons'.[159] Lord Denning MR was instrumental in the creation of both, and he has subsequently described them as 'the greatest piece of judicial law reform in my time'.[160]

---

[157] [1992] 3 All ER 504.
[158] See Chapter 6. See also Stevens 'Equity's Manhattan Project' [1999] Denning Law J 25.
[159] *Bank Mellat v Nikpour* [1985] FSR 87, at 91–92, CA.
[160] *The Due Process of Law* (1980), p 134; *The Closing Chapter* (1983), p 225.

(b) Extension and development of existing principles

Outside of the general flexibility of the trust to meet changing family, financial, and commercial circumstances, existing principles of equity have been extended and developed to meet modern social needs in a number of specific areas.

(i) Resulting and constructive trusts

As has been noted, the traditional concepts of resulting and constructive trusts have been developed and extended to form the foundations for dealings with the shared acquisition of residential property by married and cohabiting couples. These developments reflected the changing needs of society as social mores shifted from the paradigm family unit of husband and wife, where the husband alone owned the matrimonial home, to modern partnerships. The fundamental principles were set down by the House of Lords in two 1970s cases, *Pettitt v Pettitt*[161] and *Gissing v Gissing*.[162] These principles and their implications are examined in detail in Chapter 11.

(ii) Proprietary estoppel

Also operating in the context of rights and interests in land, the doctrine of proprietary estoppel has been developed from nineteenth-century principles,[163] to create proprietary interests in circumstances which do not otherwise meet the criteria for establishing a resulting or constructive trust. Proprietary estoppel is also considered in Chapter 11.

(c) Rejected new rights and remedies

Some proposed new rights and remedies have been aborted by the higher courts after a brief tentative life. It has already been noted how the House of Lords rejected Lord Denning's notion of the existence of a deserted wife's right to occupy her matrimonial home. Similarly, the Court of Appeal has regarded the 'new model' constructive trust as inconsistent with orthodox principles because of its inherent uncertainty, and in *Ashburn Anstalt v Arnold*[164] rejected Lord Denning's concerted judicial effort to confer the status of equitable proprietary interests on contractual licences.[165] In *Great Peace Shipping Ltd v Tsavliris Salvage (International) Ltd*[166] the House of Lords rejected a supposed equitable jurisdiction to grant rescission of a contract on the grounds of mistake wider than that available at common law,[167] which Lord Denning had propounded in the case of *Solle v Butcher*.[168]

---

[161] [1970] AC 777.   [162] [1971] AC 886.
[163] *Dillwyn v Llewelyn* (1862) 4 De G F & J 517; *Willmott v Barber* (1880) 15 Ch D 96.
[164] [1989] Ch 1.   [165] *Binions v Evans* [1972] Ch 359.
[166] [2002] 4 All ER 689.
[167] *Bell v Lever Brothers Ltd* [1932] AC 161. Etherton LJ, writing extra-judicially, has suggested that the 'remedial constructive trust' may have been introduced to English law through the House of Lords' decision in *Stack v Dowden* [2007] 2 WLR 831—'Constructive Trusts and Proprietary Estoppel: The Search for Clarity and Principle' [2009] Conv 104. This is discussed further in Chapter 11, at pp 387–391.
[168] [1950] 1 KB 671.

(d) Potential for future development

It is perhaps somewhat ironic that where the proposed 'new model' constructive trust led to rigorous doubt as to the creative ability of equity, the House of Lords has subsequently indicated the possible future adoption into English law of the 'remedial constructive trust', which, as a trust imposed on property by the court as a remedial response to effect restitution, shares some characteristics of the 'new model' constructive trust. In *Westdeutsche Landesbank Girozentrale v Islington London Borough Council* Lord Browne-Wilkinson remarked:

Although the resulting trust is an unsuitable basis for developing proprietary restitutionary remedies, the remedial constructive trust, if introduced into English law, may provide a more satisfactory road forward...However, whether English law should follow the United States and Canada by adopting the remedial constructive trust will have to be decided in some future case when the point is directly in issue.[169]

Although subsequent cases have chosen not to take this step,[170] the willingness of Lord Browne-Wilkinson to anticipate the ability of equity to incorporate such a remedy into English law is a strong reminder that equity's potential for childbearing has not yet passed.

[169] [1996] 2 All ER 961, at 999.
[170] *Re Polly Peck International (No 5)* [1998] 3 All ER 812.

3

Equity and the law of property

We have seen that 'equity' is more than a concept of fairness or justice in English law. It is a body of law which developed separately from the common law in England and which recognizes and protects different rights and interests. Nowhere is this more important than in relation to the law of property. The English law of property comprises a synthesis of legal and equitable rights and interests. Despite the separate genesis of the two sets of legal rules, they work together to make one coherent body of law.

Most of this book is concerned with the contribution equity has made to the law of property, in particular through the trust. This chapter provides an introduction to the influence and role of equity in the law of property. Much that is explained here will be familiar if you have already studied land law.

1 What is property?[1]

(1) The basic concept

At its most basic, the term 'property' is simply a more technical expression describing 'things'. Things can readily be distinguished from 'persons'. Persons are either individual human beings or abstract entities, such as companies or corporations, which are treated as separate legal persons for the purposes of the law. In general, persons are capable of owning things, whereas things have no capacity to own other things. Since the abolition of slavery, human persons are incapable of being owned as such. Body parts are also incapable of ownership.[2] Companies are owned by their shareholders, but the separate identity of the company is maintained so that it is not treated as synonymous with its shareholders. Animals are regarded as things and are capable of being owned, whereas they are not capable of owning.

---

[1] See Lawson and Rudden, *The Law of Property* (1982), pp 1–38; (1998) 18 LS 41 (Rotherham); McFarlane, *The Structure of Property Law* (Oxford: Hart, 2008).

[2] See Skene, 'Proprietary rights in human bodies, body parts and tissue: regulatory contexts and proposals for new laws' (2002) 22 LS 102.

Lawson and Rudden have commented that 'the law of property deals with the legal relations between people with regard to things'.[3] It addresses such questions as the following: Who owns the thing? What is the owner entitled to do with the thing he owns? How can the owner of the thing transfer it to someone else so that they become the owner in his place? Can the owner continue to assert his ownership of the thing even when a third person has taken it from him without permission, or against a person who has acquired the thing from such a third person?

For example, imagine that Kevin is the owner of a car. He purchased the car from the manufacturers and is therefore the owner of the car. If he allows his friend Leon to use the car for the weekend, does Leon become the owner of the car? If Leon gives the car to Michael while he is borrowing it, does Michael become the owner of the car thus depriving Kevin of his ownership? Does it make any difference if Leon sells the car to Michael, who believed that it belonged to Leon? The answers to these issues are determined by the law of property.

(2) Classification of types of property

Although property comprises 'things', the law differentiates between different types, or categories, of thing. The law applicable to a particular item of property will be dependent upon its nature.

(a) Real and personal property

English law distinguishes between what are termed 'real' and 'personal' property. Real property comprises land and interests in land, whereas personal property comprises everything which is not land. Items of tangible personal property, for example cars or furniture, are termed chattels. If chattels are attached to land so as to become part of the land, they lose their identity as personal property and become 'fixtures'.[4] Historically, the distinction between real and personal property was extremely significant, as the rules of succession, which determine what happens to property on the death of its owner, were different.[5]

(b) Movable and immovable property

Many continental legal systems, based on Roman law, distinguish not between real and personal property but between 'movable' and 'immovable' property—terms which speak for themselves. Although similar to the English distinction between real and personal property, this classification is not synonymous with it, as some interests

---

[3] Lawson and Rudden, *The Law of Property* (1982), p 1.

[4] See Jackson, Stevens, and Pearce, *Land Law* (4th edn, 2008), pp 17–25.

[5] Realty would pass to the surviving heir or heirs, personalty would be divided between a larger group of beneficiaries. In addition, there were different mechanics for the transfer of property. Realty passed directly to the heir, but personalty vested in the personal representatives of the estate (hence their name). This distinction is now gone, as all property passes to the personal representatives of the estate and is divided between the same group of beneficiaries—Administration of Estates Act 1924, s 1.

only does this internationally

that English law would regard as personal would be characterized as immovable.[6] For the purposes of private international law English law abandons its domestic classification and distinguishes between movable and immovable property.[7]

(c) Tangible and intangible property

A further distinction is drawn between things which are tangible and those which are not. A thing which is tangible is physical in nature, whereas intangible property only exists in abstract, comprising a bundle of rights and entitlements. Intellectual property rights, such as copyrights, patents, and trademarks, are good examples of intangible property. Others include negotiable instruments,[8] debts, and shares. These types of property are also described as choses in action.

2 **Proprietary rights**[9]

rights over things

Proprietary rights are those rights and entitlements which exist in reference to things. The most important and absolute right is that of ownership, but there are many lesser interests that may be enjoyed in respect of an item of property. It has been said that the law of property is about the relationship persons enjoy with things:

> For serious students of property, the beginning of truth is the recognition that property is not a thing but a *power relationship*—a relationship of social and legal legitimacy existing between a person and a valued resource (whether tangible or intangible). To claim 'property' in a resource is, in effect, to assert a significant degree of control over that resource.[10]

More accurately, the law of property is about the relationship which one person has with other persons in regard to things. In our example above, where Kevin bought a car, his ownership is manifested not just by his power to drive the car—a thief could do that—but more by his right, through the legal system, to control the use which others may make of it.

(1) **Ownership**

A person who owns a thing in which nobody else has any interests is the absolute owner thereof. Such ownership is the 'greatest possible interest in a thing which a mature

---

[6] For example, the interest of a leaseholder is regarded as personal rather than real, whereas it is immovable rather than movable: *Freke v Lord Carbery* (1873) LR 16 Eq 461; *Duncan v Lawson* (1889) 41 Ch D 394.

[7] *Re Hoyles* [1911] 1 Ch 179, CA. See Cheshire and North, *Private International Law* (12th edn, 1992), pp 779–783.

[8] Bills of exchange, promissory notes, and cheques.

[9] See Eleftheriadis 'The Analysis of Property Rights' (1996) 16 OJLS 31; Chambers 'Proprietary Interests in Commercial Transactions' (1998) 18 OJLS 363.

[10] Gray and Gray, *Elements of Land Law* (5th edn, 2009), p 88.

system of law recognises'.[11] The rights of an owner are best understood in terms of the legal powers which are conferred in relation to the thing. Lawson and Rudden identify three main elements of ownership:

(a) the right to make physical use of a thing;

(b) the right to the income from it, in money, in kind, or in services; and

(c) the power of management, including that of alienation.[12]

By virtue of ownership a person is entitled to do as he wishes with his property. He can possess, use, enjoy, and exploit it as he pleases. He is even free to destroy it. He can give it away, or sell it to a third person. The person who owns property is said to have 'title' to it, a term derived from the fact that he is 'entitled' to it. Of course, that ownership may be constrained by other rules of law, so, for example, a landowner may not lawfully build on his land without applying for planning permission. In many cases the ownership of property will be more complex. For example, there may be multiple owners of the thing, termed co-owners, who enjoy concurrent ownership, or there may be multiple owners with successive interests.

(2) Other rights in property

Although the most important right in property is ownership, there is a large range of other proprietary rights that a person may enjoy over a thing. The complexity of property law follows from the fact that, often, a number of persons may have different, sometimes competing, rights in the same thing. Such subsidiary rights may qualify or limit the absolute entitlement of the owner to do as he chooses with the thing. This multiplicity of proprietary rights in the same thing is most clearly illustrated in the context of land. Assume that Norman is the owner of a piece of house, Blackacre, which he purchased with the help of a Building Society loan secured by a mortgage. He has leased the house to Owen for twenty-five years. He has granted his next-door neighbour, Penelope, the right to walk to her garage across his back garden, and reached an agreement with his other next-door neighbour, Quentin, that he will not use the land for business purposes. In this simple scenario Norman, Owen, Penelope, Quentin, and the Building Society all have different proprietary interests in the same land.[13]

---

[11] Honoré, 'Ownership', in Guest (ed), *Oxford Essays in Jurisprudence* (1961).

[12] Lawson and Rudden, *The Law of Property* (1982), p 8.

[13] The nature of these rights is considered in detail in the relevant land law texts, but the salient features are outlined here. The mortgage to the Building Society gives it ultimately a right to sell the house if the loan is not repaid. Owen as a tenant can claim the exclusive right to the use of the house for the twenty-five-year duration of his lease. Penelope's right of way may be an easement, which is a binding entitlement which Norman, his tenants, and any future owners cannot interfere with. Finally, Quentin and Norman may have entered into a restrictive covenant, which is a right attaching to Quentin's land, controlling the use of Norman's land, as detailed in the agreement.

[handwritten annotations: "over the thing / no names involved → who's" "→ one person"]

(3) **Proprietary and personal rights**

(a) The need to distinguish proprietary and personal rights

While noting that there is a wide range of rights that might be enjoyed in relation to an item of property, it is important to draw a more fundamental distinction between those rights and interests recognized and enforced by the law which are proprietary in nature and those which are personal. The essence of a proprietary interest is that it is a right subsisting in relation to a thing, and not as against a particular individual or small group of individuals. For example, if Kevin owns a car, his ownership is a right which subsists in relation to the car itself. In the event that his car is stolen, and sold by the thief to Michael, his entitlement to that particular car persists. He can demand that it be returned to him. It has remained his throughout, irrespective of the fact that his possession was interrupted.

In contrast, a personal right is a right which is only enforceable against a specific individual.[14] For example, a contract creates a purely personal right enforceable only against the person who made the relevant promise. If Kevin contracted to buy a specific car from a garage, and before the sale was completed the garage sold the car to Michael, Kevin would have no rights in that car itself[15] which he could enforce against Michael. The car would not be his but Michael's and his only right would lie against the garage for breach of contract. Proprietary rights are described as rights in rem,[16] whereas personal rights are rights in personam. *[handwritten: this]*

(b) The defining characteristic of proprietary rights

While it is possible to point to the differing characteristics which attach to a right, depending upon whether it is personal or proprietary, it is much more difficult to identify any conceptual principle which operates to determine whether particular rights or entitlements enjoy proprietary status. To some extent, the characterization of rights as either proprietary or personal has been a process of historical accident. For example, leases, which are in many respects merely contracts by which an owner of land agrees to allow a tenant to occupy and use it, have long been regarded as conferring a proprietary right to the land on the tenant.[17] Similarly, a covenant entered into by the owner of land with a neighbouring land owner whereby he promises to restrict the potential use to which he may put his land is regarded as a species of proprietary right known as a restrictive covenant. Because such covenants enjoy proprietary status, they

---

[14] For a detailed treatment of the law relating to personal property, see Bridge, *Personal Property Law* (3rd edn, 2002).

[15] Unless the contract was specifically enforceable, in which case he would acquire an interest in the property by way of a constructive trust: see Chapter 10. There would be no such constructive trust in the case of a contract to purchase a readily available model of car where there would be alternatives available in the market place.

[16] Meaning 'in the thing', from the Latin word 'res', meaning 'thing'.

[17] Leases have enjoyed a strange relationship as rights of property, and are often referred to as 'chattels real'; a classification following between the boundary of everyday chattels (which are personal property) and real property (which refers to rights in land).

are capable of binding a successor in title to the original covenantor, thus circumventing the doctrine of privity of contract that prevents the enforcement of personal contractual obligations against anyone but the person who originally made the promise. These rights have both made the transition from mere contract into property, but other contractual obligations concerning things have not made this transition. For instance, a person leasing a car or a computer must rely on contract and has no proprietary interest in the car or computer which he is renting.

In this century, the courts have shown a marked reluctance to accord proprietary status to rights traditionally characterized as personal. In *National Provincial Bank Ltd v Ainsworth*[18] a husband had deserted his wife, leaving her living in their former matrimonial home, which he owned. He subsequently mortgaged the house to a bank, realizing its value for himself. The House of Lords held that although the deserted wife enjoyed a right to occupy her husband's house, known as the 'deserted wife's equity', this right was purely personal and not proprietary. Thus, it did not subsist in the house itself but only as against her husband. It was therefore incapable of detracting from the rights of the bank which had taken a mortgage.[19] In the course of his judgment Lord Wilberforce identified the essential characteristics of a property right:

Before a right or an interest can be admitted into the category of property, or of a right affecting property, it must be definable, identifiable by third parties, capable in its nature of assumption by third parties, and have some degree of permanence or stability.[20]

The central characteristic of a proprietary right is therefore that it is *capable* of enduring though changes in the ownership of the property to which it relates.

(c) Examples contrasting personal and proprietary rights

(i) Leases and licences[21]

Although leases and licences are functionally similar, in that they both confer a right to occupy land owned by another, leases are proprietary interests, whereas licences are purely personal.[22] For example, if David owns a house, grants Edward a lease and subsequently sells the house to Fiona, Edward's lease will be capable of enduring through the change of ownership so that it will detract from Fiona's ownership. She will not be entitled to evict Edward and he will still be able to enjoy his rights as tenant

---

[18] [1965] AC 1175.

[19] As an overriding interest under the Land Registration Act 1925, s 70(1)(*g*). See now Land Registration Act 2002, s 29.

[20] [1965] AC 1175 at 1248.

[21] See Jackson, Stevens, and Pearce, *Land Law* (4th edn, 2008) Ch 9; *Street v Mountford* [1985] AC 809; *Bruton London & Quadrant Housing Trust* [2001] 1 AC 406.

[22] See *Ashburn Anstalt v W. J. Arnold & Co* [1989] Ch 1. There is a separate issue relating to the title or right of the landlord to create the lease. In *Bruton London & Quadrant Housing Trust* [2001] 1 AC 406 the House of Lords acknowledged that a lease could be created by a landlord whose own title to the land was derived only from a licence. This decision has been subject to considerable criticism—see further Gray and Gray, *Elements of Land Law* (5th edn, 2009), pp 313–315.

of the land.[23] Subject to any statutory rules, his right is as effective against the land in her hands as it was when David was the owner. However, if instead David had granted Edward a mere licence to occupy the house, he would have had no proprietary interest in the land but a personal right to occupy enforceable only against David. Such a right could not detract from Fiona's ownership rightfully acquired from David. Vis-à-vis Fiona, Edward would be a trespasser, and his only remedy would be an action for damages for breach of contract against David.[24] As has already been noted, the courts have rejected the suggestion that contractual licences should be elevated to the status of proprietary rights.[25]

(ii) Retention of title clauses[26]

When one party enters into a contract for the supply of goods to another, an important question is the time at which the title to the goods passes from the buyer to the seller. Once the title to the goods has passed the seller retains no entitlement to the goods themselves, but has only a personal contractual claim against the buyer for the payment of the price. However, if the contract contains a 'retention of title clause' the seller will retain a proprietary interest in the goods supplied even after they have been delivered, until the price has been paid. Such entitlement will be of particular importance if the buyer becomes insolvent after delivery but before payment. If the property in the goods has passed he will rank only as one of the buyer's creditors, and is likely to receive only a small percentage of the amount owed. However, if he has retained his proprietary interest in the goods he will be able to claim them as his own, and they will not form part of the buyer's assets available for distribution among his general creditors. For example, in *Aluminium Industrie Vaassen BV v Romalpa Aluminium Ltd*[27] the plaintiffs supplied the defendants with aluminium foil, of which the defendants had stock worth £50,000. Under the terms of the contract, title was not to pass to the defendants until they had paid all that was owing to the plaintiffs, and they were required to store the foil in such a way that it could be identified as the plaintiffs' property. It was held that the plaintiffs were entitled to the foil in the defendants' hands. This has been followed in subsequent cases, for example *Hendy Lennox (Industrial Engines) Ltd v Grahame Puttick Ltd*.[28] Here, the plaintiffs sold engines to the defendants with the contract containing a retention of title clause until the full purchase price had been paid. The defendants became insolvent, and owed the plaintiffs some £46,000. They were unlikely to recover anything in an insolvency, as the defendants owed the debenture holders some £700,000. However, they were held entitled to claim one engine remaining on the defendants' premises which had not been appropriated

---

[23] In some instances the lease will not be binding owing to special registration rules of land law, which are beyond the scope of this book. See further, Jackson, Stevens, and Pearce, *Land Law* (2008), Ch 9.
[24] Unless Fiona was bound by a constructive trust: see Chapter 10 and *Ashburn Anstalt v Arnold* [1989] Ch 1. See also *Strand Securities v Caswell* [1965] Ch 958, CA.
[25] *Ashburn Anstalt v Arnold* [1989] Ch 1.
[26] See Worthington, *Proprietary Interests in Commercial Transactions* (1996), pp 7–42.
[27] [1976] 1 WLR 676.   [28] [1984] 1 WLR 485.

to any contract of sub-sale. This proprietary right stands in contrast to the purely personal right to the repayment of the money owed.[29]

(iii) Loans and trusts

Retention of title clauses apply to the delivery of physical goods. Similar principles have also been developed where a loan of money was made. If one person loans money to another, their relationship as creditor and debtor respectively is one of contract only. For example, if a bank lends £10,000 to a company, and the company uses the money to buy a car for its managing director, the bank can have no claim to the car. Instead, it enjoys a purely personal right to repayment of the debt by the company. However, in some circumstances where a loan has been made, it has been held that the lender retains a proprietary interest in the money lent. This is particularly important if the creditor subsequently becomes insolvent. For example, if a bank makes a loan to a company for a specific purpose, such as for the payment of a dividend declared on its shares[30] or the purchase of new machinery,[31] with a stipulation that the money is only to be used for that purpose, the bank retains a proprietary interest in the money lent by way of a resulting trust.[32] If the purpose fails and the company goes into liquidation, the bank will be able to claim the return of the specific money lent. In the absence of such a proprietary right, the money would form part of the general assets of the company to be distributed on insolvency, and the bank would be limited to a personal claim for repayment, ranking as one of the company's general creditors.

(d) Proprietary and personal rights in the context of insolvency[33]

As has been evident in the last two examples, the significance of the distinction between personal and proprietary rights is especially important where the person against whom a right is claimed is insolvent. If it can be shown that the claimant enjoys a proprietary right to some specific asset in the bankrupt's possession, it will not form part of the bankrupt's general assets for distribution among his creditors. As such he will gain priority over all the other creditors, and avoid the basic principle that all unsecured creditors should share their losses pari passu (ie equally). The practical importance of proprietary claims in such cases is well illustrated by the facts of *Chase Manhattan Bank NA v Israel-British Bank (London) Ltd*.[34] Chase Manhattan owed the defendants $1m, which they paid. Unfortunately, due to a clerical error, they paid the same amount again a day later. The Israel-British Bank subsequently became insolvent and Chase Manhattan sought to recover the $1m that

---

[29] See also *Borden (UK) Ltd v Scottish Timber Products Ltd* [1981] Ch 25; *Re Peachdart Ltd* [1984] Ch 131; *Re Andrabell Ltd* [1984] 3 All ER 407; *Clough Mill Ltd v Martin* [1985] 1 WLR 111; *Armour v Thyssen Edelstahlwerke AG* [1991] 2 AC 339, HL; *Re Weddell New Zealand Ltd* (1995) 5 NZBLC 104.555; *Chaigley Farms Ltd v Crawford, Kaye & Grayshire Ltd* [1996] BCC 957; [1997] CLJ 28 (Sealey).

[30] *Barclays Bank plc v Quistclose Investments Ltd* [1970] AC 567, HL.

[31] *Re EVTR Ltd* [1987] BCLC 646.   [32] See Chapter 9.

[33] See Oakley 'Proprietary Claims and their Priority in Insolvency' [1995] CLJ 377.

[34] [1981] Ch 105.

had been overpaid. There was no doubt that Chase Manhattan was entitled to return of the money paid by mistake by way of a claim to restitution. Such a restitutionary claim was personal in nature, imposing an obligation on the payee to return the mistaken payment to the payor. A personal claim would not enable Chase Manhattan to recover the whole of the money paid because Chase Manhattan would have to share any assets with the other creditors in the insolvency. The court held that Chase Manhattan was entitled to assert a proprietary claim to the overpaid $1m which was still held by the insolvent bank by way of a constructive trust, and was thus entitled to the return of the sum mistakenly paid in full. As the $1m did not form part of the insolvent bank's assets, it was not to be divided among their creditors. In this way, Chase Manhattan was able to gain priority over the rights of the other creditors of the Israel-British Bank.

It is by no means clear the court was right to find that Chase Manhattan enjoyed a proprietary right by way of a trust in the money mistakenly paid, but this is an issue that will be examined in the context of the creation of trust interests. For the moment it is sufficient to illustrate the importance of establishing a proprietary right where a person against whom a claim is maintained is insolvent. The automatic priority gained over general creditors where a proprietary right can be asserted has been a major factor motivating plaintiffs to assert, and the courts to recognize, equitable proprietary interests in commercial contexts where previously it might have been thought that no such rights existed.

(e) Proprietary rights in the context of land[35]

English land law comprises a special body of rules concerning the regulation of competing interests in and over land. This special treatment arises, as noted by McFarlane, from special features of permanence, uniqueness, limited availability, social importance, and land's capacity for multiple simultaneous use.[36] Many land rights are created by contract, such as the lease and restrictive covenant explored above, but the contract not only creates obligations enforceable between the original parties, it also creates rights that are attached to or imprinted on the land so that they may endure against third parties as proprietary interests.[37] Not every right over or concerning land is proprietary. Many less formal non-proprietary rights over land are enjoyed in everyday life. These include licences and permissions to cross or occupy land, such as the right for customers to enter a shop, for university students to sit in the library or in teaching rooms on University premises, or for employees to park at work and use their offices at their employer's place of business.

Ownership rights in land law are granted through a system of 'estates' in land, and other rights, termed 'interests in land' are enjoyed on or over these estates by

---

[35] See further Jackson, Stevens, and Pearce, *Land Law* (4th edn, 2008).
[36] *The Structure of Property Law* (2008), pp 7–11.
[37] Whether rights bind third parties is dependent in land law on statutory schemes of registration, and whether such rights are proprietary. See further Jackson, Stevens, and Pearce, *Land Law* (4th edn, 2008), Chs 4–8.

others. Estates in land are the broadest rights and nowadays comprise freehold ownership or leasehold ownership.[38] Freehold ownership is the closest to absolute ownership and for historical reasons is technically known as a 'fee simple absolute in possession'. The freehold estate of a fee simple absolute in possession allows for the normal rights associated with ownership for an unlimited period of time.[39] The leasehold estate, for historical reasons sometimes also known as a 'term of years absolute', confers similar rights for a defined period of time. The parcel of land over which these rights are enjoyed comprises not only the surface of the land but also a right to reasonable use of airspace above the land and into the depths of the earth. The leasehold estate differs from the freehold in that the duration of the ownership has a definite limit, and the bundle of rights given to the leaseholder or lessee is usually smaller than that of the freeholder. This is because the grant of the estate is regulated by the terms of the lease, known as covenants, which control and restrict the use of the land by the lessee and which are themselves proprietary rights and obligations capable of passing with the sale or gift of the lease to another person. This sophistication of ownership rights helps to facilitate the use and occupation of land.[40]

Interests in land, by comparison, are defined, specific rights that one person enjoys in or over the estate of another. They fall into two categories. The first comprises a group of rights which are directly enforceable over or against the land. These include rights of way or rights to light, mortgages, restrictive covenants, and contracts to purchase property in the future. These interests are important features of everyday commerce over land. The second group of interests over land are the sometimes complex arrangements under which the right to enjoy land or the profits from land can be shared between several individuals at the same time (concurrent interests) or by several individuals enjoying the land in turn (successive interests). Concurrent and successive interests may be combined. As a simple example, Fred and Norma may both be concurrent co-owners of an estate in Whiteacre for the duration of their lives, with cousin Gerald entitled on their death. Concurrent and successive interests all require a trust of land to come into existence. This simplifies sales and dealings with the land. Land law also provides a system for dealing with the priority of the multiplicity of sometimes competing rights, but that is beyond the scope of this book.[41]

---

[38] The right to land for life used to be considered an estate but by statute can now only exist as an interest under a trust.

[39] The property will endure after death, provided it is either left to other persons by will or passes to next of kin if the landowner dies intestate. Otherwise, the estate will come to an end and the property will pass to the Crown.

[40] Land law is also concerned with making it easy to buy, sell, and gift land, termed the free alienability of land, which allows the economic value of land to be exploited as part of the wider economy. This is one of the reasons for the systems of land registration, which control how and when interests in land might bind purchasers or people creating interests in land.

[41] The general system of priorities of equitable interests is considered below at p 60.

3 Equitable proprietary rights[42]

Proprietary rights described as 'equitable' are those which were historically recognized and enforced by the Courts of Chancery,[43] or that have been developed by process of extension from such rights. In contrast, legal proprietary rights are those which were historically recognized and enforced by the common law courts. As has been seen, following the Judicature Acts[44] the courts are required to give effect to both legal and equitable proprietary rights, and legal and equitable rights together form a coherent law of property. By far the most important of the proprietary rights developed by equity is the trust, which allows a split in ownership between management and enjoyment that is unique to common law systems.

(1) Equitable proprietary rights corresponding to legal rights

The common law only recognized the creation of proprietary rights if appropriate formalities were satisfied. This generally required the grant of the right using the special formality of a deed.[45] For example, under the Real Property Act 1845, a legal lease would not be created unless made by deed.[46] Today, a legal mortgage must be created by means of a charge by deed.[47] Similarly, a legal easement will only be created by an express or implied grant by deed.[48] However, equity, which looks to the substance rather than the form of transactions, was prepared to recognize and enforce proprietary interests even if the requisite formalities for creation at law had not been observed. Equity regards a mere contract for a lease as creating an equitable lease despite the absence of a deed.[49] Similarly, a contract to create an easement will give rise to an equitable easement[50] and a contract to create a legal mortgage will generate an equitable mortgage if the money advanced is paid to the mortgagor.[51] The difference between the legal and equitable form of these rights affects the quality of the right, not the nature of it. Thus, a legal and equitable mortgage, for example, give the mortgage holder the same rights and obligations. However, while both are proprietary interests capable of binding third parties, the circumstances in which they may bind third parties are different.[52]

---

[42] See (1955) 19 Conv 343 (Crane), cited by Lord Upjohn in *National Provincial Bank Ltd v Ainsworth* [1965] AC 1175, at 1238.

[43] See Chapter 2.   [44] See above, p 19.

[45] This originally required the document to be 'signed, sealed, and delivered'. Because of this, the grant was sometimes said to be made 'under seal'. See now Law of Property (Miscellaneous Provisions) Act 1989, s 1.

[46] See now Law of Property Act 1925, s 2(1). By s 52(2)(d) and s 54(2) there is no need for a deed for the creation of a legal lease for less than three years at the best rent which can reasonably be obtained.

[47] Law of Property Act 1925, s 85(1). Where title to land is registered, it must also be completed by registration to be effective—Land Registration Act 2002, s 27.

[48] A legal easement may also be acquired by statute or prescription.

[49] *Parker v Taswell* (1858) 2 De G & J 559; *Walsh v Lonsdale* (1882) 21 LR Ch D 9.

[50] *McManus v Cooke* (1887) 35 Ch D 681; *May v Belleville* [1905] 2 Ch 605.

[51] *Tebb v Hodge* (1869) LR 5 CP 73.

[52] See below under durability of property rights.

(2) Equitable proprietary rights without a legal equivalent

The creativity of equity also allowed it to develop proprietary interests that were not parasitic equivalents of corresponding common law rights. For example, in law the burden of a covenant affecting the use of freehold land is enforceable only against the original covenantor because of the doctrine of privity of contract.[53] However, following *Tulk v Moxhay*,[54] equity elevated freehold covenants restrictive of the owner's use of his land to the status of proprietary interests, with the consequence that they are capable of passing with the title of the land so as to bind subsequent purchasers.[55] Other contracts concerning rights over land have also been given the status of proprietary interests rather than merely personal rights. An equitable mortgage could be created by the simple deposit of the title deeds to the property with the mortgagee.[56] Similarly, a contract to purchase an interest in land is an equitable proprietary interest known as an 'estate contract', which will be binding against subsequent purchasers of the land, subject to any legislative requirements of registration.[57]

(3) Equitable ownership

Alongside equitable proprietary interests such as leases, mortgages, and restrictive covenants, equity spawned a general right of ownership of property through the development of the trust. Where property is subject to a trust, equity treats the persons for whose benefit the trust exists as the owners of the property, even though they are not the owners of it at law. Where property is subject to a trust, there is a duality of ownership, or 'double dominium', and a distinction must be drawn between the legal ownership and the equitable ownership. This capacity for dual ownership at law and in equity is the most distinctive feature of English property law. It emerged as a product of the historical divide between equity and the common law. Duality of ownership of property is the essential characteristic of a trust. A person enjoying the legal ownership of the trust property is referred to as a 'trustee', and a person enjoying the equitable ownership is a 'beneficiary'. The majority of this book will be devoted to an examination of the modern trust, and in particular to the means by which such a relationship can be brought into existence and the nature of the rights and duties of trustees and beneficiaries.

The remainder of this sub-section will consider the genesis of the trust in the Chancery courts, as well as the importance of splitting beneficial and legal ownership.

---

[53] *Austerberry v Oldham Corpn* (1885) 29 Ch D 750, CA; *Rhone v Stephens* [1994] 2 AC 310.

[54] (1848) 2 Ph 774.

[55] For some reason, English law has failed to recognize restrictions on the use of land as capable of existing as easements, the nearest equivalent right recognized by the common law.

[56] *Russel v Russel* (1783) 1 Bro CC 269. Following the Law of Property (Miscellaneous Provisions) Act 1989, the contract supporting this equitable mortgage must be made in writing.

[57] See *Midland Bank Trust Co Ltd (No 1) v Green* [1981] AC 513, HL.

Figure 3.1 Separation of ownership

(a) The importance of separation of ownership

What is important about separating the rights to property into legal and equitable ownership (strictly legal title and equitable ownership) is that it enables the powers of management to be split from the beneficial enjoyment (see Figure 3.1). In addition, it allows much greater complexity in the division of beneficial enjoyment. The relationship between the legal owner and the equitable owner does, of course, have to be regulated, and equity does this through the trust.

(b) History of the trust[58]

(i) The feudal system of land holding[59]

An understanding of the origins of the trust requires an elementary grasp of the feudal system of landowning operative during the medieval period. All land was technically owned by the King, while others enjoyed the right to use it as tenants. Individuals were granted 'tenure' of land by their 'over-lord', who would himself enjoy tenure from his 'over-lord'. These levels of tenure formed a feudal pyramid of landholdings stretching from the King (who was at its pinnacle because he had no 'over-lord') downwards. The terms of 'tenure' defined the conditions under which the tenant was entitled to enjoy the land, generally requiring the performance of services on behalf of his lord. These might include the provision of military forces,[60] religious functions,[61] or agricultural services.[62] On the death of a tenant, the person who succeeded to his tenure and thereby inherited his position on the feudal ladder was required to make a payment to his over-lord. These medieval inheritance taxes, termed 'feudal incidents', provided the Crown with a significant source of revenue. While the doctrine of tenure defined the terms under which land was held, the parallel doctrine of 'estates' determined the

---

[58] See Holdsworth, *History of English Law* (7th edn, 1956), pp 407–480; Baker, *Introduction to English Legal History* (2nd edn, 1979), pp 210–219 and 242–244. See also (1998) 61 MLR 162 (Pottage).

[59] See Gray and Gray, *Elements of Land Law* (5th edn, 2009), pp 64–68.

[60] Eg the tenure of 'Knight's service', which required the provision of armed horsemen for battle.

[61] 'Spiritual tenure'.   [62] Tenures in socage.

duration for which a grant of tenure was to last.[63] An estate in fee simple[64] was a grant of tenure for ever, and within the feudal structure the right to tenure of land in fee simple was tantamount to absolute ownership.

(ii) Development of the 'use'

In the context of this feudal structure, the 'use', the ancestor of the modern trust, was developed by the Chancery courts. If land was conveyed to X 'to the use of Y' this had the effect that, while X became the owner of the land, X was obliged to apply it for the benefit of Y and was prevented from treating it as his own. X was termed the 'feoffee' and Y the 'cestui que use'. The common law did not recognize, and would not enforce, a 'use' of land, but rather regarded the feoffee, in whom the legal estate was vested, as the absolute owner. From the perspective of equity, however, the feoffee was bound in conscience to apply the property for the benefit of the cestui que use, because of the undertaking he had given. The Court of Chancery was therefore prepared to enforce the use in personam, requiring the feoffee to apply the property vested in him to the benefit of the cestui que use. Equity did not deny the reality of the ownership of the feoffee at common law, but instead prevented him from exercising the entitlements concomitant with his legal ownership in a manner inconsistent with the interests of the cestui que use. Thus, the use shared a central characteristic of the modern trust, namely that the formal ownership of the property subject to it was separated from the right to enjoy the benefit derived from such ownership (see Figure 3.2). The use evolved as a popular mechanism for landholding because of the positive advantages it offered. It provided a means of making gifts to charities that were technically unable to own property. For example, the monastic order of St Francis was forbidden to own property by its rule, but land could be given to feoffees for its use. Though technically it would not 'own' the property, it would be entitled to derive the benefits flowing from such ownership. A landowner could avoid the strict legal rules of inheritance by directing feoffees in his will to hold the land as he wished. The use also offered a mechanism for primitive tax-planning through the avoidance of feudal dues. If land was vested in a group of feoffees, who would never die as a group because each individual feoffee would be replaced on death, the legal title would never have to be passed by way of succession. The feudal incidents payable on inheritance would thus be avoided altogether.

(iii) The development of the trust

The financial advantages attendant upon a use were so attractive to landowners that by 1500 the majority of land in England was held in use.[65] This inevitably led to a

[63] See *Walsingham's Case* (1579) 2 Plowd 547 at 555: 'the land itself is one thing, and an estate in the land is another thing, for an estate in the land is a time in the land, or land for a time, and there are diversities of estates, which are no more than diversities of time...'

[64] To be distinguished from a 'fee tail' (or 'entailed interest'), which was only to last for so long as the grantee had lineal descendants, and the life interest, which was only to last for the length of the grantee's life.

[65] YB Mich 15 Hen VII, 13, p 1, per Frowyk Sjt.

Figure 3.2 Separation of ownership and the use

serious diminution in the King's feudal revenue. In order to close this tax-avoidance loophole, legislation (the Statute of Uses 1535) was introduced to abolish uses by 'executing' them, ie vesting the legal estate in the cestui que use. However, it did not take the ingenuity of lawyers long to find ways around the Statute of Uses and, indeed, to turn it to their advantage. The statute did not apply to uses where the feoffee had active duties to perform, for example the collection and distribution of profits and the management of an estate.[66] A further means to avoiding 'execution' of a use under the statute was to create a double use, termed a 'use upon a use', whereby the legal estate in land would be conveyed 'to X, to the use of Y, to the use of Z'. Although the first use would be executed by the Statute of Uses, so that Y would be treated as the legal owner, the second use remained unexecuted. The Court of Chancery would then enforce the second use, requiring Y to hold the land for the benefit of Z. This second use was termed a 'trust', providing the modern terminology.[67] The 'use upon a use' was accepted as valid by the latter part of the sixteenth century,[68] by which time it had come to serve different social functions than the mere avoidance of feudal dues. Common objectives were to protect estates from spendthrift sons, and to enable married women to enjoy property independently of their husbands. The effect of the trust to avoid the execution of uses was so successful that in 1739 Lord Hardwicke was able to observe that the Statute of Uses 'has had no other effect than to add at most, three words to a conveyance'.[69] Although the trust had emerged as a recognized legal instrument by the end of the sixteenth century, it flourished in the nineteenth century, when it served as the foundation for property holding by families and as a device to preserve family estates.

---

[66] A use of leasehold land, a term of years, was also not executed.
[67] In fact, the term was also used for a single 'use' prior to the development of the 'use upon a use'.
[68] See (1966) 82 LQR 215 (Barton); (1977) 93 LQR 33 (Baker).
[69] *Hopkins v Hopkins* (1739) 1 Atk 581.

Figure 3.3 Separation of ownership and the trust

(c) The modern trust

The cardinal features of a modern trust are very much the same as those of the early use from which it has developed. Under a trust, the legal and equitable ownership of the trust property are separated and held by different persons.[70] A trust arises where property is conveyed to or vested in the trustee by a settlor in such circumstances that equity will compel the trustee to administer the property for the benefit of the beneficiary.

(i) Separation of title under a trust

The legal title is vested in the trustee, who must apply the property for the benefit of someone else, the cestui que trust, more commonly termed the 'beneficiary', who is regarded as the equitable owner (see Figure 3.3). It follows from this separation of the legal and equitable ownership of the trust property that there is also a separation between the management responsibilities arising in connection with the property and the enjoyment thereof.

(ii) Trustee as legal owner

The trustee looks like the outright owner of the property. He has legal title vested in him, and as legal owner, the trustee controls the property.[71] He is usually entitled to decide whether it should be retained or sold, and how it should be invested. In some types of trust the trustee even has the right to determine how the property should be distributed among a class of defined beneficiaries. However, he is compelled by equity to exercise this control over the property strictly for the benefit of the beneficiaries.

---

[70] *Selby v Alston* (1797) 3 Ves 339.

[71] It is possible that the trustee may have an equitable title only, which occurs where the property settled on the trust is equitable (technically, this is usually referred to as a sub-trust). In this case, the key points about control and separation of the benefit are exactly the same as where a trustee has legal title.

Thus, he must not exercise his rights to deal with the trust property for his own personal advantage, and equity will prevent him applying the trust property inconsistently with the terms of the trust, which define the entitlement of the beneficiary or beneficiaries. Similarly, he must consider the interests of all the beneficiaries collectively, and not favour any one of them, sometimes referred to as his duty to consider the trust as a whole. This is particularly important where persons are entitled to the beneficial interest in succession, so that someone entitled for life does not get all the benefits of ownership to the exclusion of those beneficiaries entitled after the death of the currently entitled beneficiary.

(iii) Beneficiary as equitable owner

The beneficiary has equitable ownership of the property, which identifies him as being entitled to the benefits of the property held under the trust.[72] The fact that the beneficiary has equitable ownership of the trust property differentiates the trust from a contract for the benefit of a third party. The beneficiary, as a property holder, has additional rights against other parties in addition to those against the trustee. The beneficiary's rights can be enforced not only against the trustee, but also against any new trustees (as the trust property will be vested in them) or against third parties who receive the trust property in breach of trust. A beneficiary does not have control of the property, so although the beneficiary has rights against the trustee to make sure he performs his duties throughout the duration of the trust, he does not have the right to instruct the trustee in performing those duties.

(iv) Impact of the trust

This capacity of the trust to separate the management of property from its enjoyment renders it a perfect vehicle to facilitate complex arrangements involving property, as will be seen in the following chapters. Its tremendous flexibility has enabled it to adapt through the centuries and into new social and commercial contexts. Maitland was of the opinion that the trust was 'the greatest and most distinctive achievement performed by Englishmen in the field of jurisprudence'.

(4) Mere equities

Equity further recognizes a category of entitlements described as 'equities' or 'mere equities'. This terminology is intended to distinguish them from complete equitable proprietary interests. They have been held to include the right to have a transaction set aside for fraud[73] or undue influence,[74] the right to have a document rectified,[75] and the

---

[72] It is possible for a person to be both trustee and one of the beneficiaries of the same property, in which case the person is compelled by equity to control the property for the benefit of all those sharing the beneficial ownership.

[73] *Ernest v Vivian* (1863) 33 LJ Ch 513.

[74] *Bainbrigge v Browne* (1881) 18 Ch D 188; *Barclays Bank v O'Brien* [1994] 1 AC 180.

[75] *Shiloh Spinners Ltd v Harding (No 1)* [1973] AC 691 at 721, per Lord Wilberforce.

deserted wife's right to occupy the matrimonial home.[76] When mere equities relate to property, they have a limited capacity to affect third parties who acquire ownership of it, but they are not true interests in the property itself.

4 The durability of proprietary rights[77]

As has been noted above, one of the defining characteristics of a proprietary right is that it is capable of enduring through changes in the ownership the thing to which it relates. However, the durability of a specific proprietary right will depend upon its character. Different rules developed in equity and the common law to govern the durability of their respective proprietary rights. In general, legal rights are more durable than their equitable equivalents. A statutory scheme has been introduced which determines issues of priority between legal and equitable rights and interests in land, the details of which are beyond the scope of this text,[78] but the traditional rules developed by equity and the common law remain operative in relation to personal property.

(1) Legal ownership

Of all types of ownership, legal ownership is the most durable, subject to a few exceptions at common law and to rather more which have been introduced by statute. The basic rule is that the ownership or rights of a legal owner will continue indefinitely until the owner has transferred them to someone else. Where two people claim legal rights to the same thing, the better rights are those of the person with the earlier claim. So, for instance, if Alf steals a car belonging to Mary and sells it to Peter, neither Alf nor Peter become the owner of the car. It continues to belong to Mary. If Peter still has the car in his hands, Mary can demand that it be returned to her, vindicating her continuing legal ownership. Only if the car is destroyed will Mary's legal ownership be terminated, as there will no longer be any subject matter in which the right can continue to subsist.

There are some other situations in which a legal owner can lose legal ownership against his will. For instance, a special rule which applies to currency (coins of the realm and banknotes) is that even a thief can pass ownership in them to someone who takes them in good faith and for value. Another special rule which applies to land is that a legal owner's right can be defeated by a person who takes physical possession without permission for a sufficient period of time. After twelve years of such 'adverse

---

[76] *National Provincial Bank Ltd v Ainsworth* [1965] AC 1175.

[77] For personal property, see Worthington, *Personal Property Law* (2000), pp 457–473. In relation to real property, see Jackson, Stevens, and Pearce, *Land Law* (4th edn, 2008).

[78] An overview of these systems is provided in the context of equitable rights in the family home, as the durability of these rights in land law is important to an understanding of equitable intervention in this area—see Chapter 11.

possession' the owner's rights are extinguished by the Limitation Act 1980, s 15, which provides that he may no longer bring an action to vindicate his rights. In effect, this allows a squatter to steal land from an owner who has failed to take steps to protect his rights. This is a special rule which applies only to unregistered land.[79] In relation to a chattel, legal ownership will only be displaced by a third party taking possession if the owner had previously abandoned it.[80] When a chattel has been lost, a finder will not acquire a right to it superior to that of the legal owner.[81]

In relation to some forms of property, such as land or shares, legal ownership is determined by means of a register. In such cases the statutory rule is that the person registered is the owner, even where that registration has wrongly been obtained. For instance, if a thief forges a transfer of land into his own name, and has himself registered, then he becomes the owner, even though the person he has swindled has the right to have the error in the register rectified. Until that rectification, by virtue of the statutory rule, the person registered is deemed to be the legal owner.

Apart from those situations where a special rule applies, the rule relating to legal ownership is therefore that 'legal rights bind the world'. In consequence, where two people can assert a claim with a lawful origin, 'the first in time prevails'.

(2) Subsidiary legal proprietary rights

Although ownership is the most significant legal proprietary interest, it has been seen that other subsidiary proprietary interests can exist with legal status. For example, if Peter, the legal owner of land, grants Lorna a legal lease, her lease will obviously bind Peter and detract from his right to enjoy the immediate possession and enjoyment of his land. If Peter sells the land to Brendan, so that Brendan becomes the legal owner, the principle that 'legal rights bind the world' ensures that Lorna's lease will equally bind Brendan. The mere fact that Brendan acquired legal title to the land from Peter is incapable of defeating Lorna's lease. Peter's rights are the first in time, but he has transferred them in part to Lorna. The sale to Brendan is subject to Lorna's rights because her rights were created before he acquired his. As between Lorna and Brendan, Lorna's rights are the first in time, and therefore prevail over Brendan's.

This simple rule that legal rights bind the world was abandoned in the context of rights and interests in land when a system of registration was introduced in 1925, now governed by the Land Registration Act 2002. In many cases, the system of registration has the effect that subsidiary proprietary rights, such as long leases and mortgages, can only be validly created with legal status if they are entered on the register of title of the

---

[79] The law of adverse possession has been fundamentally altered in relation to land to which title is registered under the Land Registration Act 2002. The registered title owner's interest is no longer extinguished and the claimant must seek registration of his adverse possession claim. The net effect of these changes is to make it more difficult for an adverse possession claim to succeed. See further Jackson, Stevens, and Pearce, *Land Law* (4th edn, 2008), pp 158–173.

[80] *The Crystal* [1894] AC 508.   [81] *Parker v British Airways Board* [1982] QB 1004.

land they affect. If not so registered they take effect in equity only. Those rights which can be created at law without the need for registration, for example leases for a period of less than seven years and easements, tend to be binding on any subsequent transferee of the land because they are accorded the status of overriding interests under the Land Registration Act 2002, s 29(2)(a)(ii). As such, their durability is statutory rather in consequence of their intrinsic legal character.

(3) Equitable proprietary rights[82]

(a) Priority between equitable interests

Equity followed the law when it was dealing with the relative status of claims based in equity. It therefore accepted the principle that competing claims should be judged on the footing that where they all had a lawful origin 'the first in time prevails'. For instance, suppose that before the rules were changed by the introduction of registration systems, Oliver, the owner of a freehold cottage, had contracted to sell it both to Anthony and to Declan, and they each sought an order for specific performance. The court would have granted the decree in favour of the first of them to have signed a binding contract with Oliver. The other would have to make do with a remedy in damages against Oliver.

(b) The doctrine of notice

When it came to dealing with the relative status of rights, some of which were legal and some equitable, equity again adopted the root philosophy that they should be judged in accordance with the time order of their creation. However, this philosophy is applied with one very important qualification. A pre-existing equitable interest will not subsist in property which is acquired by a bona fide purchaser of a legal interest who was not aware at the time of its acquisition of the earlier equitable interest. This principle is known as the 'doctrine of notice'. To pursue the example used above, if Peter had granted Lorna an equitable rather than a legal lease, and subsequently sold the legal title of his land to Brendan, Lorna's equitable lease would not have been binding against the land in Brendan's hands if he had not known of its existence when he purchased the legal title. An equitable interest which is so defeated by the operation of the doctrine of notice is extinguished and no longer exists.

The operation of the doctrine of notice to destroy equitable proprietary interests is rooted in concepts of good conscience, which lies at the heart of the equitable jurisdiction. In the view of equity, a person who was aware of a pre-existing interest subsisting in property cannot acquire it free from such interest. He has no grounds for complaint when equity requires him to continue to give effect to it because he knew what he was getting. Only if he purchased the property without knowing of its existence is his

---

[82] *London and South Western Rly Co v Gomm* (1882) 20 Ch D 562; *Re Nisbet and Potts' Contract* [1906] 1 Ch 386.

conscience unaffected so as to justify the conclusion that he should not be bound by it. As Lord Browne-Wilkinson explained in *Barclays Bank plc v O'Brien*:[83]

> The doctrine of notice lies at the heart of equity. Given that there are two innocent parties, each enjoying rights, the earlier right prevails against the later right if the acquirer of the later right knows of the earlier right (actual notice) or would have discovered it had he taken proper steps (constructive notice). In particular, if the party asserting that he takes free of the earlier rights of another knows of certain facts which put him on enquiry as to the possible existence of the rights of that other and he fails to make such enquiry or take such other steps as are reasonable to verify whether such earlier right does or does not exist, he will have constructive notice of the earlier right and take subject to it.

(c) Requirements of the equitable doctrine of notice

The equitable doctrine of notice only operates in favour of a person who can demonstrate that he was the bona fide purchaser of the legal ownership of the property for value without notice. Because a purchaser who meets this test takes free of any equitable interests in the property acquired, such a person is also referred to as 'equity's darling'. Each component element of this formula must be satisfied.

(i) Bona fides

The doctrine of notice only operates in favour of a person who acted in good faith. However, this requirement adds little to the element that he must not have notice of the equitable interests in the property.

(ii) Purchase for value

The doctrine of notice will only operate in favour of a person who purchased the property in which there was a pre-existing equitable interest for valuable consideration. The concept of consideration in equity is different to that at common law. In equity, nominal consideration, which would be sufficient to establish an enforceable contractual obligation at common law,[84] is insufficient. It follows from this requirement of valuable consideration that the doctrine of notice will never operate in favour of a volunteer. Thus, a person who receives property by way of gift or succession will always acquire the legal ownership subject to any pre-existing equitable interests.

(iii) Of the legal title

The doctrine of notice only protects a purchaser of the legal title to the property. In the case of land, the purchase must be of a legal estate or interest.[85] A person who purchases an equitable interest in property will therefore take subject to all other

---

[83] [1994] 1 AC 180.

[84] For example, a peppercorn. However, there is no need for the consideration to be 'adequate', as equity only insists that the consideration be valuable. Marriage consideration is also regarded as valuable consideration in equity.

[85] Under the Law of Property Act 1925, s 1 this means a fee simple absolute in possession (freehold) or a terms of years absolute (leasehold) or one of the subsidiary legal interests listed in the section.

pre-existing equitable interests, since between competing equitable entitlements 'the first in time prevails'.

(iv) Without notice[86]

This is the most important of the requirements. It concerns the extent to which the purchaser was aware or ignorant of the existence of any pre-existing equitable interests subsisting in the property acquired. Clearly, he will have 'notice' of such interests if he consciously knew of their existence, for example if the seller had informed him. Such awareness is termed 'actual notice'. However, the concept of notice has been given a wider ambit in equity, so that a person is treated as if he was actually aware of all pre-existing equitable interests that he would have discovered if he had taken all reasonable steps to investigate the property concerned by making 'such inquiries and inspections ... as ought reasonably to have been made'.[87] This prevents a person claiming the benefit of the doctrine of notice simply by seeking to avoid receiving actual notice of such rights. Such deemed notice is termed 'constructive notice'. A person will also be treated as having notice if the purchase was conducted by an agent acting on his behalf if the agent had actual or constructive notice of the existence of the equitable interest. Such notice is termed 'imputed notice'.

(d) Destruction of equitable proprietary interests by the doctrine of notice

Where all the requisite elements of the doctrine of notice are satisfied, it operates so as to completely destroy any subsisting equitable interests in the property concerned. Even if the property is subsequently transferred to a person with notice of the relevant interest, it will not revive. This can be seen from the facts of *Wilkes v Spooner*.[88] Spooner was the tenant of a pork butcher's shop. Wilkes was the beneficiary of an equitable restrictive covenant, affecting the shop, preventing its use as a general butcher's. Spooner surrendered his lease of the shop to the landlord.[89] As the landlord was unaware of the restrictive covenant, he was protected by the doctrine of notice, with the consequence that his legal ownership was not encumbered by it. Subsequently, the landlord granted a new lease of the shop to Spooner's son, who had actual notice of the restriction. Since the doctrine of notice had operated so as to destroy the right altogether, he too acquired the shop free from the restriction.

(4) Trusts and the doctrine of notice

It has been noted above that when property is subject to a trust the beneficiaries enjoy the equitable ownership thereof. As proprietary rights with equitable character,

to go back
to p.53
here.

---

[86]   See Law of Property Act 1925, s 199.

[87]   Law of Property Act 1925, s 199(1)(ii)(*a*). See *Jones v Smith* (1841) 1 Hare 43; *Northern Bank Ltd v Henry* [1981] IR 1.

[88]   [1911] 2 KB 473.

[89]   The surrender of the lease satisfied the requirement that the landlord be a purchaser of a legal estate for value.

such beneficial interests arising under a trust are equally subject to the operation of the doctrine of notice. If the trustee transfers the trust property to a bona fide purchaser who was unaware that it was subject to a trust, that person will acquire his legal title free from the entitlements of the beneficiaries. He will be the absolute and unencumbered legal owner of the property. The beneficiaries will be entitled to a personal remedy for breach of trust against the trustee if the trust property was wrongfully transferred, but they will have no continuing proprietary entitlements in the erstwhile trust property.

(a) Trusts of personal property

Where personal property is subject to a trust, the doctrine of notice operates, so that a bona fide purchase of the trust property will entirely destroy the proprietary interest of the beneficiaries. For example, if Robert holds shares on trust and sells and transfers them to Kevin, the equitable entitlement of the beneficiaries will be destroyed if Kevin had no knowledge, actual or constructive, that Robert was holding the shares as a trustee. The extension of the principles of constructive notice to commercial transactions involving personal property rather than land has sometimes been questioned. In *Manchester Trust v Furness* Lindley LJ stated:

The equitable doctrines of constructive notice are common enough in dealing with land and estates with which the Court is familiar; but there has always been repeated protest against the introduction into commercial transactions of anything like an extension of those doctrines and the protest is founded on perfect good sense. In dealing with estates in land title is everything and it can be leisurely investigated; in commercial transactions possession is everything and there is no time to investigate title; and if we were to extend the doctrine of constructive notice to commercial transactions we should be doing infinite mischief and paralyzing the trade of the country.[90]

However, the better view seems to be that the principle of constructive notice operates even where a commercial purchaser acquired legal title to personal property. In *Macmillan Inc v Bishopsgate Investment Trust plc*[91] shares were held on trust for Macmillan by Bishopsgate Investment Trust (BIT), an investment trust controlled by Robert Maxwell. In breach of trust, and without the consent or knowledge of Macmillan, BIT transferred legal title to the trust shares to various banks and financial institutions as security for the debts of other Maxwell companies. Millett J held that, if English law applied,[92] the transferees of these shares would only have acquired them free from the equitable interests of Macmillan if they had no constructive notice that they were trust shares:

It is true that many distinguished judges in the past have warned against the extension of the equitable doctrine of constructive notice to commercial transactions...but they were obviously referring to the doctrine in its strict conveyancing sense with its many refinements and its

---

[90] [1895] 2 QB 539 at 545.   [91] [1995] 3 All ER 747.

[92] In the event, he concluded that the priority of proprietary rights to the shares was to be determined by the law of New York. See: Stevens 'Restitution or Property? Priority and Title to Shares in the Conflict of Laws' (1996) 59 MLR 741.

Figure 3.4 The doctrine of notice: *Pilcher v Rawlins*

insistence on a proper investigation of title in every case. The relevance of constructive notice in its wider meaning cannot depend on whether the transaction is 'commercial': the provision of secured overdraft facilities to a corporate managing director is equally 'commercial' whether the security consists of the managing director's house or his private investments. The difference is that in one case there is, and in the other there is not, a recognized procedure for investigating the mortgagor's title which the creditor ignores at his peril.[93]

While this affirms the relevance of constructive notice to transactions involving personal property, it makes clear that the level of inquiry and investigation reasonably to be expected from a purchaser varies in relation to the nature and context of the transaction in issue. Where there is no recognized procedure for investigation into the title of the type of property offered for sale, a bona fide purchaser will satisfy the requirements of the doctrine of notice unless he had actual knowledge of the existence of the trust, was suspicious that the seller did not have the right to transfer, or had reason to know or be suspicious. If there is a recognized procedure, the purchaser will not be protected by the doctrine of notice if he has failed to follow it.

(b) Trusts of land

(i) Priority determined by the doctrine of notice

Historically, issues of priority between competing interests in land were also governed by application of the twin principle that the first in time prevailed, subject to the equitable doctrine of notice. A bona fide purchaser for value without notice of a legal estate in land would take free from any pre-existing equitable interests. For example, in *Pilcher v Rawlins*[94] trustees held £8,373 on trust for Jeremiah Pilcher, which they

---

[93] Ibid. 769.   [94] (1871–72) LR 7 Ch App 259.

Figure 3.5 The doctrine of notice: *Kingsnorth Trust v Tizard*

lent to Rawlins by way of a mortgage (see Figure 3.4). The mortgage was secured by the transfer of the legal title to the mortgaged land to the trustees. The trustees subsequently re-conveyed the legal title to Rawlins to enable him to fraudulently borrow a further £10,000 by granting a mortgage to Stockwell and Lambe. Jeremiah Pilcher, as beneficiary of the trust, claimed that Stockwell and Lambe were bound to observe the trust. However, the Court of Appeal held that they were bona fide purchasers without notice of the existence of the trust. They had therefore acquired their legal mortgage free from his equitable interest. James LJ explained:

I propose simply to apply myself to the case of a purchaser for valuable consideration, without notice, obtaining, upon the occasion of his purchase, and by means of his purchase deed, some legal estate, some legal right, some legal advantage; and according to my view of the established law of this court, such a purchaser's plea of a purchase for valuable consideration without notice is an absolute, unqualified, unanswerable defence, and an unanswerable plea to the jurisdiction of this court.

In contrast, a purchaser with notice, whether actual or constructive, will be required to yield priority to a beneficiary of a pre-existing trust. In *Kingsnorth Trust v Tizard* (see Figure 3.5)[95] a husband held the legal title to his matrimonial home on trust for himself and his wife (see Figure 3.5). After they separated she no longer lived at the house, although she visited for part of each day. He mortgaged the house and absconded with the money raised. Prior to accepting a mortgage, the mortgage company had sent a surveyor to inspect the house. He visited on a Sunday afternoon, a time arranged by the husband when he knew that his wife would not be present. He

---

[95] [1986] 1 WLR 783; Thompson 'The Purchaser as Private Detective' [1986] Conv 283.

told the surveyor that he and his wife had separated many months before and that she had no interest in the property. The court held that in these circumstances the mortgage company was bound by the wife's equitable interest under the trust. It had not made all the inquiries that were reasonably required from a potential mortgagee, and it was therefore affixed with constructive notice. Judge John Finlay, QC concluded that the inspection had been inadequate:

What is such an inspection 'as ought reasonably to be made' must, I think, depend on all the circumstances. In the circumstances of the present case I am not satisfied that the pre-arranged inspection on a Sunday afternoon fell within the category of 'such inspections which ought reasonably to have been made', the words in s 199 of the Law of Property Act 1925 ... [96]

(ii) Priority determined by statute

Statutory reform, starting in 1925 and culminating in the Land Registration Act 2002, has largely displaced the doctrine of notice as a means of determining whether a purchaser of land acquires his legal title free from pre-existing equitable trust interests. The Law of Property Act 1925 provides that where land is held on trust the interests of the beneficiaries are automatically eliminated if it is transferred to a purchaser who pays any purchase moneys arising to two or more trustees holding the legal title. This process is called 'overreaching', and it operates irrespective of whether the purchaser had knowledge, actual or constructive, of the existence of the trust. When overreaching occurs, the beneficiaries' equitable interests are not eliminated altogether, but they are displaced from the land and continue to subsist as rights in rem only in the purchase moneys paid to the trustees. Where overreaching occurs, a purchaser of land need not be concerned by the possible existence of any trusts affecting the land he acquires. He can be sure that, provided any purchase money arising from the transaction is paid to two trustees, no pre-existing trust interests will endure in the land to affect his legal ownership.

The operation and effect of overreaching were considered in *City of London Building Society v Flegg* (see Figure 3.6).[97] A house had been purchased in the name of Mr and Mrs Maxwell-Brown with the financial help of Mrs Maxwell-Brown's parents, Mr and Mrs Flegg. Mr and Mrs Maxwell-Brown therefore held the house on trust for themselves and Mr and Mrs Flegg. The Maxwell-Browns subsequently mortgaged the house to the building society without the Fleggs' consent or knowledge. The House of Lords held that since Mr and Mrs Maxwell-Brown were trustees for sale, and since the mortgage company had advanced the money borrowed to them, the Fleggs' equitable interest had been overreached.

Where trust interests in land are not overreached by a transfer of the legal title, for example if the land was owned by a sole trustee so that the qualifying condition of payment to two or more trustees was not satisfied,[98] the question whether

---

[96] [1986] 1 WLR 783, at 795.

[97] [1988] AC 54.

[98] See *Williams & Glyn's Bank Ltd v Boland* [1981] AC 487, HL; *Kingsnorth Trust v Tizard* [1986] 1 WLR 783.

Figure 3.6 Overreaching: *City of London Building Society v Flegg*

the trust subsists in the land in the hands of the transferee is determined by the relevant rules under the provisions of the Land Registration Act 2002.[99] If title to the land is already registered, and a registered disposition takes place, for example where the land is sold, a lease for more than seven years is granted, or the land is mortgaged, the beneficial interest will enjoy priority if it is an overriding interest.[100] The trust interest will only be overriding if the beneficiary was in actual occupation of the land at the date of the disposition, and either the occupation would have been obvious from a reasonably careful inspection of the land or the person to whom the disposition was made had actual notice of it.[101] The interest will cease to be over-riding if the purchaser had made enquiry of the beneficiary before the disposition took place, and the beneficiary had failed to disclose his beneficial interest when he could reasonably have been expected to do so. If the land is unregistered at the time of a disposition, and has to be registered for the first time, other special rules are applicable.[102] In this increasingly less common situation a trust interest affecting the land will bind the first registered proprietor as an overriding interest if the beneficiary was in actual occupation of the land.[103]

[99] See Jackson, Stevens, and Pearce, *Land Law* (4th edn 2008), Ch 7.
[100] Land Registration Act 2002, s 29(2)(a)(ii).
[101] Land Registration Act 2002, Sch 3, para 2.
[102] Ibid., s 11(4)(b) and s 12(4)(c).
[103] Ibid., Sch 1, para 2.

(5) **Mere equities**

Whereas it has been seen that equitable interests are only destroyed if the legal title to the property in which they subsist is acquired by a bona fide purchaser for value without notice, mere equities relating to property are incapable of binding a person who purchases an interest in it, whether legal or equitable, irrespective of whether they have notice. As Lord Upjohn stated in *National Provincial Bank Ltd v Ainsworth*:

I myself cannot see how it is possible for a 'mere equity' to bind a purchaser unless such an equity is ancillary to or dependent upon an equitable estate or interest in the land...a 'mere equity' naked and alone is, in my opinion, incapable of binding successors in title even with notice; it is personal to the parties.[104]

---

[104] [1965] AC 1175 at 1238.

4

Equitable obligations: trusts and powers

The previous chapters have charted the importance and genesis of the trust, in particular in relation to English property law. This chapter will examine the fundamental characteristics of the modern trust, and draw comparisons between it and other equitable obligations relating to property.

1 Fundamental characteristics of trusts[1]

(1) The hybrid nature of trusts

It is difficult to categorize the essential nature of a trust. As a legal concept a trust does not fit neatly into either the category of 'obligations' or of 'proprietary rights'. Rather, the trust shares some characteristics of obligations and some characteristics of proprietary rights. In this sense it is a hybrid, and can best be regarded as a sui generis 'proprietary obligation'. Despite difficulties of classification, three essential characteristics of trusts can be identified. First, a trust can only exist in relation to specific property. Second, this property must be held by trustees, who are subject to mandatory obligations governing how it should be used and applied. Third, the trustees must owe these mandatory obligations to legal persons who are entitled to enforce them. These persons are termed the beneficiaries of the trust, and they are entitled to the trust property in equity. These three elements all appear in the definition of a 'trust' in art 2 of the Hague Convention on the Law Applicable to Trusts and on their Recognition, incorporated into English law by the Recognition of Trusts Act 1987:

For the purposes of this Convention, the term 'trust' refers to the legal relationship created—inter vivos or on death—by a person, the settlor, when assets have been placed under the control of a trustee for the benefit of a beneficiary or for a specified purpose.

---

[1] See Bartlett 'When is a "Trust" Not a Trust? The National Health Service Trust' [1996] Conv 186; Hayton 'Developing the Obligation Characteristics of the Trust' (2001) 117 LQR 96; Parkinson 'Reconceptualising the Express Trust' [2002] 61 CLJ 657.

A trust has the following characteristics—

(a) the assets constitute a separate fund and are not part of the trustee's own estate;

(b) title to the trust assets stands in the name of the trustee or in the name of another person on behalf of the trustee;

(c) the trustee has the power and the duty, in respect of which he is accountable, to manage, employ or dispose of the assets in accordance with the terms of the trust and the special duties imposed upon him by law.

The reservation by the settlor of certain rights and powers, and the fact that the trustee may himself have rights as a beneficiary, are not necessarily inconsistent with the existence of a trust.

(2) Property subject to the trust

(a) A trust can only exist in relation to specific property

A trust can only exist in relation to specific property, whether land or personal property. As Lord Browne-Wilkinson stated in *Westdeutsche Landesbank Girozentrale v Islington London Borough Council*: 'In order to establish a trust there must be identifiable trust property.'[2] This requirement is reflected in a number of principles limiting the circumstances in which there will be a valid trust. A trust cannot be effectively created over 'future property', which is property not yet in existence but merely expected as a possibility in the future. For example, a trust cannot be created over property that a person expects to receive under the will of a relative who has not yet died,[3] or over money that a person might win from the national lottery. In both cases it is uncertain whether the alleged property will ever materialize. It is possible to promise to create a trust of such future property in the event that it materializes, which may create a contractual obligation so to do, but this is essentially different from the creation of an immediate trust. Similarly, a trust cannot be created over unascertained property. For example, in *Re Goldcorp Exchange Ltd (In Receivership)*[4] a company received money from customers which it invested in the purchase of gold and other precious metals. The Privy Council held that customers could not establish that the company was holding the metal on trust for them because it was impossible to identify the specific metal derived from each customer's individual investment. The customers, unable to establish a trust, were therefore limited to a contractual claim against the company for the return of their investment. A trust will also cease to exist if all the property subject to it is destroyed or dissipated.[5]

(b) The concept of a 'trust fund'[6]

Although a trust may exist in relation to a single specific asset, for example a sum of money, a piece of land, or shares in a company, often the property to which the

---

[2] [1996] 2 All ER 961, at 988.   [3] See *Re Ellenborough* [1903] 1 Ch 697.

[4] [1994] 2 All ER 806.

[5] See *Re Diplock* [1948] Ch 465; *Bishopsgate Investment Management v Homan* [1995] 1 All ER 347.

[6] See Nolan 'Property in a Fund' (2004) 120 LQR 108.

trust relates will comprise a wide range of different assets. In both cases, the trustees may be permitted to sell the assets and exchange them for new ones. For this reason the property subject to the trust is generically identified as the trust 'fund'. Often the precise content of the fund will be fluid, because the individual assets comprising the fund are frequently being substituted by means of sale and reinvestment. For example, if trustees hold capital under a trust requiring them to invest it and pay any income to the beneficiaries, the capital need not necessarily remain in the same investments throughout the life of the trust. Indeed, there will be some instances, such as with unit trusts and pension schemes, where the benefits of collective investment would largely be lost without a regular review of the investment portfolio. The trustees therefore have powers of disposition over the investments held and they will move or change those investments from time to time. Provided that the proceeds from the realization of any investment are immediately reinvested, the value of the investment portfolio will remain unchanged, apart from any gains or losses which have been made on individual investments within the portfolio. This fluidity of the trust assets was recognized in *Re Earl of Strafford (Deceased)*, where the discussion concerned a disputed claim which formed part of the trust assets. Buckley LJ said:

The trustees may enforce the claim, sell it, compromise it or compound it, or (if it be worthless) abandon it. In any case but the last, the fruit of enforcing, selling or compromising the claim will replace the claim as an asset of the trust. None of these transactions involves any variation of the trusts or of the beneficial interests under them; there is merely a change in the composition of the trust fund. If the trustees compromise the claim at an unduly low level, they may be liable for breach of trust, but no variation of the trusts is involved. The trust fund will thenceforth comprise, in addition to other assets, the fruit of the compromise plus a claim against the culpable trustees.[7]

This concept of trust assets forming a collective investment fund is a core principle in equity. It lies at the root of unit trusts and pension funds. In more domestic contexts, it provides a means by which parents with sufficient money to invest can make provision for their children, preserving wealth within the family, but giving flexibility to the trustees as to how it will be managed and invested. The fund concept has also been employed in a corporate context, where equity has recognized that it is possible to create a floating charge over the assets of a company.[8] This operates to use the assets of the company as security for an obligation, in a similar way to that in which a house can be mortgaged to secure the repayment of a loan. Instead of freezing any particular asset, however, a floating charge treats all the assets of the company as a fund, and applies to the fund as a whole. So long as it continues to trade in the ordinary course of business, so that assets disposed of are balanced by assets acquired, the company retains freedom of disposition over individual assets. Should the company cease to trade in the ordinary way, or if some other specified event occurs, then the

---

[7] [1980] Ch 28, CA.

[8] In principle, it should also be possible for an individual to create a floating charge. See also the possibility of creating a floating trust in cases of mutual wills, discussed in Chapter 12.

charge settles and crystallizes by attaching to the specific assets then forming part of the fund.[9]

(c) Property that is the product of trust property will also be trust property

A feature of a fund is that it includes accretions as well as substitutions. Property produced by trust property itself becomes subject to the trust. For example, if the trust property includes shares in a company, any dividends paid on such shares will also comprise trust property. It has already been noted that property acquired by the sale and reinvestment of trust property will belong to the trust fund.[10] As an extension of this principle, any unauthorized profits earned by the exploitation of opportunities arising from the trust property will also be trust property. For example, where the trust property comprises shares in a company, those shares inevitably carry voting rights in the company general meeting, which are controlled by the trustees by virtue of their legal title to the shares. If a trustee is then appointed director through the use of those voting rights any personal remuneration he receives in that capacity will *prima facie* constitute trust property.

(3) Trustees subject to the obligations of the trust

(a) The trust as a species of obligation

The essence of a trust is that the owner of specific property is subject to mandatory personal obligations governing how it should be used and applied. A trustee is therefore someone who owns property subject to personal obligations to manage and apply it in accordance with the terms of the trust to the advantage of the beneficiaries thereof. As such, he does not enjoy the right to treat the property as if it were his own. The precise nature of the trustee's obligations and duties in relation to the trust property are dependent upon the terms of the particular trust. His rights and duties may be both positive and negative. In other words, there may be some things that a trustee should do in relation to the trust property, and others that he should not. The obligations imposed by a trust are not such as to limit the capacity of the trustee to deal with the property. His unencumbered capacity to deal with the trust property derives simply from the fact that he owns it. The trust obligations merely dictate what he should or should not do, and dealings with the trust property in contravention of these obligations are not *ultra vires* and void. A trustee who deals with the trust property inconsistently with the terms of the trust will instead become personally liable to the beneficiaries for 'breach of trust' and, in the absence of any defences, will be required to compensate them for any loss they suffer in consequence. The relationship between the capacity of the trustee to deal with the trust property and the trust obligations

---

[9] *Governments Stock and Other Securities Co v Manila Railway Co* [1897] AC 81, at 86, per Lord MacNaghten; *George Barker (Transport) Ltd v Eynon* [1974] 1 All ER 900, at 905, per Edmund Davies LJ.
[10] See further Chapter 23.

was summarized by Lord Browne-Wilkinson in *Hammersmith and Fulham London Borough Council v Monk*:

The fact that a trustee acts in breach of trust does not mean that he has no capacity to do the act he wrongly did.[11]

(b) The source of the trust obligations

A trust arises when property is held by trustees subject to obligations owed in favour of beneficiaries. Such obligations will arise where the outright owner of property delib orately subjects it to a trust, is presumed to have subjected it to a trust, or if a trust is imposed by law.

(i) Express intention to impose trust obligations[12]

Property may be subjected to a trust obligation by the deliberate act of its owner. An outright owner[13] of property may create a trust either by subjecting himself to trust obligations, by declaring that he holds it for specified beneficiaries, or by transferring the ownership to someone else, specifying that they are intended to hold it on trust. For example, if Mike owns shares in a company and wishes to create a trust of them in favour of Norma, he can either declare himself a trustee of the shares or transfer them to Owen, directing him to hold them on trust for her. In either case the trust is said to be express, as it was created by the deliberate intention of the owner. The person creating an express trust is described as the 'settlor', as he is said to 'settle' the property on trust for the benefit of the beneficiaries.

(ii) Implied intention to impose trust obligations

While the paradigm source of trust obligations is the express intention of the settlor, there are some circumstances in which equity presumes that a person intended to subject property to a trust, even though in fact no such intention was expressed. If a presumption of a trust arises, and it is not rebutted by counter-evidence that no trust was intended, the property will be subject to what is known as a resulting trust.[14] Resulting trusts arise in two main circumstances, which were identified by Lord Browne-Wilkinson in *Westdeutsche Landesbank Girozentrale v Islington London Borough Council*:

Under existing law a resulting trust arises in two sets of circumstances:

(a) where A makes a voluntary payment to B or pays (wholly or partly) for the purchase of property which is vested either in B alone or in the joint names of A and B, there is a presumption that A did not intend to make a gift to B; the money or property is held on trust for A (if he is the sole provider of the money) or in the case of a joint purchase by A and B in shares proportionate to their contributions...

---

[11] [1992] 1 AC 478, at 493.   [12] See further Chapters 7 and 8.

[13] This is where the owner has legal and equitable title to the property in his own right. If the owner only has equitable title, it is still possible to create a trust, normally referred to as a sub-trust.

[14] See Chapter 9.

(b)   where A transfers property to B on express trusts, but the trusts declared do not exhaust the whole beneficial interest.[15]

(iii) Imposed trust obligations

In some cases property will be regarded as subject to trust obligations despite the lack of either express or presumed intention on the part of the owner because his unconscionable conduct demands that he be required to hold the property for the benefit of others. In such circumstances, the law imposes a constructive trust.[16]

(c) The content of the trustees' obligations under the trust

The precise obligations imposed on any particular trustee will vary with the terms of the trust. In many cases the obligations of the trustees will be specified in the trust instrument by the settlor creating the trust. However, in the absence of any contradictory express terms, some powers and duties are granted and imposed by statute. Two main categories of obligation can be identified.

(i) The obligation to allocate the trust property

The most important obligation imposed by a trust is the obligation of the trustees to apply the trust property for the benefit of the beneficiaries in accordance with the terms of the trust. Under some trusts, the trustees have no part to play in deciding how the trust property should be allocated among the beneficiaries because the terms of the trust stipulate how the beneficial interest is to be shared. Such a trust is described as a 'fixed trust' because the settlor who created it has specified the respective entitlements of the beneficiaries in the terms of the trust, and the trustees' duty is merely to carry out his instructions. In other cases, the trustees have a role to play in determining how the beneficial interest is to be allocated. Rather than fixing the specific entitlements of the beneficiaries, the settlor may confer on the trustees the right to decide how the trust property should be allocated among a class of beneficiaries. Such a trust is called a 'discretionary trust' because the entitlement of any individual beneficiary to share in the trust fund is at the discretion of the trustees. Where the terms of a discretionary trust require the trustees to distribute the whole of the trust property among the beneficiaries, the trust is said to be 'exhaustive', whereas if the trustees have the power to decide not to distribute the whole of the trust property, but rather to retain and invest all or some of it, the trust is said to be 'non-exhaustive'. Where property is held on trust for children who have not yet reached the age of majority, so that they do not enjoy vested interests in the trust property or the income generated from it, the trustees may enjoy the power to apply such income to their benefit, or even to allow them to receive part of the trust property itself ahead of time. These powers are respectively termed the power of 'maintenance' and the power of 'advancement'. These powers may be granted expressly to the trustees by the settlor creating the trust,

---

[15] [1996] 2 All ER 961, at 990.

[16] See Chapter 10. Constructive trusts have also been held to arise on the (implied) common intention of the parties owning a family home, which is discussed in Chapter 11.

but in the absence of an express grant they are conferred by statute under the Trustee Act 1925, ss 31 and 32.

(ii) The obligation to manage the trust property

The second category of trustees' obligations concerns their duties to manage the trust property and to maintain the integrity of the fund. The trustees enjoy complete control of the trust property by virtue of their legal ownership of the assets which comprise the fund. Management functions include decisions on how the trust fund should be invested, and on whether assets held should be realised and the proceeds of sale reinvested. The precise scope of the trustees' management powers are determined by the terms of the particular trust. For example, the terms of the trust may expressly specify the investment powers that the trustees are to enjoy in relation to the trust property, perhaps limiting the type of investments that the trustees are entitled to pursue. In the absence of such express powers of investment, statute intervenes to grant the trustees standard investment powers.[17] The trust may also specify the means by which new or replacement trustees can be appointed, and statute empowers the trustees to delegate some of their functions to an agent acting on their behalf.

(d) The mandatory character of the trustees' obligations under the trust

The obligations of a trustee are mandatory in nature. This means that trustees are required to carry the terms of the trust into effect. In the event that they fail to carry out their obligations, especially the obligation to allocate the trust fund among the beneficiaries, the court will intervene to ensure that the trust is carried out, either by ordering them to act as required by the terms of the trust, or, if necessary, by finding an alternative means of enforcing the trust, for example by appointing new trustees. In this sense trust obligations can be distinguished from powers of appointment, which are discretionary rather than mandatory in character. The mandatory character of trust obligations is also seen in the operation of the maxim that 'equity will not allow a trust to fail for want of a trustee'. If a settlor transfers property to a person who refuses to accept the office of trustee, or if he leaves property by will to a trustee who predeceases him, equity will not allow the trust to fail but will instead find an alternative person to act as trustee.

(e) The trustees' liability for breach of trust[18]

As has been noted above, trustees do not lack capacity to deal with the trust property in a manner inconsistent with the terms of the trust. However, if they do act inconsistently with the terms of the trust, their breach of obligation will render them personally liable to compensate the beneficiaries for any loss caused by the breach.[19] The trustees may commit a breach of trust in three circumstances. First, they commit a

---

[17] Trustee Act 2000. See Chapter 23 below.   [18] See Chapter 29.
[19] The beneficiaries may also have a claim against someone who receives the trust property knowing of the breach, or who dishonestly assists in the breach. See Chapter 31.

breach of trust if they act in a manner inconsistent with the terms of the trust by doing something they were not authorized to do. Second, they commit a breach of trust by omission if they fail to do what the terms of the trust require them to do. Third, they commit a breach of trust if they fail to act with the requisite objective standard of care expected of them, namely that of 'the ordinary prudent man of business'.

(f) The ability of the beneficiaries to override the terms of the trust

Although trustees are placed under personal obligations as to how the trust property should be allocated and managed, the terms of the trust stipulated by the settlor are not sacrosanct, and can be overridden by the wishes of the beneficiaries. If the trustees act in breach of trust with the authorization of the beneficiaries, they will not be liable to them for any losses that ensue from the breach. The trustees will only enjoy complete immunity from liability if all the beneficiaries authorize the breach, and they remain liable to any beneficiaries who do not give valid authorization.[20] Valid authorization can only be given by beneficiaries who are of age and legally competent. The power of the beneficiaries to override the terms of the trust is most vividly illustrated by the operation of the rule in *Saunders v Vautier*,[21] by which the beneficiaries are entitled to insist that the trust is brought to an end by requiring the trustees to transfer the legal title to the trust property to them. The erstwhile beneficiaries would become the outright owners of the trust property and it will be free from the control of the trustees. In *Saunders v Vautier*, property was held on trust for a beneficiary who was aged 21. The terms of the trust required the trustees to accumulate the income generated by the trust fund for the beneficiary, who was only to be entitled to receive it on reaching the age of 25.[22] It was held that, as the beneficiary had attained the age of majority, he was entitled to demand that the trustees transfer the trust property to him, thus negating the age restriction imposed by the settlor. Similarly, the beneficiaries of a trust can countenance variations in its terms, again potentially undermining the wishes of the settlor embodied therein. The Variation of Trusts Act 1958 even permits the court to grant approval to variations on behalf of beneficiaries who are incapable of consenting for themselves, either because they lack the capacity to consent, are not yet in existence or cannot be ascertained, provided that the proposed variations are for their 'benefit'.[23]

(g) The fiduciary obligations of trustees

While the trustees are subject to the specific obligations imposed by the terms of the trust, they are also subject to a general fiduciary duty imposed by equity. Equity recognizes that trustees may be tempted to take advantage of their position as the legal

[20] This helps to prevent any particular beneficiary dictating to the trustees how to exercise their powers in relation to the trust.

[21] (1841) 4 Beav 115.

[22] The beneficiary had a vested right to the fund. In other words, there was only a direction to postpone payment. The beneficiary's entitlement was not conditional on reaching the age specified.

[23] See Chapter 18.

owners of the trust property and utilize it to their own advantage, rather than in the interests of their beneficiaries. It therefore imposes a strict duty of exclusive loyalty on trustees, obliging them to act solely in the interests of their beneficiaries, and assumes that any personal profit derived from their position as trustee was only obtained by allowing their own interests to prevail over those of their beneficiaries. Trustees are therefore obliged to make restitution to the beneficiaries of any unauthorized profits that they received by virtue of their position, or in circumstances where there was a mere possibility of a conflict of interest between their duty and their personal interests. Trustees will be entitled to retain such profits received in breach of their fiduciary duty if they acted with the informed consent or authorization of the beneficiaries.

The fiduciary obligations are owed to *all* the beneficiaries of a trust, whether they are entitled immediately to an interest, or whether they are entitled in remainder.

(4) Beneficiaries entitled to the benefit of the trust

The third essential characteristic of a trust is that there must be persons for whose benefit the property is held, and to whom the obligations of the trustees are owed, often referred to as the 'objects' of the trust. With the exception of trusts for charitable purposes, and a very small number of other anomalous trusts for purposes, trusts must exist for the benefit of persons rather than purposes. The reason for this limitation is that only legal persons, whether human individuals, companies, or corporations, possess the necessary capacity to enjoy and enforce the obligation of the trustees. Therefore, a trust cannot be validly created for the abstract purpose of 'promoting good journalism' because there is no person to whom the obligation is owed, and no one who possesses sufficient *locus standi* to complain to the court if the trustees fail to apply the trust property to the specified purpose. In the case of charitable trusts, the trustees' obligations are supervised on behalf of the Crown by the Attorney-General and the Charity Commission.

(a) The beneficiaries have the right to enforce the trust obligations

The prime entitlement of the beneficiaries of a trust is that the trustees carry out the terms of the trust. They are entitled to enforce the trust, either by preventing the trustees acting in breach or by requiring them to perform their obligations if they are refusing to do so. In effect, they are entitled to require full performance of the trust in their favour. Once property has been validly subjected to a trust in their favour, the beneficiaries are entitled to enforce it irrespective of whether or not they provided consideration in return for the creation of the trust.

(b) The beneficiaries have the right to override the terms of the trust

As has already been noted, the beneficiaries enjoy the right to override the terms of the trust as stipulated by the settlor. They can authorize and require the trustees to act in a way which would otherwise be a breach of trust, or a breach of their fiduciary duty, and if they are all of age and legally competent they can demand that the trust be brought to an end in accordance with the rule in *Saunders v Vautier*.[24] They may not dictate to the trustees, however, as to the exercise of all or any of the trustees' powers under the terms of the trust.[25] Hence, the beneficiaries could not require a trustee to retire or a new trustee of their choice to be appointed, unless they did this by way of terminating the existing trust and creating a new one.

(c) The beneficiaries enjoy a proprietary entitlement to the trust fund

The beneficiaries of a trust enjoy more than merely personal rights to have the trust obligations carried out in their favour by the trustees. Despite some historical debate, the better view is that beneficiaries are also entitled to proprietary rights in the trust property.

(i) The beneficial interest as a mere interest in personam

Some have argued that the fact that the beneficial interest behind a trust is destroyed by the bona fide purchase of the trust property proves that it is a mere interest in personam. Maitland stated that equity had never regarded the beneficiary as 'owner' of the trust property, but only as entitled to enforce the personal obligation of the trustee to carry out the terms of the trust:

[the trustee] is the owner, the full owner, of the thing, while the cestui que trust has no rights in the thing...[26]

More recent support for the view that beneficial interests behind a trust are mere rights in personam can be derived from the decision in *Webb v Webb*,[27] where the central issue was whether a father's assertion that his son held a holiday home in France on resulting trust for him, was a claim founded on a right in rem for the purposes of art 16(1) of the Convention on Jurisdiction and the Enforcement of Judgments in Civil and Commercial Matters 1968. Following the advice of Advocate-General Damon, the Court of Appeal held that the father's claim was not founded on a right in rem but merely on the existence of a personal fiduciary relationship. However, little weight should be placed upon this decision, as the classification of the nature of claims for the purposes of settling whether the English courts have jurisdiction when the property in dispute is situated abroad should not be determinative of the jurisprudential character of beneficial interests for domestic purposes.

(ii) The beneficial interest as a proprietary interest in rem

In reality, it seems that the beneficial interest behind a trust is more than a mere personal interest enforceable against the trustee. A beneficiary's interest is enforceable against anyone acquiring the trust property except a bona fide purchaser for value, who is protected by the doctrine of notice. In this sense the beneficial interest shares

---

[24] (1841) 4 Beav 115.   [25] *Re Brockbank* [1948] Ch 206.
[26] Maitland, *Equity* (1936), p 17.
[27] [1994] QB 696; MacMillian 'The European Court of Justice agrees with Maitland: Trusts and the Brussels Convention' [1996] Conv 125. See pp 34–35 above.

the essential characteristic of proprietary rights identified by Lord Wilberforce in *National Provincial Bank Ltd v Ainsworth*,[28] namely that they are capable of enduring through changes in ownership. Beneficial interests are certainly not as durable as legal ownership, but the mere fact that in some circumstances they are defeated by superior rights should not prevent the recognition that they are essentially proprietary in nature. Even Maitland later acknowledged that a beneficiary was entitled to more than a merely personal obligation:

I believe that for the ordinary thought of Englishmen 'equitable ownership' is just ownership pure and simple, though it is subject to a peculiar, technical and not very intelligible rule in favour of bona fide purchasers ... so many people are bound to respect these rights that practically they are almost as valuable as if they were *dominium*.[29]

The proprietary nature of the beneficial interest under a trust is also supported by the fact that the beneficiary is entitled to deal with it in ways characteristic of property owners. He can transfer his equitable interest by assignment, either by way of sale or as a gift. He can dispose of it by will, or in the event of his dying intestate it passes to his heirs under the rules governing intestate succession. It can be used to provide security for a loan. He may be required to pay tax on its value. His rights, if he has a beneficial interest in land, are enforceable against third parties, subject to the limitations contained in the land registration rules. The proprietary character of the beneficial interest under a trust was clearly stated in *Westdeutsche Landesbank Girozentrale v Islington London Borough Council*,[30] where Lord Browne-Wilkinson said:

Once a trust is established, as from the date of its establishment the beneficiary has, in equity, a proprietary interest in the trust property, which proprietary interest will be enforceable in equity against any subsequent holder of the property (whether the original property or substituted property into which it can be traced) other than a purchaser for value of the legal interest without notice.[31]

2 Powers of appointment[32]

The trust is not the only mechanism which has been developed by equity to facilitate the management and allocation of property. A person may be granted a power of appointment in respect of specific property or a fund of property. This enables him to decide who should receive the property. The holder of the power (the donee) is able to allocate the property by exercising his power and making appointments thereof to the objects of the power. Unlike a trust, the donee of a power of appointment is under no obligation to exercise the power conferred upon him. It is discretionary rather than mandatory in character. A power of appointment may form part of a will, in which case it allows the donee to nominate beneficiaries to whom the personal representatives must give the property concerned. Alternatively, the power

---

[28] [1965] AC 1175.   [29] Collected papers, Vol III, p 349.
[30] [1996] AC 669.   [31] Ibid. 705.   [32] Thomas, *Powers* (1999).

may be used to give similar instructions to trustees holding property on trust to give effect to the directions of the donee. Finally, a power may be given to the trustees themselves.

(1) Classification of powers by reference to the donee's duties

Where a power is not held by the donee in a fiduciary capacity it is termed a 'bare' or 'mere' power. The donee of such a mere power enjoys an absolute discretion whether or not to allocate the fund, or part of the fund, to the objects of the power by making appointments. He is under no enforceable duty to do so, and the courts will only intervene if he makes a wrongful allocation. The objects cannot complain to the court if the donee fails to make any allocations, and the court will not compel him to do so. The donee is not even under a duty to consider whether allocations should be made. Where the donee holds the power in a fiduciary capacity, often because he is a trustee of the property to which it relates, the power is termed a 'fiduciary power'. This duty arises from the status of the donee as a fiduciary; this status transforms what would otherwise be considered a mere power into a fiduciary power. While such a power remains substantively discretionary in character, the donee is subject to a duty to consider from time to time whether he should exercise it in favour of the objects and to make appointments in their favour.

(2) Classification of powers by reference to the range of objects

A power of appointment is described as a 'general power' if the donee is entitled to appoint the relevant property to anyone in the world, including himself. For example, 'to such person or persons as Reginald may appoint'. There is no specified restricted class of objects. If a power is general in nature, it is impossible for the donee to make an appointment to someone who is outside of the scope of the power, since by definition there is no one in such a position. In contrast, a 'special power' can only be exercised in favour of an identified class of persons. For example, 'to such of my children, as Reginald may appoint'. The donee can only make valid appointments to persons who fall within that class. A 'hybrid power' arises where a donee is authorized to make appointments to anyone except the members of a specified class. For example, 'to such person or person, not being one of my children, as Reginald may appoint'. Unlike the beneficiaries of a trust, the objects of a power enjoy no proprietary entitlement to the property over which the power is enjoyed by the donee. The rule in *Saunders v Vautier*[33] has no application in the context of powers, so that the objects cannot demand that the property be transferred to them. No object is entitled to any interests in the fund unless and until the donee exercises the power and makes an appointment in his favour.

---

[33] (1841) 4 Beav 115.

3 Classification of equitable obligations

In the trust and the power, equity has developed two mechanisms which facilitate a separation between the three functions of the management and allocation of property and the right to the enjoyment of property. In the absence of either a trust or a power, these entitlements are enjoyed in a unitary manner by the owner of the property. With trusts and powers one or more of these functions is separated from the others. However, despite a degree of functional similarity between trusts and powers, it was historically important to draw a sharp distinction between them. Conceptually, a power is purely discretionary, imposing no obligations upon the donee and conferring no proprietary rights upon the objects. In contrast, a trust is mandatory in character, imposing an obligation to act upon the trustees and conferring a proprietary entitlement to the trust fund upon the beneficiaries. Equity at one time tended to differentiate between trusts and powers by examining any given situation and characterizing the mechanism created as either a trust or a power. The rights and duties of the parties were thus determined by that characterization. Traditionally, the two mechanisms were therefore clearly distinguishable from each other. However, over time such a simple bifurcation proved insufficiently flexible, and equity extended the boundaries of existing obligations and developed new obligations. As a result, the distinction between different categories of equitable mechanism may be extremely fine and very difficult to draw in practice. In the light of these developments, although convenient from the point of view of analysis, it is questionable whether it is still valid to regard the law as comprising a fixed group of categories of obligation into which each fact situation must be fitted, with the inevitable result that the categorization will determine the rights and duties. Instead, a 'scale' of equitable obligations has emerged, and the courts will be willing to construe any particular fact situation as falling somewhere along the scale, not necessarily within a fixed traditional category, and then finding the appropriate rights and duties. The shift has been from a 'black and white' categorization of equitable obligations as either trusts or powers, to a recognition that there is a 'greyscale' with an almost infinite variation between the two extremes.

(1) A traditional categorization

(a) Trust or power

As has been described, the two main classes of obligation traditionally recognized in equity were the trust and the power. They were seen as being conceptually distinct, with only a limited scope for overlap. In construing a document, it was therefore simply a question of determining whether an obligation fell within the category of a trust or power. This would be determined by a consideration of the language used in the instrument creating it. In some circumstances the characterization of an arrangement as a trust or a power would determine whether the arrangement was valid or invalid.

For both trusts and powers it is necessary for the court to supervise the arrangement by ensuring that the fund is allocated only to those who fall within the terms of the original disposition. This requires that the beneficiaries of the trust, or the objects of the power, be defined with sufficient clarity and certainty. If this certainty of objects is lacking, then the whole arrangement will be void. Until the decision of the House of Lords in *McPhail v Doulton*,[34] the test of certainty of objects for powers was more generous than the test of certainty for trusts. Thus, it was often the case that an arrangement would be valid if characterized as a power but invalid if it was a trust.

(b) Limitations of a traditional categorization

One major limitation of the traditional categorization was the difficulty of determining whether a particular obligation was to be classed as a trust or a power, which could have such significant consequences for all the parties involved. The mere use of the words 'trust' or 'power' would not necessarily be conclusive, since what was important was the intention of the property owner creating the arrangement. If he intended to impose mandatory obligations, indicating that he expected the obligations to be carried out, a trust would be created, but if he intended to give discretion without imposing an obligation, then a power would be conferred. The difficulty lay in the fine distinction between these two alternatives. As Lord Wilberforce acknowledged in *McPhail v Doulton*, this is an area of 'delicate shading'.[35] No particular words were (or are) needed to create a trust or a power. There is therefore no easy way of telling whether a particular disposition (even if professionally drafted) creates a trust or a power, and the law reports are full of cases where even the courts have found it difficult to decide which is created in a given case. In *McPhail v Doulton* itself, the judge at first instance and the Court of Appeal found that the settlor had intended to create a power. These conclusions were influenced by the fact that the arrangement would be valid if characterized as a power, but void for want of certainty if it was a trust. The House of Lords ultimately held that the mandatory character of the language used indicated an intention to create a trust, but proceeded to revise the test of certainty applicable to trusts to ensure that it was not invalidated.

(c) Trusts combined with powers

The difficulty of making a distinction between trusts and powers is compounded by the fact that a power will always be associated with a trust. This is because a power of appointment is essentially the right to give directions to trustees as to how or for whom they are to hold trust property. This can happen in one of several ways. First, trustees could be directed to hold property for whomever the donee of the power selects. In the absence of the power being exercised, there may be a defined trust in default of appointment. Second, there might be a fixed trust, subject to the donee of a power

---

[34] [1971] AC 424.
[35] [1970] 2 All ER 228, at 240. See also Sir Richard Arden MR in *Brown v Higgs* (1800) 5 Ves 495, at 505, citing *Duke of Marlborough v Lord Godolphin* (1750) 2 Ves Sen 61.

being able to divest the beneficiaries of their interests by exercising the power. Finally, there might be an obligation to make a selection, so that the 'power' is really itself a trust. In each case, the power of selection could either be held by the trustees of the trust fund themselves, or by a separate donee.

(2) The evolution of intermediate obligations

The development of trusts and powers by equity was driven by the desire to enable property owners to deal with their property as they wish. The power enabled a property owner to delegate to another the control over the distribution of his property, within the limits he had specified. The trust enabled the owner of property to distribute his property to predetermined individuals by giving the legal title to a trustee and specifying the beneficial interests. However, as owners' intentions changed with time and they sought to distribute their property in more complex ways, a simple analysis of equitable obligations proved inadequate. Equity was able to develop new obligations which combined aspects of both the power and the trust. The prime example is the emergence of the discretionary trust. Despite its lengthy heritage the effect of the development was not fully felt until the decision of the House of Lords in *McPhail v Doulton*.[36]

(a) Early developments akin to discretionary trusts

The existence of hybrid obligations was recognized by Lord Eldon LC in the leading case of *Brown v Higgs*:[37]

There are not only a mere trust and a mere power, but there is also known to the court a power which the party to whom it is given is entrusted and required to execute; and with regard to that species of power, the court considers it as partaking so much of the nature and qualities of a trust, that if the person who has that duty imposed on him does not discharge it, the court will to a certain extent discharge the duty in his room and place.

A relatively early example of such an arrangement is *Crockett v Crockett*.[38] A testator had left his entire estate to 'be at the disposal of his most true and lawful wife, Caroline Crockett, for herself and children'. Sir James Wigram V-C held this to confer equal shares on Caroline and the children, so that when the eldest child came of age he could call for his share.[39] Lord Cottenham LC, on appeal, disagreed. He did not need to categorize the arrangement exactly, but in his view one possible interpretation of the will was that Caroline was 'a trustee, with a large discretion as to the application of the fund'.[40] Sir John Romilly, who had been counsel in *Crockett v Crockett*, followed the case in *Hart v Tribe*,[41] after his appointment as Master of the Rolls. He gave a similar interpretation to a gift by will to the testator's wife Maria 'to be used for her own and the children's benefit, as she shall in her judgment and conscience think fit'. Within

---

[36] [1971] AC 424.   [37] (1799) 4 Ves 708; rehear (1800) 5 Ves 495; affd (1803) 8 Ves 561.

[38] (1848) 2 Ph 553.   [39] (1842) 1 Hare 451; (1847) 5 Hare 326.

[40] (1848) 2 Ph 553, at 561.   [41] (1854) 18 Beav 215.

just a few years the concept was sufficiently clearly established for Thomas Smith MR, in the Irish Court of Chancery, to describe it as a discretionary trust.[42]

However, as might be expected, the early development was uncertain. This is evident in the decision in *Burrough v Philcox*.[43] John Walton left property to his two children for life and granted them a power to dispose of it by will in favour of his nephews and nieces. His two children died without making any appointment and the question arose whether the nephews and nieces could claim the property or whether it would pass to the residuary legatees of John Walton's will. The arrangement was clearly a power, but the court found that there was a general intention in favour of the class by John Walton and since that intention had failed because a selection had not been made by his children, the court would carry into effect the general intention and divide the property equally between the nephews and nieces. The court chose to analyse this disposition as a power with a trust in favour of the class should the power fail to be exercised. It could equally well have been treated as a discretionary trust.

(b) The enforcement of hybrid obligations

While equity seemed willing to contemplate the emergence of mechanisms which were hybrid in nature, in that they were not exclusively mandatory or exclusively discretionary, there was uncertainty as to how the court could intervene if a trustee failed to exercise his discretion under a discretionary trust. In *Hart v Tribe* Sir John Romilly had said:

> There is no question but that this court will sometimes execute a trust, where a fund is originally given to a trustee to be disposed of in favour of certain objects, according to his judgment and discretion...I am of opinion that the court will not control this discretion, when it sees that it is *bona fide* exercised. I am far from saying, that this court would not compel the wife duly to perform the condition on which the gift was made to her, if it found that one child was really left destitute and in want, nothing being applied for its benefit—that the objects contemplated by the testator were disregarded, and the benefits which he intended the children to receive, were, in point of fact, withheld.[44]

Were any such neglect to occur, Romilly MR said that an application could be made to the court 'and I shall know how to deal with it'. An application was subsequently made on behalf of one of the children for whom Maria had made no provision.[45] Sir John Romilly ordered Maria to make an annual payment from the income of the fund to meet the majority of the boy's school fees.[46] There are other cases in which the court compelled a trustee under a discretionary trust to act,[47] or substituted its own judgment for that of a discretionary trustee who had failed to act.[48]

---

[42] *Gray v Gray* (1862) 13 I Ch R 404.   [43] (1840) 5 My & Cr 72.

[44] (1854) 18 Beav 215, at 217–218.

[45] The child, Frederick, had been informally adopted by the testator. Maria had hoped that he would remain with her, but he was taken away by his blood relatives.

[46] (1854) 19 Beav 149.

[47] See *Gisborne v Gisborne* (1877) 2 App Cas 300, HL; *Tempest v Lord Camoys* (1882) 21 Ch D 571.

[48] *Mosely v Mosely* (1673) Cas temp Finch 53; *Clarke v Turner* (1694) Freem Ch 198; *Warburton v Warburton* (1702) 4 Bro Parl Cas 1; *Richardson v Chapman* (1760) 7 Bro Parl Cas 318.

In other cases, though, the court disclaimed the ability to substitute its own opinion for that of the trustee. An example is *Gray v Gray*,[49] where Thomas Smith MR, ironically following a dictum of Romilly MR in *Hart v Tribe*, held that the only means by which the court could execute a discretionary trust where the trustee had failed to do so was by ordering equal division between all the objects. A similar view was taken by Sir Richard Arden MR in *Kemp v Kemp*.[50] The cases adopting a more flexible approach were condemned as anomalous by the Court of Appeal in 1954 in *IRC v Broadway Cottages Trust*.[51] The orthodox view adopted in that case was that the court had no right to substitute its discretion for that of the designated trustees should they fail or refuse to act. The discretion being conferred on and exercisable by the trustees alone, the court could not do other than authorize a distribution in equal shares. To this there might have been a limited exception that where the testator or settlor had laid down pointers or guides to the exercise of the discretion, this could form a basis for the exercise of a more flexible order by the court.[52]

(3) *McPhail v Doulton*: a modern watershed

Despite the early developments outlined above, the decision in the House of Lords in *McPhail v Doulton* marks the major break from the traditional dichotomy between trust and powers. Mr Bertram Baden settled property on trust to enable the trustees to make grants in favour of the staff of Matthew Hall and Co Ltd and their relatives and dependants. It was obvious that Mr Baden did not intend each and every member of staff and their dependants and relatives to have a share in the property left on trust, as there would simply not be enough for them each to receive any meaningful sum. The trustees were to have discretion which of the members of staff and their relatives and dependants were to benefit. The House of Lords held by a majority that this was a trust and not a power. Most significantly, it held that if the trustees failed to exercise their discretion, the court could intervene to compel them, or to ensure by some other means that the trust was carried out. Lord Wilberforce stated that:

The court, if called upon to execute the trust power, will do so in the manner best calculated to give effect to the settlor's or testator's intentions. It may do so by appointing new trustees, or by authorising or directing representative persons of the classes of beneficiaries to prepare a scheme of distribution, or even, should the proper basis for distribution appear by itself directing the trustees so to distribute.

(4) The contemporary classification of equitable obligations

McPhail v Doulton[53] overturned the orthodox view that there were a limited number of categories of equitable obligation and that regard would be had to the wishes of the

---

[49] (1862) 13 I Ch R 404.   [50] (1795) 5 Ves Jr 849.

[51] [1955] Ch 20, [1954] 3 All ER 120.

[52] See the dissenting judgment of Lord Hodson in *McPhail v Doulton* [1970] 2 All ER 228, at 234.

[53] [1971] AC 424.

settlor by allocating the arrangement that he had created into the most appropriate box or category. Some of the categories recognized before *McPhail v Doulton* did, of course, contain the potential for fine-tuning. The settlor could specify what discretions he was conferring upon his trustees, but the lack of anything but the crudest form of enforcement through equal division in the case of a failure by his trustees to exercise a discretion meant that the settlor's freedom of invention was comparatively limited. *McPhail v Doulton*[54] marked a watershed not merely because it changed the certainty requirement for discretionary trusts, but also because it altered the basis on which the courts would enforce fiduciary obligations. By recognizing that equal division was not the only remedy available where a trustee failed to act, the House of Lords opened the possibility of more varied and sophisticated obligations in equity. The possibilities opened up by the case have been confirmed and exploited since.

(a) Blurring distinctions

The historic categories of the mandatory fixed trust, discretionary trust, and mere power provided the beginnings of a broader scale of obligations developing as grey shades between the black and white of trusts and powers. *McPhail v Doulton* has led to the exploitation of more intermediate shades of grey. This has happened both by the evolution of new mechanisms filling the gaps between the old constructs, and also by expansion within the categories themselves (see Figure 4.1).

(i) Exhaustive and non-exhaustive discretionary trusts

Within the category of discretionary trust, it is possible to distinguish between those under which the trustees are obliged to distribute the assets of the trust, and those where there is no such obligation. Since *McPhail v Doulton* the difference matters. The way in which the court is likely to intervene may differ markedly according to whether the trustees' obligation does or does not require the exhaustion of the trust fund.

(ii) Enforcing fiduciary powers

In a similar vein, it has long been recognized that some powers are fiduciary, in the sense that the donee is unable to agree voluntarily or by contract not to exercise the power. It is said, to use the technical term, that the power cannot be released. That was as far as the court was willing to intervene when the traditional dichotomy between mandatory trusts and permissive powers held sway. However, in *Mettoy Pension Trustees Ltd v Evans*[55] Warner J held that in some circumstances the courts might be willing to compel the donee of a fiduciary power to exercise it using the same methods of enforcement that were suggested by Lord Wilberforce as applicable to discretionary trusts in *McPhail v Doulton*.[56] The case is fully discussed in a later chapter,[57] but at this stage it is sufficient to recognize that this runs against the tenor of previous cases,

---

[54] Ibid.   [55] [1991] 2 All ER 513.   [56] [1971] AC 424.   [57] See Chapter 16.

Figure 4.1 A scale of equitable obligations

which have maintained the orthodox position that the exercise of fiduciary powers[58] cannot be enforced by the courts.[59]

(iii) Blurring of the traditional categories of trust and power

Discretionary trusts themselves represent a blurring between the distinct categories of the trust and power. The House of Lords in *McPhail v Doulton* described the arrangement which Bertram Baden had set up as a 'trust power'. That phrase encapsulates the hybrid nature of the discretionary trust, which draws in elements both of trusts, in the obligation which is placed upon the trustees, and of power, in relation to the discretions which are conferred upon the trustees and the lack of defined rights, even in default, upon the part of the beneficiaries. The decision in the *Mettoy Pension* case suggests a further blurring. Rather than there being a sharp conceptual distinction between discretionary trusts and fiduciary powers, the case recognizes that there is a 'grey area' where obligations are neither distinctly one nor the other, but where they enjoy characteristics of both. Consider the difference between the fiduciary power, where following *Mettoy*[60] the donee has a discretion whether or not to exercise the power but an obligation to consider whether to do so which may be enforced by the court, and a non-exhaustive discretionary trust, where the trustee has a mandatory duty to distribute the fund subject to a power to accumulate the income. It is almost impossible to discern a clear conceptual distinction between these different obligations. The subsequent decision of the Privy Council in *Schmidt v Rosewood Trust Ltd*[61] further confirms the blurring of the traditional distinction between trusts and powers. In this case it was held that no distinction should be drawn between the rights of the

---

58 As opposed to the consideration of the exercise of the power.
59 *Re Gulbenkian's Settlement Trusts (No 1)* [1968] Ch 126; *McPhail v Doulton* [1971] AC 424; *Re Hay's Settlement Trusts* [1981] 3 All ER 786.
60 [1991] 2 All ER 513.   61 [2003] 3 All ER 76.

object of a discretionary trust or of a fiduciary power in regard to the entitlement to the disclosure of trust documents. Thus, a right that was formerly predicated upon the proprietary right of the beneficiary to the trust property was extended to the objects of a power of appointment who have no proprietary interest. In reaching this conclusion Lord Walker referred to the way in which Lord Wilberforce had demonstrated in *McPhail v Doulton* that the differences between trusts and powers were 'a good deal less significant than the similarities'.[62]

(iv) Blurring in practice: pension schemes

The increasingly sophisticated use of trusts and powers further suggests the inevitability of a blending and melding between some of the old categories. Take, for instance, the pension scheme. The trustees of a pension fund will generally be under a binding obligation to pay pension benefits to the widow or dependant children of a contributing member if he dies in service, that is, while still in employment. A capital sum will usually also be available. With most pension schemes, the trustees hold any capital sum upon discretionary trusts to distribute it among a class of beneficiaries including the member's near family, any dependants and any person the member may have nominated. The trustees may also have powers to establish trusts containing discretions and powers where they are applying a lump sum on death in service. In considering what to do, the trustees may have received directions from the member. In one typical scheme, it is stated: 'In the exercise of their discretionary powers the Trustees may have regard to but shall not be bound by any wishes notified to them by the member.' In a single arrangement, therefore, one can find fixed trusts, discretionary trusts, powers and directions with no express binding force alongside each other.

(b) Determining rights and duties

Given the blurring of the distinctions between the recognized equitable mechanisms and the difficulty of drawing conceptual distinctions between them, the traditional approach of categorizing obligations into a small number of well-defined categories seems inappropriate. In the past, there was a temptation to allow the classification of an arrangement to dictate the parties' rights and duties. However, this is a circular activity and the fallacy of it is evident by examining an illustration. In *Re Gestetner Settlement*,[63] Harman J indicated that in addition to a discretionary trust where the trustees were under an obligation to distribute, there could also be a situation where trustees were simply under an obligation to consider whether a power to distribute should be exercised, without being obliged to part with any income or capital. This is sometimes described as a non-exhaustive discretionary trust, to distinguish it from the case where the trustees are under a duty to distribute and exhaust the fund (an exhaustive discretionary trust). In *McPhail v Doulton*, Lord Wilberforce drew a distinction between a discretionary trust (which he described as a trust power) and a mere power which was conferred on trustees. In the latter case he stated that 'although the trustees may, and normally will, be under a fiduciary duty to consider whether or

---

[62] Ibid. [66].   [63] [1953] Ch 672; [1953] 1 All ER 1150.

in what way they should exercise their power, the court will not normally compel its exercise'. Lord Wilberforce did not consider this to be a discretionary trust (or a trust power, in the terminology which he used in the case), but it is difficult to see how it differs in any real respect from a non-exhaustive discretionary trust.[64]

The extent of the obligation to review the range of objects can also vary. Again, in *McPhail v Doulton* Lord Wilberforce said that:

as to the trustees' duty of enquiry or ascertainment, in each case the trustees ought to make such a survey of the range of objects or possible beneficiaries as will enable them to carry out their fiduciary duty. A wider and more comprehensive range of enquiry is called for in the case of trust powers than in the case of powers.

Earlier in his opinion, he had indicated that the distinction was a functional one:

Such distinction as there is would seem to lie in the extent of the survey which the trustee is required to carry out; if he has to distribute the whole of a fund's income, he must necessarily make a wider and more systematic survey than if his duty is expressed in terms of a power to make grants ... The difference may be one of degree rather than of principle; in the well-known words of Sir George Farwell,[65] trusts and powers are often blended, and the mixture may vary in its ingredients.

(c) A scale of equitable obligations

The mix of trusts and powers, and the nature of the obligations which can be imposed on the donee of a fiduciary power, makes it undesirable to insist upon a rigid classification. There are, moreover, difficulties in locating some arrangements clearly under one category or another. As the litigation in *McPhail v Doulton* indicates, what one person sees as a trust in favour of a class with a power to accumulate may by another be seen as a trust to accumulate with a power to make grants in favour of a class. The House of Lords recognized that not only are the distinctions fine, but also that they are not determinative of the obligations of the donee or trustee. In the words of Lord Wilberforce:

It is striking how narrow and in a sense artificial is the distinction ... between trusts ... and powers ... And if one considers how in practice reasonable and competent trustees would act, and ought to act, in the two cases, surely a matter very relevant to the question of validity, the distinction appears even less significant. To say that there is no obligation to exercise a mere power and that no court will intervene to compel it, whereas a trust is mandatory and its execution may be compelled, may be legally correct enough, but the proposition does not contain an exhaustive comparison of the duties of persons who are trustees in the two cases.[66]

This marks a fundamental shift from a simple conceptual framework of equitable obligations, where characterization as either a trust or a power determines the rights and duties of the parties, to a functional analysis, where the courts will construe an arrangement in the way best capable of fulfilling the intention of the owner of the property. The absence of a rigid hierarchy of equitable obligations means that there is instead a wide spectrum of arrangements, the characteristics of which depend upon

---

[64] See, however, Hayton's definition of a non-exhaustive discretionary trust as one in which 'the trustees must distribute the income amongst class "A" only if they fail to exercise a power to withhold the income for some purpose such as accumulating it or using it for class "B" ': Hayton and Marshall, *Cases and Commentary on the Law of Trusts* (11th edn, 2001), p 152, n 90.

[65] *Farwell on Powers* (3rd edn, 1916), p 10.   [66] [1970] 2 All ER 228, at 240.

the terms and circumstances of their creation. Any classification can be adopted only as a matter of convenience as a way of describing, rather than prescribing, the incidents of any particular arrangement. It is possible to describe some of the principal kinds of equitable obligation which are found in practice, although it is impossible to draw up a definitive list. However, some features of the scale of equitable obligations can usefully be identified.

(i) The mandatory extreme

At one end of the spectrum of equitable mechanisms for property management and holding is the bare trust. The trustee may well have no independent powers of management or investment, and the shares in which the property is to be enjoyed are predetermined. The freedom of the trustee is constrained, and control is at its highest. But even here the position may be qualified. For instance, it is not unusual for a trust providing for fixed successive interests to contain a power enabling the trustee to draw down some of the capital and to pay it by way of an advancement to a beneficiary who has only a presumptive interest in the fund. There may also be a power to make applications of income (and sometimes capital) for the education and maintenance of an infant beneficiary who would otherwise have only a deferred right to those funds.

(ii) The discretionary extreme

At the other end of the spectrum is a mere power, the donee of which enjoys an unfettered discretion whether to exercise it and, if it is exercised, how to exercise it. Even here, however, the donee does not have complete freedom, for the court will ensure that the power is exercised only within its terms.

(iii) Intermediate points on the scale

Between the black and white extremes of the bare fixed trust and the mere power there lies an almost infinite variety of intermediate arrangements. These include: trusts in favour of a fixed class, but with a power to make a selection between them in unequal shares;[67] a discretionary trust where the trustee is under an obligation to make a selection and which will be exercised by some means by the court if the trustee fails to exercise it;[68] a fiduciary power where the donee need not make a distribution but must at least consider periodically whether it should be exercised;[69] and a power or discretionary trust in favour of a class with a power to extend that class by appointing new members of the class.[70] Most of these possibilities can be combined in one form or another, creating a nearly infinite range of shades of grey.

---

[67] *Wilson v Duguid* (1883) 24 Ch D 244 (where the gift to the class in equal shares was implied); *Burroughs v Philcox* (1840) 5 My & Cr. 72 *Re Llewellyn's Settlement* [1921] 2 Ch 281; *Re Arnold* [1947] Ch 131.

[68] *Brown v Higgs* (1803) 8 Ves 561; *McPhail v Doulton* [1971] AC 424.

[69] *Re Manisty's Settlement Trusts* [1974] Ch 17; *Re Hay's Settlement Trusts* [1982] 1 WLR 202.

[70] *Re Hay's Settlement Trusts* [1982] 1 WLR 202.

5

Equity and the management
of property

In the previous chapter the key characteristics of trusts and powers were examined. It is the purpose of this chapter to sketch some of the more important practical usages of trusts. Like Molière's character in *The Bourgeois Gentilhomme* who exclaimed 'Good Heavens! For more than forty years I have been speaking prose without knowing it', the way in which trusts underpin much of the modern law of property is often unseen or unnoticed.

1 The modern significance of trusts

Trusts, and to a lesser extent powers, have evolved to enable property owners to accomplish objectives that they wish to achieve in respect of their property. While they first emerged in an entirely different social environment, where their primary use was as a means of ensuring that property remained within a family, they have proved extremely adaptable to modern family and commercial contexts. The majority of people enjoy some interaction with trusts, even though they may not be aware of it. Every person who is a co-owner of land is a beneficiary under a trust. Every person who has a pension fund, or who has investments in a unit trust or an ISA will find that the underlying assets behind their investment are held under a trust. Persons with considerable wealth may utilize trusts as a means of efficient tax planning. Every person who makes a donation to a charitable organization will in many cases unknowingly interact with the law of trusts.

2 Hiding the identity of the true owner of property

The fact that a trust enables the separation of the legal and beneficial ownership of property means that it can be used as an effective mechanism for hiding the identity of the true owner of property. If property is held on trust, it may appear to the world that the trustee is in fact the absolute legal owner, and others will have no knowledge of the existence of a trust. There is no obligation to publicly disclose the existence of a trust and therefore this mechanism will be particularly important where the legal ownership is made public, for example in the case of land where ownership is constituted by registration on a public register. For example, if a famous rock star wishes to purchase a cottage in a village without attracting attention, he may arrange for the house to be purchased on his behalf by a trustee, which would create what is known as a 'bare trust'.[1] Similarly, if a man wishes to make provision for his mistress on his death without members of his family discovering that she exists, he can leave the property he intends to give her in his will to a trusted friend who will take it as trustee on behalf of the mistress. There is no need for the identity of the mistress to appear in the will, which would become a public document as a consequence of the probate procedure, and nor is there any need for the will to make mention of the trust. Such trusts are known as secret trusts and are discussed fully in Chapter 8.

3 Transferring the ownership of property

One of the simplest dealings with property is an outright transfer of ownership, whether by gift or sale. The requirements for effective transfer of ownership vary with the type of property involved. Some forms of property, including banknotes and ordinary goods like books and furniture (referred to as 'chattels'), can be transferred simply by handing over possession with the intention of transferring ownership. Other forms of property require more. The transfer of land, for instance, requires the transfer to be made in a prescribed form, and the transferee must then be registered as the new owner by the Land Registry.[2]

Equity normally has no role to play in outright transfers, except where the form of property concerned is recognized only in equity, for example a transfer of a beneficial share in a trust fund. In some cases equity will treat an attempted transfer as effective, even though some of the special formal requirements for the transfer of that form of property have not been used. Equity will, for instance, treat a transfer of land as being effective for some purposes after all the necessary documents have been completed and signed, even though the statutory rules require the transfer to be registered.[3] Conversely, in some special cases the principles of equity may become involved to deprive an apparent transfer of its full effect by imposing a resulting or constructive trust so that the original owner retains the equitable interest in the property transferred. For example, in *Bannister v Bannister*[4] Mrs Bannister sold two cottages to her brother-in-law for one-third less than their full market value. He promised orally to let Mrs Bannister stay on in one of the cottages rent-free for the rest of her life, but four years later he

---

[1] See Chapters 14 and 21.   [2] See p 201.
[3] *Mascall v Mascall* (1985) 50 P & CR 119 and see pp 203 *et seq.*   [4] [1948] 2 All ER 133.

sought to evict her. The oral promise could not be enforced as a contract since it was not in writing, or proved in writing, as the statutory rules at the time required.[5] The Court of Appeal held, however, that in view of the promise that the brother-in-law had made, he acquired the cottage as trustee during the life of Mrs Bannister. He could not evict her so long as she desired to occupy the cottage. Similarly, in *Hodgson v Marks*,[6] Mrs Hodgson, an 83-year-old widow, had been persuaded by her lodger, Mr Evans, to transfer her house to him to prevent him from being evicted by her nephew. The transfer was not intended to be a gift, but to leave Mrs Hodgson as the effective owner Although on the surface it appeared that Mr Evans was the owner because his name had been entered as proprietor in the register kept by the Land Registry, equity imposed a trust on him to give effect to the intention that Mrs Hodgson was to remain entitled to the full benefit of the property. Mrs Hodgson's interest was protected against a purchaser to whom Mr Evans fraudulently sold the house.

4 Sharing ownership of property

(1) Concurrent ownership of property

Trusts also provide a mechanism by which the ownership of property can be shared between a number of persons. Their interests are said to be concurrent because they are enjoyed at the same time. Co-ownership can be effected by means of either a joint tenancy or a tenancy-in-common.

(a) Joint tenancy[7]

Where the ownership of property is shared by means of a joint tenancy, all of the co-owners have identical rights to the property. Taken together, they are entitled to the whole of the co-owned property, but they do not have specific shares in it. In the event of the death of one joint tenant, his interest passes automatically to the other remaining joint tenants under the principle of survivorship. A joint tenancy can be converted into a tenancy-in-common in equity by means of severance,[8] where the joint tenant severs his 'share', and the rules of survivorship no longer apply.

(b) Tenancy-in-common[9]

Where the ownership of property is shared by means of a tenancy-in-common the co-owners enjoy 'undivided shares' in the co-owned property. This means that they

---

[5] Law of Property Act 1925, s 40.   [6] [1971] Ch 892.
   [7] See Jackson, Stevens, and Pearce, *Land Law* (4th edn, 2008), pp 361–370; Gray and Gray, *Elements of Land Law* (5th edn, 2009), pp 914–923.
   [8] See Jackson Stevens, and Pearce, *Land Law* (4th edn, 2008), pp 373–392; Gray and Gray, *Elements of Land Law* (5th edn, 2009), pp 940–963.
   [9] See Jackson, Stevens, and Pearce, *Land Law* (4th edn, 2008), pp 364–367, 370–372; Gray and Gray, *Elements of Land Law* (5th edn, 2009), pp 923–927.

have specific notional shares in the property, which may be equal or unequal, and survivorship has no application. However, all the co-owners enjoy the right to use and enjoy the property, and no co-owner can regard part of it as representing his 'share' alone.

(c) Trusts and co-ownership

In relation to some property, the ownership can be shared concurrently by means of a joint tenancy or a tenancy-in-common without the need for a trust. For example, two students who purchase a car together may become the joint owners thereof and no trust is involved. In the case of personal property, the legal title may be held by co-owners either as joint tenants or tenants-in-common. Where the chattels of two owners are commingled to form an indistinguishable whole (for instance because their oil has been mixed in the same tank), they share the whole as tenants-in-common in proportion to their contributions.[10] However, in general the common law preferred the mechanism of a joint tenancy, and thus a tenancy-in-common is relatively rare without a trust. Where the property concerned is land, any form of co-ownership will inevitably give rise to a trust of land.[11] By statute the legal title to land can only be held by individuals or joint tenants,[12] and therefore a tenancy in common can only exist in equity. The only situation in which land will not be held on trust is where there is a single outright owner. This means that the trust is the foundation of most land holding under English law.

(2) Successive ownership of property

It has been seen how the trust can provide a mechanism to facilitate the shared concurrent ownership of property. An owner of property may wish to divide the ownership of property so that it is enjoyed successively rather than concurrently. For example, imagine that Alice, an elderly lady with a significant shareholding, has one daughter, Claire, and three grandchildren. On her death she wants Claire to enjoy the benefit of the shares, but ultimately she wants to ensure that they pass to her grandchildren. Alice can grant Claire a life interest in the shares that will entitle her to receive the income they produce for the duration of her life, but without any right to their capital value. On her death the shares will become the property of the grandchildren (see Figure 5.1). Such an arrangement, sharing the enjoyment of the property successively, can only be achieved by means of a trust, irrespective of whether the property concerned is land or personal property.[13]

---

[10] See *Spence v Union Marine Insurance Co* (1868) LR 3 CP 427; *Indian Oil Corpn Ltd v Greenstone Shipping SA* [1987] 3 All ER 893; cf *F S Sandeman & Sons v Tyzack and Branfoot Shipping Co* [1913] AC 680, HL.

[11] See Trusts of Land and Appointment of Trustees Act 1996, ss 1–5.

[12] Law of Property Act 1925, ss 1(6), 36(2).

[13] It was once possible to create limited interests in land without using a trust, but since the Law of Property Act 1925, a trust is now required whenever limited interests in land are created. It has always been the case that limited interests in property other than land can only be created by means of a trust. See Jackson, Stevens, and Pearce, *Land Law* (4th edn, 2008), pp 431–457.

Figure 5.1 Creating successive interests using a trust

5 Delegating management functions

Many of the most significant uses of trusts arise because they enable an owner to delegate some of the management responsibilities attendant upon the ownership of property to a third person who will become the trustee. In some cases such delegation will be chosen for reasons of convenience, while in others it may be a matter of necessity because the owner of property is incapable of managing it for himself.

(1) Delegation for reasons of convenience

The owner of property may choose to create a trust of his property for reasons of convenience. Thus, a person owning a substantial share portfolio may transfer his shares to his stockbroker or a professional trustee to facilitate dealing transactions. In the case of such a bare trust, the trustee may not enjoy any active powers of management over the trust property but will act on the instructions of the beneficiary.

(2) Delegation of allocation

An owner may know that he wants to transfer the ownership of his property but not yet know who he wants to transfer it to. By means of a trust, combined with a power of appointment, the owner can effectively delegate the responsibility for choosing who should receive the ultimate benefit of his property to someone else, the donee of the power. Often, the donee of the power or the trustee of the discretionary trust will be in a better position than the original owner to determine how it should be distributed, either by reason of the time at which they can make the decision, or because of their superior knowledge. For example, imagine that Henry has no children of his own but has a large number of nieces and nephews. He only has a small estate and he wants to ensure that his property goes to those who really need it. In his will, he can leave his property to his sister Frances for life, giving her a power of appointment to choose which of his nephews and nieces are to receive the property on her death. By doing so, Henry is able to delegate the task of selecting who is to benefit, while at the same time stipulating the class of persons among whom allocations can be made. Alternatively, Henry could leave his estate to Frances on trust for such of his nephews and nieces in such shares as she determines. By means of this discretionary trust, Henry has imposed a mandatory obligation on Frances to allocate the property among the class of his nephews and nieces, but has left her the decision as to which specific members of that class should benefit and to what extent.

Again, a discretionary trust or a power of appointment can be used on a larger scale. For instance, William is the owner of a large business with some 10,000 employees. He wishes to establish a fund to provide for the education of the children of his employees. Obviously, he cannot provide for them all, so he is able to create a trust in which the fund is transferred to trustees who have the discretion to select which of his employees' children should receive this benefit. The result is that only some of the 10,000 will benefit, but William has delegated to others the task of deciding those who will benefit.[14]

McPhail v Doulton provides an example of such delegated allocation.[15] Bertram Baden wanted to give property for the benefit of the employees and ex-employees, and their relatives and dependants, of a company he owned. Rather than determining how the property should be allocated, he left the property to trustees, giving them the discretion as to which of the potential beneficiaries should actually receive a share of the property. In this way he delegated to them the task of allocating the property (see Figure 5.2). Similarly, in *Re Diplock*,[16] Caleb Diplock left his residuary estate to his executors to be applied to 'such…charitable or benevolent objects' as they shall 'in their absolute discretion select'. Again, this was an attempt to delegate the decision as to how the property should actually be allocated to others, namely the executors.[17]

(3) Providing for vulnerable individuals

An owner may want to take deliberate advantage of the possibility of separating the legal and equitable ownership of property through a trust to gain the advantage of ensuring that the beneficial owner does not have control of the management of the property. There are a number of reasons why this may be the case.

(a) The beneficiary cannot manage the property

An owner may wish someone to enjoy the benefit of property who is not capable of managing it adequately for himself. The device of the trust enables the owner to

---

[14] For example, *Oppenheim v Tobacco Securities Trust Co Ltd* [1951] AC 297.
[15] [1971] AC 424.   [16] [1948] Ch 465.
[17] In fact, the gift failed because it was not exclusively charitable: see Chapter 19.

Figure 5.2 Delegating allocation using a trust: *McPhail v Doulton*

transfer the legal title, and therefore the management responsibility, to someone who is capable of looking after the interests of the beneficiary.

(i) Infancy

An owner may want to create a trust because the intended beneficiary is an infant, and is therefore incapable of managing the property for himself. This would be the case, for example, if parents die leaving their property to infant children. The trustee will have the control of the property, which will be invested and managed for their benefit until they reach the age of majority.

(ii) Incapacity

A trust may also be employed where the intended beneficiary lacks the capacity to conduct his own affairs for reasons other than infancy. Suppose that John has a handicapped adult son for whom he wishes to make provision in his will. John knows that his son is unable to make decisions for himself. By means of a trust, John can nominate a trustee to hold the property for his son. The trustee will have the legal ownership of the money and will be able to decide how it should be invested and used. John's son will enjoy the equitable or beneficial ownership in the money.

(b) The beneficiary should not manage the property

An owner may also want to create a trust if he is concerned that it would be unwise to permit the beneficiary, although legally competent, to manage the property. In the Victorian period, the trust was often used to preserve the integrity of family estates from spendthrift heirs. A classic example can be found in Trollope's Victorian novel, *Dr Thorne*. There, a wealthy baronet, Sir Richard Scatcherd, dies leaving a vast estate of some £300,000. His son, Sir Louis, was 21, a drunkard and a spendthrift. In order to protect the estate Sir Richard left his property to his close and trusted friend,

Dr Thorne, so that the son would not have control of it but rather that Dr Thorne would manage the estate until Sir Louis reached 25, with the hope that by such age he would be a reformed character. Somewhat fortunately for the story he died before reaching that age, leaving the heroine, Miss Thorne, to inherit the estate!

Similarly, if Alexander wanted to leave his property to a son whom he knew was a drug addict and therefore liable to waste the money in that way, he could leave it on some form of trust so that the son would be entitled to receive an income but not to rapidly dissipate the property.

(c) Protective trusts

A spendthrift may also be protected from the dangers of his own bankruptcy by a special type of trust, the protective trust. Under such a trust, property is held by the trustees with a direction that the beneficiary is to receive the income from the trust. In the case of a conventional trust, if the beneficiary becomes insolvent his trustee in bankruptcy will be entitled to receive the income from the trust. However, the terms of a protective trust provide that in the event of insolvency the beneficiary's entitlement to the income automatically fails or determines, so that he is no longer entitled to it as of right. Instead, the income is to be held by the trustees under a discretionary trust to be used for the support of a range of persons, including the original beneficiary. This means that the trustee in bankruptcy will only receive the income if the trustees of the settled fund make an appointment to the bankrupt beneficiary. By means of this device, the trust property and income are protected from the consequences of the beneficiary's bankruptcy.

It has been held that a settlor cannot create a trust to protect himself from his own bankruptcy.[18] However, a trust created by a third party that will protect the beneficiary from the consequences of his bankruptcy has been held to be valid.[19] Although a protective trust may be created expressly, a statutory form has been introduced. Section 33(1) of the Trustee Act 1925 provides that where any income is directed to be held on 'protective trusts' for the benefit of any person, then the property is to be held upon the terms set out in the section. These provide for a primary trust, and then a secondary trust that will only come into being if the primary trust fails.

(i) The terms of the primary trust

Section 33(1)(i) provides that the income will be held:

Upon trust for the principal beneficiary during the trust period or until he...does or attempts to do anything, or until any event happens...whereby, if the said income were payable during the trust period to the principal beneficiary absolutely during that period, he would be deprived of the right to receive the same or any part thereof, in any of which cases...this trust of the said income shall fail or determine.

---

[18] *Re Burroughs-Fowler* [1916] 2 Ch 251.
[19] *Billson v Crofts* (1873) LR 15 Eq 314; *Re Aylwin's Trusts* (1873) LR 16 Eq 585; *Re Ashby, ex p Wreford* [1892] 1 QB 872 QBD.

This primary trust entitles the principal beneficiary to receive the income from the trust, which entitlement determines automatically if he for any reason loses the right to retain it, for example if he becomes bankrupt, in which case his trustee in bankruptcy would be entitled to the income from the trust.[20] Other events have included the sequestration of the income[21] and the trustees impounding the income to repay capital wrongly advanced to the beneficiary.[22] In contrast, the fact that a beneficiary was resident in enemy-occupied territory, with the consequence that income could not be paid to her, was held not to be sufficient to determine the trust,[23]

(ii) The terms of the secondary trust

If the primary trust is determined, then the income is to be held on the terms of a secondary trust set out in s 33(1)(ii):

If the trust aforesaid fails or determines during the subsistence of the trust period, then, during the residue of that period, the said income shall be held upon trust for the application thereof for the maintenance or support, or otherwise for the benefit, of all or any one or more exclusively of the other or others of the following persons—

(a) the principal beneficiary and his or her wife or husband, if any, and his or her children or more remote issue, if any; or

(b) if there is no wife or husband or issue of the principal beneficiary in existence, the principal beneficiary and the persons who would, if he were actually dead, be entitled to the trust property or the income thereof or to the annuity fund, if any, or arrears of the annuity, as the case may be;

as the trustees in their absolute discretion, without being liable to account for the exercise of such discretion, think fit.

This secondary trust takes the form of a discretionary trust, so that the principal beneficiary no longer has the right to the income of the trust, but the trustees may at their discretion give him some or even all of that income, or otherwise use it for the support of his family. At any event, it will be possible to ensure his family's support without the income being seized by his trustee in bankruptcy.[24]

6 Gifts to be applied for purposes

It is a general principle of property that only a legally recognized person[25] may be an owner. The owner of property might, however, wish to transfer it not to specified individuals, but for the carrying out of a specified purpose. Clearly, an owner

---

[20] *Trappes v Meredith* (1871) 7 Ch App 248; *Re Evans* [1920] 2 Ch 304; *Re Walker* [1939] Ch 974; *Re Forder* [1927] 2 Ch 291.

[21] *Re Baring's Settlement Trusts* [1940] Ch 737.

[22] *Re Balfour's Settlement* [1938] Ch 928.   [23] *Re Hall* [1944] Ch 46.

[24] In some circumstance the trustee in bankruptcy will be entitled to income that is received by the bankrupt principal beneficiary as the assignee of his interests under the discretionary trust. See *Re Coleman* (1888) LR 39 Ch D 443; *Re Neil* (1890) 62 LT 649; *Re Ashby, ex p Wreford* [1892] 1 QB 872.

[25] This includes a company which is treated as having legal personality and therefore the capacity to hold property.

can apply his own property in the furtherance of whatever purpose he chooses, but the problem arises when he wishes to oblige a transferee of the property so to apply it. While it might be thought that a trustee could be obliged to use trust property in furtherance of a specified purpose, equity has adopted the general rule that, subject to limited exceptions, a trust can only be validly created in favour of persons rather than purposes.[26] A trust for the benefit of a pure purpose will be void. For example, in *Re Astor's Settlement Trusts*[27] a trust was established for the purpose of the 'maintenance of…good understanding sympathy and co-operation between nations' and 'the preservation of the independence and integrity of newspapers'. This was held to be invalid, as it was a gift for a purpose and not persons.

The most important exception to this principle is that property can be transferred on trust for purposes that are regarded as charitable in law, and the facilitation of charitable giving is one of the most important functions of the trust today. For example, in *Re Delius*[28] the widow of the composer Frederick Delius left her residuary estate[29] to trustees to promote the musical works of her late husband. This was upheld as a charitable gift, even though there was no person who would directly benefit from this gift. Where the trust is charitable in status, it attracts certain privileges, both legal and financial. Charitable trusts are examined in detail in Chapter 19.

7 Collective investment

Trusts are an effective vehicle by which individuals can pool their resources for collective investment, because the trust both enables the responsibilities for the management of property to be severed from its ownership and enjoyment and enables the ownership of property to be shared concurrently. One example of how trusts may be used in this way is the formation of a syndicate to enter the national lottery. Rather than entering as single individuals, a number of persons may come together to pool their resources and increase their chances of winning by financing the purchase of multiple combinations of numbers that they could not afford individually. Fundamental to the operation of such a syndicate would be the collection of the 'stakes' from the members, the purchase of the tickets and the distribution of any winnings. Since the ticket will be purchased in the name of only one member, that member will hold any winnings on trust for the members of the syndicate who have contributed, in proportion to the size of their stake.[30] More significantly, the ability of equity to facilitate collective investment lies at the heart of two important institutions, the unit trust and some pension schemes.

---

[26] See Chapter 13.   [27] [1952] Ch 534.   [28] [1957] Ch 299.

[29] The residuary estate is the balance of a deceased person's assets after their debts have been paid and all specific gifts by will have been made.

[30] See Wilkinson 'Running a Lottery Syndicate' (1995) NLJ 217.

(1) Unit trusts

Unit trusts have grown in significance since the middle of this century as a means of making modest investments on the stock exchange or in other securities. Suppose that Adrian has £1,000 to invest. He wishes to invest in stocks and shares, rather than to deposit his money with a bank or building society, because he believes that he will be better protected against the ravages of inflation. He knows the dangers of dealing on the stock market and wants to be able to spread the risk of his investment over a variety of securities, but his investment is too small to enable that. By buying units in a unit trust, Adrian is able to join together with other investors so that collectively they can spread their investments across the market. A management company, acting as a trustee, takes subscriptions from Adrian and other individual investors. They are allocated units in the trust assets in proportion to the sums that they have contributed. The subscriptions are pooled and used to purchase shares or to make other investments. The investors are thus able to share in a far wider portfolio than if they were to invest alone. Although the management company is responsible for making investment decisions, it is the investors collectively who have beneficial entitlement. Sophisticated provisions enable Adrian or the other investors to withdraw from the trust by being paid back a sum that represents the proceeds of their initial investment. New investors may buy into the trust at a price that reflects the current value of units.

(2) Pension schemes

Pension schemes can work in a very similar way to unit trusts, enabling members of the scheme to pool their contributions for the purpose of making investments that will later pay the pensions. Individuals pay into a collective investment fund managed by trustees, knowing that they will receive better returns than if they each attempted to invest individually. It is the separation of ownership from the management of property that makes this possible. Not all pension schemes work in this way. Most state old-age pension and many public sector pension schemes, however, are unfunded. This means that instead of the pensions being paid out of investments made by the pension scheme trustees, the pensions are paid directly by the government or the employer.

(3) The interface with contract

Although unit trusts and pension schemes are able to operate through mechanisms developed by the law of equity, the rights of individual investors and contributors may be dependent on the law of contract, not equity. For example, when a contributor to a pension scheme retires, he may have a contractual entitlement to receive a pension throughout his retirement based upon his final salary, rather than receiving back that proportion of the investments which represents his contributions. If he dies soon after retirement, he may draw less in pension than he has contributed. If he lives to a ripe old age, he may draw significantly more by way of pension than he has contributed. The contractual aspect of the arrangement is just as important as the trust or property aspects. Chapter 24 analyses the interrelationship between equity and contract in this area.

8 Property holding by clubs and societies

Clubs and societies that are not incorporated as companies are not capable of owning property in their own right since they lack the necessary legal personality. This raises the question as to how the funds of the society are to be held. In most cases they can be treated as belonging to the whole membership of the club, subject to the rules of the club.[31] Where the assets are vested in the members of the committee or some other group of individuals on behalf of the members of the club, those holding the club assets will be trustees for the members.

9 Trusts arising to protect legitimate expectations

Most of the situations examined concern the deliberate choice of a trust or power by an owner to achieve his objective. However, not every trust arises as a result of the owner's overt intention. For example, trusts commonly arise informally where a couple pool their resources in order to buy a home together, but the legal ownership of the home is put in the name of one of them alone. Often the couple will have given no thought as to how their arrangement would be characterized by the law. Provided that there is some common understanding that both of the couple were intended to have a share in the ownership of the property, the court will impose a trust to give effect to this intention.[32] Even in cases where there is no clear agreement, a trust will be imposed if the contributions made by each of the couple are such that the only reasonable inference is that, if asked, the couple would have said they intended to be joint owners.[33] *Grant v Edwards*[34] is a clear example. Mrs Linda Grant left her husband and moved in with Mr George Edwards. A modest house was purchased with the aid of a mortgage to provide a home for the couple. The purchase was made in the name of George Edwards and his brother, Arthur. Mrs Grant's name was not included in the purchase, since Mr Edwards suggested that it might complicate her divorce proceedings. Mrs Grant helped with the purchase by contributing to the repayment of the mortgage and in other ways. The court imposed a trust on George and Arthur to give effect to the understanding that Mrs Grant would be entitled to a half-share in the net value of the house. Chapter 11 looks in detail at how equity supports the acquisition of rights in the family home in this and other ways.

---

31 *Re Recher's Will Trusts* [1972] Ch 526.   32 See Chapter 11.
33 *Lloyds Bank plc v Rosset* [1991] 1 AC 107.   34 [1986] Ch 638.

10 Trusts that are remedial in effect

The examples above illustrate how equity enables a property owner to achieve more complicated objectives than making a simple outright transfer of his property. Those dealing with informal situations also show how equity sometimes acts to protect legitimate expectations. Equity also serves a powerful remedial function, however, by protecting the rights that it creates. In some situations equity protects an existing proprietary right, whereas in others it generates a new proprietary right. Although not universally accepted, some writers would characterize these proprietary rights as remedial or restitutionary trusts.[35] The use of remedial trusts has proved especially significant in the context of commercial transactions.

(1) Misappropriated property

Where property is subject to a trust, the proprietary rights of the beneficiaries to the trust property will not be defeated unless the property is acquired by a bona fide purchaser for value. The trust property can be traced through mixtures and substitutions. However, where property is not subject to an express trust, the rights of the owner have traditionally been governed by the common law. These rights have proved less than adequate because the common law has not developed a sophisticated means of identifying the proceeds and substitute-products thereof. Thus, where property has been misappropriated, owners may instead seek relief in equity by the demonstration that a constructive trust relationship has come into being. Where, for example, money has been misappropriated from a company by one of its senior employees, the fiduciary relationship between the company and the employee fastens a constructive trust on the stolen funds in favour of the company, and thus the company can seek remedies in equity against the recipients of the money even though it has passed through a mixed bank account.[36] In *Westdeutsche Landesbank Girozentrale v Islington London Borough Council*,[37] Lord Browne-Wilkinson suggested that a constructive trust would arise whenever money was stolen, irrespective of whether there was a fiduciary relationship or not.

(2) Avoiding the effects of insolvency

Creditors have also sought to use trusts as a means of avoiding the consequences of the insolvency of their debtors. If a creditor can demonstrate that he enjoys an equitable proprietary interest in some property in the bankrupt's hands, in other words, that the bankrupt debtor was holding it on trust for him, then, as has been seen, it will not form part of the bankrupt's assets to be distributed among his general creditors and

---

[35] See Oakley, *Constructive Trusts* (3rd edn, 1996); Birks, *An Introduction to the Law of Restitution* (1985).

[36] *Agip (Africa) Ltd v Jackson* [1992] 4 All ER 451.   [37] [1996] AC 669.

the beneficiary will gain priority in the insolvency as if he were a protected creditor. Thus, where one bank made a mistaken payment to another bank that became insolvent, it was held that the payee bank held the payment on trust for the bank making the payment.[38] Similarly, where a loan is made for a specific purpose, the money advanced will be held on trust for the creditor if the purpose has failed.[39] Where a customer has ordered goods from a supplier, they may be held on trust for him if they have been separated from the bulk so as to be identifiable as his property.[40] Where a fiduciary has earned an illegitimate profit at the expense of his principal, his duty to account for the profit received will give rise to a constructive trust in favour of the principal, thus ensuring that the principal would obtain priority over the fiduciary's other creditors in the event of his insolvency.[41]

11 Trusts and tax avoidance

Trusts have evolved to enable owners to deal with their property flexibly. However, one of the major motivations for the use of trusts is that they can be used effectively and creatively to reduce taxation. They are an essential aspect of tax planning, which aims to achieve legitimate tax avoidance.[42] As Lord Tomlin said in *IRC v Duke of Westminster*:

Every man is entitled if he can to order his affairs so that the tax attaching under the appropriate Act is less than it otherwise would be. If he succeeds in ordering them so as to secure that result, then, however unappreciative the Commissioners of Inland Revenue or his fellow taxpayers may be of his ingenuity, he cannot be compelled to pay an increased tax.[43]

This general principle has been qualified by more recent House of Lords' decisions which have held that where steps are inserted into a pre-ordained series of transactions which have no commercial or business purpose but are inserted solely to avoid tax, the transaction will be treated as a single whole and taxed as such.[44] This limitation applies to trusts.[45]

A detailed consideration of taxation is outside the scope of this book,[46] but it is essential to have an elementary grasp of the tax structure. Trusts have historically

---

[38] *Chase Manhattan Bank NA v Israel-British Bank (London) Ltd* [1981] Ch 105.

[39] *Barclays Bank Ltd v Quistclose Investments Ltd* [1970] AC 567.

[40] *Re Goldcorp Exchange* [1995] 1 AC 74.   [41] *A-G of Hong Kong v Reid* [1994] 1 AC 324.

[42] Tax avoidance is to be distinguished from illegitimate tax evasion.

[43] [1936] AC 1. See also *IRC v Willoughby* [1997] 1 WLR 1071.

[44] *W T Ramsay Ltd v IRC* [1982] AC 300; *Furniss v Dawson* [1984] AC 474; *Craven (Inspector of Taxes) v White (Stephen)* [1989] AC 398; *Ensign Tankers (Leasing) Ltd v Stokes (Inspector of Taxes)* [1992] 1 AC 655; *IRC v McGuckian* [1997] STC 908; *MacNiven (HM Inspector of Taxes) v Westmoreland Investments Ltd* [2003] 1 AC 311. See Lord Walker, 'Ramsay 25 Years on: Some Reflections on Tax Avoidance' (2004) 120 LQR 412.

[45] *Countess Fitzwilliam v IRC* [1992] STC 185.

[46] For further reading see: Whitehouse, *Revenue Law—Principles and Practice* (20th edn, 2003); Moffat, *Trusts Law* (5th edn, 2009), Chs 3 and 8; Maudsley and Burn, *Trusts and Trustees: Cases and Materials* (7th edn, 2008), Part II; Tiley, *Revenue Law* (6th edn, 2008).

been used to minimize liability to taxation. In consequence there has been an ongoing 'battle' with the government seeking to raise revenue. As a result, tax laws have become ever more complicated, and the scope to use trusts to reduce tax liabilities has diminished. There are still some instances where trusts can be used as part of tax planning, but expert advice or knowledge is required. There are three main types of taxation that will affect a trust: income tax, capital gains tax, and inheritance tax. Each will be briefly examined and their applicability to trusts considered.

(1) Income tax

(a) Definition of income tax

Income tax, as Lord Macnaghten somewhat unnecessarily pointed out,[47] 'is a tax on income'. However, income tax is not payable on a person's whole income, but only his 'taxable income'. There are a number of basic principles. Taxpayers can set some expenses against their income, and only the net figure is subject to tax. Most taxpayers are then given a personal allowance, which means that the first part of their income is not subject to any income tax. The rate of tax that is paid on the remainder of their income then increases, with higher rates of tax being paid on higher 'slices' of income. The levels of personal allowance, the percentage tax rate, and the levels at which these tax rates come into effect are varied frequently, often annually. Different types of income may be subject to different rates of tax, and some income is taxed before being received by the taxpayer. For instance, banks paying interest deduct a sum for income tax before paying the interest to the investor.

(b) Income tax and trusts

In order to prevent trusts being used to avoid the payment of income tax, trustees are liable to pay income tax on the income of the trust. There is no personal allowance. The rate of tax depends upon the type of trust and the type of income.

(c) The receipt of trust income by trust beneficiaries

Complicated provisions govern the payment of income tax by beneficiaries receiving trust income. In most cases the beneficiaries are able to set off any income tax paid by the trustees against their own liability for income tax. In some cases it is possible for a beneficiary to claim a refund of tax paid by the trustees where this exceeds the beneficiary's own liability for tax.

(d) Trusts as a means of avoiding income tax

Trusts have in the past been used as an effective means of avoiding income tax. The scope for doing this has been much reduced by changes to the tax regime, with measures such as the introduction of a high rate of tax for discretionary trusts, which had

---

[47] *LCC v A-G* [1901] AC 26, at 35.

previously been used by some settlors to allow the trustees to distribute income to beneficiaries who the settlor might otherwise have wanted to support out of taxed income, but who had a lower rate of taxation than the settlor. To further limit tax avoidance, income under a trust is treated as the income of the settlor unless the income arises from property in which the settlor has no interest. A settlor is treated as having an interest in property if that property or any property derived from it can or might be payable to or for the benefit of the settlor or the settlor's spouse in any circumstances whatsoever.

(2) Capital gains tax

(a) Definition of capital gains tax

Capital gains tax is payable on the increase in value of 'chargeable assets' when they are realized. What is taxable is the difference in value of the asset between the date of acquisition and of disposal. Taxpayers are allowed an annual exemption, the amount of which is varied from time to time.

(b) Capital gains tax and trusts

Capital gains tax cannot be avoided by settling property on trust. A settlor will be liable to pay capital gains tax personally when he settles property on trust, as this is considered a disposal.[48] In addition, trustees pay capital gains tax on disposals by the trust. The trustees will be liable when they dispose of assets as part of the administration of the trust, and where the beneficiary becomes absolutely entitled to the property held on trust, other than by the death of the life tenant, which is a 'deemed disposal'.[49] This deemed disposal means that capital gains tax is payable whenever a settlement is brought to an end and the property resettled, which increases the costs of terminating or resettling property.[50]

(3) Inheritance tax

(a) Definition and history of inheritance tax

Inheritance tax is, in essence, a tax payable on capital that passes on death, but it also applies to inter vivos gifts that were made less than seven years before the death occurred. It is something of a combination of two earlier taxes: estate duty and capital transfer tax. Prior to 1974 there was just one tax, estate duty, which was payable on death.[51] Transfers inter vivos would be liable to estate duty if made seven years before the death.[52] Estate duty was payable on the whole trust fund on the death of a life tenant, but was easily avoided by the creation of a discretionary trust where the

---

[48] Taxation of Chargeable Gains Act 1992, s 53.   [49] Ss 54(1), 71.
[50] See Chapter 18.   [51] Finance Act 1894, ss 1, 2.
[52] Finance Act 1968, s 35.

beneficiaries had no interest in the fund itself.[53] In 1974 estate duty was replaced by capital transfer tax, which was to be payable on any transfer of capital either inter vivos or on death, although higher rates applied to transfers on death. In 1986 capital transfer tax was replaced by inheritance tax.

(b) The operation of inheritance tax

Section 1 of the Inheritance Tax Act 1984 provides that 'Inheritance Tax shall be charged on the value transferred by a chargeable transfer.' The tax is charged on 'transfers of value', in other words, transfers which diminish the value of the transferor's estate. Some transfers are 'exempt transfers' that are not liable to tax. These include most transfers between spouses and relatively small gifts up to a specified annual limit. Where 'chargeable transfers' have been made, tax is payable on the cumulative total of all such transfers made within seven years of the taxpayer's death, but taper relief has the effect of reducing the rates of tax that apply to transactions made between three and seven years before death. Where a transfer has been made more than seven years before the taxpayer's death, the transfer is not subject to inheritance tax.

(c) Inheritance tax and trusts

The rules relating to inheritance tax and trusts are complicated. There are four main occasions when inheritance tax may apply to trusts: when assets are transferred into a trust; when a trust reaches a ten-year anniversary; when property is transferred out of a trust or the trust comes to an end; and when someone dies and a trust is involved when sorting out their estate. Inheritance tax rules were changed in 2006 and different rules may apply to existing trusts.

(i) Transfers into the trust

Where a settlor transfers funds into a trust, and that transfer, together with any other transfers he has made during the previous seven years exceed a specified threshold, a charge arises to inheritance tax. The rate of tax is lower than the rate payable on death, but if the settlor dies within seven years of making the gift, a further tax charge is made. Transfers into a trust for a disabled person do not carry an immediate tax charge, but are still subject to a tax charge on the death of the settlor.

(ii) Ten-year anniversary charge

Some trusts are subject to an inheritance tax 'periodic charge' on every tenth anniversary.

(iii) Charges on transfers out of the trust

An inheritance tax exit charge is levied on certain transactions when assets are distributed to beneficiaries, where a beneficiary becomes absolutely entitled, when the trust comes to an end, and in certain other situations.

---

[53] *Gartside v IRC* [1968] AC 553; see Chapter 17.

(iv) Charges on a beneficiary's death

The value of assets within a trust can be treated as part of a beneficiary's estate, and therefore be subject to inheritance tax on the beneficiary's death. This is most obviously so where the beneficiary is a beneficiary under a bare trust. There are certain other instances where the value of a beneficiary's rights may be treated as part of the beneficiary's estate for inheritance tax purposes.

(v) Charges on the settlor's death

It has already been noted above that where a settlor dies within seven years of establishing a trust, and the inter vivos rate of inheritance tax has been paid, a further charge arises to bring the total inheritance tax rate up to the rate payable on death. Even if no inheritance tax were payable when the trust was first set up, the value of all transfers to trusts with seven years of the settlor's death have to be taken into account in valuing the deceased's estate for inheritance tax purposes.

12 Distinguishing other mechanisms that facilitate a separation between the management and ownership of property

Much of the practical usage of trusts derives from their ability to separate the management responsibilities from the ownership of property. However, this ability is not unique to trusts. This section will provide a brief examination of some situations where such a separation may be facilitated by other means.

(1) Companies

One means by which a separation between management and ownership of property can be made in practice is through public companies.[54] The capital for establishing a public company is provided by the shareholders who originally subscribed to the shares. They own the company. If it is wound up, any surplus funds remaining after the payment of the company's creditors will be distributed among them. Any profits that the company makes which are not capitalized by being retained to develop the business will also be distributed by way of a dividend to the shareholders. In a very real sense, therefore, the company belongs to the shareholders. It is they who benefit from its capital value and from the income that it produces. Yet the shareholders of a public company will very rarely be involved in its day-to-day management. Instead, they will appoint directors at a general meeting to whom they delegate the everyday

---

[54] The analysis given here applies equally to private companies, although it is more likely with private companies that the same individuals will be both shareholders and directors.

management of the enterprise. The directors (unless they are also shareholders) will not themselves have a stake in the assets of the company, although within the limits of the authority given to them they will be able to decide how the assets of the company should be used. The directors will, of course, be under an obligation to exercise their powers of management honestly and properly. This is a duty that they owe, through the company, to the shareholders.

(?) Agency

(a) The agency relationship

The relationship of agency is the major means by which the common law enables the management and enjoyment of property to be separated. For example, Jake is the owner of a car he wishes to sell. Rather than arranging a contract of sale himself, he can delegate the task to another. He could authorize a garage to display the car on their forecourt and to sell the car to any purchaser prepared to pay more than a price arranged in advance. Here, Jake would be the principal and the garage would be acting as his agent. The relationship between the principal and the agent is contractual, and under this contract ownership in the car never passes to the agent. The agent is empowered to enter a contract with the purchaser on the principal's behalf, and property in the car will pass directly from the principal to the purchaser under that contract. Although he was not a party to the contract, the essence of agency is that it brings about a contract that is binding on the principal. For example, if the garage agreed to sell the car to Keith, this would bring about a contract with Jake, and if he refused to deliver the car for personal reasons, Keith would be entitled to maintain an action against him for breach of contract. Again, subject to any special arrangement between them, the agent owes a duty to his principal to act honestly and properly. An agent will be liable to his principal under the tort of negligence even where the agent is acting gratuitously.[55]

Agency is most commonly found in commercial situations. All company directors are treated as agents of the company, authorized to make decisions and to enter into engagements on behalf of the company. The manager of a shop, and the sales staff in the shop, will be agents of the proprietor, whether that proprietor is an individual or a company. Agency is less commonly found in non-commercial contexts,[56] and where it is, it is most likely to be used to support a single transaction.

(b) Automatic termination of agency

In an agency relationship the agent represents his principal for the limited purposes for which the principal has granted him authority. However, the agent cannot enjoy a greater authority than the principal has given him, or than the principal himself

---

[55] *Chaudhry v Prabhakar* [1988] 3 All ER 718, CA.

[56] Although see *Conservative & Unionist Central Office v Burrell* [1982] 1 WLR 522, discussed below, Chapter 24.

enjoys. For this reason, if the principal loses his contractual capacity, the agent automatically loses his authority to enter into contracts with third parties that are binding on the principal. He cannot enjoy the capacity to enter into contracts that the principal could not have entered himself. Thus, if the principal dies, or loses mental capacity, the authority of the agent is automatically terminated, whether or not the agent is aware of the principal's situation.[57]

(c) Powers of attorney

Where a principal wishes an agent to be empowered to enter into a transaction requiring a deed, the authority must itself be conferred by way of deed termed a power of attorney. An agent so appointed is described as an attorney. The phrase 'power of attorney', as well as describing the deed and arrangement under which an agent is permitted to execute a deed on the principal's behalf, is also used to describe a general authority given by a principal permitting an agent to undertake any business concerning property on behalf of the principal. Such an authority could be given by a principal who was expecting to spend some time abroad, during which it would be impracticable for him to manage his own affairs.

(d) Lasting powers of attorney[58]

(i) The need for lasting powers of attorney

Since a power of attorney is a form of agency, it will also terminate automatically if the principal loses his capacity. This poses particular difficulties for a society with an increasingly large elderly population, many of whom may go on to develop senile dementia, or other types of mental incapacity. An older person may wish to grant someone she trusts, perhaps a child or other relative, a comprehensive power of attorney over her affairs because she may feel that she is no longer able to cope. However, although the power of attorney will be effective as long as she retains capacity, if she becomes mentally incapable, the authority will automatically terminate and the attorney will no longer be able to deal with her property. For this reason, the enduring power of attorney was introduced by the Enduring Powers of Attorney Act 1985. This mechanism was replaced by the lasting power of attorney under the Mental Capacity Act 2005, ss 9–14, which is more comprehensive, as it allows the donor to choose someone to not only manage their financial affairs and property, but also to make decisions concerning their health and welfare.[59]

---

[57] See *Drew v Nunn* (1879) 4 QBD 661; *Yonge v Toynbee* [1910] 1 KB 215.

[58] From 1 October 2007, enduring powers of attorney (under the Enduring Powers of Attorney Act 1985) were replaced by lasting powers of attorney under the Mental Capacity Act 2005. Enduring powers of attorney granted before that period may still be used (Mental Capacity Act 2005, s 66 and Sch 4), provided they have already been registered (Mental Capacity Act 2005, Sch 5, para 11), or they are registered under the 2005 Act (Mental Capacity Act 2005, Sch 4, Pt 4).

[59] Mental Capacity Act 2005, s 9(1). It is also possible for the donor to appoint different persons to look after their property and their personal welfare.

(ii) Creation of lasting powers of attorney

A lasting power can only be created in accordance with the requirements set out in the Mental Capacity Act 2005, s 9(2); namely that it must be created using the prescribed form and be registered with the Public Guardian,[60] the donees of the power must be properly appointed,[61] and the donor must have the capacity to execute the power.[62] The instrument creating the lasting power of attorney must be certified—this replaces the requirement to have the signature of the donor and donee witnessed as under the enduring power of attorney,[63] The certifier must confirm that, in his opinion, the donor understands the purpose and scope of the document they are signing.

(iii) Supervision by the court

Clearly, the lasting power of attorney gives the attorney tremendous power over the affairs of the person who created it, and there is a real danger of abuse, particularly after the creator has become incapable and is not able to supervise the exercise of the power. For this reason, the Court of Protection[64] exercises a supervisory function and this explains why the lasing power of attorney must be registered to be effective. By ss 22 and 23, the court has powers in relation to the validity and operation of lasting powers of attorney, respectively.

(iv) Notice to named persons

When the attorney applies to the court for the power to be registered, he is under a duty to give notice to named persons in accordance with Sch 1 to the Act.[65] The Act allows the donor to nominate the 'named persons' he or she wishes to be notified,[66] and this will normally be used to allow relatives to be notified.[67] This would enable the relatives or other named persons (who will normally include those most likely to be affected by the way that the attorney deals with the donor's property), to object to the registration.[68]

(e) Agency and equity

Agency and powers of attorney are common law concepts, but both are supported by equity. The common law remedies for a failure by an agent or attorney to act in

---

[60] S 2(2).9(2)(b). The requirements for registration are set out in Sch 1 of the Act. Part 1 of Sch 1 (paras 1–3) relates to the form of the power of attorney and include the requirement that the document creating the power contains explanatory information of the general effect of the power to make clear the effect to both the principal and to the attorney (see para 2(2)). Part 2 (paras 4–17) sets out the registration regime.

[61] Mental Capacity Act 2005, s 10.

[62] Capacity is presumed under the Act (s 1), but the court has power to act where the donor lacks capacity (see s 23).

[63] Mental Capacity Act 2005, Sch 1, para 2(e).

[64] The Court of Protection is an office of the Supreme Court of Justice responsible for administering the affairs of those who are incapable of doing so for themselves by virtue of mental incapacity. See Mental Capacity Act 2005, Pt 2.

[65] Para 6.   [66] Para (2)(c)(i).

[67] The donor does not have to name any persons, and this is permissible under para (2)(c)(ii) of Sch 1.

[68] Mental Capacity Act 2005, Sch 1, para 13.

accordance with the terms of the authority conferred, or to break the duty of loyalty and care owed to the principal, are to deprive a purported but improper transaction of effect[69] and to impose on the agent or attorney an obligation to compensate the principal in damages for any loss. In some cases a third party suffering loss will have a right of redress against the agent by way of damages for breach of warranty of authority. Equity recognizes agency by treating agents or attorneys, and company directors, as fiduciaries,[70] standing in such a position of trust with regard to their principal that they can be held liable to account for any abuse of their position. Thus, if they make an unauthorized profit, they can be obliged to hand the benefit over to their principal. In this respect, there is a clear analogy between the position of an agent and the position of a trustee.

(f) Agency and ownership

Although agency provides a means by which powers of management can be divorced from the rights of enjoyment of property, it is generally considered to leave ownership in the principal unless the agent exercises his authority to pass ownership to himself or a third party. Even though the principal has conferred rights of disposal on the agent, this does not normally deprive him of his own rights of management and disposal. The agency is simply an authority which the principal gives to someone else to do some of those things which he can do himself. Moreover, apart from some limited exceptions, the principal retains the right to give instructions to the agent and to terminate the agency. The divorce between management and enjoyment is accordingly neither complete nor permanent.

(g) Mandate

Agency is normally used to permit someone entrusted by the principal to enter into contracts on behalf of the principal. The common law recognizes, however, a form of agency in which an agent is permitted to dispose of property belonging to the principal. This form of agency is known as mandate. For instance, Howard might authorize his wife, Winnie, to sign cheques payable from his own bank account. Similarly, Elizabeth, wishing to distribute a sum of money to the poor, might give a sum in cash to Philip, authorizing him to choose the recipients. In each case, the agent may not be entering into contracts with third parties but is given authority to transfer title in the principal's property to a third party. Unless and until this authority is exercised, the title in the property remains with the principal.

---

[69] This will be the case both where the transaction lies outside the limits of the agent's authority and where there has been some procedural impropriety.

[70] See Chapter 30.

6

Equitable remedies in modern English law

The previous chapters have charted the historical development of the Court of Chancery, of equity, and of equity's creation, the trust. The trust is not the only way in which equity has contributed to legal development. Equity also created remedies that were not available at common law. This chapter will examine the most significant of these remedies and show how equitable remedies have continued to evolve and how they contribute to enforcing legal rights, on occasions creating new rights and obligations.

1 Introduction to equitable remedies

Equitable remedies apply in all fields of law, from disputes over property or entitlement in contract and intellectual property, to preventing harm, or to the proceeds of wrongdoing being dissipated before a claim can be made against them. Equity evolved these remedies in the Court of Chancery to provide alternative relief to the common law remedy of damages. Perhaps the most fundamental principle concerning equitable remedies is that they are not available as of right, but are discretionary, it lying within the powers of the judge to decide not to award a remedy even if a strong prima facie case has been established. An equitable remedy is a personal remedy against the defendant, as equity acts in personam, and disobeying any remedy is therefore classified as a contempt of court.[1]

2 Specific performance

At common law the only remedy for breach of contract was damages. A defendant who had breached his contract could not be compelled to perform, but was liable to compensate the claimant for any loss he suffered as a consequence of the breach.[2] This

---

[1] See, for example, *Mid Suffolk DC v Clarke* [2007] 1 WLR 98, where it was confirmed that the failure of the defendant to comply with an order of specific performance is a contempt of court, not a breach of contract.
[2] *Tai Hing Cotton Mills Ltd v Kanmsing Knitting Factory* [1979] AC 91.

might be his 'expectation loss' or 'reliance loss'. The claimant was expected, at common law, to use his compensation to purchase alternative performance. He could buy replacement goods on the open market, or find an alternative supplier of services. As Lord Diplock observed in *Photo Production Ltd v Securicor Transport Ltd*, this means the defendant has the option of either performing the contract, or breaching the contract and paying damages:

> Every failure to perform a primary obligation is a breach of contract. The secondary obligation on the part of the contract-breaker to which it gives rise by implication of the common law is to pay monetary compensation to the other party for the loss sustained by him in consequence of the breach... [3]

In effect, the defendant can buy his way out of performance of the contract. However, equity intervened where the common law remedy was inadequate,[4] because it would have been unjust to allow the defendant to avoid performance and merely pay damages. By means of an order of specific performance the court can compel the defendant to perform his contractual obligations. The court is also willing to order specific performance of a contract to confer benefits on third parties.[5] Specific performance is an order made personally against the defendant. It illustrates how equity acts in personam.[6] If the defendant fails to comply, he will be in contempt of court and faces the possibility of imprisonment.

(1) When is specific performance available?

Specific performance is not generally available as a remedy for breach of contract. As Lord Selbourne LC said in *Wilson v Northampton and Banbury Junction Rly Co*:

> The court gives specific performance instead of damages, only when it can by that means do more and complete justice.[7]

In *Co-operative Insurance v Argyll Stores*,[8] this perspective was reiterated by the House of Lords. Lord Hoffmann stated:

> Specific performance is traditionally regarded in English law as an exceptional remedy, as opposed to the common law damages to which a successful plaintiff is entitled as of right... by the nineteenth century it was orthodox doctrine that the power to decree specific performance was part of the discretionary jurisdiction of the Court of Chancery to do justice in cases in which the remedies available at common law were inadequate.[9]

There are a number of well-recognized circumstances in which it is recognized that damages would not provide an adequate remedy so that specific performance is ordinarily available.

---

[3] [1980] 1 All ER 556.   [4] *Hutton v Watling* [1948] Ch 26; affd [1948] Ch 398.
[5] *Beswick v Beswick* [1968] AC 58; *Gurtner v Circuit* [1968] 2 QB 587.
[6] See *Penn v Lord Baltimore* (1750) 1 Ves Sen 444; *Richard West & Partners (Inverness) Ltd v Dick* [1969] 1 All ER 289.
[7] (1874) 9 Ch App 279, at 284.   [8] [1997] 3 All ER 297.   [9] Ibid., at 301.

(a) Contracts concerning land

Land is always deemed to be unique as it is assumed that there is no identical market alternative.[10] Therefore, as Lord Diplock observed in *Sudbrook Trading Estate Ltd v Eggleton*, damages would:

constitute a wholly inadequate and unjust remedy for the breach. That is why the normal remedy is by a decree of specific performance…[11]

Specific performance is therefore available in respect of a contract for the sale of land, for the grant of an interest in land, or even for the grant of a licence to occupy land.[12] A contract for the sale of land, or the disposition of an interest in land, must be made in writing in accordance with the provisions of s 2 of the Law of Property (Miscellaneous Provisions) Act 1989. Specific performance will not therefore be available to enforce an oral contract in respect of an interest in land, although such an agreement might give rise to a remedy by way of proprietary estoppel.[13]

(b) Contracts for the sale of unique personal property

Specific performance will not normally be granted to enforce a contract for the sale of personal property because a market substitute can readily be obtained. However, if the item is unique and there is no available alternative the court may grant a decree of specific performance. For example, in *Falcke v Gray*,[14] Kindersley V-C would have granted specific performance of a contract for the sale of two oriental jars which were of 'unusual beauty, rarity and distinction' if he had not found that the consideration was inadequate.[15] A contract to sell shares may also be specifically enforceable if they are not available in the general market.[16]

(c) Practical unavailability of market substitutes

Specific performance has also been granted of contracts for the sale of goods that are not unique and are normally readily available in the market where special circumstances have meant that substitutes are in fact unobtainable. In *Sky Petroleum Ltd v VIP Petroleum Ltd*,[17] the plaintiff sought an injunction to prevent the defendants

---

[10] Equity treated land as unique before the practice developed in Georgian and later periods of building large estates of houses of identical or near-identical design.

[11] [1983] 1 AC 444, at 478.

[12] *Verrall v Great Yarmouth Borough Council* [1981] QB 202. This is so even though a contractual licence does not create an interest in the land capable of binding successors in title of the licensor: *Ashburn Anstalt v Arnold* [1989] Ch 1.

[13] *Yaxley v Gotts* [2000] Ch 162. See Chapter 11, at p 391 *et seq.*   [14] (1859) 4 Drew 651.

[15] See also *Pearne v Lisle* (1749) Amb 75 (slaves could be compelled to return to plantations by their master); *Thorn v Public Works Commissioners* (1863) 32 Beav 490 (removal of unspecified building materials under a tender for the whole); *Bohnke v Bede Shipping Co Ltd* [1927] 1 KB 649 (contract for the sale of a steamship, which had unique and special value to the plaintiff); *Phillips v Lamdin* [1949] 2 KB 33. Contrast *Cohen v Roche* [1927] 1 KB 169 (eight 'Heppelwhite' chairs, which were not considered of any special value or interest by the court).

[16] *Duncuft v Albrecht* (1841) 12 Sim 189; *Oughtred v IRC* [1960] AC 206; *Neville v Wilson* [1997] Ch 144.

[17] [1974] 1 All ER 954. Compare also *Howard E Perry & Co Ltd v British Railways Board* [1980] 1 WLR 1375.

from breaching their contract as the exclusive supplier of petrol and diesel for the plaintiff's garages. Goulding J granted the injunction,[18] which had the same practical effect as specific performance of the contract, because the market in petroleum had changed considerably since the contract had been entered and the plaintiff had no market alternative:

the petroleum market is in an unusual state in which a would-be buyer cannot go out into the market and contract with another seller, possibly at some sacrifice as to price. Here, the defendant company appears for practical purposes to be the plaintiff company's sole means of keeping its business going…[19]

(d) Contracts where the quantification of damages would be difficult[20]

Specific performance has been ordered of contracts to sell or pay annuities because the value of the rights is uncertain,[21] and of contracts to execute a mortgage for money already lent because the value of having security for the loan cannot be quantified.[22] Specific performance has also been awarded where the loss is difficult to prove,[23] or where the defendant is unlikely to be able to pay damages.[24]

(e) Claimant entitled only to nominal damages

Specific performance has been ordered where the claimant would only be entitled to recover nominal damages for his loss. In *Beswick v Beswick*,[25] Mr Beswick had made a contract with his nephew to pay a pension to his wife. On his death the nephew refused to pay. Although Mrs Beswick could not sue in her own right because she was not privy to the contract, she was entitled to sue in her capacity as Mr Beswick's personal representative. The court ordered the nephew to perform the contract because damages would be an inadequate remedy. Mr Beswick had not personally suffered any loss and would therefore have been entitled only to nominal damages. That would not have compensated his widow, who had suffered a substantial loss.

(2) Contracts where specific performance is not available

In some well-recognized situations it is clear that the court will not enforce a contract by means of a decree of specific performance.

---

[18] An injunction is an order of the court prohibiting the person enjoined from a particular course of conduct. It is considered more fully later in this chapter.

[19] [1974] 1 All ER 954, at 956.

[20] *Société des Industries Metallurgiques SA v Bronx Engineering Co Ltd* [1975] 1 Lloyd's Rep 465, CA.

[21] *Ball v Coggs* (1710) 1 Bro Parl Cas 140, HL; *Kenney v Wexham* (1822) 6 Madd 355; *Adderly v Dixon* (1824) 1 Sim & St 607; *Clifford v Turrell* (1841) 1 Y & C Ch Cas 138; *Beswick v Beswick* [1968] AC 58.

[22] *Ashton v Corrigan* (1871) LR 13 Eq 76; *Swiss Bank Corpn v Lloyds Bank Ltd* [1982] AC 584h.

[23] *Decro-Wall International SA v Practitioners in Marketing Ltd* [1971] 1 WLR 361.

[24] *Evans Marshall & Co v Bertola SA* [1973] 1 All ER 992.

[25] [1968] AC 58.

(a) Contracts of personal service

Equity will not specifically enforce a contract of personal service requiring the defendant to work for the claimant because this would infringe his liberty.[26] As Fry LJ observed in *De Francesco v Barnum*:

The courts are bound to be jealous, lest they should turn contracts of service into contracts of slavery.[27]

The court will also normally refuse to grant an injunction to give effect to a contractual provision that the defendant is not to work for anyone else, as this would indirectly amount to specific performance of the contract.[28] For instance, in *Page One Records Ltd v Britton*[29] a pop group entered into an exclusive management agreement. As part of this, they agreed not to work for any other manager. Stamp J refused to grant an injunction to enforce this contractual term. In some cases it has been questioned whether equity will always decline to order specific performance of contracts for personal services, particularly given the radical change in the nature of employment over the century and a half since the rule was adopted. In *CH Giles & Co Ltd v Morris*,[30] Megarry J was at pains to emphasize that there was no absolute 'rule' that there could never be specific performance of a contract for personal services. He reconsidered the basis upon which it has been justified:

Such a rule is plainly not absolute and without exception ... The reasons why the court is reluctant to decree specific performance of a contract for personal services (and I would regard it as a strong reluctance rather than a rule) are, I think, more complex and more firmly bottomed in human nature. If a singer contracts to sing, there could no doubt be proceedings for committal if, ordered to sing, the singer remained obstinately dumb. But if instead the singer sang flat, or sharp, or too fast, or too slowly, or too loudly, or too quietly ... the threat of committal would reveal itself as a most unsatisfactory weapon: for who could say whether such imperfections of performance were natural or self-induced.[31]

He considered that 'not all contracts of personal service ... are as dependant as this on matters of opinion and judgment, nor do all such contracts involve the same degree of the daily impact of person upon person'. Therefore in some circumstances specific performance might be available because 'the matter is one of the balance of advantage and disadvantage in relation to the particular obligations in question'.[32]

In *Hill v C A Parsons & Co Ltd*,[33] the court prevented an employer from dismissing an employee shortly before the date at which he was due to retire. His dismissal

---

[26] *Lumley v Wagner* (1852) 1 De GM & G 604; *Johnson v Shrewsbury and Birmingham Rly* (1853) 3 De GM & G 914; *Brett v East India and London Shipping Co Ltd* (1864) 2 Hem & M 404; *Britain v Rossiter* (1879) 11 QBD 123; *Rigby v Connol* (1880) 14 Ch D 482; *De Francesco v Barnum* (1890) 45 Ch D 430. See also Trade Union and Labour Relations Act 1974, s 16.

[27] (1890) 45 Ch D 430.

[28] See, however, *Warner Bros Picture Inc v Nelson* [1937] 1 KB 209, where the film star Bette Davis was compelled to work for Warner Brothers for the remainder of her contractual period with the movie studio.

[29] [1967] 3 All ER 822.   [30] [1972] 1 WLR 307.   [31] Ibid., at 318.

[32] See also *Hill v CA Parsons & Co Ltd* [1972] Ch 305; *Powell v London Borough of Brent* [1987] IRLR 446; *Hughes v London Borough of Southwark* [1988] IRLR 55.

[33] [1972] Ch 305.

would have had serious implications for his entitlement to a pension which could not adequately be compensated in damages. However, in *Scandinavian Trading Tanker Co AB v Flota Petrolera Ecuatoriana, The Scaptrade*,[34] the House of Lords, in the context of a shipping time charter, reaffirmed the equitable principle that a contract for services will not normally be specifically enforced.[35] It is noteworthy that, under employment legislation, an employee may be entitled to reinstatement. This may give cause to believe that in future the courts will be less reluctant to order specific performance of contracts of employment.

(b) Contracts requiring constant supervision

In *Ryan v Mutual Tontine Westminster Chambers Association*,[36] it was held that the court will not grant specific performance of a contract where constant supervision would be required, as the court is unable to supervise the performance of a contract. The defendants, who were the lessors of a block of residential flats, covenanted to provide a resident porter who would be in constant attendance. The Court of Appeal held that this covenant could not be specifically enforced because 'the execution of it would require constant superintendence by the Court, which the Court in such cases has always declined to give'.[37] The rationale for the refusal of specific performance in such circumstances was examined by the House of Lords in *Co-operative Insurance v Argyll Stores (Holdings) Ltd*.[38] Lord Hoffmann held such refusal was not because the court would have to literally supervise the execution of the order, but because the court might have to give an 'indefinite series of rulings' whether the order had been kept or broken.[39] He emphasized that the only means by which the court could enforce the order was through the 'quasi-criminal procedure of punishment for contempt', and that given the seriousness of a finding of contempt litigation would be likely to be 'heavy and expensive'. Thus, he held that:

The possibility of repeated applications over a period of time means that, in comparison with a once and for all inquiry as to damages, the enforcement of the remedy is likely to be expensive in terms of costs to the parties and the resources of the judicial system.[40]

The refusal to grant specific performance where constant supervision was required had been followed in many cases.[41] However, in *Tito v Waddell (No 2)*,[42] Megarry V-C considered that the prohibition was not absolute. He suggested that the real issue 'is whether there is a sufficient definition of what has to be done in order to comply with

---

[34] [1983] 2 AC 694.   [35] Ibid., at 700–701, per Lord Diplock.
[36] [1893] 1 Ch 116.   [37] Ibid., at 123, per Lord Esher MR.
[38] [1997] 3 All ER 297; Phang 'Specific Performance—Exploring the Roots of "Settled Practice"' (1998) 61 MLR 421; Jones 'Specific Performance: A Lessee's Covenant to Keep Open a Retail Store' [1997] CLJ 488.
[39] [1997] 3 All ER 297, at 302.   [40] Ibid., at 303.
[41] *Rayner v Stone* (1762) 2 Eden 128; *Blackett v Bates* (1865) 1 Ch App 117; *Powell Duffryn Steam Coal Co v Taff Vale Rly Co* (1874) 9 Ch App 331; *Phipps v Jackson* (1887) 56 LJ Ch 550; *Dominion Coal Co v Dominion Iron & Steel Co Ltd and National Trust Co Ltd* [1909] AC 293; *Dowty Boulton Paul Ltd v Wolverhampton Corpn* [1971] 1 WLR 204; *Braddon Towers Ltd v International Stores Ltd* [1987] 1 EGLR 209.
[42] [1977] Ch 106.

the order of the court'.[43] In *Posner v Scott-Lewis*,[44] Mervyn Davies J was therefore prepared to grant an order for specific performance where the defendant landlords had covenanted to employ a resident porter solely for the purposes of keeping the common parts clean, looking after the central heating, and carrying rubbish to the dustbins. He held that the key questions determining whether an order should be granted were:

(a) is there a sufficient definition of what has to be done in order to comply with the order of the court? (b) Will enforcing compliance involve superintendence by the court to an unacceptable degree? (c) What are the respective prejudices or hardships that will be suffered by the parties if the order is made or not made?[45]

However, in *Co-operative Insurance v Argyll Stores (Holdings) Ltd*,[46] the House of Lords held that Megarry V-C was wrong to dismiss the difficulty of supervision as an objection to specific performance. It held that in such cases specific performance should be refused. Lord Hoffmann explained:

This is a convenient point at which to distinguish between orders which require a defendant to carry on an activity, such as running a business over a more or less extended period of time, and orders which require him to achieve a result. The possibility of repeated applications for rulings on compliance with the order which arises in the former case does not exist to anything like the same extent in the latter. Even if the achievement of the result is a complicated matter which will take some time, the court, if called upon to rule, only has to examine the finished work and say whether it complies with the order.[47]

This distinction explains why the courts have decreed specific performance of building contracts[48] and repairing covenants,[49] since the performance of such obligations requires a result to be achieved. However, Lord Hoffmann held that even a contract requiring mutual supervision may be enforced by way of specific performance if a defendant had committed a gross breach of personal faith in breaching his obligation.[50]

(c) Contracts to carry on a business

In *Co-operative Insurance v Argyll Stores (Holdings) Ltd*,[51] the House of Lords held that specific performance should not be granted of a contract to carry on a business. The defendants were a company that leased a retail unit in a Sheffield shopping centre, where they operated a Safeway supermarket. In their lease they had covenanted to keep the premises open for 'retail trade'. Following a review of their national operations, the defendants decided to close the store, along with other loss-making supermarkets. The plaintiff landlords sought specific performance of the

---

[43] See also *Wolverhampton Corpn v Emmons* [1901] 1 KB 515.   [44] [1987] Ch 25.

[45] Ibid., at 36.   [46] [1997] 3 All ER 297.   [47] Ibid., at 303.

[48] *Wolverhampton Corp v Emmons* [1901] 1 KB 515, where Romer LJ awarded specific performance of a building contract on the basis that the building work was clearly defined, damages would have been an inadequate remedy and the defendant had possession of the relevant land.

[49] *Jeune v Queens Cross Properties Ltd* [1974] Ch 97.

[50] [1997] 3 All ER 297, at 307–308. He held that the defendant had not in fact acted in such a way. See also *Greene v West Cheshire Rly Co* (1871) LR 13 Eq 44.

[51] [1997] 3 All ER 297.

covenant for the remainder of the lease, which had over nineteen years left to run. The first instance judge refused to order specific performance on the grounds that the authorities revealed a 'settled practice' that orders would not be made requiring a defendant to run a business. The majority of the Court of Appeal held that specific performance should be decreed, arguing that any objection on the grounds that such an order would require constant supervision was outmoded.[52] The House of Lords granted the defendant's appeal and held that specific performance should not be ordered, reiterating that there was a 'settled practice'[53] to this effect and that such an order requiring the defendant to conduct an activity would require constant supervision by the court. Lord Hoffmann also considered that the grant of an order might 'cause injustice by allowing the claimant to enrich himself at the defendant's expense' by requiring the defendant to run a business at a loss far greater than the claimant would suffer by reason of the breach of contract,[54] and that from the wider perspective of public policy it was not in the public interest 'to require someone to carry on business at a loss if there is any plausible alternative by which the other party can be given compensation'.[55]

(d) Agreements made without consideration

It is an established principle that equity will not assist a volunteer. A volunteer is someone who has not provided valuable consideration for the benefit they are seeking equity to enforce.[56] As specific performance is an equitable remedy, it may only be obtained by a person who has provided valuable consideration under the contract. Accordingly, specific performance may not be obtained by a volunteer who is a party to a covenant, even though a promise made by deed may be binding and enforceable at common law due to the presence of a deed.[57]

Although the Contracts (Rights of Third Parties Act) 1999 provides that a third party who is entitled to enforce a contract may obtain any remedy 'that would have been available to him in an action for breach of contract if he had been a party to the contract', it seems that a volunteer third party will still be unable to obtain specific performance. Section 1(5) provides that the 'rules relating to... specific performance... shall apply accordingly', thereby incorporating the long established rule that a volunteer may not obtain specific performance.[58]

---

[52] [1996] Ch 286. The majority felt that the obligations of the parties were sufficiently defined to allow the defendant to know what it was necessary to do to comply with the order and also suggested that specific performance was a more suitable remedy on the instant facts, as the loss in damages would be difficult to quantify.

[53] [1997] 3 All ER 297, at 301, citing *Braddon Towers Ltd v International Stores Ltd* [1987] 1 EGLR 209.

[54] Ibid., at 304, approving the comments of Millet LJ who dissented in the Court of Appeal [1996] Ch 286, at 303–305.

[55] Ibid., at 305.   [56] See Chapter 7.

[57] Equity does not consider the presence of the seal on a deed to provide valuable consideration for any of the promises contained therein—see *Jefferys v Jefferys* (1841) Cr & Ph 138; *Cannon v Hartley* [1949] Ch 213.

[58] See Hanbury & Martin, *Modern Equity* (18th edn, 2009), at pp 734, 762.

(e) Contractual terms are insufficiently precise

A contractual obligation will not be enforced by way of specific performance if its terms are insufficiently precise to enable an order to be drawn that will clearly define what the defendant must do to comply therewith.[59] The scope of this limitation was examined by Lord Hoffmann in *Co-operative Insurance v Argyll Stores (Holdings) Ltd*:

If the terms of the court's order, reflecting the terms of the obligation, cannot be precisely drawn, the possibility of wasteful litigation over compliance is increased. So is the oppression caused by the defendant having to do things under threat of proceedings for contempt. The less precise the order, the fewer the signposts to the forensic minefield which he has to traverse. The fact that the terms of a contractual obligation are sufficiently definite to escape being void for uncertainty, or to found a claim for damages, or to permit compliance to be made a condition of relief against forfeiture, does not necessarily mean that they will be sufficiently precise to be capable of being specifically performed.[60]

The degree of certainty of the obligation in question is only a factor to be taken into account by the court in relation to the exercise of its discretion, and where the claimant's merits are strong the courts have 'shown themselves willing to cope with a certain degree of imprecision in cases of orders requiring a result'.[61]

(f) Contracts for transient interests

Traditionally, equity would not specifically enforce agreements for transient interests, such as tenancies at will or short tenancies.[62] In *Lavery v Pursell*,[63] the court would not grant specific performance of an agreement for a tenancy for one year because it was normally impossible to get the action heard within that period.[64] However, in the modern case of *Verrall v Great Yarmouth Borough Council*,[65] the Court of Appeal upheld an order for the specific performance of a contract to grant a licence for two days. Roskill LJ stated that, in his judgement:

the old view...that courts of equity would not protect a so-called transient interest can no longer be supported, at any rate to its full extent.[66]

(g) Contracts for partnership

Such contracts will not be specifically enforced unless the partners have begun to act upon their agreement.[67]

---

[59] *Wolverhampton Corpn v Emmons* [1901] 1 KB 515, at 525, per Romer LJ; *Redland Bricks Ltd v Morris* [1970] AC 652, at 666, per Lord Upjohn.

[60] [1997] 3 All ER 297, at 303.   [61] Ibid., at 304.

[62] *Glasse v Woolgar and Roberts (No 2)* (1897) 41 Sol Jo 573: tenancy for a day.

[63] (1888) 39 Ch D 508.

[64] See *Lever v Koffler* [1901] 1 Ch 543; *Manchester Brewery Co v Coombs* [1901] 2 Ch 608 (agreement for a tenancy from year to year is specifically enforceable).

[65] [1981] QB 202.   [66] Ibid., at 220.

[67] *England v Curling* (1844) 8 Beav 129; *Sichel v Mosenthal* (1862) 30 Beav 371; *Scott v Rayment* (1868) LR 7 Eq 112.

(h) Contracts to transfer goodwill

The court will not specifically enforce a contract to transfer merely the goodwill of a business,[68] unless annexed to an agreement to sell the premises or other assets of the business.

(i) Contracts to exercise a testamentary power of appointment[69]

The court will not grant specific performance of a contract to exercise a testamentary power in favour of a specific person because this would undermine the intention of the person who had granted the power (the donor) that the donee should be able to exercise it until his death.[70]

(j) Indivisible contracts

The court will not specifically enforce some only of the obligations under a contract if they cannot be separated from other obligations in the contract that may not be specifically enforced. In *Ogden v Fossick*,[71] there was an agreement to grant the plaintiffs a lease of a wharf and to appoint the defendant as manager. The court would not specifically enforce the contract for the lease because it could not be separated from the agreement to appoint the defendant manager. The management agreement could not be specifically enforced because this was a contract for personal services. If the obligations under a contract can be separated, the court may enforce the relevant obligations, but not the remaining obligations.[72]

(k) Contracts referring to arbitration

The court will not specifically enforce a contract to refer a matter to arbitration,[73] but it may stay proceedings under s 9 of the Arbitration Act 1996. This will indirectly enforce the agreement because the claimant will have no option other than to seek arbitration if he wishes to obtain a remedy. A decision made by an arbitrator can be enforced by means of specific performance.

(l) Illegal or immoral contracts

The court will not grant specific performance if the contract is illegal or contrary to public policy.[74] In *Wroth v Tyler*,[75] for example, specific performance was refused by

---

[68] *Baxter v Conolly* (1820) 1 Jac & W 576; *Darbey v Whitaker* (1857) 4 Drew 134: the reason is because of the uncertainty of the subject matter.

[69] See Chapter 16.   [70] *Re Parkin* [1892] 3 Ch 510; *Re Coake* [1922] 1 Ch 292.

[71] (1862) 4 De GF & J 426.

[72] See *Lewin v Guest* (1826) 1 Russ 325 (contract for the sale of two plots of land); *Wilkinson v Clements* (1872) LR 8 Ch App 96 (contracts to grant leases could be enforced without the plaintiff having to assume other contractual obligations under the original contract); *Odessa Tramways Co v Mendel* (1878) 8 Ch D 235 (allotment of shares could be enforced as it was divisible from other fraudulent elements of the contract).

[73] *Re Smith and Service and Nelson & Sons* (1890) 25 QBD 545; *Doleman & Sons v Ossett Corpn* [1912] 3 KB 257.

[74] *Ewing v Osbaldiston* (1837) 2 My & Cr 53 (a contract of partnership which concerned the enactment of plays without the proper licence from the King); *Sutton v Sutton* [1984] Ch 184 (an ante-nuptial agreement to settle property on divorce was not enforced as it would be against public policy to do so).

[75] [1974] Ch 30.

Megarry J on the ground that it would offend public policy to compel the defendant husband to take legal proceedings against his own wife for an order terminating her statutory rights of occupation of the matrimonial home.

(3) Mutuality

Historically, it was thought that the court could not grant specific performance in favour of a claimant unless it could also have granted specific performance in favour of the defendant. For example, the court would not grant specific performance in favour of a minor, because it would not have specifically enforced the contract against him.[76] The relevant date was thought to be the date that the contract was made.[77] However, in more modern cases it has been held that lack of mutuality is not an absolute bar to specific performance. In *Price v Strange*,[78] Goff LJ stated the 'true principle':

one judges the defence of want of mutuality on the facts and circumstances as they exist at the hearing, albeit in the light of the whole conduct of the parties in relation to the subject matter, and in the absence of any other disqualifying circumstances the court will grant specific performance if it can be done without injustice or unfairness to the defendant.[79]

The defendant had agreed to grant the plaintiff a new lease of premises he occupied if he carried out some internal and external repairs. At the time of trial, the plaintiff had completed the internal repairs and had only been prevented from completing the external repairs by the defendant, who had done them herself. In these circumstances, the Court of Appeal ordered specific performance, even though at the date of the agreement the defendant could not have compelled the plaintiff to carry out his promises to repair. There was no risk of hardship to the defendant in granting specific performance because the plaintiff's contractual undertakings had been performed.

(4) Defences to specific performance

Even though the contract may be one where specific performance would be available, there are a number of defences available to a defendant.

(a) Absence of necessary formalities

Specific performance will not be available to a claimant where a contract was entered without the necessary formalities. Section 40 of the Law of Property Act 1925 required a contract for the sale or disposition of land or an interest in land to be in writing, or for there to be a memorandum or note of the agreement. The absence of such writing would be a defence to an action for specific performance, unless the defendant was

---

[76] *Flight v Bolland* (1828) 4 Russ 298; *Lumley v Ravenscroft* [1895] 1 QB 683.
[77] Fry, *Specific Performance* (6th edn, 1921), p 219. See also *Clayton v Ashdown* (1714) 2 Eq Cas Abr 516; *Hoggart v Scott* (1830) 1 Russ & M 293; *Wilkinson v Clements* (1872) 8 Ch App 96.
[78] [1978] Ch 337; (1978) 128 NLJ 569 (Glover). See also *Sutton v Sutton* [1984] Ch 184.
[79] [1978] Ch 337, at 357.

guilty of fraud[80] or the claimant had partly performed the contract.[81] However, for contracts made after 26 September 1989, s 40 of the Law of Property Act 1925 has been abolished and replaced by s 2 of the Law of Property (Miscellaneous Provisions) Act 1989, which requires that the contract must be made in writing. There is no longer any place for the doctrine of part-performance.

(b) Misrepresentation by the plaintiff

Any misrepresentation by the plaintiff to the defendant, whether innocent or fraudulent, which would entitle the defendant to rescind the contract, will be a defence to an action seeking specific performance.[82]

(c) Mistake

Where the defendant has made a mistake, which does not prevent the formation of a contract, this will generally be no defence to specific performance. However, the court may refuse the order if it would cause the defendant 'a hardship amounting to injustice'.[83] In *Webster v Cecil*,[84] for example, the defendant vendor offered to sell land for £1,250 by mistake instead of £2,250. The plaintiff purchaser must have known that it was a mistake, because earlier the defendant had refused to sell for £2,000. The plaintiff accepted the offer of £1,250 by return of post. The defendant realized his mistake and immediately told the plaintiff. The plaintiff claimed specific performance of the contract, but the court refused specific performance.

(d) Hardship

Specific performance is a discretionary remedy,[85] and the courts may refuse to grant it if it would cause great hardship to the defendant[86] or a third party.[87] In *Patel v Ali*,[88] Mr and Mrs Ali had entered into a contract to sell their house to Mr and Mrs Patel. Mr Ali was then adjudicated bankrupt and spent a year in prison. Mrs Ali was diagnosed as having bone cancer, had a leg amputated just before the birth of her second child, and then subsequently had a third child. In these circumstances, Goulding J refused an order for specific performance on the grounds of the hardship to the plaintiffs. He stressed that:

---

[80] *Maxwell v Lady Mountacute* (1719) Prec Ch 526; *Wakeham v Mackenzie* [1968] 1 WLR 1175.

[81] Law of Property Act 1925, s 40(2); *Lester v Foxcroft* (1701) Colles 108, HL; *Steadman v Steadman* [1976] AC 536.

[82] *Walker v Boyle* [1982] 1 WLR 495.

[83] *Tamplin v James* (1880) LR 15 Ch D 215, at 221, per James LJ. Compare *Malins v Freeman* (1836) 2 Keen 25.

[84] (1861) 30 Beav 62.   [85] *Co-operative Insurance v Argyll Stores* [1997] 3 All ER 297, at 299.

[86] *Denne v Light* (1857) 8 De GM & G 774; *Pegler v White* (1864) 33 Beav 403; *Tamplin v James* (1880) 15 Ch D 215; *Warmington v Miller* [1973] QB 877; *Mountford v Scott* [1975] Ch 258; *Francis v Cowcliff Ltd* (1977) 33 P & CR 368; *Shell UK Ltd v Lostock Garage Ltd* [1977] 1 All ER 481; *Cross v Cross* (1983) 12 Fam Law 182.

[87] *Earl of Sefton v Tophams Ltd* [1965] Ch 1140; *Sullivan v Henderson* [1973] 1 WLR 333; *Watts v Spence* [1976] Ch 165; *Cedar Holdings Ltd v Green* [1981] Ch 129.

[88] [1984] Ch 283.

The important and true principle...is that only in extraordinary and persuasive circumstances can hardship supply an excuse for resisting performance of a contract for the sale of immoveable property...[89]

(e) Misdescription of the property

If the property has been misdescribed in a contract for sale, the defendant will be entitled to rescind the contract[90] and resist a claim for specific performance if the property he would be forced to buy was different in substance. For example, if the contract was for the grant of a lease, the purchaser would not be compelled to take an underlease.[91] Similarly, if the contract was for the sale of 'registered freehold property', the purchaser would not be compelled to take a merely possessory title.[92] The purchaser may, however, choose to take the interest under the contract subject to an abatement of the purchase price in compensation.[93] If the misdescription is slight, so that the purchaser receives substantially what he is entitled to under the contract, the court will order specific performance, subject to the vendor compensating the purchaser, as for example in *Scott v Hanson*,[94] where there was a contract for the sale of fourteen acres of water meadow, but only twelve could be so described.[95]

(f) Delay

Equity does not regard time as of the essence of a contract[96] and therefore specific performance may be granted after the due date for performance. Although there is no statutory time limit to a claim for specific performance,[97] the claimant must not delay unduly. Thus, in *Huxham v Llewellyn*[98] a delay of five months prevented specific performance.[99] However, in *Lazard Bros & Co Ltd v Fairfield Properties Co (Mayfair) Ltd*[100] Megarry V-C rejected a strict approach and held that if it was just that between the claimant and the defendant, the claimant should obtain the remedy, the court

---

[89] Ibid., at 288. See also *Co operative Insurance v Argyll Stores* [1997] 3 All ER 297, where one of the reasons the House of Lords refused to allow an order for specific performance was that to force the defendants to carry on business at a loss might well have caused greater hardship to them than it did to the plaintiffs, especially as the lease had a number of years left to run and may have led them to trading into insolvency. The court also seemed concerned that the general effect of such orders on the business community as a whole would be of similar detrimental effect.

[90] *Flight v Booth* (1834) 1 Bing NC 370; *Charles Hunt Ltd v Palmer* [1931] 2 Ch 287. See below, p 160.

[91] *Madeley v Booth* (1848) 2 De G & Sm 718; *Re Russ and Brown's Contract* [1934] Ch 34.

[92] *Re Brine and Davies' Contract* [1935] Ch 388.

[93] *Mortlock v Buller* (1804) 10 Ves 292, at 315–316, per Lord Eldon LC; *Hill v Buckley* (1811) 17 Ves 394; *Barnes v Wood* (1869) LR 8 Eq 424; *Horrocks v Rigby* (1878) 9 Ch D 180; *Basma v Weekes* [1950] AC 441.

[94] (1829) 1 Russ & M 128.

[95] See also *M'Queen v Farquhar* (1805) 11 Ves 467; *Re Fawcett and Holmes Contract* (1889) 42 Ch D 150.

[96] *United Scientific Holdings Ltd v Burnley Borough Council* [1978] AC 904.

[97] The normal six-year limitation period under the Limitation Act 1980 does not apply, even where the specific performance claim includes claims for damages for breach of contract—*P&O Nedlloyd BV v Arab Metals Co (No 2)* [2007] 1 WLR 2288.

[98] (1873) 21 WR 570.

[99] See also *Milward v Earl of Thanet* (1801) 5 Ves 720n; *Walker v Jeffreys* (1842) 1 Hare 341; *Mills v Haywood* (1877) 6 Ch D 196; *Cornwall v Henson* [1900] 2 Ch 298.

[100] (1977) 121 Sol Jo 793; [1978] Conv 184.

ought not to withhold it merely because the claimant had been guilty of delay. Delay will be no defence where the claimant has entered into possession of the property and is simply seeking a transfer of the legal title.[101] For example, in *Williams v Greatrex*[102] specific performance was granted where there had been a delay of ten years. A failure to perform a contract by its due date is a breach for which common law damages may be payable whether or not specific performance is available.[103]

(5) Damages in lieu of specific performance

(a) Jurisdiction to award damages

The Court of Chancery was given the power to award damages in lieu of specific performance by s 2 of the Chancery Amendment Act 1858.[104] This had the procedural advantage that if a plaintiff was not awarded specific performance, he would not have to start a separate action for damages in the common law courts. After the Judicature Acts of 1873 and 1875 there was no need to rely on the earlier provision, except where damages would not have been available at common law. The Chancery Amendment Act 1858 has been repealed, but its provisions are preserved in the Supreme Court Act 1981, s 50.

(b) Assessment of damages

In *Wroth v Tyler*,[105] Megarry J held that the measure of damages awarded in lieu of specific performance need not be the same as that at common law. He refused an order for specific performance of a contract for the sale of a bungalow, and calculated damages as the difference between the contract price and the value at the date of the judgment, which was £5,500. This was more than the common law measure, which would be the difference between the contract price and the value at the date of the breach, which would have been £1,500. This approach was doubted by the House of Lords in *Johnson v Agnew*,[106] where Lord Wilberforce held that the award of damages under the Chancery Amendment Act was not to be calculated on a different basis than common law damages. However, the result in *Wroth v Tyler*[107] is supportable on the basis that it is not a fixed rule that common law damages must be assessed as at the date of breach.[108] This approach has been approved by the House of Lords in *AG v Blake*,[109] where Lord Nicholls explained that the jurisdiction under Lord Cairns' Act enables a court to assess damages to include losses likely to follow from the anticipated future continuance of the wrong, in addition to losses already suffered.

---

[101]   *Crofton v Ormsby* (1806) 2 Sch & Lef 583; *Shepheard v Walker* (1875) LR 20 Eq 659.
[102]   [1957] 1 WLR 31.
[103]   *United Scientific Holdings Ltd v Burnley Borough Council* [1978] AC 904.
[104]   Lord Cairns' Act.   [105]   [1974] Ch 30.   [106]   [1980] AC 367.
[107]   [1974] Ch 30.
[108]   *Horsler v Zorro* [1975] Ch 302; *Radford v de Froberville* [1978] 1 All ER 33; *Malhotra v Choudhury* [1980] Ch 52; *Johnson v Agnew* [1980] AC 367; *Suleman v Shahsavari* [1989] 2 All ER 460.
[109]   [2001] 1 AC 268.

3 Injunctions

By means of an order of specific performance the court may compel a person to do what he has promised: to perform his contractual obligations. In contrast, by means of an injunction the court may order a person[110] to refrain from doing something. In *Taittinger SA v Allbev Ltd*,[111] for example, the Court of Appeal granted an injunction preventing the defendants from selling their non-alcoholic drink under the name 'Elderflower Champagne'[112] because this would amount to passing off their product as genuine 'champagne'. In some exceptional circumstances, an injunction can have a mandatory effect, operating like specific performance to compel the defendant to do something. Failure to comply with an injunction will constitute a contempt of court, which may lead to sanctions including imprisonment, sequestration of property, or a fine. A third party who aids and abets a breach of an injunction will also be guilty of contempt,[113] and third parties who nullify the effect of a injunction, for example by publishing information which others have been ordered not to publish, will be in contempt of court by virtue of their knowing interference with the administration of justice.[114] The power to grant injunctions, which was originally inherent in the judiciary, is now regulated by statute. Section 37 of Supreme Court Act 1981 provides that the court can grant an injunction if 'just and convenient'. The discretion given to the judges by this provision must be exercised on settled principles. The grant of injunctions is now also governed by the Civil Procedure Rules 1998.[115]

(1) Types of injunction

(a) Prohibitory and mandatory

A prohibitory injunction orders a person to refrain from, or to discontinue, a wrongful act. A mandatory injunction requires a person to perform some act, and is often given after the wrong has been done and orders its reversal. For example, if a defendant is about to build a structure in circumstances that would be wrongful, a prohibitory injunction would order him not to build. However, if the structure had already been built, a mandatory injunction would order the building to be pulled down. Historically all injunctions had to be given in a prohibitory form, but since *Jackson v Normanby Brick Co*,[116] an injunction which is mandatory in substance will be given in a mandatory form.

---

[110] An injunction may also be granted against an unnamed person (*Bloomsbury Publishing Group plc v News Group Newspapers* [2003] 1 WLR 1633) or against the members of a class or organization (*M Michaels (Furriers) Ltd v Askew* (1983) The Times, 25 June).

[111] [1994] 4 All ER 75.

[112] Recipes for a home-made version are readily available on the Internet.

[113] *Acro (Automation) Ltd v Rex Chainbelt Inc* [1971] 1 WLR 1676.

[114] *AG v Times Newspapers Ltd* [1992] 1 AC 191; *AG v Punch* [2003] 1 AC 1046.

[115] The Woolf Reforms.   [116] [1899] 1 Ch 438.

(b) Perpetual and interlocutory

A perpetual injunction is granted to defend a claimant's rights after a full hearing. It is a final remedy, even if it does not last for ever as its name might suggest. An interlocutory injunction is granted in order to preserve the status quo pending a full trial and before the parties' rights have finally been established.

(c) Injunctions without notice

In urgent cases a claimant will be able to apply for an injunction without giving notice to the defendant (formerly called an ex parte injunction).[117] Where such an injunction is granted, the defendant will subsequently have the opportunity to have the order set aside or varied.[118]

(d) Quia timet[119] injunction

This is an injunction to prevent a threatened infringement of the claimant's rights that has not yet taken place.[120]

(2) **General principles governing the grant of a perpetual injunction**

(a) Damages would be an inadequate remedy

An injunction will only be awarded if damages would prove an inadequate remedy.[121] They are generally available as a response to continuing infringements of the claimant's rights, for example nuisance or trespass. An injunction is not available for a past infringement that will not be repeated. Damages may be inadequate simply because the defendant is a pauper.[122] It has been argued that an injunction should not be granted against a person without means because of the difficulty of enforcing the injunction. This argument was rejected in *Secretary of State for Environment, Food and Rural Affairs (Respondent) v Meier*.[123] The Supreme Court approved the grant of an injunction to prevent travellers trespassing on Forestry Commission land even though it was unlikely that the injunction would be enforced by imprisonment or sequestration of assets. Lord Rodgers observed:

Admittedly, if the present defendants did fail to comply with the injunction, sequestration would not be a real option since they are unlikely to have any substantial assets. And, of course, there are potential difficulties in a court trying to ensure compliance with an injunction by committing to prison defendants who are women with young children. Nevertheless, as Lord Bingham of Cornhill observed in *South Buckinghamshire DC v Porter* [2003] 2 AC 558, 580, para 32, in connexion with a possible injunction against gypsies living in caravans in breach of planning controls:

---

117 The change was introduced by the Civil Procedure Rules (CPR) 1998.
118 CPR 23.9, 23.10, 25.3.
119 The name comes from the Latin and means 'he who fears'.
120 See *Redland Bricks Ltd v Morris* [1970] AC 652.
121 *London and Blackwall Rly Co v Cross* (1886) 31 Ch D 354.
122 *Hodgson v Duce* (1856) 28 LTos 155.   123 [2009] UKSC 11.

'When granting an injunction the court does not contemplate that it will be dis-
obeyed...Apprehension that a party may disobey an order should not deter the court
from making an order otherwise appropriate: there is not one law for the law-abiding
and another for the lawless and truculent.'

Taking that approach, we should, in my view, be slow to assume that an injunction is a worthless remedy in a case like the present and that only the intervention of a bailiff is likely to be
effective. If that is indeed the considered consensus of those with experience in the field, then
consideration may have to be given to changing the procedures for enforcing injunctions of
this kind.[124]

(b) An infringement of the claimant's rights

In *Paton v British Pregnancy Advisory Service Trustees*, Sir George Baker P stated:

the first and basic principle is that there must be a legal right enforceable in law or in equity
before the applicant can obtain an injunction from the court to restrain an infringement of that
right.[125]

It is necessary that the claimant demonstrate that he is entitled to a legal or equitable
right that the courts can protect by means of an injunction.[126] In *Day v Brownrigg*,[127]
the Court of Appeal refused to grant an injunction restraining the defendant from
giving his house the same name as the plaintiff, his next door neighbour, had given to
his, because there was no infringement of any legal or equitable right of the plaintiff.
In *Paton v British Pregnancy Advisory Service Trustees*,[128] the court refused to grant a
husband an injunction to prevent his pregnant wife having a lawful abortion because
he had no right that was thereby infringed.[129]

(c) Grant of an injunction is discretionary

The award of an injunction is at the court's discretion, like any equitable remedy,
although as a general rule a party who establishes an infringement of his right will
usually be granted an injunction if it is sought.[130]

(i) Prohibitory injunctions

Some prohibitory injunctions are in practice available almost as of right. For example,
with reference to an injunction to restrain a breach of a negative contract, Lord Cairns
LC said in *Doherty v Allman*:

it is not a question of the balance of convenience or inconvenience, or of the amount of
damage or injury—it is the specific performance, by the Court, of that negative bargain which
the parties have made, with their eyes open, between themselves.[131]

---

[124] Ibid., at [17].   [125] [1979] QB 76.
[126] *North London Rly Co v Great Northern Rly Co* (1883) 11 QBD 30, CA; *Re C* [1991] 2 FLR 168.
[127] (1878) 10 Ch D 294.   [128] [1979] QB 276.   [129] See also *C v S* [1988] QB 135.
[130] *Imperial Gas Light and Coke Co v Broadbent* (1859) 7 HL Cas 600; *Fullwood v Fullwood* (1878) LR 9 Ch
D 176; *Pride of Derby and Derbyshire Angling Association Ltd v British Celanese Ltd* [1953] Ch 149, at 181, per
Evershed MR; *Harrow London Borough Council v Donohue* [1995] 1 EGLR 257.
[131] (1878) 3 App Cas 709, at 720.

The fact that a claimant has only suffered nominal or very small damage from the infringement of his right does not prevent the court awarding an injunction,[132] although it is a factor to be taken into account. In *Society of Architects v Kendrick*,[133] the members of the Society placed the letters MSA after their name. Joyce J refused to grant them an injunction against the defendant, who placed the letters after his name even though he was not a member of the society, because he considered the matter 'too trivial for the granting of an injunction'. In *Behrens v Richards*,[134] Buckley J refused an injunction against the defendants who were trespassing on the plaintiff's land because their use of a path caused no damage. However, a more strict approach to trespass seems to have been taken in *Patel v WH Smith (Eziot) Ltd*,[135] where the Court of Appeal held that only in very rare cases would an injunction be refused to restrain a continuing trespass.[136]

(ii) Mandatory injunctions

Lord Upjohn stated the principle in *Redland Bricks Ltd v Morris*:

the grant of a mandatory injunction is...entirely discretionary and unlike a negative injunction can never be 'as of course'. Every case must depend essentially upon its own particular circumstances.[137]

He held that the question of the cost to the defendant to do the works necessary was an element to be taken into account in determining whether an injunction should be granted. For this reason, the House of Lords refused to grant a mandatory injunction requiring the defendants to perform remedial work costing some £35,000 to their land, to provide support for the plaintiff's land which was only worth £1,500. In *Wrotham Park Estate Co Ltd v Parkside Homes Ltd*,[138] Brightman J refused to grant a mandatory injunction requiring the demolition of houses which had been built in contravention of a restrictive covenant because he felt that it would be 'an unpardonable waste of much needed houses'.[139] Obviously, the defendant's conduct is a major factor that will be taken into consideration in determining whether a mandatory injunction should be awarded. As Lord Upjohn said in *Redland Bricks Ltd v Morris*:

where the defendant has acted without regard to his neighbour's rights and has tried to steal a march on him or has tried to evade the jurisdiction of the court or...has acted wantonly and quite unreasonably in relation to his neighbour he may be ordered to repair his wanton and unreasonable acts by doing positive work to restore the status quo even if the expense to him is out of all proportion to the advantage thereby accruing to the plaintiff.[140]

---

[132] *Rochdale Canal Co v King* (1851) 2 Sim NS 78; *Wood v Sutcliffe* (1851) 2 Sim NS 163; *Marriott v East Grinstead Gas and Water Co* [1909] 1 Ch 70; *Woollerton & Wilson Ltd v Richard Costain Ltd* [1970] 1 WLR 411.

[133] (1910) 26 TLR 433. See also *Society of Accountants and Auditors v Goodway* [1907] 1 Ch 489.

[134] [1905] 2 Ch 614.

[135] [1987] 2 All ER 569. See also *Trenberth (John) Ltd v National Westminster Bank Ltd* (1980) 39 P & CR 104.

[136] Trespass to land is a tortious wrong—see further Rodgers, *Winfield & Jolowicz on Tort* (17th edn, 2006).

[137] [1970] AC 652, at 665.   [138] [1974] 1 WLR 798.   [139] Ibid., at 811.

[140] [1970] AC 652, at 666. See *Woodhouse v Newry Navigation Co* [1898] 1 IR 161, CA.

The courts are reluctant to grant mandatory injunctions in the context of industrial disputes, as Geoffrey Lane J said in *Harold Stephen & Co Ltd v Post Office*:

It can only be in very rare circumstances and in the most extreme circumstances that this court should interfere by way of mandatory injunction in the delicate mechanism of industrial disputes and industrial negotiations.[141]

(d) Delay and acquiescence

The court may refuse an injunction if the claimant has delayed for an inordinate time,[142] although where an injunction is refused for reasons of delay, a claimant may be entitled to damages in lieu.[143] His failure to seek interlocutory relief may also be relevant to a refusal to grant an injunction.[144] Equally, there will be no injunction if the claimant has acquiesced and waived his rights.[145] In *Shaw v Applegate*,[146] Goff LJ expressed the opinion that it was easier to establish acquiescence in the case of an equitable rather than a legal right. In *Fisher v Brooker*[147] one of the composers of Procol Harum's iconic song 'A Whiter Shade of Pale' (which was first released in 1967) sought to enforce his rights in 2005. His rights as a co-composer had never previously been acknowledged, and he had therefore received no royalties. The House of Lords held that he was not debarred by the significant length of time from bringing an action, although the delay would be relevant in deciding whether to grant an injunction against future exploitation of the work. The Lords' view was that in order for delay to justify a denial of equitable relief, some sort of detrimental reliance would usually be needed.[148]

(e) Claimant must come with 'clean hands'

A claimant will only be granted an injunction if he himself comes seeking the aid of equity with 'clean hands'. Breach of his own obligations or unfair conduct[149] will disentitle him to relief, as will his own refusal to carry out his future obligations.[150]

---

[141] [1977] 1 WLR 1172, at 1180. See *Parker v Camden London Borough Council* [1986] Ch 162, CA, where the court was willing to grant a mandatory injunction for the defendants to turn on boilers where tenants had no heat or hot water, because of a boilermen's strike. There is thus a strong element of public policy to this decision.

[142] *H P Bulmer Ltd and Showerings Ltd v J Bollinger SA* [1977] 2 CMLR 625, CA (where, technically, the opinions expressed were obiter). Cf *Newport Association Football Club Ltd v Football Association of Wales Ltd* [1995] 2 All ER 87, where, on the facts, there was not felt to be unreasonable delay.

[143] *Shelfer v City of London Electric Lighting Co (No 1)* [1895] 1 Ch 287; *Bracewell v Appleby* [1975] Ch 408; *Ketley v Gooden* [1996] EGCS 47.

[144] See *Shaw v Applegate* [1977] 1 WLR 970, CA.

[145] *Parrott v Palmer* (1834) 3 My & K 632; *Johnson v Wyatt* (1863) 2 De G J & Sm 18, *Blue Town Investments Ltd v Higgs and Hill plc* [1990] 1 WLR 696.

[146] [1977] 1 WLR 970, at 979.   [147] [2009] 1 WLR 1764.

[148] Ibid., at [64] per Lord Neuberger.

[149] *Shell UK Ltd v Lostock Garage Bros Ltd* [1977] 1 All ER 481. The conduct must concern the subject matter of the dispute in relation to which the injunction is sought: *Argyll v Argyll* [1967] Ch 302.

[150] *Measures v Measures* [1910] 2 Ch 248; *Chappell v Times Newspapers Ltd* [1975] 1 WLR 482.

(f) Damages in lieu of an injunction

Under the Chancery Amendment Act 1858 (Lord Cairns' Act) the court has jurisdiction to award damages in substitution for the award of an injunction. The jurisdiction remains, despite the repeal of this Act.[151] In general, the courts will only award damages in substitution in exceptional circumstances.[152]

(i) When damages will be awarded

A 'good working rule' as to when damages should be awarded in substitution was set out by AL Smith LJ in *Shelfer v City of London Electric Lighting Co (No 1)*:

(1) If the injury to the plaintiff's legal rights is small; and

(2) is one which is capable of being estimated in money; and

(3) is one which can be adequately compensated by a small money payment; and

(4) the case is one in which it would be oppressive to the defendant to grant an injunction.[153]

It must be stressed that these guidelines were given in the context of the understanding that where the claimant's legal right has been invaded he is prima facie entitled to an injunction.[154] Although the rule has at times been severely criticized, it has been applied in many cases and was accepted by the Court of Appeal in *Kennaway v Thompson*,[155] where the court reversed the decision of the judge at first instance to award damages in substitution because the first three criteria of the rule had not been met. Similarly, it was applied by the Court of Appeal in *Jaggard v Sawyer*,[156] although Millett LJ emphasized that it provided 'only a working rule and does not purport to be an exhaustive statement of the circumstances in which damages may be awarded instead of an injunction'.[157] In *Woollerton & Wilson Ltd v Richard Costain Ltd*,[158] Stamp J doubted that the criteria would be satisfied where there was a trespass which founded a claim to nominal damages only as the payment of damages in lieu of an injunction would amount to the award of a licence to continue trespassing. However, this approach was rejected by the Court of Appeal in *Jaggard v Sawyer*,[159] which held that the principles identified in *Shelfer v City of London Electric Lighting Co*[160] are applicable to cases of trespass. The principles set out in *Shelfer* have also been approved in recent Court of Appeal decisions, both dealing with nuisance, and both suggesting that the principles in *Shelfer* have not been altered or reduced by any subsequent decisions.[161]

---

[151] Supreme Court Act 1981, s 50; *Leeds Industrial Co-operative Society Ltd v Slack* [1924] AC 851, HL.

[152] *Imperial Gas Light and Coke Co v Broadbent* (1859) 7 HL Cas 600; *Shelfer v City of London Electric Lighting Co (No 1)* [1895] 1 Ch 287, CA; *Leeds Industrial Co-operative Society v Slack* [1924] AC 851, HL; *Achilli v Tovell* [1927] 2 Ch 243; *Sefton v Tophams Ltd* [1965] Ch 1140.

[153] [1895] 1 Ch 287.

[154] See *Slack v Leeds Industrial Co-operative Society Ltd* [1924] 2 Ch 475, CA.

[155] [1981] QB 88. See also *Wakeham v Wood* (1982) 43 P & CR 40, CA.

[156] [1995] 2 All ER 189.   [157] Ibid., at 208.   [158] [1970] 1 WLR 411.

[159] [1995] 2 All ER 189.   [160] [1895] 1 Ch 287.

[161] See *Watson v Croft Promosport Ltd* [2009] 3 All ER 249; *Regan Paul Properties DPF No 1 Ltd* [2007] Ch 125.

(ii) The measure of damages

The quantum of damages that may be awarded in lieu of an injunction has been a matter of some controversy. In *Johnson v Agnew*,[162] the House of Lords held that, where damages would have been available at common law, the court only possessed the jurisdiction to award damages on the same compensatory basis. However, in some cases the courts awarded damages in lieu of an injunction or specific performance even where there had been no loss. In *Wrotham Park Estate Co Ltd v Parkside Homes Ltd*,[163] for example, Brightman J refused an injunction to demolish houses built in breach of covenant but granted the plaintiff damages in substitution. The plaintiff had suffered no loss in terms of a reduction in value of his land, so at common law damages would have been purely nominal. Nevertheless, substantial damages were awarded, equivalent to the sum of money that might reasonably have been demanded by the plaintiffs for relaxing the restrictive covenant. In *Surrey County Council v Bredero Homes Ltd*,[164] Dillon LJ questioned whether this measure of compensation was consistent with *Johnson v Agnew*, but in *Jaggard v Sawyer*[165] the Court of Appeal held that the assessment of damages in *Wrotham Park Estate Co Ltd v Parkside Homes Ltd*[166] had been conducted on a compensatory basis and that it represented an appropriate means by which a judge could assess damages where he declined to prevent the commission of a future wrong by the award of an injunction.[167] The issue was re-examined by the House of Lords in *A-G v Blake*.[168] Lord Nicholls explained that although Lord Cairns' Act did not alter the measure to be employed in assessing damages, it did enable the court to award damages in respect of the future as well as the past, so that the damages awarded in lieu of an injunction could include losses likely to follow from the anticipated future continuance of the wrong as well as losses already suffered. He summarized as follows:

> The measure of damages awarded in this type of case is often analysed as damages for loss of a bargaining opportunity or, which comes to the same, the price payable for the compulsory acquisition of a right. This analysis is correct. The Court's refusal to grant an injunction means that in practice the defendant is thereby permitted to perpetuate the wrongful state of affairs he has brought about.[169]

The House of Lords has therefore approved *Wrotham Park Estates* and doubted *Surrey County Council v Breredo Homes*.[170]

(g) Suspension of injunctions

In some circumstances the court will suspend an injunction so that it does not have immediate effect.[171] This may be because it may not be possible to immediately

---

162 [1980] AC 367.   163 [1974] 1 WLR 798.   164 [1993] 3 All ER 705.
165 [1995] 2 All ER 189.   166 [1974] 1 WLR 798.
167 [1995] 2 All ER 189, at 201–202, per Sir Thomas Bingham MR.
168 [2000] 4 All ER 385.   169 [2000] 4 All ER 385, at 394.
170 See *Tamares (Vincent Square) Ltd v Fairpoint Properties (Vincent Square Ltd)* [2007] 1 WLR 2148, where similar principles were applied in deciding the measure of damages to be awarded for interference with a right to light to a building.
171 *A-G v Birmingham Borough Council* (1858) 4 K & J 528; *A-G v Colney Hatch Lunatic Asylum* (1868) 4 Ch App 146; *Jones v Llanrwst UDC* [1911] 1 Ch 393; *Stollmeyer v Petroleum Development Co Ltd* [1918] AC 498n, PC; *Pride of Derby and Derbyshire Angling Association Ltd v British Celanese Ltd* [1953] Ch 149, CA;

cease the infringing activity. In *Pride of Derby and Derbyshire Angling Association Ltd v British Celanese Ltd*,[172] for example, the Court of Appeal suspended an injunction made against the defendants who polluted a river with sewerage, giving them time to remedy the nuisance they were causing. In *Waverley Borough Council v Hilden*[173] Scott J suspended an injunction requiring gypsies to remove their caravans from an unauthorized site for three months to give them 'a reasonable time to comply with the order'. However, the courts have disapproved of the suspension granted in *Woollerton and Wilson Ltd v Richard Costain Ltd*,[174] which amounted to a licence for the defendants to continue trespassing in the plaintiff's airspace.[175]

(h) Declarations

In *Greenwich Healthcare National Health Service Trust v London and Quadrant*,[176] Lightman J held that the court has power to grant a declaration that a defendant will not be entitled to an injunction if the claimant engages in a particular course of conduct. The claimants wanted to redevelop their hospital, but this would involve a realignment of a private right of way. The owners of the private right of way had been informed of the proposals and had raised no objection; but neither had they given any positive consent.[177] The claimants were afraid that an injunction might be sought in the future. Lightman J was prepared to make the declaration that no future injunction would be granted, and that the defendants would in the future be limited to redress by means of damages. This was because the realignment was no less commodious than the original route (indeed, it constituted an improvement); the potential dominant owners had been informed and had raised no objection; and the realignment was necessary to achieve an object of substantial public and local importance and value. Lightman J observed:

The jurisdiction of the court to grant declarations must extend to entitlement both to proprietary rights and to particular remedies. Circumstances may exist when a declaration, e.g. that a defendant is not entitled to specific performance, rectification or an injunction, is necessary if a period of damaging (or indeed paralyzing) uncertainty is to be voided, and indeed the occasion for an unwarranted ransom demand is to be removed. The law is sufficiently adaptable to grant declarations which are necessary to dispel uncertainties and remove obstacles to progress and legitimate activities.[178]

Halsey v Esso Petroleum Co Ltd [1961] 1 WLR 683; *Miller v Jackson* [1977] QB 966, CA; *Waverley Borough Council v Hilden* [1988] 1 WLR 246.

[172] [1953] Ch 149.   [173] [1988] 1 WLR 246.   [174] [1970] 1 WLR 411.

[175] Disapproved in *Charrington v Simons & Co Ltd* [1971] 1 WLR 598, CA; *Trenberth (John) Ltd v National Westminster Bank Ltd* (1980) 39 P & CR 104; *Jaggard v Sawyer* [1995] 2 All ER 189, at 199. Contrast *Kelsen v Imperial Tobacco Co of Great Britain and Ireland Ltd* [1957] 2 QB 334.

[176] [1998] 3 All ER 437.

[177] This ownership was by means of an easement, which is an interest in land, enjoyed by one landowner (the dominant owner) over the land of another landowner (the servient owner). See further Jackson, Stevens, and Pearce, *Land Law* (4th edn, 2008), pp 461–503.

[178] [1998] 3 All ER 437, at 444.

(3) General principles governing the grant of an interlocutory injunction

Unlike permanent injunctions, which are granted to protect a claimant's established rights, an interlocutory injunction is granted to preserve the status quo between the claimant and the defendant before their respective rights can be determined at trial. As Lord Wilberforce said in *Hoffmann-La Roche (F) & Co AG v Secretary of State for Trade and Industry*:

The object is to prevent a litigant, who must necessarily suffer the law's delays, from losing by that delay the fruit of his litigation.[179]

(a) When should an interlocutory injunction be granted?

The principles by which the court should determine whether to grant an interlocutory injunction were outlined by Lord Diplock in the leading case of *American Cyanamid Co v Ethicon Ltd*.[180] Subsequent cases have held that the principles are not 'rules', but rather guidelines with room for flexibility.[181] Until recently, the orthodox interpretation was that in *American Cyanamid* the House of Lords had rejected earlier authorities holding that a claimant was required to demonstrate a prima facie case before an interlocutory injunction could be granted[182] in favour of a lower threshold which required the claimant to merely demonstrate that there was a 'serious question to be tried'. However, in *Series 5 Software Ltd v Clarke*,[183] Laddie J questioned this orthodoxy and provided a reinterpretation of *American Cyanamid* requiring the court to take into account the strength of the parties' respective cases on the evidence. He especially pointed to the decision of the House of Lords in *Hoffmann-La Roche (F) & Co AG v Secretary of State for Trade and Industry*,[184] which had been decided a few months before *American Cyanamid*, but was not cited in the subsequent case. There, Lord Diplock had suggested that the award of an interlocutory injunction was conditional upon the claimant demonstrating a 'strong prima facie case that he will be entitled to a final order'.[185] Having concluded that the prospects of success at trial were relevant, Laddie J indicated the matters that he thought the court should take into account in deciding whether to grant an injunction:

(1) The grant of an interlocutory injunction is a matter of discretion and depends on all the facts of the case.

(2) There are no fixed rules as to when an injunction should or should not be granted. The relief must be kept flexible.

---

[179] [1975] AC 295, at 355.

[180] [1975] AC 396, HL; (1975) 91 LQR 168 (Prescott); (1975) 38 MLR 672 (Gore); (1976) 35 CLJ 82 (Wallington); (1981) 40 CLJ 307 (Gray).

[181] See, for example. *Fellowes & Son v Fisher* [1976] QB 122, CA; *Cayne v Global Natural Resources plc* [1984] 1 All ER 225, CA; *Cambridge Nutrition Ltd v BBC* [1990] 3 All ER 523, CA; *Factortame Ltd v Secretary of State for Transport (No 2)* [1991] 1 All ER 70; *Kirklees MBC v Wickes Building Supplies Ltd* [1993] AC 227.

[182] *Preston v Luck* (1884) 27 Ch D 497; *Smith v Grigg Ltd* [1924] 1 KB 655, CA; *JT Stratford & Son Ltd v Lindley* [1965] AC 269. Compare also *Fellowes & Son v Fisher* [1976] QB 122; *Hubbard v Pitt* [1976] QB 142.

[183] [1996] 1 All ER 853. [184] [1975] AC 295. [185] Ibid., at 360–361.

(3) Because of the practice adopted on the hearing of applications for interlocutory relief, the court should rarely attempt to resolve complex issues of disputed fact or law.

(4) Major factors the court can bear in mind are (a) the extent to which damages are likely to be an adequate remedy for each party and the ability of the other party to pay (b) the balance of convenience (c) the maintenance of the status quo, and (d) any clear view the court may reach as to the relative strengths of the parties' cases.[186]

He refused to award an interlocutory injunction despite the fact that the plaintiff's case was 'arguable in the sense that it is possible that the facts at the trial may support the allegation it makes' because he was 'not impressed with its strength'.[187] It is unclear whether this general reinterpretation will be adopted.[188] However, as will be seen, there are a number of special cases where there is a long-standing practice of considering the strength of the claimant's case. In addition, Laddie J's view has been praised as restoring judicial discretion to an area that was in danger of becoming 'so encrusted with expectations as to how that discretion should be exercised that it too had established a tyranny'.[189]

(b) The orthodox interpretation of *American Cyanamid*

Under the orthodox interpretation of *American Cyanamid*, the following factors must be taken into account by the court to determine whether an interlocutory injunction should be granted.

(i) 'A serious question to be tried'

Although the claimant does not need to establish a prima facie case, Lord Diplock held that 'the court...must be satisfied that the claim is not frivolous or vexatious; in other words that there is a serious question to be tried'. Only if the plaintiff fails to show any real prospect of succeeding in his claim at trial should the court refuse the injunction without going on to consider the balance of convenience.

(ii) The 'balance of convenience'

Once the claimant has shown that there is a serious issue, the court must weigh the balance of convenience between granting and refusing an injunction, and the effect that this would have on the respective parties if the issue was determined in favour of that party at trial. The court must assess the adequacy of damages as a remedy for any loss they may suffer in consequence of the grant or refusal of an injunction. Lord Diplock explained the issues to be considered:

---

[186] [1996] 1 All ER 853, at 865.   [187] Ibid., at 867.

[188] See also *Cream Holdings Ltd v Banerjee* [2004] 4 ALL ER 617, where the House of Lords said that a claimant will have to satisfy the court that he is 'more likely than not' to win at trial in order to obtain an interim injunction, though the court can dispense with this where particular circumstances make it necessary. It is suggested this is not the same test as that set out by Laddie J in *Series 5 Software*, but it is a higher threshold than the *American Cyanamid* test.

[189] Phillips [1997] JBL 486, at 487, reviewing the cases decided since *Series 5 Software*.

[T]he court should first consider whether, if the plaintiff were to succeed at the trial in establishing his right to a permanent injunction, he would be adequately compensated by an award of damages for the loss he would have sustained as a result of the defendant's continuing to do what was sought to be enjoined between the time of the application and the time of the trial. If damages in the measure recoverable at common law would be adequate remedy and the defendant would be in a financial position to pay them, no interlocutory injunction should normally be granted, however strong the plaintiff's claim appeared to be at that stage. If, on the other hand, damages would not provide an adequate remedy for the plaintiff in the event of his succeeding at the trial, the court should then consider whether, on the contrary hypothesis that the defendant were to succeed at the trial in establishing his right to do that which was sought to be enjoined, he would be adequately compensated under the plaintiff's undertaking as to damages for the loss he would have sustained by being prevented from doing so between the time of the application and the time of the trial. If damages in the measure recoverable under such an undertaking would be an adequate remedy and the plaintiff would be in a financial position to pay them, there would be no reason upon this ground to refuse an interlocutory injunction.[190]

He concluded that where the factors appear to be evenly balanced 'it is a counsel of prudence to take such measures as preserve the status quo'. This exercise of weighing the 'balance of convenience' has also been described as the 'balance of the risk of doing an injustice',[191] or, in other words, finding the balance of convenience requires that the balance of inconvenience between the parties be considered.

(iii) 'Other special factors to be taken into consideration'

Lord Diplock also recognized that there 'may be many other special factors to be taken into consideration in the particular circumstances of individual cases'.[192] For example, in *American Cyanamid*[193] itself, where the plaintiffs sought an interlocutory injunction to prevent the defendants launching a surgical product claimed to be in breach of the plaintiffs' patent, a number of additional factors were taken into account, including the fact that the defendants as yet had no business which would be brought to a stop by the injunction; that the launch of the defendants' product would prevent the plaintiffs' patented product becoming established in the market; and that if the defendants' product was allowed on the market before trial and patients and doctors became used to it, it might be impracticable for the plaintiffs to insist on a permanent injunction at trial. For these reasons the House of Lords held that an interlocutory injunction should be granted. The public interest, and the interests of the public in general may also be factors to be taken into account in determining whether an interlocutory injunction should be granted.[194] In *Themehelp Ltd v West*,[195] the Court of Appeal was asked to

---

[190] [1975] AC 396, at 408.

[191] *Cayne v Global Natural Resources plc* [1984] 1 All ER 225, at 237, per May LJ.

[192] *Bryanston Finance Ltd v de Vries (No 2)* [1976] Ch 63, *Dunford and Elliot Ltd v Johnson and Firth Brown Ltd* [1977] 1 Lloyd's Rep 505, CA; *Roussel-Uclaf v G D Searle & Co Ltd* [1977] FSR 125; *A-G v Guardian Newspapers Ltd* [1987] 1 WLR 1248.

[193] [1975] AC 396.

[194] See *Smith v Inner London Education Authority* [1978] 1 All ER 411, CA; *Factortame Ltd v Secretary of State for Transport (No 2)* [1991] 1 All ER 70, at 118–119, per Lord Goff.

[195] [1995] 4 All ER 215.

grant an interlocutory injunction preventing the enforcement of a performance bond pending a fraud trial. The court was prepared to grant the order, but recognized that the situations in which such orders should be granted had to be considered with care lest they disturb the mercantile practice that performance bonds should normally be treated as autonomous guarantees that could be enforced regardless of any problems extraneous to the guarantee itself.

(iv) 'Real prospect of trial'

Although an interlocutory injunction is intended to preserve the status quo before the final determination of the issue at trial, it is inevitable that in many cases the matter will go no further and the parties will settle on the basis of the injunction granted.[196] With the rejection of the requirement that the claimant must establish a prima facie case, there is now no need for the court to inquire too deeply into the merits of the claimants' claim, and the consequence is that the claimant may force the defendant to settle without ever having to prove his case. To address this problem the Court of Appeal held in *Cayne v Global Natural Resources plc*[197] that a future trial must be likely to take place. Kerr LJ stated the limitation:

The second pre-requisite ... is that a trial is in fact likely to take place, in the sense that the plaintiff's case shows that they are genuinely concerned to pursue their claim to trial, and that they are seeking the injunction as a means of a holding operation pending the trial.[198]

(v) Freedom of expression

The principles by which it is determined whether an interlocutory injunction should be granted are different in cases involving a breach of confidence, privacy, or libel because of the effect of the Human Rights Act 1998, which incorporates into English Law art 10 of the European Convention on Human Rights protecting freedom of expression. Section 12(3) of the Human Rights Act provides that the court should not grant relief unless the court 'is satisfied that the applicant is likely to re-establish that the publication should not be allowed'. It follows that in such cases the courts must look at the strength of the claimant's case before granting an interlocutory injunction, and not simply apply the usual 'balance of convenience' test. An interlocutory injunction will therefore only be granted if the claimant can show that he would probably succeed at trail, unless the consequences of publication would be especially serious.[199] Even where the claimant can demonstrate the likelihood of success, the court may refuse an injunction and leave the claimant to a remedy in damages if the 'balance of convenience' favours refusing the award of an injunction.[200]

---

[196] See *Fellowes & Son v Fisher* [1976] QB 122, at 133, per Lord Denning MR, who suggested that 99 cases out of 100 go no further than the grant of an interlocutory injunction. Reasons include the expense of litigation in both time and money.

[197] [1984] 1 All ER 225.

[198] Ibid., at 234. See also *Transfield Shipping Inc v Chiping Xinta Huaya Alumina Co Ltd* [2009] EWHC 3642 (Comm) at [51]–[52].

[199] *Cream Holdings Ltd v Banerjee* [2004] 3 WLR 918.

[200] *Douglas v Hello! Ltd* [2001] QB 967. See Morgan, 'Confidence and Horizontal Effect; "Hello" Trouble' [2003] 62 CLJ 444.

(c) Undertaking in damages

On the grant of an interlocutory injunction the claimant is generally required to give an undertaking in damages to the defendant. By this undertaking, made to the court,[201] the claimant is liable to pay the defendant damages for any loss he has suffered as a result of the grant of the interlocutory injunction prior to the full hearing if at the subsequent trial it appears that the injunction should not have been granted.[202] There is no need for an undertaking in damages in matrimonial proceedings,[203] or where the crown seeks an injunction to enforce the general law[204] rather than its own proprietary right.[205]

(d) Mandatory interlocutory injunctions

The courts are more reluctant to award mandatory interlocutory injunctions, and it seems that a higher test may have to be satisfied than that set out in *American Cyanamid*,[206] which involved a prohibitory injunction. In *De Falco v Crawley Borough Council*,[207] Lord Denning MR held that a mandatory interlocutory injunction should not be granted unless the plaintiffs made out a 'strong prima facie case',[208] and in *Shepherd Homes Ltd v Sandham*[209] Megarry J held that 'the case has to be unusually strong and clear before a mandatory injunction will be granted'. His suggestion that 'the court must...feel a high degree of assurance that at the trial it will appear that the injunction was rightly granted'[210] was approved and applied by the Court of Appeal in *Locabail International Finance Ltd v Agroexport & Atlanta (UK) Ltd*,[211] which felt that the statements of principle relating to mandatory interlocutory injunctions were not affected by *American Cyanamid*.[212] Where the requirements are met the court will grant such an injunction.[213]

(e) Interlocutory injunctions in the context of trade disputes

By s 221(2) of the Trade Union and Labour Relations Act 1992, in determining whether to grant an interlocutory injunction the court must have regard to the likelihood of the defendant establishing at trial that the action was in contemplation of a trade dispute and therefore entitled to statutory immunity. The defendant must be able to show a

---

[201] Therefore, any breach is a contempt and not merely a breach of contract: *Hussain v Hussain* [1986] Fam 134, CA; *Mid Suffolk DV v Clarke* [2007] 1 WLR 980. Compare *Balkanbank v Taher* [1994] 4 All ER 239.

[202] See *Chappell v Davidson* (1856) 8 De G M & G 1; *Smith v Day* (1882) 21 Ch D 421; *Digital Equipment Corpn v Darkcrest* [1984] Ch 512.

[203] *Practice Direction (Injunction: Undertaking as to Damages)* [1974] 1 WLR 576.

[204] *Hoffman La Roche (F) & Co AG v Secretary of State for Trade and Industry* [1975] AC 295.

[205] See *A-G v Wright* [1988] 1 WLR 164.   [206] [1975] AC 396, HL.

[207] [1980] QB 460, CA.   [208] Ibid., at 478.   [209] [1971] Ch 340, at 349.

[210] Ibid., at 351.   [211] [1986] 1 WLR 657.

[212] See also *Films Rover International Ltd v Cannon Film Sales Ltd* [1987] 1 WLR 670, where Hoffmann J held that a mandatory interlocutory injunction could be granted where refusal carried a greater risk of injustice than granting it, even though the 'high degree of assurance' test was not met.

[213] *NWL Ltd v Woods* [1979] 1 WLR 1294, HL.

high degree of probability that the statutory defence will succeed if the consequences of refusing the injunction will be severe damage to the claimant.[214]

(f) Interlocutory injunctions in the context of libel

The courts will generally refuse to award an interlocutory injunction in cases of alleged libel if the defendant intends to justify (ie to prove the truth of the defamatory statement).[215] This has not been altered by *American Cyanamid*.[216]

(4) General principles governing the grant of a quia timet injunction

Quia timet injunctions are available where, although there has as yet been no infringement of the claimant's rights, such an infringement has been threatened or is apprehended. In *Redland Bricks Ltd v Morris*, Lord Upjohn distinguished two circumstances in which a quia timet injunction would be appropriate:

first, where the defendant has as yet done no hurt to the plaintiff but is threatening and intending (so the plaintiff alleges) to do works which will render irreparable harm to him or his property if carried to completion . . . Secondly, the type of case where the plaintiff has been fully compensated both at law and in equity for the damage he has suffered but where he alleges that the earlier actions of the defendant may lead to further causes of action.[217]

In order for the court to grant a quia timet injunction the plaintiff must satisfy a relatively high burden of proof that the threatened or apprehended infringement will occur. As Lord Dunedin said in *A-G for the Dominion of Canada v Ritchie Contracting and Supply Co Ltd*,[218] 'no one can obtain a quia timet order by merely saying "Timeo" '.[219] In *A-G v Manchester Corpn*, Chitty J stated:

The principle which I think may be properly and safely extracted from the quia timet authorities is, that the plaintiff must show a strong case of probability that the apprehended mischief will, in fact, arise.[220]

In *Redland Bricks Ltd v Morris*,[221] Lord Upjohn said that 'a mandatory injunction can only be granted where the plaintiff shows a very strong probability upon the facts that grave damage will accrue to him in the future'.[222] Russell LJ suggested a different formulation in *Hooper v Rogers*:

---

[214] See *Smith v Peters* (1875) LR 20 Eq 511; *Esso Petroleum Co Ltd v Kingswood Motors (Addlestone) Ltd* [1974] QB 142; *Sky Petroleum v VIP Petroleum Ltd* [1974] 1 WLR 576; *Astro Exito Navegacion SA v Southland Enterprise Co Ltd (No 2)* [1982] QB 1248; *Parker v Camden London Borough Council* [1986] Ch 162; *Hemingway Securities Ltd v Dunraven Ltd* [1995] 1 EGLR 61.

[215] *Bonnard v Perryman* [1891] 2 Ch 269, CA.

[216] *Bestobell Paints Ltd v Bigg* (1975) 119 Sol Jo 678; *J Trevor & Sons v P R Solomon* [1978] 2 EGLR 120; *A-G v BBC* [1981] AC 303; *Gulf Oil (GB) Ltd v Page* [1987] Ch 327.

[217] [1970] AC 652, at 665.   [218] [1919] AC 999, at 1005.

[219] 'Timeo' means 'I am afraid' and comes from the same Latin verb as quia timet.

[220] [1893] 2 Ch 87, at 92.   [221] [1970] AC 652.

[222] See also *A-G v Manchester Corpn* [1893] 2 Ch 87; *A-G v Rathmines and Pembroke Joint Hospital Board* [1904] 1 IR 161.

In different cases differing phrases have been used in describing circumstances in which...quia timet injunctions will be granted. In truth it seems to me that the degree of probability of future injury is not an absolute standard: what is to be aimed at is justice between the parties having regard to all the relevant circumstances.[223]

Where the defendant cannot demonstrate a strong probability of the threatened or apprehended infringement, the court will refuse to grant an injunction. In *A-G v Nottingham Corpn*,[224] for example, an application for a quia timet injunction to prevent the defendant using a building as a smallpox hospital on the grounds that it would constitute a public and private nuisance was refused because the plaintiff had failed to show 'a strong probability almost amounting to moral certainty' that there would be an actionable nuisance.[225] In contrast in *Goodhart v Hyett*,[226] the plaintiff owned, by virtue of an easement, a pipe running across the defendant's land. North J granted a quia timet injunction to prevent the defendant building a house above the pipe, because the plaintiff had shown that this would prevent him repairing the pipe.[227]

(5) Rights which will be protected by the grant of an injunction

Having examined the general requirements governing the grant of perpetual, inter-locutory, and quia timet injunctions, it is appropriate to consider the most important practical circumstances in which they are available as a remedy.

(a) Trespass

A landowner will normally[228] be entitled to a prohibitory injunction to prevent tres-passers entering his land, and a mandatory injunction ordering trespassers to be removed. These remedies are available even though he has suffered no damage from the trespass.[229]

(b) Nuisance

An injunction is an important remedy available to the occupier of land where the defendant is causing a private nuisance, or to a private individual who suffers particu-lar damage from a public nuisance.[230]

---

[223] [1974] 3 WLR 329, at 334.

[224] [1904] 1 Ch 673. See also *Worsley v Swann* (1882) 51 LJ Ch 576; *Fletcher v Bealey* (1885) 28 Ch D 688; *A-G v Manchester Corpn* [1893] 2 Ch 87; *Draper v British Optical Association* [1938] 1 All ER 115.

[225] See also *A-G v Rathmines and Pembroke Joint Hospital Board* [1904] 1 IR 161.

[226] (1883) 25 Ch D 182.

[227] See also *Emperor of Austria v Day* (1861) 3 De G F & J 217; *Dicker v Popham, Radford & Co* (1890) 63 LT 379; *Torquay Hotel Co Ltd v Cousins* [1969] 2 Ch 106.

[228] *Jaggard v Sawyer* [1995] 2 All ER 189 is an example of an exception.

[229] See *Kelsen v Imperial Tobacco* [1957] 2 QB 334; *Patel v WH Smith (Eziot) Ltd* [1987] 1 WLR 853, CA; *Trenberth (John) Ltd v National Westminster Bank Ltd* (1980) 39 P & CR 104; *Harrow London Borough Council v Donohue* [1995] 1 EGLR 257.

[230] *Lyon v Fishmongers' Co* (1875–76) 1 App Cas 662, HL; *Vanderpant v Mayfair Hotel Co Ltd* [1930] 1 Ch 138.

(c) Waste

Waste is a tort committed when by any action or inaction, a tenant under a lease of land or a tenant of land with a life interest permanently alters the physical character of land in his possession.[231] An injunction will be granted to restrain voluntary[232] and equitable waste,[233] but not ameliorative[234] or permissive waste.[235]

(d) Libel

The court possesses the jurisdiction to award an injunction to prevent the publication of defamatory material.[236] However, an injunction will only be granted if it is clear that the material to be published is false, since the court is concerned to protect the public interest in knowing the truth.[237] As was noted above, since the award of an injunction to prevent a libel may affect the right to freedom of expression, where an interlocutory injunction is sought the principles identified in *American Cyanamid* are inapplicable.[238] An injunction will rarely be granted if the defendant intends to justify statements published.[239] In *Greene v Associated Newspapers*,[240] the Court of Appeal held that the Human Rights Act 1998 had not changed the rule in *Bonnard v Perryman*[241] that a court would not impose a prior restraint on publication unless it was clear that no defence would succeed at trial. A quia timet injunction may be granted to prevent a threatened libel, but in *British Data Management plc v Boxer Commercial Removals plc*,[242] the Court of Appeal held that such an injunction should only be granted if the claimant could demonstrate with 'reasonable certainty' the threatened words that are allegedly defamatory.[243] In the case of *Holley v Smyth*,[244] the Court of Appeal held that an interlocutory injunction should not be granted to restrain the threatened publication of an allegedly libellous allegation that the plaintiff had caused a loss of £200,000 from a trust through a fraudulent misrepresentation, unless it could be shown that the allegation was 'plainly untrue' at the interlocutory stage. Where the untruthfulness of a statement has not been proved the law will allow publication. If it is subsequently proved that the allegation was libellous, then the claimant would be entitled to receive

---

[231] See Gray and Gray, *Elements of Land Law* (5th edn, 2009), p 62.

[232] Any acts which positively diminish the value of the land, for example quarrying or cutting timber.

[233] Equitable waste is malicious or wanton destruction of the land or buildings exceeding the licence conferred by a clause exempting the tenant from liability for voluntary waste: *Vane v Lord Barnard* (1716) 2 Vern 738; *Weld-Blundell v Wolseley* [1903] 2 Ch 664.

[234] Where the land is improved: *Doherty v Allman* (1878) 3 App Cas 709.

[235] Defaults of maintenance and repair: *Powys v Blagrave* (1854) 4 De GM & G 448; *Re Cartwright* (1889) 41 Ch D 532.

[236] *Quartz Hill Consolidated Gold Mining Co v Beall* (1881–82) LR 20 Ch D 501; *Bonnard v Perryman* [1891] 2 Ch 269; *Hubbard v Pitt* [1976] QB 142; *Gulf Oil (Great Britain) Ltd v Page* [1987] Ch 327; *Femis-Bank (Anguilla) Ltd v Lazer* [1991] Ch 391.

[237] *Fraser v Evans* [1969] 1 QB 349; *Woodward v Hutchins* [1977] 1 WLR 760; *A-G v BBC* [1981] AC 303.

[238] *Herbage v Pressdram Ltd* [1984] 1 WLR 1160; *Kaye v Robertson* [1991] FSR 62.

[239] *Bonnard v Perryman* [1891] 2 Ch 269.   [240] [2005] 1 All ER 30.

[241] [1891] 2 Ch 269.   [242] [1996] 3 All ER 707.

[243] Ibid., at 717, per Hirst LJ. The claimant does not therefore need to be able to plead the actual words that the defendant has threatened to use.

[244] [1998] 2 WLR 742.

compensation. This could include an award of aggravated damages,[245] if warranted, to punish a malicious defendant for publishing.[246]

(e) Breach of contract

An injunction is an appropriate remedy against a party who is in breach of a negative contractual term.[247] In *Nordenfelt v Maxim Nordenfelt Guns and Ammunition Co Ltd*,[248] for example, the House of Lords granted an injunction to enforce a contractual stipulation that the defendant would not engage in the business of manufacturing guns or ammunition for 25 years after he had sold his patents and business to the plaintiffs.[249] The court will also grant injunctions to enforce the terms of partnership agreements.[250] The court will not normally grant an injunction to enforce a contractual term in a contract for personal services that would indirectly amount to specific performance of the contract because the employee will have no option but to perform the contract or remain idle.[251]

(f) Restrictive covenants

The court may grant an injunction to enforce a restrictive covenant[252] over land. In *Wakeham v Wood*,[253] for example, a mandatory injunction was granted requiring the defendant to demolish a building that obstructed the view of the sea from the plaintiff's house, contrary to a restrictive covenant.

(g) Breach of trust

The court will grant an injunction to restrain trustees from committing a breach of trust.[254]

(h) Breach of confidence[255]

In *Campbell v MGN Ltd*, the House of Lords held that a duty of confidence arises 'whenever a person receives information he knows or ought to know is fairly and reasonably

---

[245] *Rookes v Barnard* [1964] AC 1129.   [246] [1998] 2 WLR 742, at 758–759, per Auld LJ.

[247] The term need not be expressed in a negative way as the court will look to the substance and not the form: *Wolverhampton and Walsall Rly Co Ltd v London and North Western Rly Ltd* (1873) LR 16 Eq 433. In exceptional circumstances breach of a negative term of a contract may give rise to the restitutionary remedy of an account of profits: *A-G v Blake* [2001] 1 AC 268; *Experience Hendrix LLC v PPX Enterprises Inc* [2003] 1 All ER (Comm) 830.

[248] [1894] AC 535.

[249] A worldwide prohibition would normally be invalid as being in restraint of trade, but it was upheld in this case because of the international scale and nature of the businesses concerned.

[250] *Hall v Hall* (1850) 12 Beav 414.

[251] See *Lumley v Wagner* (1852) 1 De GM & G 604; *Rely-a-Bell Burglar and Fire Alarm Co v Eisler* [1926] Ch 609; *Warner Bros Pictures Inc v Nelson* [1937] 1 KB 209; *Page One Records Ltd v Britton* [1967] 3 All ER 822; *Evening Standard Co Ltd v Henderson* [1987] IRLR 64.

[252] See Gray and Gray, *Elements of Land Law* (5th edn), p 291.

[253] (1982) 43 P & CR 40, CA.

[254] *Fox v Fox* (1870) LR 11 Eq 142; *Dance v Goldingham* (1872–73) 8 Ch App 902; *Waller v Waller* [1967] 1 All ER 305.

[255] See Chapter 30.

to be regarded as confidential'.[256] The court may grant an injunction to prevent a breach of confidence by restraining the publication of confidential information.[257] For example, in *Prince Albert v Strange*[258] the Prince obtained an injunction to prevent the publication of etchings that had been obtained in breach of confidence. In *Duchess of Argyll v Duke of Argyll*,[259] an injunction was granted to prevent the plaintiff publishing details of her marriage to the defendant. In the *Spycatcher* case, an interlocutory injunction was granted to prevent the publication of a book on the basis of the public interest of maintaining confidentiality.[260] An injunction may also be available in a commercial context where a company has received confidential information. In *Peter Pan Manufacturing Corpn v Corsets Silhouette Ltd*,[261] for example, the plaintiffs were granted an injunction to prevent the defendants manufacturing a brassiere to a design which they had been shown in confidence. The right to confidence can extend to preventing the publication of photographs[262] or of tape recordings of private conversations.[263]

Protection of confidential information is now seen as part of a rapidly developing law of privacy,[264] and the protection of such information involves consideration of the relationship between the right to privacy and the right to freedom of expression under arts 8 and 10 of the European Convention on Human Rights, incorporated into English Law by the Human Rights Act 1998. In *Campbell v MGN Ltd*,[265] the House of Lords held that neither art 8 nor art 10 were to be given pre-eminence, so that the right of the media to provide information to the public had to be balanced against the respect to be given to private life. The difficulty of determining where the balance between these competing rights should lie is well illustrated by the fact that the Law Lords were split 3:2 as to whether publication of photographs of Naomi Campbell attending Narcotics' Anonymous meetings infringed her right to privacy. The majority[266] held that details of her treatment should be protected, since they considered that the assurance of privacy was essential to the effectiveness of the therapy being received. However, the minority[267] held that the disclosure of the nature of the treatment she was receiving was unremarkable, and followed consequentially from the fact that it was in the public interest to disclose the fact that she was receiving treatment for drug addiction because she had previously denied using drugs. In developments since, the House of Lords has held that an injunction could be

[256] [2004] 2 All ER 995, at [14], per Lord Nicholls.

[257] See *Lord Ashburton v Pape* [1913] 2 Ch 469, CA; *Foster v Mountford* [1978] FSR 582; *Woodward v Hutchins* [1977] 1 WLR 760, CA; *Lion Laboratories v Evans* [1985] QB 526, CA; *X (HA) v Y* [1988] 2 All ER 648; *W v Egdell* [1990] Ch 359.

[258] (1849) 1 Mac & G 25.   [259] [1967] Ch 302.

[260] *A-G v Guardian Newspapers Ltd* [1987] 1 WLR 1248; *A-G v Guardian Newspapers Ltd (No 2)* [1990] 1 AC 109.

[261] [1964] 1 WLR 96.   [262] *Douglas v Hello* [2003] 3 All ER 996; *D v L* [2003] EWCA Civ 1169.

[263] *D v L* [2003] EWCA Civ 1169.

[264] See Phillipson, 'Transforming Breach of Confidence? Towards a Common Law Right of Privacy under the Human Rights Act' (2003) 66 MLR 726; Caddick 'Show Me the Money!' (2007) 157 NLJ 805.

[265] [2004] 2 All ER 995. See also *Douglas v Hello! Ltd* [2003] 3 All ER 996 and [2005] EWCA Civ 595.

[266] Lord Hope, Baroness Hale, Lord Carson.   [267] Lord Nicholls, Lord Hoffmann.

granted to restrain a breach of confidence to enforce an agreement giving a magazine exclusive photographic rights to a celebrity wedding ceremony (Michael Douglas and Catherine Zeta-Jones), on the basis that there was no public policy reason not to protect such an agreement under the law of confidence.[268] On the other hand, in *Mosley v News Group Newspapers Ltd*[269] an injunction was refused. Max Mosley, the son of Sir Oswald Mosley, and President of the FIA (which controls Formula 1 Grand Prix motor racing), had sought to prevent the *News of the World* showing video footage of him engaging in a private party involving prostitutes and sado-masochistic activities. Although Eady J considered the publication to be in breach of confidence, the footage had been so widely accessible that it had entered the public domain, and granting an injunction 'would merely be a futile gesture'.[270] As was noted above, as a result of the Human Rights Act 1998 the award of an interlocutory injunction to restrain publication of information on the grounds of breach of confidence will not be determined by the application of the usual *American Cyanamid* principles, so that an injunction will only be granted if the claimant can demonstrate a likelihood of success at trial.[271]

(i) Intellectual property rights

An injunction will be granted to prevent a defendant passing off a product so that it appears to be the plaintiff's,[272] using his trade mark or infringement of his patent, registered design or copyright.[273]

(j) Expulsion from clubs and societies

The court will grant an injunction to restrain the wrongful expulsion of a member from a club or professional association, for example where the rules of natural justice have been breached.[274] The court will clearly act if the member has a proprietary interest in the club,[275] but even where there is no proprietary interest[276] an injunction is available to protect his right to work[277] or if a matter of public importance is involved.[278] One particular area where injunctions have been granted is to prevent wrongful expulsion from trade unions.[279]

---

[268] *Douglas v Hello! Ltd (No.3)* [2008] AC 1.   [269] [2008] EWHC 687.

[270] Ibid., at [36].   [271] See above p 140.

[272] *GG Spalding & Bros v AW Gamage Ltd* (1915) 32 RPC 273, HL; *Erven Warnick BV v J Townend & Sons (Hull) Ltd* [1979] AC 731; *Taittinger SA v Allbev Ltd* [1994] 4 All ER 75, CA.

[273] See Trade Marks Act 1938; Patents Act 1949; Registered Designs Act 1949; Patents Act 1977; Copyright, Design and Patents Act 1988.

[274] *Labouchere v Earl of Wharncliffe* (1879–80) 13 Ch D 346.

[275] *Rigby v Connol* (1880) 14 Ch D 482.

[276] See *Baird v Wells* (1890) 44 Ch D 661, CA, *Rowe v Hewitt* (1906) 12 OLR 13; *Lee v Showmen's Guild of Great Britain* [1952] 2 QB 329; *Gaiman v National Association for Mental Health* [1971] Ch 317.

[277] *Edwards v Society of Graphical and Allied Trades* [1971] Ch 354.

[278] *Woodford v Smith* [1970] 1 WLR 806.

[279] *Osborne v Amalgamated Society of Railway Servants* [1911] 1 Ch 540; *Edwards v Society of Graphical and Allied Trades* [1971] Ch 354; *Breen v Amalgamated Engineering Union* [1971] 2 QB 175; *Shotton v Hammond* (1976) 120 Sol Jo 780.

(k) Judicial review

An injunction is one remedy[280] available where the decision of a public body is subject to 'judicial review', for instance because it has acted outside the scope of its powers. The House of Lords held in *O'Reilly v Mackman*[281] that an application for judicial review claiming a public body has infringed public rights must be brought under RSC Ord 53. However, where a private law right is infringed an injunction may be sought in the ordinary way.[282]

(l) Family matters

The court has statutory jurisdiction under the Family Law Act 1996[283] to grant injunctions excluding a spouse or partner from the matrimonial home, and to restrain one spouse molesting the other. Injunctions may also be used to protect minors. An injunction cannot, however, be obtained by a husband or partner to prevent a woman having an abortion.[284] A detailed consideration of these issues is outside the scope of this text.

4 Freezing injunctions

(1) Definition

Although basically an injunction similar to those considered in the preceding section, the freezing injunction is sufficiently important to merit a consideration of its own. If granted, it prevents a defendant (or a third party holding a defendant's assets)[285] from dissipating or removing his assets from the jurisdiction so that there will be nothing remaining to satisfy a judgment that might be obtained against him at trial.[286] Previously, freezing injunctions were known as 'Mareva' Injunctions, taking their name from the case in which they were first exercised, *Mareva Compania Naviera SA v International Bulk Carriers SA*.[287] The new nomenclature was introduced in the Civil Procedure Rules.[288]

---

[280] Others are a declaration or prerogative order.   [281] [1983] 2 AC 237.

[282] *R v BBC, ex p Lavelle* [1983] 1 WLR 23; *Law v National Greyhound Racing Club Ltd* [1983] 1 WLR 1302; *R v East Berkshire Health Authority, ex p Walsh* [1985] QB 152; *R v Derbyshire County Council, ex p Noble* [1990] ICR 808.

[283] Extending and replacing earlier legislation, including the Matrimonial Causes Act 1973 and Matrimonial and Family Proceedings Act 1984.

[284] *Paton v Trustees of British Pregnancy Advisory Service* [1979] QB 76; *C v S* [1988] QB 135.

[285] See Devonshire 'Third Parties Holding Assets Subject to a Mareva' [1996] LMCLQ 268.

[286] It has been suggested that the jurisdiction extends to future assets of a defendant as well as those in existence at the date that the injunction is granted: *Soinco SACI v Novokuznetsk Aluminium Plant* [1998] QB 406, per Coleman J.

[287] [1975] 2 Lloyd's Rep 509.   [288] CPR 25.1(1)(f).

(a) Nature of the freezing injunction

A freezing injunction is granted in an interlocutory form and is usually obtained ex parte (i.e. on the application of the claimant without hearing the defendant). As Kerr LJ stated in *Z Ltd v A–Z*:

> Mareva injunctions should be granted...when it appears to the court that there is a combination of two circumstances. First, when it appears likely that the plaintiff will recover judgment against the defendant for a certain or approximate sum. Secondly, when there are also reasons to believe that the defendant has assets within the jurisdiction to meet the judgment, in whole or in part, but may well take steps designed to ensure that there are no longer available or traceable when judgment is given against him.[289]

As Lord Donaldson MR said in *Derby & Co v Weldon (Nos 3 & 4)*,[290] the fundamental principle underlying the jurisdiction to grant a freezing injunction is that 'no court should permit a defendant to take action designed to ensure that subsequent orders of the court are rendered less effective than would otherwise be the case'.[291] Where a freezing injunction is granted the defendant is entitled to draw upon his assets to fund his legitimate expenses,[292] including his reasonable legal expenses in defending the subsequent action. Where the claimant seeks to assert a proprietary claim to property in the defendant's hands, for example asserting that he was a constructive trustee, and a freezing injunction has been granted, the defendant may still be in breach of trust if the proprietary claim is upheld and the property has been wholly or partial dissipated. It is no defence that the injunction did not prohibit expenditure on his expenses.[293] Similarly, the recipients of such property, for example solicitors whose legal fees are paid from it, will not be protected from possible future claims on the grounds that they had knowingly received trust property.[294]

(b) History

The freezing injunction is a relatively recent creation of equity.[295] It was traditionally thought that *Lister & Co v Stubbs*[296] prevented the court from granting the claimant such an injunction, but in *Nippon Yusen Kaisha v Kaageorgis* and *Mareva Compania Naviera SA v International Bulkcarriers SA*[297] the Court of Appeal held that the court enjoyed the jurisdiction to grant just such an order under the predecessor to s 37(1) of

---

289 [1982] QB 558, at 585.   290 [1990] Ch 65, at 76.

291 See also *Camdex International Ltd v Bank of Zambia (No 2)* [1997] 1 All ER 728, at 733, per Sir Thomas Bingham MR.

292 Cf *Fitzgerald v Williams* [1996] 2 All ER 171, where the Court of Appeal held that a defendant was not permitted to draw on frozen funds, to which the plaintiff asserted a proprietary claim unless he had no other funds on which he could draw.

293 *United Mizrahi Bank Ltd v Doherty* [1998] 2 All ER 230. For the nature of a proprietary claim against the trust property, see further Chapter 31 in this book.

294 See further Chapter 31 pp 983–1010.

295 However, in *The Siskina* [1979] AC 210 Lord Denning MR suggested that the Mareva injunction was a 'rediscovery' of the earlier procedure of 'foreign attachment'.

296 (1890) LR 45 Ch D 1.

297 [1980] 1 All ER 213, [1975] 2 Lloyd's Rep 509. A 'Mareva' injunction was first granted in the earlier case of *Nippon Yusen Kaisha v Karageorgis* [1975] 1 WLR 1093.

the Supreme Court Act 1981.[298] Lord Denning MR described the development of the order as 'the greatest piece of judicial law reform in my time'.[299] A freezing injunction may be granted in aid of proceedings within the jurisdiction or of proceedings in a foreign jurisdiction.[300]

(c) Practical illustrations

Two cases illustrate the practical application of the freezing injunction. *Re BCCI SA (No 9)*[301] concerned the collapse of the BCCI banking group as the consequence of a massive fraud. A worldwide Mareva injunction was granted against 'Mahfouz', a director of BCCI and 'Kahlon', an employee, whom the liquidators sought to make personally liable for the debts of BCCI on the basis of their allegedly fraudulent management. In *Balkanbank v Taher*,[302] a bank was granted a worldwide Mareva injunction against the defendants, who were alleged to have acted fraudulently in respect of a joint venture, an allegation which later failed in the Irish courts.

(2) Guidelines for the grant of a freezing injunction

In *Re BCCI SA (No 9)*,[303] following the judgment of Parker LJ in the Court of Appeal in *Derby & Co Ltd v Weldon*,[304] Rattee J stated that there were 'three issues on which the court has to be satisfied before granting a Mareva injunction'.

(a) 'Has the applicant a good arguable case?'

Although the freezing injunction is generally interlocutory, a stricter standard is applied concerning the strength of the claimant's claim. Under the orthodox test set down in *American Cyanamid Co v Ethicon Ltd*,[305] a claimant merely has to demonstrate that there is a serious question to be tried. Before a freezing injunction will be granted, he must demonstrate that he has a 'good arguable case'.[306] In *Third Chandris Shipping Corpn v Unimarine SA*,[307] Lord Denning MR said that a claimant seeking a Mareva injunction 'should make full and frank disclosure of all matters in his knowledge which are material for the judge to know',[308] and 'give particulars of his claim against the defendant, stating the grounds of his claim and the amount thereof, and fairly stating the points made against it by the defendant'. If subsequently it appears that he had not made full disclosure, the injunction will normally be discharged.[309] In

---

[298] Supreme Court of Judicature (Consolidation) Act 1925, s 45(1).

[299] *The Due Process of Law* (1980), p 134.

[300] Civil Jurisdiction and Judgments Act 1982, s 25. See *The Siskina* [1979] AC 210; *Rosseel NV v Oriental Commercial and Shipping (UK) Ltd* [1990] 3 All ER 545; *Mercedes-Benz AG v Leiduck* [1996] AC 284.

[301] [1994] 3 All ER 764.   [302] [1994] 4 All ER 239; on appeal [1995] 2 All ER 904, CA.

[303] [1994] 3 All ER 764, at 785.   [304] [1990] Ch 48, at 57.

[305] [1975] AC 396, HL.   [306] A distinction which Parker LJ said was 'incapable of definition'.

[307] [1979] QB 645.

[308] See *Negocios Del Mar SA v Doric Shipping Corpn SA, The Assios* [1979] 1 Lloyd's Rep 331; *Brinks-MAT Ltd v Elcombe* [1988] 3 All ER 188; *Tate Access Floors Inc v Boswell* [1990] 3 All ER 303.

[309] *Ali & Fahd Shobokshi Group Ltd v Moneim* [1989] 2 All ER 404; *Dubai Bank Ltd v Galadari* [1990] 1 Lloyd's Rep 120, CA.

the decision of the House of Lords in *Fourie v Le Roux*,[310] no substantive proceedings had actually been brought against the defendant at the time the freezing order was applied for, and Lord Scott held that at least an undertaking that an action would be filed was necessary before such an order could be granted.[311]

(b) 'Has the applicant satisfied the court that there are assets within and, where an extra-territorial order is sought, without the jurisdiction?'

A freezing injunction is available against both movable[312] or immovable property,[313] Originally, it was only available against assets within the jurisdiction, but may an order may be made with worldwide effect.[314]

(c) 'Is there a real risk of dissipation or secretion of assets so as to render any judgment which the applicant may obtain nugatory?'

The claimant should give some grounds for believing that there is a real risk that the assets of the defendant will be removed or dissipated before the judgment or award is satisfied.[315] In *Camdex International Ltd v Bank of Zambia (No 2)*,[316] the Court of Appeal held that it was inappropriate to grant a Mareva injunction against the Zambian government freezing a large quantity of new banknotes which had been printed for Zambia in England because the notes were of no value to the claimant (or other creditors of the defendant) on the open market. Thus, they were not an asset that might be dissipated so as to avoid satisfaction of a judgment debt. It was inappropriate to use a Mareva injunction merely to hold a defendant to ransom in the hope that he would be compelled to satisfy the judgment debt.

(3) Undertakings in damages

When a freezing injunction is granted the claimant must also give an undertaking in damages. As Lord Denning MR explained in *Third Chandris Shipping Corpn v Unimarine SA*:

The plaintiff must, of course, give an undertaking in damages—in case he fails in his claim or the injunction turns out to be unjustified. In a suitable case this should be supported by a bond or security.[317]

---

[310] [2007] UKHL 1.

[311] See Capper 'Asset Freezing Orders—Failure to State the Cause of Action' (2007) CJQ 181.

[312] 'Assets' includes a wide range of chattels. See *Allen v Jambo Holdings Ltd* [1980] 1 WLR 1252 (aeroplanes); *The Rena K* [1979] QB 377 (ships); *Rasu Maritima SA v Persuahaan Pertambangan Minyak Dan Gas Bumi Negara* [1978] QB 644 (machinery); *CBS United Kingdom Ltd v Lambert* [1983] Ch 37 (jewellery, *objects d'art*, other valuables, and choses in action); *Darashah v UFAC (UK) Ltd* (1982) Times, 30 March, CA (goodwill of a business).

[313] *Derby & Co Ltd v Weldon (Nos 3 and 4)* [1990] Ch 65 (disposition of a freehold interest in a house).

[314] See below, p 152.

[315] In *Ketchum International Plc v Group Public Relations Holdings Ltd* [1996] 4 All ER 374, at 383 the Court of Appeal, per Stuart-Smith LJ, held that there was no need to demonstrate that a defendant intends to deal with his assets so as to ensure that a judgment remains unsatisfied.

[316] [1997] 1 All ER 728.

[317] [1979] QB 645.

The undertaking in damages follows from the fact that the freezing injunction is an interlocutory injunction. If the claimant fails to establish his case at trial, the defendant may then be entitled to damages. However, as was made clear in *Balkanbank v Taher*,[318] the undertaking is made to the court and not the defendant and the 'court has a discretion whether to order the plaintiff to pay damages where the defendants have sustained loss caused by the injunction'.[319] The court is not bound to order damages, and whether it does will depend on the circumstances of the case.

(4) Disclosure of assets

In *Derby & Co Ltd v Weldon*,[320] the Court of Appeal made clear that the court has jurisdiction to grant a 'disclosure' order against the defendant in respect of assets both within and without the jurisdiction, as ancillary to a Mareva injunction. This 'disclosure' order may be made both before[321] and after[322] judgment. The court will protect the position of the defendant by requiring the claimant to grant an undertaking that he will not use information so obtained to start civil or criminal proceedings in other jurisdictions.[323] In *Den Norske Bank ASA v Antonatos*,[324] the Court of Appeal held that a defendant would be entitled to refuse to provide information on the grounds that such disclosure would infringe his privilege against self-incrimination.[325] This privilege is available in respect of any piece of information or evidence on which the prosecution might wish to rely in establishing guilt or in making their decision whether to prosecute or not.

(5) The 'worldwide' freezing injunction

(a) Development of the jurisdiction[326]

Initially, the Mareva injunction was only granted to prevent the defendant from removing assets that were within the jurisdiction of the court.[327] However, in a number of cases the court has held that it possesses the jurisdiction to grant a Mareva injunction with worldwide effect.[328] In *Derby & Co Ltd v Weldon (Nos 3 and 4)* Neill LJ concluded:

the time has come to state unequivocally that in an appropriate case the court has power to grant an interlocutory injunction even on a world-wide basis against any person who is

---

[318] [1994] 4 All ER 239.   [319] Per Clarke J.   [320] [1990] Ch 48.

[321] *Republic of Haiti v Duvalier* [1990] 1 QB 202.

[322] *Interpool Ltd v Galani* [1988] QB 738; *Maclaine Watson & Co Ltd v International Tin Council (No 2)* [1989] Ch 286, CA.

[323] See *Practice Direction* [1994] 4 All ER 52.   [324] [1998] 3 All ER 74.

[325] See also below, where the availability of the privilege against self-incrimination in the context of Anton Pillar orders is discussed.

[326] See Capper, 'The Transnational Effects of Mareva Injunctions' (1996) 15 CJQ 221.

[327] See *Ashtiani v Kashi* [1987] QB 888; *South Carolina Insurance Co v Assurantie Maatschappij De Zeven Provincien NV* [1987] AC 24.

[328] *Babanaft International Co SA v Bassatne* [1990] Ch 13; *Republic of Haiti v Duvalier* [1990] 1 QB 202, CA; *Derby & Co Ltd v Weldon* [1990] Ch 48; *Derby & Co v Weldon (Nos 3 and 4)* [1990] Ch 65.

properly before the court, so as to prevent that person by the transfer of his property frustrating a future judgment of the court. The jurisdiction to grant such injunctions is one which the court requires and it seems to me that it is consistent with the wide words of Supreme Court Act 1981, s 37(1).[329]

(b) Circumstances where the jurisdiction will be exercised

Although the court recognized the jurisdiction to grant worldwide freezing injunctions in *Derby & Co Ltd v Weldon*,[330] May LJ emphasized that 'it will only be in an exceptional case that the court will make such an order'. On the facts, which involved claims that the defendants, who were directors of the plaintiff company, had dealt in commodities on their own behalf, causing the company huge trading losses,[331] the Court of Appeal held that a worldwide injunction was justified. As Parker LJ summarized:

The defendants are clearly sophisticated operators who have amply demonstrated their ability to render assets untraceable and a determination not to reveal them. In those circumstances it appears to me that there is every justification for a world-wide Mareva...[332]

Similarly, in *Re BCCI SA (No 9)*[333] Rattee J, granting a worldwide injunction, held that the case was 'exceptional...having regard, in particular, to the complex international nature of the financial dealings in the past to both respondents and that both claim not to be resident in this country'. Where a freezing injunction is sought in aid of proceedings in a foreign jurisdiction, the Court of Appeal has also held that the order should not be worldwide except in 'very exceptional circumstances'.[334] However, in the subsequent case of *Crédit Suisse Fides Trust v Cuoghi*,[335] the Court of Appeal questioned whether it was necessary to demonstrate such exceptional circumstances, and suggested that the sole question was whether 'it would be inexpedient to make the order'.[336]

(c) Safeguards for the defendant when a worldwide injunction is granted

Although the court may grant a worldwide order, such an order is of so potentially devastating an effect that it insists that certain safeguards are built into the order in

---

[329] [1990] Ch 65, at 93. The fact that such orders act in personam avoids many potential jurisdictional issues over assets of persons overseas, because if the court can claim jurisdiction over an individual, it can make an order against that person. See, however, the difficulties caused where EU law applies—see Merrett, 'Worldwide Freezing Orders in Europe' [2008] LMCLQ 71.

[330] [1990] Ch 48, at 55, CA.

[331] The grounds of the plaintiff's claim included: breach of contract, negligence, breach of fiduciary duty, deceit, and conspiracy to defraud.

[332] [1990] Ch 48, at 57.   [333] [1994] 3 All ER 764, at 787.

[334] *Rosseel NV v Oriental Commercial and Shipping (UK) Ltd* [1990] 3 All ER 545, at 546, per Lord Donaldson MR. See *S & T Bautrading v Nordling* [1997] 3 All ER 718, where the Court of Appeal held that the circumstances were not sufficiently exceptional to justify the grant of a worldwide Mareva order.

[335] [1997] 3 All ER 724.

[336] Ibid., at 732, per Millett LJ, citing s 25(2) of the Civil Jurisdiction and Judgments Act 1982.

the form of undertakings by the claimant. In *Derby & Co Ltd v Weldon*, Parker LJ stated that the order should contain the following protection:

(a) oppression of the defendants by way of exposure to multiplicity of proceedings is avoided (b) the defendants are protected against the misuse of information gained from the ordinary order for disclosure in aid of the Mareva, and (c) the position of third parties is protected.[337]

These limitations were approved by the Court of Appeal in *Re BCCI SA (No 9)*,[338] where the key issue was whether the form of the order granted by Rattee J contained sufficient protection against the multiplicity of proceedings in foreign jurisdictions. The usual protection is an undertaking by the claimant not to seek to enforce the freezing injunction in any country other than England and Wales without the leave of the court. The defendants argued that this was insufficient and that the plaintiff should also undertake not to start any fresh proceedings in foreign courts arising out of the same subject matter. Dillon LJ stated the principle:

It does not automatically follow, as a matter of logic, that if a person obtains a worldwide Mareva injunction and to prevent oppression in the enforcement of the injunction he is required to give an undertaking not to make any application to a foreign court to enforce the injunction without first obtaining the leave of the English court, he must also be required to give a further undertaking as a safeguard against a somewhat different form of possible oppression, not to issue any fresh proceedings in a foreign court arising out of the same subject matter without first obtaining the leave of the English court. But it may none the less be reasonable that he should be required to give such an undertaking if it seems prima facie oppressive that he should be free to start further proceedings in other jurisdictions founded on the same facts as are the basis of the English proceedings.

In the circumstances the court felt that it was reasonable that the plaintiff give an undertaking not to start fresh civil proceedings in foreign courts.[339]

The standard form for the worldwide freezing injunction or order contains undertakings that the claimant 'will not without the permission of the court use any information obtained as a result of this order of the court for the purpose of civil or criminal proceedings, either in England and Wales or in any other jurisdiction' and 'will not without the permission of the court, seek to enforce this order in any country outside England and Wales [or seek an order of a similar nature including orders conferring a charge or other security against the respondent or the respondent's assets]'.[340]

In *Dadourian Group International Inc and others v Simms and others (No 2)*,[341] the Court of Appeal laid down some guidance on the factors the court should consider in deciding whether to grant permission to enforce a worldwide freezing order (WFO).[342]

---

337 [1990] Ch 48.   338 [1994] 3 All ER 764.
339 With the exception of Luxembourg, where BCCI was being liquidated.
340 PD10 *Practice Direction on Interim Injunctions* (1 October 2009), para 6.1.
341 [2006] 1 WLR 2499; Meisel 'Worldwide Freezing Orders—The Dadourian Guidelines' (2007) 26 CJQ 176.
342 [2006] 1 WLR, at 2502–2508.

These are to be referred to as 'the Dadourian guidelines'.[343] Given the complexity and length of this guidance, any 'attempt to paraphrase her ladyship's guidance is bound to misrepresent'.[344] The guidelines in full are as follows, and demonstrate that the central concerns have not changed in requiring this safeguard:

Guideline 1. The principle applying to the grant of permission to enforce a WFO abroad is that the grant of that permission should be just and convenient for the purpose of ensuring the effectiveness of the WFO, and in addition that it is not oppressive to the parties to the English proceedings or to third parties who may be joined to the foreign proceedings.

Guideline 2. All the relevant circumstances and options need to be considered. In particular consideration should be given to granting relief on terms, for example terms as to the extension to third parties of the undertaking to compensate for costs incurred as a result of the WFO and as to the type of proceedings that may be commenced abroad. Consideration should also be given to the proportionality of the steps proposed to be taken abroad, and in addition to the form of any order.

Guideline 3. The interests of the applicant should be balanced against the interests of the other parties to the proceedings and any new party likely to be joined to the foreign proceedings.

Guideline 4. Permission should not normally be given in terms that would enable the applicant to obtain relief in the foreign proceedings which is superior to the relief given by the WFO.

Guideline 5. The evidence in support of the application for permission should contain all the information (so far as it can reasonably be obtained in the time available) necessary to make the judge to reach [sic] an informed decision, including evidence as to the applicable law and practice in the foreign court, evidence as to the nature of the proposed proceedings to be commenced and evidence as to the assets believed to be located in the jurisdiction of the foreign court and the names of the parties by whom such assets are held.

Guideline 6. The standard of proof as to the existence of assets that are both within the WFO and within the jurisdiction of the foreign court is a real prospect, that is the applicant must show that there is a real prospect that such assets are located within the jurisdiction of the foreign court in question.

Guideline 7. There must be evidence of a risk of dissipation of the assets in question.

Guideline 8. Normally the application should be made on notice to the respondent, but in cases of urgency, where it is just to do so, the permission may be given without notice to the party against whom relief will be sought in the foreign proceedings but that party should have the earliest practicable opportunity of having the matter reconsidered by the court at a hearing of which he is given notice.[345]

It is submitted these guidelines will doubtless assist the court in seeking to grant such permission.[346]

---

[343] Ibid., at 2502 [25].

[344] 'Evidence Undertakings in Freezing Orders' (2001) 1 CPN 8, at 9.

[345] [2006] 1 WLR 2499 at 2502–2503.

[346] See further Pettitt, *Equity and the Law of Trusts* (11th edn, 2009), Ch 27. These directions now fall under the Civil Procedures Rules 2005.

(6) Uniformity of orders

In *Re BCCI SA (No 9)*,[347] Dillon LJ expressed the view that it was desirable that 'the practice in these matters should develop uniformly' and suggested that there was no good reason why the form of the order granted in *Derby & Co Ltd v Weldon*[348] should not be followed. On 28 July 1994, the Lord Chief Justice issued a *Practice Direction*,[349] including standard forms for worldwide Mareva injunctions and those limited to assets within the jurisdiction: 'These forms of order should be used save to the extent that the judge hearing a particular application considers there is a good reason for adopting a different form.' The most recently revised form of order was introduced on 1 October 2009.[350]

(7) Limits to the grant of freezing orders

Freezing injunctions can be granted in support of prospective proceedings in the superior courts, but as the jurisdictional limits of the inferior courts are increased, it becomes important to know how far they can be used in support of cases brought in other courts. An order can almost certainly be made in support of proceedings in a magistrates' court,[351] but no order will be issued in aid of a comprehensive statutory scheme such as that set out in the Child Support Act 1991 and which implicitly excludes other enforcement mechanisms.[352]

5 Search orders[353]

(1) Definition

Whereas a freezing injunction restrains a defendant from dissipating his assets, a search order prevents a defendant from destroying vital evidence before an issue comes to trial by requiring him to allow the plaintiff to enter his premises and search for, examine, remove, or copy articles specified in the order. Previously, such injunctions were known as Anton Piller orders, and the new nomenclature was introduced by the Civil Procedure Rules. The rationale for the order was explained by Lord Denning MR in *Anton Piller KG v Manufacturing Processes Ltd*:

such an order can be made by a judge ex parte, but it should only be made where it is essential that the plaintiff should have inspection so that justice can be done between the parties: and

---

[347] [1994] 3 All ER 764.   [348] [1990] Ch 48.   [349] [1994] 4 All ER 52.

[350] PD10 *Practice Direction on Interim Injunctions* (1 October 2009), para 6.1.

[351] [1997] 1 All ER 288, [1996] 1 WLR 1552.

[352] *Department of Social Security v Butler* [1995] 4 All ER 193, at 204–205.

[353] See *Snell's Principles of Equity* (31st edn, 2005), pp 345–379; Treitel, *The Law of Contract* (12th edn, 2007) Ch 21; Hanbury and Martin, *Modern Equity* (18th edn, 2009), pp 870–873; Pettitt, *Equity and the Law of Trusts* (11th edn, 2009), Ch 27.

when, if the defendant were forewarned, there is a grave danger that vital evidence will be destroyed, that papers will be burnt or lost or hidden.[354]

The first such order was granted in *EMI Ltd v Kishorilal Pandit*,[355] and the first by the Court of Appeal in *Anton Piller KG v Manufacturing Processes Ltd*.[356] They were approved by the House of Lords in *Rank Film Distributors Ltd v Video Information Centre*.[357] Search orders have been particularly appropriate in cases where it is suspected that 'pirating' of music or films has taken place.[358]

(2) Preconditions to the grant of a search order

Search orders are granted ex parte, as the element of surprise is essential to prevent defendants destroying or hiding the evidence. As was said in *Rank Film Distributors Ltd v Video Information Centre*:[359]

If the stable door cannot be bolted, the horse must be secured...If the horse is liable to be spirited away, notice of an intention to secure the horse will defeat the intention.[360]

Given the powerful effect of the order, as well as the fact that it will be granted without hearing the defendant, the court has laid down relatively strict criteria that the claimant must satisfy. In *Anton Piller KG v Manufacturing Processes Ltd*,[361] Ormrod LJ said that there are 'three essential pre-conditions' for the granting of an order. To these a fourth requirement suggested by Lord Denning MR can be added.

(a) Strong prima facie case

There must be 'an *extremely* strong prima facie case'. This represents a much higher standard than that required for interlocutory injunctions following *American Cyanamid*.

(b) Serious potential damage

The damage, potential or actual, must be very serious for the applicant.

(c) Real possibility evidence will be destroyed

There must be clear evidence that the defendants have in their possession incriminating documents or things, and that there is a real possibility that they may destroy such material before any application inter partes can be made.

(d) No real harm to the defendant

Lord Denning held that an order should only be granted when it 'would do no real harm to the defendant or his case'. In *Coca-Cola v Gilbey*,[362] Lightman J held that the

---

[354] [1976] Ch 55, at 61.   [355] [1975] 1 All ER 418.
[356] [1976] Ch 55.   [357] [1982] AC 380.
[358] Eg *Ex p Island Records Ltd* [1978] Ch 122, CA; *Rank Film Distributors Ltd v Video Information Centre* [1982] AC 380; *Columbia Picture Industries Ltd v Robinson* [1986] 3 All ER 338.
[359] [1982] AC 380.   [360] Ibid., at 418 per Templeman LJ.   [361] [1976] Ch 55, at 62.
[362] [1995] 4 All ER 711.

risk of violence against a defendant if forced to disclose information will not generally justify the refusal to award an Anton Piller order. An order had been granted against the defendant, who had been involved in an operation to counterfeit Coca-Cola products, but he refused to disclose information concerning the operation because such disclosure would jeopardize his safety and that of his family. Lightman J held that such threats were 'a factor' to be considered when deciding whether to grant an order, but that in most cases it would be outweighed by the interests of justice:

I cannot think that in any ordinary case where the plaintiff has a pressing need for the information in question, the existence of the risk of violence against the potential informant should outweigh the interest of the plaintiff in obtaining the information. In case of any unlawful threat or action directed at a party, a witness or their families, the rule of law requires that the law should in no wise be deflected from following its ordinary course and the court should proceed undeterred. Police protection is the appropriate remedy...[363]

(3) Protection for the defendant

Because of the 'draconian and essentially unfair nature of search orders from the point of view of the defendant'[364] there are a number of limitations and restrictions as to its execution intended to protect the defendant. Many of these were stated by Dillon LJ in *Booker McConnell plc v Plascow*[365] and Scott J in *Columbia Picture Industries v Robinson*, who recognized that:

a decision whether or not an Anton Piller order should be granted requires a balance to be struck between the plaintiff's need that the remedies allowed by the civil law for the breach of his rights should be attainable and the requirement of justice that a defendant should not be deprived of his property without being heard.[366]

Many of these limitations are incorporated in the standard form order issued under a *Practice Direction* under the Civil Procedure Rules 2005.[367]

(a) Service and explanation by a solicitor

The order must be served by an independent supervising solicitor accompanying the plaintiff,[368] who must also explain what it means to the defendant in everyday language.[369] If the premises are likely to be occupied by an unaccompanied woman and the supervising solicitor is a man, one of the persons accompanying him must be a woman.

(b) Times of service

The order may normally only be served between 9.30 am and 5.30 pm on a weekday. This is to allow the respondent of the order to seek legal advice.

---

[363] Ibid., at 716.
[364] *Columbia Picture Industries Ltd v Robinson* [1986] 3 All ER 338, at 371. See also *Lock International plc v Beswick* [1989] 1 WLR 1268; *Bhimji v Chatwani* [1991] 1 WLR 989.
[365] [1985] RPC 425, CA.   [366] [1986] 3 All ER 338.
[367] PD10 *Practice Direction on Interim Injunctions* (1 October 2009) Para 7.1.
[368] *ITC Film Distributors Ltd v Video Exchange Ltd* [1982] Ch 431.
[369] *Bhimji v Chatwani* [1991] 1 WLR 989.

(c) Application to vary or discharge

The defendant may apply to the court at short notice for variation or discharge of the order, provided that the plaintiff and his solicitor, and the supervising solicitor have been allowed to enter the premises, although not commenced the search.

(d) Items to be removed

No item may be removed from the premises until a list of the items to be removed has been prepared, and a copy of the list has been supplied to the person served with the order, and he has been given a reasonable opportunity to check the list.

(e) Search in the presence of the defendant

The premises must not be searched, and items must not be removed from them, except in the presence of the defendant or a person appearing to be a responsible employee of the defendant.

(f) Undertaking in damages

The claimant must make an undertaking in damages to compensate the claimant for any loss he suffers as a result of the carrying out of the order if the court decides that he should be compensated.

(4) The privilege against self-incrimination

In *Rank Film Distributors Ltd v Video Information Centre*,[370] the House of Lords held that a claimant would not be granted a search order requiring the defendants to answer questions or disclose documents that would have the effect of incriminating him, as he is entitled to the privilege against self-incrimination.[371] In *IBM United Kingdom Ltd v Prima Data International Ltd*,[372] Sir Mervyn Davies, QC refused to set aside sections of a search order made against a company director from whom IBM sought damages for conspiracy to extract goods without payment because the solicitor serving the order had adequately explained his right to claim privilege against self-incrimination. However, this privilege was removed as regards proceedings for the infringement of intellectual property rights and passing off by s 72 of the Supreme Court Act 1981.[373] In *Cobra Golf Ltd v Rata*,[374] Rimer J therefore held that a defendant had no right to assert an entitlement to the privilege against self-incrimination where proceedings for civil contempt had been commenced by a manufacturer of golf equipment alleging that he had infringed their trade marks.

---

[370] [1982] AC 380.
[371] See also *Tate Access Floors Inc v Boswell* [1991] Ch 512; *IBM United Kingdom Ltd v Prima Data International Ltd* [1994] 4 All ER 748; *Cobra Golf Ltd v Rata* [1997] 2 All ER 150; *Den Norske Bank ASA v Antonatos* [1999] QB 271.
[372] [1994] 4 All ER 748.   [373] See *Istel (AT & T) Ltd v Tully* [1993] AC 45, HL.
[374] [1998] Ch 109.

6 Rescission

Rescission is the right of a party to a contract[375] to have the contract set aside and to be restored to his former position, which is known as *restitutio in integrum*. The House of Lords held in *Johnson v Agnew*[376] that this is to be distinguished from the situation also described as 'rescission', where a contract is treated as never having come into existence in law, for example because of mistake, fraud, or lack of consent, where there is *rescission ab initio*. The right of a party to rescind a contract may be wider in equity than at common law. By defining the circumstances in which a contract may be rescinded, equity serves the very important function of setting the standards of acceptable behaviour in commercial transactions, thus protecting the vulnerable from exploitation at the hands of those who are more capable but lack scruples.[377]

(1) Rescission of contracts entered under mistake[378]

(a) Mistake at common law

The position at common law was stated in *Bell v Lever Bros Ltd*,[379] where the House of Lords held that only a very narrow range of mistakes shared between the parties to a contract would render it void ab initio. In essence, only those mistakes that would make the performance of the contract as agreed impossible render the contract void. This was well summarized by Denning LJ in *Solle v Butcher*:

The correct interpretation of that case... is that, once a contract has been made, that is to say, once the parties, whatever their inmost state of mind, have to all outward appearances agreed with sufficient certainty in the same terms on the same subject matter, then the contract is good unless and until it is set aside for failure of some condition on which the existence of the contract depends, or for fraud or on some equitable ground.[380]

Therefore, a contract will be void at common law if the subject matter of the contract no longer existed at the time of contracting,[381] if the purchaser is in fact already the owner of the property to be transferred under the contract,[382] or where the mistake is such that one party would be unable to perform so as to amount to a total failure of consideration. Shared mistakes relating only to the quality of the subject matter of the contract would not render it void. Thus, in *Leaf v International Galleries*[383] a contract

---

[375] Or a voluntary deed: *Gibbon v Mitchell* [1990] 1 WLR 1304; *Dent v Dent* [1996] 1 WLR 683; *Wolff v Wolff* [2004] STC 1633.

[376] [1980] AC 367, at 392.

[377] For a consideration of the proprietary consequences of rescission, see Worthington [2002] RLR 28.

[378] See Treitel, *The Law of Contract* (12th edn, 2007), Ch 18; Goff and Jones, *The Law of Restitution* (7th edn, 2006).

[379] [1932] AC 161.   [380] [1950] 1 KB 671, at 691.

[381] *Couturier v Hastie* (1856) 5 HL Cas 673; *Strickland v Turner* (1852) 7 Exch 208; *Galloway v Galloway* (1914) 30 TLR 531; *Associated Japanese Bank (International) Ltd v Crédit du Nord SA* [1988] 3 All ER 902.

[382] *Cooper v Phibbs* (1867) LR 2 HL 149.   [383] [1950] 2 KB 86, CA.

for the sale of a painting believed to be a 'Constable', but in fact by a different artist, was not void for mistake.[384]

(b) Mistake in equity

In *Solle v Butcher*,[385] Denning LJ suggested the existence of a wider jurisdiction in equity, supplemental to the narrow common law jurisdiction of *Bell v Lever Bros Ltd*, which would allow a party to rescind a contract that was entered under a shared fundamental mistake. He stated the basis of this jurisdiction as follows:

A contract is also liable in equity to be set aside if the parties were under a common misapprehension either as to facts or as to their relative and respective rights, provided that the misapprehension was fundamental and that the party seeking to set it aside was not himself at fault.[386]

It is to be noted that the two main requirements of this supposed equitable jurisdiction are that the mistake must be 'mutual', in the sense that it is shared by both parties, and that it must be 'fundamental'. Unlike mistake at common law, which renders the contract void ab initio, the right to rescind in equity would only render the contract voidable at the behest of the injured party. A number of cases accepted the existence of this more generous equitable jurisdiction.[387] The Court of Appeal has now, in *Great Peace Shipping v Tsavliris Salvage (International) Ltd*,[388] disapproved of the decision in *Solle v Butcher* and doubted the existence of any equitable jurisdiction to rescind a contract wider than that granted at common law. The Court of Appeal did not find it conceivable that the House of Lords had overlooked an equitable right to rescind the agreement in *Bell v Lever Bros*, notwithstanding that the agreement was not void for mistake at common law,[389] and concluded that there was no authority for the proposition that there are two categories of mistake, one that renders a contract void at law and one that renders it voidable in equity.[390] The Court of Appeal further found that it was impossible to distinguish between the requirement of a 'fundamental' mistake, as stated to be the basis of the equitable jurisdiction in *Solle v Butcher*, and a mistake as to quality which 'makes the thing contracted for essentially different from the thing that it was believed to be', which is the basis of the common law right in *Bell v Lever Bros Ltd*.[391] The Court of Appeal held that the decision in *Solle v Butcher* had been an unwarranted intrusion of equity where the common law had clearly drawn the line as to when relief might be given for common mistake, such that the effect was not

---

[384]   See also *Frederick E Rose (London) Ltd v William H Pim Jnr & Co Ltd* [1953] 2 QB 450.
[385]   [1950] 1 KB 671, CA. Denning LJ relied on *Cooper v Phibbs* (1867) LR 2 HL 149 and *Huddersfield Banking Co Ltd v Henry Lister & Sons Ltd* [1895] 2 Ch 273, CA.
[386]   [1950] 1 KB 671.
[387]   *Grist v Bailey* [1967] Ch 532; *Magee v Pennine Insurance Co Ltd* [1969] 2 QB 507; *Associated Japanese Bank (International) Ltd v Credit du Nord SA* [1988] 3 All ER 902; *West Sussex Properties Ltd v Chichester District Council* [2000] NPC 74.
[388]   [2003] QB 679; [2002] 4 All ER 690; [2002] LMCLQ (McMeel); (2003) 119 LQR 177 (Reynolds); (2003) 62 CLJ 29 (Hare); [2003] Conv 247 (Phang); [2003] 1 RLR 93 (Cartwright).
[389]   Ibid., at [118].   [390]   Ibid., at [153].   [391]   [1932] AC 161, at 218, per Lord Atkin.

to supplement or mitigate the common law, but to say that *Bell v Lever Bros Ltd* was wrongly decided. Lord Phillips MR therefore summarized:

> Our conclusion is that it is impossible to reconcile *Solle v Butcher* with *Bell v Lever Bros Ltd*. The jurisdiction asserted in the former case has not developed. It has been a fertile source of academic debate. But in practice it has given rise to a handful of cases that have merely emphasised the confusion in this area of our jurisprudence... If coherence is to be restored to this area of our law, it can only be by declaring that there is no jurisdiction to grant rescission of a contract on the ground of common mistake where that contract is valid and enforceable on ordinary principles of contract law.[392]

Having rejected the existence of the equitable jurisdiction, the Court of Appeal did express sympathy for the desire for the greater flexibility that it would give to grant rescission on terms where a common fundamental mistake has induced a contract, in contrast to the common law doctrine which holds the contract void in such circumstances. However, the introduction of such a jurisdiction would require legislation.[393]

(2) Rescission of contracts induced by misrepresentation

(a) Meaning of misrepresentation

In *Behn v Burness*,[394] Williams J defined a representation as 'a statement or assertion, made by one party to the other before or at the time of the contract, of some matter or circumstance relating to it'. A misrepresentation does not render a contract void, but the other contracting party may be entitled to rescind it. The representation must be of fact,[395] and not simply an expression of intention[396] or opinion.[397] Although there is no general duty on a contracting party to reveal all known relevant facts, in the case of some contracts, known as contracts *uberrimae fidei*, there is such a duty. These include contracts for insurance[398] and family settlements.[399]

(b) Fraudulent misrepresentation

A party is entitled to rescind a contract he entered on the basis of a fraudulent misrepresentation by the other, which means a false statement made knowingly, or without belief in its truth, or reckless whether it is true or not.[400]

(c) Innocent misrepresentation

Innocent misrepresentation occurs where the party making the misrepresentation honestly believes it to be true. The other party has the right to rescind the contract,[401]

---

[392] [2002] 4 All ER 689, at [157].   [393] Ibid., at [161].   [394] (1863) 3 B & S 751.

[395] *Ship v Crosskill* (1870) LR 10 Eq 73.

[396] *Edgington v Fitzmaurice* (1885) 29 Ch D 459, CA.

[397] *Bisset v Wilkinson* [1927] AC 177, PC.

[398] See *Lambert v Co-operative Insurance Society* [1975] 2 Lloyd's Rep 485, CA.

[399] *Gordon v Gordon* (1816) 3 Swan 400.   [400] *Derry v Peek* (1889) 14 App Cas 337.

[401] *Reese River Silver Mining Co v Smith* (1869) LR 4 HL 64; *Torrance v Bolton* (1872) 8 Ch App 118; *Redgrave v Hurd* (1881) 20 Ch D 1, CA; *Walker v Boyle* [1982] 1 All ER 634. By s 2(1) of the Misrepresentation Act 1967 he is also entitled to recover damages unless the defendant had reasonable grounds to believe that

although by s 2(2) of the Misrepresentation Act 1967 the court has the discretion to award damages in lieu of rescission and declare the contract subsisting.

(3) Rescission of contracts entered under undue influence

(a) Meaning of undue influence

Rescission in equity is available whenever a contract has been entered by one party acting under the undue influence of the other. The essence of undue influence is that the party making the contract was dominated by the other so that he was not acting of his own free choice.[401a]

(b) Actual undue influence

Actual undue influence arises where one party has in fact applied improper pressure to the other, which falls short of that necessary to constitute duress.[402] In *Bank of Credit and Commerce International SA v Aboody*,[403] the court held that it was also necessary for the party alleging actual undue influence to demonstrate that they had suffered a 'manifest disadvantage' from the transaction, but this requirement was rejected by the House of Lords in *CIBC Mortgages plc v Pitt*.[404]

(c) Presumed undue influence

In some circumstances, the nature of the relationship between the parties itself gives rise to the presumption of undue influence, and the burden falls on the defendant to demonstrate that no such influence was exercised.[405] Examples of relationships where influence will be presumed include parent and child,[406] spiritual adviser and disciple,[407] doctor and patient,[408] married and cohabiting couples,[409] or couples in a close, stable, sexual, and emotional relationship,[410] or between solicitor and client.[411] In the case of other relationships, for example bank and customer[412] and pop artist and

---

his statement was true: *Esso Petroleum v Mardon* [1976] QB 801; *Royscot Trust Ltd v Rogerson* [1991] 2 QB 297; *Smith New Court Securities Ltd v Scrimgeour Vickers (Asset Management) Ltd* [1997] AC 254.

[401a] Merely failing to (rather than deliberately) conceal material facts is insufficient by itself to amount to undue influence: *Royal Bank of Scotland v Chandra* [2010] EWHC 105 (Ch) at [140]. See, however, *Hewett v First Plus Financial Group plc* [2010] EWCA Civ 312, where failure to disclose a secret affair did effect undue influence.

[402] See eg *Re Craig* [1971] Ch 95; *Cheese v Thomas* [1994] 1 All ER 35.

[403] [1990] 1 QB 923, CA.

[404] [1994] 1 AC 200. See also *Barclays Bank v O'Brien* [1994] 1 AC 180.

[405] See *Allcard v Skinner* (1887) 36 Ch D 145. See also *Hammond v Osborn* [2002] WTLR 1125; [2003] LMCLQ 145 (Scott); (2003) 119 LQR 34 (Birks).

[406] [1934] 1 KB 380, CA.

[407] *Allcard v Skinner* (1887) 36 Ch D 145; *Tufton v Sperni* [1952] 2 TLR 516, CA; *Roche v Sherrington* [1982] 1 WLR 599.

[408] *Dent v Bennett* (1839) 4 My & Cr 269.   [409] *Barclays Bank v O'Brien* [1994] 1 AC 180.

[410] *Massey v Midland Bank plc* [1995] 1 All ER 929.

[411] *Wright v Carter* [1903] 1 Ch 27, CA.   [412] *Lloyds Bank v Bundy* [1975] QB 326, CA.

manager,[413] it may be possible to show that there was in fact a relationship of influence. Undue influence has increasingly been presumed where a relationship of confidence has been shown to have existed between family members or relations.[414] Similarly, the fact that a person agrees to act as surety of the debts of another will give rise to a presumption of a relationship of confidence if the surety gained no personal advantage from so acting.[415] In *Crédit Lyonnais Bank Nederland NV v Burch*,[416] the Court of Appeal held that an abuse of a relationship of confidence was presumed from the mere fact that a junior employee had executed an 'extravagantly improvident' unlimited guarantee of all her employer's debts, and that there was no need to show any sexual or emotional tie. In *National Westminster Bank Plc v Morgan*,[417] the House of Lords held that a party relying on presumed undue influence must also demonstrate that he had suffered a manifest disadvantage from the transaction. In the now leading case of *Royal Bank of Scotland v Etridge (No 2)*,[418] the House of Lords held that the requirement of 'manifest disadvantage' was ambiguous and should be discarded.

(d) Influence exercised by third parties[419]

In an ever expanding number of recent cases it has been held that a transaction can be set aside where the circumstances are such that the person benefiting from the transaction was aware of circumstances in which the other party may have been acting under the undue influence of a third party. Most typically this has occurred where a wife has executed some kind of financial guarantee of her husband's debts in favour of a bank. For example, in *Barclays Bank v O'Brien*,[420] a husband whose business was in difficulties executed a second mortgage over the family home he jointly owned with his wife to provide additional security for the company's debts. The House of Lords held that the wife had signed the mortgage documents acting under the undue influence of her husband. Given that the bank had failed to take reasonable steps to satisfy itself that she had entered the transaction freely, it had constructive notice of the undue influence and she was therefore able to set the transaction aside.[421] A person will not be affixed with constructive notice of such undue influence if they ensure that the party they contract with received independent advice as to the effect of the transaction.[422] A

---

413   *O'Sullivan v Management Agency and Music Ltd* [1985] QB 428.

414   *Simpson v Simpson* [1992] 1 FLR 601; *Cheese v Thomas* [1994] 1 WLR 129; *Langton v Langton* [1995] 2 FLR 890; *Mahoney v Purnell* [1996] 3 All ER 61.

415   *Barclays Bank v O'Brien* [1994] 1 AC 180; *CIBC v Pitt* [1994] 1 AC 200; *Massey v Midland Bank plc* [1995] 1 All ER 929; *Allied Irish Bank plc v Byrne* [1995] 2 FLR 325; *Banco Exterior Internacional SA v Thomas* [1997] 1 All ER 46; *Dunbar Bank plc v Nadeem* [1998] 3 All ER 876. But cf *Mumford v Bank of Scotland* 1996 SLT 392.

416   [1997] 1 All ER 144; Hooley and O'Sullivan 'Undue Influence and Unconscionable Bargains' [1997] LMCLQ 17.

417   [1985] AC 686.   418   [2001] 4 All ER 449.

419   See Jackson, Stevens, and Pearce, *Land Law*, pp 585–600.   420   [1994] 1 AC 180.

421   See also *Massey v Midland Bank plc* [1995] 1 All ER 929; *Banco Exterior Internacional SA v Mann* [1995] 1 All ER 936; *TSB Bank plc v Camfield* [1995] 1 All ER 951. In Scotland constructive notice is insufficient and the transaction will only be set aside if the contracting party had actual notice of the undue influence: *Mumford v Bank of Scotland* 1996 SLT 392.

422   *Barclays Bank plc v O'Brien* [1994] 1 AC 180; *Midland Bank plc v Kidwai* [1995] NPC 81; *Banco Exterior Internacional v Mann* [1995] 1 All ER 936; *Massey v Midland Bank plc* [1995] 1 All ER 929; *Bank of Baroda*

creditor may also be put on notice where the undue influence has been exercised by a co-surety of the mortgagor, rather than the debtor.[423]

Following an explosion of litigation, the House of Lords clarified the circumstances in which such surety transactions may be set aside on the grounds of undue influence in *Royal Bank of Scotland v Etridge (No 2)*.[424] The Lords looked at eight cases in which a wife had agreed to a charge in favour of a bank to secure debts owed by her husband or a company that he controlled. In seven of these cases the wife claimed that the charge was unenforceable against her because it was tainted by undue influence. In the eighth case, the wife who had agreed to a similar arrangement was suing a solicitor for breach of duty concerning the advice that he gave her. The House of Lords held that a bank would be put on inquiry whenever a wife offers to stand surety for her husband's debts. To avoid the transaction being impugned on the grounds of undue influence the bank must merely take reasonable steps to satisfy itself that the practical implications of the proposed transaction have been brought home to the wife, especially the risks involved, so that she is able to enter the transaction with her eyes open as to its basic elements. This does not require a meeting between the bank and the wife. The bank is entitled to rely upon confirmation from a solicitor acting for the wife that he has advised her appropriately.

If a mortgage is executed to replace an earlier mortgage which could be set aside because the mortgagee had constructive notice that it was effected by undue influence, the subsequent mortgage could also be set aside, even if relates to another property. The two mortgages are inseparable, and the principle that a contract of insurance can be set aside for misrepresentation if it has been renewed, even though each renewal constitutes a fresh contract, can be applied by analogy.[425]

(4) Setting aside unconscionable bargains

(a) A bargain is not unconscionable merely because its terms are unfair

Equity will set aside bargains[426] that have been entered in circumstances that can be regarded as 'unconscionable'. The scope of the doctrine is relatively narrow, and in *National Westminster Bank plc v Morgan*,[427] the House of Lords rejected the comprehensive principle of 'inequality of bargaining power' advocated by Lord Denning

---

v Rayarel [1995] 2 FLR 376; *Hemsley v Brown (No 2)* [1996] 2 FCR 107; *Banco Exterior Internacional SA v Thomas* [1997] 1 All ER 46; *Crédit Lyonnais Bank Nederland NV v Burch* [1997] 1 All ER 144.

[423] *First National Bank v Achampong* [2003] EWCA Civ 487; [2003] LMCLQ 307 (Enonchong).

[424] [2001] 4 All ER 449. See Capper, 'Banks, Borrowers, Sureties and Undue Influence—A Half-Baked Solution to a Thoroughly Cooked Problem' [2002] RLR 100; Bigwood 'Undue Influence in the House of Lords: Principles and Proof' (2002) 65 MLR 435; Phang and Tijo, 'The Uncertain Boundaries of Undue Influence' [2002] LMCLQ 231.

[425] *Yorkshire Bank plc v Tinsley* [2004] 3 All ER 463; Gravells 'Undue Influence and Substitute Mortgages' [2005] 64 CLJ 42.

[426] The jurisdiction does not extend to gifts: *Langton v Langton* [1995] 2 FLR 890.

[427] [1985] AC 686.

MR in *Lloyds Bank Ltd v Bundy*.[428] In *Boustany v Piggott*,[429] the Privy Council stated that a bargain will not be held to be unconscionable merely because it was 'hard, unreasonable or foolish', and Lord Templeman adopted a number of propositions outlining the circumstances in which relief would be available:[430]

(1) It is not sufficient to attract the jurisdiction of equity to prove that a bargain is hard, unreasonable or foolish; it must be proved to be unconscionable, in the sense that 'one of the parties to it has imposed the objectionable terms in a morally reprehensible manner, that is to say, in a way which affects his conscience'.[431]

(2) 'Unconscionable' relates not merely to the terms of the bargain but to the behaviour of the stronger party, which must be characterised by some moral culpability or impropriety.[432]

(3) Unequal bargaining power or objectively unreasonable terms provide no basis for equitable interference in the absence of unconscientious or extortionate abuse of power where exceptionally, and as a matter of common fairness, 'it was not right that the strong should be allowed to push the weak to the wall'.[433]

(4) A contract cannot be set aside in equity as 'an unconscionable bargain' against a party innocent of actual or constructive fraud. Even if the terms of the contract are 'unfair' in the sense that they are more favourable to one party than the other ('contractual imbalance'), equity will not provide relief unless the beneficiary is guilty of unconscionable conduct.[434]

(5) In situations of this kind it is necessary for the plaintiff who seeks relief to establish unconscionable conduct, namely that unconscientious advantage has been taken of his disabling condition or circumstances.[435]

Parliament has intervened with a regime of consumer protection, which extends to the regulation of terms in contracts,[436] and unconscionable terms in credit arrangements, such as hire purchase agreements, are now regulated by the Consumer Credit Act 1974, as amended by the Consumer Credit Act 2006.[437]

(b) Factors, that render a bargain unconscionable

(i) A personal disadvantage

A bargain will only be set aside if the party contracting was subject to some personal disadvantage which rendered him substantially less capable than ordinary members of society. This may include a mental incapacity such as senile dementia,[438] illiteracy, or unfamiliarity with a language or culture,[439] age,[440] or youth and inexperience.

---

[428] [1975] QB 326, CA.

[429] (1993) 69 P & CR 288. See Bamforth 'Unconscionability as a Vitiating Factor' [1995] LMCLQ 538.

[430] (1995) 69 P & CR 288, at 303.   [431] *Multiservice Bookbinding Ltd v Marden* [1979] Ch 84.

[432] *Alec Lobb (Garages) Ltd v Total Oil (Great Britain) Ltd* [1983] 1 WLR 87, at 94.

[433] Ibid., at 183.   [434] *Hart v O'Connor* [1985] AC 1000; *Nichols v Jessup* [1986] 1 NZLR 226.

[435] *Commercial Bank of Australia Ltd v Amadio* (1983) 46 ALR 402, at 413, per Mason J.

[436] See, for example, the Unfair Terms in Consumer Contracts Regulations 1999.

[437] See further, Dobson and Stokes, *Commercial Law* (7th edn, 2008), Chs 10 (consumer contracts); 20 (credit arrangements).

[438] *Archer v Cutler* [1980] 1 NZLR 386; *Hart v O'Connor* [1985] AC 1000.

[439] *Commercial Bank of Australia Ltd v Amadio* (1983) 46 ALR 402.

[440] *Watkin v Watson-Smith* (1986) The Times, 3 July.

Equity has also long recognized that a transaction may be set aside if it was entered by a person who was 'poor and ignorant'. This principle was stated by Kay J in *Fry v Lane*, where the court set aside a sale of a reversionary interest of land at an undervalue:

where a purchase is made from a poor and ignorant man at a considerable undervalue, the vendor having no independent advice, a court of equity will set aside the transaction.[441]

This principle was translated into a modern context in *Cresswell v Potter*,[442] where a wife, who was a telephonist, released her interest in the matrimonial home for inadequate consideration on divorce. Megarry J stated.

Eighty years ago, when *Fry v Lane* was decided, social conditions were very different from those which exist today. I do not, however, think that the principle has changed, even though the euphemisms of the 20th century may require the word 'poor' to be replaced by 'a member of the lower income group' or the like, and the word 'ignorant' by 'less highly educated'...[443]

In the more recent case of *Crédit Lyonnais Bank Nederland NV v Burch*,[444] Millett LJ speculated that the principle could have operated in favour of a junior employee who had entered a contract to act as unlimited surety of her employer's debts.

(ii) Conscious exploitation of vulnerability

A transaction will only be regarded as unconscionable if the one contracting party was aware of the personal disadvantage of the other, so that his conscience was affected by actual or constructive notice thereof.[445] Such exploitation will not be demonstrated if the contracting party received independent legal advice before entering the bargain.[446]

(iii) Objective unfairness of the bargain

A bargain will only be set aside if it was actually unfair. This will most easily be demonstrated if the contracting party has received no personal advantage from a transaction,[447] or if his property has been purchased at a substantially lower price than might reasonably have been expected in the market place.[448]

(5) Limitations on the availability of rescission

There are a number of circumstances where it will not be possible for a claimant to rescind a contract.

---

[441] (1888) 40 Ch D 312, at 322.   [442] [1978] 1 WLR 255n.
[443] Ibid., at 257. See also *Boustany v Pigott* (1993) 69 P & CR 288, where the Privy Council held that a contract would be set aside as unconscionable if the party was 'poor or ignorant'.
[444] [1997] 1 All ER 144.
[445] *Hart v O'Connor* [1985] AC 1000.
[446] *Fry v Lane* (1888) 40 Ch D 312; *Butlin-Sanders v Butlin* [1985] Fam Law 126.
[447] *Crédit Lyonnais Bank Nederland v Burch* [1997] 1 All ER 144.
[448] *Fry v Lane* (1888) 40 Ch D 312.

(a) Restitutio in integrum is impossible

When a contract is rescinded the parties must be returned to their former positions as far as is practically possible.[449] As Lord Blackburn said in *Erlanger v New Sombrero Phosphate Co*:

It is...clear on principles of general justice, that as a condition to a rescission there must be *restitutio in integrum*. The parties must be put in *status quo ante*...[450]

For example, in *Clarke v Dickson*[451] the court held that a party could not rescind a contract to purchase shares in a partnership that had been converted into a limited liability company.[452] Equity approaches the question flexibly, and is particularly ready to grant rescission where there was fraud.[453] In granting rescission the court may impose terms,[454] for example to account for profits or allow for deterioration.[455] The overall objective is for the courts to do 'what is practically just'.[456] Thus, in *O'Sullivan v Management Agency and Music Ltd*[457] a contract for the management of a popular singer (Gilbert O'Sullivan) was rescinded on the grounds of undue influence. The managers were allowed to retain a reasonable remuneration for the work they had done which had contributed to his success. In *Cheese v Thomas*,[458] an uncle and his great-nephew had purchased a house for £83,000. The uncle had contributed £43,000 and the remainder had been borrowed by the nephew by way of a mortgage. The uncle was held entitled to set the transaction aside on the grounds of undue influence exercised by the nephew. However, when the house was sold its value had fallen considerably and only £55,000 was received. This was sufficient to discharge the mortgage but even if the balance was paid to the uncle he would remain £25,000 out of pocket. The Court of Appeal rejected the uncle's submission that his nephew should repay him the entire £43,000 he had contributed to the property. Nicholls V-C explained that, although the transaction was to be reversed on the grounds of undue influence, it was impossible to restore the parties to the precise position they were in before the contract had been entered. The court would thus 'do what is practically just' by restoring the uncle 'as near to his original position as is now possible'. It was thus held that the uncle was entitled to receive a share of the net proceeds of sale received from the property proportionate to his original contribution; 43/83 on the facts. Thus, he would bear a proportionate share of the loss caused by the fall in value thereof.

---

[449] *Spence v Crawford* [1939] 3 All ER 271, HL; *Cheese v Thomas* [1994] 1 All ER 35, at 412, per Nicholls V-C. See also *Maguire v Makaronis* (1997) 71 ALJR 781; Moriarty 'Equitable Compensation for Undue Influence' (1997) 114 LQR 9.

[450] (1878) 3 App Cas 1218, at 1278. See Halson 'Rescission for Misrepresentation' [1997] RLR 89.

[451] (1858) EB & E 148.

[452] See also *Thorpe v Fasey* [1949] Ch 649; *Butler v Croft* (1973) 27 P & CR 1.

[453] *Spence v Crawford* [1939] 3 All ER 271, HL.

[454] See Proksch 'Rescission on Terms' [1996] RLR 71.

[455] *Lagunas Nitrate Co v Lagunas Syndicate* [1899] 2 Ch 392; *Armstrong v Jackson* [1917] 2 KB 822; *Wiebe v Butchart's Motors Ltd* [1949] 4 DLR 838. See *TSB Bank plc v Camfield* [1995] 1 All ER 951.

[456] *Spence v Crawford* [1939] 3 All ER 271, at 288, per Lord Wright; *Cheese v Thomas* [1994] 1 All ER 35, at 412, per Nicholls V-C; *Vadasz v Pioneer Concrete* (SA) Pty Ltd (1995) 130 ALR 570.

[457] [1985] QB 428.   [458] [1994] 1 All ER 35.

(b) Affirmation

A party cannot rescind a contract that he has subsequently affirmed. In *Long v Lloyd*,[459] a purchaser was taken to have affirmed a contract for the sale of a lorry when he used it a second time having discovered there were faults. He could not rescind on the grounds of the seller's misrepresentation. Similarly, a person cannot rescind a contract entered under undue influence if he affirms it after the influence has stopped.[460]

(c) Third-party rights

The right to rescind is lost once third parties have acquired rights in the property in good faith for value.[461]

(d) Delay

In *Allcard v Skinner*,[462] the plaintiff was held not to be entitled to rescind gifts of stock to a religious order five years after she left because of her delay. Lindley LJ stated that the victim must 'seek relief within a reasonable time after the removal of the influence'.[463] Similarly, in *Leaf v International Galleries*[464] a plaintiff was not entitled to rescind a contract for innocent misrepresentation after a delay of five years.

7 Rectification

Rectification is a discretionary[465] equitable remedy that allows for the correction of a document so that it reflects the real intention of the parties. It is an exception to the 'parol evidence rule' so that oral evidence may be admitted to demonstrate that a written instrument is incorrect. For example, in *Joscelyne v Nissen*[466] the Court of Appeal ordered the rectification of an agreement between a daughter and her father which they intended should include a provision that she was to pay the household expenses, which she had refused to pay, claiming that she was not required to do so on a true construction of the written agreement they had entered. A wide range of documents have been rectified, including a conveyance,[467] a bill of exchange,[468] a marriage settlement,[469] a transfer of shares[470] and, by statute, wills.[471]

---

[459] [1958] 2 All ER 402, CA.   [460] *Mitchell v Homfray* (1881) 8 QBD 587.
[461] See *Oakes v Turquand* (1867) LR 2 HL 325; *Bainbrigge v Browne* (1881) 18 Ch D 188; *Re Scottish Petroleum Co (No 2)* (1883) 23 Ch D 413; *Coldunell Ltd v Gallon* [1986] 1 All ER 429.
[462] (1887) 36 Ch D 145.   [463] Ibid., at 187.   [464] [1950] 2 KB 86.
[465] *Re Butlin's Will Trusts* [1976] Ch 251.   [466] [1970] 2 QB 86.
[467] *Beale v Kyte* [1907] 1 Ch 564.   [468] *Druiff v Lord Parker* (1867–68) LR 5 Eq 131.
[469] *Bold v Hutchinson* (1855) 5 De GM & G 558.
[470] *Re International Contract Co* (1872) 7 Ch App 485.
[471] Administration of Justice Act 1982, s 20(1). See *Wordingham v Royal Exchange Trust Co* [1992] Ch 412; *Re Segelman* [1996] Ch 171, [1995] 3 All ER 676.

(1) **Requirements for rectification**

(a) Mistake in written document

Rectification is only possible where a written document mistakenly fails to state what the parties had intended to agree. It is not necessary that the parties had actually entered a contract orally prior to the incorrect instrument. In *Joscelyne v Nissen*,[472] the Court of Appeal held that all that is necessary is a prior common intention as to what the written agreement was to be.[473] There are grounds for rectification if that common intention does not appear in the written document.[474] Rectification is only available for a mistake of the actual terms of the parties' agreement. Thus, in *Frederick E Rose (London) Ltd v William Pim Jnr & Co Ltd*[475] rectification was not possible where the parties had entered a written contract for the sale of 'horsebeans', which they had mistakenly believed were the same as 'feveroles'. The contract was a correct record of their agreement.

(b) Common mistake

Generally, an instrument will only be rectified if it records the agreement contrary to the intentions of both parties.[476]

(c) Unilateral mistake

Rectification is not normally available where a mistake is unilateral.[477] However, rectification will be available if the party who was not mistaken had acted fraudulently[478] or is estopped from resisting rectification. In *Thomas Bates & Son Ltd v Wyndham's (Lingerie) Ltd*,[479] Buckley LJ set out the circumstances in which a person will be estopped from resisting rectification:

it must be shown: first, that one party, A, erroneously believed that the document sought to be rectified contained a particular term or provision which, mistakenly, it did contain; second, that the other party, B, was aware of the omission or the inclusion and that it was due to a mistake on the part of A; third, that B has omitted to draw the mistake to the notice of A. And I think there must be a fourth element involved, namely, that the mistake must be one calculated to benefit B. If these requirements are satisfied, the court may regard it as inequitable to allow B to resist rectification to give effect to A's intention on the ground that the mistake was not . . . a common mistake.[480]

A line of authorities which suggested that the party who was not mistaken has the option of accepting rectification or rescission of the contract has been disapproved by the Court of Appeal in *Riverlate Properties Ltd v Paul*.[481]

---

[472] [1970] 2 QB 86.   [473] *Crane v Hegeman-Harris Co Inc* [1939] 1 All ER 662.
[474] *Earl v Hector Whaling Ltd* [1961] 1 Lloyd's Rep 459.   [475] [1953] 2 QB 450.
[476] *Murray v Parker* (1854) 19 Beav 305; *Fowler v Fowler* (1859) 4 De G & J 250.
[477] *Sells v Sells* (1860) 1 Drew & Sm 42.
[478] *Ball v Storie* (1823) 1 Sim & St 210; *Lovesy v Smith* (1880) LR 15 Ch D 655.
[479] [1981] 1 All ER 1077, CA.   [480] Ibid., at 1086.
[481] [1975] Ch 133.

(d) Burden of proof

For rectification the mistake must be established with 'a high degree of conviction'.[482] In *Joscelyne v Nissen*,[483] Russel LJ said that there must be 'convincing proof' of the mistake. Thus, in *Re Segelman*[484] Chadwick J held that a testator's will should be rectified where extrinsic evidence of his intentions demonstrated convincingly that it had failed to carry out his intentions.

(2) Defences to rectification

Rectification will not be granted where it would affect the position of third parties who have acquired rights bona fides for value.[485] Delay may also bar a claim.[486]

8 Account

Where someone has obtained a benefit to which they are not entitled, or has incurred an expense which should be payable by another, an account in equity may be ordered, either on its own, or as an adjunct to another substantive remedy. An account may be ordered, for instance, where equitable co-owners are entitled to share the occupation of residential property, but only one of them has been paying the bills,[487] or where land held by co-owners has been let or exploited for profit.[488] Similarly, a fiduciary who has made improper use of information acquired as adviser to a trust may be obliged by means of an account to give up to the beneficiaries any profits which he has made.[489]

(1) Ancillary orders in support of legal rights

In some instances, the order for account will not be sought in its own right, but to make effective some other remedy of the plaintiff. The claimant owed a debt might seek an account, for instance, to verify the amount owing. There were some instances where an account of this kind could be ordered at common law, but the superior

---

[482] *Crane v Hegeman-Harris Co Inc* [1939] 4 All ER 68, CA. See also *Countess of Shelburne v Earl of Inchiquin* (1784) 1 Bro CC 338; *Fowler v Fowler* (1859) 4 De G & J 250.

[483] [1970] 2 QB 86, CA. See *Brimican Investments Ltd v Blue Circle Heating Ltd* [1995] EGCS 18; *Racal Group Services Ltd v Ashmore* [1995] STC 1151; *Re Segelman* [1995] 3 All ER 676.

[484] *Re Segelman* [1995] 3 All ER 676, at 684.

[485] *Garrard v Frankel* (1862) 30 Beav 445; *Smith v Jones* [1954] 1 WLR 1089; *Thames Guaranty Ltd v Campbell* [1985] QB 210.

[486] *Beale v Kyte* [1907] 1 Ch 564.

[487] *Leake v Bruzzi* [1974] 1 WLR 1528; *Leigh v Dickeson* (1884) 15 QBD 60. See also *Henderson v Eason* (1851) 17 QB 701, at 721, per Parke B.

[488] *Henderson v Eason* (1851) 17 QB 701; *Job v Potton* (1875) LR 20 Eq 84; *Jacobs v Seward* (1872) LR 5 HL 464.

[489] *Boardman v Phipps* [1967] 2 AC 46, HL. See Chapter 30.

procedures of equity[490] meant that the equitable order largely displaced the common law jurisdiction.[491] Following the amalgamation of the courts of law and the courts of equity, and the prevailing judicial view about the effect of that fusion,[492] there is now probably no reason to distinguish between the legal and equitable jurisdictions.[493]

An order for account may be used as an adjunct to the obligation of an agent to answer to his principal under a contract of agency. The principal could, by means of account, obtain disclosure of any sums owing to him by his agent.[494] Equity was prepared to intervene because a principal places confidence in his agent, and without disclosure by the agent, may have no means of knowing what is owing.[495] For similar reasons, an inventor seeking by injunction to prevent the infringement of a patent[496] may use an account in order to discover what profits have been made from the unauthorized exploitation of the invention. Equity also offered aid through an action in account where the affairs of the parties were especially complicated[497] or where mutual accounts were involved.[498]

(2) Ancillary orders in support of equitable rights

Equity would, of course, order an account where this was necessary to support a purely equitable right, such as the right of a beneficiary against a trustee in respect of trust property, the right of a landlord against a tenant for equitable waste,[499] or the right of a mortgagor to obtain the best return reasonably possible from property of which the mortgagee has taken possession. In this last instance, the mortgagee is held accountable not only for what has in fact been received, but also for the sums that he ought to have received if he had fulfilled his duty. The mortgagee would thus be accountable for rents which could have been obtained if the property had been let as it ought[500] and for the full market rent which could have been obtained if the property had not been let subject to a disparaging condition.[501]

---

[490] *See A-G v Dublin Corpn* (1827) 1 Bli NS 312, at 337; *Beaumont v Boultbee* (1802) 7 Ves 599.

[491] *Sturton v Richardson* (1844) 13 M & W 17; *Shepard v Brown* (1862) 4 Giff 203.

[492] See above, Chapter 2.

[493] The distinction could, before the fusion of the courts of law and of equity, be of significance. For instance, equity would not order an account in favour of a customer against his banker, since the relationship between them was in the nature of a simple contract without any fiduciary character: *Foley v Hill* (1848) 2 HL Cas 28.

[494] *Beaumont v Boultbee* (1802) 7 Ves 599; *Mackenzie v Johnston* (1819) 4 Madd 373.

[495] That would not generally be the case where the agent brings an action against the principal: *Padwick v Stanley* (1852) 9 Hare 627.

[496] *Price's Patent Candle Co v Bauwen's Patent Candle Co Ltd* (1858) 4 K & J 727; *De Vitre v Betts* (1873) LR 6 HL 319. See Patents Act 1977, s 61.

[497] *O'Connor v Spaight* (1804) 1 Sch & Lef 305; *Taff Vale Rly Co v Nixon* (1847) 1 HL Cas 111; *North-Eastern Rly Co v Martin* (1848) 2 Ph 758.

[498] *Phillips v Phillips* (1852) 9 Hare 471.

[499] *Duke of Leeds v Earl of Amherst* (1846) 2 Ph 117. Equitable waste is deliberate and malicious injury to land or buildings affecting its permanent value.

[500] *Noyes v Pollock* (1886) 32 Ch D 53, at 61

[501] *White v City of London Brewery Co* (1889) 42 Ch D 237.

Where a trustee's inaction amounts to a breach of duty[502] (for instance, where a trustee has taken inadequate steps to recover sums owing to the trust fund),[503] the trustee can be held liable, by means of account, for the losses which have arisen through this failure to act, or 'wilful default' as it is described.[504] As with any action for breach of trust, at least one breach must be proved or admitted,[505] but if there is reason to believe that there may have been other instances of default, the court may order a general account, rather than limiting it to the particular instance proved.[506]

(3) Substantive orders to account

There are some instances in which the order to account appears to be used as a substantive remedy: that is, it is ordered even though there is no separate remedy such as damages in respect of which the order is sought.[507] The order of account both quantifies the measure of profit or loss, and also imposes a liability to pay it.[508] The absence of any separate remedy may reflect the absence of an antecedent and independent cause of action apart from the taking of an account. Whether the payment of the sum owing should be described as 'damages' or 'compensation' or 'restitution' is a matter of debate, and for most purposes the description of the obligation is a matter of no significance. What is significant is that the order for account is being used in some situations as a remedy in its own right. It has long been a feature of English law that the availability of a remedy has been a key feature in the development of new rights. As account is used in novel situations, we are therefore observing the development of new rights, some of which in due course will be absorbed either into existing classifications of rights and obligations, or into the developing autonomous doctrine of restitution based on unjust enrichment.

Three principal examples can be given of the use of account in a substantive way. First, an obligation to account will be imposed on a fiduciary who has made a profit from a breach of confidence. Second, a formally appointed or constructive trustee will be obliged to account for any personal advantage gained through a position of trust. Finally, an agent will be obliged to account for an illicit bribe. These cases can all be subsumed under the general rubric of unauthorized profits made by a fiduciary, although it is not clear how far the existence of a fiduciary relationship is an essential requirement.

---

[502]   *Re Stevens, Cooke v Stevens* [1898] 1 Ch 162, CA. See Chapter 29.
[503]   See *Re Vickery* [1931] 1 Ch 572.
[504]   See Stannard 'Wilful Default' [1979] Conv 345.
[505]   *Sleight v Lawson* (1857) 3 K & J 292; *Re Youngs* (1885) 30 Ch D 421.
[506]   *Re Tebbs* [1976] 2 All ER 858.
[507]   For example, in *Mouat v Clark Boyce* [1992] 2 NZLR 559, at 566 Sir Robin Cooke included an account of profits in a list of remedies available to the court alongside other remedies such as damages.
[508]   For a discussion of the extent to which equity is able to award damages or compensation for the breach of purely equitable rights see Capper 'Damages for Breach of the Equitable Duty of Confidence' (1994) 14 LS 313–334, especially, at pp 313–328.

(a) Accounting for profits from breach of confidence

We have already observed that equity was prepared to lend support, by means of taking an account, to an action for infringement of a patent. Similarly, where the originator of an idea or invention has disclosed it in confidence to a manufacturer who has exploited it without permission, the courts have been prepared to intervene by means of an injunction or an account of profits.[509] The same remedies have been given to actresses whose idea for a television series was used without their consent.[510] The remedies are available independently of any contract or other substantive basis for a remedy. In *Coco v AN Clark (Engineers) Ltd*,[511] it was said that three requirements had to be met: (i) that the information imparted was of a confidential nature; (ii) that it was communicated in circumstances importing an obligation of confidence; and (iii) that there has been an unauthorized use of the information. In the *Spycatcher* case,[512] the House of Lords agreed that the obligation to account could be extended to a newspaper that had published extracts from a book written by a former member of the British secret service. There was no doubt that Peter Wright, the member of MI5 concerned, had acted in breach of confidence. It appears to have been considered by the Lords that it was enough that the newspaper was aware of this to impose on it an obligation to account for any profits made from its publication. Lord Goff would have gone further and imposed a duty to keep confidence independently of the circumstances in which the information was acquired. He was prepared to contemplate applying an obligation to keep confidence in certain situations 'beloved of law teachers, where an obviously confidential document is wafted by an electric fan out of a window into a crowded street, or when an obviously confidential document, such as a private diary, is dropped in a public place, and is then picked up by a passer-by'.[513] The opinions come close to according the status of property to confidential information.

(b) Accounting for personal advantage from breach of trust

The second situation in which the order of account appears to be used as a substantive remedy, namely in cases of personal advantage gained through a position of trust, is discussed more fully in Chapter 30. A person who is appointed director of a company through the use of a shareholding of which he is trustee may be obliged to account to the trustees for any fees which he receives in that capacity,[514] unless the trust instrument authorizes the trustee to retain it.[515] This liability arises in order to prevent any potential conflict between the self-interest of a trustee and the proper administration of the trust. It is not clear from the cases whether the obligation is personal, or whether proprietary. The mere fact that the obligation is phrased in the language of account does not mean that any fees received by the trustee-director are trust property and are

---

[509] *Coco v A N Clark (Engineers) Ltd* [1969] RPC 41; *Seager v Copydex Ltd (No 1)* [1967] 1 WLR 923; (No 2) [1969] 1 WLR 809.

[510] *Fraser v Thames Television Ltd* [1984] QB 44.   [511] [1969] RPC 41.

[512] *A-G v Guardian Newspapers Ltd (No 2)* [1988] 3 All ER 545.

[513] [1988] 3 All ER 545, at 658–659.   [514] *Re Gee* [1948] Ch 284.

[515] *Re Llewellin's Will Trusts* [1949] Ch 225.

recoverable by the beneficiaries for that reason. It is equally possible that equity uses the mechanism of account as a means of imposing a personal obligation on the trustee to pay to the beneficiaries either the sum that he has received in fees or a sum of equal value. The remedy of account is therefore being used as a means of enforcing a money payment.[516]

(c) Accounting for bribes or secret profits

A long line of authority holds that where an agent[517] or other person in a fiduciary position, such as a company director[518] or trustee,[519] receives a bribe or makes some other secret profit, he must account for the sum received to his principal. In the case of the accountability of agents for bribes or secret profits that they have received, it used to be thought, on the authority of *Lister & Co v Stubbs*,[520] that the obligation of the agent was personal only. The court held that an employee of a company who had received bribes for favouring a third party in negotiating contracts on behalf of his employer was liable to account to his employers for the sums he had received, but only as a debtor to them, not as a trustee. Similarly, in *A-G's Reference (No 1 of 1985)*,[521] the Court of Appeal held that the manager of a public house who was permitted to sell only beverages supplied by his employers was under an obligation to account for profits which he made by selling drinks obtained from other sources, but that he was not a trustee of the sums which he received. The Court of Appeal held that the employer has no proprietary interest in the illicit profits that the manager makes.[522] In the words of Lord Lane CJ, delivering the opinion of the court:

The fact that A may have to account to B for money he has received from X does not mean necessarily that he received the money on account of B.

However, in *A-G for Hong Kong v Reid*,[523] the Privy Council considered that the decision in *Lister & Co v Stubbs* was wrong in principle in holding that a bribe received by an agent did not belong to his principal. Charles Reid, a New Zealander working in the government legal service in Hong Kong, supplemented his income by taking illicit payments in return for obstructing the prosecution of certain criminals. The Attorney General for Hong Kong, acting on behalf of the Crown, sought to assert a right to three freehold properties in New Zealand which it was alleged had been acquired with the bribes. The Privy Council held that the Crown was entitled, not merely to an account from Charles Reid, but that, provided that the assets derived from the bribes were separately identifiable, the Crown could claim proprietary rights over them.

---

[516] In other words, the equitable remedy of account is being used as equity's equivalent of the common law action for debt.

[517] *Lister & Co v Stubbs* (1890) LR 45 Ch D 1, CA.

[518] *Regal (Hastings) Ltd v Gulliver* [1942] 1 All ER 378, HL; *Industrial Development Consultants Ltd v Cooley* [1972] 2 All ER 162.

[519] See Chapter 30.   [520] (1890) LR 45 Ch D 1.   [521] [1986] 2 All ER 219.

[522] Unless, perhaps, the profit can be identified as a separate piece of property rather than as part of a mixed fund: [1986] 2 All ER 219, at 225.

[523] [1994] 1 All ER 1. See also Chapter 30.

Two reasons were given. First, if the fiduciary is not to benefit from his wrong, he must be accountable not only for the value of any property received by way of bribe, but also for any profits made through its retention in kind if it appreciates in value, or for any profits made through its advantageous reinvestment. Second, the maxim 'equity considers as done that which ought to have been done' applied. As soon as the bribe was received by the 'bribee', it should have been paid over to the person injured. The false fiduciary was therefore a constructive trustee of it. It was no objection that by giving the Crown employer a proprietary right to the bribe, it would not be available to any of Charles Reid's creditors. The bribe was money that he should never have received.

There is a sharp division of opinion as to whether the conclusion reached by the Privy Council in Reid is correct, but there is some support in *A-G v Guardian Newspapers (No 2)*[524] (the *Spycatcher* case) for conferring proprietary rights on claimants entitled to seek an account from a wrongdoer. There are indications in the House of Lords opinions that they would have been prepared to give the Crown proprietary rights in order to deprive Peter Wright of the benefits he received by publishing confidential information acquired during his employment in the security service.[525] Similarly, the House of Lords held in *Lord Napier and Ettrick v Hunter*,[526] that a stop-loss insurer of a Lloyd's underwriter had an equitable lien over money recovered by the underwriter,[527] to the extent that they represented sums paid by the insurer under the stop-loss insurance.

A problem that remains to be resolved is when a wrongdoer who receives an illicit benefit will be held personally liable only, and when the courts will consider that the injured party has proprietary rights to the sums received by the wrongdoer. No clear guidance on this matter is to be found in any of the recent decisions.

(4) Settled accounts

The essence of all the cases in which an account is sought is that the defendant owes a sum of money to the claimant, and the purpose of the taking of an account is to ascertain that sum. It is accordingly a defence to the request for an account either that nothing is due, or that the sum due has already been agreed between the parties. The agreement as to the sum owing does not need to be in any particular form,[528] but

---

[524] [1988] 3 All ER 545.

[525] See Lord Keith, at 645, Lord Griffiths, at 654 and Lord Goff, at 664. See also Scott J, at first instance, at 567 and Dillon LJ in the Court of Appeal, at 621, explaining more fully the reasons for imposing a constructive trust. These remarks are directed at the question of whether the Crown has an equitable copyright in a book written in breach of confidence by a crown servant, but Scott J also says, at 584, that the profit made through the use of confidential information 'in equity, belongs to the owner of the information'.

[526] [1993] 1 All ER 385, at 402.

[527] That is, a first right to payment from those funds. An equitable lien of this kind is a proprietary right falling short of full ownership. Liens are discussed in the context of the right to trace in Chapter 32.

[528] *Yourell v Hibernian Bank* [1918] AC 372, HL; *Phillips-Higgins v Harper* [1954] 1 All ER 116; affd [1954] 2 All ER 51n, CA.

if the nature of the settlement of account involves the making of concessions, it will not be binding unless it has effect as a contract supported by consideration. That will usually be the case where there are mutual dealings. In the words of Romer J in *Anglo-American Asphalt Co v Crowley Russell & Co:*[529]

Where A owes, or may owe, B money, and B owes, or may owe, A money, and in their accounts they strike a balance and agree that balance, that truly represents the financial result of their transactions. There is mutuality in it, and...they expressly or by implication agree to a conventional position which is established by striking a balance, and that results in what is called a settled account. But that has no application...where the whole accounting is to be rendered by one party to another.

Where the agreement on a settled account has been reached as a result of fraud, then the agreement may be set aside and the accounts reviewed.[530] Similarly, the accounts may be reviewed where there has been a mistake or oversight.[531] In the case of fraud or serious error, the court will normally reopen the account and order that it be taken anew. Where the error or mistake is less substantial, the court may direct that the account stands, subject to 'surcharge and falsification',[532] that is, subject to the addition (surcharge) of items wrongly omitted and to the deletion (falsification) of items wrongly included. A settled account will not exclude the statutory jurisdiction to reopen extortionate credit bargains.[533]

(5) Delay

The right to an account lapses after the expiration of the statutory time limit applicable to the cause of action which it supports.[534] In other cases, no express limitation period applies, although it might be expected that the general six-year limitation period would apply by analogy with other claims, subject to the ordinary general exceptions.

---

[529] [1945] 2 All ER 324, at 331.

[530] *Vernon v Vawdrey* (1740) 2 Atk 119; *Oldaker v Lavender* (1833) 6 Sim 239; *Millar v Craig* (1843) 6 Beav 433; *Gething v Keighley* (1878) 9 Ch D 547; *Allfrey v Allfrey* (1849) 1 Mac & G 87.

[531] *Pritt v Clay* (1843) 6 Beav 503; *Williamson v Barbour* (1877) 9 Ch D 529.

[532] *Pit v Cholmondeley* (1754) 2 Ves Sen 565.

[533] Consumer Credit Act 1974, ss 137–140.   [534] Limitation Act 1980, s 23.

PART II

CREATING THE RELATIONSHIP

7

Substantive and formal requirements for the creation of express trusts

The preceding section has examined the history of equity, its contribution to English law and in particular outlined the nature of the trust relationship. This section will consider how the trust relationship is created. This chapter will consider the creation of express trusts, which are trusts brought into existence by the deliberate act of the owner of property. Implied trusts, which arise other than by the deliberate act of the owner, will be considered in Chapters 9 and 10, and the application of trusts to the family home will be considered in Chapter 11.

1 Creating a valid trust

A trust only arises where there is a separation of the legal and beneficial ownership of property; in other words, where a trustee holds property on trust for beneficiaries or recognized purposes.

(1) Two ways of creating an express trust

An express trust can be created in two ways (see Figure 7.1), which were identified by the Court of Appeal in *Milroy v Lord*.[1]

(i) Declaration of self as trustee

A trust will be created if the person who holds the legal title to property[2] effectively declares himself trustee of it in favour of specified beneficiaries. From the moment of the declaration he will hold the property on trust, and, although he retains the legal

---

[1] (1862) 4 De GF & J 264.
[2] If there is no trust already in existence, the person holding the legal title also holds the full beneficial title to the property, as the owner of the property. See Chapter 3.

(i) The absolute owner declares himself trustee

(ii) The absolute owner transfers the property to a trustee on trust

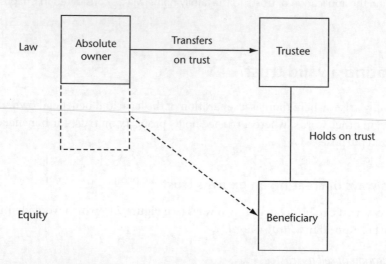

Figure 7.1 Creating a valid trust

title, the beneficiaries will enjoy the equitable interest in the property. If a trust is created by such a declaration, there is no need for any transfer of the property. Instead, the owner has simply changed his status vis-à-vis the property from that of absolute legal owner to that of trustee. The owner is known as the settlor, because he settles the property on trust.

(ii) Transfer of the property on trust to trustees

If the legal owner of property, the settlor, wishes to subject it to a trust in favour of beneficiaries, but does not wish to serve as trustee himself, he can create a trust by transferring the property to someone else, requiring them to hold it as trustee for the intended beneficiaries. In such circumstances, the original owner ceases to have any interest in the property and the transferee of the property receives it as trustee subject to the trust obligations. After the transfer has occurred, the beneficiaries enjoy the equitable interest in the property.

(2) **Requirements of an express trust**

Whichever method is used to create the trust, a number of requirements must be satisfied.

(a) Intention

An express trust will only be created if the owner of property wishes it to be subjected to a trust obligation. Therefore, he must clearly intend to create the trust, whether by declaration or by transfer.

(b) Trust property

A trust obligation can only subsist in relation to specific property which is to be subject to the trust. Mere intention to create a trust will be of no effect if the settlor does not also make it clear what property is to be held on trust.

(c) Beneficiaries

It is a consequence of what is known as 'the beneficiary principle' that a trust can only exist in favour of individuals or legal persons. With some exceptions, the most notable of which is a trust for a charitable purpose, it is not possible to create a trust for abstract purposes with no ascertainable human beneficiaries.[3] Where the owner of property has indicated an intention to create a trust but has not specified who the beneficiaries are to be, no trust will come into existence and, if the property has been transferred to a third party as trustee, the equitable interest will revert back to the settlor by means of a resulting trust.[4] The 'beneficiary principle' is examined in detail in Chapter 13.

(d) Constitution[5]

A trust will only come into existence if the intended separation between the legal and equitable title has in fact occurred. In the case of an express trust created by the owner of the property declaring himself to be a trustee, this will only be so if the declaration was effective. Alternatively, if the trust was intended to be created by transferring the property to the trustee, then the trust will only come into existence if the property was effectually transferred and the intention to impose a trust communicated. Provided

---

[3] See below, pp 458 *et seq.*   [4] See Chapter 9.   [5] See below, p 196.

that such a transfer and declaration are effective, the trust relationship comes into being and the trust is described as completely constituted. If there was no effective transfer, the trust relationship will not have come into being, and the trust is described as incompletely constituted. Constitution is thus concerned with the appropriate vesting of legal title in the trustees, and thus the separation of legal and equitable ownership.

(e) Formalities

Where the owner of property intends to create a trust of it during his lifetime, it may be necessary for him to comply with statutory provisions requiring the declaration to be made or evidenced by certain formalities. This is especially so if the intended trust property is land.[6] If these formalities are not followed, then the inter vivos declaration of trust may be void or unenforceable and the trust will not come into existence. Where the owner intends to make a trust of property on his death, he must comply with the statutory formalities required for a valid will. Formalities also apply where an existing equitable interest under a trust is transferred to new beneficiaries.

(f) Capacity

The settlor must also have the legal capacity to settle property on trust. This requires the settlor to be of sound mind in relation to the transaction involved, and where a transfer is involved, to have the legal standing to make it.[7]

2 The requirement of certainty

(1) The three certainties

An express trust will not be validly created unless the 'three certainties'[8] are present. These classic requirements for a valid trust were identified by Lord Langdale MR in *Knight v Knight*,[9] where he said that a trust would only come into existence if there was certainty of words, certainty of subject matter, and certainty of objects.[10] If a trust is uncertain in any of these respects it will be invalid. In the case of a purported declaration of trust, the owner of the intended trust property will remain the outright owner thereof. If the property was transferred to a trustee, the equitable ownership will revert to the original owner by means of an automatic resulting trust.[11]

---

6 Law of Property Act 1925, s 53.   7 See further p 99 above.

8 See *Re Kayford Ltd (In Liquidation)* [1975] 1 All ER 604, at 607; *Hunter v Moss* [1994] 3 All ER 215, at 219.

9 (1840) 3 Beav 148, at 173.   10 See *Wright v Atkyns* (1823) Turn & R 143, at 157, per Lord Eldon.

11 See Chapter 20, at pp 661–675. A failure to communicate any trust on a transfer will give the transferee title free from the trust.

(2) Certainty of intention

(a) Meaning of the requirement

The term 'certainty of words' was used by Lord Langdale MR in *Knight v Knight*,[12] but the modern meaning is probably better captured by the term 'certainty of intention'. The essence of the requirement is that an express trust will only arise if the owner of the property can be shown to have intended to subject it to a trust obligation. Where the trust is created by a document, the intention is deduced by examining the words used in the document purporting to create the obligation. As Megarry J said in *Re Kayford Ltd (In Liquidation)*:

the question is whether in substance a sufficient intention to create a trust has been manifested.[13]

Hence, there is no special formula or technical phrasing necessary to create a trust. A trust can be created without ever using the word 'trust'. In *Re Kayford Ltd (In Liquidation)* itself, a mail-order company was in financial difficulties and used a separate bank account to deposit money received from customers whose goods had not yet been delivered. When the company became insolvent the question arose whether the money in that account was held on trust for the customers, in which case it would not form part of the general assets of the company. Megarry J held that a trust had been created, stating:

As for the requisite certainty of words, it is well settled that a trust can be created without using the words 'trust' or confidence or the like...[14]

Similarly, the use of the word 'trust' will not of itself indicate the existence of an intention to create a trust, since the word may not have been used as a technical legal term.[15]

Since there is no requirement for a particular formula or phrase to be used to create a trust, an intention to create a trust must instead be deduced from the use of language that makes it clear that the recipient does not hold property for his own benefit, but holds it for the benefit of others. The words must demonstrate an intention to impose a mandatory obligation on the recipient of property as opposed to a purely moral obligation; an intention that the objects of the trust will benefit come what may. Finding an intention to create a trust is a question of fact that varies in every case on the construction of the particular language employed. However, some examples are useful to illustrate the approach of the courts. In *Re Snowden (Deceased)*,[16] an elderly lady who could not decide how to leave her property among her nephews and nieces left it all to her brother, Bert, telling him that he would 'know what to do'. It was held that she had not intended to impose a mandatory obligation on him to hold the property on trust for her nephews and nieces, but merely expressed a moral obligation to distribute the

---

[12] (1840) 3 Beav 148.   [13] [1975] 1 WLR 279, at 282.
[14] [1975] 1 All ER 604, at 607.   [15] See *Tito v Waddell (No 2)* [1977] Ch 106.
[16] [1979] 2 All ER 172.

property among her family. This can be contrasted with *Gold v Hill*,[17] where it was held that a man who orally directed the beneficiary of his life insurance policy to 'look after Carol [his former wife] and the kids' had intended to impose a mandatory obligation and created a trust. In *McPhail v Doulton*,[18] the House of Lords held that the mandatory character of the language used in a deed establishing a fund to provide for the benefit of the employees and ex-employees of a company, and their relatives and dependants, meant that the deed created a trust and not a mere power. The deed stated that the 'trustees shall apply the net income of the fund in making at their absolute discretion grants' to the specified class. The presence of the word 'shall' demonstrated that the recipients were under a mandatory duty to make grants, although they had a discretion in deciding to whom the grants would go. In *R v Clowes*,[19] it was held that a trust had arisen where an investment company had declared in its brochure that all monies received from clients would be held in a designated client account and only used to purchase specified government stock. In *Duggan v Governor of Full Sutton Prison*,[20] however, no trust was found to have been created where a prison governor held money in an account for a life prisoner in accordance with r 43(3) of the Prison Rules 1999. These rules provide that any cash which a prisoner had at a prison should be paid into an account under the control of the governor and the prisoner should be credited with the amount in the books of the prison. Hart J concluded that the language of the rules did not disclose an intention to create a trust, with a concomitant duty to 'invest' the money, but only to create the relationship of debtor and creditor. This must surely be correct, as it is unlikely that the draftsmen behind the rules intended a trust to arise in such circumstances.

Even if the language used in an agreement is inadequate in itself to create a trust, a trust may be held to have been created if this would fulfil the settlor's overriding intention. In *Don King Productions Inc v Warren (No 1)*,[21] Lightman J held that such an intention could be deduced as a 'matter of business common sense' from the commercial background and the commercial purpose of agreements for the assignment of promotion and management of a number of boxers.[22]

(b) Precatory words

In older authorities it was held that if a settlor or testator used certain key words or phrases, called 'precatory words', this would create a trust.[23] For example, if a testator had expressed his 'confidence', 'desire', 'wish', or 'hope' that a gift in his will be used in a particular way, this would be held to impose a trust on the recipient of the gift. The difficulty with this approach is that such words do not seem to impose any obligation on the recipient of the property, but merely express the wish of the transferor

---

17 [1999] 1 FLR 54.   18 [1971] AC 424.   19 [1994] 2 All ER 316.
20 [2003] 2 All ER 678.   21 [1998] 2 All ER 608; affd [2000] Ch 291, CA.
22 Ibid., at 625.
23 Even if the terms of the gift seemed to be absolute: *Malim v Keighley* (1795) 2 Ves 529; *Gully v Cregore* (1857) 24 Beav 185; *Curnick v Tucker* (1874) LR 17 Eq 320. The Court of Chancery originally held that such words created a trust, because of historical reasons relating to the possibility of abuse by executors of wills.

or testator as to how he would like to see the property used. They imply a purely moral obligation[24] and not the legally enforceable mandatory obligation which is the essential characteristic of a trust.

The lack of an intention to impose a legally binding obligation was recognized in a number of late-nineteenth-century cases, and it was held that a trust could no longer be created merely through the use of 'precatory words'.[25] In *Re Adams and Kensington Vestry*,[26] for example, a testator left all his property to his wife 'in full confidence that she would do what was right as to the disposal thereof between his children'. The question was whether this language was effective to create a trust in favour of the children, or whether the wife took the property absolutely. The Court of Appeal held that the precatory words alone were insufficient to give rise to a trust. The position was summarized by Cotton LJ:

I think that some of the older authorities went a deal too far in holding that some particular words appearing in a will were sufficient to create a trust. Undoubtedly confidence, if the rest of the context shows that a trust is intended, may make a trust, but what we have to look at is the whole of the will which we have to construe, and if the confidence is that she will do what is right as regards the disposal of the property, I cannot say that that is, on the true construction of the will, a trust imposed upon her.[27]

The consequence of these decisions is not that precatory words can never create a trust, but that such words are now just part of the evidence used to discover an intention to create a trust. A trust will be created if, on the proper construction of the whole instrument purporting to create a trust, including any precatory words, an intention can be found to subject the property to mandatory obligations.[28]

In the rather unusual case of *Re Steele's Will Trusts*,[29] it was held that precatory words were sufficient to create a trust. A testatrix left a diamond necklace to her son by will. Her will contained a clause intended to make the necklace a family heirloom that ended with the expression 'I request my said son to do all in his power by his will or otherwise to give effect to this my wish.' This form of words had been copied exactly from the will at issue in the earlier case of *Shelley v Shelley*,[30] where they had been held effective to create a trust. Wynn-Parry J concluded that although subsequent cases had held that mere precatory words were not sufficient to create a trust, in the circumstances a trust had been created. The very fact that the precedent of *Shelley v Shelley* had been followed verbatim afforded the strongest indication that the testatrix had intended to create a trust. Thus, the rationale for this decision was not the use of the precatory words per se, but the intention evidenced by following an established

---

[24] In *Mussoorie Bank Ltd v Raynor* (1882) 7 App Cas 321, at 331 the use of precatory words such as 'confidence' was described simply as an 'appeal to the conscience of the taker'. See also *Re Snowden (Deceased)* [1979] Ch 528.

[25] See *Lambe v Eames* (1871) 6 Ch App 597; *Re Hutchinson and Tenant* (1878) 8 Ch D 540; *Mussoorie Bank Ltd v Raynor* (1882) 7 App Cas 321; *Re Diggles* (1888) LR 39 Ch D 253; *Re Hamilton* [1895] 2 Ch 370; *Re Johnson* [1939] 2 All ER 458.

[26] LR (1884) 27 Ch D 394.   [27] Ibid., at 410.

[28] *Comiskey v Bowring-Hanbury* [1905] AC 84, HL.   [29] [1948] Ch 603.

[30] (1868) LR 6 Eq 540.

precedent for the creation of a trust of a family heirloom. It is unlikely that anyone would now be sufficiently foolish to attempt to create a trust in the same way.

(c) 'Sham' intention

Although an express intention will usually be effective to create a trust, provided that the appropriate formalities have been observed, the court may refuse to find that a trust was validly created if such an intention was a 'sham' and at the time it was made the owner had no real intention to subject his property to a trust. In *Midland Bank plc v Wyatt*,[31] Mr and Mrs Wyatt were the joint legal owners of their matrimonial home. In 1987 they executed a formally valid declaration of trust of the house in favour of Mrs Wyatt and their daughters. The trust deed was dated 17 June 1987 and signed by both husband and wife, although Mrs Wyatt had not been aware of its effect. The declaration of trust was not acted upon in any way but was placed in a safe. Subsequently, Mr Wyatt obtained loans to finance his business, secured by his interest in the house. The banks were unaware of the existence of the declaration. The declaration was only produced after the business had gone into receivership and the secured creditors sought a charging order against the house. D E M Young, QC held that in these circumstances the purported declaration of trust in favour of the wife and children was a sham and had therefore been ineffective to divest the husband of the entire beneficial interest in the house:

> I do not believe that Mr Wyatt had any intention when he executed the trust deed of endowing his children with his interest in Honer House, which at the time was his only real asset. I consider the trust deed was executed by him, not to be acted upon but to be put in the safe for a rainy day…As such I consider the declaration of trust was not what it purported to be but a pretence or, as it is sometimes referred to, a 'sham'…Accordingly, I find that the declaration of trust sought to be relied upon by Mr Wyatt is void and unenforceable.[32]

Midland Bank plc v Wyatt concerned a situation where a settlor purported to declare himself a trustee. Where the settlor and the trustee are distinct, the trust will only be invalidated on the basis of a sham intention if the trustee shared the intention of the settlor.[33]

(d) Failure of intention

If the words used in the instrument purporting to create a trust do not evince an intention to create a trust, then a trust cannot be created. If the words alleged to create a trust were associated with a transfer of the property inter vivos or by will, then in most cases the transfer or will gift remains effective to transfer the property and the recipient acquires the property free of any trust. If the words were alleged to constitute a declaration of the settlor himself as trustee, but show no such intention, then the settlor remains the outright owner. In some cases, where there is no disclosed intention to create a trust, the words used may confer on a third party a power of appointment

---

[31] [1995] 1 FLR 697.   [32] Ibid., at 707.
[33] *Shalson v Russo (Tracing Claims)* [2003] WTLR 1165; *Re Esteem Settlement* [2004] WTLR 1.

giving the donee of the power a discretion to distribute property to other named individuals or a class of potential objects.[34]

(3) Certainty of subject matter

A trust only exists if a separation of the legal and equitable ownership of property was brought about. Specific property must be identified which is intended to be subject to the trust obligation. An imprecise definition of the intended trust property will render the trust invalid for uncertainty of subject matter.

(a) No specific property has been indicated

Since a trust cannot exist in abstract, but only in relation to specific assets, the failure to identify any specific property as the trust property will prevent the creation of a valid trust. In *Hemmens v Wilson Browne (a firm)*,[35] which primarily concerned the duty of care owed by a solicitor, it was held that an agreement allowing a person to call for a payment of £110,000 at any time could not create a trust of such a sum arising over their general assets because no specific property had been identified as the subject matter of the obligation. As Judge Moseley, QC observed: 'there was no identifiable fund to which any trust could attach'.[36]

(b) A definition is too vague

A trust will fail for uncertainty if it is impossible to ascertain the property intended to be subject to it from the definition given. In essence, there must be no 'conceptual uncertainty' as to the subject matter of the trust. In *Palmer v Simmonds*,[37] for example, a testatrix attempted to create a trust of 'the bulk of my said residuary estate'. Kindersley V-C held that this did not create a trust because the term 'bulk' did not identify a definite, clear, and certain part of her estate. Similarly, in *Re Jones*,[38] it was held that a gift by a testator of the parts of his residuary estate which were not spent or disposed of by his wife did not create a trust.[39] In *Anthony v Donges*,[40] a husband made a gift to his wife by will of 'such minimal part of my estate of whatsoever kind and wheresoever situate save as aforesaid she may be entitled to under English law for maintenance purposes'. Lloyd J held that this provision was void for uncertainty on the grounds that it was impossible to determine what she was entitled to under English law for maintenance purposes.

In contrast, if the property is capable of being ascertained from the definition used a valid trust will be created. So, Herman can create a trust by his will of 'the residue of my estate' because the residue can be calculated. It is what is left of the estate after other bequests or testamentary gifts have been made. A more sophisticated operation

---

[34] See further, Chapter 16.   [35] [1995] Ch 223.   [36] Ibid., at 232.

[37] (1854) 2 Drew 221.   [38] [1898] 1 Ch 438.

[39] See also *Sprange v Barnard* (1789) 2 Bro CC 585; *In the Estate of Last* [1958] P 137. The authorities on mutual wills are developing in a way which suggests that (at least in some cases) a valid trust can exist where a beneficiary has a limited entitlement to draw down capital. See Chapter 12.

[40] [1998] 2 FLR 775.

of this principle is illustrated, in *Re Golay's Will Trusts*.[41] Here, a testator provided in his will that a legatee was to receive a 'reasonable income' from his properties. Ungoed-Thomas J held that this was not uncertain because the term 'reasonable income' was sufficiently objective to be capable of quantification, noting that the court is regularly required to make objective assessments of what is reasonable.[42] In *T Choithram International SA v Pagarani*,[43] the Privy Council expressed no view as to whether a settlor's gift of 'all my wealth' was void for uncertainty, as the particular assets at issue in the case had been clearly identified by the settlor as being included in the gift, and they were therefore held on trust.

(c) No means of identification has been provided

A trust will fail for uncertainty if it is impossible to identify the property subject to the trust. In *Boyce v Boyce*,[44] a testator bequeathed his two houses to trustees, one to be held on trust for each of his two daughters. The terms of the trust required the trustees to convey to Maria whichever house she chose and then to convey the other house to Charlotte. However, as Maria had died during his lifetime the court held that no valid trust of either house was created in favour of Charlotte because it was impossible to ascertain which should comprise the trust property. Uncertainty could also arise where identifiable property is to be shared unequally between several beneficiaries, but the size of each share has not been quantified. Where there is a discretionary trust, and the trustees have the discretion to determine the extent of the beneficiaries' entitlement to the trust property, no such uncertainty will occur.[45]

(d) The trust property has not been earmarked or segregated[46]

Where only part of a larger bulk of property is to be held on trust, the trust may fail if there has been insufficient earmarking or segregation of the trust property. In *Re London Wine Co (Shippers) Ltd*,[47] a wine merchant held large stocks of wine in various warehouses. When a customer ordered a consignment, it was intended that the bottles ordered should become the property of the customer and that from that moment they would be held on trust for him by the company. However, there was no segregation of the bottles ordered from the general stocks until actual delivery to the customer. No beneficiary was able to identify which of the bottles were his or hers. In these circumstances, Oliver J held that the intended express trust of wine in favour of customers whose orders had not yet been delivered failed for lack of certainty of subject matter because the wine had not been appropriated from the general stock.[48] The same

---

[41] [1965] 2 All ER 660.   [42] See *Jackson v Hamilton* (1846) 3 Jo & Lat 702.

[43] [2001] 2 All ER 492 [2001] 1 WLR 1.   [44] (1849) 16 Sim 476.

[45] See Chapter 17.

[46] See Parkinson, 'Reconceptualizing the Express Trust' [2002] 61 CLJ 657, at 667–676.

[47] (1975) 126 NLJ 977.

[48] Compare *Re Stapylton Fletcher Ltd (In Administration Receivership)* [1995] 1 All ER 192, where a legal tenancy in common was found because bottles of wine for a group of customers had been segregated from the bulk.

requirement was affirmed and applied by the Privy Council in *Re Goldcorp Exchange Ltd (In Receivership)*,[49] where a company dealing in gold and other precious metals had used investors' money to acquire bullion. The company had not appropriated or segregated any specific parcels of bullion to the individual purchasers, but rather held it in bulk. The Privy Council held that it was not held on trust for the investors. Thus, when the company became insolvent they ranked merely as general unsecured creditors. A comparable problem arose in *MacJordan Construction Ltd v Brookmount Erostin Ltd*,[50] where a builder's employer was entitled by contract to retain 3 per cent of the contract price as trustee for a builder, to ensure that the work done was satisfactory. The employer became insolvent, but had failed to earmark or put aside a separate retention fund of specific money due under the contract. The trust failed because it was impossible to identify any specific money as subject to the trust obligation.

A rather different view was taken in *Hunter v Moss*.[51] The Court of Appeal held that an oral declaration of trust by Mr Moss, who owned 950 shares in a private company, of 5 per cent of the issued share capital in favour of Mr Hunter, was not void for want of certainty of subject matter because the shares had not been segregated or appropriated. The issued share capital was 1,000 shares, so Moss held 50 of his shares on trust for Hunter. Since the shares had been sold, he was accountable for an equivalent percentage of the consideration received. The reason for this decision is not entirely clear. One interpretation is that the requirement of the appropriation of the trust property from a common stock only applies in the case of tangible property but has no application to intangible property, provided that there is an identifiable bulk from which the property allegedly subject to the trust can be drawn. This interpretation is inconsistent with the *MacJordan Construction* case. Another, more plausible, interpretation is that the declaration of trust was to be treated as of a fractional share of Mr Moss's holding, like a tenancy in common. While it could be objected that, even in this situation, the shares could have been segregated, there could be technical problems with segregating the shareholding into two separate holdings—it was likely, for instance, that Mr Moss's holding was represented by a single share certificate. An analogy could be drawn with trusts of land, where it is abundantly clear that the legal owner of land can declare a trust of a proportional share of the beneficial ownership without needing physically to divide the land in any way.

Hunter v Moss had been argued and decided before the decision had been given in *Re Goldcorp Exchange Ltd*. It has therefore been subjected to criticism[52] on the grounds that it is inconsistent with the ringing endorsement by the Privy Council of *Re London Wine Co (Shippers) Ltd*. However, in *Re Harvard Securities Ltd (In Liquidation)* Neuberger J held that he was required to follow the decision in *Hunter*, and that it

---

[49] [1995] 1 AC 74. See Birks 'Establishing a Proprietary Base' [1995] RLR 83.

[50] [1992] BCLC 350.

[51] *Hunter v Moss* [1994] 1 WLR 452; Hayton 'Uncertainty of Subject-Matter of Trusts' (1994) 110 LQR 335; Martin 'Validity of Trust of Unidentified Shares' [1996] Conv 223.

[52] See, for example, Underhill and Hayton, *Law Relating to Trusts and Trustees* (16th edn, 2003), at p 79. See also Goode 'Are Intangible Assets Fungible?' [2003] LMCLQ 379.

could be distinguished from the earlier cases on the grounds that it concerned shares and not chattels.[53] It is submitted that this is not a strong ground for distinguishing the two cases, and that the better basis for making a distinction is that property is sufficiently identified if a trust is declared of a defined fractional share of a clearly identified whole. It should be noted that as a consequence of the Sale of Goods (Amendment) Act 1995 purchasers of unascertained goods held in bulk become tenants in common of the legal title if the goods are interchangeable. Although this does not generate a trust, it ensures that the purchaser enjoys a proprietary interest in the goods purchased, with the consequence that they will enjoy priority over other general creditors if the seller subsequently becomes insolvent before the goods are segregated from the bulk.

(e) Future property

It is impossible for a settlor to create a presently existing trust of future property. 'Future property' means property which a person does not presently own, but which he hopes or expects will come into his ownership sometime in the future. Examples of future property include: the interest a person hopes to receive under the will or on the intestacy of a living person;[54] property a person may receive under the exercise of a special power of appointment;[55] future royalties;[56] a part, rather than a share, of future income;[57] and damages expected to be recovered in future litigation.[58] Future property should be distinguished from a residuary interest where a property right has already been conferred subject to the expiry of some prior right. A person with a vested or contingent right to property at some future date has an immediate proprietary interest in the property. Since it is not 'future property', he may subject it to an immediate trust.[59] For example, the person entitled to the remainder interest of property subject to a life interest may create a trust of his remainder interest.

In *Re Ellenborough*,[60] Miss Emily Towry Law, who was the sister of Lord Ellenborough, had executed a settlement in 1893 granting trustees any property to which she might become entitled on the deaths of her brother and sister. When her brother died in 1902 she decided not to transfer the property to the trustees. Buckley J held that no trust had been created by the execution of the settlement. It amounted rather to a mere promise to create a trust. The trustees could not compel her to transfer the property to the trustees because no consideration had been given for the promise and 'equity will not assist a volunteer'.[61] Similarly, in *Re Brooks' Settlement Trusts*[62] in 1929 a son assigned to trustees all the property which he might receive under the exercise of a power of appointment by his mother over property held on her marriage settlement.

---

[53] [1997] 2 BCLC 369, 381–384.   [54] *Re Ellenborough* [1903] 1 Ch 697; *Re Lind* [1915] 2 Ch 345.

[55] *Re Brooks' Settlement Trusts* [1939] Ch 993. See Chapter 16.

[56] *Re Trytel* [1952] 2 TLR 32.

[57] *Williams v CIR* [1965] NZLR 395: the settlor assigned the first £500 of his income to a charitable purpose. The New Zealand Court of Appeal held that this was future property, because it was not certain there would be such income. If he had assigned a proportion of his annual income, this would have been valid.

[58] *Glegg v Bromley* [1912] 3 KB 474.

[59] *Re Midleton's Will Trusts* [1969] 1 Ch 600; *Re Ralli's Will Trusts* [1964] Ch 288.

[60] [1903] 1 Ch 697.   [61] See pp 196–225 below.   [62] [1939] Ch 993.

An appointment of £3,517 was made in his favour in 1939. Farwell J held that no trust had been created in 1929 because the property was a 'mere expectancy' and that since the settlement had been voluntary it could not be enforced.[63]

(f) The interrelationship between certainty of intention and of subject matter

Although the certainties of 'intention' and 'subject matter' refer to different aspects of the trust relationship, they are not to be considered independently of each other. Doubt over the certainty of the subject matter of a trust will exacerbate any doubt over the certainty of intention. This was recognized by the Privy Council in *Mussoorie Bank Ltd v Raynor*,[64] where the question at issue was whether the use of precatory words had been effective to create a trust:

> Now these rules are clear with respect to the doctrine of precatory trusts, that the words of gift used by the testator must be such that the court finds them to be imperative...If there is uncertainty as to the amount or nature of the property that is given over, two difficulties at once arise...the uncertainty in the subject of the gift has a reflex action upon the previous words and throws doubt upon the intention of the testator, and seems to show that he could not possibly have intended his words of confidence, hope, or whatever they may be...to be imperative words.[65]

(g) Effect of uncertainty of subject matter

Uncertainty as to the subject matter of a trust prevents the trust taking effect. If it has been claimed that a settlor has declared himself to be a trustee, the settlor will remain outright owner free of any trust. If the uncertainty relates to property which has already effectively been given to a third party (for instance where a gift of the settlor's entire estate has been made to a third party with a direction which applies only to an unascertained part), the effect of the trust failing will be to make the gift outright and free from a trust. Finally, if the uncertainty defines not only the property subject to a trust, but also the property contained in a transfer, the uncertainty will prevent the transfer taking effect.

(4) Certainty of objects

(a) General

With the exception of charitable trusts (and the small number of anomalous unenforceable trusts which are valid as exceptions to the beneficiary principle) a trust will only be valid if it exists for the benefit of identified legal persons who possess the locus standi to enforce the trust obligations, and for whom the property is held. If an owner of property attempts to declare himself trustee without specifying any valid beneficiaries, he will retain the outright ownership of his property. If, instead, he attempts to create a trust by transferring the property to a trustee without specifying any valid

---

[63] See also *Norman v Federal Comr of Taxation* [1964] ALR 131; *Williams v CIR* [1965] NZLR 395.
[64] (1882) 7 App Cas 321.   [65] Ibid., at 331.

beneficiaries, the equitable interest in the property transferred will revert back to him by means of a resulting trust.[66] The beneficiaries must be defined in such a way that it is possible for the trustees, or in the event of their default the court, to know who they are. The trustee will only be capable of performing his functions, by allocating and transferring the trust property to the beneficiaries, if they are capable of certain identification. Problems of uncertainty generally arise where the beneficiaries are defined by means of a 'class definition'. Such a definition must be sufficiently certain, and the criterion used to identify the class sufficiently objective, to enable determination of who is within, and who is outside, the class, thus ensuring that allocations of trust property are only made to genuine beneficiaries. There are two elements to sufficient certainty of objects.

(i) Conceptual certainty[67]

This concerns the precision of language used to define the class of persons the settlor intends to benefit. It can be a difficult question, as it is concerned with linguistics and semantics. 'Nobel Prize winners' would be one example of a conceptually certain class, as it would be easy to determine whether someone was or was not within that class. Similarly, 'David's descendants' would be conceptually certain. By contrast, 'persons leading a good life' would be conceptually uncertain.

(ii) Evidential certainty[68]

This describes the extent to which the evidence in a particular case enables specific persons to be identified as members of a particular class of objects. For example, one could prove that one was a 'Nobel Prize winner' by providing the necessary documentary evidence that the prize had been awarded. In the case of 'David's descendants', although the test is conceptually certain—you are either one of David's children or grandchildren or you are not—until the advent of DNA fingerprinting there could have been evidential difficulties in individual cases of proving paternity. If the children have moved away from home and not kept in touch, there could also be difficulties in finding all of the descendants, although this is not strictly a question of certainty. The requirement of certainty of objects will be fully considered in Part III, with reference to the different types of equitable obligation.[69] This section will only briefly review the relevant tests of certainty applying to trusts.

(b) Fixed trusts[70]

In the case of a fixed trust, where the beneficial interests of each beneficiary have been predetermined by the settlor, it must be possible to draw up a 'complete list' of all the beneficiaries.[71] This is sometimes referred to as the 'class ascertainability' test. This

---

[66] See Chapter 9.   [67] See further Chapter 13, at pp 453–456.
[68] Ibid.   [69] Certainty is also required for powers of appointment, for example.
[70] See Chapter 14.
[71] *IRC v Broadway Cottages Trust* [1955] Ch 20, CA. Note, what is required is that the total number of beneficiaries are known—they need not be individually named.

means that the definition of the beneficiaries must be both conceptually certain and that there must also be evidential certainty of who is within the class. The reason for this is obvious: an obligation to divide the property in equal shares between the members of the class requires that the trustees should know how many there are in the class.

(c) Discretionary trusts[72]

In the case of discretionary trusts, the trustees enjoy the discretion to determine how the trust property should be allocated among the class of potential beneficiaries. Originally, the test for certainty of objects was the same as for fixed trusts, but in *McPhail v Doulton*,[73] the House of Lords held that the test for certainty of beneficiaries in discretionary trusts should be 'similar' to that used for the certainty of objects of powers,[74] namely that it must be possible to say of any given individual that he is, or is not, within the class. This is known as the 'individual ascertainability' test. This requires that the class be specified with conceptual certainty. The disposition in question in *McPhail v Doulton* was 'to or for the benefit of any of the officers and employees or ex-officers or ex-employees of the company or to any relatives or dependants of any such persons'. The House of Lords held that the class had been specified with appropriate certainty, despite the potential problems raised by the words 'dependants' and 'relatives'. The case was remitted to the Chancery Division to apply the new test to the facts, and the application reached the Court of Appeal as *Re Baden's Deed Trusts (No 2)*.[75] They confirmed that the class was conceptually certain, and said that the requirement of certainty would be fulfilled if:

as regards at least a substantial number of objects, it can be said with certainty that they fall within the trust, even though, as regards a substantial number of others it could not be proven whether they are in or out.

Thus, what was needed was not complete conceptual certainty, but enough certainty in the language for distribution to be made to identifiable persons.[76] The Court of Appeal also held that, if there was conceptual certainty, a discretionary trust would not be invalidated by the absence of evidential certainty. In order to distribute the funds, the trustees of a discretionary trust do not need to know the identity of every member of the class, nor the exact number of the beneficiaries.

A discretionary trust will also be invalid if it is administratively unworkable because of the sheer size of the class of potential beneficiaries.[77] This means that an otherwise valid trust can be invalidated if it would be too difficult, expensive, or time-consuming for the trustees to make distributions within the class, even though the class is both conceptually and evidentially certain.

---

[72] See Chapter 17.   [73] [1971] AC 424.

[74] *Re Gulbenkian's Settlement Trusts (No 1)* [1968] Ch 126. See Chapter 16.

[75] [1972] Ch 607.   [76] See further Chapters 16 and 17.

[77] *McPhail v Doulton* [1971] AC 424; *R v District Auditor, ex p West Yorkshire Metropolitan County Council* [1986] RVR 24.

(d) Uncertainty of objects

If there are no certain objects, and property has left the hands of the settlor, the equitable title must revert to the settlor or the settlor's estate by means of a resulting trust.

3 Constitution of trusts

(1) The meaning of constitution

(a) Fully constituted trusts

We have already seen that there are two methods by which the owner of property, termed the settlor, can create a trust over it. He may either declare himself to be the trustee of the property, or alternatively transfer it to a third party who is intended to hold it on trust for the specified beneficiaries and not to enjoy the benefit himself. If such a declaration is made, or transfer occurs, the trust is brought into existence, and from that moment the trustee holds the legal title to the property subject to the trust obligations, and the beneficiaries enjoy the equitable ownership of the trust property, provided the three certainties are also present. Such a trust is described as 'fully constituted', meaning simply that the trust has in fact come into existence, because legal title to the property has been properly vested in the trustees and beneficial title in the proposed beneficiaries. Because a perfect trust has been created, the settlor cannot reclaim the property at a later date.

(b) Incompletely constituted trusts

In contrast, if for any reason the settlor fails effectively to declare himself trustee of the intended trust property, or if the property is never transferred by the settlor to the intended trustee, the trust does not come into being. The settlor remains the owner of the property and it is not held by him subject to the trust obligations. In consequence, the beneficiaries have no proprietary entitlement to the intended trust property. Legal title has not vested in the trustees, to be held for the benefit of the beneficiaries in equity. In such circumstances, the trust is described as 'incompletely constituted'. This terminology may be confusing, as in fact no trust exists.

(c) Beneficiaries' remedies

If a trust has been completely constituted, the beneficiaries have an equitable interest in the property, and may enforce the trust obligations. However, where a trust remains incompletely constituted, the reality is often that a settlor has previously promised that he will create a trust in favour of the proposed beneficiaries, but he has not fulfilled his promise by making an effective declaration or transfer. In such circumstances, the main concern of the proposed beneficiaries will be whether they have any means of requiring the settlor to constitute the trust in their favour. The basic position is that the beneficiaries cannot force the settlor to constitute the trust if they are volunteers, due to the rule that 'equity will not assist a volunteer'. Potential beneficiaries will be volunteers if they have not provided valuable consideration in return for the settlor's promise to settle the property on trust for them. It is worth noting that the majority of potential beneficiaries will be volunteers, as it is rare that a beneficiary pays for the benefit acquired under a trust. However, it will be seen that the general restriction against enforcing a promise to create a trust is subject to a number of limited exceptions. Alternatively, even if the beneficiaries are volunteers and not entitled to any equitable remedies, they may be able to seek common law remedies to compensate them for the loss they have suffered because the trust has not been constituted.

(2) Constituting the trust by declaration

(a) Requirements of effective declaration

In *Re Cozens*, Neville J indicated what would be required by the court to establish that a settlor had declared himself trustee of his property:

in each case where a declaration of trust is relied on the Court must be satisfied that a present irrevocable declaration of trust has been made.[78]

This emphasizes that an expression of intent to create a trust in the future does not create an immediate fully constituted trust. In *Richards v Delbridge*, Jessel MR made clear that the settlor does not need to use particular words or technical expressions to create a trust by declaration:

he need not use the words 'I declare myself a trustee', but he must do something which is equivalent to it, and use expressions which have that meaning.[79]

In *Paul v Constance*, Scarman LJ accepted as a statement of principle that 'there must be clear evidence from what is said or done of an intention to create a trust'.[80]

(b) Formalities[81]

In general, an inter vivos declaration of trust will be valid and effective to create a fully constituted trust, even though it is made orally and without consideration.[82] No transfer of property is necessary; the settlor is simply changing the nature of his ownership of the property from owning it as himself to owning it as a trustee acting for named beneficiaries. The legal title does not move anywhere; the effective declaration of a trust separates the legal and equitable ownership of the property.

However, in the case of land, s 53(1)(b) of the Law of Property Act 1925 provides:

a declaration of trust respecting any land or any interest therein must be manifested and proved by some writing signed by some person who is able to declare such trust or by his will.

---

[78] [1913] 2 Ch 478, at 486.   [79] (1874) LR 18 Eq 11, at 14.
[80] [1977] 1 WLR 527, CA.   [81] See below, pp 226 *et seq.*
[82] See *Jones v Lock* (1865) LR 1 Ch App 25, at 28, per Lord Cranworth LC: 'a parol declaration of trust of personality may be perfectly valid even when voluntary'.

A purported declaration of a trust of land which is not evidenced in writing will generally be ineffective, although this general rule is subject to exceptions, which are discussed below in the context of the formalities required for the creation of express trusts.

(c) Cases illustrating effective declaration

It is ultimately a question of fact whether in any particular case an effective declaration of trust has occurred. A number of general indications can be drawn from the authorities:

(i) Loose conversation

Jones v Lock[83] suggests that words spoken in what was merely 'loose conversation' will not amount to an effective declaration of trust because the necessary intention to create a trust is lacking. Jones was an ironmonger who had returned from a business trip to Birmingham. The nurse of his infant son complained that he had not brought anything back as a present for the baby. Jones then produced a cheque for £900, payable to himself, which was the result of his business negotiations and handed it to the baby saying: 'Look you here, I give this to baby; it is for himself, and I am going to put it away for him, and will give him a great deal more along with it.' A few days later he died. The question was whether in the circumstances the father had created a trust of the money represented by the cheque for the son. The cheque had not been effectively transferred to the son, as this would have required the father's endorsement (naming the son on the back of the cheque and signing it to confirm the transfer). Lord Cranworth LC held that there was equally no effective declaration of trust:

the case turns on the very short question whether Jones intended to make a declaration that he held the property in trust for the child; and I cannot come to any other conclusion than that he did not. I think it would be of very dangerous example if loose conversation of this sort, in important transactions of this kind, should have the effect of declarations of trust.[84]

(ii) Words repeated over a period of time

Although isolated 'loose conversation' will not alone effect a valid declaration of trust, *Paul v Constance*[85] suggests that the repetition of similar words in conversation over a period of time may be sufficient to create a trust. Dennis Constance was separated from his wife and living with Doreen Paul. In 1974 he received £950 damages as compensation for an injury he had sustained at work. He deposited the money in a bank account and on a number of occasions told Paul that the money was 'as much yours as mine'. Constance died without leaving a will and his wife, from whom he had not been divorced, claimed that she was entitled to the money in the account on the grounds that it formed part of his estate, to which she was entitled by the rules of intestate succession. The Court of Appeal held that she was not entitled to the money because it was held upon a validly declared express trust in favour of Paul. Scarman LJ said that

---

[83] (1865) LR 1 Ch App 25.   [84] Ibid., at 28–29.   [85] [1977] 1 WLR 527.

although 'it is not easy to pin-point a specific moment of declaration' the 'use of those words on numerous occasions' between Constance and Paul was sufficient to constitute an express declaration of trust. Nevertheless, Scarman LJ indicated that this was very much a borderline case.

Paul v Constance has since been followed in *Rowe v Prance*.[86] Mr Prance and Mrs Rowe had conducted a relationship over many years. Although Prance had promised to divorce his wife to live with Mrs Rowe, he had remained married. He purchased a yacht where he said he would live with Mrs Rowe, and in which they could sail the world. The yacht was registered in his sole name, allegedly because Mrs Rowe did not have an Ocean Master's certificate. Over a period of time Mr Prance regularly used the word 'our' in relation to the yacht. Nicholas Warren, QC held that in these circumstances the yacht was held on trust by Mr Prance for himself and Mrs Rowe in equal shares.

(iii) Words of gift by the settlor to himself

In *Choithram (T) International SA v Pagarani*,[87] the Privy Council was forced to consider what appeared to be a novel situation that did not fall squarely within either of the methods of constitution identified in *Milroy v Lord*. The case concerned a wealthy philanthropist ('TCP') who wished to set up a charitable foundation to receive much of his wealth, consisting of company shares and deposit balances, when he died. In February 1992, knowing that he was dying, he signed a trust deed establishing the foundation. The deed stated that he was the settlor, and appointed seven trustees, of which he was one. After signing the deed he orally stated that he was giving all his wealth to the foundation. He died a month later, but had not executed any share transfers to the foundation, nor had he executed a formal declaration of trust. The judge at first instance, and the Court of Appeal of the British Virgin Islands, held that no trust had been created because of the absence of either an effective declaration or an effective transfer. The Privy Council allowed an appeal, advising that the settlor had constituted the trust. Lord Browne-Wilkinson explained that his words of gift to the foundation could only have been intended to establish a trust:

Although the words used by TCP are normally appropriate to an outright gift—'I give to X'—in the present context there is no breach of the principle in *Milroy v Lord* if the words of TCP's gift (ie to the foundation) are given their only possible meaning in this context. The foundation has no legal existence apart from the trust declared by the foundation trust deed. Therefore the words 'I give to the foundation' can only mean 'I give to the trustees of the foundation trust deed to be held by them on the trusts of the foundation trust deed.' Although the words are apparently words of outright gift they are essentially words of gift on trust.[88]

In effect the settlor made a gift of the intended trust property to himself in his capacity as trustee, which had the effect of constituting the trust. The trust was enforceable even though the trust property had only been vested in one of the trustees. Since it is somewhat artificial to regard the settlor as having made a gift to himself, as there was

---

86 [1999] 2 FLR 787.   87 [2001] 1 WLR 1.   88 Ibid., at 11–12.

no need for any transfer of the assets concerned, it might be better to treat the settlor as having declared himself a trustee of the assets which were already his.[89] Thus, words of gift by the settlor to himself on trust should be regarded in substance as a declaration of self as trustee.

(iv) Declaration by conduct

It seems an effective declaration of trust may also be inferred from conduct, even though no words approximating to such a declaration are actually used. In *Re Vandervell's Trust (No 2)*,[90] the Vandervell Trust Company held a share option on trust for Mr Vandervell. The option was exercised using £5,000 that the trust company held on separate trusts for Vandervell's children. Thereafter, the trustees wrote to the Inland Revenue saying that the shares would be held on trust for the children's settlement, and dividends arising from the shares were henceforth paid into the children's settlement. Given that this was all done with the full assent of Mr Vandervell, the Court of Appeal held that the evidence of the intention to declare a trust was clear and manifest and that the trustee company held the shares on trust for the children. Unless the trustees can be treated as acting as agents for Mr Vandervell in declaring the trust, the reasoning in this case is unconvincing, as passive assent by Mr Vandervell does not suggest a clear and present irrevocable declaration of trust, or, indeed, unequivocal conduct suggesting such a declaration.[91] This aspect of effective declaration of a trust should therefore be treated with caution.

(v) Overarching intention to create a trust

In *Don King Productions Inc v Warren (No 1)*,[92] Lightman J was faced with the task of interpreting two multi-million pound contracts between the leading boxing promoters in the UK and the USA. The judge remarked that 'the drafting of the first agreement is somewhat primitive for a transaction of this size and importance for the parties'.[93] By the agreements, Frank Warren, the UK boxing promoter, purported to assign his promotion, management, and associated contracts ('PMA contracts') to a partnership with Don King, the 'larger than life' American promoter. The contracts related to personal services, so no assignment could take place. However, Lightman J held that the benefit of the PMA contracts had been subjected to a trust in favour of the partnership since this had been the overriding intention of the parties:

the clear intent of the parties manifested in the first and second agreements was that the promotion management and associated agreements should be held by the partnership or by the partners for the benefit of the partnership absolutely, and that this intent should be given the

---

[89] See Ricketts 'Completely Constituting an Inter Vivos Trust: Property Rules?' [2001] Conv. 515, where it is suggested that this was not a novel set of facts at all, and should have been considered as a transfer of property to trustees, given that title was being transferred to third parties.

[90] [1974] Ch 269.

[91] See also Battersby 'Formalities for the Disposition of Equitable Interests under a Trust' [1979] Conv 17.

[92] [1998] 2 All ER 608.   [93] Ibid., at 615.

fullest possible effect. The agreements have accordingly at all times been held by the partners as trustees for the partnership.[94]

(3) Constituting the trust by transfer

(a) Requirements for effective transfer

Where a settlor wishes to create a trust of which a third party is the trustee, the trust will only be constituted if the trust property is vested in the trustee by means of an effective transfer of his legal or beneficial title. In *Choithram (T) International SA v Pagarani*, the Privy Council held that where the settlor intends to establish a trust with a body of trustees it will be sufficient to constitute the trust if the property is transferred to at least one of the intended trustees, since that recipient will be bound by the trust and must give effect to it by transferring the trust property into the name of all the trustees.[95] The requirements for an effective transfer of the settlor's title vary, depending on the type of property that has to be transferred.

(i) Land

By s 52 of the Law of Property Act 1925 all conveyances of land, or of interests in land, are void unless made by deed. An attempted oral transfer of land, a transfer by mere writing, or even granting the trustees physical possession of the land will thus be insufficient to create a constituted trust. In *Richards v Delbridge*,[96] a grandfather attempted to create a trust of a leasehold interest for his grandson by assigning the lease to the boy's mother. Although the assignment was in writing, it was not made by deed. There was therefore no effective transfer of the lease and the trust remained incompletely constituted. With some exceptions for short leases, the transfer of the legal title to land must be perfected by the registration of the transferee as the 'registered proprietor' at the Land Registry.[97]

(ii) Shares

Shares are owned at law by the person who is registered as the owner thereof on the 'share register' of the company to which they relate. The legal ownership of shares can only be validly transferred by means of the registration of the transferee on the share register of the company issuing them. The possession of share certificates is merely evidence of the ownership of the shares but does not itself constitute ownership. Registration of a transferee as legal owner of the shares may occur either following the completion of an appropriate share transfer form,[98] or by means of an appropriate instruction if the shares are held electronically in the CREST system.[99] In either

---

[94] Ibid., at 635.
[95] [2001] 2 All ER 492, at 502. See also *Re Ralli's Will Trust* [1964] Ch 288, considered below.
[96] (1874) LR 18 Eq 11.
[97] See Land Registration Act 2002; *Mascall v Mascall* (1984) 50 P & CR 119, CA.
[98] Companies Act 1985, ss 182, 183; Stock Transfer Act 1963, s 1.
[99] Pinner 'CREST—The New Settlement System' (1996) 146 NLJ 964.

case, simple delivery of the share certificates by the settlor to an intended trustee will not create a completely constituted trust. This was established in the leading case, *Milroy v Lord*.[100] Thomas Medley attempted to create a trust of 50 shares in the Bank of Louisiana in favour of the plaintiffs by transferring them on trust to Samuel Lord. By the constitution of the bank, the shares were only transferable in the books of the company. Although Medley had executed a deed of assignment and delivered the share certificates to Lord, the view of the court was that title had not been effectively transferred and the trust remained incompletely constituted.

(iii) Copyrights

By s 1 of the Copyright, Designs and Patents Act 1988, a copyright must be transferred in writing.

(iv) Chattels

Title to chattels, i.e. tangible personal property, may be effectively transferred by means either of a deed or gift, or delivery of possession of the chattel to the intended transferee.

(v) Bills of exchange and cheques

A bill of exchange or cheque may only be transferred by endorsement, namely by the holder of the bill of exchange or cheque writing the name of the person to whom the debt is transferred and signing to confirm the transfer. Mere physical delivery to the intended trustee will not constitute the trust. This was evident in *Jones v Lock*,[101] where the mere fact that the father had handed his cheque to his infant son was insufficient to transfer title to him.

(vi) Equitable interests

If the intended trust property is an equitable interest enjoyed in property by the settlor, it can only be transferred to the trustee by writing, as required by s 53(1)(c) of the Law of Property Act 1925, which provides:

a disposition of an equitable interest or trust subsisting at the time of the disposition, must be in writing signed by the person disposing of the same, or by his agent thereunto lawfully authorised in writing or by will.[102]

(b) Transfers where registration by a third party is required

The legal title to some forms of property such as shares or land can only be transferred by registration of the transferee as the new legal owner. Prior to the decision of the Court of Appeal in *Pennington v Waine*,[103] it was thought that the mere completion of the relevant transfer documents by the transferor would be ineffective to transfer any

---

100   (1862) 4 De GF & J 264.   101   (1865) LR 1 Ch App 25.

102   See below, p 228.

103   [2002] 1 WLR 2075; [2002] LMCLQ 296 (Tijo & Yeo); (2003) 17 TLI 35 (Ladds); (2003) 62 CLJ 263 (Doggett); [2003] Conv 364 (Garton); [2003] Con 192 (Halliwell).

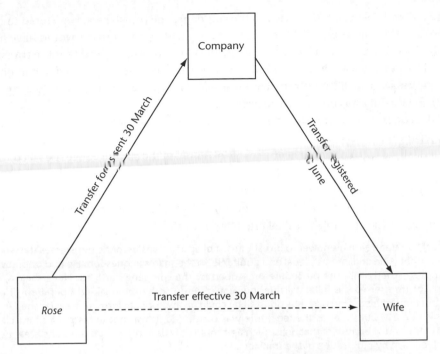

Figure 7.2 The settlor has done everything within his power to transfer the property: *Re Rose*

interest to a volunteer transferee, since equity would not act to perfect an imperfect gift. The only exception, known as the rule in *Re Rose*, was that equity would treat a transfer as complete if the transferor had done everything in his power to transfer the property to the transferee. However, in *Pennington v Waine* the Court of Appeal held that mere completion of the relevant transfer documents may be capable of giving rise to an equitable assignment of the property concerned, even where the transferor has not strictly done everything in his power to transfer the property.

(i) Transfer complete in equity when the transferor has done everything in his power to transfer the legal title to the transferee[104]

It is well established that where the legal title to property can only be effectively transferred by registration of the transferee as the substitute owner on a register maintained by a third party, equity will treat the transfer as complete from the moment that the transferor has done 'everything within his power' to facilitate the transfer of the property. This principle emerged in *Re Rose (Deceased)*,[105] where Eric Rose had transferred 10,000 shares to his wife. The share transfer form was completed

---

[104] See [1998] CLJ 46 (Lowrie and Todd). See also *Hunter v Moss* [1994] 3 All ER 215, 220; *Re Harvard Securities Ltd (In Liquidation)* [1997] 2 BCLC 369, 375.

[105] [1952] Ch 499.

on 30 March 1943 and forwarded to the company. The transfer was registered in the books of the company on 30 June. To avoid estate duty the transfer would have had to have been completed prior to 10 April. The Court of Appeal held that the transfer had in fact been completed on 30 March, since at that time the transferor had done everything within his power to divest himself of his interest in the shares (see Figure 7.2). Estate duty was not therefore payable.

The concept of the transferor having done 'everything within his power' to transfer legal title to his property does not merely mean that he had done all that he was practically able to do, or had been capable of doing, in the circumstances he faced. The rule in *Re Rose* operates where the only acts which remain to achieve the transfer of the legal title to the transferee are those of third parties. The transferor must have gone beyond the point of no return so that he is no longer able to prevent the transfer being completed. The principle was explained by Jenkins LJ:

[Rose] had done all in his power to divest himself of and to transfer to the transferees the whole of his right, title and interest, legal and equitable, in the shares in question. He had, moreover, complied strictly with the procedure prescribed by the company's articles. Nevertheless, he had not transferred the full legal title, nor could he do so by the unaided operation of any instructions of his . . . [He] had thus done all he could, in appropriate form, to transfer the whole of his interest, but so far as the legal title was concerned, it was not in his power himself to effect the actual transfer of that, inasmuch as it could only be conferred on the transferees in its perfect form by registration of the transfers.[106]

The rule did not operate in *Re Fry*[107] because in that case the transferor had failed to do everything which was necessary to transfer title. The owner of shares in an English company, who was domiciled in America, had executed a share transfer form and sent it to England to be registered. Under wartime legislation in force, the company was prohibited from registering the transfer without the consent of the Treasury. Although the transferee had obtained, completed, and returned the appropriate forms seeking such consent, he had died before it was given. In these circumstances, Romer J held that he had not done everything within his power to transfer title to the shares, and that they therefore remained his at the date of his death:

Now I should have thought it was difficult to say that the testator had done everything that was required to be done by him at the time of his death, for it was necessary for him to obtain permission from the Treasury for the assignment and he had not obtained it. Moreover the Treasury might in any case have required further information of the kind referred to in the questionnaire which was submitted to him, or answers supplemental to those which he had given in reply to it.[108]

The rule in *Re Rose* was applied to a transfer of registered land in *Mascall v Mascall*.[109] William Mascall wanted to transfer his house to his son. He filled in all the relevant parts of a form of transfer supplied by the Land Registry to effect a transfer of the land and handed it to his son. The son completed those parts that the intended transferee

---

[106] Ibid., at 515.   [107] [1946] Ch 312.

[108] Ibid., at 317–318. See also *Zeital v Kaye* [2010] EWCA Civ 159, where handing over an incomplete but signed share transfer form was held to be insufficient.

[109] (1984) 50 P & CR 119.

was required to complete and sent the form to the Stamp Office, a necessary step prior to sending the form for registration. He then had a row with his father, who sought a declaration that the transfer was void. The transfer form had not yet been sent to the Land Registry. The Court of Appeal held that the father had done everything in his power to transfer the title to his son, and that the transfer was therefore completed when he handed the transfer form to him, having completed all the parts that were required of the transferor. Although it had not yet been sent to the Land Registry, this was the responsibility of his son as transferee, and therefore the father had done everything within his power, or more precisely everything that was necessary by him, to transfer the title. All that remained were the acts of third parties, the son sending the form to the Land Registry and their registering him as the proprietor, which were out of the father's control. The principle was stated by Browne-Wilkinson LJ:

A gift is complete as soon as the settlor or donor has done everything that the donor has to do, that is to say, as soon as the donee has within his control all those things necessary to enable him, the donee, to complete his title.[110]

The rule has also been held to apply to an assignment of a lease which must be completed by registration.[111]

Re Rose[112] and *Mascall v Mascall*[113] concerned absolute transfers of property by way of outright gift, but the rule would equally operate in favour of a transferee who was intended to acquire the legal title as a trustee. In such a case, the trust would be completely constituted from the very moment that the settlor had done everything within his power to transfer title. Technically, this is not an exception to the rule that 'equity will not assist a volunteer', because there is no need for the court to intervene and order the trust to be constituted on behalf of the beneficiaries. Nevertheless, in practical terms the rule in *Re Rose*[114] does indirectly operate to assist volunteers by widening the circumstances in which equity will regard a trust as having come into existence.

(ii) Transfer complete in equity when it would be unconscionable for the transferor to recall the gift to the transferee

It used to be considered that an attempted transfer of shares would only be regarded as complete if the strict requirements of the rule in *Re Rose* were satisfied. However in *Pennington v Waine*[115] the Court of Appeal held that, in appropriate circumstances, the execution of a share transfer form might in itself be sufficient to give rise to an equitable assignment of the beneficial interest in the shares. The result would be that the transferor would hold the shares on trust for the transferee, even though the completed form has not been delivered to the transferee or the company's registrar. The facts are important to consider what these appropriate circumstances might be.

In September 1998, Ada Crampton executed a share transfer form in favour of her nephew, Harold Crampton, in respect of 400 shares in a family company. The

---

[110] Ibid., at 126.
[111] *Brown & Root Technology Ltd v Sun Alliance and London Assurance Co Ltd* [1996] Ch 51.
[112] [1952] Ch 499.   [113] (1984) 50 P & CR 119.
[114] [1952] Ch 499.   [115] [2002] 1 WLR 2075.

share transfer form had been drawn up for her by a partner in the Company's auditors. She returned the form to him and it was placed on the company's file. Ada also wanted Harold to become a director of the company, and the auditor wrote to him enclosing instructions to complete form 288A (a prescribed form of consent to act as a director), and also stating that Ada had instructed him to arrange the transfer to him of 400 shares in the company, adding that this did not require any action on his part. The auditor took no further action to transfer the shares prior to Ada's death in November 1998. It was clear that Ada had not done everything in her power to effect transfer of the shares, because the transfer form had not been delivered to Harold or submitted to the company for registration. Nevertheless, the Court of Appeal held that the gift of the shares was effective in equity. Arden LJ, with whom Schiemann LJ agreed, held that the gift was complete because Ada had intended to make an immediate gift and it would have been unconscionable for her to recall the gift.[116] Clarke LJ instead held that the execution of the share transfer form could be taken as a complete assignment of her equitable interest in the shares, thus generating a trust under which she could have been compelled to procure the registration of the shares in Harold's name.[117]

In the view of the majority, the crucial element that renders a transfer complete in equity is that it would be unconscionable for the transferor to recall the gift. Arden LJ identified the circumstances which she considered had made it unconscionable for Ada to recall the gift:

> There can be no comprehensive list of factors which makes it unconscionable for the donor to change his or her mind: it must depend on the court's evaluation of all the relevant considerations. What then are the relevant facts here? Ada made the gift of her own free will: there is no finding that she was not competent to do this. She not only told Harold about the gift and signed a form of transfer which she delivered to Mr Pennington for him to secure registration; her agent also told Harold that he need take no action. In addition Harold agreed to become a director of the Company without limit of time, which he could not do without shares being transferred to him. If Ada had changed her mind on (say) 10 November 1998, in my judgement the court could properly have concluded that it was too late for her to do this as by that date Harold signed the form 288A.[118]

It is submitted that this case dangerously undermines the established principles that equity will not act to perfect an imperfect gift nor assist a volunteer. A finding that a donor intended to make an immediate gift does not mean that an immediate gift was made. The established equitable principles enable a transferor to change his or her mind whether to make a gift even after they have completed many of the steps necessary to effect a transfer. While it might have been clear on the particular facts in *Pennington v Waine* that Ada had not changed her mind about the intended transfer, in other cases the evidence will be more equivocal. The effectiveness of alleged transfers of property should not be determined by the vagaries of whether the court

---

[116] Ibid., at [66].

[117] Ibid., at [110]. It is submitted that this seems to directly contravene *Re Rose* itself, where no such trust was found, and is therefore dubious reasoning.

[118] Ibid., at [64].

considers that it would be 'unconscionable' for the transferee to change his or her mind.[119]

Arden LJ held that if she had been wrong to hold that the delivery of the share transfers to the company or donee was not required, then the case could have been decided the same way by finding that Ada and the Company auditor had become agents for Harold for the purpose of submitting the share transfer to the company.[120] It is submitted that this analysis would have been preferable to the amelioration of the strict requirements of the rule in *Re Rose*, although it may be stretching the concept of agency somewhat to accommodate it.[121] Alternatively, it might have been argued that Harold had provided valuable consideration by agreeing to become a director of the company without limit of time in return for the gift of shares, thus entitling equity to act on his behalf. It still remains to be seen whether the new approach founded on unconscionability finds favour with higher courts.

(4) Constitution of a trust through coincidental receipt of the trust property by the trustee

In most cases, a trust will only be fully constituted if the trust property is transferred to the trustee by the deliberate act of the settlor. However, in some very rare cases it seems that a trust will be fully constituted if the trustee received the legal title to the trust property as a matter of coincidence. In *Re Ralli's Will Trusts*,[122] a number of trusts were created by the members of a family (see Figure 7.3). The patriarch, Ambrose Ralli, died in 1899. Under his will his wife was to enjoy a life interest of his residuary estate which was to be held on trust, and on her death it would pass to his daughters, Helen and Irene, in equal shares. In 1924 Helen executed a marriage settlement, under which she promised to settle any after-acquired property for the benefit of the beneficiaries of the settlement. This would include the remainder interest in her father's estate to which she would become entitled on the death of her mother. The beneficiaries under the marriage settlement were her sister Irene's children. Helen died in 1956 and the testator's widow in 1961. The plaintiff, who had been appointed a trustee of Ambrose Ralli's will in 1946, was at that date the sole surviving trustee of the trusts established under the will. He was, coincidentally, also the sole surviving trustee of Helen's marriage settlement. On Ambrose's widow's death, the remainder interest in his residuary estate was vested in him as trustee under the will. The central question was whether he held Helen's half share as part of Helen's estate, in which case it would pass under

---

[119] See further Halliwell 'Perfecting Imperfect Gifts and Trusts: Have We Reached the End of the Chancellor's Foot?' [2003] Conv 192. Cf Garton 'The Role of the Trust Mechanism in the Rule in *Re Rose*' [2003] Conv 364, who favours the flexibility and conceptual clarity that an approach based on unconscionability might bring over the existing equitable principles.

[120] [2002] 1 WLR 2075 at [67].

[121] See Halliwell 'Perfecting Imperfect Gifts and Trusts: Have We Reached the End of the Chancellor's Foot?' [2003] Conv 192.

[122] [1964] Ch 288.

Figure 7.3 *Re Ralli's Will Trusts*

her will, or whether he held it under the terms of her marriage settlement, in which case it would pass to Irene's children. Although there had been no intentional transfer of the property to the plaintiff in his capacity as trustee of the marriage settlement, Buckley J held that the fact that he had received it in his capacity as the trustee of the will was sufficient to constitute the trust, and the property was therefore held on the terms of the marriage settlement. He concluded that it did not matter how the trustee had come to receive the legal title to the trust property, it was sufficient that the title had vested in him:

In my judgment the circumstance that the plaintiff holds the fund because he was appointed a trustee of the will is irrelevant. He is at law the owner of the fund, and the means by which he became so have no effect on the quality of his legal ownership. The question is: For whom, if anyone, does he hold the fund in equity?[123]

In the circumstances that transpired, it was a fortuitous coincidence that the plaintiff had enjoyed a double capacity as trustee of both the will and of the marriage settlement. It meant that Helen could not claim the property from him without breaking

[123] Ibid., at 301.

her promise to give it to him on trust. On a narrow reading of the case this was an essential part of the decision. On a wider reading, the case supports the view that it is not essential for a trustee to obtain the legal title to the trust property by way of a deliberate transfer from the settlor.

As with the principle in *Re Rose*[124] examined above, *Re Ralli's Will Trusts*[125] does not provide an example of equity assisting a volunteer. The trust is completely constituted, so there is no need for equity to assist the beneficiaries. Again, the practical effect of the principle is to broaden the circumstances in which equity will regard a trust as having been constituted, which indirectly assists the position of volunteers

(5) Relationship between constitution by transfer and constitution by declaration

It has been seen that a fully constituted trust may be created either by an effective declaration of self as trustee, or by an effective transfer of the property to the trustee on trust. If there was an intention by the settlor to create a trust in favour of the beneficiaries by transferring the trust property to trustees, but an attempt to constitute the trust was ineffective because the property has not been transferred, the question arises whether equity should treat the settlor as holding the property on trust. This would have the advantage of ensuring that the beneficiaries were able to enforce their equitable entitlement to the trust property, which seems to have been the settlor's intention. However, in such circumstances equity will not construe an ineffective transfer as a declaration of trust by the settlor. This was made clear in *Milroy v Lord*[126] where, as was noted above, the settlor who intended to create a trust of shares had failed to transfer title to the intended trust, because he had merely handed the share certificates to him and he had not been registered as the owner thereof on the company share register. The Court of Appeal held that there had been no effective declaration of trust by the settlor. The principle was stated by Turner LJ:

> it is plain that it was not the purpose of this settlement, or the intention of the settlor, to constitute himself a trustee of the bank shares. The intention was that the trust should be vested in... Samuel Lord, and I think therefore that we should not be justified in holding that by the settlement, or by any parol declaration made by the settlor, he himself became a trustee of these shares for the purposes of the settlement. By doing so we should be converting the settlement or the parol declaration to a purpose wholly different from that which was intended to be created by it, and, as I have said, creating a perfect trust out of the imperfect transaction.[127]

In *Choithram (T) International SA v Pagarani*,[128] which was also discussed above, the Privy Council dealt with a situation which did not easily fit into the two categories identified in *Milroy v Lord*. The decision does not, however, undermine the traditional principle that a failed transfer will not be construed as a declaration of trust. Instead

---

[124] [1952] Ch 499.
[125] [1964] Ch 288. [126] (1862) 4 De GF & J 264.
[127] Ibid., at 275. [128] [2001] 1 WLR 1.

it is submitted that the highly unusual situation of a settlor's words of gift to himself should be construed in substance as a declaration of trust.

(6) Enforcing a trust

(a) Enforcing fully constituted trusts

Where a trust has been fully constituted, whether in consequence of a settlor's declaration or through an effective transfer of the intended trust property to trustees, the beneficiaries are immediately entitled to the equitable interest in the property held on trust for them. They can seek the aid of equity to compel the trustees to perform the trust obligations by virtue of their interest as beneficiaries, irrespective of whether they were volunteers or whether they had provided consideration to the settlor in return for the creation of the trust. Once the trust has been created, the settlor cannot change his mind.[129]

This can be seen from the following two cases. *Paul v Paul*[130] concerned a marriage settlement executed by parties who had since separated. Under the terms of the settlement as husband and wife, they were entitled to enjoy the income derived from the trust property for life, with the remainder interest passing on their deaths to the children of the marriage. If there were no children and the wife predeceased her husband she enjoyed a general power to appoint over the trust property by will, subject to an express provision in default of appointment in favour of her next of kin. As there were no children, the husband and wife applied to have the capital of the trust paid over to themselves, arguing that the only other persons with any interest in it were the next of kin, who were volunteers. The Court of Appeal held that although the next of kin were volunteers, they enjoyed an immediate equitable interest in the capital because the trust was fully constituted and they were beneficiaries under it. As such, the trust could not be brought to an end without their consent. In *Re Bowden*,[131] Catherine Bowden agreed to settle any property to which she might become entitled under her father's will on trust. Her father died in 1869, and between 1871 and 1874 the property to which she was entitled under his will was transferred to the trustees. In 1935 she requested that the trustees transfer the trust funds to her absolutely. Bennett J held that she was not entitled to the transfer because the property had become impressed with the trust the moment that it had been received by them.

(b) Enforcing incompletely constituted trusts

As mentioned above, where a settlor has neither declared himself trustee of the trust property nor transferred it to trustees, the trust is said to be incompletely constituted. In reality, no trust exists. The trust property is not subject to any obligations, and the

---

[129] See *Jefferys v Jefferys* (1841) Cr & Ph 138; *Bentley v Mackay* (1851) 15 Beav 12; *Kekewich v Manning* (1851) 1 De GM & G 176; *Milroy v Lord* (1862) 4 De GF & J 264; *Richardson v Richardson* (1867) LR 3 Eq 686; *Henry v Armstrong* (1881) 18 Ch D 668.

[130] (1882) 20 Ch D 742, CA.   [131] [1936] Ch 71.

legal and equitable ownership are not separated. The settlor remains the owner of the property. The intended beneficiaries enjoy no entitlement to the putative trust property, nor can they enforce the trust obligations against the intended trustees, because there is no trust. In substance, the intended beneficiaries are merely the victims of the settlor's unfulfilled promise to create a trust in their favour. In such circumstances, the question arises as to whether there are any means by which the intended beneficiaries can compel the settlor to carry out his promise to subject the property to a trust in their favour, by in effect requiring specific performance thereof. The basic principle is that if the intended beneficiaries have provided valuable consideration in return for the settlor's promise to create a trust in their favour, then equity will compel the settlor to constitute the trust. However, if they are volunteers the rule that 'equity will not assist a volunteer' operates to prevent them compelling the settlor to constitute the trust.

(i) Beneficiaries of an incompletely constituted trust who have given valuable consideration

Where the potential beneficiaries have given valuable consideration, equity will come to their assistance and compel the settlor to constitute the trust.[132] Equity does not take the same view of consideration as the common law and will not enforce a promise made in return for merely nominal consideration. Instead, equity requires 'valuable consideration'. 'Valuable consideration' is a technical term requiring either 'money or money's worth'[133] or marriage consideration.[134] As well as excluding nominal consideration, it also excludes a deed (a covenant) which is enforceable at common law by the covenantee even where no consideration at all has been provided. The ability of equity to compel the creation of trusts which are not completely constituted on behalf of those who have provided valuable consideration can be illustrated from the context of marriage settlements. In *Pullan v Koe*,[135] a wife covenanted to settle after-acquired property of a value greater than £100 on the trusts established under her marriage settlement. She subsequently received a gift of £285 from her mother, which she failed to transfer to the trustees and which was instead invested in bonds. On the death of her husband, the bonds were in the possession of his executors. Swinfen Eady J held that the trustees were entitled to enforce the trust on behalf of her children because they were within the scope of the marriage consideration and not mere volunteers. (It may be a surprising concept nowadays, but it is well accepted that a contract made in expectation of marriage can be enforced by the parties to the marriage and any of their

---

132 See *Donaldson v Donaldson* (1854) Kay 711; *Lee v Lee* (1876) 4 Ch D 175.

133 If value was given, it is irrelevant whether the consideration was adequate: *Bassett v Nosworthy* (1673) Cas temp Finch 102.

134 Marriage consideration exists where gifts are made in contemplation of, or at the time of, marriage of the potential beneficiaries. Only the husband, wife, and direct issue (children) of the marriage are within the marriage consideration: *De Mestre v West* [1891] AC 264; *A-G v Jacobs-Smith* [1895] 2 QB 341, CA; *Rennell v IRC* [1962] Ch 329; *Re Cook's Settlement's Trusts* [1965] Ch 902.

135 [1913] 1 Ch 9.

children.) The bonds were held on the terms of the marriage settlement, even though they had not been transferred to the trustees.

(ii) Volunteer beneficiaries of an incompletely constituted trust

In contrast, where the beneficiaries of an incompletely constituted trust are volunteers who have provided no valuable consideration in return for the settlor's promise to create a trust, equity will not compel the constitution of the trust.[136] This is an application of a more general principle that equity will not act to complete an imperfect gift, which was explained by Page-Wood V-C in *Donaldson v Donaldson*:

[Where there is an imperfect gift] which requires some other act to complete it on the part of the assignor or donor, the court will not interfere to require anything else to be done by him.[137]

This limitation prevented the enforcement of a trust in *Re Plumptre's Marriage Settlement*,[138] which, like *Pullan v Koe* above, also concerned a wife's covenant in her marriage settlement to transfer any after-acquired property to the trustees. She was subsequently given certain stocks by her husband, but they were never transferred to the trustees of the marriage settlement. On her death her next of kin sought to enforce the trust. It was held that they were unable to do so because they were outside of the scope of the marriage consideration and volunteers in equity. The stocks therefore remained free of the marriage settlement trusts and formed part of her estate. Similarly, in *Re Cooks' Settlement Trusts*,[139] it was held that volunteer beneficiaries were not entitled to enforce a settlor's promise to create a trust, even though other beneficiaries had given consideration. Sir Francis Cook executed a covenant that he would settle the proceeds of sale of any picture he had received from his father, and which he sold in his lifetime, on trust for members of his family. The beneficiaries provided no consideration for this covenant. During his lifetime he gave Rembrandt's 'Titus' to his wife, which she wished to sell. The trustees sought the opinion of the court as to the steps they should take if the picture was sold and the proceeds were not paid over to them. Buckley J held that since the potential beneficiaries were volunteers, equity would not enforce the trust if it was not completely constituted by the promised transfer of the proceeds of sale.[140]

(iii) Volunteer beneficiaries of an incompletely constituted trust who are able to obtain specific performance of a contract to create a trust

Where a settlor has entered a contract with a third party promising to settle specified property on trust for beneficiaries, the potential beneficiaries will generally be unable

---

[136] See *Jefferys v Jefferys* (1841) Cr & Ph 138; *Dening v Ware* (1856) 22 Beav 184; *Re D'Angibau* (1880) LR 15 Ch D 228; *Harding v Harding* (1886) 17 QBD 442; *Re Earl of Lucan* (1890) 45 Ch D 470.

[137] (1854) Kay 711, at 718.   [138] [1910] 1 Ch 609.

[139] [1965] Ch 902.

[140] The abrogation of the doctrine of privity of contract by the Contracts (Rights of Third Parties) Act 1999 would enable the beneficiaries to obtain common law damages for breach of contract in such a situation, but does not enable them to obtain specific performance. This is discussed more fully below, at p 221.

to obtain specific performance because they are volunteers. However, in exceptional circumstances, the potential beneficiaries might be able to stand in the position of the third party to whom the contractual promise was made and obtain specific performance to enforce the trust. In *Beswick v Beswick*,[141] Peter Beswick contracted to transfer his business to his nephew, John, in return for his promise to pay an annuity of £5 per week to his wife. The business was transferred, but after Peter died John refused to pay the annuity. The House of Lords held that Mrs Beswick, although a volunteer who was not privy to the contract, was entitled to an order of specific performance to compel the nephew to pay the annuity. She was not, however, entitled to this remedy in her own right, but rather because she stood in the shoes of her husband as she was the administrator of his estate. It was therefore as if Peter Beswick himself were seeking the remedy. *Beswick v Beswick* did not in fact involve a trust, but if the nephew had agreed to settle property on Mrs Beswick, as administratrix, she would have been similarly able to obtain an order of specific performance, enforcing the trust. Her status as administratrix meant she was able to obtain indirectly what she was not entitled to obtain directly.

(7) Exceptions to the rule that 'equity will not assist a volunteer'

(a) Importance of the exceptions

In limited circumstances equity is prepared to assist a volunteer transferee of property where a transferor has failed effectively to transfer the legal title to him. These exceptions to the rule that 'equity will not assist a volunteer' operate whether the ineffective transfer was intended as an absolute gift or whether the property was intended to be held by the transferee on trust for third party beneficiaries. If the transferee was intended to hold the property as trustee, the effect of equity compelling the perfection of the imperfect transfer is to constitute the trust.

(b) The rule in *Strong v Bird*[142]

If a donor makes an imperfect gift during his lifetime, so that the donee does not receive the legal title to the property, the rule in *Strong v Bird* operates to perfect the gift if the donee is appointed the donor's executor, or becomes his administrator on intestacy. The gift is perfected because the donee receives legal title to all the donor's property in his capacity as executor or administrator, including the property that was the intended subject matter of the gift. This has the effect of completing the imperfect transfer, by vesting the necessary legal title in the trustee.[143] *Strong v Bird*[144] concerned an incomplete release of a debt. Strong had borrowed £1,100 from his step-mother, who lived in his house and paid board to him. It was initially agreed that he would repay the sum to her by means of a deduction of £100 from the board she paid quarterly. After

---

[141] [1968] AC 58.
[142] (1874) LR 18 Eq 315; Kodilinye, 'A Fresh Look at the Rule in *Strong v Bird*' [1982] Conv 14.
[143] See *Re Ralli's Will Trusts* [1964] Ch 288.   [144] (1874) LR 18 Eq 315.

two quarters where the deduction was made, she told him that she did not want the money returned and reverted to paying full board. This was not effective as a release of the debt at common law, which required a deed, and Strong had not provided any consideration for the release. Four years later, the step-mother died. Strong was appointed sole executor in her will. The court held that his appointment operated to perfect the imperfect release of the debt, so that Strong was not liable to repay the loan to the estate. The principle was stated by Jessel MR:

it appears to me that there being a continuing intention to give, and there being a legal act which transferred the ownership or released the obligation—for it is the same thing—the transaction is perfected, and he does not want the aid of a court of equity to carry it out, or to make it complete, because it is complete already, and there is no equity against him to take the property away from him.[145]

This principle was subsequently applied in *Re James*.[146] Sarah James had been the housekeeper of James for some nineteen years. Although she received no payment, he told her that his house and furniture were to be hers on his death. When he died his son John inherited the property and gave Sarah the title deeds of the house, where she continued to live with her husband. John later died intestate and Sarah was granted letters of administration. Farwell J held that this had the effect of perfecting the gift of the house, which was imperfect because there had been no conveyance to her. He held that:

by her appointment as one of the administratrixes she got the legal estate vested in her...she needs no assistance from equity to complete her title.[147]

A number of conditions must be satisfied before the rule in *Strong v Bird* will operate to perfect an imperfect gift—these are considered in the following sections.

(i) The donor must have intended to make an inter vivos gift

The rule will only apply if an immediate inter vivos gift of the property had been intended by the donor, which failed because the transfer was ineffective given the nature of the property. The rule has no application where the donor intended to make a gift which would only take effect on his death.

(ii) The donor's intention to make the gift must have continued until his death

The rule will only operate if the donor who had failed to make an effective gift of the property had a 'continuing intention' to make the gift at the time of his death. This was emphasized in *Strong v Bird*[148] and also in *Re James*,[149] where Farwell J concluded that he was 'completely satisfied that there was a continuing intention in the donor up to the time of his death to give the property to the defendant'.[150] In contrast, in *Re Gonin*[151] it

---

[145] Ibid., at 319.   [146] [1935] Ch 449.   [147] Ibid., at 451.

[148] (1874) Lr 18 Eq 315.   [149] [1935] Ch 449.

[150] See also *Re Freeland* [1952] Ch 110; *Re Wale* [1956] 1 WLR 1346; *Choithram (T) International SA v Pagarani* [2001] 2 All ER 492.

[151] [1979] Ch 16; (1977) 93 LQR 488.

was held that the donor had no continuing intention, and the rule could not operate. The plaintiff, Lucy Gonin, had returned home in 1944 to look after her parents. They promised that in return she should have their house when they died. Because Lucy had been born illegitimate, her mother mistakenly believed that she could not leave the property to her by will. In 1962 she drew a cheque for £33,000 in Lucy's favour, which she left in an envelope that was discovered after her death. Lucy claimed that in these circumstances the imperfect gift of the house was perfected when she was granted letters of administration over her mother's estate. Walton J held that the rule in *Strong v Bird* could not apply because her mother had not had a continuing intention to make a gift of the house at the time of her death:

so far as the land is concerned no such continuing intention can be found...I think that the intention changed by the latest in 1962 when the deceased drew her cheque in favour of her daughter. I find it impossible to think that from then on what she really had in mind was anything other than that the plaintiff would inherit the cheque on the deceased's death—no immediate gift, and no gift of land.[152]

(iii) The donee must have been appointed an executor or granted letters of administration

The perfection of an imperfect gift by the rule in *Strong v Bird* is only effected by the vesting of the legal title to the intended subject matter in the donee in his capacity as the executor or administrator of the donor. It is irrelevant whether the donee is a sole executor, or one of several joint executors.[153] Some doubts were expressed in *Re Gonin*[154] as to whether the rule should apply to administrators, because 'it is often a matter of pure chance which of many persons equally entitled to a grant of letters of administration finally takes them out'.[155] However, Walton J was unwilling to determine the issue and noted that the rule was applied to an administrator in *Re James*,[156] which had been cited without dissent by Buckley J in *Re Ralli's Will Trusts*.[157]

(iv) The intended subject matter of the gift must have been capable of enduring the death of the donor

Most property, whether tangible or intangible, is capable of enduring past the death of its owner. However, a cheque which has not been endorsed by the payee constitutes nothing more than a revocable mandate of the customer on whose account it was drawn, to his bank, requesting them as his agents to make payment to the payee. On the death of the customer, this mandate is automatically terminated. It follows that a cheque which remains uncashed at the date of death of the drawer will be incapable of passing title to the money instructed to be transferred, even if the payee is appointed the executor or administrator of the estate. Thus, in *Re Gonin*[158] the daughter had no entitlement to the £33,000 cheque her mother had left for her. If, however, a cheque is

---

152 [1979] Ch 16, at 35.
153 *Re Stewart* [1908] 2 Ch 251.
154 [1979] Ch 16.
155 Ibid., at 35.
156 [1935] Ch 449.
157 [1964] Ch 288, at 301.
158 [1979] Ch 16.

endorsed by its payee, it becomes a negotiable instrument and is a species of property capable of enduring despite the death of the drawer.

Although the rule in *Strong v Bird*[159] is commonly cited as an example of an exception to the rule that equity will not assist a volunteer, it is questionable whether this is genuinely the case. Instead, like the principles identified in *Re Rose*[160] and *Re Ralli's Will Trusts*,[161] it may be viewed as an example of widened circumstances in which equity is willing to find that a transfer has in fact been completed.

(c) Donatio mortis causa (gift on account of death)

The donatio mortis causa (sometimes referred to as a 'deathbed' gift) provides a genuine exception to the principle that equity will not assist a volunteer. It operates where an owner wants to make a gift of property to the donee that is only intended to take effect if he dies. If, in such circumstances, the donor failed to make an effective transfer of the property to the donee during his lifetime, equity will act to compel his executors, or administrators, to perfect the donee's imperfect title. It does not matter that the donee is a volunteer. If the donee was intended to receive the property as a trustee, the operation of the donatio mortis causa will have the effect of constituting the trust.

In its simplest form, a donatio mortis causa is merely a gift which is conditional upon death. Where the intended subject matter of a gift is personal property, a straightforward gift (such as a birthday present) is normally made by handing the property to the recipient with the intention to make a gift. The intention will normally be unconditional. However, it is possible for the intention to be subject to some condition being satisfied. For instance, a doting father might lend a car to his daughter, telling the daughter that she can keep it if she passes her examinations. If the daughter does pass, then the gift is completed. Where the condition which has to be satisfied is the death of the donor, the gift could be described as a donatio mortis causa. In extended forms of the donatio mortis causa the gift may go beyond the simple characteristics of such a conditional gift, as will be seen from the cases described below.

The essential conditions of a valid donatio mortis causa were stated by Lord Russell CJ in *Cain v Moon*:[162]

(i) 'The gift or donation must have been made in contemplation, though not necessarily in expectation of death'

The special treatment granted to the donee of a donatio mortis causa is only warranted because of the unique circumstances in which the gift was made. Only if the donee made the gift in contemplation of death can a valid donatio occur. This requires something more specific than a realization of the general truth that we are all going to

---

[159] (1874) LR 18 Eq 315.   [160] [1952] Ch 499.   [161] [1964] Ch 288.
[162] [1896] 2 QB 283. See also *Re Johnson* (1905) 92 LT 357, per Farwell J; *Re Craven's Estate (No 1)* [1937] Ch 423, per Farwell J; *Delgoffe v Fader* [1939] Ch 922, per Luxmore LJ; *Birch v Treasury Solicitor* [1951] Ch 298.

die eventually. As Hale J said in the Australian case, *Smallacombe v Elder's Trustee & Executor Co Ltd*:

the donor must have been contemplating a comparatively early death from some cause or other, whether it be an existing illness, a dangerous journey[163] or even extreme old age. While an immediate expectation of immediate death is not required, nevertheless something more is required than a mere recognition of the inevitability of death itself.[164]

Where a gift is made by a donor in contemplation of death from a specific cause, it is irrelevant if he in fact dies from different causes, and this does not prevent the validity of the donatio. In *Wilkes v Allington*[165] the donor was diagnosed as suffering from cancer in 1922. Although he continued to farm, he considered himself under a sentence of death. He therefore made several incomplete gifts to his nieces. In January 1928, after coming home in a bus from Worcester market, he caught a chill and died of pneumonia. Lord Tomlin held that there was a valid donatio, even though the precise cause of death was different to the contemplated cause.

It seems that a gift made in contemplation of suicide will not operate as a valid donatio mortis causa.[166] However, the Irish case *Mills v Shields*[167] held that a gift in contemplation of death by natural causes was a valid donatio even if the donor subsequently committed suicide.

(ii) 'There must have been delivery to the donee of the subject matter of the gift'

An imperfect inter vivos gift will only be perfected as a donatio mortis causa if the donor had delivered the property intended to be the subject matter of the gift to the donee before his death.[168] The requirement is delivery, not a transfer of title, so any formalities necessary validly to transfer title to the property in question are not necessary. In the case of chattels, delivery can usually be achieved by handing physical possession of the property to the donee.[169] However, by way of one extension of the simple concept of a conditional gift, it will also be sufficient if the donor hands the donee 'dominion' over the property by granting him the means to control it. Such dominion would have been given, for example, if the property had been kept in a locked box and the donor had handed the key to the donee.[170] In *Re Lillingston*,[171] the donor gave the donee the key to a trunk, which contained the key to a safe deposit at Harrods, which in turn contained the key to a safe deposit at the National Safe Deposit and Trustee Co. It was held that there was a valid donatio mortis causa of jewellery in the trunk and the contents of the two safe deposit

---

[163] See *Thompson v Mechan* [1958] OR 357: the ordinary risks of air travel are not sufficient for a valid donatio.

[164] [1963] WAR 3, at 4–5.   [165] [1931] 2 Ch 104.

[166] *Agnew v Belfast Banking Co* [1896] 2 IR 204, CA; *Re Dudman* [1925] Ch 553. This is because the act of suicide is an illegal act,

[167] [1948] IR 367.   [168] *Ward v Turner* (1752) 2 Ves Sen 431.

[169] *Miller v Miller* (1735) 3 P Wms 356.

[170] See *Re Wasserberg* [1915] 1 Ch 195; *Re Cole (A Bankrupt)* [1964] Ch 175; *Sen v Headley* [1991] Ch 425, CA.

[171] [1952] 2 All ER 184.

boxes. In *Woodard v Woodard*,[172] the Court of Appeal held that there was a valid donatio of a car where the donor had given the donee a set of keys, since these constituted sufficient dominion.

When the intended subject matter of the gift is land or intangible property it is impossible for the donor to physically deliver it to the donee, or grant him dominion over it. Here, the prerequisite of a valid donatio is that the donor delivered the 'essential indicia or evidence of title'[173] to the donee, or gave him dominion over such indicia. For money held in a bank deposit account,[174] post office saving account,[175] or national saving certificates,[176] the relevant pass-book or certificates are the necessary indicia. In *Sen v Headley*,[177] the Court of Appeal held that in the case of unregistered land the deeds were the essential indicia of title, and that the passing of dominion over the deeds effected a valid donatio mortis causa of the land. Presumably, the 'land certificate' would be sufficient indicia of title of registered land. In respect of shares in a public company, *Staniland v Willott*[178] suggests that handing the donee an executed share transfer form is sufficient for a valid donatio of the shares, even though the formal transfer of such rights requires the appropriate form of assignment. It is unclear whether mere delivery of a share certificate will suffice, although Australian authority suggests that it will,[179] as does reasoning by analogy from *Sen v Healey*.

A second extension to the concept of the simple conditional gift is that where there is a valid donatio mortis causa of property such as land, or money in a deposit account, where the transfer of dominion is purely symbolic, equity will intervene to compel the personal representatives of the deceased's estate to do whatever is necessary to complete the formal transfer of the property.

(iii) 'The gift must be made under such circumstances as show that the thing is to revert to the donor in case he should recover'

There will be no valid donatio unless the donor only intended the gift to take effect in the event of his death. Otherwise, the gift is simply an ineffective inter vivos transfer. Thus, there will be no effective donatio mortis causa if the donor intended the donee to have the property at all events. As Wynn-Parry J said in *Re Lillingston*:

The gift should be conditional, ie, on the terms that, if the donor should not die, he should be entitled to resume complete dominion of the property the subject matter of the gift.[180]

---

[172] [1991] Fam Law 470.   [173] *Birch v Treasury Solicitor* [1951] Ch 298, CA.

[174] *Re Dillon* (1890) 44 Ch D 76; *Birch v Treasury Solicitor* [1951] Ch 298.

[175] *Re Thompson's Estate* [1928] IR 606; *Re Weston* [1902] 1 Ch 680.

[176] *Darlow v Sparks* [1938] 2 All ER 235.   [177] [1991] Ch 425.

[178] (1852) 3 Mac & G 664.

[179] *Duffcy v Mollica* [1968] 3 NSWR 751. Compare the Irish case of *Mills v Shields (No 2)* [1950] IR 21, where Gavan Duffy P held that delivery of share certificates was not sufficient to constitute a valid donatio of the shares.

[180] [1952] 2 All ER 184, at 187.

A donatio will not be invalid merely because the donor knows that he will not recover, and in such cases the intention to make a revocable gift is implied.[181] Where the donatio has been made in contemplation of death from an illness, the gift is automatically revoked by the donor's recovery.[182] The donor may also revoke the gift at any time during his lifetime, for example by retaking dominion over the property,[183] or giving the donee notice of revocation.[184] However, he cannot revoke the gift by will, since his death completes the gift.[185]

A fourth requirement may be added to the three set out by Lord Russell:[186]

(iv) The property must be capable of forming the subject matter of a donatio mortis causa

Even if the preceding three conditions are satisfied, it has been held that some types of property are not capable of forming the subject matter of a valid donatio mortis causa. A cheque payable to the donor is capable of forming the subject matter of a donatio,[187] but a cheque written by the donor cannot,[188] because it is merely a revocable mandate to his bank which automatically terminates on death. Similarly, the donor's promissory note is incapable of forming the subject matter of a donatio.[189] A conflict of authorities renders it unclear whether shares are capable of forming the subject matter of a donatio. Some cases adopt the view that shares cannot be the subject of a valid donatio,[190] but in *Staniland v Willott*[191] it was held that there could be a valid donatio of shares in a public company. There seems to be no reason in logic or principle why shares should not be able to form the subject matter of a donatio mortis causa.[192]

Following dicta of Lord Eldon in *Duffield v Elwes*,[193] land was traditionally regarded as incapable of forming the subject matter of a valid donatio mortis causa because it was not thought possible to grant dominion to the donee. In *Sen v Headley*,[194] the Court of Appeal held that it was possible to part with dominion over the essential indicia of title of unregistered land, namely the title deeds, and that to refuse to permit a

[181] *Wilkes v Allington* [1931] 2 Ch 104; see also *Sen v Headley* [1991] Ch 425, where the gift was made by the donor two days after he had been readmitted to hospital, when he knew he did not have long to live and when there could have been no practical possibility of his ever returning home.

[182] *Gardner v Parker* (1818) 3 Madd 184; *Staniland v Willott* (1852) 3 Mac & G 664; *Keys v Hore* (1879) 13 ILT 58.

[183] *Bunn v Markham* (1816) 7 Taunt 224; *Staniland v Willott* (1852) 3 Mac & G 664.

[184] *Bunn v Markham* (1816) 7 Taunt 224.

[185] *Jones v Selby* (1710) Prec Ch 300; White and Tudor, *Leading Cases in Equity* (7th edn, 1897) Vol 1, p 403.

[186] *Cain v Moon* [1896] 2 QB 283.

[187] *Re Mead* (1880) LR 15 Ch D 651; *Re Mulroy* [1924] 1 IR 98.

[188] *Re Beaumont* [1902] 1 Ch 886.   [189] *Re Leaper* [1916] 1 Ch 579.

[190] *Ward v Turner* (1752) 2 Ves Sen 431 (South Sea annuities); *Moore v Moore* (1874) LR 18 Eq 474 (railway stock); *Re Weston* [1902] 1 Ch 680 (building society shares).

[191] (1852) 3 Mac & G 664.

[192] See Samuels 'Donatio Mortis Causa of a Share Certificate' (1966) 30 Conv 189.

[193] (1823) 1 Sim & St 239. See also *Wilkes v Allington* [1931] 2 Ch 104.

[194] [1991] Ch 425; [1991] Conv 307 (Halliwell); (1991) 50 CLJ 404 (Thornely); All ER Rev 1991, p 207 (Clarke); (1991) 1 Carib LR 100 (Kodilinye); (1993) 109 LQR 19 (Baker).

valid donatio of land would create an anomalous exception.[195] Mrs Sen had lived with Mr Hewitt for ten years and had remained very close to him after this. When he was dying he told her that his house, title to which was unregistered, was hers, and he gave her the keys to a steel box which contained the deeds. It was held that in these circumstances a valid donatio had been made in her favour, and she was therefore entitled to compel the administrator of his estate to transfer the legal title of the house into her name. Although the case concerned unregistered land, where title is constituted by the title deeds, there seems no reason why the same principle should not apply to registered land where a land certificate has been issued, particularly as the object of the court was to avoid anomalous exceptions. Although the land certificate to registered land is only evidence of title,[196] it is sometimes treated as the equivalent of the title deeds to unregistered land.[197] However, it is no longer the practice to issue a land certificate, and this will therefore have the effect of preventing a donatio mortis causa of registered land.

(8) Common law remedies which may be available to the beneficiary of an incompletely constituted trust

(a) Significance of common law remedies

If a volunteer is unable to get help from equity to enforce the settlor's promise to create a trust, he may instead be entitled to sue the settlor at common law and recover compensatory damages for the failure to constitute the trust. Where damages at common law are available, the measure recoverable will be the quantum of loss suffered in consequence of the settlor's failure to constitute the trust, which will generally be the value of the promised trust property. Historically, the possibility of obtaining common law damages arose because equity and the common law treated the concept of consideration differently. At common law, a promise to create a trust would be enforceable if it was contained in a covenant (ie a deed)[198] or was accompanied by even nominal consideration. In neither instance would equity treat the agreement as enforceable. Such a contract or covenant might have been entered between the settlor and the intended beneficiaries, or between the settlor and the intended trustees. The ability of volunteer beneficiaries to obtain a remedy at common law has recently been significantly widened by the Contracts (Rights of Third Parties) Act 1999, which has had the effect of abrogating the doctrine of privity of contract. This will prove especially significant where a settlor has covenanted or contracted to create a trust with the intended trustees but not the beneficiaries. The new regime applies to contracts entered into on or after 11 May 2000.[199]

---

195   [1991] Ch 425, at 440, per Nourse LJ.
196   Land Registration Act 2002, Sch 10, para 4.
197   See, for example. Land Registration Act 1925, s 66; *Thames Guaranty Ltd v Campbell* [1985] QB 210, at 233; Jackson, Stevens and Pearce, *Land Law* (4th edn, 2008), p 579.
198   See Law of Property (Miscellaneous Provisions) Act 1989, s 1.
199   Contracts (Rights of Third Parties Act) 1999, s 10(2).

It is important to realize that the beneficiaries' entitlement to claim damages at common law is not a means by which they can constitute the trust, thus circumventing the rule that equity will not assist a volunteer. Any damages recovered are compensation for the fact that no trust was ever created in their favour, and they will receive such damages absolutely and free from any trust. By contrast, where a beneficiary who has given consideration recognized by equity brings a suit, the remedy will normally be to compel the constitution of the trust which will, of course, also work to the advantage of the beneficiaries who have provided no consideration. Whether beneficiaries are in fact able to recover damages for the settlor's breach of covenant will depend on the circumstances of the case.

(b) Common law compensation on or after 11 May 2000

(i) Settlor covenanted or contracted with the beneficiary to create a trust

Where a settlor has entered into a covenant to create a trust with the intended beneficiary, or has entered into a contract with the beneficiary for nominal consideration, the beneficiary will be entitled to sue to recover damages at common law if he fails to fulfil his promise to constitute the trust. As the intended beneficiary is a party to the covenant or contract, there is no difficulty of privity. Such situations will be rare, as most settlors do not enter into contracts with beneficiaries to create trusts.

(ii) Settlor covenanted or contracted with the trustee to create a trust

The Contracts (Rights of Third Parties) Act 1999, s 1(1) provides that a third party is entitled to enforce a term of a contract if it expressly provides that he may, or if it purports to confer a benefit on him. Where a settlor enters into a covenant[200] or contract to create a trust with the intended trustee, the beneficiary will be entitled to sue to recover damages at common law if he fails to fulfil his promise, unless the contract made clear that it was not intended to be enforceable by him.[201] Although s 1(5) provides that a third party is entitled to obtain any remedy that would have been available to him in an action for breach of contract if he had been a party to the contract, the better view appears to be that this does not mean that the beneficiary can obtain specific performance, as the rule that equity will not assist a volunteer has not been abrogated.[202]

(c) Common law compensation where the settlor covenanted to create a trust before 11 May 2000

The Contracts (Rights of Third Parties) Act 1999 does not apply to covenants granted prior to 11 May 2000. The rights of the beneficiaries to enforce such a covenant will continue to be determined by the traditional rules.

---

[200] S 7(3).   [201] S 1(2).

[202] Hanbury and Martin, *Modern Equity* (18th edn, 2009), p 762. See also Andrews 'Strangers to Justice No Longer: The Reversal of the Privity Rule under the Contracts (Rights of Third Parties) Act 1999' (2001) 60 CLJ 353.

(i) Beneficiary was a party to the settlor's covenant to create a trust

If a beneficiary is a party to a settlor's covenant to create a trust in his favour, it is clear from *Cannon v Hartley*[203] that he can recover damages for breach of covenant against the settlor if the latter subsequently fails to constitute the trust. Bernard Hartley executed a covenant on his separation from his wife, to which his wife and daughter were parties. He agreed that he would settle any money or property worth more than £1,000 which he subsequently received on the death of his parents on trust for his daughter. When his parents died, he received a substantial amount of money but refused to transfer it to trustees. Romer J held that although the daughter was a volunteer, and therefore unable to enforce the incompletely constituted trust in equity, she was entitled to receive damages for breach of covenant:

The plaintiff, although a volunteer, is not only a party to the deed of separation but is also a direct covenantee under the very covenant upon which she is suing. She does not require the assistance of the court to enforce the covenant for she has a legal right herself to enforce it. She is not asking for equitable relief but for damages at common law for breach of covenant.[204]

(ii) Common law compensation where the trustee was party to the settlor's covenant to create a trust

The proposed beneficiary's position is much less certain if the intended trustee of the settlement was a party to the settlor's covenant to create a trust, but he himself was not. The beneficiary cannot sue the settlor for breach in his own right, as he has no privity of contract to do so. Unless the intended trustees hold the benefit of the covenant on trust for him[205] he similarly cannot compel them to bring an action for breach against the settlor. The central question in these cases is whether the intended trustee is able to sue the settlor if he so wishes and, if so, as to the quantum of damages recoverable.

It is well established that where a trustee who is party to the settlor's covenant seeks the court's direction whether he should sue, he will be directed not to take proceedings to enforce the covenant. In *Re Pryce*,[206] Eve J directed the trustees of a marriage settlement to take no proceedings to enforce a covenant to settle after-acquired property. In *Re Kay's Settlement Trusts*,[207] Simonds J followed the decision in *Re Pryce* and held that where a spinster had failed to perform her voluntary covenant to settle after-acquired property, the trustees should be directed not to take any proceedings to enforce the covenant by an action for damages for breach. These authorities were approved in *Re Cook's Settlement Trusts*,[208] where Buckley J held that volunteer beneficiaries could not compel the trustees to sue on the settlor's covenant to settle the proceeds of sale of certain paintings, even though other beneficiaries had given consideration. The rationale underlying these decisions is that to allow trustees to recover under the settlor's deed at common law would indirectly assist volunteers who are not entitled to the direct assistance of the court in equity.[209]

---

[203] [1949] Ch 213.   [204] Ibid., at 223.   [205] See below, pp 223 *et seq.*
[206] [1917] 1 Ch 234.   [207] [1939] Ch 329.   [208] [1965] Ch 902.
[209] See *Re Pryce* [1917] 1 Ch 234, at 241, per Eve J.

If an intended trustee were to decide to sue the settlor on their own initiative, rather than asking the court for a direction, it is debatable whether they would be entitled to recover substantial damages. One view, supported by the Canadian decision of *Re Cavendish Browne's Settlement Trusts*,[210] is that the trustee in such circumstances should be entitled to recover damages equivalent to the value of the property that was to be settled on trust, and hold those damages on trust for the beneficiaries.[211] The case concerned a covenant entered into with the intended trustees to settle land on beneficiaries who were volunteers, and the court held that the trustees were entitled to damages to the value of the land, to be held on trust for the intended beneficiaries.[212]

In the English cases, it has been argued that, as a matter of principle, a covenantee is only entitled to recover damages as compensation for his own personal loss[213] resulting from breach of the covenant to which he was a party. It follows that, as a trustee derives no personal gain from a trust, the personal loss suffered is minimal, so the intended trustee would be entitled to recover only nominal damages from the settlor. Furthermore, even if a trustee were held entitled to recover substantial damages, it has been suggested that he should hold them on a resulting trust for the settlor, rather than for the volunteer beneficiaries.[214] It is suggested that it would be a brave trustee who decided to sue on their own initiative, knowing that the English court would not direct such an action if asked. This perhaps explains why the questions over the action remain unanswered.

(iii) Common law compensation where the trustees hold the benefit of the settlor's covenant on trust for the beneficiary

It is accepted that beneficiaries who are not party to the settlor's covenant to settle cannot compel trustees who are parties to take proceedings. However, if the trustees can be shown to hold the 'benefit of the covenant' on trust for the beneficiaries, they can sue in their own right as the beneficiaries of a completely constituted trust of the covenant, and the trustees can either join their action as co-plaintiffs or be joined as co-defendants. Such a trust of the benefit of the covenant is possible because a covenant is a 'chose in action', which is a form of intangible property. Given that it is property, it is capable of forming the subject matter of a trust. It can be held on a completely constituted trust, as no particular formalities are required to vest title to a chose in action in the trustees and beneficiaries. The possibility of a trust of the benefit of a covenant therefore provides a clever device to avoid the restrictive implications of

---

[210] [1916] WN 341; (1979) 32 CLP 1 (Rickett).

[211] See (1960) 76 LQR 100 (Elliott); (1975) 91 LQR 236 (Barton); [1982] Conv 280 (Friend); [1988] Conv 18 (Goddard).

[212] However, *Re Cavendish Browne's Settlement Trusts* is distinguishable from *Re Pryce, Re Kay* and *Re Cook* as it involved a covenant to settle identified specific property rather than after-acquired property.

[213] *Woodar Investment Developments Ltd v Wimpey Construction UK Ltd* [1980] 1 WLR 277; *Panatown Ltd v Alfred McAlpine Construction Ltd* [2000] 4 All ER 97.

[214] Lee 'Public Policy of *Re Cook's Settlement Trusts*' (1969) 85 LQR 213.

the privity doctrine, which prevents an intended beneficiary suing in his own right. This type of situation is sometimes referred to as the trust of a promise.

The concept of a 'trust of the benefit of a covenant', which enables a beneficiary to enforce a settlor's covenant with the trustees, was accepted by Wigram V-C in the mid-nineteenth-century case, *Fletcher v Fletcher*:

One question made in argument has been whether there can be a trust of a covenant the benefit of which shall belong to a third party; but I cannot think there is any difficulty in that... The proposition, therefore, that in no case can there be a trust of a covenant is clearly too large, and the real question is whether the relation of trustee and [beneficiary] is established in the present case.[215]

Ellis Fletcher had executed a voluntary covenant to settle £60,000 on trust for his illegitimate sons, John and Jacob, if they survived him. He retained the deed and did not make known its existence either to the trustees with whom it was made or to his sons. The deed was found among his papers after his death. Jacob, who had survived his father and attained the age of 21, sued the executors of his father's estate for £60,000. Wigram V-C held that although Jacob was not a party to the deed himself he was entitled to recover the £60,000 from the executors because the trustees held the benefit of the covenant on trust for him. The legitimacy of the concept of a 'trust of a promise' has been confirmed by the courts in a large number of cases;[216] including *Don King Productions v Warren*,[217] where Lightman J cited the dicta of Lord Shaw in *Lord Strathcona Steamship Co Ltd v Dominion Coal Co Ltd*:

The scope of the trusts recognized in equity is unlimited. There can be a trust of a chattel, or of a right or obligation under an ordinary legal contract, just as much as a trust of land.[218]

However, while *Fletcher v Fletcher*[219] clearly establishes that the benefit of a covenant may form the subject matter of a trust, such trusts are not commonplace. There is great difficulty is establishing that such a trust has come into existence. There is a marked reluctance to find that such trusts have been created because they are capable of undermining the doctrine of privity of contract. *Fletcher v Fletcher* is open to criticism in that there was no evidence on the facts of an intention to create a trust of the benefit of the covenant. There was no evidence that Fletcher intended to create such a trust, and the trustees and beneficiaries were unaware of the existence of the covenant. How could the trustees be said to be holding the benefit of a covenant, the existence of which they were unaware of, on trust for beneficiaries for whom they did not know they were trustees? In more recent cases the courts have held that a trust of a covenant will only be created by clear express intention. In *Vandepitte v Preferred Accident Insurance Corpn of New York*,[220] the Privy Council held that to

---

[215] (1844) 4 Hare 67.
[216] See *Lloyd's v Harper* (1880) 16 Ch D 290, CA; *Vandepitte v Preferred Accident Assurance Corpn of New York* [1933] AC 70, PC; *Re Schebsman (Decd)* [1944] Ch 83, CA; *Re Cook's Settlement Trusts* [1965] Ch 902; *Swain v Law Society* [1983] 1 AC 598, HL.
[217] [1998] 2 All ER 608.   [218] [1926] AC 108, at 124.
[219] (1844) 4 Hare 67.   [220] [1933] AC 70.

establish a trust of the benefit of an insurance contract 'the intention to constitute the trust must be affirmatively proved', and that such an intention could not necessarily be inferred from the words of the policy. There was therefore no intention that the policy holder had any intention to create a trust in favour of the plaintiff. Similarly, in *Re Schebsman*[221] Lord Greene MR held that it was 'not legitimate to import into the contract the idea of a trust when the parties have given no indication that such was their intention'.[222] These cases suggest that a trust of the benefit of a promise will not be implied merely from the fact that a promise has been made between two parties for the benefit of a third. Such a trust will only arise if there is clear evidence of an intention on the part of the parties to the promise to create such a trust.[223] It clearly cannot arise if the contract contains a term prohibiting such a declaration.[224]

One further anomalous restriction on the scope of the concept of a trust of the benefit of a covenant is that it has been held that a covenant to settle future property is incapable of forming the subject matter of a trust. In *Re Cook's Settlement Trusts*[225] Sir Francis Cook covenanted to settle the proceeds of sale of certain pictures sold during his lifetime. This covenant did not create a property right that would have been capable of being the subject matter of an immediate trust, so Buckley J held that no trust of the covenant could have been created:

> this covenant upon its true construction is...an executory contract to settle a particular fund or particular funds of money which at the date of the covenant did not exist and which might never come into existence. It is analogous to a covenant to settle an expectation or to settle after-acquired property. The case, in my judgment, involves the law of contract, not the law of trusts.[226]

This limitation has been severely criticized,[227] since although the covenant concerns future property, which could not itself form the subject matter of a trust,[228] it is no less a valid chose in action than a covenant to settle existing property. The promise itself is the subject matter of a trust of the benefit of a covenant, not the property to which the promise relates.

The mechanism of a trust of a promise may become of increasingly marginal utility given the requirement of a clearly demonstrated intention to create a trust, which is not something a settlor is often likely to do, and the impact of the enactment of the Contracts (Rights of Third Parties) Act 1999.

---

[221] [1944] Ch 83.   [222] Ibid., at 89.
[223] *Swain v Law Society* [1983] 1 AC 598.
[224] *Don King Productions v Warren* [1998] 2 All ER 608, at 632–633.
[225] [1965] Ch 902.   [226] Ibid., at 914.
[227] (1965) 24 CLJ 46 (Jones); (1969) 85 LQR 213 (Lee); (1979) 32 CLP 1 and (1981) 34 CLP 189 (Rickett); (1982) 98 LQR 17 (Feltham); [1982] Conv 280 (Friend); [1982] Conv 352 (Smith).
[228] See above.

4 Formalities required for the creation of trusts

A valid trust may be created either by the self-declaration of the legal owner, or by the transfer of the legal title to trustees upon trust. The trust may be created either inter vivos or by will. In some circumstances, legislation requires the observance of specified formalities to create a valid or enforceable trust.

(1) Inter vivos declarations of trust

(a) Trusts of land[229]

(i) Formalities required

Section 53(1)(b) of the Law of Property Act 1925[230] provides:

a declaration of a trust respecting any land or any interest therein must be manifested and proved by some writing signed by some person who is able to declare such a trust or by his will.

Formalities are required for declarations of trusts of land to prevent the disputes and inconvenience which would result if purely oral declarations were allowed. In essence s 53(1)(b) imposes an evidential safeguard. It is important to note that a purported oral declaration of a trust of land is not void, but only unenforceable.[231] The requirement of writing applies whether the trust is created by the land owner declaring himself trustee or transferring the land to trustees. It is not necessary that the actual declaration of the trust be made in writing, nor need the writing which evidences the declaration be contemporaneous with the declaration of the trust.[232] However, the written evidence must contain all the material terms of the trust, namely the beneficiaries, the trust property, and the nature of the trust.[233] Unlike the parallel provision s 53(1)(c), s 53(1)(b) will not be satisfied if the writing was signed by an agent. However, if the land is transferred subject to a trust, the transferee of the land may sign the written evidence of the declaration.[234]

(ii) The rule in Rochefoucauld v Boustead[235]

Although s 53(1)(b) renders an orally declared trust of land unenforceable in the absence of substantiating writing, this requirement is not always strictly enforced.

---

[229] Youdan 'Formalities for Trusts of Land, and the Doctrine in *Rochefoucauld v Boustead*' [1984] CLJ 306.

[230] Re-enacting the Statute of Frauds 1677, s 7.

[231] *Gardner v Rowe* (1828) 5 Russ 258; *Gissing v Gissing* [1969] 2 Ch 85, at 99; *Cowcher v Cowcher* [1972] 1 WLR 425, at 430–431; *Midland Bank plc v Dobson* [1986] 1 FLR 171, at 175.

[232] *Forster v Hale* (1798) 3 Ves 696; *Rochefoucauld v Boustead* [1897] 1 Ch 196.

[233] *Smith v Matthews* (1861) 3 De GF & J 139; *Rochefoucauld v Boustead* [1897] 1 Ch 196.

[234] *Gardner v Rowe* (1828) 5 Russ 258; *Smith v Matthews* (1861) 3 De GF & J 139.

[235] See Youdan 'Formalities for Trusts of Land, and the Doctrine in *Rochefoucauld v Boustead*' [1984] CLJ 306; McFarlane, 'Constructive Trusts Arising on a Receipt of Property *Sub Conditione*' (2004) 120 LQR 667.

The courts have held that where insistence upon writing would allow the statute to be used as 'an instrument of fraud' the trust will be enforced, irrespective of the lack of writing. A fraud arises if a person to whom land was conveyed, subject to an oral understanding that it was to be held on trust, seeks to deny the trust, and claims to be absolutely entitled to the land because the requisite formalities are lacking. In *Rochefoucauld v Boustead*[236] the Comtesse de la Rochefoucauld owned the Delmar Estates in Ceylon, subject to a mortgage of £25,000. The land was sold by the mortgagee to the defendant, who was intended to take as trustee for the Comtesse. He subsequently mortgaged the land for a further £/1,000 without her consent. The Comtesse sought a declaration that the defendant had acquired the land subject to a trust in her favour. The defendant claimed that the alleged trust had not been proved by any writing signed by him, as required by the Statute of Frauds, s 7.[237] The Court of Appeal held that, despite the lack of formalities compliant with the statutory provision, evidence other than writing signed by the defendant would be admitted to prove the trust, since otherwise the defendant would be committing a fraud against the Comtesse. The principle was stated by Lindley LJ:

the Statute of Frauds does not prevent the proof of a fraud; and it is a fraud on the part of a person to whom land is conveyed as a trustee, and who knows it was so conveyed, to deny the trust and claim the land himself. Consequently, notwithstanding the statute, it is competent for a person claiming land conveyed to another to prove by parol evidence that it was so conveyed upon trust for the claimant, and that the grantee, knowing the facts, is denying the trust and relying upon the form and conveyance and the statute, in order to keep the land himself.[238]

Although the principle applies where a third party seeks to deny that he received the legal title to land as a trustee, it is less likely that a fraud will be committed if the owner of land orally declares himself a trustee in favour of a volunteer beneficiary. In such a case there is no justification for finding that a fraud had been perpetrated against the purported beneficiary.

The principle adopted in *Rochefoucauld v Boustead* has the merit of justice, but clearly runs contrary to the wording of the statute. Subsequent cases have tended to treat the principle as an example of where a constructive trust is imposed, so that the intended trustee cannot rely on the absence of writing to deny the trust because he is already a constructive trustee of the land for the intended beneficiary.[239] In *Bannister v Bannister*, for example, Scott LJ described the principle as:

the equitable principle on which a constructive trust is raised against a person who insists on the absolute character of a conveyance to himself for the purpose of defeating a beneficial interest.[240]

This analysis of the rule in *Rochefoucauld v Boustead* has the attraction of not seeming to contradict the wording of s 53(1)(b) of the Law of Property Act 1925, as s 53(2)

---

[236] [1897] 1 Ch 196.   [237] Predecessor of s 53(1)(b) of the Law of Property Act 1925.
[238] [1897] 1 Ch 196, at 206.
[239] *Bannister v Bannister* [1948] 2 All ER 133; *Neale v Willis* (1968) 19 P & CR 836; *Re Densham (A Bankrupt)* [1975] 1 WLR 1519.
[240] [1948] 2 All ER 133.

provides that formalities are not required for the creation of 'resulting, implied or constructive trusts'. Therefore, if a constructive trust of the land can be found, the court will not be seen to be enforcing a trust that the clear words of s 53(1)(b) render unenforceable. However, in *Rochefoucauld v Boustead*[241] itself, the Court of Appeal was of the view that an express trust was being enforced, despite the lack of statutory formalities. Lindley LJ stated that 'the trust which the plaintiff has established is clearly an express trust'. Given this, it seems more satisfactory to regard *Rochefoucauld v Boustead* as authority for the proposition that the court will enforce an express trust of land, despite an absence of writing, where to do otherwise would be to allow the statute to facilitate a fraud.

(b) Trusts of personal property

Section 53(1)(b) has no application to declarations of trusts of personal property. An absolute owner may orally declare himself the trustee of such property without the need for any further formalities.[242]

(c) Declaration of a sub-trust

Where property is already held on trust, the beneficiary enjoys an immediate proprietary interest in the trust property. Since equitable proprietary interests are themselves capable of forming the subject matter of a trust, the beneficiary is entitled to declare himself a trustee of his interest under the trust, creating a sub-trust. If the property held under the head trust is land, any declaration of a sub-trust will only be enforceable by the sub-beneficiary if it is evidenced in writing in compliance with s 53(1)(b), since the trust property consists of an 'interest in land'. If the property held under the head trust is personalty, formalities will only be required to create the sub-trust if s 53(1)(c) applies.[243] This section stipulates that dispositions of subsisting equitable interests can only be made in writing. The central question is whether a declaration of a sub-trust is to be characterized as effecting a 'disposition' of the original beneficiary's equitable interest under the head trust. If so, any purported declaration which is not effected in writing will be of no effect. In addressing this question, it seems that the courts have drawn a distinction between genuine declarations of a sub-trust, and transactions which, though in the form of a declaration of sub-trust, are in substance a disposition of the beneficiary's equitable interest. If the sub-trust declared is a bare trust,[244] so that the sub-trustee has no active duties to perform because the sub-beneficiary's entitlement to the trust property is identical to his own, he will be regarded as having effected a disposition of his interest. The sub-trust would merely amount to a duplication of the head-trustee's duties, so the sub-trustee is said to drop out of the picture and the head trustee holds the property on trust for the newly declared beneficiary (see Figure 7.4). This principle was recognized in *Grainge v*

---

[241] [1897] 1 Ch 196.
[242] See, for example, *Re Kayford Ltd* [1975] 1 WLR 279; *Paul v Constance* [1977] 1 WLR 527, CA.
[243] See below, p 229.   [244] See Chapters 14 and 21.

(i) Declaration   (ii) Disposition

Figure 7.4 The declaration of a 'sub-trust'

Wilberforce.[245] More significantly, it was accepted in *Grey v IRC*,[246] where Upjohn J used the language of a sub-trustee 'disappearing from the picture'[247] when a sub-trust is declared. Where a beneficiary who declares a sub-trust 'drops out of the picture' in this manner, the reality of the transaction is that he has effected a disposition of his equitable interest under the trust to the intended sub-beneficiary, and therefore the transaction will be ineffective unless the declaration is effected in writing.

In contrast, if an intended sub-trustee has active duties to perform under the sub-trust, he does not drop out of the picture and there is no disposition. Instead, a genuine sub-trust arises. This would be the case, for example, if a beneficiary created a life-interest of his interest under the trust in favour of a sub-beneficiary. Provided that the trust property is not land, in such circumstances there is no need for the declaration to be made in writing under s 53(1)(c). A purely oral declaration of the sub-trust will be sufficient.[248]

---

[245] (1889) 5 TLR 436. See also: *Re Lashmar* [1891] 1 Ch 258, CA; Law Com No 260, *Trustees' Powers and Duties* (1999), para 5.4, fn 3.

[246] [1958] Ch 375.   [247] [1958] Ch 375, at 382, per Upjohn J.

[248] Green '*Grey, Oughtred* and *Vandervell*—A Contextual Reappraisal' (1984) 47 MLR 385.

(2) Declarations of trusts by will

A valid declaration of trust can be made by will for any property, whether land or personalty.[249] The requirements of a valid will are set out in s 9 of the Wills Act 1837. A will is only valid if it is made in writing,[250] which is signed by the testator (or by some other person acting at his direction in his presence)[251] in the presence of two witnesses, who themselves attest and sign the will (or acknowledge their signature) in the presence of the testator.[252]

(3) Dispositions of subsisting equitable interests[253]

(a) The requirement of writing

It has already been noted in the context of the difficulties associated with the declaration of sub-trusts above that a different formality requirement applies to dispositions of existing equitable interests. Section 53(1)(c) of the Law of Property Act 1925 provides that:

a disposition of an equitable interest or trust subsisting at the time of the disposition must be in writing signed by the person disposing of the same, or by his agent thereunto lawfully authorised in writing or by will.

This section applies whenever the beneficiary of a trust attempts to transfer his equitable interest in the trust property to someone else. In *Vandervell v IRC*, Lord Upjohn provided an explanation of why formalities are required to effect such dispositions of a beneficiary's interest under a trust:

the object of the section, as was the object of the old Statute of Frauds, is to prevent hidden oral transactions in equitable interests in fraud of those truly entitled, and making it difficult, if not impossible, for the trustees to ascertain who are in truth his beneficiaries.[254]

It is questionable whether it is truly correct that the requirement of writing prevents hidden oral transactions, as there is no obligation on the part of the transferor or transferee to bring the transfer to the attention of the trustees. Writing is required because, as in the case of other forms of intangible property such as copyrights, there is no other means of effecting a transfer, as the property cannot be physically possessed or delivered. Unlike s 53(1)(b), where the effect of a lack of written evidence is merely to render an oral declaration of a trust of land unenforceable, a failure to comply with s 53(1)(c) renders the purported disposition void.[255] As such, the transferee-beneficiary will have failed to divest himself of his equitable interest in the trust property.

The following aspects of the requirement deserve attention.

(i) 'Disposition'

Section 53(1)(c) only applies to dispositions of subsisting equitable interests. It therefore has no application to declarations of trust, otherwise s 53(1)(b) would be redundant

---

[249] S 53(1)(b) and (c).   [250] S 9(a).   [251] S 9(a).
[252] S 9(c) and (d).   [253] See Harris (1975) 38 MLR 557.
[254] [1967] 2 AC 291, at 311.   [255] See *Grey v IRC* [1960] AC 1; *Oughtred v IRC* [1960] AC 206.

in requiring a declaration of a trust of land to be evidenced in writing. It is clear that an assignment of a subsisting equitable interest must be made in writing, as was held in *Re Danish Bacon Co Ltd Staff Pension Fund Trusts*.[256] Nevertheless, the meaning of the term 'disposition' has been the subject of much debate, as beneficiaries have sought to avoid compliance with the requirement of writing for tax reasons. The tax in question in many of the cases before the courts was ad valorem stamp duty.[257] This tax, which was calculated as a proportion of the value of the subsisting equitable interest being transferred, was payable if and only if the equitable interest was transferred in writing. Stamp duty was levied not on the transaction, but on a written document of transfer. Accordingly, if the transfer could be effected orally, and was later evidenced in writing, no tax was payable. The fact that only a 'disposition' of a subsisting equitable interest was required to be in writing, and the fact that no statutory definition of 'disposition' was provided in the Law of Property Act 1925, led to many ingenious methods which sought to effect transfers of interest without them being classed as 'dispositions' required to be in writing and subject to tax.[258]

The scope of a 'disposition' was considered by the House of Lords in *Grey v IRC* (see Figure 7.5),[259] where it was held that it should be given its 'natural meaning'.[260] The appellants held 18,000 shares on a bare trust as nominees for Mr Hunter. On 18 February 1955, Hunter orally directed them to henceforth hold the shares under six trusts, of 3,000 shares each, in favour of his grandchildren. On 25 March, the trustees executed a declaration of trust to that effect. The central question was whether the oral direction of 18 February was effective to transfer the equitable interest in the shares to the grandchildren. The Revenue argued that without writing the oral direction was void and ineffective to transfer the equitable interest in the shares. The trustees responded that the transaction did not require a written instrument because there had been no 'disposition' within the meaning of s 53(1)(c). They alleged that the Law of Property Act 1925 was merely a consolidating act, and that the word 'disposition' should be given no wider meaning than that accorded to the words 'grants and assignments' in the Statute of Frauds.[261] The House of Lords rejected this argument and held that the word 'disposition' should be given its natural meaning, in which case the oral direction to the trustees had been a disposition and was void and ineffective to transfer the equitable interest in the shares to the children. Lord Radcliffe stated:

if there is nothing more in this appeal than the short question whether the oral direction that Mr Hunter gave to his trustees on February 18th 1955 amounted in any ordinary sense to a 'disposition of an equitable interest or trust subsisting at the time of the disposition', I do not feel any doubt as to my answer. I think that it did. Whether we describe what happened in technical or in more general terms the full equitable interest in the 18,000 shares concerned, which

---

[256] [1971] 1 WLR 248.   [257] Finance Act 1910, s 74

[258] Stamp duty was abolished by the Finance Act 2003 in respect of shares, though stamp duty land tax was introduced in respect of land. The incentive to arrange matters to be effected without writing is now greatly reduced.

[259] [1960] AC 1; (1960) CLJ 31 (Thornely); see also *Re Danish Bacon Co Ltd Staff Pension Fund Trusts* [1971] 1 WLR 248, at 254, per Megarry J; *Halley v The Law Society* [2003] WTLR 845.

[260] [1960] AC 1, at 13, 15, per Lord Simmonds.

[261] Statute of Frauds 1677, s 9.

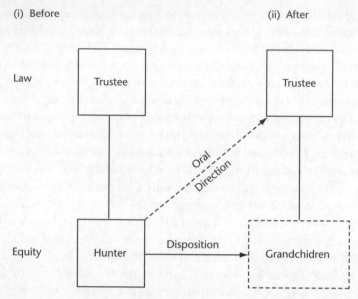

(i) Before   (ii) After

Figure 7.5 *Grey v IRC*

at that time was his, was...diverted by his direction from his ownership into the beneficial ownership of [his grandchildren]...[262]

As the oral directions of 18 February were ineffective because of the absence of writing, the transfer of the equitable interest in the shares had only been effected by the deed executed on 25 March. This written declaration was instead the disposition and therefore liable to ad valorem stamp duty. It is worth considering whether the decision in this case might have been different if the spectre of illegitimate tax avoidance had not haunted the minds of their Lordships. This was not a case where it could be suggested that there was a hidden oral transaction which could give rise to a fraud. All parties concerned were aware from the oral direction of the proposed change of ownership. Hunter may have dropped out of the picture, but the trustees and Hunter were aware of this.

A disclaimer of an equitable interest will not be regarded as a 'disposition' requiring writing,[263] whereas a surrender of an equitable interest is a disposition and will fall within the ambit of s 53(1)(c).[264]

(ii) Of an equitable interest or trust subsisting at the time of the disposition

Section 53(1)(c) only applies to beneficial interests which actually exist at the date of the disposition. In *Re Danish Bacon Co Ltd*,[265] an employee had nominated someone to receive pension benefits if he died in pensionable service. Megarry J suggested that

---

[262] [1960] AC 1, at 15.   [263] *Re Paradise Motor Co Ltd* [1968] 1 WLR 1125.
[264] See *Newlon Housing Trust v Al-Sulaimen* [1999] 1 AC 313 in the context of Matrimonial Causes Act 1973, s 37.
[265] [1971] 1 WLR 248.

in these circumstances s 53(1)(c) did not apply because the employee had been dealing with something that could never be his. He had no subsisting equitable interest in the benefits he was allocating.

(iii) In writing

Unlike s 53(1)(b), which only requires that a declaration of trust be evidenced in writing, s 53(1)(c) requires that a disposition actually be made in writing. This writing must obviously be contemporaneous with the intended disposition, although the disposition may be found in two or more separate documents provided they are sufficiently connected.[266] The requirements of writing and signing may be satisfied by an electronic document.[267] This will be important where, for example, shares are held in trust and are traded electronically.

(iv) Signed by the person disposing of the same or his agent

Again, in contrast to s 53(1)(b), the written instrument effecting a disposition need not be personally signed by the beneficiary or other person disposing of the equitable interest. It will be effective if signed by his lawfully authorized agent (such as the trustees in *Grey v IRC*).

(v) By will

A disposition of a subsisting equitable interest may be effected by will. The requirements of a valid will were considered above.

(b) Exceptions to s 53(1)(c)

Although the requirement of writing under s 53(1)(c) appears comprehensive, in a number of situations the courts have concluded that writing was not required to effect a transaction which was in substance a disposition of an equitable interest. These cases have largely arisen in the context of taxation, where, as we have seen, transferees have sought to avoid stamp duty by effecting transfers of their equitable interest without using a written instrument that will attract duty. In some cases, the courts have held that writing was not necessary to effect the transfer, but generally they have also found that tax remained payable.

The cases suggest that writing will not be required to effect a transfer of a subsisting beneficial interest in the following circumstances.

(i) The beneficiary of a bare trust directs the trustees to transfer the legal title

In *Vandervell v IRC*,[268] the House of Lords held that s 53(1)(c) did not have to be satisfied where a beneficiary with a subsisting equitable interest under a bare trust directed

---

[266] *Re Danish Bacon Co Ltd Staff Pension Fund Trusts* [1971] 1 WLR 248, at 254–255.

[267] See Electronic Communications Act 2000, s 8; Pt 3 of the Advice from the Law Commission, *Electronic Commerce: Formal Requirements in Commercial Transactions* (2001).

[268] [1967] 2 AC 291; (1966) 24 CLJ 19 (Jones); (1967) 31 Conv (NS) 175 (Spencer); (1967) 30 MLR 461 (Strauss); (1975) 38 MLR 557 (Harris). Nolan has argued that the decision can be explained on the basis of overreaching: '*Vandervell v IRC*; A Case of Overreaching' [2002] 61 CLJ 169.

Figure 7.6 *Vandervell v IRC*

the trustees to transfer the legal title to a third party and the transaction was completed (see Figure 7.6). The facts are complicated but important. Mr Vandervell was
the sole beneficiary of a bare trust of shares in his company, Vandervell Products Ltd,
of which Vandervell Trustees Ltd was the trustee. He decided to endow a chair of
pharmacology at the Royal College of Surgeons. At the time income tax (surtax) rates
were very high and there was no tax relief for gifts to charity. Mr Vandervell wished
to save tax on his gift. His scheme was to transfer shares in his company to the Royal
College of Surgeons, and to fund the new professorship by declaring a sufficiently
large dividend on the shares. He therefore directed the trustee company to execute
a share transfer form for the shares and to pass it to him, leaving the name of the
transferee blank. The trustees duly completed the transfer form and handed it to Mr
Vandervell, who entered the name of the Royal College of Surgeons as transferee. The
College was then registered as the owner of the shares on the company share register. In return for the transfer of the shares, the college granted the trustees an option
to repurchase the shares for £5,000. Dividends of some £250,000 were subsequently
declared on the shares to provide the endowment for the chair. The Revenue claimed
that Mr Vandervell was liable to pay surtax on these dividends, arguing that the transaction amounted to a settlement of property in which the settlor had not absolutely
divested himself of his interest in the property.[269] One ground of the Revenue's case
was that Vandervell had failed to divest himself of his equitable interest in the shares
because the disposition had not been effected in writing.

---

[269] Income Tax Act 1952, Pt XVIII.

Addressing this argument, the House of Lords held that, in the circumstances, writing had not been necessary to effect a transfer of Vandervell's equitable interest in the shares to the college. As the beneficiary of a bare trust he was entitled to direct the trustee to transfer the legal title to the trust property, and there was no need for a separate disposition to transfer the equitable title. As Lord Wilberforce said: 'No separate transfer... of the equitable interest ever came to or needed to be made and there is no room for the operation of the subsection.'[270] The rationale was more fully explained by Lord Upjohn:

I cannot agree... that prima facie a transfer of the legal estate carries with it the absolute beneficial interest in the property transferred; this plainly is not so, e.g., the transfer may be on a change of trustee; it is a matter of intention in each case. But if the intention of the beneficial owner in directing the trustee to transfer the legal estate to X is that X should be the beneficial owner I can see no reason for any further document or further words in the document assigning the legal estate also expressly transferring the beneficial interest; the greater includes the less. X may be wise to secure some evidence that the beneficial owner intended him to take the beneficial interest in case his beneficial title is challenged at a later date but it certainly cannot, in my opinion, be a statutory requirement that to effect its passing there must be some writing under section 53(1)(c).[271]

He also held that a transfer without writing in such circumstances would not offend against the policy underlying the formality requirement noted above, namely to prevent hidden oral transactions in equitable interests in fraud of those truly entitled and which might make it difficult or impossible for the trustees to ascertain their beneficiaries:

when the beneficial owner owns the whole beneficial estate and is in a position to give directions to his bare trustee with regard to the legal as well as the equitable estate there can be no possible ground for invoking the section where the beneficial owner wants to deal with the legal estate as well as the equitable estate.[272]

This does make perfect sense, as in this situation, the trust itself is coming to an end, as both Vandervell and his trustees dropped out of the picture. Had it not been for the option to repurchase the shares, Vandervell would have had no rights to recover any interest in the shares, as the Royal College of Surgeons were the outright owners in law and equity of the shares. This dealt with the issue of formalities under s 53(1)(c). Nevertheless, while Vandervell was able to avoid ad valorem stamp duty on the transfer of his equitable interest in the shares, the majority of the House of Lords went on to find Vandervell liable to surtax on the dividends declared. They held that the option to repurchase the shares granted by the College to the trustee company was, in the absence of an express declaration of trust, held on an automatic resulting trust for Vandervell himself.[273] Since he was the beneficiary of the option he had failed to fully divest himself of all interest in the shares, thus attracting liability to surtax.

---

[270] [1967] 2 AC 291, at 330.   [271] Ibid., at 311.
[272] Ibid.   [273] See Chapter 9.

(ii) A specifically enforceable contract for the transfer of the subsisting equitable interest

Where a beneficiary enters a specifically enforceable contract to transfer a subsisting equitable interest under a trust, that interest passes to the intended transferee immediately on the making of the contract by means of a constructive trust. Since the transferee obtains the equitable interest by means of the constructive trust arising from the contract, there is no need for further writing under s 53(1)(c). In *Oughtred v IRC*,[274] shares in a private company were held on trust for Mrs Oughtred for life with remainder to her son, Peter (see Figure 7.7). On 18 June, they entered an oral contract in which Peter agreed to release his interest in the shares subject to the settlement, so that his mother would be absolutely entitled to them, in return for which she would transfer 72,700 shares, of which she was already the absolute owner, to nominees for him. A deed of release was executed on 26 June. The central question before the House of Lords was whether ad valorem stamp duty was payable on this deed, which depended on whether the deed was a 'transfer on sale' within the provisions of the Stamp Act 1891.[275] The Oughtreds argued that the deed was not a 'transfer on sale' because the equitable remainder interest in the shares had passed to Mrs Oughtred by virtue of the contract to transfer, since, from the moment of the agreement, Peter held his interest on constructive trust. The majority of the House of Lords[276] held that irrespective of any constructive trust the deed of 26 June was a 'transfer on sale' for the purposes of the Stamp Act, and that stamp duty was therefore payable.[277] However, Upjohn J at first instance, and Lord Radcliffe in the House of Lords, took the view that the oral contract had given rise to a constructive trust which effected a transfer of the remainder interest in the shares to Mrs Oughtred without the need for further writing. Lord Radcliffe explained:

The reasoning of the whole matter, as I see it, is as follows: On June 18 1956 the son owned an equitable reversionary interest in the settled shares: by his oral agreement of that date he created in his mother an equitable interest in his reversion, since the subject-matter of the agreement was property of which specific performance would normally be decreed by the court. He thus became a trustee for her of that interest sub modo: having regard to subsection (2) of section 53 Law of Property Act 1925, subsection (1) of that section did not operate to prevent that trusteeship arising by operation of law...[278]

There has been some question whether Lord Radcliffe's comments establish that a specifically enforceable contract to transfer a subsisting equitable interest passes the interest by way of a constructive trust without the need for further writing, because the other members of the House of Lords did not express an opinion. However, his approach seems to have been adopted as correct in subsequent cases. It was accepted

---

[274] [1960] AC 206.
[275] Stamp Act 1891, s 54, Sch 1. Note that stamp duty was abolished by the Finance Act 2003.
[276] With the exception of Lord Denning.
[277] Per Lords Keith, Denning and Jenkins, Lords Radcliffe and Cohen dissenting.
[278] [1960] AC 206, at 227.

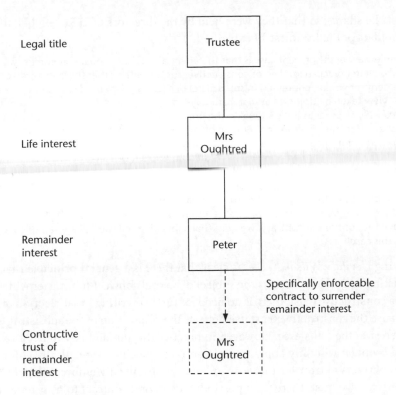

Figure 7.7 *Oughtred v IRC*

by Megarry J in *Re Holt's Settlement*[279] and by the Court of Appeal in *Neville v Wilson*.[280] This case concerned a trust of 120 shares in a company (U Ltd), which were held by the directors of the company as nominees for a separate family company (J Ltd). In 1969 J Ltd had been struck off the register because it had become defunct. It was claimed that in 1969 an oral agreement had been reached between the shareholders of J Ltd that the assets of the company should be divided among the shareholders rateably. The central question was whether this oral agreement gave rise to a constructive trust of the 120 shares in favour of the shareholders of J Ltd or whether it was void for failure to comply with the requirements of s 53(1)(c). If no such constructive trust had arisen, the shares would pass to the Crown as bona vacantia. The Court of Appeal held that the oral agreement of the shareholders had produced a constructive

---

[279] [1969] 1 Ch 100. See *DHN Food Distributors Ltd v London Borough of Tower Hamlets* [1976] 3 All ER 462 (1977) 93 LQR 170 (Sugarman and Webb); *Chinn v Collins (Inspector of Taxes)* [1981] 1 All ER 189, HL.

[280] [1997] Ch 144; (1996) 55 CLJ 436 (Nolan); [1996] Conv 368 (Thompson); (1997) 113 LQR 213 (Milne). See also *Bishop Square Ltd v IRC* (1999) 78 P & CR 169, where the Court of Appeal applied *Oughtred v IRC* to a very similar fact situation.

trust of the shares, so that they were held by the directors of U Ltd on behalf of the shareholders of J Ltd. Nourse LJ explained:

> The simple view of the present case is that the effect of each individual agreement was to constitute the shareholder an implied or constructive trustee for the other shareholders, so that the requirement for writing contained in sub-s (1)(c) of s 53 was dispensed with by sub-s (2). That was the view taken by Upjohn J at first instance and by Lord Radcliffe in the House of Lords in *Oughtred v IRC*... So far as it is material to the present case, what sub-s (2) says is that sub-s (1)(c) does not affect the creation or operation of implied or constructive trusts. Just as in *Oughtred v IRC* the son's oral agreement created a constructive trust in favour of the mother, so here each shareholder's oral or implied agreement created an implied or constructive trust in favour of the other shareholders. Why then should sub-s (2) not apply? No convincing reason was suggested in argument and none has occurred to us since. Moreover, to deny its application in this case would be to restrict the effect of the general words when no restriction is called for, and to lay the ground for fine distinctions in the future. With all the respect which is due to those who have thought to the contrary, we hold that sub-s (2) applies to an agreement such as we have in this case.

Following *Neville v Wilson*, it seems clear that there is a general principle that where a subsisting equitable interest is the subject of an oral contract to transfer which gives rise to a constructive trust, there is no need for further writing in satisfaction of s 53(1)(c) because the constructive trust itself effects the disposition of the subsisting equitable interest to the transferee. However, in practice this possibility will be of relatively limited scope. It will only apply to oral contracts which are specifically enforceable. While contracts to transfer interests in land are specifically enforceable, giving rise to a constructive trust, there is no possibility of an oral contract to transfer a subsisting equitable interest under a trust of land avoiding formality provisions altogether, because the contract itself must be in writing.[281] In the case of personal property, contracts are not specifically enforceable unless the subject matter of the contract is unique because no market substitute is available. For example, a contract to transfer shares in a public company is not usually thought to give rise to a constructive trust.[282] In *Oughtred v IRC*,[283] the contract was specifically enforceable because the shares were in a private company and were not freely available in the market.

(iii) Extinction of a subsisting equitable interest under a resulting trust

It further seems that there is no need for writing in satisfaction of s 53(1)(c) if the act of a third party has the effect of extinguishing a subsisting equitable interest which has arisen under an automatic resulting trust.[284] It has already been seen how, in

---

[281] Law of Property (Miscellaneous Provisions) Act 1989, s 2.

[282] See, however, *Chinn v Collins (Inspector of Taxes)* [1981] AC 533, which provides some authority that even in the case of shares in a public company a constructive trust will arise. Lord Wilberforce considered the effect of a contract to transfer the equitable interest in shares in a public company quoted on the London Stock Exchange which were held on trust by a nominee. He regarded the agreement as giving rise to a constructive trust so that dealings with the equitable interest did not require formalities. He seemed to regard it as irrelevant whether the contract would have been specifically enforceable. However, *Oughtred v IRC* was not cited.

[283] [1960] AC 206.   [284] See Chapter 9.

Vandervell v IRC,[285] Mr Vandervell failed to divest himself absolutely of his interest in shares transferred to the Royal College of Surgeons because the option to repurchase was held on resulting trust for him by the Vandervell Trustee Company. The trustee company subsequently exercised this option using money they held on other trusts for Vandervell's children. They then informed the Revenue that they held the re-acquired shares on trust for the children, and all dividends deriving from those shares were paid to the children's settlement. In *Re Vandervell's Trusts (No 2)* (see Figure 7.8),[286] the Revenue claimed that Vandervell was liable to pay surtax on these dividends as well, on the grounds that he had still not divested himself absolutely of his interest in the shares. Their argument that there had been no effective declaration of trust in favour of the children was accepted by Megarry J, at first instance, but rejected by the Court of Appeal, which held that the conduct of the trustees was sufficient to amount to a declaration of trust in favour of the children. The Revenue further argued that Vandervell had never effectually disposed of his equitable interest under the resulting trust of the option, because he had never done so in writing as required by s 53(1)(c). The Court of Appeal also rejected this argument, holding that there had been no need of a written instrument to extinguish Vandervell's resulting trust interest. Lord Denning MR based his conclusion on the nature and function of the resulting trust:

A resulting trust for the settlor is born and dies without any writing at all. It comes into existence whenever there is a gap in the beneficial ownership. It ceases to exist whenever that gap is filled by someone becoming beneficially entitled. As soon as the gap is filled by the creation or declaration of a valid trust, the resulting trust comes to an end. In this case, before the option was exercised, there was a gap in the beneficial ownership. So there was a resulting trust for Mr Vandervell. But as soon as the option was exercised and the shares registered in the trustee's name, there was created a valid trust of the shares in favour of the children's settlement...[287]

Lawton LJ took the view that the declaration of the trust of the shares in favour of the children's settlement had the effect of extinguishing Vandervell's interest under the resulting trust of the option. An extinction was not a 'disposition' and therefore writing was not required:

The exercise of the option and the transfer of the shares to the trustee company necessarily put an end to the resulting trust of the option. There could not be a resulting trust of a chose in action which was no more. The only reason why there ever had been a resulting trust of the option was the rule that the beneficial interest in property must be held for some one if the legal owner is not entitled to it. The legal but not the beneficial interest in the option had vested in the trustee company. The beneficial interest had to be held for some one and as the trustee company had declared no trusts of the option, the only possible beneficiary was Mr Vandervell. Once the trustee company took a transfer of the shares the position was very different. The legal title to them was vested in the trustee company and by reason of the facts and circumstances to which I have already referred it held the beneficial interest for the trusts of the children's settlement. There was no gap between the legal and beneficial interests and in consequence no need for a resulting trust in favour of Mr Vandervell to fill it. Neither the extinction of the resulting trust of the option resulting from its exercise nor the creation of a beneficial interest in

285 [1967] 2 AC 291.   286 [1974] Ch 269; (1975) 38 MLR 557 (Harris).
287 [1974] Ch 269, at 320.

Figure 7.8 *Re Vandervell's Trusts (No 2)*

the shares by the declaration of trust amounted to a disposition of an equitable interest or trust within the meaning of sections 53(1)(c) and 205(1)(ii) of the Law of Property Act 1925.[288]

The precise impact of the decision in *Re Vandervell's Trusts (No 2)*[289] is open to question, as is the reasoning within it. It is doubtful whether, in reality, the acts of the trustee company were of themselves sufficient to divest Vandervell of his resulting trust of the option. As Megarry J had commented at first instance:

That issue is, in essence, whether trustees who hold an option on trust for X will hold the shares obtained by exercising that option on trust for Y merely because they used Y's money in exercising the option. Authority apart, my answer would be an unhesitating no. The option belongs to X beneficially, and the money merely exercises rights which belong to X. Let the shares be worth £50,000 so then an option to purchase those shares for £5,000 is worth £45,000, and it will be at once seen what a monstrous result would be produced by allowing trustees to divert from their beneficiary X the benefits of what they hold for him merely because they used Y's money instead of X's.

More significantly, it is questionable whether the mere fact that the beneficial interest in the option arose under a resulting trust should provide a justification for the inapplicability of s 53(1)(c). There is no conceptual imperative for treating a disposition of a subsisting equitable interest which has arisen by way of a resulting trust any differently from a disposition of an interest arising under an express trust. The court's reasoning that the resulting trust is somehow eliminated by the act of the trustee identifying new beneficiaries is spurious. While it is true that the original resulting trust

---

[288] [1974] Ch 269, at 326.   [289] [1974] Ch 269.

arose because Vandervell had failed to specify who was to be the beneficial owner of the option, the trust is only a 'resulting trust' to the extent that it was not expressly created, and this characterization should not colour its nature for the whole of its existence. The prime duty of a trustee, whether of a bare or active trust, is to preserve the trust fund for the beneficiary. The beneficiary's interest cannot be transferred to different beneficiaries by the mere act of the trustees without assignment by the beneficiary, otherwise the trustee would be able to dispose of the beneficial interests under the trust without reference to the beneficiary. For example, if two friends (X and Y) contributed equally to the purchase of shares valued at £100,000 acquired in the name of X alone, surely X should not be able to eliminate Y's beneficial half-interest under a resulting trust merely by declaring that henceforward he regards himself as holding the shares on trust for Z. To conclude that interests subsisting behind resulting trusts can be disposed of without writing would also provide an easy means of evasion of the ruling in *Grey v IRC*, which concerned an equitable interest subsisting under an express bare trust. If a settlor were to transfer property to a nominee, without specifying a beneficiary and thus giving rise to a resulting trust in his favour, he could then transfer the equitable interest to new beneficiaries by merely orally directing the trustees to declare new trusts.

If any general principle can be construed from *Re Vandervell's Trusts (No 2)* it would therefore seem that it should be limited to a case where the extinction of the equitable interest arising under a resulting trust is the act of a third party, and not of the person who enjoys the interest. It was only because the declaration of trust was made by the trustees that there was no need for writing. If Vandervell himself had sought to transfer his equitable interest under the resulting trust, writing would surely have been required in satisfaction of s 53(1)(c).

(4) Resulting and constructive trusts

The formality requirements of s 53(1) only apply in respect of declarations of express trusts and dispositions of existing equitable interests. As will be evident in the following chapters, they have no application to resulting[290] or constructive trusts.[291] This is the effect of s 53(2), which provides:

This section does not affect the creation or operation of resulting, implied or constructive trusts.

---

[290] See Chapter 9.   [291] See Chapter 10.

8

Secret trusts

It is a simple truth that a man cannot take his property with him when he dies. He may, however, wish to decide to whom it should pass when he no longer has any need of it. Secret trusts provide a mechanism by which an owner can direct how his property should be distributed on death. While English law provides a number of other means by which an owner can determine the destiny of his worldly goods on his demise, they generally involve some element of public scrutiny to prevent fraud or abuse, with the inevitable consequence that the identity of the ultimate recipient of the property becomes public knowledge. The cardinal feature of secret trusts is that the ultimate recipient of the property may be kept entirely secret by not being disclosed in the will.

1 Distributing property on death

(1) The function of secret trusts

Secret trusts are probably most often used today to provide for a beneficiary who has been forgotten, and in some cases because the testator was unsure as to who should be the ultimate beneficiary when he made his will. They have historically been used by owners wishing to leave property to persons whose existence they would prefer to conceal, for example mistresses or illegitimate children.[1] Rather than leaving property directly to such a person by will, the testator instead leaves it to a trusted friend, who has agreed in advance to pass it on to the secret beneficiary. If such an arrangement is established, the face of the will simply suggests that a bequest is made to the friend, whereas the reality behind the scenes is that provision is made secretly for the unrevealed beneficiary.

(2) Mechanisms for distributing property on death

(a) General

Since 'we brought nothing into the world, and we can take nothing out of it',[2] the question arises as to what should happen to a man's property on death. The law provides a

---

[1] Eg, *Re Boyes* (1884) LR 26 Ch D 531; *Blackwell v Blackwell* [1929] AC 318.
[2] St Paul, First Letter to Timothy, Ch 6, v 7.

number of mechanisms that enable the owner of property to determine who should receive his property after death.

It is necessary to examine these mechanisms and their operation to gain a full appreciation of the advantages offered by secret trusts and the policy motivations that led to their acceptance and enforceability.

(b) Testamentary dispositions

(i) Formalities required

The most important mechanism by which an owner can stipulate how his property should be distributed on his death is through a valid will. A document is only a valid will if it complies with the provisions of the Wills Act 1837. The formalities there prescribed are intended to prevent fraud and to ensure that the genuine intentions of the owner are carried out. Section 9 provides that a will is only valid if it is in writing and properly attested and witnessed:

No will shall be valid unless—

  (a) it is in writing, and signed by the testator, or by some other person in his presence and by his direction; and

  (b) it appears that the testator intended his signature to give effect to the will; and

  (c) the signature is made or acknowledged by the testator in the presence of two or more witnesses present at the same time; and

  (d) each witness either—

    (i)   attests and signs the will; or

    (ii) acknowledges his signature, in the presence of the testator (but not necessarily in the presence of any other witnesses).

Although it is obviously necessary to have a general requirement that wills must be executed in a specified form, the law recognizes that in some circumstances it is unfair or impracticable to expect a testator to comply with such requirements. In limited cases a testator is therefore entitled to make a privileged will without the need to comply with the formality provisions of s 9. Section 11 provides that 'any soldier[3] being in actual military service'[4] or 'any mariner or seaman[5] being at sea'[6] can make a valid will without any formalities.

(ii) The process of probate

Where a person has died leaving a valid will, this does not automatically effect a distribution of his property to the named beneficiaries, nor can the beneficiaries simply seize the property left to them. Instead, on death the totality of the testator's assets

---

[3] *Re Donaldson's Goods* (1840) 2 Curt 386; *Re White's Application* [1975] 2NSWLR 125. See also Wills (Soldiers and Sailors) Act 1918, s 5(2) (members of the RAF to be treated as soldiers).

[4] *White v Repton* (1844) 3 Curt 818; *Re Spark's Estate* [1941] P 115; *Re Gibson's Estate* [1941] P 118n; *Re Rowson's Estate* [1944] 2 All ER 36; *Re Wingham* [1949] P 187; *Re Jones* [1981] 1 All ER 1.

[5] See *Re Yate's Estate* [1919] P 93; *Re Knibb's Estate* [1962] 2 All ER 829; *Re Hale's Goods* [1915] 2 IR 362.

[6] *Re Barnes' Goods* (1926) 96 LJP 26; *Re Rapley's Estate* [1983] 1 WLR 1069.

pass to his executors. The executors are not entitled to distribute the property comprising the estate until they have been granted probate. Probate will only be granted once the executor has 'proved' the will, demonstrating that it was the last effective will of the deceased. During the process of obtaining probate the will becomes a public document and is open to public scrutiny. This means that details of the value of the testator's estate, and the identity of those to whom it was left, enter the public sphere. For this reason it was possible for reporters to discover the exact details of the will of Diana, Princess of Wales. This publicity is an essential part of the probate process as it ensures effective scrutiny of the will. Interested parties can examine the will and then challenge its authenticity if the terms suggest that it is not genuine. It is the public nature of this probate process that prevents a testator making secret bequests of his property by will. The very people he would most wish to keep from discovering that he had made provision for a mistress or illegitimate child, namely his family, would be those most likely to examine the will.

(c) Incorporation by reference

While a valid testamentary disposition must comply with the appropriate formalities identified above, there is in fact no need for a will to contain all the terms specifying how the deceased's property should be distributed on death. Under the doctrine of 'incorporation by reference' documents which are not themselves signed, attested, and witnessed may be incorporated into a will. Where a document is effectively incorporated into the will, it 'becomes part of the will'.[7] As such, the incorporated document must also be admitted to probate, and thereby becomes a public document in the same way as the will itself. The doctrine of incorporation by reference does not, therefore, enable a testator to make secret dispositions of his property on death.

A document will only be incorporated by reference into a will if the conditions stated by Gorell-Barnes P in *Re Smart's Goods*[8] are met.

(i) Incorporated document was in existence at the date of the will

Only a document that was in existence at the date the will was executed can be incorporated by reference, thus becoming part of the will.[9] A document may be incorporated if it was written after the will was executed provided that a subsequent properly executed codicil is added confirming that it is to be incorporated.

(ii) Incorporated document is referred to in the will

To be incorporated into a will a document must not only exist at the date of the will, but it must also be referred to in the will as existing at that date. In *Re Smart's Goods*[10] the testatrix, Caroline Smart, executed a will in 1895 leaving her property to the friends she might designate in a book or memorandum. At the time that the will was executed no such book or memorandum existed. A book was written between 1898 and 1899,

---

[7] *Re Smart's Goods* [1902] P 238, at 240.   [8] [1902] P 238.
[9] *Singleton v Tomlinson* (1878) 3 App Cas 404, HL.   [10] [1902] P 238.

and in 1900 a codicil was added to the will. However, although this book was in existence at the date of the execution of the codicil it was held that it was not incorporated into the will because the codicil made no reference to it as existing at the date that it was executed. The will continued to refer to the book as a future document.[11]

(iii) Incorporated document must be clearly identified in the will

A document will only be incorporated by reference if it is clearly identified in the will.[12]

(d) Non-testamentary mechanisms

(i) Intestacy

If the owner of property dies without leaving a valid will he is said to die 'intestate'. Since he has not left a valid will indicating how his property should be allocated after his death, it will be distributed on the basis of the rules of intestacy. For those dying after 31 May 1987 the rules of intestacy are found in the Administration of Estates Act 1925 and the Family Provision (Intestate Succession) Order 2009.

(ii) Donatio mortis causa

The principle of donatio mortis causa, which was examined in detail in the previous chapter,[13] provides a means by which an owner can allocate property on his death. He can make an inter vivos conditional gift that is only intended to become an absolute gift in the event of his death. A donatio will only occur if the donor transferred dominion of the property to the donee in contemplation of death. Provided the requirements are met, the donor's executors or administrators will be obliged to make good any defects in the donee's title.

(iii) Secret trusts

As has been noted, secret trusts provide a further means by which an owner can determine who is to benefit from his property after his death outside of the terms of his will.

(iv) Inter vivos settlements

The owner of property can settle it during his lifetime by creating a trust under which he retains only a life estate, the remainder passing to the person he desires to benefit on his death. Such a settlement confers an immediate proprietary interest on the beneficiaries that can be varied only in accordance with the terms of the trust or with the consent of all the beneficiaries.

---

[11] See also *University College of North Wales v Taylor* [1908] P 140; *Re Bateman's Will Trusts* [1970] 3 All ER 817.

[12] See *Croker v Marquis of Hertford* (1844) 8 Jur 863; *Re Balmes' Goods* [1897] P 261; *Re Saxton's Estate* [1939] 2 All ER 418; *Re Mardon's Estate* [1944] P 109.

[13] See above, pp 216 *et seq.*

2 Introduction to secret trusts

(1) Types of secret trust

English law recognizes two categories of secret trust, namely 'fully secret trusts' and 'half-secret trusts'. The central difference between these categories is the extent to which the testator's will discloses that the person named as the recipient of a bequest is intended to take the property as a trustee rather than for himself. While the difference might appear slight, for a long period of time it was held that only fully secret trusts should be recognized as valid, and even though half-secret trusts are now accepted, the rules governing their creation are somewhat more restrictive.

(a) Fully secret trusts

A fully secret trust is created when a testator bequeaths property to a specified person in his will who has agreed that he will hold the property left to him on trust for a third party. In a fully secret trust, neither the fact of the trust nor the identity of the beneficiary under the trust are revealed in the will. For example, imagine that George has a mistress, Henrietta, for whom he wishes to make provision on his death without his wife discovering her existence. He therefore leaves £50,000 in his will to his close friend, Ian, having told him of his intention, and Ian having agreed that he will ensure that Henrietta receives the money. On the face of George's will, it appears that Ian is the absolute beneficiary of the bequest, whereas in fact, behind the scenes, Henrietta is intended to benefit. This arrangement would give rise to a fully secret trust. On the death of George, Ian will receive the money under the terms of the will, but he will not be entitled to retain it for himself. Instead, he will be required to hold it as trustee for Henrietta. Ian is therefore the trustee of the secret trust, and Henrietta the beneficiary.

(b) Half-secret trusts

The performance of a fully secret trust is to some extent dependent on the integrity of the beneficiary who has agreed to act as the secret trustee. There is always a danger that the secret trustee will ignore the trust and take the property left to him by will for his own benefit and refuse to apply it to the intended secret beneficiary. This danger will be avoided if the testator indicates in his will that the recipient of the bequest is not intended to take the property absolutely, but as a trustee. By this means the identity of the ultimate beneficiary remains concealed, but the beneficiary named in the will is clearly seen to be a secret trustee. Amending the example used above, if George were to leave £50,000 to Ian in his will 'on trust', without disclosing that Henrietta was the ultimate beneficiary, a half-secret trust would have been created. The trust is described as 'half-secret' because the fact that the property is subject to a trust obligation appears on the face of the will, although its terms, and especially the identity of the intended beneficiary, remain secret. In the case of a half-secret trust the secret trustee cannot ignore the trust and take the property absolutely for himself because the fact of the trust appears on the face of the will and it is clear to the court that he is not intended to take the property absolutely.

(c) Secret trusts arising on intestacy

Although secret trusts generally arise in the context of a testamentary disposition, a secret trust may arise in a case of intestacy,[14] provided that the person entitled to the deceased's estate on his intestacy had agreed that he would receive the specified property as a trustee and not for himself absolutely. As Romer J stated in *Re Gardner (No 2)*:

> The principle has been applied . . . where the owner of property refrains from making a will and so allows the property to pass to the donee as on an intestacy.[15]

Therefore, if, under the rules of intestacy, Ian was entitled to receive a share of George's estate, George could ask him to hold that share for the benefit of Henrietta. Provided that Ian agreed, and George died without making a will, Ian would hold whatever he received from the administration of George's estate on trust for Henrietta.

(d) Secret trust arising on transfer by survivorship in joint tenancy

A secret trust can probably also arise where a person acquires an enlarged interest in property through survivorship to a joint tenancy. In *Healey v Brown*[16] David Donaldson, QC (sitting as a Deputy High Court Judge) held that a constructive trust applied to the half interest in a flat to which Mr Brown had succeeded as a joint tenant on the death of his wife, to whom he had promised to leave the flat to a named beneficiary on his own death, David Donaldson observed that 'the present case differs from the ordinary case of secret trusts, since the property passed outside the will and by operation of law rather than pursuant to a bequest. But to my mind that is a matter of form without substantive significance.'[17]

(2) Why does equity enforce secret trusts?

The enforcement of secret trusts seems at odds with the policy of public regulation and scrutiny of testamentary dispositions embodied in the Wills Act and probate process. Superficially, the enforcement of a secret trust even seems to be inconsistent with the terms of s 9, since such enforcement appears to permit a testamentary disposition without satisfaction of the requisite formalities. Historically, equity justified the enforcement of secret trusts on the ground that to refuse to uphold them because of a lack of formality would be to allow the Wills Act to be used as an instrument of fraud. This historic explanation has been eclipsed by a more fashionable alternative, which is

---

[14] *Stickland v Aldridge* (1804) 9 Ves 516.
[15] [1923] 2 Ch 230, at 233. [16] [2002] EWHC Ch 1405.
[17] Ibid., at [29]. While this remark referred to secret trusts, most of the judgment concerns mutual wills—see Chapter 12.

that a secret trust is an inter vivos trust, declared by the testator and the secret trustee, which remains incompletely constituted until the death of the testator, at which time it is constituted through the operation of the will passing title to the trust property to the secret trustee. This explanation has the advantage that it does not presuppose a conflict between the enforcement of the secret trusts and the requirements of s 9 of the Wills Act. The secret trust arises altogether outside of the will, which simply operates according to its terms. These rival explanations will be examined in detail below.

3 Requirements for the creation of secret trusts

The essential requirements of 'intention, communication and acceptance' must be satisfied to create a valid fully secret, or half-secret, trust. It has been questioned whether the creation of a secret trust requires a contract between the testator and the intended trustee, whereby the trustee agrees to hold the property bequeathed to him on trust for the indicated beneficiary. In *Re Goodchild (Decd)*[18] Morritt LJ suggested that the 'principles applicable to cases of a fully secret trust do, in substance, require the proof of a contract', although he accepted that they do not 'require exactly the same degree of agreement as does a contract at law'.[19] While many of the authorities elucidating the meaning of these requirements are applicable to both categories of secret trust, it should be noted in advance that there are significant differences regarding the application of the requirement of communication to half-secret trusts.

(1) Fully secret trusts

The leading authority stating the requirements of a fully secret trust is *Ottaway v Norman*.[20] Harry Ottaway cohabited with Miss Hodges in his house, 'Ashcroft'. On his death, 'Ashcroft' was left to Miss Hodges in his will, and she left it in her will to Mr and Mrs Norman. Harry's son, William, claimed that the house had been left to Miss Hodges on the understanding that she would leave it to him on her death. He claimed that a secret trust had been created in his favour, so that Miss Hodges held the house on trust for him and that it had not therefore formed part of her estate. Although the case is open to criticism on the grounds that it did not really involve a secret trust, as Miss Hodges was not subjected to an immediate obligation to hold the house on trust for William on the death of Harry, it was argued and decided on the basis that the existence of a secret trust was at issue. Having examined the facts, Brightman J concluded that a fully secret trust had been created. In the course of his judgment he referred to the secret trustee as the 'primary donee' (who would take the property under the will) and the secret beneficiary as the 'secondary donee'.[21] He held that

---

[18] [1997] 3 All ER 63.   [19] Ibid., at 75.
[20] [1972] Ch 698; (1972) 36 Conv 129.   [21] Ibid., at 711.

subjection of property to a fully secret trust required the three elements of intention, communication, and acceptance.

(a) Intention

Brightman J stated that a secret trust would not be created unless it was 'the intention of the testator to subject the primary donee to an obligation in favour of the secondary donee'.[22] This requirement is no different from the requirement that conventional express trusts must demonstrate sufficient 'certainty of intention' to create a trust.[23] It must be shown that the testator intended to subject the secret trustee to a mandatory obligation to hold the property for the benefit of the secret beneficiary. An intention to impose a purely moral obligation is insufficient, as can be seen in *Re Snowden (Decd)*,[24] where an elderly testatrix left her entire residuary estate to her older brother because she was uncertain as to how she should leave her property among her relatives, and she said that her brother would 'know what to do'. She died without changing her will, and six days later her brother also died, leaving all his property to his only son. The question was whether the brother had taken Mrs Snowden's residuary estate on secret trust for her nephews and nieces equally. Megarry V-C concluded that she had not possessed the necessary intention to impose a trust on her brother in favour of the nephews and nieces, but that she had merely intended to impose on him a 'moral obligation' to do what he thought best. As a result no secret trust was established, and the brother's son was entitled to the entire residue absolutely.

(b) Communication

The mere fact that a testator intends to create a secret trust is alone insufficient to subject the recipient of the trust property under his will to an enforceable secret trust. As Brightman J stated in *Ottaway v Norman*, creation of a valid secret trust requires 'communication of that intention to the primary donee'.[25] The conscience of a beneficiary under the will is only affected, so as to justify the imposition of a trust, if the testator made him aware that he was to receive the property bequeathed as a trustee.

Communication will only be effective to create a fully secret trust if it satisfies the following criteria.

(i) Communication of both the fact of the trust and the terms of the trust

A fully secret trust will only arise if the testator makes the intended trustee aware of both the fact that he is to hold the property bequeathed to him on trust, and the identity (or the means of discovering the identity) of the intended beneficiary thereof. Where either of these elements is missing, the property will not be held on trust. For example, in *Re Boyes*[26] George Boyes left his entire estate by will to his solicitor, Frederick Carritt. Prior to his death Boyes had informed Carritt that he was to hold

---

[22] Ibid.
[23] See above, p 184.
[24] [1979] 2 All ER 172.
[25] *Ottaway v Norman* [1972] Ch 698, at 711.
[26] (1884) LR 26 Ch D 531.

the property on trust, the terms of which he said he would communicate to him by letter. No communication of the terms of the trust was made during the testator's lifetime, but after his death papers were discovered directing Carritt to hold the property for his mistress and illegitimate child. Kay J held that in these circumstances a secret trust had not been established in favour of the mistress and child. However, as the solicitor had admitted that he had agreed to receive the property left to him as a trustee, he was not entitled to take it absolutely for himself, and therefore he held it on a resulting trust for Boyes' next of kin. While a complete failure to communicate the terms of the trust before the testator's death prevents the creation of a valid secret trust, it seems that communication of the terms of the trust by means of a sealed envelope, given to the trustee during the testator's lifetime with the stipulation that it was not to be opened until after his death, will be sufficient to create a secret trust. This was accepted by the Court of Appeal in *Re Keen*,[27] where Lord Wright MR considered such communication analogous with that of a ship sailing under sealed orders, which he considered is 'sailing under orders though the exact terms are not ascertained by the captain till later'. He held that a sealed envelope containing the terms of the trust that had been given to the trustee could constitute sufficient communication to create a secret trust.

(ii) Communication of the extent of the trust

A secret trust will only affect property bequeathed to the intended trustees to the extent that effective communication had been made. In *Re Cooper*[28] a testator left £5,000 by will to two trustees. He had previously communicated the terms of the trust to them both. He subsequently added a codicil to his will, increasing the amount of the gift to £10,000, but without communicating this alteration to the trustees. The Court of Appeal held that only £5,000 of the money bequeathed to the trustees was subject to the secret trust.[29]

(iii) Communication must be made before the death of the testator

A valid fully secret trust will be created provided that effective communication was made to the trustee at any time prior to the death of the testator. It has already been seen how failure to communicate the terms of the intended trust before the testator's death prevented the finding of a secret trust in *Re Boyes*.[30] In *Wallgrave v Tebbs*[31] William Coles left property by will to the defendants. From a letter he had written it appeared that he had intended that it should be applied by them for the charitable purpose of endowing a church. However, as this intention had not been

---

[27] [1937] Ch 236. See also *Re Boyes* (1884) LR 26 Ch D 531, at 536; *Re Bateman's Will Trusts* [1970] 1 WLR 1463.

[28] [1939] Ch 811.

[29] As it was a half-secret trust, the remaining £5,000 was held on resulting trust for the testator's residuary legatees. If it had been an attempted fully secret trust, the intended trustees would have been entitled to the remaining £5,000 absolutely.

[30] (1884) LR 26 Ch D 531.   [31] (1855) 2 K & J 313.

communicated to them during his lifetime, Page-Wood V-C held that no trust had been created, and that the defendants were entitled to take the property bequeathed to them absolutely.

(iv) Communication to joint trustees

Particular difficulties of communication emerge if a testator intends to subject property to a secret trust bequeathed to two or more persons jointly in his will. The question arises whether the joint beneficiaries under the will are bound by the secret trust if communication had only been made to some of them. In answering this dilemma the law distinguishes between bequests made to the intended trustees as joint tenants, and bequests made to them as tenants-in-common. The principles were stated by Farwell J in *Re Stead*.[32] Where the intended trust property is bequeathed to two or more persons as tenants-in-common, a secret trust will only bind the respective shares of those tenants-in-common to whom the testator had communicated the terms of the trust. Those to whom the trust had not been communicated are entitled to receive their respective shares of the bequeathed property absolutely.[33] In *Re Stead*, Mrs Stead had left property to Mrs Witham and Mrs Andrews as tenants-in-common. She informed Mrs Witham that £2,000 was to be held on trust for John Collett, but made no communication to Mrs Andrews. It was held that Mrs Andrews took her share of the property free from any trust. Where the intended trust property is bequeathed to joint tenants, a further distinction is made on the grounds of the timing of any communication of the trust. Farwell J held that if a testator made effective communication to any one of the joint tenants before executing the will, they would all be bound by the secret trust.[34] However, he held that where communication occurred after the will had been executed, only those to whom communication had been made would be bound by the trust, and that therefore those tenants-in-common to whom no communication had been made would be entitled to take their respective shares of the bequeathed property absolutely.[35] Although clearly representing the present law, it has been persuasively argued that the rules expounded in *Re Stead*[36] are incorrect because Farwell J developed his reasoning from a misunderstanding of earlier cases cited as authority.[37] It is suggested that, rather than distinguishing between joint tenants and tenants-in-common (and in the latter case also between communication before and after the execution of the will), the question in each case should be whether the testator was induced to make the joint bequest only because of the promise of some of those entitled that the property would be held on trust.[38] Clearly, it will be more difficult to

[32] [1900] 1 Ch 237.
[33] See *Tee v Ferris* (1856) 2 K & J 357; *Rowbotham v Dunnett* (1878) LR 8 Ch D 430; *Re Young (Deceased)* [1951] Ch 344. Compare also *Geddis v Semple* [1903] 1 IR 73.
[34] *Russell v Jackson* (1852) 10 Hare 204; *Jones v Badley* (1868) 3 Ch App 362.
[35] *Burney v Macdonald* (1845) 15 Sim 6; *Moss v Cooper* (1861) 1 John & H 352.
[36] [1900] 1 Ch 237.
[37] Perrins 'Can You Keep Half a Secret?" (1972) 88 LQR 225.
[38] Applying the principle of *Huguenin v Baseley* (1807) 14 Ves 273 that 'No man may profit by the fraud of another.'

show that the gift was so induced if it was made to tenants-in-common, or if the promise was only made after the will had been executed.

(c) Acceptance

A secret trust is not imposed on property bequeathed to an intended secret trustee merely because the testator effectively communicated his intention that it should be held on trust. The property will only be subject to a secret trust if the intended trustee accepted that he would hold it on trust. As Brightman J said in *Ottaway v Norman*,[39] the third essential element for the creation of a fully secret trust is 'the acceptance of that obligation by the primary donee either expressly or by acquiescence'. Such acceptance does not need to be active. It has been held that if the terms of the trust have been communicated to the intended trustee, his silence will be taken to be an acceptance of the trust. In *Moss v Cooper*[40] John Hill left property in his will to James Gawthorn, William Sedman, and James Owen. He communicated his intention to all three that the property should be used for the benefit of certain charities. The trust was accepted by Gawthron and Sedman. However, Owen remained silent. Page-Wood V-C held that, having learned of the testator's intention, such silence amounted to an acceptance of the trust. He justified this conclusion on the grounds that 'the legatees, as soon as they learned the intention of the testator, would be bound to elect whether they would undertake the trust or not'.

(2) Half-secret trusts

The creation of a valid half-secret trust is dependent upon satisfaction of the same three elements of intention, communication, and acceptance. However, there are significant differences concerning the application of the requirement of communication. The leading case stipulating the requirements for half-secret trusts is *Blackwell v Blackwell*,[41] where Lord Sumner stated that the essential criteria were 'intention, communication and acquiescence'.[42] As the criteria of intention and acceptance are identical to those required for a valid fully secret trust, which have been discussed above, only the element of communication will be examined.

(a) Communication must be made before the execution of the will

It has already been seen that property bequeathed to an intended trustee will be subject to a fully secret trust if the testator made effective communication of the trust at any time before his death. In contrast, in the case of half-secret trusts it has been held that the testator must make communication to the intended trustee before his will is executed. Communication subsequent to the execution of the will, even though prior to the testator's death, will not subject the bequeathed property to an enforceable

---

39 [1972] Ch 698, at 711.   40 (1861) 1 John & H 352.
41 [1929] AC 318, HL.   42 Ibid., at 334.

half-secret trust. This follows from the judgment of Lord Sumner in *Blackwell v Blackwell*,[43] who stated:

A testator cannot reserve to himself a power of making future unwitnessed dispositions by merely naming a trustee and leaving the purposes of the trust to be supplied afterwards...

His comments in this respect were strictly obiter, because the trust in question had been communicated to the intended trustee before the testator's will was executed. However, the limitation was accepted by the Court of Appeal in *Re Keen*,[44] and followed in *Re Bateman's Will Trusts*.[45] It is hard to see the logic for this differentiation between fully and half secret trusts.[46] The justification provided for this insistence on communication before the execution of the will appears to arise by analogy between the doctrine of half-secret trusts and the principle of incorporation by reference. As was explained above, a document can only be incorporated into a will if it was in existence when the will was executed. It is submitted that this analogy is false, and that there is no reason for maintaining a distinction between the rules of communication applicable to fully and half-secret trusts. A document incorporated by reference becomes part of the will itself, whereas according to the prevailing theory a secret trust, whether fully or half-secret, arises wholly outside of the terms of the will.[47] It may yet be open to the House of Lords to find that a half-secret trust can be validly created by communication at any time before the death of the testator, and other jurisdictions have rejected the distinction and held that the same rule applies to both fully and half-secret trusts.[48] In the Irish case *Riordan v Banon*,[49] Chatterton V-C seems to have suggested that a valid half-secret trust can be created by communication after the date of the will but before the testator's death, and this has been supported by later cases.[50]

(b) Evidence will not be admissible of communication inconsistent with the face of the will

Even if a testator communicates the trust to the intended trustee of a half-secret trust before executing his will, evidence of such communication will not be admitted to establish the trust if it is inconsistent with the face of the will. Therefore, evidence of a communication inconsistent with the manner in which the will stated that communication would be made will not be admissible to prove the existence of a half-secret trust. The application of this rule had the effect of preventing the creation of a

---

[43] Ibid., at 339. [44] [1937] Ch 236. [45] [1970] 1 WLR 1463.

[46] Holdworth, 'Secret Trusts' (1937) 53 LQR 501. In *Gold v Hill* [1999] 1 FLR 54, a man who had separated from his wife nominated a solicitor as the beneficiary of a life insurance policy, having communicated to him that the proceeds were to be held on trust for his partner and her children. This nomination and communication had taken place after the execution of his will, which had left his estate to his wife. Carnwath J held that the situation was analogous to that of a half secret trust, but held that any doubts as to the effectiveness of communication after the execution of a will were derived from the particular rules applying to wills and should not create difficulties for nominations.

[47] See below, p 260. [48] See Scott, *Law of Trusts* (4th edn, 1988), para 55.8.

[49] (1876) 10 IrR Eq 469.

[50] See *Re King's Estate* (1888) 21 LR Ir 273; *Re Browne* [1944] IrR 90; *Re Prendeville* (5 December 1990, unreported) (Irish High Court). See [1992] Conv 202 (Mee).

half-secret trust in *Re Keen*.[51] While the terms of the trust had in fact been communicated to the trustee before the execution of the will, by means of a sealed envelope, the Court of Appeal held that evidence of the communication was inadmissible because clause 56 of the will anticipated that communication would only be made after the will had been executed. Therefore, evidence of the prior communication was inconsistent with the face of the will. In *Re Spence*[52] a testator had communicated the trust to some of the four trustees to whom he had jointly bequeathed the intended property. While such communication would have been sufficient to establish a fully secret trust, it was held that evidence of the communication was inadmissible to establish a half-secret trust. It was inconsistent with the terms of the will, which stated that communication had been made to them all.

The validity of this restriction should also be questioned. It is inconsistent with the approach applied to fully secret trusts, where parol evidence of communication is admissible to prove the secret trust, despite the fact that it is always inconsistent with the face of the will, which suggests that an absolute gift has been made. The inconsistency should only be material where it casts significant doubt upon whether the testator had intended the communication to be an effective expression of his wishes.

(3) The burden of proof required to establish a secret trust

In order to establish a secret trust, there must be evidence to show that the necessary requirements have been satisfied. The level of proof necessary to establish a secret trust has been a matter of some debate. Traditionally, secret trusts were thought to be imposed by the court to prevent the secret trustee committing a fraud by denying the existence of the trust. In *McCormick v Grogan*[53] Lord Westbury therefore held that an extremely high burden of proof must be discharged before the court would impose a secret trust:

Now, being a jurisdiction founded on personal fraud, it is incumbent on the court to see that a fraud, a malus animus, is proved by the clearest and most indisputable evidence…You are obliged, therefore, to show most clearly and distinctly that the person you wish to convert into a trustee acted mala animo. You must show distinctly that the testator or the intestate was beguiled and deceived by his conduct…

As will be seen below, this view of secret trusts imposed to prevent personal fraud has been rejected by more modern cases in favour of the theory that they are inter vivos trusts arising wholly outside of the testator's will.[54] It is therefore illogical to require the same special standard of proof as that which applies to an allegation of fraud. In *Ottaway v Norman*,[55] Brightman J suggested that what was required was a standard of proof 'analogous to that required before the court would rectify a written instrument'. This is higher than the usual civil law standard of proof on the balance of probabilities. However, in *Re Snowden*[56] Megarry V-C considered that even this was inappropriate, since it demanded a higher threshold than the ordinary civil standard of proof, and it

---

[51] [1937] Ch 236.   [52] [1949] WN 237.   [53] (1869) LR 4 HL 82.
[54] See below, p 260.   [55] [1972] Ch 698, at 699.   [56] [1979] 2 All ER 172.

was founded upon a false analogy between rectification of documents and the operation of secret trusts. He concluded that the standard of proof required to establish a secret trust was simply the 'ordinary standard of evidence required to establish a trust'.[57] The higher standard appropriate for fraud would only need to be satisfied in circumstances where the secret trust could only be established by holding the legatee guilty of fraud.

4 Failure of secret trusts

Where a testator has bequeathed property in his will intending that it should be subject to a secret trust, but having failed to satisfy the requisite criteria, the ultimate location of the ownership of the intended trust property will depend upon whether the trust was fully or half-secret.

(1) Failure of a fully secret trust

If a testator fails to establish a valid fully secret trust, the intended secret trustee will be entitled to take the property for himself absolutely. This is nothing other than his entitlement under the will because the fact of the trust does not appear from the face of the will.[58] The intended trustee will only be required to hold the property on resulting trust for the testator's residuary legatees or next of kin[59] if he admits that he was intended to receive the property as a trustee.

(2) Failure of a half-secret trust

Unlike a fully secret trust, a half-secret trust is evident from the face of the will. If the trust fails for any reason the trustee will therefore be prevented from retaining the property bequeathed to him by the will. Instead, he will hold it on resulting trust, either for the residuary legatees under the will or, if the bequest is of the residuary estate, for the testator's next of kin.[60]

5 Death or disclaimer of the secret trustee

A secret trust does not come into existence until the death of the testator who has bequeathed the trust property in his will to the intended secret trustee. Inevitably there is therefore a period of time, which in some cases may be substantial, between

---

[57] Ibid., at 178.

[58] Eg *Wallgrave v Tebbs* (1855) 2 K & J 313; *Jones v Badley* (1868) 3 Ch App 362; *McCormick v Grogan* (1869) LR 4 HL 82; *Re Pitt Rivers* [1902] 1 Ch 403.

[59] *Re Boyes* (1884) LR 26 Ch D 531.   [60] See *Re Cooper* [1939] Ch 811, CA.

the communication and acceptance of the trust and the death of the testator. This time interval will give rise to practical difficulties if the intended secret trustee predeceases the testator, or disclaims the trust on the death of the testator. In either event, the question will arise whether the intended trust property is subjected to a valid trust on the death of the testator. The answer will be determined primarily by the nature of the secret trust concerned.

(1) Death of the secret trustee

(a) Secret trustee predeceases the testator

(i) Fully secret trust

Under the law of succession, a bequest lapses and fails if the beneficiary predeceases the testator.[61] As a matter of logic, the predecease of a trustee of a fully secret trust should therefore cause the trust to fail. This was accepted in *Re Maddock*,[62] where Cozens-Hardy LJ stated that a fully secret trust will fail if the trustee dies during the lifetime of the testator. This is consistent with the modern explanation of the operation of secret trusts discussed below, namely that a secret trust is an expressly declared inter vivos trust which remains unconstituted until the testator's will operates to transfer the legal title to the trust property to the trustee. Since the predecease of the trustee causes the gift to lapse, the testator's will fails to effect a constitution of the trust.

(ii) Half-secret trusts

In the case of a fully secret trust, the existence of the intention to subject the property bequeathed to a trust is entirely absent from the face of the will. In contrast, where the trust is half-secret, the fact that the property bequeathed was intended to be subject to a trust is apparent from the will itself. It is therefore clear that the legatee was never intended to enjoy the property left to him absolutely. If the intended trustee of a half-secret trust predeceases the testator, equity will not allow the trust to fail for want of a trustee. The testator's personal representative will act as trustee in his place.[63] Provided that it is still possible to identify the terms thereof, the half-secret trust will not fail.

(b) Death of the secret trustee subsequent to the death of the testator

If the trustee of a secret trust, whether half- or fully secret, dies after the testator, the trust will not fail. In both cases the testator's will operates according to its terms to transfer the legal title of the property bequeathed to the secret trustee at the moment of the testator's death, thus constituting the trust. As the trust is fully constituted from the death of the testator, it will not fail for want of a trustee. However, if the death of the secret trustee renders it impossible to identify the beneficiary of the trust, the property will pass by resulting trust to the testator's residuary legatees or next of kin.

---

[61] *Elliott v Davenport* (1705) 1 P Wms 83; *Mabank v Brooks* (1780) 1 Bro CC 84.
[62] [1902] 2 Ch 220, at 231.   [63] See *Mallott v Wilson* [1903] 2 Ch 494.

(2) Secret trustee disclaims the trust

(a) Revocation of acceptance before the death of the testator

It has been seen that a secret trust will only be established if the intended trustee accepts that he will hold the property bequeathed to him on trust. His acceptance, however, is not irrevocable. A secret trustee is entitled to revoke a previous acceptance of the trust at any time before the death of the testator. If the trust was fully secret, a trustee who has revoked the trust will be entitled to take the property bequeathed to him in the will absolutely for his own benefit. In contrast, if the trust was half-secret, the intended trust property will be held on resulting trust for the testator's residuary legatees or next of kin. To be effective, the trustee must communicate his change of mind to the testator. He will otherwise be estopped from asserting his revocation of the agreement to hold upon trust.

(b) Disclaimer after the death of the testator

While a secret trustee may revoke his acceptance of the secret trust at any time before the death of the testator, in principle disclaimer after the will has taken effect should not invalidate the trust. Despite dicta to the contrary by Cozens-Hardy LJ in *Re Maddock*,[64] dicta of Lord Buckmaster and Lord Warrington in *Blackwell v Blackwell*[65] suggest that a secret trust will not fail if the trustee disclaims the trust subsequent to the testator's death. This is logical because the trust is constituted by the operation of the testator's will, thus crystallizing the secret beneficiary's equitable entitlement to the trust property. Since the trust has come into existence, it should not be allowed to fail for want of a trustee.

6 Can a secret trustee benefit from a secret trust?

In some cases, the trustee of a secret trust will enjoy no personal entitlement to the trust property and will hold it entirely for others. However in others the testator may also wish to grant the trustee some entitlement to the trust property, either as a joint beneficiary of the secret trust, or by way of a right to retain any surplus funds remaining after the beneficiaries have been allocated their interests. In *Irvine v Sullivan*[66] it was held that the trustee of a fully secret trust was entitled to retain the surplus of the trust property remaining after the trusts had been carried out. In contrast, in *Re Rees' Will Trusts*[67] the Court of Appeal held that the trustee of a half-secret trust was not entitled to assert any entitlement to such a surplus because this would be inconsistent with the terms of the will, which suggested that all the property bequeathed to him was subject to the trust. This decision was doubted by Pennycuick J in *Re Tyler's*

---

[64] [1902] 2 Ch 220.   [65] [1929] AC 318, at 328, 341.
[66] (1869) LR 8 Eq 673.   [67] [1950] Ch 204.

Fund Trusts[68] and there is no logical justification for maintaining this differentiation between fully secret and half-secret trusts.[69] It may be significant that in *Re Rees' Will Trusts* the trustee was the testator's solicitor and a beneficial gift was therefore inherently less likely.[70]

7 Justifying the enforcement of secret trusts

While it is easy to appreciate the practical advantages that have contributed to the evolution of secret trusts as mechanisms for allocating property on death, it is less easy to provide an adequate explanation of the legal principles justifying their enforcement. They appear to operate in contradiction of the clear policy of the Wills Act requiring testamentary dispositions to be executed in the specified form. Equity's effort to provide an adequate explanation for the enforcement of secret trusts is an *ex post facto* rationalization of a mechanism that had already developed. It has already been noted that historically, equity enforced secret trusts on the grounds that to fail to do so would allow the Wills Act to be used as an instrument of fraud. Cases after the decision of the House of Lords in *Blackwell v Blackwell*[71] have held that they are enforced as valid inter vivos trusts arising outside (dehors) the will. The advantage of this explanation is that it does not predicate a conflict between the enforcement of secret trusts and the provisions of the Wills Act. However, even this theory is not wholly satisfactory.

(1) Secret trusts enforced to prevent fraud

In the nineteenth century equity accepted that secret trusts were enforced in order to prevent fraud. The secret trustee had induced the testator to leave property to him on the understanding that he would apply it for the benefit of the secret beneficiary. If the secret trustee were permitted to deny the trust, because of a lack of testamentary formalities, and to assert a personal entitlement to the property bequeathed to him in the testator's will, he would be using the Wills Act as an instrument of fraud. To prevent such a fraud, equity would allow the admission of parol evidence on behalf of the beneficiary to prove that the bequest had been subject to a trust. This rationale was accepted by the House of Lords in *McCormick v Grogan*,[72] where Lord Hatherley LC described the enforcement of secret trusts as:

a doctrine which involves a wide departure from the policy of . . . the [Wills Act] and it is only in clear cases of fraud that this doctrine has been applied—cases in which the court has been persuaded that there has been a fraudulent inducement held out on the part of the apparent

---

[68] [1967] 1 WLR 1269.   [69] See Oakley, *Constructive Trusts* (3rd edn, 1997), p 259.
[70] See [1950] Ch 204, at 211, per Lord Evershed MR.
[71] [1929] AC 318.   [72] (1869) LR 4 HL 82.

beneficiary in order to lead the testator to confide to him the duty which he so understood to perform.[73]

Lord Westbury also emphasized that the enforcement of secret trusts was 'founded altogether on personal fraud'.[74]

However, despite the early acceptance of the fraud explanation by the House of Lords, it came to be thought that the fraud theory was inadequate as a justification for the enforcement of secret trusts.[75] A number of defects were identified. First, the fraud theory accepts that the enforcement of secret trusts is in direct conflict with the provisions and policy of the Wills Act. Although such conflict has been tolerated in other areas, for example where the principle of *Rochefoucauld v Boustead*[76] operates to enforce an oral declaration of a trust of land despite the lack of writing, the courts today are reluctant to adopt an analysis so directly opposed to the terms of legislation. Second, a major defect of the fraud theory was that it did not provide an adequate justification for the enforcement of half-secret trusts. In the case of a half-secret trust, the fact of the trust is evident from the face of the will, so that there is no possibility of fraud. The secret trustee cannot take the property absolutely for himself. Fraud would easily be avoided by the secret trustee holding any property received under the will on resulting trust for the residuary legatees or the testator's next of kin. Third, it is questionable whether the fraud theory is also capable of explaining why a fully secret trust should be enforced in favour of the secret beneficiary. While it might justify the refusal to allow the secret trustee to take the property bequeathed to him by the testator absolutely, it is less easy to see why the possibility of fraud justifies enforcement of the trust in favour of the secret beneficiary. Any fraud could equally be prevented if the trustee was required to hold the property on resulting trust for the residuary legatees under the will or the testator's next of kin. This would prevent the trustee benefiting by his fraud, but would not contradict the provisions of the Wills Act. Fourth, as has been noted above, adoption of the fraud theory had the effect that an unduly high burden of proof needed to be discharged if a beneficiary was to establish that property was held on secret trust. In consequence of these inadequacies, the fraud analysis has been rejected in more modern cases in favour of a theory that secret trusts arise entirely outside of the operation of the testator's will by express inter vivos declaration.

However, the fraud theory continues to enjoy the support of some academics. Critchley has argued that the modern theory that secret trusts arise outside of the will is implausible, and argues that secret trusts are upheld to prevent fraud where this is demanded by legal policy.[77] Such enforcement will only be justified where there is a combination of personal wrongdoing on the part of the trustee, and harm would be caused to beneficiary and/or testator if the trust were not enforced. The requisite element of personal wrongdoing would only be satisfied if 'the trustee was fully

---

[73] Ibid., at 89.   [74] Ibid., at 99.

[75] See Hodge 'Secret Trusts: the Fraud Theory Revisited' [1980] Conv 341.

[76] [1897] 1 Ch 196, CA. See above p 226.

[77] 'Instruments of Fraud, Testamentary Dispositions, and the Doctrine of Secret Trusts' (1999) 115 LQR 631.

aware that the property was only to be transferred to him on trust, but that he took no steps to deny this understanding until the transfer was completed beyond the recall of the testator'.[78] However, this argument does not address all of the problems identified above. Critchley concludes that while the fraud maxim might justify the enforcement of a fully secret trustee where the trustee actively seeks to deny the trust, it is 'less overwhelmingly supportive' of justifying the enforcement of other fully and half-secret trusts. She therefore suggests that these other secret trusts must be allowed to tag along in the wake of those which can be justified on the basis of fraud, since otherwise further problems, such as the increase of opportunities for fraud, or of litigation over the construction of the will, seem likely, if not bound, to emerge.[79] It is submitted that this concedes that the fraud theory, even articulated in a more sophisticated form, is incapable of adequately justifying the enforcement of secret trusts.

(2) Secret trusts arise outside of the testator's will

The modern justification of the enforcement of secret trusts was neatly summarized by Megarry V-C in *Re Snowden*:[80]

the whole basis of secret trusts, as I understand it, is that they operate outside the will, changing nothing that is written in it, and allowing it to operate according to its tenor, but then fastening a trust on to the property in the hands of the recipient.

This explanation evolved from the decision of the House of Lords in *Cullen v A-G for Ireland*, where Lord Westbury said:

I think it very material to point out that where there is a secret trust...the title of the party claiming under the secret trust...is a title dehors the will, and which cannot be correctly termed testamentary.[81]

It was utilized and developed by the House of Lords in *Blackwell v Blackwell*[82] to justify the enforceability of half-secret trusts. Its overwhelming advantage is that it does not presuppose a contradiction between the enforcement of secret trusts and the Wills Act.[83]

The essence of this modern justification for the enforcement of secret trusts is that they come into existence entirely outside of the operation of the will to which they relate, so that the equitable interest enjoyed by the secret beneficiary is not a species of testamentary disposition. The modern theory postulates two distinguishable stages in the creation of a valid secret trust. First, the testator communicates to the secret trustee his intention to subject the property bequeathed to a trust, at which point the secret trustee accepts the trust obligation. However, at this point the secret trust has not yet come into existence. The intended subject matter of the trust remains the absolute property of the testator, and the legal title to it has not been transferred to the trustee. In effect the testator and trustee have agreed that the property will be subject to a trust

---

[78] Ibid., at 647.　　[79] Ibid., at 653.　　[80] [1979] 2 All ER 172, at 177.
[81] [1866] LR 1 HL 190, at 196.　　[82] [1929] AC 318.　　[83] Ibid., at 340.

(i) The trust is declared inter vivos but remains unconstitued

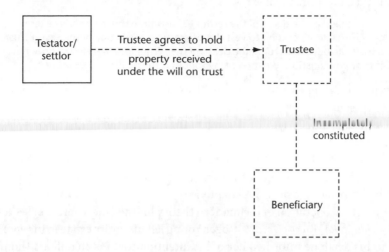

(ii) The trust is constituted by the operation of the settlor's will

Figure 8.1 The operation of secret trusts

when it comes into the hands of the trustee but at present the trust remains incompletely constituted. Second, when the testator dies his will operates according to its terms to transfer the legal title to the property bequeathed to the secret trustee. His receipt of the property in this way has the effect of constituting the incompletely constituted trust.[84] He henceforth holds the property on trust for the secret beneficiary (see Figure 8.1).

---

[84] Critchley, however, argues that this analysis is 'implausible': (1999) 115 LQR 631, at 634.

The secret trust does not therefore arise completely independently of the testator's will. As Kincaid has commented:

A secret trust relies on the death of the settlor to constitute the trust and the terms of the will or the rules of intestate succession to vest the property in the hands of the secret trustee or legatee. The trust can be revoked until the death of the settlor and therefore it does not stand alone until it is properly constituted either *inter vivos* or on the death of the settlor.[85]

This explanation appears to involve no element of conflict between the enforcement of a secret trust and the provisions of the Wills Act. The testator's will operates according to its terms, transferring ownership of the bequeathed property to the legatee. The trust is enforced not under the will, but because the legatee has previously agreed that he will observe the terms of the trust which were communicated to him by the testator. In a sense the secret trust is constituted by a mechanism similar to the rule in *Strong v Bird*[86] examined in the previous chapter.

The practical operation of the modern theory for the enforcement of secret trusts is clearly seen in *Re Young (Decd).*[87] Roger Young left his entire estate to his wife, Eveleen. Prior to his death he informed her of his intention that his chauffeur, Thomas Cobb, should receive a legacy of £2,000. This prima facie established a fully secret trust in Cobb's favour. However, Cobb was coincidentally one of the witnesses to Roger's will. By s 15 of the Wills Act 1837 a legacy to a person attesting a will is forfeit. The central question was, therefore, whether Cobb's entitlement to the £2,000 subject to the secret trust should be characterized as a legacy under the will, in which case it would be void. Danckwerts J held that the chauffeur was entitled to receive the money because his entitlement was by way of a secret trust which had arisen wholly outside of the will:

The whole theory of the formulation of a secret trust is that the Wills Act has nothing to do with the matter because the forms required by the Wills Act are entirely disregarded, since the persons do not take by virtue of the gift in the will, but by virtue of the secret trusts imposed upon the beneficiary, who does in fact take under the will.[88]

(3) Date of accrual of the beneficial interest under a secret trust

A further practical problem that has arisen relates to the time at which the beneficiary of a secret trust accrues the equitable interest in the bequeathed property intended as the subject matter thereof. In principle, because a secret trust is only fully constituted when the testator's will operates to transfer the bequeathed property to the trustee, a secret beneficiary should not be entitled to any interest in the putative trust property until the death of the testator. Prior to his death, the testator retains the right to change his will, enabling him to subvert the trust by bequeathing the property to someone other than the secret trustee, thus ensuring that the trust is never constituted.[89] The logic of this argument was not, however, followed in *Re*

---

[85] 'The Tangled Web: The Relationship between a Secret Trust and the Will' [2000] Conv 420, at 442.
[86] (1874) LR 18 Eq 315   [87] [1951] Ch 344.   [88] Ibid., at 350.
[89] Pawlowski and Brown argue, however, that an estoppel equity may arise from the moment that the testator departs from his promise to benefit the secret beneficiary and changes his will: 'Constituting a Secret Trust by Estoppel' [2004] Conv 388.

Gardner (No 2).[90] A testatrix made a will leaving all her property to her husband for life, with the remainder subject to a secret trust in favour of her two nieces and nephew. At the date of the testatrix's death she had been predeceased by one of her nieces. The court was required to decide whether the personal representative of the niece was entitled to a third share of the remainder interest by way of the secret trust. Romer J held that, as a secret beneficiary, the niece had been entitled to her share of the trust property from the moment that the husband had accepted the terms of the trust. Her third share was therefore held on trust for her personal representative, notwithstanding that she had predeceased the testator. This case is open to the criticism that the niece cannot have gained an interest in the testatrix's estate until her death, since a secret trust remains unconstituted until the will operates to transfer the trust property to the trustee. Prior to the testator's death, the trust does not exist. It is therefore submitted that the decision in *Re Gardner (No 2)* is incorrect and that a secret beneficiary enjoys no entitlement to the putative trust property until the trust is fully constituted through the operation of the testator's will.

(4) Problems associated with the modern theory

The currently fashionable theory for explaining secret trusts is less elegant than it may seem and has attracted academic criticism. There appears to be no reason why the testator should not change his mind about the creation of the trust prior to his death, either by informing the trustee that he no longer wishes to create a trust, or by an amendment to his will. The secret trust therefore shares one of the characteristics of a testamentary gift, namely that it is revocable at any time prior to the testator's death. Furthermore, secret trusts are clearly intended to become operative only on the testator's death, so that they do not in any way inhibit the testator's power to deal as he wishes with his property during his lifetime. This is also a characteristic of a testamentary gift. Finally, in *Re Maddock*[91] a gift by way of a secret trust was treated as if it had been made by will in a case where the estate was insufficient to meet all the specific gifts made by the testator. The case for treating gifts under a half-secret trust in this way would be even stronger.

Critchley has therefore argued that the *dehors* (outside) the will theory cannot justify the enforcement of secret trusts.[92] She submits that secret trusts are testamentary dispositions because they possess the characteristics of ambulatoriness and revocability, in that they do not take effect until the death of the testator, and the testator can change his mind:

the *dehors* theory seems to be fatally flawed. In essence the mistake is to confuse 'outside the will' with 'outside the *Wills Act*'. The *dehors* theory needs—and fails—to demonstrate the trust of the latter and too often ends up resting merely upon the former, which is wholly inadequate as a justificatory argument.[93]

---

[90] [1923] 2 Ch 230. [91] [1902] 2 Ch 220.

[92] 'Instruments of Fraud, Testamentary Dispositions, and the Doctrine of Secret Trusts' (1999) 115 LQR 631.

[93] Ibid., at 641.

However, in the light of the admitted inability of the rival fraud theory to justify the enforcement of all the well-established categories of secret trusts, it is submitted that the modern theory that secret trusts arise outside of the will remains the most convincing justification.[94] It is certainly the explanation that commands the support of the authorities. While the fashionable modern theory explaining their operation is imperfect, it has the merit of pragmatism.

(5) The juridical nature of secret trusts

The accepted modern justification for enforcement of secret trusts is that they arise inter vivos outside of the will. However, the acceptance of this theory does not of itself answer the question whether secret trusts should be characterized as express or constructive trusts. This is not an entirely esoteric academic question. If secret trusts are characterized as express in nature, practical difficulties arise where the intended trust property is land or an interest in land, as s 53(1)(b) of the Law of Property Act 1925 renders an oral declaration of a trust of land unenforceable without substantiating evidence in writing. In contrast, if they are characterized as constructive in nature, a secret trust of land will be enforceable without the need for further formalities as s 53(2) exempts all constructive trusts from the need of writing.

(a) Secret trusts characterized as express trusts

The modern theory that secret trusts arise inter vivos outside of the testator's will would logically suggests that they are express in nature. The acceptance of the trust by the secret trustee amounts to an express inter vivos declaration of trust. This view has been favoured in the past by most academic writers.[95] However, such a characterization could produce the unsatisfactory implication of rendering an oral agreement to hold land subject to a secret trust unenforceable through the absence of writing, as required by s 53(1)(b) of the Law of Property Act 1925.[96] Thus, in *Re Baillie*[97] North J held a secret trust of land unenforceable because the Statute of Frauds applied and the trust had not been indicated in writing. In other cases, for example *Ottaway v Norman*,[98] orally declared secret trusts of land have been enforced without question. Of itself the enforcement of the trusts in such cases fails to prove the point, since a trust will not fail for lack of formalities unless the absence of writing is specifically pleaded as a ground of invalidity.[99] However, even if secret trusts are characterized as express

---

[94] Emma Challinor has argued that no logical rationale for the enforcement of secret trusts may be discerned, and that they are covert devices by which the courts avoid the statutory formalities of the Wills Act 1837, thus subverting the policy of the Wills Act: 'Debunking the Myth of Secret Trusts?' [2005] Conv 493. She therefore proposes abolition or fundamental revision of the law relating to secret trusts.

[95] See Snell, *Principles of Equity* (30th edn, 2000), pp 132–136; Pettit, *Equity and the Law of Trusts* (12th edn, 2009); Oakley, *Constructive Trusts* (3rd edn, 1997), p 263; (1991) 5 Tru LI 69 (Caughlon). See also Sheridan 'English and Irish Secret Trusts' (1951) 67 LQR 314—where half-secret trusts are held to be express, but fully secret trusts to be constructive.

[96] See Chapter 27.   [97] (1886) 2 TLR 660.   [98] [1972] Ch 698.

[99] *North v Loomes* [1919] 1 Ch 378.

trusts, it is submitted that an orally declared secret trust of land should not fail merely because of the lack of writing. The court should invoke the well-established doctrine of *Rochefoucauld v Boustead*,[100] namely that equity will not allow the statute requiring trusts of land to be evidenced in writing to be used as an instrument of fraud, to prevent the secret trustee denying the trust because of the absence of writing. This would not mark a reversion to the fraud explanation of the enforcement of secret trusts in conflict with the terms of the Wills Act, as the rule in *Rochefoucauld v Boustead* would only be employed to prevent the use of s 53(1)(b) of the Law of Property Act as an instrument of fraud.

(b) Secret trusts characterized as constructive trusts

Despite traditional academic consensus that secret trusts are express in nature, in *Re Cleaver*[101] Nourse J characterized them as constructive trusts. As the case concerned the doctrine of mutual wills, his expression of opinion is strictly obiter. A number of commentators have adopted the view that secret trusts are gratuitous promises enforced as constructive trusts on the grounds of fraud or unconscionability.[102]

---

[100] [1897] 1 Ch 196, CA.   [101] [1981] 1 WLR 939.

[102] McFarlane, 'Constructive Trusts Arising on a Receipt of Property *Sub Conditione*' (2004) 120 LQR 667. See also Hanbury and Martin, *Modern Equity* (18th edn, 2009), pp 174–175, which concludes that secret trusts can be enforced as either express trusts or constructive trusts, and suggests that the area be made subject to a statutory scheme.

9

Resulting trusts

The previous two chapters have examined the circumstances in which a trust relationship may be created by the deliberate intention and act of the settlor. Such trusts are known as 'express trusts'. However, in some situations property will be regarded as subject to a trust despite the absence of any express intention on the part of the settlor. In English law 'resulting trusts' are one of the two main categories of such informal trusts, the other being that of 'constructive trusts' (considered in the next chapter). In general, resulting trusts arise to give effect to the implied intention of the owner of property that someone else should not enjoy the benefit of it.

1 Introduction to resulting trusts

(1) What are resulting trusts?[1]

The circumstances in which property will become subject to a resulting trust were examined by the House of Lords in *Westdeutsche Landesbank Girozentrale v Islington London Borough Council.*[2] Lord Browne-Wilkinson identified two circumstances in which a resulting trust would arise:

Under existing law a resulting trust arises in two sets of circumstances: (A) where A makes a voluntary payment to B or pays (wholly or in part) for the purchase of property which is vested either in B alone or in the joint names of A and B, there is a presumption that A did not intend to make a gift to B; the money or property is held on trust for A (if he is the sole provider of the money) or in the case of a joint purchaser by A and B in shares proportionate to their contributions. It is important to stress that this is only a *presumption,* which presumption is easily rebutted either by the counter presumption of advancement or by direct evidence of A's intention to make an outright transfer... (B) Where A transfers property to B *on express trusts*, but the trusts declared do not exhaust the whole beneficial interest.[3]

---

[1] See Chambers, *Resulting Trusts* (1997).
[2] [1996] AC 669. See Birks 'Trusts Raised to Avoid Unjust Enrichment: The *Westdeutsche* Case' [1996] RLR 3.
[3] [1996] AC 669, at 708.

Resulting trusts of the second type will be examined in Chapter 20, where it will be seen that they operate to 'fill the gap' in the beneficial ownership of property where an express trust fails. This chapter will be concerned largely with resulting trusts of the first type, commonly termed 'presumed resulting trusts'.

(2) Distinguishing resulting and constructive trusts

In some cases, the House of Lords seem to have used 'resulting' and 'constructive' trusts as interchangeable terms,[4] suggesting that it is not necessary to distinguish between them. However, it is submitted that they are fundamentally different, operating on different principles, and that they need to be strictly differentiated.

Constructive trusts[5] are imposed by the court as a consequence of the conduct of the party who becomes a trustee. Resulting trusts are not imposed as a response to the conduct of the trustee, but to give effect to the implied intentions of the owner. Where a transfer of property has occurred and the legal title has been transferred, but the transferor has failed to show an intention to divest himself fully of all his interest in that property, the transferee will not be permitted to receive the property absolutely for his own benefit. Instead, he will hold it on trust for the transferor. The equitable interests are said to 'result back' to the transferor, thus ensuring that he retains his interest in the property. Practical imperatives may also demand that a distinction be drawn between beneficial entitlements taking effect under resulting and constructive trusts. *Re Densham (A Bankrupt)*[6] concerned a dispute as to the ownership of a matrimonial home. While the husband was the sole legal owner of the house, his wife had contributed towards the purchase price and they had also agreed that the ownership should be jointly shared. Goff J held that, in consequence of the agreement, the wife was prima facie entitled to a beneficial half share in the ownership of the house by way of a constructive trust, and that through her direct financial contribution to the purchase price she was also entitled to a ninth share of the beneficial ownership by way of a resulting trust. However, because the husband was bankrupt, she was held unable to assert any entitlement by way of the constructive trust, because it was not a settlement made for 'valuable consideration' and therefore void against his trustee in bankruptcy.[7] Nevertheless, she was able to assert her entitlement by way of the resulting trust.

Re Densham therefore illustrates the need to distinguish between the operation of resulting and constructive trusts. This need was reiterated by the Court of Appeal in *Drake v Whipp*,[8] where the central issue was as to the proportion of the equitable interest that the plaintiff enjoyed in a barn owned by her erstwhile partner by virtue of her contributions to the purchase price and work done, where there was also a

---

[4] For example, *Gissing v Gissing* [1971] AC 886, at 905, per Lord Diplock; *Tinsley v Milligan* [1993] 3 All ER 65, at 86–87, per Lord Browne-Wilkinson.

[5] See Chapter 10.   [6] [1975] 1 WLR 1519.

[7] Bankruptcy Act 1914, s 42.   [8] [1996] 1 FLR 826.

common intention that she was to enjoy a share of the ownership. Peter Gibson LJ remarked:

A potent source of confusion, to my mind, has been suggestions that it matters not whether the terminology used is that of the constructive trust, to which the intention, actual or imputed, of the parties is crucial, or that of the resulting trust which operates as a presumed intention of the contributing party in the absence of rebutting evidence of actual intention.[9]

Thus, while by means of a resulting trust the plaintiff would only be entitled to a share of the beneficial interest directly equivalent to the proportion of her contribution to the purchase price of the barn (which was 19.4 per cent), by way of a constructive trust she was entitled to a third interest.[10]

Most cases involving resulting trusts have involved the family home. In this context, there has been some blurring of the distinction between resulting trusts and constructive trusts. In some recent decisions the courts have treated any financial contribution to the family home as opening up to the court the option to confer on the contributor a share of ownership which is not calculated arithmetically by reference to the financial contribution, but which is a 'fair share' on the basis of all the parties' dealings with the property. An illustration is provided by the decision of the Court of Appeal in *Oxley v Hiscock*.[11] Ms Oxley had contributed 22 per cent of the cost of acquiring the family home, but the Court of Appeal held that she was entitled to a 40 per cent share of the value of the home even though there had never been any discussion about what share she should have. It would be unwise to see such cases as this as establishing a general principle applicable in all situations. What is happening in reality is the development of a special jurisprudence applicable to cohabiting couples. This jurisprudence is explored in Chapter 11.

(3) **Rationale of resulting trusts**

In *Westdeutsche Landesbank Girozentrale v Islington London Borough Council*[12] Lord Browne-Wilkinson stated that resulting trusts arise to fulfil the implied intentions of the parties:

Both types of resulting trust are traditionally regarded as examples of trusts giving effect to the common intentions of the parties. A resulting trust is not imposed by law against the intentions of the trustee (as is a constructive trust) but gives effect to his presumed intention.[13]

However, this formulation is open to question. While it is certainly the case that a presumed resulting trust arises in consequence of the presumed intention of the transferor of the trust property (or contributor to its purchase, as the case may be) it is not necessarily the case that the trustee who received the legal title intended the property to be held on trust. In many cases, a resulting trust has been found in circumstances where the transferee of the legal title anticipated that a gift had been made divesting the transferor of his entire interest in the property. This can be seen from the fact that

---

[9] Ibid., at 827.   [10] See also *Midland Bank Plc v Cooke* [1995] 4 All ER 562.
[11] [2004] EWCA Civ 546.   [12] [1996] AC 669.   [13] Ibid., at 708.

many cases involve a dispute as to whether a presumption of resulting trust has been rebutted. As Lord Browne-Wilkinson himself observed, a resulting trust of the first type arises because 'there is a presumption that A did not intend to make a gift to B'.[14] A resulting trust will arise in favour of A in such circumstances even though B anticipated that he was the beneficiary of an absolute gift, and in this sense B will be required to hold the property on resulting trust against his intentions. More significantly, a resulting trust may even arise where the transferee of property was unaware that the transfer had occurred.[15] Therefore, it should not be thought that a resulting trust will only arise on the basis of the mutual intention of the parties. Instead, a resulting trust should arise whenever a transferee (or contributor) cannot be shown to have possessed the intention to make a gift. As Lord Goff stated, a presumed resulting trust arises when there are:

voluntary payments by A to B, or for the purchase of property in the name of B or in his and A's joint names, where there is no presumption of advancement or evidence of intention to make an out-and-out gift.[16]

A number of earlier cases provide a less confusing analysis of the rationale for the creation of resulting trusts. In *Re Sick and Funeral Society of St John's Sunday School, Golcar*[17] Megarry V-C stated that:

A resulting trust is essentially a property concept: any property that a man does not effectually dispose of remains his own.

This clearly recognizes that a resulting trust arises because of the failure of the transferor to make an absolute gift of his property. As Lord Reid observed in *Vandervell v IRC*:

where it appears to have been the intention of the donor that the donee should not take beneficially, there will be a resulting trust in favour of the donor.[18]

A more nuanced understanding of the operation of resulting trusts was provided by the Privy Council in *Air Jamaica Ltd v Charlton*, where Lord Millett stated:

Like a constructive trust, a resulting trust arises by operation of law, although unlike a constructive trust it gives effect to intention. But it arises whether or not the transferor intended to retain a beneficial interest—he almost always does not—since it responds to the absence of any intention on his part to pass a beneficial interest to the recipient.[19]

2 Presumed resulting trusts[20]

Presumed resulting trusts arise where the transferor of property did not intend to dispose of his entire ownership interest in the property transferred. Under English law there is a rebuttable presumption that a transferor of property does not intend

---

[14] [1996] AC 669, at 708.
[15] As, for example, in *Re Vinogradoff* [1935] WN 68. See Chambers, *Resulting Trusts* (1997), p 37.
[16] [1996] AC 669, at 689.   [17] [1973] Ch 51.   [18] [1967] 2 AC 291, HL.
[19] [1999] 1 WLR 1399, at 1412.   [20] See Chambers, *Resulting Trusts* (1997), pp 11–39.

to make a gift of it, and unless this presumption is rebutted the transferee will hold it on resulting trust for the donor. However, in some circumstances the nature of the relationship between the transferor and the transferee gives rise to an opposite presumption, namely that the transferor did intend to benefit the transferee, in which case unless the presumption of a gift is rebutted there will be no resulting trust. This counter-presumption is known as the 'presumption of advancement'.

(1) The basic presumption of resulting trust

English law adopts two basic presumptions about the intentions of property owners, both of which are rebuttable by evidence of a contrary intention.

(a) A presumption against gifts

First, it is presumed that, outside of certain relationships, an owner of property never intends to make a gift. If an owner voluntarily transfers the legal title of his property to a third party without receiving any consideration in return, he is presumed to have intended to retain the equitable interest for himself. The transferee will therefore hold the property on resulting trust for him. This presumption was invented by equity to defeat the misappropriation of property as a consequence of potentially fraudulent or improvident transactions.[21]

(b) A presumption in favour of the provider of purchase money

By extension of this first presumption, it is also presumed that a person who provides the money required to purchase property intends to obtain the equitable interest in the property acquired. Therefore, when the property is purchased in the name of someone who did not provide the purchase money, he will be presumed to hold the legal title on trust for the provider thereof. This presumption is long established and was recognized in *Dyer v Dyer*, where Eyre CB stated:

the trust of a legal estate...whether taken in the names of the purchasers and others jointly, or in the names of others without that of the purchaser; whether in one name or several; whether jointly or successive, results to the man who advances the purchase-money.[22]

Where a person has only contributed a part of the purchase price of property, a resulting trust will be presumed in his favour of an equivalent proportion of the equitable interest.[23] *Tinsley v Milligan*[23a] (see Figure 9.2) provides an example.

(2) Voluntary transfers of property

Where an owner makes a voluntary transfer of property, either into the sole name of the transferee or into the joint names of himself and the transferee, without receiving any consideration in return, a resulting trust will be presumed in his favour unless

---

[21] *Lynch v Burke* [1995] 2 IR 159, per O'Flaherty J.　　[22] (1788) 2 Cox Eq Cas 92, at 93.

[23] *Midland Bank plc v Cooke* [1995] 4 All ER 562; *Drake v Whipp* [1996] 1 FLR 826.

[23a] [1993] 3All E R 65. See below, p 280.

Figure 9.1 *Re Vinogradoff*

rebutted by evidence that he intended to make a gift. The presumption of a resulting trust clearly operates in the context of voluntary transfers of personal property, but it is less certain whether it operates in respect to voluntary transfers of land.

(a) Operation of the presumption of resulting trust in the context of personal property

The operation of the presumption of a resulting trust is well illustrated by *Re Vinogradoff* (see Figure 9.1).[24] Mrs Vindogradoff transferred £800 War Loan stock into the joint names of herself and her infant granddaughter. Farwell J held that the stock was held on resulting trust for her,[25] and that therefore on her death it belonged in equity to her estate. In *Thavorn v Bank of Credit and Commerce International SA*[26] a resulting trust was found to exist where a woman opened a bank account in favour of her infant nephew. In 1981 Mrs Thavorn opened an account with some £20,000 in her nephew's name. She had directed the bank that she alone was to operate the account. Lloyd J held that in these circumstances there was no evidence to rebut the presumption of a resulting trust:

There was not the slightest evidence on which I could hold that, by opening the account in his name, she intended to transfer any beneficial interest to him during her lifetime.[27]

The bank was therefore liable to pay damages when they paid the money into his current account. A presumption of resulting trust will also arise where a person transfers money into a bank account in joint names. In *Aroso v Coutts*[28] it was held that the presumption of resulting trusts operated when Sr Aroso transferred money into a joint

---

[24] [1935] WN 68. See also *Re Muller* [1953] NZLR 879.

[25] The granddaughter was held to be a trustee of the resulting trust despite her minority. See Law of Property Act 1925, s 20.

[26] [1985] 1 Lloyd's Rep 259. Compare also *Re Howes* (1905) 21 TLR 501.

[27] [1985] 1 Lloyd's Rep 259, at 263.   [28] [2002] 1 All ER (Comm) 241.

Figure 9.2 *Tinsley v Milligan*

account opened in the names of himself and his nephew, although the presumption was held to have been rebutted by evidence that a gift had been intended.

(b) Operation of the presumption of resulting trust in the context of land

While the presumption of resulting trust clearly operates in respect of voluntary transfers of personal property, a more difficult question is whether the presumption against gifts continues to apply in the context of voluntary transfers of land. Section 60(3) of the Law of Property Act 1925 provides:

In a voluntary conveyance a resulting trust for the grantor shall not be implied merely by reason that the property is not expressed to be conveyed for the use or benefit of the grantee.

There has been much debate as to whether this provision was enacted to remove the presumption of resulting trust where land is conveyed voluntarily,[29] or whether it was merely intended to remove a conveyancing inconvenience. Prior to the enactment of s 60(3), it was necessary to declare in a voluntary conveyance that land was granted 'unto and to the use of' the grantee to ensure an effective transfer. It has therefore been argued that s 60(3) was intended to render such a declaration unnecessary, so that the mere absence of it will not alone lead to a resulting trust, while leaving the operation of the presumption intact.[30] The true effect of s 60(3) has not fallen for determination by the higher courts. In *Tinsley v Milligan*[31] Lord Browne-Wilkinson commented that it was 'arguable that the position has been altered by the 1925 property legislation',[32] and

---

[29] Chambers, *Resulting Trusts* (1997), pp 18–19.

[30] See Cheshire and Burn, *Modern Law of Real Property* (15th edn, 1994), p 161.

[31] [1993] 3 All ER 65, HL.

[32] See also *Hodgson v Marks* [1971] Ch 892, where Russell LJ described the proposition that s 60(3) has put an end to the presumption, resulting trusts of land as 'debatable'.

in *Hodgson v Marks*[33] the Court of Appeal held that a resulting trust arose in favour of an elderly lady who had transferred the legal title to her house to her lodger on the basis of an oral understanding that he would look after her affairs. However, in *Lohia v Lohia*,[34] Nicholas Strauss, QC held that although both proposed interpretations of s 60(3) could reasonably be adopted by the court, on a 'plain reading' the presumption of resulting trust had been abolished in respect of a voluntary conveyance of land. Thus a presumption of resulting trust will only arise if there is some fact in addition to the lack of consideration, such as that the parties are strangers. In the light of this interpretation, he held that no resulting trust had arisen where a son had conveyed his share in the family home to his father. The mere fact that there was no evidence of any sensible reason why he had so conveyed his share in the house to his father, and that he had continued to share mortgage payments and rental income, was not sufficient to lead to the inference of a resulting trust.

It remains to be seen whether this interpretation is supported by the higher courts. It is submitted, however, that the alternative interpretation is preferable. As Nicholas Strauss, QC himself indicated, it is doubtful whether the differences between land and personalty, and between methods of making apparent gifts, provide meaningful bases for distinction. The presumptions of resulting trust and advancement operate in practice primarily to allocate the burden of proof where property has been transferred and there is a dispute as to the effect of the transfer. To eliminate the presumption of resulting trust in relation to land is, in effect, to introduce something akin to the presumption of advancement where land has been voluntarily conveyed. The transferor will therefore have to bring forward evidence to show that the beneficial interest was not intended to be transferred. The facts of *Lohia v Lohia* demonstrate that it may prove difficult to discharge such a burden. It is clearly desirable that any transfer of land where no consideration is paid should make it explicit whether or not a gift is intended.

(3) Purchase money resulting trusts

The presumption of a resulting trust in favour of a contributor to the purchase price of property applies to both personal property and land.

(a) Purchase money resulting trust of personal property

The presumption of a resulting trust of personal property was raised in *Fowkes v Pascoe*.[35] John Pascoe was the grandson of Sarah Baker. Over a period of some five years, Sarah Baker purchased annuities totalling £7,000 in the joint names of herself and John Pascoe. The Court of Appeal accepted that there was thus a presumption of a resulting trust in favour of Sarah Baker, but held the evidence rebutted

---

[33] [1971] Ch 892. This decision has been quite contentious—see, for example, Swadling in Birks and Rose, *Resulting Trusts and Equitable Compensation* (2000, Oxford), p 61, where it is suggested that the decision should have been reached on an application of express trust principles.

[34] [2001] WTLR 101.   [35] (1875) 10 Ch App 343.

this presumption and demonstrated that a gift had been intended. In *The Venture*,[36] a resulting trust was held to have arisen in favour of a contributor to the purchase price of a yacht. In *Abrahams v Trustee in Bankruptcy of Abrahams*,[37] it was held that a presumption of resulting trust operated where a wife, who was separated from her husband, contributed to a syndicate purchasing National Lottery tickets in the names of her husband. Since the presumption was not rebutted the husband held his share of the winnings, some £242,000, on resulting trust for his wife.

The important case of *Foskett v McKeown*[38] concerned the question whether a contributor to the premiums of a life insurance policy thereby gained a proportionate share of the proceeds of the policy. Mr Murphy had taken out a life insurance policy in 1986 that would provide a death benefit of £1 million. He paid the annual premiums for the first two years using his own money, but paid subsequent premiums using misappropriated trust money. He committed suicide in 1991, at which point at least 40 per cent of the premiums had been paid using trust money. The question was whether the beneficiaries were entitled to a proportionate share of the proceeds of the policy. While there was no doubt that the trust money had been used to pay premiums, under the terms of the policy the death benefit would still have been payable even if they had not been made, due to the payment of the earlier premiums. In *Re Policy No 6402 of the Scottish Equitable Life Assurance Society*[39] Joyce J had held that resulting trust principles were applicable to a life policy. In the Court of Appeal[40] Scott V-C held that this case was distinguishable because the contributions giving rise to the resulting trust had been made from the outset of the policy, so that it did not apply in favour of contributors of later premiums which would have the effect of divesting those already entitled to the proceeds of the policy.[41] Morritt LJ dissented and, while he was unwilling to decide whether a resulting trust could arise from the payment of some premiums due on an insurance policy taken out in the name of another,[42] he held that contributions to the purchase of property by instalments could give rise to a resulting trust:

in principle if property is acquired by a series of payments a resulting trust in respect of the due proportion may arise from the payment of one or more in the series; hire purchase or instalment payment transactions would be examples.[43]

The majority of the House of Lords approved the dissenting judgment of Morritt LJ, and held that the beneficiaries were entitled to a proportionate share of the proceeds of the policy. Lord Millett explained:

It is true that the last two premiums were not needed to provide the death benefit in the sense that in the events which had happened the same amount would have been payable even if those premiums had not been paid...But the fact is that Mr Murphy, who could not foresee the future, did choose to pay the last two premiums, and to pay them with the purchaser's money; and they were applied by the insurer towards the payment of the internal premiums needed to fund the death benefit. It should not avail his donees that he need not have paid the premiums,

36 [1908] P 218.   37 [1999] BPIR 637.   38 [2001] 1 AC 102.
39 [1902] 1 Ch 282.   40 [1997] 3 All ER 392.   41 Ibid., at 406.
42 Ibid., at 424–425.   43 Ibid., at 423.

and that if he had not then (in the events which happened) the insurers would have provided the same death benefit and funded it differently.[44]

Contribution to the premiums required under an insurance policy will therefore entitle the contributor to a proportionate share of the proceeds.

However, *Foskett v McKeown*[45] also illustrates the potential problems of determining the exact extent of an interest acquired by resulting trust where contributions have been made to a purchase by instalments. Lords Hoffman and Browne-Wilkinson held that the extent of the interest in the proceeds of the policy should be proportionate to the contributions the parties had made to the premiums. Lord Millett considered that, since the policy was unit-linked in nature, the appropriate division was in proportion to the number of units that were acquired by the respective premiums.

(b) Purchase money resulting trust of land[46]

In the context of the acquisition of land it is clear that a presumed resulting trust will arise in favour of a contributor to the purchase price. The general principle was stated by Lord Reid in *Pettitt v Pettitt*:

in the absence of evidence to the contrary effect, a contributor to the purchase-price will acquire a beneficial interest in the property.[47]

This was reiterated by Lord Pearson in *Gissing v Gissing*, where the issue was whether a wife was entitled to a share of the ownership of her matrimonial home, which had been purchased in the sole name of her husband:

If [the wife] did make a contribution of a substantial amount towards the purchase of the house, there would be a resulting trust in her favour. That would be the presumption as to the intention of the parties at the time or times when she made and he accepted the contributions. The presumption is a rebuttable presumption: it can be rebutted by evidence showing some other intention...[48]

It is in relation to the ownership of the family home that presumed resulting trusts have most often been employed to allow a non-legal owner to acquire a beneficial interest, and their operation in this context is considered in detail in Chapter 11. What follows is an overview of the major areas of interest in the application of these trusts to the acquisition of interests in land generally.

(i) Nature of contributions

The major area of controversy has concerned the nature of 'contributions' sufficient to give rise to the presumption. While 'indirect' contributions may constitute sufficient detriment to call for the imposition of a constructive trust if there was an express common intention to share the ownership of the land,[49] only 'direct' contributions to the purchase price will give rise to a presumption of resulting trust in favour of the contributor. Thus, paying for the cost of renovations or repairs to a property may give

---

[44] [2001] 1 AC 102, at 138.   [45] [2001] 1 AC 102.
[46] See Gray and Gray, *Elements of Land Law* (5th edn, 2009), pp 836–861. Jackson, Stevens and Pearce, *Land Law* (4th edn, 2008), pp 301–315.
[47] [1970] AC 777, at 794. See Chapter 11.   [48] [1971] AC 886.   [49] See Chapter 11.

rise to the presumption,[50] while contributing to the household expenses[51] or working for a low wage[52] will not, but may lead to the imposition of a constructive trust. Mortgage payments have caused considerable difficulties, and yet most properties are now purchased with the help of a mortgage loan. Quite apart from the practical difficulties of quantifying the beneficial share from mortgage repayments,[53] unless there is a repayment agreement made before the mortgage was entered into, payment of the mortgage instalments on a property will not give rise to the presumption of resulting trust, as they are technically not payments to the purchase price, but the reduction of an existing monetary debt.[54]

(ii) Quantification of beneficial share

The issue of quantification has been of major significance in this area of the law. The application of a strict resulting trust analysis would, as we have seen, fix the share of the beneficial interest in property in direct proportion to the money advanced towards the purchase price. In cases involving the family home, the courts have often conferred a larger share. In *Midland Bank v Cooke*[55] the wife had contributed only 6.74 per cent of the purchase cost of the family home through a direct contribution, but the Court of Appeal held that she was entitled to one-half share on the basis of a 'common intention' constructive trust. The Court of Appeal went even further in *Oxley v Hiscock*[56] and suggested that the size of a beneficial share awarded by means of a resulting trust should represent a 'fair share' on the basis of all the parties' dealings with the property. While a forthright judicial determination of a fair interest has been disapproved in the latest House of Lords' decision of *Stack v Dowden*,[57] a holistic approach to determine the interest has not.

(iii) Special rules for the family home

There were suggestions in the House of Lords' decision in *Stack v Dowden* that the purchase money resulting trust has either been subsumed into the concept of constructive trusts, such that it ceases to have a separate existence in the acquisition of a beneficial interest in the family home, or is no longer applicable.[58] The comments of their Lordships in *Stack v Dowden* were obiter on this issue,[59] but in any event were directed only to the acquisition of interests in the family home. It is clear that the purchase money resulting trust will continue to operate in commercial situations. Even in the domestic context, where it can be shown that the family home was bought as an investment for the family, rather than primarily as its home, it may be possible to use

---

[50]   *Drake v Whipp* [1996] 1 FLR 826.   [51]   *Burns v Burns* [1984] Ch 317.

[52]   *Ivin v Blake* (1994) 67 P&CR 263 (no resulting trust where daughter worked in her mother's pub).

[53]   See *Marsh v Von Steinberg* [1986] 1 FLR 526.

[54]   *Curley v Parkes* [2004] EWCA Civ 1515.   [55]   [1995] All ER 562.

[56]   [2004] EWCA Civ 546,   [57]   [2007] 2 AC 432.

[58]   Ibid., at [25]–[31] per Lord Walker.

[59]   It was held that there was presumption of beneficial co-ownership that arose from the property having been acquired in joint names, so that acquisition of an interest by means of a resulting trust was not at issue. See further Chapter 11.

resulting trust principles to determine the ownership of the property on the dissolution of the relationship.[60]

(4) Rebutting the presumption of resulting trust

In *Pettitt v Pettitt* Lord Diplock observed that the presumptions of resulting trust and advancement are:

no more than a consensus of judicial opinion disclosed by reported cases as to the most likely inference of fact to be drawn in the absence of any evidence to the contrary.[61]

It therefore follows that they can be rebutted by evidence that in a specific situation the 'most likely inference' was not, in fact, intended. The presumption of a resulting trust, whether arising from a voluntary transfer or a contribution to the purchase price of property, will be rebutted by evidence that the transferor or contributor had no intention to retain any beneficial interest in the property. The strength of the evidence required to rebut the presumption of a resulting trust will depend upon the strength of the presumption, which will in turn depend upon the facts and circumstances which gave rise to it.[62]

(a) Circumstances rebutting the presumption of resulting trust

(i) Evidence a gift was intended[63]

It was noted above that in *Fowkes v Pascoe*[64] a presumption of a resulting trust was raised when Sarah Baker purchased annuities in the joint names of herself and John Pascoe. However, this presumption was rebutted by evidence indicating that a gift had been intended. Two initial purchases of stock were made by Sarah, one of £250 in the joint names of herself and John Pascoe, and another of £250 in the joint names of herself and her companion. She also held large quantities of the same stock in her own name, besides other property. The court considered this 'absolutely conclusive' that a gift was intended. As James LJ said:

Is it possible to reconcile with mental sanity the theory that she put £250 into the names of herself and her companion, and £250 into the names of herself and [John Pascoe], as trustees upon trust for herself? What... object is there conceivable in doing this?[65]

In *Re Young*[66] it was similarly held that the presumption of a resulting trust had been rebutted. Colonel and Mrs Young had a joint bank account, which contained money derived from Mrs Young's separate income. The account was used to pay for household expenses, and Colonel Young, with his wife's consent, withdrew money to purchase investments in his own name. Pearson J held that the evidence showed that the money

---

[60] *Laskar v Laskar* [2008] EWCA Civ 347 (CA).   [61] [1970] AC 777, at 823.

[62] *Vajpeyi v Yijsaf* [2003] EWHC 2339, per Peter Prescott, QC, at [71].

[63] See *Sekhon v Alissa* [1989] 2 FLR 94, where there was insufficient evidence of a gift to rebut the presumption of a resulting trust.

[64] (1875) LR 10 Ch App 343.   [65] Ibid., at 349.   [66] (1885) 28 Ch D 705.

in the account was intended to be joint, and that the investments purchased in his own name were his own property, and were not held on resulting trust for his wife.

In *Arosos v Coutt's & Co*[67] Collins J held that the presumption of resulting trust was rebutted where a wealthy Portuguese gentleman had transferred money into a joint account in the names of himself and his nephew. The evidence, primarily the mandate establishing the account that clearly stated that the beneficial interest was to be held jointly and the evidence of the bank client relationship officer who had explained the effect of the account, established that he had intended the nephew to take the property beneficially.

It appears that a presumption of resulting trust may be rebutted even where money has been paid into a joint bank account with the intention that the transferee is not allowed to draw on the account until the death of the transferor. This approach was adopted in *Russell v Scott*,[68] where an aunt had opened a joint account in the names of herself and her nephew, but did not intend her nephew to benefit during her lifetime. The Australian High Court held that she had nevertheless conferred an immediate beneficial interest on him that would only fall into possession on her death through the operation of the right of survivorship. Because of her control over the account, the interest that she conferred on him remained revocable by her during her lifetime. This decision was followed in England in *Young v Sealey*.[69] In contrast, in Ireland it was held in *Owens v Greene*[70] that the presumption of resulting trust could not be rebutted in such cases because the transferor's intention amounted to an intention to make a testamentary gift, and that evidence of this intention was not admissible, since otherwise the requirements for making a will would be avoided. However, as many commentators have observed,[71] rebutting the presumption of resulting trust in such circumstances is no more offensive to the policy of the Wills Act than the recognition of secret trusts. *Owens v Greene* has since been overruled by the Irish Supreme Court in *Lynch v Burke*.[72] In *Arosos v Coutt's & Co*[73] Collins J indicated that he would have followed *Russell v Scott* and *Young v Sealey*, but the point did not arise for decision.

(ii) Evidence a loan was intended

The presumption of a resulting trust will also be rebutted where evidence shows that money was advanced by way of a loan. In *Re Sharpe (a bankrupt)*[74] Mr and Mrs Sharpe lived in a maisonette with their 82-year-old aunt, Mrs Johnson. The property had been purchased in the name of Mr Sharpe for £17,000. Mrs Johnson had contributed £12,000 towards the purchase price, while the remainder was raised by way of a mortgage. Mr and Mrs Sharpe were subsequently declared bankrupt and Mrs Johnson claimed to be entitled to a proprietary interest in the maisonette by means of a resulting trust

---

[67] [2002] 1 All ER (Comm) 241.   [68] (1936) 55 CLR 440.
[69] [1949] Ch 278.   [70] [1932] IR 225.
[71] See Delaney, *Equity and Trusts in the Republic of Ireland* (1995), p 133.
[72] [1995] 2 IR 159. See (1996) ILSI Gazette March, p 70 (Mee).
[73] [2002] 1 All ER (Comm) 241.
[74] [1980] 1 WLR 219. See also *Blue Sky One Ltd v Blue Airways LLC* [2009] EWHC 3314 (Comm) at [255]–[257].

presumed from her contribution to the purchase price. Browne-Wilkinson J held that the money had in fact been advanced by way of a loan, with the intention that it would be repaid. She was not therefore entitled to any share of the equitable interest of the property. A presumption of a resulting trust was also rebutted by evidence that a loan was intended in *Vajpeyi v Yijaf*.[75] In this case, the claimant provided the defendant, who was her lover, with £10,000 to enable him to purchase a house in his sole name. At the time of the purchase in 1980 the defendant was a young man of limited means. The claimant alleged that by virtue of this payment she was entitled to a 33.89 per cent share of the equitable ownership of the property on the basis of a presumed resulting trust, whereas the defendant claimed that the money had been advanced by way of a loan, which he had repaid. Peter Prescott, QC held that the following factors had rebutted the presumption of a resulting trust in favour of a loan: the fact that the defendant had been a young man of limited means who was anxious to get on the property ladder whereas the claimant was a lady who was already on the property ladder, when the money was advanced; the fact that the claimant had tolerated the defendant collecting rents from the property and keeping them for himself for some twenty-one years; the fact that the claimant had failed to propound her claim to an interest for twenty-one years, and the fact that she had never said anything about her alleged interest in the house when it was mortgaged by the defendant to enable him to purchase her matrimonial home some years previously.

(b) Evidence required to rebut the presumption of resulting trust

Fowkes v Pascoe[76] makes clear that the quality of evidence required to rebut a presumption of a resulting trust will vary depending on the circumstances in question, because the presumption of resulting trust will be given varying weight depending upon the context. As Mellish LJ stated:

the presumption must...be of very different weight in different cases. In some cases it would be very strong indeed. If, for instance, a man invested a sum of stock in the name of himself and his solicitor, the inference would be very strong indeed that it was intended solely for the purpose of a trust, and the court would require very strong evidence on the part of the solicitor to prove that it was intended as a gift; and certainly his own evidence would not be sufficient. On the other hand, a man may make an investment of stock in the name of himself and some person, although not a child or wife,[77] yet in such a position to him as to make it extremely probable that the investment was intended as a gift. In such a case, although the rule of law, if there was no evidence at all, would compel the Court to say that the presumption of trust must prevail, even if the court might not believe that the fact was in accordance with the presumption, yet, if there is evidence to rebut the presumption, then, in my opinion, the court must go into the actual facts.[78]

(c) Admissibility of evidence to rebut a presumption of resulting trust

Any acts or declarations by the parties forming part of the transaction to which the presumption of a resulting trust relates will be admissible in favour of, or against, the

---

[75] [2003] EWHC 2339. [76] (1875) LR 10 Ch App 343.
[77] Where the presumption of advancement would apply. See below, p 283.
[78] (1875) LR 10 Ch App 343, at 352–353.

parties performing them. However, in *Shephard v Cartwright*[79] the House of Lords held, in the context of the rebuttal of a presumption of advancement, that subsequent acts and declarations are admissible only as evidence against the party who made them, and not in his favour.

(5) Presumed resulting trust arising in the context of an illegal purpose[80]

In *Tinsley v Milligan*[81] the House of Lords was faced with the question whether a plaintiff was entitled to rely on a presumption of resulting trust arising in the context of a transaction entered to facilitate an illegal purpose. A house had been purchased in the sole name of Tinsley, using money which both Tinsley and Milligan, a cohabiting lesbian couple, had raised from the sale of a previous property, augmented by a mortgage loan. The reason for this was to enable Milligan to appear to be a mere lodger in the property, rather than a co-owner, so that she could make false claims for various state social welfare benefits. After the breakdown of their relationship, Milligan claimed that Tinsley held the house on trust for them in equal shares. Tinsley claimed that the court should not enforce Milligan's claim because of the illegal purpose underlying the transaction, demanding a strict application of the maxim that 'he who comes to equity must come with clean hands'. This would obviously have the consequence that Tinsley was solely entitled to the house, despite the fact that she had been as much party to the illegality as Milligan. While this might have seemed a harsh result between the specific parties, especially given that the falsely claimed social security money had been repaid, the strict rule was intended to operate as a deterrent to those who might be tempted to involve themselves in illegal transactions.

The majority of the Court of Appeal rejected the application of such a strict principle in favour of the adoption of a 'public conscience test', which would vest the court with a discretion to balance the consequences of either granting or refusing relief to the person seeking to claim an interest.[82] The House of Lords in turn rejected this discretionary approach, favouring the application of a strict rule to determine when a plaintiff could assert an interest. However, it was divided as to the appropriate rule. Lord Goff and Lord Keith held that the equitable maxim requiring clean hands should be strictly applied. Lord Goff explained how this would operate:

> once it comes to the attention of a court of equity that the claimant has not come to the court with clean hands, the court will refuse to assist the claimant, even though the claimant can prima facie establish his claim without recourse to underlying fraudulent or illegal purpose.[83]

In contrast, the majority adopted an evidential approach, whereby a claimant is entitled to enforce an equitable interest provided that he or she did not have to rely on the

---

[79] [1955] AC 431.

[80] See J D Davies, 'Presumptions and Illegality' in Oakley, *Trends in Contemporary Trust Law* (1996); Halliwell, 'Equitable Property Rights, Discretionary Remedies and Unclean Hands' [2004] Conv 439.

[81] [1994] 1 AC 340.   [82] [1992] 2 All ER 391.   [83] [1993] 3 All ER 65, at 75.

fact of the illegal purpose in order to establish that interest. Lord Browne-Wilkinson stated the principle:

In my judgement the time has come to decide clearly that the rule is the same whether a plaintiff founds himself on a legal or equitable title: he is entitled to recover if he is not forced to plead or rely on the illegality, even if it emerges that the title on which he relied was acquired in the course of carrying through an illegal transaction.[84]

He explained how this principle applied where the alleged equitable interest had arisen through the operation of a presumption of a resulting trust:

The presumption of resulting trust is...crucial in considering the authorities. On that presumption...hinges the answer to the crucial question: does a plaintiff claiming under a resulting trust have to rely on the underlying illegality? Where the presumption of resulting trust applies, the plaintiff does not have to rely on the illegality. If he proves that the property is vested in the defendant alone but that the plaintiff provided part of the purchase money, or voluntarily transferred the property to the defendant, the plaintiff establishes his claim under a resulting trust unless either the contrary presumption of advancement displaces the presumption of resulting trust or the defendant leads evidence to rebut the presumption of resulting trust. Therefore, in cases where the presumption of advancement does not apply, a plaintiff can establish his equitable interest in the property without relying in any way on the underlying illegal transaction.[85]

Applying this principle it was therefore held that Milligan was entitled to assert her entitlement to a half-share of the equitable ownership of the house, since all she needed to do to establish her interest was to prove that she had contributed to the purchase price. This would give rise to a presumption of resulting trust in her favour, and she did not need to rely on the illegal purpose underlying the transaction.

The evidential approach adopted in *Tinsley v Milligan* has been applied in subsequent cases. In *Silverwood v Silverwood*[86] an elderly lady had transferred money to her grandchildren to enable her to claim income support to contribute towards the costs of her residential care. The Court of Appeal held that the plaintiff, who was a beneficiary under her will, was entitled to maintain that the money was held on resulting trust by the recipients, as he did not need to rely on the illegality to establish the resulting trust. Peter Gibson LJ also stated that it would be absurd and unjust if he could not lead evidence of fraud in order to disprove a spurious defence by the recipients. In *Lowson v Coombes*[87] a man had purchased a flat together with his mistress, but it was conveyed into her sole name so that his wife would not be able to maintain any claim to it. The Court of Appeal held that he was entitled to assert a half-interest by way of a resulting trust, despite the illegal purpose of frustrating any potential claim under Matrimonial Causes Act 1973, because he did not need to rely on the illegal purpose to establish his entitlement. In *Zabihi v Janzemini & Ors*[88] Blackburne J held that it was no defence to a claim for the return of jewellery

---

[84] Ibid., at 91.   [85] Ibid., at 87.   [86] (1997) 74 P & CR 453.
[87] [1999] Ch 373.   [88] [2008] EWHC 2910.

entrusted by the claimant to the defendant that the jewellery might have been imported illegally:

> The illegal importation of the jewellery, assuming that to have happened, is irrelevant to the claim against Mr Janzemini in that it is not necessary to the establishment of Mr Zabihi's title to the jewellery and thus to his claim to recover it or its value that he should have to rely on its illegal importation.[89]

However, it has also been subjected to criticism. In *Silverwood v Silverwood*[90] itself, Nourse LJ described the principle adopted in *Tinsley v Milligan* as a 'straitjacket' and indicated that he would have preferred a more flexible approach. In particular the approach adopted by the House of Lords arbitrarily differentiates between situations where a presumption of resulting trust and a presumption of advancement are operative. While Milligan was held able to assert her interest by way of a presumed resulting trust without the need to rely on the fact of her illegal conduct, a more difficult problem would have arisen if the countervailing presumption of advancement had applied between Tinsley and herself. In such circumstances she would only have been entitled to assert her interest if she could rebut the presumption, which would require evidence of the illegal purpose of the transaction. The Court of Appeal was forced to grapple with such a difficulty in *Tribe v Tribe*,[91] where a presumption of advancement did arise between the parties. As Nourse LJ observed in *Silverwood v Silverwood*:

> It is not at all easy to understand or to see any public or other policy or advantage behind a rule which regulates the claimant's right of recovery solely according to whether the other party to the transaction is his wife, child or fiancée on the one hand or his brother, grandchild or anyone else on the other.[92]

Lord Goff, in his dissenting judgment, also pointed to the arbitrary consequences that might follow from the application of the principle adopted by the majority in *Tinsley v Milligan*:

> But it is not to be forgotten that other cases in this category will not evoke the same sympathy on the part of the court. There may be cases in which the fraud is far more serious than that in the present case, and is uncovered not as a result of a confession but only after a lengthy police investigation and a prolonged criminal trial. Again there may be cases in which a group of terrorists, or armed robbers, secure a base for their criminal activities by buying a house in the name of a third party not directly implicated in those activities. In cases such as these there will almost certainly be no presumption of advancement. Is it really to be said that criminals such as these, or their personal representatives, are entitled to invoke the assistance of a court of equity in order to establish an equitable interest in property?[93]

In the light of such criticisms the law regarding illegality, alongside defences to illegality in contract and tort, has been reviewed by the Law Commission, who have recommended the abandonment of the 'reliance principle' adopted in *Tinsley v Milligan* in favour of granting the court a discretion to determine that a beneficiary ought not to

---

89 Ibid., at [286].   90 (1997) 74 P & CR 453.   91 [1996] Ch 107.
92 (1997) 74 P & CR 453, at 458.   93 [1993] 3 All ER 65, at 79.

be allowed to enforce the equitable interest.[94] The operation of this proposed discretion is discussed in more detail below in the context of the operation of the presumption of advancement, since this has provided the context for the more serious difficulties.

3 The presumption of advancement

(1) Nature of the presumption

In some circumstances where a person voluntarily transfers property into the name of another, or contributes to its purchase, the law presumes that a gift was intended and that the transferor/contributor did not intend to retain any interest in the property concerned. This presumption, known as the 'presumption of advancement', displaces the presumption of resulting trust. The presumption of advancement arises as a consequence of a pre-existing relationship between the parties to the transfer or acquisition, where the transferor/contributor is regarded as morally obliged to provide for the person benefiting. As Lord Eldon stated in *Murless v Franklin*:

The general rule that on a purchase by one man in the name of another, the nominee is a trustee for the purchaser, is subject to exception where the purchaser is under a species of natural obligation to provide for the nominee.[95]

The range of relationships where equity recognizes a presumption of advancement reflects a nineteenth-century understanding of family responsibility, and it is clear that, today, the strengths of the presumptions vary to reflect differing social circumstances. However, the state of the law in this area remains far from satisfactory.

(2) Relationships giving rise to a presumption of advancement

(a) Father and child

Traditionally, there was a strong presumption of advancement between a father and his child.[96] In *Re Roberts (Decd)*[97] Evershed J held that the presumption of advancement applied where a father had made payments on a policy of assurance taken out on his son's life. He said that:

It is well established that a father making payments on behalf of his son prima facie, and in the absence of contrary evidence, is to be taken to be making and intending an advance in favour of the son and for his benefit.[98]

---

[94] 'The Illegality Defence. Law Com No. 320, following 'Illegal Transactions: The Effect of Illegality on Contracts and Trusts' (1999), Law Comm CP No 154.

[95] (1818) 1 Swan 13, at 17.

[96] See *Shephard v Cartwright* [1955] AC 431. In *Oliveri v Oliveri* (1995) 38 NSWLR 665 Powell J suggested that a presumption of advancement could operate between a stepfather and stepchild.

[97] [1946] Ch 1.   [98] Ibid., at 5.

In *B v B*[99] a Canadian court held that the presumption of advancement applied where a father had purchased a winning lottery ticket in the name of his 12-year-old daughter. She was therefore entitled to the winnings absolutely. The rationale for the presumption of advancement between a father and child is that a father, by the very nature of his position, is under a duty to provide for his child.[100] This may include the child's mother if she stands in loco parentis. There is no presumption of advancement in the case of other family relationships.[101]

The strength of this presumption of advancement between a father and child was questioned by the Court of Appeal in *McGrath v Wallis*,[102] where Nourse LJ stated:

Ever since the decision in *Pettitt v Pettitt* it has been my understanding that, in its application to houses acquired for joint occupation, the equitable presumption of advancement has been reclassified as a judicial instrument of last resort, its subordinate status comparable to that of the contra proferentem rule in the construction of deeds and contracts...For myself, I have been unable to recollect any subsequent case of this kind in which the presumption has proved decisive...[103]

(b) Persons standing in loco parentis

A presumption of advancement also arises between a child and a person standing in loco parentis.[104] The rationale for this extension of the presumption was stated by Jessel MR in *Bennet v Bennet*:

as regards a child, a person not the father of the child may put himself in the position of loco parentis to the child, and so incur the obligation to make provision for the child...[105]

(c) Husband and wife

The presumption of advancement also arises between a husband in favour of his wife (but not vice versa). The principle was stated in *Re Eykyn's Trusts*, by Malins V-C:

The law of this court is perfectly settled that when a husband transfers money or other property into the name of his wife only, then the presumption is, that it is intended as a gift or advancement to the wife absolutely at once, subject to such marital control as he may exercise. And if a husband invests in money, stocks, or otherwise, in the names of himself and his wife, then also it is an advancement for the benefit of the wife absolutely if she survives her husband...[106]

The operation of the presumption in this context reflects a nineteenth-century social understanding of a husband's obligation to provide for his wife.

---

[99] (1976) 65 DLR (3d) 460.

[100] *Bennet v Bennet* (1879) LR 10 Ch D 474, at 476, per Jessel MR. This has led some other jurisdictions to hold the presumption of advancement inapplicable to children of adult age, as they are not in need of support—see Glister 'The Presumption of Advancement to Adult Children' [2007] Conv 370; Low 'Apparent Gifts: Re-Examining The Equitable Presumption' (2008) 124 LQR 369.

[101] Eg sister (*Noack v Noack* [1959] VR 137; *Gorog v Kiss* (1977) 78 DLR (3d) 690); son-in-law (*Knight v Biss* [1954] NZLR 55); and nephew (*Dury v Dury* (1675) 75 SS 205; *Russell v Scott* (1936) 55 CLR 440).

[102] [1995] 2 FLR 114.   [103] Ibid., at 115.

[104] *Hepworth v Hepworth* (1870) LR 11 Eq 10; *Re Orme* (1883) 50 LT 51; *Shephard v Cartwright* [1955] AC 431; *Re Paradise Motor Co Ltd* [1968] 1 WLR 1125, CA.

[105] (1878–79) LR 10 Ch D 474.   [106] (1877) 6 Ch D 115, at 118.

Although these comments were cited in *Pettitt v Pettitt*,[107] the House of Lords acknowledged that the presumption between husband and wife had reduced in significance.[108] Lord Reid suggested that the only reasonable basis for the presumption had been the economic dependence of wives on their husbands, and that given the changes in social circumstances 'the strength of the presumption must have much diminished'.[109]

Lord Diplock considered that it was not appropriate that transactions between married couples should be governed by presumptions 'based upon inferences of fact which an earlier generation of judges drew as to the most likely intentions of earlier generations of spouses belonging to the propertied classes of a different social era'.[110] The presumption of advancement also applies between a man and his fiancée.[111] In recent cases, the operation of the presumption in this context has come under further attack,[112] and Arden LJ has suggested in *Gibson v Revenue and Customs Prosecution Office* that the presumption of advancement no longer has any application where legal title to property is co-owned:

the function of the presumption of advancement is now performed by the presumption of equal beneficial ownership of property held in joint names laid down in *Stack v Dowden*.[113]

(3) Relationships where no presumption of advancement arises

(a) Mother and child[114]

No presumption of advancement arises between a mother and her child, and therefore if a mother transfers property voluntarily to her child the counter presumption of resulting trust will apply.[115] In *Bennet v Bennet*[116] Jessel MR explained the absence of the presumption on the basis that 'there is no moral legal obligation...no obligation according to the rules of equity—on a mother to provide for her child'.[117] Again, such reasoning reflects nineteenth century concepts of the family, and in modern social conditions mothers almost invariably share the responsibility to provide for their children.[118] Despite the socially archaic rationale, more modern cases have confirmed

---

[107] [1970] AC 777, at 815, per Lord Upjohn.

[108] See *Silver v Silver* [1958] 1 All ER 523, at 525, per Evershed MR. The presumption of advancement between husband and wife also applies in Ireland and Australia: *Heavey v Heavey* [1971] 111 ILTR 1; *M v M* [1980] 114 ILTR 46; *Doohan v Nelson* [1973] 2 NSWLR 320; *Napier v Public Trustee (Western Australia)* (1980) 32 ALR 153.

[109] [1970] AC 777, at 792.   [110] Ibid.

[111] *Moate v Moate* [1948] 2 All ER 486; *Silver v Silver* [1958] 1 WLR 259; *Tinker v Tinker (No 1)* [1970] P 136; *Mossop v Mossop* [1989] Fam 77.

[112] *Stack v Dowden* [2007] 2 AC 432, at [16] per Lord Walker and at [101] per Lord Neuberger.

[113] [2008] EWCA Civ 645, at [27].

[114] See Dowling 'The Presumption of Advancement between Mother And Child' [1996] Conv 274.

[115] *Re De Visme* (1863) 2 De GJ & Sm 17; *Bennet v Bennet* (1878–79) LR 10 Ch D 474. See also: *Sayre v Hughes* (1867–68) LR 5 Eq 376; *Gore-Grimes v Grimes* [1937] IR 470.

[116] (1878–79) LR 10 Ch D 474.   [117] Ibid., at 478.

[118] Compare *Dullow v Dullow* [1985] 3 NSWLR 531.

that there continues to be no presumption of advancement between a mother and child. The presumption of resulting trust was applied by the Court of Appeal in *Gross v French*,[119] and by Hoffmann J in *Sekhon v Alissa*.[120] In the latter case, a mother had provided £22,500 to help her daughter purchase a house. In the absence of sufficient evidence to rebut the presumption of a resulting trust, the mother was held entitled to an interest in the property.

Despite the absence of a presumption of advancement between mother and child, the presumption of resulting trust arising in default is relatively weak and easily rebutted. As Jessel MR said in *Bennet v Bennet*:

> We arrive then at this conclusion, that in the case of a mother . . . it is easier to prove a gift than in the case of a stranger: in the case of a mother very little evidence beyond the relationship is wanted, there being very little additional motive required to induce a mother to make a gift to her child.[121]

In *Nelson v Nelson*[122] the Australian High Court has held that a presumption of advancement should operate between a mother and child.[123] In England the decision in *Re Cameron (Decd)*[124] suggests a possible avenue by which it might be found that the presumption should operate between a mother and child. Lindsay J held that, in the light of the difference between Victorian and modern attitudes to the ownership and ability to dispose of property, it would be appropriate nowadays to take both parents to be in loco parentis for the purposes of the succession rule against double portions unless the contrary is proved.[125]

(b) Wife and husband

Similarly, no presumption of advancement operates between a wife and her husband, so that in orthodox theory if a wife voluntarily transfers property into the name of her husband, or contributes to the purchase of property in his name, a presumption of resulting trust arises. Thus, in *Re Curtis*,[126] in the absence of evidence that a gift was intended, a wife was presumed to enjoy the equitable interest in shares, which she had voluntarily transferred into the name of her husband, by way of a resulting trust.[127] The absence of the presumption seems to have been accepted in the more recent case of *Mossop v Mossop*,[128] and led to the presumption

---

[119]   (1975) 238 Estates Gazette 39.   [120]   [1989] 2 FLR 94.

[121]   (1879) 10 Ch D 474, at 480. See, however, *Sekhon v Alissa* [1989] 2 FLR 94, where Hoffmann J held that the evidence was inconsistent with there being a gift.

[122]   (1995) 132 ALR 133.

[123]   In *Re Dreger Estate* (1994) 97 Man R (2d) 39 it was held that in modern conditions the presumption of advancement ought to be applicable between mother and child.

[124]   [1999] 2 All ER 924.   [125]   Ibid., at 939.

[126]   (1885) 52 LT 244.

[127]   See also *Mercier v Mercier* [1903] 2 Ch 98; *Pearson v Pearson* (1965) The Times, 30 November; *Pettitt v Pettitt* [1970] AC 777; *Heseltine v Heseltine* [1971] 1 WLR 342; *Northern Bank Ltd v Henry* [1981] IR 1; *Allied Irish Banks Ltd v McWilliams* [1982] NI 156.

[128]   [1988] 2 All ER 202, at 206, where Lawton LJ cited the relevant principles from Snell, *Principles of Equity* (28th edn, 1982), p 183.

of a resulting trust in *Abrahams v Trustee in Bankruptcy of Abrahams*,[129] where a wife contributed to a syndicate purchasing National Lottery tickets in the name of her husband.

The absence of the presumption of advancement between a wife and her husband reflects nineteenth-century social circumstances. As was noted above,[130] in *Pettitt v Pettitt*[131] the House of Lords held that the presumption of resulting trust between a wife and her husband was of much diminished strength and would be rebutted by very slight evidence that a gift was intended. Following *Stack v Dowden*,[132] no presumption of resulting trust arises where a property is acquired in the joint names of husband and wife as their family home since this now gives rise to a presumption of ownership in equal shares. Even outside this narrow context, the jurisprudence being developed by the courts in relation to the family home has regard to such a wide range of factors that there will rarely be any place for the application of classical presumptions of advancement in this context.[133]

(c) Co-habiting couples/mistresses

There is no presumption of advancement between cohabiting couples (whether heterosexual or homosexual),[134] nor between a man and his mistress.[135] The presumption of resulting trust will therefore apply if property is voluntarily transferred in such cases, except where the jurisprudence relating to the acquisition of a family home produces a different result.

(4) Rebutting a presumption of advancement

(a) Evidence required to rebut a presumption of advancement

A presumption of advancement will be rebutted by evidence that the transferor (or contributor) did not intend to make a gift but wished to retain an interest in the property transferred or acquired. In *Re Gooch*[136] Sir Daniel Gooch transferred shares into the name of his eldest son. The son paid the dividends from the shares to his father, who also retained the share certificates. Kay J held that the presumption of advancement was rebutted by evidence that the shares had been transferred to qualify the son to become a director of the company, and that no gift had been intended. In *Warren v Gurney*,[137] a father purchased a house in the name of his daughter prior to her wedding. He retained the title deeds until his death. The Court of Appeal held that the presumption of advancement was rebutted by evidence that at the time of the transaction the father had intended her husband to repay the money. The retention

---

129 [1999] BPIR 637.   130 See above, p 285.   131 [1970] AC 777.
132 [2007] 2 AC 432.   133 This is considered in detail in Chapter 11.
134 *Rider v Kidder* (1805) 10 Ves 360; *Soar v Foster* (1858) 4 K & J 152; *Allen v Snyder* [1977] 2 NSWLR 685; *Calverly v Green* (1984) 56 ALR 483.
135 *Diwell v Farnes* [1959] 1 WLR 624.   136 (1890) 62 LT 384.
137 [1944] 2 All ER 472. See also *Webb v Webb* [1992] 1 All ER 17; refd [1994] 3 All ER 911.

of the title deeds was considered a very significant fact, as 'one would have expected the father to have handed them over either to [his daughter] or her husband, if he had intended the gift'.[138] In *McGrath v Wallis*[139] a house was acquired for joint occupancy by a father and son in the sole name of the son. The purchase price was provided partly by the proceeds of sale of the father's previous house and partly by means of a mortgage. The Court of Appeal held that the presumption of advancement was rebutted by evidence that the father had intended to retain an interest in the ownership of the house, including an unsigned declaration of trust which would have shared the beneficial ownership in the proportions represented by the deposit and mortgage, respectively.

The mere fact that any rents and profits generated from the property concerned are returned to the purchaser or transferor will not conclusively rebut a presumption of advancement. In *Stamp Duties Comrs v Byrnes*[140] a father had purchased property in Australia in the name of his sons. They paid over to him the rents received from the properties, and he paid for rates and repairs. The Privy Council held that as it was not unusual for a father to transfer property to a son while continuing to receive any rents and profits during his lifetime, the presumption of advancement had not been rebutted:

Having regard to the state of the family and the relations subsisting between Mr Byrnes and his two sons who were living at home, it seems very natural that the sons receiving advances should yet feel a delicacy in taking the fruits during their father's lifetime. They had all they wanted as things were, and if they were unduly favoured it might possibly have created some feeling of jealousy among the rest.[141]

Although the opening of a bank account by a husband in the joint names of himself and his wife will lead to the presumption of a joint tenancy of the money therein,[142] the presumption of advancement operating between them may be rebutted. In the nineteenth-century case of *Marshal v Crutwell*[143] it was held that the presumption of advancement was rebutted where a husband had transferred his bank account into the joint names of himself and his wife. The court held that the transfer was merely for convenience, since the husband was in ill health and could not draw cheques himself. His wife was not therefore entitled to the balance in the account on his death. In *Anson v Anson*[144] the presumption of advancement was rebutted where a husband had entered a guarantee of an overdraft on a bank account in his wife's name. After their divorce he was called to pay £500 to the bank under the guarantee, and demanded repayment from the wife. Pearson J held that the intention was that the debt would remain her debt, and the guarantee to the bank was not intended to relieve her of her obligation but merely to solve her immediate banking emergency.

---

138 [1944] 2 All ER 472, at 473, per Morton LJ.   139 [1995] 2 FLR 114.
140 [1911] AC 386.   141 Ibid., at 392.
142 See *Re Bishop* [1965] Ch 450; *Re Figgis* [1969] 1 Ch 123.
143 (1875) LR 20 Eq 328.   144 [1953] 1 QB 636.

(b) Rebuttal of a presumption of advancement by evidence of an illegal purpose[145]

(i) The general rule

It has been seen above that, as a general rule, a plaintiff will not be permitted to rely on evidence of his own illegal conduct to rebut a presumption of resulting trust.[146] He will similarly be prevented from relying on evidence of an illegal purpose to rebut a presumption of advancement. In *Gascoigne v Gascoigne*[147] a husband took a lease of land in his wife's name. The judge at first instance held that the presumption of advancement was rebutted by evidence that he had not intended to make a gift of the lease to his wife because it had been taken in her name only to defeat the claims of his creditors. However, the Court of Appeal held that he was not entitled to rebut the presumption by raising evidence of the illegal purpose underlying the transaction:

what the learned judge has done is this: He has permitted the plaintiff to rebut the presumption which the law raises by setting up his own illegality and fraud, and to obtain relief in equity because he has succeeded in proving it. The plaintiff cannot do this...[148]

This restriction was followed by the Court of Appeal in *Tinker v Tinker (No 1)*,[149] where a husband had purchased a house in the name of his wife, on the advice of his solicitor, again with the intention of preventing the house being seized by creditors if his business failed. On the breakdown of the marriage it was held that he could not rebut the presumption of advancement. Lord Denning MR stated:

he cannot say that the house is his own and, at one and the same time, say that it is his wife's. As against his wife, he wants to say that it belongs to him. As against his creditors, that it belongs to her. That simply will not do. Either it was conveyed to her for her own use absolutely; or it was conveyed to her as trustee for her husband. It must be one or the other. The presumption is that it was conveyed to her for her own use: and he does not rebut that presumption by saying that he only did it to defeat his creditors...[150]

In *Re Emery's Investments Trusts*[151] a husband was held unable to rebut a presumption of advancement when he had purchased American stock in the name of his American wife to avoid taxation under American Federal law, and in *Chettiar v Chettiar*[152] a father could not rebut a presumption of resulting trust where he had purchased a rubber estate in the name of his son to avoid a provision restricting the maximum area of land in a rubber plantation that an individual could own.

(ii) A modified approach

While the policy objective of this strict approach is to discourage persons from entering illegal transactions, in the more recent case of *Tribe v Tribe*[153] the Court of

---

[145] See J D Davies, 'Presumptions and Illegality' in Oakley, *Trends in Contemporary Trust Law* (1996).
[146] See *Tinsley v Milligan* [1993] 3 All ER 65, at 90.   [147] [1918] 1 KB 223.
[148] Ibid., at 226.   [149] [1970] P 136.   [150] Ibid., at 141.
[151] [1959] Ch 410.   [152] [1962] 1 All ER 494.
[153] [1995] 4 All ER 236; (1996) 112 LQR 386 (Rose); [1996] CLJ 23 (Virgo); (1997) 60 MLR 102 (Creighton). See also (1995) 111 LQR 135 (Enonchong); [1996] RLR 78 (Enonchong).

Appeal demonstrated a marked reluctance to disallow a father from rebutting the presumption of advancement arising when he had transferred property voluntarily to his son to achieve an illegal purpose. The father was the owner of a majority shareholding in a family company and the tenant of two properties occupied by the company as licensee. The landlord of these premises served notice of various alleged dilapidations on the father, requiring him to carry out substantial repairs. The father was advised by his solicitor that, if the claims were valid, he might be forced to sell the company shares to pay for the repairs. He therefore transferred them to his son as a means of safeguarding his assets. The transfer was stated to be made for a consideration of £78,030, but no money was ever paid. In the event, the father was never required to carry out the repairs and he sought to recover the shares from his son. The son refused to retransfer them to him, and the father alleged that he held them on bare trust for him. The son argued that the presumption of advancement applied in his favour and that the father could not rebut it by evidence of the illegal attempt to evade his creditors. While accepting that the decision of the House of Lords in *Tinsley v Milligan*[154] had the general effect that a presumption of advancement cannot be rebutted by evidence of an underlying illegal purpose, the Court of Appeal held that this general rule was subject to an exception if the 'illegal purpose has not been carried into effect'. As Nourse LJ explained:

The judge found that the illegal purpose was to deceive the plaintiff's creditors by creating an appearance that he no longer owned any shares in the company. He also found that it was not carried into effect in any way. [Counsel for the defendant] attacked the latter finding on grounds which appeared to me to confuse the purpose with the transaction. Certainly the transaction was carried into effect by the execution and registration of the transfer. But *Wright's*[155] case shows that that is immaterial. It is the purpose which has to be carried into effect and that would only have happened if and when a creditor of the plaintiff had been deceived by the transaction. The judge said there was no evidence of that and clearly he did not think it appropriate to infer it. Nor is it any objection to the plaintiff's right to recover the shares that he did not demand their return until after the danger had passed and it was no longer necessary to conceal the transfer from his creditors. All that matters is that no deception was practised on them. For these reasons the judge was right to hold that the exception applied.[156]

Millett LJ reached the same conclusion but stated the principle more broadly, holding that a person is entitled to recover property transferred for an illegal purpose if he withdrew from the transaction before it was carried out. He attempted to formulate a single unitary principle derived from the equitable doctrines regarding the rebuttal of presumptions of resulting trust and advancement and common law cases where it had been held that a party was entitled to withdraw from an illegal contract. While he made clear that effectual withdrawal from a transaction did not require 'genuine repentance' on the part of the wrongdoer, he held that he must have withdrawn

---

154 [1993] 3 All ER 65.
155 *Perpetual Executors and Trustees Association of Australia Ltd v Wright* (1917) 23 CLR 185.
156 [1995] 4 All ER 236, at 248.

voluntarily. There would therefore be no effective withdrawal if 'he is forced to [with-draw] because his plan has been discovered'.[157]

Despite the superficial attraction of simplicity, this proposed general approach is inadequate because it is unclear when a transaction has been carried into effect so as to prevent withdrawal. As Millett LJ noted, early common law cases indicated that a party to an illegal contract could withdraw only so long as it has not been completely performed, whereas later decisions held that any recovery under the contract was barred once partial performance had occurred.[158] He formulated his general propos-ition in the following terms:

The transferor can lead evidence of the illegal purpose whenever it is necessary for him to do so provided that he has withdrawn from the transaction before the illegal purpose has been *wholly or partly* carried into effect.[159]

It is suggested that this is extremely confusing, as it does not clarify whether with-drawal is possible in cases where the transaction was partially carried into effect.

(iii) Explaining the modified approach

Tribe v Tribe should only be considered good authority to the extent that it decides that evidence of an illegal purpose may be admitted to rebut a presumption of advance-ment if the illegal purpose has not been carried into effect at all. Nonetheless, even when assessed in the light of this limited proposition, the decision remains unsatis-factory. The conclusion that the illegal purpose had not been carried into effect was artificial, as in reality the act which was intended to achieve the illegal purpose was the transfer of the legal title of the shares to the son, thus on the face of it divesting the father of any interest. It is arguable that the illegal object was carried into effect at the very moment that the legal title was effectually transferred to the son. Far from rebut-ting the presumption of advancement, the very act of transferring the shares to the son with the illegal aim of defeating the creditors actually reinforces the presumption of a gift to the son. As Millet LJ stated:

The only way in which a man can protect his property from his creditors is by divesting himself of all beneficial interest in it. Evidence that he transferred the property in order to protect it from his creditors, therefore, does nothing by itself to rebut the presumption of advancement; it reinforces it. To rebut the presumption it is necessary to show that he intended to retain a beneficial interest and conceal it from his creditors.[160]

The reality is that, in both *Tribe v Tribe* and *Tinsley v Milligan*,[161] the respective courts were attempting to avoid the perceived unfairness that would result from the appli-cation of a strict rule against illegality intended to serve a general public policy of deterring wrongdoers. It would seem unfair if Milligan were to be prevented from asserting any entitlement to an equitable share of the house owned at law by Tinsley when they were both parties to the illegal purpose, and the consequence would be that Tinsley received a large windfall gain at Milligan's expense. The majority of the

---

[157] Ibid., at 259. [158] *Kearley v Thomson* (1890) 24 QBD 742.
[159] [1995] 4 All ER 236, at 259. [160] [1995] 4 All ER 236, at 259. [161] [1994] 1 AC 340.

House of Lords was conveniently able to avoid such a result by exploiting the logic that Milligan merely needed to prove that she had contributed to the purchase price of the house to raise a presumption of resulting trust in her favour. While achieving justice between the parties, the decision represented a departure from the traditional position that a transferor could not recover property transferred in pursuit of an illegal purpose irrespective of whether the presumption of advancement or the presumption of resulting trust applied. *Tinsley v Milligan* therefore introduced an arbitrary distinction, whereby the general rule would apply where there was a presumption of advancement between the parties, but not where there was a presumption of resulting trust. As has been noted above, the circumstances in which a presumption of advancement arises are largely derived from out-dated conceptions of family responsibility. They are riddled with inconsistency, to such an extent that the courts have tended to treat them as of relatively little weight and easily rebutted. Given the inadequacy of the law determining the circumstances in which a presumption of advancement arises, any differentiation between the effects of illegality on such grounds is highly unsatisfactory. As Judge Weekes stated at first instance in *Tribe v Tribe*:

Finally, it is not for me to criticise their Lordship's reasoning, but with the greatest respect I find it difficult to see why the outcome in cases such as the present one should depend to such a large extent on arbitrary factors, such as whether the claim is brought by a father against a son, or a mother against a son, or a grandfather against a grandson.[162]

It is also worth noting that, if the facts of *Tinsley v Milligan* were to be retried following the decision of the House of Lords in *Stack v Dowden*,[163] it is by no means clear that the presumption of a resulting trust could have been used to facilitate Milligan's entitlement to an interest. It was suggested in that case that the resulting trust analysis should be abandoned in cases relating to interests in the family home, and the matter is still in some doubt, as noted above.

(iv) The call for reform

The arbitrary operation of the rules on illegality established by *Tinsley v Milligan* can hardly be considered satisfactory.[164] One solution would be an approach which operates consistently, irrespective of the nature of the presumption applicable. Such consistency could have been obtained by retention of the traditional rule that an equitable interest cannot be asserted by a transferor of property if the purpose of the transfer was to give effect to an illegal purpose, irrespective of any presumption, be it advancement, resulting trust, or any other.[165] Instead, the estate would 'lie where it falls'. However, this approach was rejected by the majority in *Tinsley v Milligan* precisely because it would lead to unfairness in individual cases. It was also rejected

---

[162] Quoted by Nourse LJ [1995] 4 All ER 236, at 244. See also *Collier v Collier* [2003] WTLR 617, at 654–655, per Mance LJ.

[163] [2007] 2 AC 432.

[164] See also *Moore Stephens (a firm) (Respondents) v Stone Rolls Limited* [2009] UKHL 39, at [130], where Lord Phillips described *Tinsley v Milligan* as 'in some ways a difficult and controversial decision'.

[165] If the parties own the legal title jointly, there is a presumption of equal beneficial ownership—see *Stack v Dowden* [2007] 2 AC 432.

by the High Court of Australia in *Nelson v Nelson*,[166] where Deane and Gummow JJ described it as a 'harsh and indiscriminate principle'. In that case, the approach of the House of Lords in *Tinsley v Milligan* was also rejected on the grounds that it generated different results which were 'entirely fortuitous being dependent upon the relationship between the parties', and therefore 'wholly unjustifiable on any policy ground'.[167] The High Court held that a person should only be prevented from asserting an equitable right if to allow him to do so would be inconsistent with the public policy applicable to the specific right claimed. Applying this test, the High Court held that public policy did not prevent a mother asserting an equitable interest in property she had transferred to her children. Mrs Nelson had provided the purchase money for a house which was transferred into the names of her two children to enable her to obtain a subsidized advance towards the purchase of another house under the Australian housing legislation. To obtain such an advance she had to declare that she did not own, or have an interest, in any other house. After she had received the advance the first house was sold, and one of the children claimed that he was entitled to half the proceeds of sale. It was held that Mrs Nelson could rebut the presumption of advancement operating in favour of the children because the policy of the particular legislation concerned would 'not be defeated if the court enforces her equitable right'. Thus, the court was willing to allow Mrs Nelson to assert her equitable entitlement even though the illegal purpose had been carried into effect, a result which would not have been possible through an application of the principles adopted in *Tribe v Tribe*. However, the majority further held that her right to assert her equitable interest should be conditional on repayment of her unlawful benefit to the state.

While there are undoubtedly problems with the current law, it should be noted that all members of the House of Lords in *Tinsley v Milligan* rejected a discretionary approach to the effect of illegality on equitable property rights, preferring strict rules which would determine whether a right could be asserted. The law regarding illegality has been reviewed by the Law Commission.[168] Given its unsatisfactory nature, the Law Commission recommended in its earlier report the abandonment of the 'reliance principle' adopted in *Tinsley v Milligan* in favour of granting the court a discretion to declare a trust illegal or invalid.[169] This discretion would be structured so that a court would have to take into account a number of specified factors in reaching its decisions:

those factors should be: (a) the seriousness of the illegality; (b) the knowledge and intention of the illegal trust beneficiary; (c) whether invalidity would tend to deter the illegality; (d) whether invalidity would further the purpose of the rule which renders the trust 'illegal'; and (e) whether invalidity would be a proportionate response to the claimant's participation in the illegality.[170]

---

[166] (1995) 132 ALR 133.   [167] Ibid., at 166, per Dawson J.
[168] 'The Illegality Defence. Law Com No. 320.
[169] '*Illegal Transactions: The Effect of Illegality on Contracts and Trusts*' (1999), Law Com CP No 154.
[170] Enonchong 'Illegal Transactions: The Future?' [2000] RLR 82, at para 8.63.

The Law Commission's final report advocates a modified and much more restrictive version of the statutory discretion scheme it had previously advocated.[171] The proposed discretion is limited to cases where a trust was created, or subsequently continued, in order to conceal the true beneficial ownership of the trust property in connection with the commission of an offence.[172] The Law Commission's view is that an illegality should only have an effect on the beneficial entitlement under the trust when the court considers that there are exceptional circumstances.[173] The draft Bill sets out a list of relevant factors.[174]

(c) Admissibility of evidence to rebut a presumption of advancement

As in the case of the rebuttal of presumptions of a resulting trust,[175] only evidence of the plaintiff's acts and declarations contemporaneous with the transaction are admissible in his favour to rebut the presumption of advancement. Evidence of subsequent acts and declarations are only admissible as evidence against him. This principle was stated and applied by the House of Lords in *Shephard v Cartwright*,[176] where Lord Simmonds approved a summary of the law in Snell's *Equity*:

The acts and declarations of the parties before or at the time of the purchase, or so imme-diately after it as to constitute a part of the transaction, are admissible in evidence either for or against the party who did the acts or made the declaration . . . But subsequent dec-larations are admissible as evidence only against the party who made them, and not in his favour.[177]

In 1929 Philip Shephard subscribed for shares in the name of his children. In 1934 the shares were sold to a company promoted by him, and the children signed the requis-ite documents at his request without knowing what they were doing. The proceeds of sale were paid into separate deposit accounts in the children's names. They later signed documents, unaware of their contents, authorizing him to withdraw money from the accounts, whereupon he withdrew money from them without their know-ledge. In an action by the children against his executors the central issue was whether the presumption of advancement had been rebutted. The House of Lords held that evi-dence of the father's acts after the transaction of 1929 were not admissible to prove the rebuttal of the presumption of advancement as they did not form part of the original transaction.[178]

---

171 'The Illegality Defence. Law Com. 320.

172 Ibid., at paras 2.24–2.35.

173 Ibid., at para 2.61.

174 Part of the reasoning behind this is to accommodate the effect of *Stack v Dowden* on acquisitions of property.

175 See above, p 277.   176 [1955] AC 431.

177 Ibid., at 445; Snell, *Principles of Equity* (24th edn, 1990), p 153.

178 Similarly, evidence of the children's acts in signing the documents at their father's request was not admissible against them, because they had been unaware of the contents.

4 Reform of presumed resulting trusts

The presumptions of resulting trusts largely operate as a mechanism for allocating the burden of proof when there is a dispute as to intended effect of a transaction on the beneficial ownership of property. As the Australian High Court stated in *Russell v Scott*:

The presumption of resulting trusts does no more than call for proof of an intention to confer beneficial ownership.[179]

Thus where the presumption of resulting trust applies, a transferee will have to discharge the burden of proof by demonstrating that a gift was intended, whereas if the presumption of advancement applies the transferor will bear the burden of proving that no gift was intended. The presumptions may serve the purpose of protecting vulnerable individuals where property has been transferred, or contributions made, in circumstances where there was very little evidence as to the intended nature of the transaction. It has already been noted that the role of the purchase money resulting trust may have irreversibly altered in relation to the acquisition of interests in the family home, and discussion of this aspect, alongside potential legislative solutions to the issue, are considered in Chapter 11.

5 Resulting trusts operating to reverse unjust enrichment?

At the beginning of this chapter it was noted that there are two categories of resulting trusts recognized in English law, historically differentiated as 'presumed' and 'automatic' resulting trusts. However, a great deal of recent debate has been addressed to the question whether a third type should be recognized, namely a restitutionary resulting trust, which arises for the purpose of reversing unjust enrichment. Although English law did not historically recognize a right to restitution founded on a general principle against unjust enrichment, in *Likpin Gorman v Karpnale Ltd*[180] the House of Lords held that 'unjust enrichment' should be recognized as a valid autonomous cause of action. This recognition has been reiterated in many subsequent decisions[181] and is now beyond doubt. A claimant will be entitled to restitution whenever he can demonstrate that the defendant was unjustly enriched at his expense. Where a claimant can demonstrate an entitlement to receive restitution from the defendant, the question arises as to the nature of the remedy available to him to effect such restitution.

---

[179] (1936) 55 CLR 440, per Dixon and Evatt JJ.
[180] [1991] 2 AC 548. See Birks 'English Recognition of Unjust Enrichment' [1991] LMCLQ 473.
[181] See *Woolwich Equitable Building Society v IRC* [1993] AC 70; *Westdeutsche Landesbank Girozentrale v Islington London Borough Council* [1996] AC 669; *Kleinwort Benson Ltd v Glasgow City Council* [1999] 1 AC 153, HL.

The claimant will generally be entitled to a personal remedy, requiring the defendant to pay over to him an amount equivalent to the enrichment that had been received, but this remedy will be of little use if the defendant is insolvent. If, however, it can be shown that property constituting the enrichment received by the defendant was subjected to a trust, the plaintiff will be able to assert a proprietary claim to any assets remaining in the defendant's hands which are the traceable proceeds of the enrichment received. Such a trust will not arise expressly and there would be no grounds for finding a presumed resulting trust.

However, in a significant article, Professor Birks argued that a resulting trust should arise whenever a defendant receives an unjust enrichment conferred by mistake or under a contract the consideration for which wholly fails.[182] If such a resulting trust were to arise from the mere fact of enrichment in such cases the claimant would be entitled to a proprietary remedy. This thesis was considered in *Westdeutsche Landesbank Girozentrale v Islington London Borough Council*,[183] where it was comprehensively rejected by the House of Lords, which preferred the critical approach of William Swadling.[184] The case involved an interest rate swap agreement entered into between the plaintiff bank and the defendant local authority. Under the agreement the bank made a payment of £2.5m to the authority. However, as a consequence of the decision of the House of Lords in *Hazell v Hammersmith and Fulham London Borough Council*,[185] the contract between the parties was ultra vires the local authority and therefore void. The bank sought restitution of the balance of the payment it had made, less the repayments the authority had already made, together with interest. In the House of Lords the sole remaining question was as to the nature of the interest payable on the award of restitution. If the bank was only entitled to restitution at common law then the court had no jurisdiction to award compound interest. However, the bank alleged that the payment had been received subject to a resulting trust, because the contract under which it was made was void, thus rooting their claim in equity and entitling the court to award compound interest. Lord Browne-Wilkinson explained that the circumstances of the payment could not have given rise to a resulting trust:

Applying these conventional principles of resulting trust to the present case, the bank's claim must fail. There was no transfer of money to the local authority on express trusts: therefore a resulting trust of type (B) above could not arise. As to type (A) above, any presumption of resulting trust is rebutted, since it is demonstrated that the bank paid, and the local authority received, the upfront payment with the intention that the moneys so paid should become the absolute property of the local authority. It is true that the parties were under a misapprehension that the payment was made in pursuance of a valid contract. But that does not alter the actual intentions of the parties at the date the payment was made...[186]

---

[182] Birks, 'Restitution and Resulting Trusts', in Goldstein (ed), *Equity: Contemporary Legal Development* (1992). See also Chambers, *Resulting Trusts* (1997), pp 93–219.

[183] [1996] AC 669; (1996) 112 LQR 521 (Cape); [1996] CLJ 432 (Jones); [1997] LMCLQ 441 (Stevens).

[184] (1996) 16 LS 133.   [185] [1992] 2 AC 1.   [186] [1996] AC 669, at 708.

He further elucidated three reasons for rejecting Professor Birks' thesis that the concept of the resulting trust should be extended to provide a plaintiff with a proprietary remedy whenever he had transferred value to a defendant under a mistake or subject to a condition which is not subsequently satisfied. First, he held that trust interests could not arise in relation to the restitutionary concept of 'value transferred' but only in relation to defined property. Second, he considered that a trust would only arise at the moment that a defendant received a payment if he was aware of the circumstances alleged to give rise to the trust. Since a recipient of a payment subsequently found void for mistake or failure of consideration will not have been aware of the circumstances rendering it void at the date of receipt, his conscience cannot have been affected so as to generate a trust. Thirdly, he noted that the thesis was flawed by the need to artificially exclude cases of partial failure to perform a contract, despite the fact that the wider concept logically led to a resulting trust in such cases.

Alongside these conceptual objections to the recognition of restitutionary resulting trusts, the House of Lords considered that the consequential expansion in proprietary entitlements would have unacceptable practical consequences for third parties.[187] For example, if money paid under a void contract was subject to a resulting trust, third parties who entered into transactions with the recipient of the payment might be affected by the trust interest of the payor, even though no one knew that the contract was void, so that they could not have been aware of the supposed trust. In the light of these considerations Lord Browne-Wilkinson concluded:

If adopted, Professor Birks' wider concepts would give rise to all the practical consequences and injustice to which I have referred. I do not think it right to make an unprincipled alteration to the law of property (ie the law of trusts) so as to produce in the law of unjust enrichment the injustices to third parties...and the consequential commercial uncertainty which any extension of proprietary interests in personal property is bound to produce.[188]

Although the House of Lords has rejected the adoption of a wider restitutionary resulting trust, this does not mean that a trust interest will never be raised for the purpose of reversing an unjust enrichment. Lord Browne-Wilkinson stated:

Although the resulting trust is an unsuitable basis for developing proprietary restitutionary remedies, the remedial constructive trust, if introduced into English law, may provide a more satisfactory road forward.[189]

The nature of the remedial constructive trust is examined in the following chapter.

---

[187] See Burrows 'Swaps and Friction between Common Law and Equity' [1995] RLR 15 for a fuller consideration of the practical implications of the adoption of restitutionary resulting trusts.

[188] [1996] AC 669, at 709.   [189] Ibid., at 716.

10

Constructive trusts

This chapter considers the operation of constructive trusts, and the situations in which such trusts are found to arise under equitable principles to counter unconscionable conduct. Constructive trusts arise in various, defined circumstances wherever justice and good conscience require it, as English law has yet to develop the concept of a 'remedial' constructive trust.

1 Introduction to constructive trusts

(1) Terminology

The major obstacle to any analysis of the English doctrine of constructive trusts is the wide number of circumstances described by the term 'constructive trust'. This has led Sir Peter Millet to comment that 'the use of the language of constructive trust has become such a fertile source of confusion that it would be better if it were abandoned'.[1] It has been used to describe a range of situations as diverse as the remedy available against a fiduciary who has made an unauthorized profit in breach of his duty, to the creation of a trust where parties make mutual wills. At its simplest, the term 'constructive trust' describes the circumstances in which property is subjected to a trust by operation of law. Unlike an expressly declared trust, a constructive trust does not come into being solely in consequence of the express intention of a settlor. Unlike a resulting trust, it is not the product of an implied or presumed intention.[2] In *Westdeutsche Landesbank Girozentrale v Islington London Borough Council*[3] Lord Browne-Wilkinson identified a constructive trust as a trust 'which the law imposed on [the trustee] by reason of his unconscionable conduct'.[4]

---

[1] McKendrick, *Commercial Aspects of Trusts and Fiduciary Obligations* (1992), p 3.
[2] But see, however, *Midland Bank plc v Cooke* [1995] 4 All ER 562, where the Court of Appeal failed to maintain a strict distinction between resulting and constructive trusts. The use of constructive trusts of common intention to provide a non-legal owner of a family home with a beneficial interest in equity does depend on an implied or imputed intention of the settlor and claimant, but does arise without the need for court intervention—this is explored further below. The operation of trust in the family home is explored in detail in Chapter 11.
[3] [1996] AC 669; (1996) 112 LQR 521 (Cape); [1996] CLJ 432 (Jones); [1997] LMCLQ 441 (Stevens).
[4] [1996] AC 669, at 705. See also *Paragon Finance plc v D B Thakerar & Co* [1999] 1 All ER 400, 409, where Millett LJ stated that a 'constructive trust arises by operation of law whenever the circumstances are such

(2) The English concept of the 'constructive trust'

Although the terminology of 'constructive trust' is used throughout common law jurisdictions, it does not describe identical concepts. Different jurisdictions have developed widely differing views as to the nature of constructive trusts and the circumstances in which they come into existence. One of the most significant conceptual distinctions is between what are described as 'institutional' and 'remedial' constructive trusts.

(a) The 'institutional' constructive trust

An institutional constructive trust is a trust that is brought into being on the occurrence of specified events, without the need for the intervention of the court. The trust comes into being if the facts that are necessary to give rise to it are proved to have occurred. It exists from the time that the relevant events occurred.[5] The court does not impose the trust, but rather recognizes that the beneficiary enjoys a pre-existing proprietary interest in the trust property. The court has no discretion to decide whether or not the property should be subject to a trust. Since an institutional constructive trust does not arise from the judgment of the court, it is capable of gaining priority over any interests acquired by third parties in the trust property during the period between the creation of the trust and its recognition by the court.

(b) The 'remedial' constructive trust

In contrast to the 'institutional' constructive trust, some other jurisdictions have come to regard constructive trusts as one of a range of remedies to facilitate restitution where a defendant has been unjustly enriched at the expense of a plaintiff. Having found that there has been an unjust enrichment, the court can, in its discretion, impose a constructive trust over assets representing any remaining enrichment in the hands of the defendant if appropriate, or alternatively award a monetary remedy. A remedial constructive trust is imposed by the court, which does not merely recognize a pre-existing proprietary right. The trust arises from the date of the court's judgment and it will not therefore gain automatic priority over the rights of third parties. These characteristics of a 'remedial' constructive trust were recognized in *Metall and Rohstoff AG v Donaldson Lufkin & Jenerette Inc*,[6] where Slade LJ stated:

the court imposes a constructive trust *de novo* on assets which are not subject to any preexisting trust as a means of granting equitable relief in a case where it considers it just that restitution should be made.[7]

that it would be unconscionable for the owner of property (usually but not necessarily the legal estate) to assert his beneficial interest in the property'.

[5] *Re Sharpe* [1980] 1 All ER 198, at 203, per Browne-Wilkinson J.

[6] [1990] 1 QB 391.

[7] Ibid., at 478. See also *Re Polly Peck (No 2)* [1998] 3 All ER 812, at 831, where Nourse LJ defined a remedial constructive trust as 'an order of the court granting, by way of remedy, a proprietary right to someone who, beforehand, had no proprietary right'.

At present English law only recognizes the 'institutional' constructive trust and has not been willing to adopt the remedial constructive trust.[8] Other jurisdictions, in particular Canada, have adopted an unjust enrichment analysis to explain the availability of constructive trusts, and the operation of the remedial constructive trust will be examined in detail at the end of this chapter.[9]

(3) The search for a coherent theory

As the terminology of constructive trusts is utilized in so many different contexts, it is difficult to provide any coherent unifying theory that will adequately explain their incidence. English law has tended to take the view that constructive trusts arise in a range of relatively well circumscribed conditions in which the trustee's conduct is considered unconscionable. A previous edition of Snell's *Equity* concluded:

For the present... constructive trusts fall for the most part in well-established categories, and it is only occasionally and in unusual circumstances that it would be necessary to take refuge in such a broad and fundamental principle [ie of unconscionability].[10]

In the case of the remedial constructive trust, the unifying fundamental principle is that of the reversal of unjust enrichment. Although superficially attractive as a touchstone, this merely shifts the goal posts, since it becomes necessary to define when an enrichment is 'unjust'. This will require the identification of common fact situations where enrichment is regarded as 'unjust', which may of themselves have no greater coherency than those regarded as giving rise to constructive trusts in English law. In this sense the restitutionary approach may simply reinvent the wheel under a different name.

Despite the difficulty of providing any single coherent theory for the enforcement of constructive trusts, the factor that appears to connect the circumstances in which the court will find that a constructive trust has arisen is an emphasis on the conduct of the party who is required to hold property subject to the constructive trust. Constructive trusts are imposed by equity in order to satisfy the demands of justice and good conscience,[11] and where it would be unjust to allow the trustee to assert an absolute entitlement to property. As Lord Denning MR observed in *Binions v Evans*,[12] quoting the words of an American judge:

A constructive trust is the formula through which the conscience of equity finds expression. When property has been acquired in such circumstances that the holder of the legal title may not in good conscience retain the beneficial interest, equity converts him into a trustee.[13]

---

[8] See *Metall und Rohstoff AG v Donaldson Lufkin & Jenrette Inc* [1990] 1 QB 391; *Westdeutsche Landesbank Girozentrale v Islington London Borough Council* [1996] AC 669; *Re Polly Peck (No 2)* [1998] 3 All ER 812.

[9] See below, p 315.   [10] Snell, *Principles of Equity* (29th edn, 1990), p 197.

[11] *Carl-Zeiss-Stiftung v Herbert Smith & Co (No 2)* [1969] 2 Ch 276, at 301, per Edmund Davies LJ.

[12] [1972] Ch 359, at 386.

[13] *Beatty v Guggenheim Exploration Co* 225 NY 380 (1919), at 386 per Cardozo J.

The concept of 'justice and good conscience' is too broad to be of direct practical value.[14] Analysis of the precise conduct justifying the imposition of a constructive trust can only realistically be attempted in the context of the common circumstances where constructive trusts have been found to arise. This chapter will therefore follow the common approach of identifying and describing the circumstances in which English law will find that a constructive trust has been created.

(4) The significance of constructive trusts

(a) Creation of proprietary interests

As a species of trust, constructive trusts inherently create equitable proprietary interests in favour of identifiable beneficiaries. A trust cannot arise in abstract, but only in respect of defined property.[15] Constructive trusts therefore provide a means by which a legal owner will be required to hold property on trust for beneficiaries, despite the lack of any express or implied intention that he should do so, or where an intention to create a trust is ineffective because it is not expressed in compliance with the appropriate statutory formalities.[16] This ability of constructive trusts to generate proprietary interests has been especially significant in the context of the ownership of land. Alongside resulting trusts, constructive trusts provide a means by which a person can obtain a share of the beneficial ownership where no formal declaration of trust has been made in their favour.[17] Where constructive trusts do give rise to proprietary interests, they may have far-reaching effects, especially by detracting from the interests that third parties may have acquired after the trust had arisen, for example if land subject to a constructive trust has been mortgaged, and by gaining automatic priority over the rights of other creditors if the trustee is insolvent. The institutional nature of the constructive trust gives the court no flexibility to consider the potential effects of the constructive trust on such third parties or creditors.

(b) Preservation of pre-existing equitable interests

Constructive trusts also operate to preserve the interest of the beneficiaries of an existing trust, however created, if the legal title to the trust property is wrongly transferred by the trustee. A third party who purchases the legal title to the trust property from a trustee will take free from the pre-existing trust interests of the beneficiaries if he was a bona fide purchaser for value without notice. However, if the requirements of the doctrine of notice are not fulfilled, either because the transferee of the legal title was

---

[14] See *Snell's Equity* (13th edn, 2000), p 221.

[15] *Westdeutsche Landesbank Girozentrale v Islington London Borough Council* [1996] AC 669, at 709, per Lord Browne-Wilkinson.

[16] *Rochefoucauld v Boustead* [1897] 1 Ch 196. See also, in this context, *Re Rose (Deceased)* [[1952] Ch 499], where it was held that a constructive trust arose once a transferor had done all he could do to transfer legal title to property—see further Chapter 7.

[17] This topic is explored fully in Chapter 11. See also Howard and Hill 'The Informal Creation of Interests in Land' (1995) 15 LS 356.

a volunteer who had not provided consideration, or because he had notice (whether actual or constructive) of the existence of the trust, the transferee will hold the property as constructive trustee for the beneficiaries. By this means their pre-existing entitlements are preserved and the recipient will not be entitled to treat the property as if he were the absolute owner.

(c) Misappropriated property

Constructive trusts have increasingly come to prominence in commercial contexts where property has been misappropriated from its true owner. If the misappropriated property was not previously subject to a trust, it may be rendered subject to a constructive trust in the hands of the recipient if it was misappropriated by a person standing in a fiduciary relationship to the owner,[18] or if it was received in circumstances generating a fiduciary relationship between the recipient and the owner.[19] By means of such a constructive trust, the entitlement of the true owner is preserved in equity. In *Westdeutsche Landesbank Girozentrale v Islington London Borough Council*[20] Lord Browne-Wilkinson held that a thief would hold the money he had stolen on constructive trust for the victim.[21]

(d) Receipt of an unauthorized profit by a fiduciary

A constructive trust will also arise whenever a fiduciary receives an unauthorized profit in breach of the duty of loyalty that is owed to his principal.[22] A person who holds such a fiduciary position is under a duty not to abuse his position by receiving any unauthorized remuneration, or to profit by allowing his duty and his interest to conflict. Equity will compel a fiduciary to hold any unauthorized profits he receives on trust for his principal, who will be entitled to claim an equitable proprietary interest in them or their traceable proceeds. The remedies available against a fiduciary will be fully considered in Chapter 30.

(e) Personal liability to account as a constructive trustee

Historically, English law utilized the concept of the constructive trust to impose a personal liability to account upon a fiduciary who had received an unauthorized profit, a stranger to a trust who had knowingly received and dissipated trust property, and a stranger who had knowingly assisted in the commission of a breach of trust. However, in *Paragon Finance plc v D B Thakerar & Co*[23] Millett LJ considered that the terminology of constructive trusts was inappropriate to describe such liability. He distinguished between two categories of constructive trusts. The first category were those situations in which a person had assumed the duties of a trustee even though he had not been expressly appointed as such. The second were circumstances in which the

---

[18] As, for example, in *Agip (Africa) v Jackson* [1991] Ch 547.
[19] *Chase Manhattan Bank NA v Israel-British Bank (London) Ltd* [1981] Ch 105.
[20] [1996] AC 669.   [21] Ibid., at 716.
[22] *A-G for Hong Kong v Reid* [1994] 1 All ER 1, PC.   [23] [1999] 1 All ER 400.

defendant was implicated in a fraud. In respect to this second category of cases he considered that the language of constructive trusts was inappropriate:

The second class of case is different. It arises when the defendant is implicated in a fraud. Equity has always given relief against fraud by making any person sufficiently implicated in the fraud accountable in equity. In such a case he is traditionally though I think unfortunately described as a constructive trustee and said to be 'liable to account as a constructive trustee'. Such a person is not in fact a trustee at all, even though he may be liable to account as if he were. He never assumes the position of a trustee, and if he receives the trust property at all it is adversely to the plaintiff by an unlawful transaction which is impugned by the plaintiff. In such a case the expressions 'constructive trust' and 'constructive trustee' are misleading, for there is no trust and usually no possibility of a proprietary remedy; they are 'nothing more than a formula for equitable relief': *Selangor United Rubber Estates Ltd v Craddock (No 3)*.[24]

While it is certainly correct that the personal liability of a person who has assisted in the commission of a breach of trust should not be characterized as the liability of a constructive trustee, as the assistor will usually never have held the trust property, it is less obvious that the terminology is inappropriate to describe the personal liability of a fiduciary who has received an unauthorized profit, or a stranger who has received and dissipated trust property. In both situations the liability arises because the fiduciary or stranger has failed to preserve the property that he held on trust. However, given the confusion of terminology, the personal liability of a fiduciary to account for unauthorized profits, or of a stranger to account for the value of trust property he has received, are better analysed as examples of claims to restitution in equity.[25] The personal remedies available against a fiduciary are considered in Chapter 30, and those against a stranger who has received trust property in Chapter 31.

2 Preventing benefit from crime[26]

(1) The principle that no criminal may benefit from his crime

It is a basic principle of English Law that no criminal should be entitled to retain a material benefit derived from his crime. As Fry LJ said in *Cleaver v Mutual Reserve Fund Life Association*:

no system of jurisprudence can with reason include among the rights which it enforces rights directly resulting to the person asserting them from the crime of that person... This principle of public policy, like all such principles, must be applied to all cases to which it can be applied without reference to the particular character of the right asserted or the form of its assertion.[27]

---

[24] Ibid., at 409. [25] As, for example, in *Re Montagu's Settlement Trusts* [1987] Ch 264.
[26] See Oakley, *Constructive Trusts* (3rd edn, 1996), pp 46–53; Goff and Jones, *The Law of Restitution* (5th edn, 1998), pp 802–814; Youdan 'Acquisition of Property by Killing' (1973) 89 LQR 235; Earnshaw and Pace 'Let the Hand Receiving It Be Ever So Chaste' (1974) 37 MLR 481.
[27] [1892] 1 QB 147, at 156.

The principle operates to prevent property coming into the hands of a criminal as a result of his crime, and instead deflects it to others who would be entitled in his place by forfeiting his entitlement. The potentially harsh operation of the rule is illustrated in *Re D W S (decd)*.[28] In this case a son had murdered his parents, who had died intestate. Clearly the son was disqualified from inheriting their estates. The Court of Appeal held that his illegitimate son was also unable to inherit his grandparent's estate because the rules of intestacy state that 'no issue shall take whose parent is living at the date of the intestate'.[29] Their estates therefore passed to more distant relatives.

Where, however, a criminal has already received property into his hands in consequence of his crime, it will be subjected to a constructive trust in favour of those who would have been entitled to it in his place. Suppose, for example, a man kills his wife and subsequently inherits property that she bequeathed to him in her will. If it is later discovered that she was murdered, he will hold what remains of the property, or its traceable proceeds, on constructive trust. The imposition of this constructive trust has the effect of depriving him of the beneficial interest in the property, although he will continue to hold the legal title as trustee.

The principle that a criminal cannot benefit from his crime could have application in two main circumstances; first, where a person receives property by theft, and second where a person acquires property (whether by succession or survivorship) from someone who has died in consequence of a crime committed by that person.

(2) Property obtained by theft

The principle has little practical application to the area of theft because a thief does not normally acquire legal title to the property that he steals.[30] Under s 28 of the Theft Act 1968 the court has power to order a person convicted of theft to return the property to its owner. The equitable rules of tracing may be helpful in following the property into the hands of a third party where the thief has disposed of it.[31] The process of tracing is considered in Chapter 32.

(3) Property acquired by a crime causing death

A person who unlawfully kills another will not be entitled to retain property received as a result of his victim's death, whether under the victim's will, on intestacy, or through the operation of survivorship in the context of jointly owned property. Similarly, an unlawful killer will not be able to recover under an insurance policy covering the consequences of the death of the unlawfully killed person. In each of these cases the courts intervene to prevent the criminal obtaining a benefit.

---

[28] [2001] Ch 568.   [29] Administration of Estates Act 1925, s 47 (1) (i).
[30] A purchaser from a thief will only obtain good title in a few cases. See Bradgate, *Commercial Law* (3rd edn, 2000).
[31] See *Westdeutche Landesbank v Islington Borough Council* [1996] AC 669.

(a) Must the criminal have used or threatened violence?

The principle of forfeiture by imposition of a constructive trust will apply where a person has received property from a victim he has unlawfully killed. Unlawful killing obviously includes murder, but forfeiture will not operate against a killer found innocent on the grounds of insanity because such a verdict constitutes an acquittal.[32] It has been less clear whether forfeiture applies where a killer has committed manslaughter. As Salmon LJ observed in *Gray v Barr*:

Manslaughter is a crime which varies infinitely in its seriousness. It may come very near to murder or amount to little more than inadvertence, although in the latter class of case the jury only rarely convicts.[33]

It remains unclear whether forfeiture operates in cases of 'involuntary manslaughter', for example where death was caused by reckless driving. The courts have shown reluctance to draw a distinction between voluntary and involuntary manslaughter.[34] For example in *Re Giles*, where a wife had been found guilty of the manslaughter of her husband on the ground of diminished responsibility, Pennycuick V-C held:

It is sufficient to state that the rule has been established and that the deserving of punishment and moral culpability are not necessary ingredients of the type of crime to which this rule applies, that is, culpable homicide, murder or manslaughter.[35]

Some evidence for the inapplicability of the forfeiture rule to cases of involuntary manslaughter can be derived from insurance cases where a driver had committed 'motor manslaughter' and killed through his reckless driving. In such cases the courts have held that an insured driver was not prevented from recovering under his insurance policy,[36] unless his conduct was wilful and culpable.[37]

However, in cases not involving motor manslaughter, the courts have historically held that forfeiture operates if the killer used violence, or threats of violence, against his victim, even if the death was accidental. In *Gray v Barr*,[38] Mr Barr confronted Mr Gray believing that his wife, with whom Mr Gray had been having an affair, was present. He involuntarily shot Mr Gray after falling backwards while threatening him with a loaded shotgun. The Court of Appeal held that in these circumstances the principle of forfeiture should apply. Salmon LJ stated:

Although public policy is rightly regarded as an unruly steed which should be cautiously ridden, I am confident that public policy undoubtedly requires that no one who threatens unlawful

---

[32] Criminal Procedure (Insanity) Act 1964, s 1.   [33] [1971] 2 QB 554, at 581.

[34] Voluntary manslaughter is where what would otherwise be murder is reduced to manslaughter by provocation or diminished responsibility, or because the death occurred in pursuance of a suicide pact. Involuntary manslaughter is where an unlawful killing is reduced to manslaughter because there was no intent to kill or to do grievous bodily harm: see *Re K* [1985] Ch 85, at 98.

[35] [1972] Ch 544, at 552. See also *R v Chief National Insurance Comr, ex p Connor* [1981] QB 758; *Re Royse* [1985] Ch 22.

[36] See *Tinline v White Cross Insurance Association Ltd* [1921] 3 KB 327; *James v British General Insurance Co Ltd* [1927] 2 KB 311.

[37] *Hardy v Motor Insurers' Bureau* [1964] 2 QB 745.   [38] [1971] 2 QB 554.

violence with a loaded gun should be allowed to enforce a claim for indemnity against any liability he may incur as a result of having so acted.[39]

At first instance, Geoffrey Lane J had held that the forfeiture rule should apply if a person was 'guilty of deliberate, intentional and unlawful violence or threats of violence'. This test was cited with approval by Vinelott J in *Re K*,[40] where a wife had shot and killed her husband following domestic violence. She had intended to frighten him with a loaded shotgun that was kept in their kitchen, but it had gone off when she removed the safety catch. At trial she was acquitted of murder but found guilty of manslaughter on the grounds of diminished responsibility. Vinelott J held that the forfeiture rule applied because she had threatened violence deliberately in order to frighten and deter her husband, even though his death had been wholly unintended. In *Re H*[41] Peter Gibson J held that the forfeiture rule did not apply where a offender convicted of manslaughter on grounds of diminished responsibility had not been responsible for his actions, which were therefore neither deliberate nor intentional.

However, in *Dunbar v Plant*[42] the Court of Appeal rejected the view that forfeiture only operates where deliberate violence, or threats of violence, have been used and concluded that it applied where a woman had aided and abetted the suicide of her fiancé. The facts of the case were tragic. Miss Plant, who was facing a trial for theft from her employers, decided to commit suicide rather than face the prospect of jail. Mr Dunbar, her fiancé, said that he could not contemplate life without her, so they agreed that they would commit suicide together. An initial attempt to gas themselves in a car failed, as did a attempt to hang themselves with cable. On a further attempt to hang themselves with sheets, Dunbar was successful but Plant survived. Further suicide attempts, including cutting her throat and jumping out of a window, were also unsuccessful. The case concerned the question whether forfeiture should operate to prevent her obtaining the benefit of Dunbar's life insurance policy, of which she was the beneficiary. Counsel for Plant argued that the forfeiture rule should not apply at all because she had not used or threatened violence against Dunbar. This was rejected unanimously by the Court of Appeal, which held that the forfeiture rule prima facie applied. Mummery LJ explained:

In my judgment...the presence of acts or threats of violence is not necessary for the application of the forfeiture rule. It is sufficient that a serious crime has been committed deliberately and intentionally. The references to acts or threats of violence in the cases are explicable by the facts of those cases. But in none of those cases were the courts legislating a principle couched in specific statutory language. The essence of the principle of public policy is that (a) no person shall take a benefit resulting from a crime committed by him or her resulting in the death of the victim and (b) the nature of the crime determines the application of the principle. On that view, the important point is that the crime that had fatal consequences was committed with a guilty mind (deliberately and intentionally). The particular means used to commit the crime (whether violent or non-violent) are not a necessary ingredient of the rule.[43]

---

[39] Ibid., at 581.   [40] [1985] 2 WLR 262, at 276.   [41] [1990] 1 FLR 441.
[42] [1998] Ch 412.
[43] [1997] 4 All ER 289, at 300. Mummery LJ cited the Canadian case *Whitelaw v Wilson* [1934] OR 415, where it had been held that the forfeiture rule applied to the survivor of a suicide pact in which a husband and wife both drank poison.

Given that violence was not required, it was held that the forfeiture rule operated where the offence of aiding and abetting suicide contrary to s 2(1) of the Suicide Act 1961 had been committed in the context of a suicide pact. Miss Plant had encouraged Dunbar to commit suicide, thus committing the offence and attracting the operation of the forfeiture rule. In *Dalton v Latham*,[44] Patten J held that *Dunbar v Plant*:

must now be taken to be a binding statement of the law as to the application of the rule of public policy. It applies to all cases of unlawful killing, including manslaughter by reason of diminished responsibility or by reason of provocation. The only possible exception is where the defendant is found to be criminally insane, which leads to an acquittal.[45]

In *Dalton v Latham*, the claimant was acquitted of murder on the grounds of diminished responsibility but pleaded guilty to manslaughter. In *Land v Land*[46] the forfeiture rule was again applied, on this occasion to a man, assessed as probably having a developmental disorder, who had pleaded guilty to manslaughter after failing to call for medical assistance to aid his domineering mother, who was terminally ill and bedridden with breast cancer. According to HHJ Alastair Norris, QC, sitting as a High Court judge:

Following *Dunbar*... it is no longer possible to discriminate in the application of the rule, only to mitigate its effects where the ends of justice require. The rule will accordingly be applied even where the public interest does not require it (and even where its application may be contrary to the public interest), but in some circumstances its effects may be mitigated.[47]

As is evident from *Dunbar v Plant*, where Miss Plant had not been convicted of the offence of aiding and abetting, the forfeiture rule will apply even though the person causing death has not been convicted of a criminal offence. This may be because it has not been possible to bring him to trial, for example because of his own suicide.[48] In *Gray v Barr*,[49] the Court of Appeal held that the forfeiture rule should apply even though Mr Barr had been acquitted at trial of both murder and manslaughter. In the civil trial the lower evidential standard of the 'balance of probabilities' applied. For this reason, Lord Denning MR was able to conclude: 'there is no doubt, to my mind, that Mr Barr was guilty of manslaughter'.[50]

(b) Forfeiture of entitlement under the victim's will

Where the forfeiture rule operates, a criminal will not be permitted to derive any benefit under the will of his victim. In *Re Sigsworth*[51] a coroner's inquest found that Mary Sigsworth had died as a result of a fractured spine caused by her son, Thomas. He subsequently committed suicide before he could be brought to trial. She had left the whole of her property to him. On the assumption that he had murdered his mother,[52]

---

[44] [2003] EWHC 796.   [45] Ibid., at [9].   [46] [2006] EWHC 2069.
[47] Ibid., at [18].   [48] See *Re Sigsworth* [1935] Ch 89.
[49] [1971] 2 QB 554.   [50] Ibid., at 568.
[51] [1935] Ch 89. See also *Re Callaway* [1956] Ch 559; *Re Peacock* [1957] Ch 310.
[52] The verdict of the coroner's jury was not conclusive, and the judge stressed that if the administrator of the estate acted upon his judgement he would have to take the risk that the assumption of fact may conceivably turn out to be erroneous.

Clauson J held that Thomas was not entitled to take any interest under the will. He stated the principle:

the claim of the [son], to the estate of the mother under her will is bound to fail by reason of the well-settled principle that public policy precludes a sane murderer from taking a benefit under his victim's will.[53]

(c) Forfeiture of entitlement arising on the victim's intestacy

Similarly, the forfeiture rule operates to preclude the criminal receiving any property to which he would ordinarily have been entitled on the intestacy of the deceased. In *Re Crippen*[54] Harvey Crippen was executed following his conviction for the murder of his wife, Cora. She had left no will. Before his execution he made a will leaving all his property to his mistress, Ethel Le Neve. The court held that Le Neve was not entitled to receive the property to which Crippen would have been entitled from his wife's estate under the rules of intestacy. The principle was again stated by Clauson J in *Re Sigsworth*:

the principle of public policy which precludes a murderer from claiming a benefit conferred on him by his victims will preclude him from claiming a benefit conferred on him, in case of his victim's intestacy, by statute.[55]

(d) Forfeiture of entitlement by survivorship

Where property is held by co-owners as joint tenants, the principle of survivorship (the *ius accrescendi*) operates, so that the property vests automatically in the surviving joint tenant or tenants. This will apply whether the joint tenancy is of the legal or the equitable title to property. Therefore, if Harry and Joan are the joint tenants of a house in law and in equity, and Harry dies, the title will vest automatically in Joan. It will make no difference if he had left all his property by will to charity, as the operation of survivorship takes precedence over the disposition by will. However, if Joan unlawfully killed Harry and survivorship were allowed to operate, she would benefit from her crime. Therefore, the forfeiture rule is applied and the principle of survivorship will not operate between the joint tenants.[56] In *Re K*,[57] Vinelott J held that the principle of forfeiture applied so that a wife who was guilty of the manslaughter of her husband was not entitled to their jointly owned matrimonial home by the operation of survivorship between them. Instead, she held the house on trust for herself and her husband's next of kin in equal shares as tenants-in-common.[58] Similarly, in *Dunbar v Plant*[59] the forfeiture rule *prima facie* excluded the operation of survivorship in respect of a jointly owned house.

---

[53] [1935] Ch 89, at 92.   [54] [1911] P 108.   [55] [1935] Ch 89, at 92.

[56] It should be noted that the rule does not deprive the killer of his or her own presumptive share under the joint tenancy.

[57] [1985] Ch 85.

[58] See also *Schobelt v Barber* (1966) 60 DLR (2d) 519; *Re Pechar* [1969] NZLR 574. Although the forfeiture rule operates simply where there are only two joint tenants, it is much more complicated where there are three or more and one joint tenant kills another. See *Rasmanis v Jurewitsch* [1970] 70 SRNSW 407.

[59] [1997] 4 All ER 289.

(4) The court's jurisdiction to grant relief from forfeiture

Although the forfeiture rule *prima facie* applies where a person has died in consequence of a crime, under the Forfeiture Act 1982 the court has the discretion to grant relief from the effects of the rule. Section 2(1) provides that where the forfeiture rule has precluded a person who has unlawfully killed another from acquiring any interest in property: 'the court may make an order…modifying the effect of that rule'. This jurisdiction applies to property in the form of beneficial interests under the deceased's will, intestacy, a donatio mortis causa, or under a trust. The section has no application to persons convicted of murder.[60] Under s 2(2) the court may only exercise its jurisdiction to grant relief if satisfied that:

having regard to the conduct of the offender and of the deceased and to such other circumstances as appear to the court to be material, the justice of the case requires the effect of the rule to be modified in that case.

The jurisdiction was exercised in *Re K*.[61] Vinelott J held that the discretion conferred by the Act requires the court to investigate the moral culpability of the killing, and he concluded that, because of the tragic circumstances of the case, and the fact that a loyal wife had suffered grave violence at the hands of her husband, it was appropriate for the court to grant relief so that she would not be deprived of the provision which her husband had made for her under his will or of the matrimonial home under the operation of survivorship. He also considered that it was relevant to take into account the relative financial position of persons claiming relief under the Act and those who would be entitled if the forfeiture rule was applied.

In *Dunbar v Plant*[62] the Court of Appeal also held that Miss Plant should be granted relief against forfeiture of the proceeds of Dunbar's life insurance policy, even though this was contested by his father. It was unanimously held that the approach of the first instance judge, who had sought to 'do justice between the parties', was an inappropriate approach to the exercise of the jurisdiction. The majority went on to conclude that, in the case of suicide pacts which were the result of irrational depression or desperation, total relief from forfeiture would be appropriate. Phillips LJ, with whom Hirst LJ agreed, concluded that there was nothing in the circumstances to require a different approach:

The desperation that led Miss Plant to decide to kill herself, and which led to the suicide pact, was an irrational and tragic reaction to her predicament. I do not consider that the nature of Miss Plant's conduct alters what I have indicated should be the normal approach when dealing with a suicide pact—that there should be full relief against forfeiture. The assets with which this case is concerned were in no way derived from Mr Dunbar's family. They are the fruits of insurance taken out by Mr Dunbar for the benefit of Miss Plant.[63]

In *Land v Land*[64] judge Alastair Norris, QC mitigated the impact of forfeiture by making an order for the claimant under the Inheritance (Provision for Family and Dependants) Act 1975 as envisaged by s 3(1) of the Forfeiture Act 1982.

---

[60] S 5.
[62] [1997] 4 All ER 289.
[61] [1985] Ch 85, Vinelott J; affd [1986] Ch 180, CA.
[63] Ibid., at 313.
[64] [2006] EWHC 2069.

(5) Reform of the forfeiture rule

Where the forfeiture rule operates, *Re DWS (Decd)*[65] establishes that neither the perpetrator of the offence nor anyone claiming through him can benefit under the will or intestacy. This harsh consequence has led the Law Commission to recommend that the rule be reformed. The Law Commission has proposed that the forfeiture rule should be replaced by a 'deemed predecease' rule, so that the property of the intestate would be distributed as if the killer had died immediately before the deceased.[66] This rule would extend to an intestacy and to situations where the deceased had made a will and the potential beneficiary is excluded because he or she claims through the person who killed the deceased.[67] The proposals would not, however, have any application to the operation of the survivorship rule in joint tenancies since the deemed predecease rule would be confined to the construction of the intestacy legislation and of wills.[68]

3 Specifically enforceable contract to sell property

From the very moment that a vendor enters a specifically enforceable contract to sell property, he holds it on constructive trust for the purchaser. The reason for the imposition of the trust in these circumstances is that the contract of sale renders the vendor subject to an obligation to transfer the property to the purchaser that will be enforced in equity by means of the remedy of specific performance. By applying the maxim that 'equity treats as done that which ought to be done', the constructive trust ensures that the purchaser is entitled to the equitable interest immediately, even though he will not become the full absolute owner until the vendor transfers the legal title in fulfilment of the contract. The operation of such constructive trusts was explained in *Lysaght v Edwards*[69] by Jessel MR:

the moment you have a valid contract for sale the vendor becomes in equity a trustee for the purchaser of the estate sold, and the beneficial ownership passes to the purchaser...[70]

Such constructive trusts will most commonly arise in the context of contracts for the purchase of land.[71] The majority of contracts for the purchase of personal property are not specifically enforceable because the subject matter is not unique. However, if specific performance would be available, a constructive trust will arise. Such a constructive trust was found to have arisen in *Oughtred v IRC*,[72] which involved a contract

---

65 [2001] Ch 568.

66 *The Forfeiture Rule and the Law of Succession*, Law Comm No 295 (2005), para 1.14–1.15.

67 Ibid., at para 1.16.   68 Ibid., at para 2.29.

69 (1876) 2 Ch D 499; see also *Haywood v Cope* (1858) 25 Beav 140.

70 Compare *Rayner v Preston* (1880–81) LR 18 Ch D 1, CA, where Brett LJ held that a trust did not arise; *KLDE Pty Ltd v Stamp Duties Comr (Queensland)* (1984) 155 CLR 288.

71 Eg *Green v Smith* (1738) 1 Atk 572; *Rose v Watson* (1864) 10 HL Cas 672; *Appleton v Aspin* [1988] 1 WLR 410, CA.

72 [1960] AC 206. See also *Re Holt's Settlement* [1969] 1 Ch 100.

for the sale of shares in a private company. This decision was reaffirmed by the Court of Appeal in *Neville v Wilson*.[73]

From the moment of contract, a genuine trust relationship is created, so that the vendor holds the title of the property on trust for the purchaser. His duties are not the same as those of an ordinary trustee,[74] for example he is entitled to retain profits arising from the property before completion of the contract.[75] However, he is under a duty to 'use reasonable care to preserve the property in a reasonable state of preservation'.[76]

4 Mutual wills

It is a fundamental principle that a man is entitled to make a will leaving his property to whomsoever he chooses. Any will he makes remains revocable until his death. However, if two persons enter into a contract to execute wills in a common form, and the survivor subsequently changes his will, the court will impose a constructive trust on the property in the hands of the executors of the survivor in favour of the beneficiaries of the mutual wills. The doctrine of mutual wills is fully considered in Chapter 12.

5 Acquisition of land expressly subject to the interests of a third party

One of the central objectives of land law is to determine whether a transferee of land is bound by third party interests in the land that were valid against the transferor. Where title to the land is registered, the equitable doctrine of notice has been replaced by a scheme of registration.[77] Lesser interests must be protected by means of an entry on the register of the title to which they relate. If an interest is unprotected, a transferee for valuable consideration of the legal title will acquire the land free from it,[78] unless it is an 'overriding interest',[79] in which case it will bind the transferee irrespective.

---

[73] [1996] 3 All ER 171; (1996) 55 CLJ 436 (Nolan); [1996] Conv 368 (Thompson).

[74] *Shaw v Foster* (1872) LR 5 HL 321; *Earl of Egmont v Smith* (1877) 6 Ch D 469; *Royal Bristol Permanent Building Society v Bomash* (1887) LR 35 Ch D 390; *Cumberland Consolidated Holdings Ltd v Ireland* [1946] KB 264; *Engelwood Properties v Patel* [2005] 3 All ER 307.

[75] *Cuddon v Tite* (1858) 1 Giff 395.

[76] *Clarke v Ramuz* [1891] 2 QB 456, at 459–460, per Lord Coleridge CJ. See also *Royal Bristol Permanent Building Society v Bomash* (1887) LR 35 Ch D 390; *Phillips v Lamdin* [1949] 2 KB 33; *Lucie-Smith v Gorman* [1981] CLY 2866.

[77] Jackson, Stevens, and Pearce, *Land Law* (4th edn, 2008), pp 111–139.

[78] Land Registration Act 2002, s 29.   [79] Land Registration Act 2002, Sch 3.

However, it has been held that if a transferee of the land expressly agrees that he will honour the rights of a third party, he will be bound by those rights under a constructive trust even though it had not been properly protected on the register. This constructive trust prevents the purchaser taking advantage of his strict rights under the statute. Such a constructive trust was held to have arisen in *Lyus v Prowsa Developments*.[80] Mr and Mrs Lyus entered a contract to purchase a house that was to be built on a new estate. The developers subsequently went into liquidation and the bank that held a mortgage of the land sold it to another developer. This second developer agreed in the contract to take the land 'subject to, but with the benefit of the contract made with Mr and Mrs Lyus'. This developer subsequently sold the land to a third, who agreed to the same terms. The contract entered between the first developer and Mr and Mrs Lyus was an interest in land which should have been protected on the register as a minor interest. Even though it had not been protected appropriately, Dillon J held that the developers who had purchased the land were bound by it. They had expressly agreed to take subject to the interest and therefore a constructive trust was raised to 'counter unconscionable conduct or fraud'.[81] Dillon J stressed that the agreement was not a general agreement to take the land subject to possible encumbrances but a positive stipulation in favour of a particular identified interest. A similar position was adopted by the Australian High Court in *Bahr v Nicolay (No 2)*.[82]

The operation of such a constructive trust was further considered in *Ashburn Anstalt v Arnold*.[83] The Court of Appeal addressed, obiter, the question whether a purchaser could be bound by a constructive trust when he had expressly agreed to acquire land subject to a third party's contractual licence. Citing *Lyus v Prowsa Developments*,[84] the court accepted that a constructive trust could arise in such circumstances, but stated that 'the court will not impose a constructive trust unless it is satisfied that the conscience of the estate owner is affected'.[85] The mere fact that land was expressly said to be conveyed 'subject to' a contractual right would not suffice alone:

We do not think it is desirable that constructive trusts of land should be imposed in reliance on inference from slender materials.[86]

It was suggested that other factors would be necessary to justify the imposition of a constructive trust, for example evidence that the purchaser paid a lower price for the land as a consequence of the express agreement to take subject to the interest. The

---

[80] [1982] 1 WLR 1044. This case deals with registered title. There is no reason to suspect that, had the facts arisen in unregistered title, the decision would have been any different—see further Jackson, Stevens, and Pearce, *Land Law* (4th edn, 2008), pp 133–135.

[81] [1982] 1 WLR 1044, at 1052.

[82] (1988) 78 ALR 1. Compare, however, *Hollington Bros v Rhodes* [1951] 2 All ER 578n, where a different conclusion was reached concerning an unregistered charge under the Land Charges Act 1925. See now the Land Charges Act 1972.

[83] [1989] Ch 1; [1988] Cov 201 (Thompson); (1988) 51 MLR 226 (Hill); (1988) 104 LQR 175 (Sparkes).

[84] [1982] 1 WLR 1044.   [85] [1989] Ch 1, at 25.   [86] Ibid., at 26.

essence of the constructive trust is the purchaser's voluntary acceptance of obligations in favour of the third party.[87]

6 Common intention to share the ownership of land[88]

One of the most significant areas of operation of the doctrine of constructive trusts in the past sixty years has been in the context of land ownership, and especially the ownership of the family home. Constructive trusts provide a means by which a person may obtain a share of the ownership of land despite the lack of any express declaration of trust in his favour.

The House of Lords affirmed the use of constructive trusts as a means to acquire an interest for the non-legal owner of property in the landmark decision of *Gissing v Gissing*:

A...constructive trust...is created by a transaction between the trustee and the [beneficiary] in connection with the acquisition by the trustee of a legal estate in land, whenever the trustee has so conducted himself that it would be inequitable to allow him to deny to the [beneficiary] a beneficial interest in the land acquired.[89]

Lord Diplock emphasized that a legal owner would only have acted so as to justify the imposition of a constructive trust:

if by his words or conduct he has induced the [beneficiary] to act to his own detriment in the reasonable belief that by so acting he was acquiring a beneficial interest in the land.[90]

This very broad principle has been developed and refined in subsequent cases, notably *Lloyds Bank v Rosset*,[91] to create the distinctive, but inaccurately named, 'common intention constructive trust'. This branch of equity has emerged in response, in part, to the changing patterns of home ownership following the Second World War, and the fact that there is no concept of 'common law' marriage for unmarried cohabiting couples that gives a non-legal owner rights over the property on the cessation of the relationship. Many couples still operate under the mistaken belief that following a period of time together they will acquire some rights in any home they share. In the absence of marriage or, in the case of same-sex couples, registering as civil partners, which give statutory powers to redistribute property at the end of a relationship, cohabiting couples do not enjoy any rights without the intervention of equity.

The principle underlying the common intention constructive trust is that the constructive trust will be imposed where the owner of land (usually the husband or the

---

[87] There is a clear analogy with cases such as *Bannister v Bannister* [1948] 2 All ER 133 and *Binions v Evans* [1972] Ch 359. See also McFarlane 'Constructive Trusts Arising on a Receipt of Property *Sub Conditione*' (2004) 120 LQR 667.

[88] See: Mee, *The Property Rights of Cohabitees* (1999); Hopkins, *The Informal Acquisition of Rights in Land* (2000); Jackson, Stevens, and Pearce, *Land Law* (4th edition, 2008) pp 315–353.

[89] [1971] AC 886, at 905.   [90] Ibid., at 905.   [91] [1971] AC 886.

male partner in a relationship) has promised his cohabitant that she will have a share of the beneficial ownership, and she has acted upon that promise, usually by making a financial contribution. In some circumstances, even where no express promise has been made, a promise can be implied from conduct. Constructive trusts of common intention are thus based on the express or implied intention of the parties. They are the counterpart, in the context of domestic property, of the trust imposed in cases like *Lyus v Prowsa Developments*,[92] discussed above.

The traditional rationale for the common intention constructive trust is that it is inequitable for the owner of land to resile from an expectation that he has created or encouraged. The courts are not inventing intention, but finding it from the express discussions of the parties, or inferring it from their actions. The actions that will suffice to establish a constructive trust, where there has been no express discussion about ownership, are very limited, and it may be that only a direct financial contribution towards the acquisition of the property will suffice. However, the cases demonstrate that once a constructive trust has been established, a much wider range of factors can be taken into account in quantifying the size of the beneficial share of the property to be awarded to the cohabitant. Household labour by one party may not, for example, support a claim to an interest, but may be used to quantify it.

The common intention constructive trust is an area of fertile litigation, both in relation to acquiring and quantifying a beneficial interest. The applicability of constructive trusts as a mechanism for allowing a cohabitant to gain an interest has attracted considerable criticism for various reasons, not least that as a method of property management it is ill-suited to protecting the financial needs of family members, which extend to children from a relationship, or that it stretches the concept of constructive trust too far.[93] The Law Commission has undertaken projects either to place the existing equitable rules on a statutory footing or to replace them with a statutory scheme, giving cohabitants similar rights to married couples and registered civil partners. To date, none of these proposals have been enacted and cohabitants must rely on equitable methods.

There is a close relationship between common intention constructive trusts and purchase money resulting trusts (discussed in Chapter 9). The decision of the House of Lords in *Stack v Dowden*[94] has suggested that resulting trusts in this context have been entirely subsumed within the common intention constructive trust. There are also strong parallels between the common intention constructive trust and the equitable doctrine of proprietary estoppel. The interaction between common intention constructive trusts, purchase money resulting trusts, and proprietary estoppel is considered in detail in Chapter 11.

---

[92] [1982] 1 WLR 1044.
[93] These opinions, and others, are explored in Chapter 11 at pp 428 *et seq*.
[94] [2007] 2 AC 432.

7 The 'remedial constructive trust'[95]

(1) Defining the 'remedial constructive trust'

The English doctrine of constructive trusts has been subjected to much criticism. As has been seen in the context of trusts of co-owned land, English law adopts an 'institutional' form of constructive trust, whereby the court merely recognizes a pre-existing equitable interest. There is little scope for flexibility, other than by manipulation of the criteria that must be satisfied for the creation of a constructive trust, and the nature of the claim predetermines the remedial outcome.[96]

In other jurisdictions, an entirely different approach towards constructive trusts has emerged. An equitable proprietary right is regarded as one possible remedial response to effect restitution where a defendant has been unjustly enriched. Restitution may be effected either by a personal remedy requiring the enriched defendant to pay a monetary sum equivalent to the value of the enrichment he received to the plaintiff, or by the award of a proprietary remedy over any assets representing the enrichment which remain in the defendant's hands. The essence of the 'remedial' constructive trust is that the court enjoys the discretion to determine whether or not a proprietary remedy should be awarded. If the court exercises its discretion to award a constructive trust, the resulting beneficial entitlement can be said to have been 'imposed' by the court, which does not merely recognize a pre-existing proprietary interest. The plaintiff's equitable proprietary interest does not therefore arise from the facts per se, which establish a cause of action in unjust enrichment, but from the exercise of its discretion to award such a remedy.

(2) Development of the remedial constructive trust

The Commonwealth approaches to resolving issues concerning the ownership of the family home suggest a movement away from the institutional approach to constructive trusts, towards a more remedial understanding. The courts of Canada seem to have taken the greatest steps towards the recognition and acceptance of a general remedial constructive trust, not merely within the context of familial or quasi-familial property, but also in commercial situations. The best description of how the remedial nature of the constructive trust came to be recognized in Canada is found in the judgment of Dickson CJC in *Hunter Engineering Co Inc v Syncrude Canada Ltd*:

The constructive trust has existed for over two hundred years as an equitable remedy for certain forms of unjust enrichment. In its earliest form, the constructive trust was used to provide a remedy to claimants alleging that others had made profits at their expense. Where the claimant could show the existence of a fiduciary relationship between the claimant and the person

---

[95] See Birks (ed), *The Frontiers of Liability* (1994) Vol 2, pp 163–223; (1998) 114 LQR 399 (Sir Peter Millett).

[96] The considerable debate over determining the size of the beneficial share does not alter the nature of the right—the court is only seeking to decide the extent of the pre-existing beneficial interest.

taking advantage of the claimant, the courts were receptive...Equity would not countenance the abuse of the trust and confidence inherent in a fiduciary relationship and imposed trust obligations on those who profited from abusing their position of loyalty. The doctrine was gradually extended to apply to situations where other persons who were not in a fiduciary relationship with the claimant acted in concert with the fiduciary or knew of the fiduciary obligations. Until the decision of this court in *Pettkus v Becker*, the constructive trust was viewed largely in terms of the law of trusts, hence the need for the existence of a fiduciary relationship. In *Pettkus v Becker* the court moved to an approach more in line with restitutionary principles by explicitly recognising a constructive trust as one of the remedies for unjust enrichment. In finding unjust enrichment the court...invoked three criteria: namely (1) an enrichment (2) a corresponding deprivation, and (3) absence of any juristic reason for the enrichment. The court then found that in the circumstances of the case a constructive trust was the appropriate remedy to redress the unjust enrichment.[97]

Several key points of this restatement of principle require examination.

(a) A restitutionary cause of action

A remedial constructive trust can only be imposed against a person who has been unjustly enriched. 'Unjust enrichment' is therefore the cause of action for which the constructive trust is available as a remedy. In the absence of an unjust enrichment, a constructive trust will not be imposed. For this reason a constructive trust was not imposed in *Hunter Engineering Co v Syncrude Canada Ltd*.[98] Syncrude ordered some specialist gearboxes from Hunter Canada Ltd, a company which fraudulently misrepresented that it acted on behalf of an American company, Hunter US. Hunter Canada placed a contract for the gearboxes with a subcontractor, Alco Sales and Engineering. When Hunter US discovered the circumstances they immediately alerted Syncrude and began an action against Hunter Canada for 'passing off'. Fearing a delay in the production of the gearboxes, Syncrude set up a trust fund into which they paid all the moneys which would have been payable to Hunter Canada, and agreed to pay Alco the contract price of the subcontract from this fund. The balance, representing the profit which Hunter Canada would have made, was to be distributed according to the outcome of the litigation between Hunter Canada and Hunter US. In these circumstances, Hunter US claimed that the balance of the fund was held on constructive trust for them, because it represented the profit that Hunter Canada would have made through passing themselves off as their authorized representatives. The majority of the Supreme Court allowed an appeal against the judgment of the Court of Appeal which had imposed a constructive trust under the principle of *Pettkus v Becker*.[99] They held that there had been no enrichment of Hunter Canada that would call for restitution, and therefore that a constructive trust could not be justified. Any claim of Hunter US could only arise as a result of Hunter Canada's actions, and Hunter Canada would only be entitled to the surplus in the trust fund on the basis of their contract with Syncrude. Since that contract had been terminated because of the fraudulent misrepresentation, Hunter Canada was no longer entitled to any payment under the contract, and

---

[97] (1989) 57 DLR (4th) 321, at 348.   [98] (1989) 57 DLR (4th) 321.
[99] (1980) 117 DLR (3d) 257.

Hunter US could not be in a better position vis-à-vis Syncrude than Hunter Canada. In conclusion, rather than reversing an enrichment received by Syncrude, Dickson CJC considered that:

> if Hunter US's claim prevailed (i) Hunter US would be enriched (ii) with a corresponding deprivation of Syncrude (iii) and for no juristic reason that I am able to detect.[100]

(b) A range of remedial responses

Once liability has been established by demonstrating an unjust enrichment which calls for restitution, the court is entitled to select the appropriate remedy to effect restitution. It may conclude that a proprietary remedy is appropriate. Alternatively, a purely personal monetary award may be made. This flexibility was recognized by the Supreme Court in *Sorochan v Sorochan*, where Dickson CJC stated:

> The constructive trust constitutes one important judicial means of remedying unjust enrichment. Other remedies, such as monetary damages, may also be available to rectify situations of unjust enrichment. We must, therefore, ask when and under what circumstances it is appropriate for a court to impose a constructive trust...[101]

This remedial flexibility was similarly adopted in *Rawluk v Rawluk*.[102] McLachlin J explained:

> The significance of the remedial nature of the constructive trust is not that it cannot confer a property interest, but that the conferring of such an interest is discretionary and dependant on the inadequacy of other remedies for the unjust enrichment in question. The doctrine of constructive trust may be used to confer a proprietary remedy, but that does not automatically presuppose a possessory property right. Thus, even where the tests for constructive trust are met—unjust enrichment, corresponding deprivation, and no juridical justification for the enrichment—the property interest does not automatically arise. Rather, the court must consider whether other remedies to remedy the injustice exist which make the declaration of a constructive trust inappropriate.[103]

The most important decision concerning the nature and function of remedial constructive trusts is that of the Supreme Court in *LAC Minerals Ltd v International Corona Resources Ltd*.[104] This case concerned the application of the remedial constructive trust to a commercial situation rather than to the specialized circumstances of the family home. Corona owned the mining rights over land, and approached LAC with a view to negotiating a joint venture to exploit mineral deposits. In the course of these negotiations Corona revealed results from their exploratory drilling, from which it was clear that adjacent land was also likely to contain mineral deposits. Corona sought to purchase the neighbouring land but were defeated by a competing bid by LAC, which proceeded to exploit the deposits alone. The court held that in these circumstances LAC had been unjustly enriched by misuse of the confidential information they had received from Corona. The central question was as to the nature of the remedy that should be awarded to effect restitution and reverse their unjust enrichment.

---

[100] (1989) 57 DLR (4th) 321, at 353. [101] (1986) 29 DLR (4th) 1.
[102] (1990) 65 DLR (4th) 161. [103] Ibid., at 185–186.
[104] (1989) 61 DLR (4th) 14.

To give some idea of the size of the claims involved, the trial judge had valued the land at \$700m. The Supreme Court emphasized that as the plaintiff's right to restitution had been established it possessed a remedial discretion:

The court can award either a proprietary remedy, namely that LAC hand over the [land], or award a personal remedy, namely a monetary award. The constructive trust does not lie at the heart of the law of restitution. It is but one remedy, and will only be imposed in appropriate circumstances.[105]

The majority of the court held that, in the circumstances, a constructive trust was appropriate, and that LAC should hold the land on trust for Corona.

(3) Difficulties associated with the remedial constructive trust

Although superficially attractive, in that it seems to provide a single coherent theory to explain the imposition of constructive trusts, as well as providing flexibility of remedies, the remedial constructive trust poses difficulties that cannot be ignored. The essential problem is one of uncertainty, which arises both at the level of the cause of action and at the level of the court's remedial discretion. For these reasons, the English courts have not yet followed the Canadian lead and adopted the 'remedial constructive trust'. Whilst some English judges have suggested that the remedial constructive trust might be introduced in the future, most cases have refused to countenance its adoption.

(a) Uncertainty as to the cause of action[106]

The remedial constructive trust is seen as one means by which restitution may be effected. The cause of action which gives rise to it is not therefore breach of fiduciary duty or inequitable conduct, which are the triggers for a constructive trust in English law, but unjust enrichment. The Canadian courts have been quick to develop and recognize a general principle of unjust enrichment, whereas in England there has been a historic reluctance to adopt what has been seen as vague and amorphous concept. In *LAC Minerals Ltd v International Corona Resources Ltd*[107] the Supreme Court stressed that unjust enrichment was not simply a vague concept of fairness. La Forest J was keen to point out that:

The determination that the enrichment is 'unjust' does not refer to abstract notions of morality and justice, but flows directly from the finding that there was a breach of a legally recognised duty for which the courts will grant relief. Restitution is a distinct body of law governed by its own developing system of rules.[108]

The remedial constructive trust is therefore dependent upon a highly developed and well-defined concept of unjust enrichment. Otherwise, it would evolve into the 'palm tree justice' that the courts have been so keen to avoid, and which was the prime reason

---

105   (1989) 61 DLR (4th) 14, at 48, per La Forest J.
106   See Delaney and Ryan 'Unconscionability: A Unifying Theme in Equity' [2008] Conv 401.
107   (1989) 61 DLR (4th) 14.   108   Ibid., at 45.

for the rejection of Lord Denning's new model constructive trust. In *Korkontzilas v Soulos*[109] the majority of the Supreme Court of Canada held that a remedial constructive trust was available even where there had been no unjust enrichment, and that it could be imposed where good conscience requires. If uncertainty is to be avoided, the view of the dissenting minority that a constructive trust may only be imposed where there has been an unjust enrichment should be preferred.

(b) Uncertainty as to the remedy

Once unjust enrichment has been established it is for the court to determine the appropriate remedy. It is therefore impossible for the parties to determine whether a constructive trust will be imposed from the fact than an unjust enrichment had been received, although precedents might provide some guidance as to the likely remedy. In *LAC Minerals v International Corona Resources Ltd* the court was aware of the problems of uncertainty attendant on the remedial constructive trust. La Forest J observed that:

There is no unanimous agreement on the circumstances in which a constructive trust will be imposed.[110]

The approach advocated by Goff and Jones, who had argued that a restitutionary proprietary remedy should be awarded when it is 'just, in the particular circumstances of the case, to impose a constructive trust',[111] was rejected unless further guidance could be given as to what those circumstances might be.[112] However, some guidelines were suggested, and it was held that there was no need to demonstrate a special relationship between the parties as a prerequisite of a constructive trust, nor that there must have been a pre-existing property right. La Forest J suggested that 'a constructive trust should only be awarded if there is reason to grant the plaintiff the additional rights that flow from the recognition of a right of property'.[113] A number of factors were identified which may be relevant in determining whether to award a proprietary remedy:

Amongst the most important of these will be that it is appropriate that the plaintiff receive the priority accorded to the holder of a right of property in a bankruptcy. More important in this case is the right of a property owner to have changes in value accrue to his account rather than to the account of the wrongdoer...The moral quality of the defendant's acts may also be another consideration in determining whether a proprietary remedy is appropriate. Allowing the defendant to retain a specific asset when it was obtained through conscious wrongdoing may so offend a court that it would deny to the defendant the right to retain the property.

Having considered these factors, La Forest J, with whom the majority concurred, concluded that a constructive trust should be imposed:

[the constructive trust] is but one remedy, and will only be imposed in appropriate circumstances. Where it could be more appropriate than in the present case, however, it is difficult to see.[114]

[109] (1997) 146 DLR (4th) 214.   [110] (1989) 61 DLR (4th) 14, at 49.
[111] Goff and Jones, *The Law of Restitution* (3rd edn, 1986), p 78.
[112] (1989) 61 DLR (4th) 14, at 51.   [113] (1989) 61 DLR (4th) 14.
[114] Ibid., at 48.

However, the absolute certainty of the rightness of a proprietary remedy in this statement only serves to emphasize the difficulty of uncertainty, for whilst La Forest J and the majority considered that the facts provided the clearest possible case for a proprietary remedy, Sopinka J and McIntyre J dissented and held that a personal monetary award of restitution was sufficient to reverse the unjust enrichment.[115] This uncertainty about the correct remedy was also evident in the more recent case of *Korkontzilas v Soulos*,[116] where the Supreme Court considered whether a constructive trust should be awarded against a gratuitous agent who had acted in breach of his fiduciary obligations. The majority held that a constructive trust should be awarded, whereas the dissenting minority held that it should not.

(c) The rise and fall of the 'new model' constructive trust

During the 1970s, Lord Denning MR advocated a novel approach whereby a constructive trust should be imposed simply to achieve perceived justice between cohabitants in the family home in acquiring an interest in land. He described this principle as a 'new model' constructive trust.[117] In *Hussey v Palmer* he expounded the nature and operation of such a trust:

> it is a trust imposed by law whenever justice and good conscience require it. It is a liberal process, founded on large principles of equity, to be applied in cases where the defendant cannot conscientiously keep the property for himself alone, but ought to allow another to have the property or a share in it. The trust may arise at the outset when the property is acquired, or later on, as the circumstances may require. It is an equitable remedy by which the court can enable an aggrieved party to obtain restitution.[118]

In essence, the 'new model' constructive trust was a trust imposed to achieve restitution, in other words to prevent the legal owner of land being unjustly enriched by refusing to acknowledge that the beneficiary was entitled to an interest. The 'new model' constructive trust was derived from the American model of constructive trusts, as stated in the Restatement of Restitution:

> Where a person holding title to property is subject to an equitable duty to convey it to another on the ground that he would be unjustly enriched if he were permitted to retain it, a constructive trust arises.[119]

Lord Denning even claimed that in advocating the 'new model' constructive trust he was merely extending the concept that had been approved by the House of Lords in *Gissing v Gissing*.[120] In *Eves v Eves* he stated:

---

[115] See also Tang 'Confidence and the Constructive Trust' (2003) 23 LS 135, who argues that a constructive trust should not have been imposed.

[116] (1997) 146 DLR (4th) 214.

[117] *Eves v Eves* [1975] 1 WLR 1338, at 1341. See also *Binions v Evans* [1972] Ch 359; *Cooke v Head (No 1)* [1972] 1 WLR 518; *Hussey v Palmer* [1972] 1 WLR 1286.

[118] *Hussey v Palmer* [1972] 3 All ER 744, at 747; (1973) 37 Conv (Hayton); (1973) 89 LQR 2; (1973) 32 CLJ 41 (Fairest); (1973) 36 MLR 426 (Ridley); (1973) 26 CLP 17 (Oakley); (1978) 8 Sydney LR 578 (Davies).

[119] Para 16.   [120] [1971] AC 886.

Equity is not past the age of child bearing. One of her latest progeny is a constructive trust of a new model. Lord Diplock brought it into the world[121] and we have nourished it...[122]

However, on careful reading, his citation of Lord Diplock's comments was extremely selective and, as will be seen below, the House of Lords did not suggest anything approximating to the 'new model' constructive trust. What Lord Denning was advocating was a form of remedial constructive trust, which arises as a remedy to correct a wrong, rather than an institutional constructive trust which arises on a particular set of legal principles.

The 'new model' constructive trust has been comprehensively rejected by the English courts. The main objection has been the absence of a coherent principle by which it can be decided whether the imposition of a constructive trust is warranted in any particular situation, which would lead to uncertainty and unpredictability in proprietary rights. After Lord Denning had retired, the Court of Appeal held in a number of cases that, whilst the actual decisions where he had advocated the 'new model' constructive trust could be justified on other grounds, Lord Denning's reasoning was inconsistent with earlier authorities. For example, in *Grant v Edwards*[123] Nourse LJ suggested that Lord Denning's decision in *Eves v Eves*[124] had been 'at variance with the principles stated in *Gissing v Gissing*'.[125]

The main objection raised against the new model constructive trust was the fear that such an approach to proprietary entitlements would create uncertainty, and that decisions would depend on the personal moral feelings of the individual judge. This danger was clearly expressed by Bagnall J in *Cowcher v Cowcher*,[126] where he considered the argument that injustice could result from the narrow criteria required for a constructive trust by the House of Lords in *Pettitt v Pettitt*[127] and *Gissing v Gissing*:[128]

In any individual case the application of these propositions may produce a result which appears unfair. So be it; in my view, that is not an injustice. I am convinced that in determining rights, particularly property rights, the only justice that can be attained by mortals, who are fallible and are not omniscient, is justice according to law; the justice which flows from the application of sure and settled principles to proved or admitted facts. So in the field of equity the length of the Chancellor's foot has been measured or is capable of measurement. This does not mean that equity is past the age of child bearing: simply that its progeny must be legitimate—by precedent out of principle. It is well that this should be so; otherwise no lawyer could safely advise on his client's title and every quarrel would lead to a law suit.

This attitude was echoed in *Springette v Defoe*,[129] where Dillon LJ proclaimed:

The court does not as yet sit, as under a palm tree, to exercise a general discretion to do what the man in the street, on a general overview of the case, might regard as fair.

The new model constructive trust was also initially rejected by some Commonwealth jurisdictions on similar grounds of uncertainty and lack of principle. In Australia,

---

[121] In *Gissing v Gissing* [1971] AC 886.
[122] [1975] 1 WLR 1338, at 1342.
[123] [1986] Ch 638, at 647.
[124] [1975] 1 WLR 1338.
[125] [1971] AC 886.
[126] [1972] 1 WLR 425, at 430.
[127] [1970] AC 777.
[128] [1971] AC 886.
[129] [1992] 2 FLR 388, at 393.

Allen v Snyder[130] doubted whether the new model constructive trust could be sup-
ported from *Gissing v Gissing*,[131] and the High Court rejected it in *Muschinski v
Dodds*.[132] In New Zealand the 'new model' constructive trust was described in *Carly v
Farrelly*[133] by Mahon J as:

a supposed rule of equity which is not only vague in its outline but which must disqualify itself
from acceptance as a valid principle of jurisprudence by its total uncertainty of application and
result.

It is somewhat ironic that, as we have seen, these jurisdictions have subsequently
adopted forms of constructive trust which are imposed as remedies to prevent 'unjust
enrichment' similar to the new model constructive trust as Lord Denning described
it.[134] Some would also argue that the broad and imprecise criteria adopted by a majority of the House of Lords in *Stack v Dowden*[135] for imputing an intention to create a
common intention constructive trust have resulted in the introduction of a new model
constructive trust in all but name.

(4) Prospects for the remedial constructive trust in England

While the remedial constructive trust developed in Canada has to some degree been
adopted in other commonwealth jurisdictions, it has yet to find a place in English
law.[136] As has been evident throughout this chapter, English law seems to have been
particularly sensitive to the difficulties of uncertainty, especially in the field of proprietary rights. The ability of a legal system to incorporate a concept such as the remedial
constructive trust may largely be determined by the prevailing legal culture and its ability to accept a degree of remedial discretion in the interests of individual justice at the
expense of absolute certainty. However, the emergence of a coherent doctrine of unjust
enrichment in England has opened the door to the possible acceptance of a remedial
style of constructive trust in the future. In *Lipkin Gorman v Karpnale Ltd*[137] the House
of Lords took the momentous step of acknowledging the existence of an autonomous
cause of action in unjust enrichment, which has been consistently affirmed in subsequent decisions.[138] The precise scope of the principle against unjust enrichment has
been the subject of intense academic scrutiny, and as restitutionary claims are more
frequently considered judicially it is inevitable that it will attain greater clarity. Whilst
some areas remain vague, for example the practical scope of the restitutionary defence

---

[130] [1977] 2 NSWLR 685.   [131] [1971] AC 886.

[132] (1985) 160 CLR 583, 62 ALR 429, at 452.

[133] [1975] 1 NZLR 356; (1978) 94 LQR 347 (Samuels). See also *Avondale Printers & Stationers Ltd v Haggie*
[1979] 2 NZLR 124.

[134] See below, p 421.   [135] [2007] 2 AC 432.

[136] The possible existence of the remedial constructive trust was left open by the Privy Council in *Re
Goldcorp Exchange Ltd (in receivership)* [1995] 1 AC 74.

[137] [1991] 2 AC 548.

[138] See *Woolwich Equitable Building Society v IRC* [1992] 3 All ER 737; *Westdeutsche Landesbank
Girozentrale v Islington London Borough Council* [1996] AC 669; *Kleinwort Benson Ltd v Glasgow City
Council* [1999] 1 AC 153.

of change of position, it seems clear that English law has developed an independent law of restitution, founded on the principle against unjust enrichment, which is the necessary prerequisite of the adoption of the remedial constructive trust. The adoption of a cause of action in unjust enrichment inevitably raises the question as to the nature of the remedies available to effect restitution. Whilst personal restitutionary remedies are available, it is less clear when restitution may be effected by the award of a proprietary remedy. Traditionally, such proprietary remedies have only been available where an enrichment has been received in breach of fiduciary duty, or if the defendant enjoyed a pre-existing proprietary right, or 'proprietary base'[139] in the property from which the enrichment was derived. It was noted in the preceding chapter how Professor Birks proposed an extension of the concept of the resulting trust as a vehicle to effect restitution, which would have led to a significant expansion in the circumstances in which a proprietary remedy was available against an enriched defendant. Although this thesis was rejected by the House of Lords in *Westdeutsche Landesbank Girozentrale v Islington London Borough Council*,[140] Lord Browne-Wilkinson took the opportunity to suggest that English law may yet decide to adopt the remedial constructive trust:

> Although the resulting trust is an unsuitable basis for developing proprietary restitutionary remedies, the remedial constructive trust, if introduced into English law, may provide a more satisfactory road forward. The court by way of remedy might impose a constructive trust on a defendant who knowingly retains property of which the plaintiff has been unjustly deprived. Since the remedy can be tailored to the circumstances of the particular case, innocent third parties would not be prejudiced and restitutionary defences, such as change of position, are capable of being given effect. However, whether English law should follow the United States and Canada by adopting the remedial constructive trust will have to be decided in some future case when the point is directly in issue.[141]

However, in subsequent cases the Court of Appeal has rejected any suggestion that English law should introduce the remedial constructive trust. In *Halifax Building Society v Thomas*[142] Peter Gibson LJ refused to impose a constructive trust where a defendant had obtained a profit by purchasing a house, which had subsequently risen in value, using a fraudulently obtained mortgage. He stated that English Law had not followed other jurisdictions where the constructive trust has become a remedy for unjust enrichment, and indicated that, in the light of Parliamentary action that presupposed that a criminal might keep the benefit of his crime without statutory intervention, the courts should not indulge in such judicial creativity.[143]

Such objections were stated even more strongly in *Re Polly Peck (No 2)*,[144] which is the only English case where the issue of the existence of the remedial constructive trust has arisen for decision. The applicants, who were the owners of land in Cyprus, applied for leave, pursuant to s 11(3)(d) of the Insolvency Act 1986, to commence proceedings

---

[139] *Lonrho plc v Al-Fayed (No 2)* [1992] 1 WLR 1.
[140] [1996] AC 669; (1996) 112 LQR 521 (Cape); [1996] CLJ 432 (Jones); [1996] LMCLQ 441 (Stevens). See [1996] RLR 3 (Birks).
[141] [1996] AC 669, at 716.   [142] [1996] Ch 217.
[143] [1995] 4 All ER 673, at 682.   [144] [1998] 3 All ER 812.

by writ against the administrators of Polly Peck International. They claimed that they were entitled to a remedial constructive trust of the profits which Polly Peck had obtained by wrongful exploitation of their land after it had been misappropriated by the Turkish Republic of Northern Cyprus. As Polly Peck was in administration, the grant of such a proprietary remedy would enable them to gain priority over other creditors. The Court of Appeal held that there was no prospect that the court would grant the order requested. It would impose a retrospective proprietary interest on the assets of the insolvent company, excluding those assets from pari passu distribution amongst the general creditors, thereby modifying the statutory scheme for the distribution of the company's assets under the Insolvency Act. Nourse LJ held that the remedial constructive trust could only be introduced into English law by an Act of Parliament.[145] Having noted that Lord Browne-Wilkinson had accepted the possibility that the remedial constructive trust may become part of English Law in *Westdeutsche Landesbank Girozentrale v Islington London Borough Council*, he continued:

such observations, being both obiter and tentative, can only be of limited assistance when the question has to be decided, as it does here. There being no earlier decision, we must turn to principle. In doing so, we must recognise that the remedial constructive trust gives the court a discretion to vary proprietary rights. You cannot grant a proprietary right to A, who has not had one beforehand, without taking some proprietary right away from B. No English court has ever had the power to do that, except with the authority of Parliament... It is not that you need an Act of Parliament to prohibit a variation of proprietary rights. You need one to permit it: see the Variation of Trusts Act 1958 and the Matrimonial Causes Act 1973.[146]

He further indicated that, in his opinion, the possibility of a remedial constructive trust would not have been seriously arguable even if Polly Peck had been solvent and there was no direct conflict with the provisions of the Insolvency Act.

In the light of these cases, some commentators have suggested that there is no prospect that the remedial constructive trust will be introduced in England.[147] However, the prospect has not disappeared. Writing extra-judicially, Etherton LJ has suggested that the recent House of Lords decision in *Stack v Dowden*[148] has introduced a remedial constructive trust in the family home by introducing a new method of acquiring a proprietary interest without the need for detrimental reliance, a change 'driven by social policy rather than strict adherence to precedent'.[149] This view almost certainly goes too far since it is based on *obiter* comments and is inconsistent with earlier decisions of the House of Lords, like *Gissing v Gissing*,[150] which have not been overruled. Lord Scott, using a technique reminiscent of Lord Denning, has also laid down a 'marker'

---

[145] This almost certainly underestimates the power of the House of Lords, and now the Supreme Court, to develop the law. No such statutory authority was required in Canada.

[146] [1998] 3 All ER 812, at 831. Nourse LJ placed particular reliance on the judgment of Lord Simmond LC in *Chapman v Chapman* [1954] AC 429.

[147] Birks 'The End of the Remedial Constructive *Trust*?' (1998) 12 *Trusts Law International* 202; Wright 'Professor Birks and the Demise of the Remedial Constructive Trust' [1999] RLR 128.

[148] [2007] 2 AC 432.

[149] Etherton 'Constructive Trusts and Proprietary Estoppel: The Search for Clarity and Principle' [2009] Conv 104.

[150] [1971] AC 886.

which could enable courts in the future to adopt the remedial constructive trust. In *Thorner v Major*,[151] the House of Lords applied the doctrine of proprietary estoppel to compel a farmer to honour his promise to leave his farm to a cousin who had provided unpaid assistance for many years. Giving his opinion, Lord Scott, whilst concurring in that view, expressed his preference for using a 'remedial constructive trust'. He said:

The possibility of a remedial constructive trust over property, created by the common intention or understanding of the parties regarding the property on the basis of which the claimant has acted to his detriment, has been recognised at least since *Gissing v Gissing*[152] (see particularly Lord Diplock, at p 905) [153]

This view is open to challenge on a number of counts. First, he has taken a view about proprietary estoppel that is not shared by his peers.[154] Second, he adopts a highly idiosyncratic view of Lord Diplock's comments, since the passage to which he refers has always been taken to relate to an institutional rather than a remedial constructive trust. Third, if Lord Scott is merely renaming the common intention constructive trust, then it is confusing and unnecessary. Finally, it is noteworthy that none of the other Law Lords passed comment on this view. It cannot be taken to be the view of the most senior court, and this attempt to create a novel mechanism is unlikely to find favour in the near future.

---

[151] [2009] UKHL 18.   [152] [1971] AC 886.   [153] [2009] UKHL 18, at [20].
[154] See the comments made by Lord Walker in *Thorner v Major* [2009] UKHL 18, at [67] on Lord Scott's observations about proprietary estoppel in *Yeoman's Row Management Ltd v Cobbe* [2008] UKHL 55. See further Chapter 11.

11

Trusts of the family home

This chapter explores how it is possible for someone living in a family home to acquire an interest in it. This can be done formally and documented in writing, but even where this is not the case; it is possible for an interest in the family home to be acquired informally through the application of equitable principles and doctrines. In view of the fact that this is a complex area, the chapter begins with an overview and a relatively brief summary of the equitable mechanisms used to confer interests in the family home, both in cases of express agreement and where the arrangements between the parties are more informal. The equitable mechanisms are then considered individually in more detail.

1 Trusts and the family home

Before the Second World War, most people in Britain rented the house in which they lived. Now most people live in houses that are owned by one of the people living there.[1] Since the average house is now worth over £150,000,[2] the family home represents the most substantial tangible asset in most households. Despite this, it is surprisingly common for very little thought to be given to the arrangements for its ownership, or for any arrangements to be informal and unrecorded. This can give rise to problems where one of the occupiers dies, or where there is a breakdown in family relationships.

The most common situation that will provide the focus of this chapter is where a couple cohabit in a property that has been acquired in the name of one of them only (historically the male partner). There are other situations at which we will be looking, such as where a person has contributed to the cost of acquiring a family home, or to the expenses of life in the family home, or where a person has been led to believe that for some other reason they are acquiring a stake in the home. In most of these cases, the problem would not have arisen if the parties had given sufficient thought to the issue and had chosen to create an express trust, declaring how the beneficial interests

---

[1] See *Cohabitation: The Financial Consequences of Relationship Breakdown* Law Comm No 207 (2007), Parts I and II.

[2] Land Registry House Price Index, May 2009.

in the property would be held.[3] Although the legal principles that are discussed below are in most cases capable of conferring rights on parties other than married or unmarried cohabiting couples, this kind of relationship is the most typical situation in which these issues arise. For convenience, the discussion therefore assumes that this is the relationship between the parties in dispute. There are, however, many reported cases in which different relationships are considered, especially in relation to proprietary estoppel. For instance there are a number of cases where someone has been persuaded to provide support for an older person by providing unpaid personal care, or by working on their farm without being fairly paid. They may be able to acquire rights using the same principles as those which apply between couples.

(1) The social and legal context[4]

(i) The emancipation of women

Changes in the pattern of home ownership and the emancipation of women have made the acquisition of an interest in the family home a matter of increasing importance since the middle of the twentieth century. Before the Married Women's Property Act 1882, a wife did not have a separate legal existence to her husband, and in consequence property vested in the husband alone. During the first half of the twentieth century, the majority of matrimonial homes were purchased in the sole name of the husband, who generally worked to provide the family income while the wife brought up their children and took care of the domestic needs of the family. Divorce was less common than it is now and it was often unnecessary to determine whether the wife had any independent interest in the property. However, the increasing recognition of the equal place of women, their growing economic contribution to marriage through their participation in the labour market, and especially the growth in divorce, made it essential to determine when a wife enjoyed a share of the ownership of her matrimonial home.[5] This was particularly important in the context of divorce, since under early divorce laws the court possessed no jurisdiction to divide the matrimonial property between the parties. If the husband was the sole owner of the matrimonial home, it would remain his on divorce. Since the Matrimonial Causes Act 1973, divorce laws do now contain provisions for the allocation of assets between married couples on the dissolution of marriage, and there is also special protection for marital relationships on the death of one of the parties.[6] There remain some situations (such as claims by a mortgage provider during the subsistence of a marriage) where the legislation is silent.

---

[3] Land Registration Rules 2003, TR 1 and Declarations form.
[4] See, for example. A J H Morris, QC, 'Equity's Reaction to Modern Domestic Relationships' in Oakley, *Trends in Contemporary Trust Law* (1996).
[5] See Cretney, *Family Law in the Twentieth Century* (Oxford, Oxford University Press, 2003).
[6] A discussion of such legislation is outside the scope of this book—see further Welstead and Edwards, *Family Law* (2nd edn, 2008), Chs 6 and 7.

(ii) Non-marital heterosexual relationships

From around the third quarter of the twentieth century there has been significant growth in the number of heterosexual people living together as a couple without marrying. The divorce legislation has no application to 'common law marriage', despite a sustained and mistaken belief of a large proportion of the population that such relationships are given special recognition.[7] There is no other legislation similar to the divorce legislation in such circumstances. Proposals to introduce legislation have been controversial, and any legislation would in any event be incapable of covering the whole range of possibilities. There has been, since 1995, limited protection for the maintenance of a cohabitant on the death of their partner under the Inheritance (Provision for Family and Dependants) Act 1975. On 29 October 2009, the Law Commission published a consultation paper on a review of the law of intestacy, entitled 'Intestacy and Family Provision Claims on Death'.[8] In Part IV of the consultation paper, the Commission proposed that certain cohabitants should have entitlements similar to those of married couples when one of the cohabitants dies intestate. This is discussed further below at p 425.

(iii) Same-sex relationships

Until the Sexual Offences Act 1967 male homosexual activity was illegal (lesbian activity has never been illegal). Since that date there has been further harmonization of same-sex relationships with heterosexual relationships, and it is now possible under the Civil Partnerships Act 2004 for same-sex couples to enter into a civil partnership, which is treated in the same way as a marriage between a heterosexual couple. A same-sex couple who have not entered into a civil partnership are treated in the same way as an unmarried cohabiting heterosexual couple.

(iv) Other situations

Disputes relating to the ownership of the family home can arise in other situations, for instance where a child is living in a house purchased by a parent,[9] or where a parent and a child are living together. The principles used to decide upon ownership of the family home can also apply in other situations, such as where a farmer has promised to leave his farm to his nephew, and the nephew, acting on this promise, has worked for him over many years without pay.

(v) Express agreement

In most of the situations which have been described, disputes about ownership of the family home would have been resolved if the parties had formally recorded their

---

[7] See, for example, *Cohabitation: The Financial Consequences of Relationship Breakdown*, Law Comm No 207 (2007), p 31 para 2.49; Probert 'Why Couples Still Believe in Common-Law Marriage' (2007) 37 Family Law 403.

[8] Consultation Paper No 191. This also includes proposals on reform of the eligibility requirements under the Inheritance (Provision for Family and Dependants) Act 1975. See pp 95–101, paras 4.112–4.137.

[9] See, for instance, *Turner v Jacob* ([2006] EWHC 1317).

understanding or agreement about ownership. This would not, of course, displace the jurisdiction of the courts to vary the arrangements on divorce or death, but it would avoid most of the difficulties that arise in other situations. The agreement would usually need to take the form of an express trust, since even where the legal ownership of the property is vested in the parties jointly, this does not automatically exclude the possibility of the beneficial interests being held in some other way or in unequal shares.

(vi) Equity fills the gap

In a surprisingly high proportion of cases the arrangements concerning rights to the family home are not formally recorded, either through inadvertence or through ignorance.[10] In the absence of any legislative provisions, the courts have had to deal with the problems to which this gives rise. Equity has filled the gap, and this is an area where the creativity of equity is ably demonstrated,[11] as equity has adapted existing principles and doctrines (with varying degrees of success) to meet a problem caused by changes in lifestyle and the family unit since the middle of the last century.

The first innovation in this area was the 'deserted wife's equity', invented by Lord Denning to prevent a husband from evicting a wife he has deserted from his home. This device was emphatically rejected by the House of Lords in *National Provincial Bank v Ainsworth*,[12] where it was insisted that conventional principles of property law needed to be applied. The subsequent case law has shown that there are three principal devices which equity can utilize to allow a cohabitant to acquire an interest—the resulting trust, constructive trust, and proprietary estoppel, though other methods have been used from time to time, such as restitution claims, based, as ever, on unjust enrichment of the legal owner at the expense of the cohabite.[13]

(vii) New rules or old?

The courts have insisted that they have not developed new or special rules, and that they have simply applied existing rules to new situations. The reality appears to be that a new jurisprudence is being created to resolve problems relating to ownership of the family home. At the very least, existing principles have been strained to their absolute limits to provide solutions in this difficult area. The issues with which the courts are dealing are complex, so it is not surprising that there have been some false starts, and that there has been uncertainty or inconsistency. The varying results for the cohabitant of each of these devices, and the different ways in which they are employed from their use in other contexts, all add to the complexity of applying the law in this area,

---

[10] See *Cohabitation. The Financial Consequences of Relationship Breakdown* Law Comm No 207 (2007); Barlow, Duncan, James, Park, *Cohabitation, Marriage and the Law* (2005). See also Cooke 'Cohabitants, Common Intention and Contributions (Again)' [2005] Conv 555.

[11] See Chapter 2, pp 35–41.   [12] [1965] AC 1175.

[13] For the application of the trust devices in other contexts see Chapter 9 (resulting trusts), Chapter 10 (constructive trusts), and Chapters 29–32 (unjust enrichment in the context of remedies for breach of trust). Proprietary estoppel is considered later in this chapter, at pp 391–421.

which is entirely undesirable. It can also make giving good advice on this area challenging; an issue for student and practitioner alike.

(viii) No easy legislative solution

The complexity of home ownership and occupation in modern British society was recognized by the Law Commission in the paper 'Sharing Homes' in 2002.[14] The Commission summarized as follows:

> By the year 2000 seven out of ten homes in England were owned by one or more of their occupiers. Over the last quarter of a century, living arrangements within those homes have become increasingly diverse, and greater numbers of people are now living together in circumstances which are characterized by informality. While marriage remains popular, cohabitation outside of marriage continues to grow, and, as has been observed, statistics based solely on the marital status of the parties give 'an increasingly incomplete picture of relationships and family circumstances'. Moreover, the notion of the 'traditional' family, based on one or two parents and their children living together in one unit, does not make allowance for multi-generational living arrangements within a family, where a home which may be legally owned by the head of the family is occupied by siblings, children, grand-children, and possibly even great grand-children, many of whom may be adults. As the population ages, there are many elderly siblings or friends who live together for comfort and companionship, and adult children who move in with their elderly parents to provide day-to-day care and support.[15]

The Law Commission has proposed a partial legislative solution,[16] but this is neither comprehensive nor uncontroversial.[17]

(2) Proprietary and personal rights

(a) When disputes arise

Disputes about the ownership of the family home most frequently occur on the breakdown of the relationship, or on the death of one of the parties. The dispute may arise simply between the parties directly involved, or it may involve a third party. In *National Provincial Bank Ltd v Ainsworth*,[18] for example, the dispute arose because after a husband had deserted his wife, he failed to meet the mortgage payments on the family home, and the bank to which the property had been mortgaged sought to evict the wife in order to sell. Since the wife's right was held by the House of Lords to be only a personal right, not a proprietary right or interest, she was unable to resist the bank's application for possession. Disputes involving third parties can also arise during the subsistence of a relationship. If a happily married couple fall on hard times because the husband's business fails, can the wife claim to have a financial interest in the family home which gives a share of the proceeds if the house has to be sold to pay

---

[14] See Mee 'Property Rights and Personal Relationships: Reflections on Reform' (2004) 24 LS 414.

[15] Law Com No 278 (2002), para 1.7.

[16] *Cohabitation: The Financial Consequences of Relationship Breakdown*, Law Comm No 207 (2007). This is explored below at pp 425–428.

[17] See, for instance, Baroness Deech of Cumnor, 'Cohabitation and the Law', Gresham Lecture, 17 November 2009.

[18] [1965] AC 1175.

her husband's debts? Only if she has a proprietary interest can she succeed with such a claim.

(b) Formally recorded agreement

If a cohabiting couple reach agreement as to how the family home is to be owned, and they formally record that agreement, there is (unless there is some fraud or mistake), unlikely to be any need to resort to the equitable mechanisms which are considered in this chapter. If a cohabitant is formally recorded as the legal owner, or as one of the legal owners of the family home, their rights will automatically be enforceable against third parties. It will not be possible for the family home to be sold or mortgaged without their knowledge and agreement. If a cohabitant is given an interest in the family home by way of an express trust, then their interest will also be enforceable against third parties, if the appropriate formal steps have been taken to protect these rights. In the absence of a formally recorded express agreement, however, it will be necessary to consider whether a cohabitant may nevertheless have rights in the family home, and if so, whether these rights constitute a proprietary interest which can be enforced against third parties. It is also possible that cohabitants may have recourse to the equitable principles, if they wish to increase their share of the beneficial ownership of the property.[19]

(c) Proprietary rights

The distinction between personal and proprietary rights has already been explored in detail.[20] Broadly, a proprietary right in the family home will provide rights akin to ownership. It will usually allow occupation of the premises, and is a valuable asset in that it can be bought and sold. A personal right to occupy the family home, by contrast, is (usually) a non-transferable licence to occupy the premises, and has no inherent asset value as it cannot be sold. The most important element of the distinction for most cohabitants is that a proprietary right is at least capable of binding a third party on sale or on the creation of an interest in the family home such as a mortgage or charge.[21] Since a bank lending money secured by a mortgage or charge has the right to sell the property concerned if there is a default under the loan agreement, an occupier without an interest binding the bank could find themselves homeless when the bank seeks to enforce its security and without any capital from the home to use as a deposit to purchase a new home.

(d) Rights arising under a trust

Where a cohabitant acquires an interest by way of a trust, this will always be a proprietary interest consisting of a beneficial share in the equitable ownership of the

---

[19] This is made possible through the decision in *Stack v Dowden* [2007] 2 AC 432, which is discussed below in the context of quantifying beneficial shares in property that is legally co-owned, at pp 374–380 and 381–384.

[20] See Chapter 3.

[21] For a detailed discussion of mortgages and charges, see Jackson, Stevens, and Pearce, *Land Law* (4th edn, 2008), Ch 17.

property. It can be bought and sold, is capable of binding purchasers or other parties involved in the sale or mortgage of the family home, and gives simultaneous rights of occupation.[22]

(e) Rights arising through proprietary estoppel

Other mechanisms, notably proprietary estoppel, will not always give the cohabitant a proprietary right in the land. Instead, no right may be granted to use or occupy the domestic premises; rights can include a monetary charge over the property or the grant of a personal licence to occupy the premises. Even where an occupation right is granted, that right may be a personal right, and may be accompanied by an order to pay rent or some other fee for continued occupation of the property.

2 Equitable mechanisms

Because this is a highly complex area of the law, this chapter contains a brief outline of the equitable mechanisms before they are individually considered in greater detail (see Figure 11.1, which provides a diagrammatic presentation).

(1) Express trusts

The most straightforward way for a cohabitant to acquire an interest in the family home is by means of a formally created express trust. An express trust arises where the parties have agreed on their shares in the property, and have recorded this agreement. This trust might be created at the time the family home is acquired, or subsequently. Because the trust relates to land, it must be declared or evidenced in writing[23] and it must also comply with the general rules that apply to express trusts.[24]

(i) When an express trust can be created

The most common form of express trust will be where there are joint legal owners, and an express declaration is made at the time of the purchase stating what their interests are. It is equally possible for a sole legal owner to create an express trust in favour of himself or herself and their partner or spouse, again declaring their interests. Although less common, there is nothing to prevent an express trust being declared after the purchase has been completed. The creation of an express trust relating to the family home

---

[22] Trusts of Land and the Appointment of Trustees Act 1995, ss 12 and 13. These sections, though badly drafted, confer on cohabitant rights to occupy the property and not to have that right excluded, unless the property is purchased for a declared purpose other than as the family home (e.g. it has been let to someone else). See further Jackson, Stevens, and Pearce, *Land Law* (4th edn, 2008), Ch 11.

[23] Law of Property Act 1925, s 53.

[24] The property must be vested in the trustee, there must be a clear intention to create a trust, and the terms of the trust must be clear. See further Chapter 7.

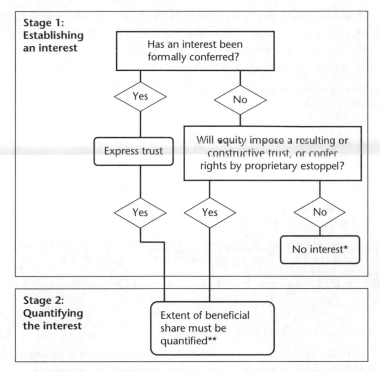

Figure 11.1 Acquiring an interest in the family home

is now encouraged in relation to registered land. For current transactions in registered land, the registration form now provides a box for the transferees to declare the trusts on which they wish to hold the property.[25] If this express declaration were made in every situation, the scope for dispute would be much diminished. However, a declaration of trusts is optional, so that a legal adviser cannot insist that trusts are declared,[26] and it has already been noted that not all couples think about their respective rights in the property at the outset, particularly where the property is to be the family home, rather than an investment.

(ii) Functions of an express trust

An express trust serves two functions: it both establishes the existence of an equitable interest, and simultaneously quantifies that interest. Where the claimant is a party

[25] Land Registry Form, TR1 (updated October 2009).
[26] See further Moran 'Anything to Declare? Express Declarations of Trust on Land Registry Form TR1: The Doubts Raised in *Stack v Dowden*' [2007] 71 Conv 364.

to the expressly declared trust, the terms of the trust will be conclusive of the interest which that party has unless there is fraud or mistake, or something has happened subsequently to change the terms of the trust. The effect of an express declaration is explained by Slade LJ in *Goodman v Gallant*:

If, however, the relevant conveyance contains an express declaration of trust which comprehensively declares the beneficial interests in the property or its proceeds of sale, there is no room for the application of the doctrine of resulting implied or constructive trusts unless and until the conveyance is set aside or rectified; until that event the declaration contained in the document speaks for itself.[27]

It was suggested, however, in *Stack v Dowden*[28] that it would be possible for the parties to vary their original shares as declared in the trust instrument, without the need for a supplemental deed of variation. However, compelling evidence would be needed to show such an intention, involving:

[D]iscussions, statements or actions, subsequent to the acquisition, from which an agreement or common understanding as to such a change could properly be inferred.[29]

These are essentially the same criteria as those used for establishing a constructive trust.

(iii) Express trust not declaring beneficial interests

It is possible for the parties buying the home to declare that they are joint legal owners and that they hold the property on trust, without defining the nature or extent of their beneficial interests. In that case, quite obviously, the declaration of trust is not conclusive about the quantification of the beneficial interests of the parties, since this is a matter on which it is silent. It is worth noting in this context that stating whether or not the survivor of the relationship can give a good receipt for capital monies on the old Land Registry form[30] where the house is registered in joint names is not evidence of an express declaration of a beneficial joint tenancy.[31]

(2) Resulting trusts[32]

(i) How resulting trusts operate

The general operation of resulting trusts has already been discussed in Chapter 9. A resulting trust is an implied trust that confers a share of beneficial ownership on a person who has contributed to the acquisition of the property, but is not named as a legal

---

[27] [1986] Fam 106, at 110–111.   [28] [2007] 2 AC 432.

[29] Ibid., at 475 [138] per Lord Neuberger, who was in dissent, but is unlikely to be doubted on this issue.

[30] This form was used for conveyances prior to 1 April 2008.

[31] It does not determine that the parties will have identical rights when one of the couple dies: the entire property passes to the survivor—see *Stack v Dowden* [2007] 2 AC 432 (HL), at 452 [51] per Baroness Hale, approving the earlier decisions of the Court of Appeal on this point—*Harwood v Harwood* [1991] 2 FLR 274; *Huntingford v. Hobbes* [1993] 1 FLR 736.

[32] See Gray and Gray, *Elements of Land Law* (5th edn, 2009), pp 836–861; Jackson, Stevens, and Pearce, *Land Law* (4th edn, 2008), pp 301–315.

owner and there has been no declaration of an express trust. The resulting trust thus seeks to 'fill the gap' in the beneficial ownership. The trust arises at the date on which a property is acquired, and in principle is based exclusively upon contributions made at that date rather than subsequently.

(ii) Resulting trust is based on a presumption

The resulting trust is based on a presumption that the purchaser would not have financed the transaction without wishing to retain a share of the beneficial ownership. The general principle was stated by Lord Reid in *Pettitt v Pettitt*:

in the absence of evidence to the contrary effect, a contributor to the purchase-price will acquire a beneficial interest in the property.[33]

This was reiterated by Lord Pearson in *Gissing v Gissing*, where the issue was whether a wife was entitled to a share of the ownership of her matrimonial home, which had been purchased in the sole name of her husband:

If [the wife] did make contribution of a substantial amount towards the purchase of the house, there would be a resulting trust in her favour. That would be the presumption as to the intention of the parties at the time or times when she made and he accepted the contributions. The presumption is a rebuttable presumption: it can be rebutted by evidence showing some other intention...[34]

The presumption can apply where a family home is bought in the name of one of the couple only, or where it is bought in their joint names and there is no express declaration of the beneficial interests.

(iii) Presumption can be rebutted

It is important to remember that the presumption of resulting trust is rebuttable, either by evidence demonstrating that other shares were intended, or that the payment was a loan, gift, or income payment, or through the contrary presumption of advancement.[35]

A loan only entitles the lender to the return of interest[36] and income payments such as rent are not 'purchase money' contributions to give rise to the presumption of resulting trust in the first place.[37] The House of Lords has held in *Stack v Dowden*[38] that where a property is acquired by a cohabiting couple in joint names, but there is no express declaration of their beneficial interests, there is a presumption that the beneficial ownership is similarly held jointly. The view of the majority was that this presumption displaces the presumption of a resulting trust. The presumption can, in turn, be rebutted by a party asserting a different share, but clear evidence will be needed to support such a claim.[39] In the past unequal contributions to the purchase of property provided evidence of an intention to create undivided shares

---

[33] [1970] AC 777, at 794. [34] [1971] AC 886.
[35] See further Chapter 9, pp 269 *et seq.* [36] *Dewar v Dewar* [1975] 1 WLR 1532.
[37] *Savage v Dunningham* [1974] Ch 181. [38] [2007] 2 AC 432.
[39] *Stack v Dowden* [2007] 2 AC 432, at 458–459 [68] per Baroness Hale.

proportionate to the contributions;[40] that is no longer the case following *Stack v Dowden*.[41]

The presumption of advancement is a presumption that in certain relationships a contribution towards the acquisition of property was intended to be an outright gift. The presumption applies in only two situations: where a husband makes a transfer to, or contributes towards the cost of purchase in the name of, his wife; and where a father does the same for a child. There is no presumption from wife to husband or between mother and child.

(iv) Presumption of advancement is extremely weak

The application of the presumption of advancement has been considerably weakened over the years. The high point in recent memory was Lord Denning's use of the presumption in *Tinker v Tinker*[42] to frustrate a husband who had conveyed property into his wife's name to shield the family assets from his creditors, and later wished to claim the property back. Subsequently, Lord Diplock referred to the presumption as a judicial instrument of last resort in *Pettitt v Pettitt*.[43] Indeed, even stronger doubt has come from the House of Lords in *Stack v Dowden*,[44] in which Lord Walker and Lord Neuberger observed that the presumption was no longer in keeping with modern life.[45] Arden LJ confirmed in *Gibson v Revenue and Customs Prosecution Office*,[46] that where legal title to property is registered in joint names, the presumption of joint ownership in equal shares displaces the presumption of advancement as:

the function of the presumption of advancement is now performed by the presumption of equal beneficial ownership of property held in joint names laid down in *Stack v Dowden*.[47]

In consequence, there is no strong reason to think that the presumption has any real use even in cases of single legal ownership. The presumption is now only likely to be employed on behalf of a claimant in the most desperate or extreme of circumstances, and even then, some supporting evidence is likely to be needed if the claim is to succeed.

(v) Resulting trusts not important in this context

The use of resulting trusts in the family home has been severely restricted by two decisions of the House of Lords. First, since *Lloyds Bank v Rosset*,[48] the concept has become commingled with the constructive trust approach, even though there have been calls that it should be treated separately as an entirely separate device.[49]

---

[40] See, for example, *Gissing v Gissing* [1971] AC 886.
[41] [2007] 2 AC 432. The reasoning in *Stack* does not allow the courts to 'second-guess' the size of the beneficial interests when these have been expressly declared in the trust instrument and there is no evidence of an agreement or understanding to vary these shares. This is discussed further below.
[42] [1970] 2 WLR 331.   [43] [1970] AC 777.   [44] [2007] 2 AC 432.
[45] Ibid., at [16] per Lord Walker; [101] per Lord Neuberger.
[46] [2008] EWCA Civ 645.   [47] Ibid., at [27].   [48] [1991] 1 AC 107 (HL).
[49] *McHardy v Warren* [1994] 2 FLR 338.

Subsequently, in *Stack v Dowden*, the House of Lords suggested that resulting trusts no longer have any part to play whatsoever in the acquisition of interests in the family home, at least in the domestic context.[50] This position, to which the courts had in any event been moving, albeit slowly, leaves the application of resulting trusts to affect property bought during a familial relationship to those cases where that property is bought as an investment rather than as the family home. These issues are discussed in greater depth below,[51] but, despite the judicial pronouncements of the death of the resulting trust, it is important to understand the contribution it has made to securing interests in the family home.

(3) Constructive trusts

(i) The use of constructive trusts

Constructive trusts were considered in Chapter 10. The form of constructive trust that has been employed in the context of the family home, and indeed that has been developed almost exclusively in the context of the family home, is the common intention constructive trust. The trust is so called because Lord Diplock in *Pettitt v Pettitt*[52] said that the approach to be adopted in cases involving the family home should be based upon seeking the common intention of the parties. This form of constructive trust has been seen as more apt for resolving disputes relating to ownership of the family home than resulting trusts. It has the advantage of greater flexibility and the ability to resolve issues about ownership both at the time of acquisition of the family home and later.

(ii) Prerequisites for the establishment of a constructive trust

Although the House of Lords held in *Gissing v Gissing*[53] that a constructive trust should be imposed whenever it is 'inequitable' for a legal owner to deny the beneficiary an equitable interest in land, the circumstances in which this test would be met were closely defined. Lord Diplock emphasized that a legal owner would only have acted so as to justify the imposition of a constructive trust:

> if by his words or conduct he has induced the [beneficiary] to act to his own detriment in the reasonable belief that by so acting he was acquiring a beneficial interest in the land.[54]

This formulation captures the essential elements of the constructive trust, namely that the court is acting to fulfil the reasonable expectations of the beneficiary, who is entitled to have his expectation fulfilled because he has acted to his detriment in the belief that they would be fulfilled. The legal owner cannot be allowed to enjoy the benefit conferred by the beneficiary's detrimental reliance without also allowing him to enjoy the expected interest.

---

[50] [2007] 2 AC 432.   [51] This is discussed below, at pp 356–360.
[52] [1970] AC 777.   [53] [1971] AC 886.   [54] Ibid., at 905.

(iii) The criteria developed

The criteria for a common intention constructive trust first set out in *Gissing v Gissing* have been subject to considerable discussion and development. For many years the classic statement of the criteria was contained in *Lloyds Bank plc v Rosset*.[55] Lord Bridge, delivering an opinion with which the other members of the House of Lords agreed, described two situations where a constructive trust would arise. The first was where there had been some 'agreement, arrangement or understanding' expressly reached between the parties, 'based on evidence of express discussions between the partners, however imperfectly remembered and however imprecise their terms may have been'.[56] Having demonstrated this, the claimant would then need to show 'that he or she has acted to his or her detriment or significantly altered his or her position in reliance on the agreement in order to give rise to a constructive trust or a proprietary estoppel'.[57]

The second situation was where there was no evidence of express agreement, and a common intention had to be inferred. Lord Bridge said:

> In this situation direct contributions to the purchase price by the partner who is not the legal owner, whether initially or by payment of mortgage instalments, will readily justify the inference necessary to the creation of a constructive trust. But, as I read the authorities, it is at least extremely doubtful whether anything less will do.[58]

(iv) Overlap with proprietary estoppel

Lord Bridge, in describing the first of the two situations in which a common intention constructive trust could arise, referred to 'a constructive trust or a proprietary estoppel'. This suggests an overlap between, or even an integration of, the two mechanisms. While there is not universal agreement about this, it is suggested that the better view is that there is an overlap rather than an integration. While there are considerable similarities between the two, the courts have held that a reasonable expectation sufficient to give rise to a constructive trust will only be found if there was an expressed or implied common intention or understanding between the parties that the ownership of the property would be shared. As Glass JA said in *Allen v Snyder*:

> when it is called a constructive trust, it should not be forgotten that the courts are giving effect to an arrangement based upon the actual intentions of the parties, not a rearrangement in accordance with considerations of justice, independent of their intentions and founded upon their respective behaviour in relation to the matrimonial home.[59]

(v) Overlap with resulting trust

The second of the situations described by Lord Bridge shares a marked similarity to a purchase money resulting trust. There is, however, one notable difference. This is that the contribution towards the acquisition of the family home need not have been made by an initial contribution, but could consist of contributions towards mortgage

---

55 [1991] 1 AC 107.   56 [1991] 1 AC 107, at 132.   57 Ibid.
58 Ibid., at 133.   59 [1977] 2 NSWLR 685, at 693.

payments. Nevertheless, Lord Bridge's description of this situation appears to be wide enough to subsume the classic resulting trust entirely within the common intention constructive trust in this context.

(vi) The impact of Stack v Dowden

The House of Lords decision in *Stack v Dowden*[60] has created a degree of uncertainty in this area. The case involved an unmarried couple who had been living together for eighteen years before they separated. A dispute arose as the ownership of the home they had most recently purchased to live in. The title had been taken in joint names, but there was no express declaration of trust. The House of Lords held that where a family home was purchased in joint names, there was a presumption that the partners intended to share the beneficial ownership jointly, unless there was evidence of a different intention. In the rather unusual circumstances of this case, the evidence supported a conclusion that Ms Dowden was intended to have the larger share of the beneficial ownership.

The House of Lords was dealing with a case where a property had been acquired in joint names. The view of the majority in this situation appears to have been that there should be a two-stage process: first, a decision whether there was an intention to share beneficial ownership; second, what the parties intended the shares of beneficial ownership to be. The first stage was met in the case of an acquisition in joint names by the presumption to which this gave rise of joint beneficial ownership. The second stage was to be determined by putting into the melting pot all relevant factors, including:

any advice or discussions at the time of the transfer which cast light upon their intentions then; the reasons why the home was acquired in their joint names; the reasons why (if it be the case) the survivor was authorised to give a receipt for the capital moneys; the purpose for which the home was acquired; the nature of the parties' relationship; whether they had children for whom they both had responsibility to provide a home; how the purchase was financed, both initially and subsequently; how the parties arranged their finances, whether separately or together or a bit of both; how they discharged the outgoings on the property and their other household expenses.[61]

The uncertainties are how much of this reasoning can be translated to the situation where a family home is acquired or bought in the name of one party only, and whether any place remains for the requirement, enunciated in *Lloyds Bank Ltd v Rosset*, for the claimant to have acted in reliance on the expectation of acquiring an interest in the family. The impact of *Stack v Dowden* will be explored in more detail later in the chapter.

(4) Proprietary estoppel[62]

(i) How proprietary estoppel operates

Proprietary estoppel is an entirely different equitable device from either the constructive or resulting trust, because it does not operate by recognizing the existence of a beneficial

---

[60] [2007] 2 AC 432.   [61] [2007] 2 AC 432, at [69] per Baroness Hale.
[62] Jackson, Stevens, and Pearce, *Land Law* (4th edn, 2008), Ch 19.

interest already created by the parties themselves, as is the case with express, resulting, and constructive trusts. Instead, it provides an equitable remedy, even though the remedy may allow a party to acquire an interest in the property. The broad basis of estoppel is that where one party makes a representation upon which another relies to his or her detriment, the party making the representation will be prevented (estopped) from later denying it. The remedies available can be greater or lesser than a share of the beneficial interest in the property. In *Dilwyn v Llewyln*,[63] for example, a son built a grand mansion on land belonging to his father in the expectation, created by his father, that the land would be transferred to him. The court ordered the transfer of the freehold to satisfy the expectation that the claimant should receive the whole of the property outright.

The doctrine of proprietary estoppel provides a means by which a person may become entitled to a proprietary right despite the absence of appropriate formalities. As Stephen Moriarty has observed:

The role of proprietary estoppel seems self-evident: it provides for the informal creation of interests in land whenever a person has acted detrimentally in reliance upon an oral assurance that he has such an interest. Oral grants of interests by themselves, therefore, are insufficient; but act in reliance upon some such assurance, and proprietary estoppel will validate what the Law of Property Act says has no effect.[64]

Proprietary estoppel does not require an express assurance. There can be circumstances in which an assurance can be implied.

(ii) The basis of proprietary estoppel

A claim by way of proprietary estoppel is not in itself a remedy. However, where a claimant can demonstrate an entitlement by way of estoppel, an appropriate remedy will be awarded. The estoppel is therefore best seen as a species of cause of action that demands an appropriate remedial response. While the general doctrine of estoppel is only capable of acting as a shield to protect against a person asserting his rights, proprietary estoppel 'may be relied on as a sword, not merely as a shield'.[65]

Recently, it was suggested by Lord Scott in the tightly reasoned but heavily criticized[66] Privy Council decision of *Cobbe v Yeoman's Row*,[67] that the basis of proprietary estoppel lay in promissory estoppel, the controversial doctrine 'discovered' by Lord Denning in the *Central London Property Trust v High Trees*[68] case. This decision also appeared to severely limit the scope of proprietary estoppel, almost to the point of destroying the utility of the doctrine in relation to domestic property.[69] Lord Scott's controversial view was rejected in the subsequent judgment of the House of Lords on proprietary estoppel in *Thorner v Major and others*.[70] It was suggested that proprietary

---

63 (1862) 4 De GF & J 517.   64 (1984) 100 LQR 376, at 381.

65 *Pascoe v Turner* [1979] 1 WLR 431, at 436, per Cumming-Bruce LJ.

66 See, for example [2009] Conv 85; [2009] Conv 104 (Etherton); [2009] Conv 141; [2009] Conv 154 (Sloan); (2008) LMCLQ 449.

67 [2008] 1 WLR 1752.   68 [[1947] KB 130.

69 Etherton 'Constructive Trusts and Proprietary Estoppels: The Search for Clarity and Principle' [2009] Conv 104.

70 [2009] UKHL 18; McFarlane and Robinson 'Apocalypse Averted: Proprietary Estoppel in the House of Lords' (2009) LQR 535.

estoppel is based on identified property, whereas promissory estoppel is based on an existing legal relationship,[71] and that there was 'some difficulty'[72] with the analysis put forward in *Cobbe*. It also confirmed that the restrictions suggested by Lord Scott in *Cobbe* were incorrect and were, in Lord Walker's view, based 'on a rather apocalyptic view'[73] of that decision.

(iii) The scope of proprietary estoppel

The principles of proprietary estoppel have been held to operate so as to create rights and interests in land, and possibly other types of property. However, it has been suggested that they do not apply in the context of public law matters, such as the grant of planning permission. In *Western Fish Products Ltd v Penwith District Council*, Megaw LJ said:

> We know of no case, and none has been cited to us, in which the principle set out in *Ramsden v Dyson* and *Crabb v Arun District Council* has been applied otherwise than to rights and interests created in or over land. It may extend to other forms of property: see per Lord Denning MR in *Moorgate Mercantile Co Ltd v Twitchings*.[74] In our judgment there is no good reason for extending the principle further. As Harman LJ pointed out in *Campbell Discount Co Ltd v Bridge*,[75] the system of equity has become a very precise one. The creation of new rights and remedies is a matter for Parliament, not the judges.[76]

Although Megaw LJ considered that the doctrine of proprietary estoppel had no application in a public law context, the developing doctrine of legitimate expectation in public law does, however, provide a close analogy with proprietary estoppel.

(iv) Establishing a claim through proprietary estoppel

There are two essential stages to the process of claiming a remedy by way of proprietary estoppel, namely establishing an estoppel 'equity' and satisfying that equity through an appropriate remedy. In order to establish the estoppel, the claimant must demonstrate (1) an assurance; (2) reliance on that assurance; (3) a change of position or detriment; and (4) that there is no bar to the establishment of the estoppel.[77] Having thus established an estoppel, the claimant is entitled to remedial relief. The court must then decide what remedy is appropriate in the circumstances to satisfy the expectation raised by the estoppel.[78] The court can select from a range of remedies, but is guided by the concept that it should award the *minimum* right or interest necessary to do justice between the parties.

---

[71] [2009] UKHL 18, at [61] per Lord Neuberger.

[72] Ibid,, at [67] per Lord Walker, though his Lordship did not elaborate what the basis should be as 'this is not the place for any prolonged discussion of terminology or taxonomy'.

[73] Ibid. See also *Thompson v Foy* [2009] EWHC 1076 (Ch), where Lewison J applied the test as explained by Lord Neuberger in *Thorner v Major* [2009] UKHL 18.

[74] [1981] 2 All ER 204, at 218. [75] [1976] QB 225, at 242.

[76] [1961] 1 QB 445, at 459.

[77] See *A-G of Hong Kong v Humphreys' Estate (Queen's Gardens) Ltd* [1987] AC 114, PC.

[78] *Plimmer v City of Wellington Corpn* (1883–84) LR 9 App Cas 699.

(v) Relationship with constructive trusts[79]

It has been illustrated that English law adopts a predominantly 'institutional' or 'substantive' approach towards constructive trusts. If the requirements for a constructive trust are demonstrated, the legal owner will be treated as having held the property subject to a trust from the time that the requirements were met. English law has not yet adopted the 'remedial constructive trust', which would allow the court the discretion to decide whether a trust should arise, and if so whether it should gain priority over other third party interests subsisting in the property affected. However, where a proprietary estoppel can be established, the court possesses a much wider discretion as to the range of remedies that it may award. It is arguable that one means by which the court can satisfy the equity is the imposition of a trust.[80]

Some have argued that any distinction between constructive trusts and proprietary estoppel is purely illusory, and that they should therefore be regarded as rooted in a common principle, for example the discretionary prevention of unconscionability.[81] However, even though there has been some blurring of the concepts of proprietary estoppel and constructive trusts in judicial statements, it is submitted that it remains important to maintain a distinction[82] between them. The criteria applied by the courts in relation to each concept are clearly different, particularly since *Stack v Dowden*. To establish a constructive trust it is essential to demonstrate that the parties shared a 'common intention' as to the ownership of the property in question, whereas in the case of proprietary estoppel a mere 'assurance' is required, which is a somewhat less definite requirement. In the case of a constructive trust (subject to the uncertain impact of *Stack v Dowden*), only a limited range of activities will be considered sufficient to constitute detriment, whereas there is a much greater willingness to regard non-financial detriment as sufficient to establish an estoppel equity. Finally, in the case of constructive trusts, the court possesses no remedial flexibility and cannot take account of the effect that the recognition of an equitable interest in the property will have on third parties, whereas under proprietary estoppel the court claims a discretion to determine how the equity should be satisfied, and any remedy only takes effect from the date that the court awards it in satisfaction of the equity. The decision in *Stack v Dowden*[83] accentuates the distinction between the two mechanisms.

(vi) Overlap with constructive trusts

There is, however, a substantial overlap between constructive trusts and proprietary estoppel. This means that the same facts might give rise either to the recognition of a constructive trust, or to the award of an estoppel remedy. This was evident in the case of *Yaxley v Gotts*,[84] where a builder had refurbished and converted a house into flats on the basis of an oral agreement with the owner that he would acquire the ground floor

---

79 See Nield 'Constructive Trusts and Estoppel' (2003) 23 LS 311.
80 See below, pp 407 *et seq.*
81 Hayton 'Equitable Rights of Cohabitees' [1990] Conv 370.
82 Ferguson 'Constructive Trusts—A Note of Caution' [1993] 109 LQR 114.
83 [2007] 2 AC 432.   84 [2000] 1 All ER 711.

flats for himself. The Court of Appeal upheld the decision of the first instance judge that the builder was entitled to an interest by way of proprietary estoppel, but also held that the facts entitled him to an interest under a constructive trust in accordance with the principles of *Lloyds Bank plc v Rosset*.[85] The overlap has in the past led the judiciary to enquire whether there is any substantive difference between the two; see, for example the *obiter* statements of Chadwick LJ in *Oxley v Hiscock*:[86]

[I]t seems to me very difficult to avoid the conclusion that an analysis in terms of proprietary estoppel will, necessarily lead to the same result [as an analysis in terms of constructive trust]; and that it may be more satisfactory to accept that there is no difference, in cases of this nature, between constructive trust and proprietary estoppel.[87]

Nevertheless, it is not unusual for a claimant to have two alternative bases of claim on the same facts.[88] Even if there may be circumstances in which both mechanisms operate, Lord Hope in *Stack v Dowden* correctly identified that the two doctrines are different in both approach and outcome:

Proprietary estoppel typically consists of asserting an equitable claim against the conscience of the 'true' owner. The claim is a 'mere equity'. It is to be satisfied by the minimum award necessary to do justice...which may sometimes lead to no more than a monetary award. A 'common intention' constructive trust, by contrast, is identifying the true beneficial owner or owners, and the size of their beneficial interests.[89]

3 **Advantages of proprietary interests**[90]

The conferment of a proprietary right through a beneficial interest in the cohabitant is particularly important because of its capacity to bind third parties. This is most clearly illustrated in the domestic context where the relationship breaks down, and the legal owner (or one owner in the case of express ownership) seeks to sell the trust property. There are two distinct issues of concern here:

- can the other cohabitant be evicted; and
- who is entitled to the proceeds of sale?

The answer to these questions is provided by an analysis of the rights of each cohabitant and then by applying the rules and principles set out in the Trusts of Land and Appointment of Trustees Act 1996 (TOLATA) and the Land Registration Act 2002. Questions can also arise where a third party is involved, for instance because the

---

[85] [1991] 1 AC 107.   [86] [2005] Fam 211.   [87] Ibid., at [66].

[88] For instance, a person injured by a defective product may have both a claim for breach of contract and a claim for negligence.

[89] [2007] 2 AC 432, at 448 [37].

[90] These issues are explored in more depth in land law texts—see further, for example, Gray and Gray, *Elements of Land Law* (5th edn, 2009); Jackson, Stevens, and Pearce, *Land Law* (4th edn, 2008).

property has been mortgaged and the bank desires to sell it because the mortgage repayments are seriously in arrears.[91]

(a) Disputes between the cohabitants.

Under TOLATA, a person with a beneficial interest in the property has a right of occupation that can be regulated by the courts, and can also apply to court to prevent a sale taking place under s 14. In making a decision on matters such as whether the property should be sold, the court has regard to various factors set out in s 15, which are:

(a) the intentions of the persons who created the trust.

(b) the purpose for which the property subject to the trust is to be held,

(c) the welfare of any child who is or might reasonably be expected to be in occupation of the property as his home,

(d) the interests of any secured creditor of any beneficiary,

(e) the circumstances and wishes of any beneficiaries of full age entitled to an interest in possession.

While this looks comprehensive, the section does not give the court any guidance about the weighting or application of the factors, and therefore how disputes should be resolved or the protection of use and occupation weighed against the other interests.[92] In the domestic context, it would be difficult to argue that the 'purpose' of the trust continues through a relationship breakdown, and the court would normally order sale in such circumstances.[93] The fact that the family home may be required for the maintenance of any children of a relationship is not a sufficient reason for the court to refuse an order for sale, unless there is a real threat of harm to the children.[94]

(b) Disputes with third parties

(i) Disputes with a lender financing the purchase

More problematic is the situation where it is not the other party in the relationship seeking sale, but a mortgagee or other secured creditor is asking that the home be sold to pay off existing debts. If the mortgage was taken out when the property was purchased, it will be binding on all the parties who agreed to it and on anyone who

---

[91] A detailed treatment of issues for purchasers is outside the scope of this text, as it is really a matter of land law—see further, for example, Jackson, Stevens, and Pearce, *Land Law* (4th edn, 2008), Chs 4, 5, and 11 (pp 354–360); Gray and Gray, *Elements of Land Law* (5th edn, 2009), pp 1083–1156.

[92] In the past, trust interests were viewed as personal property, not interests in land, as land was held under a trust for sale, which included a duty to sell on the trustees. Various methods were adopted to postpone sale where the supposed 'purpose' of the trust was continuing, under s 30 of the Law of Property Act 1925. The methods for postponing sale have substantially been re-enacted in s 15. See further Gray and Gray, *Elements of Land Law* (5th edn, 2009), pp 967–1020.

[93] See, however, *Holman v Kingston Howes* [2005] EWHC 2824 (Ch), where the purchase of the property as a home for one of the beneficiaries led to the court postponing sale.

[94] See *First National Bank plc v Achampong* [2003] EWCA Civ 487, [2004] 1 FCR 18.

acquired an interest simultaneously with or after the date of purchase.[95] On the basis that they have acquired their rights subject to the mortgage, the use and occupation of the property by the homeowners is not protected. Indeed, in the absence of hardship to children as a factor to be taken into consideration, it seems from the case law that the rights of mortgagees and other creditors will be given precedence, and at best sale will only be postponed to allow for alternative arrangements for accommodation to be made.[96] Nevertheless, it remains true that a party granted an interest in land is still better off than someone without a proprietary interest in the home, as no such discussion even arises in relation to personal interests.

(ii) Subsequent transactions

Let us take a case where the sole legal owner of property holds it on a constructive trust to give effect to a proprietary interest in favour of his partner. Suppose, for instance, that Darby and Joan purchase a house together, having agreed that they will both enjoy an interest in it. They both contribute to the purchase, and they do not require a mortgage. For some reason the house is purchased in the name of Joan alone. Joan will almost certainly hold the property on constructive trust for herself and Darby in the shares they have agreed. If Joan later mortgages or sells the house without Darby's knowledge or approval, can Darby's rights be enforced against the bank or purchaser? The answer is relatively complicated. It depends upon whether the land was unregistered or registered, and whether there is a single legal owner, or there are joint legal owners.

(iii) Sole legal owner of unregistered land

In the now relatively rare situation where the land is not registered (because the property was purchased some time ago),[97] Darby will be protected against subsequent mortgages and sales by the equitable doctrine of notice.[98] This means that any subsequent purchaser (a word which includes a mortgagee)[99] will have to respect Darby's rights if they had actual, constructive, or imputed notice of them. In other words, Darby's rights are protected against later sales and mortgages if the buyer or the bank knew of his rights or could have discovered them. One of the ways in which Darby's rights could be discovered is by inspecting the land. If Darby is living there, the buyer

---

[95] See, for example, *Abbey National v Cann* [1991] 1 AC 56 (registered title); *Bristol & West BS v Henning* [1985] 1 WLR 778 (unregistered title).

[96] In *Mortgage Corporation v Shaire* [2000] 1 FLR 273, for example, where sale was not immediately ordered, the creditor mortgagee was entitled to be paid interest as the price of not making an order for sale, and the order was postponed, not suspended. For an excellent exposition of the competing interests at work between occupiers and mortgagees, see McFarlane, *The Structure of Property Law* (2008), pp 11–13.

[97] Unregistered title is of diminishing importance, as the triggers requiring land to be registered have been greatly extended under ss 4–5 of the Land Registration Act 2002. See generally, Jackson, Stevens, and Pearce, *Land Law* (4th edn, 2008), Ch 4.

[98] See further Gray and Gray, *Elements of Land Law* (5th edn, 2009), pp 1150–1156.

[99] See the definition of a purchaser in s 205(1)(xxi) of the Law of Property Act 1925 and s 11 of the Land Charges Act 1972. In registered land, a mortgage is classed as a registered disposition under s 27 of the Land Registration Act 2002 (the definition includes transfer and other purchases of estates in land).

or the bank (acting usually through a surveyor) is expected to have discovered this and to have asked Darby to confirm whether or not he has any rights. If Darby's rights have arisen, not by virtue of a constructive trust, but through proprietary estoppel, it is unclear whether they will be binding on a subsequent purchaser.[100] Technically, the interest granted through estoppel is crystallized by court order, so that in many cases it will postdate the creation of competing interests in the land. Despite this, there is some authority that suggests that rights arising by proprietary estoppel can be enforced against purchasers of the land. Although there is little authority, it has also been argued that proprietary estoppel might give rise to a continuing personal liability even after the land or property to which it relates has been sold.[101]

(iv) Sole legal owner of registered land

The position is different if land is registered. A sale or mortgage is treated as a registered disposition. A registered disposition takes effect in precedence or priority to all earlier rights unless they have been recorded or protected on the register, or those rights constitute an overriding interest. Darby could protect his rights by registering a restriction on the register, preventing any sale taking place without his consent.[102] If he does not do this, then he will only be protected if his rights constitute an overriding interest.[103] The most relevant category of such rights are the rights of a person 'in actual occupation' of the land. That includes a person who is living at the property unless the 'occupation would not have been obvious on a reasonably careful inspection of the land at the time of the disposition'.[104] The protection extends to include rights arising by proprietary estoppel.[105]

(v) Joint legal owners

Where legal title is vested in two or more legal owners, the land legislation permits trust interests to be overreached. This is a process in which, after a sale, the equitable beneficial interests which were previously enforceable against the land instead can be enforced only against the proceeds of the sale. For overreaching to apply, the sale (or mortgage) must be agreed by all the legal owners, and any restrictions on the register (when the title is registered) must be complied with.[106] Since in most jointly owned family home cases the cohabitants are registered as legal owners, this means that their

---

[100] See Gray and Gray, *Land Law* (5th edn, 2009), pp 1234–1240; Jackson, Stevens, and Pearce, *Land Law* (4th edn, 2008), pp 668–671; *Sledmore v Dalby* (1996) 72 P & CR 196; (1997) LQR 232 (Pawlowski).

[101] Bright and McFarlane 'Personal Liability in Proprietary Estoppel' [2005] Conv 14.

[102] For the operation of restrictions, see Land Registration Act 2002, Part IV, ss 40–47. See further Gray and Gray, *Elements of Land Law* (5th edn, 2009), pp 200–202.

[103] Land Registration Act 2002, ss 29 and 30.

[104] Land Registration Act 2002, Sch 3. The rights of a person in actual occupation are protected even if their occupation is not obvious if the rights are known to the purchaser.

[105] Land Registration Act 2002, s 116.

[106] An overreaching sale requires the capital purchase money or the sum raised by the mortgage to be paid to or by the direction of two trustees. See further Gray and Gray, *Elements of Land Law* (5th edn, 2009) pp 989–997.

rights cannot be converted by overreaching without their knowledge and approval. In the fairly rare circumstances where legal title is held by joint legal owners but equitable beneficial interests are held by other people as well (for instance, where a married couple are registered as legal owners, but their parents have kept an equitable interest in return for helping to finance the purchase), it is possible for overreaching to take place without the knowledge and approval of all the beneficial owners. The way in which the beneficial owners can protect themselves against this possibility is by registering a restriction requiring their consent to any registered disposition.

4 Resulting trusts

A convenient approach when considering how an interest in the family home can be acquired through a resulting trust is to look at two stages: first, whether the claimant has an interest, and second, what is the extent of that interest (see Figure 11.2)? This distinction is not always applied, so in the discussion that follows it will be seen that the two issues sometimes run together. However, the division has been adopted in some of the cases, so it is a help to understanding to bear the distinction in mind.

(a) Acquiring the interest

As we have seen, the acquisition of the interest under a presumed resulting trust is based on a contribution to the purchase price of land. The major area of controversy has concerned the nature of the 'contributions' sufficient to give rise to the presumption. While 'indirect' contributions may constitute sufficient detriment to support claims based on constructive trust or proprietary estoppel, only 'direct' contributions to the purchase price have been held to give rise to a presumption of resulting trust in favour of the contributor. In *Ivin v Blake*[107] the Court of Appeal therefore held that a daughter who had helped her mother to run a pub, drawing only weekly pocket money from the business, had not acquired any interest in a house purchased by her mother by way of a resulting trust because she had not made a direct contribution to the purchase price.

(i) Contribution to the purchase price

A direct contribution to the purchase price of the land will give rise to a presumed resulting trust, prima facie in proportion to the amount of the contribution. In *Tinsley v Milligan*[108] a lesbian couple purchased a house in the sole name of Tinsley. The purchase price of £29,000 was raised by way of a mortgage of £24,000, with the remainder derived from the sale of a car that they owned jointly. The House of Lords held that this direct contribution of half the deposit gave rise to a presumption of a resulting trust in favour of Milligan of one-half share in the house.[109]

---

[107] (1994) 67 P & CR 263.   [108] [1994] 1 AC 340.
[109] The mortgage was repaid from the proceeds of their joint business.

(ii) Contribution to mortgage repayments

In the majority of cases land is not purchased outright but with the help of a mortgage. In such circumstances it might be thought that a person who contributes to the mortgage repayments should be treated as having contributed to the purchase price, thus raising a presumption of resulting trust in his or her favour in proportion to his contributions. However, the principle traditionally taken as a starting point is that the amount paid through mortgage is treated in the same way as a cash contribution by the person taking out the mortgage, since that person has a legal liability to repay it. That principle can be modified if there is an agreement at the time the mortgage is taken out that the sum raised by mortgage will be treated as a joint contribution to the purchase price. In this case the payment of mortgage instalments will be taken to give rise to a resulting trust. This was explained in *Cowcher v Cowcher*, where Bagnall J considered the consequences of a conveyance of a house to A for £24,000, where A had provided £8,000 of his own money and the remainder was provided by a mortgage taken out in the name of B:

suppose that at the time A says that as between himself and B he, A, will be responsible for half the mortgage repayments... Though as between A and B and the vendor A has provided £8,000 and B £16,000, as between A and B themselves A had provided £8,000 and made himself liable for the repayment of half the £16,000 mortgage namely a further £8,000, a total of £16,000; the resulting trust will therefore be as to two-thirds for A and one-third for B.[110]

Applying this principle, Bagnall J held that a resulting trust was presumed in favour of a wife who had made some of the repayments on a mortgage taken out by her husband. Similarly in *Tinsley v Milligan*[111] the House of Lords held that there was evidence to support finding a resulting trust where the parties had agreed that the mortgage repayments would be made from an account containing the proceeds of their joint business operation, even though this was in the sole name of Tinsley.

(iii) Mortgage contributions not referable to agreement prior to purchase

In the absence of any agreement prior to purchase that the mortgage is to be treated as finance provided by both parties, the payment of mortgage instalments subsequent to the initial acquisition of the property will not give rise to any interest by way of a resulting trust, since they are not regarded as being contributions to the purchase price of the property. This was so held by the Court of Appeal in *Curley v Parkes*.[112] In this case Mr Curley and Miss Parkes were living together. A house was purchased in 2001 in the sole name of Parkes. The purchase was funded exclusively by the proceeds of sale of her previous solely owned house, cash she provided and a mortgage of £138,000 which was taken out in her sole name. Curley subsequently paid some £9,000 into Park's bank account, from which the mortgage instalments were paid, as a way of assisting her with the huge commitments she was taking on. Curley claimed that these payments entitled him to an 8.5 per cent share of the equitable ownership of the house by way of a resulting trust. The Court of Appeal rejected his claim to an interest

---

[110] [1972] 1 WLR 425.   [111] [1994] 1 AC 340.   [112] [2004] EWCA Civ 1515.

on this basis, holding that the payments could not be regarded as a contribution to the purchase price. Peter Gibson LJ explained the relevant principles:

> The relevant principle is that the resulting trust of a property purchased in the name of another, in the absence of contrary intention, arises once and for all at the date on which the property is acquired. Because of the liability assumed by the mortgagor in a case where monies are borrowed by the mortgagor to be used on the purchase, the mortgagor is treated as having provided the proportion of the purchase price attributable to the monies so borrowed. Subsequent payment of the mortgage instalments are not part of the purchase price already paid to the vendor, but are sums paid for discharging the mortgagor's obligations under the mortgage.[113]

Since it will frequently be the case that there is no direct evidence of an agreement to treat mortgage payments as a joint contribution to the cost of acquiring the family home, it may be possible for the payments themselves to be treated as evidence from which such an agreement can be inferred. This may be the correct interpretation of *McQuillan v Maguire*,[114] where a wife was held to be entitled to a 50 per cent share of a matrimonial home bought in the husband's name because she had subsequently contributed indirectly to the discharge of the mortgage.

(iv) Impact of excluding mortgage contributions

The importance of resulting trusts in determining the ownership of the family home is very much diminished by the decision to exclude payments subsequent to the date of purchase, except where these can be referred back to an agreement at the date of purchase. On the other hand, it avoids the need for difficult calculations to determine the proportion of the ownership of property acquired by way of subsequent contributions to mortgage payments, a difficulty which was acknowledged by the House of Lords in *Gissing v Gissing*, and for which no easy solution had been found.[115] However, even though such contributions may be insufficient to gain an interest by way of a resulting trust, they may be relevant for the purposes of a constructive trust, whether by way of establishing an implied common intention to share the ownership of the property, or as a 'detriment' on the part of the contributor where there was an express common intention between the parties to share the ownership of the land.[116] If such a constructive trust can be established, the contributor may be entitled to a share of the beneficial ownership of the land far in excess of the exact mathematical equivalent of their contributions.

---

[113] Ibid., at [14].

[114] [1996] 1 ILRM 394. Where there is no clear intention at the date of purchase, and a share of the ownership arises from subsequent contributions to repaying a mortgage, an alternative interpretation is that backward tracing is operating: see Chapter 32, p 1051.

[115] [1971] AC 886, at 987, per Lord Reid. 'where [the contributor] does not make direct payments towards the purchase it is less easy to evaluate her share. If her payments are direct she gets a share proportionate to what she has paid. Otherwise there must be a more rough and ready evaluation. I agree that this does not mean that she would as a rule get a half-share...There will of course be cases where a half-share is a reasonable estimation, but there will be many others where a fair estimate might be a tenth or a quarter or something even more than a half.'

[116] See below, at pp 360 *et seq*.

(v) Contribution by qualification for a discount in the purchase price

If a house is purchased at a discounted price, the amount of the discount is regarded as a contribution to the purchase price. Therefore, the person who qualified for the discount will be presumed to be the beneficiary of a resulting trust to that extent in the property. In *Marsh v Von Sternberg*[117] Bush J held that a discount gained on the market value of a long lease because one of the parties was a sitting tenant was to be treated as a contribution to the purchase price in assessing their respective interests under a resulting trust. In *Springette v Defoe*[118] a discount of 41 per cent of the market value of a council flat obtained because the plaintiff had been a tenant for more than eleven years was counted as a contribution to the purchase price by the Court of Appeal.

(vi) Contributions to the cost of repairs or renovation

Where, contemporaneously with the purchase, the property is repaired or renovated, and its value is thereby increased, a person who contributes towards the cost of such repairs or renovations will be entitled to an interest in the land by way of a resulting trust proportionate to the extent to which the increase was attributable to their contribution.[119] Improvements made much later than the date of purchase may give rise to a constructive trust.

(vii) Contributions to general household expenses

In contrast to indirect contributions to the purchase price of land, it seems that contributions made to general household expenses will not give rise to a presumption of resulting trust in favour of the contributor because they are not sufficiently referable to the purchase price. In *Burns v Burns*[120] Mr and Mrs Burns began living together as man and wife in 1961. In 1963 a house was purchased in the sole name of Mr Burns, who financed the purchase by way of a mortgage. Mrs Burns began to work in 1975. She used part of her earnings to pay the rates and telephone bills and to buy various domestic chattels for the house. When they split up in 1980, she claimed to be entitled to an equitable interest in the house by reason of her contributions. The Court of Appeal held that she was not entitled to an interest by way of resulting trust because she had 'made no direct contribution to the purchase price'.[121] It should be noted that although such contributions to family expenses will not give rise to a presumption of resulting trust, they may, if substantial, constitute sufficient detriment to lead to the imposition of a constructive trust.[122]

(viii) Contributions to removal expenses

In *Curley v Parkes*[123] the Court of Appeal held that neither the payment of solicitor's fees and expenses, nor the payment of removal costs, were capable of giving rise to a

---

117   [1986] 1 FLR 526.
119   *Drake v Whipp* [1996] 1 FLR 826.
121   Ibid., at 326, per Fox LJ.
123   [2004] EWCA Civ 1515.

118   [1992] 2 FLR 388.
120   [1984] Ch 317.
122   See below, at p 371.

resulting trust. Although such costs might be substantial, they do not form any part of the purchase price of the property itself, and hence do not give rise to a presumption of resulting trust. They may, however, be relevant for the purposes of a constructive trust.[124]

(ix) Contributions otherwise explained as loans

Even where there is a direct contribution towards the cost of acquiring a property which would normally lead to a resulting trust, the presumption of a resulting trust will be rebutted where evidence shows that money was advanced by way of a loan. In *Re Sharpe (a bankrupt)*[125] Mr and Mrs Sharpe lived in a maisonette with their 82-year-old aunt, Mrs Johnson. The property had been purchased in the name of Mr Sharpe for £17,000. Mrs Johnson had contributed £12,000 towards the purchase price, while the remainder was raised by way of a mortgage. Mr and Mrs Sharpe were subsequently declared bankrupt and Mrs Johnson claimed to be entitled to a proprietary interest in the maisonette by means of a resulting trust presumed from her contribution to the purchase price. Browne-Wilkinson J held that the money had in fact been advanced by way of a loan, with the intention that it would be repaid. She was not therefore entitled to any share of the equitable interest of the property. A presumption of a resulting trust was also rebutted by evidence that a loan was intended in *Vajpeyi v Yijaf.*[126] In this case the claimant provided the defendant, who was her lover, with £10,000 to enable him to purchase a house in his sole name. At the time of the purchase in 1980 the defendant was a young man of limited means. The claimant alleged that by virtue of this payment she was entitled to a 33.89 per cent share of the equitable ownership of the property on the basis of a presumed resulting trust, whereas the defendant claimed that the money had been advanced by way of a loan, which he had repaid. Peter Prescott, QC held that the following factors had rebutted the presumption of a resulting trust in favour of a loan: the defendant had been a young man of limited means who was anxious to get on the property ladder, whereas the claimant was a woman who was already on the property ladder when the money was advanced; the claimant had tolerated the defendant collecting rents from the property and keeping them for himself for some twenty-one years; the claimant had failed to propound her claim to an interest for twenty-one years; and she had never said anything about her alleged interest in the house when it was mortgaged by the defendant to enable him to purchase her matrimonial home some years previously.

(x) Contributions otherwise explained as gifts

The normal presumption that a contribution to the purchase price of property creates a resulting trust will also be rebutted where there is evidence that the payment was made by way of gift. There has traditionally been a presumption (known as the presumption of advancement) that transfers by a husband to his wife, or by a man to his children are intended as gifts. That presumption has over recent years been heavily

---

[124] See below, at p 371.   [125] [1980] 1 WLR 219.   [126] [2003] EWHC 2339.

condemned as anachronistic, dating as it does from the patriarchal attitudes and legal system of the nineteenth century and earlier. The gender bias of the presumptions may also contravene the European Convention on Human Rights.[127] The presumption will not apply if there is any evidence at all of what was really intended.[128] The presumption does not apply where a wife conveys property into the name of her husband, or when property is purchased in the name of the husband with money provided by the wife. As Lord Upjohn observed in *Pettitt v Pettitt*:

> If a wife puts property into her husband's name it may be that in the absence of all other evidence he is a trustee for her, but in practice there will in almost every case be some explanation (however slight) of this (today) rather unusual course. If a wife puts property into their joint names I would myself think that a joint tenancy was intended, for I can see no other reason for it.[129]

The difficulties of the old presumption of advancement were recognized by the Law Commission in its report, *Family Law: Matrimonial Property*.[130] It concluded that the present law was unsatisfactory, but its recommendations for change have not been implemented.

(b) Quantifying the interest

The normal method of quantifying an interest arising out of a resulting trust, is, as we have seen, an arithmetical calculation, so that the share of the beneficial ownership attained is proportionate to the share of the purchase price contributed. This was one of the weaknesses of the resulting trust approach when compared to the common intention constructive trust, which allows a wider range of factors to be considered in determining a share of the beneficial interest. This has not gone unnoticed in the case law, and there have been some instances where different approaches to quantification have been adopted. These alternative approaches have been questioned by the House of Lords in *Stack v Dowden*,[131] as will be explored below.[132]

(i) Utilizing the constructive trust analysis

In *Midland Bank plc v Cooke*[133] the Court of Appeal found that the circumstances which established a resulting trust also sufficed to establish a constructive trust, allowing a different approach to quantification to be adopted. A house was purchased in the sole name of a husband for £8,500. While the majority of the purchase price was raised by way of a mortgage, the deposit was provided largely by a wedding gift of £1,100 from the husband's parents. As this gift had been made to the husband and wife jointly, it was held that she had contributed £550 to the purchase price, and that this gave rise to a presumption of a resulting trust in her favour. Where such a direct contribution has been made to the purchase price, the classic approach is that the

---

127 Law Commission Discussion Paper, *Sharing Homes* (2002), para 2.60.
128 *Stack v Dowden* [2007] 2 AC 432.   129 [1970] AC 777, at 815.
130 Law Com No 175 (1988).   131 [2007] 2 AC 432.   132 [1970] AC 777.
133 [1995] 4 All ER 562 (1995) 27 HLR 733; (1997) 60 MLR 420 (O'Hagan); [1997] Conv 66 (Dixon). See also *McHardy and Sons (A firm) v Warren* [1994] 2 FLR 338.

contributor will be entitled to a proportionate share of the beneficial interest mathematically equivalent to the proportion of her contribution. In *Midland Bank plc v Cooke*,[134] Mrs Cooke's contribution of £550 to the purchase price would have entitled her to a 6.74 per cent share of the beneficial interest of the house by way of a presumed resulting trust. A contributor will only be able to demonstrate an entitlement to a share of the beneficial interest greater than the exact mathematical equivalent of her contribution if she can demonstrate that the land was held on constructive trust.[135] The Court of Appeal held that there was sufficient evidence to conclude that Mrs Cooke was entitled to a 50 per cent share of the property by way of a constructive trust, as her financial contribution was sufficient to give rise to the inference of a common intention. In determining the interest, Waite LJ explained that the court was entitled to take account of all the circumstances of the parties' relationship:

> The general principle to be derived from *Gissing v Gissing* and *Grant v Edwards* can in my judgement be summarised in this way. When the court is proceeding, in cases like the present where the partner without legal title has successfully asserted an equitable interest through direct contribution, to determine (in the absence of express evidence of intention) what proportions the parties must be assumed to have intended for their beneficial ownership, the duty of the judge is to undertake a survey of the whole course of dealing between the parties relevant to their ownership and occupation of the property and their sharing its burdens and advantages. That scrutiny will not confine itself to a limited range of acts of direct contribution of the sort that are needed to found a beneficial interest in the first place. It will take into consideration all conduct which throws light on the question what shares were intended. Only if that search proves inconclusive does the court fall back on the maxim that 'equality is equity'.[136]

On the basis that Mrs Cooke had looked after their children and maintained the property, contributed to household bills from her own salary, and consented to a second mortgage of the house to guarantee her husband's business debts, Waite LJ concluded:

> One could hardly have a clearer example of a couple who had agreed to share everything equally: the profits of his business while it prospered, and the risks of indebtedness suffered through its failure; the upbringing of their children; the rewards of her own career as a teacher; and most relevantly, a home into which he put his savings and to which she was to give over the years the benefit of the maintenance and improvement contribution. When to all this there is added the fact (still an important one) that this was a couple who had chosen to introduce into their relationship the additional commitments which marriage involves, the conclusion becomes inescapable that their presumed intention was to share the beneficial interest in the property in equal shares.[137]

Although criticized by some commentators, this more holistic approach certainly had the benefit of enabling the court to take into account non-financial conduct in determining the extent of the beneficial interests of a claimant arising by way of a constructive trust, and the approach was followed in subsequent cases.[138]

---

[134] [1995] 4 All ER 562 (1995) 27 HLR 733. [135] See *Drake v Whipp* [1996] 1 FLR 826.
[136] (1995) 27 HLR 733, at 745. [137] Ibid., at 747.
[138] See, for example, *Le Foe v Le Foe* [2001] 2 FLR 970.

(ii) Giving the claimant a 'fair' share

Oxley v Hiscock[139] was similarly a case that ostensibly dealt with common intention constructive trusts, but where the acquisition of an interest was based on a contribution to the purchase price such as would have given rise to a presumed resulting trust. The Court of Appeal again rejected an argument that quantification should be based on the arithmetical contribution alone and also moved away from dealing with the assumed intention of the parties. It was contended on the facts that Ms Oxley, who had contributed 22 per cent of the financial purchase price of the family home, realized through the sale of a previous property, was entitled to one-half share of the proceeds of sale on the property, although the parties had never discussed the extent of their respective beneficial interests. This argument was successful at first instance, and Chadwick LJ conducted an extensive review of existing authorities relating to quantification of interests. He dismissed the assumed intention approach in *Midland Bank v Cooke*[140] as unsatisfactory and a pretence and instead adopted a new broad principle that the beneficial interests of the parties should be determined by the court on the basis of what seemed 'fair' in the light of all the circumstances:

> It must now be accepted (at least in this Court and below) the answer is that each is entitled to that share which the court considered fair having regard to the whole course of dealing between them in relation to the property. And, in that context, the 'whole course of dealing between them in relation to the property' includes the arrangements which they make from time to time in order to meet the outgoings (for example, mortgage contributions, council tax and utilities, repairs, insurance and housekeeping) which have to be met if they are to live in the property as their home.[141]

On the facts, Ms Oxley was awarded a 40 per cent share to reflect the fact that Mr Hiscock had contributed nearly twice as much to the purchase price of the home and that the parties' conduct was:

> consistent with an intention to share the burden of the property (by which she must, I think, have meant the outgoings referable to ownership and cohabitation), it would be fair to treat them as having made approximately equal contributions to the balance of the purchase price (£30,000).[142]

(iii) Applying the fairness test

The principles adopted in *Oxley v Hiscock* have been applied in a number of subsequent cases[143] that illustrate how the discretion will be exercised in practice. In *Cox v Jones*[144] two barristers in a relationship purchased a mill in Essex, which they intended to renovate as a home, in the sole name of Mr Jones. The initial purchase price was raised by way of a small financial contribution from both parties and a mortgage of £450,000. The mortgage was paid exclusively by Mr Jones, who also paid virtually all

---

[139] [2005] Fam 211.   [140] [1995] 4 All ER 562 (1995) 27 H.L.R. 733.
[141] [2005] Fam 211, at [69].   [142] Ibid., at [74].
[143] For example, *Lightfoot v Lightfoot-Browne* [2005] EWCA Civ 201, although in this case it was held that a common intention could not be inferred.
[144] [2004] EWHC 1486; Probert 'Land, Law and Ex-Lovers' [2005] Conv 168.

of the costs of the renovation, which were some £163,000. Miss Cox spent £1,000 on the renovations, £4,000 on services and insurance, and £6,800 on furniture. She also performed a large planning, management, and coordination role in the renovation, did a small amount of physical work, and lived at the mill for the period of the works which caused her work and earnings to decline. Mann J held that the parties had had an express common intention to share the property, but that there was no express agreement as to the share that Miss Cox would be entitled to. He therefore applied *Oxley v Hiscock* and concluded that it would be fair in all the circumstances for Miss Cox to receive a 25 per cent share of the beneficial ownership. He reasoned as follows:

> I do not consider that a 50% share for Miss Cox would be fair in these circumstances. Mr Jones funded the entirety of the purchase and the works, and the mortgage payments (though those have fallen into arrears). Miss Cox paid virtually nothing. She did, of course, forego the income from her practice, and contributed very materially to the project, but I do not think that that entitles her to as much as 50% of the equity in the property. Scientific analysis is impossible in these cases; what the court has to do is to form an overall assessment. I think that 25% is a proper figure for her share, reflecting everything she has put in but giving due weight to Mr Jones's own considerable contributions.[145]

In *Pinfield v Eagles*[146] Mr Eagles and Mrs Pinfield, who were living together, formed a company and went into business purchasing and managing care homes. The majority of the finance for the purchase of the care homes was raised by a commercial loan, with Mr Eagles providing the remainder. Mrs Pinfield did not contribute directly to the purchase price, but was appointed a director of the company, gave up a flower-arranging business that paid her a modest income, and ran the homes. For six months she drew no salary, but enjoyed the benefit of a company car and expenses. Thereafter she drew a salary of £20,000. Hart J held that although there was an express agreement that she was to have an interest in the business, there was no express agreement that she was to have one-half share. He therefore applied *Oxley v Hiscock* and held that she should be entitled to a 39 per cent share, on the basis that this represented the financial contribution she had made to the initial purchase:

> 'What would be a fair share for each party having regard to the whole course of dealings between them in relation to the [companies]?' My answer to that question is arrived at by looking at the contributions made by each of them to the initial financing. I think they should be treated as having contributed equally to the procurement of the commercial finance (£1,436,000). The balance of approximately £415,000 was procured by the efforts of Mr Eagles alone. On that basis Mr Eagles can be treated as having contributed 61% and Mrs Pinfield 39%. Those are the proportions in which I would declare the parties are respectively entitled to share in the net equity of the companies.[147]

(iv) 'Fair shares' rejected

In *Stack v Dowden*,[148] the majority in the House of Lords cast severe doubt on whether resulting trusts should be used at all in the family home and also unanimously suggested that 'the court's view of fairness is not the correct yardstick for determining

---

[145] Ibid., at [80]–[81].   [146] [2005] EWHC 447.   [147] Ibid., at [38]–[39].
[148] [2007] 2 AC 432.

the parties' shares'.[149] Instead, the majority believed that once an entitlement to a beneficial interest had been established, its quantification should be based on common intention constructive trust principles. A new system of quantification was proposed, listing a series of different factors (discussed below under constructive trusts), which, in effect, involves imputing an intention to the parties. The extent of the parties' financial contributions to the purchase was only one of a number of factors.

(c) The scope of resulting trusts after *Stack v Dowden*

(i) Is there a continuing role for resulting trusts of the family home?

Lord Neuberger was alone in *Stack v Dowden* in considering that there was a continuing role for resulting trusts in relation to the family home. He agreed with the conclusion of the majority in *Stack*, but dissented on the reasoning, he felt that the resulting trust approach was to be favoured as part of the process of determining the rights of parties acquiring a family home. In his view, which provided a masterly reconciliation of the legal principles, one should start by identifying the parties' shares at the time of acquisition. This would be done by applying a presumption of sole or joint ownership (depending on how legal title was acquired), and then modifying this by an application of classic resulting trust principles to give the parties (in the absence of express agreement) beneficial interests proportionate to their contributions. This starting point could then be subject to further modification using constructive trust principles if there was evidence of a contrary intention, inferred not imputed, as imputation would be 'not only be wrong in principle... but it would also involve a judge in an exercise which was difficult, subjective and uncertain'.[150]

(ii) Common intention to be found by constructive trust alone

In *Stack v Dowden*,[151] the majority of the House of Lords dismissed resulting trusts as no longer an appropriate tool to discover common intention.[152] This approach has been affirmed by Arden LJ in the Court of Appeal in *Fowler v Barron*,[153] a case that, like *Stack v Dowden*, involved joint legal owners:

> The legal technique that the court will use to ascertain whether both joint owners who had been cohabitees had a beneficial interest is that of the common intention constructive [trust], rather than that of resulting trust.[154]

Lord Walker in *Stack* itself was equally emphatic, although extending his views to cases of sole legal ownership as well:

> In a case about beneficial ownership of a matrimonial or quasi-matrimonial home (whether registered in the names of one or two legal owners) the resulting trust should not in my opinion operate as a legal presumption, although it may (in an updated form which takes account of

---

149 Ibid., at [127] per Lord Neuberger, affirming the view expressed by Lady Hale at [61].
150 Ibid., at [127] per Lord Neuberger.   151 [2007] 2 AC 432.
152 Ibid., at [60] per Baroness Hale, citing with approval Lord Walker's discussion at [19]–[31].
153 [2008] EWCA Civ 377 (CA).   154 Ibid., at [24].

all significant contributions, direct or indirect, in cash or kind) happen to be reflected in the parties' common intention.[155]

(iii) Reaction to Stack v Dowden

The view of resulting trusts adopted by the majority in *Stack v Dowden* has attracted criticism, notably from Swadling. He argues that the dismissal of the resulting trusts basis for acquiring an interest in the family home by Baroness Hale in *Stack* was:

made with the benefit of almost no reasoning, and even a mistaken view of their nature, for she said that the 'presumed resulting trust' reflected equity's presumption 'against gifts' without explaining why equity took that stance.[156]

It is also important to note that neither the House of Lords, nor Arden LJ, sought to overrule or even distinguish *Gissing v Gissing*,[157] which suggested that resulting trusts had a role to play in the family home. Given that both *Stack* and *Fowler* were cases of *joint* legal ownership, so that the enquiry related to the size of the beneficial share, not its acquisition, it is submitted that it is highly doubtful that the decision has any value in removing resulting trusts as a method of establishing an interest in the family home in cases of sole legal ownership.

(iv) A continuing role for resulting trusts

Lord Neuberger's dissenting analysis also suggests that the resulting trust still has some life,[158] particularly in situations where *Stack v Dowden*[159] has no influence, which is in acquiring an interest, rather than in quantifying it. In *Stack* and subsequent cases that have followed it, the question before the court has been the quantification of a beneficial interest, not whether such an interest has been acquired. It follows that *Stack* does not alter the law on the *acquisition* of interests by means of a resulting trust. Since the circumstances which give rise to a presumed resulting trust can also support the conclusion that there is a common intention to share the premises giving rise to a constructive trust (*Stack* is silent on this), it is submitted that the resulting trust still has a life, albeit disguised by the language of constructive trust. On this basis, Bailey-Harris has argued:

In essence, the judgement clarifies the method by which the extent of each party's beneficial interest is quantified, once the existence of those interests has been established... In effect and for practical purposes, the constructive trust 'overrides' the resulting trust.[160]

(v) Property purchased as an investment

Where property is bought as a family home, it seems from *Stack* that the constructive trust analysis prevails. However, where property is bought in a domestic relationship as an investment, the correct approach is to apply the presumption of resulting trust.

---

[155] [2007] 2 AC 432, at [31].
[156] Swadling 'The Common Intention Constructive Trust in the House Of Lords: An Opportunity Missed' [2007] LQR 511, at 518.
[157] [1971] AC 886.   [158] [2007] 2 AC 432, at [110]–[132].
[159] [2007] 2 AC 432.   [160] 'Property' [2004] Fam Law 569.

In *Laskar v Laskar*[161] property was bought by a mother and her daughter primarily as an investment, not as a home in which to live together. According to Lord Neuberger (sitting as a Lord Justice of Appeal in the Court of Appeal), the correct approach to determine the beneficial ownership of the investment asset on the breakdown of the relationship is to apply the presumption of resulting trust:

It would not be right to apply the reasoning in *Stack v Dowden* to such a case as this, where the parties primarily purchased the property as an investment for rental income and capital appreciation, even where the relationship is a familial one.[162]

(vi) Use of resulting trusts to quantify the interest

In *Laskar v Laskar* Lord Neuberger opined that even if (contrary to his view) the presumption of joint beneficial ownership applied even to predominantly investment purchases in a domestic context, nevertheless resulting trust reasoning could be used to rebut that presumption and to quantify the nature of the interest:

I can see no reason not to fall back on the resulting trust analysis, namely that in the absence of any relevant discussion between the parties their respective beneficial shares should reflect the size of their contributions to the purchase price subject to any subsequent actions or discussions having the effect of varying those shares.[163]

Whist this appears to be correct in logic and in principle, it remains to be seen whether any subsequent decisions follow up on this proposition, given the possibility that *Stark v Dowden* could be interpreted as sweeping the resulting trust away entirely, even beyond the context of familial acquisitions of a property to be shared as a home. Mark Pawlowski has argued as follows:

it is apparent that the resulting trust still remains an important tool for determining beneficial ownership...the resulting trust will still perform an important role in cases where the only relevant contributions are those made by either (or both) parties at the time of acquisition (see *Arogundale v Arogundale*),[164] or where there is no firm evidence of any agreement or understanding between the parties so as to support an express common intention constructive trust and the court is asked not to approach the question in two stages by inferring a common intention in the light of all the relevant circumstances (see *Day v Day*).[165] The mechanism of the resulting trust, it seems, will also operate where there is an absence of common intention to benefit the claimant despite his (or her) participation in a joint mortgage liability. Here, the presumed intention in favour of the sole joint contributing party to own the beneficial interest exclusively will prevail, see *Carlton* and *McKenzie*.[166]

(vii) The future of resulting trusts

So, where does that leave the resulting trust in relation to the family home? The answer is not entirely clear, but it does seem that it has not been completely eclipsed in operation, even in its purest form that allows mathematical quantification only, rather than as one of the factors in identifying a common intention based on conduct (see Figure 11.2).

---

161 [2008] EWCA Civ 347.　　162 Ibid., at [17]
163 Ibid., at [21].　　164 [2005] EWHC 1766 (Ch); [2005] All ER (D) 61 (Jul).
165 [2005] EWHC 1455 (Ch); [2005] All ER (D) 268 (Jun), at para 43.
166 Pawlowski 'Resulting Trusts, Joint Borrowers and Beneficial Shares' [2008] Fam Law 654.

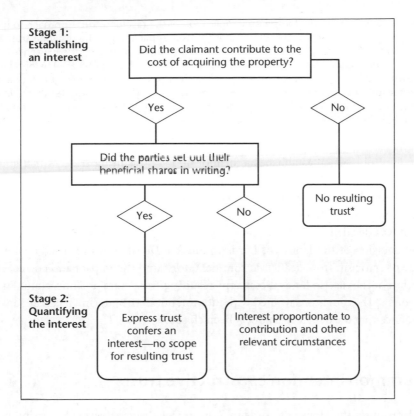

Stage 1:
Establishing
an interest

Did the claimant contribute to the
cost of acquiring the property?

Yes

No

Did the parties set out their
beneficial shares in writing?

Yes

No

No resulting
trust*

Stage 2:
Quantifying
the interest

Express trust
confers an
interest—no scope
for resulting trust

Interest proportionate to
contribution and other
relevant circumstances

*The claimant may have a remedy in constructive trust, proprietary estoppel,
or unjust enrichment.

Figure 11.2 Resulting trusts of the family home

There is good reason to suggest that a resulting trust, free of the shackles of constructive trust language, should continue to exist, not least Lord Neuberger's intelligent and compelling dissenting reasoning in *Stack* which permits both the arithmetical calculation and the ability to look to other factors to rebut the arithmetical formula when it is necessary to take a wider range of circumstances into account. Nevertheless, there is a tenable argument that if *Stack* and *Fowler* are followed, the resulting trust no longer has a role to play in acquiring an interest in the family home, except in so far as it forms part of the analysis of constructive trusts. However, as noted by Piska, none of the cases since *Stack* actually exclude the resulting trust:

However, there is not yet direct authority on the point. Both *Stack* and *Fowler* were joint legal owner cases concerned with the quantum of the interest, and whilst *Abbott*[167] and *Holman v Howes*[168] were sole legal owner cases, in both the legal owner had conceded the existence of a beneficial interest and the sole issue was the quantification of that interest. *Abbott* and *Holman*

[167] [2007] UKPC 53. [168] [2007] EWCA Civ 877.

therefore stand as authority for the non-application of the resulting trust approach to quantification in sole legal owner cases, but not for the non-application of the resulting trust at the existence hurdle. Although *James v Thomas*[169] and *Morris*[170] did concern the existence hurdle, they can be distinguished on the basis that the properties had been purchased before the non-legal owner had met the legal owner, and so there was no possibility of an argument based on the presumption of resulting trust. Moreover, the statement in *Fowler* indicates that a different approach may apply in the sole legal owner context, as Arden LJ is always careful to restate the ratio of *Stack* in terms of 'joint owners' alone.[171]

Piska has also suggested, with some force, that *Stack* is really a resulting trusts decision, albeit one which establishes a form of updated resulting trust, which allows a holistic quantification of the beneficial interest by the courts.[172] This would essentially be following the view of Lord Neuberger in dissent. It is suggested while this is a compelling analysis, it provides a critical analysis of the reasoning, rather than a statement of what was decided.

The decision of the House of Lords in *Stack v Dowden* has received an unusual degree of criticism from academic commentators, and the impact and correct interpretation of the case so far as it concerns resulting trusts remains uncertain. Further decisions of the courts are awaited with interest, but in the interim, it can be said with confidence that the debate has not yet been closed.

5 Common intention constructive trusts

The decision of the House of Lords in *Stack v Dowden* creates a real possibility that different approaches need to be adopted to cases where legal title is acquired in joint names, and those where there is a sole legal owner. These two situations are therefore considered separately. In the summary above, it was explained how a common intention constructive trust is imposed when it would be inequitable for a legal owner not to accept that he holds the property on trust; and that the classic view is that a trust is required if there was a common intention that the claimant would have an interest, and the claimant has acted in reliance on that understanding or expectation. In the classic analysis, there are therefore three stages: has an interest been acquired or conferred; what is the extent of that interest; and has there been reliance?

(1) Common intention constructive trusts: sole legal owner

(a) Acquisition of the interest

We begin by looking at the acquisition of an interest by constructive trust in cases of sole legal ownership.

---

[169]　[2007] EWCA Civ 1212.　　　[170]　[2008] EWCA Civ 257.

[171]　Piska 'Two Recent Reflections on the Resulting Trust' [2008] Conv 441.

[172]　Piska 'Intention, Fairness and the Presumption of Resulting Trust after *Stack v Dowden*' (2008) 71 MLR 120, at 129.

(i) A 'common intention' is an essential element

A constructive trust will only be established if it can be demonstrated that there was a common intention between the parties that the ownership of the land was to be shared. Where such a common intention was present, the constructive trust arises to ensure that it is carried into effect in equity, even though legal title to the land was vested in only one of the parties.

(ii) Establishing a common intention

Establishing the presence of a common intention is often the greatest hurdle to establishing a constructive trust. In *Grant v Edwards*[173] Nourse LJ observed that in most cases 'the fundamental, and invariably the most difficult, question to decide is whether there was the necessary common intention'.[174] In *Lloyds Bank plc v Rosset*[175] Lord Bridge recognized that one barrier to the establishment of a common intention is that 'spouses living in amity will not normally think it necessary to formulate or define their respective interests in the property in any precise way'.[176] Although the expectation of the parties to a happy marriage is generally that they will share the practical benefits of occupying the matrimonial home, whoever owns it, he maintained that this is not identical to a common intention to sharing the ownership of the property. A true common intention to share ownership sufficient to found a constructive trust may be established either from the expressed sentiments of the parties or by inference from their conduct.

(iii) Lloyds Bank plc v Rosset

The classic decision concerning the operation of constructive trusts of the family home is *Lloyds Bank plc v Rosset*,[177] in which the House of Lords provided a framework for determining when such trusts will arise. The case concerned a married couple, and the central issue was whether the wife had acquired an interest in her matrimonial home by way of a constructive trust that was capable of gaining priority over a legal mortgage of the house that the husband had granted to a bank. Mr and Mrs Rosset were married in 1972. In 1982 Mr Rosset became entitled to a substantial sum of money under a trust fund established by his grandmother in Switzerland. They found a house that required complete renovation. It was purchased for £57,500 in the sole name of Mr Rosset because the Swiss trustee had refused to advance the money for a purchase in joint names. The cost of the renovation work was also provided by Mr Rosset alone, so that his wife made no direct financial contribution to the purchase. Mrs Rosset had, however, helped with the renovation work. She had decorated some bedrooms and prepared others for decoration. She had also supervised the work of builders who were carrying out the renovation work. In the light of this she claimed to be entitled to a share of the ownership by way of a constructive trust.[178] The judge at first instance held

---

[173] [1986] Ch 638. [174] Ibid., at 647. [175] [1991] 1 AC 107.
[176] Ibid., at 127–128. [177] [1991] 1 AC 107.
[178] The issue did not arise on a divorce of the parties, where it would have been open to the court to adjust their interests in the property. Instead, Mr Rosset had mortgaged the property without his wife's consent, and she was seeking to establish an overriding interest which would bind the bank and therefore prevent

that, although there was no express agreement that Mrs Rosset was intended to enjoy a share of the beneficial ownership, he could infer a common intention to share from the fact that she had assisted with the renovations, as this had been work 'upon which she could not reasonably have been expected to embark unless she was to have an interest in the house'. However, the House of Lords held that no such intention could be inferred from the work she had done, and that, in the absence of an express common intention, no constructive trust had arisen in her favour and Mr Rosset remained the absolute owner of the house. In consequence, Mrs Rosset had no proprietary interest that could take priority over the rights of the mortgagee bank.

The significance of the decision lies beyond the mere conclusion that Mrs Rosset did not enjoy any interest by way of a constructive trust. Lord Bridge, with whom the other members of the House of Lords agreed, expounded the meaning and practical requirements of the concepts of 'common intention' and 'detriment', thus delimiting the scope of the constructive trust.

(iv) Express common intention

Lord Bridge in *Lloyds Bank v Rosset* stated that a constructive trust can be established where the parties expressly agreed that the ownership of the land was to be shared:

The first and fundamental question which must always be resolved is whether independently of any inference to be drawn from the conduct of the parties in the course of sharing the house as their home and managing their joint affairs, there has at any time prior to acquisition, or exceptionally at some later date, been any agreement, arrangement or understanding reached between them that the property is to be shared beneficially.[179]

It will be harder to establish such an intention if there are circumstances which make such an express agreement unlikely. For example, Mrs Rosset claimed that in conversations with her husband it had been expressly agreed that the house was to be jointly owned. Lord Bridge considered that, given that Mr Rosset's family trust had provided the whole purchase price and the cost of renovation, a high standard of evidence would have been required to establish this claim:

Mrs Rosset would...have encountered formidable difficulty in establishing her claim to joint beneficial ownership...In these circumstances, it would have required very cogent evidence to establish that it was the Rossets' common intention to defeat the evident purpose of the Swiss trustee's restriction by acquiring the property in Mr Rosset's name alone but to treat it nevertheless as beneficially owned jointly by both spouses.[180]

The judge at first instance had held that there was no express agreement and the House of Lords merely confirmed this. The agreement must, of course, be operative at the relevant date. In *Clarke v Corless*[181] three landowners had made an express agreement to acquire a strip of land that provided an access to their properties. Two of them

---

them from enforcing the sale of the house. To establish the overriding interest, Mrs Rosset would have to show that she had an interest in the property, which she claimed to have by way of a constructive trust. See Jackson, Stevens, and Pearce, *Land Law* (4th end, 2008), pp 326–344.

[179] [1991] 1 AC 107, at 132.   [180] Ibid., at 128.   [181] [2009] EWHC 1636 (Ch).

later acquired parts each in their own right, and the third objected to one of these purchases. Proudman J held that there was no constructive trust because at the time of the purchase the agreement had been abandoned, and also had not been relied upon by the claimants.

(v) Express agreement to share ownership amounts to a declaration of trust

Where a genuine express agreement to share the ownership of land is found, in substance the legal owner has expressly declared, or agreed to declare, a trust in favour of the claimant. However, such a declaration would be merely oral and therefore ineffective to create an enforceable trust due to the absence of compliance with the formality requirements of s 53(1)(b) of the Law of Property Act 1925.[182] Although there is no enforceable express declaration of trust, a constructive trust will be imposed if the claimant acted to her detriment on the basis of the express agreement, as it would be inequitable to allow the legal owner to deny a trust which would give effect to his intentions.

(vi) Examples of 'common intention'

Lord Bridge considered that the earlier cases of *Eves v Eves*[183] and *Grant v Edwards*[184] were 'outstanding examples'[185] of constructive trusts created through an express common intention. In *Eves v Eves*[186] an unmarried couple, Janet and Stuart Eves,[187] moved to a new house. It was purchased solely in the name of Stuart, who told Janet that it was to be their house, and a home for themselves and their children. He also told her that the purchase could not be completed in their joint names because she was under 21, but that if she had been of age it would have been purchased in their joint names. In *Grant v Edwards*[188] a man purchased a house in his name alone to provide a home for himself and his lover. He told her that he had not purchased it in their joint names because that would prejudice her divorce proceedings.

However, in both of these cases the supposed 'common intention' was in reality merely an appearance of common intention. Neither of the male parties genuinely wished their partners to enjoy a share of the ownership of their respective houses. Better examples of a true common intention can be found in the subsequent cases of *Yaxley v Gotts* and *Banner Homes plc v Luff Developments Ltd*. In *Yaxley v Gotts*,[189] a case that was in fact decided on the grounds of proprietary estoppel, the Court of Appeal held that a constructive trust could have been established where a builder had carried out work to convert and refurbish a house into flats on the basis of an oral understanding that he would acquire the ground floor flat. In *Banner Homes plc v Luff*

---

182 Law of Property Act 1925.   183 [1975] 1 WLR 1338.   184 [1986] Ch 638.
185 [1991] 1 AC 107, at 133. See also *Hammond v Mitchell* [1992] 2 All ER 109.
186 [1975] 1 WLR 1338.
187 Although they shared the same name, they were unmarried. She had changed her name to his by deed poll.
188 [1986] Ch 638.   189 [2000] Ch 162.

Developments Ltd[190] the Court of Appeal held that a constructive trust arose where two development companies reached an understanding that they would acquire a site as a joint venture, but one went ahead and developed the site alone. These cases also demonstrate that the principles of constructive trusts are not confined to domestic situations, but are of general application. A recent example of what constitutes an agreement can be found in *HSBC Bank plc v Dyche*.[191] Here, when Mr Collelldevall had been made bankrupt, he had (with the consent of his trustee in bankruptcy) transferred his jointly owned family home to his daughter and son-in-law (Mr and Mrs Dyche) for much less than its open market value. The Collelldevalls remained in the house, and alleged that an agreement had been reached that the property would be held by the Dyches for them and that it would be transferred back when a loan taken out to finance the transfer had been repaid. Judge Purle, QC (sitting as a High Court judge) found an agreement on the evidence which gave rise to a common intention constructive trust. The claimant had agreed to transfer the property upon faith of a clear agreement or understanding that it would thereafter be held for him and his wife (who had since died). That agreement had been acted upon by his transferring the property, at a price that bore no relationship to its true value, to his daughter and son-in-law and by making repayments to his son corresponding broadly to the sums falling due under the mortgage. The requisite common intention was to be inferred also from the simple fact that the claimant had continued to have sole beneficial use of the property as his home.

(vii) Agreement on shares is not essential

In *Drake v Whipp*,[192] the Court of Appeal stressed that the principles identified in *Lloyds Bank plc v Rosset* did not require the parties to have reached a common intention 'as to the respective shares to be taken by the beneficial owners'.[193] Peter Gibson LJ stated:

All that is required for the creation of a constructive trust is that there should be a common intention that the party who is not the legal owner should have a beneficial interest and that that party should act to his or her detriment in reliance thereon.[194]

(viii) Agreement is not imputed

While the evidence needed to support a finding of a 'common intention' falls short of that needed to support the finding that there was a legally binding contract,[195] the courts have been clear that they are finding an express agreement that the parties had, not imputing an agreement to them. In *Gissing v Gissing*, Lord Morris stated categorically:

The courts cannot devise agreements which the parties never made. The court cannot ascribe intentions which the parties in fact never had.[196]

---

190 [2000] 2 All ER 117.   191 [2009] EWHC 2954 (Ch).
192 [1996] 1 FLR 826.   193 Ibid., at 830, per Peter Gibson LJ.
194 [1971] AC 886, at 898.   195 *Clarke v Corless* [2009] EWHC 1636 (Ch), at [22].
196 [1996] 1 FLR 826, at 830.

This proposition is illustrated by *James v Thomas*.[197] A couple separated after fifteen years together. Ms James worked unpaid for Mr Thomas, in a business run from home. The profits went into Thomas's bank account and all payments were made from this account. Later, they entered into a partnership, which was dissolved, and then became joint account holders of the bank account. To demonstrate a common intention, Ms James relied on improvements made to the property and the fact that Mr Thomas had said she would be well provided for in the event of his death. The Court of Appeal held that Ms James had no interest under an express common intention constructive trust. In relation to the improvements, they held that the improvements made to the property, using money from the joint account, were not referable to the acquisition of an interest in the property, but were instead about the quality of life of the parties inhabiting the property, and the assurance about provision after death was made on the 'common assumption' that the parties would be living together on the occurrence of that (unfortunate) event.[198] Moreover, clear evidence of Mr Thomas' evasiveness when Ms James asked about transferring title to the property into joint names was adduced as evidence that he did not intend to share the beneficial interest. In the words of Chadwick LJ:

> Although it is possible to envisage circumstances in which the fact that one party began to make contributions to capital repayments due under a mortgage might evidence an agreement that the party was to have a share in the property, the circumstances of this case are not of that nature... That is not to undervalue her contribution; which, as Mr Thomas recognised, was substantial. But it is to recognise that what she was doing gives rise to no inference that the parties had agreed (or had reached a common understanding) that she was to have a share in the property: what she was doing was wholly explicable on other grounds.[199]

This approach has already drawn criticism from Greer, noting the distinction between this and cases such as *Eves v Eves*:

> In all of these cases, including *James [v Thomas]*, the clear intention of the male partner was to avoid joint ownership of the property, yet in all but this case the claimant succeeded. Ms James would have been more successful if Mr Thomas had simply lied to avoid putting the property in joint names, rather than evaded the issue, which seems to make nonsense of the law.[200]

(ix) Is the evidence for an agreement adequate?

Although the courts have repeatedly indicated that they are not imputing an agreement or common intention to the parties, it is worth noting that one of the major criticisms of the common intention constructive trust is that, whether intentionally or otherwise, the court is devising an agreement from scraps of conversation between the parties and construing their words out of context.[201] Indeed, there is much force in the contention that if the parties had expressly agreed to share the beneficial interest,

---

[197] [2007] EWCA Civ 1212.
[198] Compare this to the approach to that adopted in *Grant v Edwards* [1986] Ch 638.
[199] [2007] EWCA Civ 1212 at [27].   [200] Greer 'Back to the Bad Old Days' (2008) 158 NLJ 174.
[201] See, for example, Clarke 'The Family Home: Intention and Agreement' [1992] Fam Law 72.

then they would probably also have decided to declare that in a trust or by deciding to share the legal title.

(x) Assurance rather than common intention?

Even more compelling, particularly when considering that an excuse to exclude a partner from the legal title was construed as an express common intention to grant an interest in *Grant v Edwards*,[202] is the suggestion that what the court is really looking for is a representation or assurance from the legal owner, or a reasonable expectation on the part of the claimant, even if the other party never meant what they said. That certainly appears to have been the case in *Eves v Eves*[203] and *Grant v Edwards*.[204] This is really at the crux of the express common intention demonstrated through an agreement, and explains the overlap with proprietary estoppel, where a detrimental reliance on a representation or assurance is part of the test (this is discussed further below).

(xi) Inferred common intention

The absence of an express common intention is not necessarily fatal to the establishment of a constructive trust. In fact, in *Midland Bank plc v Cooke*[205] the Court of Appeal held that it was possible to infer a common intention even where the evidence proved that the parties had made no express agreement concerning the ownership property. Waite LJ explained that a wife was able to establish an interest in her matrimonial home by way of a constructive trust even though there had been no discussions between herself and her husband as to how the property should be owned when it was purchased in his name alone:

It would be anomalous...to create a range of home-buyers who were beyond the pale of equity's assistance in formulating a fair presumed basis for sharing of beneficial title, simply because they had been honest enough to admit that they never gave ownership a thought or reached any agreement about it.[206]

In *Lloyds Bank plc v Rosset*, Lord Bridge made clear that in some circumstances the parties' conduct alone will entitle the court to infer that they held a common intention to share the ownership of property:

where there is no evidence to support a finding of an agreement or arrangement to share...the court must rely entirely on the conduct of the parties both as the basis from which to infer a common intention to share the property beneficially and as the conduct relied on to give rise to a constructive trust.[207]

The claimant's conduct may thus be relevant in two distinct senses. First, it may constitute the evidence from which it can be inferred that there was a common intention to share the beneficial ownership. Second, it will also constitute the detrimental reliance which is required if that intention is to be carried into effect by the court recognizing that the land is subject to a constructive trust.

---

202 [1986] Ch 638.   203 [1975] 1 WLR 1338.   204 [1986] Ch 638.
205 [1995] 4 All ER 562.   206 Ibid., at 575.   207 [1991] 1 AC 107, at 132–133.

(xii) What conduct can be used to infer a common intention?

Since the conduct of the parties may on its own lead to the establishment of a constructive trust, it is vitally important to determine the type of conduct which the court will consider sufficient to give rise to the inference of a common intention. In *Lloyds Bank plc v Rosset*, the House of Lords significantly concluded that a common intention should only be inferred where a claimant had made direct contributions to the purchase price of the property concerned. Lord Bridge stated that in circumstances where a common intent would have to be inferred:

direct contributions to the purchase price by the partner who is not the legal owner, whether initially or by payment of mortgage instalments, will readily justify the inference necessary to the creation of a constructive trust. But, as I read the authorities, it is at least extremely doubtful whether anything less will do.[208]

A common intention can be inferred from such a direct contribution to the purchase price because it is assumed that the contributor would not have made a contribution unless he was expecting to gain a share of the ownership of the property. This requirement of a direct financial contribution has not been altered by subsequent decisions, such as *Oxley v Hiscock*,[209] *Fowler v Barron*,[210] or the House of Lords' judgment in *Stack v Dowden*,[211] as these decisions relate only to the quantification of the beneficial interest where a common intention has been established, and not to the issue of whether a common intention may be inferred in the first place.[212] Nevertheless, there are strong pronouncements in *Stack* that this approach is outdated and outmoded. Baroness Hale, who delivered the leading speech, pointed out that Lord Bridge's statements were themselves strictly obiter, but she did not go as far as to overrule the decision.[213] Lord Walker opined that the law should take a wide view of what is capable of counting as a contribution towards the acquisition of a residence, while remaining sceptical about the value of alleged improvements that are really insignificant, or elaborate arguments (suggestive of creative accounting) as to how the family finances were arranged.[214] He added:

Whether or not Lord Bridge's observation was justified in 1990, in my opinion the law has moved on, and your Lordships should move it a little more in the same direction, while bearing in mind that the Law Commission may soon come forward with proposals which, if enacted by Parliament, may recast the law in this area.[215]

Nevertheless, it is clear that Lord Bridge's requirements on direct contributions appear to have emerged unscathed. In *Morris v Morris*,[216] the Court of Appeal held that no common intention arising from conduct arose on the facts of the case as no direct contribution had been made to the purchase price, either direct or indirect. They opined that Lord Bridge's statement still had force of law, despite the obiter remarks in *Stack*, that Lord Bridge could be ignored or his 'test' softened. Chadwick LJ, in *James v*

---

208 Ibid., at 133. See *Burns v Burns* [1984] Ch 317.   209 [2005] Fam 211.
210 [2008] EWCA Civ 377.   211 [2007] 2 AC 432.
212 This is discussed further below, pp 387–391.   213 [2007] 2 AC 432, at [63].
214 Ibid at [34].   215 Ibid at [26].   216 [2008] EWCA Civ 257.

Thomas,[217] a case dealing with express rather than inferred common intention, none-theless agreed that *Stack* had not altered the law relating to acquisition of interests:

Her interest in the property (if any) must be determined by applying principles of law and equity which (however inadequate to meet the circumstances in which the parties live together in the twenty-first century) must now be taken as well-established. Unless she can bring herself within those principles, her claim must fail.[218]

It is therefore clear that a common intention will be inferred in circumstances where a presumption of resulting trust might have arisen. A common intention will be inferred where a person has made a financial contribution to the purchase of the property, has enabled the property to be purchased at a discounted price,[219] or had increased the value of the property by undertaking or contributing to the cost of significant improvements.[220]

(xiii) Contributions after the date of purchase

A difference between resulting trusts and the common intention constructive trust is that a common intention can be inferred from a contribution referable to the acqui-sition or improvement of the family home made after the date of its purchase. For instance, a wife who pays for the construction of a house on land, which has been inherited by her husband should, in principle, be able to make a claim on the basis of an intention inferred from conduct. However, relatively insignificant improvements will not be sufficient to give rise to an inference of a common intention. In *Lloyds Bank plc v Rosset* itself, the House of Lords held that Mrs Rosset's assistance with the decora-tion of the house 'could not possibly justify' the inference of a common intention that she was to gain a share of the ownership thereof:

Mrs Rosset was extremely anxious that the new matrimonial home should be ready for occupa-tion before Christmas if possible. In these circumstances it would seem the most natural thing in the world for any wife, in the absence of her husband abroad, to spend all the time she could spare and to employ any skills she might have, such as the ability to decorate a room, in doing all she could to accelerate progress of the work quite irrespective of any expectation she might have of enjoying a beneficial interest in the property.[221]

The monetary value of her work, in the light of a total purchase price exceeding £70,000, was also said to have been 'so trifling as to be almost de minimis'.[222] Cases

---

[217] [2007] EWCA Civ 1212.   [218] Ibid., at [38].

[219] As was the case in *Oxley v Hiscock* [2005] Fam 111.

[220] Note that s 65 of the Civil Partnerships Act 2004 expressly provides that a civil partner who contrib-utes in money or money's worth to the improvement of property will be entitled to a share, or an increased share, of the beneficial ownership of the property, either on the basis of what may have been agreed between the parties, or in default of such agreement on the basis of what may seem just to the court in all the circumstances.

[221] [1991] 1 AC 107 at 131.

[222] See also *W v G* (1996) 20 Fam LR 49; (1997) 113 LQR 227 (Bailey-Harris)—where the NSW Supreme Court held that a contribution of $500 towards the deposit of a house was de minimis and therefore incap-able of establishing an interest by way of a constructive trust. Contrast, however, *Midland Bank plc v Cooke* [1995] 4 All ER 562, where a small contribution to the purchase price of property derived from a joint gift was sufficient to establish a common intention.

subsequent to *Lloyds Bank plc v Rosset* have also held that the words of Lord Bridge requiring a 'direct financial contribution to the purchase price' should not be interpreted so strictly as to exclude the possibility of an inference of a common intention where a person has contributed to the payment of household expenses and this has enabled the legal owner to pay the mortgage. In *Le Foe v Le Foe*[223] Nicholas Mostyn, QC held that the financial contributions of a couple to the acquisition of their home should be viewed as a whole, so that a wife's contributions towards the household expenses could be regarded as an indirect contribution to the purchase price of the property:

Although I am sure that H earned more than W...I have no doubt that the family economy depended for its function on W's earnings. It was an arbitrary allocation of responsibility that he paid the mortgage, service charge and outgoings, whereas W paid for day-to-day domestic expenditure. I have clearly concluded that W contributed indirectly to the mortgage repayments, the principal of which furnished part of the consideration of the initial purchased price.[224]

Thus contributions to the purchase price that are, strictly speaking, indirect may still be capable of leading to the inference of a common intention if they enabled the other party to make a direct contribution.

(xiv) Contributions towards mortgage payments

Despite some cases suggesting that direct or indirect contributions towards mortgage payment can be relevant in inferring a common intention, the decision of the Court of Appeal in *Curley v Parkes*[225] has called into question whether contributions to the payment of a mortgage, whether direct or indirect, made subsequent to the acquisition of the property can be regarded as a contribution to the purchase price at all. The case itself concerned a claim to an interest by way of a resulting trust. The Court of Appeal held that contributions made toward the payment of mortgage instalments subsequent to the acquisition of a property are simply sums paid to discharging the mortgagor's obligations under the mortgage, and as such are not a contribution to the purchase price.[226] It is unclear whether the same principle will apply in the context of constructive trusts. There is no theoretical reason why contributions subsequent to the purchase should be ignored, even if not envisaged at the time of purchase, since the theory which underpins a constructive trust is different from that which underpins a resulting trust. A resulting trust adopts the principle that a person is entitled to keep what they have paid for, unless there is some other explanation for their payment. A constructive trust is based on the undertaking by a legal owner, evidenced by the common intention, to confer an interest on the other party. In some cases since *Curley v Parkes* the possibility of a common intention being inferred from contributions to mortgage payments has been entertained without question.[227] However, in *Driver v Yorke*[228] it was held that occasional contributions to the mortgage instalments made by

---

[223] [2001] 2 FLR 970.   [224] Ibid., at 973.   [225] [2004] EWCA Civ 1515.
[226] See above p 348.   [227] *Lightfoot v Lightfoot-Browne* [2005] EWCA Civ 201.
[228] [2003] 2 P & CR 210.

the two sons of the purchaser of a flat would not give rise to an inference of a common intention because the payments did not have sufficient connection with the purchase to be treated as a contribution to the purchase price. If the dicta in *Curley v Parkes* are strictly applied, a claimant who moved in with an owner of a mortgaged property and then contributed to the mortgage instalments—even paying them all—would not be able to establish an inferred common intention to share the ownership from the payments alone, and so would only be able to maintain a constructive trust if the payments were made on the basis of an express common intention to share the ownership. Since this is one of the most common scenarios in which cohabitation may occur without the parties giving any express consideration to their respective property rights, such an application would severely reduce the ability of home sharers to establish an interest by way of a constructive trust.

(xv) Financial contribution alone may not establish common intention

The mere fact that a financial contribution has been made towards the purchase price of property does not in itself guarantee that a common intention will be inferred. No constructive trust will arise if the contribution is made in circumstances that demonstrate that there was no intention on the part of the contributor to obtain an interest in the property. A common intention will not therefore be inferred if the parties have merely done what spouses or partners would ordinarily do. As Lord Diplock observed in *Pettitt v Pettitt*:[229]

It is common enough nowadays for husbands and wives to decorate and to make improvements in the family home themselves, with no other intention than to indulge in what is now a popular hobby, and to make the home pleasanter for their common use and enjoyment. If the husband likes to occupy his leisure by laying a new lawn in the garden or building a fitted wardrobe in the bedroom while the wife does the shopping, cooks the family dinner or bathes the children, I, for my part, find it quite impossible to impute to them as reasonable husband and wife any common intention that these domestic activities or any of them are to have any effect upon existing proprietary rights in the family home on which they are undertaken.[230]

In *Lloyds Bank plc v Rosset*[231] the decisions of the Court of Appeal in *Eves v Eves* and *Grant v Edwards* were reviewed. In *Eves v Eves*[232] Lord Denning had considered that Janet had done 'a great deal of work to the house and garden...much more than many wives would do',[233] including stripping the hall of wallpaper, painting the woodwork in the lounge and kitchen, painting the kitchen cabinets, painting the brickwork, breaking up concrete in the front garden, and demolishing a shed. In *Grant v Edwards*[234] Linda Grant had made a substantial contribution to housekeeping expenses. However,

---

229 [1970] AC 777, at 826.

230 See also *Burns v Burns* [1984] Ch 317 at 344, where May LJ said: 'The court is only entitled to look at the financial contributions or their real and substantial equivalent to the acquisition of the house; that the husband may spend this weekend redecorating or laying a patio is neither here nor there, nor is the fact that the woman has spent so much of her time looking after the house, doing the cooking and bringing up the family.'

231 [1991] 1 AC 107.   232 [1975] 1 WLR 1338.

233 Ibid., at 1340.   234 [1986] Ch 638.

Lord Bridge concluded that the conduct of neither of the respective claimants had been sufficient to infer a common intention. The constructive trusts in each case were only justifiable on the basis of an express common intention. In *Driver v Yorke*[235] it was held that a person who had acted as a guarantor of the mortgage on behalf of the purchaser of a flat had not made any contribution to the purchase price because he had not shown any intention of being liable for the mortgage instalments. Similarly, a contribution to the purchase of property by way of a loan or a gift cannot give rise to an inference of a constructive trust.[236] Nor will a common intention be inferred where a person has made a contribution to the purchase price within the knowledge of the legal owner. In *Lightfoot v Lightfoot-Browne* a claimant who had made a payment of £41,000 towards the mortgage of a property without knowledge of the sole legal owner was therefore held unable to establish a common intention by inference from the payment.[237]

(xvi) Payments not referable to acquisition of home

Payments that do not contribute to the purchase price of property, for example the payment of removal costs or solicitors' fees,[238] will clearly be insufficient to generate an inferred common intention, as they are not regarded as a contribution to the purchase price. Nor will a constructive trust be inferred from conduct that, though costly in time and effort, does not contribute financially at all. Thus a constructive trust will not be inferred in favour of a person who undertakes domestic responsibilities, bears children, provides child care or looks after sick or elderly relatives. However, such non-financial contributions are not entirely irrelevant, as they can be taken into account in determining the extent of the beneficial interest that will arise under a constructive trust established on the basis of a common intention inferred from a direct financial contribution. Thus, such non-financial conduct will only be irrelevant in a case where a person has acted in the absence of an express common intention and they have not made any financial contribution of any kind, no matter how small, to the purchase price of the property.

(b) Reliance or detriment

The mere fact of a 'common intention' will not alone give rise to a constructive trust. The criteria as set out by Lord Bridge in *Lloyds Bank v Rosset*,[239] following a similar requirement described in *Gissing v Gissing*,[240] is that a constructive trust will only arise in favour of a person who acted to his detriment, or substantially changed his position in reliance on the common intention. The constructive trust arises because it would be inequitable to allow the legal owner to refuse to give effect to the intention

---

[235] [2003] 2 P & CR 210.   [236] See *Re Sharpe (A Bankrupt)* [1980] 1 WLR 219.
[237] [2005] EWCA Civ 201. Note that in the light of *Curley v Parkes* [2004] EWCA Civ 1515 such a contribution to the discharge of the mortgage might not have been considered a contribution to the purchase price in any event.
[238] *Curley v Parkes* [2004] EWCA Civ 515.   [239] [1991] 1 AC 107.
[240] [1971] AC 886.

when the claimant has acted in a personally detrimental manner. It is absolutely essential to grasp that the standard of conduct sufficient to establish detrimental reliance is different from the standard of conduct required to justify an inference of a common intention. While only a direct contribution to the purchase price will justify the inference of a common intention, a much wider range of conduct will constitute sufficient detriment to lead to the imposition of a constructive trust if there was an express common intention.

(i) Detriment where there was an express common intention

In *Lloyds Bank plc v Rosset*[241] Lord Bridge summarized what was required in the way of detriment to establish a constructive trust founded upon an express common intention to share the ownership of the property:

it will only be necessary for the partner asserting a claim to a beneficial interest against the partner entitled to the legal estate to show that he or she has acted to his or her detriment or significantly altered his or her position in reliance on the agreement in order to give rise to a trust...[242]

This clearly adopts a much lower standard than the restrictive threshold of conduct from which it is possible to infer a common intention. The cases clearly support the proposition that conduct other than a direct contribution to the purchase price of the property will suffice to establish a constructive trust if there was an express common intention that the ownership of the land be shared. In *Lloyds Bank plc v Rosset*[243] itself the House of Lords held that there was no express common intention between the husband and wife as to the ownership of the house and therefore the question whether Mrs Rosset's activities would have been sufficient detriment or change of position was not addressed. The leading authority therefore remains *Grant v Edwards*,[244] where it was held that there was an express common intention that Linda Grant was to enjoy a share of the ownership of the house she cohabited with George Edwards. While Edwards paid the mortgage instalments, Grant made a substantial contribution from her own wages to the housekeeping and bringing up the children. The Court of Appeal held that her conduct amounted to sufficient detriment to justify a constructive trust.

(ii) Must the conduct be referable to the expected interest?

A difference of opinion appears in the judgments in *Grant v Edwards* as to whether the conduct alleged to represent reliance or detriment needed to be directly linked to the interest claimed. Nourse LJ addressed the question as to the nature of conduct required and concluded:

In my judgment it must be conduct on which the woman could not reasonably have been expected to embark unless she was to have an interest in the house.[245]

He held that Grant's contribution to the housekeeping amounted to an indirect contribution to the mortgage instalments, as it enabled Edwards to pay them from his

---

241 [1991] 1 AC 107.   242 Ibid., at 132.   243 [1991] 1 AC 107.
244 [1986] Ch 638.   245 Ibid., at 648.

own wages. This was conduct that could not have been reasonably expected unless she was to have an interest in the house. Sir Nicholas Browne-Wilkinson V-C took a more liberal view:

Once it has been shown that there was a common intention that the claimant should have an interest in the house, any act done by her to her detriment relating to the joint lives of the parties is, in my judgment, sufficient detriment to qualify. The acts do not have to be referable to the house.[246]

He emphasized the practical difficulties attendant on a test that required the court to find that the claimant's conduct could only be explained on the basis that a beneficial interest in the property would be thereby acquired:

In many cases of the present sort, it is impossible to say whether or not the claimant would have done the acts relied on as a detriment even if she thought she had no interest in the house. Setting up house together, having a baby, making payments to general housekeeping expenses (not strictly necessary to enable the mortgage to be paid) may all be referable to the mutual love and affection of the parties and not specifically referable to the claimant's belief that she has an interest in the house.[247]

Given that Lord Bridge indicated in *Lloyds Bank plc v Rosset*[248] that 'a significant change of position by the claimant' was sufficient detriment to support a constructive trust in fulfilment of an express common intention, it seems that the more liberal approach of Browne-Wilkinson V-C is to be preferred. This also follows from the growing recognition that the detriment required in the case of a constructive trust based on an express common intention is analogous to that required to sustain a claim to a remedy under the principles of proprietary estoppels.[249] This is considered further below.

(iii) Is detriment necessary?

In *Banner Homes Group plc v Luff Developments Ltd*[250] the Court of Appeal suggested that a constructive trust might be established even where the claimant had suffered no detriment through his reliance on a common intention or agreement, if the defendant had obtained an advantage. The case concerned an understanding between two developers that they would form a joint venture to acquire a development site. The site was to be acquired by a company owned by Luff Developments. In the event, Luff acquired the site, and then informed Banner Homes that it was withdrawing from the joint venture. The Court of Appeal held that Banner Homes was entitled by way of a constructive trust to over half the shares in the company that had purchased the land. Chadwick LJ held that Banner Homes had suffered a detriment because, on the basis of the understanding with Luff Developments, it had stayed out of the market for the

---

246 Ibid., at 657. Compare the similar debate on part performance in *Steadman v Steadman* [1976] AC 536.
247 [1986] Ch 638, at 657.   248 [1991] 1 AC 107.
249 *Lloyd's Bank plc v Rosset* [1991] 1 AC 107, at 132. See also *Grant v Edwards* [1986] Ch 638, at 656, where Browne-Wilkinson V-C thought that 'useful guidance may in future be obtained from the principles underlying the law of proprietary estoppel which in my judgment are closely akin to those laid down in *Gissing v Gissing*'.
250 [2000] 2 All ER 117.

site. However, he also opined that the trust would have arisen even if it could not have been held that Banner Homes had suffered detriment:

It may be just as inequitable to allow the defendant to treat the property as his own when it had been acquired by the use of some advantage which he has obtained under the agreement or understanding as it is to allow him to treat the property as his own when the plaintiff has suffered some detriment under the arrangement or understanding.[251]

(iv) Detriment where a common intention is inferred

Where there was no express common intention but the criteria are satisfied to entitle the court to infer a common intention, the element of detriment presents much less difficulty. Given that the court can only infer a common intention from conduct constituting a direct contribution to the purchase price of the property,[252] the contributor will clearly have acted to his detriment sufficiently to justify a constructive trust. Indeed, it is this essential fact which demonstrates how resulting trusts can be clothed in the language and trappings of common intention, as the necessary payment to the purchase price which gives rise to the presumption of resulting trust provides both the intention and necessary detriment to be awarded a constructive trust. The nature of the detriment will, however, be crucial to the determination of the extent of the beneficial interest thereby acquired and it is here that the attractiveness of arguing an inferred common intention rather than resulting trust manifests itself.[253]

(c) Quantifying the beneficial interest under a common intention constructive trust

(i) When is it necessary for the court to quantify the beneficial interests?

Where the evidence establishes that the parties had reached an express agreement as to the ownership of the property, the constructive trust will operate to fulfil that agreement. In many cases the parties will have expressly agreed to share the property equally, and the claimant will be entitled to one half-share of the equitable interest. However, where there is no express common intention as to the respective shares of the parties in the property, either because they had an express common intention to share the ownership of the property but had not discussed the specific proportions in which the ownership was to be shared,[254] or because the common intention to share has had to be inferred from a contribution to the purchase price, the extent of the equitable interest arising under the constructive trust will have to be determined by the court. The decision of the House of Lords in *Lloyds Bank plc v Rosset*[255] failed to address conclusively the way in which the respective shares of the parties in the beneficial interest

---

251 Ibid., at 141.   252 *Lloyds Bank plc v Rosset* [1991] 1 AC 107, at 133.
253 See above pp 352–356.
254 As in *Cox v Jones* [2004] EWHC 1486 and *Pinfield v Eagles* [2005] EWHC 477.
255 [1991] 1 AC 107.

should be determined in such cases. The relevant principles have now been set out in *Stack v Dowden*.[256]

(ii) How should the court quantify the beneficial interests?

The starting point for analysis is the basic principle that constructive trusts arise to fulfil the intentions of the parties, so as Browne-Wilkinson V-C stated in *Grant v Edwards*,[257] 'prima facie the interest of the claimant will be that which the parties intended'. This fundamental link between the intention of the parties and the quantum of the interest arising was identified by Lord Diplock in *Gissing v Gissing*.

> the court must first do its best to discover from the conduct of the spouses whether any inference can reasonably be drawn as to the probable common understanding about the amount of the share of the contributing spouse upon which each must have acted in doing what each did even though that understanding was never expressly stated by one spouse to the other or even consciously formulated in words by either of them independently. It is only if no such inference can be drawn that the court is driven to apply as a rule of law, and not as an inference of fact, the maxim 'equality is equity', and to hold that the beneficial interest belongs to the spouses in equal shares.[258]

(iii) Approach is not based on relative size of contributions

The approach to the quantification of an interest in a constructive trust can be distinguished from the resulting trust. In the case of a presumed resulting trust, the extent of the claimant's beneficial entitlement will be determined solely by the amount of contribution made to the purchase price of the property, whereas in the case of a constructive trust the claimant may gain a share of the equitable interest far in excess of the proportion they have contributed to the purchase price, or of the value of their action which constitutes the necessary detriment. This difference is neatly illustrated by *Midland Bank plc v Cooke*,[259] where a wife who had contributed 6.74 per cent of the purchase price of a property was held to be entitled to one-half share by way of a constructive trusts arising on the basis of a common intention to share inferred from her contribution, though, it is fair to say, the boundary line between the two concepts is elastic from the perspective of a claimant; if they clothe the direct contribution to the purchase price giving rise to a resulting trust in the language of conduct sufficient to show a common intention, they can reap the benefits of the constructive trust analysis.

(iv) Principles to be adopted

We have already explored under resulting trusts the alternative methods of quantification suggested in *Midland Bank plc v Cooke*[260] and *Oxley v Hiscock*,[261] to permit the court to take into account all the aspects of the parties' relationship. In *Cooke* the basis was imputed agreement, in *Oxley*, what the court adjudged to be a fair

---

[256] [2007] 2 AC 432.   [257] [1986] Ch 638, at 657.
[258] [1971] AC 886, at 908.   [259] [1995] 4 All ER 562.
[260] Ibid.; O'Hagan 'Quantifying Interests under Resulting Trusts' (1997) 60 MLR 420.
[261] [2005] Fam 211.

376 Trusts of the family home

share in all the circumstances of the case. We have also seen how the courts struggled to apply the concept of 'fairness' in subsequent cases.[262]

These decisions have both been subject to academic and judicial criticism, not least that the determination of the beneficial interest arising under a constructive trust will ultimately turn on subjective value judgements rather than legal principles.

The leading authority on quantification of beneficial interests is now *Stack v Dowden*.[263] Here, a couple had lived together for twenty-five years, and had four children. The original family house had been purchased by Ms Dowden alone, using £8,000 savings and a mortgage of £22,000. Ms Dowden paid all the mortgage repayments and Mr Stack helped with improvements. On sale, title to the new house was registered in both names. The purchase was funded 65 per cent from Ms Dowden (proceeds of sale and savings) and the remainder from an endowment mortgage loan. Mr Stack paid the interest on the loan. Capital was repaid by lump sums, of which Mr Stack contributed £27,000, and Ms Dowden the remaining £38,000. The parties kept their financial affairs entirely separate throughout their relationship together. On the breakdown of the relationship, Mr Stack sought an order for sale and equal division of any proceeds of sale. Following the decision in *Oxley v Hiscock*, the Court of Appeal had divided the proceeds of sale 65 per cent to Ms Dowden, 35 per cent to Mr Stack as representing a fair share of the course of dealings between the parties. The House of Lords approved the finding of fact, but for very different reasons.

In delivering the leading speech, Baroness Hale said that in determining the size of a beneficial share in the property, the court should have recourse to the following indicative list of factors:

any advice or discussions at the time of transfer which cast light on their intentions then; the reasons why the home was acquired in their joint names; the reasons why (if it be the case) the survivor was authorised to give a receipt for the capital moneys; the purpose for which the home was acquired; the nature of the parties' relationship; whether they had children for whom they both had responsibility to provide a home; how the purchase was financed, both initially and subsequently; how the parties arranged their finances, whether separately or together or a bit of both; how they discharged their outgoings on the property and their other household expenses.[264]

Lady Hale stressed that the list was not exhaustive, but also suggested that the court was not to consider what it felt to be fair in the circumstances:

[The court must not] abandon that search [for common intention] in favour of the result which the court itself considers fair. For the court to impose its own view of what is fair upon the situation in which the parties find themselves would be to return to the days before *Pettit v Pettit*.[265]

The reasoning in *Oxley* was therefore expressly disapproved, even though a holistic approach was required to be taken. Her Ladyship was also keen to stress that the court

---

[262] See above, pp 354–356.   [263] [2007] 2 AC 432.
[264] Ibid., at [69] and [70].   [265] Ibid., at [61].

must be careful in making findings of fact, and must keep a watchful eye to make sure that the parties are not misrepresenting evidence:

The parties' individual characters and personalities may also be a factor in deciding where their true intentions lay. In the cohabitation context, mercenary considerations may be more to the fore than they would be in a marriage, but it should not be assumed that they always take pride of place over natural love and affection.[266]

The court is looking to 'search to ascertain the parties' shared intentions, actual, inferred or imputed, with respect to the property in the light of their whole course of conduct in relation to it'.[267]

It is interesting that the court is admitting to imputing an intention, which seems inconsistent with the view expressed that 'fairness' is inappropriate. It is clear that Lady Hale was suggesting that imputation could only take place on very definite factors, including those outlined.[268]

In practical terms, this creates a great stress on the findings of fact; something their Lordships criticized the first instance judge for not doing as well as they would have liked. Nevertheless, their Lordships found for Ms Dowden on the basis that (a) Ms Dowden had contributed far more to the purchase price than Mr Stack; (b) although Mr Stack would pay the interest on the mortgage and the insurance premiums, there was a clear understanding that they planned to reduce the mortgage as quickly as possible; (c) all other commitments were undertaken by Ms Dowden. In Lady Hale's mind, it was clear that the simple fact that the financial accounts were kept entirely separate was an important factor in making the award.[269]

(v) Applying the criteria

At the very least, the principles outlined in *Stack v Dowden* structure the discretion used in quantifying the beneficial interest, however it is attained. It is clear that all the circumstances of the relationship are to be considered once an entitlement to a beneficial share has been established, irrespective of how the interest was granted. The clear stress on findings of fact is, it is suggested, likely to add to the expense and time taken in deciding such cases, but this is perhaps unavoidable.

Subsequent cases have demonstrated how this test will be applied by the courts. In *Fowler v Barron*,[270] Mr Barron was the 'breadwinner' and paid all property-related expenses, whereas Ms Fowler paid for the 'extras', such as school trips for the children, holidays, and clothing. Arden LJ affirmed that the emphasis of the courts' approach is on finding the parties' shared intentions. On the instant facts, the lack of financial contributions was only one factor, and not necessarily a 'critical factor'[271] in determining the beneficial share, and it was decided that the property should be shared equally. Other factors to which Arden LJ had recourse included that the property was the only

---

[266] Ibid., at [69]

[267] Ibid., at [60]. Summarized as an 'holistic approach': *Hapeshi v Allnatt* [2010] EWHC 392 (Ch) at [18] and [50].

[268] The case considers more than this in relation to common intention.

[269] [2007] 2 AC 432, at [92].   [270] [2008] EWCA Civ 377.   [271] Ibid., at [41].

real asset of the parties, and the mortgage liability was joint even though it was discharged by one of them.

The Privy Council (constituted by many of the members who had decided *Stack*) also addressed the issue in *Abbott v. Abbott*.[272] Here the husband's mother transferred the plot of land on which the matrimonial home was later built to the husband, who held title as sole legal owner. The construction costs were paid by the husband and wife taking out a bridging loan and then a mortgage, and the husband's mother also contributed. Following acquisition, the wife made herself jointly and severally liable for the repayment of principal and interest on the mortgage. The couple had a joint bank account and all payments were made from it. The wife did not work for a period of nearly nine years. The parties ultimately divorced, and the question before the court was to consider the extent of the wife's beneficial interest. The Court of Appeal of Antigua and Barbuda, following *Rosset*, had taken a view that the wife could only acquire an interest proportionate to her contributions to the purchase price, which amounted to an 8.31 per cent share of the property. In deciding that the parties shared the beneficial ownership equally, the Privy Council disapproved *Rosset* and said that the parties' whole course of conduct in relation to the property had to be taken into account in determining their shared intentions as to its ownership, as with *Stack v Dowden*. Equal division was the correct inference (without more) from the fact that gift by the husband's mother was intended for both of them, and that was backed up by the conduct of the couple throughout their marriage, as they arranged their finances jointly and undertook joint liability on the mortgage.

In *Jones v Kernott*,[273] 'very unusual circumstances' were considered by Nicolas Strauss, QC in approving a 90:10 split of the ownership in favour of Ms Jones. It was not contested that both parties had a beneficial interest, and the only dispute was as to their shares. Mr Kernott had paid the initial deposit, for a valuable extension to the property, and had made some of the mortgage repayments. Against this, he had left the property fifteen years previously (and had not made any mortgage repayments since then), had treated his finances separately, and had made a capital gain on property he had purchased with proceeds from a joint life insurance policy.[274] All of these factors, taken holistically, suggested that the original inference of the parties that the original property should be shared equally should be altered. However, in conducting an analysis of *Stack* and subsequent cases, Nicolas Strauss, QC was clearly of the opinion that the concept of 'fairness' had a major role to play in determining what the parties' common intention as to their beneficial share would be:

The court was not entitled to disregard that evidence of what the parties probably intended and substitute what it might consider, without taking account of it, to be fair. But that does not mean that, while respecting the parties' intentions so far as they were apparent, the court could not consider what was fair so as to supply any missing elements.[275]

---

[272] [2008] Fam Law 215 (PC).   [273] [2009] EWHC 1713 (Ch).
[274] Without the issue of the capital gains, the balance of the value of Mr Kernott's contributions to the family home as against Ms Jones were considered 4:1 in favour of Ms Jones. The capital gains, arising as they did from proceeds of the joint insurance policy, there had a considerable influence on the facts. See [2009] EWHC 1713 (Ch), at [51].
[275] Ibid., at [32].

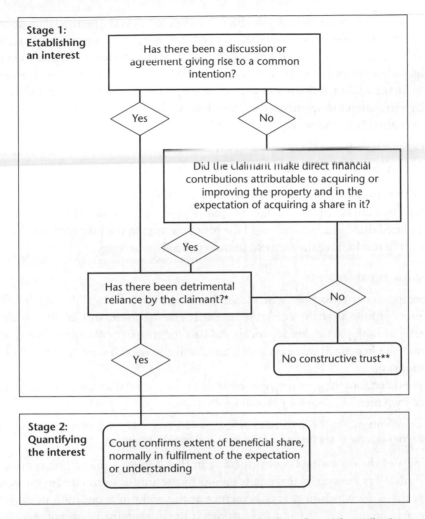

Stage 1: Establishing an interest

Has there been a discussion or agreement giving rise to a common intention?

Yes   No

Did the claimant make direct financial contributions attributable to acquiring or improving the property and in the expectation of acquiring a share in it?

Yes

Has there been detrimental reliance by the claimant?*

No

Yes

No constructive trust**

Stage 2: Quantifying the interest

Court confirms extent of beneficial share, normally in fulfilment of the expectation or understanding

* In cases where there has been no agreement, the direct financial contribution may also provide the necessary detrimental reliance.

**The claimant may have a remedy in proprietary estoppel or unjust enrichment.

Figure 11.3 Constructive trusts of the family home: the classic formulation

(vi) The search for intention

Whatever else is happening in the law, it now appears settled that once an interest has been acquired, whether through express or inferred common intention, the quantification of that interest is now based upon a discovery of the parties' 'common intention' deduced from all the circumstances surrounding the case (see Figure 11.3). The court is thus making value judgements, not on the basis of what it considers to be a fair division of the equitable ownership, but on an analysis of the surrounding circumstances to consider what the parties are thought to have agreed as to the beneficial ownership. A realist might question whether there is any difference of substance between an analysis of what is fair in all the circumstances and what the parties can be considered by a judge to have intended when there is no direct evidence of that intention. The extent of any financial contribution now appears to play a very small role in quantification: small contributions to acquiring the family home as in *Abbott* can lead to a finding of a 50 per cent stake in the beneficial ownership.

(2) Common intention constructive trusts: joint legal owners

One of the key characteristics of *Stack v Dowden*[276] is that legal title to the family home was held by both Mr Stack and Ms Dowden as legal joint tenants. However, they had not declared on what trusts they held the beneficial title to the property and the issue was thus to resolve how they were to share beneficial ownership.

(a) Acquiring an interest

According to Baroness Hale, where, as in *Stack v Dowden*,[277] legal title is joint, there is a presumption that the equitable title will also be joint, so that the beneficial interests of both parties are identical, and it is for the party disputing this (claiming that the beneficial ownership deviates from the legal ownership) to rebut the presumption.

The existence of the presumption, elevated to the status of a 'default rule' was confirmed by Arden LJ in *Fowler v Barron*:

[The presumption] provides a default rule that, unless and until the contrary is proved, joint tenants in this context are treated as joint legal and beneficial owners.[278]

This part of the reasoning is not surprising in that it follows the orthodox principle encapsulated in the maxim that equity follows by presuming a joint tenancy in equity, unless there are words or acts of severance at the point of acquisition to suggest a tenancy in common.[279] What is less justified is the unexplained assumption that the existence of this presumption means that the first stage in establishing a constructive trust—demonstrating an express or implied common intention—has been satisfied. The presumption simply creates a starting point based on imputed intention, not actual intention. It could be argued that even though the starting point is a presumption of equality, departing from this still requires the same kind of evidence of an express or implied agreement to share the property differently as is required in cases of sole legal ownership.

---

[276] [2007] 2 AC 432.   [277] Ibid.

[278] [2008] EWCA Civ 377, at [34]. See also *Jones v Kernott* [2009] EWHC 1713 (Ch), at [26] where Nicolas Strauss, QC cited this statement with approval.

[279] See further Jackson, Stevens, and Pearce, *Land Law* (4th edn, 2008), Ch 12.

(b) Reliance or detriment

(i) No requirement of detriment to support the presumption of equality

In *Stack v Dowden* there is no reference to any requirement of reliance or detriment. It is implicit in the presumption of joint beneficial ownership that there is no element of detriment required to found the interest.[280] It follows from the legal ownership.

(ii) Shared beneficial ownership is conceded

Where it is conceded that both parties share beneficial ownership, even when title is vested in a sole legal owner, there is no requirement of detriment. The concession will be sufficient, at least so far as it extends. However, since *Stack v Dowden* suggests that there is a presumption of equality wherever shared beneficial ownership is conceded, it is unclear whether the concession will also mean that there is no requirement of reliance or detriment up to and including an equal share, even if only less than this has been conceded by the legal owner.

(iii) Detriment needed where the presumption of equality is challenged?

Since *Stack v Dowden* did not overrule earlier House of Lords' decisions in which the requirement of reliance or detriment was laid down, this presumably remains a requirement where it is alleged that the shares are other than the presumed equal shares. That is, however, something which has not yet been confirmed.

(c) Quantifying the interest

(i) Burden of proof lies on person seeking to rebut presumption of equality

Where, applying *Stack v Dowden*,[281] there is a presumption of equal shares, it is for the party asserting a greater share to bear the burden of proof in adducing evidence to rebut the presumption of equality. This was followed and applied in *Fowler v Barron*,[282] where Toulson LJ said:

> The burden rests on the party challenging that presumption to show that the parties should be taken to have intended that their beneficial interests should be different from their legal interests.[283]

In deciding whether the burden has been discharged, the court must apply the 'civil standard of proof'.[284]

It is apparent from the judgments in *Stack v Dowden* that it will be rare that the presumption of equality arising from a transfer of ownership into joint names will be rebutted. As Lady Hale said:

> cases in which the joint legal owners are to be taken to have intended that their beneficial interests should be different from their legal interests will be very unusual.[285]

---

[280] See Etherton 'Constructive Trusts and Proprietary Estoppels: The Search for Clarity and Principle' [2009] Conv 104.

[281] [2007] 2 AC 432.   [282] [2008] EWCA Civ 377.   [283] Ibid., at [51].

[284] Ibid., at [35] per Arden LJ.   [285] [2007] 2 AC 432, at [69].

In *Stack v Dowden* itself, the House of Lords considered that the normal presumption had been rebutted, but the circumstances were exceptional because:

> There cannot be many unmarried couples who have lived together for as long as this, who have had four children together, and whose affairs have been kept as rigidly separate as this couples' affairs have been kept. This is all strongly indicative that they did not intend their shares, even in the property which was put in both their names, to be equal (still less that they intended a beneficial joint tenancy with the right of survivorship should one of them die before it was severed). Before the Court of Appeal Ms Dowden contended for a 65% share and in my view she has made good her case for that.[286]

(ii) What is exceptional?

It has been suggested that 'independent money-management is not uncommon among cohabiting couples, and would hardly mark *Stack* as an exceptional case'.[287] *Fowler v Barron*[288] is also instructive on this issue. It is to be remembered that Mr Barron failed to rebut the presumption in this case, and the property was divided equally, in spite of no financial contribution having been made by Ms Fowler. As Sarah Greer has commented: a claimant wishing to establish anything other than equal beneficial ownership will have a far from easy task.[289]

Nick Piska is more critical.[290] He argues that it is difficult to see the distinction on the material facts between *Fowler* and *Stack*, given that the outcomes are so different, beyond the fact that in *Stack*, the parties had recourse to other assets, while in *Fowler*, the house was the sole asset. It remains unclear what will be considered necessary to rebut the presumption, but there are some indicators that can be gleaned from the emerging case law.

(iii) Inferred and imputed intentions

It has already been mentioned that Lady Hale referred in *Stack v Dowden* to an imputed intention, which is really an invented intention. Lord Neuberger, in dissent on the reasoning in *Stack*, suggested that the court's role in this area (as in *Lloyds Bank v Rosset*) was, in the absence of express intention, to infer, not impute, intention:

> An inferred intention is one which is objectively deduced to be the subjective and actual intentions of the parties, in the light of their actions and statements. An imputed intention is one which is attributed to the parties, even though no such actual intention can be deduced from their actions and statements, and even though they had no such intention.[291]

An imputed intention is thus 'one found—that is, invented—by the court where C and D neither discussed the matter nor proceeded on the basis of a shared assumption, but the court deals with the case as though they had done so'.[292]

---

286 Ibid., at [92] per Baroness Hale.
287 Probert 'Equality in the Family Home' (2007) 15 *Feminist Legal Studies* 341, at 347.
288 [2008] EWCA Civ 377, at [2]–[8].   289 Greer 'No More Nonsense' 158 NLJ 1055.
290 Piska 'Two Recent Reflections on the Resulting Trust' [2008] Conv 441.
291 Ibid., at [126].   292 Gardner 'Family Property Today' [2008] LQR 422.

(iv) The relevant factors

In applying the new test for determining the beneficial ownership of a home which is legally co-owned, Lady Hale in *Stack v Dowden*[293] stressed that the court was looking for what the parties reasonably understood as to the beneficial ownership from their words and actions (see above). It is for this reason that her Ladyship listed the factors to which the court was to have recourse when deciding the extent of any common intention and the importance of a clear finding of fact on these matters. The factors included:

- any evidence from discussions about intention;
- the reasons why the home was acquired in joint names;
- whether they had responsibility to provide for children;
- the financing of the purchase, initially and subsequently; and
- the arrangement of the relationship finances generally.

(v) Balancing and evaluating the factors

In *Stack*, it seems that the critical element was the degree to which the parties had separated their financial affairs and assets. Looking at *Fowler v Barron*,[294] monetary contributions were not a critical factor; instead it appears important that the home was the only significant asset, and that it was thus unlikely that the parties would have intended, if their relationship broke down, that Fowler would be homeless and 'dependent on state benefits and housing support'.[295] However, there is a fallacy in this reasoning, as suggested by Piska:

Such an inference as to the parties' intentions is tenuous. Moreover, elsewhere in her judgment Arden L.J. draws the inference that the parties' never gave family finances any thought, so it is interesting to find that she is happy to draw an inference as to the parties' intentions on the basis of the hypothetical consequences of a hypothetical relationship breakdown.[296]

It suggests that, despite the indicative factors set out in *Stack*, there is wide latitude in how they are applied, and the courts are taking holistic views in imputing a common intention, rather than going through a list of factors and weighing them against one another. It is hard to avoid the conclusion that, where the parties themselves have not reached an express understanding between themselves as to the beneficial ownership of the family home, the task of discovering what the parties themselves would have decided if they had reached agreement is an impossible one, and that the courts are therefore forced to substitute their own judgment of what is appropriate. In *Jones v Kernott*,[297] Nicolas Strauss, QC considered this very question, and admitted that, where the parties have not themselves clearly

---

[293] [2007] 2 AC 432.   [294] [2008] EWCA Civ 377.
[295] Ibid., at [46] per Arden LJ.
[296] Piska 'Two Recent Reflections on the Resulting Trust' [2008] Conv 441, at 458–9.
[297] [2009] EWHC 1713 (Ch).

shown their intention, the court was imputing to them the intention it thought they should have:

In my view, what the majority in *Stack* held was only that the court should not override the intention of the parties, in so far as that appears from what they have said or from their conduct, in favour of what the court itself considers to be fair. The key words used by Baroness Hale are that the court must not impose its view. To the extent that the intention of the parties cannot be inferred, the court is free . . . to impute a common intention to the parties. Imputing an intention involves, as Lord Neuberger points out, attributing to the parties an intention which they did not have, or at least did [not] express to each other. The intention is one which the parties 'must be taken' to have had. It is difficult to see how this process can work, without the court supplying, to the extent that the intention of the parties cannot be deduced from their words or conduct, what the court considers to be fair.[298]

(vi) The 'ambulatory' constructive trust

It was suggested by Lord Hoffmann in argument in *Stack v Dowden*[299] that a beneficial interest arising under a constructive trust could be 'ambulatory' in nature, which means that the parties' intentions about their beneficial ownership may change over the course of time. Hence, when considering the parties words and actions in applying the factors set out by Lady Hale (above) in quantifying their beneficial entitlement, it is important to recognize that the parties' intentions may have changed over the period they owned the property. Lord Neuberger referred to this as an 'elegant characterisation',[300] which indeed it is. It enables a court to take account of the fact that the parties' intentions may evolve and change as their relationship develops and their circumstances change. This appears to have been the view of Nicolaus Strauss, QC in *Jones v Kernott*, who, finding that the presumption of equality had been displaced in that case, said that:

The parties' interests were 'ambulatory': their respective interests could be quantified at any given time, but until this was done they changed over time to take account of the increasing contribution of Ms. Jones and the ever more distant relationship between Mr. Kernott and the property.[301]

A recognition that the intentions of the parties may change over time, and are not fixed immutably at the date a property is acquired, accords with reality. However, it does not make the task of the court any easier, and indeed may even make it more difficult, since less reliance can be placed upon explicit discussions or even a formally recorded declaration of trust at an early point in a relationship. It adds a further dimension and concomitantly additional uncertainty to a process which the court is already being asked to undertake.[302]

---

[298] Ibid., at [30]–[31].

[299] [2007] 2 AC 432. Lord Hoffmann did not deliver a speech in the House of Lords, but the concept is picked up in the leading speech of Lady Hale (at [62]) and the dissenting speech of Lord Neuberger (at [138]).

[300] Ibid., at [138]. Nevertheless, he felt that it did 'not justify a departure from the application of established legal principles any more than such a departure is justified, at the time of acquisition'.

[301] [2009] EWHC 1713 (Ch), at [49].

[302] See also Nicolas Strauss, QC, at [26], where he suggests that while *Stack* confirms the existence of an ambulatory trust, it provides 'little guidance . . . as to the circumstances in which the presumption of equality will be displaced or how, if it is, the altered amounts are to be assessed'.

(3) Common intention constructive trusts: a common approach?

(i) Why is there a presumption of shared ownership in cases of joint legal title?

The House of Lords in *Stack v Dowden*[303] assumed that the decision to put a property in joint names was a conscious decision from which the inference or imputation of an intention to share the beneficial ownership could fairly be drawn. Lady Hale said that 'it will almost always have been a conscious decision to put the house into joint names'.[304] Even Lord Neuberger, dissenting on the reasoning, stated that 'the fact that a property is taken in joint names is some evidence that both parties were intended to have some beneficial interest'.[305] However, there could be a range of other reasons why the property is put into joint names, which could include the need to secure a joint mortgage if the earnings of both parties are needed to achieve a mortgage loan of the extent needed to finance the purchase, even though both parties intend only one of them to make all the repayments; it could also be to facilitate transfer on death but without affecting the beneficial interests during the parties' lives. That is a practice which is not uncommon in relation to bank accounts. If the only evidence relating to beneficial ownership is the registration of a family home in joint names, the view that equal shares are presumed owes as much to the maxim 'equity follows the law' as it does to any inferred intention, and more to 'what reasonable parties would have agreed' than to 'what these parties have actually agreed'. The presumed intention to share beneficial ownership in such circumstances is more accurately described as imputed than it is as inferred.

(ii) Imputing an intention to share ownership to all cases

Why should a similar imputation not be made in relation to family homes registered in the name of a sole legal owner? Some commentators have a very strongly held view that the current property-based approach to identifying the interests of cohabitants in the family home has a discriminatory effect, since it is said to be more common for the sole legal owner to be the male partner in a heterosexual relationship than the female partner. To redress this discrimination they would support a presumption in favour of shared ownership in all cases involving the home in which a cohabiting couple live. Mark Tattershall has said:

> If an intention can be imputed in a joint names case, is there any reason in logic or in principle why it cannot be imputed in a sole name case?[306]

But what imputed intention should this be? One argument is that since relationships are, by definition, about sharing lives, both parties are likely also to have intended to share their property, whoever happens to be the legal owner (see Figure 11.4). The converse argument is that the choice of sole legal ownership is indicative of an intention to keep the assets separate. It is the latter view that Lady Hale espoused in *Stack*.

---

[303] [2007] 2 AC 432.   [304] Ibid., at [66].   [305] Ibid., at [116].
[306] '*Stack* v *Dowden*: Imputing an Intention' [2008] Fam Law 249, at 250.

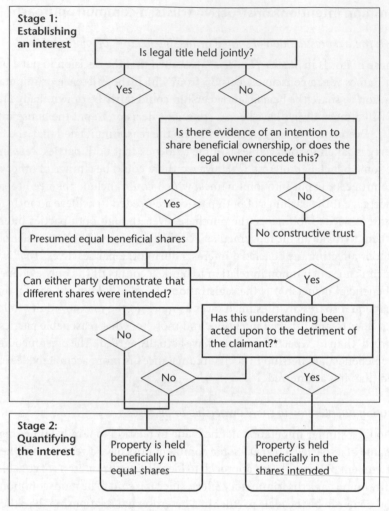

Stage 1:
Establishing
an interest

Is legal title held jointly?

Yes

No

Is there evidence of an intention to share beneficial ownership, or does the legal owner concede this?

Yes

No

Presumed equal beneficial shares

No constructive trust

Can either party demonstrate that different shares were intended?

Yes

Has this understanding been acted upon to the detriment of the claimant?*

No

No

Yes

Stage 2:
Quantifying
the interest

Property is held beneficially in equal shares

Property is held beneficially in the shares intended

* The need for this test has been doubted.

Figure 11.4 Constructive trusts of the family home: presumed common intention

(iii) Rebutting a presumption of sole beneficial ownership

Baroness Hale in *Stack v Dowden* stated that the presumption of equality of ownership in a case of joint legal title was a very strong presumption that could only be rebutted in exceptional circumstances. If her reasoning is to be followed, the presumption that the sole legal owner is the sole beneficial owner would also be a strong one, and rebutting the presumption would not be easy. Rebutting the presumption would depend upon the same group of factors as those used for rebutting the presumption of shared beneficial ownership.[307] The great bulk of the modern case law, however, suggests that

---

[307] *Stack v Dowden* [2007] 2 AC 432, at [69] per Baroness Hale.

rebutting the presumption of sole beneficial ownership is comparatively easy, and some would say, almost to the extent that the slightest indication of an intention to share results in equality being the default position. This is still not enough for some commentators. One commentator has suggested that:

Whatever perceived advance there might have been in 2007 with respect to quantifying a share it is plain that there has been no real advance in the law in establishing a share. Even contributions to the mortgage may not be enough if they can be explained away, for example as payments in lieu of a rent or licence fee.[308]

(iv) The need for detriment

On the basis that the House of Lords in *Stack v Dowden* made no reference to a requirement for reliance or detriment to support a finding in a case involving joint legal title that the shares are other than equal, some commentators have assumed that the case dispenses with the need for proof of reliance or detriment in such cases. The better view, already expressed, is that because earlier cases have not been overruled, the requirement for reliance or detriment remains, if the claimant is put to proof. However, if the case is correctly interpreted as dispensing with the requirement, then similarly, there should be no requirement of detriment in cases involving a sole legal owner, and it is here that the greatest change in the law would be occasioned. A non-legal owner would be being given an interest on the imputation of a common intention by the courts, without having to prove any detrimental reliance to establish the interest, something that Etherton LJ (writing extra-judicially) suggests:

if more than simple accident, is 'driven by social policy rather than strict adherence to precedent.[309]

(4) Criticism of the 'common intention' constructive trust[310]

(i) Is finding a common intention an artificial exercise?

Although the common intention approach to constructive trusts was firmly entrenched by *Lloyds Bank plc v Rosset*,[311] building on the foundation laid in *Pettit v Pettit*[312] and *Gissing v Gissing*,[313] it has been subjected to extensive criticism.[314] The major objection is that the whole process of finding, and then enforcing, the 'common intention' of the parties, is highly artificial, and that despite their protestations to the contrary, the courts are effectively 'inventing' or 'discovering' an intention

---

308 Ralton 'Establishing a Beneficial Share: *Rosset* Revisited' [2008] Fam Law 424.

309 Etherton 'Constructive Trusts and Proprietary Estoppel: The Search for Clarity and Principle' [2009] Conv 104, at 110.

310 Gardner 'Rethinking Family Property' (1993) 109 LQR 263; Riniker 'The Fiction of Common Intention and Detriment' [1998] Conv 202.

311 [1991] 1 AC 107.   312 [1970] AC 777.   313 [1971] AC 886.

314 Gardner 'Rethinking Family Property' (1993) 109 LQR 263; Glover and Todd 'The Myth of Common Intention' (1996) 16 LS 325; Riniker, 'The Fiction of Common Intention and Detriment' [1998] Conv 202; Mee, *The Property Rights of Cohabitees* (1999) pp 117–173; Rotherham, 'The Property Rights of Unmarried Cohabitees: The Case for Reform' [2004] Conv 268.

where they feel that a trust should arise. As Tipping J said in *Lankow v Rose* in the New Zealand Court of Appeal:

English jurisprudence appears still to be concerned with notions of express or imputed intention or understanding. That approach, essentially contractual or quasi-contractual, is in my view unnecessarily artificial. It is better to acknowledge openly that a constructive trust is being imposed in equity without the consent, express, implied or imputed, of the constructive trustee. The trust is imposed because equity will not allow the legal owner to deny the claimant a beneficial interest.[315]

Thus whereas Lord Bridge described *Eves v Eves*[316] and *Grant v Edwards*[317] as 'outstanding' examples of express common intention, the facts would suggest that there was no real agreement between the parties to share the ownership of the property concerned. In both cases the men concerned had no real intention that their partners should enjoy an interest in the property. Stuart Eves refused to put Janet on the title of the house, using the excuse that she was under 21. Grant would not put Edwards on the title because he said that it would prejudice her forthcoming matrimonial proceedings. Both of these excuses covered the real intention of the men that their partners were not to receive any proprietary interest in the house. They were to remain the owners and to enjoy the power and control that are necessarily commensurate with such ownership. If the relationship broke down, they wanted to be able to remove their erstwhile partner and not to be encumbered by their presence in the house. To describe the parties in these cases as enjoying a 'common intention' to share the ownership is nothing short of a fiction. The inference of common intention is similarly fraught with the danger that the court is merely inventing a justification for imposing a constructive trust. In *Westdeutsche Landesbank Girozentrale v Islington London Borough Council*[318] Lord Browne-Wilkinson suggested that, unlike a resulting trust, a constructive trust is imposed on a trustee by law against his intentions,[319] which is undoubtedly true of some forms of constructive trust. The inevitable implication of this greater realism is that the language of 'common intention' is inappropriate as a description of the true rationale for establishing a constructive trust of the family home.

(ii) Is the real purpose of a common intention constructive trust to achieve fairness?

As Gardner[320] points out, the central difficulty is that the common intention analysis focuses on the parties' own thinking as the basis for the imposition of a constructive trust, when in fact they will often have given little or no thought to the question of ownership, as was evident in *Midland Bank plc v Cooke*.[321] If the principle of a common intention were applied literally, constructive trusts would arise in virtually no domestic circumstances. It also fails to take account of the nature of the relationship between the parties, which should arguably be the main factor in determining the location of the ownership of the property held by the partners. Mee goes so far as

315　[1995] 1 NZLR 277, 293.　　316　[1975] 1 WLR 1338.
317　[1986] Ch 638.　　318　[1996] AC 669.
319　Ibid., at 708.　　320　(1993) 109 LQR 263, at 282.
321　[1995] 4 All ER 562.

to conclude that the English 'common intention constructive trust' is theoretically indefensible:

The English courts have thrown into the pot three distinct doctrines (resulting trusts, estoppel and the principle in *Rochefoucauld v Boustead*[322]) and have sealed over this unpalatable mixture with a thick crust of confusion, in the form of the misleading phrase 'common intention' (with its implications of bargains and subjective consensus). Not surprisingly, even after twenty-five years in the oven, the 'common intention' analysis remains stubbornly half-baked... Furthermore, there is the great irony that, despite the liberties it takes with legal principle, the common intention trust analysis can boast very few advantages at a practical level: it is difficult and expensive to apply and provides a remedy for claimants in only a narrow range of cases. Clearly, this ill conceived doctrine should find no place in the law of England.[323]

The decision of the Court of Appeal in *Oxley v Hiscock*[324] in relation to the quantification of the beneficial interest arising under a constructive trust at least has the merit of eliminating the need for the court to identify an artificial assumed intention where there was no express intention between the parties as to the sharing of the property, but the reintroduction of a broad discretion for the court to decide what share would be 'fair' in all the circumstances opens the door to the equally dangerous problems of legal uncertainty and inconsistency. The House of Lords in *Stack v Dowden*[325] has, at least ostensibly, moved away from the approach of fairness, by suggesting that the role of the court is to discover, not invent, the common intention of the parties,[326] although by referring to the imputation of intention, it contradicts its own position.[327] As Lord Neuberger, in dissent on the reasoning in *Stack*, said:

Imputation involves concluding what the parties would have intended, whereas inference involves concluding what the parties did intend.[328]

(iii) Are the courts' decisions easily predicted?

If the criteria by which the court is to make a judgment, as enumerated in *Stack*, provided a clear and predictable guide to the outcome, this would at least present a more constrained and therefore less objectionable concept of social justice than the unfettered approach of fairness suggested in *Oxley v Hiscock*. However, the indicative range of factors listed by Baroness Hale to which the courts are to have regard when deciding the extent of the common intention have also been subject to criticism as being too wide and open to uncertainty. In the words of Dixon, these factors may become:

the property lawyer's equivalent of a Pandora's box—everything included with only a small hope that this will not lead to endemic uncertainty.[329]

Much will depend on the development of the application of these principles in subsequent cases, but if the range of factors is construed too widely, it is suggested that ultimately they will simply be a mask to conceal what a particular judge on a particular day felt was 'fair' or appropriate between the parties on the facts before him.

---

[322] [1897] 1 Ch 196.
[324] [2005] Fam 211.
[326] Ibid.
[328] Ibid., at [126].

[323] *The Property Rights of Cohabitees* (1999), pp 173–174.
[325] [2007] 2 AC 432.
[327] Ibid., at [60] per Baroness Hale.
[329] Dixon [2007] 71 Conv 353.

In a dual call for some clarity in the law and a criticism on what he perceived as the creation of a new form of 'new model'[330] constructive trust in *Stack v Dowden*, Swadling summarized the current position of the law:

> What we have instead is more unfocused tinkering with Lord Denning's (not Lord Diplock's) mutant child, and the creation of even finer and more unintelligible distinctions. Until a fundamental analysis of this subject is undertaken, we will never properly understand the common intention constructive trust, nor its relationship to the remedial constructive trust, the resulting trust, or even proprietary estoppel, a doctrine which merited only a passing reference in the case . . . until such an enquiry is undertaken, we are doomed to continue lurching from one seemingly arbitrary precedent to another.[331]

(iv) Alternative approaches

However, despite the acknowledged deficiencies of the 'common intention' constructive trust, it has proved difficult to identify an alternative that is not equally problematic. This is explored below in the section on reform,[332] but is worth noting here that the Law Commission[333] has not recommended the replacement of the common intention constructive trust as a means of acquiring beneficial interests, but advocated in 2002 that a wider range of monetary contributions should suffice to establish an interest,[334] such as indirect contributions enabling repayment of mortgages and a holistic approach to quantifying the interest granted.[335] These recommendations have already arguably been achieved, at least in relation to quantification of interests,[336] by *Stack v Dowden*.

Interestingly, the most recent scheme suggested by the Law Commission seeks to give the courts similar rights to distribute assets of unmarried couples on the breakdown of the relationship to those available under the Matrimonial Causes Act 1973 to married couples,[337] but suggests that common intention constructive trusts be retained for those parties who do not meet the threshold of the scheme. It is clear that the common intention constructive trust is unlikely to disappear from English law soon.

(v) Renaming the common intention constructive trust

Intellectual integrity would perhaps be better served by the rejection of 'common intention' as the touchstone for constructive trusts and replacement with some other description and associated principles, such as the fulfilment of the claimant's 'reasonable or legitimate expectation' arising in the light of the parties' relationship

---

[330] Such trusts were a creation of Lord Denning, which met with almost universal criticism and have been rejected by the courts—see Chapter 10, at pp 320–322.

[331] Swadling 'The Common Intention Constructive Trust in the House of Lords: An Opportunity Missed' [2007] LQR 511, at 518.

[332] See below, pp 421–428.

[333] *Sharing Homes* Law Com No 278 (2002).

[334] Ibid., para 4.26.   [335] Ibid., para. 4.27.

[336] Contrast the position in *Le Foe v Le Foe* [2002] 2 FLR 970 about inference of a common intention from indirect contributions with the more orthodox approach in *James v Thomas* [2007] EWCA Civ 1212.

[337] Law Comm *Cohabitation: The Financial Consequences of Relationship Breakdown* No 307 (2007), discussed below, at pp 425–428.

and conduct. A number of Commonwealth jurisdictions have rejected the 'common intention' analysis in favour of such alternative explanations for the imposition of constructive trusts—these are discussed in the section on reform, as alternatives only really make sense once English law's 'alternative approach' through proprietary estoppel has been discussed.

6 Proprietary estoppel[338]

(1) Acquiring an interest: establishing the equity

(a) The essence of proprietary estoppel

The essence of proprietary estoppel is that if the legal owner of property (almost invariably land) has so conducted himself (whether by encouragement or representations) that the claimant believes that he has, or will obtain, some rights in respect of the land, and he has acted to his detriment on the basis of his induced belief, it would be unconscionable for the legal owner to assert his strict legal entitlement to the property, and equity with therefore intervene to prevent this.[339] The remedy granted in satisfaction of the estoppel equity is therefore awarded because the claimant has experienced a 'frustrated expectation'.[340]

(b) When will conduct be 'unconscionable'?

Although the principle of proprietary estoppel has a long historical pedigree, dating from before the nineteenth century,[341] it was only towards the end of the twentieth century that the full scope of the doctrine was recognized and that the courts formulated the key requirements in a general way. The most important question is to identify the circumstances in which a legal owner's conduct can be regarded as 'unconscionable', thus calling for the court to provide the claimant with a remedy and preventing him from asserting his legal rights. The courts have recognized that at the moment the circumstances in which the equity will be established are 'ill defined'.[342]

(i) Strict criteria: the 'five probanda'

In the late nineteenth century, the courts held that there were strict and rigid criteria that must be met before an estoppel equity was raised. Despite earlier and broader

---

[338] See Hopkins, *The Informal Acquisition of Rights in Land* (2000); Finn, *Equitable Estoppel*, in Finn (ed), *Essays in Equity* (1905), Welstead, 'Proprietary Estoppel and the Family Home' (unpublished PhD thesis), Cambridge University Library; Denning Law Library, University of Buckingham; (1997) 17 LS 258 (Cooke).

[339] See Snell, *Principles of Equity* (29th edn, 1990), pp 573–574.

[340] Gray, *Elements of Land Law* (2nd edn, 1993), p 356.

[341] See *Bridges v Kilburne* (1792) (referred to in *Jackson v Cator* (1800) 5 Ves 688); *Dillwyn v Llewelyn* (1862) 4 De G F & J 517; *Ramsden v Dyson* (1866) LR 1 HL 129.

[342] *Walker v Walker* (12 April 1984, unreported), per Browne-Wilkinson LJ.

statements of principle in *Ramsden v Dyson*,[343] in *Willmott v Barber* Fry J stipulated five essential elements which had to be established before the court would restrain a defendant from asserting his legal rights over property:

> A man is not to be deprived of his legal rights unless he has acted in such a way as would make it fraudulent for him to set up those rights. What, then are the elements or requisites necessary to constitute fraud of that description? In the first place the plaintiff must have made some mistake as to his legal rights. Second, the plaintiff must have expended some money or must have done some act (not necessarily upon the defendant's land) on the faith of his mistaken belief. Thirdly, the defendant, the possessor of the legal right, must know of the existence of his own right which is inconsistent with the right claimed by the plaintiff. If he does not know of it he is in the same position as the plaintiff, and the doctrine of acquiescence is founded upon conduct with a knowledge of your legal rights. Fourthly, the defendant, the possessor of the legal right, must know of the plaintiff's mistaken belief of his rights. If he does not, there is nothing which calls upon him to assert his own rights. Lastly, the defendant, the possessor of the legal right, must have encouraged the plaintiff in his expenditure of money or in the other acts which he has done, either directly or by abstaining from asserting his legal right. Where all these elements exist, there is fraud of such a nature as will entitle the court to restrain the possessor of the legal title from exercising it, but, in my judgment, nothing short of this will do.[344]

These five 'probanda' came to be regarded as essential requirements of estoppel, and claims failed where it was not possible to establish all five.[345] In *Crabb v Arun District Council*[346] Scarman LJ considered that the five requirements were 'a valuable guide as to the matters of fact which have to be established in order that a plaintiff may establish this particular equity', and in *Coombes v Smith*[347] Jonathan Parker, QC, sitting as a deputy High Court judge, addressed the question of whether an equity had been established by considering whether each of the five requirements were met on the facts.

Despite such judicial approval, the requirements in *Willmott v Barber*[348] should not be regarded as a comprehensive statement of the essentials of an estoppel claim. They were stipulated in the context of a situation where the claimant had acted under a mistake as to his existing rights. This should be distinguished from cases where the claimant founded his claim upon an 'expectation' created or encouraged by the legal owner. This concept of estoppel by encouragement had found expression in the judgment of Lord Kingsdown in *Ramsden v Dyson*, where he had suggested a less restrictive approach:

> If a man, under a verbal agreement with a landlord for a certain interest in land, or what amounts to the same thing, under an expectation, created or encouraged by the landlord, that he shall have a certain interest, takes possession of such land, with the consent of the landlord, and upon the faith of such promise or expectation, with the knowledge of the landlord, and without objection by him, lays out money upon the land, a Court of equity will compel the landlord to give effect to such promise or expectation.[349]

---

[343] (1866) LR 1 HL 129, at 152 (Lord Cranworth LC) and at 170 (Lord Kingsdown).

[344] (1880) 15 Ch D 96, at 105–106.

[345] See *Kammins Ballroom Co Ltd v Zenith Instruments (Torquay) Ltd* [1971] AC 850, at 884; *E and L Berg Homes Ltd v Grey* (1979) 253 Estates Gazette 473.

[346] [1976] Ch 179.   [347] [1986] 1 WLR 808.   [348] (1880) 15 Ch D 96.

[349] (1866) LR 1 HL 129, at 170.

(ii) A broader understanding of what is unconscionable

The restrictive approach of *Willmott v Barber*[350] has largely given way to a much broader understanding of proprietary estoppel.[351] *In Taylor Fashions Ltd v Liverpool Victoria Trustees Co Ltd*[352] Oliver J restated the requirements of proprietary estoppel in a manner which means that not all the 'probanda' of *Willmott v Barber*[353] are necessarily applicable to every case of proprietary estoppel:

the recent cases indicate,[354] in my judgment, that the application of the *Ramsden v Dyson* principle—whether you call it proprietary estoppel, estoppel by acquiescence or estoppel by encouragement is really immaterial—requires a very much broader approach which is directed rather at ascertaining whether, in particular individual circumstances, it would be unconscionable for a party to be permitted to deny that which, knowingly or unknowingly, he has allowed or encouraged another to assume to his detriment than to inquiring whether the circumstances can be fitted within the confines of some preconceived formula serving as a universal yardstick for every form of unconscionable behaviour.[355]

Therefore, rather than determining whether an equity had been established by application of a rigid list of requirements which must be satisfied, he held that the appropriate inquiry was simply whether the defendant's conduct had been, in all the circumstances of the case, 'unconscionable'.[356]

This modern approach was also adopted by the Privy Council in *Lim Teng Huan v Ang Swee Chuan*,[357] where Lord Browne-Wilkinson stated:

The decision in *Taylor Fashions Ltd v Liverpool Victoria Trustees Co Ltd* showed that, in order to found a proprietary estoppel, it is not essential that the representor should have been guilty of unconscionable conduct in permitting the representee to assume that he could act as he did: it is enough if, in all the circumstances, it is unconscionable for the representor to go back on the assumption which he permitted the representee to make.[358]

In *Gillett v Holt*, Robert Walker LJ similarly emphasized that the prevention of 'unconscionability' is the essence of proprietary estoppel:

Moreover, the fundamental principle that equity is concerned to prevent unconscionable conduct permeates all the elements of the doctrine. In the end the court must look at the matter in the round.[359]

---

[350] (1880) 15 Ch D 96.
[351] However, in the recent case of *Taylor v Dickens* [1998] 1 FLR 806, Judge Weeks, QC rejected the notion of a broad doctrine of estoppel founded on the principle of 'unconscionability' and said that the existence of such a doctrine would mean that 'you might as well forget the law of contract and issue every judge with a portable palm tree'. His comments appear to be inconsistent with the majority of modern cases and have been severely criticized: [1998] Conv 213 (Thompson).
[352] [1982] QB 133; *McMahon v Kerry County Council* (1981) ILRM 419; (1985) 79 ILSI Gaz 179 (Pearce).
[353] (1880) 15 Ch D 96.
[354] See *Inwards v Baker* [1965] 2 QB 29; *ER Ives Investment Ltd v High* [1967] 2 QB 379; *Crabb v Arun District Council* [1976] Ch 179; *Moorgate Mercantile Credit Co Ltd v Twitchings* [1976] QB 225, CA; *Shaw v Applegate* [1977] 1 WLR 970, CA.
[355] See also *Amalgamated Investment and Property Co Ltd (in liquidation) v Texas Commerce International Bank Ltd* [1982] QB 84.
[356] [1982] QB 84, at 155.   [357] [1992] 1 WLR 113.
[358] Ibid., at 117.   [359] [2000] 2 All ER 289, at 301.

(iii) Residual significance of the 'probanda'?

While the five requirements stipulated in *Willmott v Barber*[360] do not provide an exhaustive statement of the circumstances in which an estoppel equity will be established, they may retain an important residual significance in cases of acquiescence. This was recognized by Cumming-Bruce LJ in *Swallow Securities Ltd v Isenberg*:

it has been recognised that the court should regard the formulation by Fry J of the requirement of five probanda as being guidelines, which will probably prove to be the necessary and essential guidelines, to assist the court to decide the question whether it is unconscionable for the plaintiffs to assert their legal rights by taking an advantage of the defendant.[361]

They were also applied in *Matharu v Matharu*,[362] where Roch LJ held that they had been satisfied.

(c) Application of the modern requirements

Although the approach taken in *Taylor Fashions*[363] explains the doctrine of proprietary estoppel on the general principle of 'unconscionability', to establish an equity the courts have held that the three key elements of 'assurance', 'reliance', and 'detriment or change of position' must be present.[364] Although these elements can be separated for analytical purposes, in *Gillett v Holt*[365] Robert Walker LJ suggested that in practice they are often interrelated because 'the quality of the relevant assurances may influence the issue of reliance' and that 'reliance and detriment are often intertwined'.[366]

(i) 'Assurance'

No estoppel 'equity' will arise unless the claimant can establish that the legal owner of land made a representation, or created or encouraged an expectation that he was presently entitled, or would become entitled,[367] to an interest in the land. An assurance may be given 'actively' through the acts of the legal owner, or 'passively' through his silence and failure to disabuse the claimant of his belief that he is entitled to an interest in the land.[368] To be valid, the assurance must be:

unambiguous and must appear to have been intended to be taken seriously. Taken in its context, it must have been a promise which one might reasonably expect to be relied upon by the person to whom it was made.[369]

---

[360] (1880) 15 Ch D 96.   [361] [1985] 1 EGLR 132, at 134.

[362] (1994) 68 P & CR 93 [1994] 2 FLR 597; [1995] Conv 61 (Welstead); (1995) 58 MLR 411 (Milne).

[363] [1982] QB 133n.

[364] See *A-G of Hong Kong v Humphreys Estate (Queen's Gardens) Ltd* [1987] AC 114, PC; *Gillies v Keogh* [1989] 2 NZLR 327, at 346, per Richardson J. There is also the requirement, rarely emphasized in the case law, that, as with other equitable remedies, there must be no bar to the equity, so that the court is free to intervene. In other words, the acts of the claimant must be free of the taint of unconscionability if they are to be provided with relief through estoppel—see below, at pp 420–421.

[365] [2000] 2 All ER 289, at 301.

[366] See also *Jennings v Rice* (2003) 1 P & CR 8 and *Henry v Henry* [2010] 1 All ER 998 at [55].

[367] *Re Basham (Decd)* [1987] 1 All ER 405.

[368] *Warnes v Headley* (31 January 1984, unreported), CA.

[369] [2009] UKHL 18, at [56] per Lord Walker, approving the words of Hoffmann LJ in *Walton v Walton* (unreported).

In some cases the assurance may take the form of an actual agreement between the parties. In others there may be a promise that falls short of an agreement, and in others again there may be no more than an understanding or even a course of dealing that shows that a particular state of affairs was assumed or accepted.

(ii) Active assurance

In *Pascoe v Turner*[370] the plaintiff made an active assurance to the defendant, a woman with whom he was living. The defendant had moved in with the plaintiff in 1964. In 1973 he left the house when he started an affair with another woman, but the evidence showed that he had visited the defendant and had declared to her that she had nothing to worry about, as the house was hers and everything in it. The Court of Appeal held that the evidence established an assurance sufficient to found an estoppel equity, and since she had acted to her detriment in reliance upon it she was entitled to a remedy by way of proprietary estoppel. In *Inwards v Baker*[371] Mr Baker's son, Jack, was intending to build a bungalow. He was persuaded by his father to build the bungalow on his land, which he subsequently did. The Court of Appeal held that this amounted to a sufficient inducement or encouragement to give rise to an estoppel. In *Griffiths v Williams*[372] the Court of Appeal held that an estoppel equity was established where a mother had assured her daughter that she would be entitled to live in her house for the whole of her life. An active assurance will certainly have been given if the legal owner of property promised that the claimant was, or would become, entitled to some interest in it.[373]

(iii) Can an agreement be enforceable if it is void as a contract?

In *Yaxley v Gotts*[374] a builder had entered into an oral agreement with the owner to refurbish and convert a house into flats in return for his acquiring the ground floor flats. The Court of Appeal held that, although this agreement was unenforceable as a contract for lack of formalities,[375] it could give rise to a claim by way of proprietary estoppel. Lord Scott suggested in *Yeomans Row v Cobbe*,[376] that 'proprietary estoppel cannot be prayed in aid in order to render enforceable an agreement that statute has declared to be void',[377] such as a contract to grant an interest in land which has not been made in writing. At face value, this would have robbed proprietary estoppel of any real utility in the family home (and beyond),[378] but the case was never likely to be decisive in domestic cases. *Yeoman's Row v Cobbe* was a commercial case where a property developer was led to believe that he would be able to contract to buy land for redevelopment if he succeeded in gaining planning permission. He spent considerable time and money in securing planning permission, only to find that the landowner then wished to increase the price that had been discussed and agreed. Lord Scott's

---

[370] [1979] 1 WLR 431. [371] [1965] 2 QB 29.
[372] (1977) 248 Estates Gazette 947. [373] *Wayling v Jones* (1993) 69 P & CR 170.
[374] [2000] 1 All ER 711. [375] Law of Property (Miscellaneous Provisions) Act 1989, s 2.
[376] [2008] UKHL 55. [377] Ibid., at [29].
[378] Etherton 'Constructive Trusts and Proprietary Estoppels: The Search for Clarity and Principle' [2009] Conv 104, at 120.

principal reason for rejecting proprietary estoppel as a basis for a remedy[379] was that, even if the developer's expectation was fulfilled, all that he would receive would have been a contract to purchase the development property, some of the important terms of which remained to be agreed. This could not found a claim in proprietary estoppel, for which, in his view, there had to be a claim to a 'certain interest in land' which the party estopped was prevented from denying. A contract to purchase a property was not a certain interest in land. In addition, the claimant knew that he was taking a risk. Lord Scott's observation about proprietary estoppel not being available to enforce a contract that is required to be made in writing was therefore not necessary for a decision in the case. Lord Walker suggests in his judgment that a distinction should be drawn between commercial cases involving individuals who are aware of their rights and who may well have taken legal advice, and domestic cases where the claimant is much less likely to be legally advised and where expectations and understandings might be much less clearly formulated.[380]

Thorner v Major[381] is a later House of Lords' decision. For nearly thirty years David Thorner worked without pay on the farm of his father's cousin, Peter. Although no express promise had been made, the clear understanding between David and Peter was that David would inherit the farm on Peter's death. In the event, Peter died without making a will. The House of Lords held that David's reasonable belief that he would inherit the farm should be fulfilled since he had acted on that belief by foregoing other opportunities. The view of the majority was that this was in most respects a straightforward instance of proprietary estoppel, although Lord Scott, while agreeing that the requirements of proprietary estoppel had been met would have found it 'easier and more comfortable to regard David's equity as established via a remedial constructive trust'.[382] Lord Walker and Lord Neuberger both indicated that the assurance or understanding on which a claimant relied did not need to be expressed with precise and exact definition.[383] Lord Neuberger was forthright in his view that Lord Scott's observations about the difficulty of using proprietary estoppel to render enforceable a contract that was void because it was not in writing had no relevance in a case with no contractual connection.[384] Some emphasis is placed in *Thorner v Major* on the commercial nature of the transaction in *Yeoman's Row v Cobbe*, the sophistication of the parties, and their awareness of the risks in undertaking work on the basis of a promise they both knew could not be enforced as a contract. Lord Walker, in a postscript, expressed his difficulty with Lord Scott's alignment in *Yeoman's Row* of proprietary estoppel with the requirements of promissory estoppel (including the requirement of a 'clear and unambiguous' representation). In *Thompson v Foy,*[385] Lewison J followed the guidance of Lords Walker and

---

[379] The claimant did not go without a remedy. It was held that he was entitled to reasonable remuneration for the time and effort which he had spent on a *quantum meruit* basis.

[380] [2008] UKHL 55, at [68], [81], and [87].   [381] [2009] UKHL 18.

[382] Ibid., at [14].   [383] See, for example, [2009] UKHL 18, at [98].

[384] [2009] UKHL 18, at [96]–[98] per Lord Neuberger.

[385] [2009] EWHC 1076 (Ch).

Scott in *Thorner v Major*. In this case, the relevant assurance related to the building of an extension to the family home by Mrs Foy. Lewison J, held that, despite there being no evidence of specific conversations between Mrs Thompson and Mrs Foy, it was 'clear enough'[386] that there was a 'mutual understanding'[387] that the extension would belong to Mrs Foy.

It seems, therefore, that the impact of *Cobbe* in the domestic context is likely to be small. At least one question, however, remains. Would it not be perverse if an assurance which has been made as an express promise intended to be acted upon cannot be enforced through proprietary estoppel because it looks too much like an unenforceable contract, but a similar expectation acquired through more oblique and circumlocutory means can be enforced? This may not be particularly important for the utility of estoppel as a means of acquiring interests in the family home, as in the majority of cases the assurance will fall far short of any formal agreement between the parties.

(iv) Passive assurance

It seems that if a legal owner merely stands by while the claimant acts to his detriment, in the belief that he is entitled to an interest in the land, this will constitute a sufficient assurance to give rise to an estoppel equity. In *Ramsden v Dyson* Lord Wensleydale said:

[if a stranger] builds on my land, supposing it to be his own, and I, knowing it to be mine, do not interfere, but leave him to go on, equity considers it to be dishonest in me to remain passive and afterwards to interfere and take the profit.[388]

Although it is not strictly essential[389] that the owner knew of the claimant's action and mistaken belief, and of his own rights to intervene,[390] these are relevant issues and it will be easier to establish an equity where they are present. In *St Pancras and Humanist Housing Association Ltd v Leonard*,[391] Mr Leonard (described by the judge as a seasoned squatter) had, for over twelve years, been in exclusive possession of a garage close to a group of houses that had been acquired from Camden Council by a cooperative of which he was a member. He attended a meeting of the cooperative in which the decision was taken to seek a lease of land, including the garage from the Council, for the benefit of all the members. He raised no objection. The trial judge, upheld by the Court of Appeal, held that Mr Leonard was later estopped from asserting his claim to exclusive rights to the garage, even though he was not aware at the time of the meeting that his adverse possession gave him a right to claim title. He did believe at the time that he had the right to prevent other cooperative members from using the garage, and his failure to assert this was enough to make his silence at the meeting an acceptance that the garage would become a communal asset.

---

[386] Ibid., at [90].   [387] Ibid., at [92].   [388] (1866) LR 1 HL 129, at 168.

[389] *Shaw v Applegate* [1978] 1 All ER 123, CA; *Taylor Fashions Ltd v Liverpool Victoria Trustees Co Ltd* [1982] QB 133; *Thorner v Major* [2009] UKHL 18.

[390] Compare *Armstrong v Sheppard & Short Ltd* [1959] 2 QB 384, CA.

[391] [2008] EWCA Civ 1442.

(v) Assurance relating to specific assets

Whether the assurance is active or passive it will only generate an equity if it is given with respect to particular assets. In a sense, this limitation operates as an equivalent of the rule that a trust can only be validly created if there was 'certainty of subject matter'. In *Layton v Martin*[392] a man had given a woman who had moved in with him a general assurance that he would provide her with 'financial security'. It was held that this assurance was too amorphous and insufficiently connected with specific property to give rise to an estoppel equity. Scott J concluded that proprietary estoppel can only arise:

in connection with some asset in respect of which it has been represented, or is alleged to have been represented that the claimant is to have some interest... The present case does not raise that question. A representation that 'financial security' would be provided by the deceased to the plaintiff, and on which I will assume she acted, is not a representation that she is to have some equitable or legal interest in any particular asset or assets.[393]

In *Re Basham (Decd)*[394] it was held that a plaintiff was able to claim a right by way of proprietary estoppel to the residuary estate of the defendant who had made an assurance to that effect, on the basis that it could extend to the 'the whole of A's estate',[395] rendering it clearly identifiable.

Appropriate identification of assets was an important issue before their Lordships in *Thorner v Major and others*.[396] Peter Thorner had led his nephew David to believe that he would inherit his farm on his death. Over the thirty-year-period in which the claimant had worked without payment on the farm there had been a number of disposals and acquisitions of parcels of land. It was argued before their Lordships that the property had not been established with sufficient certainty. Their Lordships, while noting the requirement of certainty, felt that the fluidity of the farm holding did not stop it being identified as the proprietary subject of the assurance. Lord Neuberger opined that:

It would represent a regrettable and substantial emasculation of the beneficial principle of proprietary estoppel if it were to be artificially fettered so as to require the precise extent of the subject of the alleged estoppel to be strictly defined in every case... focusing on technicalities can lead to a degree of strictness—inconsistent with the fundamental aims of equity.[397]

His Lordship was responding, in part, to the contention in the earlier speech of Lord Scott in *Yeoman's Row v Cobbe*[398] which suggested that a contractual level of certainty as to assets identified was required in estoppel claims.

(vi) Assurance relating to a grant of future rights

An estoppel equity can arise when an assurance is made concerning the future grant of rights in specific property. This will most commonly occur where an owner had made assurances that he will leave property to the claimant in his will. For example, an estoppel equity was established in *Wayling v Jones*,[399] where the owner of a hotel

---

[392] [1986] 2 FLR 227.   [393] [1986] 2 FLR 227, at 238–239.   [394] [1986] 1 WLR 1498.
[395] Ibid., at 1510.   [396] [2009] UKHL 18.   [397] Ibid., at [98].   [398] [2008] UKHL 55.
[399] (1993) 69 P & CR 170. See also *Gillett v Holt* [1998] 3 All ER 917, where it was held that an assurance that the defendant would leave his estate to the plaintiff was capable of founding an entitlement by way of

had promised his partner that he would leave it to him by will on his death. *Thorner v Major and Others*[400] is another example.

However, in *Taylor v Dickens*[401] it was held that there was no claim by way of proprietary estoppel where an elderly lady had said that she would leave her estate to her gardener, but changed her mind without telling him after he had stopped charging her for his help. Judge Weeks, QC held that, in light of the inherent revocability of testamentary dispositions, such an assurance would only give rise to an estoppel equity if it created or encouraged the claimant to believe that the owner would not exercise her right to change her will. This decision was subjected to severe academic criticism,[402] which was accepted by the Court of Appeal in *Gillett v Holt*.[403] In this case Gillett had worked for Holt, who was a gentleman farmer, for nearly forty years. On seven separate occasions Holt had assured him that he would leave his entire estate to him, and that he and his family could therefore be sure of a secure future. Robert Walker LJ explained that these assurances were sufficient to give rise to an estoppel equity, even though they did not include an explicit assurance that the owner would not alter his will:

> But the inherent revocability of testamentary dispositions (even if well understood by the parties, as Mr Gillett candidly accepted that it was by him) is irrelevant to a promise or assurance that 'all this will be yours'... Even when the promise of assurance is in terms linked to the making of a will...the circumstances may make clear that the assurance is more than a mere statement of present (revocable) intention, and is tantamount to a promise.[404]

(vii) Assurance not required to have been intended to be acted upon

It is not necessary for the party making the assurance to intend that the assurance be acted upon. This was confirmed by Lord Scott in *Thorner v Major*:

> If it is reasonable for a representee to whom representations have been made to take the representations at their face value and rely on them, it would not in general be open to the representor to say that he or she had not intended the representee to rely on them.[405]

(viii) Resolving ambiguity in an assurance

It has been noted that an assurance must be sufficiently clear and relate to specific assets. Nevertheless, as the House of Lords indicated in *Thorner v Major and others*,[406] the requirement of clarity must not be used to defeat otherwise meritorious claims.

---

proprietary estoppel. However, in the event Carnwath J held that a claim failed because the defendant had only expressed a mere intention to leave his estate by will to the plaintiff and not an irrevocable promise that he would inherit regardless of any changes in circumstances.

[400] [2009] UKHL 18.   [401] [1998] 3 FCR 455.

[402] Thompson 'Emasculating Estoppel' [1998] Conv 220; Swadling 'Case Note on *Taylor v Dickens*' [1998] RLR 455.

[403] [2000] 2 All ER 289.

[404] Ibid., at 304. Pawlowski and Brown argue that an estoppel equity would also arise where a testator promises to create a secret trust and then subsequently changes his will so that the property is not left to the secret trustee: 'Constituting a Secret Trust by Estoppel' [2004] Conv 388.

[405] [2009] UKHL 18, at [17].   [406] [2009] UKHL 18.

Lord Neuberger, exploring this issue in detail,[407] opined that any assurance needs to be adjudged according to three separate (though related) criteria: (i) in context;[407a] (ii) without rigidity;[408] and (iii) that any ambiguity, such as where the assurance has more than one possible meaning, should be taken into account in quantifying the estoppel interest, rather than to negative the assurance.

(ix) Assurances and common intention

It has already been seen that the courts have at times confused the devices of the common intention constructive trust and proprietary estoppel, despite their clear differences. One of the reasons is that there is significant overlap between the requirements necessary to demonstrate an express common intention to acquire an interest by means of a constructive trust and a representation or assurance to found a claim through proprietary estoppel. Neither requires a contractual style of agreement in the family homes context and both require that the understanding or assurance relates to a right in particular property. An important distinction is that in proprietary estoppel the courts are focusing on finding an assurance or representation by the representor; in the constructive trusts context the courts are supposedly seeking the common intention of the parties. That distinction may be narrower than appears at first blush since analysis of the case law on common intention suggests that the courts are in fact concerned only with a representation from the legal owner which the claimant relies upon, and since *Stack v Dowden*,[409] not even this. It would be rare for circumstances which give rise to the finding of an express common intention to not also give rise to an assurance in proprietary estoppel.[410]

(d) 'Reliance'[411]

(i) Requirement of reliance

An essential element of proprietary estoppel is that the claimant must have acted in reliance upon the assurance in relation to which the claim is being made. It is not unconscionable to make an assurance if it is not acted upon.

(ii) 'Reliance' as a causal connection

Reliance connects the assurance with the detriment. It demonstrates that the assurance caused the claimant to act to his detriment. As Balcombe LJ stated in *Wayling v Jones*:

> There must be a sufficient link between the promises relied upon and the conduct which constitutes the detriment.[412]

---

407 Ibid., at [84]–[86].

407a See *Cook v Thomas* [2010] EWCA Civ 227 at [99].

408 Ibid., at [85]: 'The court should not search for ambiguity or uncertainty, but should assess the question of clarity and certainty practically and sensibly, as well as contextually.'

409 [2007] 2 AC 432.

410 Dixon 'Invalid Contracts, Estoppel and Constructive Trusts' [2005] Conv 247.

411 See further Robertson 'The Reliance Basis of Proprietary Estoppel Remedies' [2008] Conv 295.

412 (1993) 69 P & CR 170, at 173. See also *Eves v Eves* [1975] 1 WLR 1338, at 1345, per Brightman J; *Grant v Edwards* [1986] Ch 638, at 648–649, 655–657, 656, per Nourse LJ and per Browne-Wilkinson V-C; *Gillett v Holt* [2000] 2 All ER 289, 306.

(iii) Burden of proving reliance

In order to establish an estoppel equity a claimant must demonstrate[413] not merely that an assurance was made by the legal owner of land, but also that he relied upon the assurance made. In *A-G of Hong Kong v Humphreys Estate (Queen's Gardens) Ltd*[414] the Privy Council stated that it was necessary for the claimants to 'show' that they had relied on an expectation that had been encouraged by the landowner. In *Lim Teng Huan v Ang Swee Chuan*[415] the Privy Council held that the requisite reliance could be established by an 'inevitable'[416] inference drawn from the facts. In *Wayling v Jones* Balcombe LJ held:

> Once it has been established that promises were made, and that there has been conduct by the plaintiff of such a nature that inducement may be inferred then the burden of proof shifts to the defendant to establish that he did not rely on the promises.[417]

(iv) Establishing reliance

A claimant will thus fail to establish an estoppel equity if it can be shown that he acted as he did for reasons other than the assurance. In *Coombes v Smith*[418] Mrs Coombes had an unhappy marriage and fell in love with Mr Smith. He bought a house where it was intended they should live together. She became pregnant by him, and moved into the house. Mr Smith never moved in with her, but visited regularly. The house was sold and another purchased, which Mrs Coombes decorated. After their relationship had broken down, Mrs Coombes claimed an interest in the house by way of proprietary estoppel. Jonathon Parker, QC held that even if an assurance had been made, Mrs Coombes had not acted in reliance on it. As to her becoming pregnant, he considered:

> it would be wholly unreal, to put it mildly, to find on the evidence adduced before me that the plaintiff allowed herself to become pregnant by the defendant in reliance on some mistaken belief as to her legal rights. She allowed herself to become pregnant because she wished to live with the defendant and bear his child.[419]

Likewise, leaving her husband was not because of any assurance that Mr Smith had made but because 'she preferred to have a relationship with...the defendant rather than continuing to live with her husband...There is no evidence that she left her husband in reliance on the defendant's assurance that he would provide for her if and when their relationship came to an end.' Even the decorating she carried out failed to demonstrate reliance, since it was done 'by the plaintiff as occupier of the property, as the defendant's mistress, and as [the child's] mother, in the context of a continuing relationship with the defendant...'[420]

---

[413] See *Greasley v Cooke* [1980] 1 WLR 1306, where Lord Denning MR considered that there is a presumption of reliance once a representation has been established.

[414] [1987] AC 114.   [415] [1992] 1 WLR 113.   [416] Ibid., at 118.

[417] (1993) 69 P & CR 170, at 173.   [418] [1986] 1 WLR 808.

[419] Ibid., at 820.

[420] Compare the House of Lords' views of the wife's activities in *Lloyds Bank plc v Rosset* [1991] 1 AC 107. For similar reasoning, see also *Stilwell v Simpson* (1983) 133 NLJ 894; *Layton v Martin* [1986] 2 FLR 227.

However, it may be that *Coombes v Smith* adopts an unduly restrictive approach to the concept of reliance and an over-optimistic confidence in the ability of the court to determine the true rationale for the claimant's actions. Motives are invariably mixed rather than pure, and it would not be unreasonable to suggest that Mrs Coombes' actions were at least partially influenced by the assurances she had received from her lover. Only with the promise of security was she prepared to continue her relationship and have a child. Subsequent cases have tended to take a more generous attitude towards questions of reliance. In *Matharu v Matharu*[421] a wife returned to live with her husband on the mistaken basis that the matrimonial home was as much hers as his. She later discovered that it was in fact owned by his father. She subsequently acted to her detriment by installing a new kitchen. The Court of Appeal held that this indicated that she had acted in reliance upon an assurance by her father-in-law, through his conduct, that he would abstain from asserting his legal rights to the house, even though the expenditure had been incurred after she was aware of her mistaken assumption as to the ownership of the property.

Similarly, in *Wayling v Jones*[422] the plaintiff and deceased defendant had cohabited in a homosexual relationship. The defendant ran a hotel business in which he was helped by the plaintiff, who acted as his companion and chauffeur in return for pocket money and the promise that the defendant would leave the business to him on his death. When the defendant died he had left the plaintiff only a motor car valued at £375. The Court of Appeal held that sufficient reliance was demonstrated and could be established by inference from the plaintiff's conduct. Balcombe LJ stated the principle:

The promises relied upon do not have to be the sole inducement for the conduct: it is sufficient if they are an inducement.[423]

Nevertheless, in *James v Thomas*,[424] the reasoning is as restrictive as in *Coombes*. Peter Thomas had acquired a cottage, previously owned by his parents, by buying out the shares of his brother and sister in 1986. In 1989, he developed a relationship with Sharon James, and she moved to live with him. Sharon worked without pay in Peter's business. She also helped with the manual work involved in carrying out improvements. Peter told Sharon that these actions 'will benefit us both' and he told her he would ensure that she was provided for if he died. The relationship broke down in 2005 and Sharon claimed an interest in the cottage. It was argued that the defendant had created an expectation that the claimant would acquire a proprietary interest in property, on which the claimant had acted to her detriment. Sir John Chadwick, in the Court of Appeal, held that the trial judge was correct to form the conclusion that Peter had not given any assurance that Sharon would acquire an interest in the cottage. He added:

for completeness, I should add that the factors which lead to the conclusion that the assurances were not intended or understood as a promise of some property interest lead, also, to the conclusion that it would be unreal to think that Miss James did what she did in reliance on

---

[421] (1994) 68 P & CR 93.

[422] Ibid.; Cooke 'Reliance and Estoppel' (1995) 111 LQR 389; Davis 'Estoppel—Reliance and Remedy' [1995] Conv 409.

[423] (1995) 69 P & CR 170, at 173.   [424] [2007] EWCA Civ 1212.

such a promise. The true position, as it seems to me, is that she worked in the business, and contributed her labour to the improvements to the property, because she and Mr Thomas were making their life together as man and wife. The Cottage was their home: the business was their livelihood. It is a mistake to think that the motives which lead parties in such a relationship to act as they do are necessarily attributable to pecuniary self-interest.[425]

Whether there has been reliance will therefore be very much a question of fact in every case, and it is relatively easy to find apparent inconsistencies in the approach of individual members of the judiciary.

(v) Reasonableness of reliance

The reliance on the assurance must be reasonable and not be so far divorced from the assurance or expectation given as to render it irrelevant. Nevertheless, whether a reliance is reasonable must be considered on a holistic appraisal of all the facts, not just those known at the time of the reliance:

Past events provide context and background for the interpretation of subsequent events and subsequent events throw retrospective light upon the meaning of past events. The owl of Minerva spreads its wings only with the falling of dusk. The finding was that [the appellant] reasonably relied upon the assurance from 1990, even if it required later events to confirm that it was reasonable for him to have done so.[426]

(e) 'Detriment or change of position'

(i) Assurance and reliance insufficient without detriment or change of position

An estoppel equity calling for a remedy will only be established if a claimant can show that he acted to his detriment in reliance upon the assurance that was made. This final element of detriment renders it 'unconscionable' for the legal owner to assert his strict rights.[427] If the owner had created an expectation on the part of the claimant, but the claimant had done nothing in response, there would be no reason why he should not be entitled to assert his rights. Rights over land are not created by mere representations, which do not amount to either a contract or a declaration of trust.[428]

(ii) Detriment and change of position

The courts have tended to express the requirement of detriment in terms of 'change of position'[429] and to highlight that 'the categories of detriment [are] not closed'.[430] In *Gillett v Holt* Robert Walker LJ summarized what detriment requires:

The overwhelming weight of authority shows that detriment is required. But the authorities also show that it is not a narrow or technical concept. The detriment need not consist of the

---

[425] Ibid., at [36].　　[426] *Thorner v Major* [2009] UKHL 18, *at* [8] per Lord Hoffmann.

[427] See *Grundt v Great Boulder Pty Gold Mine Ltd* (1937) 59 CLR 641.

[428] It will be remembered that in the case of a declaration of a trust of land there is a need for evidence in writing under s 53(1)(b) of the Law of Property Act 1925. A contract for the creation of an interest in land must be made in writing in accordance with s 1 of the Law of Property (Miscellaneous Provisions) Act 1989.

[429] See *ER Ives Investment Ltd v High* [1967] 2 QB 379, CA; *Bhimji v Salih* (4 February 1981, unreported), CA; In *Re Basham (Decd)* [1986] 1 WLR 1498, at 1504, *Lloyds Bank v Rosset* [1991] AC 107, at 132.

[430] *Watts v Storey* (1983) 134 NLJ 631.

expenditure of money or other quantifiable financial detriment as long as it is something substantial. The requirement must be approached as part of a broad inquiry as to whether repudiation of an assurance is or is not unconscionable in all the circumstances.[431]

This detriment must therefore be considered together with the question of unconscionability, such that a change of position will only be sufficiently substantial if it means it would be unjust or inequitable to withdraw the assurance or expectation. This has been criticized by Wells, on the basis that it is destroying existing categories and principles of detriment and thereby creating uncertainty.[432] Nevertheless, Robert Walker LJ's words have been affirmed directly in *Campbell v Grifffin*[433] and *Parker v Parker*[434] and tacitly by the House of Lords in their most recent decision in *Thorner v Major.*[435]

The cases have found that a wide range of conduct is sufficient 'detriment' to give rise to an equity. It is also worth noting that the requirement of change of position is similar to the level of detriment required to give effect to an express common intention to found an interest by means of a constructive trust,[436] but, as will be seen, the range of factors which may be taken into account in demonstrating change of position are wider, as they do not have to relate directly to the purchase of the family home.

(iii) Improvement of the legal owner's land

Sufficient detriment will be demonstrated if the claimant had expended money improving the land in respect of which an assurance was given.[437] For example, in *Inwards v Baker*[438] it was a held that a son had acted to his detriment by building a bungalow on his father's land in reliance on an assurance he had received. In *Pascoe v Turner*[439] an equity was raised where the claimant had spent money on redecoration, improvements, and repairs to a house that was owned by her former lover, while he passively assured by his acquiescence that she had an interest in the house. In *Matharu v Matharu*[440] it was held that a wife had acted to her detriment when she installed a new kitchen in a house owned by her father-in-law in reliance upon an assurance that it belonged to her husband and that she would have an interest in it. In *Gillett v Holt*[441] one of the ways in which the claimant had acted to his detriment was by incurring substantial expenditure improving the farmhouse he occupied. In *Thompson v Foy,*[442] the claimant had acted to her detriment by building and paying for an extension to the family home.

(iv) Improvement of the claimant's own land

A claimant will also be held to have acted to his detriment if he improved his own land in reliance upon an assurance that he is to enjoy a right over the land of the

---

[431] [2000] 2 All ER 289, at 308.
[432] 'The Element of Detriment in Proprietary Estoppel' [2001] Conv 13.
[433] [2001] WTLR 981   [434] [2003] EWHC 1846.   [435] [2009] UKHL 18.
[436] [1970] AC 777.   [437] See *Voyce v Voyce* (1991) 62 P & CR 290, CA.
[438] [1965] 2 QB 29.   [439] [1979] 1 WLR 431.   [440] (1994) 68 P & CR 93.
[441] [2000] 2 All ER 289, at 309–310.   [442] [2009] EWHC 1076 (Ch).

legal owner. In *Rochdale Canal Co v King*[443] a mill owner built a mill on his own land after having applied to the canal company to take water from the canal to operate his steam engines. The company did not refuse the application and pipes were laid in the presence of their engineers. The court held that, due to their acquiescence, they were not entitled to an injunction restraining the mill owner from drawing water from the canal.[444]

(v) Acquisition of new land by the claimant

In *Salvation Army Trustees Co Ltd v West Yorkshire Metropolitan County Council*[445] the council informed the Salvation Army that the site of their hall would be required for a proposed road-widening scheme. Although there was no contract for the sale of the hall to the council, the Salvation Army acquired a new site and built a new hall. The council subsequently informed them that the proposed scheme would not be adopted for some years and that they would not therefore be acquiring the old site. Woolf J held that the Salvation Army was entitled to a claim on the basis of proprietary estoppel. He held that the principle of proprietary estoppel was:

capable of extending to the disposal of an interest in land where that disposal is closely linked by an arrangement that also involves the acquiring of an interest in land.[446]

(vi) Working without adequate remuneration

In *Wayling v Jones*[447] it was held that an estoppel equity was established where the claimant had helped his homosexual partner to run a cafe and hotel in reliance upon the assurance that it would be left to him by will. The fact that he received 'little more than pocket money' as remuneration for his work was sufficient to constitute the necessary element of detriment. Similarly, in *Thorner v Major and others*[448] the House of Lords held that the claimant had acted to his detriment by doing substantial farm work for thirty years without pay, for most of that time in reliance on an assurance that he would inherit the farm. Along similar lines, giving up a job and moving to a new area has been held to be a sufficient change of position.[449]

(vii) Personal disadvantage

A claim may arise by way of proprietary estoppel even if the claimant did not act to his detriment financially by incurring the expenditure of money. In a number of cases purely personal disadvantage, such as being 'deprived...of the opportunity of a better life elsewhere',[449a] has been held sufficient to give rise to an equity. A classic example is

---

[443] (1853) 16 Beav 630.   [444] See also *Cotching v Bassett* (1862) 32 Beav 101.
[445] (1980) 41 P & CR 179.   [446] Ibid., at 192.
[447] (1993) 69 P & CR 170. See also *Gillett v Holt* [1998] 3 All ER 917, where Carnwath J accepted that a 'lower salary than would otherwise have been appropriate would have been sufficient detriment to establish a claim by way of proprietary estoppel'. However, there was no evidence to prove that the plaintiff had received a lower salary and the claim therefore failed.
[448] [2009] UKHL 18
[449] See *Jones v Jones* [1977] 1 WLR 438.   [449a] *Henry v Henry* [2010] UKPC 3 at [61].

Greasley v Cooke.[450] Doris Cooke moved into the house of Arthur Greasley as a maid-servant in 1938. She lived with one of his sons, Kenneth from 1946. Throughout that time she looked after the son and his mentally disabled sister, Clarice. When Kenneth died in 1975 the members of the family who had inherited the house asked her to leave. The trial judge found that she 'reasonably believed and was encouraged by members of the family to believe that she could regard the property as her home for the rest of her life', but held that she had not acted to her detriment. The Court of Appeal allowed her appeal. Lord Denning MR stated that it was not necessary that the change of position take the form of expenditure of money. He held that:

It is sufficient if the party, to whom the assurance is given, acts on the faith of it in such circumstances that it would be unjust and inequitable for the party making the assurance to go back on it.[451]

The importance of cumulative detriment was emphasized in *In Re Basham (decd)*,[452] in which acts such as refraining from taking a job outside the area, paying legal expenses for boundary disputes, and spending time and money on the upkeep of the property, while individually not particularly significant, collectively demonstrated acts beyond 'normal love and affection' that supported a finding of detrimental reliance as the claimants had 'subordinated their own interests to the wishes of the deceased'.[453] Similar evidence of personal detriment was approved to support financial detriment by the Court of Appeal in *Gillett v Holt*,[454] including the claimant and his wife performing tasks beyond the normal scope of an employee's duties and subordinating their wishes to those of Holt, such as the decision as to the school their son would attend.

The most important comments regarding the relevance of non-monetary detriment were made by Browne-Wilkinson V-C in *Grant v Edwards*.[455] The case concerned a common intention constructive trust[456] but he considered that 'useful guidance may … be obtained from the principles underlying the law of proprietary estoppel'. On the question of detriment he stated:

In many cases of the present sort, it is impossible to say whether or not the claimant would have done the acts relied on as a detriment even if she thought she had no interest in the house. Setting up house together, having a baby, making payments to general housekeeping expenses (not strictly necessary to enable the mortgage to be paid) may all be referable to the mutual love and affection of the parties and not specifically referable to the claimant's belief that she has an interest in the house. As at present advised, once it has been shown that there was a common intention that the claimant should have an interest in the house, any act done by her to her detriment relating to the joint lives of the parties is, in my judgment, sufficient detriment to qualify.[457]

---

450 [1980] 1 WLR 1306.
451 Ibid., at 1311.   452 [1986] 1 WLR 1498.
453 [1970] AC 777.   454 [2000] 2 All ER 289, at 309–310.
455 [1986] Ch 638; Hayton 'Equity and the Quasi-Matrimonial Home'[1986] CLJ 394; Warburton 'Interested or Not?' [1986] Conv 291.
456 See Chapter 10.
457 [1986] Ch 638, at 657.

Applying the test of 'any act done by her relating to the joint lives of the parties' to proprietary estoppel claims,[458] a whole range of non-monetary detriment would be sufficient to raise an equity.

However, as has been noted above, some cases have taken a much narrower attitude towards non-monetary detriment. In particular, in *Coombes v Smith*[459] Jonathon Parker, QC held that a woman who had left her husband to live with her lover, became pregnant by him, gave birth to their child, and looked after the shared property and their daughter had not 'acted to her detriment' in reliance on an assurance that she was entitled to an interest in the house. As has been discussed above, this may be because these acts could not be seen as performed 'in reliance' on an assurance, rather than because they were not detrimental per se.[460]

(viii) Weighing detriment against any benefits derived

It appears that the court should weigh any detriment that the claimant has suffered against any benefit that he has received.[460a] In *Watts v Storey*[461] the claimant was persuaded by his grandmother to give up a tenancy of a house in Leeds and move into her home, Apple House, in Nottinghamshire, following her move to the Isle of White. He gave up his prospects of finding employment in Leeds. Although the Court of Appeal found that there was an assurance that Apple House would be left to him by will, it held that there was insufficient detriment to found a claim by way of proprietary estoppel:

> when the benefits derived by him from his rent-free occupation...are set against any detriments suffered by him as a result of making the move from his Rent Act protected flat in Leeds, he has not on balance suffered any detriment in financial or material terms.

(2) Quantification: satisfying the equity

(a) A range of remedial responses

(i) Court must identify the appropriate remedy

Once a claimant has established an estoppel equity by demonstrating the elements of assurance, reliance, and detriment, the question arises as to his remedial entitlement. The mere fact that he has established an equity does not entitle him to any particular remedy, or even to a remedy at all. It is for the court to determine, in its discretion, whether the estoppel equity requires the award of a remedy, and if so the type

---

[458] Although Browne-Wilkinson J did not rest his judgment on the analogy between common intention constructive trusts and proprietary estoppel because the point had not been fully argued.

[459] [1986] 1 WLR 808.

[460] In the Australian case *W v G* [1996] 20 Fam LR 49, the NSW Supreme Court held that a lesbian partner had acted to her detriment where she had agree to have a child by way of artificial insemination on the basis of an assurance that her partner would assist in the upbringing of the child. The court did not, however, find that having a child per se was a detriment: see Bailey-Harris 'Equity Still Childbearing in Australia?' (1997) 113 LQR 227.

[460a] See *Henry v Henry* [2010] UKPC 3 at [59].

[461] (1983) 134 NLJ 631.

of remedy that would be appropriate to achieve justice between the parties. This process of determining the appropriate remedial response is described as 'satisfying the equity'. This terminology is long established, as in *Plimmer v Wellington Corpn* the Privy Council stated that:

the court must look at the circumstances in each case to decide in what way the equity can be satisfied.[462]

Where an estoppel equity has been established, the courts have awarded a wide range of remedies in satisfaction. The process and criteria by which the court determines the appropriate remedy will be examined below, but this emphasises that the creation of any right is by court order. The right granted may be lesser or greater than the parties expected or might have wished.

(ii) Transfer of the legal ownership of land

The most powerful remedy by which the court may satisfy an estoppel equity is to order the legal owner to transfer his land to the claimant. In *Dillwyn v Llewelyn*[463] and *Pascoe v Turner*[464] the legal owner was ordered to convey the fee simple in his house to the claimant.[465] In *Gillett v Holt*[466] the court ordered Holt to transfer the freehold of the farm they occupied to the claimant in part satisfaction of his estoppel interest. The court may also be able to award a conditional or determinable fee simple, specifying the conditions on which the right will come to an end. In *Williams v Staite*[467] Goff LJ stated that:

the court . . . might hold in any proper case, that the equity is in its nature for a limited period only or determinable upon a condition certain. In such a case the courts must then see whether, in the events which have happened, it has determined or it has expired or been determined by the happening of that condition.[468]

More recently, Lewison J in *Thompson v Foy*,[469] emphasized that the satisfaction of an equity was a remedy for the courts,[470] and therefore granted ownership of an extension built by Mrs Foy, rather than a licence to occupy it, which, it was argued by Mrs Foy's mother, was the minimum equity to do justice between the parties. This was in line with what his Lordship considered the underlying expectation between the parties.

(iii) Transfer of an undivided share in the land

Where land is held on trust the court may order one joint tenant to transfer his undivided share in the land to another in satisfaction of an estoppel equity. In *Lim Teng*

---

[462] (1883–84) LR 9 App Cas 699, at 714.   [463] (1862) 4 De GF & J 517.
[464] [1979] 1 WLR 431.
[465] See also *Thomas v Thomas* [1956] NZLR 785; *Cameron v Murdoch* [1983] WAR 321; *Riches v Hogben* [1986] 1 Qd R 315; *Re Basham (Decd)* [1987] 1 All ER 405; *Voyce v Voyce* (1991) 62 P & CR 290, CA; *Durant v Heritage and Hamilton* [1994] NPC 117; *Walton v Walton* (20 July 1994, unreported), Ch Div.
[466] [2001] Ch 210.   [467] [1979] Ch 291.   [468] Ibid., at 300.
[469] [2009] EWHC 1076 (Ch).
[470] *Thompson v Foy* [2009] EWHC 1076 (Ch), at [96].

Huan v Ang Swee Chuan[471] the plaintiff and the defendant were the equitable joint tenants of land in Brunei. The defendant built a house on the land believing (wrongly) that a contract had been entered between himself and the plaintiff. The Privy Council held that the plaintiff was therefore estopped from claiming his title to the land, and that the land should belong outright to the defendant, subject to him paying compensation for the value of the land.

(iv) Grant of a lease

In some cases the court has awarded a leasehold estate in satisfaction of proprietary estoppel, as for example in *Siew Soon Wah v Yong Tong Hong*.[472] In *Grant v Williams*[473] a daughter who had lived for most of her life in her mother's house and had cared for her and incurred expenditure improving the property on the basis of a representation that she would be entitled to live in it for the rest of her life was granted a long lease at a nominal rent, determinable on death, in satisfaction of her estoppel equity. In *Yaxley v Gotts*[474] the Court of Appeal upheld the grant of a long lease in satisfaction of an estoppel equity where a builder had refurbished and converted a house into flats in reliance upon an assurance from the owner that he would thereby acquire the ground floor flats.

(v) Right of occupancy

In the majority of cases the courts have stopped short of awarding a claimant full ownership of the property and have granted some form of a right of occupancy. For example, in *Greasley v Cooke*,[475] the Court of Appeal held that the claimant should be entitled to remain in the house rent free for as long as she wished. Similarly, in *Inwards v Baker*[476] the son, who had built his bungalow on his father's land, was held entitled to remain there as long as he wanted. In *Matharu v Matharu*[477] the Court of Appeal held that a claimant was entitled to 'a licence...to remain in this house for her life or such shorter period as she may decide'.[478] Such rights of occupation virtually amount to the grant of a 'life interest'. Prior to the introduction of trusts of land under the Trusts of Land and Appointment of Trustees Act 1996, such a right would have tended to create a strict settlement under the provisions of the Settled Land Act 1925.[479] The grant of a lease in *Griffiths v Williams*[480] was a means of avoiding the unsatisfactory consequences of a strict settlement.[481] With the introduction of the trust of land, the courts may become more willing to utilize the equitable life interest as a means of satisfaction of an estoppel equity. Unlike the Irish courts, the English courts have not recognized rights of residence not conferring exclusive possession as proprietary interests in land.

---

[471] [1992] 1 WLR 113. [472] [1973] AC 836. [473] (1977) 248 Estates Gazette 947.
[474] [2000] 1 All ER 711. [475] [1980] 1 WLR 1306. [476] [1965] 2 QB 29.
[477] (1994) 68 P & CR 93. [478] Ibid., at 103.
[479] See *Dodsworth v Dodsworth* (1973) 228 Estates Gazette 1115; *Ungurian v Lesnoff* [1990] Ch 206; *Costello v Costello* (1994) 70 P & CR 297.
[480] (1977) 248 Estates Gazette 947.
[481] See Jackson, Stevens, and Pearce, *Land Law* (4th edn, 2008), pp 695–696.

(vi) Financial compensation

In some other cases, the courts have awarded a claimant only financial reimbursement in satisfaction of his estoppel equity. In *Dodsworth v Dodsworth*[482] the legal owner of a bungalow allowed the claimants, her brother and his wife, to live in it on their return from Australia. They spent £700 on improvements in the expectation that they would be able to remain in the bungalow as long as they wished. After a breakdown in the relationship between the parties, the Court of Appeal held that the claimants were not entitled to occupy rent-free for life, but were entitled to be repaid their outlay on improvements. The court may award the claimant a lien or a charge over the property to the value of the improvements made.[483] In *Wayling v Jones*[484] the Court of Appeal held that the claimant should be entitled to recover the proceeds of sale of the hotel that his partner had promised to leave him by will. In *Jennings v Rice*[485] the Court of Appeal held that a gardener who had acted to his detriment by looking after an elderly lady in reliance upon her assurance that she would 'see to it' that he would be alright in her will should receive £200,000 from her estate.

(vii) Grant of easement

Where appropriate, the courts have held that a claimant is entitled to the grant of an easement over the land of the person estopped, as, for example, in *ER Ives Investment Ltd v High*[486] and *Crabb v Arun District Council*.[487] The loss of an easement is also possible, as in *Lester v Woodgate*.[487a]

(viii) Composite remedy

On occasion, the court has awarded a composite remedy combining. For example, in *Re Sharpe (a bankrupt)*[488] Dorothy Johnson moved into a house, with her nephew Thomas Sharpe, which had been purchased in his name. She provided £12,000 of the purchase price of £17,000 by way of a loan to him. Browne-Wilkinson J held that since the payment was made by way of loan, there was no possibility of a resulting trust, but that she was entitled to an interest under the principles of proprietary estoppel. He held that she should have the right to live in the house until her loan was repaid.[489] As has been seen, in *Gillett v Holt*[490] the Court of Appeal awarded the claimant the freehold of the farm he occupied. In addition he was also awarded a sum of £100,000 to compensate him for his exclusion from the rest of the farming business carried on by Holt.

---

[482] (1973) 228 Estates Gazette 1115.

[483] *Unity Joint Stock Mutual Banking Association v King* (1858) 25 Beav 72; *Taylor v Taylor* [1956] NZLR 99.

[484] (1995) 69 P & CR 170.　　[485] 2002 WL 45443, [2002] NPC 28.　　[486] [1967] 2 QB 379, CA.

[487] [1976] Ch 179, CA.　　[487a] [2010] EWCA Civ 199 (acquiescence in blocking of right of way).

[488] [1980] 1 WLR 219.

[489] See also *Dodsworth v Dodsworth* (1973) 228 Estates Gazette 1115, CA; *Stratulatos v Stratulatos* [1988] 2 NZLR 424.

[490] [2001] Ch 210.

(ix) Imposition of a constructive trust

Although the courts have not yet awarded an interest by way of a constructive trust in satisfaction of an estoppel equity, there appears to be no reason in principle why this would not be possible. The effect would be similar to an order to transfer the legal ownership of land, in that the claimant would receive an ownership interest in the property, only in the form of a share of the beneficial ownership behind a trust of land. There are indications in dicta that a constructive trust may be awarded as a remedy. Originally, these came from Lord Denning MR in *Hussey v Palmer*,[491] in which his Lordship suggested his now discredited new model constructive trust.[492] However, in *Re Basham (Decd)*[493] Edward Nugee, QC also took the view that a constructive trust was an appropriate remedy for cases of proprietary estoppel:

> The plaintiff relies on proprietary estoppel, the principle of which, in its broadest form, may be stated as follows: where one person, A, has acted to his detriment on the faith of a belief, which was known to and encouraged by another person, B, that he either has or is going to be given a right in or over B's property, B cannot insist on his strict legal rights if to do so would be inconsistent with A's belief... But in my judgment at all events where the belief is that A is going to be given a right in the future, it is properly to be regarded as giving rise to a species of constructive trust...[494]

In *Matharu v Matharu*[495] the first instance judge held that the claimant was entitled to a share of the beneficial ownership of her matrimonial home by way of proprietary estoppel. This could only take effect by means of a trust.

If the court does possess the jurisdiction to award an equitable interest by way of a constructive trust in satisfaction of an estoppel equity, such a constructive trust would be radically different to the 'institutional' common intention constructive trust generated under the principles set out in *Lloyds Bank plc v Rosset*.[496] A constructive trust imposed by the court by way of proprietary estoppel would be akin to the remedial constructive trust adopted in other jurisdictions, since the claimant's equitable interest would only arise at the date of judgment, and not at the date of the assurance, reliance, and detriment.[497] We have already seen that in some recent cases the courts have considered that estoppel and trusts are interchangeable methods of quantifying an interest. Indeed, in the House of Lords' decision in *Thorner v Major and others*,[498] Lord Scott talked in terms of the overlap between constructive trusts and estoppel, and suggested that a set of facts which he agreed gave rise to a proprietary estoppel could also give rise to a 'remedial constructive trust'.[499] Any suggestion that the principles of constructive trusts and proprietary estoppel have melded to create a remedial trust should be treated with extreme caution, as this does not yet reflect the orthodox view.[499a] Lord Scott's preference for circumscribing resulting

---

[491] [1972] 3 All ER 744   [492] See above, at p 320.   [493] [1986] 1 WLR 1498.
[494] Ibid., at 1503–1504.   [495] (1994) 68 P & CR 93.   [496] [1991] 1 AC 107.
[497] If an equitable proprietary interest was created as an automatic consequence of the assurance, reliance and detriment, the constructive trust would similarly arise automatically and would be recognized, rather than created, by the court.
[498] [2009] UKHL 18.
[499] Ibid., at [18].   [499a] See *Cook v Thomas* [2010] EWCA Civ 229 at [105].

trusts and proprietary estoppel in favour of a remedial constructive trust doctrine has yet to receive majority support.

(x) No remedy because the claimant has already received 'full satisfaction'

In some cases it appears that the courts may find that a claimant does not require the award of any remedy at all in order to satisfy an estoppel equity because he has already received advantages which have fully satisfied his claim. In *Sledmore v Dalby*[500] Mr Dalby had lived in a house owned by his parents-in-law since 1965. Initially, he and his wife paid rent, but in 1976 they ceased to do so because his wife became seriously ill. He subsequently substantially improved the property, having been encouraged to do so by Mr and Mrs Sledmore. Following the death of his wife, he continued to live in the house, which was then owned by Mrs Sledmore alone, rent free. In 1990 she gave him notice to quit. At first instance Mr Dalby was held entitled to a non-assignable licence to occupy the house for life on the grounds of proprietary estoppel, but the Court of Appeal held that, although he was entitled to an estoppel equity, it had been fully met. Although he had spent money on the property, he had enjoyed the benefits of that expenditure through more than fifteen years' rent-free occupation. Roch LJ also took account of the parties' respective situations, weighing the fact that Mrs Sledmore was a widow dependent upon benefit, who urgently wanted to sell the house, against the fact that Mr Dalby was employed and currently making minimal use of the house because he enjoyed accommodation elsewhere.

(b) Determining the appropriate remedy[501]

(i) Is the court's discretion narrow or broad?

As is clear from the preceding section, the courts have awarded a wide range of remedies in satisfaction of estoppel equities. The central question is therefore whether there is any coherent principle underlying the process by which the remedy is selected in each case. Two main opposing views have been advocated to explain the function of the court in the determination of the appropriate remedy. The narrow approach considers that the court is simply required to carry into effect the parties' own 'reasonable expectations'. Under this view, the court is left with a highly circumscribed discretion as to the remedy that is appropriate. The flexible approach argues that the court has a wide discretion to decide the appropriate remedy in the circumstances. In *Jennings v Rice*[502] the Court of Appeal considered the merits of these alternatives and concluded that a composite approach should be adopted which would ensure that there was proportionality between the remedy awarded and the detriment experienced.

---

[500]   (1996) 72 P & CR 196; Pawlowski 'Proprietary Estoppel—Satisfying the Equity' (1997) 113 LQR 232.

[501]   See especially Gardner 'The Remedial Discretion in Proprietary Estoppel' (1999) 115 LQR 438; Bright and McFarlane 'Proprietary Estoppel and Property Rights' [2005] 64 CLJ 449.

[502]   2002 WL 45443, [2002] NPC 28.

(ii) Fulfilment of the claimant's 'reasonable expectation'

A number of academics have argued that when the court satisfies an estoppel equity, it invariably selects the remedy which as far as possible fulfils the reasonable expectations of the claimant.[503] It is alleged that this analysis is capable of rationally explaining the apparent conflict in outcome between *Dillwyn v Llewelyn*[504] and *Pascoe v Turner*,[505] where the court ordered the transfer of the fee simple to the claimant, and *Inwards v Baker*[506] and *Williams v Staite*,[507] where only a lesser right of occupancy was awarded. The crucial distinguishing feature is said to be the nature of the claimant's expectation raised by the assurance of the legal owner. In *Pascoe v Turner*[508] the assurance given to Mrs Turner was that 'the house is yours and everything in it'. Therefore, her reasonable expectation was that she owned the house and, having acted to her detriment in reliance on that assurance, the court acted to fulfil her expectation. In contrast, in *Inwards v Baker*[509] the father's representation to his son was simply 'Why not put the bungalow on my land and make the bungalow a little bigger?' Although this amounted to a clear indication that the son would be entitled to remain on the land, it cannot be taken as an assurance that the son would own the land. The award of a right to occupy for as long as he wished therefore fulfilled the reasonable expectation raised by the assurance he received. Similarly, in *Williams v Staite*[510] the representation was merely that 'you can live here as long as you like', and on the basis of such a representation there could be no reasonable expectation of ownership.

(iii) How can financial remedies be explained?

Slightly more difficult to analyse on this 'expectation model' are cases where the claimant was awarded merely monetary compensation for detriment suffered, as for example in *Dodsworth v Dodsworth*.[511] However, in these cases financial compensation seems to operate as a default remedy when the circumstances prevent the fulfilment of the claimant's legitimate expectation. In *Dodsworth*[512] the plaintiff's brother and sister-in-law moved into her bungalow with her on their return from Australia, and spent £700 on improvements in reliance on the assurance by the plaintiff that they would be able to remain in the bungalow as their home for as long as they wished. Obviously, this representation is comparable to that made in *Williams v Staite*[513] and a similar remedy of a right of occupancy would be expected. However, the

---

[503] See (1984) 100 LQR 376 (Moriarty); (1997) 17 LS 258 (Cooke). However, in *Sledmore v Dalby* (1996) 72 P & CR 196, Hoffmann LJ adopted the view that there must be 'proportionality' between the detriment experienced and the remedy awarded, so that the claimant's expectations will not be fulfilled if to do so would be disproportionate to the amount of detriment he had experienced: see (1997) 113 LQR 232 (Pawlowski). See also [1998] Conv 213, where Mark Thompson suggests that there is no need for an expectation to be satisfied in full where an estoppel equity is raised.

[504] (1862) 4 De GF & J 517.   [505] [1979] 1 WLR 431, CA.

[506] [1965] 2 QB 29, CA.   [507] [1979] Ch 291, CA.   [508] [1979] 1 WLR 431, CA.

[509] [1965] 2 QB 29, CA.   [510] [1979] Ch 291, CA.

[511] (1973) 228 Estates Gazette 1115: see also *Taylor v Taylor* [1956] NZLR 99; *Re Sharpe* [1980] 1 WLR 219.

[512] (1973) 228 Estates Gazette 1115.   [513] [1979] Ch 291, CA.

court awarded the defendants only monetary compensation for their improvements. The explanation may well be that it was impossible to fulfil the claimants' reasonable expectation, namely the right to reside in the bungalow with the plaintiff, because the relationship between them had broken down.[514] As Russell LJ observed, the consequence of awarding the defendants a right of occupancy would be that the plaintiff:

would...have to continue sharing her home for the rest of her life with the defendants with whom she was, or thought she was, at loggerheads.

The award of monetary compensation is therefore a default remedy given where a reasonable expectation of shared occupation is no longer a realistic possibility. This analysis is also capable of explaining the award of monetary compensation in *Hussey v Palmer*;[515] *Re Sharpe*;[516] and *Burrows and Burrows v Sharp*.[517] Moriarty summarizes the argument as follows:

The remedies granted [for proprietary estoppel]...are not the product of an unpredictable discretion; but are selected in accordance with well-established principles of English property law. Normally, therefore, a remedy will be chosen which gives the party precisely what he has been led to expect, but occasionally, where joint rights to land have been represented, he may get money instead.[518]

(iv) Criticism of expectation analysis

Although the 'fulfilment of the reasonable expectation' analysis has the attractive merit of certainty, a number of criticisms may be made. First, it ignores a large number of judicial statements that emphasize the court's flexibility in determining the appropriate remedy.[519] Second, it assumes that it is possible to correctly identify the reasonable expectations of the claimant, whereas the reality is often that the assurance, and therefore the derived expectation, are ambiguous. The informal circumstances and terms in which the assurance is given cannot always be taken as sufficiently certain to determine the remedy. To some extent, the court is engaged in the business of rationalizing the claimant's expectation, and an element of discretion is simply built into that process. For example, is it strictly accurate to conclude from the language used by the father in *Inwards v Baker*[520] that the son's expectation was only of a right to remain on the land rather than to own it? The extent of his detriment, building a house, could surely indicate that something more substantial than a right of occupancy was expected. As Lord Westbury LC said in *Dillwyn v Llewelyn*:

---

[514]　See *Thompson v Park* [1944] KB 408.

[515]　[1972] 1 WLR 1286, CA. Although the plaintiff was only claiming monetary compensation, there had been a breakdown of the sharing relationship between the mother-in-law and son-in-law.

[516]　[1980] 1 WLR 219. Although the sharing relationship between aunt and nephew had not broken down, it was the nephew's trustee in bankruptcy who was seeking to evict the aunt.

[517]　[1991] Fam Law 67; [1992] Conv 54.　　[518]　(1984) 100 LQR 376, at 412.

[519]　See *Plimmer v Wellington Corpn* (1883–84) LR 9 App Cas 699; *Crabb v Arun District Council* [1976] Ch 179, CA; *Griffiths v Williams* (1977) 248 Estates Gazette 947; *Denny v Jensen* [1977] 1 NZLR 635; *Greasley v Cooke* [1980] 1 WLR 1306, CA; *Morris v Morris* [1982] 1 NSWLR 61.

[520]　[1965] 2 QB 29.

No one builds a house for his own life only, and it is absurd to suppose that it was intended by either party that the house at the death of the son, should become the property of the father.[521]

The heart of the problem is that, in the informal (and often family) context, the parties rarely formulate precisely the extent of the entitlement being represented, and it is only after the events that the court is called to analyse what has taken place. Determining the claimant's expectation is not therefore an exact science. Moriarty's claim that 'we can get quite some way...towards explaining the court's intuitive choice of remedy by merely paying closer attention to the precise content of the representation'[522] is an overstatement.

(v) Composite approach

In the light of such criticisms the Court of Appeal held in *Jennings v Rice*[523] that a pure 'fulfilment of expectations' approach was not the appropriate means of determining the remedy to satisfy an estoppel equity. The case concerned a gardener who had taken care of an elderly lady without remuneration, relying upon her assurance that she would 'see to it' that he was alright, and her statements to him that her house would 'all be yours one day'. At first instance Judge Weeks held that he was entitled to a claim by way of proprietary estoppel, but that he should receive a sum of £200,000 rather than the freehold of the house and its furniture, which was worth considerably more. On appeal it was argued that he should have been entitled to the house and furniture on the grounds that an estoppel equity should be satisfied by making good the expectation of the claimant. The Court of Appeal held that while the nature of the expectation was a relevant consideration, it did not alone determine the appropriate remedy. The court was rather required to do justice by ensuring that there was proportionality between the remedy and the detriment. The importance of proportionality was emphasized in *Malik v Kalyan*[523a] and *Henry v Henry*.[523b]

(vi) Broad discretion approach

In contrast to the 'expectation' analysis, other academics have argued[524] that the court possesses a broad discretion to select whichever remedy it feels is appropriate in the circumstances of each case. The 'equity' of the claimant arises as a result of the assurance, reliance, and detriment, and that equity remains 'inchoate' until the court determines a remedy to satisfy it. In this sense, the court is acting in a similar way to the courts of other jurisdictions where the remedial constructive trust is recognized.[525] The cause of action is proprietary estoppel, and, if established, the court selects the appropriate remedy.

Dicta in a significant number of cases support the suggestion that the court possesses a wide discretion to determine the appropriate remedy. In *Plimmer v Wellington*

---

[521] (1862) 4 De GF & J 517, at 522. [522] (1984) 100 LQR 376, at 383.
[523] 2002 WL 45443, [2002] NPC 28. [523a] [2010] EWCA Civ 113. [523b] [2010] UKPC 3 at [65].
[524] See Thompson 'Estoppel and Clean Hands' [1986] Conv 406; Dewar 'Licences and Land Law: An Alternative View' (1986) 49 MLR 741.
[525] See Chapter 10.

Corpn[526] Sir Arthur Hobhouse stated that 'the court must look at the circumstances in each case to decide in what way the equity can be satisfied'. In *Crabb v Arun District Council*[527] Lord Denning MR emphasized that in answering the question how an established equity should be satisfied, 'equity is displayed at its most flexible'. He also restated the principle in *Greasley v Cooke*:

The equity having thus been raised…it is for the courts of equity to decide in what way that equity should be satisfied.[528]

Such flexibility was also emphasized in *Griffiths v Williams*,[529] where Goff LJ answered the question 'What is the relief appropriate to satisfy the equity?' in this way:

the…question is one upon which the court has to exercise a discretion. If it finds that there is an equity, then it must determine the nature of it, and then, guided by that nature and exercising discretion in all the circumstances, it has to determine what is the fair order to make between the parties for the protection of the claimant.[530]

The wide discretion of the court was also stressed in New Zealand in *Stratulatos v Stratulatos*,[531] where McGehan J said that 'the range of available remedies should not be cluttered by arbitrary rules'.

(vii) Criticism of discretionary approach

As with any area in which the court possesses a wide remedial discretion, the key criticism has been that of uncertainty.[532] If the remedy is entirely within the choice of the courts, without any defined criteria as to how that choice will be made, it will not be possible to advise accurately on the likely remedy, which could range from a transfer of the fee simple to mere monetary compensation. The courts seem to be aware of the danger of uncertainty, as was indicated by Browne-Wilkinson J in *Re Sharpe*.[533] Having held that the claimant entitled to occupy the property until the loan was repaid, he noted:

I reach this conclusion with some hesitation since I find the present state of the law very confused and difficult to fit in with established equitable principles. I express the hope that in the near future the whole question can receive full consideration in the Court of Appeal, so that, in order to do justice to the many thousands of people who never come into court at all but who wish to know with certainty what their proprietary rights are, the extent to which these irrevocable licences bind third parties may be defined with certainty. Doing justice to the litigant

---

526 (1883–84) LR 9 App Cas 699, at 714.   527 [1976] Ch 179, at 189.
528 [1980] 1 WLR 1306, at 1312.   529 (1977) 248 Estates Gazette 947.
530 See also *Williams v Staite* [1979] Ch 291, at 298, where Goff LJ said: 'In the normal type of case…whether there is an equity and its extent will depend…simply upon the initial conduct said to give rise to the equity, although the court may have to decide how, having regard to supervening circumstances, the equity can best be satisfied.'
531 [1988] 2 NZLR 424.
532 See *Cowcher v Cowcher* [1972] 1 WLR 425, at 430, where Bagnall J said: '[justice] flows from the application of sure and settled principle for proved or admitted facts'; *Taylor v Dickens* [1998] 1 FLR 806; [1998] Conv 210 (Thompson).
533 [1980] 1 WLR 219.

who actually appears in the court by the invention of new principles of law ought not to involve injustice to the other persons who are not litigants before the court but whose rights are fundamentally affected by the new principles.[534]

Such fears of uncertainty also lead the Court of Appeal to reject a purely discretionary approach in *Jennings v Rice*.[535] While it was accepted that equity acts flexibly to do justice by preventing unconscionability, Robert Walker LJ rejected any notion of an unfettered discretion:

It cannot be doubted that in this as in every other area of the law, the court must take a principled approach, and cannot exercise a completely unfettered discretion according to the individual judge's notion of what is fair in any particular case.

(viii) Proportionality between the remedy and the detriment[536]

It has now been recognized that it is a false dichotomy to set the two views explained above against each other as if only one were correct. In *Jennings v Rice*[537] the Court of Appeal has confirmed that elements of both are discernible in the decided cases, so that although the courts articulate a flexibility to determine the appropriate remedy to satisfy an estoppel equity, they do so in a circumspect way that takes account of the claimant's expectations. Robert Walker LJ stated the underlying principle as follows:

once the elements of proprietary estoppel are established an equity arises. The value of that equity will depend upon all the circumstances including the expectation and the detriment. The task of the court is to do justice. The most essential requirement is that there must be proportionality between the expectation and the detriment.[538]

In applying this underlying principle he drew a distinction between a situation where the assurance and reliance related to specific property and had a consensual character falling not far short of an enforceable contract,[539] and a situation where the claimant's expectation was more uncertain and did not focus on any specific property. In cases falling within the first category, he considered that the court should act to fulfil the expectation of the claimant, on the grounds that the 'consensual element of what has happened suggests that the claimant and the benefactor probably regarded the expected benefit and the accepted detriment as being (in a general, imprecise way) equivalent, or at any rate not obviously disproportionate'.[540] He suggested that the situation where an elderly benefactor reaches a clear understanding with the claimant that, if the claimant resides with and cares for the benefactor, the claimant will inherit the benefactor's house, was a typical case where the expectations should be fulfilled. However, in cases falling within the second category, where the expectations are uncertain and do not relate to specific property, he considered that the claimant's

---

[534] Ibid., at 226.   [535] [2003] 1 P & CR 8.
[536] See Bright and McFarlane 'Proprietary Estoppel and Property Rights' [2005] 64 CLJ 449.
[537] [2003] 1 P & CR 8.   [538] Ibid., at [36].
[539] As, for example, in *Yaxley v Gotts* [2000] Ch 162.   [540] [2003] 1 P & CR 8, at [45].

expectations should be regarded as 'no more than a starting point' for the determination of the remedy:

> But if the claimant's expectations are uncertain, or extravagant, or out of all proportion to the detriment which the claimant has suffered, the court can and should recognise that the claimant's equity should be satisfied in another (and generally more limited) way.[541]

In such cases the court must exercise 'a wide judicial discretion'[542] to determine the appropriate remedy. While the claimant's expectations remain relevant, the court must also consider the detriment suffered and exercise its discretion so as to ensure that a disproportionate remedy is not awarded. While unwilling to provide a comprehensive enumeration of the factors relevant to the exercise of the court's discretion, Robert Walker LJ did indicate a number of factors which should be taken into account: the misconduct of the claimant; particularly oppressive conduct on the part of the defendant; the court's recognition that it cannot compel people who have fallen out to live peaceably together; alterations in the benefactor's assets and circumstances; the likely effects of taxation; and (to a limited degree) the other claims (legal or moral) on the benefactor or his or her estate.[543]

Having established the appropriate principles, the Court of Appeal concluded that the first instance judge had exercised his discretion correctly in awarding the claimant £200,000 rather than ownership of the benefactor's house and its furniture. He had been unaware of the extent of her wealth, the actual value of her estate was out of all proportion to what he might reasonably have charged for the services he had provided free, and the nature of the house was such that it was unsuitable for him to reside in on his own.

(ix) Confirmation of the intermediate approach

Other cases also illustrate that the court neither possesses an unbridled discretion, nor determines remedies on a purely mechanistic formula. In *Burrows and Burrows v Sharp*[544] an equity was established when the plaintiff and her family moved in with her grandmother. The relationship broke down and it fell to the court to determine how the equity should be satisfied. The judge at first instance had held that the plaintiff was entitled to continue to reside in the house. The Court of Appeal held that this was unworkable, and instead ordered that the grandmother make financial compensation for the expenditure the plaintiff had incurred. In discussing the appropriate remedy, Dillon LJ emphasized that the court 'had a discretion as to how the equity should be satisfied',[545] and that the appropriate remedy 'had to be decided in the light of the circumstances at the date of the hearing, taking into account, if appropriate, the conduct of the parties up to that date'. As a prime principle he held that it was often appropriate to satisfy the equity by granting the claimant the interest he was intended to have.

---

[541] Ibid., at [50].   [542] Ibid., at [51].   [543] Ibid.
[544] [1991] Fam Law 67.   [545] Citing *Griffiths v Williams* (1977) 248 Estates Gazette 947, CA.

This emphasizes that the claimant's 'reasonable expectation' is the key factor which circumscribes the court's discretion. However, he admitted that in some cases it was not practicable for the court to order that the intention be fulfilled and that in such cases the court must do the best it could. This might mean that 'the way in which an equity should be satisfied might take a wholly different form from what had been intended when the parties were on good terms'. Along with the nature of the claimant's expectations, other factors which should be taken into account in determining the remedy include: the extent of reliance; the relative wealth of the parties; the existence of children; and inequitable conduct by either party.[546]

A similar approach was taken by the Court of Appeal in *Gillett v Holt*.[547] Having concluded that an estoppel equity was established, Robert Walker LJ stated that the 'court must decide what is the most appropriate form for the relief to take'.[548] While this might suggest a broad discretion, he proceeded to undertake a two-stage process to determine appropriate relief. First he identified the extent of the owner's property in respect of which the equity was established. This, it appears, was determined by the expectations that had been generated by the assurances given, namely Holt's farming business. However, having established the maximum extent of the equity he held that the court should determine the 'minimum required to satisfy it and do justice between the parties'.[549] Thus the court does not possess an unbridled discretion, but is required to exercise its discretion to determine an appropriate remedy within the limits of the expectations that have been created by the assurances. In exercising its discretion to determine the minimum required he held that the court should look at all the circumstances, including the need to achieve a 'clean break' between the parties and to avoid or minimize future friction. Another good example is *Parker v Parker*,[550] where the court had to consider the right of Lord Macclesfield to live in Shirburn castle. There had been a representation by the company owning the castle that it would negotiate and agree terms for Lord Macclesfield's occupation of the castle, in reliance on which Lord Macclesfield gave up the tenancy of a farm. By the time of the action, relationships between the parties had broken down to such an extent that the court felt ordering them to live together would have been inadvisable. Instead, they held that Lord Macclesfield was entitled to occupation until given at least two years notice to quit, to allow his Lordship the time necessary, from the evidence, to catalogue and remove his chattels and find alternative accommodation.

(x) The impact of the constructive trust cases

There may be a temptation, to look to the constructive trust cases for illustrations of how the court might exercise its discretion in estoppel cases, and, particularly, to adopt the indicative list of factors proposed by Lady Hale in *Stack v Dowden*.[551] It is suggested that this temptation should be resisted. The exercise being undertaken in

---

[546] Thompson 'Estoppel and Clean Hands' [1986] Conv 406.   [547] [2000] 2 All ER 289.
[548] Ibid., at 311.   [549] Ibid., at 312.   [550] [2003] EWHC 1846.
[551] [2007] 2 AC 432, at [69].

Figure 11.5 Proprietary estoppel

Stack v Dowden was to ascertain the 'common intention' of the parties. In proprietary estoppel, ascertaining the assurance or expectation is only the starting point. A relatively clear and settled practice has arisen in the jurisprudence on proprietary estoppel. If proprietary estoppel and constructive trusts are to merge into a remedial rather than substantive form of constructive trust in the family home, a clear decision of the House of Lords, reversing earlier decisions inconsistent with this premise, will be required.

(3) Bars to a remedy

It follows from the fact that proprietary estoppel is an equitable remedy, based on the conscience of the parties, that there must be no bar in any given case to the claimant seeking to rely on an estoppel to found an interest (see Figure 11.5). Hence, the claimant must 'come with clean hands', so that if the original representation was procured through any falsehood on the part of the claimant, no claim to an interest by estoppel will be supported by the courts.[552] Similarly, unreasonable delay in bringing an action under estoppel may bar a claim to a remedy.[553]

7 Alternative approaches and reform

(1) Alternative judicial approaches

The mechanisms used by equity to deal with the problem of ownership of the family home all have flaws and drawbacks. Is there a better way of approaching this problem? What follows is a brief outline of two of the approaches used in other jurisdictions to determine interests in the family home, and a brief evaluation of them. The treatment is not exhaustive, but provided for comparative purposes to the approach of the English jurisdiction. This section concludes by looking at proposals for legislative reform.

(a) Reversing unjust enrichment

The approach which has been adopted in Canada to resolve disputes about ownership of the family home is the use of a remedial constructive trust to effect restitution through the reversal of unjust enrichment. The principles were stated in *Pettkus v Becker*,[554] where the Supreme Court outlined the three elements that must be satisfied to justify the imposition of a constructive trust:

an enrichment, a corresponding deprivation and absence of any juristic reason for the enrichment.[555]

The court held that a woman who had lived with a man for 14 years and worked with him on his honey farm was entitled to one-half share by way of a constructive trust. This rationale has been accepted and followed by subsequent cases.[556]

(i) An enrichment

This element is satisfied when the legal owner of the land has been benefited (enriched) by the actions of the claimant of a constructive trust. In *Sorochan v Sorochan*[557] Mary and Alex Sorochan lived together as man and wife for forty-two years, jointly working a farm. The Supreme Court held that Alex had been enriched because he had derived a benefit from the appellant's many years of labour in the home and on the farm. This

---

[552] See further Chapter 2, pp 30–31.
[553] See, e.g., *Voyce v Voyce* (1991) 62 P&CR 290, where, on the facts, there was no unreasonable delay.
[554] (1980) 117 DLR (3d) 257.   [555] Ibid., at 274.
[556] See, for example, *Sorochan v Sorochan* (1986) 29 DLR (4th) 1; *Rawluk v Rawluk* (1990) 65 DLR (4th) 161; *Peter v Beblow* (1993) 101 DLR (4th) 621.
[557] (1986) 29 DLR (4th) 1.

enrichment included the valuable savings he had made as a result of having essential farm services and domestic work performed without remuneration.

(ii) A corresponding deprivation

This element is often simply the inverse of the requirement of enrichment. One party has been enriched and as a result the other has been deprived. As Cory J said in *Peter v Beblow*,[558] 'as a general rule, if it is found that the defendant has been enriched by the efforts of the plaintiff there will, almost as a matter of course, be deprivation suffered by the plaintiff'. In that case a woman was held to have been deprived of any compensation for her labour when she had devoted the majority of her time and energy, and some money she earned, towards the benefit of her partner, his children, and his property.

(iii) The absence of any juristic reason for the enrichment

This final element means that the claimant must not have been obliged to provide the services or other activity that constituted an enrichment. This element is closely connected to the concept of 'reasonable expectation'. In *Pettkus v Becker* Dixon J stated:

> I hold that where one person in a relationship tantamount to spousal prejudices herself in the reasonable expectation of receiving an interest in property and the other person in the relationship freely accepts benefits conferred by the first person in circumstances where he knows or ought to have known of that reasonable expectation, it would be unjust to allow the recipient of the benefit to retain it.[559]

The Canadian approach is more willing to look to the reality of the relationship between the parties, and to assess their consequent expectations than the traditional English constructive trust. As Cory J observed in *Peter v Beblow*:

> in today's society it is unreasonable to assume that the presence of love automatically implies a gift of one party's services to another. Nor is it unreasonable for the party providing the domestic labour required to create a home to expect a share in the property of the parties when the relationship is terminated. Women no longer are expected to work exclusively in the home. It must be recognised that when they do so, women forgo outside employment to provide domestic services and child care. The granting of relief in the form of a personal judgment or a property interest to the provider of domestic services should adequately reflect the fact that the income earning capacity and the ability to acquire assets by one party has been enhanced by the unpaid domestic services of the other.[560]

A further aspect of the Canadian approach is that if the three elements are satisfied, thus establishing an unjust enrichment, it is not inevitable that a constructive trust will arise. The court enjoys discretion to decide whether a constructive trust should be imposed, or whether some alternative remedy, for example a monetary entitlement, would be more appropriate.

---

[558] (1993) 101 DLR (4th) 621, at 632.   [559] (1980) 117 DLR (3d) 257, at 274.

[560] (1993) 101 DLR (4th) 621, at 633–634. See also *Single v Macharski Estate* (1996) 107 Man R (2d) 291.

Although the Canadian approach is commendable for its more enlightened approach to the reality of relationships, it is still open to criticism,[561] not least as a restitutionary device. Mee argues that the language of restitution has been misappropriated by the courts to justify a discretion to adjust the property rights of cohabitants. In his view the Canadian courts have violated restitutionary theory in three ways: by failing to adequately justify why restitution should be available in such cases; by taking into account detriments incurred by a claimant which do not enrich the land owner; and by awarding remedies which have no reference to the enrichment conferred.[562]

(b) Unconscionability[563]

The Australian courts now[564] favour the imposition of constructive trusts on the grounds of 'unconscionability'. This approach to the constructive trust was explained by Deane J in *Muschinski v Dodds*:

Viewed in its modern context, the constructive trust can properly be described as a remedial institution which equity imposes regardless of actual or presumed intention...to preclude the retention or assertion of beneficial ownership of property to the extent that such retention or assertion would be contrary to equitable principle.[565]

He went on to say that the content of the principle was that where there was a joint endeavour and joint contributions to the purchase of property, 'equity will not permit [a party]...to assert or retain the benefit of the relevant property to the extent that it would be unconscionable for him to do so'.[566]

'Unconscionability' has been recognised as the explanation not merely of constructive trusts, but also of the doctrine of proprietary estoppel. These doctrines, which are treated as distinct in English law, operate as aspects of one common principle.[567] One consequence of this is that whether a beneficial interest under a constructive trust arises retrospectively on the acts of the claimant (as it must with the English institutional approach) or prospectively on the order of the court (as with a remedy granted in English law as a result of a claim in proprietary estoppel) is a matter at the discretion of the Australian courts.[568]

The approach of 'unconscionability' has the merit of doing away with the highly artificial concept of 'common intention'. However, in reality, the court is still required to decide whether the parties' conduct was 'unconscionable', so as to justify the imposition of a constructive trust. It involves the same sort of value judgements as the English law approach, and one of the key issues that has confronted the courts is what circumstance are necessary to found an action, in the absence of financial contributions to

---

[561] See (1993) 109 LQR 263 (Gardner), pp 269–275.

[562] *The Property Rights of Cohabitees* (1999), p 226.

[563] See Hayton 'Equitable Rights of Cohabitees' [1990] Conv 370; Bailey-Harris 'Equity Still Childbearing in Australia' (1997) 113 LQR 227.

[564] See *Allen v Snyder* [1977] 2 NSWLR 685—the courts initially adopted a common intention approach, based on the actual or subjective intentions of the parties; *Baumgartner v Baumgartner* (1988) 164 CLR 137.

[565] (1985) 160 CLR 583, at 614, 62 ALR 429, at 451.   [566] Ibid., at 455.

[567] See *Waltons Stores (Interstate) Ltd v Maher* (1988) 62 ALJR 110 (Aust HC).

[568] *Muschinki v Dodds* (1985) 160 CLR 583.

the purchase of the property. The Australian approach has also attracted academic criticism. Wong, for example, argues that it is only marginally more flexible than the English common intention constructive trust, and that there are remnants of gender bias in that, by requiring some evidence of commercialism in the relationship, it ignores the impact of sexual division of labour on women's employment and earning patterns.[569]

(c) Comparisons

What is clear, with every approach, is that in grappling with the issues raised by partners, married or cohabiting, who have not specified how the property is to be held, there are three major issues that need to be addressed:

(a) the extent to which the parties' thinking is relevant;

(b) the relevance of non-financial contributions to the relationship;

(c) identifying the appropriate remedy.

It is suggested that whatever the solution adopted, there is unlikely to be a conclusive response to these three issues. It is the difficulty of having any firm and preordained answer to these very issues that means that no single approach is necessarily better than any other. English law, like the other approaches, is not necessarily internally coherent or clear, but presents a no less laudable attempt to deal with the issues than the other jurisdictions identified. The problem, it is suggested, is that this is judge-made law, and the judiciary are being asked to evolve the law—to socially engineer existing equitable principles—to meet the issues raised in the context of the family home. It is to be expected that they do not find an easy solution when social practices are in flux and variable, and attempts at legislative solutions have proved controversial and difficult to identify.

(d) Encouraging cohabitants to formalize their arrangements

Although equitable devices have been evolved so as to enable cohabitants to gain a beneficial interest of the home they share, the courts have stressed the need for parties embarking upon cohabitation to think carefully about the proprietary implications, and to execute an express declaration of trust so as to avoid having to rely on the vagaries of the principles of resulting and constructive trusts or proprietary estoppel. Practitioners who are involved in home purchases also bear a responsibility to try to ensure that the parties clarify their intentions with respect to the ownership. As Ward LJ stated in *Carlton v Goodman*:

I ask in despair how often this court has to remind conveyancers that they would save the clients a great deal of later difficulty if only they would sit the purchasers down, explain the difference between a joint tenancy and a tenancy in common, ascertain what they want and then expressly declare in the conveyance of transfer how the beneficial interest is to be held

---

[569] 'Constructive Trusts over the Family Home: Lessons to Be Learned from other Commonwealth Jurisdictions' [1998] 18 LS, at 369, 382.

because that will be conclusive and save all argument. When are conveyancers going to do this as a matter of invariable standard practice? This court has urged that time after time. Perhaps conveyancers do not always read the law reports. I will try one more time: ALWAYS TRY TO AGREE ON AND THEN RECORD HOW THE BENEFICIAL INTEREST IS TO BE HELD. It is not very difficult to do.[570]

Sadly, experience demonstrates, through the steady stream of cases before the lower and appellate courts, that a practical solution is currently wanting.

(2) Legislative reform

The tortured search for a satisfactory mechanism by which cohabitants can obtain an interest in land highlights the difficulty of utilizing strict property concepts to solve what is essentially a social problem. Some jurisdictions have therefore adopted a legislative solution, granting the courts a discretion to adjust the property rights of cohabitants, in much the same way as the courts in England have been granted the right to adjust the property rights of married couples on divorce. For example, the New South Wales Property (Relationships) Act 1984 grants the court the discretion to adjust the property rights of those who are party to a domestic relationship.[571] Section 20 provides:

(1) On an application by a party to a domestic relationship for an order under this Part to adjust interests with respect to the property of the parties to the relationship or either of them, a court may make such order adjusting the interests of the parties in the property as it seems just and equitable having regard to:

    (a) the financial and non-financial contributions made directly or indirectly by or on behalf of the parties to the relationship to the acquisition, conservation or improvement of any of the property of the parties or either of them or to the financial resources of the parties or either of them, and

    (b) the contributions, including any contributions made in the capacity of homemaker or parent, made by either of the parties to the relationship to the welfare of the other party to the relationship or to the welfare of the family constituted by the parties and one or more of the following, namely:

        (i) a child of the parties,

        (ii) a child accepted by the parties or either of them into the household of the parties, whether or not the child is a child of either of the parties.

One problem with such legislative solutions is the difficulty of formulating an adequate definition of a 'domestic' or 'de facto' relationship. Thus in New South Wales a 'de facto relationship' is defined as a relationship between two adult persons, who live together as a couple, and who are not married to one another or related by family. To determine whether two persons are in a de facto relationship, all the circumstances of the relationship are to be taken into account, including: the duration of the relationship, the nature and extent of common residence; whether or not a sexual relationship exists; the degree of financial dependence or interdependence; any arrangements for

---

[570] [2002] EWCA Civ 545 AT [44].
[571] Other examples include: Victoria Property Law (Amendment Act) 1987; Northern Territory De Facto Relationships Act 1991; ACT Domestic Relationships Act 1994.

financial support between the parties; the ownership, use and acquisition of property; the degree of mutual commitment to a shared life; the care and support of children; the performance of household duties; and the reputation and public aspects of the relationship.[572]

No equivalent legislation extending to all cohabitation relationships has yet been introduced in English law, although various proposals for such a reform have been made. The greatest legislative change has been the Civil Partnerships Act 2004, which has accorded many of the rights of married couples to same-sex couples who register as civil partners.[573] In particular, the court may adjust the property rights of the partners on the dissolution of the civil partnership in the same way that they can adjust the property rights of married couples on divorce.[574] The legislation does not extend to heterosexual cohabiting couples, or to homosexual couples who choose to keep their relationship informal rather than registering it as a civil partnership. Since couples who choose to enter a formal civil partnership are those most likely to have given express consideration to their respective property rights in their shared home, the legislation will make little practical difference to the application of constructive trusts in determining the beneficial ownership of shared homes. The principles of resulting and constructive trusts, together with the parallel doctrine of proprietary estoppel, are thus not rendered irrelevant.

In 2007 the Law Commission suggested a statutory scheme for cohabiting couples, albeit on a different basis to that proposed in New South Wales. This would allow for the determination of the property rights of cohabitants on a similar basis to married couples and registered civil partners. This arose from a consultation exercise in 2006,[575] which lead to a full report in July 2007.[576]

The scheme is outlined in paras 4.26–4.42 of the Report. It rejects common intention as a basis of claim, but as the scheme is voluntary, parties may opt out of it by a written agreement made at any time. It also requires parties to meet some basic qualifying criteria for the scheme to operate, so that there will be a residual importance for the equitable devices in determining property rights on relationship breakdown. Nevertheless, where the scheme operates the parties would have access to the statutory property adjustment regime, to the exclusion of claims based on implied trusts, estoppel, and contract.

To qualify for protection, cohabitants must either have had a child (or children), or meet a minimum qualifying period of occupation instead. This is not set in the proposals, but is unlikely to be above five years. The parties also need to have made

---

[572] Section 4. See also s 5, where a 'domestic relationship' is defined as a de facto relationship, or a close personal relationship (other than a marriage or a de facto relationship) between two adult persons, whether or not related by family, who are living together, one or each of whom provides the other with domestic support and personal care.

[573] Civil Partnership Acts 2004, s 1.

[574] Civil Partnership Acts 2004, s 72 and Sch 5, para 1.

[575] Law Commission, Consultation Paper No. 179 (2006) *Cohabitation: The Financial Consequences of Relationship Breakdown.*

[576] Law Commission 'Cohabitation: The Financial Consequences of Relationship Breakdown' No 307.

contributions, defined as 'any contribution arising from the cohabiting relationship which is made to the parties' shared lives or to the welfare of the members of their families', 'giving rise to certain enduring consequences at the point of separation'.[577] This is designed to cover situations where the legal owner has retained a benefit, or that claimant had a continuing economic disadvantage, as a result of contributions made to the relationship. What qualifies as contributions includes the financial, non-financial, and future contributions (those that would have been made if the relationship had continued). 'Retained benefit' would include capital, income, or earning capacity that has been acquired, retained, or enhanced, and an economic disadvantage' would be a present or future loss, such as diminution of savings, lost future earnings, or the future cost of paid child care.

On relationship breakdown, unless the parties have, by a written agreement, excluded the proposed statutory scheme, the court is empowered to make a property adjustment award that reflects the extent of contributions, as well as the following factors:

- the financial needs and obligations of the parties;
- the extent and nature of the financial resources which either party has or is likely to have in the foreseeable future;
- the welfare of any children who live with, or might reasonably be expected to live with, either party; and
- the conduct of each party.

This is intended as a balancing exercise, and a wide range of remedies are available, including a share in property, a lump sum payment, property transfer, orders for sale, and pension sharing. There is no proposed power to make periodic payments, except in relation to child maintenance. Any written agreement to exclude the statutory scheme would be enforceable unless it was manifestly unfair at the time it was made or there had been a change of circumstances since that date.

If enacted, this would meet many of the current concerns of the use of the equitable devices, not least in terms of clarity and flexibility, both as to the contributions necessary for non-married couples to claim the assistance of the courts and the practical remedies available to meet their needs on relationship breakdown.[578] Sadly, despite the careful examination given by the Law Commission to developing its proposals, the report seems destined to gather dust on a shelf. The issue is both politically sensitive and unlikely to gain votes for any party supporting it. Moreover, as has already been observed, the solution would in any event be only partial, for there are many situations with which the courts have had to grapple which would fall outside the terms of the proposed legislation.

---

[577] Ibid.

[578] There are concerns over the implementation of proposals—see, for example, Douglas, Pearce, and Woodward 'The Law Commission's Cohabitation Proposals: Applying Them in Practice' [2008] Fam Law 351.

In a much more limited context, the Law Commission have recently suggested proposals for reform of the law of intestacy, which include an entitlement for cohabitants where the other cohabitant dies intestate.[579] The 'cohabitant'[580] must meet a five-year minimum duration requirement to become fully entitled under the proposals,[581] or have children from the relationship, in which case no qualifying period is required.[582] The proposed share of the estate would be the same as the same share of a partner's estate as a spouse would receive on intestacy on the basis of the 'essential functional similarity between marriage or civil partnership and an interdependent cohabiting relationship'.[583] The consultation period, which opened on 29 October 2009, closed on 28 February 2010.

For the foreseeable future, the plight of cohabitants remains in the hands of the judiciary and their common law solutions.

8 Overview and critique

There have been many criticisms of the equitable mechanisms that have been examined in this chapter. Some of these criticisms are directed at the adequacy of the equitable mechanisms to operate as tools of social justice; others at the way they operate; and others at the validity of their historical and juridical roots.

(i) The scope of the equitable mechanisms

Some commentators have argued that the equitable mechanisms operate badly as tools for dealing with the breakdown of relationships, particularly where children are involved. The devices are concerned principally with ascertaining entitlement to property. Although the resulting trust, the constructive trust, and proprietary estoppel are all capable of applying to other assets (and we have explored many cases in which they have done so), most disputes have involved entitlement to the family home. This will in most instances be because the family home represents the single largest asset within any relationship, and frequently also the most important. It may also be because couples are clearer about the allocation of ownership of their other assets—there is unlikely, for instance, to be much argument about who owns the clothes. The equitable devices have no application to the breakdown

---

579 Consultation Paper 191 (2009) 'Intestacy and Family Provision Claims on Death', Part IV.

580 CP No 191, p84 para 4.59. 'Cohabitant' is to be defined as two people living together in a joint home (para 4.60).

581 Ibid., paras 4.79–4.80. It is also proposed that cohabitation of between two and five years could lead to a 50 per cent entitlement (p 90, para 4.85).

582 Ibid., p 86, para 4.68.

583 Ibid., p 85 para 4.64. Special rules are proposed in relation to personal chattels, which would follow the normal rules of intestacy—see p 92, paras 4.95–4.96.

of a relationship when no assets are involved. In cases where a couple live in rented accommodation and have no investments, there is almost no scope for the equitable mechanisms to apply.

(ii) Redistribution of assets

The equitable mechanisms all look to ascertain how the parties intended to divide the assets concerned between themselves, even where the starting point for that enquiry is a presumption or set of presumptions. The evidence at which the courts look is generally designed to ascertain what the parties themselves intended or what the claimant could reasonably be expected to understand or believe. The courts are not seeking to redistribute the family assets on the basis of need, length of relationship, whether there are children, or other considerations. As Stephen Cretney has said:

> The general principles of law and equity do not in the main operate as a means of resource distribution, i.e. they do not transfer entitlement from one party to another in order to achieve a just result. Thus their very nature and origins render these doctrines imperfect vehicles for achieving social justice in the context in which they are now commonly invoked, namely the resolution of property disputes on the breakdown of unmarried relationships.[584]

(iii) Identifying what the parties intended

Other criticisms of the current approach centre on the inadequacies of common intention as a concept to capture and compensate a domestic cohabiting relationship. According to John Eekelaar:

> The theoretical basis of the trusts mechanism, common intention, is inappropriate to handle the domestic issues under consideration, partly because authority precludes the most significant form of domestic behaviour as evidence to establish such intentions, and partly because the character of the intentions attributed to the parties in the domestic sphere is unreal.[585]

The presumption of shared beneficial ownership deduced from purchase in joint names applied in *Stack v Dowden* can be seen as an endeavour to reflect more accurately current social values and mores in the presumptions about the intention of parties at the time the family home is acquired, but this presumption does not operate to a purchase in one party's name only, or where the parties cohabit after what becomes the family home has already been purchased.

(iv) Gender imbalance

It has also been argued that women are denied fair shares in property, due to the traditional sexual division of labour, the lack of financial value accorded to housework and childcare, unequal access to capital, and pay inequalities. Some have

---

[584] *Family Law in the Twentieth Century: A History*, at p 113.
[585] 'A Woman's Place—A Conflict between Law and Social Values' [1987] Conv 93, at p 101.

suggested that a gendered basis for intervention is needed, giving women special treatment as:

If women continue to suffer structural social and economic disadvantage at the hands of men, then the removal of a gendered basis for intervention can place them at a legal disadvantage too.[586]

By contrast, it has been argued that the current system, which allows for parties to declare their legal interests (and gain a presumption of an equal share of the property by means of the presumption in *Stack v Dowden*)[587] is preferable to any gendered intervention, as although it relies on knowledge, it attributes autonomy rather than stereotyping familial roles and appropriate behaviour.[588]

(v) A more flexible family-centred approach?

What is clear is that, for many family lawyers, the equitable devices are inappropriate. Even when it comes to quantifying an interest gained through an equitable solution, there are problems. Miles, for example, argues that economic difficulties following relationship breakdown 'cannot be solved without express reference to the nature, or effects of, the relationship between the parties and an express policy aimed at dealing specifically with the problems encountered in such relationships'.[589] For these critics, a flexible, family-law based approach is therefore required. This might require legislative intervention, but the genius of equity has been its ability to evolve, and it is possible that further evolution of existing mechanisms is possible in the light of changes in social values. One such change might be a wider presumption of equality of shares in family home cases. This is already the starting point, following *Stack v Dowden*,[590] where the home has been purchased in joint names, and it is also the starting point for property division on divorce under s 25 of the Matrimonial Causes Act 1973 (MCA 1973). It has been proposed that this approach should be extended to cases where a family home is held in the sole name of one party.[591] The House of Lords in *White v White*[592] and *McFarlane v McFarlane*[593] has established that the discretionary factors to which the court has regard when adjusting property rights under s 25 MCA 1973, are implicitly underpinned by the principles of fairness and equal division. Equal division between the former spouses is the overall aim of the court. However, in 'everyday cases' of property division on divorce, the focus on equal division is of very little relevance as the courts focus on the immediate housing needs of the parent with care of dependent

---

[586] Auchmuty, 'Unfair Share for Women: The Rhetoric of Equality and the Reality of Inequality' in Lim and Bottomley *Feminist Perspectives on Land Law* (Routledge-Cavendish, Oxford, 2007), at p 180.

[587] [2007] 2 AC 432.

[588] Bottomley, 'Women and Trust(s): Portraying the Family in the Gallery of Law' in Bright and Dewar, *Land Law: Themes and Perspectives* (OUP, 1998), p 221.

[589] Miles 'Property Law v Family Law: Resolving the Problems of Family Property' (2003) 23 LS 624, at 648.

[590] [2007] 2 AC 432.

[591] George '*Stack v Dowden*—Do as We Say, Not as We Do' (2008) 30 *Journal of Social Welfare and Family Law* 41, at 59.

[592] [2001] Fam LR 21.   [593] [2009] EWHC 891 (Fam).

children.[594] This needs-based approach is focused on the practicalities, rather than on the more abstract notion of equality, that is only a factor in 'mid-money' cases (those where the parties have significant assets but cannot be described as wealthy).[595]

Translating a similar approach to the equitable jurisdiction, the equality approach in *Stack v Dowden* is also a starting point, a presumption that can be displaced. The courts could extend the presumption of equality, and take account of a range of factors like those used in the statutory divorce jurisdiction to modify the presumption. There would, however, be very substantial problems with such an approach. It would require an identification of the circumstances in which a relationship was close enough to apply a principle of equality. What factors would be taken into account? Would the duration of the relationship be relevant? Would it be relevant if the parties were related as family members, such as brothers or sisters? Would it be relevant if the relationship was platonic rather than sexual? These are normally matters to be resolved by the legislature, not by the courts. And if the approach was to be based on needs, not ownership, then, as the Law Commission has observed in specifically rejecting the possibility of extending the MCA 1973 approach to cohabitation cases:

cohabitants, have not given each other the legal commitment, or accepted status, of marriage.'[596]

(vi) Property rights

In most negotiations, it is helpful to have a clear starting point. Clarity is also important when dealing with proprietary interests, because of their capacity to bind third parties.[597] In providing an institutional set of methods to provide for cohabitants seeking an interest in the family home, English law is involved in a search for fairness balanced by clarity, however flawed that search may be. If the balance swings too far in favour of fairness, there is not only a problem in deciding what factors are relevant and what weight they should carry, there is also a problem of lack of clarity and certainty, particularly when strangers to the relationship are involved. It can be argued that if English law is to develop a process that promotes social justice through adjustments in property rights, or through an enlarged jurisdiction to take account of a wide range of factors in 'discovering' entitlements to property, it should do so by adopting a remedial rather than institutional approach. If this argument is correct, then the observations of Lord Scott in *Thorner v Major and others*[598] about a 'remedial constructive trust' have merit. Those observations, have not yet, however, received majority support, but what may be developing is a new form of implied trust. If so, it is suggested that the judiciary would do well to abandon any attempts to mask this with clever language, and should instead consider the limits of this

---

[594] Hitchings 'Everyday Cases in the Post-*White* Era' [2008] Fam Law 873, at 877.

[595] Ibid.

[596] Law Commission, 'Cohabitation: The Financial Consequences of Relationship Breakdown' No 207 (2007), at para 4.2.

[597] *National Provincial Bank v Ainsworth* [1965] AC 1175.   [598] [1970] AC 777.

new implied trust. In doing so they should take care to respect both the restrictions imposed by statute on the informal creation of rights in land, and by the established jurisprudence which has required detriment or change of position to make enforceable informal representations or understandings concerning property rights. Rights over land are not created by mere representations, which do not amount to either a contract or a declaration of trust.[599] Whatever results, this area is likely to remain a fertile area of litigation for many years to come.

---

[599] A transfer on an interest in land by way of gift requires a deed: Law of Property Act 1925 s 52. In the case of a declaration of a trust of land, there is a need for evidence in writing under the Law of Property Act 1925 s 53(1)(b). A contract for the creation of an interest in land must be made in writing in accordance with s 1 of the Law of Property (Miscellaneous Provisions) Act 1989.

12

Mutual wills

When an owner of property dies, English law permits him to dictate how it should be distributed by means of a will. The cardinal feature of a will is that it remains revocable until the death of the testator, who thus remains free to alter its terms at any time before his demise. The doctrine of 'mutual wills' evolved in equity to overcome the problems presented by the revocability of wills, and to allow binding mutual wishes as to the distribution of property by two or more people to be given legal effect.

1 The nature of mutual wills[1]

(1) The practical problem

In English law, wills are revocable at any point up until the death of the testator. As was said in *Vynior's Case*:

If a man makes his testament and last will irrevocably, yet he may revoke it; for his acts or his words cannot alter the judgement of the law, to make that irrevocable which, of its own nature, is revocable.[2]

The potential revocability of a will presents a significant obstacle if an owner wishes to leave property to one person absolutely, subject to a requirement that the recipient bequeaths it to an agreed third person. For example, if a husband and wife have one child the husband may want his wife to enjoy all his property if he predeceases her, but also to ensure that it is ultimately left to their daughter. If he simply executes a will leaving his property to his wife, it will become her absolute property on his death and she will be free to execute her own will leaving the property to whomever she chooses, perhaps to the children of a second marriage or to some charitable object. To try to avoid such difficulties they may decide to execute wills with identical terms, leaving their property to each other in the event that they predecease, but to their daughter

---

[1] See Oakley, *Constructive Trusts* (3rd edn, 1997), pp 264–274; Burgess 'A Fresh Look at Mutual Wills' (1970) 34 Conv (NS) 230; Youdan 'The Mutual Wills Doctrine' (1979) 24 U Tor LJ 390; McFarlane 'Constructive Trusts Arising on a Receipt of Property *Sub Conditione*' (2004) 120 LQR 667.

[2] (1610) 8 Co Rep 80a.

if they survive. However, even where identical wills have been executed, the survivor will remain free to revoke the former will and leave the property to others.

These practical difficulties are well illustrated by the facts of *Re Cleaver*.[3] Arthur and Flora Cleaver had married in 1967, when he was 78 and she was 74. He had three children by a previous marriage and she had none. They executed identical wills, leaving the bulk of their estates[4] to the survivor absolutely, and in default of their survival to the three children.[5] Arthur died in 1975. The will was proved and Florence became entitled to his estate absolutely. She subsequently executed a new will leaving her entire estate, which included the property she had inherited from Arthur, to only one of the children. While Arthur had clearly intended that the property bequeathed to his wife should ultimately be left by her to the children equally,[6] it was impossible to prevent his widow revoking her will and executing a replacement with different terms. If the terms of the new will were allowed to operate, Arthur's intentions would have been defeated by his wife's subsequent change of mind.

While these difficulties can be avoided by bequeathing property directly to the intended ultimate beneficiaries, or through the use of a life interest that will ensure that the survivor is only entitled to utilize the income derived from the property but not the capital, in reality these are often impracticable solutions. Where the testators do not possess great wealth, the survivor may need to make use of the property bequeathed to them, for example to provide retirement income or to pay for nursing care if needed, and solutions which do not enable them to do so are inadequate to fulfil their intentions.[7] What is required is a mechanism which enables the survivor to enjoy the property inherited from the first to die, if necessary, but which prevents the survivor from making an effective bequest of any of that property remaining at the date of their death to anyone other than the agreed beneficiary. Equity provides such a mechanism through the doctrine of 'mutual wills'.

(2) The doctrine of mutual wills

The doctrine of 'mutual wills' evolved in equity to overcome the problems presented by the revocability of wills. The essence of this doctrine was stated by Morritt J in *Re Dale (Decd)*:

The doctrine of mutual wills is to the effect that where two individuals have agreed as to the disposal of their property and have executed mutual wills in pursuance of the agreement, on the death of the first (T1) the property of the survivor (T2), the subject matter of the agreement is held on an implied trust for the beneficiary named in the wills. The survivor may thereafter alter his will, because a will is inherently revocable, but if he does his personal representatives will take the property subject to the trust.[8]

---

[3] [1981] 2 All ER 1018.　　[4] The remainder after certain specific legacies.

[5] Two of the children were to receive one-third shares absolutely, with the daughter receiving only a life interest in the remaining third.

[6] [1981] 2 All ER 1018, at 1029. Nourse J described him as 'a very determined man' and that 'everything suggests that he would, so far as he could, have wanted to ensure that anything which was left at [his wife's] death should go back to his side of the family'.

[7] See Stevens 'Avoiding Disinheritance' (1996) NLJ 961.　　[8] [1993] 4 All ER 129, at 132.

Where mutual wills have been executed, equity does not prevent the survivor from changing his will.[9] Instead, the executors of the new will hold any property that was intended to be left to the beneficiary of the mutual wills on constructive trust. By means of this trust the property will be held for the beneficiary named in the original mutual wills, and will not pass to those named in the new will. As the Privy Council stated in *Gray v Perpetual Trustee Co Ltd*:

If two persons simultaneously make wills to the same effect, and in that sense mutually, a second will be made by one of them after succeeding to the other's estate under the originally made will is precluded from being treated as effective to interfere in equity with the existing disposition.[10]

Returning to the example of *Re Cleaver*,[11] it was held that the wills executed by Arthur and his wife had been 'mutual wills', so that the equitable doctrine applied and a constructive trust had come into existence. The widow's executors therefore held the property she had received under her husband's will on constructive trust for the three children in equal shares.

(3) Rationale for the imposition of a constructive trust

A constructive trust will be imposed if the testators executed mutual wills on the basis of an agreement not to revoke. The rationale for imposing a constructive trust in such circumstances is that equity will not permit the survivor to commit a fraud by going back on his agreement. Since the property he received on the death of the first testator had only been bequeathed to him on the basis of the agreement not to revoke his own will, it would be a fraud for him to take the benefit while failing to observe the agreement, and equity intervenes to prevent this fraud.[12] This rationale is evident from the judgment of Lord Cottenham LC in the early case of *Dufour v Pereira*:

The parties by the mutual will do each of them devise, upon the engagement of the other, that he will likewise devise in manner therein mentioned. The instrument itself is the evidence of the agreement; and he, that dies first, does by his death carry the agreement on his part into execution. If the other then refuses, he is guilty of a fraud, can never unbind himself, and becomes a trustee of course. For no man shall deceive another to his prejudice. By engaging to do something that is in his power, he is made a trustee for the performance, and transmit that trust to those that claim under him . . . [13]

The principle was stated in a more modern way by Dixon J in the Australian case *Birmingham v Renfrew*,[14] which was cited with approval in *Re Cleaver*:

It has long been established that a contract between persons to make corresponding wills gives rise to equitable obligations when one acts on the faith of such an agreement and dies leaving his will unrevoked so that the other takes property under its dispositions. It operates to impose

---

9 See *Re Hey's Estate* [1914] P 192.
10 [1928] AC 391, at 399.   11 [1981] 2 All ER 1018.
12 See *Re Dale (Decd)* [1993] 4 All ER 129, at 142, per Morritt J.
13 (1769) 2 Hargreave's Juridical Arguments 304, cited by Morritt J in *Re Dale (Decd)* [1993] 4 All ER 129, at 135–136.
14 (1937) CLR 666.

upon the survivor an obligation regarded as specifically enforceable. It is true that he cannot be compelled to make and leave unrevoked a testamentary document and if he dies leaving a last will containing provisions inconsistent with his agreement it is nevertheless a valid testamentary act. But the doctrines of equity attach the obligation to the property. The effect is, I think, that the survivor becomes a constructive trustee and the terms of the trust are those of the will which he undertook would be his last will and testament.[15]

In *Re Dale (Decd)*, Morritt J reiterated the fraud justification for the imposition of a constructive trust:

There is a contract between the testators which on the death of T1 is carried into effect by him, that T1 dies with the promise of T2 that the agreement will stand and that it would be a fraud on T1 to allow T2 to disregard the contract which became irrevocable on the death of T1.[16]

The reasoning in *Re Dale (Decd)* was cited with approval by the Court of Appeal in *Olins v Walters*.[17]

Given that the mutual wills operate to prevent the survivor acting fraudulently, the question has arisen whether the doctrine of mutual wills operates if the surviving testator gains no personal benefit under the will of the first testator who predeceases him. In the majority of cases this problem will not arise because the mutual wills provide that the survivor is to inherit the estate of the predeceasing party absolutely, or receive a life interest in it. However, the problem did arise in *Re Dale (Decd)*.[18] Norman and Monica Dale executed mutual wills in September 1988. They had two children, a son Alan and a daughter Joan. Under the terms of the mutual wills all their property, real and personal, was to be divided equally between their children. They left nothing to each other. Norman died in November 1988 and his estate was worth about £18,500. Monica died in 1990, having made a new will earlier that year leaving £300 to Joan and everything else to Alan. Her estate was valued at £19,000. Joan claimed that the doctrine of mutual wills applied so that Alan, as executor, held Monica's estate on constructive trust in accordance with the terms of the mutual wills. Alan argued that the doctrine could not operate because Monica had derived no personal benefit under Norman's will. After reviewing the authorities, Morritt J concluded that the doctrine of mutual wills could operate even where the surviving testator received no benefit under the first testator's will:

As all the cases show the doctrine applies when T2 benefits under the will of T1. But I am unable to see why it should be any the less a fraud on T1 if the agreement was that each testator should leave his or her property to particular beneficiaries, for example their children, rather than to each other. It should be assumed that they had good reason for doing so and in any event that is what the parties bargained for. In each case there is the binding contract. In each case it has been performed by T1 on the faith of the promise of T2 and in each case T2 would have deceived T1 to the detriment of T1 if he, T2, were permitted to go back on his agreement. I see no reason why the doctrine should be confined to cases where T2 benefits when the aim of the principle is to prevent T1 from being defrauded...[19]

---

15   [1981] 1 WLR 939, at 946.

16   [1993] 4 All ER 129, at 136; Brierley 'Mutual Wills—Blackpool Illuminations' (1995) 58 MLR 95.

17   [2009] Ch 212, at 221 [37].   18   [1993] 4 All ER 129; O'Hagan 'Mutual Wills' [1994] NLJ 1272 .

19   [1993] 4 All ER 129, at 142. In the Canadian case *Lynch Estate v Lynch Estate* (1993) 8 Alta LR (3d) 291, it was held that a 'disposition agreement' was generally only enforceable against someone who had taken a benefit under it.

2 Establishing that wills were mutual

(1) A contract not to revoke

(a) Necessity of a contract

The doctrine of mutual wills will only operate if the testators had agreed that their wills would not be revoked. In the absence of such an agreement there will be no fraud if the surviving testator revokes his will. As Lord Loughborough LC indicated in *Walpole v Lord Orford*,[20] the principal difficulty in establishing that wills were intended to be mutual is determining whether the testators had entered a legally binding obligation not to revoke their wills rather than a mere 'honourable engagement'. In *Re Cleaver* Nourse J stated:

I would emphasise that the agreement or understanding must be such as to impose on the donee a legally binding obligation to deal with the property in the particular way.[21]

More recent cases have held that this agreement between the parties must take the form of a valid contract. In *Re Dale (Decd)*[22] Morritt J held that 'there is no doubt that for the doctrine to apply there must be a contract at law'. The requirement of a contract was reiterated in *Goodchild v Goodchild*,[23] where it had been argued that a contract should not be required because it was not an essential element of the establishment of a constructive trust. The Court of Appeal rejected the purported analogy between the operation of mutual wills and secret trusts and concluded that a contract was required. Morritt LJ stated:

As Leggatt LJ has pointed out, a consistent line of authority requires that for the doctrine of mutual wills to apply there must be a contract between the two testators. In delivering the advice of the Privy Council in *Gray v Perpetual Trustee Co Ltd*[24] such requirement was made abundantly clear by Viscount Haldane. Counsel . . . suggests that this test is too high. He does so by reference to the requirements for a secret trust or for the imposition of a constructive trust. I do not accept that there is any justification to be found in those areas of equity such as would justify departing from the clear statement of Viscount Haldane.[25]

While critics have suggested that Morritt LJ misrepresented the earlier cases cited in support of his conclusion that a contract is required,[26] and argued that the doctrine of mutual wills should operate whenever testators have reached an agreement or understanding not to revoke their wills,[27] subsequent decisions make clear that

---

[20] (1797) 3 Ves JR 402, at 419. Cited by Nourse J in *Re Cleaver* [1981] 2 All ER 1018, at 1024.
[21] [1981] 2 All ER 1018, at 1024.   [22] [1993] 4 All ER 129, at 133.
[23] [1997] 3 All ER 63; Grattan 'Mutual Wills and Remarriage' [1997] Conv 153.
[24] [1928] AC 391, at 400.   [25] [1997] 3 All ER 63, at 75
[26] *Dufour v Pereira* (1769) 1 Dick 419; *Walpole v Lord Orford* (1797) 3 Ves JR 402; *Gray v Perpetual Trustee Co Ltd* [1928] AC 391; *Birmingham v Renfrew* (1937) CLR 666; *Re Cleaver* [1981] 2 All ER 1018.
[27] Harper 'A Retreat from Equitable Mutuality?' [1997] Conv 182; Grattan 'Mutual Wills and Remarriage' [1997] Conv 153.

a contract will be required.[28] The courts have enjoyed ample opportunity to adopt a lower threshold but have pointedly, and repeatedly, chosen not to do so. For example, in *Olins v Waters*,[29] Mummery LJ reiterated that it 'is a legally *necessary* condition of mutual wills that there is clear and satisfactory evidence of a contract between two testators'. This decision must in principle be correct. The effect of a finding that there are mutual wills is to impose a binding legal obligation in respect of the property affected. To give rise to this, even if a contract is not required, there must be an agreement intended to have legal effect. The difference between such an agreement and a contract is no more than semantic.

(b) Necessity of consideration

In order to establish that the testators had entered into a binding contract not to revoke their wills, it is necessary to show that consideration was provided. In *Re Dale (Decd)*[30] the defendants argued that consideration was only given for the promise not to revoke if the first testator to die had provided a benefit to the survivor other than his promise not to revoke his own will, because otherwise he would simply bequeath his property in the way that he wished while remaining able to change his mind and revoke his will at any time before his death. Morritt J rejected this submission and held that a testator has acted sufficiently to his detriment to constitute consideration where he has performed his promise by executing the mutual will, and not subsequently taken advantage of his legal right to revoke it.

(c) Absence of any contract

In the absence of a contract the testators' wills will not be mutual, and a constructive trust cannot arise. In *Re Oldham*,[31] Mr and Mrs Weldon executed similar wills in 1907. In 1914 the husband died. As a result his estate passed to his wife absolutely. In 1921 she married Mr Oldham, who was some 35 years her junior, and altered her will to grant him a life interest in a large portion of her estate. She died in 1922, leaving some £108,000, all but £10,000 of which had come from her first husband's estate. Astbury J held that there was no evidence of an agreement that the 'mutual' wills should be irrevocable, and therefore there was no trust raised in favour of the beneficiaries named in them.

In *Healey v Brown*,[32] a question arose about the effect of s 2 of the Law of Property (Miscellaneous Provisions) Act 1989 (which requires contracts relating to interests in land to be made in writing). Thomas and Mary Theresa Brown had made identical mutual wills. By these wills the survivor left the flat which they occupied as their family home to Mary's niece, Jacqueline (the claimant), and the remainder of the estate to Paul, Thomas's son by a previous marriage. Mary died in 1997 and Thomas shortly thereafter transferred the flat into the joint names of himself and Paul. Following

---

[28] *Birch v Curtis* [2002] FLR 1158. In New Zealand it was held that the doctrine of mutual wills may be founded either on the basis of contract or restitution: *Re Newey* [1994] 2 NZLR 590.

[29] [2009] Ch 212, at 221 [36].   [30] [1994] Ch 31.

[31] [1925] Ch 75.   [32] [2002] EWHC 1405 (Ch).

Thomas's death in 1999 Jacqueline claimed the flat from Paul. David Donaldson, QC, sitting as a Deputy High Court judge, concluded that Jacqueline's claim based on the mutual wills was precluded by the fact that there was no written contract signed by both Thomas and Mary. In his view if there was no enforceable contract, the mutual wills doctrine could not apply. He was, however, prepared to hold that Paul was subject to a constructive trust—akin to either a secret trust or a common intention constructive trust—of the half-share in the flat which represented the half-interest which his father Thomas had acquired from Mary. With respect, this decision takes the requirement of an enforceable contract too far. Section 2 of the 1989 Act preserves the effect of implied, constructive, or resulting trusts. Since mutual wills agreements are enforced as constructive trusts of the property subject to the agreement, they should not be rendered unenforceable merely by the absence of a single document signed by both parties. This is an issue which would merit reconsideration by a higher court.

(d) Breach of contract by revocation

As mutual wills are executed on the basis of a contract not to revoke, a testator who unilaterally revokes his will before either has died will have acted in breach of his contractual obligations. As such, he will be prima facie liable to pay damages to his fellow testator, and if he has died his estate will be liable to the survivor.[33] There will be no liability for breach if the revocation occurred by operation of law, for example where the testator married or divorced, but the relevant property may still be subject to a constructive trust.

(2) Establishing a contract not to revoke

(a) The standard of proof

In *Re Cleaver*[34] Nourse J held that the agreement not to revoke the mutual wills can only be established by 'clear and satisfactory evidence' and that the burden of proof is the ordinary civil standard of the balance of probabilities.

(b) Mere fact of identical wills

In *Dufour v Pereira*[35] Lord Cottenham LC had suggested that, where identical wills had been executed, it was possible to infer that the parties had agreed that they should not be revoked because 'the instrument itself is the evidence of the agreement'. However, it seems clear from more recent cases that the necessary contract not to revoke will not be construed from the mere fact that the testators simultaneously executed identical wills. In *Gray v Perpetual Trustee Co Ltd*[36] the Privy Council concluded that:

the mere simultaneity of the wills and the similarity of their terms do not appear, taken by themselves, to have been looked on as more than some evidence of an agreement not to revoke. The

---

[33] *Robinson v Ommanney* (1883) 23 Ch D 285.   [34] [1981] 2 All ER 1018, at 1024.
[35] (1769) 1 Dick 419; see also *Walpole v Lord Orford* (1797) 3 Ves JR 402.
[36] [1928] AC 391, at 400.

agreement . . . was a fact which had in itself to be established by evidence, and in such cases the whole of the evidence must be looked at.[37]

This statement of principle was approved by Nourse J in *Re Cleaver*.[38] For this reason, no constructive trust was established in *Re Oldham*,[39] the facts of which were noted above. The only evidence of an agreement came from the fact that the wills had been executed and Astbury J held that this was insufficient. He explained that it was impossible to construe the true intentions of the testators from the mere fact of their identical wills:

> The plaintiff contends that no such agreement need be proved outside the facts of the form of the mutual wills. I regret that I am unable in the circumstances of this case to give effect to that contention, and all the more so because I have no doubt at all that if the husband in 1907 had foreseen that his wife after seven years' survivorship would marry a young man and leave the whole of her first husband's property to that young man and her own relatives he would have made a very different testamentary disposition.[40]

His rationale for insisting upon a high degree of proof of an agreement is instructive as to the unwillingness of the courts to impose trusts on property in the absence of any clear intention:

> The plaintiff says that each was satisfied to trust the other and made the arrangement only in respect of the property taken by the survivor and not disposed of in the survivor's lifetime. Now this question must be answered. Could these parties have acted as they did with any other object or intent than that the plaintiff asserts? It is impossible to deny that they could. I cannot build up a trust on conjecture, and there are many reasons which may have operated on the minds of these mutual will makers. Each may have thought it quite safe to trust the other, and to believe that, having regard to their ages, nothing was likely to occur in the future substantially to diminish the property taken by the survivor, who could be trusted to give effect to the other's obvious wishes. But that is a very different thing from saying that they bound themselves by a trust that should be operative in all circumstances and in all cases [. . .] Putting it shortly I have no sufficient means for deciding with certainty what, among many possible inferences, is the sole inference that ought to be drawn from the circumstances of this case.[41]

Although the mere fact of the execution of mutual wills is not alone sufficient to prove the necessary contract, it may provide a strong indication that a contract had been concluded between the testators.[42] This was recognized even in *Re Oldham*.[43]

(c) Additional evidence of agreement

Since a contract will not be inferred from the mere execution of identical wills, additional evidence will have to be provided to demonstrate that the testators had concluded a contract not to revoke. A constructive trust will be established if the mutual wills themselves contain a statement that they have been executed on the basis of an

---

[37] Ibid., at 400.   [38] [1981] 2 All ER 1018, at 1022.   [39] [1925] Ch 25.
[40] Ibid., at 87.   [41] [1925] Ch 25, at 88–89.
[42] Ibid., at 87, where Astbury J said: 'Of course it is a strong thing that these two parties came together, agreed to make their wills in identical terms and in fact so made them. But that does not go nearly far enough.' The approach of Astbury J was approved by the Privy Council in *Gray v Perpetual Trustee Co Ltd* [1928] AC 391, at 400.
[43] [1925] Ch 75.

agreement, as was the case in *Re Hagger*.[44] Written evidence outside of the wills, for example a memorandum stating the testators' intentions, will also support the establishment of a mutual wills constructive trust. In *Olins v Walters*,[45] a statement in the wills that they were intended to be mutual wills was supported by an attendance note from the testators' solicitor (who was also their grandson and a beneficiary), and by his oral evidence.

A number of cases have concerned the difficulties of establishing that there was a constructive trust in the absence of any written evidence concerning the testator's intentions. While oral evidence of the testators' intentions may suffice, it is difficult to establish the existence of the essential contract not to revoke. In *Re Cleaver*,[46] Nourse J held that evidence of family conversations entitled him to conclude that that there was 'clear and satisfactory evidence that the testator and the testatrix did make an agreement which they intended should impose mutual legal obligations as to the disposal of their property'.[47] This evidence included conversations of Mr Cleaver with his children when Mrs Cleaver was present, and the attitude of Mrs Cleaver after his death, which seemed to suggest that she was aware that she was under an obligation to dispose of her estate in accordance with the terms of their mutual wills, and not merely an honourable engagement.[48] It was only later that she adopted the attitude that she did not have to worry about promises made to her husband because he was dead and could do nothing about it.[49] In *Olins v Walters*,[50] there was sufficient evidence to support the finding of a legally binding mutual wills agreement, despite the testator subsequently alleging that he had no recollection of the meeting on which his solicitor gave evidence or of the codicils which contained the clauses evidencing the agreement.

In contrast, in *Goodchild v Goodchild*[51] it was held that the evidence had failed to establish that the testators had contractually agreed not to revoke their wills. Dennis Goodchild and his wife Joan executed similar wills in 1988, leaving the majority of their estates to their son Gary. Joan died in 1991 and in 1992 Dennis married Enid, his second wife. He subsequently executed a new will leaving his entire estate to Enid. He died in 1993. Gary claimed that his parents had executed mutual wills in 1988, and that a constructive trust should be imposed over the property left to Enid deriving from his mother. Carnwath J[52] held that there 'was no clear agreement that they were to be mutually binding', a conclusion which was upheld by the Court of Appeal on the grounds that there was inadequate evidence to justify holding that a binding contract had been made.

A variety of evidence had been given in the case. Gary gave evidence from a meeting with his parents that led Carnwath J to conclude that he had no doubt 'he was led to believe by both his parents that he would inherit everything',[53] Other family

---

44 [1930] 2 Ch 190.   45 [2009] Ch 212.   46 [1981] 2 All ER 1018.
47 Ibid., at 1028.   48 Ibid., at 1027.   49 Ibid., at 1027–1028.
50 [2009] Ch 212.   51 [1997] 3 All ER 63.   52 [1996] 1 All ER 670.
53 Ibid., at 678.

friends gave evidence that the wills were intended to be mutually binding.[54] Their housekeeper gave evidence that Joan had wanted to ensure that Gary would 'be all right'. However, this body of anecdotal evidence was weighed against the evidence of the family solicitor who had drawn up the wills in question. He claimed that it was not his normal practice to draw up mutually binding wills, but rather to grant a life interest to the survivor. He claimed to have discussed the matter with them and that they clearly intended the survivor to be free to deal with the property during his or her lifetime. Carnwath J summarized the solicitor's evidence:

He claimed to have discussed this specifically with them. His normal approach was to make something of a joke of the point, for example to ask the wife whether she accepted that, if her husband went off with a blonde nurse he would be able to give her everything (or conversely to ask her husband if he would mind if his wife went off with the milkman). He remembers the visit to the Goodchilds on 13 January, because he had known the house under previous occupants and was interested to see it. He also remembers Mr Goodchild being busy looking after both his wife and her mother, who was also ill and staying with them. His attendance note is in summary form, because as far as he was concerned it was a perfectly straightforward transaction. Had there been instructions to make some form of unusual provision, then he would have noticed that.[55]

Faced with this conflict of evidence, Carnwath J placed greater weight on the evidence of the solicitor. He concluded that in the circumstances no agreement had been proved:

Faced with this conflict of evidence, I have to bear in mind that the onus of proof lies on the plaintiffs, and that, as the cases show, there must be established evidence of a specific agreement outside the wills, not just some loose understanding or sense of moral obligation...The evidence in this case also shows how difficult it is to rely on the evidence of lay witnesses, when one is dealing with the somewhat technical issue as to whether there has been an agreement for mutually binding wills...[56]

He distinguished *Re Cleaver* on the grounds that the evidence for an agreement in that case had been stronger.[57] The Court of Appeal upheld his conclusion that there was insufficient evidence to establish anything beyond a mere moral obligation that the testators' estates would be left to Gary. Leggatt LJ stated:

Two wills may be in the same form as each other. Each testator may leave his or her estate to the other with a view to the survivor leaving both estates to their heir. But there is no presumption that a present plan will be immutable in the future...Dennis and Joy executed wills in the same terms save that each left his or her estate to the other. Thus the survivor was to have both estates. They wanted Gary to inherit the combined estates. But there was no express agreement not to revoke the wills. Nor could any such agreement be implied from the fact that the survivor was in a position to leave both estates to Gary. The fact that each expected that the other would leave them to him is not sufficient to impress the arrangement with a floating trust, binding in equity. A mutual desire that Gary should inherit could not of itself prevent the survivor from resiling from the arrangement. What is required is a mutual intention that both wills should remain unaltered and that the survivor should be bound to leave the combined estate to the son. That is what is missing here.[57a]

---

[54] Ibid., at 679.   [55] Ibid., at 681.

[56] [1996] 1 All ER 670, at 681–682.

[57] Ibid., at 683.   [57a] [1997] 3 All ER 63, at 71.

It should be noted that the overriding difference between the evidence presented in the cases of *Re Cleaver* and *Goodchild v Goodchild* was as to the evidence of the respective solicitors. In *Re Cleaver* the solicitor's evidence was relatively weak. In contrast, in *Goodchild* the solicitor was adamant that no agreement had been intended, and that he had expressly outlined to the testators the various options as to how they could ensure that the estate passed to the son, and that they had decided to opt for the identical, but not mutual, wills, which he had explained would mean that the survivor was still free to dispose of the property freely as they chose. Thus, in the earlier case the solicitor's evidence was inadequate to rebut the indication from the other oral evidence that an agreement had been intended, but of which he had not been made aware, whereas in the latter the solicitor's evidence fully rebutted any inference of an agreement that could be drawn from the other oral evidence presented. In *Olins v Walters*,[58] the evidence of the testators' solicitor was also considered to be important.

(3) Certainty of subject and objects

In *Re Cleaver*,[59] Nourse J also emphasized that there must be certainty of subject matter and of objects for a constructive trust to arise on the basis of mutual wills. He considered that these requirements 'are as essential to this species of trust as they are to any other'. It is not necessary, however, that the mutual wills agreement should deal with every eventuality. In *Olins v Walters*[60] counsel argued that there was no binding mutual wills agreement because there were some unanswered questions, such as the extent to which the survivor could use any property they inherited for their own purposes. This argument about insufficiency of terms was roundly rejected by Mummery LJ, who said:

Possible, and as yet unexplored, legal consequences of the application of the equitable principles do not negative the existence of the foundation contract or prevent a constructive trust from arising by operation of law on the death of the Deceased.[61]

3 The operation of mutual wills

While English law clearly accepts the doctrine of mutual wills, there are many theoretical and practical difficulties concerning the nature of the trust interest established thereby. In *Goodchild v Goodchild*[62] Morritt LJ emphasized that 'the doctrine of mutual wills is anomalous',[63] and for this reason uncertainties and inconsistencies are tolerated which would render a more conventional trust void.

---

58 [2009] Ch 212.   59 [1981] 2 All ER 1018.   60 [2009] Ch 212.
61 Ibid, at 221 [41].   62 [1997] 3 All ER 63.   63 Ibid., at 76.

(1) Date of creation of the constructive trust[64]

When it is established that wills were intended to be mutual, it has been seen that a constructive trust will arise to prevent the survivor disposing of his property in contravention of his contractual agreement not to vary his will. While it is clear that equity imposes a constructive trust, it is less clear when the trust arises. A number of alternatives present themselves.

(a) Date the mutual wills are executed

As a matter of logic, this cannot be the date at which the constructive trust arises. The parties remain free to revoke their wills by agreement at any time before the death of the first testator.[65] It may even be that a revocation without agreement will prevent a constructive trust arising. As Sir Gorell Barnes P held in *Stone v Hoskins*,[66] the survivor has no claim to a constructive trust where the testator who has died revoked his mutual will and executed another in a different form.

(b) Date of the death of the survivor

The date of death of the surviving testator cannot be the relevant date for the establishment of the constructive trust, as it has been held that the interest of a beneficiary of a mutual will who survives the first testator but predeceases the second does not lapse. In *Re Hagger*[67] John and Emma Hagger executed mutual wills leaving one-sixth interests in their estates to Edward Adams, Eleanor Palmer, and Alice Young. All three survived Emma's death in 1904, but predeceased John, who died in 1928. Clauson J held that their respective interests had not lapsed because the trust took effect from the date of the wife's death.

(c) Date of the first testator's death

It therefore seems that a constructive trust imposed on the basis of the doctrine of mutual wills arises on the date of the death of the first of the testators who executed them. In *Thomas and Agnes Carvel Foundation v Carvel*,[68] Thomas and Agnes Carvel made mutual, identical wills, each leaving their estate on trust to the other for life, with the remainder on trust for the claimant, an American corporation. By a reciprocal will agreement they agreed not to alter the provisions of their wills without the consent of the other, and that the survivor would not make any alterations. Following the death of Thomas in America, Agnes made two further wills, the last of which revoked all previous wills. When Agnes died in England the claimant instituted proceedings in the United States of America to enforce the reciprocal will agreement. By the time the case reached the English High Court, the main issue before the court was the potential removal of Agnes' personal representative for failing to administer the estate as

---

[64] See (1951) 14 MLR 137 (Mitchell).

[65] However, if the testator revokes his will before death, he will have committed a breach of contract and his estate will be liable to the survivor in damages: see *Robinson v Ommanney* (1883) LR 23 Ch D 285.

[66] [1905] P 194.   [67] [1930] 2 Ch 190.   [68] [2008] Ch 395.

required by the mutual will. Lewison J had to determine whether the claimant foundation had any interest under the will, to determine whether the personal representative was acting improperly. He concluded that the mutual will arose on the time of the first testator's death, therefore binding Agnes from that point. In his view:

> The essential point, to my mind, is that the trust does not arise under the will of the surviving testator. Nor does it arise under any previous will of the surviving testator. It arises out of the agreement between the two testators not to revoke their wills, and the trust arises when the first of the two dies without having revoked his will. In so far as there is an 'operative will', it seems to me that it is the will of the first testator (and his death with that will unrevoked) which brings the trust into effect. That being so, I do not consider that a person who claims under the doctrine of mutual wills is a person beneficially interested in the estate *under the will of the deceased*.[69]

(2) The beneficial interest under the constructive trust

(a) The property subject to the constructive trust

Although it seems clear that a constructive trust arises on the death of the first testator, it is more difficult to identify the precise nature and extent of the beneficial interest subsisting behind the trust. The property subject to the trust must be determined by the agreement of the testators.[70] One possibility is that the trust only affixes to the property inherited by the survivor under the will of the first testator. In that case it would be possible to hold that, from that moment, the survivor holds it as trustee for the ultimate beneficiary and has no power to dispose of it himself. This view seems to have been accepted in *Re Hagger*,[71] where Clauson J held that from the moment the property came into the hands of the survivor it was held on trust for the beneficiary with the survivor enjoying only a life interest. However, the testators may agree that all of their property, including that owned by the survivor, is covered by the agreement. In *Goodchild v Goodchild*[72] the Court of Appeal indicated that this was a crucial distinguishing feature of the doctrine of mutual wills. The constructive trust arising on the death of the first testator not only affected the property inherited by the survivor, but also the property owned absolutely by the survivor. Morritt LJ explained that for this reason the doctrine of mutual wills was to be distinguished from that of secret trusts, thus explaining the need for a contractual agreement:

> The principles applicable to cases of a fully secret trust do, in substance, require the proof of a contract...But if those principles do not require exactly the same degree of agreement as does a contract at law there is no reason to import that lesser requirement into the doctrine of mutual wills. Secret trusts affect the property of the donor not that of the primary donee. Where there are mutual wills the doctrine affects the property of both testators, in particular that of the second to die. If he is to be subjected to an obligation with regard to the property of his own not derived from the other then an agreement should be required.[73]

[69] [2008] Ch 395, at 404 [27].   [70] *Re Cleaver* [1981] 2 All ER 1018.   [71] [1930] 2 Ch 190.
[72] [1997] 3 All ER 63.   [73] Ibid., at 75.

It therefore seems that, whenever the essential requirement of a contractual agreement not to revoke is present, a constructive trust will arise at the date of death of the first testator over all the property in the hands of the survivor which it was agreed would be bequeathed to the ultimate beneficiaries of the mutual wills, irrespective of whether it was derived from the first testator's estate or was the survivor's own property. It is unclear whether the trust should extend to encompass property acquired by the survivor after the death of the first testator, for example through receipt of a windfall profit such as gambling winnings. Presumably, this is also a matter which is governed by the terms of the agreement giving rise to the mutual wills and therefore to the trust.[74]

(b) The beneficiaries' entitlement to the property subject to the constructive trust

Given that a constructive trust arises at the date of death of the first testator over all the property in the hands of the survivor which it was agreed would be bequeathed to the beneficiaries of the mutual wills, the question arises as to the precise nature of that trust interest. It does not seem that the beneficiaries should enjoy the immediate equitable ownership of the trust property in the conventional sense, which would entitle them to compel the survivor to transfer it to them in accordance with the principle of *Saunders v Vautier.*[75] The practical reality is that, in most cases, the underlying intention of the mutual wills is to allow the survivor to use the property inherited for his own support and maintenance during his lifetime. This could be achieved simply by giving the survivor the right to income under a life interest. However, in most cases it will be intended that the survivor can utilize the capital if necessary, but that the residue remaining at his death will be bequeathed to the agreed beneficiaries, rather than to others. As Nourse J observed in *Re Cleaver,*[76] Mr Cleaver wanted Mrs Cleaver to enjoy 'the security after his death which a free power of disposal over his estate would give her' and at the same time 'to ensure that anything which was left at her death should go back to his side of the family'. This means that the property rights of the beneficiaries of the mutual wills cannot crystallize until the date of the death of the survivor. If the trust were to fix unconditionally on the death of the first testator, ludicrous and unintended results could follow. While the issue was not considered in *Re Dale (Decd),*[77] it is obvious that a trust cannot have been intended to crystallize on the death of the first testator. If the beneficiaries' interests had crystallized at the date of their father's death, their mother would have held all her property, which was the subject matter of the trust, on trust for the children in equal shares, and she would in effect have no longer owned anything absolutely. At most, she would have enjoyed a right to a life interest thereof.

---

[74] The issue was raised in *Olins v Walters* [2009] Ch 212, but had not been pleased on the facts, so neither the trial judge nor the Court of Appeal expressed any binding view on the matter.

[75] (1841) Cr & Ph 240.   [76] [1981] 2 All ER 1018, at 1029.

[77] [1994] Ch 31.

An alternative model is therefore required to explain the nature of the entitlement of the beneficiaries of a constructive trust arising under mutual wills. The cases have therefore suggested that the property in the hands of the survivor affected by the mutual wills is rendered subject to a floating trust which arises as the date of death of the first testator, but which does not crystallize in favour of the beneficiaries until the death of the survivor. The possibility of such a 'floating trust' was raised by Dixon J in the Australian case *Birmingham v Renfrew*:

The purpose of an arrangement for corresponding wills must often be, as in this case, to enable the survivor during his life to deal as absolute owner with the property passing under the will of the party first dying. That is to say, the object of the transaction is to put the survivor in a position to enjoy for his own benefit the full ownership so that, for instance, he may convert it and expend the proceeds if he chooses. But when he dies he is to bequeath what is left in the manner agreed upon. It is only by the special doctrines of equity that such a floating obligation, suspended, so to speak, during the lifetime of the survivor can descend upon the assets at his death and crystallise into a trust.[78]

The concept of such a 'floating', uncrystallized, trust was raised in England in *Ottaway v Norman*[79] in the context of a fully secret trust.[80] Harry Ottaway left his bungalow by will to Eva Hodges, a woman he had been living with, having communicated his intention that on death she should leave it to his son, William. Although argued and decided on the basis that a fully- secret trust had been created, this does not easily accord with the facts. It was not the intention of Harry that Eva should hold the bungalow on trust for William from the moment of his death. Nor were there mutual wills. Despite an expectation that Eva would leave the bungalow by will to William, she made no simultaneous will alongside Harry. Having held that a secret trust had arisen, Brightman J considered the nature of the beneficiary's rights during the lifetime of Eva, the trustee:

I am content to assume for present purposes but without so deciding that if property is given to the primary donee on the understanding that the primary donee will dispose by his will of such assets, if any, as he may have at his command at his death in favour of the secondary donee, a valid trust is created in favour of the secondary donee which is in suspense during the lifetime of the primary donee, but attaches to the estate of the primary donee at the moment of the latter's death.[81]

It therefore seems best to regard mutual wills as creating some type of floating trust, which allows the survivor to dispose of the property subject to it if necessary but crystallizing over whatever remains at his death[82] or on any asset subject to an unauthorized voluntary disposition prior to death.[83] This approach was also assumed by Astbury J in *Re Oldham*.[84] Most significantly, in *Goodchild v Goodchild*[85] Leggatt

---

[78] (1937) CLR 666.   [79] [1972] Ch 698.
[80] See Chapter 8.   [81] [1972] Ch 698, at 713.
[82] As has been seen in Chapter 7, a number of cases hold that such a trust, if created expressly, would fail for lack of certainty.
[83] *Healey v Brown* [2002] EWHC 1405 (Ch), at [13].
[84] [1925] Ch 25, at 88.   [85] [1997] 3 All ER 63.

LJ assumed that mutual wills operated to create a floating trust. In the course of his comments concerning the need for a contractual agreement between the testators, he stated:

The fact that each expected that the other would leave them to him is not sufficient to impress the arrangement with a floating trust.[86]

(c) Use of the property subject to the 'floating' trust by the survivor

Where the doctrine of mutual wills operates so that property in the hands of the surviving testator is subject to a floating constructive trust, the question arises as to duties of the survivor as trustee. The doctrine of mutual wills clearly operates to prevent the survivor disposing of the trust property by will in a manner inconsistent with the mutual wills, but the more significant issue is whether he is prevented from disposing of it during his lifetime. In *Re Oldham*[87] Astbury J was of the opinion that the survivor could dispose of the property inter vivos. However, it is clear that there must be limits to the power of the survivor to dispose of the property subject to the trust, otherwise the entire purpose of the arrangement could easily be defeated. This difficulty was recognized by Dixon J in *Birmingham v Renfrew*:

No doubt gifts and settlements, inter vivos, if calculated to defeat the intention of the compact, could not be made by the survivor and his right of disposition, inter vivos, is, therefore, not unqualified. But, substantially, the purpose of the arrangement will often be to allow full enjoyment for the survivor's own benefit and advantage upon condition that at his death the residue shall pass as arranged.[88]

Adopting this analysis, the position would be very similar to a floating charge over the assets of a company.[89] So long as the survivor continued to behave in an ordinary way that was in accordance with his means and circumstances, he would continue to have freedom of disposition over the assets subject to the inchoate trust. The trust would, however, crystallize and settle on the assets upon his death, and even during his lifetime he could be called upon to account for any extraordinary transaction inappropriate to his circumstances. If a purported extraordinary transaction was identified in time, a beneficiary affected by it could presumably take steps to restrain it. If the transaction has already taken place, the recipient could be held subject to a constructive trust. For instance, in *Healey v Brown*[90] Thomas Brown put into joint names with his son a flat which Thomas had agreed with his wife to leave to her niece (the claimant) on his death. The deputy High Court judge took the view that, if a mutual wills agreement had been established, Thomas's son would have held the flat on constructive trust for the niece. The judge, David Donaldson, QC, observed:

Had Mr Brown sold the flat and used the proceeds to fund a place in a nursing home, there would have been no basis for complaint. But to give away the flat to his son—with immediate

---

[86] Ibid., at 71.   [87] [1925] Ch 25, at 88.   [88] (1937) CLR 666.
[89] *Re Panama, New Zealand and Australian Royal Mail Co* (1870) 5 Ch App 318.
[90] [2002] EWHC 1405 (Ch).

effect as to a 50% undivided share, and with effect on death as to the remainder by operation of the doctrine of survivorship—could scarcely run more directly and fully counter to the intention of the mutual will compact that the flat should pass to his deceased's wife niece on his own death. Subject therefore to the impact of the 1989 Act I have no doubt that the mutual wills doctrine would apply in the present case so as to impose in favour of the Claimant a constructive trust attaching to the flat.[91]

[91] Ibid., at [14]–[15].

PART III

ALLOCATION OF BENEFIT

13

Introduction to allocation

In the preceding chapters it has been seen how the separation of the management of property from its beneficial ownership using equitable mechanisms enables owners to deal with their property with great flexibility. Part II has examined the circumstances in which property will be subjected to a trust relationship. In this section, the focus of attention shifts to a consideration of the allocation of the trust fund, in other words how it is decided who has the rights of enjoyment over it.

1 General

The nature of the allocation of a trust fund will be dependent upon the type of equitable obligation which has been created, whether a power of appointment, fixed trust, or discretionary trust. The original owner may have specified how the fund should be allocated himself or, alternatively, he may have given to someone else the task of deciding how the allocation should be made by granting a discretion. Each of these mechanisms will be examined in detail in the following chapters. This chapter will sketch some of the recurrent themes that run through the area.

2 Certainty of objects

(1) Nature of the problem

Whenever an equitable mechanism is used to allocate the ownership of a fund, it must be possible for the allocation to be carried out in practice. If it cannot, then the mechanism will fail and the property returns from the fund to the original owner, or his successor in title, by means of a resulting trust.[1] It must also be possible for the court to be able to supervise allocations from the fund to ensure that the owner's

---

[1] See Chapter 20.

wishes are followed and that the fund is not allocated to persons who were never intended to benefit from it. The problem arises particularly where the original owner has defined the potential objects as a class, using a generic description rather than naming them as individuals. For example, if George was to leave £10,000 to his wife, Mildred, to be divided equally among his 'good friends', it would be impossible for his directions to be carried out. How would Mildred know what was meant by a 'good friend'? The concept is not capable of objective definition. To allocate the fund according to his instructions she would have to ascertain the identity of all George's 'good friends' before she could know how much to allocate to each 'good friend'. No doubt there would be many obvious candidates, but that would not be sufficient to make the gift workable. There is bound to be a grey area where it is unclear whether someone is a 'good friend' or not. The rights of any specific 'good friend' cannot be determined until the entire class is known.

If George had given Mildred a discretion to allocate the fund among 'whichever of my good friends she chooses', the problem remains, although in a less extreme form. Clearly, the terms of the gift only permit allocation to 'good friends', and to prevent fraud the court must ensure that it is so allocated. If Mildred were to make an allocation of £1,000 to Brian, who was a childhood friend of George but has not seen him for twenty years, how could the court decide whether she had acted within the terms of the discretion? Is Brian a 'good friend' or not?

The very fact that this question is unanswerable is the problem addressed by the requirement that the objects of an equitable obligation to allocate the fund must be certain.[2] This means that the class of people who are potential recipients from the fund are capable of being identified sufficiently clearly for the allocator to carry out his duty and the court effectively to scrutinize any allocations made. Such a term as 'good friends' would not be regarded as sufficiently certain, because it has no clear objective meaning.[3] The precise requirement of certainty of objects differs with the variety of equitable obligation in issue.[4] The test for powers of appointment and discretionary trusts is different from that for fixed trusts. Although the details differ, the principle is the same, namely that the objects (or potential objects) of allocation must be certain.

(2) Types of certainty

In *Re Baden's Deed Trusts (No 2)*[5] the Court of Appeal drew a distinction between 'conceptual' certainty and 'evidential' certainty. Understanding this distinction is an essential prerequisite to understanding the requirements of certainty applicable to different equitable obligations.

---

[2] See below for what is meant by certainty in this context.
[3] See *Re Baden's Deed Trusts (No 2)* [1973] Ch 9.   [4] See *McPhail v Doulton* [1971] AC 424, HL.
[5] [1973] Ch 9.

(a) Conceptual certainty

Conceptual certainty refers to the semantic clarity of the description of beneficiaries. If there is any ambiguity in the words used to define a class of objects or if the definition is not objective, so that the court or the allocator cannot determine without a doubt whether a person is within the class or not, it will be conceptually uncertain. For example, 'tall men' is conceptually uncertain because there is no way of telling what is 'tall'. 'Men over 6 ft' would be conceptually certain, because it is possible to say clearly of every man whether he is over 6 ft and within the class, or 6 ft or under and outside it. Similarly, a class of 'old ladies', 'good friends' or 'regulars' at a local pub would be conceptually uncertain. In *Re Baden's Deed Trusts (No 2)*[6] Sachs LJ gave as examples of conceptually certain classes 'first cousins', 'members of the X trade Union', and 'those who have served in the Royal Navy'. Browne-Wilkinson J expressed the problem clearly with regard to the word 'friends' in *Re Barlow's Will Trusts*:

> ['Friends'] has a great range of meanings; indeed its exact meaning probably varies from person to person. Some would include only those with whom they had been on intimate terms over a long period; others would include acquaintances who they liked. Some would include people with whom their relationship was primarily one of business; others would not. Indeed, many people, if asked to draw up a complete list of their friends, would probably have some difficulty in deciding whether certain of the people they knew were really 'friends' as opposed to 'acquaintances'...[7]

No equitable mechanism, whether a power, trust or discretionary trust, is valid if the class of objects is not conceptually certain.[8]

(b) Evidential certainty

Evidential certainty is concerned with proving whether a person falls within the specified class of objects of an equitable obligation. The class may be conceptually certain, as for example 'relatives', but unless some scientific process such as genetic fingerprinting can be used, it may be difficult or impossible for some persons to prove whether they are relatives or not. Thus, it may be conceptually certain that any given individual 'is or is not' a relative, but it is impossible to prove to which category a specific person belongs. Fixed trusts require every beneficiary to be identified in fact, and are invalid if evidential certainty is lacking.[9] Powers and discretionary trusts do not require evidential certainty.[10]

---

[6] Ibid., at 20.   [7] [1979] 1 WLR 278, at 298.

[8] *Re Baden's Deed Trusts (No 2)* [1973] Ch 9. See also Emery 'The Most Hallowed Principle: Certainty of Beneficiaries of Trusts and Powers of Appointment' (1982) 98 LQR 551.

[9] *IRC v Broadway Cottages Trust* [1954] 3 WLR 438; affd [1955] Ch 20, sub nom *Broadway Cottages Trust v IRC* [1954] TR 295, C; *O T Computer Ltd v First National Tricity Finance Ltd* [2007] WTLR 165. See below, pp 480 *et seq*.

[10] *Re Gulbenkian's Settlement Trusts* [1970] AC 508; *McPhail v Doulton* [1971] AC 424; *Re Baden's Deed Trusts (No 2)* [1973] Ch 9. See below pp 507 *et seq* and 536 *et seq*.

Obligation	Test of certainty	Authority	Requirements
Power	It must be possible to say whether any given individual is or is not a member of the class	*Re Gulbenkian* [1968] Ch 126	Conceptual certainty
Discretionary trusts	It must be possible to say whether any given individual is or is not a member of the class	*McPhail v Doulton* [1971] AC 424; *Re Baden* (No 2) [1972] Ch 607	Conceptual certainty
Fixed trusts	Complete list of all beneficiaries	*OT Computers Ltd v First National Tricity Finance Ltd* [2003] EWHC 1010 (Ch); [2007] WTLR 165	Conceptual and evidential certainty
Conditional gifts (conditions precedent)	Condition valid for those who can prove they satisfy the condition	*Re Barlow's Will Trust* [1979] 1 WLR 278	Individual proof

Figure 13.1 Tests for certainty of objects

(3) Summary

As has been noted above, different requirements of certainty are applied to different types of equitable obligation. Figure 13.1 summarizes the appropriate test for the main varieties of obligation. These will be examined in more detail in the following chapters.

3 Beneficial entitlement and ownership

A second recurrent theme is the question of the nature of the rights enjoyed by the potential objects of allocation in the fund. This will again depend on the exact nature of the equitable mechanism that has been created, and will range from a subsisting property interest in a share of the fund, to no property right at all in the fund. For example, Oliver has four children, Peter, Quentin, Robert, and Stuart. He leaves £100,000 to their godparents, Tristan and Una, to be allocated between them. The exact rights that the children have in the fund will depend on the type of equitable obligation that has been created.

(1) Fixed trust

At one end of the scale is the fixed trust, where Oliver stipulates that Tristan and Una are to hold the fund on trust for the children in equal shares. From the very moment that the trust is created, when the property comes into the hands of the trustees, the children have an immediate proprietary interest in the fund. They are each the owners in equity of a quarter of the trust property. They are liable for tax on their interest,[11] and it will be protected as against third parties who are not bona fide purchasers for value of a legal estate without notice.[12] The important decision of *Saunders v Vautier*[13] states that, as a consequence of having an immediate proprietary interest in the fund, the beneficiaries of a fixed trust can together demand that the legal title is transferred to them by the trustee. This means that if the four children were all of age and mentally competent they could demand that Tristan and Una convey the legal title to them.

(2) Power of appointment

At the other end of the scale is the power of appointment. If Oliver provides that Tristan and Una are to hold the property and that they have the power to appoint it in favour of such of his children as they may choose, then the children have no immediate proprietary interest in the fund at all.[14] None of them has any interest in the fund unless and until Tristan and Una exercise their power and make an appointment in favour of all or some of them.[15] If they make an appointment of £50,000 in favour of Robert, then Robert will have a proprietary right in the proportion of the fund that has been allocated to him, but he and the others continue to have no interest in the £50,000 comprising the other half of the fund. If there are no appointments the fund will pass by resulting trust[16] to the residuary legatees under Oliver's will.[17]

(3) Discretionary trust

Between these two extremes lies the discretionary trust, where the exact nature of the potential beneficiaries' right is unclear. The beneficiaries do not have immediate proprietary rights to specific shares of the fund, but they are not without any proprietary right in the fund as a whole. Oliver may have left the fund to Tristan and Una on trust to 'distribute among my children as they in their discretion think fit'. As a class, the children have proprietary rights to the fund, but as individuals they could not identify any particular share of the fund as their own, unless and until it was allocated to them by the trustee

---

[11] See Chapter 5.   [12] See Chapter 3.   [13] (1841) 4 Beav 115.
[14] *Vestey v IRC* [1980] AC 1148, HL.   [15] *Re Brooke's Settlement Trusts* [1939] Ch 993, at 997.
[16] See Chapter 9.
[17] Unless the rule in *Burroughs v Philcox* (1840) 5 My & Cr 72 applies. See Chapter 16.

They can, if they all come together, call for the transfer of the legal title under the rule in *Saunders v Vautier*,[18] as was done in *Re Smith*.[19] In practice, this would be almost impossible if the class were a large group, for example in the case of a discretionary trust for the benefit of 'all the employees and ex-employees' of a company. The position taken in *Gartside v IRC*[20] and *Sainsbury v IRC*[21] was that the potential beneficiary of a discretionary trust has no actual proprietary interest in the fund. Instead, he or she merely has a right to be considered as a beneficiary by the trustees. Once a selection has been made, the beneficiary has entitlement to the share allocated to him or her. This means that under a discretionary trust the beneficial interest in the property is held 'in the air' without a specific group who have proprietary rights in the fund, until allocations are made by the trustee.

4 Purpose trusts[22]

Since a trust creates a proprietary interest in favour of the beneficiaries, it is a cardinal principle that it must have beneficiaries who are capable of owning property and enforcing the trust. For this reason, the law insists that trusts must be for the benefit of legal persons[23] and not merely for the object of carrying out purposes. This limitation is not, however, absolute. By far the most significant exception to this rule is the area of charity, where purpose trusts are upheld as valid and a mechanism to supervise and enforce them is provided by the state for reasons of public policy.[24] There are also several minor exceptions that are considered below.

(1) The beneficiary principle

The rule against purpose trusts is long established. In *Morice v Bishop of Durham* Sir William Grant MR stated that:

Every . . . trust must have a definite object. There must be somebody, in whose favour the court can decree specific performance.[25]

Similarly, in *Bowman v Secular Society*[26] Lord Parker of Waddington said that 'for a trust to be valid it must be for the benefit of individuals'.[27]

---

18 (1841) 4 Beav 115.   19 [1928] Ch 915.

20 [1968] AC 553.   21 [1970] Ch 712.

22 See Matthews 'The New Trust: Obligations without Rights?' in Oakley, *Trends in Contemporary Trust Law* (1996).

23 See Naffine 'Who are Law's Persons? From Cheshire Cats to Responsible Subjects' (2003) 66 MLR 346.

24 See Chapter 19.   25 (1804) 9 Ves. Jr. 399 at 405.

26 [1917] AC 406, at 441.

27 See also *Leahy v A-G for New South Wales* [1959] AC 457, per Viscount Simmonds: 'a trust may be created for the benefit of persons as cestui que trust but not as a purpose or object unless the purpose or object be charitable'.

(a) Rationale for the beneficiary principle

There are three main problems with the validity of purpose trusts that have led to the adoption of the beneficiary principle.

(i) Without beneficiaries there is no owner

In its simplest form, a trust makes the beneficiaries into equitable owners. However, as has been seen, the principle that a trust fund 'belongs' to the beneficiaries is not absolute. There are many cases where property may—at least for a time—have no owner in equity. For instance, a trust in favour of Sandra's grandchildren will have no ascertained beneficiaries before at least one grandchild has been born. Similarly, a trust to invest and accumulate a fund for the first woman to land on the moon has no owner in equity until the condition has been satisfied.[28] A discretionary trust in favour of a large class defined in a conceptually certain way, but too large to list, has no identifiable owner. Yet again, it has been held that there is no beneficial owner of the estate of a deceased person until the completion of the administration of the estate. In *Stamp Duties Comr (Queensland) v Livingston*[29] a husband had died, leaving all his property by will to his wife, who had died shortly thereafter, and before the administration of her husband's estate had been completed. The Privy Council held that the wife's estate was not liable to pay death duties on the property she was expected to receive on the completion of the administration of her husband's estate because, until the administration was complete, she had no equitable title to the property. The personal representatives were the legal owners and there was no separate equitable owner; the personal representatives merely owed enforceable duties to the 'beneficiaries' of the will or intestacy to see that the administration of the estate was conducted properly. Since the personal representatives had no beneficial interest in the property—they could not keep it for their own use—it follows that, during administration of a deceased's estate, there is no equitable beneficial owner. The concept of property being subject to enforceable obligations but having no immediate beneficial owner is thus well established. This should not be an objection to purpose trusts.

(ii) The trust cannot be enforced by the court

Where a trust is created to carry out a purpose there is no person with locus standi to apply to the court to ensure that the terms of the trust are being carried out and that the trustees do not act in breach of trust, for example by misappropriating the trust property for themselves. The supervision of trusts relies first and foremost on the beneficiaries, as the persons most interested in the proper administration of the trust, bringing abuses to the attention of the court.[30]

---

[28] The rule against perpetuities requires a perpetuity period to be specified.

[29] [1965] AC 694.

[30] See Chapter 28. See also *Re Astor's Settlement Trusts* [1952] Ch 534, at 549; *Re Shaw* [1957] 1 WLR 729, at 744–746.

(iii) The trust will violate the rule against perpetuity

The law has always been reluctant to allow property to become subject to restrictions that would unduly prevent its free marketability. Where property is subject to a trust, it is not freely available and the terms of the trust may prevent its most efficient use. For this reason the law provides that property may not be subject to a trust for an excessive period of time. A private trust (as opposed to a charitable trust) must not exceed the perpetuity period, which has been defined to consist of the duration of a human life in being at the date that the trust was established plus an additional period of twenty-one years. If a trust were created for the carrying out of a purpose, there is no guarantee that the purpose would ever be completed so as to bring the trust to an end. The property would therefore be perpetually held on trust. If property is subject to a trust for persons, the perpetuity period is less likely to be violated, as the beneficiary will be a life in being and the trust will not endure beyond his death, although problems may occur if successive interests are created behind a trust. If a trust offends against the perpetuity period it is void ab initio.[31]

(b) Application of the beneficiary principle

The beneficiary principle was applied so as to invalidate the trust in *Re Astor's Settlement Trusts*.[32] A settlement was made by Viscount Astor of all the issued shares of the *Observer* newspaper. The terms of the trust were that the income was to be applied for the 'maintenance ... of good understanding between nations' and 'the preservation of the independence and integrity of the newspapers', purposes which were considered not to be charitable. Roxburgh J held that the trust was invalid on two grounds, first that it offended against the beneficiary principle, and second that the purposes were uncertain. He examined the principle laid down by Lord Parker in *Bowman v Secular Society*[33] and concluded that it was not susceptible to attack from a base of principle,[34] and that it was well established in authority.[35] He referred to *Re Wood*,[36] where Harman J had asserted the orthodox position that 'a gift on trust must have a cestui que trust'.[37] Since the purposes did not fall within any of the exceptions to the beneficiary principle, the trust was void.

In *Re Shaw*[38] George Bernard Shaw left his residuary estate to trustees to apply the income to purposes including research into a proposed 40-letter alphabet, and the transliteration of one of his plays into such an alphabet. These were held not to be charitable purposes, and they failed as purpose trusts. Harman J indicated some dissatisfaction with the 'beneficiary principle',[39] but felt himself bound by the higher authority of the House of Lords and Court of Appeal.[40] In *Re Endacott*[41] Harman LJ

---

[31] The more relaxed rules in the Perpetuities and Accumulations Act 1964 only apply to the rule against remoteness of vesting, not to the rule against perpetual trusts.

[32] [1952] Ch 534.   [33] [1917] AC 406.   [34] Ibid., at 541.

[35] Ibid., at 546.   [36] [1949] Ch 498.   [37] Ibid., at 501.

[38] [1957] 1 WLR 729.   [39] Ibid., at 745.

[40] *Bowman v Secular Society* [1917] AC 406; *Re Diplock* [1941] Ch 253, at 259; *IRC v Broadway Cottages Trust* [1955] Ch 20, CA.

[41] [1960] Ch 232.

in the Court of Appeal applied the beneficiary principle to a gift by Albert Endacott to the North Tawton Devon Parish Council 'for the purposes of providing some useful memorial to myself'. He did not indicate any of the doubts he had mentioned in *Re Shaw*[42] but instead applauded the 'orthodox sentiments expressed by Roxburgh J in the *Astor* case'.[43] The Court of Appeal held that the gift was a non-charitable purpose trust that did not fall within any of the exceptions to the beneficiary principle.

(2) Exceptions to the beneficiary principle

Whilst the cases cited above confirm the existence of the 'beneficiary principle' rendering non-charitable purpose trusts void, English law recognizes a number of exceptions where pure non-charitable purpose trusts will be upheld despite the lack of beneficiaries. There is no logical rationale for these exceptions, and in this sense they are said to be anomalous. In *Re Astor's Settlement Trusts*, Roxburgh J reviewed the exceptions and commented that they were 'anomalous and exceptional…concessions to human weakness or sentiment'.[44] In *Re Endacott*[45] Harman LJ confirmed their anomalous nature, and indicated that the number of exceptions should not be increased. They are decisions:

which are not really to be satisfactorily classified, but are perhaps merely occasions where Homer has nodded, at any rate these cases stand by themselves and ought not to be increased in number, nor indeed followed, except where the one is exactly like the other.[46]

Even where a trust falls within the ambit of one of the anomalous exceptions, it will be void if it offends the rule against perpetual trusts because it might exceed the perpetuity period. Opinion differs as to the exact juridical status of the exceptions but they are best regarded as valid unenforceable trusts ('trusts of imperfect obligation').[47] As such, they are not void, but the trustees cannot be required to carry out the trust, though the court will prevent them from misapplying the trust property.

(a) Care of particular animals

A trust for the welfare of animals in general, or of a particular class of animals, will be charitable. A trust for the maintenance of a specific animal is not charitable but may be upheld as an anomalous exception to the beneficiary principle, provided that it does not offend against the perpetuity period. In *Pettingall v Pettingall*[48] a gift by a testator of £50 per annum for the upkeep of his favourite black mare was upheld. In *Mitford v Reynolds*[49] a gift for the upkeep of the testator's horses was upheld. In *Re Dean*[50] William Dean left his eight horses and his hounds to his trustees, and charged

---

[42] [1957] 1 WLR 729.   [43] *Re Endacott* [1960] Ch 232, at 250.

[44] [1952] Ch 534, at 547.   [45] [1960] Ch 232, CA.   [46] Ibid., at 250–251.

[47] See (1953) 17 Conv (NS) 46 (Sheridan); (1953) 6 CLP 151 (Marshall); Morris and Leach, *The Rule Against Perpetuities* (2nd edn, 1962) Ch 12; Maudsley, *The Modern Law of Perpetuities* (1979), pp 166–178; (1970) 34 Conv (NS) 77 (Lovell); (1973) 37 Conv (NS) 420 (McKay); (1971) 87 LQR 31 (Harris); (1970) 40 MLR 397 (Gravells); (1977) 41 Conv (NS) 179 (Widdows).

[48] (1842) 11 LJ Ch 176, at 177.   [49] (1848) 16 Sim 105.

[50] (1889) 41 Ch D 552.

his freehold estates with an annuity of £750 per year for fifty years, if they should live that long, to be paid to the trustees for their upkeep. North J held that this was a valid non-charitable trust. However, he seemed to reject the 'beneficiary principle' entirely, stating that he did not assent to the view that a trust is not valid if there is no cestui que trust to enforce it.[51] Although *Re Dean* has been taken as authority for the upholding of trusts for the maintenance of particular animals, the reasoning is incompatible with the beneficiary principle.

Another difficulty with *Re Dean*[52] is that it seems to offend against the perpetuity period. A non-charitable trust must not last beyond the period of lives in being plus twenty-one years. In *Re Dean* the gift to the horses and hounds was for a maximum of fifty years, which exceeds the perpetuity period. One possible solution would be to measure the perpetuity period by reference to an animal life, but this was rejected by Meredith J in *Re Kelly*,[53] who said 'there can be no doubt that "lives" means lives of human beings, not of animals or trees in California'. In some cases the courts have taken judicial notice that an animal's lifespan is less than twenty-one years,[54] or that the particular animal has less than twenty-one years to live. Again, this approach was questioned in *Re Kelly*.[55] It would still leave problems with animals that clearly have a life expectancy beyond twenty-one years.

The most common circumstance in which a trust will be established for a particular animal is where a testator leaves property for the benefit of his favourite pet.[56] It should not be forgotten in such circumstances that the animal also constitutes property and ownership of it will also devolve on the testator's death. The new owner will have the prime responsibility to care for the animal and failure of the trust does not necessarily mean that there is no one to care for the animal.

It must not be forgotten, either, that a gift to an individual with a statement that it is to be used for a particular purpose will often be treated as an absolute gift. The expression of the purpose is considered to be no more than the motive for the gift, imposing a moral obligation rather than a legally binding trust obligation.

(b) Maintenance of specific graves and monuments

Trusts to provide for the maintenance of specific graves and monuments have been upheld as valid and unenforceable despite the lack of a beneficiary who can enforce

---

[51] Ibid., at 556–557.   [52] (1889) 41 Ch D 552.

[53] [1932] IR 255, at 260–261.

[54] See *Re Haines* (1952) The Times, 7 November, where Danckwerts J took judicial notice that a cat would not live for more than twenty-one years and upheld the gift.

[55] Meredith J: 'It was suggested that the last of the dogs could in fact not outlive the testator by more than twenty-one years. I know nothing of that. The court does not enter into the question of a dog's expectation of life. In point of fact neighbours' dogs and cats are unpleasantly long lived...'

[56] See Brown 'What Are We To Do with Testamentary Trusts of Imperfect Obligation?' [2007] Conv 148, where a survey of probate practitioners demonstrated that such trusts are still common, along with testamentary trusts for the maintenance of specific graves or monuments.

them.[57] In *Mitford v Reynolds*[58] a gift for the erection of a monument was upheld as valid. In *Pirbright v Salwey*[59] a gift of £800 for the upkeep of the burial enclosure of a child in a churchyard for 'as long as the law permitted' was upheld for at least twenty-one years from the testator's death. In *Re Hooper*[60] a testator left £1,000 to his executors to use the income for the upkeep of various family graves and monuments for 'so long as they legally can do so'. Following *Pirbright v Salwey*[61] Maugham J held that the trust was valid for twenty-one years from the testator's death. If the purpose exceeds the perpetuity period, the trust will be void. In *Mussett v Bingle*[62] a testator gave £300 for the erection of a monument and £200 to provide income for its upkeep. This second gift was held void for perpetuity.[63]

This exception did not apply in *Re Endacott* because no specific memorial was identified: 'some useful memorial' was too vague. Even though suitable projects like a bus shelter, a park bench, or public conveniences might come to mind, there was insufficient guidance to enable the trustees to direct the property to a specific project.

(c) Saying masses for the dead

According to Catholic theology, on death the soul does not go direct to heaven but to purgatory, a place of punishment where unforgiven sins must be paid for before the soul can go to heaven. The saying of masses for the dead soul may reduce the length of time that must be spent in purgatory. Thus, testators may seek to leave money to provide for the saying of masses for the benefit of their own souls, or those of their relatives. The saying of masses for the dead was held to be a charitable activity for the advancement of religion in *Re Hetherington (Decd)*,[64] provided they are celebrated in public. Thus, a trust for the saying of masses may be valid as a charity. However, it is possible that a gift for the saying of masses in private will be a valid unenforceable purpose trust even though it is not charitable. Such an approach is suggested by the decision of the House of Lords in *Bourne v Keane*.[65] Again, the duration of the gift must not exceed the perpetuity period.

The exception may also extend to the provision of other non-charitable rites. In *Re Khoo Cheng Teow*[66] a gift for the performance of ceremonies called Sin Chew to perpetuate the testator's memory during the perpetuity period was upheld by the Supreme Court of the Straits settlement.

---

[57] See *Trimmer v Danby* (1856) 25 LJ Ch 424 (testator gave £1,000 to his executors to erect a monument to himself in St Paul's Cathedral).

[58] (1848) 16 Sim 105.   [59] [1896] WN 86.   [60] [1932] 1 Ch 38.

[61] [1896] WN 86.   [62] [1876] WN 170.

[63] By s 1 of the Parish Councils and Burial Authorities (Miscellaneous Provisions) Act 1970 a burial authority may agree, for the payment of a sum, to maintain a grave or monument for a period not exceeding 99 years.

[64] [1990] Ch 1.

[65] [1919] AC 815; see also *Re Hetherington (Decd)* [1989] 2 All ER 129, at 132.

[66] [1932] Straits Settlements LR 226.

(3) Policy limitations on purpose trusts

Even if a purpose trust falls within the anomalous exceptions, it appears that it will be invalid if it is for capricious or useless purposes. In *Brown v Burdett*[67] a trust to block up all the rooms of a house for twenty years was held void. The Scottish courts have been astute to hold that trusts for useless purposes are invalid on grounds of public policy. In *M'Caig v University of Glasgow*[68] a trust to erect statues of the testator and 'artistic towers' on his estates was set aside. In *M'Caig's Trustees v Kirk-Session of United Free Church of Lismore*[69] a trust to erect bronze statues of the testatrix's parents and their children was void on grounds of public policy, since it involved 'a sheer waste of money'.[70]

(4) Trusts for purposes that will benefit an identifiable class of persons

Whilst a non-charitable purpose trust will generally be void unless it falls within the limited categories of the anomalous exceptions, a trust will not be void merely because it is expressed to be for the carrying out of a purpose if it will in fact benefit identifiable individuals who possess sufficient locus standi to enforce it. The central question is whether the carrying out of the specified purpose directly or indirectly benefits an ascertainable and certain group of individuals.

(a) The rule in *Re Denley's Trust Deed*[71]

In *Re Denley's Trust Deed*[72] the court upheld a gift that appeared to establish a purpose trust. Charles Denley had transferred land to trustees to be maintained and used as a sports field for the employees of a company. Goff J took the view that, although the trust was expressed to be for a purpose, it was in fact for the benefit of individuals (the employees of the company) because they would benefit, directly or indirectly, from the carrying out of the purpose. As such, it was outside the mischief of the beneficiary principle.[73] Since the employees were an ascertainable and certain class, they had locus standi to apply to the court to enforce the trust. He emphasized that the employees gained a direct benefit from the carrying out of the purposes, and warned that if the benefit was not so direct or intangible the beneficiary principle would invalidate the trust.[74] The trust was therefore upheld because the court could act to enforce it at the suit of the beneficiaries, either negatively by restraining any improper disposition

---

[67] (1882) 21 Ch D 667.   [68] 1907 SC 231.   [69] 1915 SC 426.

[70] Per Lord Salvesen. Other cases include *Aitken's Trustees v Aitken* 1927 SC 374 (erection of a massive bronze equestrian statue); *Lindsay's Executor v Forsyth* 1940 SC 568 (£1,000 on trust to provide weekly supply of flowers to own and mother's graves).

[71] For comment on *Re Denley's Trust Deed* see Jaconelli 'Independent Schools, Purpose Trusts and Human Rights' [1996] Conv 24; Matthews, 'The New Trust: Obligations without Rights' in Oakley, *Trends in Contemporary Trust Law* (1996), pp 13–15.

[72] [1969] 1 Ch 373.   [73] Ibid., at 383–384.   [74] Ibid., at 383.

or use of the land, or positively by ordering the trustees to allow the employees to use the land for recreation.[75]

Although the decision prevents the trust falling foul of the beneficiary principle by finding that the employees can enforce the trust, it does not answer the problem of the beneficial ownership of the land. Do the trustees hold the land on trust for the employees? If so, the employees could together demand the transfer of the land to them under the principle of *Saunders v Vautier*,[76] for example if they wanted to sell it to a supermarket for a lucrative development. If that were the case, it would defeat the settlor's intention in establishing the trust. The only other logical conclusion from the decision is that the beneficial interest is suspended for the duration of the trust, which must be limited to the perpetuity period.

(b) Application of the principle to an unincorporated association

Re Denley's Trust Deed was applied in slightly different circumstances by Oliver J in *Re Lipinski's Will Trusts*.[77] Harry Lipinski left his residuary estate to the Hull Judeans (Maccabi) Association in memory of his wife, to be used solely in constructing new buildings for the association. As the gift was made to an unincorporated association the only way it could be upheld was if it was a gift to the individual members of the association.[78] However, it would be difficult to construe a gift for a purpose as a gift to the individual members. Oliver J adopted *Re Denley's Trust Deed* with approval, and concluded that although this gift was expressed as a gift for a purpose (the new buildings) it was directly for the benefit of the members of the Association and could be construed as a gift to them as individuals. He summarized the principle of the case:

A trust which, though expressed as a purpose, was directly or indirectly for the benefit of an individual or individuals was valid provided those individuals were ascertainable at any one time and the trust was not otherwise void for uncertainty.[79]

In conclusion, this means that although a gift may be expressed as a gift to a purpose, the court can find that it is really a gift for the benefit of individuals if there is a certain and ascertainable class who will benefit sufficiently directly from its performance. Provided it is not void for perpetuity, it will be upheld.

(c) Inapplicability of the *Denley* principle to an administratively unworkable class

The principle in *Re Denley's Trust Deed* will not apply if the class of beneficiaries is administratively unworkable through being too wide to form anything like a class. In *R v District Auditor, exp West Yorkshire Metropolitan County Council*[80] a trust was established to assist economic development, youth, and community projects and encourage ethnic and minority groups for 'the benefit of all or any or some of the inhabitants of West Yorkshire'. It was held invalid as a private purpose trust, and it

---

[75] Ibid., at 388. [76] (1841) 4 Beav 115. [77] [1976] Ch 235.

[78] See Chapter 24. [79] [1976] Ch 235, at 248.

[80] [1986] RVR 24.

could not be upheld on the basis of the *Denley* principle. This is because there were no 'ascertained or ascertainable beneficiaries', as the court had also held that with some 2.5 million potential beneficiaries, the trust was administratively unworkable.[81]

(5) Criticism of the beneficiary principle[82]

The central reason for the beneficiary principle is that if a trust does not have beneficiaries then the court will not be able to enforce and supervise it. As Roxburgh J said in *Re Astor's Settlement Trusts*:

a court of equity does not recognise as valid a trust which it cannot both enforce and control.[83]

Where there is no beneficiary, there is no one in whose favour the court can order performance. There is also no one who is interested in the performance of the trust to apply to the court if the obligation is not being appropriately performed. The court relies on the self-interest of beneficiaries to police trusts and bring any wrongdoing on the part of the trustees to their attention.

However, the force of these objections may have been overstated. Where a trust is made for a purpose, there is always someone who will be entitled to the property in default if the purpose is not carried out,[84] whether the residuary legatee under a will or the owner of the property himself under a resulting trust. Such a person would have sufficient interest to apply to the court if the property were being misapplied by the trustee. This would provide a potential mechanism for control and enforcement.[85] Roxburgh J noted in *Re Astor's Settlement Trusts* that in many of the cases of exceptions to the beneficiary principle there was a residuary legatee who would be able to ensure that the purpose was carried out.[86] Such a mechanism for enforcement seems to have been applied in *Re Thompson*.[87] The testator bequeathed £1,000 to his friend, George Lloyd, to be applied for the promotion of fox hunting.[88] The residuary legatee under the will was Trinity Hall, University of Cambridge. Clauson J ordered that the executors pay the money to Lloyd, on his giving an undertaking that he would so apply the money. Trinity Hall would be at liberty to apply to the court if the property

---

[81] See Harpum 'Administrative Unworkability and Purpose Trusts' (1986) 45 CLJ 391.

[82] See Hayton 'Developing the Obligation Characteristic of the Trust' (2001) 117 LQR 96.

[83] [1952] Ch 534, at 549.

[84] Although that person will not always be immediately ascertainable, as where the residuary beneficiary is whoever happens to be the Vice-Chancellor of the University of Buckingham twenty-one years from the death of the testator.

[85] See Brown 'What are We to Do with Testamentary Trusts of Imperfect Obligation?' [2007] Conv 148, at pp. 159–160.

[86] *Pettingall v Pettingall* (1842) 11 LJ Ch 176; *Mitford v Reynolds* (1848) 16 Sim 105; *Re Dean* (1889) 41 Ch D 552; *Re Hooper* [1932] 1 Ch 38; *Pirbright v Salwey* [1896] WN 86. See also *Re Astor's Settlement Trusts* [1952] Ch 534, at 542–545.

[87] [1934] Ch 342.

[88] Such a gift could no longer be upheld, as fox hunting with hounds is now illegal, following the Hunting Act 2004.

was misapplied. Although this seems to offer a way of avoiding the beneficiary principle, the case is of limited value. The case was uncontested, and both parties wanted
to see the gift upheld. The court only granted the order that they together requested.
The result would have been different if the residuary legatee had not wanted to see the
purpose performed, but had wanted to see the gift fail so that they would receive the
£1,000 as part of the residue.

The problem with this mechanism for enforcement is that in most cases the residuary legatees, who would be able to apply to the court to prevent misapplication of
the funds, are the very people who will benefit if the purpose is not carried out and
therefore have no incentive to ensure that the testator's wishes are followed. In fact, in
most cases they are actively challenging the validity of the purpose trust because they
will be entitled to the property in default. Under a trust, the beneficiaries stand to gain
if the trust is properly administered, but the residuary legatee under a purpose trust
will not gain from the performance of the purpose. The motivation of self-interest is
the key to the proper supervision of trusts, and in the case of purpose trusts that self-
interest is not present. This mechanism for enforcement would only be able to ensure
that the property was not misapplied, but would not be able to ensure that the trustee
carried out his duty to perform the trust.

In the light of these difficulties, other jurisdictions have introduced statutory
schemes that facilitate the enforcement of non-charitable purposes trusts.[89] The
essence of many such schemes is the introduction of a third party 'enforcer' who is
empowered to act to ensure that the trustees carry out their duties. For example, under
the Cayman Islands Special Trusts (Alternative Regime) Law 1997[90] the 'enforcer' of
a trust, who may not himself enjoy any interest in the trust property, is granted 'the
same personal and proprietary remedies against the trustee and against third parties
as a beneficiary of an ordinary trust'.[91] The enforcer therefore performs a similar function to that of the Crown in relation to the oversight and enforcement of charitable
trusts. Whilst such regimes have been adopted in many offshore jurisdictions,[92] no
equivalent has yet been adopted in England.[93]

(6) The beneficiary principle and certainty of objects

There is a very close relationship between the beneficiary principle and the requirement that the objects of a trust must be certain. In both cases, the requirement follows from the fact that the court must be able to supervise and enforce the operation

---

[89] For example, Jersey, Bermuda, Isle of Man, Cayman Islands, British Virgin Islands.

[90] See Duckworth, *STAR Trusts* (1998, Gostick Hall Publications).

[91] S 7(1).

[92] Note also that the Ontario Perpetuities Act 1966 enacts that trusts for non-charitable purposes should
be construed as powers, thus overcoming the beneficiary principle, and that the US Uniform Trust Code
permits purpose trusts for twenty-one years.

[93] See Pawlowski and Summers 'Private Purpose Trusts—A Reform Proposal' [2007] Conv 440, advocating proposals for statutory reform of private purpose trusts along similar lines to those found in the offshore
jurisdictions listed.

of the trust. It is possible to re-analyse the cases that have offended against the beneficiary principle as cases of uncertainty. Where the purpose is so uncertain that the court could not properly supervise or enforce its execution, then it will not be valid. If the purpose is sufficiently certain and its performance is capable of judicial scrutiny, then it should be valid and upheld.

In *Re Thompson*[94] Clauson J emphasized that the purpose was 'defined with sufficient clearness and is of a nature to which effect can be given'.[95] Similarly, the anomalous exceptions that have been recognized are all sufficiently certain to enable a court to determine whether the property is being applied to the purpose specified. The court can objectively assess whether specified graves are being maintained, animals cared for, or masses said. In contrast, *Re Astor's Settlement Trusts*,[96] *Re Shaw*[97] and *Re Endacott*[98] are all explicable on the basis of uncertainty. It would have been impossible for the court to scrutinize whether the trust property was being applied to the 'maintenance...of good understanding...between nations', or 'the preservation of the independence and the integrity of newspapers', because these concepts are themselves uncertain.[99] Similarly, a trust to provide 'some useful memorial to myself' is unenforceable because it is uncertain.[100] How would the court be able to decide whether the terms of the trust had been carried out?

Although this analysis on the basis of certainty is attractive, and would eliminate the beneficiary principle as an independent requirement, it is not supported by present authority. Uncertainty was a secondary ground for the decision in *Re Astor's Settlement Trusts*[101] and the objection that there were no beneficiaries was treated separately. In *Re Endacott* Lord Evershed MR made absolutely clear that there was a separate 'beneficiary principle':

No principle perhaps has greater sanction or authority behind it than the general proposition that a trust by English law, not being a charitable trust, in order to be effective must have ascertained or ascertainable beneficiaries.[102]

5 Charitable and benevolent giving

Although purpose trusts are not as a general rule valid, it is often the case that owners wish to allocate their property to purposes rather than to specific individuals. This is particularly so when owners want to support causes that they consider to be worthy. The law provides that certain purposes are charitable and gifts and trusts for these purposes are valid, even though there are no beneficiaries

---

94 [1934] Ch 342.   95 [1934] Ch 342, at 344.   96 [1952] Ch 534.
97 [1957] 1 WLR 729.   98 [1960] Ch 232.   99 See [1952] Ch 534, at 548.
100 [1960] Ch 232, at 247, per Lord Evershed MR: 'though this trust is specific, in the sense that it indicates a purpose capable of expression, yet it is of far too wide and uncertain a nature...'
101 [1952] Ch 534.   102 [1960] Ch 232, at 246.

as such. The purposes considered charitable are those that have come to be recognized as for the 'public good', and which are now listed in the Charities Act 2006.[103]

Charitable trusts are not only valid but also enjoy extensive financial support through government grants and tax exemptions.[104] The state provides a mechanism by which they can be enforced and supervised, thus preventing their invalidity under the beneficiary principle. They are enforced by the Attorney General or Charity Commission in the name of the Crown. The general administration of charities is supervised by the Charity Commission. All this State support of purpose trusts is provided in the interests of encouraging giving to worthy causes. The definition of 'charity' is fully considered in Chapter 19 and the control of charities in Chapter 28.

6 The duty to act even-handedly

(1) A general duty

Where a trust has been created for the benefit of multiple beneficiaries, the trustees who have the task of allocating the property have a duty to act even-handedly between them, so that they are all treated impartially and no favouritism is shown to one beneficiary or category of beneficiaries. In *Lloyds Bank plc v Duker*[105] John Mowbray, QC stated that there was a general principle that:

trustees are bound to hold an even hand among their beneficiaries and not to favour one as against another.[106]

This clearly means that a trustee must not be partisan to the interests of one beneficiary at the expense of others.[107] The Law Reform Committee in its 23rd Report[108] recommended that trustees be under a statutory duty to hold a fair balance between beneficiaries.[109]

The need to maintain even-handedness between beneficiaries is particularly acute in two contexts: first, in the context of discretionary trusts where the trustee is entitled to decide how the trust property should be allocated among the class of beneficiaries; and, secondly, where a trust creates successive interests so that a life tenant is to enjoy the income generated by the trust property for his lifetime, but the person entitled to the remainder interest will receive the capital of the fund on his death.

---

[103] Charities Act 2006, s 2. See Chapter 19   [104] See Chapter 19.
[105] [1987] 1 WLR 1324.
[106] Ibid., at 1330–1331, citing *Snell's Principles of Equity* (28th edn, 1982), p 225.
[107] See *Simpson v Bathurst* (1869) 5 Ch App 193, at 202.   [108] Cmnd 8733.
[109] Ibid., at para 3.36.

(2) **The duty to act even-handedly in the context of a discretionary trust**

The trustees' duty to act even-handedly in the context of a discretionary trust was examined by the Court of Appeal in *Edge v Pensions Ombudsman*.[110] The case concerned a decision by the trustees of a pension scheme to increase the benefits payable to members in service on a particular date. Pensioners who had been in service prior to this date complained to the ombudsman that the changes in the rules introduced were unjust. At first instance, Scott V-C concluded that the trustees were under a duty to act impartially between the different beneficiaries, and that they had acted with 'undue partiality' towards those preferred by the rule change. He rejected any notion of a general duty to act impartially in the context of a discretionary trust as the very essence of the trust is that the trustees select some to benefit from the wider class of potential beneficiaries. Instead, he held that the trustees were under a duty not to take into account irrelevant, irrational, or improper factors. Chadwick LJ, delivering the opinion of the Court of Appeal, cited Scott V-C's words with approval and agreed that the trustees had properly exercised their discretion and had in fact considered the position of those pensioners who would not benefit. The Pensions Ombudsman and the court had no right to interfere in the proper exercise of a discretionary trust. He concluded:

Properly understood, the so-called duty to act impartially…is no more than the ordinary duty which the law imposes on a person who is entrusted with the exercise of a discretionary power: that he exercises the power for the purpose for which it is given, giving proper consideration to the matters which are relevant and excluding from consideration matters which are irrelevant. If pension fund trustees do that, they cannot be criticised if they reach a decision which appears to prefer the claims of one interest—whether that of employers, current employees or pensioners—over others. The preference will be the result of a proper exercise of the discretionary power.[111]

(3) **The duty to act even-handedly in the context of successive interests**

Where property is subject to a life interest behind a trust it is important to ensure that both the life tenant and those entitled to the remainder receive a fair share of the fruits of the trust fund, and that the fund is not invested and allocated in such a way that income is generated at the expense of the preservation of the capital, or that the capital is preserved but no income is generated. Equity has tackled this problem by means of rules designed to ensure that the trust fund is invested in such investments as by their very nature will operate fairly in producing income whilst preserving capital.

(a) The duty to convert investments

(i) The rule in Howe v Earl of Dartmouth

As will be seen in Chapter 23, the trustees may be under a duty to convert unauthorized investments. This duty may be expressly imposed in the trust instrument or,

---

[110] [2000] Ch 602. [111] Ibid., at 627.

in the case of a residuary bequest in a will, implied[112] under the rule in *Howe v Earl of Dartmouth*.[113] This has the effect that the trustee must sell unauthorized investments that by their very nature operate unfairly between the life tenant and the remainderman and then reinvest the realized funds in authorized investments. For example, if the trust fund consists of wasting assets, for example copyrights,[114] the consequence of retaining them would be that they would generate a large income for the life tenant, but would be of rapidly depreciating capital value, leaving perhaps little or nothing for the remainderman. The introduction of a general power of trustees to invest as if absolutely entitled to the assets of the trust in the Trustee Act 2000 has vastly extended the range of authorized investments, so that the circumstances in which the rule in *Howe v Earl of Dartmouth* will apply have been significantly restricted.[115]

(ii) Reform of the rule in Howe v Earl of Dartmouth

In May 2009, the Law Commission issued a report recommending that the rule in *Howe v Earl of Dartmouth* requiring the trustees to convert unauthorized investments (as well as some other equitable rules) be abolished in all new trusts.[116] Originally, the Commission had also proposed the adoption of a new statutory power for trustees to allocate investment returns and trust expenses as income or capital in so far as in necessary to maintain a balance between income and capital.[117] This no longer forms part of their recommendations.[118] The Commission also recommends that the implied trust for sale that exists where a trustee is under an obligation to convert unauthorized or hazardous wasting assets would be abolished.[119] This proposal is discussed more fully below.

(b) Apportionment between income and capital

(i) The general rules

Where the trustees are subject to a duty to convert the trust property, it is inevitable that there will be some delay between the time that the trustee receives the property as comprising part of the fund and when he is able to convert it. When the property has been converted and its value realized, the question arises as to how it should then be allocated between the life tenant and the remainderman. It would not be fair for the whole of the proceeds of the converted assets to be applied entirely to capital, since if it

---

[112] Unless it is excluded by contrary intention of the testator: *Hinves v Hinves* (1844) 3 Hare 609; *Re Pitcairn* [1896] 2 Ch 199.

[113] (1802) 7 Ves JR 137.   [114] *Re Sullivan* [1930] 1 Ch 84.

[115] *Capital and Income in Trusts: Classification and Apportionment*, Law Comm CP No 175 (2004), para 3.8.

[116] *Capital and Income in Trusts: Classification and Apportionment*, Law Comm No 319 (2009) para 6.65.

[117] *Capital and Income in Trusts: Classification and Apportionment*, Law Comm CP No 175 (2004) para 1.21.

[118] *Capital and Income in Trusts: Classification and Apportionment*, Law Comm No 319 (2009) para 5.81.

[119] Ibid. (2009), para 6.53.

was a non-income-generating asset the life tenant would have been entitled to receive some income from it during the period of time that it had not yet been converted. The rules of apportionment determine how an allocation is to be made of the realized value of the converted asset between income and capital. Obviously, any express intentions of the testator or settlor will take priority over the implied rules of apportionment. The exact application of the rules will depend upon the type of property that was converted.

The basic position is that when unauthorized investments are converted, the life tenant is entitled to receive the income that he would have received if they had been authorized investments all along. This has been held to an income of 4 per cent per annum on the value of the converted asset from the date of the death of the testator to the date of the conversion.[120] The remainder of the value realized by the conversion is to be reinvested as capital of the fund. For example, if the asset was of a wasting nature that created a large income, it is possible that the actual income generated between the death of the testator and the conversion would be greater than 4 per cent of the value of the asset. In such a case, the life tenant would only be entitled to receive the equivalent of 4 per cent and the remainder would be applied to capital. However, if the asset did not generate income equivalent to 4 per cent, the life tenant would be entitled to receive such an amount from the realized value, and the remainder would then be applied to capital.

One crucial question is the date at which the value of the converted asset is to be calculated, so as to enable apportionment to take place. This will depend on whether the trust instrument grants the trustees an express power to postpone conversion. Where there is no power to postpone conversion, the trustees are expected to convert the assets within the 'executor's year'. If the assets are converted within the year, the relevant value is the actual amount realized on conversion.[121] However, if they are not sold within the year, the relevant value is the value one year from the date of death.[122] The life tenant is then entitled to the equivalent of 4 per cent per annum interest on that value and the remainder will be applied to capital. Where the trustees have the power to postpone the conversion, the relevant date for valuing the asset is the date of the testator's death.[123]

The operation of these rules is neatly illustrated by the facts of *Brown v Gellatly*.[124] An estate consisted of several unauthorized assets to which a duty to convert applied, including some ships. With respect to the ships, there was a power to postpone the conversion. Therefore, the relevant date for valuation of the ships was the date of death, but the relevant date for the other unauthorized investments was a year from the testator's death.

---

[120]   *Re Fawcett* [1940] Ch 402.   [121]   [1940] Ch 402.

[122]   *Dimes v Scott* (1828) 4 Russ 195.

[123]   *Brown v Gellatly* (1867) 2 Ch App 751; *Re Owen* [1912] 1 Ch 519; *Re Parry* [1947] Ch 23; *Re Berry* [1962] Ch 97.

[124]   (1867) 2 Ch App 751.

(ii) Rules applicable to a reversionary interest

Where the assets of the trust include a reversionary interest and there is a duty to convert by selling and reinvesting in authorized investments, a different rule of apportionment applies. In *Re Earl of Chesterfield's Trusts*[125] it was held that the sum to be allocated to capital was the sum which, if it had been invested at 4 per cent per annum compound interest, taking account of income tax, would have produced the sum which was actually realized by the sale of the interest. The remainder of the realized value is then to be paid to the life tenant as income. This rule may be displaced, and if the will demonstrates the testator's intention that the life tenant was to receive the actual income generated, he will receive nothing by way of income.[126]

(iii) Rules applicable to leaseholds

The rule in *Howe v Earl of Dartmouth*[127] originally applied to leaseholds. However, these are now authorized investments under the Trusts of Land and Appointment of Trustees Act 1996, s 6(3).

(iv) Reform of apportionment

The current equitable rules governing apportionment can be criticized on the grounds that they are rigid, technical, and outdated.[128] They require very complex calculations affecting small amounts of money. The rate of interest used to calculate the respective allocations to income or capital may also be criticized. A figure of 4 per cent may be appropriate in times of low inflation and low interest rates, but is wholly inappropriate when there is high inflation. In other areas a more flexible approach has been developed, for example the interest payable by a trustee for breach of trust is the same as that paid on the court's short-term investment account. In the light of these criticisms a number of proposals for reform have been made. The Law Commission has now issued a report and Draft Bill, proposing the abolition of all existing equitable rules of apportionment in all new trusts, subject to any contrary provision in the trust instrument.[129] If the Bill were to be enacted, existing trusts would therefore be unaffected. Moreover, in new trusts, settlors and testators would be able to make express provision in the trust instrument if they wished to replicate the effect of the existing equitable rules.

The Commission proposes that, in place of the existing equitable rules, the sale and reinvestment of trust property should form part of a trustee's general

---

[125] (1883) LR 24 Ch D 643.

[126] *Mackie v Mackie* (1845) 5 Hare 70; *Rowlls v Bebb* [1900] 2 Ch 107, CA.

[127] (1802) 7 Ves Jr 137.

[128] *Capital and Income in Trusts: Classification and Apportionment*, Law Comm No 319 (2009), para A.6: 'Professionally drafted trust instruments generally exclude them. In most trusts where they have not been excluded they are either ignored or cause considerable inconvenience by requiring complex calculations in relation to very small sums of money.'

[129] *Capital and Income in Trusts: Classification and Apportionment*, Law Comm No 319 (2009), paras 6.54–6.65 and cl 1(2)(a)-(2b) (*Howe v Early of Dartmouth* rules) and cl.1(3) (*Re Earl of Chesterfield's Trusts* rule).

investment duties under the Trustee Act 2000.[130] The creation of a general discretion or power simply to replace the equitable rules was considered and rejected for tax considerations.[131] The Commission also felt unable to provide a series of limited discretions to cover the circumstances existing under the existing equitable rules of allocation, as, while desirable, they would be too cumbersome and likely to be excluded in trust instruments.[132]

If implemented, the Draft Bill would allow for a more flexible approach to investment, but the absence of any power to apportion could in some (probably rare) instances lead to a lack of balance between the competing interests of income and capital beneficiaries. It remains to be seen whether these proposals will meet with favour by the legislature.

(c) Corporate receipts received as a 'windfall' by the trust

Problems of allocation between the life tenant and remainderman may arise if the trust receives a 'windfall' because of the assets held. This is particularly the case when the trust holds shares in a company which either makes cash payments to shareholders as a 'capital profits dividend', capitalizes its profits and issues bonus or scrip dividend shares to the existing shareholders, or demerges and gives shares in the new company to the original shareholders.[133] The question arises whether these payments or shares should be allocated to capital or income. In the event of liquidation, all payments to the trustees who hold shares are regarded as capital.[134]

(i) Cash payments

If a company decided to distribute some form of cash bonuses to shareholders, any payments received by trustees who hold shares as part of trust assets are to be regarded as income and therefore allocated to the life tenant. In *Re Bates*[135] a company distributed cash bonuses to shareholders after selling some vessels at prices exceeding their value in the company balance sheets. Eve J held that the life tenant of a trust holding shares in the company was entitled to receive the entire payment as income.[136]

(ii) Bonus shares

If the company decides to capitalize its profits and issue bonus shares to the present shareholders and they are received by the trustees, then they are to hold them as part of the capital of the trust. This was so held by the House of Lords in *Bouch v Sproule*,[137] where it was emphasized that the decision whether to distribute cash or to capitalize

---

[130] *Capital and Income in Trusts: Classification and Apportionment*, Law Comm No 319 (2009), para 6.63.

[131] Ibid. para. 6.61. The potential tax problems included the re-categorization of trusts with the statutory power as non-interest in possession trusts for the purposes of Income Tax and Inheritance Tax. See further para 5.79.

[132] Ibid. para 6.63.   [133] See *Sinclair v Lee* [1993] Ch 497.

[134] *Re Armitage* [1893] 3 Ch 337; *IRC v Burrell* [1924] 2 KB 52.   [135] [1928] Ch 682.

[136] See also *Re Whitehead's Will Trusts* [1959] Ch 579.   [137] (1887) 12 App Cas 385.

was for the company alone. The result would no doubt be different if the trustees were entitled to elect to take a dividend either in cash or in the form of additional shares.[138]

(iii) Demergers

The allocation between capital and income where a company demerges is complex, and a distinction may be drawn between a direct and an indirect demerger. A direct demerger occurs where the original company allocates the shares in the new company to its shareholders. In such cases the Inland Revenue views the shares distributed as income. An indirect demerger occurs where the new company allocates its own shares to the shareholders of the original company. In *Sinclair v Lee*[139] it was held that new shares were to be treated as capital assets.

(iv) Reform of the allocation of corporate receipts

The Law Commission issued a report suggesting reforms in 2009.[140] It considers that the current law regarding the classification of corporate receipts as capital or income does not rest on principle, and fails to deliver either certainty or fairness. The Law Commission would have liked to propose an abolition of the existing rules and the introduction of a more appropriate regime allowing more flexible treatment of trust receipts, but it felt it was constrained from doing so by the tax implications of these changes.[141] It therefore proposed only that the distinction between direct and indirect demergers should be abolished, a measure which would be tax neutral. It also proposed further changes which could be introduced if the tax regime were amended to permit it, and further recommended a dialogue between HM Revenue and Customs, the Treasury, and the trust industry, to consider facilitating a move towards total investment return accompanied by percentage trusts. This combination would allow trustees to invest for the best overall combination of income and capital growth. Instead of receiving the actual income, the income beneficiaries would receive a defined percentage of the total fund value each year. This percentage would be defined by the trust or by legislation. The Law Commission's report demonstrates how much trust law has become dominated by tax considerations.

---

[138] For the treatment of scrip dividend shares, see *Pierce v Wood* [2009] EWHC 3225 (Ch).
[139] [1993] Ch 497.
[140] Capital and Income in Trusts: Classification and Apportionment, Law Comm No 319 (2009).
[141] Ibid. para 5.83.

14

Defined interests

This chapter considers the mechanisms for the distribution of a trust fund where the trustees have no discretion as to how the fund is to be allocated. The interests of the objects of the fund, that is who is to benefit and in what proportions, have already been fixed, or defined, by the creator of the trust. The role of the trustees is merely to carry out those instructions, and carry into effect the owner's intentions.

1 Introduction

(1) Meaning of defined interests

The type of equitable obligation where the interests in the fund are already defined is the fixed trust. The settlor of the trust himself defines the beneficial interests which the beneficiaries under the trust are to enjoy in the trust instrument. The trustee must carry out those terms and distribute the fund as has been specified.

(a) Example of fixed trusts

If David leaves 10,000 shares in a public company to Elizabeth on trust for his three children, Frieda, Graham, and Henrietta, in equal shares, Elizabeth has no discretion as to how the fund is to be allocated as the beneficial interests of the three children have already been defined by David. They will each have an immediate beneficial entitlement to a third of the fund (see Figure 14.1). It is Elizabeth's duty to allocate them their respective shares. If David provides that the children should take in unequal proportions, for example that Frieda should be entitled to 5,000 shares and the others 2,500 each, Elizabeth would have to allocate in those defined shares.

(b) Fixed trusts in favour of a class of beneficiaries

The interests granted under a fixed trust may also be specified by means of a class definition rather than by listing each individual who is intended to benefit. Instead of naming Frieda, Graham, and Henrietta as beneficiaries, David could have left the shares to Elizabeth 'on trust for such of my children who survive me', or alternatively

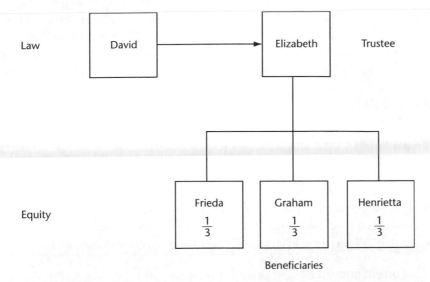

Figure 14.1 An example of fixed trusts

'to all the present employees at the date of my death' of a particular company. The presumption would be that the members of the class would take the property in equal shares. If such a class definition is used, the trust will only be valid if the objects of the trust are sufficiently certain to enable the trustee, or if necessary the court, to carry out the trust. The trust must, in addition, be administratively workable.

2 Defined interests under trusts

(1) Bare trusts

A bare trust arises where there is a trustee who holds the trust property on trust for the benefit of a single beneficiary. In a bare trust the trustee has no active duties to perform but merely holds the property on trust for the benefit of the person entitled. The trustee acts exclusively at the direction of the beneficiary, who is able to demand the legal title to be conveyed to him at any time under the principle of *Saunders v Vautier*.[1] The trustee is, in effect, the nominee of the beneficiary and acts at his discretion. For example, in *Vandervell v IRC*[2] the National Provincial Bank held stock in Vandervell Products Ltd for Mr Vandervell. This was a bare trust, and the bank was acting as his nominee. It was obliged to follow his directions, and thus when he asked them to complete a share transfer form to enable him to transfer the shares to

---

[1] (1841) 4 Beav 115.   [2] [1967] 2 AC 291, HL.

the Royal College of Surgeons they acted at his request. The allocation of the fund is not necessarily the prime purpose of a bare trust. It is a very simple mechanism for hiding the true owner of property from the world. The trustee appears to be the legal owner and the beneficiary can remain hidden from the management of the property. In practice, the trustee acts at the beneficiary's direction, who therefore himself keeps control of the management of the property.

(2) Fixed trusts

Unlike a bare trust, the prime purpose of a fixed trust is to allocate the trust fund, or limited interests in the fund, to others. The flexibility of the trust, and the equitable interests in property which subsist behind it, facilitate such allocation. Interests in the fund can be allocated concurrently between two or more beneficiaries, or consecutively, so that different beneficiaries will enjoy the property at different times.

(a) Concurrent interests

The fixed trust can be used to allocate concurrent interests in the same assets. Often the property comprised in a fund is physically indivisible, and the only way that more than one person can enjoy shares in it is through the allocation of the beneficial interest. For example, it is not possible for people to enjoy shared ownership of land other than behind a trust. If Robert wanted to leave his house to his sons, Steven and Timothy, in equal shares, it is unlikely to be possible for the house to be physically divided between them. Instead, he can leave it to them on trust as tenants-in-common in equity of equal shares. From the moment that the trust comes into being, they enjoy equal shares of the equitable interest in the house under a trust of land.[3] The fixed trust can also be used to delay allocation of concurrent interests in the trust fund until the future. Rashid, who is dying, has two small children, Khalid and Fatima, and wants to make provision for them. He leaves his property to his brother, Karim, on trust for them until they reach the age of 21. Here Karim would hold the legal title and enjoy the powers of management over the property described in the previous section, but he would be under a duty to allocate the fund to the children equally when they reach the stated age. Whatever the terms of the trust for the timing of the allocation, the trustee must follow them. Karim cannot allocate the fund to his own children when they reach 21, and to do so would be a breach of trust that the court would intervene to prevent or remedy.

(b) Consecutive interests

Fixed trusts also enable interests in the property to be divided by time, so that one person may enjoy the use of the property for the present, but another has an interest for the future. Alexander dies and leaves his property to trustees on trust for his wife, Becky, for life, and then to his children, Charles and Delia, in equal shares. His wife

---

[3] Trusts of Land and Appointment of Trustees Act 1996, s 1.

enjoys an immediate life interest in the property, which will entitle her to the income from it. His children do not have any immediate entitlement to the capital of the fund so they cannot demand that the trustees transfer the legal title to them now, but they enjoy a remainder interest in the fund and will be entitled to the capital in equal shares on the death of their mother. This is a proprietary right that they can sell or assign to others, and if they die it will pass to their own heirs. The task of the trustees is to obey the terms of the trust by investing the fund and by paying the income to Becky, and when she dies by allocating it equally between the children. If they fail to do so they have committed a breach of trust.

3 Beneficial entitlement to defined interests

The beneficiaries under a fixed trust may be either immediately ascertainable or ascertainable only in the future. In the example just given, Alexander identified all of the beneficiaries of his trust by name. They are immediately ascertainable. However, if Sandra creates a trust for her grandchildren equally, the beneficiaries are not yet ascertainable since, even if Sandra already has some grandchildren, she might have more who have not yet been born.

Beneficiaries under a fixed trust may also have vested or contingent interests. They have vested interests where they are immediately ascertainable, and do not have to satisfy any conditions in order to benefit. An interest can be vested even if enjoyment is postponed to a future date. For instance, in Alexander's trust, Charles and Delia have vested interests even though they will only get the capital of the fund when Becky dies. If they die before Becky, they may not be able to enjoy their capital share personally, but it will form part of their estate to be dealt with by will or intestacy. A contingent interest, by contrast, is one where, even though a beneficiary is immediately ascertainable, some further condition has to be satisfied. For instance, if Alexander specified that Charles and Delia had to be living when Becky died in order to take a share of capital, their rights to the capital would be contingent during Becky's life, and would vest only on her death (if they survived her). This is because surviving Becky has been made a condition of taking the gift.

Immediately ascertainable beneficiaries with a vested interest under a fixed trust have immediate proprietary interests in the assets of the fund. If they are of full age, mentally competent and entitled to an immediate interest in the property, they can require the trustee to transfer the legal title to them under the principle of *Saunders v Vautier*.[4] If the beneficiaries are not immediately entitled but have a vested or contingent future interest, they will have to wait until they have an immediate entitlement before they can exercise this right. Thus, a remainder interest behind a life interest in the trust fund does not entitle the beneficiary to call for the legal title. However, when

---

[4] (1841) 4 Beav 115.

the life tenant dies he becomes the sole beneficiary and can demand the conveyance of the legal title.

As the holder of a proprietary interest in the fund, a beneficiary with an immediate vested interest is liable to taxation on his interest.[5] If he dies it will form part of his estate and be subject to inheritance tax. If the property comprising the fund is wrongfully transferred to others by the trustee, not only will all the beneficiaries have personal remedies against the trustee for breach of trust, but their proprietary rights over the fund will be preserved into the hands of all except a bona fide purchaser for value of the fund.[6]

4 Certainty of objects

It has already been seen that a valid trust requires certainty of intention,[7] certainty of subject matter, and certainty of objects.[8] It is also a cardinal principle that the court must be able to carry out the trust if the trustee is unable and unwilling to do so. This reflects the mandatory nature of the trust obligation. If the objects of the trust are not sufficiently certain, it is impossible for the trustee to carry out his duty of allocation, nor can the court carry out the trust in the event of his default if necessary.

Under a fixed trust the beneficial interests of each and every beneficiary are pre-defined by the settlor. If these are named then there is no uncertainty. The problem arises where the beneficiaries are defined by means of a 'class definition'. Imagine that Wendy leaves £20,000 to Lucy on trust for 'my children in equal shares'. To be able to carry out the trust it must be possible to identify each and every person who falls within the class of 'Wendy's children', because the share of each child in the fund cannot be determined until the full extent of the class is identified. If Lucy were to distribute the fund in equal shares to the first three people who showed themselves to be children of Wendy, she would be in breach of trust if it subsequently came to light that there was a fourth child who should also have received a share. If it fell to the court to carry out the trust and allocate the fund they would also have to be able to identify each and every child.

The problem of uncertainty is generally slight in the context of fixed trusts because they are usually only appropriate for small, well-defined, classes. For larger classes, for example 'all the employees and ex-employees' of a company, a discretionary trust would tend to be used. However, if a fixed trust was intended in such circumstances it would not be possible to carry out the trust and allocate the fund unless each and every employee and ex-employee were identified.

[5] See Chapter 5.   [6] See Chapter 3.
[7] See Chapter 7.   [8] *Knight v Knight* (1840) 3 Beav 148.

(1) The 'complete list' test

In order to carry out the terms of the trust and allocate the fund in accordance with the settlor's intentions, the trustee must be able to ascertain each and every person who is entitled to a defined interest in the fund. If he cannot do so then he cannot carry out the terms of the trust. Wynn-Parry J stated in *IRC v Broadway Cottages Trust*[9] that the class must be 'capable of ascertainment'.[10] He took this to mean that the trustee must be able to draw up a 'complete list'[11] of all the beneficiaries of the trust, and that the trust will fail if such a list cannot be drawn up.[12]

The 'complete list' test is almost universally accepted as the requisite test of certainty of objects for fixed trusts.

However, it has been argued that the 'complete list' test is a 'heresy' that has grown from a misunderstanding of judicial statements,[13] and that the test for fixed trusts should be the same as that for discretionary trusts.[14] This argument runs against principle, logic, and authority, and fails to take sufficient account of the differences between the duty of trustees of a fixed trust to allocate the fund and that of trustees under a discretionary trust.[15] The 'complete list' test is, supported both in principle and in logic. The very nature of the fixed trust where the beneficiaries are defined as a class requires that a 'complete list' be drawn up before the trustee can allocate the fund. If such a list cannot be drawn up, it is absolutely impossible for the trustee to carry out his duty to allocate the fund, or for the court to act on his default. Lord Upjohn expressed the problem clearly in *Re Gulbenkian's Settlement*:

Suppose the donor directs that a fund be divided equally between 'my old friends', then unless there is some admissible evidence that the donor has given some special 'dictionary' meaning to that phrase which enables the trustees to identify the class with sufficient certainty, it is plainly bad as being too uncertain. Suppose that there appeared before the trustees (or the court) two or three individuals who plainly satisfied the test of being among 'my old friends', the trustees could not consistently with the donor's intentions accept them as claiming the whole or any defined part of the fund. They cannot claim the whole fund for they can show no title to it unless they prove they are the only members of the class, which they cannot do, and so, too, by parity of reasoning they cannot claim any defined part of the fund and there is no authority in the trustees or the court to make any distribution among a smaller class than that pointed to by the donor.[16]

[9] [1954] 1 All ER 878.   [10] [1954] 1 WLR 659, at 664.

[11] [1954] 1 All ER 878, at 881.

[12] See Hopkins 'Continuing Uncertainty as to Certainty of Objects of Trust Powers' (1971) 29 CLJ 68 at 81.

[13] Matthews 'A Heresy and a Half in Certainty of Objects' [1984] Conv 22.

[14] Requiring only 'conceptual certainty' and not a 'complete list' to be in fact drawn up. See also Matthews 'The Comparative Importance of the Rule in *Saunders v Vautier*' (2006) LQR 268 at 276: 'there is no sensible basis for applying a different test of certainty for different kinds of equitable owners. The size or stability of the equitable interest concerned is not a sufficient reason. All interests having a *Saunders v Vautier* value (however big or small) should be judged by the same criteria of certainty.'

[15] Martin 'Certainty of Objects—What Is Heresy?' [1984] Conv 304; Hayton 'Certainty of Objects—What Is Heresy?' [1984] Conv 307.

[16] [1970] AC 508, at 524.

Re Gulbenkian's Settlement involved a power, not a trust, so the observations do not form part of the ratio decidendi. Other cases supporting the 'complete list' test[17] pre-dated the decision of the House of Lords in *McPhail v Doulton*,[18] which rejected this test for discretionary trusts. The cases themselves also involved discretionary trusts. This meant that there was a lack of direct authority. It now seems that the matter is settled, as the 'complete list' test was applied to a fixed trust in *OT Computers Ltd v First National Tricity Finance Ltd.*[19] Pumphrey J, in considering that a proposed fixed trust of a supplier's deposit account was uncertain, stated that a complete list of beneficiaries was necessary so that the property could vest immediately under the trust:

> At this point, it is important to remember that the trust which is proposed is a fixed trust. Accordingly, it must be possible to identify each member of the class of beneficiaries. It is not sufficient to be able to say whether or not any identified person is or is not a member of the class entitled to be considered: the purpose of the trust in the present case is to vest an immediate interest in the suppliers in question.[20]

Significantly, Pumphrey J cited *McPhail v Doulton*[21] as authority for this statement of the law, demonstrating that the 'complete list' test has survived that decision. In the absence of a contrary decision of a higher court, the law now accords with principle and logic.

(2) Application of the 'complete list' test[22]

Application of the 'complete list' test means that a fixed trust will be void unless the objects are defined with conceptual certainty *and* can be identified with evidential certainty. Provided that these two elements of certainty are present, it is not necessary that the beneficiaries be immediately ascertainable.

(a) 'Conceptual certainty'

If a 'complete list' of beneficiaries must be drawn up, it is essential that any class is defined in conceptually certain terms. As was mentioned in the previous chapter,[23] this means that there must be a clear objective definition that will enable the trustee or court to determine whether any given individual falls within the class or is outside it. Without such 'conceptual certainty' it is impossible for a 'complete list' to be drawn up. This was emphasized in the example provided by Lord Upjohn in *Re Gulbenkian's Settlements* above. A trust to divide a fund equally between 'my old friends' is void for uncertainty, because the class is 'conceptually uncertain'. It is impossible to define what is mean by an 'old friend', and it is impossible for the trustee or the court to say of

---

[17] *IRC v Broadway Cottage Trust* [1954] 1 All ER 878 affirmed by the Court of Appeal [1955] Ch 20 and followed by Upjohn J in *Re Sayer* [1957] Ch 423 at 430.

[18] [1971] AC 424.   [19] [2003] EWHC 1010 (Ch); [2007] WTLR 165.

[20] [2003] EWHC 1010 (Ch) at [21].   [21] Referred to as *Re Baden* [1971] AC 424.

[22] Emery 'The Most Hallowed Principle: Certainty of Beneficiaries of Trusts and Powers of Appointment' [1982] 98 LQR 551.

[23] See above, pp 453–456.

any individual whether he is, or is not, an 'old friend' because they have no criteria on which to make such a judgement.

In *OT Computers Ltd v First National Tricity Finance Ltd*,[24] a proposed trust in favour of 'urgent suppliers' failed as it did not create a conceptually certain class. The case concerned the collapse of the Tiny Computer retailer, owned by the claimant, OT Computers Ltd. To protect its customers and suppliers from creditors in difficult trading conditions, the claimant had instructed the defendant bank to set up two separate bank accounts, one for customers and one for monies owed to its suppliers. The company also created two schedules, which listed the names of its customers and a selection of its suppliers, respectively. When the claimant company went into receivership, the defendant sought to reclaim a loan due to it from the money in the two deposit accounts. The claimant argued that trusts had been validly declared of the monies in the bank accounts. Pumphrey J upheld a fixed trust of the customer account, as all the beneficiaries could be clearly identified due to the payments made by them to the claimant company. However, in relation to the supplier account, the schedule did not list all suppliers, but referred instead to 'urgent suppliers'. Pumphrey J held that the term 'urgent suppliers' was an insufficiently conceptually certain description of a class, so that the trustees could not draw up a complete list. The term 'urgent' was simply too vague. The money in the suppliers account remained part of the company assets.

(b) 'Evidential certainty'

A 'complete list' of beneficiaries can only be drawn up if it is possible to identify each and every member of the class in fact. This means that there must be absolute 'evidential certainty'. If the trust is created in favour of all the 'employees and ex-employees' of a company, it must be possible to identify each and every employee and ex-employee. In *Re Sayer*[25] a trust in favour of the employees and ex-employees of Sayers (Confectioners) Ltd was held void for uncertainty[26] because it was impossible to draw up a complete list of the persons employed by the company since its incorporation. The company had found it impossible to keep accurate records of its ex-employees.[27] Lord Upjohn also gave an example of a fixed trust void for evidential uncertainty in *Re Gulbenkian's Settlements*:

If a donor...directs trustees to make some specified provision for 'John Smith', then to give legal effect to that provision it must be possible to identify 'John Smith'. If the donor knows three John Smiths then by the most elementary principles of law neither the trustees nor the court in their place can give effect to that provision; neither the trustees nor the court can guess

---

[24] [2003] EWHC 1010 (Ch); [2007] WTLR 165.   [25] [1957] Ch 423.

[26] *Re Sayer* involved what today would be regarded as a discretionary trust and the test adopted in the House of Lords in *McPhail v Doulton* [1971] AC 424, HL would now be applied. As interpreted in *Re Baden (No 2)* [1973] Ch 9 the trust would be upheld, as for a discretionary trust the class of beneficiaries must be 'conceptually' certain but need not be 'evidentially' certain. See further Chapter 17.

[27] [1957] Ch 423, at 430: because of its large number of shops (seventy), and the nature of its workforce, which consisted of a large number of female shop assistants who tended to change employment frequently.

at it. It must fail for uncertainty unless of course admissible evidence is available to point to a particular John Smith as the object of the donor's bounty.[28]

The relevant date for the drawing up of the complete list is the date of execution of the trust, not the date of its creation.[29]

(c) 'Ascertainability'

A class may enjoy 'evidential certainty', so that it is possible to draw up a 'complete list' of the beneficiaries, even though it may be impossible to ascertain where some of those who appear on the list are, or whether they are still alive. If Francis leaves all her property to Eric on trust to be divided equally among her cousins, this will create a valid fixed trust. The class is conceptually certain, and it is known that Francis had seven cousins. One of the seven, Graham, left for South America in 1987 and has not been seen or heard from since. Would the fact that it is not known whether he is alive or cannot be found, invalidate the trust? Although this looks similar to the problem of 'evidential uncertainty', it is a quite different problem, one of 'ascertainability'.[30] The distinction was drawn by Lord Upjohn in *Re Gulbenkian's Settlements*, where he said:

If the class is sufficiently defined by the donor the fact that it may be difficult to ascertain the whereabouts or continued existence of some of its members at the relevant time matters not.[31]

Lord Wilberforce echoed this distinction in *McPhail v Doulton*:

as to the question of certainty, I desire to emphasise the distinction clearly made and explained by Lord Upjohn, between linguistic or semantic uncertainty ... and the difficulty of ascertaining the existence or whereabouts of members of the class ... [32]

Problems of the 'ascertainability' of beneficiaries will not render the trust void for uncertainty. This is consistent with principle. If a complete list can be drawn up, then the minimum share to which each beneficiary is entitled is known and the fund can be allocated on that basis. In our example, because it is known that Francis had seven cousins, each cousin is certainly entitled to a seventh share in the fund, and Eric can allocate it on that basis. As to the seventh share to which Graham may be entitled, Eric can 'apply to the court for directions or pay a share into court'.[33] In the case of unascertainable beneficiaries who are thought to be dead, the court can make a 'Benjamin order'. This entitles the trustees to allocate the fund on the presumption that the beneficiary had predeceased the testator. In *Re Benjamin*[34] David Benjamin left his residuary estate to his children in equal shares. He had twelve children surviving him,

---

[28] [1970] AC 508, at 523.

[29] See, for example, *Swain v Law Society* [1981] 3 All ER 797. Thus a trust may be created now for the benefit of persons as yet unborn or unascertained, but it must be possible to draw up a complete closed list on the due date of execution.

[30] See Emery 'The Most Hallowed Principle: Certainty of Beneficiaries of Trusts and Powers of Appointment' [1982] 98 LQR 551, at 556.

[31] [1970] AC 508, at 524.   [32] [1971] AC 424, at 457.

[33] *Re Gulbenkian's Settlement Trusts* [1970] AC 508, at 524, per Lord Upjohn.

[34] [1902] 1 Ch 723.

but one had disappeared while on holiday in France a year before the testator's death. Joyce J held that, in the absence of any evidence to the contrary, he must be presumed to be dead and his share was to be allocated accordingly. If it subsequently turns out that the unascertained beneficiary is alive, he may trace his share of the fund into the hands of those who received it,[35] and the trustees are not liable for breach of trust. The court order protects them.

(3) Resolving uncertainty

There are some ways in which a gift that would otherwise fail on grounds of uncertainty might be found to be valid. What might appear to be a gift to an ill-defined group such as 'my old friends' might perhaps be treated as a series of separate gifts that can be considered as if they stood alone. For instance, in *Re Barlow's Will Trusts*,[36] Helen Alice Dorothy Barlow died leaving a valuable collection of paintings. She gave instructions in her will that 'any members of my family and any friends of mine' could buy any of the paintings at the prices contained in a catalogue of valuations made some five years before her death. These prices were significantly below the value of the paintings after her death. Browne-Wilkinson J held that the instruction was not invalid for uncertainty. This was not a gift to a class. It was properly to be regarded as a series of individual gifts to persons answering the description of friend or family member. The test which applies to class gifts 'has no application to a case where there is a condition or description attached to one or more individual gifts; in such cases, uncertainty as to some other persons who may have been intended to take does not in any way affect the quantum of the gift to persons who undoubtedly possess the qualification'.[37] Accordingly, 'anyone who can prove that by any reasonable test he or she must have been a friend' of Helen Barlow would be entitled to purchase a picture. Anyone who did not satisfy this stringent test would not be entitled to take advantage of the option created by the will. Similarly, anyone who could prove a blood relationship to Helen Barlow would qualify as a family member. The fact that there might be considerable areas of uncertainty did not defeat the provision for those who clearly satisfied it.

Another way in which problems of uncertainty can be resolved is where the gift itself provides a mechanism for resolving that uncertainty. Thus, a gift to 'intelligent people' would normally fail for lack of certainty because there is no clear definition of intelligence. However, a gift to people who, in the opinion of the President of Mensa, are intelligent, would probably be held to be valid. For instance, in *Re Tuck's Settlement Trusts*,[38] Sir Adolf Tuck, a Jew, was made a baronet in 1910. He wanted to make sure that future descendants inheriting the title of baronet remained in the Jewish faith. To this end, he specified that future baronets would inherit the funds he left by will only if they married a wife of Jewish blood who at the time of her marriage 'continues to

---

[35] Subject to the Limitation Act 1980, ss 18, 21(3), 22.   [36] [1979] 1 WLR 278.
[37] Ibid., at 281–282.   [38] [1978] Ch 49, [1978] 1 All ER 1047.

worship according to the Jewish faith'. He added that in case of dispute 'the decision of the Chief Rabbi in London shall be conclusive'. Eveleigh LJ in the Court of Appeal had some doubt as to whether the condition as to the Jewish faith would in itself have been sufficiently clear. However, the reference to the Chief Rabbi operated to make it clear: 'Different people may have different views or be doubtful as to what is "Jewish faith" but the Chief Rabbi knows and can say what meaning he attaches to the words.'[39]

There has been some debate about the reasoning lying behind this decision. Eveleigh J suggested that the Chief Rabbi would have a clear understanding of what was meant by the Jewish faith and could provide it if asked. But it is more than likely that, even for the Chief Rabbi, there could be areas of conceptual doubt. In that case, does reference to him for a decision resolve any uncertainty? It may be that providing for a decision to be made by a third party means that an inherently uncertain concept (for instance, who is intelligent?) is replaced by the certain test (eg those persons stated by the President of Mensa to be intelligent). In that case, what can be done if a decision is taken by the third party arbitrarily—for instance, if the President of Mensa states that someone is intelligent when they are clearly not? The courts are reluctant to see their jurisdiction ousted. If they retain a supervisory jurisdiction, then they need to be able to control the arbitrary exercise of the decision-making authority conferred on the third party. Yet they can only decide if the decisions he or she makes have been properly made if the test itself is sufficiently certain to be applied by the court. That takes us back to where we began.[40]

The answer to this problem is contained in the common-sense judgment of Lord Denning. Even if there is conceptual uncertainty, it can be cured by a provision stating that any uncertainty may be resolved by the decision of a competent third party:

> So long as he does not misconduct himself or come to a decision which is wholly unreasonable, I think his decision should stand...As this very case shows, the courts may get bogged down in distinctions between conceptual uncertainty and evidential uncertainty...The testator may want to cut out all that cackle, and let someone decide it who will really understand what the testator is talking about, and thus save an expensive journey to the lawyers and the courts. For my part, I would not blame him. I would give effect to his intentions.[41]

5 Policy limits

Although a prime purpose of the law of equity is to enable owners to deal with their property as they wish, there are certain policy-motivated limits which constrain their freedom. The rule against perpetuities prevents owners tying their property up outside

---

[39] [1978] 1 All ER 1047, at 1057.

[40] It may be possible to classify this decision as one of evidential uncertainty, rather than conceptual uncertainty, but doing so does not resolve the issues raised above, as the same concerns about arbitrary decision-making by the nominated third party remain.

[41] [1978] 1 All ER 1047, at 1053–1054.

of the market for too long a period of time. Conditional and determinable interests, where the conditions are designed to influence the beneficiaries' behaviour in a way that is contrary to public policy, are also restricted. These limitations are equally applicable to varieties of equitable obligations other than the fixed trust. Legislation also provides that trusts may be set aside if they are established with the object of defrauding the creditors of the settlor.

(1) The rule against perpetuities

(a) Remoteness of vesting[42]

The law requires that gifts of property vest within a certain period of time, the perpetuity period. This prevents property being tied up, and hence kept outside the economy, for long periods. At common law, if the property might vest outside of the perpetuity period, the gift would be void. The relevant perpetuity period is a life in being plus twenty-one years. This means that the gift must not vest outside of a period of twenty-one years after the lifetime of a human person living at the date of the creation of the interest.[43]

The rule preventing remoteness of vesting was reformed by the Perpetuities and Accumulations Act 1964. Under s 1, a settlor may specify the relevant perpetuity period in the trust instrument instead of a perpetuity period of a life in being plus twenty-one years, up to a period of eighty years. This is obviously simpler than the requirement of a life in being and is a more attractive option than the 'royal lives' clauses previously regularly used in trust instruments.[44] Where no perpetuity period is specified under s 1, and the trust would have been invalid under the common law rule because it might have vested outside of the perpetuity period,[45] s 3 provides a 'wait and see' procedure. The trust will only be void if it does not in fact vest within the perpetuity period.[46] Section 3 provides its own list of statutory lives by which the perpetuity period is to be measured. It is a great pity that the common law principle with all its complexity was not abolished altogether and replaced by the principle of 'wait and see'.[47] It has been proposed that the rule against perpetuities should be simplified and reformed.[48]

---

[42] See Gray, *The Rule Against Perpetuities* (4th edn, 1942); Morris and Leach, *The Rule Against Perpetuities* (2nd edn, 1962); Maudsley, *The Modern Law of Perpetuities* (1979).

[43] Gray on *Perpetuities*, §201.

[44] These clauses defined the perpetuity period by reference to the lives of the living descendants of a member of the royal family such as Queen Victoria.

[45] It will be invalid, even though it may be highly likely in fact to vest within the perpetuity period.

[46] In other words, it is not sufficient to invalidate the gift that it might not vest within the perpetuity period; it must actually fail to vest.

[47] Virtually all trusts that are void under the common law principle are covered by the 'wait and see' provisions of s 3. However, because the statutory lives of s 3 are not identical to common law lives, it is theoretically possible to have a trust which would be valid under the common law principle, but to which the 'wait and see' provisions of s 3 would not apply. For this reason, the common law principle is not entirely irrelevant.

[48] Law Com. No 251, *The Rules against Perpetuities and Excessive Accumulations* (1998).

(b) Rule against inalienability

As well as the rule against remoteness of vesting for reasons of public policy, the law does not allow property to be tied up, and hence become inalienable,[49] forever. A trust must not have a duration longer than the perpetuity period of a life in being plus twenty-one years. This has already been examined in the previous chapter in the context of non-charitable purpose trusts.[50] Charitable trusts are exempt from this requirement and may be perpetual,[51] as are most pension funds.[52] The Perpetuities and Accumulations Act 1964 has not affected the rule against inalienability (or 'the rule against perpetual trusts', as it is sometimes known).

(c) Reform of the rule against perpetuities

The rule against perpetuities has been examined by the Law Commission, which has recommended significant legislative reform.[53] The Law Commission recommends that the rule be retained so as to ensure that there is 'some restriction on the freedom of one generation to control the devolution of property at the expense of the generations that follow'. The rule would continue to apply to property held on trust, although it is recommended that it should not apply to pension schemes.[54] However, it recommends that the current complex perpetuity period be replaced by a fixed period of 125 years.[55] In respect of the rule against remoteness of vesting the 'wait and see' principle would continue to operate. Any such change would only operate prospectively, so that trusts created prior to the introduction of such a scheme would continue to be governed by the current law. However, the trustees of such a trust would be able to elect by deed that the trust be subject to the new statutory perpetuity period if the trust contains an express perpetuity period of lives in being plus twenty-one years and they believe that it is difficult or impracticable to ascertain the existence or whereabouts of the measuring lives.[56]

The Law Commission's recommendations were accepted by the Government in 2001, but no time was found to implement them. In 2008, the Bill was proposed as the first in the trial of the new House of Lords' procedure for Law Commission Bills,[57] and the Bill was introduced to the House of Lords under this procedure on 1 April 2009.[58] At the time of writing, the Bill has yet to become law.[59]

---

[49] This means that the property cannot be transferred or sold (alienated) and enter the general property market.

[50] See above, p 460.   [51] See below, Chapter 19, p 577.

[52] Pensions Schemes Act 1993, s 163.

[53] Law Com No 251, *The Rules Against Perpetuities and Excessive Accumulations* (1998). See T P Gallanis 'The Rule Against Perpetuities and the Law Commission's Flawed Philosophy' [2000] 59 CLJ 284.

[54] Para 7.36.   [55] Para 8.13.   [56] Para 8.20.

[57] HL Paper 63, *1st Report of Session 2007–08: Law Commission Bills*. In essence, this sets out a streamlined procedure for enacting uncontroversial Law Commission Bills that allows them to be taken in Committee off the floor of the House.

[58] Under this procedure, the Ministry of Justice carried out a targeted consultation process in Summer 2008, and subsequently undertook updating work on the Bill.

[59] The Third reading took place in the House of Lords on 20 July 2009. The Bill will now go to the Commons.

The new scheme will not have retrospective effect, so that wills executed before the new legislation comes into effect will continue to be administered under the current scheme.[60]

(2) Conditional and determinable interests

Owners may choose not to make absolute gifts to others, but instead to make gifts that are subject to conditions subsequent or determinable on the happening of a particular event. For example, Terrance may leave his cottage to trustees on trust for his mistress, Joyce, on the condition that she does not marry. This is a very powerful method of controlling a donee's behaviour, since he has a strong financial incentive not to breach the condition and forfeit the interest. However, if the condition is illegal, or one that would constrain the donee's behaviour in a way contrary to public policy, it will be void.

(a) Conditions void for uncertainty

If the condition or determining event is uncertain, then it will be void. Lord Cranworth stated the principle in *Clavering v Ellison*[61] that the court must be able to 'see from the beginning, precisely and distinctly, upon the happening of what event it was that [the gift] was to determine'.[62] Conditions which have been held void for uncertainty include: a requirement that the donee 'conform to' the Church of England;[63] not marry a person 'not of Jewish parentage';[64] not have a 'social or other relationship with a named person',[65] 'continue to reside in Canada'[66] or 'take up permanent residence in England'.[67]

(b) Conditions void as contrary to public policy

Certain types of condition have also been held to be void because they offend against public policy.

(i) Conditions restricting alienation

If a condition attached to a gift is tantamount to a complete restriction on alienation or transfer of the property, it will be void as contrary to public policy.[68] In *Re Brown*[69] a father bequeathed his freehold properties to his four sons in equal shares, with a condition that they were not to alienate their shares other than to each other. Harman J held that this amounted to a general prohibition on alienation because they were a small and diminishing class, and the condition was void.[70]

---

[60] There are limited opt-in opportunities for existing trusts, so that they may be administered under the new scheme.

[61] (1859) 7 HL Cas 707.   [62] Ibid., at 725.   [63] *Re Tegg* [1936] 2 All ER 878.

[64] *Clayton v Ramsden* [1943] AC 320, HL.   [65] *Re Jones* [1953] Ch 125.

[66] *Sifton v Sifton* [1938] AC 656.   [67] *Re Gape* [1952] Ch 743.

[68] *Muschamp v Bluet* (1617) J Bridge 132; *Hood v Oglander* (1865) 34 Beav 513; *Re Rosher* (1884) 26 Ch D 801; *Corbett v Corbett* (1888) 14 PD 7; *Re Dugdale* (1888) LR 38 Ch D 176; *Re Cockerill* [1929] 2 Ch 131.

[69] [1954] Ch 39.

[70] Contrast *Re Macleay* (1875) LR 20 Eq 186, where a restriction to alienation within 'the family' was upheld. Harman J considered that this was a large and indeterminable group of people that may increase.

(ii) Conditions restraining marriage

Marriage has always been the fundamental building block of society, and conditions which seek to undermine marriage are void as contrary to public policy.[71] Conditions that completely restrain the donee's freedom to marry are void.[72] However, conditions that restrain the donee's freedom to *remarry* have in the past been upheld.[73]

Conditions that restrain marriage to particular individuals[74] or classes are also valid. In *Jenner v Turner*[75] a testatrix left property to her brother on condition that he did not marry a 'domestic servant'. This was held to be a valid condition by Bacon V-C. In *Duggan v Kelly*[76] a condition not to marry a 'Papist' was upheld, as was a condition not to marry a 'Scotchman' in *Perrin v Lyon*.[77] Conditions that encourage separation or divorce of husband and wife are void.[78] Thus, in *Re Johnson's Will Trusts*[79] a donor established a trust in favour of his daughter which would pay her £50 per year as long as she continued to be married to her husband, but would pay her the full income from the fund if she were divorced or separated. Buckley J held that the condition was void as it amounted to an incentive to the break-up of the marriage.[80]

(iii) Conditions restraining religion

Conditions that restrict the choice of religion of a beneficiary have never been regarded as void because they offend against public policy.[81] In *Blathwayt v Baron Cawley*[82] a condition that a beneficiary forfeit his interest if he 'be or become a Roman Catholic' was upheld by the House of Lords. It was neither uncertain nor contrary to public policy. Lord Wilberforce explained that:

to introduce for the first time a rule of law which would go far beyond the mere avoidance of discrimination on religious grounds...would bring about a substantial reduction of another freedom, firmly rooted in our law, namely that of testamentary disposition. Discrimination is not the same thing as choice: it operates over a larger and less personal

---

[71]   See *Long v Dennis* (1767) 4 Burr 2052, at 2059, per Lord Mansfield: 'conditions in restraint of marriage are odious...'.

[72]   *Low v Peers* (1770) Wilm 364, at 372: an absolute restraint on marriage 'tends to evil and the promoting of licentiousness; it tends to depopulation, the greatest of all political sins...'.

[73]   *Jordan v Holkham* (1753) Amb 209: provision of testator's will that his wife would forfeit her interest if she remarried was upheld. Contrast the Irish case of *Duddy v Gresham* (1878) 2 LR Ir 442, where a condition in the testator's will that his wife not remarry but enter a convent of her choice was held void.

[74]   *Re Bathe* [1925] Ch 377; *Re Hanlon* [1933] Ch 254: a gift by testator to her daughter subject to the condition that she does not 'intermarry with AB' upheld by Eve J.

[75]   (1880) 16 Ch D 188.   [76]   (1848) 10 I Eq R 473.

[77]   (1807) 9 East 170.

[78]   *Wren v Bradley* (1848) 2 De G & Sm 49; *Re Moore* (1888) 39 Ch D 116; *Re Caborne* [1943] Ch 224; *Re Johnson's Will Trusts* [1967] Ch 387; *Re Hepplewhite Will Trust* [1977] CLY 2710.

[79]   [1967] Ch 387.   [80]   [1967] Ch 387, at 396.

[81]   The boundary between race and religion is uncertain. In *Mandla v Dowell Lee* [1983] 2 AC 548 Sikhs were held to be a racial group, and in *King-Ansell v Police* [1979] 2 NZLR 531 Jews were also held to be a racial group. However, the distinction is of no practical importance for the law of trusts since conditions on grounds of neither religion nor of race are invalid.

[82]   [1976] AC 397, HL.

area, and neither by express provision nor by implication has private selection yet become a matter of public policy.[83]

However, if the condition restrictive of religion is uncertain it will not be binding. In *Clayton v Ramsden*[84] a provision forfeiting the beneficiary's interest on marriage to a person 'not of Jewish parentage' was held void for uncertainty.[85]

The Equality Act 2006, which prohibits discrimination on the grounds of religion or belief, has no application to private trusts.[86] The impact of the Human Rights Act has yet to considered.

(iv) Conditions affecting parental duties

Conditions which seek to separate parent from child are void as contrary to public policy.[87] In *Re Sandbrook*[88] the condition that a gift of the income of a fund was to be forfeited if children lived with their father was held void. Such a condition is void even if the parents are divorced.[89] Some cases have suggested that conditions that interfere with the exercise of parental duties are void. In *Re Borwick*[90] a condition that a minor forfeit an interest if she 'become a Roman Catholic or not be openly or avowedly Protestant' was held void as it operated to interfere with the exercise of a parent's duty in the religious instruction of his children.[91] In *Blathwayt v Baron Cawley*[92] the House of Lords limited the range of this principle, holding that:

To say that any condition which in any way might affect or influence the way in which a child is to be brought up, or in which parental duties are exercised, is void seems to me to state far too wide a rule.[93]

(v) Conditions discriminatory on grounds of race

The Race Relations Act 1976, s 1 renders discrimination on grounds of colour, race, nationality, or ethnic or national origins unlawful. This applies especially in the fields of employment,[94] provision of goods and services, and the disposal of property. It does not have any application to private trusts.[95] The reasoning of Lord Wilberforce in *Blathwayt v Baron Cawley*[96] that legislation against general discrimination had not

---

[83] Ibid., at 426.   [84] [1943] AC 320, HL.

[85] See also *Re Tegg* [1936] 2 All ER 878, where a condition 'to conform' to the Church of England was held void for uncertainty.

[86] Charitable trusts are covered under s 58 of the Act. It is permissible for charities to provide for benefits only to persons of a particular religion or belief.

[87] See *Re Morgan* (1910) 26 TLR 398; *Re Boulter* [1922] 1 Ch 75.

[88] [1912] 2 Ch 471.

[89] *Re Piper* [1946] 2 All ER 503, which concerned a gift by will to children provided they do not live with their father before attaining the age of 30. Mother had divorced father before the date of the will.

[90] [1933] Ch 657.   [91] The condition was also held void on the grounds of uncertainty.

[92] [1976] AC 397.   [93] Ibid., at 426, per Lord Wilberforce.

[94] Ss 4–9.

[95] Charitable trusts are covered by s 34 of the Act. It is permissible to provide for benefits for a class defined by race, nationality, or ethnic or national origin, but not to provide for a class defined by colour.

[96] [1976] AC 397.

impinged upon individual selection and choice[97] would be equally applicable to this area. This is reflected in the Race Relations Act, where it is not lawful to discriminate on grounds of race when employment for the purposes of a private household is concerned.[98]

(vi) Conditions discriminatory on grounds of sex

The Sex Discrimination Act 1975 has no application to private trusts.[99]

(vii) Impact of the Human Rights Act

Many of the decisions in this area date from the nineteenth century, and some may be open to reconsideration in the light of changing social mores and more specifically as a consequence of the incorporation of the European Convention on Human Rights Act 1998 into British law by the Human Rights Act 1998. Whilst the Act, and therefore the Convention, are not directly applicable to private trusts, the fundamental rights and freedoms set out in the Convention are very likely to have an impact upon judicial views of public policy.

(c) Effect of an invalid condition

The exact consequences of a condition being found to be void will depend on whether the gift was made subject to a condition subsequent or was a determinable interest.

(i) Determinable interests

If the gift is characterized as 'determinable' and the determining event is unlawful for reasons of public policy, the gift will fail and the property reverts to the original owner. Thus, in *Re Moore*[100] a trust to pay a weekly sum to a woman 'whilst...living apart from her husband' was held to be a determinable interest and the gift was void.

(ii) Conditional interests

If the gift is subject to a condition subsequent and the condition is unlawful, the gift is not void and the condition is merely struck out. The gift will thus become absolute.[101] In *Re Beard*[102] a testator made a gift of his estates to his nephew, Herbert, 'provided that he does not enter into the naval or military services of the country'. As the condition was held contrary to public policy,[103] it was struck out and the nephew took an absolute interest in the estates.

---

[97] See above, p 490.   [98] S 4(3).

[99] S 43 provides that charities may provide benefits for one sex only.

[100] (1888) 39 Ch D 116.

[101] See *Re Croxon* [1904] 1 Ch 252; *Re Turton* [1926] Ch 96.

[102] [1908] 1 Ch 383.

[103] [1908] 1 Ch 383, at 387, per Swinfen Eady J: 'there can be few, if any, provisions more against public good and the welfare of the State than one tending to deter persons from entering the naval or military service of the country'.

(d) Distinguishing conditional and determinable gifts

Given the different consequences for determinable and conditional gifts, if the condition or determining event is unlawful, it is necessary to distinguish between them. The distinction is notoriously difficult to pin-point and has been described as 'little short of disgraceful to our jurisprudence'.[104] The essence of the distinction is that a determinable gift is defined as lasting only for the duration of a certain state of affairs, whilst a conditional gift is one which may be cut short if a given event occurs. For instance, a gift to Myfanwy 'whilst she remains a widow' would be a determinable gift; on the other hand a gift to Myfanwy 'provided that she does not remarry' would be a gift subject to a condition subsequent.

Put another way, in a determinable gift the gift is never contemplated as being absolute, but only as lasting until the determining event occurs.[105] Thus, a gift to George 'until he becomes a brain surgeon' will be a determinable gift. If the determining event occurs, the gift will automatically revert to the original donor. In a conditional gift, the gift is contemplated as being absolute from the very beginning, but the occurrence of the condition brings it to an end. A gift to George 'unless he becomes a brain surgeon' would be a conditional gift. In cases concerning conditional gifts of land, it has been held that a gift does not end automatically when the condition occurs, but that the donor or his successor in title must 're-enter' by taking steps to terminate the interest.[106] This dogma has no application to a conditional gift by way of trust, where the condition represents a direction to trustees that they will carry out without any further intervention by the original donor.

---

[104] Porter MR in *Re King's Trusts* (1892) 29 LR Ir 401, at 410.

[105] If the determining event becomes impossible in fact, the gift automatically becomes absolute: *Re Leach* [1912] 2 Ch 422.

[106] See Challis's *Real Property* (3rd edn, 1911), pp 219, 261.

15

Powers of advancement and maintenance

When a settlor creates interests under a fixed trust which are contingent upon the happening of a future event, the question arises what to do with the income generated by the trust until the interest vests in the beneficiaries. There may be good reason to allow the contingent beneficiaries to receive the income or a share of the capital, as for example where the beneficiaries may need income to meet living expenses. This is permitted in certain circumstances by the use of inherent, statutory, or express powers of maintenance (income) and advancement (capital).

1 Introduction

In Chapter 14 it was seen that a settlor can create interests under a fixed trust which are contingent upon the happening of some future event. For example, a testator with young children may leave his estate to them subject to a stipulation that they will only become entitled to the property on attaining the age of 21. Although the trustees will hold the fund on trust for them from the time of his death, they will not be entitled to the capital until they attain the specified age and the trustees will be under no duty to transfer it to them. However, whilst the settlor may have created such a contingent interest with the object of preventing his children receiving their inheritance before they are sufficiently mature to manage it for themselves, such an arrangement may cause practical difficulties. In our example, the children may have no actual income on which to live in the interim period before they are entitled to their share of the fund.

To overcome such difficulties, the law grants trustees powers that enable them to apply the fund on behalf of beneficiaries even where they have not yet satisfied the specified contingency. The power of maintenance allows the trustees to apply the income generated by the fund on behalf of the beneficiary, and the power of advancement allows the trustees to apply part of the capital from the fund. Although both such powers can be granted expressly in a trust deed, the Trustee Act 1925 grants trustees powers of maintenance[1] and advancement[2] which are usually sufficient. The court also possesses an inherent jurisdiction to provide advancement and maintenance.

2 The trustees' power of maintenance

(1) Express powers of maintenance

A settlor may include express powers of advancement in the trust instrument. However, given the width of the statutory powers it is not usually necessary to do so.

(2) Trustee Act 1925, s 31[3]

Section 31 of the Trustee Act 1925 draws a distinction between the position of a minor who is contingently interested under a trust, and the position of an adult who is similarly contingently interested.[4]

(a) The position of a contingently interested minor—s 31(1)(i)

Section 31(1)(i) grants the trustees of every trust where property is held for any person, whether their interest is vested or contingent, the power to apply the whole or the part of the income generated by the fund to his parent or guardian for his 'maintenance education or benefit'.[5] This power is to be exercised solely at their discretion.

(b) The position of a contingently interested adult—s 31(1)(ii)

Section 31(1)(ii) directs that if the beneficiary has reached the age of majority,[6] the trustees are to pay the income generated by the fund to him, until his interest either vests or fails. Payment of such income is not a matter for the trustees' discretion, although it may be excluded if there is a counter-intention indicated by the testator in the trust document.[7]

It has been held that the power to pay over the income to an adult beneficiary who is contingently interested in the fund is excluded if there is a direction in the trust

---

[1] Trustee Act 1925, s 31.   [2] Trustee Act 1925, s 32.

[3] Trustee Act 1925, s 31 replaces the Conveyancing Act 1881, s 43 (which still applies to instruments coming into force before 1926), which itself replaced a provision in Lord Cranworth's Act of 1860.

[4] By s 31(4) the same principles are applied to income generated by an annuity vested in a minor, with the exception that s 31(2)(ii) has no application and the accumulated income is the absolute property of the infant.

[5] S 31(1)(i). See *Fuller v Evans* [2000] 1 All ER 636.   [6] That is, 18 years of age.

[7] As the Trustee Act 1925 makes clear by s 69(2): 'All the powers conferred by this Act on trustees are in addition to the powers conferred by the instrument, if any, creating the trust, but those powers unless otherwise stated, apply, if and so far only as a contrary intention is not expressed in the instrument, if any, creating the trust, and have effect subject to the terms of that instrument.'

instrument to accumulate the income.[8] Thus, in *Re Turner's Will Trusts*[9] the Court of Appeal held that a beneficiary who was 24 was not entitled to the income from a fund in which he would obtain a vested interest on attaining the age of 28 because the settlor had directed that the income be accumulated.[10] Similarly, in *Re Erskine's Settlement Trusts*[11] a direction to accumulate the income from a fund was held to exclude the power under s 31, even though the direction was itself void under s 164 of the Law of Property Act 1925. Even in the absence of a direction to accumulate, the obligation to pay over the income under s 31(1)(ii) may be excluded. In *Re McGeorge*[12] a gift of agricultural land by a testator to his daughter, which was not to take effect until the death of his wife, was held to express a contrary intention because 'by deferring the enjoyment of the devise until after the widow's death the testator has expressed the intention that the daughter shall not have the immediate income'.[13]

(c) Gifts carrying intermediate income[14]

By s 31(3) the powers of maintenance granted to trustees under s 31(1) are only available if the contingent interest 'carries the intermediate income'. This means that the beneficiary must be entitled to the income earned by the share of the fund to which he is contingently entitled between the date of the gift and the date when his share is paid over to him. Whether a gift carries the intermediate income depends on a series of technical rules, derived from both statute and cases.

(i) Vested gifts

A gift that is vested carries the intermediate income unless there is a contrary intention, for example if the income is directed to be applied to someone else.[15]

(ii) Contingent gifts of residuary personalty

A contingent gift of residuary personal property[16] made by will always carries the intermediate income from the date of the testator's death.[17] This was explained in *Re Adams*,[18] where North J stated that since the income was 'undisposed of'

---

[8] See *Re Watt's Will Trusts* [1936] 2 All ER 1555; *Re Turner's Will Trusts* [1937] Ch 15; *Re Ransome* [1957] Ch 348; *Re Erskine's Settlement Trusts* [1971] 1 WLR 162.

[9] [1937] Ch 15.

[10] Although he had granted the trustees an express power to apply the income for the 'maintenance, benefit and education' of the beneficiaries, and it was the surplus income which was to be accumulated.

[11] [1971] 1 WLR 162.   [12] [1963] Ch 544.

[13] Ibid., at 552–553, per Cross J. He also held that s 31 did not apply because the daughter's interest was not contingent, but rather subject to being divested.

[14] (1953) 17 Conv 273 (Ker); PVB 'Carrying the Intermediate Income' (1963) 79 LQR 184.

[15] A direction to accumulate merely indicates an exclusion of the power of maintenance, and not that the gift does not carry the intermediate income.

[16] This includes leasehold property, which ranks as personal property: *Guthrie v Walrond* (1883) 22 Ch D 573; *Re Woodin* [1895] 2 Ch 349.

[17] *Countess of Bective v Hodgson* (1864) 10 HL Cas 656; *Re Taylor* [1901] 2 Ch 134.

[18] [1893] 1 Ch 329.

it would itself become part of the residue. However, if the gift is deferred to 'a future date which must come sooner or later',[19] it does not carry the intermediate income.[20]

(iii) Specific devises or bequests

Section 175 of the Law of Property Act 1925 provides that contingent or future specific devices or bequests of property, whether personal or real, carry the intermediate income from the date of the death of the testator unless that income has been otherwise expressly disposed of.[21] The section has been held not to apply to pecuniary legacies.[22]

(iv) Contingent pecuniary legacies

Since pecuniary legacies are not included within the scope of s 175, as a general principle a contingent pecuniary legacy will not carry the intermediate income.[23] There are three exceptions to this principle. First, gifts by fathers to their children. If a pecuniary legacy is left by a father to his child, the gift carries the intermediate income if there is no other fund provided for the child's maintenance,[24] and the contingency is the child attaining the age of majority.[25] The rationale behind this exception is clearly similar to that which reveals itself in the presumption of advancement which rebuts an inference of a resulting trust when a gift is made by a father to his child,[26] namely the obligation of the father to provide. The exception will also apply when a gift of a contingent pecuniary legacy is made by a person standing in loco parentis to the minor.[27] Second, gifts made with the intention of providing maintenance. If the will expressly or impliedly indicates that the income be used for the maintenance of the minor, the gift will carry the intermediate income. In *Re Churchill*[28] a gift of a pecuniary legacy to a grandnephew was held to carry the intermediate income where the will directed the trustees at their discretion to pay any part of it 'towards the advancement in life or otherwise for the benefit' of the legatee.[29] It is not necessary that the legacy be contingent upon the attainment of majority.[30] Third, 'set aside' gifts. Where a pecuniary legacy is set aside by the testator[31] as a segregated fund for his benefit, to be available on the happening of the contingency, the gift will carry the intermediate income.[32]

---

[19] *Re McGeorge* [1963] Ch 544, at 551, per Cross J.

[20] *Re Gillett's Will Trust* [1950] Ch 102; *Re Geering* [1964] Ch 136; *Re McGeorge* [1963] Ch 544; *Re Nash* [1965] 1 All ER 51. Compare also *Re Lindo* (1888) 59 LT 462.

[21] *Re Reade-Revell* [1930] 1 Ch 52; *Re Stapleton* [1946] 1 All ER 323.

[22] *Re Raine* [1929] 1 Ch 716.   [23] *Re George* (1877) 5 Ch D 837, CA.

[24] *Re Moody* [1895] 1 Ch 101; *Re George* (1877) 5 Ch D 837; *Re West* [1913] 2 Ch 345.

[25] *Re Abrahams* [1911] 1 Ch 108.   [26] See Chapter 9.

[27] *Re Eyre* [1917] 1 Ch 351.   [28] [1909] 2 Ch 431.

[29] See also *Re Selby-Walker* [1949] 2 All ER 178.   [30] *Re Jones* [1932] 1 Ch 642.

[31] *Re Judkin's Trusts* (1884) 25 Ch D 743.

[32] *Re Medlock* (1886) 54 LT 828; *Re Clements* [1894] 1 Ch 665; *Re Woodin* [1895] 2 Ch 349, CA. Compare also *Re Judkin's Trusts* (1884) 25 Ch D 743.

(d) Undistributed income

Since s 31(1)(i) grants the trustee a discretion to pay maintenance out of the intermediate income to the parent or guardian of a minor who has a contingent interest, the
question arises as to what should happen to any surplus income the trustees decide not
to apply for the beneficiary's maintenance. Such eventuality is covered by the provisions of s 31(2).

(i) Accumulation of surplus income

Under s 31(2) the trustees are directed to accumulate and invest any income from the
fund which has not been applied to a beneficiary's maintenance. Such accumulated
income is then available to be distributed for the beneficiary's maintenance, and may
be applied as if it were income arising in the current year.

(ii) Beneficiary's entitlement to accumulated surplus income

Section 31(2)(i)(b) provides that if the beneficiary is entitled to a vested interest in the
capital of the fund on attaining his majority (or on marriage under that age), he will
be entitled to the accumulated surplus income. If, however, his interest is not vested,
or liable to be determined, he will not be entitled to the accumulated income.[33] One
anomalous result of the wording of s 31(2)(i)(b) is that a distinction is drawn between
determinable gifts of realty and personalty. The section states that the beneficiary
must be entitled to the property from which the income arose 'in fee simple, absolute or determinable, or absolutely…' In *Re Sharp's Settlement Trusts*[34] it was held
that the words 'in fee simple, absolute or determinable' apply only to realty, and the
word 'absolute' applies exclusively to 'personalty'. This means that a beneficiary has
no entitlement on reaching majority to the accumulated income on a fund of personal
property in which he has only a determinable interest. On the facts, a beneficiary who
had attained the age of 21 was not entitled to the accumulated income from the fund
because his contingent interest was liable to be defeated by the exercise of a power of
appointment.[35]

(iii) Death of a minor before attaining a vested interest

Where a beneficiary dies before attaining majority (or earlier marriage) and income
has been accumulated on his behalf, s 31(2)(ii) provides that the accumulated income
should be added to the capital of the fund, and not pass as part of the minor's
estate.[36] This provision will not apply if a contrary intention is shown from the trust
instrument.[37] Thus in *Re Delamere's Settlement Trusts*[38] the trustees of a settlement
appointed the income from a trust fund to six infant beneficiaries 'in equal shares

---

[33] *Re Sharp's Settlement Trusts* [1973] Ch 331.
[34] [1973] Ch 331; (1972) 36 Conv 436 (Hayton).
[35] See also *Phipps v Ackers* (1842) 9 Cl & Fin 583; *Re Heath* [1936] Ch 259; *Re Kilpatrick's Policies* [1966]
Ch 730; *Brotherton v IRC* [1978] 1 WLR 610.
[36] *Re Joel's Will Trusts* [1967] Ch 14.   [37] Trustee Act 1925, s 69(2).
[38] [1984] 1 WLR 813; [1985] Conv 153 (Griffith).

absolutely'. The Court of Appeal held that this excluded the operation of s 31(2)(ii) and that the infant beneficiaries had indefeasible interests in the accumulated income.

(3) The court's inherent jurisdiction

The court has an inherent jurisdiction to allow trust income to be used for a minor's maintenance,[39] and in exceptional circumstances the court may even allow capital to be so used.[40] The courts have generally refused to allow trust income to be used for a child's maintenance where the father has sufficient means to provide for the child.[41] The width of the general statutory power of maintenance has rendered the court's inherent jurisdiction insignificant.

3 The trustees' power of advancement

(1) Meaning of advancement

A power of maintenance enables the trustees to apply the income generated by a trust fund for the maintenance of the beneficiaries, even where they are not as yet entitled to the capital of the fund. A power of advancement enables the trustees to advance part of the capital to beneficiaries who are contingently interested in the trust fund. As Lord Radcliffe observed in *Pilkington v IRC*, the purpose of a power of advancement is that the trustees can in a proper case:

anticipate the vesting in possession of an intended beneficiary's contingent or reversionary interest by raising money on account of his interest and paying or applying it immediately for his benefit. By so doing they released it from the trusts of the settlement and accelerate the enjoyment of his interest . . .[42]

(2) Express powers of advancement

A settlor may grant the trustees express powers of advancement in the trust instrument. However, since the enactment of a statutory power,[43] which grants the trustees of a power of advancement modelled on the standard form of such express powers, express powers are only necessary if a settlor wishes the trustees to have wider powers than those granted by the statute.[44]

---

[39] *Wellesley v Wellesley* (1828) 2 Bli 124, at 133–134, per Lord Redesdale.

[40] *Ex p Green* (1820) 1 Jac & W 253; *Ex p Chambers* (1829) 1 Russ & M 577; *Robinson v Killey* (1862) 30 Beav 520.

[41] *Douglas v Andrews* (1849) 12 Beav 310, at 311.

[42] [1964] AC 612, at 633.   [43] Trustee Act 1925, s 32.

[44] For example, the power to advance more than half a beneficiary's presumptive share. See also Trustee Act 1925, s 32(1)(a).

(3) Trustee Act 1925, s 32

(a) Scope of the statutory power of advancement

Section 32(1) grants trustees the power, in their absolute discretion, to apply the capital of a trust fund on behalf of any beneficiary who has an absolute or contingent interest in the fund. It makes no difference that the beneficiary's contingent interest may at some later date be defeated, for example by the exercise of a power of appointment, or that his precise share of the fund may diminish because of an increase in the number of a class to which he belongs.[45] The section introduces some practical limitations on the trustee's power of advancement:

(i) Proportion of share which may be advanced

Section 32(1)(a) provides that the trustees must not advance to a beneficiary more than a half of his presumptive or vested interest under the fund.[46]

(ii) Accounting for advancements in the final distribution of the trust fund

Where a beneficiary is contingently entitled to a share of the trust fund, s 32(1)(b) provides that any property advanced be taken into account in calculating the size of any share to which he becomes absolutely entitled.[47] This obviously prevents unfairness between the beneficiaries.

(iii) Protection of those with a prior interest in the trust fund

Where an advancement would be to the prejudice of those who have a prior life or other interest in the fund, s 32(1)(c) requires that they give consent in writing to any advancement.[48] This protects, for example, a life tenant, who is entitled to the income of the fund during his lifetime. Clearly, if an advancement of capital is made to a contingently entitled remainderman, the life tenant will suffer as the income generated by the fund will decrease with the reduction in the capital.

(b) Type of fund where capital may be advanced

Section 32(2) provides that the power of advancement does not apply to funds consisting of capital money under the Settled Land Act 1925.

---

[45] For example, a trust may grant contingent interests to the children of the settlor, and the class may subsequently increase with the birth of further children.

[46] See *Re Marquess of Abergavenny's Estate Act Trusts* [1981] 1 WLR 843; [1982] Conv 158 (Price). The court may be willing to approve a variation of trusts which will allow the advancement of more than a half of the trust fund if this would be of 'benefit' to the beneficiary: *CD (A Child) v O* [2004] 3 All ER 780. See below, Chapter 18.

[47] See *Re Fox* [1904] 1 Ch 480.

[48] The court cannot dispense with the need for consent: *Re Forster's Settlement* [1942] Ch 199. A member of a discretionary class does not need to give consent: *Re Harris's Settlement* (1940) 162 LT 358; *Re Beckett's Settlement* [1940] Ch 279.

(c) The requirement of benefit

The most important restriction of the trustees' power of advancement is the requirement that the application of capital must be for the 'advancement or benefit' of the beneficiary. The meaning of this phrase was considered by Lord Radcliffe in *Pilkington v IRC*, where he held that the phrase 'advancement and benefit':

means any use of the money which will improve the material situation of the beneficiary.[49]

The case concerned a proposed advancement of part of the contingent share of an infant beneficiary, Penelope Pilkington. She was entitled to a share of a fund established by her great uncle, provided she reached the age of 21, but the trustees wanted to advance £7,600, to be settled on different trusts in her favour, to avoid death duties. The House of Lords held that this was a proper exercise of the statutory power of advancement, and that there was a benefit to the infant in the avoidance of taxation. Lord Radcliffe observed:

if the advantage of preserving the funds of a beneficiary from the incidence of death duty is not an advantage personal to that beneficiary, I do not see what is.[50]

It did not matter that the advanced money was to be resettled on different trusts for the infant.[51]

A wide range of purposes have been held to be sufficiently beneficial to permit an advancement. In the nineteenth century, typical examples included the provision of an apprenticeship, the purchase of a commission in the army, or an interest in a business.[52] Benefits have included the discharge of the beneficiary's debts,[53] an advancement to a wife who helped her husband set up in business,[54] an advancement to a girl on her marriage,[55] and an advancement to provide for the beneficiary's maintenance and education.[56] In *Re Halstead's Will Trusts*[57] the court approved an advancement to a man so that he could make provision for his wife and child in the future by settling a sum upon himself for life; and after his death for his wife for life, remainder to his children. Farwell J held that this was within the 'very wide terms in which the word "benefit" has been construed in the past'. The purchases of house and furniture have also been held to be for the benefit of a beneficiary.[58]

In *Re Clore's Settlement Trusts*[59] an advancement to enable a contingently entitled beneficiary to make a donation to charity which they felt morally obliged to make was held to be a benefit. However, in *X v A*,[60] it was held that an advancement of the whole of the trust fund to enable a charitable donation was not of benefit. Hart J reasoned that

---

[49] [1964] AC 612, at 635.   [50] [1964] AC 612, at 640.
[51] *Roper-Curzon v Roper-Curzon* (1871) LR 11 Eq 452; *Re Halstead's Will Trusts* [1937] 2 All ER 57; *Re Ropner's Settlement Trusts* [1956] 1 WLR 902.
[52] *Pilkington v IRC* [1964] AC 612, at 634.   [53] *Lowther v Bentinck* (1874) LR 19 Eq 166.
[54] *Re Kershaw's Trusts* (1868) LR 6 Eq 322.   [55] *Lloyd v Cocker* (1860) 27 Beav 645.
[56] *Re Breed's Will* (1875) 1 Ch D 226; *Re Garrett* [1934] Ch 477.
[57] [1937] 2 All ER 57.   [58] *Re Pauling's Settlement Trust* [1964] Ch 303, CA.
[59] [1966] 1 WLR 955.   [60] [2006] 1 WLR 741.

the extent of the gift meant that the contingently entitled beneficiary would not have their material situation improved by the advancement as required under *Pilkington v IRC*, as the beneficiary would not have been able to meet the moral obligation from their own resources.

(d) Fiduciary nature of the power of advancement

A power of advancement is a fiduciary power, and must therefore be exercised by the trustee in a fiduciary manner. In *Re Pauling's Settlement Trusts*,[61] in the context of an express power, the Court of Appeal held that this means that before exercising the power the trustees must 'weigh on the one side the benefit of the proposed advancee, and on the other hand the rights of those who are or may hereafter become interested under the trusts of the settlement'.[62] The trustees are also subject to a duty to ensure that money advanced is applied by the beneficiaries for the purposes for which it was advanced.[63]

(4) **The court's inherent jurisdiction**

The court possesses an inherent jurisdiction to apply capital[64] for the maintenance or advancement of an infant. For example, in *Clay v Pennington*[65] the court advanced a sum of £125 to cover the cost of an infant's passage to India.[66]

---

[61] [1964] Ch 303. [62] Ibid., at 333, per Willmer LJ.
[63] Ibid., at 334. [64] *Barlow v Grant* (1684) 1 Vern 255.
[65] (1837) 8 Sim 359. [66] See also *Re Mary England's Estate* (1830) 1 Russ & M 499.

16

Powers of appointment and redistribution

Powers of appointment are one of the key distributive mechanisms offered by equity. They enable a person who is not the owner of property to identify who will benefit from it. Such powers may be held by trustees or independently. The key feature of a power of appointment is that it is discretionary in character. Except in cases where the power is subject to fiduciary duties, the donee of a power is under no enforceable obligation to consider the power or to exercise it. The court, however, does exercise a supervisory jurisdiction to ensure that, if the donee decides to exercise the power, he does so properly. There are, in addition, cases where the power is fiduciary, and the donee is subject to additional duties and restrictions. This chapter explores in detail the creation, use, and obligations imposed by powers of appointment.

1 The nature of powers of appointment

Powers of appointment confer on a person who does not own property the authority to choose who shall become the owner. Powers of appointment are one of the equitable mechanisms which facilitate the management and allocation of property. The key feature of a power of appointment is that it is discretionary in character. Unlike a fixed trust or a discretionary trust, the donee of a power is under no enforceable obligation to make any appointments of the fund at all. Even if the donee were never to make any appointments at all, he would not be in breach of a duty owed either to the donor or to the potential objects of the power. The court will not step in to compel the exercise of the power, but it will exercise a supervisory jurisdiction to ensure that, if the donee does decide to exercise the power, he does so properly. Powers of appointment are commonly used as a mechanism to determine the allocation of the surplus remaining in a trust fund after the beneficiaries have received their defined interests. Many older cases concern family trusts where the property of a testator was left on trust for a spouse for life, with a power of appointment granted over the remainder interest (see Figure 16.1).[1] This

---

[1] *Re Weekes' Settlement* [1897] 1 Ch 289.

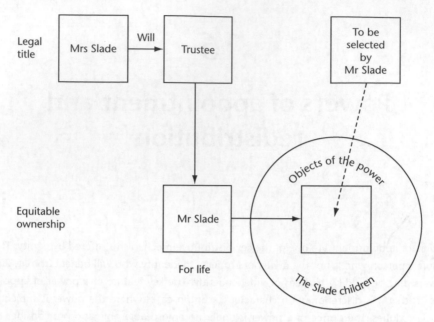

Figure 16.1 An example of powers of appointment: *Re Weekes' Settlement*

allows the donee of the power to decide how the capital of the fund should be allocated on the death of the life tenant. The discretionary nature of the power means that the testator does not have to predetermine how the remainder interest should be distributed, and allows the donee of the power to take account of changing circumstances between the death of the testator and the death of the life tenant. Later cases have tended to concern pension funds, where the donee is given a power of appointment over any surplus that remains after the contributors have received their contractual entitlements.[2] Although the position has now changed, with many pension funds operating in deficit, in the 1990s some pension funds had assets exceeding their liabilities. The power to allocate the surplus by exercise of a power of appointment, whether to the pensioners or the company, was therefore an extremely valuable right.

(1) Classification of powers of appointment

Though all powers of appointment share their discretionary character, several sub-categories of power can be identified, which are differentiated by the nature of the class of potential objects and by the exact duties of the donee.

---

[2] *Mettoy Pension Trustees Ltd v Evans* [1990] 1 WLR 1587; *Hillsdown Holdings plc v Pensions Ombudsman* [1997] 1 All ER 862; *Edge v Pensions Ombudsman* [1998] 2 All ER 547.

(a) Classification by the nature of the class of objects

There are three types of power of appointment: general, special, and hybrid powers. They are differentiated by the range of potential objects in whose favour the power may be exercised:

(i) General powers

Under a general power of appointment the donee enjoys the right to allocate the property by appointment to anyone he wishes. The donee may even appoint the property to himself. This extremely wide power is tantamount to absolute ownership by the donee.

(ii) Special powers

Where the donor of a power has specified that it should only be exercised in favour of a class of people, it is said to be a special power. The donee has absolute discretion whether to make any appointments of the property but any appointments made must be to persons within the specified class. In *Re Weekes' Settlement*,[3] Mrs Slade granted a life interest of her estate to her husband and gave him a power of appointment over the reversionary interest in favour of their children (see Figure 16.1). This created a special power in favour of the class of their eight surviving children. Mr Slade had discretion whether to make appointments at all, but he could only make appointments to those who fell within the class of potential objects (see Figure 16.1).

(iii) Hybrid powers[4]

A hybrid, or intermediate,[5] power is the inverse of a special power. The donee is entitled to make appointments in favour of anyone except the members of a specified class. In *Re Byron's Settlement*[6] a power of appointment was given by the testatrix to her daughter in favour of anyone except 'her present husband or any friend or relative of his'. In *Re Lawrence's Will Trusts*[7] Mr Lawrence granted his wife a power of appointment over his residuary estate in favour of anyone except her relatives.[8]

(b) Classification by donee's duties

Powers may also be divided into those where the donee owes no duty of a fiduciary nature to the potential objects of the power, and those where some fiduciary duties are owed. Although in both cases the power remains essentially discretionary, there is a

---

3 [1897] 1 Ch 289. See also *Re Gestetner Settlement* [1953] Ch 672 (wide class including named persons, named charitable bodies, and employees and ex-employees of the settlor's company); *Re Sayer* [1957] Ch 423 (class in favour of employees, ex-employees, and widows and infant children of Sayers Confectionary Ltd).

4 See *Re Lawrence's Will Trusts* [1972] Ch 418, at 423.

5 See *Re Manisty's Settlement* [1974] Ch 17, where Templeman J described a power to appoint anyone in the world except the settlor, his wife and other excepted persons as an 'intermediate power'.

6 [1891] 3 Ch 474.   7 [1972] Ch 418.

8 See also *Re Park* [1932] Ch 580; *Re Abrahams' Will Trusts* [1969] 1 Ch 463; *Re Manisty's Settlement* [1974] Ch 17.

slight difference in the duties owed. This difference normally arises because the donee is also a trustee.

(i) Bare or mere powers[9]

If the donee of the power does not hold the power in a fiduciary capacity, then he owes no duties to the objects concerning its exercise. He is under no duty to exercise it, and need not even consider whether he should exercise the power. He can completely forget that he has it, and never apply his mind to the question whether he should exercise it. This type of power is known as a bare or mere power.

(ii) Fiduciary powers[10]

If the donee holds the power of appointment in a fiduciary capacity, most commonly because it is a power which arises under a trust of which he is the trustee, then he owes limited fiduciary duties to the potential objects of the powers.[11] He must periodically consider whether to exercise the power, although it remains entirely discretionary and he is under no enforceable obligation to make appointments.[12] If he does decide to exercise the power, he must first survey the range of potential objects before making particular appointments. The fact that the donee has fiduciary obligations does not mean that he is a trustee. Although there is a wide spectrum of fiduciary duties, some of which are analogous to or akin to the duties of a trustee,[13] there can be 'considerable differences between the office or the capacity of a trustee and the position of a donee of a fiduciary power'.[14]

(2) **Duties of the donee of a power**

The donee of a bare power is under no duty to exercise the power because it is entirely discretionary. If he makes no appointments at all he is not in breach of any duty. In *Re Weekes' Settlement*,[15] Mr Slade failed to make any appointments in favour of his children and had not committed any breach thereby. The donee does not even have to consider whether or not to exercise the power. By way of exception, if the power is held by someone who is also a trustee, then he holds the power in a fiduciary capacity,[16] and he must from time to time consider whether or not to exercise the power in favour of the objects.[17] If the donee of a mere power does choose to exercise the power, he must not act outside of the terms of the power and appoint in favour of non-objects. Such

---

[9] See below, pp 514 *et seq*.   [10] See below, pp 521 *et seq*.

[11] See *Re Hay's Settlement Trusts* [1982] 1 WLR 202.

[12] See *Re Allen-Meyrick's Will Trusts* [1966] 1 WLR 499, where the court refused to intervene to compel trustees to exercise a power that they held over a fund in favour of the settlor's husband.

[13] See *Gomez and others v Gomez-Monche Vives and others* [2008] EWCA Civ 1065; [2009] Ch 245 (CA), at [94].

[14] Ibid.   [15] [1897] 1 Ch 289.   [16] See below, p 521.

[17] See *Re Abrahams' Will Trusts* [1969] 1 Ch 463, at 474 per Cross J; *Re Hay's Settlement Trusts* [1982] 1 WLR 202.

an appointment to non-objects is known as 'excessive exercise' because it exceeds the scope of the power. He must exercise the power honestly and not fraudulently.[18]

(3) **Rights of the objects of powers**

In Chapter 13 it was seen that the beneficiaries of a fixed trust have an immediate proprietary interest in the share of the fund which is earmarked for them and, if of age and legally competent, they can demand that the trustees transfer the property to them.[19] The potential objects of a power of appointment have no immediate proprietary interest in the property over which the donee has power.[20] An object only gains a proprietary interest in any property which is allocated to him by the donee. In *Re Brooks' Settlement Trusts* Farwell J said of the position of a son who was a potential object of a special power under his mother's marriage settlement:

it is...impossible to say that until an appointment has been made in favour of this son that the son had any interest under his mother's settlement other than an interest as one of the people entitled in default of appointment.[21]

2 **The validity of powers of appointment**

(1) **Certainty of objects**

(a) Comparison with fixed trusts[22]

In the case of a fixed trust it must be possible to draw up a 'complete list' of each and every beneficiary.[23] If this is not possible, the trust is void for uncertainty because neither the trustee nor the court could carry out the trust. If the beneficiaries are defined as a class, then a complete list can only be drawn up if the class is both conceptually and evidentially certain. In the case of powers, the test of certainty is less stringent. There is no need for the donee to be able to draw up a complete list of every potential object to exercise the power properly. In the case of a general power, such a requirement would entail the production of a list of the entire population of the world! Equally, the court will not step in to exercise the power if the donee defaults because it is purely discretionary. However, the court must be able to supervise any exercise of the power. In the case of a special power, this means that the court must be able to determine whether any person selected by the donee was within the class, and therefore entitled to enjoy the benefit of the exercise. As Lord Upjohn observed in *Re Gulbenkian's Settlement*:

those entitled to the fund in default [of appointment] must clearly be entitled to restrain the trustees from exercising it save amongst those within the power. So the trustees, or the court, must be able to say with certainty who is within and who without the power.[24]

---

18 See below, p 515.
20 *Vestey v IRC* [1980] AC 1148, HL.
22 See Chapter 14.
24 [1970] AC 508, at 525.

19 *Saunders v Vautier* (1841) 4 Beav 115.
21 [1939] Ch 993, at 997.
23 See above, p 480.

If an appointment is made to a person who is outside the class of objects, then the exercise is excessive and void. The test for certainty of objects for powers of appointment has developed to meet this necessity.

(b) The 'is or is not' test

The test of certainty for powers of appointment was laid down by the House of Lords in *Re Gulbenkian's Settlement (No 1)*.[25] A special power of appointment was granted in favour of a class consisting of Nubar Gulbenkian, his wife and children, and 'any person or persons in whose house or apartments or in whose company or under whose care or control or by whom or with whom he may from time to time be employed or residing'. This was upheld as sufficiently certain. Lord Upjohn stated the relevant test of certainty:[26]

a mere or bare power of appointment among a class is valid if you can with certainty say whether any given individual is or is not a member of the class: you do not have to be able to ascertain every member of the class.[27]

This test had been propounded by Harman J in *Re Gestetner Settlement*[28] and approved by the Court of Appeal in *IRC v Broadway Cottages Trust*.[29] Lord Upjohn rejected[30] a broader test of certainty put forward by Lord Denning MR in the Court of Appeal that a power of appointment would be valid if it could be said with certainty of any one person that he was clearly within the class, even if it may be difficult to say in other cases whether a person is within the class or not.[31] In *Re Gresham*[32] Harman J had held that a power with similar terms to that in *Re Gulbenkian* was void for uncertainty, but the Court of Appeal and House of Lords overruled the decision. Mere difficulty in determining whether an individual is within or without the class is not sufficient to invalidate the power, and the Court can rule on borderline cases.[33] It is only insuperable difficulty that will render the power void for uncertainty.

The *Gulbenkian* test is consistent with established principle and logic. It requires that the court must be able to determine with absolute certainty whether any given individual is or is not a member of the class of potential objects. This is essential if the court is to determine whether the power has been exercised properly. If Toby grants Stephanie a power of appointment over his residuary estate in favour of 'old men', it would be impossible for the court to determine if an appointment in favour of Robert, who is 64, was excessive. It is not possible to say of every individual whether they are

---

[25] [1970] AC 508.

[26] Lord Hodson and Lord Guest agreed with Lord Upjohn; Lord Reid delivered a similar opinion; Lord Donovan agreed with Lord Upjohn but reserved his opinion on whether the test proposed by the Court of Appeal that the power should be valid if it could be said of any one person that he was within the class, although he was 'inclined to share' Lord Upjohn's view.

[27] [1970] AC 508, at 521.

[28] [1953] Ch 672; followed by Roxburgh J in *Re Coates (Decd)* [1955] Ch 495 and Upjohn J in *Re Sayer* [1957] Ch 423.

[29] [1955] Ch 20. See also *Re Hain's Settlement* [1961] 1 WLR 440, at 445, per Lord Evershed MR.

[30] [1970] AC 508, at 134.   [31] [1968] Ch 126, at 134.

[32] [1956] 1 WLR 573.   [33] [1970] AC 508, at 523.

'old' or not, because 'old' has no clear objective meaning. A power in favour of 'men aged over 65' is clearly valid because it is possible to say of every man whether he is over 65 or not.

(c) Application of the 'is or is not' test[34]

The test for certainty of objects for powers laid down in *Re Gulbenkian*[35] was adopted for discretionary trusts by the House of Lords in *McPhail v Doulton*.[36] It was subsequently examined and applied by the Court of Appeal in *Re Baden's Deed Trusts (No 2)*.[37] It follows that, although these cases concerned discretionary trusts, they are the main authorities considering the implications of the *Re Gulbenkian* test for powers of appointment. They indicate that while the 'is or is not' test requires conceptual certainty, a special power will not be invalid for reasons of evidential uncertainty.

(i) 'Conceptual certainty'

The class of a special power must be defined with conceptual certainty.[38] This means that the class must be defined by objective criteria by which the court can judge whether any given individual is within the class. Thus, a power of appointment in favour of 'my good friends' or 'my business associates' would be void for uncertainty. In contrast, a power of appointment in favour of 'the fellows of Oriel College, Oxford University' or 'members of the National Union of Students' would create an objectively certain class.

(ii) 'Evidential certainty'

In *Re Baden's Deed Trusts (No 2)*[39] the majority of the Court of Appeal held that a discretionary trust which was conceptually certain was not defeated by evidential uncertainty. In other words, provided the class criteria are clear-cut it does not matter that it is not possible to prove of every individual whether they meet the criteria or not.[40] For example, a class defined as 'Medwin's children' is conceptually certain, even though before DNA profiling it might have been difficult to prove paternity for every child. Since the test is the same for powers of appointment, it is not necessary that the class of a special power be evidentially certain. The lack of a requirement of strict evidential certainty follows from the fact that the donee of the power does not have to consider every single potential object in exercising his discretion to appoint the property. His complete discretion means that his only duty is to ensure that any appointments are made to persons within the class of objects and not to exercise the power excessively.[41]

---

[34] See Hopkins 'Continuing Uncertainty as to the Certainty of Trust Powers' [1971] CLJ 68; Emery 'The Most Hallowed Principle: Certainty of Beneficiaries of Trusts and Powers of Appointment' (1982) 98 LQR 551.

[35] [1970] AC 508.   [36] [1971] AC 424 (also referred to as *Re Baden's Deed Trusts* (No 1)).

[37] [1973] Ch 9.   [38] See Chapter 13.   [39] [1973] Ch 9.   [40] See Chapters 13 and 17.

[41] With the exception of a fiduciary power, where the trustee who holds the power of appointment is under a duty to have an appreciation of the width of the field of potential objects when he exercises it. See *Re Hay's Settlement Trusts* [1982] 1 WLR 202.

(d) Criticism of the 'is or is not' test

Following *Re Gulbenkian*,[42] *McPhail v Doulton*,[43] and *Re Baden (No 2)*,[44] the same requirement of conceptual certainty applies to fixed trusts, discretionary trusts, and powers of appointment. Equitable obligations of any of these types will be void if there is no conceptual certainty. This could lead to some unsatisfactory results, and it remains questionable whether the same strict test should apply to powers of appointment, which are discretionary, and trusts, which are in essence mandatory equitable obligations. There is much to commend a modified version of the broader proposition of Lord Denning MR in the Court of Appeal, who proposed that:

> if the [donees] can say of a particular person: 'He is clearly within the category', the gift is good, even though it may be difficult in other cases to say whether a person is or is not within the category.[45]

In *Re Gibbards Will Trusts*[46] a testator gave his trustees a power of appointment over his residuary estate in favour of 'any of my old friends'. Plowman J concluded that 'there is not a sufficient degree of uncertainty about the expression'[47] to hold the power void for uncertainty. Similarly, in *Re Coates (Decd)*[48] a power to appoint a specified sum to 'friends' was upheld as valid. Roxburgh J held that the word 'friend' was not too vague, although he recognized that 'friendship' was a phrase 'particularly blurred in outline'.[49] It is unclear whether these cases could be decided similarly today. Definitions such as 'old friends' would probably not be sufficiently conceptually certain[50] under the test propounded in *Re Baden (No 2)*.[51] A fixed trust for 'my old friends' would certainly not be valid as it would not be possible to identify the full extent of the class. *Re Gibbard*[52] was decided on the basis of the test rejected by the House of Lords in *Re Gulbenkian* that it must be possible to say of at least some persons that they are certainly within the class, even if it were not possible to say of others whether they are or not.

(e) An alternative to the 'is or is not' test for powers?

Ultimately, it is a question of policy whether a purely discretionary power should fail for lack of complete conceptual certainty. If a donor grants a power to appoint his property in favour of his 'old friends', there are clearly some people who are without question within the class. Should the power fail and the donor's intention be defeated merely because there are others about whom it cannot be definitely stated whether they are 'old friends' or not? It would be more in keeping with the donor's intentions that appointments can be made in the donee's discretion to those who are definitely objects. An analogy can be drawn from the requirement of certainty applicable to a

---

42 [1970] AC 508.   43 [1971] AC 424.   44 [1973] Ch 9.
45 *Re Gulbenkian's Settlement* [1968] Ch 126, at 134.
46 [1966] 1 All ER 273.   47 Ibid., at 281.
48 [1955] Ch 495.   49 Ibid., at 499.
50 See *Re Barlow's Will Trusts* [1979] 1 WLR 278, at 298, per Brown-Wilkinson J: '["Friends"] has a great range of meanings; indeed, its exact meaning probably varies slightly from person to person…'.
51 [1973] Ch 9.   52 [1966] 1 All ER 273.

gift subject to a condition precedent. In *Re Barlow's Will Trusts*[53] Browne-Wilkinson J held that, if such gifts are made to a class, then they are valid if 'it is possible to say of one or more persons that he or they undoubtedly qualify even though it may be difficult to say of others whether or not they qualify'.[54] The case concerned a testatrix who directed her executor to sell valuable paintings at a considerable undervalue to her family and 'friends'. These gifts were valid because it was possible to say of some people that 'on any reasonable basis' they were friends, and would therefore be entitled to purchase. Provided a potential purchaser satisfied the condition of proving that he was definitely a friend, it did not matter that it was impossible to say whether others were friends or not.

If this approach was applied to powers of appointment it might provide a better balance between upholding the donor's intentions and ensuring that the court can supervise the execution of the power. The court will not intervene if the power is not exercised, so there is no possibility of the court exercising the power itself.[55] The court could prevent excessive exercise by upholding only appointments to those shown definitely to be within the class on any reasonable basis. In cases of doubt, the donee of the power could apply to the court for determination whether a person falls indisputably within the class. Such an approach would be entirely inappropriate for fixed or discretionary trusts, where the court may have to carry out the terms of the trust. For powers of appointment it would provide a less stringent test than that declared by the House of Lords in *Re Gulbenkian*,[56] and would be similar to the rejected test applied by the Court of Appeal in that case. One disadvantage is that it would again create a distinction between the test of certainty applying to discretionary trusts and powers, which would make the question of whether a particular instrument creates a trust or a power far more significant, since that may determine its validity. That danger could be prevented by the court taking a strict view and not succumbing to the temptation of construing an invalid trust as a valid power.[57]

(2) Capriciousness

Even if a special power of appointment is sufficiently certain, it will be invalid if it is capricious in nature. The principle of capriciousness was considered applicable to special powers in *Re Manisty's Settlement*,[58] where Templeman J suggested that a special power in favour of the 'residents of Greater London' would be capricious 'because the terms of the power negated any sensible intention on the part of the settlor'.[59] Capriciousness does not invalidate a power merely because of its width of the power, as a general power is valid even though the donee has the discretion to make appointments to anyone in the whole world. Instead, it invalidates a special power because there is no rational reason why the donor selected the specified class, and consequently

---

[53] [1979] 1 WLR 278.   [54] Ibid., at 281, following *Re Allen* [1953] Ch 810.
[55] Unlike a discretionary trust. See *McPhail v Doulton* [1971] AC 424.
[56] [1970] AC 508.   [57] As was taken in *McPhail v Doulton* [1971] AC 424.
[58] [1974] Ch 17.   [59] Ibid., at 27.

the donee has no rational basis on which he can exercise his discretion.[60] 'Residents of Greater London' would be capricious because the class was 'an accidental agglomeration of persons who have no discernible link with the settlor or with any institution'.[61] If there were a link between the donor of the power and the class of potential objects, the power would not be open to the charge of capriciousness. In *Re Hay's Settlement Trusts*[62] Megarry V-C suggested that a power in favour of 'the residents of Greater London' would not be capricious if the donor were a former chairman of the Greater London Council. In *R v District Auditor ex p West Yorkshire Metropolitan County Council*[63] it was held that a discretionary trust created by the council for the benefit of the residents of West Yorkshire was not capricious.[64]

Where a power is found to be capricious it will be rendered void. Capriciousness will only invalidate a special power, and the principle has no application to a general power, or a hybrid power.[65] As both *Re Manisty's Settlement* and *Re Hay's Settlement Trusts* concerned fiduciary powers,[66] where the donee of the power has additional fiduciary duties, the principle may not apply to bare powers where the donee has no obligations of a fiduciary nature.

3 Exercise of powers of appointment

(1) Formalities

As a general rule, no special formalities are required for the valid exercise of a power of appointment. However, the donee of the power must intend to allocate the fund or part of the fund to an object of the power. Where the power is granted in relation to land an appointment must be evidenced in writing signed by the donee, in accordance with s 51(1)(b) of the Law of Property Act 1925. In some circumstances additional formalities may be required.

(a) Formalities required by the terms of the power

The terms of the power may require it to be exercised in a particular form, for example by deed. If so, the power can only be exercised in that form. Where it is stipulated that a power must be exercised by deed, a purported exercise by will will be ineffective.[67] Similarly, a power which can only be exercised by will cannot be exercised inter vivos.[68]

---

[60] Ibid. 'A capricious power negatives a sensible consideration by the trustees of the exercise of the power.'
[61] Ibid.   [62] [1982] 1 WLR 202.   [63] [1986] RVR 24.
[64] It was, however, found to be 'administratively unworkable', demonstrating that 'capriciousness' and 'administrative unworkability' are distinct concepts. See below, p 526.
[65] See *Re Manisty's Settlement* [1974] Ch 17, at 27; *Re Hay's Settlement Trusts* [1982] 1 WLR 202, at 212.
[66] See below, p 521.   [67] *Re Phillips* (1889) LR 41 Ch D 417.
[68] *Re Evered* [1910] 2 Ch 147, at 156, per Cozens-Hardy MR.

(b) Limitations on additional formalities

Although the terms of the power may specify additional formalities, legislation has limited the range of stipulations which must be observed to effect a valid exercise. Under s 159(1) of the Law of Property Act 1925, where a power is exercised inter vivos the exercise will be valid if the donee executed by a valid deed,[69] even though the terms of the power required some 'additional or other form of execution or attestation or solemnity'. This does not exclude the necessity for the donee to comply with any terms of the power requiring him to gain the consent of another individual, or performing an act not relating to the mode of executing the deed.[70] In the case of a will, s 10 of the Wills Act 1837 provides that the exercise of a power by a valid will is effective notwithstanding the absence of any additional formalities required by the terms of the power.[71]

(2) Defective exercise

In general, a defective exercise of a power is void, and the purported appointment of the fund does not take place. However, equity may validate a defective exercise if the donee 'in discharge of moral or natural obligations shows an intention to execute [a] power'.[72] This will only apply in favour of purchasers for value, creditors, charities, and persons to whom the donee is under a natural or moral obligation to provide. Some key elements must be proved if the defective exercise is to be upheld:

the intention to pass the property...the persons to be benefited...the amount of the benefit...good consideration.[73]

(3) Contracts to exercise

A contract to exercise a power of appointment will operate in equity as a valid exercise of the power, provided that the contract is specifically enforceable. This is an application of the maxim that 'equity treats as done that which ought to be done'. Since a contract to exercise a testamentary power is not specifically enforceable,[74] it does not operate as an effective exercise of the power, and the only remedy available to the disappointed object is an action for damages for breach of contract against the estate.

(4) Excessive exercise

The exercise of the power will be excessive if the donee makes an appointment to a person outside of the potential objects of the power. In the case of a special power,

---

[69] Executed in the presence of and attested by two or more witnesses (Law of Property (Miscellaneous Provisions) Act 1989, s 1).

[70] Law of Property Act 1925, s 159(2).   [71] See also Wills Act 1963, s 2.

[72] *Farwell on Powers* (3rd edn, 1916), p 378; *Chapman v Gibson* (1791) 3 Bro CC 229.

[73] *Farwell on Powers* (3rd edn, 1916), p 379.

[74] *Re Bradshaw* [1902] 1 Ch 436; *Re Cooke* [1922] 1 Ch 292.

appointments can only be made to members of the specified class, while in the case of a hybrid power, appointments must not be made to members of the excluded class. Any such excessive appointments are void and of no effect.

If an appointment is made which is partly good and partly bad, the court will sever the good from the bad if possible. In *Re Kerr's Will Trusts*[75] Maria Young had a special power of appointment over a fund in favour of the children of her marriage. By will, she appointed the fund to two of her children, Charlotte and Catherine. Catherine was a child of the marriage and within the power, but Charlotte was an illegitimate child of Maria before she married. The exercise was thus excessive, but the court applied severance and Catherine took the share of the fund appointed to her. The remainder of the fund was divided equally among those entitled in default of appointment. In *Re Holland*[76] an appointment was made with attached conditions which rendered the exercise excessive. The conditions were severed from the appointment and it was upheld as a valid exercise.[77] If it is impossible to sever the condition from the appointment, the exercise will be excessive and void.[78]

(5) Effect of valid exercise

The effect of a valid exercise of the power is to allocate the share of the fund appointed to the person in whose favour the donee has exercised the power. The appointee will then be entitled to an immediate proprietary interest in the share of the fund which has been allocated.[79] In *Churchill v Churchill*,[80] Lord Romilly MR held that the effect of an appointment by Sir Orford Gordon under a special power of a fund to his three daughters in equal shares was to vest in them absolute interests in the appointed fund.

4 Duties of the donee of a mere power of appointment

(1) No duty to exercise the power

The donee of a mere power of appointment is under no duty to exercise the power and make appointments in favour of the potential objects. He has complete discretion and the court will not compel him to exercise the power, nor even to consider periodically whether he should exercise the power. If he fails to make any appointments at all he is not in breach of any duty owed either to the donor of the power or to the potential objects, and they in turn have no cause for complaint against him.

---

[75] (1878) 4 Ch D 600.   [76] [1914] 2 Ch 595.

[77] See also *Churchill v Churchill* (1866–67) LR 5 Eq 44; *Price v William-Wynn* [2006] EWHC 788 (Ch) (a clause inserted into deeds of appointment and revocation, which was held to exceed the powers given to trustees under a settlement, was therefore severed from each of the affected deeds so that they could validly be read without the offending clause).

[78] *Re Cohen* [1911] 1 Ch 37.   [79] See *Vestey v IRC* [1980] AC 1148, HL.

[80] (1866–67) LR 5 Eq 44.

(2) No duty to consider the width of the field

If the donee of the mere power does decide to exercise it, he has no duty to survey and consider the range of potential objects of the power before exercising his discretion in favour of any one object. He may appoint to whomsoever he wishes, provided they are within the class, without having to take account of others who could benefit if he were to exercise his discretion in their favour. If he is within the scope of the power, the donee may appoint the fund entirely to himself without even considering the other potential objects. Thus, in *Re Penrose*[81] an exercise of a special power of appointment by the donee in favour of himself, where he was an object, was upheld.

(3) Duty not to delegate the exercise of the power

The donee must not delegate the power of appointment to others except in so far as this is authorized by the terms of the grant: *delegatus non potest delegare* (a delegate has no power to delegate).

(4) Duty not to exercise the power excessively

The donee of the power is under a duty to make appointments only to those who are objects of the power. As has been seen, any appointments which are excessive will be void.

(5) Duty not to exercise the power fraudulently

Even if the donee exercises the power and makes appointments which appear to be within the scope of the power, they will be void if the exercise amounts to a 'fraud on the power'. The power must be exercised honestly, and the court will look to the motives and intentions of the donor of the power to ensure that they are not improper. As Lord Parker of Waddington observed in *Vatcher v Paull*:

> The term fraud in connection with frauds on a power does not necessarily denote any conduct on the part of the appointor amounting to fraud in the common law meaning of the term or any conduct which could be properly termed dishonest or immoral. It merely means that the power has been exercised for a purpose or with an intention, beyond the scope of or not justified by the instrument creating the fraud...[82]

Thus, in *Hillsdown Holdings plc v Pensions Ombudsman*[83] an exercise of a power was held to constitute a 'fraud', despite the fact that the donee and all parties had acted honestly and with good intentions. In *Edge v Pensions Ombudsman*[84] Scott V-C held that pension trustees were required to 'exercise their discretionary power honestly and for the purpose for which the power was given and not so as to accomplish any ulterior purpose'.

---

[81] [1933] Ch 793. [82] [1915] AC 372, at 378.
[83] [1997] 1 All ER 862. [84] [1998] 2 All ER 547, at 569.

Where the exercise of a power is held invalid on the grounds of fraud, the court acts to protect the interests of those who would be entitled to the fund if no appointments are made. They are the victims of the fraud if appointments are made with improper motives, since they are thereby divested of an interest in the fund to which they would otherwise have become entitled.[85] The effect of fraud is to render the exercise of the power void, not merely voidable.[86]

In *Vatcher v Paull*[87] Lord Parker indicated three circumstances in which the exercise of a power would amount to a fraud. The essence of each is that the benefit is not exclusively conferred upon objects of the power.[88] Clearly, these limitations apply only to special powers and not to general powers, since in the case of a general power there are no persons outside of the scope of the power and the donee may even appoint in his own favour.

(a) Where the exercise is due to some bargain between the appointor and the appointee

If an appointment is made on the basis of a prior agreement between the donee/appointor and the appointee as to how the appointed share of the fund should be used, the appointment is void. The purpose of the bargain may be for the donee to gain some benefit for himself, or for a non-object of the power. The objection to such a bargain is 'that the power is used not with the single purpose of benefiting its proper objects'.[89] In *Hillsdown Holdings plc v Pensions Ombudsman*,[90] Hillsdown plc participated in a pension scheme (the FMC scheme) which had accumulated an actuarial surplus of some £20m. The scheme contained no power allowing the trustees to repay any surplus to employers participating in the scheme, and the scheme could not be amended to confer such a power. After an agreement had been negotiated between Hillsdown and the FMC trustees to augment the benefits of FMC pensioners and to transfer to the company £11m of the surplus, the trustees exercised a power under the scheme to transfer the entire fund to another scheme (the HF scheme), the rules of which were changed to allow the surplus to be paid to Hillsdown. Knox J held that the FMC trustees' exercise of the power, transferring the assets to HF was a fraud on the power as it amounted to 'an improper use of the power for a collateral purpose'[91] of paying the surplus to Hillsdown.

There is no objection to an appointment made on the basis of a bargain with those who are entitled in default of any appointment being made.[92] Where an appointment is a fraud because it was made on the basis of such a bargain, the court may sever the good from the bad provided that it:

can clearly distinguish between the quantum of the benefit bona fide intended to be conferred on the appointee and the quantum of benefit intended to be derived by the appointor or to be conferred on a stranger.[93]

85 *Re Brooks' Settlement Trusts* [1939] Ch 993.
86 *Cloutte v Storey* [1911] 1 Ch 18, CA.
87 [1915] AC 372, at 378.
88 See *Re Merton* [1953] 1 WLR 1096.
89 *Vatcher v Paull* [1915] AC 372, at 379.
90 [1997] 1 All ER 862.
91 Ibid., at 883.
92 [1915] AC 372, at 379.
93 Ibid., at 378.

(b) The appointor's purpose and intention is to secure a benefit for himself

Even where there was no explicit bargain between the donee/appointor and appointee, the exercise will constitute a fraud if the purpose of the appointment was to enable the appointor to receive a benefit. Thus, if an appointor makes an appointment in favour of a child they know to be dying, with the intention that they will gain the benefit of that sum on the death of the child, the appointment is a fraud on the power. In *Lord Hinchinbroke v Seymour*[94] a father appointed £10,000 in favour of his daughter who was fourteen and dying of consumption. The intention of the appointment was that the father would take the money as administrator of the child. It was 'as plain a case of gross fraud on a power as can well be imagined', and 'it was quite obvious what the motive was. It could not have been for the benefit of the child, because she was already provided for.'[95] An appointment made to a child who is healthy is not a fraud, even though the appointor stands to gain if the child subsequently dies.[96]

(c) The appointor's purpose is to benefit for some other person not an object of the power

An appointment in favour of an object of the power will be fraudulent if the real intention of the donee/appointor was to benefit a non-object. In *Re Dick*,[97] Mrs Sherman was the donee of a special power of appointment over property left on trust by her father in favour of her brothers or sisters and their issue. She exercised the power by will in favour of her sister, Miss Dick, but contemporaneously with the will executed a formal memorandum desiring her sister provide an annuity of £800 per annum for her gardener Mr Claydon, who was not an object. The memorandum expressly stated that it did not impose a 'trust or legal obligation' on Miss Dick, so that there was no bargain between the appointor and appointee. Nevertheless, the Court of Appeal held that this amounted to an excessive exercise of the power. Evershed MR stated that the central question was:

whether the right inference is that what Mrs Sherman intended to do, her real deliberate purpose which she wanted and set out by all means that were possible to achieve, was to benefit the Claydons via her relations...or whether her purpose was really to benefit her relations subject only to this, that she had indicated to them that she hoped...they would so something for the Claydons on the lines she had suggested.[98]

The court held that in all the circumstances the real intention was to benefit the non-object. This case suggests that the court will weigh the appointor's motives and intentions from all the available evidence, a principle that was established by Cohen LJ in *Re Crawshay (Decd) (No 2)*.[99] This is notoriously difficult, as evidenced by the large number of indications and counter-indications considered by the Court of Appeal in *Re Dick*.

---

[94] (1784) 1 Bro CC 395.   [95] *Henty v Wrey* (1882) LR 21 Ch D 332, at 342, per Jessel MR.
[96] (1882) LR 21 Ch D 332.   [97] [1953] Ch 343.
[98] Ibid., at 363.   [99] [1948] Ch 123.

5 Failure to exercise the power

Since a power of appointment is purely discretionary in nature, a donee is under no obligation to exercise it, and the objects have no rights to the fund unless it is appointed to them. If the power is not exercised, the fund passes to those entitled in default. Usually this will occur where a donee has been granted a power but has died without making any valid appointments, either inter vivos or by will (see Figure 16.2).

(1) Express gift over in default of appointment

The power of appointment may itself contain an express stipulation of who is to receive the fund if no appointments are made. Such an express provision will determine how the fund should be distributed.

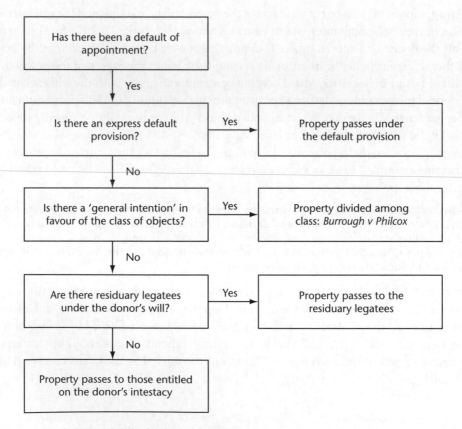

Figure 16.2 Effect of default of appointment

(2) No express gift over in default

If the power does not contain an express gift over in default, the fund will fall to be distributed according to the general principles governing the distribution of surplus funds.[100] If the fund was created by will, the property passes to those entitled to the residuary estate under the will. If the fund was created by an inter vivos settlement, it will result back to the settlor, or his heirs, by a resulting trust. There may, however, be an implied trust producing a different result.

(3) An implied trust in default

In some circumstances, even though no appointment has been made, the court may hold that the fund should be divided among the objects rather than passing to the residuary legatees or by resulting trust. This will only be possible if the court can find that there was a 'general intention' by the donee of the power to benefit a class. The leading case is *Burrough v Philcox*.[101] John Walton granted his surviving daughter, Ann, a power of appointment over his property in favour of his nephews and nieces. The power contained no express gift over in default and Ann died without making any appointments. Under the rules of succession, the testator's next of kin would be entitled to the fund. However, Lord Cottenham LC held that the effect of the arrangement was to create a trust in favour of the nephews and nieces subject to Ann's power of selection, so that when Ann died without having made any appointments, they each took an equal share in the fund. The principle was stated by Lord Cottenham:

where there appears a general intention in favour of a class, and a particular intention in favour of individuals of a class to be selected by another person, and the particular intention fails, from that selection not being made, the court will carry into effect the general intention in favour of the class.[102]

The key element is the finding of a general intention in favour of the class. In effect, the court is concluding from the circumstances of the creation of the power that if it has not been exercised the donor would have wanted the fund to go to the objects. In this sense the operation of the implied trust in default is somewhat similar to an application cy-près, where a charitable gift has failed initially on the grounds that the donor had an overriding charitable intention.[103]

(a) Demonstrating a general intention

An implied trust in default will only arise if it can be shown that the donor of the power possessed a general intention to benefit the objects thereof. If the power contained an express gift in default, then the court cannot conclude that there was a general intention in favour of the class of objects because the donee had already expressed

---

[100] See Chapter 20.   [101] (1840) 5 My & Cr 72.
[102] Ibid., at 92.   [103] See Chapter 20, pp 681 *et seq*.

his intention vis-à-vis the fund in default of any appointments.[104] It is not inevitable that the absence of an express gift over in default will lead to the finding of a general intention in favour of the objects. In *Re Weekes' Settlement*[105] Mrs Slade granted her husband a power of appointment over a fund established under her marriage settlement. Mr Slade died without making any appointments, and the children of the marriage claimed to be equally entitled to the fund. Romer J held that there was no general intention in favour of the class, and the fund therefore passed to the eldest son, who was Mrs Slade's heir at law. He stated:

> The authorities do not show...that there is a hard and fast rule that a gift to A for life with a power to appoint among a class and nothing more must, if there is no gift over in the will, be held a gift by implication to the class in default of the power being exercised...you must find in the will an indication that the testatrix did intend the class or some of the class to take—intended in fact that the power should be regarded in the nature of a trust.[106]

No general intention in favour of the class was found in *Re Combe*[107] or *Re Perowne (Decd).*[108] Such a general intention is only likely to be found where the power is in favour of a small and well-defined class, especially a close family group.

(b) Juridical nature of the implied trust in default

There remains confusion as to the basis under which the fund subject to a power is distributed to the objects under the rule in *Burrough v Philcox*. One analysis is that the power is in fact a discretionary trust under which the donee is under an obligation to make an appointment. Thus, in *Burrough v Philcox* Lord Cottenham LC cited the dictum of Lord Eldon in *Brown v Higgs*[109] that the power is given so as to:

> make it the duty of the donee to exercise it; and, in such case, the court will not permit the objects of the power to suffer by the negligence or conduct of the donee, but fastens upon the property a trust for their benefit.[110]

Similarly, in *Re Weekes' Settlement*[111] Romer J considered that if there had been a general intention in favour of the class this would have rendered the power in the nature of a trust.

A second analysis is that the general intention in favour of the class creates a fixed trust in favour of the whole class, so that from the very beginning the objects/beneficiaries enjoy equal shares in the fund, but that the donor of the power is entitled to divest them of their interests by the exercise of the power.

A third analysis is that the trust in favour of the whole class applies only in default of appointment, just as would be the case if the trust had contained an express gift over in default of appointment. In this situation the beneficiaries of the trust in default of appointment do not have vested, but only contingent, interests which depend for their vesting and fulfilment on the power not being exercised.

---

104 *Re Mills* [1930] 1 Ch 654.
105 [1897] 1 Ch 289.
106 Ibid., at 292.
107 [1925] Ch 210.
108 [1951] Ch 785.
109 (1803) 8 Ves 561.
110 (1840) 5 My & Cr 72, at 92.
111 [1897] 1 Ch 289.

The confusion has arisen because the rule only comes into play after there has been a failure on the part of the donee to exercise the power. If appointments had been made, no difficulties would arise. It is better to regard the court as acting *ex post facto*, and implying a trust in favour of the objects of power in the event of no appointment being made, rather than to construe a trust in their favour from the beginning. This was the approach taken by Buckley J in *Re Wills' Trust Deeds*.[112] He considered that a trust in favour of the objects only arose in the event of default:

> A perusal of these cases... leads to the conclusion that they really turn on the question whether on the particular facts of each case it was proper to infer that there was a trust in default of appointment for the objects of the power. The court did not, and I think, could not compel the donee personally to exercise the power but carried what it conceived to be the settlor's intention into effect by executing an implied trust in default of appointment.[113]

It therefore seems that the best analysis is that a power is given to the donee, which he is under no duty to exercise, but that in the event of there being no exercise the court implies a trust in favour of the class on the basis of a general intention in their favour on the part of the donor. The objects thus have no beneficial entitlement to the fund until the trust is implied and the donee of the power has no enforceable duties and is not in breach by failing to make appointments.

6 Fiduciary powers

(1) Definition

If a power of appointment is held by the donee in a fiduciary capacity, the power is a 'fiduciary power'. This will normally occur because the donee is also a trustee of the property subject to the power. In *Re Hay's Settlement Trusts*[114] David Greig and Colin Oliver were the trustees of a settlement made by Lady Hay. As part of the settlement they enjoyed a general power of appointment over the property subject to the trust. As they were trustees, they held their power in a fiduciary capacity.[115] In *Mettoy Pension Trustees Ltd v Evans*[116] Warner J described such an obligation as a 'fiduciary power in the full sense',[117] which he defined as:

> comprising any power conferred on the trustees of the property or any other person as a trustee of the power itself.[118]

The case concerned the pension fund of a company, Mettoy plc, which had gone into liquidation. After the fund had met the fixed entitlements of pensioners, there was

---

[112] [1964] Ch 219.   [113] Ibid., at 230.
[114] [1982] 1 WLR 202.   [115] See also *Breadner v Granville-Grossman* [2001] Ch 523.
[116] [1991] 2 All ER 513. See Martin [1991] Conv 364, Gardner 'Fiduciary Powers in Toytown' (1991) 107 LQR 214.
[117] Using the language of Chitty J in *Re Somes* [1896] 1 Ch 250.   [118] [1991] 2 All ER 513, at 545.

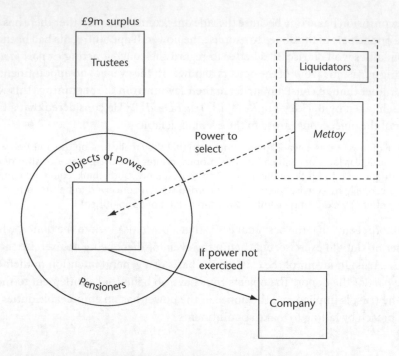

Figure 16.3 Fiduciary powers: *Mettoy Pension Trustees v Evans*

a surplus of some £9m remaining in the fund. Rule 13(5) of the fund's rules granted a power of appointment over any surplus, which could be exercised to increase the entitlements of the pensioners. This power was held by the company and not by the separate trustee of the fund. If the power was not exercised, an undistributed surplus would pass to the company itself (see Figure 16.3). In these circumstances Warner J concluded that the power was a fiduciary power, even though the trustee was not the donee. He relied on two main factors to reach this conclusion. First, he considered that if the power were a mere power and not a fiduciary power, any supposed discretion by the company to appoint increased entitlements to the pensioners would be 'illusory', since the company would in effect only be making ex gratia gifts from property which they owned absolutely.[119] Second, the objects of the power were not volunteers, as the fund surplus had arisen partially from their own pension contributions and not from successful investment or over-contribution by the company alone.[120]

(2) Duties of the donee of fiduciary powers

The key difference between a 'fiduciary power' and a 'mere power' is that the donee of a fiduciary power owes limited duties to the objects. The scope of these additional duties

---

[119] Ibid., at 547.
[120] Ibid., at 550–551. See also *Thrells Ltd v Lomas* [1993] 1 WLR 456; *Re William Makin & Sons Ltd* [1993] OPLR 171.

was considered in *Re Hay's Settlement Trusts*[121] and *Mettoy Pension Trustees Ltd v Evans*.[122] In *Re Hay's Settlement Trusts*[123] Sir Robert Megarry V-C held that there were three additional duties owed by the donee to the objects of a fiduciary power. These duties point to the fact that the donee of a fiduciary power must have a greater sensitivity to the nature of the discretion that he holds.

(a) Duty periodically to consider whether or not he should exercise the power

Unlike a mere power, which the donee need never consider whether or not to exercise, Megarry V-C held that the donee of a fiduciary power cannot simply fold his hands and ignore it, for normally he must from time to time consider whether or not to exercise the power'.[124] This duty is enforceable by the court, which may direct the donee to consider whether he should exercise the power.[125]

(b) Duty to consider the range of objects of the power

The fiduciary nature of the position of the donee also affects the manner in which a donee makes appointments. Following the decision of the House of Lords in *McPhail v Doulton*,[126] which concerned the duties of trustees of a discretionary trust, Megarry V-C held that the donee of a fiduciary power must 'make such a survey of the range of objects' as will enable him to carry out his fiduciary duty.[127] This does not mean that he has to identify every single member of the class of objects before making any allocations of the fund, but that he must find out 'the permissible area of selection'. He cannot make an appointment to the first object who comes to mind.

(c) Duty to consider the appropriateness of individual appointments

Having considered the range of potential objects, the donee of a fiduciary power must 'then consider responsibly, in individual cases, whether a contemplated beneficiary was within the power and whether, in relation to other possible claimants, a particular grant was appropriate'.[128]

(d) Duty to make trust documents available to the objects

In *Schmidt v Rosewood Trust Ltd*[129] the Privy Council held that the objects of a fiduciary power of appointment may be entitled to seek disclosure of trust documents of the trust to which the power relates, so as to ensure the proper administration of the trust. However, this right is not absolute as disclosure is ordered under the inherent jurisdiction of the court, and the entitlement to disclosure may be limited or safeguarded so as to protect personal or commercial confidentiality, or to balance the competing

---

[121] [1982] 1 WLR 202.   [122] [1991] 2 All ER 513.   [123] [1982] 1 WLR 202.
[124] Ibid., at 209.   [125] Ibid.   [126] [1971] AC 424.
[127] Per Lord Wilberforce, quoted by Sir Robert Megarry V-C in *Re Hay's Settlement Trusts* [1982] 1 WLR 202, at 209.
[128] *McPhail v Doulton* [1971] AC 424, at 457, quoted by Sir Robert Megarry in *Re Hay's Settlement Trusts* [1982] 1 WLR 202, at 209.
[129] [2003] 2 AC 709.

interests of different beneficiaries, trustees, or third parties. At all events, the object of a power of appointment will not be granted access to trust documents which would reveal the trustees' reasons for exercising, or not exercising, the power.[130]

(e) Different duties in different contexts

There is a degree of circularity in identifying whether a power is fiduciary and what duties are imposed on the donee. The power is fiduciary because the donee is subject to duties; but it follows that if the power is fiduciary, the donee is subject to duties. Sir Robert Megarry's analysis in *Re Hay's Settlement Trusts*[131] of the duties of a donee of a fiduciary power tends to assume that all fiduciary powers involve the same duties. The decision of the Court of Appeal in *Gomez and others v Gomez-Monche Vives*[132] accepts that there is a wide range of fiduciary duties, some analogous to those of a trustee, and some less so. This means that a more sophisticated analysis of fiduciary powers is required: a power will be fiduciary if the donee is subject to duties, but the nature of those duties will depend upon an analysis of the instrument creating the power and any other relevant circumstances.

(3) Supervision by the court of fiduciary powers

Since the donee of a fiduciary power owes duties to the objects, the court will ensure that these duties are properly performed.

(a) Appointments made without due consideration

If appointments are made by the donee without proper consideration of the range of objects and the appropriateness of the particular appointments being made, then such appointments will be void as an invalid exercise of the power. In *Turner v Turner*[133] the trustees of a settlement made appointments by deed under a power of appointment they held in their capacity as trustees. They had executed the deeds at the request of the solicitors acting for the settlor without reading or understanding what they were signing, and without making a decision to appoint. Mervyn Davies J held that these appointments should be set aside because they had been made 'in breach of their duty, in that it was their duty to "consider" before appointing, and this they did not do'.[134]

(b) Failure to exercise the power

Where the donee of a fiduciary power has failed to make any appointments, the question arises whether the court can intervene to compel them to carry out their duties. In *Re Hay's Settlement Trusts*[135] Sir Robert Megarry V-C indicated that the courts would compel the donee of a fiduciary power to consider exercising it.[136] However, the courts

---

[130] See also *Foreman v Kingstone* [2004] 1 NZLR 841. See below p 834 *et seq* for a fuller discussion of the right to disclosure of trust documents.

[131] [1982] 1 WLR 202.   [132] [2008] EWCA Civ 1065; [2009] Ch 245 (CA).

[133] [1983] 2 All ER 745.   [134] Ibid., at 752.   [135] [1982] 1 WLR 202.

[136] Ibid., at 209.

have been reluctant to suggest that they would compel the donee to *exercise* the power, as this is inconsistent with its discretionary character. In *McPhail v Doulton*[137] Lord Wilberforce cited the judgment of Lord Upjohn in *Re Gulbenkian's Settlement*[138] and stated:

although the trustees may ... be under a fiduciary duty to consider whether or in what way they should exercise their power the court will not normally compel its exercise.[139]

However, in the *Mettoy*[140] case Warner J considered that in some circumstances the court might be willing to step in and compel the exercise of a fiduciary power. As has been seen, the power was held by Mettoy plc, a company in liquidation. Therefore, the donee was incapable of exercising the power itself, and it was held by the liquidators. They would be unable to exercise it because of a conflict between their duty to give proper consideration to exercising it in favour of the pensioners and their duty to the company's creditors, which would require them to exercise the power to enable the company to take the surplus in default. Warner J held that, since there was no one remaining who could exercise the power, the court should step in. He held that in such circumstances the court could exercise the fiduciary power in the same way that it was entitled to intervene if the trustees of a discretionary trust were failing to carry out their duties. He cited *McPhail v Doulton*,[141] where Lord Wilberforce had suggested a number of means by which the court could intervene to compel the performance of a discretionary trust:

by appointing new trustees, or by authorising or directing representative persons of the classes of beneficiaries to prepare a scheme of distribution, or even, should the proper basis for distribution appear, by itself directing the trustees to so distribute.[142]

He then suggested that 'the methods [Lord Wilberforce] indicated could be equally appropriate in a case where the court was called upon to intervene in the exercise of a [fiduciary power]'.[143] He therefore held that the court would execute the power of appointment itself, but that, before doing so, further evidence was required to enable it to determine the basis on which an allocation of the surplus fund should be made between the pensioners and the company.[144]

Mettoy Pension Trustees Ltd v Evans marks a trend toward the assimilation of discretionary trusts and powers of appointment. The traditional distinction between trusts, which the court will enforce, and powers, which it will not, is all but abolished if the courts are willing to enforce fiduciary powers in exactly the same way that they will enforce discretionary trusts. The limitation seems to be the recognition that this procedure is only available in the limited exceptional circumstances where the power cannot be exercised because there is no donee able to make any appointments.

A different problem arises where the donee of a fiduciary power has failed to make any appointments because he has not fulfilled his duty to consider whether or not to

---

137 [1971] AC 424.   138 [1970] AC 508.   139 [1971] AC 424, at 456–457.
140 [1991] 2 All ER 513.   141 [1971] AC 424.   142 Ibid., at 457.
143 Ibid., at 549.   144 Ibid., at 562.

exercise the power. In *Breadner v Granville-Grossman*[145] the two trustees of a discretionary trust were granted a power of appointment in 1976. Under the terms of the trust this power had to be exercised before a specified date, namely 2 August 1989. At a late stage one of the trustees prepared a deed appointing the entire beneficial interest to one beneficiary, which he only explained to his co-trustee on the day that the deed was executed, which was 2 August 1989, in other words after the last day for exercising the 1976 power. The beneficiary claimed that the appointment was still effective in equity, on the grounds that the trustees had failed to comply with their duty to consider exercising it. Park J held that, while the trustees had failed to perform their duty to consider exercising the power, the court could not intervene because the power had ceased to be exercisable, even though they would have made the appointment if they had performed their duty. He explained that the willingness of the court to intervene in *Mettoy Pension Trustees Ltd v Evans* did not extend to such a situation:

> In my judgement, however, there is a very big difference between, on the one hand, the courts declaring something which the trustees have done to be void, and on the other hand, the courts holding that a trust takes effect as if the trustees had done something which they had never done at all ... In the *Mettoy Pension Trustees Ltd* case Warner J observed that, if a case arose where the trustees had done something but, if they had taken all relevant factors into account, would have done something quite different, the court should declare void what they have done. There is no suggestion that the court would or might substitute the different thing which it thinks that the trustees would have done themselves ... I do not think that Warner J would have done it, and I will not do it either.[146]

(4) Validity of fiduciary powers

(a) Certainty

The test for certainty of objects of a fiduciary power is the same as that for a mere power, namely the 'is or is not' test.[147]

(b) Capriciousness

It is clear from *Re Manisty's Settlement*[148] and *Re Hay's Settlement Trusts*[149] that a fiduciary power will be void if it is capricious in nature.[150]

(c) Administrative unworkability[151]

In *McPhail v Doulton*[152] Lord Wilberforce suggested that a discretionary trust which is not void for uncertainty may yet be void for 'administrative unworkability'[153] if the class is 'too wide to form anything like a class'.[154] In *Re Hay's Settlement Trusts*[155] Sir Robert Megarry V-C considered that the principle of 'administrative unworkability' was directed only towards discretionary trusts and had no application to

---

[145]   [2000] 4 All ER 705.   [146] Ibid., at 723.   [147] See above pp 507–511.
[148]   [1974] Ch 17.   [149] [1982] 1 WLR 202.   [150] See above, p 511.
[151]   See Gardner 'Fiduciary Powers in Toytown' (1991) 107 LQR 214.
[152]   [1971] AC 424.   [153] Ibid., at 444.   [154] [1971] AC 424, at 457.
[155]   [1982] 1 WLR 202.

fiduciary powers. However, following the greater assimilation of fiduciary powers and discretionary trusts in *Mettoy Pension Trustees Ltd v Evans*[156] and the willingness of the court to compel their exercise in exceptional circumstances, it may be that the principle will also apply to fiduciary powers. The fiduciary power in the *Mettoy* case would not, however, have been invalidated for 'administrative unworkability' because the class of objects was small and well defined, ie the pension fund members.

7 Release of powers

The donor of a power of appointment, whether a bare power or a fiduciary power, may wish to release it. As a consequence of release he will cease to be able to make any appointments of the fund. This has the same effect on the ownership of the property subject to the power as if the power had not been exercised. Therefore, on release those entitled in default will automatically become entitled to the property previously held subject to the power. Sometimes a power may be released to remove persons from the class of potential recipients of the property if the possibility of their receiving a benefit would result in tax disadvantages. For example, it may be advantageous to exclude the settlor from the class of objects of a power to avoid inheritance tax under the 'reservation of benefit' rules.[157] Similarly, a settlement may be liable to income tax if the settlor or his wife may benefit from the exercise of a power of appointment in their favour. In *Muir v IRC*[158] the Court of Appeal held that the trustees had released their power to pay income from the trust towards the payment of premiums of insurance policies held by persons including the settlor, and that therefore the settlor had no interest in the income from the settlement and was not liable to surtax. In *Re Wills' Trust Deeds*[159] property was held on trust for such of the issue of the testator or charitable institutions as the trustees should appoint. The trustees sought to release the power in favour of the testator's issue so that the trust would be for exclusively charitable objects.

(1) The consequences of release

If property is gifted to persons subject to a power of appointment which may divest them of their interest, on the release of the power their interests will become indefeasible. This was seen in *Re Mills*,[160] which concerned the will of Algernon Mills. His residuary estate was to be held for the benefit of such of his father's children and remoter issue that his brother should appoint or, in default of any such appointment, for his brother absolutely. The brother made a number of appointments and then released

---

[156] [1991] 2 All ER 513.   [157] See Chapter 5.   [158] [1966] 1 WLR 1269.
[159] [1964] Ch 219.   [160] [1930] 1 Ch 654, CA.

the power by deed. The Court of Appeal held that this was a valid release, and the consequence was that the brother became absolutely entitled to the property under the default provision.

(2) **Authority to release**

Not every power is capable of being released by the donee. The leading authority concerning the circumstances in which a power may be released is the judgment of Buckley J in *Re Wills' Trust Deeds*.[161] Generally, a donee will only be able to release a power which he is under no obligation to exercise or to consider exercising.

(a) Mere powers

In the case of a bare or mere power, which is not held in any fiduciary capacity and where there is no express or implied trust in favour of the objects in default of appointment, the donee may release the power. As Buckley J said:

Where a power is conferred on someone who is not a trustee of the property to which the power relates or, if he is such a trustee, is not conferred on him in that capacity, then in the absence of a trust in favour of the objects of the power in default of appointment, the donee is, at any rate prima facie, not under any duty recognisable by the court to exercise a power such as to disenable him from releasing the power.[162]

Mere powers fall within the ambit of s 155 of the Law of Property Act 1925, which provides:

A person to whom any power, whether coupled with an interest or not, is given, may by deed release, or contract not to exercise, the power.[163]

(b) Mere powers with a trust in favour of the objects in default of appointment

Where there is a trust in default of appointment under the power, according to Buckley J, the donee is not entitled to release the power so as to defeat the trust. This will be so whether the trust in default is express or implied under the rule in *Burrough v Philcox*.[164] This was explained by Buckley J:

if a power is granted to appoint among a class of objects and in default of appointment there is a trust, express or implied, in favour of the members of that class, the donee of the power cannot by failure to appoint or by purporting to bind himself not to appoint or, which comes to the same thing, by purporting to release his power, defeat the interests of the members of the class of objects. This proposition really needs only to be stated to be accepted. The problem in such cases, where there is no express trust in default of appointment, is whether such a trust should be inferred . . . [A] power of the kind just mentioned cannot be released, for the donee is under a duty to exercise it, notwithstanding that the court may not be able to compel

---

[161] [1964] Ch 219.   [162] Ibid., at 237.
[163] Law of Property Act 1925, s 160 provides that s 155 applies to 'powers created or arising either before or after the commencement' of the Act.
[164] (1840) 5 My & Cr 72.

him personally to perform that duty, and can remedy his default only be executing the trust in default of appointment.[165]

Buckley J's view that a power cannot be released in this situation is based on the assumption that the trust in favour of the members of the class arises from an obligation to exercise the power. As has already been explained, this may not be the best interpretation of *Burrough v Philcox*. Despite his view to the contrary, the logic of his statement that the power cannot be released also cannot apply to an express trust by way of gift over in default in favour of the class of objects. Such release will accelerate the gift in favour of the class. In *Re Radcliffe*[166] a father held a power of appointment in favour of the class of objects of his children, with an express trust in favour of them equally in default of appointment. One of the three children had died in infancy, and the father was entitled as his administrator. The father released the power of appointment by deed and demanded that the trustees pay a third of the trust property to him. The Court of Appeal, following the earlier case of *Smith v Houblon*,[167] held that there had been a valid release and that, subject to the father surrendering his life-interest over the trust, he was entitled to the third to be transferred to him.

(c) Fiduciary powers

(i) Fiduciary powers with no authorization to release

Where a power is held in a fiduciary capacity, whether by a trustee or other fiduciary, the donee may not release it unless release is authorized by the instrument creating the power. When the predecessor to s 155 of the Law of Property Act 1925 was enacted in 1881,[168] the courts held that it did not apply to trusts held in a fiduciary capacity.[169] This was followed by the Court of Appeal in *Re Mills*[170] and in *Re Wills' Trust Deeds*, where Buckley J said:

[W]here a power is conferred on trustees virtute officii in relation to their trust property, they cannot release it or bind themselves not to exercise it...[T]he same is true if the power is conferred on persons who are in fact trustees of the settlement but is conferred on them by name and not by reference to their office, if on the true view of the facts they were selected as donees of the power because they were the trustees.[171]

This principle was applied by Millett J in *Re Courage Group's Pension Schemes*,[172] where he held that a committee of management of a pension scheme could not release their powers or discretion so as to deprive their successors of the right to exercise them as they were vested in the committee in a fiduciary capacity. This restriction will also apply where the power is held in a fiduciary capacity, even though the donees are not trustees. As has been seen in *Mettoy Pension Trustees v Evans*,[173] the company,

---

[165] [1964] Ch 219, at 236.   [166] [1892] 1 Ch 27.
[167] (1859) 26 Beav 482.   [168] Conveyancing Act 1881, s 52.
[169] See *Weller v Kerr* (1866) LR 1 Sc & Div 11; *Re Eyre* (1883) 49 LT 259; *Saul v Pattinson* (1886) 55 LJ Ch 831.
[170] [1930] 1 Ch 654.   [171] [1964] Ch 219.   [172] [1987] 1 WLR 495.
[173] [1991] 2 All ER 513.

although not a trustee of the fund, held a power of appointment in a fiduciary capacity. Warner J therefore held that it could not be released.

(ii) Fiduciary powers with authorization to release

The donee of a fiduciary power will be entitled to release it if the instrument creating the power gives him the authority to do so. The principle was stated by Harman LJ in *Muir v IRC*,[174] where he commented on the judgment of Buckley J in *Re Wills' Trusts Deeds*:[175]

I would agree that, if a power is conferred on trustees virtute officii, that is to say, if it be a [fiduciary] power which the trustees have the duty to exercise, they cannot release it in the absence of words in the trust deed authorising them to do so...[176]

On the facts he found that the trust instrument did authorize a release.[177]

(d) Discretionary trusts

Due to the evolutionary development of concepts and terminology, some early cases referring to 'trust powers'[178] would today be recognized as 'discretionary trusts'. Clearly, these cannot be released because the obligation is in the nature of a trust, and the court will compel its exercise.

(3) Means of release

It seems clear that a purely oral release will be ineffective to release a power.[179] However, if a donee of a power of appointment possesses the jurisdiction to release the power, he may do so by deed, as provided in s 155 of the Law of Property Act 1925. Alternatively, a power may be released by the donee entering into a contract not to exercise the power, as also provided in s 155. It seems that a power will also be released where there has been any dealing with the property subject to it which is inconsistent with the exercise of the power. In *Foakes v Jackson*[180] a power was held jointly by a husband and wife, and the survivor had a separate power. A deed was executed in 1886 by the husband, wife, and those beneficially entitled to the property assigning it to one of the objects. In 1899, after the wife's death, the husband purported to appoint the property to a different object. Farwell J held that the earlier deed which, with the intention of the donees and the parties entitled in default, had the effect of passing the property absolutely to the object operated as a release of the power. Similarly, in *Re Courtauld's Settlement*[181] Plowman J held that where there had been an application to vary a settlement so that a power was extinguished, there was no need to execute a separate deed

---

174 [1966] 1 WLR 1269.   175 [1964] Ch 219.
176 [1966] 1 WLR 1269, at 1283.   177 See also *Blausten v IRC* [1972] Ch 256, CA.
178 See Chapter 17.
179 See *Re Christie-Miller's Settlement Trusts* [1961] 1 All ER 855n; *Re Courtauld's Settlement* [1965] 2 All ER 544n.
180 [1900] 1 Ch 807.   181 [1965] 2 All ER 544n.

of release. Trustees may surrender their trusts and powers by paying the trust property into court, as provided in s 63 of the Trustee Act 1925.

(4) Release and fraud on a power

The equitable doctrine that will invalidate the fraudulent exercise of a power examined above[182] has no application to the release of a power of appointment, and therefore a donee may release a power even though he thereby derives a personal benefit. In *Re Somes*[183] a father held a power of appointment over property held on his marriage settlement. In default, his daughter was absolutely entitled. He was suffering financial difficulties and therefore released the power and he and his daughter then mortgaged their interests in the fund for £10,000, which was paid to the father. Chitty J held that this was a perfectly valid release:

it appears to me that there is a fallacy in applying to a release of a power of this kind the doctrines applicable to the fraudulent exercise of such a power. There is no duty imposed on the donee of a limited power to make an appointment; there is no fiduciary relationship between him and the objects of the power beyond this, that if he does exercise the power of appointment, he must exercise it honestly for the benefit of an object or the objects of the power, and not corruptly for his own personal benefit; but I cannot see any ground for applying that doctrine to the case of a release of a power; the donee of the power may, or he may not, be acting in his own interest, but he is at liberty, in my opinion, to say that he will never make any appointment under the power, and to execute a release of it.[184]

Obviously, this will only apply if the power is of a type which may be released, and the court finds that the power is not subject to fiduciary duties excluding such a release.

---

[182] See p 515.   [183] [1896] 1 Ch 250.   [184] Ibid., at 255.

17

Discretionary trusts

This chapter considers the key features of a discretionary trust, which look similar to powers of appointment covered in Chapter 16, in that it is another of the equitable mechanisms that facilitate the management and allocation of property. However, unlike a power of appointment, a trustee must make a distribution to the identified class, and the court will step in to compel the exercise of a discretionary trust. This chapter explores in detail the nature, creation, use and rights, and obligations imposed by discretionary trusts.

1 Introduction

(1) The nature of discretionary trusts

(a) The definition of discretionary trusts

Discretionary trusts were defined by Warner J in *Mettoy Pension Trustees Ltd v Evans* as:

> cases where someone, usually but not necessarily the trustee,[1] is under a duty to select from among a class of beneficiaries those who are to receive, and the proportions in which they are to receive, income or capital of the trust property.[2]

They are mechanisms by which an owner of property can grant to others the power to allocate a fund among a defined group of individuals. As in a power of appointment, the allocator has complete discretion how the fund should be allocated, either or both in terms of the persons who should receive shares of the fund, and the size of the shares they should receive. However, unlike powers of appointment, the allocator is under a mandatory duty to make allocations in accordance with the terms of the trust. The court will intervene to ensure that this duty is discharged.

---

[1] This exception is probably intended to recognize the possibility of there being separate management and custodian trustees.
[2] [1991] 2 All ER 513.

Figure 17.1 The *Baden* discretionary trust (*McPhail v Doulton*)

(b) The flexibility of discretionary trusts

The discretionary trust is therefore an extremely flexible mechanism for the distribution of property. It combines all the advantages of the power of appointment in permitting the owner of property not merely to delegate the task of transferring his property to others, but also of delegating the responsibility for deciding how that property should be distributed. Yet it avoids the potential pitfalls of the mere power because the trustees are under a duty to distribute according to the terms of the trust, which is enforceable by the court. This inherent flexibility, coupled with the security of enforcement by the court, has made the discretionary trust ideal as a means of allocating large funds among large potential classes of beneficiaries. For example, in the leading case of *McPhail v Doulton*,[3] Bertram Baden established a trust in 1941 to provide benefits for the staff of Matthew Hall & Co Ltd and their relatives and dependants (see Figure 17.1). Clause 9(a) of the deed stated that:

> The trustees shall apply the net income of the fund in making at their absolute discretion grants to or for the benefit of any of the officers and employees or ex-officers and ex-employees of the company or to any relative or dependants of any such person in such amounts... as they think fit.

In 1941 the company employed some 1,300 people. By 1962 the fund contained assets valued at £163,000, which had risen to £463,000 in 1972. Clearly, it was never the

---

[3] [1971] AC 424.

intention of Mr Baden that each and every member of the specified class should receive payments from the fund, but that those appointed trustees should have the discretion to select some to benefit. Equally, it was not his intention that the trustees be able to sit idly by and fail to make any allocations at all. The language of the deed clearly indicated an obligation, or duty, to distribute the income of the fund. The House of Lords held that a discretionary trust had been created. Although the trustees had complete discretion which particular members of the class specified were to receive shares of the income produced by the fund, they had no freedom to refuse to carry out the trust.

(2) The development of the discretionary trust[4]

Although the terminology of the 'discretionary trust' is a more recent development, the underlying concept of an equitable obligation which is discretionary in part while remaining predominantly mandatory is well established and has a strong historical pedigree. In *Brown v Higgs*[5] Lord Eldon, the Lord Chancellor, held that equitable obligations could not simply be categorized as trusts or powers:

> But there are not only a mere trust and a mere power, but there is also known to this court a power which the party to whom it is given is entrusted and required to execute; and with regard to that species of power the court consider it as partaking so much of the nature and qualities of a trust that, if the person who has that duty imposed upon him does not discharge it, the court will, to a certain extent, discharge the duty in his room and place.[6]

In essence, he was describing what today would be termed a discretionary trust. The older cases often use the phrase 'trust power'. This term has been the source of some confusion, since it is used interchangeably in the cases to describe both a trust implied in default of the exercise of a power of appointment under the principle of *Burrough v Philcox*,[7] and an obligation which would today be characterized as a discretionary trust.

In *Crockett v Crockett*,[8] Lord Cottenham found that a possible construction of a will where a husband left all his property 'at the disposal of his wife, for herself and children', was that she was 'as between herself and her children...a trustee, with a large discretion as to the application of the fund'.[9] This analysis was followed by Sir John Romilly MR in *Hart v Tribe*.[10] Even in the leading case of *McPhail v Doulton*[11] the House of Lords spoke of the obligation created by Baden's deed as a 'trust power',[12] although when the case returned to the Court of Appeal as *Re Baden's Deed Trusts (No 2)*[13] the term 'discretionary trust' was used. It is important to be alive to the different terminology used.[14]

---

4 See also Chapter 4.   5 (1800) 5 Ves 495.   6 Ibid., at 570.
7 (1840) 5 My & Cr 72.   8 (1848) 2 Ph 553.   9 Ibid., at 561.
10 (1854) 18 Beav 215.   11 [1971] AC 424.
12 Lord Wilberforce did on one occasion refer to 'discretionary trusts': see [1971] AC 424, at 452.
13 [1973] Ch 9.
14 See also *Mettoy Pensions v Evans* [1991] 2 All ER 513, for a discussion of the various terminologies used in the cases, and the potential for confusion between trusts and powers.

(3) **Types of discretionary trusts**

There are two types of discretionary trust: 'exhaustive' and 'non-exhaustive'.

(a) Exhaustive discretionary trusts

In an exhaustive discretionary trust the trustees are subject to a duty to distribute the whole of the trust fund, or its income, to the potential beneficiaries. They have no power to decide not to distribute part of the fund. An example of an exhaustive discretionary trust is found in *Re Lockers Settlement Trusts*,[15] where a discretionary trust was established in favour of a class of individuals, charities, and other institutions. The trustees were regarded as being in breach of trust when they failed to distribute the trust income within a reasonable period of time.[16]An exhaustive discretionary trust will arise, as in *Re Gourju's Will Trusts*,[17] whenever the trustees are not given an express power to retain all or part of the income from the fund.

(b) Non-exhaustive discretionary trusts

In a non-exhaustive discretionary trust the trustees are not obliged to distribute the whole of the trust fund income among the class of beneficiaries but may, in their discretion, decide to accumulate it. This is only possible if the trustees are expressly given the power to retain and accumulate the income, or part of the income, from the trust fund by the terms of the trust. *McPhail v Doulton*[18] is an example of a non-exhaustive discretionary trust. The trust deed did not require the trustees to distribute all the income generated by the fund to the employees, ex-employees, relatives, and dependants, but granted them the power to retain and accumulate it.[19] In many ways a non-exhaustive discretionary trust is extremely similar in practice to a fiduciary power. In neither case is the allocator of the fund obliged to distribute the fund or its income to the class of potential objects or beneficiaries. This leads to the question whether there is any real distinction between them.[20] Analytically, a distinction can be drawn on the basis of the nature of the duties owed by the allocator in each case. Under a non-exhaustive discretionary trust, the prime duty of the trustee is to distribute the fund income among the class of beneficiaries, although there is a power to retain and accumulate.[21] Whether the trustee has exercised that power properly is open to the supervision of the court under an objective test, that he must have acted in the best interests of the class of beneficiaries. In the case of a power of appointment, the donee of the power has no prime duty, as it is purely

---

[15] [1977] 1 WLR 1323.   [16] Ibid., at 1325.
[17] [1943] Ch 24.   [18] [1971] AC 424.
[19] Clause 9(b) of the deed creating the Matthew Hall Staff trust fund stated: 'The trustees shall not be bound to exhaust the income of any year or other period in making grants...' and granted them a power to invest the undistributed surplus under clause 6(a).
[20] See [1970] ASCL 187 (Davies); Grbich 'Baden: Awakening the Conceptually Moribund Trust' (1974) 37 MLR 643; (1976) 54 CBR 229 (Cullity).
[21] Compare eg a trust for sale of land, where the trustees are under a duty to sell but have a power to postpone sale. See Chapter 3.

within his discretion whether he allocates the property subject to the power. He owes no objective duties that the court can supervise, but purely a subjective duty to act as he thinks best. Provided he acts genuinely, the court cannot question his decision.[22] This is a fine distinction, but it demonstrates that the non-exhaustive discretionary trust remains in essence a trust, although it is extremely close on the scale of equitable obligations to the fiduciary power.[23] A further distinction is that, under a discretionary trust, the legal title to the trust fund will normally be vested in the trustees, who will thus also be required to invest and manage the trust property. In contrast, a fiduciary power may be held by a person with no rights of ownership to the fund. Thus, in *Mettoy Pension Trustees Ltd v Evans*[24] a power of appointment over a pension fund surplus was held in a fiduciary capacity by a company which was not simultaneously the trustee thereof. However, in the majority of cases a fiduciary power will be held by a trustee, since the donee's status as a trustee invests the power with fiduciary characteristics.

2 Essential validity of discretionary trusts

A discretionary trust will only be validly created if it satisfies the requirements for the validity of trusts in general. It must have certainty of subject matter and objects, and it must comply with the beneficiary principle. The trust must not exist for a period exceeding the duration of the perpetuity period.[25] Some aspects of these general requirements warrant detailed attention in the context of discretionary trusts, and there are also some additional requirements which are specific to such trusts, especially that they must not be 'administratively unworkable'.

(1) Certainty of objects

(a) The test for certainty prior to *McPhail v Doulton*[26]

When the trust fund is subject to a fixed trust, the trustees hold the fund on trust for the beneficiaries in the shares and proportions determined by the settlor who created the fund. They have no discretion as to how the fund should be allocated. Where the beneficiaries are defined as a class, a fixed trust will be void for uncertainty unless it is possible to draw up a 'complete list' of each and every person who is a member of the specified class. This is because the trustee (or the court in the event of his default) must know the full extent of the class before he is able to determine the individual shares of each beneficiary and carry out the trust. Prior to the leading

---

[22] See Chapter 16.   [23] See Chapter 4.

[24] [1991] 2 All ER 513: see Martin [1991] Conv 364; Gardner 'Fiduciary Powers in Toytown' (1991) 107 LQR 214.

[25] *Re Coleman* [1936] Ch 528.   [26] [1971] AC 424.

case of *McPhail v Doulton*,[27] this test was also applied to discretionary trusts. Thus, in *IRC v Broadway Cottages Trust*[28] the Court of Appeal held that a discretionary trust in favour of a class of beneficiaries that could not be completely ascertained at any one moment was void for uncertainty. There were two essential rationales for the application of the 'complete list' test to discretionary trusts:

(i) The court must be able to exercise the trust

In *Morice v Bishop of Durham*,[29] Lord Eldon stated that a trust is only valid if the court is able to execute it in the event of a failure by the trustee to carry out their obligation so to do, whether through death, neglect, or refusal. The 'complete list test' was applied to discretionary trusts because it was thought that the only method the court could employ to carry out the trust in the event of the trustee's default was to order equal division of the fund between all the potential beneficiaries. Obviously, such equal division would require a complete list of the beneficiaries. However, some early cases had adopted a more flexible approach, holding that the court could exercise its discretion in the event of the trustee's failure. In *Mosely v Mosely*[30] an estate was held on trust by two trustees for such of the testator's relatives as they should think fit. When the trustees failed to exercise their discretion to allocate the property, the court ordered that it be conveyed into court, rather than divided equally among the class of potential beneficiaries.[31] In *Warburton v Warburton*[32] trustees held a fund on discretionary trust for the testator's children. The House of Lords ordered that the eldest child be given a double share. In *Hart v Tribe*[33] a testator's wife held £4,000 on discretionary trust for herself and his children. She refused to award any of the income from the fund for the education and maintenance of his son by another marriage. Sir John Romilly MR directed that the boy receive £30 a year from the fund. Although explicable as a case where the trustees' discretion had not been exercised bona fides, this decision does seem to amount to an exercise of the discretion by the court. In earlier proceedings[34] the Master of the Rolls had indicated that, although the normal means by which the court can execute the trust is equal division between the beneficiaries, this is only one method, and that the court can compel the trustees to exercise their discretion.[35] However, the orthodox position was reiterated in *Gray v Gray*,[36] where Thomas Smith MR held that the only way the court could exercise a discretionary trust where the trustee had failed to do so was by ordering equal division between all the members of the class, and a similar view was taken by Sir Richard Arden in *Kemp v Kemp*.[37] The cases which adopted a more flexible approach were condemned as anomalous by the Court of Appeal in *IRC v Broadway Cottages Trust*.[38] Jenkins LJ asserted the principle that 'a trust for such members of a given class of objects as the trustees shall select is void for uncertainty, unless the whole range of objects eligible for selection is

---

[27] Ibid.   [28] [1955] Ch 20.   [29] (1805) 10 Ves 522, at 539–540.
[30] (1673) Cas temp Finch 53.   [31] See also *Clarke v Turner* (1694) Freem Ch 198.
[32] (1702) 4 Bro Parl Cas 1.   [33] (1854) 19 Beav 149.   [34] *Hart v Tribe* (1854) 18 Beav 215.
[35] See also *Richardson v Chapman* (1760) 7 Bro Parl Cas 318.   [36] (1862) 13 I Ch R 404.
[37] (1801) 5 Ves Jr 849.   [38] [1955] Ch 20.

ascertained or capable of ascertainment'.[39] The court rejected the view that it could execute the trust in any way other than by the equal division of the fund among all the potential beneficiaries:

it might be assumed that the trustees for some reason or other might fail or refuse to make any distribution, and see whether the court could execute the trust in that event. Consideration of the case on that assumption shows that the most the court could do would be to remove the inert or recalcitrant trustees and appoint others in their place. That, however, would not be execution of the trust by the court, but a mere substitution for one set of trustees invested with an uncontrollable discretion of another set of trustees similarly invested, who might be equally inert or recalcitrant.[40]

(ii) The trustee must be able to exercise his discretion

In the case of a discretionary trust the trustee is subject to an obligation to exercise his discretion to distribute the fund among the class of potential beneficiaries.[41] An underlying assumption of the cases prior to *McPhail v Doulton*[42] was that the trustee would not be able properly to exercise his discretion without drawing up a complete list of the class before making decisions as to how he should allocate the fund. Unlike the donee of a mere power of appointment, who owes no fiduciary duty to the objects, the trustee of a discretionary trust owes the class of beneficiaries fiduciary duties and for this reason would be expected to consider them individually before exercising his discretion. This would require a complete list.

(b) Criticism of the 'complete list' test

The 'complete list' test applied to discretionary trusts in *IRC v Broadway Cottages Trust*[43] was open to two major criticisms. First, it failed to take account of the developing social function of discretionary trusts. While it might have been appropriate for 'family'-style discretionary trusts, where there was a small class of potential beneficiaries, so that in the event of default by the trustee equal division would be a sensible and fair solution, it was entirely inappropriate for discretionary trusts designed to allocate benefits from a fund among a large class of potential beneficiaries. The 'complete list' test was simply unworkable for trusts such as that established in *McPhail v Doulton*,[44] since it would never be possible to draw up a list of every single individual who fell within the class of employees, ex-employees, and relatives and dependants. The continued application of the 'complete list test' would stagnate the developing social function of the discretionary trust as a means of allocating property. Secondly, it placed too much emphasis on the distinction between trusts and powers of appointment. An inevitable consequence of the adoption of the complete list test for discretionary trusts was that it became essential to tell if a particular obligation was a trust or a power. If it were characterized as a power, then it would probably be valid, as the test of certainty

---

[39] Ibid., at 36.   [40] Ibid., at 31.
[41] Although in the case of a non-exhaustive discretionary trust he has the power to accumulate rather than distribute.
[42] [1971] AC 424.   [43] [1955] Ch 20, CA.   [44] [1971] AC 424.

in *Re Gulbenkian's Settlement Trusts*[45] would apply. If it were characterized as a trust, then the much more demanding complete list test would render it void. This placed an undue significance to the question of characterization, especially since the obligations are in essence very similar to each other. This problem is well illustrated by the history of the litigation in *McPhail v Doulton*.[46] Goff J, at first instance, and the majority of the Court of Appeal, held that a valid power had been created. This was despite the fact that the language creating the obligation was clearly of a mandatory character, and therefore the House of Lords unanimously held that it was a discretionary trust. The factor that had influenced the decisions of the lower courts was the problem that, as a result of the *Broadway Cottages*[47] test, to characterize the obligation as a trust would be to render it completely void for uncertainty, as indeed the minority of Lord Hodson and Lord Guest held. It was clearly unsatisfactory that the question of the validity of an obligation should depend upon the fine distinction between powers and discretionary trusts. As Lord Wilberforce observed:

> It is striking how narrow and in a sense artificial is the distinction, in cases such as the present, between trusts or as the particular type of trust is called, trust powers, and powers . . . It is only necessary to read the learned judgment in the Court of Appeal to see that what to one mind may appear as a power of distribution coupled with a trust to dispose of the undistributed surplus, by accumulation or otherwise, may to another appear as a trust for distribution coupled with a power to withhold a portion and accumulate or otherwise dispose of it. A layman and, I suspect, also a logician would find it hard to understand what the difference is.[48]

Given this artificiality, the majority of the House of Lords radically altered the test of certainty applicable to discretionary trusts.

(c) *McPhail v Doulton*[49]

The effect of the decision of the majority of the House of Lords in *McPhail v Doulton*[50] was briefly summarized by Lord Wilberforce:

> the rule recently fastened upon the courts by *IRC v Broadway Cottages Trust* ought to be discarded and the test for the validity of [discretionary trusts][51] ought to be similar to that accepted by this House in *Re Gulbenkian's Settlement* for powers, namely, that the trust is valid if it can be said with certainty that any given individual is or is not a member of the class.[52]

Thus, it is no longer necessary that it be possible to draw up a 'complete list' of potential beneficiaries. To reach this conclusion Lord Wilberforce, with whom Lord Reid and Viscount Dilhorne concurred, had to overcome the perceived obstacles which had led to the adoption of the 'complete list test'.

(i) *Equal division was inappropriate if the trustee defaulted in his duty*

The rationale for the adoption of the 'complete list' test was that the court could only intervene to enforce the trust by 'equal division' of the fund between the class of potential beneficiaries. While conceding the applicability of equal division to 'family

---

[45] [1970] AC 508.   [46] [1971] AC 424.   [47] [1955] Ch 20.
[48] *McPhail v Doulton* [1971] AC 424, at 448.   [49] [1971] AC 424.   [50] Ibid.
[51] Lord Wilberforce actually used the term 'trust powers'.   [52] [1971] AC 424, at 456.

trusts', Lord Wilberforce demonstrated how it was wholly inappropriate to large-scale discretionary trusts of the type in issue:

As a matter of reason to hold that a principle of equal division applies to trusts such as the present is certainly paradoxical. Equal division is surely the last thing the settlor ever intended: equal division among all may, probably would, produce a result beneficial to none...[53]

This represents a recognition that the social function of discretionary trusts had evolved to enable property owners to 'confer benefits on deserving cases among large constituencies—in the same sort of way as charitable trusts'.[54] Clearly, there was never any intention by Bertram Baden that every single employee, ex-employee, relative, and dependant should benefit from the fund he had established in their favour, but that the nominated trustees should choose some from that class to receive substantial benefits. The settlor's purpose in creating the fund would be completely defeated if, in the event of the trustees' default, each and every member of the class were to receive an insignificant payment which was far outweighed by the administrative costs of determining the full extent of the class.

(ii) The court could enforce the trust other than by ordering equal division

Although 'equal division' might be inappropriate, cases such as *Gray v Gray*[55] and *Kemp v Kemp*[56] suggested that the courts had no alternative. In *McPhail v Doulton*[57] Lord Wilberforce noted the early cases where the courts had taken a more flexible approach,[58] and concluded that:

the court, if called upon to execute the [discretionary trust],[59] will do so in the manner best calculated to give effect to the settlor's or testator's intentions...

He suggested three alternative means by which the court is able to ensure that the trust is enforced:

It may do so by appointing new trustees, or by authorising or directing representative persons to the classes of beneficiaries to prepare a scheme of distribution, or even, should the proper basis for distribution appear by itself directing the trustees so to distribute.

(iii) The trustee does not need a 'complete list' of the potential beneficiaries to exercise his discretion

The suggestion that the trustee must have a complete list of all the potential beneficiaries of the discretionary trust before he can exercise his discretion in favour of any particular beneficiary was also rejected by Lord Wilberforce:

a trustee with a duty to distribute, particularly among a potentially very large class, would surely never require the preparation of a complete list of names, which anyhow would tell him little that he needs to know.[60]

---

[53] Ibid., at 451.   [54] Gardner, *An Introduction to the Law of Trusts* (2nd edn 2003), pp 199–200.
[55] (1862) 13 I Ch R 404.   [56] (1795) 5 Ves 849.   [57] [1971] AC 424, at 457.
[58] Ibid., at 451. See also *Moseley v Moseley* (1673) Cas temp Finch 53; *Clarke v Turner* (1694) Freem Ch 198; *Warburton v Warburton* (1702) 4 Bro Parl Cas 1; *Richardson v Chapman* (1760) 7 Bro Parl Cas 318, HL.
[59] Lord Wilberforce used the term 'trust powers'.
[60] [1971] AC 424, at 449.

Instead, the trustee has a duty of 'inquiry or ascertainment' so 'in each case the trustees ought to make such a survey of the range of objects or possible beneficiaries as will enable them to carry out their fiduciary duty'.[61]

(d) Application of *McPhail v Doulton*

The House of Lords in *McPhail v Doulton*[62] settled the theoretical question: namely, which test for certainty of objects should govern discretionary trusts? The case was remitted to the Chancery Division for consideration as to whether the terms of the Baden trust met the new requirements, and the case reached the Court of Appeal under the name *Re Baden's Deed Trust (No 2)*.[63] The central question was whether the application of the 'is or is not' test adopted by the House of Lords from *Re Gulbenkian's Settlement Trusts*[64] requires positive proof of the negative limb, so that it can be categorically stated that any individual in the world 'is not' a member of the given class. Counsel[65] for Baden's personal representatives, who claimed the trust was void for uncertainty, argued that as 'relative' in its widest sense means 'descended from a common ancestor' it is impossible to prove that any given individual is not a 'relative'. Therefore, the trust should fail, since it is impossible to say with certainty of any given individual that 'he is not' a member of the class.

The majority of the Court of Appeal took the view that this was not the intended effect of the *Gulbenkian* test, and that it is not necessary to be able to prove that any given individual is not within the class. Sachs and Megaw LLJ distinguished 'conceptual' and 'evidential' certainty,[66] and said that the test is satisfied provided the class is conceptually certain. As Sachs LJ observed:

'the court is never defeated by evidential uncertainty', and it is in my judgment clear that it is conceptual certainty to which reference was made when the 'is or is not a member of the class' test was enunciated... The suggestion that such trusts could be invalid because it might be impossible to prove of a given individual that he was not in the relevant class is wholly fallacious...[67]

Both Sachs and Megaw LLJ took the view that since the words 'relatives' and 'dependants' were conceptually certain in their widest possible meanings, the trust was valid and not void for uncertainty. However, they took slightly differing approaches to the problem of 'evidential certainty' (see Figure 17.2).[68] Sachs LJ took the view that if a class was 'conceptually certain' then there was in essence no evidential difficulty because of the operation of a presumption that anyone not positively proved to be within the class is outside of it. The burden falls on potential claimants to prove they fall within the class. Megaw LJ did not employ such a simple evidential presumption, but considered that there were three groups of persons: ie those positively proved within the class; those positively proved to be outside the class; and those about whom, if they were to be considered, it would have to be said they are not proven to be inside or outside

---

[61] Ibid., at 457.   [62] [1971] AC 424.   [63] [1973] Ch 9.
[64] [1970] AC 508.   [65] John Vinelott, QC and Rupert Evans.
[66] See above, p 454.   [67] [1973] Ch 9, at 20.
[68] Criticized Hopkins 'Continuing Uncertainty as to Certainty of Objects of Trust Powers' [1973] CLJ 36; (1972) 36 Conv (NS) 351, 352.

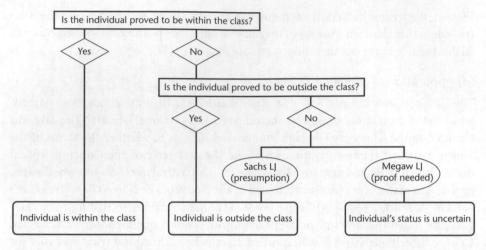

Figure 17.2 Dealing with evidential certainty

the class. He concluded that the trust would be valid provided 'as regards a substantial number of objects, it can be said with certainty that they fall within the test'.[69] Stamp LJ took a differing view to that of the other members of the Court of Appeal. He accepted the argument that it must be possible to say of any individual that 'he is not a member of the class' and on that basis alone would have found the trust void for uncertainty.[70] However, he followed *Harding v Glyn*,[71] a previous authority where 'relations' had been treated by the court as meaning next of kin. He applied this to the Baden trust and concluded that 'relations' meant 'next of kin', which was sufficiently certain.[72]

To summarize, the effect of the decision of the Court of Appeal in *Re Baden's Deed Trusts (No 2)*[73] is that the application of the 'is or is not' test merely requires that the class of potential beneficiaries is conceptually certain. If the class is not conceptually certain, then the trust will be void, but it will not be rendered void merely by evidential uncertainty.[74]

(2) Administrative unworkability

(a) Definition

Even though a discretionary trust has sufficiently certain objects, it may still be void if it is 'administratively unworkable'. This concept was first proposed by Lord Wilberforce in *McPhail v Doulton*, where he suggested there may be classes where:

---

[69] [1973] Ch 9, at 24.   [70] Ibid., at 28.   [71] (1739) 1 Atk 469.
[72] [1973] Ch 9, at 28–29.   [73] [1973] Ch 9.
[74] See Emery 'The Most Hallowed Principle: Certainty of Beneficiaries of Trusts and Powers of Appointment' (1982) 98 LQR 551.

the meaning of the words used is clear but the definition of the beneficiaries is so wide as to not form 'anything like a class' so that the trust is administratively unworkable...[75]

He hesitated to give any example, but suggested that a discretionary trust in favour of 'all the residents of Greater London' would fall within the category of administratively unworkable trusts. The principle has been criticized because it is not clear precisely what evil it is seeking to prevent.[76] However, the cases suggest that the sheer size of the class is the most relevant factor. If a class is too vast in number, it is impossible for the trustees to carry out their duty to survey the range of the beneficiaries of the trust in any real sense, and in the event of their default the court would likewise be unable to carry out the distribution of the fund.

(b) Application

In *Re Hay's Settlement Trusts*[77] Sir Robert Megarry V-C considered obiter that a discretionary trust with a class similar to that of an intermediate power, namely for all the people in the world except for an excluded class, would be administratively unworkable. In *R v District Auditor ex p West Yorkshire Metropolitan County Council*[78] the Council attempted to create a discretionary trust over a fund of £400,000 in favour of the 'inhabitants of the County of West Yorkshire'. The Council's purpose was to defeat government legislation which prevented them incurring expenditure prior to their being abolished. The Divisional Court held that, although the class was conceptually certain the range of objects, comprising some 2.5 million potential beneficiaries, was so wide as to be 'incapable of forming anything like a class'. It was thus administratively unworkable and void. Drawing from Lord Wilberforce's example of 'all the residents of Greater London', and the facts of this case, it can be surmised that 'administrative unworkability' will only render discretionary trusts void which have a class ranging in the magnitude of millions. Where the line is to be drawn between trusts falling foul of the principle and those which are valid is impossible to predict. It is easier to understand the concept of administrative unworkability in the context of a fixed trust. There, in the case of a small gift to a large class, the costs of ascertainment and distribution could easily take up the whole, or a disproportionately large part, of the fund. With a discretionary trust it must be rare that a fund would be so small that no rational scheme could be devised. However, it is possible that with a small gift to a large class it might prove impossible to devise any scheme that could have sufficient regard to the interests of the class as a whole, to which the trustees owe fiduciary duties. That would surely then be a case of administrative unworkability. Unworkability could be avoided if, despite the smallness of the gift, the settlor gave some instruction as to the principles upon which the trustees should exercise their discretion.

---

[75] [1971] AC 424, at 457.
[76] See Harris 'Trust, Power and Duty' (1971) 87 LQR 31; McKay '*Re Baden* and the Third Class of Uncertainty' (1974) 38 Conv 269.
[77] [1982] 1 WLR 202.
[78] [1986] RVR 24; Harpum 'Administrative Unworkability and Purpose Trusts' [1986] CLJ 391.

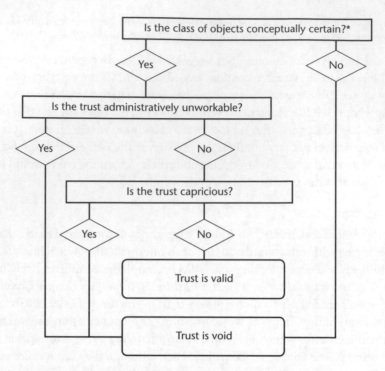

*Evidential uncertainty does not affect the validity of the trust.

Figure 17.3 The validity of discretionary trusts

(3) Capriciousness[79]

A discretionary trust will also be void if it is capricious (see Figure 17.3). This principle was suggested in *Re Manisty's Settlement*[80] in the context of fiduciary powers, when Templeman J indicated that a power in favour of the 'residents of Greater London' might be capricious. The concept was developed in *Re Hay's Settlement Trusts*,[81] where Sir Robert Megarry V-C suggested that a power in favour of the 'residents of Greater London' would not be void for capriciousness if the donor of the power were, for example, a former mayor of the Greater London Council. It seems that a gift to members of a class will be capricious if there is absolutely no rational reason for making the gift to that class, and that the person charged with allocating the fund has no rational basis on which to make allocations. It is clear that capriciousness is a principle which applies to discretionary trusts and that it is a concept distinct from administrative unworkability. The discretionary trust in *R v District Auditor ex p West Yorkshire Metropolitan County Council*[82] was not regarded as capricious because the Council had every reason to create a fund in favour of its residents.

79 See above, p 511.   80 [1974] Ch 17.
81 [1982] 1 WLR 202.   82 [1986] RVR 24.

3 Rights of beneficiaries of discretionary trusts

(1) A proprietary interest in the fund

In the case of a power of appointment, it is clear that the objects of the power have no proprietary interest in the fund unless an appointment is made in their favour.[83] In the case of a fixed trust the beneficiaries have equitable title to the property held on trust for them, and may compel the trustees to transfer the legal title to them under the rule in *Saunders v Vautier*.[84] The position of the beneficiaries of a discretionary trust is not so clear cut, and has led some commentators to suggest that they have a 'quasi-proprietary' right.[85] The rights of the class as a whole are essentially different from the rights of any individual members of the class.

(a) A proprietary right for the class as a whole

By analogy with fixed trusts, since a discretionary trust is a mandatory equitable obligation and the trustees must distribute the fund among the beneficiaries, it would seem logical that the equitable title to the property is vested in the class of potential beneficiaries as a whole. This approach was taken in *Re Smith*,[86] where property was held by trustees on discretionary trust for Mrs Aspinall and her three children. Romer J, following the Court of Appeal decision in *Re Nelson*,[87] held that the class as a whole could have come to the trustees and demanded the transfer of the legal title. He suggested that the principle for the class of such a discretionary trust was to 'treat all the people put together just as though they formed one person, for whose benefit the trustees were directed to apply the whole of a particular fund'.[88] However, despite its credentials in logic, this proprietary interest approach was rejected by the House of Lords in *Gartside v IRC*.[89] The case concerned a non-exhaustive discretionary trust in favour of John Gartside and his wife and children. The central question was whether estate duty was payable on the trust fund, which had not yet been distributed at the date of John's death. The relevant legislation[90] would render the fund liable to estate duty if he was regarded as having an 'interest' in the fund. In these circumstances, the House of Lords held that the deceased beneficiary had no 'interest' in the fund and that estate duty was not payable. To reach this conclusion it rejected any possibility of a 'group interest' in the fund. Lord Reid said that 'two or more persons cannot have a single right unless they hold it jointly or in common. But clearly objects of a discretionary trust do not have that: they each have individual rights: they are in competition with each other and what the trustees give to one is his alone.'[91] Lord Wilberforce echoed this thinking,

---

[83] See above, p 457. [84] (1841) Cr & Ph 240.
[85] [1982] Conv 118. [86] [1928] Ch 915.
[87] [1928] Ch 920. [88] Ibid.
[89] [1968] AC 553. [90] Finance Act 1940, s 43(1).
[91] [1968] AC 553, at 605–606.

stating that although it was correct that a beneficiary had more than a mere hope[92] of a right:

that does not mean that he has an interest which is capable of being taxed by reference to its extent in the trust's income: it may be a right, with some degree of concreteness or solidity, one which attracts the protection of a court of equity, yet it may still lack the necessary quality of definable extent which must exist before it can be taxed.[93]

The case is therefore best understood as a reaction against the prospect of the taxation of the entire balance of the fund which has not yet been allocated every time that a member of the class who is a potential beneficiary dies. This would have been the consequence of holding that the members of the class had a group 'interest' in the trust property.

While the analysis adopted in *Gartside v IRC*[94] was applied to exhaustive discretionary trusts in *Re Weir's Settlement*[95] and *Sainsbury v IRC*,[96] it is arguable that the root problem lay with the drafting of the relevant taxing provisions, which would lead to a ludicrous result, rather than with the suggestion that the class of beneficiaries of a discretionary trust hold the equitable title to the property. As Lord Reid observed in *Gartside*, 'it may be that in 1894 discretionary trusts were not so common that the draughtsman of the legislation must have had them in mind'.[97] The tax has now been abolished. It is submitted that, despite the authority of the House of Lords, the equitable interest of property subject to a discretionary trust does not remain inchoate, or 'in the air', but vests in the class of potential beneficiaries as a whole. There is support for this view in the approach which is taken in relation to the variation of trusts with the consent of the beneficiaries.[98] In the case of an exhaustive discretionary trust, the class would theoretically be able to demand the transfer of the legal title by the trustees. In reality, this will often be impossible, as the class may be incapable of complete ascertainment.

(b) A proprietary right for individual beneficiaries

Although the class of beneficiaries of a discretionary trust may be regarded as having a collective proprietary entitlement to the fund, it is clear that members of the class cannot claim an individual proprietary entitlement to the fund or any part of the fund unless the trustees exercise their discretion to appoint property in their favour. As Lord Reid observed in *Gartside v IRC*:

you cannot tell what any one of the beneficiaries will receive until the trustees have exercised their discretion.[99]

---

[92] Lord Wilberforce used the Latin word 'spes' in his speech.

[93] [1968] AC 553, at 618.   [94] [1968] AC 553.

[95] [1969] 1 Ch 657, at 682. Cross J stated: 'I do not think that Lord Reid was intending to suggest that the distinction [between exhaustive and non-exhaustive discretionary trusts] was relevant to his discussion of the "group theory". Even if the trust is exhaustive and there is no power to withhold income, the objects have individual competing interests, not concurrent interests in the income.'

[96] [1970] Ch 712.   [97] [1968] AC 553, at 606.   [98] See Chapter 18.

[99] *Gartside v IRC* [1968] AC 553.

(2) The right to be considered as a potential beneficiary

The most concrete right that the members of a class of beneficiaries of a discretionary trust possess is the right to be considered as potential recipients from the fund by the trustees.[100] They also have the right to have the trustees exercise their discretion 'bona fides',[101] 'fairly', 'reasonably', or 'properly'.[102]

4 The duties of trustees of discretionary trusts

The prime obligation of the trustee of a discretionary trust is to carry out the terms of the trust and allocate the fund among the class of potential beneficiaries. In the case of an exhaustive discretionary trust, the trustees must allocate the whole of the fund or its income, whereas in the case of a non-exhaustive discretionary trust they have the power to retain and accumulate all or part of the fund or income.[103] The central issues concern the question how the trustees should go about their obligation to allocate in practice.

(1) The duty to conduct a survey of the range of the objects

The trustees of a discretionary trust are subject to a duty to consider the members of the class as potential recipients of benefit from the trust fund. In the case of a trust with a fairly small class of beneficiaries it may be practicable for the trustees to consider the circumstance of each and every member of the class before deciding on any allocations of benefit. However, in the case of discretionary trusts with a large class it is impossible for the trustees to consider the circumstances of each and every member of the class of potential beneficiaries. For example, the trustees of the Baden trust could not have considered the position of each employee, ex-employee, or their relatives and dependants, particularly since many within the class would remain unknown to the trustees at the moment they exercised their discretion.

The requirement that the trustees 'consider' allocations in favour of members of the class of beneficiaries has thus been developed in a way which reflects what can reasonably be expected of them in practice. The exact degree of consideration required of the trustees will depend on the type of the discretionary trust concerned, and in particular the size of the class of potential beneficiaries. The larger the class, the less onerous the duty to consider becomes. In *McPhail v Doulton*[104] Lord Wilberforce stated that trustees must 'make such a survey of the range of objects or possible beneficiaries as

---

[100] Ibid., at 606, per Lord Wilberforce.
[101] [1968] AC 533, at 606, per Lord Reid.
[102] Ibid., at 618, per Lord Wilberforce.
[103] See above, p 535.
[104] [1971] AC 424 at 457.

will enable them to carry out their fiduciary duty'. In the course of his judgment he sought to elucidate what that duty required:

Any trustee would surely make it his duty to know what is the permissible area of selection and then consider responsibly, in individual cases, whether a contemplated beneficiary was within the power, and whether, in relation to other possible claimants, a particular grant was appropriate.[105]

In the case of a discretionary trust with a large class of beneficiaries, the factors that will be taken into account in determining the extent of the trustees' duty to survey the range of objects include the size of the class and the size of the fund available for distribution. As Lord Wilberforce observed:

a trustee with a duty to distribute, particularly among a potentially very large class, would surely never require the preparation of a complete list of names, which anyhow would tell him little that he needs to know. He would examine the field by class and category; might indeed make diligent and careful enquiries, depending on how much money he had to give away and the means at his disposal, as to the composition and needs of particular categories and of individuals within them; decide upon certain priorities or proportions, and then select individuals according to their needs or qualifications.[106]

The test is therefore extremely flexible, and appropriate to the modern usage of discretionary trusts as a mechanism to distribute relatively small funds among selected members of a potentially vast class. As Sachs LJ observed in *Re Baden's Deed Trusts (No 2)*:

The word 'range'...has an inbuilt and obvious element of elasticity, and thus provides for an almost infinitely variable range of vision suitable to the particular trust to be considered. In modern [discretionary] trusts...it may be sufficient to know whether the range of potential postulants runs into respectively dozens, hundreds, thousands, tens of thousands or even hundreds of thousands...Assessing in a businesslike way 'the size of the problem' is what the trustees are called on to do.[107]

In practical terms, what this means is that the trustee must not make an allocation from the fund to an individual beneficiary without first assessing the appropriateness of that allocation in the light of the claims of other possible beneficiaries. It would be inappropriate for the trustees of a fund of £1m held on an exhaustive discretionary trust for a class of ten beneficiaries to allocate only to three or four individuals without first considering the claims of all the members of the class. In the case of a fund of £1m to be divided among a class of a hundred thousand, the trustees would not need to consider the case for each member of the class, provided they bear in mind the number of potential claimants from the class and the purposes of the fund when deciding whether to make any individual allocations.

---

[105]   Ibid., at 449.
[106]   [1971] AC 424, at 449.
[107]   [1973] Ch 9, at 20. See also *Re Hay's Settlement Trusts* [1982] 1 WLR 202, at 210, where Sir Robert Megarry V-C considered that the analogous duties of the trustee of a fiduciary power are to: 'consider the range of the objects of the power; and...consider the appropriateness of individual appointments'.

(2) The duty not to make allocations outside of the class of potential objects

The trustees must not allocate the trust fund to persons who do not fall within the class of beneficiaries. Any such allocations will be held void by the court because they fall outside of the terms of the trust, and the trustees will be in breach of trust. If such an allocation is made the beneficiaries may enforce remedies against the trustees[108] and the wrongful recipient of the trust property.[109]

---

[108] See Chapter 29.   [109] See Chapters 31 and 32.

18

Variation of beneficial interests[1]

The original terms of a trust may no longer serve the purposes of the beneficiaries of a trust or operate as intended by the settlor. It is possible in some cases to amend the trusts by varying the beneficial interests. Variation of existing beneficial interests normally requires the consent of all the current and prospective beneficiaries. The general principles and the exceptions are explored in this chapter.

1 Introduction

(1) Allocation of beneficial interests under trusts

In the case of discretionary trusts the allocation of benefit in the trust fund is within the discretion of the trustee. The original owner of the property who created the trust has not specified precisely how the fund is to be allocated among the class of beneficiaries. In the case of a fixed trust the interests of the beneficiaries have been specified by the settlor, and the trustee's obligation is merely to carry out the trust according to its terms. However, it may well be that it is in the interests of the beneficiaries that the trust be carried out in a way which is different to that specified by the settlor. For example, circumstances may have changed since the trust was created so that what was once a tax-advantageous settlement now has disastrous tax consequences.[2] This chapter examines how the allocation of benefit under a trust can be altered from what was originally specified by the settlor.

(2) The primacy of the settlor's intention?

It is a basic principle that a trust must be carried out according to its terms, and that any deviation from them constitutes a breach of trust. In *Re New*, Romer LJ stated that:

---

[1] See Harris, *Variation of Trusts* (1975).
[2] As Lord Denning MR observed in *Re Weston's Settlements* [1969] 1 Ch 223, at 245: 'Nearly every variation that has come before the court has tax avoidance as its principal object.'

As a rule, the court has no jurisdiction to give, and will not give, its sanction to the performance by the trustees of acts with reference to the trust estate which are not, on the face of the instrument creating the trust, authorised by its terms.[3]

This 'primacy to the settlor's intention' was also expressed by Farwell J in *Re Walker*,[4] where he declined 'to accept any suggestion that the court has an inherent jurisdiction to alter a man's will because it thinks it beneficial'. However, this commitment to the primacy of the settlor's intention has to be balanced against giving effect to the present wishes and interests of the beneficiaries, and it has never been a principle which has been rigidly applied. Instead, the wishes of the beneficiaries are given primacy over the intentions of the settlor. In *Goulding v James*,[5] the Court of Appeal held that the beneficiaries were entitled to vary a trust in a way that entirely undermined the intentions of the settlor.

(3) The primacy of the beneficiaries' wishes

It has long been recognized that the beneficiaries of a trust can consent to the execution of the trust in a manner other than that specified by the settlor. A trustee will not be liable for breach of trust if he acts at the request, or with the consent, of the beneficiaries.[6] If the trustees so act and in effect vary the trust by performing it inconsistently with the settlor's intentions, the court will not intervene. At its most dramatic, this enables the beneficiaries to bring the trust to an end. Under the principle of *Saunders v Vautier*[7] the beneficiaries, provided they are absolutely entitled, sui juris and of age, may call for the legal title to the trust property.[8] In *Re Smith*[9] the beneficiaries of a discretionary trust were held able to compel the trustees to transfer the legal title to them. In *Saunders v Vautier*,[10] Daniel Vautier was the sole beneficiary of a trust of East India stock established by Richard Wright. The settlor directed in the terms of the trust that dividends from the stock be accumulated by the trustees until Daniel attained the age of 25. The court held that as he was solely entitled to the fund, and the accumulation was for his benefit alone, he entitled to the fund at the age of twenty-one. In effect, primacy was given to the beneficiary's wishes, rather than the settlor's expressed intentions. In *Goulding v James*, Mummery LJ identified the principle embodied in the rule in *Saunders v Vautier*:

The principle recognises the rights of beneficiaries, who are sui juris and together entitled to the trust property, to exercise their proprietary rights to overbear and defeat the intention of a

---

[3] [1901] 2 Ch 534, at 544.   [4] [1901] 1 Ch 879, at 885.

[5] [1997] 2 All ER 239, at 247; Luxton 'Variation of Trusts: Settlors' Intentions and the Consent Principle in *Saunders v Vautier*' (1997) 60 MLR 719. See below p 565.

[6] *Re Pauling's Settlement Trusts* [1964] Ch 303, CA. See Chapter 29.

[7] (1841) Cr & Ph 240.

[8] See *Re Chardon* [1928] Ch 464; *Re Smith* [1928] Ch 915; *Re Nelson* [1928] Ch 920n; *Re Beckett's Settlement* [1940] Ch 279; *Re AEG Unit Trusts (Managers) Ltd's Deed* [1957] Ch 415.

[9] [1928] Ch 915.   [10] (1841) Cr & Ph 240.

testator or settlor to subject property to the continuing trusts, powers and limitations of a will or trust instrument.[11]

(4) Limits to consensual variation

The primacy of the beneficiaries' wishes established by *Saunders v Vautier*[12] enables them to vary the beneficial entitlements under a trust. However, their right to do so is subject to severe practical restrictions and is often inadequate to authorize a variation of the beneficial interest. A consensual variation of trust can only take place where there is the unanimous consent of all the actual and potential beneficiaries of the trust, since if any beneficiary fails to give consent the trustees will remain open to liability for breach of trust to any who have not consented. Therefore, consensual variation will not be possible if some of the beneficiaries are minors and unable to give consent, or alternatively unidentifiable or not yet in existence, for example if the class of beneficiaries includes children as yet unborn or the future spouses of present beneficiaries. This will often be the case if the trust creates successive interests, as in *Goulding v James*,[13] itself, where the potential beneficiaries of the remainder interest behind a life interest were the as yet unborn great-grandchildren of the testator. To overcome these limitations the law has developed various means by which the court can approve a variation of trust when the beneficiaries are not able to do so themselves.

2 Variation under the inherent jurisdiction of the court

In *Chapman v Chapman*,[14] the House of Lords recognized that in four situations the court possesses an inherent jurisdiction to authorize a variation of the terms of a trust.[15] However, even in these situations the court has no real jurisdiction to alter the beneficial interests under the trust.

(1) Conversion jurisdiction

The court has the power to authorize the conversion of property in which an infant has an equitable interest from personalty or realty.[16] Lord Morton emphasized that even this limited jurisdiction was exceptional in nature,[17] and its exercise would in no way

---

11 [1997] 2 All ER 239, at 247.   12 (1841) Cr & Ph 240.
13 [1997] 2 All ER 239, at 247.   14 [1954] AC 429.
15 Ibid., at 445, per Lord Simmonds LC.
16 See *Earl of Winchelsea v Norcloffe* (1686) 1 Vern 435; *Pierson v Shore* (1739) 1 Atk 480; *Bridges v Bridges* (1752) 12 App Cas 693n; *Inwood v Twyne* (1762) Amb 417; *Lord Ashburton v Lady Ashburton* (1801) 6 Ves 6.
17 *Re Jackson* (1882) 21 Ch D 786; *Glover v Barlow* (1831) 21 Ch D 788n.

affect the infant's beneficial entitlement.[18] The very wide powers of investment now given to trustees mean that this jurisdiction will very rarely be required.

(2) Emergency jurisdiction

The court has jurisdiction to authorize transactions involving the trust property which are not authorized by the trust if a 'peculiar set of circumstances arises'[19] for which no provision was made in the trust instrument. In *Re New*,[20] the trust fund consisted of ordinary shares in a private limited company. A company reorganization was proposed in which ordinary shares would be transferred for preference shares and debentures. As the trust instrument did not give the power to invest in such securities, the Court of Appeal authorized the investment acting under their inherent jurisdiction. Romer LJ emphasized that the variation must be for the 'benefit' of the beneficiaries. As in the case of the 'conversion jurisdiction', this 'emergency jurisdiction' does not give the court power to vary the interests of the beneficiaries. The wider powers of investment now enjoyed by trustees will similarly make the exercise of this jurisdiction exceedingly rare.

(3) Maintenance jurisdiction

Where the settlor directed that income from the trust fund should be accumulated for the beneficiaries, the court has the jurisdiction to authorize the advancement of the income to provide for their maintenance. Usually, although not necessarily, this will be in the case of infant beneficiaries.[21] The maintenance jurisdiction does not give the court the power to alter the beneficial interests of the beneficiaries.[22] The statutory powers of advancement and maintenance (considered in Chapter 15) make this power less significant than it was in the nineteenth century and before.

(4) Compromise jurisdiction

The court also has inherent jurisdiction to approve on behalf of those who cannot consent for themselves[23] a compromise agreement between the beneficiaries where there has been a 'genuine dispute' about the extent of the rights of the beneficiaries. Prior to the decision of the House of Lords in *Chapman v Chapman*,[24] this 'compromise jurisdiction' had been given a wide meaning so that it could be used to authorize variations in the beneficial interest of the beneficiaries. For example, in *Re Downshire*

---

18 [1954] AC 429, at 451.   19 *Re New* [1901] 2 Ch 534, at 534, per Romer LJ.

20 [1901] 2 Ch 534. See also *Re Tollemache* [1903] 1 Ch 955, CA.

21 See *Revel v Watkinson* (1748) 1 Ves Sen 93; *Cavendish v Mercer* (1776) 5 Ves 195n; *Greenwell v Greenwell* (1800) 5 Ves 194; *Errat v Barlow* (1807) 14 Ves 202; *Haley v Bannister* (1820) 4 Madd 275; *Havelock v Havelock* (1881) 17 Ch D 807; *Re Collins* (1886) 32 Ch D 229.

22 *Chapman v Chapman* [1954] AC 429, at 456, per Lord Morton.

23 [1954] AC 429, at 457, per Lord Morton, the jurisdiction had been exercised on behalf of 'infants interested under a will or settlement and on behalf of possible after-born beneficiaries'.

24 [1954] AC 429.

Settled Estates[25] the Court of Appeal authorized a scheme restructuring the beneficial interests of a settlement for tax reasons. Evershed MR took the view that 'the word "compromise" should not be narrowly construed so as to be confined to "compromises" of disputed rights'.[26] In his dissenting opinion Denning LJ advocated a very general jurisdiction to vary:

> The jurisdiction is not confined to cases where there is a dispute about the extent of the beneficial interests, nor to cases of emergency or necessity, but extends wherever there is a bargain about the beneficial interests which is for the benefit of the infants or unborn persons.[27]

However, in *Chapman v Chapman*[28] the House of Lords asserted that the court only has the inherent jurisdiction to approve a compromise altering beneficial interests if there is a 'genuine dispute' as to the beneficial entitlements of the beneficiaries. In essence, this means that the court does not possess any jurisdiction to 'vary' the beneficial entitlement of beneficiaries, but merely a jurisdiction to clarify them when there is a dispute about their extent. In the words of Lord Morton:

> ... the court's jurisdiction to sanction a compromise in the true sense, when the beneficial interests are in dispute, is not a jurisdiction to alter these interests, for they are still unascertained. If, however, there is no doubt as to the beneficial interests, the court is, to my mind, exceeding its jurisdiction if it sanctions a scheme for their alteration... [29]

The decision in *Chapman v Chapman*[30] thus deprived the courts of any real jurisdiction to authorize variations in the beneficial interests under trusts. For example, in *Re Powell-Cotton's Resettlement*[31] an alleged dispute over an investment clause in the trust instrument was held not to be a 'genuine dispute' and the Court of Appeal refused to authorize a compromise agreement.[32] The restriction of the court's inherent jurisdiction led to the enactment of the Variation of Trusts Act 1958, which gives the court a 'very wide and, indeed, revolutionary discretion'[33] to approve variations of trusts, including the variation of beneficial interests.

3 Statutory powers of variation other than the Variation of Trusts Act 1958

(1) Trustee Act 1925, s 57[34]

By this section the inherent 'emergency jurisdiction' is extended to cases where a transaction is merely 'expedient' in the opinion of the court. The section is expressly

---

[25] [1953] Ch 218.   [26] Ibid., at 239.   [27] Ibid., at 274.   [28] [1954] AC 429.
[29] Ibid., at 461.   [30] [1954] AC 429.   [31] [1956] 1 WLR 23.
[32] See also *Allen v Distillers Co (Biochemicals) Ltd* [1974] QB 384; *Mason v Farbrother* [1983] 2 All ER 1078.
[33] *Re Steed's Will Trusts* [1960] Ch 407, at 420–421, per Evershed MR.
[34] See *Re Beale's Settlement Trusts* [1932] 2 Ch 15; *Re Thomas* [1930] 1 Ch 194; *Re Harvey* [1941] 3 All ER 284; *Re Power* [1947] Ch 572; *Re Cockerell's Settlement Trusts* [1956] Ch 372; *Re Shipwrecked Fishermen and Mariners' Royal Benevolent Society* [1959] Ch 220.

limited to matters of 'the management and administration' of the trust property, and does not enable the variation of beneficial interests under the trust.[35]

(2) Settled Land Act 1925, s 64(1)

This section enables the court to authorize 'any transaction affecting or concerning the settled land' by the tenant for life, provided that the transaction is, in the opinion of the court, for 'the benefit of the settled land'. Although limited to settled land, this provision allows the court to authorize alterations in beneficial interests, as for example in *Re Downshire Settled Estates*.[36] It has not been possible to create new settlements governed by the Settled Land Act 1925,[37] so this provision is of limited and decreasing importance.

(3) Trustee Act 1925, s 53[38]

This section extends the court's inherent 'maintenance jurisdiction' in favour of infants and gives the court power to order the application of the capital or income from the trust for the 'maintenance, education or benefit of the infant'.

(4) Matrimonial Causes Act 1973

This Act grants the court wide powers to make orders concerning the parties to matrimonial proceedings. By s 24 this includes the powers to order the making of a settlement for the benefit of the 'other party to the marriage and of the children of the family',[39] and to vary the beneficial interests under 'any ante-nuptial or post-nuptial settlement'.[40] This power was exercised by the court in *E v E (Financial Provision)*,[41] where the court ordered that £200,000 should be paid to a wife, on her divorce, from a post-nuptial settlement of the matrimonial home on discretionary trusts in favour of the husband, wife, and children, thus varying the beneficial interests. It was also exercised in *Brooks v Brooks*,[42] where the House of Lords held that a husband's pension scheme constituted a 'post-nuptial' settlement, thus bringing it within the scope of s 24(1)(c) and allowing the court to vary it so that his ex-wife was entitled to receive a pension from its surplus. However, Lord Nicholls was at pains to stress that this

---

[35] *Re Downshire Settled Estate* [1953] Ch 218 and *Sutton v England* [2009] EWHC 3270 (Ch).

[36] [1953] Ch 218. See also *Hambro v Duke of Marlborough* [1994] Ch 158.

[37] The creation of new Settled Land Act settlements is prohibited under the Trusts of Land And Appointment of Trustees Act 1996, s 2(1).

[38] See *Re Meux* [1958] Ch 154; *Re Gower's Settlement* [1934] Ch 365; *Re Bristol's Settled Estates* [1964] 3 All ER 939; *Re Lansdowne's Will Trusts* [1967] Ch 603; *Re Heyworth's Contingent Reversionary Interest* [1956] Ch 364.

[39] S 24(1)(a)–(b).

[40] S 24(1)(c)–(d). *C v C (Ancillary relief: Nuptial Settlement* [2005] 2 WLR 241; Bennett 'Variation of Ante and Post Nuptial Settlements' (2007) Fam Law 916.

[41] [1990] 2 FLR 233.   [42] [1996] AC 375; Thomas 'Divorce and Pension Funds' [1997] Conv 52.

approach did not provide a solution to the problem of splitting pension rights on divorce:

This decision should not be seen as a solution to the overall pensions problem. Not every pensions scheme constitutes a marriage settlement. And even when a scheme does fall within the court's jurisdiction to vary a marriage settlement, it would not be right for the court to vary one scheme member's rights to the prejudice of other scheme members...A feature of the instant case is that there is only one scheme member and, moreover, the wife has earnings of her own from the same employer which will sustain provision of an immediate pension for her. If the court is to be able to split pension rights on divorce in the more usual case of a multi-member scheme where the wife has no earnings of her own from the same employer, or to direct the taking out of life insurance, legislation will still be needed.[43]

(5) Mental Capacity Act 2005, s 18(1)(h)

This section, which came into force in October 2007,[44] gives the court power to make a settlement on behalf of a person who lacks capacity, and to vary it if any material fact was not disclosed when the settlement was made, or if there has been any substantial change in circumstances.

4 The Variation of Trusts Act 1958

(1) Introduction

The Variation of Trusts Act was passed in the aftermath of the decision of the House of Lords in *Chapman v Chapman*,[45] which severely restricted the 'compromise jurisdiction' that the courts had construed to give themselves a wide jurisdiction to vary trusts. The matter was referred to the Law Reform Commission, which concluded that:

...the only satisfactory solution to the problem is to give the court the unlimited jurisdiction to sanction such changes which it in fact exercised in the years preceding the decision in *Chapman v Chapman*.

The subsequently enacted Variation of Trusts Act gives the court a 'very wide... discretion'[46] to authorize the variation of trusts, including the adjustment of the beneficial interests thereunder.[47]

(2) Scheme of the Variation of Trusts Act

The Variation of Trusts Act operates alongside the principle of consensual variation, by which the beneficiaries can consent to the trust being performed in a manner

---

[43] [1996] AC 375, at 396. See Pensions Act 1995; Family Law Act 1996.
[44] This section replaces a similar provision under the Mental Health Act 1983.
[45] [1954] AC 429.   [46] *Re Steed's Will Trusts* [1960] Ch 407, at 420–421, per Evershed MR.
[47] The problem of whether an English court might vary a trust governed by a foreign law is examined by Harris in the light of *Charalambous v Charalambous* [2004] EWCA Civ 1030: (2005) 121 LQR 16.

different to that stipulated by the settlor in the trust instrument. The court is given the power to approve 'any arrangement[48] ... varying or revoking all or any of the trusts, or enlarging the powers of the trustees of managing or administering any of the property subject to the trusts',[49] on behalf of the categories of persons specified in s 1 who are not able to consent on their own behalf.[50] In this sense, the court acts as a 'statutory attorney'[51] for those who cannot consent for themselves, and it enjoys no power to consent on behalf of persons who are able to consent for themselves.[52] As a safeguard to ensure that the interests of those on whose behalf the court can approve a variation are not prejudiced, the arrangement approved must be for their benefit. Thus the Act achieves flexibility, by allowing trusts to be varied to take account of changing circumstances, while preserving the right of parties who can consent on their own behalf to make their own decisions, and protecting the interests of those who cannot. The operation of the jurisdiction was most recently considered by the Court of Appeal in *Goulding v James*,[53] where Mummery LJ explained the role of the court and the relationship between the statutory jurisdiction and the rule in *Saunders v Vautier*:

First, what varies the trust is not the court, but the agreement or consensus of the beneficiaries. Secondly, there is no real difference in principle in the rearrangement of the trusts between the case where the court is exercising its jurisdiction on behalf of the specified class under the 1958 Act and the case where the resettlement is made by virtue of the doctrine in *Saunders v Vautier* and by all the adult beneficiaries joining together. Thirdly, the court is merely contributing on behalf of infants and unborn and unascertained persons the binding assents to the arrangement which they, unlike an adult beneficiary, cannot give. The 1958 Act has thus been viewed by the courts as a statutory extension of the consent principle embodied in the rule in *Saunders v Vautier*.[54]

While the Variation of Trusts Act enables the courts to approve a proposed variation of the allocation of benefit behind a trust, it has been held that the courts do not possess the jurisdiction to approve a 'resettlement' of the trusts, so that the trust is completely reshaped. There is a line to be drawn somewhere between what amounts to a genuine variation and what is a resettlement.

(a) A 'resettlement' rather than a 'variation'

On one side of the line falls *Re T's Settlement Trusts*.[55] A trust provided that an infant would become entitled to a quarter of the trust income on attaining her majority. The child was irresponsible and immature, and the court's consent was sought to a variation which would transfer her share of the trust fund to new trustees to be held on

---

[48] In *Re Steed's Will Trusts* [1960] Ch 407 Evershed MR held that the word 'arrangement' should be given the 'widest possible sense ... to cover any proposal ... put forward'. See also *Ridgwell v Ridgewll* [2007] EWHC 2666 (Ch), where Behrens J confirmed this wide interpretation in considering whether the addition of a life interest was an arrangement within s 1.

[49] S 1(1).   [50] See *Re Holt's Settlement Trusts* [1969] 1 Ch 100.

[51] *Goulding v James* [1997] 2 All ER 239, at 249, per Mummery LJ.

[52] S 1(1) specifically states that the court's power to approve is given irrespective of 'whether or not there is any other person beneficially interested who is capable of assenting thereto'. See also *IRC v Holmden* [1968] AC 685, at 701, per Lord Reid.

[53] [1997] 2 All ER 239, at 247.   [54] Ibid., at 247.   [55] [1964] Ch 158.

protective trusts for her life, with remainder to her issue. Wilberforce J held that he did not have jurisdiction to approve this arrangement:

It is obviously not possible to define exactly the point at which the jurisdiction of the court under the Variation of Trusts Act stops or should not be exercised. Moreover, I have no desire to cut down the very useful jurisdiction which this act has conferred upon the court. But I am satisfied that the proposal as originally made to me falls outside it. Though presented as a 'variation' it is in truth a complete new resettlement. The former trust funds were to be got in from the former trustees and held upon wholly new trusts such as might be made by an absolute owner of the funds. I do not think that the court can approve this.[56]

(b) A genuine variation

Re Holts Settlement[57] falls on the other side of the line. A trust had been created for Mrs Wilson for life, with remainder to her children who attained the age of twenty-one. A variation was proposed under which Mrs Wilson would surrender her life interest in a half of the income in favour of the children, but also to postpone the children's entitlement to capital until each child attained the age of thirty.[58] Megarry J felt that this amounted to a genuine variation and not a resettlement:

It is not, of course, for the court to draw the line in any particular place between what is a variation and what, on the other hand, is a completely new settlement. A line may, perhaps, one day emerge from a sufficiently ample series of reported decisions; but for the present all that is necessary for me to say is whether the particular case before me is on the right side or the wrong side of any reasonable line that could be drawn. In this case I am satisfied that the arrangement proposed falls on the side of the line which bears the device 'Variation'.[59]

In the later case of *Re Ball's Settlement Trusts* Megarry J laid down a general test to distinguish between 'variations' and 'resettlements', namely the 'substratum test':

If an arrangement changes the whole substratum of the trust, then it may well be that it cannot be regarded merely as varying the trust. But if an arrangement, while leaving the substratum, effectuates the purpose of the trust by other means, it may still be possible to regard that arrangement as merely varying the original trusts, even though the means employed are wholly different and even though the form is completely changed.[60]

In *Wyndham v Egremont*,[61] Blackburne J did not find this statement particularly helpful, since it left unanswered what was meant by the 'substratum'. He had been asked to approve a variation of a trust made concerning the ancestral estates around Petworth House in West Sussex. The variation was intended to defer a very considerable tax liability and to ensure that the ancestral estates continued to devolve down the senior male line with the baronies of Egremont and Leconfield. Blackburne J concluded that this was not a resettlement and that he could and should approve it. He referred to a

---

[56] Ibid., at 162.   [57] [1969] 1 Ch 100.

[58] See also *Goulding v James* [1997] 2 All ER 239, where the Court of Appeal approved a variation in which the life tenant and remainderman agreed that 90 per cent of the trust capital should be divided between themselves, thus defeating the life interest under the trust.

[59] [1969] 1 Ch 100, at 118.   [60] [1968] 1 WLR 899, at 905.

[61] [2009] EWHC 2076 (Ch).

statement of Lord Wilberforce, in a different context (whether a new settlement had been created giving rise to a capital gains tax liability):

I think that the question whether a particular set of facts amounts to a settlement should be approached by asking what a person, with knowledge of the legal context of the word under established doctrine and applying this knowledge in a practical and common-sense manner to the facts under examination, would conclude.[62]

Applying this test (which can scarcely be considered to be any clearer than the substratum test), Blackburne J concluded that he was being asked to approve only a variation:

The trustees remain the same, the subsisting trusts remain largely unaltered and the administrative provisions affecting them are wholly unchanged. The only significant changes are (1) to the trusts in the remainder, although the ultimate trust in favour of George and his personal representatives remains the same, and (2) the introduction of the new and extended perpetuity period.[63]

The restriction that the court cannot approve a resettlement is a remaining vestige of the 'primacy of the settlor's intention'.

(3) Persons on whose behalf the court may approve an arrangement

The court may approve a variation of trust on behalf of four groups of persons identified in s 1 of the Variation of Trusts Act 1958.

(a) Persons incapable of consenting for reasons of infancy or incapacity

By s 1(1)(a) the court can consent on behalf of:

...any person having, directly or indirectly, an interest, whether vested or contingent under the trusts who by reason of infancy or other incapacity is incapable of assenting.

(b) Unascertained persons

By s 1(1)(b) the court may consent on behalf of:

any person (whether ascertained or not) who may become entitled, directly or indirectly, to an interest under the trusts as being at a future date or on the happening of a future event a person of any specified description or a member of any specified class of persons, so however that this paragraph shall not include any person who would be of that description, or a member of that class, as the case may be, if the said date had fallen, or the said event had happened at the date of the application to the court.

This complicated section is designed to cover the case of beneficiaries who are unascertainable, in the sense that it is not known who they are because the circumstances that would bring them within the class have not yet occurred. Since they are unascertainable, they cannot give consent to variations which affect their position, and the court can consent on their behalf. In *Re Clitheroe's Settlement Trust*,[64] for

---

[62] *Roome v Edwards* [1982] AC 279, at 292–293.   [63] [2009] EWHC 2076 (Ch), at [24].
[64] [1959] 1 WLR 1159.

example, a variation of a discretionary trust was approved by the court. The trust was established by Lord Clitheroe in favour of 'the descendants of Sir Ralph Cockayne Assheton [his father] or the spouse of any of them'. Consent was given to a tax advantageous variation by the court under s 1(1)(b) on behalf of any future wife that Lord Clitheroe might have, who would thereby become a beneficiary of the trust. Two features of this section are worthy of special attention.

(i) The court has no jurisdiction on behalf of persons who have an existing contingent interest in the trust

The court only has jurisdiction under s 1(1)(b) to grant approval on behalf of persons who 'might become entitled...to an interest' under the trust in the future. In *Knocker v Youle*[65] it was held that this means that the court cannot consent for persons who have a current interest in the trust, no matter how remote, even though it is impracticable to seek their consent. The case concerned a trust created in 1937 in favour of the settlor's daughter, with default clauses that could cause the property to be held on trust for her cousins. As Warner J noted, these were very numerous[66] and some lived in Australia, so that it was not practical to get their approval to a proposed variation. However, he held that he did not have the jurisdiction to grant approval on their behalf because 'a person who has an actual interest directly conferred upon him or her by a settlement, albeit a remote interest, cannot properly be described as one who "may become" entitled to an interest',[67] and is therefore not within the scope of s 1(1)(b).

(ii) Section 1(1)(b) implies a 'double contingency' test

The second part of the definition in s 1(1)(b) adds a 'proviso'[68] that the court cannot consent on behalf of persons who would have interests in the trust if the event that would render them a beneficiary had in fact occurred at the date of the application. This means that the court only has jurisdiction to approve variation on behalf of persons who become entitled in the event of a 'double contingency'. This perceived 'proviso' was applied in *Re Suffert*.[69] A trust was established for Elaine Suffert for life, with the remainder to such of her issue as she should appoint, and in the event of default to those who would be entitled if she died intestate. She was a spinster, without issue, and had three adult cousins. She sought to vary the trust, one cousin consented, and the approval of the court was sought on behalf of all unascertained persons who might become entitled under the trusts. Buckley J held that he could not grant approval on behalf of the two adult cousins because they fell within the proviso to s 1(1)(b), since if the event under which they would become entitled, namely the death of Elaine Suffert, had occurred at the date of the application, they would have been beneficiaries

---

[65] [1986] 1 WLR 934; Riddall 'Does It or Doesn't It?—Contingent Interests and the Variation of Trusts Act 1958' [1987] Conv 144.

[66] There were 17.   [67] [1986] 1 WLR 934, at 937.

[68] Ibid., at 937, per Warner J.   [69] [1961] Ch 1.

of the trust. Similarly, in *Re Moncrieff's Settlement Trusts*[70] a trust was established in favour of Anne Moncrieff, then for such of her issue as she appointed, and in default of appointment, to those entitled on intestacy. The court's approval to a variation was sought on behalf of her adopted son and her next of kin. Buckley J held that there was no jurisdiction to grant approval on behalf of the adopted son, as he fell within the limitation to s 1(1)(b), and would have been entitled at the date of the application if his mother had died. However, the court could consent on behalf of the other next of kin since they would only be entitled on the occurrence of a 'double-contingency', meaning both the death of the mother and the predecease of the adopted son. If the mother alone had died at the date of the application, they would still not have been entitled. *Re Suffert*[71] and *Re Moncrieff's Settlement Trusts*[72] were cited and followed by Warner J in *Knocker v Youle*.[73]

(c) Persons unborn

By s 1(1)(c) the court can consent on behalf of 'any person unborn'. If it is clearly the case that a person is past the age of childbearing and the chance of further beneficiaries arising is an impossible contingency, it is inappropriate to apply to the court to approve a variation under the Variation of Trusts Act. Thus, in *Re Pettifor's Will Trusts*[74] Pennycuick J refused to approve a variation on behalf of the unborn children of a woman of seventy-eight.

(d) Persons contingently interested under protective trusts[75]

By s 1(1)(d) the court can consent on behalf of:

...any person in respect of any discretionary interest of his under protective trusts where the interest of the principal beneficiary has not failed or determined.

The important feature of this paragraph is that the court's jurisdiction is not limited to variations which are 'for the benefit' of the person on whose behalf approval is given. If a person falls within the scope of either paras (a)–(c), where the requirement of benefit applies, or para (d), where there is no need to prove benefit, the court may act under paragraph (d).[76]

(4) The requirement of benefit

Under s 1 the court may only grant approval to a scheme of variation on behalf of a person within the categories set out in s 1(1)(a)–(c) if: 'the carrying out thereof would be for the benefit of that person'.

[70] [1962] 1 WLR 1344. [71] [1961] Ch 1.
[72] [1962] 1 WLR 1344. [73] [1986] 1 WLR 934.
[74] [1966] Ch 257. [75] See p 100 for an explanation of protective trusts.
[76] *Re Turner's Will Trusts* [1968] 1 All ER 321.

(a) Recognized benefits

The courts have recognized that a variety of different types of benefit will be sufficient to allow them to authorize variations:

(i) Financial benefit

There is no doubt that the court will grant approval on behalf of persons who would benefit financially from a proposed variation. In *CD (A Child) v O*,[77] for example, Lloyd J approved a variation which would insert a power of advancement into a trust allowing the advancement of the whole capital of the fund to an infant beneficiary to be applied to pay school fees. However, the financial benefit sought in most cases has been a reduction in tax liability. As Lord Denning MR observed in *Re Weston's Settlement*, 'nearly every variation that has come before the court has tax-avoidance for its principal object'.[78] In *Re Weston's Settlement*[79] Stamp J did seem to suggest that the court would not sanction 'illegitimate tax avoidance'. He described the proposed variation in a family trust as 'a cheap exercise in tax avoidance which I ought not to sanction, as distinct from a legitimate avoidance of liability to taxation'.[80] However, the Court of Appeal in *Chapman v Chapman*[81] had not objected to a variation which had as its prime object the reduction of tax liability. In principle all attempts to avoid tax, provided they are lawful, should be legitimate and a 'benefit'. This approach was approved and followed in *Ridgwell v Ridgwell*,[82] which concerned variations that sought to defer the date at which any current and future children of the life tenant under a trust fund would obtain a vested interest in the fund. Behrens J, in approving the arrangement, held that the changes would confer a benefit on the current and unborn children, due to the savings in Capital Gains Tax and inheritance tax arising from the variations.[83]

(ii) Non-financial benefits

The courts have also approved variations where the benefit derived is of a social or moral nature. In *Re T's Settlement Trusts*[84] Wilberforce J held that the advantage of postponing the age at which a minor who was irresponsible and immature would become entitled to an interest under the trust was 'the kind of benefit...which seems to be within the spirit of the Act'.[85] In *Re Holt's Settlement*[86] Megarry J granted approval to a variation which deferred the interests of the infant beneficiaries until

---

[77] [2004] 3 All ER 780. This would introduce a power of advancement into the trust wider than that conferred by s 32 of the Trustee Act 1925, which gives the trustees discretion to advance up to one-half of the presumptive interest of the beneficiary. See above, Chapter 15.

[78] [1969] 1 Ch 223, at 245.   [79] [1969] 1 Ch 223.   [80] [1969] 1 Ch 223, at 234.

[81] [1953] Ch 218.   [82] [2007] EWHC 2666.

[83] Ibid., at [36]. There was also a possibility of cheaper life insurance being obtained through the variation.

[84] [1964] Ch 158.

[85] Ibid., at 162. Wilberforce J held on the facts he did not have the jurisdiction to approve the proposed variation.

[86] [1969] 1 Ch 100.

they attained the age of thirty. He considered that 'the word "benefit" ... is ... plainly not confined to financial benefit, but may extend to moral or social benefit',[87] and that it would therefore be a benefit to the children not to receive an income from the trust which would make them independent of the need to work before they had become reasonably advanced in their careers and settled in life. In *Re Remnant's Settlement Trusts*[88] a family trust contained a forfeiture clause which would forfeit the interests of members of the family who became, or married, Roman Catholics. A variation removing this clause was approved by the court, which found a benefit to the children in that they would no longer be deterred from marrying a Roman Catholic if they so chose, and that the clause could be a source of future family dissension.[89] Facilitating the administration of the trust will also amount to a benefit, so in *Re Seale's Marriage Settlement*[90] Buckley J approved on behalf of an infant the transfer of a trust to a Canadian trustee where the family had moved permanently to Canada.

(b) Conflicting benefits

The court may be faced with a situation where the proposed variation is beneficial in some ways but disadvantageous in others. For example, there may be great social or moral benefits, but financial disadvantages. In such circumstances the court will weigh the benefits to determine whether the variation is 'for the benefit' of the persons on whose behalf the court is asked to consent. In *Re Weston's Settlement*[91] the court's approval was sought on behalf of the infant beneficiaries of a marriage settlement to a variation which would transfer the trust to Jersey. Although this would produce a financial benefit of some £800,000, the Court of Appeal held that this was outweighed by the social benefits of the children remaining in England. Lord Denning MR explained how he had weighed the different benefits:

The court should not consider merely the financial benefit to the infants or unborn children, but also their educational and social benefit. There are many things in life more worthwhile than money. One of these things is to be brought up in this our England, which is still "the envy of less happier lands". I do not believe it is for the benefit of children to be uprooted from England and transported to another country simply to avoid tax.[92]

This weighing of 'benefit' obviously involves a value judgement on the part of the court of the relative merits of the benefits and disadvantages associated with a proposed variation. In *Ridgwell v Ridgwell*,[93] for example, Behrens J considered that the long-term tax benefits of a proposed variation outweighed any disadvantage of a postponement of the current and unborn children's entitlement to interests in remainder under a settlement.[94]

---

[87] Ibid., at 121.   [88] [1970] Ch 560.
[89] There was also a financial benefit to the children in having their interests under the trust advanced.
[90] [1961] Ch 574.   [91] [1969] 1 Ch 223.   [92] Ibid., at 245.
[93] [2007] EWHC 2666.   [94] Ibid., at [36].

(5) A discretion to vary

The Variation of Trusts Act provides that the court 'may if it thinks fit' approve a proposed variation. This clearly gives the court a discretion, and the court is not obliged to approve a variation, even if the requisite element of benefit can be shown. In some recognized circumstances the court will not exercise its discretion to approve a variation.

(a) Fraud on a power[95]

The court will not approve a variation which amounts to a fraud on a power. Megarry J stated the principle in *Re Wallace's Settlements*:

> If it is clear that a fraud on the power is involved, then plainly the court ought to withhold its approval. The power of the court under the Act is a discretionary power exercisable if the court 'thinks fit'; and I cannot conceive that it would be fitting for an arrangement to be approved if that arrangement had been made possible by a manifest fraud on a power, or was in some way connected with such a fraud.[96]

Difficulty arises where a life tenant holds a life interest over a fund and special power of appointment over the remainder interest. To avoid inheritance tax the life tenant has exercised the power in favour of the objects, and then sought the court's approval to bring the life interest to an end, and divide the fund between himself and the objects of the power. The danger is that the life tenant himself benefits by receiving a share of the capital of the fund, and this may be the prime motivation for exercising the power. In determining whether there has been a fraud on the power an important factor has been the extent to which the life tenant benefits by a division of the fund. If the life tenant receives a share of the fund which is greater than the actuarial value of his life interest[97] then this suggests a fraud on a power. In *Re Brook's Settlement*[98] Stamp J took a very strict approach and held that if the purpose of the exercise of a power of appointment was that the life tenant should gain a share of the fund, then there was a fraud on the power even though the life tenant may gain a share of the fund lower than the market value of his life interest.[99] However, a more flexible approach was adopted by Megarry J in *Re Wallace's Settlements*,[100] where he approved a variation when there had been an exercise of a power of appointment, even though the life tenant received a share of the fund slightly greater than the actuarial value of her life interest. On the facts, he held that the exercise of the power had been long intended and was for the benefit of the beneficiaries, and therefore there was no fraud.

(b) Undermining protective trusts[101]

It seems that the courts will not approve a proposed variation that would have the effect of reducing the protection enjoyed by the beneficiary of a protective trust. In *Re*

---

[95] See Chapter 16.   [96] [1968] 1 WLR 711, at 717–718.
[97] The actuarial value of the life interest is the sum that would be necessary to purchase an annuity producing the same annual income.
[98] [1968] 1 WLR 1661.   [99] Ibid., at 1669.   [100] [1968] 1 WLR 711.
[101] See above, p 100.

Steed's Will Trusts[102] the Court of Appeal refused to approve a variation which would effectively remove the protective element from a protective trust of property left by a testator to his housekeeper. The court took the view that the protective element was part of the 'testator's scheme' and it had been his desire and intention that she enjoy that protection.[103]

(c) Manifest benefit

It is not enough that those on whose behalf the court is asked to grant approval to a proposed variation gain a benefit from the variation. The extent of their benefit must reflect that they are bargaining from a position of strength. This requirement prevents their position being exploited. In *Re Van Gruisen's Will Trusts*,[104] Ungoed Thomas J held that it would not be sufficient for the infants and unborn children on whose behalf he was asked to consent merely to receive the actuarial value of their remainder interest in the trust fund. Instead, the court must make 'a practical and business-like consideration of the arrangement including the total amounts of the advantages which the various parties obtain and their bargaining strength'. On the facts, he held that the share of the infants and unborn did adequately exceed their actuarial value.

(d) Relevance of the settlor's intentions

Where the court is requested to grant approval of a variation for persons unable to consent on their own behalf, it is not entitled to refuse a variation which would be for their benefit merely because the variation would contravene the intentions of the original settlor. In such circumstances the intentions and wishes of the original settlor are of 'little, if any, relevance or weight'[105] to the question whether approval should be given. In *Goulding v James*,[106] the testatrix left her residuary estate on trust for her daughter for life, with remainder to her grandson on his attaining the age of 40. It was further provided that if he failed to attain the age of 40 the residuary estate should pass to such of his children (ie her great-grandchildren) as were living at the date of his death. She had established this trust with the express object of preventing her daughter touching the capital of her estate, because she did not trust her son-in-law. She had postponed her grandson's interest until he was 40 because he was presently living with an artistic community in Nantucket and she considered him a 'free spirit' who had not yet settled down. The daughter and grandson sought to vary the trusts under the will so that they would receive a 45 per cent share each of the residuary estate absolutely, with the remaining 10 per cent on trusts for any great-grandchildren. As they were adults, the daughter and grandson were perfectly entitled to agree to such variation, but they sought the approval of the court on behalf of the as yet

---

[102] [1960] Ch 407.
[103] [1960] Ch 407, at 421–422: the purpose of the protection was to prevent the housekeeper being 'sponged upon' by her brothers.
[104] [1964] 1 All ER 843n.
[105] *Goulding v James* [1997] 2 All ER 239, at 251–252, per Mummery LJ.
[106] [1997] 2 All ER 239.

unborn great-grandchildren. Although the variation was for their benefit, because actuarial valuation showed that the current value of the contingent interest of the great-grandchildren was only 1.85 per cent of the residuary estate, Laddie J held that the court should refuse to exercise its discretion to grant approval because the object of the arrangement was the complete opposite of what the testatrix had intended.[107] However, the Court of Appeal held that approval should have been forthcoming. Mummery LJ held that the testatrix's intentions were all but irrelevant in deciding whether the discretion should be exercised:

In my judgment the legal position is as follows. (1) The court has a discretion whether or not to approve a proposed arrangement. (2) That discretion is fettered by only one express restriction. The proviso to s 1 prohibits the court from approving an arrangement which is not for the benefit of the classes referred to in (a) (b) or (c). The approval of this arrangement is not prevented by that proviso, since it is plainly the case that it is greatly for the benefit of the class specified in s 1(1)(c).[108]

Ralph Gibson LJ similarly explained that the settlor's original intention was irrelevant:

Where there is an application under the Variation of Trusts Act 1958 for approval of an arrangement agreed by the beneficiaries, capable of giving assent, it is not clear to me why evidence of the intention of the testator can be of any relevance whatever if it does no more than explain why the testator gave the interests set out in the will and the nature and degree of feeling with which such provisions were selected...The fact that a testator would not have approved or would have disapproved very strongly does not alter the fact that the beneficiaries are entitled in law to do it and, if it be proved, that the arrangement is for the benefit of the unborn. If, of course, it can be shown that the arrangement put forward constitutes, for example, a dishonest or inequitable or otherwise improper act on the part of one or more of the beneficiaries, then such evidence would clearly be relevant to the question whether the court would 'think fit' to approve it on behalf of a minor or unborn persons. In this case, the evidence of intention of this testatrix seems to me to have been of no relevance.[109]

The decision in *Goulding v James*[110] is at odds with the decision in *Re Steed's Will Trusts*,[111] where the court refused to vary a protective trust because, among other reasons, this was part of the testator's scheme. While the decision in *Goulding v James* may be better founded in logic, the power of the court to approve a variation is discretionary, and it is hard to see why the testator's motives should be wholly disregarded. On the other hand, treating the court as the 'statutory attorney' for those on whose behalf it consents, its task is not to adjudicate on the merits of the scheme as a whole, but only on its impact on those for whom the court acts as a surrogate. From this point of view, why should those beneficiaries lose the benefits in kind they would receive from a variation unless those benefits are more than compensated by the non-pecuniary benefits of knowing that the testator's wishes have been respected?

---

107 [1996] 4 All ER 854.   108 [1997] 2 All ER 239, at 249.
109 [1997] 2 All ER 239, at 252.
110 Ibid., per Mummery LJ. See Luxton 'Variation of Trusts: Settlors' Intentions and the Consent Principle in *Saunders v Vautier*' (1997) 60 MLR 719.
111 [1960] Ch 407.

(e) Widening powers of investment

The Variation of Trusts Act is not limited to the variation of beneficial interest, but may also be used to vary the powers of the trustees under the trust deed. In the past the courts held that they would not grant approval to a variation of the trustee's powers of investment which were wider than those contained in the Trustee Investment Act 1961.[112] However, the courts came to recognize that the Act was outdated and approved variations granting wider investment powers.[113] The Trustee Investment Act 1961 has now been replaced by the Trustee Act 2000, which grants trustees the power to make any kind of investment. This new legislative framework is likely to free the courts from any residual unwillingness to grant variations in the trustees' power of investment. The trustees' power of investment is discussed in Chapter 23.

(6) Effect of an order to vary

The question has arisen as to how precisely a variation of the beneficial interests under a trust take place. Does it occur by the order of the court, or as a result of the arrangement that is consented to by those who are able, and by the court on those who cannot consent for themselves? The difficulty is not merely theoretical because of the implications of s 53(1)(c) of the Law of Property Act, which requires that a disposition of a subsisting equitable interest 'must be in writing signed by the person disposing of the same'.[114] If the variation is considered a 'disposition',[115] and takes effect as a consequence of the arrangement and not the court order, is it necessary that all those who can consent for themselves do so in writing? Although there is some authority to the contrary,[116] the House of Lords has held that the variation takes effect through the arrangement and not by the order of the court. The principle was stated by Lord Reid in *IRC v Holmden*:

Under the Variation of Trusts Act the court does not itself amend or vary the trusts of the original settlement. The beneficiaries are not bound by variations because the court has made the variation. Each beneficiary is bound because he has consented to the variation. If he was not of full age when the arrangement was made he is bound because the court was authorised to act on his behalf and did so by making an order. If he was of full age and did not in fact consent he is not affected by the order of the court and he is not bound. So the arrangement must be regarded as an arrangement made by the beneficiaries themselves. The court merely acted on behalf of or as representing those beneficiaries who were not in a position to give their own consent and approval.[117]

---

[112] See *Re Kolb's Will Trusts* [1962] Ch 531.

[113] See *Mason v Farbrother* [1983] 2 All ER 1078; *Trustees of the British Museum v A-G* [1984] 1 WLR 418; *Steel v Wellcome Custodian Trustees Ltd* [1988] 1 WLR 167.

[114] See Chapter 7.

[115] *Grey v IRC* [1960] AC 1, HL.

[116] *Re Viscount Hambleden's Will Trusts* [1960] 1 All ER 353n, per Wynn-Parry J.

[117] [1968] AC 685, at 701; *Re Joseph's Will Trusts* [1959] 1 WLR 1019.

Whether the consenting beneficiaries must comply with s 53(1)(c) was considered by Megarry J in *Re Holt's Settlement*,[118] where he adopted two possible solutions to avoid the difficulty. First, he accepted that the express granting of the power to vary trusts to the courts by Parliament in the Variation of Trusts Act has 'provided by necessary implication an exception from s 53(1)(c)'.[119] Second, if the arrangement is an agreement made for valuable consideration, then because it is specifically enforceable the 'beneficial interests pass to the respective purchasers on the making of the agreement', by means of a constructive trust.[120] By virtue of s 53(2), writing is therefore not required.

---

[118] [1969] 1 Ch 100. It is worth noting that *Re Holt's Settlement Trusts* was decided prior to the House of Lords' decision in *Re Holmden's Settlement Trusts* and that Megarry J proceeded on the basis that it was the court order which varied the trusts.

[119] [1969] 1 Ch 100, at 115: Megarry J accepted that this was not the most natural construction and that he was 'straining a little at the wording in the interests of legislative efficiency'.

[120] [1969] 1 Ch 100, at 116, following *Oughtred v IRC* [1960] AC 206, HL.

19

Charities[1]

Charity has a legal meaning, well beyond the everyday concept of helping the underprivileged in society. Trusts set up for recognized charitable purposes and other legally recognized forms of charities receive financial benefits from the state in the form of tax exemptions, and also legal advantage over trusts set up for private beneficiaries. The restrictions of charity law mean that many activities that the public may consider 'charitable' are not so in law, but are instead carried out by non-charitable voluntary organizations. Charities do not have named beneficiaries, so the law is enforced by the Attorney-General and the Charity Commission on behalf of the public. Charities must demonstrate that they carry out their activities for the benefit of the public at large. This chapter considers the nature and benefits of an organization gaining charitable status, as well as an in-depth look at the legal requirements to be granted charitable status.

Schemes for dealing with surplus property for charities are detailed in Chapter 20, and specific restrictions on charity trustees in the discharge of their duties, particularly in relation to investment, and the regulation of charitable activity by the Charity Commission, are considered in the relevant chapters of Part IV of this book.

1 Introduction

The majority of trusts and equitable mechanisms examined so far are used by owners to allocate their property to individuals, whether by mechanisms which allocate fixed shares, or those which grant others the discretion how the property should be allocated. Owners do not always wish to dispose of their property to individuals, but may also wish to give to purposes that they consider worthy, whether to their church, their school parent-teachers' association, the local animal refuge, an appeal following a major disaster, or to a political party which they support. In Chapter 13 it has already been seen that, except for some anomalous exceptions, gifts for purposes will fail by virtue of the 'beneficiary principle'.[2] The most significant exception to this is the area

---

[1] Lloyd, *Charities—The New Law 2006: A Practical Guide To The Charities Acts* (2007).
[2] See above, p 458.

of charitable trusts, where the law upholds and encourages giving to purposes that are regarded in law as charitable. Some, but not all, of the purposes outlined above would be considered to be charitable.

(1) The social context of charitable giving

The significance of charity to society is self-evident, but the extent and value of charitable activity is worth noting. There is a point at which many people have real, if unknowing, contact with the law of trusts, whether they are putting a small donation into collection boxes or envelopes, putting something into a collection at church, signing a Gift Aid declaration on admission to zoological gardens or National Trust properties, contributing regularly through payroll giving schemes, or responding to major 'Band Aid'-type disaster appeals. Charity and charitable giving is a growth area. Both the number of charities and the income they receive is increasing, indicating a continued expansion of the charitable sector. The number of charities has been expanding rapidly. A high proportion of total charity funds are held by a small number of very large charities, such as the Wellcome Trust (the UK's largest charity), which has investments of £13 billion and spends £600 million each year on scientific research. At the other end of the scale there are a large number of charities with very small funds, or even no investments at all. When the Nathan Committee reported in 1952 there were some 111,000 charitable trusts,[3] but by 1986 this had grown to 157,902 registered charities, with a suspected further 110,000 unregistered.[4] By the end of March 2008, there were over 190,000 registered charities,[5] with an annual income of over £48bn. Donations to charities by individuals and corporations are also increasing. An Ipsos MORI survey in mid-2008 for the Charity Commission suggested that an overall increase in charitable giving was beginning to emerge:

In 2008, a comparable figure of 85% of the public, as in 2005, donates money to charity. The proportion of people donating time and goods has, however, increased significantly since 2005 with 47% of the public donating goods, compared with 37% in 2005; whilst a third have given time to charity compared with 23% as in 2005.[6]

Whether this continues in the global economic slowdown, prevalent at the time of writing, remains to be seen, but it is clear that demand for charitable activity and services has, perhaps unsurprisingly, increased as a result of the prevailing economic conditions.[7]

---

[3] *Report of the Committee on the Law and Practice relating to Charitable Trusts* (1952) Cmd 8710), para 103.

[4] *Home Office and HM Treasury, Efficiency Scrutiny of the Supervision of Charities* (1987), Annex E.

[5] Charity Commission Annual Report *2008–2009*.

[6] Ipsos MORI/Charity Commission, Charity Commission Study into Public Trust and Confidence in Charities (May 2008), p 21.

[7] Charity Commission, *Economic Survey of Charities* (prepared by Carol Goldstone Associates) (March 2009), where 20 per cent of charities surveyed reported a major increase in demand for their services.

(2) Mechanisms for charitable giving

Owners of property may decide to apply it for the furtherance of charitable purposes in a variety of ways.

(a) Outright gifts to charitable organizations

An owner may make a gift to an organization which enjoys charitable status, whether an unincorporated association, or a charitable corporation. Charitable corporations may be established by Royal Charter (as is the case with many of the older universities); as a company limited by guarantee; by virtue of specific legislation (as is the case with Further Education Corporations); or, following the Charities Act 2006, as a charitable incorporated organization registered as such by the Charity Commission.[8] The organization will receive the property, and apply it to its charitable purposes. A gift to Cancer Research UK, Oxfam GB (both companies limited by guarantee), or to a particular educational establishment would be such a gift.

(b) Fixed trusts in favour of charitable objects

Alternatively, an owner may transfer property to trustees to be used for specified charitable purposes. In such a case the trustees will be subject to a duty to apply the funds to those purposes only. A gift by will to trustees to be applied for the education of the testator's poor relations would be an example.

(c) Discretionary trusts in favour of charitable objects

An owner may alternatively transfer the property to trustees granting them the discretion as to the charitable purposes to which the fund may be applied. This may be a wide discretion, for example a gift of '£100,000 to trustees to be applied to such charities as they see fit', or the owner may place limits on the width of the discretion, for example 'for such educational charities as they see fit'.

(d) All charitable institutions are treated similarly

Whether a charity exists as an incorporated or unincorporated body, or as a trust, it is governed by essentially similar rules.[9]

(3) The unity of charity

Although there are numerous charitable organizations, and distinct charitable purposes covering wide ranges of human activity, in some senses the law regards all

---

[8] Charities Act 2006, s 34 and Sch 7. The operation, regulation, and potential benefits of the CIO are beyond the scope of this text, but in essence the structure seeks to provide the advantages of a corporate structure (including limited liability) without the burden of regulation under company law. See Charity Commission, *Charitable Incorporated Organisation (CIO)* (March 2009).

[9] This chapter is concerned with charitable trusts, though many of the rules also apply to charitable corporations. Charitable companies are also subject to the rules of company law, which means that they are subject to two regulatory regimes.

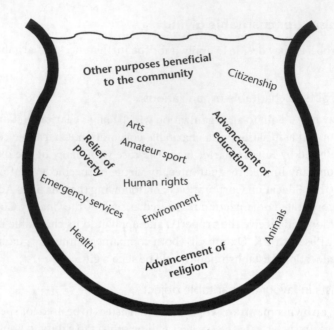

Figure 19.1 The common pot of charity

property dedicated to charity as comprising a single fund, a 'common pot' (see Figure 19.1). This is evident in the way that a gift 'to charity' will be upheld, despite the absence of any indication of the giver's intention as to how it should be used. In such circumstances, the Crown disposes of the property to charitable purposes by sign manual. Similarly, if a charity fails, or a charitable purpose comes to an end, any property dedicated to that charity or purpose will be applied to other similar charitable purposes under the principle of cy-près.[10] The property, once dedicated to charity, is seen as placed into the 'common pot', and cannot be removed from it, but will be applied to other purposes. Hence, it is not possible for an organization that has become a charity to voluntarily cease operating as a charity, taking with it its assets, as the property is held for charitable purposes.

(4) Regulation and control of charities

Given both the quantity of money concerned and the dangers of abuse and misuse,[11] the area of charities is regulated by the government. The Attorney-General enforces charitable trusts in the name of the Crown, but they are regulated and overseen by the

---

[10] Discussed in Chapter 20, at pp 681–694.

[11] See, for example, the case of the Hospital Fund, where some £2.7m of the charity's funds were stolen by the chief fundraiser, reported by the Charity Commissioners in their Report for 1992, paras 91–96.

Charity Commission,[12] which plays the predominant role in the supervision and regulation of charities. This regulation and supervision will be examined in Chapter 28. The law concerning the regulation of charities was consolidated and amended by the Charities Act 1993, which itself has been amended by the Charities Act 2006.[13] Regulation also provides an important public validation of charitable organizations, and a safeguard for those contributing to worthy causes. Thus, it is said that 'trust is the voluntary sector exchange rate',[14] so that an effective charity 'is accountable to the public and other stakeholders in a way that is transparent and understandable'.[15]

Most charities are required to be registered,[16] and the Charity Commission also undertakes the process of registration and the maintenance of the register.

(5) Charities and the Third Sector

Charities form a very significant part of a wider Third Sector,[17] which includes 'not for profit', voluntary and community sector, social enterprise, and mutual societies or organizations, cooperatives, and non-governmental organizations all working independently of direct governmental direction. This grouping of organizations is often referred to as the voluntary sector, of which charities form a major section. The voluntary sector has its own support organizations, such as the National Council for Voluntary Organisations (NCVO), itself a registered charity.[18] In 2006, the sector's importance was further recognized through the establishment of a new Office for the Third Sector within the Cabinet Office, and the appointment of a Minister for the Third Sector.

Charities, as part of the Third Sector, are also perceived to be an essential component of social provision,[19] as they encourage and create 'new services... [plug] gaps in delivery... and often focus on meeting the needs of the disadvantaged and socially excluded'.[20] The current welfare system in Britain, which includes the National Health Service and free school education for all, developed as a state system following

---

[12] Prior to the Charities Act 2006 that constituted the Charity Commission as an incorporated body, the functions of the Commission were vested in the Charity Commissioners.

[13] On 11 September 2009, the Office of the Third Sector (Cabinet Office) announced a Draft Charities Consolidation Bill. This seeks not to alter the law, but 'to make the legislation simpler, better structured, and more accessible to the lay person'. A consultation process on this draft Bill ended on 4 December 2009. Enactment of the Bill in 2010 is unlikely.

[14] NCVO, 'Blurred vision' in Research Quarterly Issue 1, January 1998.

[15] Charity Commission, CC10, *The Hallmarks of an Effective Charity* (July 2008), p 11.

[16] Each registered charity is given a unique registration number. The register is open to public inspection, and is now computerized.

[17] The other two sectors are referred to as the private sector and public sector.

[18] The NCVO itself defines a voluntary sector organization as '[a]n independent, self-governing body of people who have joined together voluntarily to take action for the benefit of the community... established otherwise than for financial gain'.

[19] See HM Treasury, *Exploring the Third Sector In Public Service Delivery and Reform: A Discussion Document* (2005), Chapter 1.

[20] FCO, 'Implementing the Cross Cutting Review on "The Role of the Voluntary and Community Sector in Service Delivery"' (2004).

the example of charitable organizations working in these fields in the nineteenth century.[21] This chapter will explore the charitable activities now recognized by the law. Such activity includes work as diverse as providing homes and appropriate care for individuals suffering from recognized mental illnesses and learning difficulties, providing cultural sites of interest such as art collections, to funding innovative and important medical research through charitable grants schemes.[22]

The success of charitable organizations in carrying out their purposes has led to a view that charities (and other voluntary organizations) should be utilized in providing front-line public services, such as council housing, rather than the traditional view of charities as providing additional or complimentary services to those for which the state had responsibility. This initiative, sometimes referred to as 'the Third Way', seeks to make charities enablers and providers of public services, and there is a political will to reduce barriers to third sector organizations that become involved in delivering and designing public services.[23] It seems there are no longer any barriers to charities undertaking such a role, following the registration decision of the Charity Commission in the *Trafford* decision,[24] where the Commission decided that charities should be free to undertake public services of whatever nature, provided the normal characteristics of a charity are present and that the charity remains independent. However, the desirability of this sort of initiative has been questioned, both at a political[25] and theoretical level.[26]

(6) Negative perceptions of charity

While the social importance of charities is self-evident and recognized by equity in allowing trusts for a charitable purpose, the concept of 'charity' is not without difficulty in modern times. Few, if any, beneficiaries of charitable endeavours would like to be referred to as 'objects of charity', as there are evident negative connotations in that status. Similarly, research undertaken for the Charity Commission suggests that a significant proportion of the populace are not inclined to donate funds, property, or time to charities.[27] The reasons provided include negative attitudes towards the helping

---

[21] See Jones, *History of the Law of Charity* (1969); Weiner (1978) 12 *Journal of Social History* 314.

[22] See Charity Commission, *Firm Foundations: A Snapshot of How Trusts and Foundations are Responding to the Economic Downturn in 2009* (July, 2009), where it was found that charitable grant-making trusts and foundations provide about 10 per cent of charity income, and are key players in providing funding for high-risk or innovative research and activities.

[23] Office of the Third Sector/Cabinet Office, *Partnership in Public Services—An Action Plan for Third Sector Involvement* (2006); followed by *Partnership in Public Services—The Public Services Action Plan One Year On* (2007).

[24] Charity Commission Decisions of the Charity Commission for England and Wales, Applications for Registration (i) Trafford Community Leisure Trust; and (ii) Wigan Leisure and Culture Trust, April 2004.

[25] See, for example. HC Public Administration Select Committee, *Public Services and the Third Sector: Rhetoric or Reality*, Eleventh Report of Session 2007–08, Vol. 1, HC 112—I, 9 July 2008.

[26] See Glover-Thomas and Barr 'Enabling or Disabling? Increasing Involvement of Charities in Social Housing' [2009] Conv 209.

[27] Charity Commission, *Charity Commission Study into Public Trust and Confidence in Charities* (2008).

of others; the concern that charitable organizations are using intrusive fundraising methods; the use of for-profit enterprises in the collection of donations; distrust of the ways in which some charitable organizations carry out their functions; and a view that charities should not be using public money to pay for a service that the public purse was already financing, as there was a duty on the government to provide the service directly through public sector organizations.

The structure of the sector, which allows considerable overlap between functions of organizations in the same geographic areas and a preponderance of smaller charities, has led to the view that:

The public thinks that there are too many charities;[28] businesses think that there are too many charities;[29] funders think that there are too many charities.[30,31]

Nevertheless, while donations to charity are no longer exclusively motivated by altruism,[32] and the nature of the sector has undoubtedly altered significantly since the Victorian era of philanthropy, the continued importance of charities cannot be denied. The Charities Act 2006, which has brought some significant changes to the regulation of charities and to the promotion of the work that they do, seeks to address some of the more negative aspects of the charity 'brand'.[33]

(7) Charities, the Charity Commission and the law

It has been noted that the Charity Commission, as well as acting as regulator of the charity sector, also maintains the register of charities. This means that it is the Charity Commission that decides whether an organization can be registered as charitable. It is important to recognize, however, that the Charity Commission does not make the law. In deciding whether an organization can be registered as a charity, the Commission is bound by the case law and must apply the law as set down by the courts, and its decisions are open to appeal to the First Tier Tribunal (Charity) and from there to the High Court. It is vital to appreciate that although the Charity Commission does interpret and apply the law on an everyday basis, it is not a law maker, and its application

---

[28] MORI/Charity Commission, *The Work of the Charity Commission. A Survey of Public Attitudes and Knowledge*, 1999; (58 per cent of those surveyed thought that there were too many charities); see also [2001–2002], Ch Com Rep, p 21.

[29] Some local authorities and health authorities are refusing to continue to fund multiple charities operating in the same area, Charity Law Unit, Liverpool University, Legal Issues in Charity Mergers, 2001, p 9 (at: www.liv.ac.uk/law/clu/projectreports.htm.).

[30] Buzzacott and Third Sector, *Major Issues Facing Charities in 2000* (75 per cent of businesses responding felt that charities with similar purposes should merge).

[31] Warburton and Barr 'Charity Mergers—Property Problems' [2002] Conv 531.

[32] See Warburton, 'Trusts: Still Going Strong 400 Years after the Statute of Charitable Uses' in Hayton (ed), *Extending The Boundaries of Trusts and Similarly Ring-Fenced Funds* (2002), Kluwer Press.

[33] The Act is concerned with the modernization of both the regulatory framework for charities and, to a lesser extent, the rationalization of the legal principles underpinning charity law. The Act has a chequered history, explored further below, but in essence it arose following a process of review undertaken by the Charity Commissioners and, more significantly, a report of the Cabinet Office Strategy Unit, *Private Action, Public Benefit, A Review of Charities and the Wider Not-For-Profit Sector* (2002).

of the law may be tested in the legal system. However, the Charity Commission does not simply 'rubber-stamp' every application that comes its way; there is a great deal of interpretation required to match the legal principles to the facts, not least because there are gaps and ambiguities in the legal framework. Indeed, the Charity Commissioners have developed the law by analogy to existing charitable purposes, a role explored in detail below. Moreover, many decisions as to registration will not be appealed, so that the decision of the Charity Commission in effect decides the issue of charitable status for many applicants. Reasons for not appealing a decision may include the cost in time and money in mounting such an action, so that important issues of charitable status may not always reach the legal system. For example, the Charity Commission extended the range of religions that it would accept as charitable long before the issue was addressed by the law courts.

Similarly, when the Charity Commission publishes guidance on legal matters, such as the requirements of registration for a charity and public benefit, such guidance does not have the force of law, and cannot change or depart from existing case law or statutory enactments on the relevant issues under discussion. The Commission is alive to this important distinction, as evidenced in its written guidance:

> The Charity Commission's public benefit guidance is guidance on what the law says on public benefit. It does not create new public benefit law. Nor does it create a new legal definition of public benefit.[34]

This must also be appreciated when reading through Charity Commission guidance, particularly when the Commission gives its views on contentious or difficult issues of law.

2 Privileges enjoyed by charitable trusts

Charities and charitable trusts are granted various privileges that are not enjoyed by other private trusts. In *Dingle v Turner*,[35] Lord Cross observed that the privileges enjoyed by charitable trusts were of 'two quite different sorts', namely privileges as to their essential validity, and financial privileges through exemption from some forms of taxation. Underlying this privileged status of charitable trusts is public policy, which seeks to encourage benevolent giving to purposes that are in the public interest.

(1) Privileges as to essential validity

Charitable trusts enjoy exemption from various requirements that would render a non-charitable trust invalid.

---

[34] *Charities and Public Benefit* (Jan 2008), p 8. See also *Catholic Care v Charity Commission* [2010] EWHC 520 (Ch) at [68].
[35] [1972] AC 601.

(a) Purpose trusts

It is a trite proposition that private non-charitable trusts must be for the benefit of persons and not purposes.[36] Charitable trusts are thus the major exception to this 'beneficiary principle'. However, since a mechanism for the enforcement of charitable trusts is provided by the state, the chief objection to purpose trusts (that there is nobody in whose favour the court can decree performance of the trust)[37] does not apply. Charitable trusts are enforced by the Charity Commission or by the Attorney-General in the name of the Crown.

(b) Certainty of objects

While non-charitable trusts must have objects that are certain,[38] gifts made exclusively for charitable purposes are valid even though the exact purposes have not been identified with certainty. Thus, a gift to trustees 'for charity' will be valid. This follows from the fact that the law regards 'charity' as if it were a single common pot, and since the gift was certainly intended for that common pot, it will be upheld. If the exact charitable purposes to which the owner of the property intends to give are uncertain, the Charity Commission[39] and the court have jurisdiction to draw up a scheme to apply the funds.

(c) Perpetuity

Charitable trusts are valid even though they may last for an indefinite period of time. They are exempt from the rule against inalienability, by which trusts requiring capital to be retained for a period longer than the perpetuity period of a life in being plus twenty-one years are invalid. However, with one exception, the rule against remoteness of vesting applies to gifts to charities as to other gifts. This rule requires that all property given to the trust must vest during the perpetuity period, again normally[40] a life in being plus twenty-one years. The exception applies where there is a gift over from one charity to another charity. The gift to the second charity will be valid even though it takes place outside of the perpetuity period. The reason for this exception is that the property has been dedicated forever to charity by the gift to the first charity which vests within the perpetuity period, and it makes no difference that it is subsequently applied for a different charitable purpose. The exception was used in *Re Tyler*[41] to give effect indirectly to a non-charitable purpose. Sir James Tyler left £42,000 of stock to the London Missionary Society, with the condition that they were to maintain his family vault. If the condition was broken, there was a gift over in favour of the Blue Coat School. The gift over did not render the gift void for perpetuity, even though it could conceivably have vested outside of the perpetuity period. Although the London

---

[36] There are a small number of anomalous exceptions, explored, at p 461 above.

[37] *Morice v Bishop of Durham* (1804) 9 Ves 399.   [38] See above, p 456.

[39] Charities Act 1960, s 18(1). Prior to the Charities Act 2006 that constituted the Charity Commission as an incorporated body, the functions of the Commission were vested in the Charity Commissioners.

[40] A statutory period of up to eighty years can also be specified.

[41] [1891] 3 Ch 252, CA.

Missionary Society could not be compelled to maintain the vault, they would have had a strong financial incentive to do so.

(2) Financial privileges

Charities and charitable trusts enjoy tremendous financial advantages over private trusts. It is difficult to be certain of the precise value of these privileges, but the Inland Revenue estimated that in the year 2007–08, the value of tax relief for charities was around £2.19bn.[42] This is likely to be a conservative estimate, and does not include the value of tax advantages (excluding Gift Aid) that are provided to donors to promote donation to charity, either corporate or as private individuals.[43] Charities are exempt from income tax on investments and corporation tax.[44] Many charities today participate in profitable trading activities, for example charity shops. These profits may be exempt from income tax.[45] Gifts to charities are exempt from inheritance tax.[46] Charities also benefit from Gift Aid donations, whereby the Charity can reclaim the basic rate of tax on the gift.[47] Charities are exempt from capital gains tax,[48] stamp duty,[49] and National Insurance Surcharge.[50] There is an 80 per cent exemption from non-domestic rates on properties they occupy.[51] Charities are not exempt from VAT. These financial privileges amount to a massive state subsidy of charitable trusts. Some charities may even enjoy exceptional financial privileges. For example, in *Scott v National Trust*[52] Robert Walker J observed that the trust, which was established by statute, is a charity 'whose special place in the affairs of the nation has been recognized by tax exemptions and reliefs (especially in connection with capital taxation) going well beyond those accorded to charities generally'.[53]

(3) Assessment of the privileges enjoyed by charities

It is clear that charitable trusts enjoy tremendous advantages over non-charitable trusts through their enjoyment of these privileges. The justification for such

[42] HMRC *Annual Report Tables & Statistics 2007–2008*, Table 10.2.

[43] These include, for private individuals, employer payroll deduction schemes, whereby employees can obtain tax relief for donations to charity deducted from their wages (see Income Tax (Earning and Pensions) Act 2003, ss 713–715). Corporate donations may be deductible from taxable profits for the purposes of corporation tax, for example, through Gift Aid (Income and Corporations Tax Act 1988, s 339).

[44] Income and Corporations Tax Act 1988, s 505 as amended (charitable companies and unincorporated associations), Income Tax Act 2007, Part V (charitable trusts).

[45] Income Tax Act 2007, s 525. The exemption applies provided that the profits are applied solely for the purposes of the charity and that the trade is exercised in the course of carrying out a primary purpose of the charity, or is mainly carried out by beneficiaries of the charity.

[46] Inheritance Tax Act 1984, ss 23, 76.

[47] See Income Tax Act 2007, ss.413–430 and 520–522; Finance Act 2008, s 60 (charitable trusts); Income and Corporations Tax Act 1988, s 339; Finance Act 2000, s 40 (company donations).

[48] Taxation of Chargeable Gains Act 1992, s 256.

[49] Finance Act 1982, s 129.   [50] Finance Act 1977, s 57.

[51] Local Government Finance Act 1988, s 43(5); under s 47 the rating authority has discretion to relieve up to the whole amount payable.

[52] [1998] 2 All ER 705.   [53] Ibid., at 710.

advantageous treatment is that charitable purposes are of sufficient importance to the community at large that they deserve both to be upheld and encouraged. It is for this reason that the definition of charity focuses on the notion of 'public benefit', for only those purposes that can be said to be of benefit to the public as a whole can be considered worthy of such special treatment. However, it is questionable whether all charities and charitable trusts need be treated alike. At the moment, every charitable trust enjoys not only the privileges as to essential validity, but also the financial privileges. There is no necessary reason why every charitable trust should automatically enjoy the financial privileges, a conclusion that Lord Cross described in *Dingle v Turner*[54] as 'unfortunate'. Obviously, all must receive the privileges as to validity; otherwise, many would fail under the beneficiary principle. The proposal that only some charities should enjoy financial privileges was made by the Radcliffe Commission in 1956[55] and, as many charities begin to act more like companies, operating in a commercial manner, running what are often multimillion pound trading operations, it is perhaps time that the question of universal financial privilege was re-examined. The financial privileges available to public schools such as Eton and Harrow are a particularly contentious issue, and were the subject of extensive debate in the progress of the Charities Act through Parliament.

It is also an open question whether the availability of financial privilege is a factor to be taken into account when the court is considering if a trust is charitable. In *Dingle v Turner*[56] Lord Cross took the view that, in considering whether a trust was for the benefit of the 'public', regard should be had to the availability of fiscal privileges. However, the other four members of the House expressed doubts as to its relevance. The issue is not resolved by the Charities Act 2006.

3 Defining charitable trusts

(1) When is a trust charitable?

For a trust to be charitable in law, it must be of a charitable character (see Figure 19.2). In other words, it must be for a purpose that is considered in law to be prima facie charitable. The purposes considered to be charitable are all purposes that in a general sense can be considered to be beneficial. In addition to this requirement, the particular application contained in the trust must be for the public benefit. The rationale is that even if a purpose can be considered in a general sense to be beneficial, it should only secure the privileges of charitable status if benefits are conferred upon the public, rather than being confined to a small group of private individuals. Finally, if it is possible for funds to be applied in ways that are not considered to be charitable, this will

[54] [1972] AC 601, HL.
[55] *Royal Commission on Taxation of Profits and Income* (1955) Cmd 9474, ch 7.
[56] [1972] AC 601, HL.

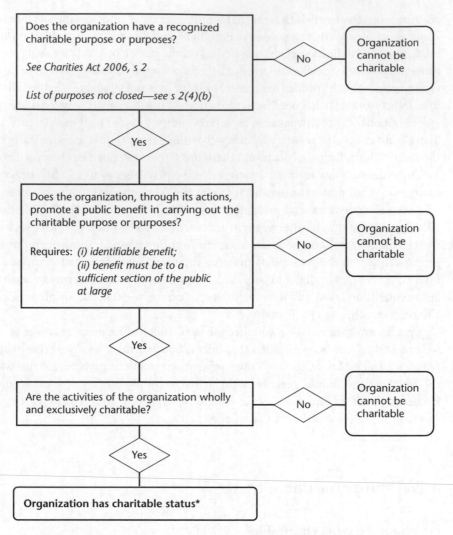

Does the organization have a recognized charitable purpose or purposes?

See Charities Act 2006, s 2

List of purposes not closed—see s 2(4)(b)

No → Organization cannot be charitable

Yes

Does the organization, through its actions, promote a public benefit in carrying out the charitable purpose or purposes?

Requires: *(i) identifiable benefit;*
(ii) benefit must be to a sufficient section of the public at large

No → Organization cannot be charitable

Yes

Are the activities of the organization wholly and exclusively charitable?

No → Organization cannot be charitable

Yes

Organization has charitable status*

*Most charities are required to be registered with the Charity Commission, unless exempt.

Figure 19.2 Requirements for an organization to be charitable

prevent the whole trust from being considered to be charitable, even if parts, taken alone, could have been held charitable. This is often referred to as the requirement that the organization's activities must be 'exclusively charitable'.

(2) Statutory definition of 'charity'

Until the Charities Act 2006, there had been no statutory definition of charity. Given the significance of the distinction between charitable and non-charitable trusts, this might be thought surprising. Until the enactment of the Charities Act into law, the meaning of 'charity' as a legal concept was therefore determined by reference to judicial precedents and the registration decisions of the Charity Commission.

The Charities Act 2006 for the first time contains a statutory definition of charity.[57] According to section 1 of the Act:

(1) For the purposes of the law of England and Wales, 'charity' means an institution which—

    (a) is established for charitable purposes only, and

    (b) falls to be subject to the control of the High Court in the exercise of its jurisdiction with respect to charities.

(2) The definition of 'charity' in subsection (1) does not apply for the purposes of an enactment if a different definition of that term applies for those purposes by virtue of that or any other enactment.

(3) A reference in any enactment or document to a charity within the meaning of the Charitable Uses Act 1601 (c 4) or the preamble to it is to be construed as a reference to a charity as defined by subsection (1).

The definition of charitable purposes is contained in s 2 of the Charities Act 2006, and has made almost no change to the law. The definition essentially consolidates the previous law by reclassifying existing recognized purposes and has the advantage of providing a greater degree of transparency about the range of purposes that are currently considered to be charitable in law. It also preserves the flexibility that was a fundamental feature of the previous categorization of charitable purposes. The main drawback with the definition is that, because it incorporates a reference to the previous law, it is impossible to draw a line at the date of the enactment of the Charities Act 2006 into law: it is also necessary to have regard to most of the case law prior to its enactment.

(a) Relevance of previous law

The Charities Act 2006, s 2(2) provides a list of purposes which are prima facie considered to be charitable, but then states that any purposes which do not fall within the specific categories in the list shall be recognized as charitable if they are 'recognised as charitable purposes under existing charity law'.[58] The statutory definition therefore adds to rather than replaces existing law.

(b) List is not closed

The Charities Act retains the dynamism of the previous concept of charitable purposes. The existing law recognized the possibility of development by analogy or because of changes in society and public attitudes. For example, in *Scottish Burial Reform and Cremation Society v Glasgow City Corpn*[59] a trust to promote cremation as a method of disposal of the dead was held charitable by the House of Lords, as it was analogous to earlier cases in which it had been held that trusts for the maintenance of

---

[57] Charities Act 2006, ss 1–5.   [58] Charities Act 2006, s 2(2)(m) and s 2(4).
[59] [1968] AC 138.

graveyards were charitable. Development was possible even where previous case law suggested that a purpose would not, in the past, have been considered to be charitable. For instance in *Funnell v Stewart*[60] Hazel Williamson, QC held that faith healing had 'become a recognized activity of public benefit' so as to be charitable, even though an earlier decision had held that a trust to promote faith healing was non-charitable.[61] Preservation of this ability to develop charitable purposes is essential, as, in the words of Viscount Simonds in *IRC v Baddeley*, 'there is no limit to the number and diversity of the ways in which man will seek to benefit his fellow man'.[62]

The concept of development by analogy is recognized by s 2(4)(b) of the Charities Act 2006, which states that charitable purposes include 'any purposes that may reasonably be regarded as analogous to, or within the spirit of, any purposes falling within' the listed categories or the provision retaining existing charitable purposes. Moreover, development by analogy upon analogy is expressly preserved under s 2(4) (c), which states that a charitable purpose includes 'any purposes that may reasonably be regarded as analogous to, or within the spirit of, any purposes which have been recognised under charity law'. This permits development by analogy from development by analogy and so on ad infinitum. The extraordinary effect of the statutory definition is therefore that it retains all the elements of the previous law. The only change effected by the statutory definition is that the list of purposes which it contains can be changed only by legislation: under the previous law it was possible for a purpose which was once considered to be charitable to cease to be charitable because of changing social conditions. As Lord Wilberforce observed in *Scottish Burial Reform and Cremation Society v Glasgow City Corpn*,[63] 'the law of charity is a moving subject' which evolves over time. This was also recognized by Lord Simmonds in *National Anti-Vivisection Society v IRC*,[64] where a society which promoted the suppression of vivisection was held not to be charitable, as the court found that the advantages of reduced cruelty to animals were outweighed by the detriments to medical research that would be caused if the purpose was accomplished. He said that:

A purpose regarded in one age as charitable may in another be regarded differently...I conceive that an anti-vivisection society might at different times be differently regarded.

This flexibility to take into account changes in society and in public attitudes is unlikely to be possible for purposes which have been entrenched by legislation, but may, it seems, be reflected in the assessment of public benefit, which is required to be demonstrated by all charitable organizations.[65]

(3) The categories of charitable purpose

Prior to the Charities Act 2006, there were three sources from which the categories of charitable trust were drawn: a long-repealed ancient Act of Parliament which

---

[60] [1996] 1 WLR 288. [61] *Re Hummeltenberg* [1923] 1 Ch 237.
[62] [1955] AC 572. [63] [1968] AC 138.
[64] [1948] AC 31, HL. [65] See below, at pp 628–655.

contained a descriptive list; the decisions of the courts, which were categorized into four groups by a leading nineteenth-century judgment; and the determinations of the Charity Commissioners. These original sources can still be discerned in the list provided by the new law.

(a) The Charitable Uses Act 1601

The Charitable Uses Act 1601[66] did not set out to define charity, but rather to correct abuses in the administration of charitable trusts. However, the preamble to the Act contained a list of the objects that the law regarded as charitable in 1601, which became a guide to which the courts referred to determine whether purposes were charitable. Although the preamble was repealed in 1960,[67] it has continued to provide guidance in defining charity until the changes made by the Charities Act 2006.

(b) *Income Tax Special Purposes Comrs v Pemsel*[68]

In this case, Lord Macnaghten provided an organizing classification of charitable purposes. He identified four 'heads' of charity:

Charity in its legal sense comprises four principal divisions; trusts for the relief of poverty; trusts for the advancement of education; trusts for the advancement of religion; and trusts for other purposes beneficial to the community, not falling under any of the preceding heads.

This classification was not an exhaustive definition of the law of charity, but a convenient grouping of the cases into areas of benefit that the law regards as charitable, with the exception of the fourth division which is obviously a 'catch-all' category. The categories themselves did not provide the answers as to whether a particular purpose was indeed charitable. In *Scottish Burial Reform and Cremation v Glasgow City Corpn* Lord Wilberforce gave three cautions about its use:

first that, since it is a classification of convenience, there may well be purposes which do not fit neatly into one or other of the headings; secondly, that the words used must not be given the force of a statute to be construed; and thirdly, that the law of charity is a moving subject which may well have evolved even since 1891.[69]

(c) The role of the Charity Commission in defining 'charity'

The Charity Commission plays an increasingly important role in shaping the development of the definition of charitable purposes. The Commission has the legal obligation to keep a register of institutions that are charitable.[70] The Commission has the power to recognize a new purpose as charitable in circumstances where it believes

---

[66] 43 Eliz, c 4.   [67] Charities Act 1960, s 38(1).
[68] [1891] AC 531.   [69] [1968] AC 138, at 223.
[70] Charities Act 1993, s 3. Under s 4(1) of the Act, the register is deemed conclusive of the charitable nature of an organization. Certain charities are not required to be registered. These include exempt charities (see s 3A(2)(a) and Sch 2) who are organizations that are subject to another form of regulatory or supervisory control, eg universities, national galleries, and museums. Small charities, defined by having a total income of less than £5,000 a year, are also not required to register (s 3A(2)(d)) but may choose to do so. See further Lloyd, *Charities—The New Law 2006: A Practical Guide To The Charities Acts* (2007), Ch 3.

that the courts of law would do so, and it therefore has in practice the same powers as the court to take into account changing social and economic circumstances in determining whether an organization is charitable or not. The Charity Commission has indicated that it will adopt a 'two-step' test to determine whether a new purpose is charitable, examining whether it is 'analogous to a purpose previously accepted as charitable' and whether it 'satisfies the requirement that the purpose benefits the public'.[71] The Commission has recognized a number of new charitable purposes (such as the promotion of urban and rural regeneration in areas of social and economic deprivation and the conservation of the environment) that have now been included in the list contained in the Charities Act 2006. The Commission has also decided that some previously charitable purposes should lose their charitable status. For example, civilian rifle and pistol clubs had historically enjoyed charitable status on the grounds that they promoted the defence of the realm by encouraging skill in shooting. However, in 1993 the Commission decided that gun clubs could no longer be regarded as a reserve for the armed forces. Following the Charities Act 2006, the Charity Commission no longer has the power to depart from any of the statutory purposes listed. Any changes in recognition of those purposes as charitable will have to come through legislative enactment.

In reaching a decision on registration, the Commission may also have to conduct an evidential investigation of an application to determine whether registration is permissible,[72] including the activities of an existing organization.[73] It is an offence for an organization to provide misleading information to the Charity Commission.[74]

The role of the Commission in determining whether a purpose is charitable confers on it the ability to develop the law, subject to the possibility of its decisions being challenged through the tribunal system and ultimately the courts. For instance, using reasoning by analogy, the Commissioners decided in 2003–2004 that the promotion of restorative justice was charitable. The Commissioners concluded that 'the promotion of restorative justice was analogous to the charitable purposes of the preservation of public order and the prevention of breaches of the peace, the protection of life and property and the promotion of the sound administration of the law, and as such was for the public benefit'.[75] The Commission has been prepared to make decisions in some potentially contentious areas. For instance, it registered religious charities that do not involve belief in a deity, before there was judicial recognition that this was possible, and even though belief in a deity had been stated as a requirement in the previous case law.[76] While it can be argued that the authority given to the

[71] RR1a, *Recognising New Charitable Purposes* (2001), para 22.

[72] Charities Act 1993, s 3B(1), which places the potential charity trustees under a duty to supply such documents and information as the Commission may require.

[73] This is contentious, as it may take the Commission into considering the activities of the organization, rather than the words used in the governing instrument. See further Mitchell, *Reviewing the Register* in Mitchell and Moody (eds), *Foundations of Charity* (2000), p 175.

[74] Charities Act 1993, s 11.

[75] *Annual Report of the Charity Commissioners for England and Wales 2003–2004*, p 11.

[76] See below p 594.

Charity Commission does not enable it to change the law since any guidance issued or decisions made on registration only have effect unless and until they are tested in the courts, it is nevertheless the case that many registration decisions will not be appealed immediately or at all.[77] In consequence, there is little choice for organizations seeking registration other than to follow existing Commission decisions in contentious areas.

(4) The new list of charitable purposes

The list is essentially an extended formulation of the classification provided by Lord Macnaghten, even to the extent of including the first three substantive categories, and after an additional group of substantive categories, a 'catch-all' category. This catch-all category includes any other purposes currently considered to be charitable, but which are not included in the previous paragraphs, as well as any other purposes which could on the basis of analogy (and by analogy from analogy) be considered to be charitable. The new list, like Lord Macnaghten's, is no more than a classification. However, being statutory, it is an authoritative classification. Like Lord Macnaghten's list, it does not follow automatically that because a trust is, for example, for the advancement of animal welfare that it will be charitable. It merely indicates that the potential purpose is recognized as charitable, as the trust must also satisfy the requirement of public benefit and its activities must be exclusively charitable.[78]

The list of charitable purposes is set out in s 2(2) of the Charities Act 2006 as follows:

(a) the prevention or relief of poverty;

(b) the advancement of education;

(c) the advancement of religion;

(d) the advancement of health or the saving of lives;

(e) the advancement of citizenship or community development;

(f) the advancement of the arts, culture, heritage or science;

(g) the advancement of amateur sport;

(h) the advancement of human rights, conflict resolution or reconciliation or the promotion of religious or racial harmony or equality and diversity;

(i) the advancement of environmental protection or improvement;

(j) the relief of those in need by reason of youth, age, ill-health, disability, financial hardship or other disadvantage;

(k) the advancement of animal welfare;

---

[77] Before the introduction of the Tribunal service, any appeal on a registration decision had to be taken to the High Court, with the attendant expense. It should come as no surprise that appeals were few and far between, particularly as organizations seeking charitable status were unlikely to have the will or resources to mount such an appeal.

[78] Charities Act 2006, s 2(1). The requirement that the purpose be exclusively charitable is often considered alongside the issue of charitable purpose. It makes sense to treat it as a separate requirement, as will be explained below.

(l) the promotion of the efficiency of the armed forces of the Crown, or of the efficiency of the police, fire and rescue services or ambulance services;

(m) any other purposes within subsection (4). [ie purposes recognised by existing charity law and developments by analogy]'

The list relies heavily upon existing case law. The Act states that where the list contains a term which 'has a particular meaning under charity law, the term is to be taken as having the same meaning where it appears in that provision'.[79] Even where this is not the case, previous case law is a guide to the scope and effect of some of the categories. In one of the first reported cases involving the Act, a case involving an animal welfare charity, Lewison J observed:

The advancement of animal welfare is now expressly recognised as a charitable purpose by section 2 (2)(k) of the Charities Act 2006. I do not, however, regard this as a significant change in the law.[80]

He later reiterated that 'I do not regard this as amounting to any change in the substance of the law.' If this view is taken by other judges, then the list of charitable purposes in the 2006 Act may have had no more impact than to have provided a useful categorization.

In considering the categories, for convenience, each will be taken separately.

4 Charitable purposes[81]

(1) Trusts for the prevention or relief of poverty

The first general head of charitable purposes identified by Lord Macnaghten and repeated in the list in the Charities Act 2006 was that of the 'relief of poverty', a description extended to include the prevention of poverty by the Charities Act 2006. In a social era when there was no welfare state and little other state provision for those at the bottom of society, it was obviously 'beneficial' for private individuals to provide for them. Thus, the law has always regarded the relief of poverty as a charitable purpose to be encouraged, and has tended to be particularly lenient in defining when a gift for the relief of poverty is for the benefit of the 'public',[82] a leniency that is altered by the Charities Act 2006.

The preamble to the Statute of Charitable Uses 1601 referred to the relief of poverty in a wider context, including the 'relief of aged, impotent [ie infirm or disabled]

---

[79] Charities Act 2006, s 2(5).

[80] *Hanchett-Stamford v Attorney-General* [2009] Ch 173, at [14] and [23].

[81] The Charity Commission has issued considerable guidance on how it will interpret charitable purposes, both before and after the enactment of the Charities Act 2006. At the time of writing the latest such publication is the *Commentary on the Descriptions of Purposes in the Charities Act 2006* (August 2009). Reference will be made to relevant guidance, where appropriate, in the following treatment.

[82] *Dingle v Turner* [1972] AC 601. See below p 648.

and poor people'. As a result, trusts dealing with the relief of problems arising from age or infirmity were recognized as charitable. Trusts for these purposes are now covered by separate categories in the 2006 list.

(a) The meaning of 'poor'

Poverty is not defined or explained in the Charities Act 2006. Case law prior to 2006 indicated that it is a relative concept, and that what a society regards as 'poor' will vary with changes in social circumstance and what is regarded as a 'normal' level of income and ownership of consumer products. As a society we are used to images of extreme poverty both at home and abroad. However, apart from these extreme examples, wealth increases through the levels of society and it is almost impossible to draw a line defining the boundary of poverty. Absolute criteria, for example a specified weekly income, would be inadequate, as they cannot take account of a person's complete circumstances. In the light of these difficulties the law has not attempted to define poverty but has taken a general, impressionistic approach, which is best illustrated by the examples given in the cases themselves.

The starting point must be *Re Coulthurst*,[83] where Sir Raymond Evershed MR made clear that from the perspective of the law of charity, 'poverty' is not synonymous with destitution:

It is quite clearly established that poverty does not mean destitution; it is a word of wide and somewhat indefinite import; it may not unfairly be paraphrased for present purposes as meaning persons who have to 'go short' in the ordinary sense of that term, due regard being had to their status in life.

This means that poverty is not to be understood as something experienced only by those at the very bottom of society, and the concept of 'going short'[84] will mean different things to people at different social levels. Those who are middle-class yet have fallen on harder times may well fall within this understanding of poverty, since they 'go short' compared to their social peers, although there may be others with similar financial circumstances who are not regarded as poor, because in the light of their social position they do not 'go short'. Thus, gifts in favour of 'distressed gentlefolk'[85] or persons of 'moderate means'[86] have been held to fall within this understanding of 'poor'. In *Re De Carteret*[87] the Bishop of Jamaica left property on trust to pay an annuity of £40 per annum to widows and spinsters in England whose income was between £80 and £120. Although this excluded widows with an income lower than £80, who seem to be poorer in an absolute sense, the gift was upheld as a valid charitable gift for the relief of poverty. Maugham J expressed some hesitation at this conclusion, and emphasized that the gift expressed the Bishop's preference that the annuities be paid

---

[83] [1951] Ch 661, CA.
[84] This term was approved by Lightman J in *IRC v Oldham Training and Enterprise Council* [1996] STC 1218, at 1233.
[85] *Re Young* [1951] Ch 344.   [86] *Re Clarke* [1923] 2 Ch 407.
[87] [1933] Ch 103.

to widows who had children dependent upon them. In contrast, in *Re Gwyon*[88] a gift for the provision of clothing for children was held not charitable since the terms of the gift did not exclude children who were from affluent backgrounds. In *Re Segelman (Decd)*,[89] Chadwick J held that the beneficiaries of a trust had been selected on the basis of potential 'poverty' where they were presently 'comfortably off—in the sense that they are able to meet their day-to-day expenses out of income—but not affluent', but where they might need financial help in the future:

> Like many others in similar circumstances, they need a helping hand from time to time in order to overcome an unforeseen crisis: the failure of a business venture, urgent repairs to a dwelling house or expenses brought on by reason of failing health.[90]

He further considered that minors who became students would be likely to experience 'relative poverty' when their income from grants or parental resources fails to cover their expenditure on 'their actual or perceived needs'.[91]

In *Re Sanders' Will Trusts*[92] money was given to provide dwellings for 'the working classes and their families'. Harman J held this was not charitable, since the term 'the working classes' did not indicate poor persons. In *Re Niyazi's Will Trusts*[93] Megarry V-C held charitable a gift of £15,000 for the construction of a 'working men's hostel' in Cyprus. He distinguished *Re Sanders' Will Trusts* on the basis that 'hostel' meant modest, temporary accommodation for those with a relatively low income, whereas 'dwellings' were ordinary houses which may be inhabited by the well-to-do as much as the relatively poor. In *IRC v Oldham Training and Enterprise Council*, Lightman J held that a trust to help the unemployed would be a charitable trust for the relief of poverty:

> So far as the object... is to set up in trade or business the unemployed and enable them to stand on their own feet, that is charitable as a trust for the improvement of the conditions in life of those 'going short' in respect of employment and providing a fresh start in life for those in need of it.[94]

A modern analogy can be drawn from how the courts have reinterpreted the meaning of 'poor' in the equitable doctrine of *Fry v Lane*.[95] The court held that there was a general jurisdiction to set aside a sale made by a 'poor and ignorant man' at a considerable undervalue. This concept was translated into the twentieth century in *Cresswell v Potter*[96] where, on divorce, a wife transferred her equitable interest in her matrimonial home to her husband for virtually no consideration. Megarry J set the transaction aside, holding that the wife, who was a Post Office telephonist, fell within the category of 'poor and ignorant'. He considered that the words must be reinterpreted to fit the twentieth-century context:

> Eighty years ago when *Fry v Lane* was decided, social conditions were very different from those which exist today. I do not, however, think that the principle has changed, even though the

---

[88] [1930] 1 Ch 255.   [89] [1995] 3 All ER 676.   [90] Ibid., at 690.

[91] [1995] 3 All ER 676, at 690. Under the current student loan system and tuition fees systems operating in the UK, which forces an undertaking of debt to pursue higher education study, students might find this a comforting concept.

[92] [1954] Ch 265.   [93] [1978] 1 WLR 910.   [94] [1996] STC 1218, at 1233.

[95] (1888) 40 Ch D 312.   [96] [1978] 1 WLR 255.

euphemisms of the twentieth century may require the word 'poor' to be replaced by 'a member of the lower income group'.[97]

Two simple propositions can be drawn from these cases. First, that the legal concept of poverty is itself a relative one, and a person's social position and circumstances will be taken into account in determining if they are 'poor'. Second, that to be a valid gift for the relief of poverty, the gift must be exclusively for the benefit of the poor. If those who are not considered poor fall within the scope of the gift, then it will not be charitable. The Charity Commission has issued guidance for trustees of charities whose purpose included the relief of the poor summarizing the law:

'People in poverty' does not just include people who are destitute, but also those who cannot satisfy a basic need without assistance…In essence, 'people in poverty' generally refers to people who lack something in the nature of a necessity, or quasi-necessity, which the majority of the population would regard as necessary for a modest, but adequate, standard of living.[98]

It is worth noting that the majority of cases that examine the concept of poverty pre-date the creation of the welfare state. It has not been suggested that those in receipt of state benefits are outside of the class of poor people, since they receive the level of income society has decided to grant them, and provision which is additional to state support will still be charitable for the relief of poverty.[99] The Charity Commission has stated that, in their view, 'people may qualify for assistance from a poverty charity whether or not they are eligible for state benefits'.[100] In previous guidance, the Commission had warned that charity resources should not be used simply to replace state benefits, as this would not make the recipients any better off.[101] This is not repeated in the current guidance, but would seem to be a sensible interpretation of the law.

In *Cawdron v Merchant Taylors' School*,[102] Blackburne J was called upon to consider, inter alia, whether the objects of a fund were charitable as being for the relief of poverty. The object in question was as follows:

(a) The creation of a fund the income or capital of which shall be employed in (1) paying for the education at the School of any son of an Old Merchant Taylor who has fallen in the war or who has been thereby disabled, whether directly or indirectly, or in (2) assisting any relative of such Old Merchant Taylor as may be dependent upon him; in every case the decision as to the eligibility of the candidates and the extent and method of assistance to be in the sole discretion of the Committee.

In holding the fund charitable, Blackburne J emphasized both the importance of reading the wording used in context, and of the legal meaning of 'poverty':

Is then object (a) to be interpreted as a gift for the relief of poverty? In considering that question, the following points are to be noted about object (a). First, the payment to be made is

---

[97] Ibid., at 257.
[98] CC4, *Charities for the Relief of the Poor* (2008) section C1, p 8. This replaced earlier guidance issued in 2001.
[99] See, generally, Dunn 'As "Cold as Charity"?: Poverty, Equity and the Charitable Trust' (2000) LS 222.
[100] CC4, *Charities for the Relief of the Poor* (2008) section C1, p 8.
[101] CC4, *Charities for the Relief of the Poor* (2001), para 1.
[102] [2009] EWHC 1722 (Ch).

described, in the words which follow the semi-colon, as 'assistance'. Second, it is not every son or dependent relative of an OMT killed or disabled in the war that is to receive the assistance; whether any eligible person is to receive any and what assistance is a matter for the Committee. Third, the eligibility of candidates for assistance in the case of relatives of OMTs killed or disabled in the war is their dependency on the OMT. When coupled with the reference to the Committee's discretion to determine the extent and means of the assistance, this suggests that financial need is the criterion ie that it is to those who would otherwise 'go short' that the assistance is to be directed. It was therefore accepted by Mr Jones, rightly, that the second limb of object (a)—the provision of financial assistance to dependent relatives of the OMTs killed or disabled in the war—is charitable in nature as being for the relief of poverty. Fourth, it is difficult to see why, if that is so in the case of dependent relatives, the criterion of financial need, because otherwise they would 'go short', is any less the criterion where eligibility depends on being the son of an OMT killed or disabled in the war.[103]

(b) The meaning of 'relief' or 'prevention'

Under the first category, a gift is not charitable merely because it is for the benefit of the poor. It must also relieve a need that they have as a result of their condition of poverty or must operate to prevent poverty. The concept of relief has been well explored in the courts, but the concept of prevention has been added by the Charities Act and has therefore not yet been tested. The requirement of relief is best explained in a wider context than that of the relief of poverty. In *Joseph Rowntree Memorial Trust Housing Association Ltd v A-G*[104] the housing association wished to build small dwellings for elderly people, who would be able to purchase them on long leases. The elderly would pay 70 per cent of the purchase price of the premises, with the remainder being paid by the housing association. To be charitable Peter Gibson J emphasized that:

there must be a need which is to be relieved by the...gift, such need being attributable to the aged...condition of the person to be benefited.

Therefore, as counsel for the Attorney-General had argued, a gift for the 'aged millionaires of Mayfair' would not be charitable as it would not relieve a need that such millionaires experienced as aged people. The fact that the housing association was providing a specialist type of accommodation for the elderly meant that a need was being relieved and the purpose was charitable.[105]

The distinction between the relief and prevention of poverty has been considered by the Charity Commission in their current guidance, as follows:

the prevention of poverty includes preventing those who are poor from becoming poorer, and preventing people who are not poor from becoming poor.[106]

Therefore, in the Commission's view, the relief and prevention of poverty are generally interchangeable terms, but, where a charity is set up purely for the prevention of

---

[103] Ibid., at para [33].   [104] [1983] Ch 159.

[105] See also the Garfield Poverty Trust, which provided interest-free loans to assist poor members of the Exclusive Brethren to purchase housing; Report of the Charity Commissioners for England and Wales 1990, para 13, App A.

[106] CC4, *Charities for the Relief of the Poor* (2008) section C1, p 8.

poverty, it will 'tend to take a very specific approach to poverty, which usually involves tackling its root causes'.[107]

Examples of purposes for the prevention of poverty are thus providing money management training to someone at actual risk of being in poverty or at risk of becoming impoverished due to natural disaster or famine.[108] There would seem to be considerable sense in this approach, and it is unlikely that the courts would take issue with this guidance.

(2) Trusts for the advancement of education

(a) A broad concept of 'education'

Under the second head of the classification of charity, gifts for the advancement of education will be charitable. The preamble to the 1601 Act included the 'maintenance of schools of learning, free schools and scholars in the universities' and 'the education and preferment of orphans'. The law takes a wide view of what may be regarded as for the advancement of education, and education is not confined to teaching in schools and colleges. In *IRC v McMullen* Lord Hailsham spoke of the education of the young as:

a balanced and systematic process of instruction, training and practice containing...both spiritual, moral, mental and physical elements.[109]

Education thus covers skills and understanding, as well as knowledge. This wide concept of education has been reflected in the cases that have held that not only gifts to advance academic study but also for research, culture, and sport may be charitable. The Charities Act 2006 contains separate heads that cover some of these areas.

(b) Teaching

The advancement of academic teaching and of institutions that provide such teaching is clearly charitable. Charitable gifts have included: the founding of a professorial chair (*A-G v Margaret and Regius Professors in Cambridge*[110]); the endowments of schools and colleges (*A-G v Lady Downing*;[111] *Abbey Malvern Wells Ltd v Ministry of Local Government and Planning*;[112] and the payment of teachers and administrative staff of an institution (*Case of Christ's College Cambridge*).[113] In *Customs and Excise Comrs v Bell Concord Educational Trust Ltd*[114] it was held that trusts endowing fee-paying schools are charitable, provided that the school is non-profit making, or uses its profits for school purposes only.[115] Purposes ancillary to teaching institutions may also be

---

[107] Ibid.

[108] Ibid. Annex A, at p 20. Usefully, this Annex contains examples of charitable purposes that would be for the relief or prevention of poverty.

[109] [1981] AC 1, HL.   [110] (1682) 1 Vern 55.   [111] (1766) Amb 550.

[112] [1951] Ch 728.   [113] (1757) 1 Wm Bl 90.   [114] [1990] 1 QB 1040, CA.

[115] The issue with fee-paying schools is more often one of public benefit, discussed below, at pp 628–654.

charitable, as for example in *A-G v Ross*,[116] where the students' union at a polytechnic was held charitable as it furthered the educational function of the institution.

(c) Industrial training and professional bodies

The advancement of industrial and technical training has also been held charitable (*Re Koettgen's Will Trusts*[117] and *Construction Industry Training Board v A-G*).[118] In *IRC v White*[119] an association with the purpose of encouraging craftsmanship and maintaining the standards of the modern and ancient crafts was held to be charitable. The Royal College of Surgeons, which exists to promote the study and practice of the art of surgery, has been held charitable,[120] as has the Royal College of Nursing, whose objects are the better education and training of nurses and to promote nursing as a profession.[121] In contrast, the General Nursing Council, which was established by statute to regulate the nursing profession, has not been held charitable[122] since its objects included the enhancement of the status of nurses, which is analogous to the objectives of trade unions to advance the interests of their members.

(d) Research[123]

The advancement of education extends beyond mere teaching to include research activity. Despite a general unwillingness to make value judgements that may be subjective, the courts have sought to distinguish research which is of truly educational value and worthy of charitable status, from that which is not. Research that is of no educational value, or of purely esoteric value to the researcher, will not be charitable. The key concept the courts have used is that of public benefit, and only research that is of benefit to the public will be charitable. This was so even though, at the time of the relevant decisions, the legal requirement of public benefit was presumed for education.[124] The three criteria laid down by Slade J in *Re Besterman's Will Trusts*[125] summarize the present state of the law. For a trust for research to be charitable:

(1) the subject matter of the research must be a useful subject of study;

(2) the knowledge acquired by the research must be disseminated to others; and

(3) the trust must be for the benefit of the public, or a sufficiently important section of the public.

The case concerned a trust for research into the works of Voltaire and Rousseau, and since the three criteria were met it was held to be charitable. In the earlier case

---

[116] [1986] 1 WLR 252.   [117] [1954] Ch 252.

[118] [1973] Ch 173, CA.   [119] [1980] TR 155.

[120] *Royal College of Surgeons of England v National Provincial Bank Ltd* [1952] AC 631, HL.

[121] *Royal College of Nursing v St Marylebone Corpn* [1959] 1 WLR 1077, CA.

[122] *General Nursing Council for England and Wales v St Marylebone Borough Council* [1959] AC 540, HL.

[123] The case law on this purpose now overlaps to some degree with the distinct purpose of the advancement of arts, culture, heritage, or science under the Charities Act 2006, s 2(2)(f).

[124] The requirement of public benefit is considered below, at pp 628–654.

[125] (1980) The Times, 21 January.

of *Re Shaw*,[126] Harman J had held that a gift by George Bernard Shaw in his will for research into a 40-letter alphabet, and translation of one of his plays into it, was not charitable. However, Harman J seems to have taken a very narrow view of education, stating that:

if the object [of the research] be merely the increase of knowledge, that is not in itself a charitable object unless it be combined with teaching or education.[127]

It is questionable whether the same result would have been reached under the principle applied in the later case of *Re Hopkins' Will Trusts*,[128] which concerned a gift to the Francis Bacon Society to be used to find manuscripts proving that the plays of Shakespeare were written by Francis Bacon. Holding the purpose charitable, Wilberforce J stated that the research 'must either be of educational value to the researcher or must be so directed as to lead to something which will pass into the store of educational material, so as to improve the sum of communicable knowledge in an area which education may cover'. This test has now evolved into the three criteria set out by Slade J in *Re Besterman's Will Trusts*.[129]

Propaganda—the promotion of a single view-point or a set of singular views—masquerading as research will not be charitable. The educational value of research comes from the presentation of a balanced argument, reaching conclusions through analysis of evidence and considering competing arguments. This does not mean that research cannot be value-driven, provided that it does not amount to campaigning for a particular view. Thus, in *Re Hopkinson*,[130] a proposed trust for educating adults in the views of a single political party was not held charitable.[131] The issue often overlaps with the promotion of political purposes or campaigning, which is discussed further below.

In summary, it is essential that the subject of proposed research must be of some usefulness. The court, or the Charity Commission, will have to make value judgements if it appears that a subject is of absolutely no worth to the educational community.

The results of the research must also enter the public domain, usually by publication, and if the information is kept purely for the benefit of the researcher alone it will not be charitable, as there is no advancement of education in non-disseminated work. Similarly, research carried out by companies and intended for their exclusive commercial use will not be charitable, as it is not publicly available. Nor will it be charitable for a university to conduct research on behalf of a corporation if the results of the research cannot enter the public domain. It is worth noting that the requirement of research being in the public domain in this context means that the research must be available to the public, not in the technical sense understood in copyright law of it being free of author's copyright.

---

126 [1957] 1 WLR 729. 127 Ibid., at 737. 128 [1965] Ch 669.
129 (1980) The Times, 21 January. 130 [1949] 1 All ER 346.
131 It is also possible to view the decision in *Re Shaw* [1957] 1 WLR 729 in this light, as the proposed bequest was for the promotion of George Bernard Shaw's alphabet, not really to research the benefits of the Shaw alphabet as compared to the existing Roman system.

(e) Advancement

It is clear from the discussion above that, whatever the broad view given to the meaning of 'education', it will only be a charitable if the proposed charitable activities actually *advance* education. In the words of guidance issued by the Charity Commission this means 'to promote, sustain and increase'[132] educational purposes. Hence, an activity which is individually or collectively edifying but does nothing to advance understanding in an area cannot be charitable. The Commission also provides a list of example purposes that they would consider to be charitable,[133] which draw upon the legal decisions reached above.

(3) **The advancement of religion**

Trusts for the advancement of religion are the third of Lord Macnaghten's categories that have been retained by the Charities Act 2006. The law has historically been liberal in granting charitable status to religious purposes and groups, and this reflects the fact that religion was central to the fabric of the nation at the time when many of the cases were decided. The law assumes that any religious activity, provided it is carried on in the public domain,[134] is charitable. There is no need at this first stage of the test as to whether a purpose is charitable for the particular religion in issue to prove its value, or for the court to weigh the validity of its beliefs. This was emphasized by Lord Reid, who stated in *Gilmour v Coats*, that:

A religion can be regarded as beneficial without it being necessary to assume that all its beliefs are true, and a religious service can be regarded as beneficial to all those who attend it without it being necessary to determine the spiritual efficacy of that service or to accept any particular belief about it.[135]

Thus, in *Funnell v Stewart*[136] a gift to further the work of a small group of faith healers was not denied charitable status merely because there was no evidence that anyone had ever been healed, as was argued by the testatrix's next of kin, who alleged that the bequest was invalid. Hazel Williamson, QC upheld the argument of the Attorney-General that there was no need to prove public benefit, as it was presumed.

It is interesting to note that in December 2008, approximately 29,000 registered charities had purposes that included religious activities.[137]

(a) The meaning of 'religion'

Although the position has now been changed, the courts originally defined religion so as to require belief in a divine being. Indeed, in *Bowman v Secular Society*[138] Lord Parker suggested that only monotheistic faiths would count as religions for the

---

132   Charity Commission, *Advancement of Education for the Public Benefit* (December 2008), at p 8.
133   *Ibid*. Annex A, at pp 23–24.   134   See *Gilmour v Coats* [1949] AC 426.
135   [1949] AC 426, at 862. See also: *Re Watson* [1973] 1 WLR 1472; *Funnell v Stewart* [1996] 1 WLR 288.
136   [1996] 1 WLR 288.
137   Charity Commission, *The Advancement of Religion for the Public Benefit* (December 2008) p 3.
138   [1917] AC 406, HL.

purposes of charity. It therefore follows that groups that merely promoted a moral lifestyle without a spiritual dimension would not be charitable for the advancement of religion. That seemed somewhat ironic given that the assumed benefit of religion is that citizens will adopt a more moral lifestyle as a result of their beliefs and not the essential validity of the spiritual truths they profess. In *Re South Place Ethical Society*[139] Dillon J expressed the view that religion is 'concerned with man's relations with God' and therefore a society that had the purpose of promoting the 'study and dissemination of ethical principles' did not advance religion.[140] Similarly, in 1999 the Charity Commission rejected the application of the Church of Scientology for registration as a charity. It held that a body would only be charitable for the advancement of religion if it engaged in the worship of the divine being.[141] While it was accepted that the Church of Scientology believed in the existence of a divine being, its activities did not exhibit the defining characteristics of worship, namely the 'reverence or veneration for that supreme being'. The activities of Scientology consisted of 'auditing', which was found to be very much akin to counselling, and 'training', which involved the detailed study of the works of L Ron Hubbard.[142]

The view that religion requires belief in a divine being would rule out the possibility of recognizing Buddhism as a religion.[143] Equally, if religion requires belief in a single god, then neither could Hinduism be recognized as a religion. This would be an odd conclusion in an open and liberal society in which differences are respected and cherished. It is therefore no surprise that the Charities Act 2006 states that:

'religion' includes—

(i) a religion which involves belief in more than one god, and

(ii) a religion which does not involve belief in a god;[144]

This confirms the practice which the Charity Commission had already adopted of registering Hindu and Buddhist trusts,[145] although in many but by no means all cases the organizations included additional objects such as the advancement of education or the relief of poverty, and could therefore have been considered charities on that basis. It is worth noting that even in *Re South Place Ethical Society*,[146] although Dillon J considered that ethics did not constitute a religion, he considered that the South Place

---

[139] [1980] 1 WLR 1565.

[140] Although it could be, and was, in this particular case, held to be charitable under Lord Macnaghten's fourth category of other purposes beneficial to the public.

[141] Decision of the Charity Commissioners for England and Wales made on 17 November 1999. See also *R v Registrar General, ex p Segerdal* [1970] 2 QB 697.

[142] See also O'Brien 'Rastafarianism as Religion' (2001) 252 NLJ 509.

[143] See the doubts expressed by Dillon J in *Re South Place Ethical Society* [1980] 1 WLR 1565.

[144] S 2(3)(a).

[145] See, for instance, *Gaudiya Mission v Brahmachary* [1997] EWCA Civ 2239; *Varsani v Jesani* [1998] EWCA Civ 630; *Muman v Nagasena* [1999] EWCA Civ 1742. A search of the register of charities discloses many more examples.

[146] [1980] 1 WLR 1565.

Ethical Society was a charity because the promotion of ethical values and philosophies are charitable as for the advancement of education.

The Charity Commission practice, if tested in the courts, would almost certainly have been approved. For instance in *Varsani v Jesani*[147] the Court of Appeal had to adjudicate on how to deal with the property of a Hindu sect established to follow the teachings of Shree Swaminarayan Bhagwan, who was believed by adherents to have been the incarnation or manifestation of the Supreme Being. The sect had become irretrievably divided. The Court of Appeal had so little doubt that the sect, and both of the divisions which had emerged from it, were charitable that the question of whether Hinduism could be recognized as charitable did not even feature in debate.

It is interesting to consider whether the definition of religion in the Charities Act 2006 expands the law further, or simply endorses the existing practices of the Charity Commission at the time of enactment. It appears that the new definition expressly enacts the recommendations of the Strategy Unit report that any statutory definition include multi-deity and non-deity faiths, where there may be no belief in a god, but there might be a belief in a supreme entity or set of spiritual principles.[148] There appears no longer to be a requirement for worship for a religious charity to be recognized. In its current guidance, the Charity Commission articulate the requirement of worship as:

a relationship between the believer and the supreme being or entity by showing worship of, reverence for or veneration of the supreme being or entity.[149]

In charities where there is no worship of a supreme being, the Commission suggest that the requirement many be fulfilled if the religion concerned instils a sense of 'connectedness' with the spiritual belief system or transcendental entities in such religions, particularly where this instils 'in followers or adherents feelings of self-worth which might motivate or be expressed through the quality of life they lead and in meaningful and purposeful activity, especially that which involves helping others and inspiring others to do likewise'.[150] The Commission cite Jainism as an example, where there is no worship of a supreme being, but the teaching of a supreme being or entity serves to inspire followers to lead better lives.[151]

Whether reliance upon a set of spiritual principles without worship or recognition of a supreme being can be considered to be a 'religion' has yet to be seen. The statutory definition is of little help, since it does not define religion as such, but only eliminates some limitations expressed in previous case law. The Charity Commission guidance seems, at present, to continue to require belief in a supreme being.

---

[147] [1999] 1 Ch 219.

[148] See Strategy Unit, *Private Action, Public Benefit* (2002), paras 4.32–4.34. See further Lloyd, *Charities—The New Law 2006: A Practical Guide to the Charities Acts* (2008), Ch 2. See also Charity Commission, *The Advancement of Religion for the Public Benefit* (December 2008), where the Commission adopts this viewpoint.

[149] Charity Commission, *The Advancement of Religion for the Public Benefit* (December 2008), p 8.

[150] Ibid. Annex A, at p 23.   [151] Ibid.

What of the fate of the Church of Scientology?[152] In contrast to the position in England, in Australia Scientology has been held to be a religion and entitled to charitable status and tax exemptions.[153] This appears to have been on the basis that Australian law does not require that there must be a belief in a deity. It is suggested that the law after the Charities Act 2006 in England and Wales would continue to exclude the Church of Scientology from registration as a charity for the advancement of religion, as the necessary 'connectedness' would not be evident in the system of audit for there to be worship of a supreme being. The law still requires some veneration, albeit obliquely, of a supreme being.

(b) Equal treatment of different religions

Given that the benefit the court assumes to derive from a trust for the advancement of religion is the benefit of an improved life through religious belief, it follows that the precise nature of the religious belief is not important, and the law does not discriminate between different faiths and traditions. This was expressed by Cross J in *Neville Estates Ltd v Madden*:

as between different religions the law stands neutral, but it assumes that any religion is at least as likely to be better than none.

The promotion of the Christian religion in all its denominational forms is clearly charitable, and despite little authority it seems that the mainstream non-Christian religions will be treated similarly.[154] In contrast to their willingness to attempt to assess the value of research or supposed art, the courts have not in the past weighed the merits of religious belief. Thus, in *Re Watson*[155] a trust to promote the works of H G Hobbs, the leader of a small group of non-denominational Christians comprising only members of his family, was held charitable despite the unanimous conclusion of expert evidence that they were of no value.

If past authority is followed, it seems that sects and cults will be charitable provided that they are not destructive to the whole concept of religion or contrary to the foundations of society, no matter how obscure or foolish their beliefs. In *Thornton v Howe*[156] a trust to promote the publication of the works of Johanna Southcote, who claimed that she was the mother of the second messiah was held charitable. The Unification Church (commonly known as the 'Moonies') has been registered as a charity.

What remains to be seen is whether there will be a change in practice following the express requirement of proof of public benefit for all charities, with no exception being made for religious charities.

---

[152] For interesting commentaries of the Charity Commission's decision from the perspective of human rights, see Quint and Spring 'Religion, *Charity Law* and Human Rights' (1999) *Charity Law and Practice Review* 153; Harding 'Trusts for Religious Purposes and the Question of Public Benefit' (2008) MLR 159.

[153] *Church of the New Faith v Comr of Pay-Roll Tax* (1983) 49 ALR 65.

[154] See the discussion above in relation to Buddhism and Hinduism. *Straus v Goldsmid* (1837) 8 Sim 614, *Re Michel's Trust* (1860) 28 Beav 39 and *Neville Estates Ltd v Madden* [1962] Ch 832 for the promotion of Judaism. The Charity Commission has also registered organizations or trusts for the promotion of Islam.

[155] [1973] 1 WLR 1472.   [156] (1862) 31 Beav 125.

(c) Purposes ancillary to religion

Purposes ancillary to the advancement of religion will also be charitable. The construction or maintenance[157] of religious buildings, and even the provision of bells,[158] have been held charitable. Provision for the benefit of religious ministers, retired missionaries,[159] and the church choir[160] have also been held charitable.

(d) Gifts to religious leaders

Gifts made to religious leaders in their capacity as such will be considered charitable gifts for the advancement of religion, provided that the gifts are exclusively for the spiritual work of the leader. In *Re Flinn*[161] a gift to the Archbishop of Westminster for 'such purposes as he shall in his absolute discretion think fit' was held charitable, as was a gift to the Bishop of the Windward Islands 'to be used by him as he thinks fit in his diocese'.[162] In *Farley v Westminster Bank*[163] a gift to a vicar for his 'work in the parish' was held charitable, but in *Re Simson*[164] a gift to a vicar for his 'parish work' was held not to be charitable, since as a matter of construction it was held that his 'parish work' may include work which was not exclusively charitable. This distinction is tenuous, if not spurious.

(e) Advancement, not merely belief

A purpose will not be charitable simply because it involves belief in a religion. It must be for the *advancement* of religion. In other words, the activities involved must in some way promote, maintain, or practice the religion or encourage or increase belief in the faith concerned.[165] In *United Grand Lodge of Ancient Free and Accepted Masons of England v Holborn Borough Council*,[166] freemasonry was held not to be charitable because it did not advance religion as such, but merely encouraged its members to lead a good moral life. Current examples of purposes that advance religion can be found in Annex B to the latest Charity Commission guidance, *The Advancement of Education for the Public Benefit*.[167]

(4) Advancement of health or the saving of lives

(a) Medical and healthcare charities

This is the first of the new categories of charitable purpose added by the Charities Act 2006. It does not represent an entirely new category, but simply a subdivision of what in Lord Macnaghten's classification would have been considered 'other purposes beneficial to the community'. The preamble to the Statute of Charitable Uses referred

---

[157] *Re Hooper* [1932] 1 Ch 38—trust to upkeep a tablet and a window in a church.
[158] *Re Pardoe* [1906] 2 Ch 184.   [159] *Re Mylne* [1941] Ch 204.
[160] *Re Royce* [1940] Ch 514.   [161] [1948] Ch 241.   [162] *Re Rumball* [1956] Ch 105.
[163] [1939] AC 430, HL.   [164] [1946] Ch 299.
[165] Charity Commission, *The Advancement of Religion for the Public Benefit* (December 2008), p 8.
[166] [1957] 1 WLR 1080.   [167] (2008), at pp 24–26.

to the relief of the 'aged, impotent and poor'. The word 'impotent' in this context does not have its modern meaning relating to sexual function, but was used in a more general archaic sense to refer to incapacity, infirmity, or illness. In *Joseph Rowntree Memorial Trust Housing Association Ltd v A-G*,[168] it was held that the words of the preamble were to be read disjunctively. It has therefore been recognized for four centuries that the provision of medical care is a charitable purpose.[169] In *Re Smith's Will Trusts*[170] the Court of Appeal held that a gift to be applied to the benefit of such hospitals as the trustees in their absolute discretion thought fit was charitable. The court considered that the testator, who had made his will before the creation of the National Health Service, had meant hospitals dependent on voluntary contributions and not nursing homes run for private profit, which would not be charitable.[171] The provision of health care is not confined to conventional treatment. In *Funnell v Stewart*[172] the court held that a trust to further the work of a group offering faith healing was charitable. The view of the Charity Commission is that the promotion of alternative and complementary therapies can be charitable, but evidence is required of its efficacy:

Assessing the efficacy of different therapies will depend upon what benefits are claimed for it (ie whether it is diagnostic, curative, therapeutic and/or palliative) and whether it is offered as a complement to conventional medicine or as an alternative. Each case is considered on its merits, but the 6th Report of the House of Lords Select Committee on Science and Technology (Session 1999–2000) on complementary and alternative medicine provides a useful guide.[173]

It also seems clear that this category of charitable purpose extends beyond formal health care to include services to ease the suffering of the sick, disabled, or infirm.[174] A hospice providing palliative care for the terminally ill would therefore fall within this category.

(b) Imposition of fees or charges for treatment[175]

Hospitals can be charitable even if they charge for the treatment they provide, even if as a result their services are only available to those who are capable of paying or have insurance. In *Re Resch's Will Trusts*[176] a gift of $8m was made to the St Vincent's Private Hospital. The Privy Council held that this was a valid charitable gift, and that there was sufficient benefit to the community resulting from 'the beds and medical staff of the general hospital, the availability of a particular type of nursing and treatment which supplements that provided by the general hospital and the benefit to the standard of medical care in the general hospital which arises from the juxtaposition

---

[168] [1983] Ch 159.
[169] See more recently the Charity Commission publication CC6—*Charities for the Relief of Sickness* (2000).
[170] [1962] 2 All ER 563.   [171] Ibid., at 564, per Lord Denning MR.
[172] [1996] 1 WLR 288.
[173] Charity Commission, *Commentary on the Descriptions of Charitable Purposes in the Charities Act 2006* (August 2009), para 25.
[174] Ibid., at para 26. There is thus likely to be some overlap between this category and the relief of those in need in s 2(2)(j) of the Charities Act 2006.
[175] See also the discussion below on the impact of fees upon public benefit.   [176] [1969] 1 AC 514.

of the two institutions'.[177] Again, it was emphasized that if the hospital was carried on as a commercial venture, with a view to making profits for individuals, then it would not be charitable.[178] This means that the majority of privately owned and run nursing homes and old people's homes will not be charitable. This is sensible, since profit-making ventures do not warrant the tax privileges granted to charities.

(c) Saving lives (and property)

Trusts for the protection of human life and property have been held to be charitable as falling within the 'spirit and intendment' of the preamble. For example, in *Re Wokingham Fire Brigade Trusts*[179] the provision of a voluntary fire brigade was held charitable. The Royal National Lifeboat Institution is also charitable.[180] Clearly, such services must not exist to make profits for individuals, which would rule out commercial organizations offering emergency services. The Charity Commission considers that a trust for the provision of emergency services or services assisting the emergency services, or for the provision of life-saving or self-defence classes, could be considered charitable purposes under this head.[181]

(d) Analogous and ancillary purposes

The Charities Act 2006 makes it clear that the advancement of health is to be given an expansive meaning. It states that it 'includes the prevention or relief of sickness, disease or human suffering'.[182] As with trusts for the advancement of education and religion, purposes ancillary to the provision of medical care are charitable, so in *Re Bernstein's Will Trusts*[183] a surgeon's gift of part of his residuary estate to provide extra comforts at Christmas for the nurses of a specified hospital was held charitable. In *London Hospital Medical College v IRC*[184] a students' union at a medical school was held charitable as being a practical necessity to the efficient functioning of the school. The Charity Commission has also decided that the General Medical Council should be registered as a charity on the grounds that it was established for the charitable propose of 'the protection, promotion and maintenance of the health and safety if the community' by ensuring proper standards in the practice of medicine.[185]

(5) Advancement of citizenship or community development

The Charity Commission considers that this head of charity covers a broad range or purposes 'directed towards support for social and community infrastructure which is focused on the community rather than the individual'.[186]

---

[177] Ibid., at 540, per Lord Wilberforce.   [178] [1969] 1 AC 514.
[179] [1951] Ch 373.   [180] *Re David* (1889) 43 Ch D 27.
[181] Charity Commission, *Commentary on the Descriptions of Charitable Purposes in the Charities Act 2006* (August 2009), para 28.
[182] S 2(3)(b).   [183] (1971) 115 Sol Jo 808.   [184] [1976] 1 WLR 613.
[185] Decision of the Charity Commissioners, 2 April 2001.
[186] Charity Commission, *Commentary on the Descriptions of Charitable Purposes in the Charities Act 2006* (August 2009), para 29.

(a) Rural or urban regeneration

Section 2(3)(c) of the Charities Act 2006 states that this head of charitable purpose 'includes rural or urban regeneration'. This is a category of charity recognized by the Charity Commission[187] before the passing of the 2006 Act and is an area of activity on which the Commission has issued guidance.[188] In order to attain charitable status, an organization must seek to maintain or improve 'the physical, social and economic infrastructure' and assist people 'who are at a disadvantage because of their social and economic circumstances'. Such purposes might include: providing financial assistance to people who are poor; providing or improving housing standards; helping people find employment; providing education, training, and retraining; providing assistance to businesses, including land and buildings on favourable terms; providing and maintaining roads and transport; providing, maintaining, and improving recreational facilities; preserving historic buildings in the area; providing public amenities.[189]

(b) Promotion of community capacity building

The Charity Commission has decided that the promotion of community capacity building in relation to communities that are socially or economically disadvantaged should be recognized as charitable.[190] Community capacity building means 'developing the capacity and skills of the members of a community in such as way that they are better able to identify, and help meet, their needs and to participate more fully in society'.[191] This might involve: equipping people with skills and competencies; realizing existing skills and developing potential; promoting people's increased self-confidence; promoting people's ability to take responsibility for identifying and meeting their own, and other people's, needs; encouraging people to become involved in their community and wider society in a fuller way.[192]

(c) Civic responsibility and good citizenship[193]

Organizations such as the Guides and Scouts would be considered charitable under this category. Another example, reported by the Charity Commission in their Annual Report for 2004–2005 is 'Funky Dragon', the Welsh youth parliament.

(d) Promoting ethical standards in business and corporate responsibility

Despite the extensiveness of the list of charitable purposes set out in the Charities Act 2006, there are many examples of charitable activity that are hard to classify. For instance, even though there was no direct judicial authority, the Charity Commission has decided to recognize as charitable organizations which promote the incorporation of ethics into business practice, and which advise and protect

[187] See *Charity Commission Annual Report 2003–2004*, p 8.
[188] RR2—*Promotion of Urban and Rural Regeneration*.
[189] Ibid., para 7.   [190] RR5—*The Promotion of Community Capacity Building* (Nov 2000).
[191] Ibid., para 7.   [192] Ibid., para 13.
[193] The promotion of civic responsibility is specifically included within this head by Charities Act 2006, s 2(3)(c)(ii).

vulnerable employees faced with ethical dilemmas in the course of their work. In the light of this, the Commission considered that the objects of the Centre of Corporate Accountability, which sought to promote safety by encouraging corporate account-ability for breaches of health and safety laws, were capable of being charitable, although the organization itself was held not to be charitable because its objects were also political.[194]

(e) Volunteering and the voluntary sector

Volunteering consists of engaging in action which is not compulsory, for which finan-cial reward is not the primary motivation, and which benefits others or society.[195] According to the Home Office Citizenship Survey in 2003, more than 50 per cent of the adult population volunteers.[196] Volunteering makes a very substantial contribution to many areas of life, including culture and the arts, sport and recreation, conservation and regeneration, health and care, and politics. Some volunteering is done on an indi-vidual basis, but much operates through what is called the voluntary sector. The volun-tary sector comprises organizations which are 'formally constituted, independent of government, self-governing, not profit distributing, primarily non-business and that benefit from voluntarism'.[197] These organizations are established for purposes that add value to the community. Some, but not all voluntary sector organizations are charit-able. For instance, housing associations providing social housing for disadvantaged groups and community care associations providing care in the community for indi-viduals with disabilities or mental health problems may be either charitable or non-charitable, depending upon their objects. Section 2(3)(c)(ii) of the Charities Act 2006 adds the promotion of volunteering and the voluntary sector to this head of charity.

(f) Promoting the efficiency of charities

Promoting the effectiveness or efficiency of charities is added to the list of charita-ble purposes under this head by s 2(3)(c)(ii) of the Charities Act 2006. While this is a slightly unusual categorization, there could be little doubt that trusts seeking to enhance the effectiveness of charities would be recognized as beneficial to the public, since they could only be encouraging the better performance of functions which have already been held, themselves, to be charitable.

[194] Decision of the Charity Commission for England and Wales, Application for Registration of the Centre for Corporate Accountability, 24 August 2001.

[195] See the definition contained in the United Nations Volunteers Report, prepared for the UN General Assembly Special Session on Social Development, Geneva, June 2004 and cited in the Russell Commission Report 2005, p 13. The Russell Commission was established in May 2004 by the then Home Secretary, David Blunkett, and the Chancellor of the Exchequer, Gordon Brown, to develop a new national framework for youth action and engagement. A new charity, 'V' (registered charity no: 1113255) was set up as a result in May 2006.

[196] Russell Commission Report 2005, p 19.

[197] RR13—*The Promotion of the Voluntary Sector for the Benefit of the Public* (September 2004), para 3.

(6) **Advancement of the arts, culture, heritage, or science**

(a) Art, culture, and education

Trusts which promote an appreciation of the arts and other cultural activities have long been held to be charitable. Prior to the re-categorization of charities by the Charities Act 2006, this was because such purposes were considered to be extensions of Lord Macnaghten's category of trusts for the advancement of education. A trust to promote the works of William Shakespeare has been held charitable,[198] as has a trust to hold exhibitions of Egyptian archaeological finds.[199] In *Royal Choral Society v IRC*[200] the society, whose purposes were 'to form and maintain a choir in order to promote the practice and performance of choral works', was held charitable by the Court of Appeal. Lord Greene MR rejected the narrow view of education as teaching that had been proposed by counsel for the Inland Revenue, and stated that 'the education of artistic taste is one of the most important things in the development of a civilised human being'. This approach was followed in *Re Delius (Decd)*,[201] where Roxburgh J held charitable a trust to promote the music of the composer Frederick Delius. In *IRC v White*[202] the Clerkenwell Green Association of Craftsmen, which existed to further crafts and craftsmanship, was held charitable. Charitable purposes within this head can include societies supporting the arts, local or national history or archaeology, the establishment or support of museums, the preservation of ancient sites or buildings, or an individual monument.[203] Purposes that are too vague and uncertain will not be held charitable. So in *Associated Artists Ltd v IRC*[204] the promotion of 'artistic dramatic works' was not considered charitable.

(b) Monuments

A trust to erect a public statue of Earl Mountbatten of Burma was considered charitable by the Charity Commissioners.[205] The chief consideration was that the person to be commemorated could be said to be a figure of historical importance. The benefit of such a statue was that it would foster patriotism and good citizenship, and act as an incentive to heroic and noble deeds. Memorials to private individuals of no such historical importance will not be charitable.[206] The Charity Commission accepted in 2003 that an appeal to provide a new statue in Banbury to celebrate the nursery rhyme 'Ride a cock horse to Banbury Cross, to see a fine lady upon a white horse' was charitable on the grounds of a trust for the enhancement of a locality and raising artistic taste, even though it was not accepted that the associated activities proposed in the

---

[198] *Re Shakespeare Memorial Trust* [1923] 2 Ch 398.
[199] *Re British School of Egyptian Archaeology* [1954] 1 WLR 546.
[200] [1943] 2 All ER 101.   [201] [1957] Ch 299.   [202] [1980] TR 155.
[203] See Charity Commission, *Commentary on the Descriptions of Charitable Purposes in the Charities Act 2006* (August 2009), para 35.
[204] [1956] 1 WLR 752.
[205] Report of the Charity Commissioners for England and Wales 1981, paras 68–70.
[206] See *Re Endacott* [1960] Ch 232, CA.

application for registration were of educational value.[207] It is suggested that this decision might now be explained as an example of the preservation of heritage,[208] as an activity 'concerned with preserving or maintaining a particular tradition where the benefit to the public in preserving it can be shown'.[209]

(c) A requirement of merit

Despite the desire to uphold gifts that genuinely advance artistic and cultural appreciation, the Charity Commission and the courts are astute to ensure that gifts that promote purposes of no artistic merit are not held charitable. The very nature of art makes it difficult for the courts to exercise objective judgments as to what is artistically valuable, and what is not. One man's masterpiece is another man's rubbish. In *Re Delius*[210] it was suggested that the subjective nature of such a judgment would mean that the court would have no option but to hold charitable a trust to promote the work of even an inadequate composer. On the facts, the issue did not arise because the high standard of Delius's work was not challenged. However, it is now clear that the court will take expert advice as to the value of work of supposed artistic merit, and if the expert advice is unanimous that it is of no value, then the courts will not find that there is a charity for the advancement of education.[211] In *Re Pinion (Decd)*[212] Harry Pinion had been a prolific collector of paintings, furniture, china, glass, and other objets d'art. On his death he left his residuary estate to trustees to open his studio as a museum housing the collection. Expert witnesses considered the merits of the collection, and were unanimous in their conclusion that it was of no value. Indeed, one expert expressed his surprise that such a voracious collector had not even managed to pick up a single meritorious piece by accident. In the light of this evidence the Court of Appeal held that the trust was not charitable. Harman LJ concluded 'I can conceive of no useful object to be served in foisting upon the public this mass of junk.'

(d) Can the vernacular and the popular have merit?

There is an increasing interest in the study of the vernacular, and of the need to preserve historical evidence of the way of life of ordinary people in the past. The National Trust, for instance, has preserved an ordinary terraced house in the North of England, using it to reflect a comparatively recently bygone way of life.[213] Industrial and folk museums have developed in recent years. No doubt all of these could be considered

---

[207] *Re The Fine Lady Upon A White Horse Appeal* [2006] WTLR 59.

[208] See Charity Commission RR9, *Preservation and Conservation* (February 2001).

[209] Charity Commission, *Commentary on the Descriptions of Charitable Purposes in the Charities Act 2006* (August 2009), para 33.

[210] [1957] Ch 299.

[211] This is reflected in the Charity Commission's review of the register, which sets out the selection requirements of such experts—Charity Commission, RR10 *Museums and Art Galleries* (August 2002) paras A12–A17.

[212] [1965] Ch 85.

[213] 20 Forthlin Road, Liverpool (Paul McCartney's former council house home) has been opened to the public by the National Trust.

charitable, even though they reflect 'ordinary' rather than 'high' culture. What the courts have yet to address specifically, however, is whether the promotion and assistance of popular culture and music can be charitable. Why should promoting opera, choral music, and the works of Delius be considered charitable if promoting the musical compositions of the Beatles or Lady GaGa is not? Are the only values that the law should uphold as charitable those which are held by the elite and not those held by the masses? The courts have not yet made this clear, nor can anything be inferred from the latest Charity Commission guidance on the issue, which simply refers to 'the arts of drama, ballet, music, singing, literature, sculpture, painting, cinema, mime, etc.'.[214]

(7) Advancement of amateur sport

(a) Promotion of sport *per se*

It was originally considered that trusts encouraging the playing of sport would not in themselves be considered charitable. The leading case was *Re Nottage*,[215] in which it was held that establishing a prize for ocean yacht racing was not charitable. There had to be some factor other than the playing of sport that justified a conclusion that the purpose was charitable. For instance, in an era when archers formed an essential part of the armed forces, a trust to promote archery practice would have been considered charitable since it helped to promote the defence of the realm by providing a cadre of skilled archers.

(b) Sport and the advancement of education

A line of authority supported the view that the promotion of sport in schools and universities would be regarded as for the advancement of education, since, as Lord Hailsham indicated in *IRC v McMullen*,[216] education includes 'spiritual, moral, mental and physical elements'. In *Re Mariette*[217] a gift to provide fives and squash courts at a specific school was held charitable. In *IRC v McMullen*[218] the Football Association had established a trust for the promotion of football and other games or sports in schools and universities. This was held charitable for the advancement of education by the House of Lords, even though the gift was not for the benefit of any specific institution. The promotion of intellectually stimulating games was also held to be charitable, and in *Re Dupree's Deed Trusts*[219] the gift of a prize for chess to boys

---

[214] See Charity Commission, *Commentary on the Descriptions of Charitable Purposes in the Charities Act 2006* (August 2009), para 35.

[215] [1895] 2 Ch 649, CA. It may be wondered whether the nature of the sport was relevant. Ocean yacht racing has sometimes been described as being as pleasurable as standing under a cold shower tearing up £50 notes. However, cases subsequent to *Re Nottage* have held that even sports of the common man, such as athletics and football, are not charitable.

[216] [1981] AC 1, HL.   [217] [1915] 2 Ch 284.   [218] [1981] AC 1.

[219] [1945] Ch 16.

and young men resident in Portsmouth was held charitable. In contrast, in 1989 the Charity Commissioners refused charitable status to the Birchfield Harriers, a leading athletic club, on the basis that there was an insufficient element of education in their activities.[220]

(c) Sport, health, and community interest

In November 2002 the Charity Commissioners decided that Community Amateur Sports Clubs (CASCs) should be recognized as charitable:

As part of our *Review of the Register* project, we have looked at the relationship between sport and charity in the light of modern social conditions. We have taken account of the enormous public interest in sport as a means of promoting health and the vital role that sport plays in improving the health of the nation. We have concluded that, within the law as it stands, we can properly recognise as charitable bodies that set out to encourage community participation in healthy sports.[221]

By the date of the Charity Commission's Annual Report for 2003–2004, 120 CASCs had been registered.[222] It is this development that has formed the basis for the head of promotion of amateur sport contained in the Charities Act 2006.

(d) Healthy recreation

The Charity Commission view was that 'it is the close and obvious connection between physical exercise and physical health that makes the provision of facilities for healthy recreation charitable'.[223] The test that the Charity Commission applied was that:

Sports that are capable of providing 'healthy recreation' are those sports which, if practised with reasonable frequency, will tend to make the participant healthier, that is, fitter and less susceptible to disease. Fitness includes elements of stamina, strength and suppleness (there may be others), but it will be enough if a sport contributes to just one of these elements.[224]

(e) Statutory extension of the promotion of sport

The Charities Act 2006 extends the category of sporting activity that can be held to be charitable. By s 2(2)(g) the promotion of amateur sport is a charitable purpose. Only sports that involve 'physical skill and exertion' are charitable under this head.[225] This reflects the similar restriction that the Charity Commission applied to the recognition of Community Amateur Sports Clubs. It is unlikely that promoting the playing of darts or snooker would be considered to be charitable under this head. More difficulty might be experienced with a game such as lawn bowls, where the extent of exertion required is modest.

---

[220] Report of the Charity Commissioners for England and Wales 1989, para 52.
[221] RR11—*Charitable Status and Sport* (April 2003), para 5.
[222] *Charity Commission Annual Report for 2003–2004*, p 5.
[223] RR11—*Charitable Status and Sport* (April 2003), para 8.
[224] Ibid., para 9.   [225] Charities Act 2006, s 2(3)(d).

(f) Not all amateur sports clubs are charitable

It does not follow that because it is possible for an amateur sports club to be charitable that all clubs will satisfy the requirements to be charitable. This might be because benefits are confined to a small, private, group of members, as may be the case with some golf clubs. It might be because the sport does not satisfy the test of promoting health or involving physical exertion and skill. It might be because the sport is insufficiently inclusive. For instance, ocean yacht racing has been described as a sport for those who enjoy tearing up £10 notes while standing under a cold shower. It is an expensive sport that is generally confined to people with significant means. Without evidence that people from all levels of society have the potential to participate, it is likely that a trust to provide an annual prize for ocean yacht racing would still not be considered to be charitable.[226] Polo and motor racing may also be considered to be 'elite' sports which fail to satisfy the test of public benefit, unless a trust to promote these sports includes measures which enable participation by people who, without the support offered by the trust, could not afford to acquire the expensive equipment needed.[227] The Charity Commissioners refused charitable status to the Birchfield Harriers, a leading athletics club, since they existed to promote competitive sport, rather than to provide sporting facilities to the public.[228] Certain amateur sports clubs can register with HM Customs & Revenue in order to gain tax-exempt status under the Finance Act 2002, Sch 18, but it is not possible following the Charities Act 2006 for a club to be both registered in this way and to be a registered charity.[229]

(8) Advancement of human rights, conflict resolution, and equality

(a) A broad category

This new head of charity contained in the Charities Act 2006 has the longest description. It comprises 'the advancement of human rights, conflict resolution or reconciliation or the promotion of religious or racial harmony or equality and diversity'. This is a category of charitable purpose that, perhaps more than any other, reflects changes in society and social attitudes. The category is clearly of considerable scope.

(b) Advancement of human rights

The advancement of human rights is now seen as being charitable by analogy with other charitable purposes,[230] a position confirmed by the Charities Act 2006. The Charity Commission has provided detailed guidance on the recognition of human

---

[226] See *Re Nottage* above.

[227] RR11—*Charitable Status and Sport* (April 2003), para 26.

[228] *Report of the Charity Commissioners for England and Wales 1989*, para 54.

[229] Charities Act 2006, s 5(4).

[230] RR12—*The Promotion of Human Rights* (January 2005), para 8: 'Given that respect for human rights is widely regarded as a moral imperative, the well-established charitable purpose of promoting the moral or spiritual welfare and improvement of the community provides a sufficient (but not the only) analogy for treating the promotion of human rights generally as charitable.'

rights charities, and revised this guidance following the recommendation of the Prime Minister's Strategy Unit in *Private Action, Public Benefit*[231] that the Commission should take a more positive approach to campaigning by charities. The problem is that the promotion of human rights may often require advocating a change in the law, and advocating such a change has been held to be a political purpose that cannot therefore be charitable.[232] By adopting a less cautionary view of what is permissible in relation to political campaigning, the Charity Commission has enabled human rights charities to be registered, even if seeking to influence government policy or to change the law may be activities that the charity will undertake. The Commission has provided what it considers a model set of objects for a human rights charity:[233]

To promote human rights (as set out in the Universal Declaration of Human Rights and subsequent United Nations conventions and declarations)[234] throughout the world by all or any of the following means:

- monitoring abuses of human rights;
- obtaining redress for the victims of human rights abuse;
- relieving need among the victims of human rights abuse;
- research into human rights issues;
- educating the public about human rights;
- providing technical advice to government and others on human rights matters;
- contributing to the sound administration of human rights law;
- commenting on proposed human rights legislation;
- raising awareness of human rights issues;
- promoting public support for human rights;
- promoting respect for human rights among individuals and corporations;
- international advocacy of human rights;
- eliminating infringements of human rights.

In furtherance of that object but not otherwise, the trustees shall have power

- to engage in political activity provided that the trustees are satisfied that the proposed activities will further the purposes of the charity to an extent justified by the resources committed and the activity is not the dominant means by which the charity carries out its objects;

(c) Advancement of conflict resolution or reconciliation

This description would include a trust seeking to resolve national or international conflicts, and also a trust promoting restorative justice 'where all the parties with a

---

[231] September 2002.

[232] Charities and political purposes are considered further below, at pp 621–627.

[233] Charity Commission RR12—*The Promotion of Human Rights* (January 2005), para 37. This is supplemented by *Commentary on the Descriptions of Purposes under the Charities Act 2006* (August 2009), paras 39–42.

[234] Since there are different codes of human rights, it is important that the objects of the charity define which code of human rights it is proposed to promote: RR12—*The Promotion of Human Rights* (January 2005), para 13.

stake in a particular conflict or offence come together to resolve collectively how to deal with its aftermath and its implications for the future'.[235]

(d) The promotion of religious or racial harmony or equality and diversity

The Charity Commission has indicated that this head will include a broad range of charitable activities, including enabling people to understand the religious beliefs of others, promoting equality and diversity by eliminating discrimination on the grounds of age, sex, or sexual orientation, as well as the promotion of good relations between different groups.[236]

The promotion of equality between men and women was held charitable in *Halpin v Steear*.[237] The promotion of good community relations has more recently come to be recognized as a charitable purpose, demonstrating that the law of charity is able to develop to meet the social needs of the day, and to reflect the current moral agenda.[238] In *Re Strakosch (Decd)*[239] a gift to be used to appease racial feeling between the Dutch- and English-speaking sections of the South African community was held not to be charitable on the basis that it was a political purpose, too vague, and might include very wide objects, some of which would not be charitable. It had been thought that this decision rendered the promotion of racial harmony a non-charitable object. However, the Charity Commissioners have taken the view that the promotion of racial harmony is analogous to other purposes that the courts have held charitable, and have accepted that 'promoting good race relations, endeavouring to eliminate discrimination on grounds of race and encouraging equality of opportunity between persons of different racial groups' are charitable purposes.[240] The promotion of religious harmony was accepted as charitable by the Charity Commission in 2002 when it registered The Friends of Three Faiths Forum, an organization intended to promote religious harmony by enabling people of one faith to understand the religious beliefs of others. The three faiths concerned were Christianity, Judaism, and Islam. The Commissioners considered that the purposes were charitable by virtue of the analogy 'to the existing purposes of promoting equality of women with men, promoting racial harmony and promoting the moral or spiritual welfare or improvement of the community'.[241]

---

[235] Charity Commission, *Commentary on the Descriptions of Charitable Purposes in the Charities Act 2006* (August 2009), para 40. The promotion of restorative justice was recognized as a charitable purpose by the Charity Commission in 2003: *Charity Commission Annual Report 2003–2004*, p 11.

[236] Charity Commission, *Commentary on the Descriptions of Charitable Purposes in the Charities Act 2006* (August 2009), para 42.

[237] (27 February 1976, unreported).

[238] RR1—*The Review of the Register of Charities* (2001), para B1.

[239] [1949] Ch 529, CA.

[240] Report of the Charity Commissioners for England and Wales 1983, paras 18–20.

[241] *Charity Commission Annual Report 2002–2003*, p 22.

(9) **Advancement of environmental protection or improvement**

The preservation of national heritage and conservation of the environment are charitable purposes under the 2006 Act. The National Trust is charitable,[242] since its objects of 'promoting the permanent preservation for the benefit of the nation of lands and tenements (including buildings) of beauty or historic interest and as regards lands for the preservation... of their natural aspect features and animal and plant life'[243] are for the public benefit. In their 1973 Annual Report the Charity Commissioners reported that they had registered as charitable the Advisory Committee on Oil Pollution of the Sea, which sought to preserve the sea in general, and especially the seas around the United Kingdom from pollution.[244] In 2001, the Charity Commission recognized the conservation of the environment as a charitable purpose in its own right, including organizations that conserve the environment by promoting biodiversity.[245] Where the organization is set up to maintain a particular building, site, or habitat, the element of public benefit will only be satisfied if the public have access. While there is a presumption that public benefit requires physical access, if there are valid reasons for limiting or excluding such access the public benefit element may be satisfied if the organization puts in place alternative means of informing the public about its activities.[246] In April 2002 the Charity Commission therefore decided that Recycling in Ottery, a company which sought to 'protect and safeguard the environment particularly through the promotion of re-use and recycling and the provision of recycling facilities', and which ran a scrap yard where members of the public could bring items for recycling, was charitable.[247] However, environmental campaign groups that have primarily political purposes will not enjoy charitable status.[248]

(10) **Relief of need**

It has already been seen that the Statute of Charitable Uses recognized that charitable purposes included the relief of poverty, infirmity, and illness. These are merely examples of need, and other (mainly now archaic) examples are contained in the preamble to the 1601 Statute. The Charities Act 2006 states that it is a charitable purpose to provide relief for those in need 'by reason of youth, age, ill-health, disability, financial hardship or other disadvantage'.[249] This 'includes relief given by the provision of accommodation or care to the persons mentioned in that paragraph'.[250]

[242] *Re Verrall* [1916] 1 Ch 100.   [243] National Trust Act 1907, s 4(1).
[244] Report of the Charity Commissioners for England and Wales 1973, para 40.
[245] RR1—*The Review of the Register of Charities* (2001), para B9.
[246] RR9—*Preservation and Conservation* (Feb 2001), paras A18–A20.
[247] Decision of the Charity Commissions for England and Wales, *Application for Registration of Recycling in Ottery*, April 2002.
[248] See below pp 621 *et seq*.   [249] Charities Act 2006, s 2(2)(j).
[250] S 2(3)(e).

(a) Examples of the relief of need

There is clearly considerable overlap between this head of charity and the head relating to the relief of poverty and the advancement of health, and many trusts that are charitable under those heads would also be charitable within this category. The category would clearly include the provision of social housing, since this is expressly included in the category. In *Joseph Rowntree Memorial Trust Housing Association Ltd v A-G*,[251] the Housing Association, which wished to build small dwellings for sale to the elderly, was considered charitable even though those who would benefit by purchasing the dwellings would not fall within the definition of 'poor'. Other forms of assistance to disadvantaged groups would also be charitable. For example, the relief of unemployment was not historically a charitable object in itself, though organizations that have helped unemployed people have been considered charitable under the categories of advancing education or relieving poverty. As part of its review of the Register, the Charity Commission decided in 1999 that an organization for the relief of unemployment would be charitable per se if it can be demonstrated that it is tackling unemployment, either generally or for a significant section of the community. Acceptable activities include the provision of: advice and training to unemployed individuals; practical support for unemployed people by way of accommodation, child care facilities, or assistance with travel; land, and buildings at below market or subsidized rents to businesses starting up; capital grants or equipment to new businesses; and payments to an existing commercial business to take on additional staff.[252]

It is not necessary that the needs relieved relate only to the United Kingdom. The Charity Commission has held the promotion of trading fairly is a charitable purpose. Thus in 1995 it registered as a charity an organization which would award a 'fair trade mark' on the packaging of goods sold in supermarkets, which would have the effect of relieving the conditions of life of third-world workers.[253]

(b) Provision of recreational facilities

Until the position was changed by the Recreational Charities Act 1958, the provision of recreational facilities was not, in itself, charitable, even if those facilities are provided to the public at large. This position was established by three decisions of the House of Lords in the mid-twentieth century. In *Williams' Trustees v IRC*[254] a trust was established to promote Welsh interests in London, including the provision of a meeting place to promote the 'moral, social, spiritual and educational welfare of Welsh people'. The House of Lords held that this was not charitable because of the 'social' purposes, although many of the other purposes of the society would be charitable. In *IRC v City of Glasgow Police Athletic Association*,[255] an association which existed 'to encourage and promote all forms of athletic sports and general pastimes' among members of the force claimed charitable status and tax exemption on the

---

[251] [1983] Ch 159.   [252] RR3—*Charities for the Relief of Unemployment* (1999).
[253] RR1—*The Review of the Register of Charities* (2001), para B17.
[254] [1947] AC 447, HL.   [255] [1953] AC 380.

grounds that it promoted the efficiency of the police force, which would be a charitable object. The House of Lords held that the provision of recreation for the members was not purely incidental to the charitable purpose of promoting the efficiency of the force, and therefore the association was not entitled to charitable status. In *IRC v Baddeley*[256] a gift of land was made to a Methodist Mission, including an area laid out as a playing field complete with a pavilion and groundsman's bungalow. The purposes of the gift included 'the provision of facilities for religious services and instruction and for the social and physical training and recreation' of persons resident in West Ham and Leyton. The House of Lords held that this was not a gift made exclusively for charitable purposes, following *Williams' Trustees v IRC*.[257]

A number of cases have held that gifts for the provision of public recreation grounds can be charitable, for example in *Re Hadden*,[258] where a gift was made for the provision of playing fields, parks, and gymnasiums in Vancouver, and in *Re Morgan*,[259] where a gift for the provision of a public recreation ground for a particular parish was held charitable. In *Brisbane City Council v A-G for Queensland*[260] a trust to provide an area for 'a park and recreation purposes' was also held charitable. Viscount Simmonds in *IRC v Baddeley* was careful to stress that the provision of recreation grounds would still be charitable.[261]

The decision in *IRC v Baddeley* gave rise to concern that Women's Institutes and similar organizations, previously considered to be charitable, would no longer qualify for that status. To eliminate any uncertainty, the Recreational Charities Act 1958 was enacted. This Act was not intended to enlarge the definition of charity,[262] but instead to give statutory recognition to purposes already recognized as charitable. The statute covers the provision of 'facilities for recreation or other leisure-time occupation'[263] and specific mention is made of facilities at 'village halls, community centres and women's institutes'.[264] The key provision of the Act is that the facilities must be provided in the 'interests of social welfare'.[265] This requirement cannot be met unless the facilities provided have the object of 'improving the conditions of life for the persons for whom the facilities are primarily intended'[266] and those persons must fall within either of the two groups specified:

1. persons needing such facilities because of their youth, age, infirmity or disability, poverty or social and economic circumstances;[267]

2. the public at large or the male[268] or female members of the public.[269]

---

[256] [1955] AC 572.   [257] [1947] AC 447.   [258] [1932] 1 Ch 133.
[259] [1955] 1 WLR 738.   [260] [1979] AC 411, PC.
[261] [1955] AC 572, at 559: 'I think it right to say that, in my opinion, a gift of land for the use as a recreation ground by the community at large or by the inhabitants of a particular geographical area may well be supported as a valid charity.'
[262] Halsbury's Statutes, Vol 5, p 801.   [263] S 1.   [264] S 2.
[265] S 1.   [266] S 1(2)(a).   [267] S 1(2)(b)(i).
[268] Male members of the public were included by Charities Act 2006, s 5(2). Prior to this, benefits could be confined to female members of the public, but not to male members of the public. While the difference in treatment would now be considered indefensible under the Human Rights Act, at the time of the original enactment of the Recreational Charities Act 1958, it was intended to protect the charitable status of women's institutes.
[269] S 1(2)(b)(ii).

Thus, private clubs, such as golf clubs, which provide facilities only for their members, will not attract charitable status and the consequent tax privileges. Only facilities provided for the public in general, for female members of the public (an early example of positive discrimination), and now male members of the public, or to groups in some way disadvantaged will attract charitable status. For example, in their 1984 Report the Charity Commissioners considered as charitable a company with the object of providing an ice-rink in Oxford that would be available to members of the public at large.[270] Although the Act does not specifically mention ethnic or minority groups, the Charity Commission has considered that it would be charitable to set up a community association or other recreational organization primarily for the use of some identifiable racial minority group.[271] The statute does not exactly define 'social welfare',[272] stating instead the essential elements that must be present. At first instance in *IRC v McMullen*[273] Walton J took the view that 'social welfare' indicates that there must be some kind of deprivation and that as a class, pupils at schools and universities cannot be described as 'deprived'.[274] In the Court of Appeal[275] Bridge LJ rejected that view, stating 'the village hall may improve the conditions of life for the squire and his family as well as for the cottagers'. This was the view of the Charity Commissioners,[276] and was approved by the House of Lords in *Guild v IRC*.[277] Lord Keith expressly stated that Walton J's approach had been incorrect, and that 'persons in all walks of life and all sorts of social circumstances may have their conditions of life improved by the provision of recreational facilities of a suitable character'.[278] A gift for use in connection with a sports centre in North Berwick was therefore held charitable. The fact that patrons must pay reasonable charges for the use of the facilities does not deprive the activity of its charitable status.

The Charity Commission has published its view as to the scope of s 1 of the Recreational Charities Act as part of its review of the Register of Charities.[279] The Commission suggests that an organization will only be charitable under the Act if it is altruistic in character, meaning that it seeks to provide something for the benefit of others, rather than for itself. Thus a social club established by a group of people for their own benefit will not gain charitable status because they are not engaged in 'social welfare'. It also suggests that it will be more difficult to accept that the provision of facilities for the playing of a single sport meets the requirement of social welfare, in contrast to multi-purpose sports facilities provided for the public at large which promote healthy recreation.[280]

---

[270] *Report of the Charity Commissioners for England and Wales for 1984*, para 19.
[271] RR1A—*Recognising New Charitable Purposes* (October 2001), para B14.
[272] See *Valuation Comr for Northern Ireland v Lurgan Borough Council* [1968] NI 104, at 126–127, per Lord MacDermott LCJ.
[273] [1978] 1 WLR 664.   [274] Ibid., at 675.   [275] [1979] 1 WLR 130.
[276] *Report of the Charity Commissioners for England and Wales 1989*, para 55.
[277] [1992] 2 AC 310, [1992] 2 All ER 10.   [278] [1992] 2 All ER 10, at 17.
[279] RR4—*The Recreational Charities Act 1958* (2000).
[280] Ibid., paras A24–A25.

(11) **Advancement of animal welfare**

Gifts to specific animals may be upheld as valid unenforceable purpose trusts since they are recognized as anomalous exceptions to the beneficiary principle.[281] In contrast, trusts that promote the welfare of animals in general are charitable. This was recognized before the 2006 Act, which according to Lewison J in *Hanchett-Stamford v Attorney-General*,[282] has not effected 'any change in the substance of the law'.[283] In *Re Wedgwood*[284] Frances Wedgwood left property to her brother on secret trust for the protection and benefit of animals. She had discussed with him the possible use of the money to forward the movement for humane slaughtering of animals, which the Court of Appeal held to be a valid charitable object. The necessary element of public benefit was not found in any benefits to the animals themselves, but in the beneficial effects that the relief of cruelty to animals was expected to have on public morality. This was emphasized by all the members of the Court of Appeal. For example, Swinfen Eady LJ explained that:

a gift for the benefit and protection of animals tends to promote and encourage kindness towards them, to discourage cruelty and to ameliorate the condition of the brute creation, and thus to stimulate humane and generous sentiments in man towards the lower animals, and by these means promote feelings of humanity and morality generally, repress brutality, and thus elevate the human race.[285]

This reasoning was accepted without question by Nourse J in *Re Green's Will Trusts*.[286] Although it is well established that trusts for the relief of cruelty to animals are charitable, it should not be necessary to justify them on such a convoluted basis. They should be charitable simply because they benefit the animals themselves, the approach taken in Ireland.[287] Such a rationale would reflect current public sentiment towards animals, and would be another example of how the law of charity should not stand trapped by precedents from a previous social era. It is, moreover, far from self-evident that 'ameliorating the condition of the brute creation' does in fact have the effect of elevating the human race through improved feelings of humanity and repressed brutality.

In *Re Moss*[288] the welfare of cats and kittens was held charitable, as was a home for lost dogs.[289] In *Tatham v Drummond*[290] the RSPCA was held charitable, and more recently in *Re Green's Will Trusts*[291] a trust for the rescue, maintenance, and benefit of cruelly treated animals was held charitable. Gifts for animal sanctuaries have been held charitable, as in *Re Murawski's Will Trusts*,[292] where a gift was made to the Bleakholt Animal Sanctuary, whose constitution adopted the objects of 'the provision of care and shelter for stray, neglected and unwanted animals of all kinds and the protection

---

281 See Chapter 13.
283 Ibid., at [22].
285 Ibid., at 122.
287 *Armstrong v Reeves* (1890) 25 LR Ir 325.
289 *Re Douglas* (1887) 35 Ch D 472.
291 [1985] 3 All ER 455.

282 [2009] Ch 173.
284 [1915] 1 Ch 113.
286 [1985] 3 All ER 455, at 458.
288 [1949] 1 All ER 495.
290 (1864) 4 De GJ & Sm 484.
292 [1971] 1 WLR 707.

of animals from ill-usage, cruelty and suffering'. However, it seems that the sanctuary must either relieve cruelty or provide access to the public to view the animals if it is to be regarded as for the benefit of the public. Thus, in *Re Grove-Grady*[293] the Court of Appeal considered that a gift to found the 'Beaumont Animal Benevolent Society' was not charitable. Its purposes were to provide a refuge where animal life of all types might be completely undisturbed by man. The court held that the public derived no benefit from such a refuge, since the purpose was not the reduction of pain or cruelty to the animals and the public could be excluded from entering the area or even looking into it. Russell LJ considered that there was no public benefit when:

all that the public need know about the matter would be that one or more areas existed in which all animals (whether good or bad from man's point of view) were allowed to live free from any risk of being molested or killed by man; though liable to be molested and killed by other denizens of the area.[294]

Again, it is questionable whether this attitude should prevail today, when there is greater awareness and concern about environmental and conservation issues (a specific category of charity following the Charities Act 2006) and of the desirability of maintaining genetic diversity. The establishment of animal sanctuaries kept free from any interference by man could well be regarded as beneficial to the public, the benefit arising simply from the knowledge that such sanctuaries are there, and the heightened awareness of environmental and conservation concerns that they would engender.

An organization promoting the welfare of animals will not be a charity if its principal purpose is to campaign for a change in the law. In *Hanchett-Stamford v Attorney-General*,[295] Lewison J held that the Performing and Captive Animals Defence League was not charitable because the achievement of its purposes required a change in the law.

(12) Promotion of the efficiency of the armed forces and the police, fire, rescue, and ambulance services

Gifts that promote the efficiency of the defence services have been held charitable under the fourth head. This was held to follow from the 'spirit and intendment' of the preamble, which mentioned the 'setting out of soldiers'. Thus, a gift of plate for an officers' mess was held charitable in *Re Good*.[296] In *Re Gray*[297] a gift for the promotion of shooting, fishing, cricket, football, and polo for a regiment was held charitable, as it promoted the physical efficiency of the army.[298] The provision of RAF playgroups and ex-servicemen's associations are also charitable.[299] By analogy, it has been held that gifts to promote the efficiency of the police force will also be charitable.[300]

---

[293] [1929] 1 Ch 557.   [294] Ibid., at 586.   [295] [2009] Ch 173.
[296] [1905] 2 Ch 60.   [297] [1925] Ch 362.   [298] Ibid., at 365, per Romer J.
[299] Charity Commission for England and Wales, Annual Report 1997, para 90.
[300] *IRC v City of Glasgow Police Athletic Association* [1953] AC 380.

However, many of the cases in this area date from the early part of the nineteenth century and the more recent cases suggest that there will only be a charity if the prime object of the purposes is to promote efficiency. In *IRC v City of Glasgow Police Athletic Association*[301] a gift to promote sport and athletic pastimes in the police force was not held charitable. Although similar to the facts of *Re Gray*,[302] this was held to be a non-charitable purpose, as the promotion of efficiency was only incidental to the promotion of sport.[303]

The Charity Commission has issued guidance on the new head, which suggests that it will be charitable 'to promote the efficiency of the police, fire, rescue or ambulance services as they exist for the prevention and detection of crime, the preservation of public order and to protect the public'.[304] This would include providing equipment or services, or encouraging recruitment to the services.[305]

(13) **Other purposes beneficial to the community**

Notwithstanding the length of the list contained in the Charities Act 2006, there are many instances of charity which do not fall under any of these categories, but which will remain charitable because of the preservation of the current law by s 2(4). For instance, a number of cases hold that the promotion of trade and industry can be charitable. In *Construction Industry Training Board v A-G*[306] the Board, which was to make provision for the training of those employed in the construction industry, was held charitable. In *IRC v Yorkshire Agricultural Society*[307] the society, which existed for the general promotion of agriculture, was held charitable, as was the provision of a 'showground'[308] that would encourage agriculture. In their annual report for 1973[309] the Charity Commissioners considered that the Council of Industrial Design, which seeks to improve the design of industrial products, was charitable, since it was clearly of benefit to the public at large. However, the promotion of the interests of individuals rather than industry in general will not be charitable. In *Hadaway v Hadaway*[310] a trust to 'assist planters and agriculturists' by the provision of loans at favourable rates of interest was held non-charitable by the Privy Council because it was directed at conferring private benefits. Similarly, in *IRC v Oldham Training and Enterprise Council*[311] Lightman J held that a trust to promote 'trade

---

[301] [1953] AC 380.   [302] [1925] Ch 362.

[303] Essentially, the gift was not exclusively charitable. This requirement is considered below, at pp 655–658.

[304] Charity Commission *Commentary on the Descriptions of Charitable Purposes in the Charities Act 2006* (August 2009), para 49. Fire and rescue services are as defined in Part 2 of the Fire and Rescue Services Act 2004.

[305] Ibid., at para 50.

[306] [1971] 1 WLR 1303. See also *Crystal Palace Trustees v Minister of Town and Country Planning* [1951] Ch 132, where a trust with the purpose of the promotion of industry commerce and art was held charitable.

[307] [1928] 1 KB 611.   [308] *Brisbane City Council v A-G for Queensland* [1979] AC 411.

[309] *Report of the Charity Commissioners for England and Wales 1973*, paras 69–70.

[310] [1955] 1 WLR 16.   [311] [1996] STC 1218.

commerce and enterprise' in the Oldham area by providing 'support services and advice to and for new businesses' was not exclusively charitable because of the private benefits. The purposes would enable the TEC to 'promote the interests of individuals engaged in trade commerce or enterprise and provide benefits and services to them'.[312]

The list provided by the Charity Commission in its *Commentary on the Descriptions of Charitable Purposes in the Charities Act 2006*[313] demonstrates both the difficulty of classifying charities and the extent to which purposes may be charitable under more than one head:

- the provision of public works and services and the provision of public amenities (such as the repair of bridges, ports, havens, causeways and highways, the provision of water and lighting, a cemetery or crematorium, as well as the provision of public facilities such as libraries, reading rooms and public conveniences);
- the relief of unemployment;
- the defence of the country (such as trusts for national or local defence)
- the promotion of certain patriotic purposes, such as war memorials;
- the social relief, resettlement and rehabilitation of persons under a disability or deprivation (including disaster funds);
- the promotion of industry and commerce;
- the promotion of agriculture and horticulture;
- gifts for the benefit of a particular locality (such as trusts for the general benefit of the inhabitants of a particular place); the beautification of a town; civic societies;
- the promotion of mental or moral improvement;
- the promotion of the moral or spiritual welfare or improvement of the community;
- the preservation of public order;
- promoting the sound administration and development of the law;
- the promotion of ethical standards of conduct and compliance with the law in the public and private sectors;
- the rehabilitation of ex-offenders and the prevention of crime.

5 Recognizing new charitable purposes

Since the list of charitable purposes is not closed, a question arises as to how new charitable purposes will be recognized. The Charities Act 2006, s 2(4) preserves as charitable those purposes 'recognised as charitable under existing charity law' and then, as has already been described, allows the recognition as charitable 'any purposes that may reasonably be regarded as analogous to, or within the spirit of' any purposes listed in the Act or recognized by existing law as charitable, and so on ad infinitum.

---

[312] Ibid., at 1235.   [313] August 2009.

(1) The 'spirit and intendment' of the Statute of 1601

The Charities Act appears to exclude a method of reasoning which has been extensively used in the past. Traditionally, the 'spirit and intendment' of the preamble to the Statute of 1601 has acted as the benchmark to determine which purposes benefit the public in ways which are charitable. In *Williams' Trustees v IRC*,[314] where the House of Lords held that a trust for promoting Welsh interests in London was not charitable, Lord Simmonds said that:

it is still the general law that a trust is not charitable and entitled to the privileges which charity confers, unless it is within the spirit and intendment of the preamble to the Statute of Elizabeth.

The continued significance of the preamble was reiterated by the Privy Council in *A-G of the Cayman Islands v Wahr-Hansen*,[315] where Lord Browne-Wilkinson took it for granted that it was necessary to decide whether a purpose specified by a donor fell within the spirit and intendment of the preamble. However, the preamble cannot possibly anticipate the needs of society in the twenty-first century, and is an inadequate vehicle for determining charitable status. As Lord Upjohn commented in *Scottish Burial Reform and Cremation Society Ltd v Glasgow City Corpn*,[316] 'the authorities show that the spirit and intendment of the preamble to the Statute of Elizabeth have been stretched almost to breaking point'.

(2) Development by analogy

The practice of development by analogy, incorporated in the Charities Act, has become the predominant means of ascertaining whether a new purpose can be considered charitable. Lord Wilberforce in the *Scottish Burial Reform* case examined how the principle of the spirit and intendment had been applied in practice:

the courts appear to have proceeded first by seeking some analogy between an object mentioned in the preamble and the object with regard to which they had to reach a decision. And then they appear to have gone further and to have been satisfied if they could find an analogy between an object already held to be charitable.[317]

The Goodman Committee in 1976 recommended that the preamble should be replaced by a modern list of purposes deemed charitable to serve as a new benchmark for further development.[318] The Committee's recommendations have now been implemented, some thirty years later.

(3) Purposes without an analogy

A new situation will occasionally arise in which, although there appears to be a public benefit, there is no obvious analogy. The problem may then arise as to whether

---

[314] [1947] AC 447.   [315] [2001] 1 AC 75, [2000] 3 All ER 642.
[316] [1968] AC 138, at 153.   [317] Ibid., at 147.
[318] Report of the Goodman Committee: *Charity Law and Voluntary Organisations* (1976), para 32.

this can be considered charitable. In *Williams' Trustees v IRC*, Lord Simmonds said, 'it is not enough to say that the trust in question is for public purposes beneficial to the community or for the public welfare; you must show it to be a charitable trust'.[319] How is this to be done in the absence of any analogy? An approach which has been suggested is that trusts which are for purposes manifestly for the public benefit should be prima facie charitable, unless there are any reasons why they should not be. In *Incorporated Council of Law Reporting for England and Wales v A-G*[320] Russell LJ recognized the inadequacies of the 'spirit and intendment' principle and proposed instead that purposes which cannot be thought otherwise than beneficial to the community and of general public utility' should be charitable in law 'unless there are any grounds for holding it to be outside of the equity of the Statute [of 1601]'. This proposal was embraced by Sachs and Buckley LJJ. Applying this principle, it was held that the Incorporated Council of Law Reporting was registrable as a charity since its object of the production of law reports, was clearly of general public utility and there were no grounds on which it should not be held charitable.

This approach has much to commend it, as the Privy Council indicated in *A-G of the Cayman Islands v Wahr-Hansen*.[321] It is an honest recognition of how the courts and the Charity Commission actually seem to go about identifying charitable purposes, and it retains the safeguard of an option for charitable status to be refused even if the object is in the public interest. However, in *Barralet v A-G* Dillon J expressed doubt whether it is consistent with the decision of the House of Lords in *Williams' Trustees v IRC*[322] and concluded:

it seems to me that the approach to be adopted in considering whether something is within the fourth category is the approach of analogy from what is stated in the preamble to the Statute of Elizabeth or from what has already been held to be charitable within the fourth category.[323]

The approach may also no longer be open in view of the way in which s 2(4) of the Charities Act 2006 is phrased, although the preservation of 'any purposes ... recognised as charitable purposes under existing charity law' by s 2(4) may be capable of being interpreted to include 'other purposes beneficial to the community' as described by Lord Macnaghten in *Pemsel's* case, and therefore allow the use of the reasoning in the *Incorporated Council of Law Reporting* case. It is suggested that the Commission will continue to take a flexible approach to registration decisions;[324] it simply remains to see what process of reasoning will be used to support decision-making in instances where there are no obvious precedents to follow.

---

[319] [1947] AC 447.   [320] [1972] Ch 73, CA.   [321] [2001] 1 AC 75, [2000] 3 All ER 642.
[322] [1947] AC 447.   [323] [1980] 3 All ER 918.
[324] Charity Commission *Commentary on the Descriptions of Charitable Purposes in the Charities Act 2006* (August 2009), para 53, where the Commission states that the process of evolving the law to meet social conditions 'continues today'.

6 Charitable purposes overseas

A trust is not denied charitable status merely because any benefit from its execution will be experienced abroad rather than within the jurisdiction. In their Annual Report for 1963 the Charity Commissioners had no doubt that the advancement of religion, the advancement of education, and the relief of poverty are charitable in any part of the world, although they indicated that in the case of trusts for the relief of poverty the poverty must be observable and the measures designed to relieve it must have reasonably direct results.[325] For charities within Lord Macnaghten's fourth head of 'other purposes beneficial to the community', they said that there must be some benefit to the community of the United Kingdom, and not merely to the foreign country, reflecting a dictum of Lord Evershed MR in *Camille and Henry Dreyfus Foundation Inc v IRC*.[326] The Commissioners suggested that this might be more easily found in benefits to a Commonwealth country.[327]

With the declining significance of the Commonwealth and the growing importance of links with Europe, Eastern Europe, and increased international concern, this distinction is artificial. In their report for 1990, the Commissioners noted the trend toward a European and international dimension in new charities illustrated by the registration of the Gdansk Hospice Fund, the Nairobi Hospice Trust, and the USSR Support Charity.[328] Examples of charities with an international dimension include: a gift to the German government for the benefit of soldiers disabled in the Great War;[329] a trust for aid to churches, hospitals, and schools and for the assistance of the poor and aged in Cephalonia;[330] a trust for planting a grove of olive trees in Israel;[331] and a trust for a working men's hostel in Cyprus.[332]

Commonwealth jurisdictions have also upheld charitable purposes that bring a benefit abroad.[333] In *Re Levy Estate*[334] the Ontario Court of Appeal held that a gift to Israel for charitable purposes under the fourth head was valid even though there was no benefit to the Canadian community. Blair JA rejected earlier English authorities and the views of the Charity Commissioners and concluded:

> The principle that gifts, which are valid for charitable purposes in Canada are equally valid for the same charitable purposes abroad, is deeply embedded in our jurisprudence and also reflects the multinational and multicultural origins of Canadians.[335]

In their Annual Report of 1992 the Charity Commissioners adopted this approach and rejected the complex concepts of tangible and intangible benefit to the community

---

[325] *Report of the Charity Commissioners for England and Wales 1963*, para 72.

[326] [1954] Ch 672, at 684.

[327] *Report of the Charity Commissioners for England and Wales 1963*, para 72.

[328] *Report of the Charity Commissioners for England and Wales 1990*, paras 32, 33.

[329] *Re Robinson* [1931] 2 Ch 122.   [330] *Re Vagliano* [1905] WN 179.

[331] *Re Jacobs* (1970) 114 Sol Jo 515.   [332] *Re Niyazi's Will Trusts* [1978] 1 WLR 910.

[333] *Re Lowin* [1967] 2 NSWR 140, CA; *Re Stone* (1970) 91 WNNSW 704 (SC); *Lander v Whitbread* [1982] 2 NSWLR 530.

[334] (1989) 58 DLR (4th) 375.   [335] Ibid., at 383.

of the United Kingdom. In future, the Commissioners indicated that a charity of any type operating abroad will be presumed charitable in the same way as if its operations were confined to the United Kingdom. This presumption will be rebutted if it would be contrary to public policy to recognize the charity.[336] There is nothing in the Charities Act 2006 that challenges this practice.

7 Trusts with political objects

The fundamental principle behind the definition of charity is that purposes that are charitable must be for the public benefit. However, even if a purpose falls within one of the categories above, and is therefore considered as beneficial, it will not be charitable if it is for political purposes. Lord Parker in *Bowman v Secular Society*[337] stated that equity had always refused to recognize as charitable 'purely political objects'. This restriction was applied by Slade J in *McGovern v A-G.*[338] Amnesty International wanted to set up a trust with four main objects:

(1) the relief of needy relatives and dependants of prisoners of conscience;

(2) attempting to secure the release of prisoners of conscience;

(3) procuring the abolition of torture or inhuman or degrading treatment or punishment;

(4) undertaking, and disseminating the results of research into the observance of human rights.

The Charity Commissioners had refused to register the trust as a charity, and their decision was affirmed by Slade J, who held that the main purpose was political.

(1) Meaning of 'political objects'

In the course of his judgment Slade J identified the circumstances in which a court would regard a trust as political. The tests he proposed were more recently approved (although in a different context) by the Court of Appeal in *R v Radio Authority, ex p Bull.*[339] According to Slade J, a trust will be regarded as political if it has as a direct or principal purpose supporting a political party, changing the law, or changing government policy.

---

[336] *Report of the Charity Commissioners for England and Wales 1992*, para 76.
[337] [1917] AC 406.
[338] [1982] Ch 321.
[339] [1998] QB 294; Stevens and Feldman 'Broadcasting Advertisements by Bodies with Political Objects, Judicial Review, and the Influence of Charities Law' [1997] PL 615.

(a) To further the interests of a political party

In *Re Ogden*[340] a trust to promote 'Liberal principles' in politics was held not to be charitable.[341] The Charity Commissioners refused to register 'Youth Training' as a charity, since its purpose was to assist the Workers' Revolutionary Party.[342]

(b) To procure changes in the laws of this country[343]

A ground for the decision of the House of Lords in *National Anti-Vivisection Society v IRC*[344] was that the society's object of the abolition of vivisection would necessitate a change in the law of the land. This, it was held, would not be charitable. Summarizing the law and the rationale for this principle, Slade J said:

> the court will not regard as charitable a trust of which the main object is to procure an altera-tion of the law of the United Kingdom for one of two or both of two reasons; first, the court will ordinarily have no sufficient means of judging as a matter of evidence whether the proposed change will or will not be for the public benefit.[345] Secondly, even if the evidence suffices to enable it to form a prima facie opinion that a change in the law is desirable, it must still decide the case on the principle that the law is right as it stands since to do otherwise would usurp the functions of the legislature.

The promotion of the present status quo by maintaining the existing law or policy is equally a political purpose,[346] unless the effect of the law or policy concerned is to pro-mote a charitable purpose.[347]

(c) To procure changes in the law of a foreign country

Although there is no obligation on the court to assume that foreign law is right as it stands, Slade J considered that it was still impossible to judge whether a change in foreign law would be beneficial to the community, and therefore such purposes are not charitable. In *R v Radio Authority, ex p Bull*[348] it was held that even the attempt to persuade countries to implement human rights in accordance with their obligations through international treaties was political.

---

[340] [1933] Ch 678.

[341] See also *Bonar Law Memorial Trust v IRC* (1933) 49 TLR 220.

[342] Charity Commissioners for England and Wales Annual Report 1982, paras 451–651.

[343] *IRC v Temperance Council of Christian Churches of England and Wales* (1926) 10 TC 748; *National Anti-Vivisection Society v IRC* [1948] AC 31.

[344] [1948] AC 31.

[345] See *Bowman v Secular Society* [1917] AC 406, at 443, per Lord Parker of Waddington: 'a trust for the attainment of political objects has always been held invalid, not because it is illegal...but because the court has no means of judging whether a proposed change in the law will or will not be for the public benefit'. See also [1973] Anglo-American Law Review 47 (Sheridan).

[346] *Re Hopkinson* [1949] 1 All ER 346; *Re Koeppler Will Trusts* [1984] Ch 243.

[347] *Re Vallance* (1876) 2 *Seton's Judgments* (7th edn) 1304; *Re Herrick* (1918) 52 ILT 213.

[348] [1998] QB 294; Stevens and Feldman 'Broadcasting Advertisements by Bodies with Political Objects, Judicial Review, and the Influence of Charities Law' [1997] PL 615.

(d) To procure a reversal of government policy or of particular decisions of governmental authorities in this country

The courts are also unwilling to encroach on the functions of the executive. Therefore, and also because it is impossible to determine whether any changes would result in a public benefit, Slade J held that such purposes would not be charitable.

(e) To procure a reversal of government policy or of particular decisions of governmental authorities in a foreign country

Similarly, the court has no satisfactory means of judging whether there is any public benefit from such a reversal.

(2) Application of the restriction

Whatever the category of charitable purpose, if a trust or organization has political purposes, it cannot be recognized as charitable. In *Re Hopkinson*[349] a gift was made for the advancement of adult education on the lines of a Labour Party memorandum. Vaisey J held that the purpose was 'political propaganda masquerading as education' and therefore not charitable.[350] In *Re Bushnell*[351] a trust for the promotion of socialized medicine through the publishing and distribution of books was held to be political, rather than for the provision of medical care. In contrast, in *Re Koeppler Will Trusts*[352] a gift to 'Wilton Park', an institution which was not party political and sought to promote greater cooperation in Europe, was held charitable. The Court of Appeal emphasized that the discussions it organized were neither party political nor propagandist. The Charity Commission has decided that the Centre for Corporate Accountability was not exclusively charitable because, although it was established for the charitable purpose of promoting public safety, it sought to do so by advocating changes to the law of corporate killing and influencing the prosecutions and investigations policy of the Crown Prosecution Service and the Health and Safety Executive.[353] Charities have been held not to be entitled to engage in public campaigning on political issues unrelated to their charitable objects. In *Baldry v Feintuck*[354] a student union was held to have applied money to a non-charitable object when it supported a campaign against the Government policy of ending free milk in schools. Similarly, in *Webb v O'Doherty*[355] support by a student union of a campaign against the Gulf War was held non-charitable. In *R v Radio Authority, ex p Bull*,[356] Lord Woolf pointed out that an activity that was not in itself political could be considered to become political

---

[349] [1949] 1 All ER 346.

[350] However, in *Re Trust of Arthur McDougall Fund* [1956] 3 All ER 867 it was held that a trust for the education of the public in forms of government and in political matters generally was charitable.

[351] [1975] 1 WLR 1596.   [352] [1986] Ch 423.

[353] Decision of the Charity Commissioners for England and Wales, *Application for Registration of the Centre for Corporate Accountability* (24 August 2001).

[354] [1972] 2 All ER 81.   [355] (1991) The Times, 11 February.

[356] [1997] 2 All ER 561.

if it had the objective of promoting a political purpose. 'It takes its nature from the principal objective.'[357]

In *Hanchett-Stamford v Attorney-General*[358] a society was established to prevent cruelty to animals by prohibiting their use for performances on stage or in films. The association had been denied the benefits of charitable status in the past, on the basis that it was campaigning for a change in the law. Lewison J held that the:

Charities Act 2006 has not changed the fundamental principle that if one of the objects or purposes of an organisation is to change the law, it cannot be charitable.[359]

(3) Ancillary political activities

Slade J's decision in *McGovern v A-G*[360] initially gave many charities cause for concern. Amnesty International had taken professional advice in drawing up their trust deed. The whole intention was 'that there should be hived off into a trust those purposes which they had been advised would be charitable'.[361] The decision of Slade J was therefore something of a surprise. It affected not just Amnesty International, but also other charities, like Oxfam or Shelter, which, in addition to fulfilling their main purpose of providing relief or care services, would also seek to influence government opinion in favour of the causes which they espoused. Slade J had recognized that a limited degree of political activity was permissible, provided that it was not a main purpose of the trust. He said:

Trust purposes of an otherwise charitable nature do not lose it merely because the trustees, by way of furtherance of such purposes, have incidental powers to carry on activities which are not themselves charitable...If all the main objects of the trust are exclusively charitable, the mere fact that the trustees may have incidental powers to employ political means for their furtherance will not deprive them of their charitable status.[362]

In *R v Radio Authority, ex p Bull,* Brooke LJ commented on the impact of this exception:

Many charitable trusts today—national charities concerned with children, or the physically or mentally disabled, or with housing the homeless, for example—are prominent in their espousal of political means to attain their ends.[363]

(4) Legitimate political activity by charities

It is obviously correct that purposes of a truly political nature should not receive the state subsidy in effect granted to charities through tax privileges. However, it is also the case that many well-established charities engage in political activity of some type, whether campaigning, lobbying Parliament, or advocating changes in the law. For example, the housing charity Shelter may challenge government housing policy, and

---

[357] Ibid., at 572.　　[358] [2009] Ch 173.　　[359] Ibid., at 181.　　[360] [1982] Ch 321.
[361] [1981] 3 All ER 493, at 500, per Slade J. Amnesty did ultimately come up with a scheme for a trust which satisfied the Charity Commissioners: see [1997] 2 All ER, at 581 and 584.
[362] [1981] 3 All ER 493, at 509 and 511.　　[363] [1997] 2 All ER 561, at 580.

relief agencies may demand a different attitude by government towards the Third World. A fine balance must be drawn between legitimate political activity by charities, and political activism that is incompatible with the retention of charitable status—any political activity must be purely ancillary to their main charitable objects. This was the theme of the advice given to charity trustees by the Charity Commissioner in guidelines published in their 1981 Report.[364]

In 1999 the Charity Commissioners provided updated comprehensive guidance to charity trustees in their publication *Political Activities and Campaigning by Charities*.[365] Their advice was further updated following the Prime Minister's Strategy Unit report, *Private Action, Public Benefit*—a review of charities and the wider not-for-profit sector.[366] This recommended that the Charity Commission's guidance on political campaigning should place a greater emphasis on the campaigning activities that charities can undertake because:

- their strong links into local communities means that charities are well placed to monitor, evaluate and comment upon policies as they are implemented;
- the high levels of public trust and confidence they command means that charities are well placed to offer alternative ways of engaging with the public policy debate and the processes of democracy; and
- the diversity of causes they represent, [enables] charities to give voice to a far wider range of political perspectives, including those of minority groups or interests, than might otherwise be heard by government.[367]

The Charity Commission's guidance was revised in September 2004 following these recommendations, and again in March 2008 following the enactment of the Charities Act 2006. This most recent guidance is far less cautionary in tone, and less directive. Instead of telling charity trustees what they are or are not permitted to do, the guidance is more general, leaving the ultimate decision on appropriateness of any given activity to the organization itself.

The Commission acknowledges that, while an organization can never be a charity if it is established solely for political purposes, so long as a charity is 'engaging in campaigning or political activity solely in order to further or support its charitable purposes, and there is a reasonable likelihood of it being effective, it may carry out campaigning and political activity'.[368] Charity trustees must consider that the methods used are lawful and an effective use of charity resources,[369] and be satisfied that the activities are permitted under the governing document of the charity.[370] A charity may seek to influence government.[371] It may provide and publish comments on possible or proposed changes in the law or government policy,[372] and advocate a

---

[364] *Report of the Charity Commissioners of England and Wales for 1981*, paras 53–56.
[365] CC9—*Political Activities and Campaigning by Charities* (September 1999).
[366] September 2002.
[367] CC9—*Political Activities and Campaigning by Charities* (September 2004), para 5.
[368] CC9—*Speaking Out: Guidance on Political Activities and Campaigning by Charities* (March 2008), para D1.
[369] Ibid., para G2.   [370] Ibid., paras D1 and D4 .   [371] Ibid., para D9.
[372] Ibid., para D7.

change in the law or public policy, provided that these activities do not become the dominant means by which it carries out its purposes.[373] The evaluation of risk is a key feature of the guidance,[374] as when considering campaigning and political activity charity trustees must carefully weigh up the possible benefits against the costs and risks in deciding whether the campaign is likely to be an effective way of furthering or supporting the charity's purposes.[375] Similarly, the decision whether to use emotive or controversial material is a value judgment for the trustees, taking into account whether it is justifiable in the context of the campaign and has a legitimate evidence base to support the claims made.[376]

Additionally, although charities may not support a political party, they may support specific policies advocated by political parties if the policy would help them achieve their charitable purpose.[377] Moreover, it appears that a charity may focus most or all of its resources on political activity for a period, if this is the best way to support the charity's purposes and does not become the reason for the charity's existence.[378]

The interpretation given by the Charity Commission of what political activities are permitted go significantly beyond the limits set out by Slade J in *McGovern v A-G*,[379] even as subsequently glossed in *Re Koeppler Will Trusts*.[380] They seek to add clarity to what is permissible activity by charity trustees. It remains to be seen, however, whether this very considerable extension is recognized by the courts if and when they are faced with such activities.

(5) Critique of the political purposes test

A larger question than the limits on political campaigning is whether the judicial aversion to political trusts is well founded. Slade J in *McGovern v A-G*[381] spoke of the difficulty of judges in identifying whether a change in the law is for the public benefit and of the danger of usurping the functions of the legislature. The objection that Slade J gives to party political purposes is that:

> Since their nature would ex hypothesi be very controversial, the court could be faced with even greater difficulties in determining whether the objects of the trust would be for the public benefit; correspondingly, it would be at even greater risk of encroaching on the functions of the legislature and prejudicing its reputation for political impartiality, if it were to promote such objects by enforcing the trust.[382]

Slade J gave almost identical reasons for objecting to trusts that sought to achieve their objective through influencing opinion. There would again be no way of telling

---

[373] Ibid., paras D3 and D7.

[374] See further Atkinson 'Charities and Political Campaigning, The Impact of Risk-based Regulation' (2008) *Liverpool Law Review* 143.

[375] CC9—*Speaking Out: Guidance on Political Activities and Campaigning by Charities* (March 2008), para F1.

[376] Ibid., para G4.   [377] Ibid., para D5.   [378] Ibid., para D8.

[379] [1982] Ch 321.   [380] [1986] Ch 423.   [381] [1982] Ch 321.

[382] [1981] 3 All ER 493, at 507.

whether a reversal of government policy was for the public benefit 'and in any event [the court] could not properly encroach on the functions of the executive, acting intra vires, by holding that it should be acting in some other manner'.[383]

The objections that Slade J sets out are almost certainly overstated. His aversion to comment on whether the changes in the law are for the public benefit does not seem to have prevented the judges shaping the law through the development of new rules and principles,[384] nor has it prevented them, on occasions, from making suggestions for law reform in their judgments. Judges have also taken a leading role in law reform through chairmanship of the Law Commission. Lord Woolf in *R v Radio Authority ex p Bull*[385] acknowledged that a campaign to seek a change in the law would be political even though it could also be commendable. Fine distinctions have also been made. Slade J had no difficulty in reconciling *Jackson v Phillips*[386] with his view of political purposes. There the Massachusetts Supreme Court had upheld as charitable a trust to campaign against slavery before slavery was prohibited in the United States. Slade J took the view that 'the pressure was to be directed by the trustees against individual persons, rather than governments with a view to obtaining the "voluntary manumission" of the slaves belonging to such individuals'.[387]

Much of the objection to the court 'taking sides' would be overcome if the court adopted the policy of accepting purposes as being for the public benefit if they are not immoral, illegal, or subversive and are adopted by a significant proportion of the public.[388] It would then be possible for opposing views both to be capable of being considered charitable. It may also be that a distinction needs to be made between propagandist trusts and those which seek to influence public and governmental opinion, and perhaps even influence changes in laws, not through any pre-ordained view of what is right and wrong (which is the position taken in many 'political' activities), but only after careful and considered debate. After all, why should a trust to promote the work of the Law Commission not be held charitable, even though the whole purpose of the Commission is to change the law?

Strong support for the view that such a distinction should be made can be found in *Re Koeppler Will Trusts*.[389] The testator had left a substantial gift to support the work of 'Wilton Park', in making 'a British contribution to the formation of an informed international public opinion and to the promotion of greater co-operation in Europe and the West in general'. The organization worked by bringing together in conferences a broad range of politicians, academics, civil servants, industrialists, and journalists to exchange views on political, economic, and social views of

---

383 Ibid., at 508.
384 See the discussion in Chapter 2.
385 [1997] 2 All ER 561, at 571.
386 96 Mass 539 (1867).
387 [1981] 3 All ER 493, at 514.
388 See the discussion below of the test used for public benefit in Ireland, at p 635.
389 [1986] Ch 423.

common interest. Peter Gibson J, at first instance, having considered the *McGovern* case, held that:

> trusts aimed at securing better international relations, including co-operation in a particular part of the world, can properly be called political causes…Whether there should be better relations and co-operation and, if so, how it should be achieved and with whom are matters for government decision, not for the court.[390]

This view was overruled by the Court of Appeal. The judgment of the court was given by Slade LJ (who had now been promoted to the Court of Appeal). He distinguished the case from his previous decision in *McGovern*:

> In the present case…the activities of Wilton Park are not of a party political nature. Nor, as far as the evidence shows, are they designed to procure changes in the laws or governmental policy of this or any other country: even when they touch on political matters, they constitute, so far as I can see, no more than genuine attempts in an objective manner to ascertain and disseminate the truth. In these circumstances I think that no objections to the trust arise on a political score…The trust is, in my opinion, entitled to what is sometimes called a 'benignant construction', in the sense that the court is entitled to presume that the trustees will only act in a lawful and proper manner appropriate to the trustees of a charity and not, for example, by the propagation of tendentious political opinions.[391]

For Slade LJ to say in this case that there was no intention to change laws or governmental policy seems rather disingenuous. A large part of the reason for bringing together distinguished conference participants capable of influencing opinion in Europe and the West must surely have been to act as a driver for cooperation between states and governments. If that is not 'political' at an international level, it is hard to see what could be. The major significance of this judgment must therefore be the recognition that a distinction can be drawn between 'the propagation of tendentious political opinions' which the court will not consider to be charitable, and 'genuine attempts objectively to ascertain and disseminate the truth', even in a political context, which can be charitable. Applying this test, a trust to promote the work of the Law Commission could be charitable, even if a trust to reform the rule against perpetuities would not.

8 The requirement of public benefit[392]

(1) General principles

It is not enough for a trust to be charitable that it demonstrates a charitable character under s 2(2) of the Charities Act 2006. It has also always been the case that the way in which that purpose is achieved must also be for the public benefit. That requirement has been given statutory force by the Charities Act 2006, s 2(1)(b) and s 3. There is no

---

[390] [1984] 2 All ER 111, at 124.
[391] [1985] 2 All ER 869, at 878.
[392] See Warburton 'Charities and Public Benefit—From Confusion to Light? (2008) *Charity Law and Practice Review* 1; Hackney 'Charities and Public Benefit' (2008) 124 LQR 347.

new statutory definition, so public benefit is defined as having the same meaning as under the previous law[393] with one major change, which is that there is no presumption that a purpose of a particular description is for the public benefit, as was the case in some instances under the previous law.

(a) Charity Commission guidance

The Charity Commission has issued guidance on its understanding of the public benefit requirement, as it is obliged to under s 4 of the Charities Act 2006. The purpose of the guidance is to promote awareness and understanding of the public benefit requirement,[394] but 'the charity trustees of a charity must have regard to any such guidance when exercising any powers or duties to which the guidance is relevant'.[395]

The guidance therefore has authoritative status. The Charity Commission is not empowered to change the law on public benefit, and its guidance is subject to oversight on appeal to the First Tier Tribunal (Charity) and thence to the courts.[396] The Charity Commission is clear in its guidance that it is following existing legal decisions, and considers that:

Our guidance sets out a framework of factors to consider when assessing public benefit based on the principles of public benefit contained in existing case law.[397]

However, there are three areas in which the Charities Act 2006 has changed the presumption of public benefit previously accorded to certain categories of charity. These are the advancement of education, the advancement of religion, and the relief of poverty. Since the case law prior to the 2006 Act applied a presumption of public benefit in these areas, it is inevitable that the guidance of the Charity Commission is treading new ground. It has already been noted that appeals from decisions of the Charity Commission are rare, so, in practice, the guidance from the Commission will have very considerable influence before it is tested through the higher courts.

The Commission is expected to carry out public and other consultation on any guidance it issues.[398] At the date of writing, guidance has been issued on fee charging and public benefit, and in relation to *The Prevention or Relief of Poverty for the Public Benefit*,[399] *The Advancement of Education for the Public Benefit*,[400] and *The Advancement of Religion for the Public Benefit*.[401] It is clear from this guidance that the requirement of public benefit may differ with the charitable purpose to be considered. As will be seen later, some of the guidance has been controversial.

(b) When does the public benefit test apply?

The public benefit test applies to new organizations or trusts seeking to be registered as a charity. It also applies to existing charities, which must continue to satisfy the

---

[393] Charities Act 2006, s 3(3).   [394] Charities Act 2006, s 4(2).
[395] Charities Act 2006, s 4(6).
[396] Charity Commission, *Charities and Public Benefit* (January 2008), para D5.
[397] Ibid., para D2.   [398] Charities Act 2006, s 4(4).
[399] December 2008.   [400] December 2008.   [401] December 2008.

public benefit test and must demonstrate that they do so. Charities are now required to report on public benefit as part of the Trustees Annual Report. This information must be set in the context of the charity's aims, and must demonstrate how in practice each purpose of the charity has been carried out for the public benefit. The change in the public benefit requirement made by the Charities Act 2006 will have an impact upon existing charities. The Charity Commission will be conducting public benefit checks on all existing charities to ensure that they can show positively that they are set up and operate for the public benefit.[402] The procedure the Commission will adopt to assess public benefit is detailed in those specific publications on the three charitable purposes considered above, namely advancement of education, the relief or prevention of poverty, and the advancement of religion. As of July 2009, the Charity Commission has carried out the review of twelve organizations.[403] The methodology adopted in each includes desk-based research of information from the last three years on the relevant charity, a questionnaire on public benefit based on the issued guidance, a visit to each charity to look at issues in greater depth, and the preparation of a draft report on which the charity concerned could check the factual accuracy.[404] More significantly for all registered charities, in addition to publishing the individual reports, the Commission has also published some emerging findings for charity trustees arising from these initial assessments.[405]

(c) Consequences of failing the public benefit test

Where a proposed charity does not meet the public benefit test, it will not be a charity and will not therefore enjoy the benefits and advantages of that status. It may be possible for the objectives or purposes of the trust or organization to be amended to satisfy the test.

Where an existing charity fails to satisfy the public benefit test, the trust or organization will have essentially one of three choices. It could challenge the Charity Commission's interpretation of the requirements of public benefit. It may amend its purposes and modify its activities in order to comply with the Charity Commission guidance,[406] and may be required to do this by the Charity Commission. Finally, if it is not possible to make such changes, it could cease to be a registered charity. The impact of the last course of action could be catastrophic for the entity concerned. Once assets have irrevocably been devoted to charitable purposes, they cannot be used for any non-charitable purposes, but must, in the event of an organization ceasing to be charitable, be applied to other charitable purposes.[407] Thus, if a public school lost its

---

[402] Charity Commission, *Public Benefit—the Charity Commission's approach* (January 2005), paras 19 and 27.

[403] Charity Commission, *The Public Benefit Assessment Reports* (July 2009). This includes 4 religious charities, 5 independent schools, and 3 care homes.

[404] Charity Commission, *Public Benefit Assessment Report—Methodology* (July 2009).

[405] Charity Commission, *Public Benefit Assessments: Emerging Findings for Charity Trustees from the Charity Commission's Public Benefit Assessment Work: 2008–09* (July 2009).

[406] Charity Commission, *Public Benefit—The Charity Commission's Approach* (January 2005), para 22.

[407] Ibid., para 23.

charitable status, and wished to operate as a private sector school, it would not be able to transfer its assets to the new non-charitable entity. The new entity would either have to purchase the assets or acquire new premises and facilities. That would inevitably have a dramatic and negative impact upon the level of fees that the new entity would need to charge, or upon the quality of the provision which it could offer.

(2) What is 'public benefit'?

It is stating the obvious to observe that public benefit has two dimensions: whether the proposed charity provides benefits; and whether those benefits are conferred upon the public. The Charity Commission further breaks this analysis down into seven more specific sub-principles:[408]

Principle 1: There must be an identifiable benefit or benefits

    1a It must be clear what the benefits are

    1b The benefits must be related to the aims [of the charity]

    1c Benefits must be balanced against any detriment or harm

Principle 2: Benefit must be to the public, or a section of the public

    2a The beneficiaries must be appropriate to the aims

    2b Where benefit is to a section of the public, the opportunity to benefit must not be unreasonably restricted:

        • by geographical or other restrictions; or

        • by ability to pay any fees charged

    2c People in poverty must not be excluded from the opportunity to benefit

    2d Any private benefits must be incidental

(a) 'Identifiable benefit'

It does not follow that because a proposed purpose falls within one of the recognized categories of charitable purpose the way in which that purpose will be implemented (or is being implemented) is charitable. It could be argued that a trust to provide training to the Taliban in making explosive devices is 'educational', but it is hardly a charitable purpose to train terrorists. There would be no public benefit from the particular form of education proposed, or to express this in the language used by the Charity Commission, there would not be any 'identifiable benefit'.

(i) Form of benefit may be practical or intangible

The public benefit may consist of practical assistance, as in most cases involving the relief of need, for instance through the provision of housing to the homeless, financial assistance to the poor, or advocacy for those who lack the mental capacity to represent themselves. The benefit may also be of an intangible or moral nature. For instance,

---

[408] Charity Commission, *Charities and Public Benefit* (January 2008), para C3. See also Charity Commission, *Analysis of the law Underpinning Charities and Public Benefit* (December 2008).

the promotion of fine music or the preservation of the cultural heritage may have no direct practical benefits, but they may help to improve the human condition in a moral or intellectual sense. It used to be considered that the provision of overseas aid was justified on moral, rather than practical grounds, although a different view is now taken. The Charity Commission has indicated that in deciding whether there are intangible benefits, it will take into account the general consensus of fair-minded and unprejudiced opinion, although public opinion cannot by itself determine what is charitable.[409]

(ii) Benefit may be direct or indirect

It is possible for indirect benefits to be taken into account in deciding whether there is public benefit. A trust to train teachers in the use of sign language provides services directly to the individuals who are trained, but the greater benefits are to the pupils who will benefit from having teachers who have the skills that they need for their education. A hospice providing care for the terminally ill confers benefits not only on the patients who may receive care more closely aligned to their needs than would otherwise be the case; it also relieves the burden which the National Health Service would need to carry, and it provides assistance to the family of the patient who might find it difficult to cope in providing the level of intensive support which a patient needs. All of these factors can be weighed in the balance in deciding whether there is a benefit to the public.

(iii) Benefit must be recognized as charitable

It is so obvious that it hardly needs saying that for a benefit to be recognized by law, it must be of a kind which promotes a purpose which has been recognized by law as charitable. Acting illegally cannot be considered to be beneficial. A proposed trust to provide cannabis to chronic sufferers of arthritis would not be charitable, even if it could be proved that the drug would improve the condition of life of those receiving the treatment. In a less extreme situation, a trust to build a private (for profit) hospital would not be charitable because even if it could be considered as for the advancement of health, doing so for profit is not considered to be charitable.

(iv) Benefit must relate to the aims of the charity

Although benefits can be indirect, they must be sufficiently related to the primary activities or purposes of the organization or trust. In *IRC v Oldham Training and Enterprise Council*[410] a TEC existed to promote 'trade, commerce and enterprise' in the Oldham area by providing 'support services and advice to and for new businesses'. It was argued that although this might involve promotion of the interests of individuals engaged in trade and commerce, this would be charitable because such efforts

---

[409] Charity Commission, *Charities and Public Benefit—The Legal Principles* (January 2008), para D8.9.
[410] [1996] STC 1218.

would 'make the recipients more profitable and thereby, or otherwise, to improve employment prospects in Oldham'. However, Lightman J held that these objects were non-charitable because the 'benefits to the community conferred by such activities are too remote'.[411] The primary purpose of the organization was not charitable, and the incidental public benefit was not sufficient to confer charitable status on the organization. Similarly, the public benefit in a charity for the advancement of education could not consist of something which has no connection whatever to education. For example, worthless education would not be redeemed because the educational institution was based in an historical building worthy of protection. This is simply an application of the principle that the activities of a charity must be consistent with the purposes of the charity.[412]

(b) Assessing benefit

Different views can be taken about what constitutes a benefit. Some purposes or activities may be beneficial in the eyes of some but detrimental in the eyes of others. For example, some members of the community may think that public health would be promoted by campaigning to promote vegetarianism, but others may think that advocating the eating of red meat would be in the public interest for similar reasons. How can the Charity Commission or the court determine whether there is a public benefit without simply making a value judgement? Different approaches are possible.

(i) Assessment of benefit can be controversial

The assessment of benefit is not free from controversy. A particularly contentious issue which took up much time in debate over the Charities Act 2006 in both Lords and Commons concerns the charitable status of public schools, which is discussed below. The Government essentially passed this thorny issue to the Charity Commission for resolution. The Charity Commission anticipated that its task would be far from straightforward:

[a]pplying principles drawn from a small number of cases involving particular charities and situations will involve difficult judgements and interpretations of the law to be made by the Commission. Quite rightly, these will be open to challenge.[413]

The Commission published its initial views, following considerable consultation, in December 2008 in three separate reports, *Public Benefit and Fee-Charging*, an *Analysis of the Law underpinning Public Benefit and Fee Charging*, and *The Advancement of Education for the Public Benefit*. It published its first Public Benefit Assessments of some independent schools in 2009.

---

[411] Ibid., at 1235.

[412] See Charity Commission, *Analysis of the Law Underpinning Charities and Public Benefit* (December 2008), at para 2.20: 'the benefit must be related to purposes and that the remoter benefits of having a charitable purpose are not enough ... The inclusion of a purpose within the list of the descriptions merely indicates that purposes falling within the classification have the potential of being for the public benefit.'

[413] *Public Benefit—The Charity Commission's Position on How Public Benefit Is Treated in the Charities Act* (July 2005).

The Charity Commission was right to consider that its task would be controversial. It was reported in October 2009 that two QCs considered that the Charity Commission's approach was unlawful. Stanley Brodie, QC was quoted as saying:

the directions given to two private schools on the basis that they have failed the test are almost certainly without lawful foundation, as is the threat to deprive them of their charitable status.[414]

The Commission has been accused by a leading independent school headmaster of making 'politically motivated' judgments and adopting 'a blinkered approach'.

(ii) The view of the public

What benefits the public could be judged by public opinion—an 'ask the audience' approach. This is not the approach used in the UK. Public opinion is not easy to measure, and it can change frequently. In the Canadian case of *Everywoman's Health Centre Society (1988) v Minister of National Revenue*[415] the court said that:

to define charity through public consensus would be a most imprudent thing to do. Charity and public opinion do not always go hand in hand...Courts are not well equipped to assess public consensus, which is a fragile and volatile concept. The determination of the charitable character of an activity should not become a battle between pollsters.

While public opinion may not be the primary test for identifying whether there is a benefit, there are instances where public views are relevant. There are some instances in which the Charity Commission acknowledges that reference to public opinion is required. It gives as an example that 'public opinion might be relevant when considering whether there is a public benefit in the general appreciation of a beautiful landscape or building'.[416] In *Funnell v Stewart*[417] it was held that a trust to advance the practice of faith healing was charitable on the grounds that it had become 'a recognised activity of public benefit'. This suggests that the attitude of the public cannot be disregarded in determining whether an activity should be characterized as for the public benefit.

(iii) A subjective assessment of benefit

Another possibility is for the court to adopt a subjective test, and uphold the gift if the donor thought the activity confers public benefit. This approach seems to have been applied by Chitty J in *Re Foveaux*,[418] where a gift to the International Society for the Total Suppression of Vivisection was held charitable. He acknowledged that vivisection was a practice over which opinion was divided, and said that it was not for the court to 'enter into or pronounce any opinion on the merits of the controversy which subsists between the supporters and opponents of the practice of vivisection'. Instead, when 'humane men and women of a high order of intelligence and education are found

[414] *Daily Telegraph* online 3 October 2009 (www.telegraph.co.uk/education/educationnews/6257886/Charity-Commission-chair-Suzi-Leather-faces-frosty-conference-over-independent-schools.html).

[415] [1992] 2 FC 52, at 68–69.

[416] Charity Commission online guidance, *Charities and Public Benefit* (January 2008), para D8.

[417] [1996] 1 WLR 288.   [418] [1895] 2 Ch 501.

in the ranks on either side the law stands neutral'. This reluctance to judge the merits of questions of morals where men's minds reasonably differ was also reflected in the Irish case of *Re Cranston*,[419] which concerned a gift to a vegetarian society. Fitzgibbon LJ took the view that it would be charitable provided the purpose was one which the founder of the society believed to be to public advantage, and that his belief 'be at least rational and not contrary either to the general law of the land or to the principles of morality'. The key factor is the subjective belief of the donor, within certain objective limits, that the purpose is beneficial. In neither of these two cases was the court willing to weigh the alleged benefits of the purpose against its alleged drawbacks.

(iv) An objective assessment of benefit

In *National Anti-Vivisection Society v IRC*[420] the House of Lords overruled the decision in *Re Foveaux*[421] and held that a gift to the society, whose object was the suppression of vivisection, was not charitable. They adopted an objective approach to the question of public benefit, and a willingness to weigh the merits of the purpose. Lord Simmonds stated:

Where on the evidence before it the court concludes that, however well-intentioned the donor, the achievement of his object will be greatly to the public disadvantage, there can be no justification for saying that it is a charitable object.[421a]

The House was faced by the decision of fact of the Special Commissioners for Income Tax that any benefit 'was far outweighed by the detriment to medical science and research and consequently to the public health which would result if the society succeeded in achieving its objects'.[422]

The *National Anti-Vivisection Society* decision suggests that the underpinning requirement for all kinds of public benefit is that the benefit must be capable of proof. The classic formulation of this requirement can be found in the judgement of Slade J in *McGovern v AG*:

The question whether a purpose will or may operate for the public benefit is to be answered by the court forming an opinion on the evidence before it...No doubt in some cases a purpose may be so manifestly beneficial to the public that it would be absurd to call evidence on this point. In many other instances, however, the element of public benefit may be much more debatable. Indeed, in some cases the courts will regard this element [as] being incapable of proof one way or the other and thus will inevitably decline to recognise the trust as being of a charitable nature.[423]

(v) Balance of benefit and detriment

Nearly all activities have both positive and negative impacts. For an activity to be charitable, it is not necessary for there to be unqualified benefits. It is sufficient if, on balance, the benefits sufficiently outweigh the disadvantages. The Charity Commission gives as an example the playing of physical sports, which inevitably involve a measure

---

[419] [1898] 1 IR 431.   [420] [1948] AC 31.
[421] [1895] 2 Ch 501.   [421a] [1948] AC 31, at 65–66.
[422] [1948] AC 31 at 65–66.   [423] [1981] 3 All ER 493, at 504.

of risk of injury. If the risk of injury is managed, it is far outweighed by the positive benefits of healthy exercise.[424] The balancing process is well illustrated in *National Anti-Vivisection Society* v *IRC*,[425] where the evidence before the House of Lords was that the benefits achievable through medical research from experimentation on animals far outweighed the moral benefits in preventing vivisection of animals.

(vi) Can benefit always be measured objectively?

The objective approach adopted in the *National Anti-Vivisection case* assumes that the court is competent to make judgments of what is in the public interest. This is questionable as a universal proposition, since there are many instances where the issue of whether there is a benefit to the public is a matter of opinion. This is especially the case if fine moral issues over which there is a real divergence of opinion in society are involved, and at best the court can only give its own value judgement on the issue. There are also some very interesting examples of activities held to be charitable despite no evidence having been provided to demonstrate public benefit. These include religious organizations engaged in public worship and societies promoting the humane treatment of animals. In both of these instances the courts have been prepared to assume public benefit without any form of proof of benefit being offered. In both cases, quantification or measurement of the benefits (if they exist) would be difficult or impossible.

(vii) Is a hybrid approach preferable?

The subjective approach, with objective limitations, suggested in *Re Cranston*[426] provides a more attractive alternative than a purportedly purely objective approach. There is no need for the court—or the Charity Commission—to make its own value judgments about relative merits. Is it not possible that both a trust for the prevention of animal experimentation and a trust for the promotion of medical research could be considered charitable, although their objects are to some extent in conflict? Similarly, could not a trust for the promotion of vegetarianism be charitable alongside a trust for the promotion of meat? All that is really needed is a test that will eliminate those purposes that are in no sense in the public interest or are of benefit only to small and obscure groups and sects. A test which upholds purposes that a substantial body of public opinion regards as beneficial would be adequate for this purpose, and more honest than a spurious claim to make all judgments objectively.

(c) Assessing benefit in the light of modern conditions

There is not the slightest doubt that the concept of what constitutes a public benefit has changed over the years, and that this is reflected in the decisions of the courts and of the Charity Commission. For instance, it is now recognized that charities that operate overseas can be justified on the basis of the benefits that they confer

---

[424] Charity Commission online guidance, *Charities and Public Benefit* (January 2008), para E4.
[425] [1948] AC 31.   [426] [1898] 1 IR 431.

on their overseas beneficiaries, without needing to show a benefit to the public in the United Kingdom.[427] Views relating to the conservation of the built and natural heritage have changed. There is now, for instance, a belief that the protection of bio-diversity could in itself be of value without needing to establish immediate practical benefits.[428]

Changes in social conditions and emerging scientific findings can change the view of what will be considered to be a public benefit. The Charity Commission gives an example:

> for a long time in the earlier part of the 20th century, the supply of cigarettes to sick people in hospital was regarded as charitable. During the First World War, major charities, in carrying out such a charitable aim, would provide cigarettes as 'useful sedatives for sick or wounded men'...Today, we would not regard the provision of cigarettes to hospital patients as being charitable for the public benefit. Any apparent benefits from the cigarettes acting as a sedative would be more than outweighed by the very real and considerable detriment caused to the patients and others by cigarette smoke.[429]

(d) Benefit to the public

It might seem fairly obvious as to whether there is a benefit to the public, but in many cases it is hard to determine whether benefits are genuinely public. For instance, the provision of a park in Lampeter is unlikely to be of much value to the residents of Birmingham, Liverpool, or Worcester. Does it therefore confer benefits on the public? If a trust provides advice and guidance to people suffering from a rare disease, can that be considered to be providing benefits on the public? The answer in both cases is likely to be that the activities concerned are for the public benefit, but they are clearly not for the benefit of the whole of the public, if by that we mean the whole population of England and Wales, or of the United Kingdom. Benefits can be public, therefore, even if they are available only to part of the public. But, if benefits are available only to part of the public, how can we determine whether those benefits are to the public or merely to a group of private individuals? The cases on public benefit have, in the past, distinguished between different heads of charity. They raise complex issues and are not always easy to reconcile. The abolition of the presumption of public benefit for some categories of charity may result in a harmonization of the principles of public benefit, but the Charity Commission considers that 'the public benefit requirement is likely in practice to look different for different groups of charities'.[430] Nevertheless, there are some recurrent themes and common principles. These include the factors set out in the Charity Commission's guidance, and can be summarized as the absence of arbitrary restrictions, and non-charitable benefits being no more than incidental.

---

[427] *Report of the Charity Commissioners for England and Wales 1992*, para 76.
[428] RR1—*The Review of the Register of Charities* (2001), para B9.
[429] *Charities and Public Benefit* (January 2008), para D6.
[430] Charity Commission: *Charities Act 2006—A Guide to the Main Provisions which Affect Charities* (November 2006).

(e) Absence of arbitrary restrictions

(i) Assumption that benefits will be available to all in need

In its guidance, the Charity Commission states that 'the beneficiaries must be appropriate to the aims' and the opportunity to benefit 'must not be unreasonably restricted... by geographical or other restrictions; or by ability to pay any fees'. It also states that 'People in poverty must not be excluded from the opportunity to benefit.'[431] The aims of a charity will largely govern the kinds of benefit which would be expected, and the general principle is that this benefit should be available to all those who have the need at which the provision is (or could be) directed.

(ii) Some restrictions may be justified

It is not inconsistent with charitable status for limits to be provided on access to benefits, provided that these limits are not irrational or unreasonable, and they can be justified by reason of the nature of the charity. It is inevitable that many charitable purposes are not available to every single member of the public. Trusts for the benefit of the blind or the disabled are not available to every member of the community because not every member of the community is blind or disabled. Trusts to provide for sea defences are not of direct benefit to members of the public living inland.[432]

There can also legitimately be limits that are not dictated simply by the nature of the benefit conferred. The provision of almshouses or sheltered accommodation could reasonably be confined to residents of a geographical area, since this is a rational way of allocating a limited provision. Participation in an orchestra might be confined to those who reach a satisfactory musical standard, since otherwise the quality of the musical experience might be affected. Membership of a debating society, while open to the public as a whole, might be limited at any one time to the number of seats in the debating chamber.

(iii) Arbitrary restrictions are not permitted

What is not permitted is a restriction that operates arbitrarily. The Charity Commission has suggested that a restriction would be inappropriate if it was unrelated to an organization's purpose, for example 'by hair colour or support for a particular football team'.[433] The bar on arbitrary restrictions is illustrated by *IRC v Baddeley*.[434] In this case a gift to a Methodist Mission in London for the promotion of the 'religious, social and physical training' of persons resident in West Ham and Leyton 'who were or were likely to become members of the Methodist Church' was held non-charitable because of the inclusion of social and recreational purposes. However, the House of Lords also held that the class of potential beneficiaries did not constitute a section of the public, so that there was insufficient 'public benefit'. There is no doubt that the residents of a

---

[431] See above p 631.   [432] See *IRC v Baddeley* [1955] AC 572.

[433] *Public Benefit—The Legal Principles* (January 2005) para 23. See also RR8—*The Public Character of Charity* (February 2001), para 11.

[434] [1955] AC 572.

particular area will be regarded as constituting a section of the public, but Viscount Simmonds drew a distinction between 'a form of relief extended to the whole community yet by its very nature advantageous only to the few and a form of relief accorded to a selected few out of a larger number equally willing and able to take advantage of it'.[435] He said that it would be charitable to provide a bridge, available to the public at large, but only used by a very small number. However, it would be different for 'a bridge to be crossed only by impecunious Methodists'. He held that the proposed gift fell within the second category because it was not available to all the residents of West Ham and Leyton but only those who were, or were likely to become, members of the Methodist Church. In effect, he ruled that a class drawn from within a class will not amount to a section of the public where the charity does not fall within one of the then substantively recognized groups (education, poverty, and religion):

a trust cannot qualify as a charity . . . if the beneficiaries are a class of persons not only confined to a particular area but selected from within it by reference to a particular creed.[436]

The scope of this particular principle is uncertain. Lord Reid dissented, holding that the members of a particular church were a section of the public and that there should not be a different standard for public benefit between different heads of charity.[437] Lord Tucker[438] and Lord Porter[439] expressed no opinion on the question whether the potential beneficiaries constituted a section of the public. The rule flows from the opinion of Viscount Simmonds, expressed not just in *IRC v Baddeley* but also in *Williams' Trustees v IRC*,[440] that the test for public benefit should be more stringent where it does not fall within a substantively recognized group of charitable purposes.

(iv) A 'class within a class' is not permitted?

The description of the limitation as preventing the creation of a 'class within a class' goes too far, since there are many cases where a charitable trust operates despite a double limitation on eligibility. For instance, a trust for poor widows in Rotherhithe was charitable despite there being three limitations on eligibility.[441] The real objection, it is submitted, is the introduction of an arbitrary limitation on eligibility. There is no objection to funding a church for the use of Methodists, or a synagogue for the use of Jews. But to limit the use of a bridge to Methodists (even poor Methodists) is an arbitrary and capricious restriction in the use of a facility that should be made available to all.

The continuing relevance of this test for charities has been affirmed by the Charity Commission. In giving guidance about charities for the relief of unemployment the Commission stated:

It may be that the people living in a particular area of high unemployment belong predominantly to a particular racial, ethnic or religious or other group, and this group will inevitably be the main beneficiary of the organisation's activities. This is unobjectionable in terms of charity

---

[435] Ibid., at 592.   [436] Ibid., at 592.   [437] Ibid., at 612.
[438] Ibid., at 614.   [439] Ibid., at 593.   [440] [1947] AC 447.
[441] *Re Faraker* [1912] 2 Ch 488.

law *as long as* the benefits are not additionally *restricted* solely to members of that group. This would constitute a 'class within a class', and is too small a beneficial class for charities set up to relieve unemployment.[442]

(v) Excluding the less well-off

There are many cases that demonstrate that it is not inimical to charitable status for charges to be made by a charity for the services which it provides. It has already been seen above that this has been held to be the case for a housing charity, a health-care charity, for a sports centre, and for educational charities. Nevertheless, there is continuing disquiet in some circles about charities such as public schools or private hospitals that impose charges for their services, with the result that benefits are only available to those who can afford to pay for these services. The fact that these organizations make no private profit, or that any profit that they do make is ploughed back into the further enhancement of their provision, does not silence their critics. In *Re Resch's Will Trusts*[443] it was made clear that the assessment of public benefit in the case of a fee-charging organization need not be confined to an assessment of the benefits to the direct recipients of the services. Indirect benefits to the public can also be taken into account. However, if an organization excludes the less well-off from both direct and indirect benefits, this is likely to affect its charitable status. In assessing whether the less well off are excluded, the Charity Commission has indicated factors that may be considered:

- The provision of concessions, subsidised or free places (for example, in the case of schools by offering scholarships, bursaries or assisted places, or in the case of theatres by offering concessionary tickets);
- The existence of accessible insurance or other benefit schemes (for example, medical insurance schemes);
- The provision of wider access to charitable facilities or services. For example some charities may provide additional facilities or services for the less well off people who would otherwise be excluded. Some charities may lend equipment or staff out to other charities or groups which provide the same facilities or services to the less well off. For example, a charitable independent school allowing a state maintained school to use its educational facilities.[444]

(vi) The creation of new principles

There is relatively little case law on how public benefit is to be measured when an organization charges fees. The illustrations given above by the Charity Commission reflects its interpretation of the law rather than a set of principles derived directly from judicial decisions. The latest guidance from the Commission on the issue of fees builds on these general principles,[445] and usefully gives examples of the types

---

[442] RR3—*Charities for the Relief of Unemployment* (March 1999), para A6. See also RR2—*The Promotion of Urban and Rural Regeneration* (March 1999), para A20.

[443] [1969] 1 AC 514.

[444] Charity Commission, *Public Benefit—The Legal Principles* (January 2005), para 36.

[445] See Charity Commission, *Public Benefit and Fee-Charging* (December 2008).

of opportunity that might suffice to offset fee charging for services, depending on the charitable purpose concerned. It is stated that the benefit conferred on someone unable to meet the fees must be 'genuine and meaningful' rather than 'nominal or minimal'.[446] So, for example, where the purpose is the advancement of education, in addition to subsidized access the formal secondment of teaching staff to other state schools or colleges, for example in specialist subjects such as individual sciences or modern languages, may be enough.[447] Similarly, for trusts concerned with the preservation of heritage, providing free information and advice on archaeology may suffice as a secondary benefit when coupled with offers of free or concessionary admission prices.[448] This whole area is highly controversial, and is one of the areas in which the Charity Commission is most exposed to accusations that its decisions are politically influenced.

(f) Non-charitable benefits must be incidental

(i) The 'exclusively charitable' rule

It has already been seen that a trust that combines both charitable and non-charitable objects will not be considered to be charitable. The same principle applies to the way in which the charity operates and the benefits which it confers. By definition, a charity exists for the public benefit. A trust which confers only private benefits cannot be a charitable trust, nor can a trust which provides a mixture of both public and private benefits, unless the private benefits can be seen as being no more than ancillary or subordinate to the public benefits. As the Charity Commission has stated, the purpose of the public benefit requirement is to ensure that 'charities are not used as a means of inappropriately conferring family benefits or fringe benefits on employees'.[449] There can therefore be issues relating to the relative balance of benefits in the case of membership organizations or trusts that confer benefits on a narrow range of beneficiaries. The essential test, as expressed by the Charity Commission, is:

it is a question of degree; does the organisation exist primarily for the advantage of its members or has the membership structure been adopted solely as an effective way of delivering charitable benefits or for administrative convenience?[450]

(ii) Incidental private or non-charitable benefits[451]

Although as a general rule a trust will only be charitable if its objects are exclusively charitable, the courts have held that there is an element of leeway such that a trust is not invalidated merely because it contains some non-charitable objects that are subsidiary or ancillary to the main charitable purposes. Thus, in *IRC v City of Glasgow Police Athletic Association*[452] Lord Cohen posed the question whether 'the main purpose of the body ... is charitable and the only elements in its constitution

---

446 Ibid., p 12.   447 Ibid., p 35.   448 Ibid., p 38.
449 RR8—*The Public Character of Charity* (February 2001), para 13.
450 Charity Commission, *Charities and Public Benefit* (January 2008), para F12.
451 See Gravells 'Public Purpose Trusts' [1978] Conv 92.   452 [1953] AC 380.

and operation which are non-charitable are merely incidental to that purpose'.[453] The House of Lords held that, in the circumstances, the promotion of sport was not purely ancillary to the purpose of promoting the efficiency of the police force. The decision would have been different if the non-charitable benefits had been only incidental. It is, for instance, possible for universities as charitable bodies to pay their teaching and support staff, even though this confers private benefits, provided that the payments made represent a fair payment for services rendered. In *Re Coxen*[454] a charitable trust was upheld despite the presence of some non-charitable elements. A previous Lord Mayor of London left some £200,000 to the Court of Aldermen on trust to apply the income to the following purposes:

(a) a sum not exceeding £100 for a dinner for the Court of Aldermen meeting on trust business;

(b) to pay one guinea to each alderman attending a committee in connection with the trust; and

(c) the balance for the benefit of orthopaedic hospitals.

If the first two purposes had not been charitable, Jenkins J would have regarded them as purely ancillary to the main charitable gift. In the event, he held that they were charitable as promoting the better administration of the charity. In *London Hospital Medical College v IRC*[455] a students' union[456] that provided social, cultural, and athletic activities for the students of a London teaching hospital was held charitable. Brightman J considered that the prime object of the union was the furtherance of the purposes of the medical college and not the private and personal benefit of the students, which was ancillary.[457] Similarly, in *Re South Place Ethical Society*[458] Dillon J regarded the organization of social activities by the society as purely ancillary to the society's main object of the promotion of ethical principles.[459] In *Funnell v Stewart*[460] the testatrix had left a substantial sum of money to a faith-healing group which held private religious services but which saw its raison d'être as 'the healing work it did for members of the community'.[461] Hazel Williamson, QC held that despite the non-charitable nature of the private services, the trust as a whole was charitable because the private services were 'clearly ancillary or subsidiary to the public faith healing part of the group's work, which was its predominant function'.[462]

(iii) Severance of non-charitable elements

In some cases it will be possible to sever the non-charitable or private elements in a trust. Where a gift is made in favour of some charitable and other non-charitable

---

[453] Ibid., at 405.   [454] [1948] Ch 747.   [455] [1976] 1 WLR 613.
[456] See also *A-G v Ross* [1986] 1 WLR 252, where the students' union of North London Polytechnic was held charitable despite some non-charitable activities which were regarded as ancillary.
[457] [1976] 1 WLR 613, at 623.   [458] [1980] 1 WLR 1565.
[459] Ibid., [1980] 1 WLR 1565, at 1569.   [460] [1996] 1 WLR 288.
[461] Ibid., at 296.   [462] Ibid.

purposes, the court may sever the good from the bad. In *Salusbury v Denton*[463] a gift to the testator's widow was to be applied partly toward charitable objects and the rest to his relatives. The widow died without making any appointments, and the court held that there could be a division of the fund between the charitable and non-charitable objects. Page-Wood V-C applied the maxim 'equality is equity' and divided the fund into two equal shares. However, where severance is possible equal division may not always be the most appropriate solution. In *Re Coxen*[464] Jenkins J held that if he had not been able to find that the object of providing a dinner for the aldermen was charitable, he would have been prepared to divide the fund unequally so as to sever the charitable from the non-charitable objects.

(g) Distinguishing between public and private benefits: the 'personal nexus' rule

It is rather more difficult than it might seem to distinguish between public and private benefits. There is, of course, no difficulty at the extremes. Funding research into a cure for cancer on terms that the research is to be made publicly available is obviously for the public benefit. Conversely, a trust for a named individual will be considered to confer only private benefits, even if the gift will transform the life of a person who is in poor health, badly housed, badly educated, and impecunious. A trust to educate the members of a single family will also be considered to confer only private benefits, even if the family is very large. One test to distinguish public from private benefits is the 'personal nexus' test, but it will be seen that this test has drawbacks.

(i) Meaning of the 'personal nexus' rule

This test has its foundation in the decision of the House of Lords in *Oppenheim v Tobacco Securities Trust Co Ltd*.[465] John Phillips was a large shareholder in British American Tobacco (BAT), and on his death he left securities to the trust company to be held upon trust and the income applied to provide for the education of the children of the employees or ex-employees of BAT. The House took the view that this group was not a section of the public but a private class, and that the trust was therefore non-charitable. The principle was stated by Lord Simmonds, who identified two characteristics that would render a class of beneficiaries a 'section of the public'. First, such a class would have to be 'not numerically negligible'. Second, the identity of the members of the class could not be defined by means of a personal nexus. He explained that:

the quality which distinquishes [the potential beneficiaries] from other members of the community, so that they form by themselves a section of it, must be a quality which does not depend on their relationship to a particular individual.[466]

---

463 (1857) 3 K & J 529.   464 [1948] Ch 747.
465 [1951] AC 297.   466 Ibid., at 306.

Thus, although the employees and ex-employees formed a class of some 110,000 persons, they were not a section of the public because they were identified by their personal contractual relationship with BAT. As Lord Simmonds said:

A group of persons may be numerous but, if the nexus between them is their personal relationship to a single propositus or to several propositi, they are neither the community nor a section of the community for charitable purposes.[467]

(ii) Impact of the personal nexus rule

The 'personal nexus' rule provides a conclusive test of whether a class should be regarded as a section of the public. If the identifying feature of the class is the members' nexus or relationship to a particular individual or group of individuals, they cannot constitute a section of the public. So the employees of a company would not constitute a section of the public, nor would the relatives of an individual[468] or the members of a trade union.[469] A strict application of the test might mean that the patients of a particular doctor or general medical practice, the clients of a firm of solicitors, and the members of a university and other similar classes would all be considered to be private groups.

(iii) Criticism of the personal nexus test

The rationale behind the personal nexus test is understandable, namely that purely private groups should not receive the tax privileges enjoyed by charities. If BAT had attempted to set up a similar trust in favour of its own employees, charitable status should not have been granted, as the company would have been seeking to provide its employees with a tax-free benefit. However, the facts of *Oppenheim*[470] were essentially different. The trust was established by a man whose only interest in the company was that he owned a substantial shareholding,[471] and in no sense was there an attempt by the company to give their employees a tax-free perk. In such circumstances, where the gift was made by an outside donor to a substantial class, it is questionable whether there is any reason for refusing charitable status.

The philosophy of providing rigid tests for public benefit is also questionable, since it is impossible to devise a rule that will cover all circumstances and not lead to anomalous results. For this reason, Lord MacDermott dissented from the decision of the other members of the House of Lords in *Oppenheim*, and rejected the personal nexus test. He pointed out that historically there had been no single conclusive test as to what constituted a sufficient section of the public, but that instead:

The usual way of approaching the issue...was...to regard the facts of each case and to treat the matter very much as one of degree.[472]

---

[467] [1951] AC 297.

[468] See *Re Compton* [1945] Ch 123, where the Court of Appeal held that a trust for the education of the descendants of three named persons was not charitable.

[469] *Re Mead's Trust Deed* [1961] 1 WLR 1244.   [470] See above, p 643.

[471] See [1951] AC 297, at 299, where it is recorded that 'no evidence was given of any connection of the grantors with the company except that John Phillips was a large stockholder'.

[472] [1951] AC 297, at 314.

Employees of the National Coal Board

Figure 19.3a Coal miners identified by a personal nexus

Coal miners in South Wales

Figure 19.3b Coal miners in a geographical area

He pointed out that far from proving conclusive, the 'personal nexus' test would produce unacceptable anomalies (see Figure 19.3):

Are miners in the service of the National Coal Board now in one category and miners at a particular pit or of a particular district in another?[473]

The force of Lord MacDermott's criticisms was felt by all members of the House of Lords in *Dingle v Turner*,[474] which is discussed below.

(iv) Continued relevance of the personal nexus test

Despite these criticisms, the personal nexus test has continued to be applied and is contained in the Charity Commission guidance on public benefit,[475] although the

---

[473] Ibid., at 318.   [474] [1972] AC 601.
[475] Charity Commission, *Public Benefit—The Legal Principles* (January 2005), para 23.

Commission has indicated that 'whilst the Commission must apply the law as set out in the *Oppenheim* decision unless and until it is over-ruled, it should be both cautious and flexible in the application of the test'.[476] Moreover, the courts have not merely looked to the definition of the class of beneficiaries but to the manner in which the purportedly charitable benefit has been allocated, thus following the time-honoured maxim that equity looks to the substance rather than the form. The personal nexus test was applied by the Court of Appeal in *IRC v Educational Grants Association Ltd.*[477] Metal Box Ltd established and funded the EGA, which had the object of advancing education by providing grants for individuals to attend university or private schools. Between 76 per cent and 85 per cent of the grants made by the EGA were made to children of employees of Metal Box, although Metal Box was not mentioned in the memorandum of association of the EGA. The Court of Appeal held that in practice there was a personal nexus, and that the EGA was not exclusively charitable. This decision seems correct, as it is clear that Metal Box was attempting to provide tax-free benefits for its employees under the cloak of charity. However, the same conclusion would surely have been reached by a more flexible test looking to all the circumstances of the case. In *Re Koettgen's Will Trusts*[478] an educational trust was open to the public at large, subject to a direction that the trustees were to give preference to the families of employees, up to a maximum of 75 per cent of the income. This was held to be valid, although Pennycuick J in *IRC v Educational Grants Association* expressed considerable difficulty with it. In *Caffoor v Income Tax Comr for Columbo*[479] it was held that a preference for the grantor's family made an educational trust non-charitable. This seems to be the better view, although it must be a question of degree in each case whether the extent of a preference is sufficient to deprive an otherwise charitable trust of its charitable status.

(v) Modified application of the personal nexus test

The Charity Commission, while noting that it must apply the law as set out in *Oppenheim*, has put forward an interpretation of the personal nexus rule that looks to the substance rather than to the form and therefore helps to modify its most extreme application.

It would appear that a class whose distinguishing feature is an impersonal quality may be a sufficient section of the public even though its constituent members also happen to share some personal characteristic (eg being tenants or related to tenants of a single landlord.[480] This means that:

- on this view there may be a sufficient section of the public in a case where (even though all potential beneficiaries might actually be connected by kin or contract):
  - on a general survey of the circumstances and considerations regarded as relevant it is clear that a public class is suggested; and

---

[476] Ibid., para A11. See also the Law Commission document, *Analysis of the Law Underpinning Charities and Public Benefit* (2008) v 1.1.1, para 3.45.
[477] [1967] Ch 993.   [478] [1954] Ch 252.   [479] [1961] AC 584.
[480] See *Re Tree* [1945] Ch 325.

- that class can be (and, as a rule, is in fact) described otherwise than by reference to kin or contractual relationship;[481]
- if it is difficult to describe a class using objective and impersonal terms, that would suggest that the body concerned is established for private rather than public benefit; and
- in those cases where the conclusion is that private benefits are intended for a group of individuals who are not together fairly describable as a section of the public or a section of the public [sic], the [personal nexus] rule applies to deny the benefits of charitable status.[482]

The Charity Commission also expresses the view that to treat groups differently on the basis simply of the way in which the group is defined by the terms of a trust or gift 'would be amenable to challenge under the Human Rights Act 1998 if it leads to an outcome which is not justifiable relationally in the public interest in terms of charity law'.[483]

(vi) The scope of the 'personal nexus' rule

The personal nexus test has not been applied to all categories of charity. *Oppenheim v Tobacco Securities Trust Co Ltd* and *IRC v Educational Grants Association* both concerned trusts for the advancement of education, and the test clearly applies to that head. It was also applied to charities within Lord Macnaghten's fourth head of 'other purposes beneficial to the community'.[484] It was not applied to trusts for the advancement of religion, provided that the religiously affected people lived their lives among the community at large (an illustration of the acceptance of indirect benefits). Most significantly, it did not apply to charities that fell under the head of relief of poverty. Thus, as Chadwick J observed in *Re Segelman (Decd)*:

a gift for the relief of poverty is no less charitable because those whose poverty is to be relieved are confined to a particular class limited by ties of blood or employment.[485]

This exception enjoyed an insurmountable historical pedigree. The special treatment of trusts for the relief of poverty does not seem to apply to trusts relieving needs of other types. Thus in *Re Mead's Trust Deed*[486] a trust to provide a home for aged members of a trade union and to provide a sanatorium for members suffering from tuberculosis was held not to be charitable because the members of a trade union are not a section of the public.

(vii) Poor relations

In *Re Compton*,[487] where the personal nexus test was first suggested, Lord Greene MR referred to a series of cases where gifts to the 'poor relations' of an individual

---

[481] See *Springhill Housing Action Committee v Commissioner of Valuation* [1983] NI 184.
[482] Charity Commission, *Analysis of the Law Underpinning Charities and Public Benefit* (December 2008), para 3.46.
[483] Charity Commission, *Public Benefit—The Legal Principles* (January 2005), para B9.45.
[484] See *Re Drummond* [1914] 2 Ch 90, where a gift to provide the holiday expenses of the workpeople of a spinning company was held not charitable, since it was not for general public purposes.
[485] [1996] Ch 171, [1995] 3 All ER 676, at 687.   [486] [1961] 1 WLR 1244.
[487] [1945] Ch 123.

had been held charitable.[488] He concluded that although these cases would fail under the personal nexus test, they were to be regarded as 'anomalous'[489] exceptions to the principle. In *Oppenheim*, Lord Simmonds was similarly unwilling to 'harmonise' and overturn the 'poor relations' cases.[490] It might be thought that members of a family are just the type of class that is private rather than public, and therefore not deserving of charitable status. The exception can only be justified on public policy grounds that the relief of poverty is such an important object to society that any gift that seeks to relieve it will be encouraged and upheld.[491] Thus, in *Re Scarisbrick's Will Trusts*[492] Bertha Scarisbrick left her residuary estate to trustees upon trust for her relations 'in needy circumstances'. The Court of Appeal held that this was a valid charitable trust. In *Dingle v Turner*,[493] this exception was confirmed by the House of Lords. Frank Dingle left his residuary estate to trustees, the income to be used to pay pensions to the 'poor employees' of E Dingle & Co, a company that he jointly owned. The House of Lords held unanimously that the personal nexus rule had no application to trusts for the relief of poverty.[494] The exemption was re-affirmed in *Re Segelman*,[495] where a testator left property in his will to be used for a period of twenty-one years for the benefit of the poor and needy members of his family. A schedule was drawn up in which he named six members of his extended family and the issue of five of them as comprising the class of beneficiaries. Chadwick J held that this created a valid charitable gift, falling within the scope of the exception, because it was 'a gift to particular poor persons, the relief of poverty among them being the motive for the gift'.[496]

The future of the anomalous exception of trusts for the relief of poverty from the personal nexus rule is uncertain. The public benefit in having a narrowly defined group of individuals kept in a lifestyle determined by reference to their former conditions of life rather than by reference to any objective assessment of poverty must be tenuous. Nor does a trust for financial provision for the members of one's own family have the characteristic of altruism that is normally the hallmark of charitable activity. It might be thought that such an anomaly could not survive the abolition of the presumption of public benefit in the Charities Act 2006. Nevertheless, the Charity Commission has accepted the continuation of this strange exception

[488] *Isaac v DeFriez* (1754) Amb 595; *A-G v Price* (1810) 17 Ves 371; *Bernal v Bernal* (1838) 3 My & Cr 559; *Browne v Whalley* [1866] WN 386; *Gillam v Taylor* (1873) LR 16 Eq 581; *A-G v Duke of Northumberland* (1877) 7 Ch D 745.
[489] [1945] Ch 123, at 139.   [490] [1951] AC 297, at 308.
[491] See *Re Scarisbrick* [1951] Ch 622, at 639, per Evershed MR: 'The "poor relations" cases may be justified on the basis that the relief of poverty is of so altruistic a character that the public element may necessarily be inferred thereby, or they may be accepted as a hallowed, if illogical, exception.'
[492] [1951] Ch 622.   [493] [1972] AC 601.
[494] Ibid., at 623, per Lord Cross: 'it must be accepted that whatever else it may hold sway the *Compton* rule has no application in the field of trusts for the relief of poverty'.
[495] [1996] Ch 171, [1995] 3 All ER 676; Bennett Histed 'Rectification of Wills and Charitable Trusts for Poor Relations: Broadening the Boundaries' [1996] Conv 379.
[496] [1995] 3 All ER 676, at 688.

to the personal nexus rule,[497] on the basis that it is bound by existing authorities. The Commission has issued some guidance about how the public benefit test will apply to the different purposes of different groups of charities. While the guidance for charities for the relief of poverty accepts that the class of beneficiaries may be defined by virtue of a family or company relationship,[498] the guidance cautions that any further restriction would not be acceptable. Using an example demonstrating a possible interaction between the rule against arbitrary restrictions and the acceptance of a family group as sufficient for the public benefit requirement for poverty, the Charity Commission says:

Preventing poverty is likely to involve addressing practices and issues within society which might have a very wide impact—for example, pursuing improvements in agricultural practices in order to address rural poverty. But it would not be appropriate to restrict the beneficial class for this aim in an artificial way, such as farmers from a particular family.[499]

The Commission also voices the general caution:

An organisation which has only the prevention of poverty as a charitable aim and which has a very narrowly defined beneficiary class, such as a family or employer connection, might have difficulties in demonstrating that its aims are for the public benefit.[500]

These comments in the guidance suggest that the Commission will try to distinguish or limit the poor relations exception where the possibility presents itself, and that its approach will be rather more restrictive than the breadth of some of the propositions in the case law could reasonably be considered to support. No such reservations were apparent, however, in *Cawdron v Merchant Taylors' School*,[501] where Blackburne J, in a case considered after the 2006 Act, saw no objection to holding charitable a gift to provide assistance (including scholarships) for the sons and other dependant relatives of Old Merchant Taylors killed or disabled in the First World War.

(h) Distinguishing between public and private benefit: a flexible approach

In contrast to the strict approach to questions of public benefit in the personal nexus test outlined above, others have advocated a more flexible response, arguing that strict tests are unworkable in practice and lead to anomalous results. They consider that each situation should be considered on its own facts, with a variety of circumstances being taken into account before an impressionistic judgment is made whether a class constitutes a section of the public or not.

As was noted above, in *Oppenheim v Tobacco Securities Trust Co Ltd* Lord MacDermott dissented from the decision of the majority and held that the personal nexus rule should not alone govern the question of public benefit. He considered that to separate the attributes dividing human beings into classes of those purely personal and those purely impersonal was a task 'no less baffling and elusive than the problem

---

[497] Charity Commission, *Analysis of the Law Underpinning Charities and Public Benefit* (January 2007), paras B9.41and B.10.

[498] Charity Commission, *The Relief and Prevention of Poverty* (December 2008), para E3.

[499] Ibid.   [500] Ibid.   [501] [2009] EWHC 1722 (Ch).

to which it is directed, namely, the determination of what is and what is not a section of the public'.[502] He also pointed out the anomalous results that would follow from such a rigid approach, so that a trust framed to provide for the education of children of those employed in the tobacco industry in a named town would be charitable, even though the class of potential beneficiaries may have been appreciably smaller than that under the trust in question. It would also call into question long-standing charities, for example gifts for the education of the daughters of missionaries or children sent to a particular school. He advocated a flexible approach whereby the court would 'regard the facts of each case and . . . treat the matter very much as one of degree', with a process of 'reaching a conclusion on a general survey of the circumstances and considerations regarded as relevant rather than of making a single, conclusive test'.[503] On such an approach he would have held the trust charitable, taking into account the numerical size of the class and the fact that it was not limited to present employees but also ex-employees. The intention of the donor was to 'advance the interest of the class described as a class rather than as a collection or succession of particular individuals'.[504]

In *Dingle v Turner*[505] Lord Cross, who delivered the leading judgment, expressed his dissatisfaction with the strict approach taken in *Oppenheim*. He accepted the force of the criticisms of Lord MacDermott, and acknowledged that he himself would 'prefer to approach the problem on much broader lines'.[506] He considered that the distinction between personal and impersonal relationships was unsatisfactory, and concluded that 'at the end of the day one is left where one started with the bare contrast between "public' and "private"'.[507] Like Lord MacDermott, he accepted that the question whether a trust was for the benefit of the public was a question of degree[508] and that a variety of factors would be taken into account. He suggested that a number of factors were significant:

(i) The size of the class

Obviously, the larger the class of potential beneficiaries the more likely it is that they will constitute a section of the public. Thus, the employees of a fairly small firm are less likely to be a section of the public than the employees of large companies like ICI and GEC, which employ many thousands of men and women who are largely unknown to each other.[509]

(ii) The purpose of the trust

The objects of the trust will exert a major influence on whether it should be regarded as charitable. Lord Cross explained that there was an intrinsic relationship between the size of the class and the objects of the trust:

---

502 [1951] AC 297, at 317.   503 Ibid., at 314.   504 Ibid., at 315.
505 [1972] AC 601.   506 Ibid., at 623.   507 Ibid.
508 Ibid., at 624.   509 Ibid.

It may well be that, on the one hand, a trust to promote some purpose, prima facie charitable, will constitute a charity even though the class of potential beneficiaries might fairly be called a private class and that, on the other hand, a trust to promote another purpose, also prima facie charitable, will not constitute a charity even though the class of potential beneficiaries might seem to some people fairly describable as a section of the public.[510]

Unfortunately, he did not give any illustration of how this principle might apply in practice.

(iii) The fiscal privileges enjoyed as a consequence of charitable status

Lord Cross further indicated that the question of charitable status cannot be determined in isolation from the benefits that such status will bring, so that regard to the fiscal privileges attendant upon charitable status cannot be avoided. He was of the view that the decisions in *Re Compton* and *Oppenheim* were influenced by the 'consideration that if such trusts as were there in question were held valid they would enjoy an undeserved fiscal immunity'.[511] However, Lord MacDermott expressed doubt whether fiscal privilege was a factor to be taken into account in determining whether a class constitutes a section of the public, and Viscount Dilhorne and Lord Hodson concurred with his reservation.

(i) The unsatisfactory state of the current law on distinguishing public and private benefit

While the judgment of Lord Cross in *Dingle v Turner*[512] highlights the deficiencies of the *Oppenheim* test, it sadly fails to eliminate the difficulties caused thereby.[513] Its status is in doubt. Although all the members of the House of Lords expressly concurred with his judgment, their comments vis-à-vis the *Oppenheim* test were purely obiter because the trust in question fell within the 'poverty' exception to the personal nexus rule. It is unfortunate that the law is in such a state of uncertainty. It is obvious that the distinction between 'public' and 'private' classes is extremely fine and impossible to capture in any single test or definition. The strict approach advocated by Lord Simmonds should therefore be rejected, and the 'impressionistic' approach advocated by Lord MacDermott and Lord Cross, which takes into account a wide range of factors, should be adopted. There is no reason why fiscal privilege should not be considered as a factor, since the very reason why the law insists that a charity must benefit the public or a section of the public is that private groups should not be entitled to massive state subsidy at the expense of the taxpayer. This awaits the opportunity for a court of sufficient seniority to consider the issue, as the Charity Commission may not resolve this issue in its guidance, as it has no power to change the existing law.

---

510 Ibid.   511 [1972] AC 601, at 625.

512 [1972] AC 601.   513 Jones 'Charitable Trusts. What is Public Benefit?' (1974) 33 CLJ 63.

(3) Public benefit in particular circumstances[514]

(a) Presumptions of public benefit

(i) The assumed public benefit of education

Prior to the Charities Act 2006, it was generally accepted that educational institutions operated for the public benefit, even if they charged fees. It has never been seriously questioned that universities are charitable institutions, even though students have to pay fees for their education. Nor, until the 2006 Act, was it questioned that not-for-profit schools such as public schools were legally charitable. The Charity Commission is now expecting independent schools registered as charities to provide affirmative proof that they meet the 'public benefit' test by demonstrating what number and level of scholarships they offer, and what other activities they undertake to provide benefits to a wider group than just fee-paying students. Some independent schools have challenged the approach being taken by the Charity Commission.[515] The Charities Act 2006 is ambiguous or even contradictory on whether a new public benefit test can be applied to educational charities. In section 3(2) it states that 'In determining whether that requirement is satisfied in relation to any such purpose, it is not to be presumed that a purpose of a particular description is for the public benefit', but in the following subsection it states 'any reference to the public benefit is a reference to the public benefit as that term is understood for the purposes of the law relating to charities in England and Wales'. While indicating that any presumption of public benefit has been abolished, it makes it clear that there has not in any other respect been a change in the law on public benefit. The implication of this has yet to be explored and tested. A similar issue arises in relation to the presumption of benefit in religion, which is considered next.

(ii) The assumed public benefit of religion

Until the Charities Act 2006, it was presumed that, provided religious organizations operated in the public domain, they met the public benefit requirement. The benefit to the public that the court assumed results from religious activity is not the spiritual benefit that a particular religion offers its adherents, but the benefit that comes to the community through the influence and example of its citizens who have adopted and attempted to put into practice the moral and ethical teaching of their religion. This is not a matter on which the courts have ever expected evidence to be presented. In *Neville Estates Ltd v Madden* this attitude was reflected by Cross J, who said:

the court is...entitled to assume that some benefit accrues to the public from the attendance at places of worship of persons who live in this world and mix with their fellow citizens.[516]

---

[514] See: RR8—*The Public Character of Charity* (February 2001).
[515] See above p 634.   [516] [1962] Ch 832.

This was echoed by Sir Nicholas Browne-Wilkinson V-C in *Re Hetherington (Decd)*:

The celebration of a religious rite in public does confer a sufficient public benefit because of the edifying and improving effect of such a celebration on the members of the public who attend.[517]

He therefore held that the saying of masses for the dead was prima facie charitable since the invariable practice is that they are said in public, 'which provides a sufficient element of public benefit'. No evidence was presented as to the nature of the benefit either to the dead or to the living.

It remains unclear what impact the abolition of the presumption of public benefit will have for religious charities.[518] The fact that the advancement of religion is recognized as a category of charitable purpose means that once a trust or organization demonstrates that it is established for this purpose, it will satisfy the first part of the twofold test for charitable status. However, it will still be necessary for the trust or organization to show that it satisfies the test of public benefit in regard to the way or ways in which it achieves its charitable purpose. Is it legitimate, if the presumption of public benefit has been abolished, for judicial notice still to be taken of the benefits allegedly conferred by the participation in public life of people who attend religious worship? As has already been seen, no presumption is made that a museum collection is of educational value to the public simply because it is available to the public. Why should a presumption be made that religious activity is of public benefit simply because members of the public participate in that activity? Since in almost all of the cases the test for public benefit in religion has been addressed exclusively using the presumption that religious worship is for the benefit of the public, it is hard to divorce the presumption from the test for benefit.

Commission guidance on the public benefit requirement of religion has been published,[519] but this guidance largely applies the assumptions that were previously made by the judiciary, such as that provided a place of worship is open to all who wish to attend, this will constitute a public benefit. There is no requirement that benefits be objectively proved or measured. Rather than providing a statement of how public benefit will be assessed, the Commission details a process:

We will do this by carrying out research studies on the extent to which different types of charity are meeting the public benefit requirement and by working with representative professional and umbrella bodies and with users of those charities.[520]

The Charity Commission has recently completed four public benefit assessments of existing religious charities.[521]

---

[517] [1990] Ch 1.
[518] See further Harding 'Trusts for Religious Purposes and the Question of Public Benefit' (2008) 71 MLR 159.
[519] Charity Commission, *The Advancement of Religion for the Public Benefit* (December 2008).
[520] Ibid., para G2.
[521] Charity Commission, *The Public Benefit Assessment Reports* (July 2009).

(iii) The assumed public benefit of animal welfare

A similar issue about presumed public benefit arises in relation to the public benefit of animal welfare charities, where judicial notice was taken *Re Wedgwood*[522] of the elevating effect on the human race of providing animal welfare. Will it be sufficient that animal welfare organizations operate in the public domain, or will it be necessary for them to demonstrate through evidence the beneficial impact of their activities? If evidence acceptable to a court of law is required to demonstrate the public benefit of a ban on experimentation on animals, why should there be no need of such proof of the benefits of the provision of animal welfare?

(iv) Public benefit in the 'poor relations' cases

The line of authority concerning 'poor relations' has already been considered. Can it really be considered, after the abolition of the presumption of public benefit in certain cases, that the public benefit requirement is satisfied where a person leaves a substantial sum of money for the relief of poverty among a class consisting exclusively of his or her immediate family? The Charities Act 2006 does not contain any specific statutory provision on this issue, and the Charity Commission appears to have adopted the view that the abolition of the presumption of public benefit has had no impact upon the continued applicability of this anomalous exception to the general requirement of public benefit.

(b) 'Cloistered' charities

If a charity has no operation in the public domain, it will be very hard for it to demonstrate public benefit. A trust to promote research will not be charitable unless the results of the research are published or otherwise disseminated. Contemplative religious orders that are cloistered and have no contact with the community at large have been held not to be charitable. In *Gilmour v Coats*[523] a gift of £500 was made to a priory of Carmelite nuns, who were cloistered and devoted their lives to prayer. The House of Lords held that they were not a charity because there was not the necessary element of benefit to the public. There was no interaction between the nuns and the community and Lord Simmonds rejected as 'too vague and intangible' any claimed edification of the public through the example of their spiritual lives and sacrifice. He also rejected the alleged benefit to the community of their intercessory prayer according to Roman Catholic doctrine, as evidenced by an affidavit of the Archbishop of Westminster. This alleged benefit was dismissed as 'manifestly not susceptible of proof', and he stated that the court does not accept as fact whatever a particular religion believes. In *Leahy v A-G of New South Wales*[524] a gift to religious orders which could have included contemplative orders would have been held invalid by the Privy Council as not being exclusively for charitable purposes if it had not been saved by the New South Wales Conveyancing Act 1919–54.

---

[522] [1915] 1 Ch 113.   [523] [1949] AC 426.   [524] [1959] AC 457.

9 Interpreting charitable gifts

(1) 'Exclusively' charitable purposes

(i) Purposes must be exclusively charitable

For a trust to be upheld as a valid charitable trust it must be for exclusively charitable purposes. None of the trust property must be applicable to non-charitable objects. Similarly, a corporation or unincorporated association will only be a charity if its purposes are exclusively charitable. If there is a combination of purposes, some charitable and others not, then it will not be charitable and will not enjoy the privileges outlined above. Thus, in *IRC v Oldham Training and Enterprise Council*[525] Lightman J held that a TEC was not a charitable body because its objects included some non-charitable elements, including the promotion of the interests of individuals rather than of the community in general. Similarly, in *McGovern v A-G*[526] the trust established by Amnesty International included some charitable objects, but also some non-charitable political purposes, and was not held charitable. In *Williams' Trustees v IRC*[527] the objects included many that were charitable, but also the promotion of social activities that are not. In *IRC v Baddeley*[528] the promotion of Methodism was a charitable purpose but the promotion of sport and recreation were not.

(ii) Benignant construction

Where the court is required to determine whether a gift was for exclusively charitable purposes, it may take a generous approach and give it a 'benignant construction'.[529] This means that, where there is an ambiguity such that a gift is capable of two constructions, one of which would make it void and the other effectual, the court will uphold it. This approach was confirmed by the House of Lords in *Guild v IRC*.[530] The precise scope of the principle permitting a benignant construction was considered by Hazel Williamson, QC in *Funnell v Stewart*.[531] She indicated that it would not save a 'dual purpose gift' where one identifiable object was clearly present but plainly not charitable, as the court could not simply ignore the non-charitable element of the trust. However, it would enable the court to save a gift which had a single purpose which was capable of being carried into effect in two different ways, one of which would be charitable and the other of which would not.[532]

(iii) Blue pencil approach

The decision of Lewison J in *Re Harding*[533] provides an extreme example of a benignant construction. This case concerned a testamentary bequest by a dying nun that

---

[525] [1996] STC 1218.   [526] [1982] Ch 321.   [527] [1947] AC 447.
[528] [1955] AC 572.
[529] *IRC v McMullen* [1981] AC 1, at 14, per Lord Hailsham LC; *Weir v Crum-Brown* [1908] AC 162, at 167, per Lord Loreburn LC.
[530] [1992] 2 AC 310, at 322.   [531] [1996] 1 WLR 288, at 296–297.
[532] See also *Re Hetherington* [1990] Ch 1.   [533] [2008] Ch 235.

suggested property be held 'in trust for the black community of Hackney, Haringey, Islington and Tower Hamlets'. In considering whether this was a valid gift to charity, Lewison J had to address the impact of s 34(1) of the Race Relation Act 1976 on the bequest. Rather than hold the gift void, he suggested that the effect of the provision was to remove any reference to colour, so that the trust became a trust for the benefit of people within the four London districts. The effect of the Act was therefore to enable Lewison J to apply a 'blue pencil' to delete the offending provision. He therefore upheld this as a valid trust, even though there were no instructions as to what the proposed trustees could do in relation to the property. Lewison J suggested that this would be met, if necessary, by the creation of a scheme by the Charity Commission.[534]

(2) Conjunctions combining or separating purposes in a list

Common problems arise where a trust is established for a variety of purposes, some of which are charitable and some of which are not. Where such a variety of purposes are listed together, the conjunctions used may determine whether the gift is to be construed as exclusively for charitable purposes. In general, the use of the word 'or' is usually given a disjunctive construction, so that 'charitable or benevolent' purposes are not exclusively charitable. In contrast, the word 'and' is usually given a conjunctive construction so that 'charitable and benevolent' purposes would be exclusively charitable. Although providing a strong prima facie indication, these are not binding rules of construction and each case must be examined in the light of the surrounding circumstances.

(a) 'And'

In *Re Sutton*[535] a gift to 'charitable and deserving' objects was held exclusively charitable. The word 'and' was given a conjunctive interpretation so that only deserving objects which were also charitable were contemplated. In *Re Best*[536] a gift to 'charitable and benevolent' institutions was similarly held exclusively charitable. The conjunctive construction is only a prima facie guide that may be displaced. In *A-G of the Bahamas v Royal Trust Co*,[537] a gift for purposes connected with the 'education and welfare' of Bahamian children was, in the light of all the circumstances, construed disjunctively and the gift therefore failed since it permitted the application of funds for educational purposes alternatively for welfare purposes, which need not necessarily be educational.[538]

---

[534] Ibid., at [27].   [535] (1885) 28 Ch D 464.
[536] [1904] 2 Ch 354.   [537] [1986] 1 WLR 1001.
[538] See also *Re Eades* [1920] 2 Ch 353, 'religious, charitable and philanthropic objects' held not exclusively charitable.

(b) 'Or'

In *Blair v Duncan*[539] a testatrix gave her trustee discretion to apply part of her residuary estate to 'charitable or public purposes'. The House of Lords held that this was to be read disjunctively, so that the gift included 'public purposes', which may fall outside the scope of charity. The gift therefore failed. A similar result was reached in *Houston v Burns*,[540] where a gift was made for 'public, benevolent or charitable purposes'. In *Chichester Diocesan Fund and Board of Finance v Simpson*[541] a gift in favour of 'charitable or benevolent objects'[542] was reluctantly held not to be exclusively charitable. The House of Lords could not find a more favourable interpretation than that the purposes were to be considered disjunctively.[543] Subsequently, in *A-G of the Cayman Islands v Wahr-Hansen*[544] the Privy Council advised that a trust established for the benefit of 'any one or more religious, charitable or educational institution or instructions or any organizations or institutions operating for the public good' was not exclusively charitable.

In some circumstances, on the construction of a gift as a whole, the word 'or' may not be read in this disjunctive way. In *Re Bennett*[545] a gift to educational purposes and 'other objects of charity, or any other public objects in the parish of Farringdon' was held to be exclusively charitable. Taken as a whole, and especially noting the word 'other', Eve J held that it was not to be construed disjunctively but to mean other public purposes that are also charitable.

(c) Charitable Trusts (Validation) Act 1954

This Act mitigates the impact of *Chichester Diocesan Fund v Simpson*.[546] It retrospectively validates trusts coming into effect prior to 16 December 1952, where the funds could be used exclusively for charitable purposes, but the terms also permit them to be used for non-charitable purposes. The Act has no application to trusts coming into effect after 15 December 1952. Apart from this, there is no legislation in England allowing a gift which is partly charitable and partly non-charitable to be upheld in so far as it is charitable.[547]

(d) Trusts for the benefit of a locality

For reasons which have now become obscure, the courts have adopted a benevolent construction towards gifts made in general terms for the benefit of a named locality or its inhabitants. Such gifts are construed to be impliedly limited to charitable purposes

---

[539] [1902] AC 37. [540] [1918] AC 337. [541] [1944] AC 341, HL.
[542] See also *Oxford Group v IRC* [1949] 2 All ER 537, CA.
[543] See also *Re Macduff* [1896] 2 Ch 451, where a gift to charitable or philanthropic purposes was held not exclusively charitable.
[544] [2001] 1 AC 75. [545] [1920] 1 Ch 305.
[546] [1944] AC 341, HL.
[547] There is legislation to this effect in the Republic of Ireland: Charities Act 1960, s 49. See also *Leahy v A-G for New South Wales* [1959] AC 457, where similar Australian legislation was applied.

in the specified community. Thus a gift to a particular parish,[548] or for the good of a particular country,[549] such as a gift for 'the benefit and advantage of Great Britain',[550] will be upheld as a valid charitable trust. However, in *A-G of the Cayman Islands v Wahr-Hansen*[551] the Privy Council advised that this generous rule of construction should not be extended to encompass all cases where there are general statements of benevolent or philanthropic objects. It is unlikely that the abolition of the presumption of public benefit will affect this principle of construction.

[548]   *West v Knight* (1669) 1 Cas in Ch 134.
[549]   *A-G v Earl of Lonsdale* (1827) 1 Sim 105; *Re Smith* [1932] 1 Ch 153.
[550]   *Nightingale v Goulburn* (1847) 5 Hare 484.
[551]   [2001] 1 AC 75.

20

Winding up of funds

When property is held as a fund for the benefit of other persons or purposes, it is inevitable in most instances that at some time the fund will come to an end. This may be a result of its exhaustion, as the property is properly applied. Alternatively, the purposes for which the fund was established may have failed or come to an end, leaving a surplus as yet undistributed. This chapter will consider the circumstances in which a fund comes to an end, and especially how the surplus of funds which have failed are applied.

1 Exhaustion and failure

Trusts can end both when the assets that are held on trust have been fully used, and also when, although assets remain, the purposes for which those assets were held on trust have become fulfilled or impossible. In the latter case, there will be a question as to who is entitled to the remaining assets.

(1) Exhaustion of a fund

Clearly, the fund will come to an end if all the property within it has been appropriately applied. The most obvious example is a bare trust where the property has been transferred to the beneficiary, thus bringing the trust relationship to an end. Similarly, the trustees of a discretionary trust, either exhaustive or non-exhaustive in character, may have distributed the whole of the fund among the class of potential beneficiaries. A charity may have spent all the money it possesses in pursuit of its purposes, and an unincorporated association may have exhausted its funds. In all such cases the fund has come to an end by process of exhaustion, and there is no longer any property left. There is no question of what should happen to an undistributed surplus, and the exhaustion of the fund brings the trust to an end.

(2) Failure of the fund

Alternatively, the fund may have to be wound up because of the failure of the purposes of the fund or the organization holding the fund. For example, a fund may have been established by the transfer of property to trustees on a trust which is subsequently found to be void for uncertainty, or a charitable institution holding funds may have closed.[1] In such circumstances, what happens to the surplus will depend on the nature of the fund and how it was held. In the event that there is no other person who is entitled to the surplus of a fund which has failed, it will pass to the Crown as bona vacantia.

(a) Failure of trusts

Where a trust fails, any surplus of the fund[2] will generally revert back to the original settlor of the property under a resulting trust.

(b) Dissolution of unincorporated associations

Where a non-charitable unincorporated association comes to an end, any property held by the association will usually be divided among the remaining members of the association in accordance with its rules.

(c) Failure of charities

When a charitable purpose or particular charitable institution or organization comes to an end, any surplus held by the charity will be applied cy-près for an alternative charitable purpose.

2 Surplus funds on the failure of trusts

(1) Operation of resulting trusts

When a trust is created, the property subject to it is held by trustees for the beneficiaries, who enjoy the equitable ownership thereof. If the trust fails, the equitable ownership will be returned, or 'result back', to those who originally owned the property. The trustees will then hold the property on trust for the original owners to whom it has resulted, and it is their duty to transfer it back to them. The essence of a resulting trust was captured by Megarry J in *Re Sick and Funeral Society of St John's Sunday School, Golcar*:

A resulting trust is essentially a property concept: any property a man does not effectually dispose of remains his own.[3]

The term 'resulting trust' is used to describe a number of different situations where property will revert back to its original owner, and it is important to distinguish the different senses in which the term is used. Resulting trusts were classified by

---

[1] *Re Slevin* [1891] 2 Ch 236, CA; *Re Rymer* [1895] 1 Ch 19, CA.
[2] Or the whole fund in the case of a trust fund void ab initio.
[3] [1973] Ch 51 at 59.

Megarry J in *Re Vandervell's Trusts (No 2)*[4] into 'presumed' and 'automatic' resulting trusts.[5]

(a) Presumed resulting trusts

Presumed resulting trusts are those which arise as the result of the presumption that a property 'results to the man who advances the purchase money'.[6] For example, in *Tinsley v Milligan*[7] a house was purchased in the sole name of Tinsley, but part of the purchase price was provided by her lesbian lover, Milligan. It was held that there was a resulting trust and that Tinsley held the house on trust for herself and Milligan as joint tenants. The presumptions that give rise to such resulting trusts are not conclusive, and may be rebutted by evidence that the contributor intended to make a gift and not to retain any interest in the property purchased. In some cases, because of the nature of the relationship between the parties, the law presumes that a gift is intended, and a resulting trust does not arise unless the presumption is rebutted by evidence that a gift was not intended.[8]

(b) Automatic resulting trusts

Megarry J suggested that 'automatic' resulting trusts arise by operation of law, and not on the basis of any presumed intention on the part of the original owner of the property. As he observed:

What a man fails effectually to dispose of remains automatically vested in him, and no question of a mere presumption can arise.[9]

Where a trust fails, unless expressly or impliedly excluded,[10] an automatic resulting trust determines how any remaining surplus should be applied.

In *Westdeutsche Landesbank Girozentrale v Islington London Borough Council*,[11] this twofold categorization of resulting trusts was broadly adopted. Both Lord Browne-Wilkinson and Lord Goff explained that resulting trusts arise in two situations corresponding to the presumed and automatic categories previously identified by trusts identified by Megarry J:

(1) voluntary payments by A to B, or for the purchase of property in the name of B or in his and A's joint names, where there is no presumption of advancement or evidence of intention to make an out and out gift; or (2) property transferred to B on an express trust which does not exhaust the whole beneficial interest.[12]

---

[4] [1974] Ch 269.   [5] Ibid. at 289 and 294–296.
[6] *Dyer v Dyer* (1788) 2 Cox Eq Cas 92, per Eyre CB.   [7] [1993] 3 All ER 65.
[8] The presumption of 'advancement'. See further Chapter 9.
[9] [1974] Ch 269 at 289.
[10] See *Davis v Richards and Wallington Industries Ltd* [1991] 2 All ER 563.
[11] [1996] AC 669. See Birks 'Trusts Raised to Avoid Unjust Enrichment: The *Westdeutsche* Case' [1996] RLR 3; Cape 'Compound Interest and Restitution' (1996) 112 LQR 521; Jones 'Ultra Vires Swaps: The Common Law and Equitable Fall-Out' [1996] CLJ 432; Stevens 'Simple Interest Only? Autonomous Unjust Enrichment and the Relationship between Equity and Common Law' [1997] LMCLQ 441.
[12] [1996] AC 669 at 689, per Lord Goff.

However, Lord Browne-Wilkinson doubted that the term 'automatic resulting trust' accurately described the trust arising in favour of the settlor where an express trust fails:

> Under existing law a resulting trust arises in two sets of circumstances...(B) Where A transfers property to B *on express trusts*, but the trusts declared do not exhaust the whole beneficial interest...Both types of resulting trust are traditionally regarded as examples of trusts giving effect to the common intentions of the parties. A resulting trust is not imposed by law against the intentions of the trustee (as is a constructive trust) but gives effect to his presumed intention. Megarry J in *Re Vandervell's Trusts (No 2)* suggests that a resulting trust of type (B) does not depend on intention but operates automatically. I am not convinced that this is right. If the settlor has expressly, or by necessary implication, abandoned any beneficial interest in the trust property, there is in my view no resulting trust: the undisposed of equitable interest vests in the Crown as bona vacantia.[13]

While these comments rightly observe that a resulting trust is not an inevitable result whenever an express trust fails, it is unlikely that Megarry J ever intended the term automatic resulting trust to carry this connotation. Such a resulting trust operates in effect as a form of trust implied in default, and while it may be rooted in the presumed intention of the settlor, there is a much reduced likelihood that evidence will be adduced that the settlor did not wish to have the equitable interest in the property to revert back to him in the event of such failure. The presumption of his intention is therefore much more resilient than that under a conventional presumed resulting trust, where evidence that a gift was intended will rebut the presumption. Thus, resulting trusts arising in the event of the failure of an express trust do tend to arise automatically in practice, if not in theory, as the trustee will only be able to show that the settlor has expressly, or by necessary implication, abandoned any beneficial interest in the trust property in exceptional circumstances. The law is very slow to recognize abandonment of property by the owner. There are many cases involving chattels on this point[14] and there is no reason to believe that the position should be different for interests behind a trust. However, in the light of Lord Browne-Wilkinson's comments, the terminology of automatic resulting trusts may have to be abandoned.[15] It remains unclear whether a similarly snappy label will emerge. Such trusts could perhaps be termed surplus-funds resulting trusts, which would be more descriptive than Type (B) resulting trusts, which is the best that is offered by Lord Browne-Wilkinson.

This chapter will be concerned with the operation of what, for want of any better term will continue to be called automatic resulting trusts. Presumed resulting trusts have already been considered in Chapter 9.

---

[13]   Ibid., at 708.

[14]   See *Simpson v Gowers* (1981) 32 OR (2d) 385; *Dennis v North Western Nat Bank* 81 NW 2d 254 (1957).

[15]   See Swadling 'Explaining Resulting Trusts' (2008) 124 LQR 72, who argues for retention of the automatic and presumed categorization of resulting trusts.

(2) When an automatic resulting trust will be implied

(a) Failure to declare the beneficial interests arising behind an express trust

If property is transferred to trustees upon trust but the settlor makes no effective declaration of the beneficial interests, so that the trustees do not know who they are to hold the property for, they will hold the property transferred on a resulting trust for the settlor, or if he is dead, for his successors in title.[16] The principle was stated by Lord Wilberforce in *Vandervell v IRC*, where an option to repurchase shares was held by a trust company but no indication had been given as to the beneficiaries thereof.

the option was vested in the trustee company as a trustee on trusts, not defined at the time, possibly to be defined later. But the equitable, or beneficial interest, cannot remain in the air: the consequence in law must be that it remains in the settlor...[17]

The option was therefore held by the trustee company on resulting trust for Mr Vandervell, who had been the original owner of the shares.

The operation of a resulting trust in such circumstances was examined by the Privy Council in *Air Jamaica Ltd v Charlton*.[18] Lord Millett explained that a resulting trust does not arise because the trustee wanted to retain a beneficial interest in the property:

Like a constructive trust, a resulting trust arises by operation of law, though unlike a constructive trust it gives effect to intention. But it does arise whether or not the transferor intended to retain a beneficial interest—he almost always does not—since it responds to the absence of any intention on his part to pass a beneficial interest to the recipient. It may arise even where the transferor positively wished to part with the beneficial interest, as in *Vandervell v IRC*...The House of Lords affirmed the principle that a resulting trust is not defeated by evidence that the transferor intended to part with the beneficial interest if he has not in fact succeeded in doing so.[19]

(b) Failure of an express trust

If a valid trust is created but subsequently fails for some reason, any trust property that remains in the hands of the trustees will be held on resulting trust for the settlor. For example, in *Re Ames' Settlement*[20] Louis Ames created a marriage settlement of £10,000 on the marriage of his son, John, to Miss Hamilton in 1908. The marriage was declared 'absolutely null and void' in 1927 by the Supreme Court of Kenya, on the grounds of the husband's incapacity to consummate the marriage.[21] Vaisey J concluded that, since the marriage had been void ab initio, there was a total failure of the consideration for the marriage settlement and the property should result back to the father's estate. A resulting trust would also arise if a settlement was created in contemplation of a marriage which never took place.[22] In

---

[16] See *Johnson v Ball* (1851) 5 De G & Sm 85; *Re Keen* [1937] 1 All ER 452 and *Re Boyes* (1884) 26 Ch D 531, where there were ineffective attempts to create secret trusts.

[17] [1967] 2 AC 291 at 329.   [18] [1999] 1 WLR 1399.   [19] Ibid., at 1412.

[20] [1946] Ch 217.   [21] See *Re d'Altroy's Will Trusts* [1968] 1 WLR 120; *Re Rodwell* [1970] Ch 726.

[22] *Essery v Cowlard* (1884) 26 Ch D 191; *Bond v Walford* (1886) 32 Ch D 238.

Re Cochrane[23] a marriage settlement was created in favour of a wife 'so long as she shall continue to reside with' her husband. They separated and the income was paid to the husband, who then predeceased her. It was held that the income should be held on resulting trust for the settlors in proportion to the contributions they had made to the fund.

Where a trust is void because it fails to comply with all the requirements necessary for the creation of a valid trust, the trust property will again be held on a resulting trust for the settlor or his estate. In *Chichester Diocesan Fund and Board of Finance Inc v Simpson*[24] Caleb Diplock created a discretionary trust in favour of charity. However, because the trust included some non-charitable objects it was invalid and the property resulted back to his estate. In *Re Astor's Settlement Trusts*[25] a trust created in 1945 for the promotion of 'good understanding between the nations' and the 'preservation of the independence and integrity of newspapers' was held void because it contravened the beneficiary principle. The property was therefore held on resulting trust.

Where property has been held on trust for a charity that has failed, it may similarly result to the settlors or donors. For example, in *Re Ulverston and District New Hospital Building Trusts*[26] a fund had been created for the purpose of building a new hospital. The fund consisted of contributions from named donors, anonymous donors, street collections, and the proceeds of entertainments. The purpose became impossible, and it was held that the fund should be held on resulting trust for its donors. However, often the application of a resulting trust will be excluded by the cy-près doctrine,[27] and the property will be applied to other charitable purposes.

(c) Trust fund has not been exhausted

Where a trust has been established for a specific purpose, any surplus funds that have not been exhausted on the completion of the purpose should in most cases be returned to the original contributors by way of a resulting trust in proportion to their contributions. The principle was stated by Harman J in *Re Gillingham Bus Disaster Fund*:

The general principle must be that where money is held upon trust and the trusts declared do not exhaust the fund it will revert to the donor under what is called a resulting trust.[28]

In *Re Abbott Fund Trusts*[29] a fund of £284 was collected and established in 1890 for the support of two deaf and dumb ladies. On their death in 1899 a surplus of £366 13s 9d remained in the fund. The court held that the surplus should be held for the benefit of those who had subscribed to the fund. Central to the decision was the finding by Stirling J that the fund was never 'intended to become the absolute property of the ladies'.[30] However, in subsequent cases the courts seem to have construed gifts with similar limited purposes as absolute gifts to their beneficiaries, excluding any possibility of a resulting trust to the contributors. In *Re Andrew's Trust*[31] the friends of a deceased clergyman subscribed to a fund for the education of his children. After

23 [1955] Ch 309.   24 [1944] AC 341.   25 [1952] Ch 534.
26 [1956] Ch 622.   27 See below, p 681.   28 [1958] Ch 300 at 310.
29 [1900] 2 Ch 326.   30 Ibid., at 330.   31 [1905] 2 Ch 48.

all the children had completed their education, there was a surplus of some £460 remaining in the fund. Kekewich J held that there should not be a resulting trust to the subscribers, because the gift was to be construed as an absolute gift to the children, with the purpose being merely a motive for the gift. He took the view that the court always[32] construed such gifts in this way.[33] *Re Andrew's Trust*[34] was followed in *Re Osoba (Decd)*,[35] which concerned a trust established by a testator 'for the training of my daughter Abiola up to university grade and for the maintenance of my aged mother'. His mother had died and the daughter had completed her university education, leaving a surplus in the fund. The question arose whether this should pass on a resulting trust to the testator's second wife and daughter, who were the residuary legatees of his estate. The Court of Appeal held that the gift was an absolute gift and the reference to the purpose 'merely a statement of the testator's motive in making the gift'.[36] It is difficult to reconcile[37] *Re Abbott Fund Trusts*[38] with *Re Andrew's Trust*.[39] Ultimately, as was recognized by the Court of Appeal in *Re Osoba*,[40] each turns on its own facts, and it is of perhaps crucial importance that in *Re Abbott Fund Trusts*[41] the beneficiaries of the fund were deceased, and could derive no further benefit from it.[42]

The question is whether, on the facts, the intention of the settlor was such as to preclude a resulting trust. It should be noted that the strictness of the beneficiary principle (which invalidates most trusts for non-charitable purposes ab intio) and the cy-près doctrine (which operates in relation to surplus funds of charities) operate to restrict the circumstances in which an express trust is able to be created for a purpose, which may subsequently be accomplished leaving an unexpended surplus. Special rules apply where an appeal has been made for funds to be applied for a charitable purpose, and there is a failure of the specific purpose for which the appeal was made. These rules are considered below in relation to surplus funds on the failure of a charity.

(d) Pension fund surplus[43]

Particular problems have arisen concerning the applicability of a resulting trust analysis to a surplus under a pension scheme trust. There is only one kind of pension

---

[32] See *Re Sanderson's Will Trust* (1857) 3 K & J 497; *Barlow v Grant* (1684) 1 Vern 255; *Webb v Kelly* (1839) 9 Sim 469; *Lewes v Lewes* (1848) 16 Sim 266; *Presant and Presant v Goodwin* (1860) 1 Sw & Tr 544.

[33] [1905] 2 Ch 48 at 52–53: 'If a gross sum be given, or if the whole income of the property be given, and a special purpose be assigned for that gift, this court always regards the gift as absolute, and holds the purpose merely as the motive of the gift, and therefore holds that the gift takes effect as to the whole sum or the whole income, as the case may be.'

[34] [1905] 2 Ch 48.

[35] [1979] 1 WLR 247; [1978] CLJ 219 (Rickett). See also *Re Lipinski's Will Trusts* [1976] Ch 235.

[36] [1979] 1 WLR 247 at 257, per Buckley LJ.

[37] See the judgment of Megarry V-C at first instance in *Re Osoba* [1978] 1 WLR 791.

[38] [1900] 2 Ch 326.   [39] [1905] 2 Ch 48.   [40] [1979] 1 WLR 247 at 251.

[41] [1900] 2 Ch 326.

[42] This was pointed out by Kekewich J in *Re Andrew's Trust* [1905] 2 Ch 48 at 52.

[43] See Pollard 'Pensions Law and Surpluses: A Fair Balance between Employer and Members?' (2003) TLI 2.

scheme where this can arise: where the scheme pays a pension based on a defined pro-portion of a member's earnings, and the pension is paid from a fund into which the member and his employer have made contributions. This type of pension is described as a funded defined benefit scheme. Most funded pension schemes pay a pension based on the value of the investments which are attributed to an individual member. By definition these cannot be in surplus. With a defined benefit scheme it is possible for there to be both a shortfall or a surplus. Falling investment returns and increased longevity have meant that few defined benefit pension schemes now have a surplus, but pension scheme surpluses were common in the 1990s and may still arise where a well-funded scheme is wound up. Although the fund has been created by the finan-cial contributions of the employees and employers, such contributions will have been made on the basis of a contractual relationship between the pension provider and the contributors. The contributions are not simply gifts, and it cannot easily be said that a contributor intended to receive his property back if the fund was wound up while in surplus. Rather, the contributor has bargained to receive a contractual benefit in return for his contributions, namely the payment of a contractually agreed pension, thus leaving him with no proprietary claim against the fund if he has received all that he bargained for. Historically, it has therefore been suggested that the contractual nature of the relationship between the contributor and the trustees excludes the pos-sibility of a resulting trust.[44] This principle was explained by A L Smith LJ in *Cunnack v Edwards*, which concerned the surplus funds of a society established to provide annuities for the widows of members who died:

As the member paid his money to the society, so he divested himself of all interest in this money for ever, with this one reservation, that if a member left a widow she was to be provided for dur-ing her widowhood. Except as to this he abandoned and gave up the money for ever.[45]

This logic was subsequently applied in *Re West Sussex Constabulary's Widows, Children and Benevolent (1930) Fund Trusts*[46] to a fund established to provide pay-ments for the widows and dependants of policemen. When the fund was wound up, leaving a surplus, Goff J held that the members who had contributed to the fund could not recover back the share of the surplus attributable to their contributions because they had received all the benefit that they had contracted to receive. He similarly held that any fund surplus attributable to the proceeds of entertainments, raffles, sweepstakes, and other such fund-raising activities, should not be subject to a result-ing trust because the participants had acted on the basis of a contractual bargain for services received:

the relationship is one of contract and not of trust; the purchaser of a ticket may have the motive of aiding the cause or he may not; he may purchase a ticket merely because he wishes to attend the particular entertainment or to try for the prize, but whichever it be, he pays his money as the price of what is offered and what he receives.[47]

---

[44] As Megarry J observed in *Re Sick and Funeral Society of St John's Sunday School, Golcar* [1973] Ch 51, many of the difficulties arise because of the confusion of property with contract.

[45] [1896] 2 Ch 679 at 683.   [46] [1971] Ch 1.   [47] Ibid., at 11.

However, in later cases it has been held that a resulting trust analysis might be adopted in respect of a pension fund surplus, despite the contractual nature of the contributions made. In *Davis v Richards and Wallington Industries Ltd*[48] Scott J held that it was not inevitable that payments into a fund on the basis of contract would exclude a resulting trust. The case concerned a company pension scheme that, after full provision had been made for pension obligations, contained a surplus of some £3m. This was derived partly from the contributions of employees, who were obliged by their contracts to contribute 5 per cent of their salaries, and partly from the contributions of the employer. On the question whether there should be a resulting trust in favour of those who had contributed, Scott J rejected any blanket principle that contractual payments exclude the possibility of a resulting trust:

> the fact that a payment to a fund has been made under contract and that the payer has obtained all that he or she bargained for under the contract is not necessarily a decisive argument against a resulting trust.[49]

Instead, he concluded that, whenever a trust fund was involved, any surplus would inevitably pass under a resulting trust unless such a trust was expressly or impliedly excluded.[50] Applying this principle, he held that the employers were entitled to claim the proportion of the surplus attributable to their overpayments by way of a resulting trust. However, in contrast, he held that the employees were excluded from claiming a resulting trust. He considered that there were 'unworkable' difficulties of calculating the shares of individual employees,[51] because he considered it necessary to value the benefits that each member had in fact received in order to ascertain his share in the surplus, and also pointed to the legislative rules under which the pension scheme took effect, which placed a maximum on the financial return from the fund to which each employee could become entitled, which would be exceeded if a resulting trust arose in their favour. In the light of these factors a resulting trust was excluded by implication, and the proportion of the surplus attributable to the employee's over-contributions passed to the Crown as bona vacantia.

Davis v Richards and Wallington Industries Ltd[52] thus establishes that where property is held on trust[53] a resulting trust of any surplus will always arise in favour of the contributors unless it is excluded by other considerations.[54] This approach was

---

[48] [1991] 2 All ER 563; [1991] Conv 366 (Martin); Gardner 'New Angles on Unincorporated Associations' [1992] Conv 41.

[49] [1991] 2 All ER 563 at 593.

[50] Ibid., at 592–593: following *Jones v Williams* (15 March 1988, unreported), per Knox J.

[51] This was because the value of the benefits of the employees would be different for each employee, depending on how long he had served, how old he was when he joined, and how old he was when he left. Two employees may have paid identical sums into the fund, but be entitled to benefits of a different value: see [1991] 2 All ER 563, 595.

[52] [1991] 2 All ER 563.

[53] As opposed to the situation where property is held by an unincorporated association.

[54] See also *Palmer v Abney Park Cemetery Co Ltd* (4 July 1985, unreported); *Kerr v British Leyland (Staff) Trustees Ltd* [1986] CA Transcript 286, Fox LJ; *Mihlenstedt v Barclays Bank International Ltd* [1989] IRLR 522.

adopted by the Privy Council in *Air Jamaica Ltd v Charlton*,[55] which also concerned a pension fund surplus attributable to the contributions of the employers and employees of a company. Lord Millett explained that employees should not be excluded from obtaining an interest in a pension fund surplus merely because they had received what they had contracted to receive:

> Their Lordships would observe that, even in the ordinary case of an actuarial surplus, it is not obvious that, when employees are promised certain benefits under a scheme to which they have contributed more than was necessary to fund them, they should not expect to obtain a return of their excess contributions.[56]

The Privy Council doubted that Scott J had been correct to exclude a resulting trust in favour of the employees. Rather than being required to value the benefits that each member had received in order to ascertain his share, the Privy Council held that the members' share of the surplus should be 'divided pro rata among the members and the estates of deceased members in proportion to the contributions made by each member without regard to the benefits each has received and irrespective of the dates on which the contributions were made'.[57] The company was also held entitled to a resulting trust of the proportion of the surplus attributable to its contributions, despite the presence of a clause in the trust deed stating that 'no moneys which at any time have been contributed by the company under the terms hereof shall in any circumstances be repayable to the company'. The Privy Council considered that this clause only operated to prevent repayments to the company under the terms of the scheme, and did not exclude the possibility of a resulting trust if the scheme came to an end:

> Consequently their Lordships think that clauses of this kind in a pension scheme should generally be construed as forbidding the repayment of contributions under the terms of the scheme, and not as a pre-emptive but misguided attempt to rebut a resulting trust which would arise dehors the scheme. The purpose of such clauses is to preclude any amendment that would allow repayment to the company.[58]

Pension trusts surpluses may be a matter of history in the present economic climate, as many defined benefit pension funds currently find themselves in deficit or are changing the terms of pension schemes to avoid such a deficit. The principles will remain important, however, should long-term conditions change.

(e) Failure of a loan made for a specific purpose[59]

One specialized application of the surplus-funds resulting trust can occur where money has been lent for a specific purpose that has failed. On the failure of the purpose the borrower may hold the money lent on a resulting trust for the lender. Such a resulting trust is extremely significant if the borrower becomes insolvent, since the lender will be entitled to assert an equitable proprietary claim to the money lent and it will not form part of the assets of the creditor. The lender will not therefore merely rank

---

[55] [1999] 1 WLR 1399.   [56] Ibid., at 1412.   [57] Ibid., at 1413.
[58] Ibid., at 1412.
[59] See Worthington, *Proprietary Interests in Commercial Transactions* (1996), pp 43–70.

among the general creditors of the borrower, which would have been his position in the absence of a trust because he would only have been entitled to a contractual claim for the repayment of the debt. It is not surprising that the principle originally evolved in cases where lenders were willing to make last-ditch loans to companies in extreme financial peril, since the added security of the resulting trust encourages them to make what would otherwise be extremely risky investments.

The implication of such a resulting trust was first recognized by the House of Lords in *Barclays Bank Ltd v Quistclose Investments Ltd*.[60] A company, Rolls Razor Ltd, was in severe financial difficulties. A financier was willing to lend them £1m if they could meet an ordinary share dividend of some £210,000. They obtained a loan for Quistclose on the agreed condition that it would only be used to pay the dividend, and for that purpose the money was to be kept in a separate bank account. Before the dividends could be paid, Rolls Razor went into voluntary liquidation. The House of Lords held that, because of the exclusive purpose for which the loan was made, the money was received by Rolls Razor in the fiduciary character of a trust to pay the dividend. Since that purpose had failed, there was a resulting trust in favour of the lenders. The principle was explained by Lord Wilberforce:

There is surely no difficulty in recognising the co-existence in one transaction of legal and equitable rights and remedies: when the money is advanced, the lender acquires an equitable right to see that it is applied for the primary designated purpose: when the purpose has been carried out...the lender has his remedy against the borrower in debt: if the primary purpose cannot be carried out, the question arises if a secondary purpose (ie repayment to the lender) has been agreed, expressly or by implication: if it has, the remedies of equity may be invoked to give effect to it...[61]

This principle has been developed and applied in subsequent cases,[62] and the House of Lords again considered whether such a trust was operative in *Twinsectra Ltd v Yardley*.[63] In this case, a finance company agreed to lend £1m to the prospective purchaser of residential land. The money was paid into the client account of the purchaser's solicitor, subject to an express undertaking that the money be utilized 'solely for the acquisition of property on behalf of our client and for no other purpose'. Contrary to the terms of this undertaking, £358,000 of the money was used for other purposes. One question was whether the arrangement had given rise to a trust of the money, a crucial prerequisite to the claim of dishonest assistance in a breach of trust that was

---

[60] [1970] AC 567. See also Mitchell 'Subrogation, Tracing and the *Quistclose* Principle' [1995] LMCLQ 451; Matthews, 'The New Trust: Obligations without Rights' in Oakley, *Trends in Contemporary Trust Law* (1996), p 16.

[61] [1970] AC 567 at 581.

[62] *Carreras Rothmans Ltd v Freeman Mathews Treasure Ltd* [1985] Ch 207 at 222, per Peter Gibson J, who explained the trust as arising from the principle 'that equity fastens on the conscience of the person who receives from another property transferred for a specific purpose only and not therefore for the recipient's own purposes, so that such person will not be permitted to treat the property as his own or use it for other than the stated purpose'. See also *Re EVTR* [1987] BCLC 646.

[63] [2002] 2 AC 164; [2002] 2 All ER 377. See [2002] RLR 111 (Ricketts); [2002] Con 387 (Thompson); (2002) 16 TLI 165 (Penner); (2002) 16 TLI 223 (Glister); (2003) 119 LQR 8 (Yeo and Tijo); (2004) 63 CLJ 632 (Glister).

being maintained by the finance company. The House of Lords held that the money was subject to a trust because it had been paid subject to an undertaking that it would only be used for a specific purpose.

While it is clearly established that a trust will arise where money is lent for a specific purpose that fails, the exact nature of such a trust has been a matter of academic controversy. In particular it has been difficult to determine when the trust comes into existence, to identify the beneficiary, and to reconcile the existence of the trust with the beneficiary principle, since it appears to require the existence of a primary trust under the terms of which money is held for the carrying out of a purpose. These theoretical problems were not explored by the House of Lords in *Quistclose* itself. There are several possibilities, none of which is free from difficulty.

(i) Primary trust for intended recipients

First, a loan for a specific purpose may be regarded as creating a primary trust in favour of the persons intended to receive payment, for example specific creditors or shareholders, which gives rise to a resulting trust when the purpose fails. This approach seems to have been adopted by Megarry V-C in *Re Northern Developments (Holdings) Ltd.*[64] However, this analysis can be criticized[65] on the grounds that such loans are made to benefit the borrower, and not for the benefit of the creditors or shareholders as such, and that it cannot explain cases where the loan was made for an abstract purpose.[66]

(ii) Primary trust for a purpose

Second, the loan might create a primary trust to use the money for a purpose, with a resulting trust arising only when the purpose, and hence the primary trust, fails. Under this approach, which was advocated by the Court of Appeal in *Twinsectra Ltd v Yardley*,[67] the equitable interest in the money might be regarded as being 'in suspense' until the stated purpose is carried out, so that neither the lender nor the borrower is, strictly speaking, the beneficiary. However, it has the difficulty of appearing to offend the beneficiary principle, and was subjected to criticism in the House of Lords on the grounds that it is unorthodox, fails to have regard to the role which resulting trusts play in equity, and fails to explain why the money is not simply held on resulting trust for the lender from the outset.[68]

(iii) No primary trust

Third, Chambers has argued that the loan does not create a primary trust at all. Rather, the borrower receives the entire beneficial ownership in the money lent, subject only to a contractual right in the lender to prevent the money being used otherwise than for

---

[64] (6 October 1978, unreported).
[65] *Twinsectra Ltd v Yardley* [2002] 2 All ER 377 [85]–[89].
[66] For example, as in *Re EVTR* [1987] BCLC 646.
[67] [1999] Lloyd's Rep Bank 438.
[68] *Twinsectra Ltd v Yardley* [2002] 2 All ER 377, [90], per Lord Millett.

the stated purpose, and a resulting trust springs into being only if the purpose fails.[69] This view has been criticized because it cannot explain cases of non-contractual payments, and it is inconsistent with the judgments in *Quistclose* that describe the borrower as under a fiduciary duty.[70]

(iv) Resulting trust throughout

Finally, the money lent for a specific purpose may be regarded as being held on resulting trust by the borrower for the lender from the very beginning, the resulting trust arising from the fact that the lender did not intend the borrower to enjoy the beneficial ownership in the money lent. This analysis has been advocated extra-judicially by Lord Millett,[71] and was therefore, unsurprisingly, adopted by him in *Twinsectra Ltd v Yardley*.[72] He explained what he considered to be the nature of the *Quistclose* trust:

> As Sherlock Holmes reminded Dr Watson, when you have eliminated the impossible, whatever remains, however improbable, must be the truth. I would reject all the alternative analyses, which I find unconvincing... and hold the *Quistclose* trust to be an entirely orthodox example of the kind of default trust known as a resulting trust. The lender pays the money to the borrower by way of loan, but he does not part with the entire beneficial interest in the money, and in so far as he does not it is held on a resulting trust for the lender from the outset. Contrary to the opinion of the Court of Appeal, it is the borrower who has a very limited use of the money, being obliged to apply it for the stated purpose or return it. He has no beneficial interest in the money, which remains throughout in the lender subject only to the borrower's power or duty to apply the money in accordance with the lender's instructions. When the purpose fails, the money is returnable to the lender, not under some new trust in his favour which only comes into being on the failure of the purpose, but because the resulting trust in his favour is no longer subject to any power on the part of the borrower to make use of the money.[73]

(v) Sui generis situation?

While this analysis has the merit of simplicity, and of avoiding any problem of any conflict with the beneficiary principle, it is submitted that it is somewhat artificial to regard a resulting trust as subsisting from the very moment that the loan is made, prior to the failure of the purpose. It might be better to acknowledge the essentially anomalous and sui generis nature of the *Quistclose* trust, rather than to search for the 'truth' as to its nature by fitting it within 'orthodox' categories. As Potter LJ suggested in the Court of Appeal, the *Quisclose*-type trust 'is in truth a "quasi-trust"'.[74]

It remains unclear whether Lord Millett's analysis was authoritatively adopted by the majority of the House of Lords. Lord Hoffmann held that the undertaking had the effect that the money paid into the solicitor's client account was held on trust until such time as it was applied for the acquisition of property in accordance with its terms. He did not specifically refer to the *Quistclose* trust, and he appears to have regarded the arrangement as more akin to an express trust created by the undertaking. Lord

---

[69] Chambers, *Resulting Trusts* (1997, OUP) pp 68–89.
[70] Ho and Smart 'Reinterpreting the *Quistclose* Trust: A Critique of Chambers' Analysis' (2001) 21 OJLS 267. See also *Twinsectra Ltd v Yardley* [2002] 2 All ER 377, [95], per Lord Millett.
[71] Sir Peter Millett 'The *Quistclose* Trust: Who Can Enforce It?' (1985) 101 LQR 269.
[72] [2002] 2 All ER 377.   [73] Ibid., at 403.   [74] [1999] Lloyd's Rep Bank 438, [76].

Slynn agreed with Lord Hoffmann. Lord Hutton agreed with both Lords Hoffmann and Lord Millett that the money was subject to a trust, but did not comment further on their reasoning. Lord Steyn agreed with both Lords Hoffmann and Lord Hutton. There therefore remains scope for further argument as to whether the trust in *Twinsectra Ltd v Yardley* should properly be regarded as a *Quistclose* trust at all.

(f) Criteria needed for *Quistclose* trusts

The precise criteria that need to be satisfied in order to give rise to a *Quistclose* trust are generally agreed, although their precise import will depend upon which theoretical understating of the nature of the trust is preferred.

(i) Loan made for a specific purpose

A *Quistclose* resulting trust will only arise if the loan was made for an agreed specific purpose that was identified with sufficient certainty. The requirement of certainty will clearly be satisfied where the money was to be used in a precisely identified way, for example for the payment of specific debts or classes of debts. In *Quistclose*, the purpose was the payment of a share dividend. In *Carreras Rothmans Ltd v Freeman Mathews Treasure Ltd (in liquidation)*[75] a resulting trust was held to arise where a loan had been made by Rothmans to their advertising agency, who were in financial difficulty, for the purpose of paying third parties with whom Rothmans' adverts had been placed. In *Re EVTR*[76] a resulting trust was found where a loan had been made to a company in financial difficulties for the purchase of new machinery. However, in *Twinsectra Ltd v Yardley* the purpose was expressed in vaguer terms, namely that the money was only to be used for the 'acquisition of property',[77] not for the acquisition of specific property. At first instance, Carnwarth J held that this purpose was insufficiently certain to generate a trust for the purpose. However, the Court of Appeal held that there was a sufficiently clear statement of purpose for the court to decide upon its ambit and whether or not, in any circumstances, it had become frustrated.[78] In the House of Lords, Lord Millett held that the undertaking was stated with sufficient certainty, and that there was no difficulty of certainty of objects:

A trust must have certainty of objects. But the only trust is the resulting trust for the lender. The borrower is authorised (or directed) to apply the money for a stated purpose, but this is a mere power and does not constitute a purpose trust. Provided that the power is stated with sufficient clarity for the court to be able to determine whether it is still capable of being carried out or whether the money has been misapplied, it is sufficiently certain to be enforced. If it is uncertain, however, then the borrower has no authority to make any use of the trust money at all and must return it to the lender under the resulting trust.[79]

(ii) Money kept in a separate bank account?

In both *Quistclose* and *Carreras Rothmans* the money lent was kept in a separate bank account. However, while this is obviously extremely clear evidence that the money is

---

[75] [1985] Ch 207.   [76] [1987] BCLC 646.   [77] [2002] 2 All ER 377.
[78] [1999] Lloyd's Rep Bank 438, [82].   [79] [2002] 2 All ER 377, [101].

intended for the specified purpose only, it is not essential. In *Re EVTR* a resulting trust was found even though the loan had been paid into the company's general account, and in *Twinsectra Ltd v Yardley*[80] a trust was found even though the money lent was held in the solicitor's general client account rather than a separate account.

(iii) The purpose has failed

In cases prior to *Twinsectra Ltd v Yardley* it was held that the resulting trust in favour of the lender only arises where the purpose, and thereby the primary trust, fails. In *Quistclose* and *Carreras Rothmans* this was when the borrower went into liquidation. The meaning of 'failure' was further considered by the Court of Appeal in *Re EVTR*. In that case, the money had been advanced to purchase new machinery. The money was paid to the manufacturers, but before the machinery could be delivered EVTR Ltd went into receivership. The machines were never delivered and the manufacturers refunded the purchase price less an amount to compensate for their loss under the breach of contract. Reversing the decision at first instance, the Court of Appeal held that the purpose had not been completed at the moment the money was paid over to the manufacturers, therefore excluding a resulting trust. As Dillon LJ pointed out:

True it is that the [money] was paid out by the company with a view to the acquisition of new equipment, but that was only at half-time, and I do not see why the final whistle should be blown at half-time.[81]

A resulting trust will also arise where only a part of the money lent for the specific purpose has been applied to it.[82]

If the explanation of the *Quistclose* trust adopted by Lord Millett in *Twinsectra Ltd v Yardley* is accepted, then it might be better to say that the trust subsists for as long as the purpose has not been carried out, since the resulting trust will simply remain in effect until the money is properly applied.

(g) Void transactions

In *Westdeutsche Landesbank Girozentrale v Islington London Borough Council*[83] the House of Lords considered whether a resulting trust would arise 'automatically' in situations other than where an express trust had failed. The case concerned an interest rate swap agreement that had been entered between a bank and a local authority, but which was ultra vires the local authority. The bank claimed that as the transaction was void the local authority was not merely subject to a personal common law obligation to make restitution but held the money received under the void contract on resulting trust. In such circumstances, the transfer of money by the bank had never been intended to be subject to an express trust, and therefore the House of Lords held that there were no grounds for finding that it was subject

[80] [2002] 2 All ER 377.   [81] [1987] BCLC 646 at 651.
[82] *Latimer v Commissioner of Inland Revenue* [2004] 2 AC 164.
[83] [1996] AC 669.

to a resulting trust merely because the contract was void. The argument for a generalized resulting trust to effect restitution was rejected. This has been examined in detail in Chapter 9.

(3) Counter-intention rebutting the implication of a surplus-funds resulting trust

As Lord Browne-Wilkinson indicated in *Westdeutsche Landesbank Girozentrale v Islington London Borough Council*,[84] the mere fact than an express trust has failed does not inevitably mean that an automatic surplus-funds resulting trust will arise in favour of the settlor/contributor. As has been noted above, where property is contributed to a fund in return for the provision of contractual benefits, this may impliedly exclude the possibility of a resulting trust in favour of the contributor. Where no contractual relationship is in issue, the presumption of an automatic resulting trust will be rebutted by evidence that the settlor had entirely abandoned his property. Thus, if he no longer intended to retain any interest in it from the moment that it was transferred by him, even by way of reverter in the event of failure of the express trust, any surplus will vest in the Crown as bona vacantia. In the absence of the settlor's express intention against a surplus-funds resulting trust, the most likely circumstance in which such a counter-intention will be implied is where an owner has made a donation which was so small as to indicate that he would not wish it returned in any event. Such cases might include trust surpluses consisting of anonymous small donations from street collections and the like. In *Re Gillingham Bus Disaster Fund*[85] a fund had been established in the aftermath of an accident, in which twenty-four Royal Marine Cadets had been killed, to defray the funeral expenses of the dead and care for the disabled. Some £9,000 was raised, largely by anonymous contributors to street collections. After providing for the funerals and care, there was a large surplus of the fund remaining, and the question before the court was whether that surplus should be returned to the donors on the basis of a resulting trust, be applied cy-près to other charitable purposes, or pass as bona vacantia to the Crown. Harman J held that as the objects of the fund were not exclusively charitable there could be no application cy-près, and the surplus should be held on resulting trust for the contributors. He recognized the tremendous practical difficulty of this solution that many of those who had contributed were unknown, but concluded that this did not make a resulting trust unworkable because the trustees could pay the money into court.[86] However, this appears to be an inappropriate solution. The individual donors surely intended to part with their money when they contributed it to the fund. As such, they should have ceased to enjoy any interest in it, even the possibility of reverter by way of a resulting trust. This more realistic approach was adopted by Goff J in *Re West Sussex Constabulary's Widows, Children and Benevolent*

---

[84] Ibid.   [85] [1958] Ch 300.

[86] Ibid., at 314. In 1993 it was announced that the money was to be paid out and used for a memorial to the victims. See Hanbury and Martin, *Modern Equity* (18th edn, 2009), p 247.

(1930) Fund Trusts[87] in the context of an unincorporated association. He declined to follow the judgment of Harman J in *Re Gillingham Bus Disaster Fund*,[88] but followed the earlier cases of *Re Welsh Hospital (Netley) Fund*[89] and *Re Hillier*,[90] which held that persons contributing to a fund through street collections parted with their money 'out-and-out'[91] and retained no interest in it. As PO Lawrence J had observed in *Re Welsh Hospital*:

It is inconceivable that any person...placing a coin in a collecting-box presented to him in the street should have intended that any part of the money so contributed should be returned to him...To draw such an inference would be absurd...[92]

In the light of this analysis it should perhaps be questioned whether a resulting trust should have arisen in favour of the donors in *Re Abbott Fund Trusts*.[93]

While the resulting trust analysis in such cases appears inappropriate, the alternative, whereby the surplus passes as bona vacantia to the Crown, is equally unattractive as an option. The contributors to the *Gillingham Bus Disaster Fund* surely would not have wanted the surplus to pass to the Crown, thus making an involuntary contribution to government income. The central problem with such cases is that they concerned non-charitable purpose trusts, and that there is no equivalent principle to that of cy-près by which any surplus can be applied to similar purposes.[94] If the donors to such purpose trusts are taken to have given their property out-and-out, it is right that a resulting trust should not be implied, but equity should provide a mechanism permitting the application of any such surplus by the trustees in a manner consistent with the original objectives of the trust.

3 Surplus funds on the dissolution of unincorporated associations

(1) Property holding by unincorporated associations

Different problems arise as to what should happen to the assets of an unincorporated association that is dissolved. Because such associations have no legal personality, the basis on which they hold property is complex, and various analyses have been suggested. The modern solution is that the officers of the association hold the assets for the members on the basis of their contract inter se, which is formed

---

[87] [1971] Ch 1.
[88] [1959] Ch 62.   [89] [1921] 1 Ch 655.
[90] [1954] 1 WLR 9; on appeal [1954] 1 WLR 700, CA.
[91] *Re Hillier* [1954] 1 WLR 9 at 21–22, per Upjohn J; [1954] 1 WLR 700 at 714, per Denning LJ.
[92] [1921] 1 Ch 655 at 660.   [93] [1900] 2 Ch 326.
[94] If *Re Gillingham Bus Disaster Fund* had concerned a charitable trust the surplus remaining after the purposes had been satisfied would have been applied cy-près: *Re Wokingham Fire Brigade Trusts* [1951] Ch 373; *Re Ulverston and District New Hospital Building Trusts* [1956] Ch 622.

by the rules of the association.[95] The members' rights over the assets are therefore governed by contract and not trust. The question of how any assets should be distributed when an association is dissolved has also been subject to a variety of approaches. Early cases decided that any surplus funds would be held on a resulting trust for those who had contributed.[96] However, cases adopting a resulting trust approach pre-date the more recent authorities adopting the contractual analysis of property holding by unincorporated associations, and the modern approach to the distribution of surplus assets is that they should be distributed to the members under that same contract.

(2) *Re West Sussex Constabulary's Trusts*: partial rejection of the resulting trust approach

In *Re West Sussex Constabulary's Widows, Children and Benevolent (1930) Fund Trusts*[97] a fund to provide benefits to the widows of members of the West Sussex police force was wound up when the force was amalgamated with others, leaving a surplus of £35,000. The club's revenue was derived from: (a) members' subscriptions; (b) legacies and donations from outsiders; and (c) proceeds of entertainments and collecting-boxes. The question arose as to how the surplus should be distributed. Goff J dealt separately with each type of revenue (see Figure 20.1).

(i) Members' subscriptions[98]

Goff J held that the members were not entitled to take any share of the surplus on the basis of resulting trusts because they had made their contributions on the basis of contract and not trust.[99] They had received all that they had bargained for from their membership of the club. Therefore this property went bona vacantia to the Crown.

(ii) Outside legacies and donations[100]

Since these were not given on the basis of contract, Goff J held there should be a resulting trust in favour of those who had contributed, in so far as the surplus was attributable to their contributions. He considered that this aspect of the case was indistinguishable from *Re Abbott Fund Trusts*.[101]

---

[95] *Leahy v A-G for New South Wales* [1959] AC 457, PC; *Neville Estates Ltd v Madden* [1962] Ch 832; *Re Recher's Will Trusts* [1972] Ch 526; *Re Lipinski's Will Trusts* [1976] Ch 235; *Re Grant's Will Trusts* [1980] 1 WLR 360. See p 653.

[96] *Re Printers and Transferrers Amalgamated Trades Protection Society* [1899] 2 Ch 184; *Re Lead Co's Workmen's Fund Society* [1904] 2 Ch 196; *Tierney v Tough* [1914] 1 IR 142; *Re Hobourn Aero Components Air Raid Distress Fund* [1946] Ch 86.

[97] [1971] Ch 1.   [98] Ibid., at 9–10.

[99] Following *Cunnack v Edwards* [1896] 2 Ch 679; *Re Gillingham Bus Disaster Fund* [1958] Ch 300.

[100] [1971] Ch 1 at 14–16.

[101] [1900] 2 Ch 326.

(iii) Proceeds of entertainments and collecting-boxes[102]

As has been considered above,[103] Goff J held that there could be no resulting trust of the surplus attributable to revenue from these sources, and it thus passed bona vacantia to the Crown.

Re West Sussex Constabulary's Widows, Children and Benevolent (1930) Fund Trusts[104] rejected a resulting trust solution in relation to members' contributions on the winding up of an unincorporated association. This had the consequence that the majority of the surplus passed bona vacantia to the Crown, with the members seeming to receive nothing for their contributions. The reason for this may be that, although the contractual analysis was argued so as to defeat any claim by the members to a resulting trust, there was no argument that the members had any contractual rights to the surplus. Goff J observed in his judgment:

> The surviving members . . . may well have a right in contract on the ground of frustration or total failure of consideration, and that right may embrace contributions made by past members, though I do not see how it could apply to moneys raised from outside sources. I have not, however, heard any argument based on contract and therefore the declarations I propose to make will be subject to . . . reservation . . .[105]

(3) *Re Bucks Constabulary Fund (No 2)*: distribution of surplus funds to the members of the association

The reasoning which denied the members any claim in *Re West Sussex Constabulary's Widows, Children and Benevolent (1930) Fund Trusts*[106] was taken a step further in *Re Bucks Constabulary Fund (No 2)*,[107] where it was held that the members of an unincorporated association enjoyed contractual rights to surplus assets (see Figure 20.1). The case concerned a society registered under the Friendly Societies Act 1896, which was wound up because of the amalgamation of the Buckinghamshire Constabulary, leaving a surplus. Given that an unincorporated association derives its existence from an 'implied contract between all the members inter se governed by the rules of the society',[108] Walton J held that this contract should govern the distribution of the surplus:

> as on dissolution there were members of the society . . . in existence, its assets are held on trust for such members to the total exclusion of any claim on behalf of the Crown.

This is entirely consistent with the reasoning that unincorporated associations hold their property on the basis of the contract between the members,[109] and that they

---

[102] [1971] Ch 1 at 11–14.   [103] See above, p 674.   [104] [1971] Ch 1.

[105] Ibid., at 10: this did not prevent the property being paid over as bona vacantia, as the Crown had offered a full indemnity to the trustees.

[106] [1971] Ch 1.   [107] [1979] 1 WLR 936.   [108] Ibid., at 943.

[109] *Re Sick and Funeral Society of St John's Sunday School, Golcar* [1973] Ch 51 at 60, per Megarry J: 'membership of a club or association is primarily a matter of contract. The members make their payments, and in return they become entitled to the benefits of membership in accordance with the rules. The sums they pay cease to be their individual property, and so cease to be subject to any concept of resulting trust. Instead, they become the property, through the trustees of the club or association, of all the members for the time being, including themselves.'

(i) *Re West Sussex*

(ii) *Re Bucks Constabulary*

Figure 20.1 Distribution of assets on the dissolution of an unincorporated association

must be able to alter the rules of the association so as to put the assets into their own pockets.[110] Since this shows that 'the money was theirs all the time',[111] they should be entitled to what is theirs on the winding-up of the association. This reasoning excludes any possibility of a resulting trust, either of the members' own contributions, or of the donations of outsiders,[112] and provides the members with a basis for entitlement to the surplus which was not found in *Re West Sussex Constabulary's Widows, Children and Benevolent (1930) Fund Trusts*.[113] Therefore, none of the assets of the association, whatever their source, should pass under a resulting trust or as bona vacantia. The only circumstances in which Walton J anticipated the surplus will pass bona vacantia

---

[110] See *Re Lipinski* [1976] Ch 235; *Re Grant's Will Trusts* [1980] 1 WLR 360.

[111] *Re Bucks Constabulary Widows' and Orphans' Fund Friendly Society (No 2)* [1979] 1 WLR 936, at 951.

[112] Since these too are held by the association on the basis of the contract for the members absolutely. See *Re Lipinski's Will Trusts* [1976] Ch 235, where Mr Lipinski's gift to the association was held to be a gift to the members subject to their contract inter se, which they could decide to distribute among themselves.

[113] [1971] Ch 1.

to the Crown is when the society is moribund by being reduced to a single member.[114] The problem with this solution is that, instead of conferring a windfall gain on the Crown (as bona vacantia), it confers a windfall gain on the members, who would never have expected to make a personal profit from a benevolent association. However, this may be no more objectionable than the windfall gains made by members of building societies which have lost their mutual status on takeover or on conversion to a bank.

(4) Last surviving member of an association

The question of what happens when an unincorporated association comes to an end because all but one of its members have died or resigned arose in *Hanchett-Stamford v A-G*.[115] The Performing and Captive Animals Defence League had been established in 1914 to seek to prevent animals being used in performances. Lewison J held that the League was not charitable because it was campaigning to change the law. The question was what should happen to its assets, which consisted mainly of a house, Sid Abbey, purchased to provide offices (worth around £675,000) and investments (worth approximately £1.77 million), with Mr Hanchett-Stamford and a Mr Hervey registered as trustees for the League. Although at one time there had been 250 members, when Mr Hervey and then Mr Hanchett-Stamford died the only traceable member was Mrs Hanchett-Stamford. Who was entitled to the assets? If Mrs Hanchett-Stamford was entitled to the funds, she intended to follow her late husband's wishes and to apply the funds to another animal charity, the Born Free Foundation. Lewison J accepted that Walton J's analysis of the way in which an unincorporated society held its assets was correct and that where no express restriction had been placed on the funds, 'the members for the time being of an unincorporated association are beneficially entitled to "its" assets, subject to the contractual arrangements between them'.[116] Lewison J saw no basis for restricting this principle to cases only where there were two members or more. It would breach human rights law to deprive the surviving member of the assets on the death of the last-but-one member. The League was still active up to the death of Mr Hanchett-Stamford. In the view of Lewison J:

I consider that the League ceased to exist upon his death in January 2006, when its membership fell below two. Since Mrs Hanchett-Stamford is the sole surviving member of the League, she is, in my judgment, entitled to its assets. She is therefore entitled to be registered as proprietor of Sid Abbey and as shareholder of the shares now held in the League's name. Her entitlement is free from any restrictions imposed by the rules of the League, which must have ceased to bind on the death of her husband. It follows that she is free, if she so chooses, to give all the former assets of the League to the Born Free Foundation.[117]

---

[114] [1979] 1 WLR 936 at 943.   [115] [2008] EWHC 330 (Ch)

[116] Ibid., at [31].

[117] Ibid., at [50]. For more information about the League, see: www.timesonline.co.uk/tol/news/polit-ics/article3599694.ece and Griffiths '*Hanchett-Stamford v Attorney General*: Another Twist in the Tale— Unincorporated Associations and the Distribution of Surplus Funds' [2009] 73 Conv 428; Panesar 'Surplus Funds and Unincorporated Associations' (2008) *Trusts and Trustees* 698.

(5) **The members' contractual rights**

The exact entitlement of each surviving member on a distribution of the surplus assets of an association depends on its rules. In the absence of express rules providing for dissolution, the surviving members at the date of dissolution will have prima facie entitlement to the surplus in equal shares, and not proportionately to their contributions.[118] This was the conclusion reached by Walton J in *Re Bucks Constabulary Fund (No 2)*.[119] However, the rules of the society may impliedly indicate that something other than equal division was intended. In *Re Sick and Funeral Society of St John's Sunday School, Golcar*[120] a society existed to provide members with sickness allowances and death benefits. Members aged five to twelve paid half-contributions and were only entitled to half-benefits. Megarry J held that since this inequality was written into the rules, dividing the members into different classes, it should be applied to the surplus funds on dissolution. Those paying half-contributions were only entitled to half-shares in the surplus.[121] The large sums involved in the dissolution of mutual associations can be extremely large: the sale of the RAC rescue service division in 1998 was expected to produce in the order of £30,000 for each of the Club's members; the assets held by the Performing and Captive Animals Defence League when it ceased to exist were worth more than £2 million.

(6) **Re-emergence of the resulting trust analysis?**

Re Bucks Constabulary Fund (No 2)[122] marks a clear rejection of the resulting trust analysis in the context of unincorporated associations. However, in the case of *Davis v Richards and Wallington Industries Ltd*,[123] Scott J applied a resulting trust analysis in the context of a company pension fund, which had the effect of denying the employees of the firm any rights to the £3m surplus. This case runs against the grain of the authorities concerned with the surplus assets of unincorporated associations. It seems that Scott J presumed that the only alternatives open to him were a resulting trust or bona vacantia, and he did not consider whether the employees of the firm had any contractual entitlement to the surplus.[124] This may be because occupational pension schemes, to which employees contribute on the basis of their contract and from which they are contractually entitled to benefits, are not analogous to unincorporated

---

[118] See *Brown v Dale* (1878) 9 Ch D 78; *Re Printers and Transferrers Amalgamated Trades Protection Society* [1899] 2 Ch 184; *Re Lead Co's Workmen's Fund Society* [1904] 2 Ch 196; *Tierney v Tough* [1914] 1 IR 142; *Feeny and Shannon v MacManus* [1937] IR 23; *Re Blue Albion Cattle Society* [1966] CLY 1274; *Re St Andrew's Allotments Association's Trusts* [1969] 1 WLR 229.

[119] [1979] 1 WLR 936 at 951–955.   [120] [1973] Ch 51.

[121] See also *Re St Andrew's Allotments Association's Trusts* [1969] 1 WLR 229.

[122] [1979] 1 WLR 936.   [123] [1991] 2 All ER 563; see also above, p 667.

[124] For example, he spoke of 'the principles to be decided between a resulting trust and bona vacantia' (at 519), and *Re West Sussex Constabulary's Widows, Children and Benevolent (1930) Fund Trusts* [1971] Ch 1 was cited in his judgment, but *Re Bucks Constabulary Widows' and Orphans' Fund Friendly Society (No 2)* [1979] 1 WLR 936 was not.

associations.[125] The employees do not have sole control of the scheme, and, unlike the members of an unincorporated association, they cannot decide to wind it up and divide the assets among themselves. The benefits payable to members are also limited by Inland Revenue rules. The essence of the decision is that the contributors are not deprived of all possible proprietary rights in the fund merely because their contributions and benefits are determined by contract, a principle affirmed by the Privy Council in *Air Jamaica Ltd v Charlton*.[126] It does not undermine the authority of *Re Bucks Constabulary Fund (No 2)*[127] in the context of unincorporated associations, where the general principle remains that the surplus will be divided among the surviving members under their contract inter se.

4 Surplus funds on the failure of a charity[128]

(1) The principle of an application cy-près

When a charity comes to an end still holding property on trust, the question arises as to what should happen to that surplus. One possibility is that it should be returned to those who donated it on the basis of a resulting trust, in much the same way as a surplus on the failure of a private trust will return to the original contributors.[129] However, charitable trusts are treated differently from private trusts because they have a public character. Although a whole range of different purposes may fall within the definition of 'charity', it is regarded as a unified area, so that property applied to any particular charitable purpose forms part of the 'common pot' of charity. The law thus regards property given for any specific charitable purpose as given not merely to that particular purpose but dedicated to charity in the general sense. If the particular purpose for which the property was given fails, it will be applied, under a scheme drawn up by the Charity Commission,[130] to other similar charitable purposes and will not return to the donor under a resulting trust. This application to alternative charitable purposes is called 'cy-près'. The principle was stated by Roxburgh J in *Re Lucas*:

once a fund has been devoted to charitable purposes, it cannot be diverted from charity by any supervening impracticality but must be applied cy-près.[131]

---

[125] Although it was argued by counsel that a pension scheme was merely a species of unincorporated association (at 589).

[126] [1999] 1 WLR 1399.   [127] [1979] 1 WLR 936.

[128] See Sheridan and Delaney, *The Cy-près Doctrine* (1959); Sheridan and Keeton, *The Modern Law of Charities* (4th edn, 1992); *Nathan Committee Report* (Cmnd 8710), Ch 9; Garton 'Justifying the Cy-Pres Doctrine' (2007) 21 *Trust Law International* 134.

[129] See above, p 663.

[130] Formerly, the scheme was drawn up by the court. This 'judicial' cy-près is to be contrasted with 'prerogative' cy-près, which is exercised by the Crown, where a gift is made to charity but not upon trust.

[131] [1948] Ch 175 at 181.

Particular difficulties arise when a testator makes a gift by will to a charity that has ceased to exist. In such circumstances the question arises whether the property bequeathed to the charity should pass to the residuary legatees under a resulting trust, or be applied cy-près to other similar charitable purposes. The principles determining whether the property will be applied cy-près are different, depending upon whether the failure of the charity concerned was 'initial' or 'subsequent'.

(a) Initial failure

An initial failure occurs if a charity to which property was bequeathed ceased to exist before the testator had died. Since the gift to the charity was never effective, the property concerned will only be applied cy-près to a similar charitable purpose if it can be shown that the testator had a 'general charitable intention'[132] when he made his bequest and not merely the intention to benefit the specific charity that has failed. If no such general charitable intention can be identified, the property will pass to the residuary legatees by way of a resulting trust.

(b) Subsequent failure

A subsequent failure occurs if a charity to which property was bequeathed ceases to exist or if a charitable purpose becomes impossible to implement between the death of the testator and the administration of the estate by the executors. Since the will operates on the death of the testator to transfer an interest in the property to the charity, it is fully dedicated to charity before the specific charity to which it was given failed. It will therefore be applied cy-près[133] without any need to demonstrate a general charitable intention. Any difficulty is only illusory, and arises because of the time gap between death and the distribution of the estate.

(c) Failure of charitable appeals

Special statutory rules apply where there is an appeal for funds for a specific charitable purpose but that purpose fails. Where a donor to the appeal cannot be identified or found after advertisement and inquiries, the funds may be applied cy-près as if the funds had been given for charitable purposes generally.[134] The same rule applies where a donor has signed a disclaimer in prescribed form. The Charities Act 2006 has extended this rule by applying the same principle even to donors who can be identified. Such donors will be treated as having disclaimed their right to have their donation returned if the solicitation by which the appeal was made stated that donors would have no right to the return of their donation in the event of the specific charitable purpose failing unless they make a declaration that they must be consulted before their donation is applied to other purposes.[135] These principles do not apply where an

---

[132] See *Re Spence* [1979] Ch 483.
[133] See *Re Slevin* [1891] 2 Ch 236, CA; *Re Wright* [1954] Ch 347, CA.
[134] Charities Act 1993, s 14.
[135] Charities Act 2006, s 17, inserting a new s 14A into the Charities Act 1993.

appeal is for non-charitable purposes, as was the case in *Re Gillingham Bus Disaster Fund*,[136] discussed above.

(2) Circumstances justifying application of surplus funds cy-près

(a) Impossibility or impracticality

Prior to the Charities Act 1960, property would only be applied cy-près if a charitable purpose had become impossible or impracticable. For example, in *A-G v London Corpn*[137] a trust for 'the propagation of the Christian religion among the infidels of Virginia' was found to have become impossible, as Lord Thurlow LC held that there were no infidels left in Virginia. Similarly, in *Ironmongers' Co v A-G*[138] a trust for the redemption of British slaves in Turkey was impossible because there were no such British slaves remaining to be redeemed. In *Re Robinson*[139] a trust had been established to endow an Evangelical church in Bournemouth, subject to a condition that the preacher always wear a black gown. Since this was alienating the congregation, PO Lawrence J held that this rendered the purpose impracticable[140] and sanctioned a scheme dispensing with the condition.[141]

In order to extend the scope of this narrow jurisdiction, the courts did not insist strictly upon impossibility or impracticality.[142] In *Re Dominion Students Hall Trust*[143] a charity maintained a hostel for male students from the British Empire, but only those of European origin. The charity sought to remove the restriction. Evershed J held that 'the word "impossible" should be given a wide significance'[144] and that in the circumstances the 'colour bar' did render the charity impossible since it would undermine its main objects. He therefore approved a scheme removing the bar. In *Re Lysaght (Decd)*[145] a testatrix left the residue of her estate to the Royal College of Surgeons (RCS) to provide medical studentships. Various limitations were placed on those eligible for the awards, including a provision that they must not be Jewish or Roman Catholic. In view of these restrictions, the RCS refused to accept the trust. Since the trustee would not accept the trust with the condition, Buckley J held that the trust had become impossible, and therefore ordered that the fund be paid to the RCS as trustees without the restriction.[146] In *Re JW Laing Trust*[147] a settlor had created a trust of shares in favour of a variety of evangelical Christian purposes. The trust contained a requirement that the fund was to be distributed during the settlor's lifetime, or within ten years of his death. He died in 1978, by which time the trust was worth some £24m. The

---

136 [1958] Ch 300.   137 (1790) 3 Bro CC 171.   138 (1844) 10 Cl & Fin 908.
139 [1921] 2 Ch 332. See also *Re Campden Charities* (1881) 18 Ch D 310, CA.
140 See also *Re Weir Hospital* [1910] 2 Ch 124.
141 In essence, he held that the paramount intention was to endow a church, and not to enforce the wearing of a black robe, and that the paramount intention would be rendered impossible by the condition. See *Re Lysaght* [1966] Ch 191 at 208.
142 See *Re Weir Hospital* [1910] 2 Ch 124.   143 [1947] Ch 183.   144 Ibid., at 186.
145 [1966] Ch 191.   146 See also *Re Woodhams* [1981] 1 WLR 493.
147 [1984] Ch 143.

types of organizations that the trust had been supporting were unsuited for receiving large sums of capital. It was held that there was no room for application cy-près, but the court removed the restriction under its inherent jurisdiction.

(b) Charities Act 1993, s 13

Given the restrictive scope of the cy-près jurisdiction, the Nathan Committee recommended that the requirements for impracticality be relaxed.[148] A wider jurisdiction was thus introduced in s 13 of the Charities Act 1960, which has been re-enacted as s 13 of the Charities Act 1993. Section 13 provides for five circumstances in which property given to charitable purposes which have not strictly failed can be applied cy-près:

(a) where the original purposes, in whole or in part,—

　(i) have been as far as may be fulfilled, or

　(ii) cannot be carried out, or not according to the directions given and to the spirit of the gift; or

(b) where the original purposes provide a use for part only of the property available by virtue of the gift; or

(c) where the property available by virtue of the gift and other property applicable for similar purposes can be more effectively used in conjunction, and to that end can suitably, regard being had to *the appropriate considerations,* be made applicable to common purposes; or

(d) where the original purposes were laid down by reference to an area which then was but has since ceased to be a unit for some other purpose, or by reference to a class of persons or to an area which has for any reason since ceased to be suitable, regard being had to *the appropriate considerations,* or to be practical in administering the gift; or

(e) where the original purposes, in whole or in part, have, since they were laid down—

　(i) been adequately provided for by other means, or

　(ii) ceased, as being useless or harmful to the community or for other reasons, to be in law charitable, or

　(iii) ceased in any other way to provide a suitable and effective method of using the property available by virtue of the gift, regard being had to *the appropriate considerations.*

The Charities Act 2006 introduced the italicized words above, in place of the original phrase 'the spirit of the gift'.[149] This change further extends the circumstances in which cy-près will be possible. Section 13(1A)[150] defines what is meant by 'appropriate considerations':

---

[148] *Report of the Committee on the Law and Practice relating to Charitable Trusts* (1952) (Cmd 8710), para 365.

[149] Charities Act 2006, s 15.　　[150] Inserted by Charities Act 2006, s 15.

(a) (on the one hand) the spirit of the gift concerned, and

(b) (on the other) the social and economic circumstances prevailing at the time of the proposed alteration of the original purposes.

This amendment facilitates a cy-près application where, for instance, a trust specified the award of an annual prize which over the years has fallen in value because of the effect of inflation, but which otherwise could still be awarded.[151]

The greater width of the cy-près jurisdiction under s 13 was evident from cases in which it has been considered, even before the amendments introduced by the Charities Act 2006. In *Re Lepton's Charity*[152] a trust established in 1716 provided for the payment of £3 per annum from the income generated by a piece of land to the minister of a dissenting church, with the remainder distributed among the poor. In 1716 the income was £5 but at the date of the case it was some £800. Pennycuick V-C held that, although the purpose of the trust had not failed, the circumstances fell within s 13(1)(a)(ii) and (1)(e)(iii) and directed that £100 per annum be paid to the minister. It is submitted that this decision would now more readily fall within the amended wording introduced by the Charities Act 2006. In *Varsani v Jesani*[153] the Court of Appeal applied s 13 in order to deal with the assets of a religious charity that had suffered an irretrievable schism. Chadwick LJ said that under the law as it stood before the Charities Act 1960, the court could not direct a scheme:

This is because it would still be possible to carry out the original purposes of the charity through the use of its property by the group who...had been found to be the adherents to the true faith; and any application of any part of the property for use by the other group would be open to attack as a breach of trust. It is for that reason that, under the old law, the court would have been required to decide the underlying question...which (if either) of the views now held by the majority group and the minority group respectively do truly reflect the teachings and tenets of Muktajivandasji.[153a]

He continued by saying that s 13 had changed the position and that it was no longer necessary to examine which group remained true to the original tenets of the faith.

The original purposes specified in the declaration of trust, that is to say the promotion of the faith of Swaminarayan as practised in accordance with the teachings and tenets of Muktajivandasji, are no longer a suitable and effective method of using the property given in 1967 (or added property held upon the same trusts) because the community is now divided and cannot worship together...to appropriate the use of the property to the one group to the exclusion of the other would be contrary to the spirit in which the gift was made.[153b]

The court ordered a scheme for the division of the funds between the two groups.

Section 13 has no application if there would have been no need for a scheme to apply the property prior to the Charities Act 1960. In *Oldham Borough Council v A-G*[154] a council owned a piece of land 'upon trust to preserve and manage the same at all times hereafter as playing fields...for the benefit and enjoyment' of local inhabitants. The

---

[151] See further Lloyd *Charities—The New Law 2006: A Practical Guide to the Charities Acts* (2008), Ch 14.

[152] [1972] Ch 276.

[153] [1999] Ch 219.   [153a] Ibid., at 237.   [153b] Ibid., at 238.   [154] [1993] 2 All ER 432.

council wished to sell the land to developers and use the proceeds to purchase a different piece of land with better facilities. The Court of Appeal held that the planned sale and reinvestment for exactly the same purposes did not involve an alternation of the 'original purposes' of the charitable gift. Therefore, since the sale and reinvestment would not have required a scheme before the Charities Act 1960, the trust was not affected by the provisions of s 13 and the court could authorize the sale under its statutory or common law power relating to charities.

(c) Administrative schemes

The jurisdiction under s 13 does not extend to administrative provisions that cannot be considered as falling within the 'original purposes' specified in s 13(1). Thus, in *Re JW Laing Trust*[155] a stipulation that all the property of the trust be distributed within ten years of the settlor's death was a purely administrative requirement and could not be altered under s 13, but it could be removed under the court's inherent jurisdiction. Similarly in *Varsani v Jesani*[156] the court held that, even if both groups remained true to the faith as prescribed in the original gift, the court had power under the inherent jurisdiction to authorize an administrative scheme 'for no alteration of the purpose of the Charity would arise'.

(3) Subsequent failure of charitable gifts

Where a testator leaves property to a charity in his will which fails after his death but before the administration of the estate is complete, it will be applied cy-près to other charitable purposes rather than resulting back to the residuary legatees, even though it was never in fact received by the charity. This is because the property was fully dedicated to charity from the very moment that the testator died. In such cases the property is applied cy-près, irrespective of whether the testator had a general charitable intention or not, provided that there was an outright and perpetual dedication to charitable purposes, rather than a dedication for a limited period.[157] A number of cases illustrate the operation of cy-près in the context of subsequent failure. In *Re Slevin*[158] a testator left a gift of £200 to St Dominic's Orphanage, Newcastle. The orphanage closed after his death but before the legacy had been paid over. The Court of Appeal held that the property should be applied cy-près, as it had become the property of the charity from the date of the testator's death. The same result was reached in a slightly more complex scenario in *Re Wright*.[159] A testatrix died in 1933, leaving property on trust to found and maintain a convalescent home, subject to a life interest. The life interest came to an end in 1942, but by that date it had become impracticable to carry out the charitable purpose. The question arose whether the property should be applied cy-près or result

---

[155] [1984] Ch 143.   [156] [1998] 3 All ER 273 at 285, per Morritt LJ.
[157] See *Re North Devon and West Somerset Relief Fund Trusts* [1953] 2 All ER 1032; *Re Cooper's Conveyance Trusts* [1956] 1 WLR 1096.
[158] [1891] 2 Ch 236.   [159] [1954] Ch 347.

back to the next of kin. The Court of Appeal decided on a cy-près application because the charity gained a right to the property, albeit subject to a life interest, at the date of the testatrix's death.[160] Property will also be applied cy-près without the need to show a general charitable intention if it was given to accomplish a charitable purpose but the purpose has been completed without the exhaustion of the property given. In *Re King*[161] property worth £1,500 was bequeathed to install a window in a church, the cost of which could not possibly exhaust that sum. Romer J held that the surplus should be applied cy-près.[162] Similarly, in *Re Wokingham Fire Brigade Trusts*[163] a surplus derived from a public appeal was held applicable cy-près without the need to demonstrate any general charitable intention on the part of the donors.[164]

(4) Initial failure of charitable gifts

A charitable gift will fail initially if the charity has ceased to exist before it receives any interest in the property donated. This will happen when a testator bequeaths property to a charity that ceases to exist before the date of his death. For example, in *Re Spence*[165] a testatrix left part of her estate to 'The Old Folk's Home at Hillworth Lodge Keighley' in a will that was executed in 1968. She died in 1972, but the Old People's Home had closed down in 1971. In cases of initial failure the testator could have changed his will to take account of the failure of the charity but has not done so, perhaps because of his health, or through lack of knowledge that the charity has ceased to exist. The question thus arises whether the property should be applied cy-près to other charitable purposes, or whether it should pass by resulting trust to his residuary legatees. Since the testator cannot be consulted, the law seeks to 'second-guess' what he would have wanted to happen to the property. If it can be shown that he had a 'general charitable intention' when he made the gift in his will, the property will be applied cy-près. Such an intention indicates that the testator would have preferred the property to be applied to another charity than result back under his will. If there is no general charitable intention, then it is presumed that the testator intended to benefit only the specific charity that has failed, and that in the event of the failure he would have preferred his property to result back to the residuary legatees rather than pass to a replacement charity.

[160] See also *Re Moon's Will Trust* (1948) 64 TLR 123; *Re Tacon* [1958] Ch 447.

[161] [1923] 1 Ch 243.

[162] See, however, *Re Stanford* [1924] 1 Ch 73, where Eve J held that a similar surplus should pass by way of a resulting trust to the residuary legatees.

[163] [1951] Ch 373. See also *Re Ulverston and District New Hospital Building Trusts* [1956] Ch 622.

[164] In *Re Welsh Hospital (Netley Fund)* [1921] 1 Ch 655 and *Re North Devon and Somerset Relief Fund Trusts* [1953] 1 WLR 1260 similar surpluses were held applicable cy-près because of the general charitable intention of the donors. However, it is doubtful that such an intention should be necessary, as the donors contributing to a public appeal surely dedicate their donation to charity at the moment it is made.

[165] [1979] Ch 483.

(a) Has the charity actually failed?

An application cy-près will only be necessary if the charity to which a bequest gift was made has actually failed. In some cases where it appears that a charity has failed the court has found a way of saving the gift by holding that charity has in some way continued. If this is the case there is no need to apply the property cy-près and it will be applied to the charitable purposes in their continuing form.

(i) Amalgamation with other charities

Where the charity nominated in the testator's will has been amalgamated with other charities it will be held to have continued in that new form, and the property will be applied to the new amalgamated charity without the need for cy-près. In *Re Faraker*[166] a testatrix left £200 to Hannah Bayly's Charity. Hannah Bayly's Charity had been founded in 1756 for the benefit of the poor widows of Rotherhithe, but had ceased to exist as a separate entity in 1905, when it was amalgamated with other charities for the benefit of the poor of Rotherhithe by the Charity Commissioners. The Court of Appeal held that there had been no failure because Hannah Bayly's Charity had not ceased to exist but continued in the form of the amalgamated charity, which encompassed its objects. The principle was applied in *Re Lucas*,[167] where a testatrix, who died in 1942, left £550 to 'the Crippled Children's Home, Lindley Moor, Huddersfield'. The 'Huddersfield Home for Crippled Children' had been founded in 1916, but was closed in 1941. However, its assets were applied to a new charity, 'The Huddersfield Charity for Crippled Children', under a scheme made by the Charity Commissioners. The Court of Appeal applied *Re Faraker*[168] and held that, rather than there being an initial failure, the legacy should pass to the new charity.[169] A more modern example might be the recent merger between the Imperial Cancer Research Fund and the Cancer Research Campaign to form Cancer Research UK. In the case of mergers of small, unincorporated charities,[170] the Charities Act 2006 introduced s 75F into the Charities Act 1993, which allows that the gift to the pre-merged charity may take effect in favour of the new charity.[171]

The principle of *Re Faraker*[172] is limited to cases where there is a genuine amalgamation so that the purposes of the charity have continued in another form. In *Re Roberts*[173] Jane Roberts, who died in 1961, left a share of her residuary estate to the 'Sheffield Boys' Working Home'. The home had closed in 1945, at which point the trustees had transferred the majority of the assets to the 'Sheffield Town

---

[166] [1912] 2 Ch 488. Expenditure is not confined to the purposes of the original charity.

[167] [1948] Ch 175; revsd [1948] Ch 24, CA.   [168] [1912] 2 Ch 488.

[169] See also *Re Lucas* [1948] Ch 175; revsd [1948] Ch 242, CA; *Re Bagshaw* [1954] 1 All ER 227; *Re Slatter's Will Trusts* [1964] Ch 512; *Re Stemson's Will Trusts* [1970] Ch 16.

[170] Such charities are defined as those having a gross income of more than £10,000 in the last financial year, and must not have land as property, to which particular rules apply—s 74, Charities Act 1993. Full treatment of small charities is outside the scope of this book—see further Lloyd *Charities—The New Law 2006: A Practical Guide To The Charities Acts* (2008, Ch 13.

[171] Charities Act 2006, s 44.   [172] [1912] 2 Ch 488.   [173] [1963] 1 WLR 406.

Trust', retaining only nominal funds themselves. Wilberforce J held that the property could not be applied to the Sheffield Town Trust on the basis of the principle of *Re Faraker*,[174] as the original charity was still in existence, although lacking the machinery to administer the legacy. It was therefore to be applied to the trustees of the home, and then applied cy-près.

Any funds received by the trustees of the amalgamated charity can be used for the general purposes of the charity. They are not limited to the specific purposes contemplated by the testator. It might therefore have surprised the testatrix in *Re Faraker* that not a penny of the funds she left need be spent on widows.

(ii) Unincorporated associations

Where a bequest is left to a charitable unincorporated association that ceased to exist before the death of the testator, the courts have held that the gift does not fail, because it should be construed as a gift to the continuing purposes of the association and not to the specific association as an entity. The rationale for this principle was considered by Buckley J in *Re Vernon's Will Trusts*:

Every gift to an unincorporated charity by name without more must take effect as a gift for a charitable purpose. No individual or aggregate of individuals could claim to take such a bequest beneficially.[175] If the gift is to take effect at all, it must be as a bequest for a purpose, viz, that charitable purpose which the named charity exists to serve. A bequest which is in terms made for a charitable purpose will not fail for lack of a trustee...[176]

Since an unincorporated charity has no independent legal personality,[177] the gift is construed as a gift to the purposes of the association, and those purposes continue even though the particular association has ceased to exist.[178] The gift will only fail if the testator's intention to make the gift was dependent upon the named association to apply the gift.[179] Under the Charities Act 2006, s 44, if a small unincorporated charity has merged, the gift will take effect in favour of the new entity.

In contrast, where a bequest is left to a charitable corporation it will be construed as a gift to that particular body, which has legal personality, and therefore if the corporation has ceased to exist the gift fails and the property will only be applied cy-près if a general charitable intention can be shown.[180] These principles were applied in *Re Finger's Will Trusts*.[181] Georgia Finger left a share of her residuary estate to a number

---

[174] [1912] 2 Ch 488.

[175] Although the usual interpretation of gifts to unincorporated associations is that the members take beneficially (see Chapter 24), this interpretation is excluded in the case of charities, since it is inconsistent with charitable status for the members of the charity to take a beneficial interest.

[176] [1972] Ch 300. See also *Re Morrison* (1967) 111 Sol Jo 758.

[177] See Chapter 24.

[178] This construction was approved by the Court of Appeal in *Re Koeppler Will Trusts* [1986] Ch 423 at 434, per Slade LJ.

[179] Eg *Re Spence* [1979] Ch 483.

[180] *Re Ovey* (1885) 29 Ch D 560; *Liverpool and District Hospital for Diseases of the Heart v A-G* [1981] Ch 193.

[181] [1972] Ch 286; (1972) 36 Conv 198 (Cotterell); (1974) 38 Conv 187 (Martin).

of charitable organizations, including The National Radium Commission (NRC), an unincorporated charity, and The National Council for Maternity and Child Welfare (NCMCW), a corporate body. Both had ceased to exist before the death of the testator. Goff J held that since the gift to the NRC was a gift to an unincorporated charity, the gift should be construed as a gift to the purposes of the Commission, which had not failed. The gift to the NCMCW had failed, but the property was applied cy-près because there was a general charitable intention.

It is noteworthy that Australian courts have rejected any difference of construction of gifts made to charitable corporate and unincorporated bodies, and have held that there is a presumption that the gift is made for the purposes of the body in either case.[182] This removes the artificiality of the distinction.

(iii) Charitable company becomes insolvent

There is no cause for an application cy-près where a testator leaves property to a charitable company that has become insolvent and entered into liquidation before the date of his death. In *Re ARMS (Multiple Sclerosis Research) Ltd*[183] testators had left property to a charity that sought to promote research into a cure for multiple sclerosis which had gone into liquidation before their deaths, with debts of just under £1.5m. Neuberger J held that although the testators would not have wanted their gifts to take effect if they had known that the company was in liquidation at the date of their deaths, their gifts took effect because the company was still in existence, even if insolvent. Their bequests were therefore available to pay creditors, and were not able to be applied cy-près to other similar charitable purposes.

(b) Application cy-près where the charity has failed

Where the charity has in fact failed, the property bequeathed to it will only be applied cy-près if it can be shown that the testator had a 'general charitable intention'. 'General charitable intention' has a technical meaning, which encapsulates the idea that the testator was not so committed to the particular charity nominated in his will that, in the event of its failure, he would have preferred his gift to result back to the residuary legatees under his will rather than to be applied to similar charitable purposes. The principle was outlined by Sir Robert Megarry V-C in *Re Spence*:

the essence of the distinction is in the difference between particularity and generality. If a particular institution or purpose is specified, then it is that institution or purpose, and no other, that is to be the object of the benefaction. It is difficult to envisage a testator as being suffused with a general glow of broad charity when he is labouring, and labouring successfully, to identify some particular specified institution or purpose as the object of his bounty. The specific displaces the general. It is otherwise where the testator has been unable to specify any particular charitable institution or practicable purpose, and so, although his intention of charity can be

---

[182]   *Sir Moses Montefiore Jewish Home v Howell & Co (No 7) Pty Ltd* [1984] 2 NSWLR 406.
[183]   [1997] 1 WLR 877.

seen, he has failed to provide any way of giving effect to it. There, the absence of the specific leaves the general undisturbed...[184]

This makes clear that whether a gift is made with general charitable intention or not is a matter of degree, and there is no single factor which will determine whether a gift falls on the 'particular' or 'general' side of the line. This will be determined in the light of all the circumstances of the gift. In assessing whether a gift was made with 'general charitable intention' the courts have taken account of the following factors.

(i) Gifts to specific institutions or bodies

Where a gift is made to a specific charitable institution or body, this is likely to indicate the absence of any general charitable intention. In *Re Rymer*[185] Horatio Rymer bequeathed a legacy of £5,000 to 'St Thomas' Seminary' in Westminster. The seminary had closed before his death, and the students had transferred to a seminary near Birmingham. The Court of Appeal held that there was no general charitable intention because the gift was a gift to a specific seminary.[186] In *Re Spence*[187] Beatrice Spence left half her residuary estate to the 'Old Folk's Home at Hillworth Lodge Keighley'. She died in 1972, and the home had closed in 1971. Megarry V-C held that this was a gift to a specific institution alone, and that there was no general charitable intention.

(ii) Gifts to a specific institution but with a clear underlying general charitable intention

Even when a gift is made to a specific institution, if the court can see a 'clear general intention underlying the particular mode' of carrying the charitable purpose out[188] they will find a general charitable intention and apply the property cy-près. Thus, in *Biscoe v Jackson*[189] a gift was made by will for the establishment of a soup kitchen and cottage hospital in Shoreditch. This had become impossible, but Kay J held that the testator had a general charitable intention in that the underlying purpose of the gift was to benefit the poor of Shoreditch through the establishment of the soup kitchen and hospital. In *Re Woodhams (Decd)*[190] the court held that a testator who had left money for the musical education of boys from specific children's homes was held to have a paramount intention to benefit musical education. In *Re Spence*[191] Megarry V-C was unable to find any such underlying general intention because the purpose was to benefit the specific patients of the specific home, and not the aged in general.

(iii) 'Charity by association'[192]

Even though a gift is made to a specific institution, the court may find a general charitable intention if the gift is one of a number of charitable bequests, and it is clear that

---

[184] [1979] Ch 483 at 493. [185] [1895] 1 Ch 19.
[186] See *Fisk v A-G* (1867) LR 4 Eq 521; *Clark v Taylor* (1853) 1 Drew 642.
[187] [1979] Ch 483. [188] *Re Spence* [1979] Ch 483 at 495, per Megarry V-C.
[189] (1887) 35 Ch D 460. See also *A-G v Boultbee* (1794) 2 Ves 380; *Cherry v Mott* (1836) 1 My & Cr 123.
[190] [1981] 1 All ER 202. [191] [1979] Ch 483.
[192] The categorization of these cases by Megarry V-C in *Re Spence* [1979] Ch 483 at 494.

the testator intended all of the property so bequeathed to go to 'charity'. In *Re Knox*[193] Dorothy Knox left her residuary estate to three hospitals and to Dr Barnardo's Homes in equal shares. One hospital, the 'Newcastle-upon-Tyne-Nursing Home', did not exist, and Luxmore J held that the quarter-share of the residuary estate should be applied cy-près. He found a general charitable intention in the context of the will, drawing from the fact that the residuary estate was divided among four beneficiaries, three of whom were undoubtedly charitable.[194] Similarly, in *Re Satterthwaite's Will Trusts*[195] a testatrix who hated all human beings left her residuary estate to be divided among nine specifically named animal charities, including the 'Animal Welfare Service'. There was no such charity. Russell LJ held that a general charitable intention could be discerned from the fact that the other eight-ninths of her estate was left to animal charities.[196] The principle of charity by association only applies where a charitable gift fails for lack of certainty or non-existence and has no application where one gift among a number of charitable gifts fails because it is non-charitable.

(iv) Specific charities that had never existed

It has been held that it is easier to find a general charitable intention where a gift is made to a specific charity that has never existed than to a charity that has ceased to exist.[197] In *Re Harwood*[198] a testatrix left bequests to a long list of charitable societies, including those devoted to peace. Among these were a gift to the 'Wisbech Peace Society', which had ceased to exist before the testator's death, and the 'Peace Society of Belfast', which the evidence suggested had never existed. Farwell J held that the gift to the Wisbech society failed, and that as it was a gift to a specific institution the testatrix had no general charitable intention. In contrast, he held that because the Belfast society had never existed, she had demonstrated a general charitable intention for the purposes of peace in Belfast, and the gift was applied cy-près. The rationale behind this analysis is probably that, as the testatrix did not check whether a particular charity existed, she must

---

[193] [1937] Ch 109.

[194] Although the case could equally be explained on the principle of *Re Harwood* [1936] Ch 285, but it was not cited, and the judge reached his conclusion by looking to the other charitable gifts in the context of the will.

[195] [1966] 1 WLR 277.

[196] However, as Megarry V-C noted in *Re Spence*, *Re Satterthwaite's Will Trusts* is not such strong authority as *Re Knox* because Harman LJ had 'the gravest doubts' whether there was general charitable intention, and Diplock LJ agreed with both other judgments.

[197] *Loscombe v Wintringham* (1850) 13 Beav 87; *Re Clergy Society* (1856) 2 K & J 615; *Re Maguire* (1870) LR 9 Eq 632; *Re Rymer* [1895] 1 Ch 19; *Re Davis* [1902] 1 Ch 876; *Re Harwood* [1936] Ch 285: This construction was rejected by the Court of Appeal of New South Wales in *A-G for New South Wales v Public Trustee* (1987) 8 NSWLR 550, where the court held that there is no rule or principle that it is more difficult to conclude that a testator had a general charitable intention where there is a gift to a named charity which existed at the date of the will but which has ceased to exist before death than in the case where the named charity never existed at all.

[198] [1936] Ch 285.

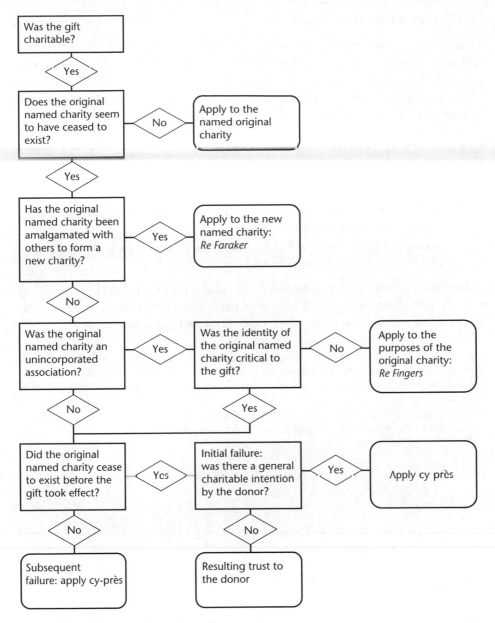

Figure 20.2 The operation of cy-près

have assumed that it did, and that her intention was therefore to benefit the purposes that the invented name suggested were being pursued.[199]

---

[199] Two difficulties arise with regard to the decision in *Re Harwood*. First, it was doubted in *Re Koeppler Will Trusts* [1984] 2 All ER 111 whether the purposes of a peace society are charitable because of their

(5) Cy-près schemes

Where charity assets are applicable cy-près, the court or the Charity Commission may make or approve a cy-près scheme (see Figure 20.2). The purposes to which those assets are applied should be as close as practicable to the original purposes. The Charities Act 2006 widened the range of possible applications. It allows the funds to be transferred to a new charity, but subject to 'a duty to secure that the property is applied for purposes which are, so far as is reasonably practicable, similar in character to the original purposes'.[200] It also requires the court or the Charity Commission in making a scheme to have regard to:

(a) the spirit of the original gift,

(b) the desirability of securing that the property is applied for charitable purposes which are close to the original purposes, and

(c) the need for the relevant charity to have purposes which are suitable and effective in the light of current social and economic circumstances.[201]

This reduces the importance of the terms and spirit of the original gift by introducing two new criteria which have equal weight. In particular, there is a requirement to consider the relevance of the terms of the scheme to present-day circumstances.

political nature. Second, in holding that there was no general charitable intention with regard to the gift to the Wisbech society the judge did not consider whether in the context of the will, and the large number of charitable bequests, there was a general charitable intention through the principle of 'charity by association'.

[200] Charities Act 1993, s 14B(4) inserted by Charities Act 2006, s 18.
[201] Charities Act 1993, s 14B(3) inserted by Charities Act 2006, s 18.

PART IV

ASSET MANAGEMENT

21

Holding trusts and nominee holdings

In Chapter 5 it was outlined how the trust can be used to enable property to be purchased by a nominee on behalf of a principal. Legal title to the property is held by the nominee or nominees as trustees, but the principal is the beneficial owner. This chapter will consider holding trusts in detail, namely the nature of such holdings, nominees' rights, and the execution and performance of holding trusts.

1 The nature of nominee holdings

The way in which a nominee arrangement will work in practice is that on any documents relating to legal ownership, it is the nominees' name that will appear. If the property concerned is land, the deed under which the land is acquired will state that it is transferred to the nominees. It is the nominees who will then be registered as owners with the Land Registry, and the Land Certificate will be issued in the name of the nominees. If the property concerned consists of stocks or shares, again the document of transfer will be made out to the nominees, and it is their names that will be recorded in the register of shareholders kept by or on behalf of the company. If the property concerned is money deposited with a bank, the names appearing on the bank account will be that of the nominees.

In consequence of the nominees having legal title, any proceeds from the property, such as rent from land, dividends on shares, or interest on bank deposits, will be payable to the nominees. Only they can give a valid receipt for the income. Similarly, any dealings with the title to the property must be authorized by the nominees. They must:

(a) authorize any withdrawal of funds from a bank account;

(b) execute any transfer of land they hold as nominees; and

(c) execute any transfer of shares.

If the property is disposed of by way of sale, the proceeds of the sale must be paid by the purchaser to the nominees, or in accordance with their instructions.

This does not mean, however, that the nominees are free to deal with the proceeds of the assets in any way they choose. The nominees hold the property on behalf of the principal, and must therefore deal with it for the principal's benefit. They must account to the principal both for the original property and for any income or capital derived from it.

Nominees therefore, like Janus, face two ways. As between themselves and the principal, it would not be misleading to describe the principal as the owner. It is he who will benefit from any gain (or bear any loss) in the value of the property. It is he who is entitled to the capital value of the assets, and to any income or revenue they produce. He may also transfer or otherwise deal with his equitable interest. This is, however, only one face of the nominees. As between the nominees and the outside world, it is the nominees who are, to most intents and purposes, the owners.

2 Rights and obligations of nominees

(1) Simple holding trusts

This twin aspect to a nominee holding is typical of the trust, and reflects the distinction that the trust permits to be made between powers of management and beneficial entitlement. The extent of the powers of management of the nominees will depend upon what was agreed at the time the relationship was established. In the usual case, the obligation of the nominees will be to act upon the instructions of the principal: the nominees therefore have no independent right to deal with the property, for instance by sale and reinvestment. An arrangement of this kind, in which the nominees or trustees must simply 'obey orders', may be described as a holding trust. It has two characteristics: the trustees have no discretion as to who will receive the benefit of the trust funds; and they have no authority to deal with the assets except upon instructions from the principal. In many cases the holding trust will be little more than a 'front' for the real beneficial owner. In *Hardoon v Belilios*,[1] for instance, shares were acquired by a firm of stockbrokers in the name of one of their employees. Similarly, in *Arrow Nominees Inc v Blackledge*[2] the 'owner' of shares in a company held his shares via a trust of which Arrow Nominees Inc was the nominee. The same result can arise even if the parties are unaware that their arrangement has created a trust. In *Pennington v Waine (No 1)*[3] the Court of Appeal held that a completed share transfer form, although never submitted to the company for registration, was nevertheless effective as an equitable assignment under which the transferor became a bare trustee for the transferee.

---

[1] [1901] AC 118.   [2] [2000] 1 BCLC 709.
[3] [2002] EWCA Civ 227, [2002] 1 WLR 2075.

Another illustration is provided by *Don King Productions Inc v Warren (No 1)*[4] where the leading boxing promoters in the USA and in the UK entered into a partnership agreement. Lightman J held that the effect of this was to make Frank Warren a trustee of promotion, management, and associated contracts (including a contract with Prince Naseem Hamed) for the benefit of the partnership.[5] There are a number of ways in which trusts of this kind can be described. A trust where the trustees hold upon trust for a single beneficiary absolutely (ie without conditions or qualifications), is generally described as a bare trust. Where there is more than one beneficiary, but the beneficial entitlements are set out in the trust documents, leaving no discretion as to the division of the property to the trustees, the trust is usually described as a fixed trust. It may also be described as an executed trust in that no further act is required to identify the rights of the beneficiaries. That there is more than one beneficiary does not necessarily affect the rights and obligations of the trustees, although it is more likely in such cases that the trustees will be given independent powers of management over the trust assets, and they must, of course, have regard to the interests of all the beneficiaries. Except where otherwise specified in the documents setting up the trusts—for instance, only where all the beneficiaries act unanimously—are they in a position to give binding instructions to the trustees.

The utility of the holding trust to conceal the identity of the 'true owner' has been greatly reduced under the Companies Act 2006. UK companies now have a right to ask any registered shareholder to disclose the beneficial ownership of shares.[6] Nevertheless, the nominee holding trust has become widely used as a means of purchasing shares. Under stock exchange rules, a person selling shares must supply the certificate for the shares sold very promptly after the sale has been made. In order to enable a shareholder to sell rapidly by telephone, many stock-broking firms will now arrange to register shares in the name of a nominee company controlled by the firm. The shares can then be sold by means of a written or oral instruction that simultaneously authorizes the nominee to release the share certificate. In some cases the nominee may consolidate the shareholdings of a number of principals under a single share certificate. Although this complicates the issue of identifying the legal title to which the principal's interest relates,[7] it does not affect the legal analysis. The position is not markedly different where ownership of shares is recorded through the new electronic CREST system, rather than in the traditional form of share certificates. Instead of the ownership of the nominee

---

[4] [1998] 2 All ER 608.

[5] The contract of partnership had purported to assign the contracts to the partnership, but the personal nature of the contracts prevented this. The judge held that because the contract of partnership manifested the clear intention that the promotion and management agreements should be held by the partnership absolutely, the agreement should be interpreted as creating a trust: [1998] 2 All ER 608, at 635.

[6] Companies Act 2006, ss 793 (notice by company requiring information about interests in its shares) and 820 (meaning of interest in shares). This would include beneficiaries behind holding trusts (see, in particular, s 820(4)(b)). It is suggested that the purpose of concealment may still be used to hide assets in the event of a hostile takeover—see Moffat, *Trusts Law* (5th edn, 2009), p 6.

[7] See Chapter 32, where the rights of a beneficiary to trace into assets acquired with his funds are discussed.

being evidenced by a share certificate, the shareholding is logged on the electronic register kept by the stock exchange. The position of the principal is not affected.

The appointment of nominees by trustees is expressly sanctioned by the Trustee Act 2000.[8] Prior to the enactment of this provision it was not clear whether trustees had the power to appoint a nominee except where there was an express provision in the trust permitting this. With the increasing use of nominees in share dealings, this change was a sensible modernization. The Trustee Act 2000 also permits the appointment of custodians by trustees.[9] Their function is to undertake safe (physical) custody of trust assets or any documents or records concerning trust assets. This could include, for instance, taking custody of valuable works of art belonging to the trust, bearer securities[10] (which must be deposited with a custodian),[11] or important documents such as share certificates or title documents relating to land. Custodians in this sense should not be confused with custodian trustees, described next. The Act authorizes the payment of nominees and custodians by trustees.[12] As with all cases of delegation (of which these are examples), the trustees must keep the arrangement under review.[13]

(2) Custodian trusts

A special form of holding trust displaying greater complexity than a nominee arrangement is a custodian trust. Whereas with a nominee arrangement the nominee holds a single asset or a single class of assets, the function of custodian trustees is to hold all the assets of the trust. The effect is to separate the legal ownership and custody of the trust assets from the function of managing those assets. The *custodian trustees* hold the assets to the order of other *management trustees* who have the powers of management (see Figure 21.1). The custodian trustees hold the legal title to the trust assets, but the management trustees make all the decisions relating to the administration of the trusts. This structure is used for the administration of unit trusts and many pension schemes.[14]

One advantage of a custodian trust is that the management trustees can be changed without the need to transfer all the trust property from the old trustees to the new.[15] Only the Public Trustee, the Official Custodian for Charities, and trust corporations[16] are authorized by statute to act as custodian trustees,[17] but there is

---

[8] Trustee Act 2000, s 16(1).   [9] Trustee Act 2000, s 17(1).

[10] I.e. securities such as investments in a company that are repayable to the person presenting the security document, unlike most investments, which are repayable to the person in whose name the investment is made.

[11] Trustee Act 2000, s 18(1).   [12] Trustee Act 2000, s 20.

[13] Trustee Act 2000, ss 21, 22. See further Chapter 25.

[14] See, for instance, *British Airways Pension Trustees Ltd v British Airways Plc* [2001] EWHC Ch 13, where Lloyd J was asked in litigation between the custodian trustees and the management trustees to resolve doubts and disagreements concerning the construction of the Airways Pension Scheme.

[15] See Maurice 'The Office of Custodian Trustee' (1960) 24 Conv (NS) 196; Pearce 'Directing the Trustee' (1972) 36 Conv (NS) 260, at 260–261.

[16] Trust corporations are companies specially authorized by statute to undertake trust business.

[17] Public Trustee Rules 1912, r 30, as substituted by the Public Trustee (Custodian Trustee) Rules 1975 (SI 1975/1189) and amended by the Public Trustee (Custodian Trustee) Rules 1976, 1981, 1984 and 1985 (SI 1976/836; SI 1981/358; SI 1984/109; SI 1985/132).

Figure 21.1 Separating management and custody by a trust

no reason why a custodian trust should not be established where this is expressly permitted by the terms of the documents establishing a trust.[18] A sports club, for instance, may have taken the lease of a sports field and clubhouse in the names of up to four trustees. The trustees can hold that land upon trust to deal with in accordance with the directions of the club committee. There is no need to change the trustees every time the composition of the committee changes.

Trustees appointed as custodian trustees under the statutory scheme[19] are obliged to follow the instructions of the management trustees, except where to do so would amount to concurring in a breach of trust. Bare trustees may not even have this freedom, for the terms of their appointment might require them to act upon any instruction of the principal.[20] Trustees appointed as custodian trustees without using the statutory scheme will not enjoy the statutory protection afforded to statutory custodian trustees, and they must use their own judgement in deciding whether to follow instructions given to them.[21] Where, however, the terms of the trust are so tightly drawn as to leave no scope for the exercise by them of their own judgement, it will not

---

[18] See *Cadogan v Earl of Essex* (1854) 2 Drew 227 (trustees subject to directions as to investments). Before the enactment of the Companies Acts permitting companies to be incorporated through a registration procedure, a commonly adopted structure for joint stock companies was one in which, under a deed of settlement, the company's assets were held by trustees on trust for the investors in the company, with the firm being managed by a separate committee of directors.

[19] Established by the Public Trustee Act 1906.

[20] See *IRC v Silverts Ltd* [1951] Ch 521, where the Court of Appeal distinguished custodian trusts from bare trusts on this ground.

[21] *Beauclerk v Ashburnham* (1845) 8 Beav 322; *Re Hart's Will Trusts* [1943] 2 All ER 557 (trustees required to be satisfied that a directed investment was purchased at a fair price).

be a breach of trust for the trustees to follow binding instructions, even if the transaction would otherwise have been imprudent and so a breach of trust.[22]

(3) Dealings with the trust assets

Even in trusts where the trustees have no powers over the allocation of beneficial entitlement it is very common for the trustees to be empowered to manage the investment of the trust fund. Such powers of management are not a normal characteristic of a nominee trust. The absence of authorization to manage the investment of the trust fund will not, however, always prevent the nominees from disposing of the property. Since they have legal title, and appear to the outside world to be the owners, a stranger dealing with them is entitled to treat them as the owners they appear. A transfer from them, by way of cheque on a bank account, or by way of a transfer of land or shares in the proper form, will be effective to give legal title to the transferee. Whether the transferee will acquire that legal title subject to the rights of the principal depends mainly upon whether the transferee was aware of any impropriety at the time of the disposition. If he was not, and the transaction is one in which the stranger gives consideration, then he will normally acquire the property free from any claim of the principal. The extent to which a nominee or other trustee can dispose of the trust property to strangers is considered in Chapters 3 and 31.

Where an unauthorized disposition has been effective to transfer the trust property to a stranger, the principal will not be left without a remedy. An unauthorized transaction on the part of nominees will be a breach of trust and will expose them to personal liability to the principal for any loss that this has occasioned. The principal may also be able to recover, in lieu of the trust property any assets for which it was exchanged. These rights are considered in Part V.

3　Execution and performance

The relationship of principal and nominee will continue for so long as the nominees hold the trust assets for the benefit of the principal. By way of agreement between the principal and the nominees (either at the time when the relationship was established, or subsequently) or, in the absence of agreement, under the rule in *Saunders v Vautier*[23] the principal can call for the nominees to transfer the trust property to him. When they do so, the principal will acquire full legal and beneficial ownership, and the trust will be said to be executed (in other words, fully carried out).[24]

---

[22]　*Re Hurst* (1890) 63 LT 665. See generally Pearce 'Directing the Trustees' (1972) 36 Conv (NS) 260.

[23]　(1841) 4 Beav 115.

[24]　Note that a trust can also be described as executed rather than executory because the precise rights of the beneficiaries have already been identified, even though legal ownership has not yet been transferred to the beneficiaries.

Similarly, by virtue of the original arrangement establishing the trust, or by sub-sequent agreement, the principal may call upon the nominees to transfer the trust property to a third party, or to deal with it in some other way. Where this is done with the intention of passing full legal and beneficial ownership to the third party, then the trust will equally come to an end. For instance, in *Vandervell v IRC*,[25] the National Provincial Bank Ltd held 100,000 'A' ordinary shares in Vandervell Products Ltd as bare trustees or nominees for the benefit of Guy Vandervell. Mr Vandervell wished to pay for the establishment of a chair in pharmacology at the Royal College of Surgeons. In a scheme devised to minimize his liability to pay tax, Mr Vandervell asked the bank, as his nominees, to transfer the shares to the college. Mr Vandervell then used his controlling interest in the company, through other share-holdings, to pay a divi-dend on the 'A' ordinary shares large enough to endow the chair in pharmacology. The Inland Revenue argued that Mr Vandervell had retained an equitable interest in the shares after the transfer, so that under the Income Tax Act 1952 he was liable to income tax and surtax (higher-rate income tax) on the dividends. The House of Lords held that the transfer of the shares to the Royal College of Surgeons was effective to give them both the legal title to the shares held by the bank, and Mr Vandervell's equitable beneficial interest. Whether the equitable beneficial interest passed on the transfer depended upon the intention of Mr Vandervell as the person entitled to the beneficial interest. There was no need for some separate transfer of Mr Vandervell's equitable rights. Mr Vandervell had not, therefore, retained an equitable interest in the shares.[26]

4 Dealing with the equitable interest

It is possible for the principal or beneficiary under a bare trust to deal with his equitable interest without terminating the trust. The same is true of a beneficiary under a fixed trust. Equity treats the beneficiary under a bare or fixed trust as having a beneficial proprietary interest, and not merely personal rights enforceable against the trustee.[27] That proprietary interest may be sold or given away, used as security for a loan, or itself held upon trust. The alienability of an equitable interest has many times been

---

[25] [1967] 1 All ER 1, HL.

[26] This was not enough, however, to enable Mr Vandervell to avoid the taxes. Because the Royal College of Surgeons had given the trustees of a Vandervell family trust an option to repurchase the shares, and there had been no declaration of who was to be the beneficiary of this option, the House of Lords considered that the trustees held the option on Mr Vandervell's behalf until he named some other beneficiary. Because Mr Vandervell therefore retained a power to control who would benefit from the shares once the option was exercised, he had sufficient power of disposition of beneficial entitlement to the shares to subject him to liability to tax. See above p 239.

[27] *Baker v Archer-Shee* [1927] AC 844. For an analysis of the debate as to whether equitable rights are properly characterized as in rem or in personam, see Waters 'The Nature of the Trust Beneficiary's Interest' (1967) 45 Can B R 219.

emphasized. According to Romer RJ in *Timpson's Executors v Yerbury (Inspector of Taxes)*,[28] an equitable interest in property in the hands of a trustee can be disposed of by the person entitled to it in favour of a third party in any one of four different ways:

The person entitled to it

(1) can assign it to the third party directly;

(2) can direct the trustees to hold the property in trust for the third party;

(3) can contract for valuable consideration to assign the equitable interest to him; or

(4) can declare himself to be a trustee for him of such interest.

(1) Direct assignment

The Law of Property Act 1925, s 136 permits the assignment of choses in action. There is some authority that the section applies to equitable rights, including interests under a trust,[29] although the matter is not entirely free from doubt.[30] For the section to operate, the assignment must be an absolute assignment of the whole interest and not an assignment of part only of the interest or a charge extending only to part of the interest.[31] It must also be made in writing and signed by the assignor, and express notice in writing must be given to the trustee.[32]

Where an assignment fails to comply with the statutory provisions, it may nevertheless be effective as an assignment in equity. An equitable assignment does not need to be in any particular form, or to use any particular set of words or language.[33] It is enough if a clear intention is manifested, by words or conduct, to transfer the benefit of a clearly identified right from the assignor to the assignee.[34] The equitable assignment need not be communicated to the trustee,[35] although if the trustee has notice of the assignment it completes the transaction as to third parties, establishes priority on the part of the assignee, and protects the assignee against any fraudulent receipt by the assignor.[36]

---

[28] [1936] 1 KB 645, at 664.

[29] *King v Victoria Insurance Co Ltd* [1896] AC 250, at 254; *Torkington v Magee* [1902] 2 KB 427, at 430–431 per Channell J (reversed on facts [1903] 1 KB 644); *Re Pain, Gustavson v Haviland* [1919] 1 Ch 38, at 44–45 per Younger J.

[30] *Snell's Principles of Equity* (30th edn, Sweet & Maxwell, 2000), pp 84–86.

[31] *Durham Bros v Robertson* [1898] 1 QB 765, CA. A charge operating by way of a mortgage by assignment of the entire interest, with a proviso for reassignment on the discharge of the loan, is, however, within this section: *Tancred v Delagoa Bay and East Africa Rly Co* (1889) 23 QBD 239.

[32] *Campania Colombiana de Seguros v Pacific Steam Navigation Co* [1965] 1 QB 101; [1964] 1 All ER 216 (notice too late if served after commencement of action against debtor).

[33] *William Brandt's Sons & Co v Dunlop Rubber Co* [1905] AC 454, at 462, per Lord MacNaghten.

[34] *Voyle v Hughes* (1854) 2 Sm & G 18. See also *Pennington v Waine* [2002] 1 WLR 2075, where it was held that a share transfer form was capable of operating as an equitable assignment because it demonstrated an immediate and unconditional intention to transfer ownership.

[35] *Kekewich v Manning* (1851) 1 De GM & G 176; *Voyle v Hughes* (1854) 2 Sm & G 18.

[36] *Kekewich v Manning* (1851) 1 De GM & G 176.

(2) **Directions to the trustees to hold on trust**

The alienation may take the form of instructions to the trustee to hold the property upon trust for some other person, as in *Tierney v Wood*.[37] Wood, the principal under a bare trust of property held by his nominee, Tierney, gave directions to his nominee by letter to hold the property upon trust for Wood's wife and daughters.[38] Where the directions impose upon the trustee an obligation more onerous than that required by the original terms of the trust, then it may be necessary for the trustee to agree to perform these obligations [39] but the alienation is valid even if no consideration has been given, provided that the beneficiary has demonstrated an unconditional intention to make an outright transfer.[40] The alienation may also be of part only of the equitable interest in the property,[41] or be in some other way less than an outright transfer.[42]

(3) **Contract to assign**

Under the principle that 'equity treats as done that which ought to be done', a contract to transfer property, if specifically enforceable, will normally be effective to pass title in equity to the beneficiary of the contract.[43] Once any conditions which relate to the transfer have been satisfied, such as the identification of the property concerned, equity treats the transfer as if it had already been made.[44] In *Collyer v Isaacs*, for instance, Jessel MR said:

A man can contract to assign property which is to come into existence in the future, and when it has come into existence, equity, treating as done that which ought to be done, fastens upon that property, and the contract to assign thus becomes a complete assignment.[45]

Where the contract is for the immediate transfer of existing and identifiable property, equity does not therefore distinguish between an equitable assignment and a contract to assign.[46]

The equitable maxim treating a contract to assign as an actual assignment applies only to contracts for value. It cannot be relied upon by volunteers who have not themselves provided any consideration,[47] possibly even if there may have been

---

[37] (1854) 19 Beav 330.
[38] Similar cases to the same effect are *Rycroft v Christy* (1840) 3 Beav 238; *Bentley v Mackay* (1851) 15 Beav 12; and *Paterson v Murphy* (1853) 11 Hare 88.
[39] *Rycroft v Christy* (1840) 3 Beav 238.
[40] *Bentley v Mackay* (1851) 15 Beav 12; *Re Chrimes* [1917] 1 Ch 30.
[41] *Rycroft v Christy* (1840) 3 Beav 238.
[42] *Tierney v Wood* (1854) 19 Beav 330 (life interest followed by entailed interest in land created out of an interest in fee).
[43] *Wright v Wright* (1750) 1 Ves Sen 409, at 412, at (Lord Hardwicke); *Legard v Hodges* (1792) 1 Ves 477, at (Lord Thurlow LC).
[44] *Tailby v Official Receiver* (1888) 13 App Cas 523; *Stephens v Green* [1895] 2 Ch 148, CA.
[45] (1881) 19 Ch D 342, at 351.   [46] *Heap v Tonge* (1851) 9 Hare 90, at 104.
[47] *Re Anstis* (1886) 31 Ch D 596; *Re D'Angibau* (1879) 15 Ch D 228, at 242; *Re Plumptre's Marriage Settlement* [1910] 1 Ch 609, at 616.

someone else who has provided consideration but who does not seek to support the assignment.[48]

(4) Declaration of subsidiary trust

Although there may originally have been some doubt as to whether a trust could be created to fasten upon a beneficial interest under an existing trust,[49] it very soon became established that there was no objection to the imposition of such a trust.[50]

As with any trust, however, the trust will come into effect only if there is a clear intention to create an irrevocable trust, and an ineffective attempt to transfer the property will not be construed as a declaration of trust.[51] As Turner LJ observed in *Milroy v Lord*:[52]

If it [a gift] is intended to take effect by transfer, the Court will not hold the intended transfer to operate as a declaration of trust, for then every imperfect instrument would be made effectual by being converted into a perfect trust.[53]

---

[48] *Re Cook's Settlement Trusts* [1965] Ch 902. This case involved a promise to create a trust of the proceeds of sale of certain paintings should they ever be sold, rather than a contract to transfer an existing equitable interest. The judge held that such a promise did not create an existing proprietary interest capable of being held upon trust. The position concerning the assignment of an existing beneficial interest under a trust is therefore distinguishable.

[49] See the discussion in Simpson, *An Introduction to the History of the Land Law* (OUP, 1961), pp 189–192.

[50] *Kekewich v Manning* (1851) 1 De GM & G 176. See also *Pulvertoft v Pulvertoft* (1811) 18 Ves 84, at 99, per Lord Eldon LC; *Meek v Kettlewell* (1842) 1 Hare 464, at 470–471, per Wigram VC. See above, Chapter 1.

[51] *Edwards v Jones* (1835) 1 My & Cr 226; *Antrobus v Smith* (1805) 12 Ves 39; *Searle v Law* (1846) 15 Sim 95; *Jones v Lock* (1865) 1 Ch App 25.

[52] (1862) 4 De GF & J 264, at 274.

[53] See further the discussion concerning the constitution of trusts in Chapter 7, at pp 196 *et seq.*

22

Management powers

This chapter considers the powers, express and implied, which are given to trustees to manage trust property. It also considers why management of trust property might be necessary, and details those trust holdings where management powers may not be necessary. In some textbooks, no distinction is made between the distributive powers of trustees to allocate equitable interests (for instance through a power of appointment and through powers of advancement and maintenance) from their management powers. The operation and effect of distributive and management powers, however, is quite different, and it is for that reason that they are considered separately in this book. Distributive powers have already been considered in Chapters 15 and 16.

1 Trusts with no management powers

With some kinds of property, such as a valuable painting which it is intended should be kept as a family heirloom, trustees might be directed to hold the property upon trust in its original form without any powers of disposition over the property. The purpose of the trust is to prevent the property—in this case, the painting—from being sold. The beneficial interests have been specified in advance by the settlor, who has left the painting on trust for his eldest child for life, and on her death for her eldest child. Since limited interests cannot be granted directly, the trust is necessary to give effect to the gift, but the trustees have no other real function. The trust can be used in a similar fashion to enable shares to be kept unsold for the benefit of future generations of a family, although in this case the trustees will receive dividend payments from the shareholding which they must pass on to the beneficiaries.

A common form of trust in which the trustee has no powers of disposition or management is a trust of a life insurance policy. When a person takes out a contract of life insurance, under which the insurance company undertakes to pay a sum of money on the death of the person insured, that sum is payable to the personal representatives of the person taking out the insurance contract, and forms part of that person's estate. Since most people taking out this form of life insurance intend their family to benefit from the proceeds of the policy, they may declare that they hold it in trust for their family.[1] The effect of this is that, on their death,[2] the insurance company may make the payment directly to the family members who have been named as beneficiaries,[3] rather than to the personal representatives. This can speed up payment. In addition, the proceeds of the policy do not form part of the estate of the deceased for inheritance tax purposes, and are not available to meet any debts which the insured may have owed. This is one of the reasons why, in *Foskett v McKeown*,[4] disappointed investors under a land investment scheme sought to trace their misused funds into an insurance policy taken out by the swindler in trust for his family. The proceeds from the policy would not otherwise have been available to meet their claim.

The disadvantages to the insured of creating a trust are that the insured will no longer be able to vary the terms of the policy without obtaining the consent of the beneficiary.[5] The insured must also act in the responsible way required of a trustee, considering the interests of the beneficiaries, for instance in considering whether to surrender the policy.[6]

2 The need for management

Unlike paintings and fully paid up insurance policies, some property cannot be left unmanaged: it requires active management. For instance, if land is held on trust, then, unless it is occupied by the beneficiary, the trustee will need to arrange for it to be let in order to produce an income. The trustee will also need to ensure that the rent is paid promptly and that proper steps have been taken to ensure that the property is properly maintained. Indeed, even a painting may need special measures to be taken to ensure that it is properly conserved, and it would be prudent to insure it. The necessary powers of management might be given to, or retained by, the beneficiaries, as is the case with nominee trusts, which were considered in the last chapter. The powers of management, though, may be conferred upon the trustees holding the title to the

---

[1] A trust arises wherever a policy of life assurance on the life assured is expressed to be made for the benefit of the spouse or children of the insured: Married Women's Property Act 1882, s 11. In other cases, there must be an express intention to create a trust: compare *Re Webb, Barclays Bank Ltd v Webb* [1941] Ch 225 (trust created) and *Re Engelbach's Estate* [1924] 2 Ch 348 (no trust created).

[2] Or, in the case of an endowment policy, the date of maturity, if earlier: see *Re Ioakimidis' Policy Trusts* [1925] Ch 403.

[3] The spouse or children may be identified by name, in which case the proceeds of the policy are payable to their estate even if they predecease the insured: *Cousins v Sun Life Assurance Society* [1933] Ch 126. If the policy is expressed to be for the insured's spouse or children (or both) without naming them, it is construed as being for the benefit of those in that category who survive the insured: *Re Browne's Policy* [1903] 1 Ch 188.

[4] [1998] Ch 265 (discussed in Chapter 32).

[5] *Re Schebsman* [1944] Ch 83, CA. The contrary view expressed in *Hill v Gomme* (1839) 5 My & Cr 250 is wrong. If the matter remains in simple contract, then the insured will remain at liberty to vary the policy: *Green v Russell* [1959] 2 QB 226.

[6] *Re Equitable Life Assurance Society of US Policy and Mitchell* (1911) 27 TLR 213.

property, or in the special case of custodian trusts (also considered in the last chapter) by a separate group of trustees.

A trust might be created expressly for the purpose of conferring responsibility for active management on the trustees, as in the case of property being left on trust for a young child, or an adult who suffers from mental impairment. In other cases, for instance where there is complex beneficial entitlement, the need for powers of management might arise incidentally.

3 The extent of the powers

The powers of management[7] conferred upon a trustee are not the same in every case. Quite obviously, the powers of express trustees are likely to differ significantly from those of constructive trustees upon whom a trust has been imposed because of their improper conduct. In the latter case, the question of the trustees' powers rarely arises. They are wrongdoers who are, by definition, acting in breach of duty. How far they are authorized to act is therefore unlikely to be in issue.

Even in the case of express trustees, however, the powers of management of the trustees will differ markedly from one situation to another. The answer to the question about the extent of the management powers of the trustees depends primarily upon the terms of the individual trust instrument. Failing this, powers may be implied by statute or common law. Finally, the court has statutory and inherent powers to authorize management transactions. It is worth noting that since the Trustee Act 2000, which came into force from 1 February 2001, very broad general powers are now conferred on trustees, so that express provision in the trust instrument may be less important than in the past.

(1) Express powers

The trust instrument may set out in considerable detail the authority of the trustees. This is particularly likely to be the case with large, professionally drawn trust deeds such as those governing pension funds or unit trusts, or even large family trusts, especially where the assets pose distinctive issues of management.[8] For example, if the property which is held upon trust is a controlling interest in a private company which it is intended should be run by the trustees, or if it consists of an author's moral rights in literary works, it would be prudent and usual for the documents establishing the trust to define in detail the powers of the trustees.

---

[7] Students must be careful not to confuse powers of management with powers of appointment, detailed in Chapters 4 and 16, or the specific powers of maintenance and advancement considered in Chapter 15.

[8] For example, in *Re Duke of Norfolk's Settlement Trusts* [1982] Ch 610, CA, the trustees had powers of management which enabled them to carry out a substantial redevelopment of the Strand Estate which formed part of the settlement trusts.

Powers of management may or may not include a power to dispose of the property and to reinvest the proceeds. In the case of a trust for sale (described below), the trustees are placed under an express obligation to sell the property and either to distribute or to reinvest the proceeds. Where the trust concerns land, the trustees will, in the absence of any express contrary intention, have both an automatic statutory power to sell the land and to postpone a sale.[9] This does not apply to trusts for sale of other kinds of property, although there can, of course, be an express power to postpone a sale.

(2) Implied powers

There are some cases where powers or duties can be implied from the context of a trust. Where a trust comprising money or quoted stocks and shares contains an express power of investment, but fails to provide express authority for sale for the purpose of reinvestment, it is reasonable to infer this power. The implication might, in some cases, go beyond the implication of a power and impose a duty on trustees.

The duty to convert under the rule in *Howe v Dartmouth*[10] is the best (although now outmoded) example of this. This rule requires trustees to sell unauthorized trust assets in order to apply the proceeds into authorized investments. With the greatly increased range of investments which trustees are now permitted to make,[11] the circumstances in which this rule might apply are now significantly reduced. There may, however, be some rare situations in which it might still operate. The first issue is whether trustees have acquired unauthorized investments. Where a settlor has transferred specific assets to trustees, as in the case of an inter vivos settlement, it can normally be assumed that he is happy for the assets to be retained in that form. It is different, however, if he has imposed an express duty to sell the assets. The retention of those assets would not then be authorized. The rule in *Howe v Dartmouth* imposes a duty to sell in a second situation. This is where the assets concerned form part of a testator's residuary estate, and, in addition, the terms of the trust provide for successive interests, so that one person is entitled to income and another to capital. In such a case there is the danger that some of the random assets which the trustees have acquired may be in a form which may result in a high income being produced at the expense of capital appreciation or capital security,[12] or conversely, that the assets might have a high or secure capital yield but produce little or no income.[13] For this reason, in order to hold a fair balance between the beneficiaries, the rule in *Howe v Dartmouth* requires the hazardous, wasting, or non-income-producing assets to be sold and converted into authorized investments.

The rule in *Howe v Dartmouth* does not fit well with modern investment conditions, where a balanced investment portfolio may well include a combination of high-yield and low-yield investments, which are intended to keep a balance between

---

[9] Trusts of Land and Appointment of Trustees Act 1996, ss 4, 6 and 8.
[10] (1802) 7 Ves 137.   [11] See Chapter 23.
[12] Such as copyrights: *Re Sullivan* [1930] 1 Ch 84.
[13] Such as reversionary interests: *Re Pitcairn* [1896] 2 Ch 199.

income generation and capital growth. The Law Reform Committee recommended[14] that the rule should be replaced with a general duty to hold a fair balance between beneficiaries. Such a rule was, in effect, introduced by s 4 of the Trustee Act 2000 under which trustees are required to keep under review the suitability of the trust investments. This could therefore be interpreted so as to overrule the anachronistic rule in *Howe v Dartmouth*. In any event, the rule can also give way to only the slightest of contrary indications, such as the inclusion of a discretionary power of sale,[15] or an indication that the income or capital beneficiary should be entitled to enjoy or receive the property in specie, as the case may be.[16] In the latter instances, the circumstances negate the duty of the trustees to sell, which is the basis of the rule. In any event, the introduction of a general power of trustees to invest as if absolutely entitled to the assets of the trust in the Trustee Act 2000 has vastly extended the range of authorized investments, so that the circumstances in which the rule in *Howe v Dartmouth* will apply have been significantly restricted.[17]

As was noted in Chapter 13, the Law Commission has issued a report recommending that the rule in *Howe v Dartmouth* be abolished in all new trusts.[18] They no longer recommend the adoption of a new statutory power for trustees to allocate investment returns and trust expenses as income or capital in so far as in necessary to maintain a balance between income and capital.[19] Instead, such matters would, it seems, be dealt with under the general powers of investment, as detailed in the Trustee Act 2000.

Other implied powers, such as the power of charity trustees to sell charity land with the consent of the court, will similarly not apply if this is inconsistent with the purpose of the trust. Thus, if a charitable trust is established to retain for the public benefit a particular house once owned by a particular historical figure or a particular building for its architectural merit, then a sale could not take place without altering the terms of the trust 'because after a sale the proceeds or any property acquired with the proceeds could not possibly be applied for the original charitable purpose'.[20]

(3) Specific statutory powers

Where a trust deed does not set out express powers of management or does not do so comprehensively, and no powers can be implied as a question of fact, the omission may be supplied by statute in one of two ways. First, there are some specific situations in which statutory powers of management are implied. The most notable of these are in trusts of land. Second, there are some general powers which are implied into all trusts by the Trustee Act 1925 and the Trustee Act 2000.

---

[14] 23rd Report (1982) Cmnd 8733.   [15] *Re Pitcairn* [1896] 2 Ch 199.

[16] *Boys v Boys* (1860) 28 Beav 436 and *Holgate v Jennings* (1857) 24 Beav 623, respectively.

[17] *Capital and Income in Trusts: Classification and Apportionment*, Law Comm CP No 175 (2004), para 3.8.

[18] *Capital and Income in Trusts: Classification and Apportionment*, Law Comm No 319 (2009), para 6.65.

[19] Ibid., para 5.81.   [20] *Oldham Borough Council v A-G* [1993] 2 All ER 432, at 439, per Dillon LJ.

(a) Trusts of land[21]

The policy of the land law reforms of the late nineteenth and early twentieth centuries was to facilitate dealings in land. The Settled Land Act 1925 and the Law of Property Act 1925 chose the mechanism of the trust as the means of achieving this. Since these Acts, a trust has been imposed wherever land is acquired for the benefit of, or transferred to, individuals who are sharing the property either consecutively or concurrently. The Acts established a complex dual system of trusts with one kind of trust (the 'strict settlement') applying in the case of most successive interests in land, and a trust for sale applying in all other cases. Thus, where a testator left the family home which he owned to his wife for life, and on her death to be divided between his children, the house would have been held on a trust, normally governed by the Settled Land Act 1925. And if a husband and wife pooled their resources to acquire jointly the house in which they intended to live, again the property would have been held upon a trust, in this case one regulated by the Law of Property Act 1925.

The rules relating to trusts of land have been considerably simplified by the Trusts of Land and Appointment of Trustees Act 1996, which substitutes a single form of trust, the 'trust of land', for the two types which could previously exist (although preserving strict settlement trusts already in existence). The detailed technical rules governing trusts of land will be found in textbooks on land law, and need not detain us here. A few important features of the trusts are, however, worth pointing out.

(b) Kinds of trusts of land

Only one kind of trust of land can be created on or after 1 January 1997. This is the trust of land governed by the Trusts of Land and Appointment of Trustees Act 1996. This Act implemented a recommendation of the Law Commission that the law should be simplified in this way.[22] Under this form of trust, the trustees have all the powers of an absolute (outright) owner, including the power to sell,[23] and they are given a power to retain the property by postponing the sale for an indefinite period.[24] The power to retain applies even to an express trust to sell land, and is not capable of being excluded.

The only other kind of trust which can still exist but can no longer be created is the strict settlement governed by the Settled Land Act 1925. Under the strict settlement, the person first entitled to a beneficial interest in the land is made a trustee of it for himself or herself and for those who will later succeed to beneficial entitlement. The trustee of the land is called a tenant for life, and in most cases will indeed be entitled to the land for life, although this is not a necessary condition.

---

[21] See Jackson, Stevens, and Pearce, *Land Law* (4th edn, 2008), pp 407–430; Gray and Gray, *Elements of Land Law* (5th edn, 2009), pp 967–1020.

[22] Law Commission No 181, *Trusts of Land* (1989); Smith 'Trusts of Land Reform' [1990] Conv 12.

[23] Trusts of Land and Appointment of Trustees Act 1996, s 6.

[24] Trusts of Land and Appointment of Trustees Act 1996, s 4.

All trusts of land other than strict settlements in existence on 1 January 1997 (the date on which the Trusts of Land and Appointment of Trustees Act 1996 came into operation) were subsumed within the new category of trusts of land.

(c) Powers of trustees of land

Before the creation of the new trust of land under the Trusts of Land and Appointment of Trustees Act 1996, trustees of land had only the limited powers set out by the Settled Land Act 1925. These included the power to sell or exchange the property,[25] to grant leases,[26] to enter into compromises,[27] to raise money by mortgage for a limited number of purposes,[28] to make certain improvements to the property,[29] and a range of other minor and ancillary powers.

As has already been indicated, the powers conferred on trustees by the Trusts of Land and Appointment of Trustees Act 1996 are very much wider since, except where the powers are expressly excluded or curtailed, the trustees have all the powers of an absolute owner.

(d) Regulating the rights of beneficiaries under trusts of land

The statutory regime established for trusts of land by the Trusts of Land and Appointment of Trustees Act 1996 contains a range of specific and special provisions applicable only to trusts of land. These provisions are discussed fully in textbooks on land law.[30] It is worth just a brief mention of one of these special provisions. The 1996 Act makes it clear that a beneficiary with an interest in possession has a prima facie right to occupy the land.[31] Whether beneficiaries under a trust for sale had rights of occupation was not clear under the previous legislation, although the courts took the common sense approach that a beneficiary with an interest in possession was entitled to occupation.[32] Nor was it clear what rights, if any, the trustees had to regulate occupation by the beneficiaries. The 1996 Act now makes the rights of occupation of the beneficiaries subject to the power of the trustees to exclude or restrict these rights of occupation.[33] Just how useful these powers will prove to be must be open to question. Like all powers exercisable by trustees, except where otherwise provided, the trustees must concur in their exercise. In most trusts of land the same people are both trustees and beneficiaries. This will almost invariably be the case with the purchase of a house by a married or unmarried couple. A need for the trustees to regulate the rights of occupation will only arise where the beneficiaries disagree. In such a case, it follows that if the trustees are the same as the beneficiaries, the disagreement cannot be resolved by the exercise of the powers given to the trustees. Just as before the

---

[25] Ss 38–40.   [26] Ss 41–48.   [27] S 58.
[28] S 71.   [29] S 83 and Sch 3.
[30] See, e.g., Jackson, Stevens, and Pearce, *Land Law* (4th edn, 2008), pp 413–430.
[31] S 12.
[32] See *Bull v Bull* [1955] 1 QB 234 and *Williams & Glyn's Bank v Boland* [1981] AC 487.
[33] S 13.

Act, it may prove necessary for the disagreement to be resolved by the court under its jurisdiction to intervene in cases of dispute.[34]

(4) General statutory powers

The Trustee Act 1925 contains a small number of powers of management which are incorporated into all trusts. Additional management powers are conferred on trustees by the Trustee Act 2000. The Trustee Act 2000 also replaces the investment provisions of the 1925 Act with a new investment regime. The investment powers are of sufficient importance to merit a separate chapter.[35] Powers given to trustees to delegate trustee management functions are also considered in a separate chapter.[36] The 1925 Act also contains a number of general powers relating to the distribution of trust funds. Since these are distributive rather than management powers, they were considered in Part III.[37]

(a) Sale

The Trustee Act 1925 contains various provisions governing sale which authorize trustees, for instance, to sell either by auction or by private contract.[38] While these provisions extend and expand upon any trust or power which a trustee may have to sell, they do not confer any authority upon the trustees to sell where it has not arisen in some other way. Similarly, the Trustee Act 2000, which extends the investment powers of trustees, does not include any provision authorizing sale except for the purpose of varying an investment.[39] There is therefore no general statutory power of sale except in the case of trusts of land.

(b) Receipts

By s 14 of the Trustee Act 1925, a trustee may give a receipt in writing 'for any money, securities, or other personal property or effects payable, transferable, or deliverable to him under any trust or power' which is a sufficient discharge to the person making the transfer and which exonerates the transferee from having to enquire into the application of the property by the trustee. This power cannot be excluded by a contrary provision in the trust instrument, if any.[40] If there is more than one trustee, they must all, it seems, concur in the receipt because of the principle that trustees must act unanimously,[41] except where the trust instrument authorizes them to act by a majority[42] or, possibly, authorizes them to act individually. Charity and pension trustees are authorized by statute to act by a majority. Where capital money arises on

---

[34] Trusts of Land and Appointment of Trustees Act 1996, s 14.   [35] See Chapter 23.
[36] See Chapter 25.   [37] Chapter 15.   [38] S 12.
[39] What constitutes investment and reinvestment is discussed in Chapter 23.
[40] S 14(3).   [41] *Attenborough v Solomon* [1913] AC 76.
[42] *Re Butlin's Settlement Trust* [1976] Ch 251, [1976] 2 All ER 483. Charitable trustees may act by a majority even if there is no express stipulation on the trust instrument: *Re Whiteley* [1910] 1 Ch 600, at 608.

a sale of land held upon trust, a minimum of two trustees are required to give a valid receipt, except where the trustee is a trust corporation.[43]

(c) Insurance

Trustees had no duty at common law to insure the trust property,[44] nor had they any power to do so. Section 19 of the Trustee Act 1925 conferred a limited power for trustees to take out insurance, and those powers were extended in 1996[45] and again by the Trustee Act 2000, which substituted a new s 19 for the original in the Trustee Act 1925. The new provision authorizes trustees to insure any trust property against the risks of loss or damage due to any event, and to pay the premiums out of the income or capital of the trust funds.[46] In the case of trusts where the beneficiaries are all of full age and capacity and together are absolutely entitled to the trust property, this power to insure is subject to any direction given by those beneficiaries.[47] If any payments are made out under the insurance policy, these payments will be treated as capital belonging to the trust, or may be used to reinstate the property lost or damaged.[48] The statutory duty to take reasonable care applies to the exercise of both the statutory and any express power to insure.[49]

(d) Compromises

A variety of powers relating to the management of property, including some enabling trustees to enter into a compromise or arrangement concerning a dispute, are contained in the Trustee Act 1925, s 15. In *Re Earl of Strafford (Decd)*[50] the sixth Earl of Strafford had left his mansion house, Wrotham Park, and his London home, together with most of his personal property, on a complex trust providing for a series of life interests. The trusts had subsequently been varied by transferring the property to Wrotham Park Settled Estates, an incorporated company.[51] In the light of evidence which emerged after the variation of trusts, there was some confusion as to whether a number of articles, amounting in value to over £170,000, belonged to the Earl of Strafford, and had been settled by him on trust so that they were potentially included in the variation, or whether they belonged to his wife, the Countess. The initial steps in litigation were taken in order to resolve the issue before the beneficiaries under the Countess's will proposed a compromise. Under this, they proposed that the trustees would abandon their claim to about half of the assets in return for the other half being held on the trusts declared by the Earl. The beneficiaries of the Countess also offered,

[43] Trustee Act 1925, s 14(2), as amended by the Law of Property (Amendment) Act 1926 and the Trusts of Land and Appointment of Trustees Act 1996, Sch 3. See Settled Land Act 1925, s 94(1) and Law of Property Act 1925, s 27(2), as amended and re-enacted by the Law of Property (Amendment) Act 1926.

[44] *Re McEacharn* (1911) 103 LT 900.

[45] By the Trusts of Land and Appointment of Trustees Act 1996.

[46] Trustee Act 1925, s 19(1), as substituted by Trustee Act 2000, s 34.

[47] Trustee Act 1925, s 19(2).   [48] Trustee Act 1925, s 20.

[49] Trustee Act 2000, s 1 and Sch 1, para 5.   [50] [1979] 1 All ER 513.

[51] Subsequently involved in a leading case concerning the award of damages in lieu of an injunction for breach of a restrictive covenant: *Wrotham Park Estate Co v Parkside Homes Ltd* [1974] 2 All ER 321.

in respect of most of those assets, to surrender their life interests under the Earl's trusts. The Court of Appeal held that the trustees were permitted by s 15 to agree to this proposed compromise even if other of their beneficiaries objected, and even though it involved a surrender of beneficial interests by those proposing the compromise. Buckley LJ said:

The language of s 15 is, it appears to me, very wide. It would, I think, be undesirable to seek to restrict its operation in any way unless legal principles require this, for it seems to me to be advantageous that trustees should enjoy wide and flexible powers of compromising and settling disputes, always bearing in mind that such a power, however wide, must be exercised with due regard for the interests of those whose interests it is the duty of the trustees to protect. I see nothing in the language of the section to restrict the scope of the power.[52]

The Court of Appeal held that the compromise could be approved provided that, when considered as a whole, it was for the benefit of all the beneficiaries in accordance with their several interests in the trust property. It is not a requirement of approving a compromise that a claim adverse to the trust would otherwise be certain to succeed.[53] There must, nevertheless, be a genuine dispute.[54] The trustees are also required to comply with the statutory duty to take reasonable care imposed by the Trustee Act 2000, s 1.

(e) Reversionary interests

Trustees are given wide powers under s 22 of the Trustee Act 1925 to enter into arrangements, agreements and other transactions concerning property to which the trust is entitled but which is not yet vested in the trustees. This would include, for instance, property which was payable to the trustees upon the winding up of a testator's estate. Once again, trustees must comply with the statutory duty to take reasonable care imposed by the Trustee Act 2000, s 1.

(5) Exceptional authority given by court

The express powers of trustees, as supplemented by the general and special statutory powers, may not cover every transaction which the trustees consider desirable. There is always the possibility of a situation arising which had not been anticipated: a valuable collection of modern art might, for instance, have started to deteriorate owing to the decomposition of some of the materials. Urgent restoration might be required in order to preserve the collection, yet no source of funds may be available to the trustees. In cases such as these, the trustees could enter into some otherwise unauthorized transaction (such as selling one piece of art to pay for repairs to the others), with the consent of all the beneficiaries. If some of the beneficiaries are unascertainable or unable to consent, or perhaps, where they decline consent, the trustees might need to apply to court for approval for an exceptional transaction.

---

[52] [1979] 1 All ER 513, at 520.   [53] *Re Ridsdel* [1947] Ch 597.
[54] *Re Earl of Strafford* [1980] Ch 28; *Chapman v Chapman* [1954] AC 429, CA.

(a) Statutory jurisdiction

The Trustee Act 1925, s 57 gives the court the jurisdiction to confer additional powers on trustees, either generally or in any particular instance. This jurisdiction may be exercised where the trustees or a beneficiary apply for authority for a transaction which is not otherwise authorized by the trust, and which 'is in the opinion of the court expedient'.[55] This statutory power does not authorize any alteration to the equitable entitlements of the beneficiaries,[56] and it does not require the consent or approval of the beneficiaries. The court would not, however, consider that conferring additional powers upon the trustees was expedient unless it could be considered to be in the interest of the trust estate as a whole.[57] The object of the section is 'to secure that the trust property should be managed as advantageously as possible in the interests of the beneficiaries'.[58] A power conferred on trustees under the section is treated as if it were an overriding power contained in the original trust instrument.[59] The section has been used to extend the investment powers of trustees;[60] to amalgamate two funds held on identical trusts;[61] to authorize a sale of a reversionary interest[62] or other trust property where there was no other power of sale[63] or a necessary consent could not be obtained;[64] and to authorize a partition of land.[65] In some cases which come close to trespassing upon the principle that beneficial interests may not be affected, sanction has been given for the release of capital to pay the debts of an income beneficiary, subject to the replacement of the capital on the income beneficiary's death by means of a policy of life assurance.[66]

(b) Inherent jurisdiction

The jurisdiction conferred upon the court by s 57 of the Trustee Act 1925 complements the inherent jurisdiction which the court has always enjoyed to ensure the good administration of trusts. Lord Morton in the House of Lords in *Chapman v Chapman*[67] suggested that there were four situations in which the court could exercise an inherent jurisdiction. These were: where it authorized the conversion of freehold property to

---

[55] A wider jurisdiction for the court to authorize specific transactions for the benefit of settled land or of the persons interested under the settlement is contained in the Settled Land Act 1925, s 64(1). This jurisdiction, which authorizes alterations in beneficial interests, applies only to settled land or land held upon trust for sale.

[56] *Re Downshire Settled Estates* [1953] Ch 218, CA.

[57] *Re Craven's Estate* [1937] Ch 423.

[58] *Re Downshire Settled Estates* [1953] Ch 218, at 248 per Evershed MR.

[59] *Re Mair* [1935] Ch 562.

[60] *Re Shipwrecked Fishermen and Mariners Royal Benevolent Society Charity* [1959] Ch 220; *Mason v Farbrother* [1983] 2 All ER 1078; *Anker-Petersen v Anker-Petersen* [1991] 16 LS Gaz R 32.

[61] *Re Harvey* [1941] 3 All ER 284; *Re Shipwrecked Fishermen and Mariners' Royal Benevolent Society Charity* [1959] Ch 220, not following the inconsistent decision in *Re Royal Society's Charitable Trusts* [1956] Ch 87.

[62] *Re Cockerell's Settlement Trusts* [1956] Ch 372.   [63] *Re Hope's Will Trust* [1929] 2 Ch 136.

[64] *Re Beale's Settlement Trusts* [1932] 2 Ch 15.   [65] *Re Thomas* [1930] 1 Ch 194.

[66] *Re Salting* [1932] 2 Ch 57; *Re Mair* [1935] Ch 562.

[67] [1954] AC 429. See also Chapter 17 above.

which an infant was beneficially entitled into personal property (which affected the devolution of the property on death until 1926 but is no longer of any significance); where it approves a compromise on behalf of an infant or an unborn beneficiary;[68] where it authorizes the use of accumulated income for the maintenance of an infant (which involves a modification of beneficial entitlement); and where 'the court has allowed the trustees of settled property to enter into some business transaction which was not authorized by the settlement'. Only this last category of the court's inherent jurisdiction is of consequence in this context.

Lord Simonds LC in *Chapman v Chapman* limited the court's inherent jurisdiction to extend the authority of trustees to cases of salvage or emergency. In one series of cases, the court had approved the sale or mortgage of an infant's property to release funds for the preservation of what was retained where such action was absolutely necessary, for instance where buildings were in imminent danger of collapse or ruin.[69] Other cases extended this principle to situations where, although there was no absolute necessity, an emergency had arisen which the creator of the trust had not foreseen or anticipated, and where the best interests of the trust required the granting of exceptional authority. Romer LJ said in *Re New*:

In the management of a trust estate...it not infrequently happens that some peculiar state of circumstances arises for which provision is not expressly made by the trust instrument, and which renders it most desirable, and it may be even essential, for the benefit of the estate and in the interest of all the cestuis que trust, that certain acts should be done by the trustees which in ordinary circumstances they would have no power to do. In a case of this kind, which may reasonably be supposed to be one not foreseen or anticipated by the author of the trust, where the trustees are embarrassed by the emergency that has arisen and the duty cast upon them to do what is best for the estate, and the consent of all the beneficiaries cannot be obtained by reason of some of them not being sui juris or in existence, then it may be right for the court, and the court in a proper case would have jurisdiction, to sanction on behalf of all concerned such acts on behalf of their trustees as we have above referred to.[70]

In that case the court authorized the trustees to agree to the reconstruction of the capital of a commercial company in which they had an interest. In *Re Tollemache*[71] the Court of Appeal said that *Re New* 'constitutes the high watermark of the exercise by the court of its extraordinary jurisdiction in relation to trusts', and refused to extend the powers of investment of the trustees to authorize the acquisition of a mortgage which would have enhanced the income of the trust. The fact that a proposed transaction would benefit one or even all of the beneficiaries is insufficient.[72] The jurisdiction which the court exercises in cases falling under the head of salvage or emergency is a jurisdiction to consent on behalf of beneficiaries who are not themselves sui juris by reason of infancy or mental incapacity. Unlike the statutory jurisdiction under s 57 of the Trustee Act 1925, which does not require the consent

---

[68] Unlike s 15 of the Trustee Act 1925, the inherent jurisdiction permits the approval of a compromise between two beneficiaries which does not directly affect the trustees.

[69] *Re Jackson* (1882) 21 Ch D 786; *Conway v Fenton* (1888) 40 Ch D 512; *Re Montagu* [1897] 2 Ch 8.

[70] [1901] 2 Ch 534, at 544.   [71] [1903] 1 Ch 955.

[72] *Re Montagu* [1897] 2 Ch 8.

of adult beneficiaries, the court is probably unable, under its inherent jurisdiction, to override or to supply consent on behalf of those who are themselves legally competent to provide it.

(c) A broader jurisdiction?

There is some authority for suggesting that the inherent powers of the court could extend beyond cases of salvage and emergency. A lengthy series of cases, reviewed in *Re Duke of Norfolk's Settlement Trusts*,[73] establishes beyond doubt that the court has an inherent jurisdiction to authorize the payment of remuneration to trustees, and even, according to the latter case, increase the level of the remuneration. Fox LJ did not consider this to be inconsistent with the principles expressed in *Chapman v Chapman*, which was concerned with the power of the court to authorize variations in beneficial interests as such. He said:

I appreciate that the ambit of the court's inherent jurisdiction in any sphere may, for historical reasons, be irrational and that logical extensions are not necessarily permissible. But I think that it is the basis of the jurisdiction that one has to consider. The basis, in my view, in relation to a trustee's remuneration is the good administration of trusts . . . [I]t is of great importance to the beneficiaries that the trust should be well administered. If therefore the court concludes, having regard to the nature of the trust, to the experience and skill of a particular trustee and to the amounts which he seeks to charge when compared with what other trustees might require to be paid for their services and to all the other circumstances of the case, that it would be in the interests of the beneficiaries to increase the remuneration, then the court may properly do so.[74]

The importance of the case in its immediate context is much reduced because the Trustee Act 2000 now allows trustees to be paid reasonable remuneration for services they provide if they are trust corporations or act in a professional capacity.[75] However, the principle of the case remains valid. The influence of the importance of the good administration of a trust is equally capable of application to administrative arrangements other than remuneration. Nor is authorization of payment for trustees the only instance in which the court enjoys jurisdiction to amend the operating arrangements for trusts. In *Re Ashton's Charity*,[76] followed in *Oldham Borough Council v A-G*,[77] Romilly MR held that, even where there is no applicable statutory authority, the Court of Chancery has a general jurisdiction to authorize the alienation of charity property where the court clearly sees that the transaction is for the charity's benefit and advantage. So, in the *Oldham* case, the Court of Appeal was prepared to authorize the sale for building development of a playing field held upon charitable trusts where the proceeds were to be used to acquire a new site with better facilities. This jurisdiction might relate only to the court's powers regarding the supervision of the administration of charities, and it almost certainly does not extend to authorizing a sale which would have the consequence of changing the nature of a

---

[73] [1981] 3 All ER 220.   [74] Ibid., at 230.
[75] Ss 28 to 30.   [76] (1856) 22 Beav 288.
[77] [1993] 2 All ER 432. See also *Re Parke's Charity* (1842) 12 Sim 329; *Re North Shields Old Meeting House* (1859) 7 WR 541.

trust, as for instance where there is a trust to retain for the public benefit a tract of land of outstanding natural beauty. Nevertheless, when taken in association with the cases on salvage and emergency, the two examples just cited may evidence a wider equitable jurisdiction for the court to sanction transactions or arrangements which have been approved by all beneficiaries capable of concurring, and which are for the benefit of the trust viewed as a whole, and more particularly for those beneficiaries for whom the court is acting as a surrogate, provided that they do not amount to a rewriting of the beneficial interests.[78]

---

[78] Compare the dissenting judgment of Lord Denning in *Re Chapman's Settlement Trusts* [1953] Ch 218.

23

Investment and reinvestment

This chapter considers the powers and duties of trustees in relation to the investment of trust funds, including the range of permitted investments, and the objectives which trustees are expected to follow. Collective investment schemes and collective asset holding structures, including pension trusts, are considered in detail in Chapter 24.

1 Introduction

Of their non-distributive functions, the powers and duties of trustees in relation to investment are undoubtedly the most important.[1] Except in the very simplest of trusts, it is the duty of the trustee to preserve the trust assets over a period for the benefit of a number of beneficiaries. In many cases, the property which is transferred to the trustee is transferred as a fund, rather than as a set of assets which are to be retained in their original form. The trustee is expected to preserve the value of that fund through proper investment. In some cases, such as with unit trusts, and to some extent with pension funds, investment is the primary purpose of the trust.

It is in the context of investment that the concept of the fund is at its most apparent. The beneficiaries are entitled to share in the wealth which the trust assets represent. The component parts of that wealth are very much less important to the beneficiaries than its aggregate value. Of course, there are exceptions. The member of the landed aristocracy who leaves the family mansion upon trust for future generations of the family will no doubt hope that the home will be preserved intact.[2] The married couple joining together in the purchase of a matrimonial home will no doubt intend to keep it as their dwelling. Even here, the land which constitutes the trust asset will be treated as a fund which can be sold and reinvested: so the new squire can sell some land on the fringe of the estate for building development and invest the proceeds in stocks and shares, or the married couple can 'up sticks' and sell to move to another area where

---

[1] Note that trustees who are conducting investment business must be authorized under s 19 of the Financial Services and Markets Act 2000, or exempted.

[2] See *Wyndham v Egremont* [2009] EWHC 2076, where the court approved a variation of trust to enable the Petworth estates to follow the titles to Leconfield and Egremont.

they will buy another house, without in either case dissolving the original trust. The case of land is, perhaps, somewhat special, since the legislature has ensured that trustees of land will always have a power of sale and reinvestment, and as we have already seen in the previous chapter, there is no general power of sale in relation to property other than land which is vested in trustees.

It has already been described how the concept of the fund enables some assets to be disposed of, so that the purchaser acquires the assets free from the trust obligations, the trust obligations instead resting upon the price paid by the purchaser, or with whatever is purchased with the proceeds of the disposal. The issues which have to be addressed in the context of investment are first, when trustees are permitted to dispose of existing trust assets in order to substitute new assets; second, what assets may be substituted for the original ones; and third, the principles upon which those investments must be chosen. Overarching these issues is a fundamental question—what is the purpose of investment? It is with that question that we need to begin.

2 The purpose of investment

(1) Even-handedness between beneficiaries

As little as a century ago, one of the more common forms of trust was the family settlement, in which a man of property would settle funds for the benefit of his spouse and children for their lives, with entitlement to the capital then passing to the next generation. The duty of the trustees in such a case was to ensure that the capital was preserved for the benefit of the capital beneficiaries, while an income was produced for the settlor's wife and children. The trustees were obliged to keep a fair balance between the two, except where they had been given other instructions by the settlor. This rule of even-handedness between beneficiaries was at the root of the rule in *Howe v Dartmouth*, discussed in an earlier chapter.[3]

(2) The purpose of the trust

Not all trusts provide for successive interests, therefore requiring both income generation and preservation of capital. It is possible that a trust will provide for the accumulation of income for a limited period, with a view to conferring a lump sum benefit on a beneficiary at a future date. In such a case, it is of greater importance that the trust fund should produce capital appreciation than that it should provide a large income. For instance, in the case of an endowment fund for a major museum and art gallery, 'the desirability of having an increase of capital value which will make possible the purchase of desirable acquisitions for the museum despite soaring prices does

[3] See above, pp 469 *et seq.*

something to justify the greater risks whereby capital appreciation may be obtained'.[4] On the other hand, the investment of a pension fund will require a combination of investments which will provide some measure of protection against the ravages of inflation[5] and of investments which will enable the payment of benefits to pensioners as and when they fall due for payment, bearing in mind always the need to make a judgement which takes account of the risks of the investments in question[6] and which has proper regard to the need for security.[7] It may even be that, in considering investment policy, the trustees will need to have regard to the circumstances of individual beneficiaries. Trustees of land, for instance, may invest or apply trust funds in the purchase of property for occupation by a beneficiary,[8] a decision which can be made only after considering the circumstances of the beneficiaries. Also, in *Nestlé v National Westminster Bank plc*,[9] Staughton LJ thought that it would be appropriate for trustees to take into account the circumstances of the beneficiaries, as, for example, 'if the life tenant is living in penury and the remainderman already has ample wealth'.[10]

Expressed in general terms, it can be said that the purpose of investment is to enable the fulfilment of the objectives of the trust. In one of the leading investment cases, Sir Robert Megarry said:

The starting point is the duty of trustees to exercise their powers in the best interests of the present and future beneficiaries of the trust, holding the scales impartially between different classes of beneficiaries. This duty of the trustees towards their beneficiaries is paramount... When the purpose of the trust is to provide financial benefits for the beneficiaries, as is usually the case, the best interests of the beneficiaries are normally their best financial interests. In the case of a power of investment, as in the present case, the power must be exercised so as to yield the best return for the beneficiaries, judged in relation to the risks of the investments in question; and the prospects of the yield of income and capital appreciation both have to be considered in judging the return from the investment.[11]

This statement does not apply only to the exercise by trustees of their powers. The influence of the policy which underlies it can be seen also in the historical approach to trustees' general powers of permitted investment, and in the approach which the courts have in the past adopted in considering extensions to trustees' powers of investment.

3 Powers of disposal

(1) Assets available for investment

Except where trustees are under an obligation to make an immediate distribution, the trustees will have assets to invest where the funds they receive are in cash or currency.

---

[4] *Trustees of the British Museum v A-G* [1984] 1 All ER 337, at 343, per Megarry V-C.
[5] *Mason v Farbrother* [1983] 2 All ER 1078, at 1086–1087.
[6] See *Cowan v Scargill* [1985] Ch 270.
[7] See Grosh 'Trustee Investment: English Law and the American Prudent Man Rule' (1974) 23 ICLQ 748.
[8] Trusts of Land and Appointment of Trustees Act 1996, s 6.   [9] [1993] 1 WLR 1260.
[10] Ibid., at 1279.   [11] *Cowan v Scargill* [1985] Ch 270, at 286, per Megarry V-C.

It would rarely be appropriate for the trustees to retain large quantities of banknotes, uncleared cheques, or similar assets. Where the assets which the trustees receive are already in some form of investment, such as shares in a public company, a landholding, or some other enduring form, then it is less clear whether there is a power or even an obligation to realize those assets for the purpose of reinvestment. It has already been noted in the last chapter that there is no general power of sale. The power of sale for the purpose of reinvestment now needs to be examined more closely.

(2) Trust for sale

In some trusts, the trustees are placed under an obligation to sell the property in the form in which it is originally received, and either to distribute or to reinvest the proceeds of sale. Such a trust is called a trust for sale. A trust for sale may be imposed expressly by the settlor. Before the Trusts of Land and Appointment of Trustees Act 1996, it was also the statutory form of a trust of land, although that is no longer the case.

A trust for sale may, finally, arise under the rule in *Howe v Earl of Dartmouth*, explained in Chapter 13,[12] where hazardous or wasting assets, or assets generating no income, and which formed part of a testator's residuary estate, are received by a trustee who is to hold the assets for beneficiaries entitled to successive interests. The Law Commission has recently recommended the abolition of the rule in *Howe v Earl of Dartmouth* and of the implied trust for sale of unauthorized, hazardous, or wasting assets generated thereby.[13] Express and statutory trusts for sale would be unaffected by this reform.

(3) Other powers of sale and reinvestment

A well-drafted trust will have anticipated the desirability of selling trust assets for the purpose of reinvestment, and will have made express provision. Trusts of land governed by the Settled Land Act 1925 confer upon the tenant for life, as trustee of the land, a power of sale,[14] with the proceeds of sale being treated as capital money which, if not otherwise required, is available for reinvestment.[15] Similarly, there is a power of sale[16] and a power indefinitely to postpone sale[17] in the case of trusts of land governed by the Trusts of Land and Appointment of Trustees Act 1996. This includes all trusts of land which are created on or after 1 January 1997, and all trusts of land arising before that date and which are not governed by the Settled Land Act 1925.

Strangely, the Trustee Act 2000, which introduced a new regime for investment of trust funds failed to make clear whether trustees had a power of sale for the purposes

---

[12] See above, pp 469 *et seq.*

[13] *Capital and Income in Trusts: Classification and Apportionment*, Law Comm No 319 (2009) para 6.65.

[14] Settled Land Act 1925, s 38: see p 713.   [15] Settled Land Act 1925, s 73.

[16] Trusts of Land and Appointment of Trustees Act 1996, s 6.

[17] Trusts of Land and Appointment of Trustees Act 1996, s 4.

of investment. The Act stated in section 3 that 'a trustee may make any kind of investment that he could make if he were absolutely entitled to the assets of the trust', but nowhere does it indicate when a trustee may or must make investments. The Trustee Investments Act 1961, which the Trustee Act 2000 largely replaces, did contain the more explicit statement that 'a trustee may invest any property in his hands, whether at the time in a state of investment or not … and may from time to time vary such investments'.[18] This omission is made all the more strange by the fact that section 8 of the Trustee Act 2000 confers a power on the trustees of personalty to purchase a legal estate in land as an investment.[19] In the absence of such a general provision, it will be a matter for the proper construction of the trust instrument as to whether the trustees are permitted or expected to invest the trust property. Such a conclusion could readily be reached if the trust assets are to be retained for any length of time, and the conferment of a statutory power of investment could be interpreted as implying a power to sell for the purpose of making an investment.[20] The indications are that the courts are likely to take a broad and common sense view of when property is available for investment. In *Gregson v HAE Trustees Ltd*[21] Henry Cohen, the founder of the Courts furniture group, set up a family trust in 1960 using company shares, with the intention that a wider family group should benefit from the success of the company. The trustees did not sell the shares and in 2004, when the Courts group collapsed, the shares became worthless. It was held that the shares constituted investments, even though it was not envisaged that they would necessarily be sold. Henry Cohen had not prohibited their sale, and indeed had given the trustees a power to sell them. The trustees should therefore have considered whether to diversify the trust's investments. The judge stated:

It seems to me that on its natural reading 'the investments of the trust' comprise any asset of the trust which happens to be invested, whether it was in that state when originally settled or it came into that state of investment later.[22]

However, as has already been explained, there could be circumstances in which the power of sale is excluded because the trust requires the retention of the assets in a particular form.[23] Although there are authorities that suggested that there must be a clear exclusion of the statutory investment powers in express terms,[24] these were cases that sought to limit and not to exclude the trustee's powers of investment. It is submitted

---

[18] S 1(1).

[19] In fact, the section allows the purchase of land for purposes other than investment such as for occupation by a beneficiary (s 8(b)) or for any other reason (s 8(a)).

[20] See Trustee Act 1925 s 16(1), which could be interpreted as conferring a power of sale in these circumstances. Compare *Hume v Lopes* [1892] AC 112; *Re Pratt's Will Trust* [1943] Ch 326.

[21] [2008] EWHC 1006 (Ch).

[22] Ibid., at [81] (Robert Miles QC sitting as a deputy High Court judge). The claim for breach of trust failed because the corporate trustees had no assets and the judge held that it was not possible for a beneficiary to make a direct ('dog leg') claim against the directors.

[23] See the now repealed s 1(3) of the Trustee Investments Act 1961, which stated that the previous statutory provisions are 'exercisable only in so far as a contrary intention is not expressed…'.

[24] *Re Rider's Will Trusts* [1958] 1 WLR 974; *Re Burke* [1908] 2 Ch 248; *Re Hill* [1914] WN 132.

that the implied statutory power to sell for the purpose of investment does not apply to property that it is the trustee's duty to retain.[25]

4 Authorized investments

(1) Principles

Except in those rare situations where a person is both trustee and beneficiary (as for instance in the case of co-ownership trusts of land), a trustee is investing property on behalf of others. This requires an approach to risk which may not be the same as that which might be adopted by a person making investments on his or her own behalf. Whilst an individual may consider it appropriate when making decisions on their own behalf to incur a high degree of risk, this is much less appropriate when dealing with the assets of others. To take an extreme example, a person can choose to gamble with their own money by buying lottery tickets, but this would not be a suitable application of trust funds. A 'turf investment' at the racecourse would not be a trustee investment.

There are two different methods which can be used to limit the investment decisions of trustees to investments which are suitable for trust funds. One is to provide a list of investments which are considered to be sufficiently secure and robust to be used for the investment of trust funds, limiting trustees to making a choice from this menu. The other is to impose a general duty on trustees only to select investments which meet the criteria of suitability. The first approach was at one time the approach adopted in Britain, but the Trustee Act 2000 implemented a sea change by sweeping away most of the previous restrictions on investment by trustees and adopting the second approach.

(2) History

The turbulence caused by the bursting of the South Sea Bubble in 1720 was the cause for a serious curtailment by the Court of Chancery of the investments which trustees were permitted to make. From the end of the eighteenth century onwards, it became the rule that a trustee would be liable to bear the deficiency if any loss resulted from making an investment in a way which was not authorized by the settlor or the beneficiaries, and which had gone beyond the range of investments contemplated by the courts or the legislature. Prior to the Trustee Act 2000, the investments authorized by

---

[25] Compare Settled Land Act 1925, s 67, under which heirlooms (defined as personal chattels settled so as to devolve with settled land) may be sold only pursuant to an order of the court, even where the purpose of sale is to invest the proceeds. In *Re Hope* [1899] 2 Ch 679 the court refused permission under this section to sell the 'Hope' diamond.

the general law were conservative, placing considerable emphasis on the security of trust funds.

The policy adopted by legislation up to and including the Trustee Investments Act 1961 was to protect beneficiaries by limiting trustees to 'safe' forms of investment. The Trustee Investments Act 1961 adopted a very much more constrained regulation of trustee investments than in some other jurisdictions, notably in North America, where the principal requirement is that in making investments, trustees should act as a prudent man would do when investing on behalf of others.[26] It also lagged substantially behind the practice of well advised settlors inserting their own express investment powers. This, of course, limited the return that trustees could achieve through investment for the beneficiaries; as safety and high-income yield rarely go hand in hand.

Precisely to avoid the limitations on the powers of investment by trustees, settlors often included an express power of investment in a settlement. The trustees could also obtain the consent of the beneficiaries to investments which would not otherwise be authorized, although this course of action was only available if all the beneficiaries were capable of giving consent. Finally, the trustees could enlarge their investment powers by means of an application to court, either under the Variation of Trusts Act 1958, where the beneficiaries who are capable of consenting concur, or where this is not practicable, under s 57 of the Trustee Act 1925.

(3) The new approach

The new approach to investment has been embraced by the Trustee Act 2000. The approach was described in a Treasury consultation paper.[27] Rather than limit the kinds of investment which trustees can make, it is seen as more sensible to give the trustees more extensive powers of investment in relation to the selection of individual investments. The interests of the beneficiaries are then protected by requiring the trustees to take such expert advice as the nature of the trust requires and by charging them with responsibility to ensure that the portfolio of investments is properly balanced.

This new approach was first adopted by the Pensions Act 1995. This permits pension fund trustees to make any kind of investment as if they were absolutely entitled to the assets.[28] However, the trustees are required to maintain a statement of investment policy,[29] including information about the policy on risk, expected returns, and realization. The trustees are expected to secure and consider professional advice, to consider the need to maintain a balanced portfolio, and to consider the merits of each individual investment proposed.[30] The same approach has now been adopted by the Trustee Act

---

[26] See Grosh 'Trustee Investment: English Law and the American Prudent Man Rule' (1974) 23 ICLQ 748.
[27] Investment Powers of Trustees (May 1996).   [28] Pensions Act 1995, s 34.
[29] Pensions Act 1995, s 35.
[30] Pensions Act 1995, s 36. See also Occupational Pensions Schemes (Investment) Regulations SI 2005/3378, which set out detailed regulations governing the exercise of the investment powers. There is special provision allowing the trustees to delegate some of these responsibilities: s 34.

2000 as the general principle for most trusts.[31] Trustees are given the same power to invest trust funds, with some narrow exceptions, as if they owned the assets outright. They are, however, subject to an obligation to act in the best interests of the beneficiaries, to consider the need for diversification of investment, to consider the suitability of individual investments, and to take advice where appropriate.

The power of investment conferred by the Trustee Act 2000, described as the *general power of investment*, extends the powers of investment which may have been conferred upon trustees by other statutory provisions or by the trust instrument, but it can be excluded or restricted by the trust instrument or by legislation.[32] The general power of investment applies to existing trusts, not just those created after the passing of the 2000 Act.[33]

(4) Express powers of investment

(a) Interpretation

The need for express powers of investment is significantly reduced by the general power of investment conferred by Trustee Act 2000. Nevertheless, it is still common practice for professionally drafted trusts to contain express investment powers. The approach to the interpretation of such powers is demonstrated *by Re Harari's Settlement Trusts*.[34] Sir Victor Harari had transferred assets to trustees which fell outside the categories authorized by the general rules for trustees. Under an express provision in the trust deed, it was declared that:

> The trustees shall hold the said investments so transferred to them as aforesaid upon trust that they may either allow the same to remain in their present state of investment so long as the trustees may see fit or may at any time or times realise the said investments and invest the money produced thereby in or upon such investments as to them may seem fit with power to vary or transpose any investments for or into others.

It was argued before the judge that the investments which the trustees could select under this clause were limited to those generally authorized by law (which, of course, at the time were much narrower than they are now), since the clause did not clearly and unambiguously extend the range of investments beyond those permitted by statute. Jenkins J held, however, that the trustees were given a wider power of investment. In his view, he was free to construe the settlement according to what he considered to be the natural and proper meaning of the words used in their context, and he saw no justification for implying any restriction on the wide construction which the words themselves were sufficient to bear.[35]

---

[31] The general investment powers do not apply to occupational pension schemes, authorized unit trusts, or certain schemes under the Charities Act 1993: see Trustee Act 2000, ss 36–38. There are special statutory rules applying to these forms of collective investment.

[32] Trustee Act 2000, s 6.   [33] Trustee Act 2000, s 7.

[34] [1949] 1 All ER 430.

[35] See, to similar effect, *Re Peczenik's Settlement* [1964] 2 All ER 339.

(b) Limits to investment powers

Although it is clear from *Re Harari's Settlement Trusts*[36] that investment clauses will not be given a restrictive interpretation, there are still pitfalls for the draftsman. If the draftsman seeks to impose a limit on the range of permissible investments, that limit should be clearly and unambiguously expressed. Difficulties have occurred in the past with clauses limiting investments to stocks in 'any British colony or dependency' because of changes in the status of Commonwealth and former Commonwealth countries.[37] A clause authorizing investment in 'blue chip' securities has also been held to be ineffective on grounds of uncertainty.[38]

(c) Meaning of 'investment'

A number of cases, discussed in relation to the Trustee Act 2000, below, have considered what is meant by the word 'investment'. The cases suggest that an application of funds will not be considered to be an investment unless the assets produce an income. It may be that in the light of changing investment practice, a different view would be taken today and that assets expected to produce a capital gain could be considered to be investments even if they were producing no income.[39] Nevertheless, good drafting will make clear that applications in non-income generating assets are permitted. The Universities' Superannuation Scheme Rules (the pension scheme for academic staff within the old universities), for instance, state that the trustee may apply its assets for the purchase of 'investments or property...whether producing income or not':[40]

All trust moneys in the fund shall either be placed on current or deposit account with a bank, or invested in the name or under the legal control of the trustee company in the purchase, or at interest upon the security, of such investments or property, whether involving liability or not, and *whether producing income or not*, or upon such personal credit, with or without security, as the trustee company shall think fit, to the intent that the trustee company shall have the same full and unrestricted powers of investing and transposing investments as if it was absolutely entitled to the fund beneficially. [emphasis added]

(d) Loans

In *Khoo Tek Keong v Ch'ng Joo Tuan Neoh*[41] the Privy Council held that trustees were not authorized to make an unsecured personal loan under a clause which permitted them 'to invest all moneys liable to be invested in such investments as they in their absolute discretion think fit'. Where security is given for the loan, it may be classed as

---

[36] [1949] 1 All ER 430.

[37] *Re Maryon-Wilson's Estate* [1912] 1 Ch 55, CA; *Re Brassey's Settlement* [1955] 1 WLR 192; *Re Rider's Will Trusts* [1958] 1 WLR 974.

[38] *Re Kolb's Will Trusts* [1962] Ch 531.

[39] See *Cook v Medway Housing Society* [1997] STC 90, at 98 for support for this view.

[40] Universities' Superannuation Scheme New Rules (1 May 2009), r 64.1. This replaced the old rules, which in r 20.8(a) allowed for a slightly wider category of 'investments or other property of whatsoever nature and wheresoever...and whether producing income or not'.

[41] [1934] AC 529.

an investment under such a clause and, again, a suitably drafted clause can authorize the application of trust funds in unsecured personal loans.[42]

(5) General power of investment under Trustee Act 2000

(a) Meaning of 'investment'

The general power of investment conferred by the Trustee Act 2000 states that 'a trustee may make any kind of investment that he could make if he were absolutely entitled to the assets of the trust'.[43] The Act does not define what is meant by an investment, and this is therefore something to be resolved by reference to general principles of interpretation. The explanatory note to the Act states that an investment is something which is expected to produce an income or capital return. The case law on the use of the word in express investment clauses shows a narrower interpretation being adopted. In *Re Wragg*,[44] P.O. Lawrence J held that a clause authorizing investment in 'stocks funds shares and securities or other investments' was wide enough to include the purchase of land that was to be rented out to produce an income. He stated that 'to invest' includes as one of its meanings:

to apply money in the purchase of some property from which interest or profit is expected and which property is purchased in order to be held for the sake of the income which it will yield.

In *Re Power*,[45] the court considered that the purchase of a house for occupation by a beneficiary was not permitted under a clause providing that 'All moneys requiring to be invested under this my will may be invested by the trustee in any manner in which he may in his absolute discretion think fit in all respects as if he were the sole beneficial owner of such moneys including the purchase of freehold property in England or Wales.' The reason for this was that land being occupied by a beneficiary would not be generating income, and it could not therefore appropriately be described as an investment.[46] Strict application of this interpretation of the meaning of 'investment' would preclude trustees from purchasing, in the absence of the conferral of an express power in the trust instrument, assets for investment which only have potential to appreciate in capital value but do not produce any income. This would include the purchase of precious metals, works of art, fine wine, or antiques. Premium bonds would also not be considered an investment.

The reason the Trustee Act 2000 is silent on a definition of 'investment' can be found in the Law Commission report on the powers and duties of trustees that preceded the Act. The Commission expressed the view that avoiding any definition of investment would permit the concept to evolve in ways which might be constrained

---

[42] *Re Laing's Settlement* [1899] 1 Ch 593. The Universities' Superannuation Scheme New Rules (1 May 2009) state that the trustee may apply funds 'upon such personal credit, with or without security, as the trustee company shall think fit' (r 64.1).

[43] Trustee Act 2000, s 3(1).   [44] [1919] 2 Ch 58.

[45] [1947] Ch 572.   [46] See also *Re Peczenik's Settlement Trusts* [1964] 1 WLR 720.

were a definition to be given.[47] The explanatory notes accompanying the Act state that the power of investment conferred by the Act permits trustees to invest so as to produce an income or capital return, but these do not form part of the Act and cannot be regarded as having overruled the definition of 'investment' in *Re Power*.[48] It would, however, be inconvenient if the word 'investment' in the Trustee Act 2000 were to be interpreted in the same restrictive way. Changing patterns of investment now mean that it is not uncommon for applications of funds to carry no rights to income. For instance, some companies adopt a policy of making no declaration of a dividend in order to reinvest profits with the intention of increasing the value of their shares. Similarly, it is possible to purchase units in authorized unit trusts where all income is reinvested rather than being paid out to investors, again with the intention of producing capital growth. It is also possible to purchase capital bonds that are redeemable after a fixed period at a value higher than the purchase price, compensating for the lack of interest by this capital growth. All of these applications of funds generate potential capital growth and can have a place in a properly constructed investment portfolio. It would be unfortunate if trustees were not able to take advantage of them. As has already been indicated, it is possible that were the issue to be addressed today, a court would adopt the view set out in the explanatory memorandum and hold that the expression 'investment' included any application of funds which produced either potential income or potential capital returns.[49]

(b) Traditional investments

There are certain types of investment which undoubtedly fall within the expression 'investment' as used in the Trustee Act 2000. These would include deposits in a bank or building society, the purchase of government stock, and the purchase of shares in publicly quoted companies. All of these forms of investment were permitted by the Trustee Investments Act 1961, which contained the list of authorized trustee investments prior to the enlargement of investment powers given to trustees by the 2000 Act. The 1961 Act was the first Act to allow trustees to invest in company shares. This was a significant step, as a short analysis of different types of investment will indicate.

Where money is invested by deposit with a bank, the bank pays annual or other periodic interest, but undertakes only to return the sum originally deposited when the account is closed. Government stock is not repayable on demand, but is usually repayable at a fixed future date. Again, interest is payable periodically, but when the date for repayment of the stock falls due, it is repaid only at face value. Pending the date of repayment, the price at which the stock is traded will fluctuate in accordance with prevailing market interest rates and the period before redemption. A stock which offers a high fixed rate of interest on its nominal value, compared with market

---

[47] Law Commission Report No 260 (1999), *Trustees Powers and Duties*, p 22.

[48] [1947] Ch 572.

[49] This view was taken in a different context in *Cook v Medway Housing Society* [1997] STC 90, at 98. See also Hicks 'The Trustee Act 2000 and the Modern Meaning Of Investment' (2001) 15 TLI 203, for the view that the 'portfolio' theory of investment permits more flexibility.

rates, will tend to trade at a premium (ie at a higher price than its nominal value), reflecting the advantage of the holder receiving the high income. Conversely, a stock which offers a low rate of nominal interest will tend to trade at a discount against its nominal value, reflecting the low yield of interest.

Shares (also referred to as 'equities') in public companies offer the advantage, compared with fixed interest securities and deposits, of offering the potential for both income and capital growth. The policy of most companies is to pay an annual dividend out of the profits which the company makes, while also retaining assets and profits which will enable the underlying capital value of the company to grow. As the net worth of the company increases, so its stock market value will tend to increase. The shareholder will thus receive an income and hope to participate in capital gains. The stock market can be volatile, particularly in the short term, so that, as investment advisers are required to warn, 'the value of your investment can fall as well as rise'. The share-market crash of October 2008 shows how dramatic the falls can be, with £93 billion wiped off the value of the FTSE 100 top companies in a day. Nevertheless, over the longer term, investments in shares have consistently outperformed bank and building society deposits and purchases of fixed interest securities. The ability of trustees, even in the absence of express extended powers of investment, to invest in shares, has been of considerable importance in enabling astute trustees to produce a reasonable income while providing a good measure of protection against inflation through capital appreciation.

(c) Financial instruments

The relatively recent past has seen an increase in the variety of financial instruments available. Some of these were created expressly for the purpose of providing investment vehicles, whilst others originated as mechanisms to help in managing the risks of exchange rate or share price fluctuations. Some appear to have evolved for purely speculative purposes. It is not clear whether all of these financial instruments would be considered to be investments permitted by the Trustee Act 2000. Some should fall within the meaning of the term, provided that it is not given too narrow an interpretation. Capital bonds, under which a company undertakes to repay a given sum at a fixed date in the future, but without any payment of interest in the meantime, have already been referred to. Since these bonds are sold at a price below their redemption value, the capital gain makes up for the loss of interest. There should be no reason why these capital bonds should not be considered valid trustee investments.

There are other financial instruments which are less readily considered to be investments within the ordinary meaning of the term. This includes, for instance, the so-called 'derivatives'. One form of derivative is the 'future' under which a person commits to the sale or purchase of shares or currency at a given date in the future at a fixed price. The other principal form is the 'option' under which the holder has the right, but not an obligation, to buy (purchase) or sell (put) at a fixed price on a future date. These instruments allow a jeweller, for instance, to reduce the risks of the price of gold going up or down by entering into an advance purchase contract or option. They would allow an exporter who knows that he will receive payment in a foreign currency in a year's time to reduce the risk of currency fluctuation by entering into a contract which effectively fixes the exchange rate. However, they also allow speculators to gamble on whether prices will go up or down.[50] There may be a place for this kind of speculation in some trusts, such as pension trusts, and banks were offering dealings in derivatives to private clients with substantial funds to invest. However, since they are extremely risky compared to most other forms of investment, they could well be considered to be outside the scope of authorized investment. Even if they were held to be 'investments' as that term is used in the Trustee Act 2000, a trustee would have to show that a properly informed decision had been made to apply trust funds in this fashion, and that the inherent risks were being managed, for instance by applying only a small part of the fund in this way.

(d) Purchase of land

The general power of investment does not in itself authorize trustees to invest in the purchase of land.[51] Section 8 of the Trustee Act 2000, however, contains authority for trustees (with some exceptions[52]) to purchase land. This extends to all trustees the power to apply trust funds to the purchase of land which was first conferred by statute on trustees of land by the Trusts of Land and Appointment of Trustees Act 1996.[53] There is now no distinction between trustees of land and trustees of personal property in this regard. Trustees may purchase land as an investment, for occupation by a beneficiary, or for any other reason. The purchase may be of a legal freehold or leasehold estate in the United Kingdom.[54] Trustees have no statutory authority to purchase land overseas, but the power to acquire such land could be conferred expressly by the trust instrument. Trustees who acquire land under the statutory power conferred by the Trustee Act 2000, s 8 have all the powers of an absolute owner in relation to the land for the purpose of exercising their functions as trustees.[55]

(e) Loans

Trustees have been permitted to invest in loans secured by way of a mortgage over the borrower's land for over one hundred years.[56] The Trustee Act 2000 continues to allow

---

[50] It is also possible to gamble on prices going up or down through 'spread betting' where a gambler stakes money against the future price of a given share. If the share falls within the agreed band or spread of prices at the set date, the betting company pays out on the bet. It is unlikely that any convincing argument could be made that spread betting constitutes an investment within the meaning of the Trustee Act 2000.

[51] Trustee Act 2000, s 3(3).

[52] The power does not apply to trustees of settled land, who have the power to apply trust funds to the purchase of land under the Settled Land Act 1925, ss 73, 75. Similarly, the power does not apply to occupational pension funds, authorized unit trusts, and certain charity investment funds: Trustee Act 2000, ss 36–38.

[53] S 6.

[54] Or the equivalent of a legal estate in the case of land in Scotland; Trustee Act 2000, s 8(2).

[55] This means, for instance, that trustees are able to grant leases, borrow against the security of the land, carry out building works, and so on.

[56] See Trustee Act 1925, s 8; Trustee Investments Act 2000, Sch 1, Pt II, para 13. Similar provisions appeared in the legislation which these Acts replaced.

trustees to invest by way of loans secured on land,[57] but there is nothing in the Act which expressly confers any power to make unsecured loans. *Khoo Tek Keong v Ch'ng Joo Tuan Neoh*[58] suggests that unsecured loans would not be considered as investments without some express authority.

(f) Modification of the general power of investment

The general power of investment conferred on trustees by the Trustee Act 2000 is in addition to any express powers which might be conferred upon trustees,[59] but may also be restricted or excluded by an express provision.[60] It goes almost without saying that the general power of investment can be modified by legislation, although, out of an abundance of caution, the Act makes this clear.[61]

As was indicated earlier, the Act applies to trusts created before the commencement of the Act as well as to those created subsequently.[62] Where a trust instrument contains a phrase such as 'the trustees may invest in any investment authorized by law for the investment of trust property', this will be treated as conferring on trustees the general power of investment, whether the trust was made before or after the 2000 Act.[63] Express provisions contained in trust instruments made before 3 August 1961 (the day on which the Trustee Investments Act 1961 came into operation) are not to be treated as restricting or excluding the general power of investment.[64]

5 Widening of powers of investment

The substantial increase in the investment powers given to trustees by the Trustee Act 2000 should mean that it will be rare that they will consider their powers to be too narrow. However, there may be some instances in which they seek wider investment powers, for instance permitting the purchase of property overseas, or clarifying whether they are permitted to invest in assets which produce no income. There are a number of ways in which this may be possible.

(1) Power of variation in trust deed

Some trust deeds contain provisions under which alterations or amendments to the deed can be made. For instance, the Universities' Superannuation Scheme Rules provide that the rules can be altered by deed, with certain restrictions concerning

---

[57] Although Trustee Act 1925, s 8 has been repealed, Trustee Act 2000, s 3(3) acknowledges that trustees may make loans secured on land.

[58] [1934] AC 529. The case is referred to above in relation to express powers of investment.

[59] Trustee Act 2000, s 6(1)(a).   [60] Trustee Act 2000, s 6(1)(b).

[61] Trustee Act 2000, s 6(1)(b).   [62] Trustee Act 2000, s 7(1).

[63] See Trustee Act 2000, s 7(3). A trust instrument made after the 2000 Act, which stated that trustees could invest in the manner authorized by the Trustee Investments Act 1961 would, however, be treated as limiting the investment powers of trustees to those permitted under the old rules set out in that Act.

[64] Trustee Act 2000, s 7(2).

maintaining the purpose of the scheme to provide pensions and other benefits for eligible employees, and subject to certain consents.[65]

(2) Consent of beneficiaries

Where all the beneficiaries of a trust are ascertainable, and, being competent to do so, give their consent, then new powers of investment proposed by the trustees may be adopted.

(3) Variation of Trusts Act 1958

Where it is not possible to obtain consent from all the beneficiaries of a trust, or some of the beneficiaries of the trust are not competent to give consent, and in certain other cases, the Variation of Trusts Act 1958 will apply. This enables the court to approve a variation of trust, including a variation of investment powers, on behalf of the unascertainable or incompetent beneficiaries.[66] The Act does not permit the court to consent to a variation on behalf of ascertainable and competent beneficiaries who have not been consulted (even where to do so would be inconvenient) or to override a refusal of consent by such a beneficiary.

(4) Trustee Act 1925, s 57

This section authorizes the court to approve a transaction, either exceptionally or generally,[67] and has been held to be wide enough in scope to authorize extended investment powers.[68] It has an advantage over the Variation of Trusts Act 1958 in that it does not require the beneficiaries to be consulted or to agree to the enlargement of the investment powers, although the court will not approve the variation unless it can be seen as being in the general interests of all the beneficiaries. In *Anker-Petersen v Anker-Petersen*[69] it was suggested that applications for extending powers of investment were more appropriately brought under s 57 than under the Variation of Trusts Act 1958. This was because it was more realistic for the court to consider the matter on behalf of the beneficiaries as a group rather than individually, as the 1958 Act required.

(5) Principles on which court grants approval

In a case decided shortly after the passing of the Trustee Investments Act 1961, *Re Kolb's Will Trusts*,[70] it was said that the investment powers in that Act should 'be taken to be

---

[65] USS New Rules (1 May 2009), s 76. See also *British Coal Corpn v British Coal Staff Superannuation Scheme Trustees Ltd* [1995] 1 All ER 912.

[66] See Chapter 18.

[67] The Act applies to private trusts. The court has similar powers in respect of charitable trusts under the Charitable Trusts Acts 1853–1925.

[68] *Mason v Farbrother* [1983] 2 All ER 1078.   [69] [1991] 16 LS Gaz R 32.

[70] [1962] Ch 531.

prima facie sufficient and ought only to be extended if, on the particular facts, a special case for extending them can be made out'.[71] Subsequent cases departed from that
view, and showed a greater willingness to entertain requests for enlarging powers of
investment. Thus, in *Mason v Farbrother*,[72] Blackett Ord V-C approved a considerable
widening of the powers of investment of the trustees of the Co-Operative Wholesale
Society pension fund, and in *Trustees of the British Museum v A-G*[73] Megarry V-C
approved the enlargement of the investment powers of the trustees of a museum of
international importance. The first case was dealt with under the provisions of the
Trustee Act 1925, s 57, and the latter under the Variation of Trusts Act 1958, but there
does not seem to have been a difference in approach. Relevant factors included the
quality of the advice available to the trustees, and the measures which were to be taken
to balance risk and safety. The division of the trust fund into separate parts with different risk profiles was considered to be an important factor in granting approval. In
Steel v Wellcome Custodian Trustees,[74] Hoffmann J approved almost unfettered investment powers, with no obligation to divide the fund into divisions for the trustees of
an extremely large charitable foundation. He had regard to the size of the fund, the
eminence and experience of the trustees, and the provisions in the proposed scheme
for obtaining advice.

It is only possible to speculate what approach would now be taken by the courts in
deciding whether to grant extended powers of investment. The width of the powers
given by the 2000 Act might mean that there would be the same kind of reluctance
to entertain an application as happened in *Re Kolb's Will Trusts*. Since the current
legislative regime does not require any division of the trust fund, it is unlikely that
a court would insist on it if granting enlarged powers, but the factors identified by
Hoffmann J would still surely be relevant in deciding whether an extension of powers
was appropriate.

6 Portfolio investment theory

(1) The responsibilities of trustees

The duties of trustees in relation to investment are considered in detail below.
Foremost in those duties is a requirement to have regard to the fact that they are
dealing with money belonging to others, and therefore have a duty to safeguard it.
They must also consider the appropriate balance between capital and income, and
the need to protect the trust assets against erosion through inflation. If the trustees
are holding only a small fund which they are expected to distribute in the near
future, then the principal consideration will be safeguarding the assets in the short

---

71 Ibid., at 540.   72 [1983] 2 All ER 1078.
73 [1984] 1 All ER 337.   74 [1988] 1 WLR 167.

term whilst keeping the ability to draw on the fund for the purposes of distribution. Investing the money by way of deposit in a bank might be the simplest and most appropriate way of doing this. However, if the funds are larger and are to be retained for a longer period, then other considerations affecting the choice of investments come into play.

(2) Risk management

The advantage of depositing money with a bank is that the bank undertakes to return the same amount as was deposited with it, together with interest. The depositor runs only a very small risk that if the bank becomes insolvent, it may not be able to meet its obligations in full. That risk is made smaller still by government deposit protection schemes and the general unwillingness of governments to see deposit-taking institutions fail. The disadvantage is that the effect of inflation reduces the purchasing power of the cash sum which the bank returns to the depositor. How then is it possible for an investor to safeguard against inflation? A traditional means of doing this is to purchase company shares, which over the long term can be expected to increase in value in money terms, as well as providing an income through the dividends which the company pays. However, the risks associated with company shares are greater. The company may not flourish: it may be badly managed, or it may be operating in a sector which is generally in decline. In consequence, the risks that a single shareholding will fall in value are much greater than is the case with a bank deposit. The greater potential return from company shares is balanced by a greater element of risk. Trustees are permitted to take risks with trust funds. No investment is entirely risk free. However, it is the function of the trustees to manage the risks so that the balance of risk and profit is appropriate for the nature of the trust.

(3) Investment portfolios

One of the principles of investment policy is that you should not 'put all your eggs in one basket'. By investing in several companies, not just one, there is less chance that all will fail (although equally less chance that all will thrive). The risks are further reduced if the investments are made in different market sectors—for instance, buying shares in companies operating in different fields such as banking, oil distribution, business services, or supplying utilities. Portfolio investment theory is that where an investment fund is large enough, different parts of the fund should be invested in different ways to provide a balance of growth or income potential, and of security and risk. Instead of evaluating the profile or risk of individual investments, what matters is the balance across the portfolio as a whole—higher risks in some parts of the fund may be balanced by lower risks, or compensating considerations, in other parts of the fund. The exact balance will vary according to individual requirements. A pension fund investing for existing pensioners needs to tilt more towards income and security than, say, a trust fund, which is designed to accumulate to pay out a sum to a beneficiary in 20 years' time. The portfolio theory of investment was examined and discussed in *Nestlé v National Westminster Bank plc*.[75]

(4) Trustee Investments Act 1961

The Trustee Investments Act 1961 espoused the portfolio investment theory, but did so in a rigid way. Investments authorized for trustees were divided into three categories, and trustees who wished to invest in the riskier categories were obliged to take advice, and for certain investments (called wider-range investments) to create a separate part of the trust fund. The enlargement of the categories of permitted investment was welcome, but the way in which the Act required trustees to allocate investments was mechanical, cumbersome, and arbitrarily inflexible.[76] Certain aspects of the operation of the Act were rightly described as 'curious'.[77]

(5) Trustee Act 2000

The rigidity and capriciousness of the investment rules in the 1961 Act have been swept away by the 2000 Act. This permits trustees to invest in the way most appropriate for the circumstances of their trust, with none of the arbitrary limitations of the 1961 Act. In reviewing whether trustees have acted properly, the courts are likely to take account of the current theory of portfolio investment.[78]

(6) Total overall return

The return on an investment consists of either or both capital growth and income return. The total return which an investment makes is the combination of both of these elements. If £1,000 is invested in company shares and at the end of the first year of investment the shares have increased in value to £1,100, and the company has paid a dividend of £50, the total overall return on the investment is £150—the sum total of the capital growth and the income. If a person were investing for their own benefit, they might aim to get the best possible overall total return, regardless of the split between capital growth and income. If they need money, they can always cash in part of the investment if the income it produces is insufficient. Conversely, they could reinvest the

---

[75] [1993] 1 WLR 1260; Martin 'Investment Duties: A Victory for Complacency' (1992) 142 NLJ 1279; Kenny 'Are a Bank Trustee's Fees Performance Related?' [1993] Conv 63; Watt and Stauch 'Is There Liability for Imprudent Trustee Investment?' [1998] Conv 352.

[76] The Act initially required a division of the trust fund into two equal parts to enable the wider powers of investment to take effect (Trustee Investments Act 1961, s 2(1)), and this was later varied by the Trustee Investments (Division of Trust Fund) Order 1996, SI 1996/845 to permit three-quarters of the fund to be applied in the wider range of investments. Trustees could not choose some other division, such as two-thirds.

[77] *Nestlé v National Westminster Bank Ltd* [1993] 1 WLR 1260, at 1278, per Staughton LJ. See also Legair 'Modern Portfolio Theory: A Primer' (2000) 14 TLI 75.

[78] See further Hicks 'The Trustee Act 2000 and the Modern Meaning of Investment' (2001) 15 TLI 203.

income if they wanted to see their overall wealth increase. The same strategy could be adopted by a trust which has no beneficiaries currently entitled to the income, such as a charitable trust. The trust invests for the best total overall return, and draws down a defined percentage of the fund each year. However, if the trust is one in which a beneficiary is entitled to the income, the strategy could operate unfairly since under current law the income is defined as the return the trust obtains through dividends and interest on its investments. Where there is an income beneficiary, the strategy would therefore only be appropriate where it is expressly envisaged by the trust instrument and a different means of identifying regular periodic sums which should be paid to the 'income' beneficiaries. This might be a fixed sum, possibly index-linked, or a fixed percentage of the value of the fund each year.

7 Duties of trustees in relation to investment

(1) The general duty of care

There is a substantial body of case law considering the duties of trustees in relation to investment, much of which remains relevant, although the Trustee Act 2000 imposes some statutory duties. The first of these statutory duties is the statutory duty of care. Trustees are required to exercise such care and skill in relation to investments as is reasonable in the circumstances.[79] As is explained elsewhere, a higher standard of care is expected from trustees acting in a professional capacity and where the trustee claims to have special knowledge or experience.[80] This is no more than a statutory restatement of the principles which had been established by the cases, with a clarification of the position of professional trustees. In *Speight v Gaunt*[81] Lord Blackburn stated that the general duty of trustees was to act honestly and fairly and to take 'all those precautions which an ordinary prudent man of business would take in managing similar affairs of his own'. In *Re Whiteley*[82] Lindley LJ refined this dictum as it applies to investment. He said:

The duty of the trustee is not to take such care only as a prudent man would take if he had only himself to consider, the duty is rather to take such care as an ordinary prudent man would take if he were minded to make an investment for the benefit of other people for whom he felt morally bound to provide.[83]

Lord Watson on appeal to the House of Lords explained:

Business men of ordinary prudence may, and frequently do, select investments which are more or less of a speculative character; but it is the duty of a trustee to confine himself to the class of

---

[79] Trustee Act 2000, s 1(1).
[80] Trustee Act 2000, s 1(1). See the discussion in Chapter 28.
[81] (1883) 9 App Cas 1.
[82] (1886) 33 Ch D 347; affd sub nom *Learoyd v Whiteley* (1887) 12 App Cas 727.
[83] (1886) 33 Ch D 347, at 355.

investments which are permitted by the trust, and likewise to avoid all investments of that class which are attended by hazard.[84]

In addition to the specific duties relating to investment, trustees remain subject to their general fiduciary duties in making investment decisions. This means that they should not act in a way which gives rise to a conflict of interest. Thus, in a Canadian case, it was held that the trustees were in breach of trust where they made a loan to a company owned by one of the trustees. Even though this application of the trust funds did not fall outside the investment powers of the trustees, the conflict of interest made the loan an improper investment.[85]

We have already seen how the rule in *Howe v Earl of Dartmouth*,[86] if it has not been superseded by the Trustee Act 2000, may require immediate disinvestment by trustees of hazardous investments received under a residuary testamentary gift which is to be held for beneficiaries with successive interests.[87] However, in accordance with portfolio investment theory, as has already been explained, trustees may be entitled to retain or to make an investment which involves a measure of risk (as most investments inevitably do), provided that the risk involved in that investment is balanced by other elements in the portfolio. That is the tenor of most recent judgments on the investment powers of trustees. In *Nestlé v National Westminster Bank plc*,[88] Hoffmann J said that 'an investment which in isolation is too risky and therefore in breach of trust may be justified when held in conjunction with other investments'.

(2) The standard investment criteria

The Trustee Act 2000, s 4 requires all trustees exercising a power of investment, including trustees exercising express investment powers, to have regard to what are described as the *standard investment criteria*.[89] There are two such criteria. First, the trustees must have regard to the suitability of the investment concerned, and second to the need for diversification. The trustees must have regard to these standard investment criteria both in making investments,[90] and also in periodically reviewing the investments.[91] The responsibilities of trustees in relation to investments are ongoing—they cannot invest funds and then forget them. They must keep the investment portfolio under periodic review. It is also clear that the duty to review extends to investments settled on the trustee at the creation of the trust, as well as investments made by trustees in pursuance of their powers of investment.[92]

---

[84] (1887) 12 App Cas 727, at 733.

[85] *Re David Feldman Charitable Foundation* (1987) 58 OR (2d) 626.

[86] See above, p 469.

[87] We have also seen that the Law Commission has suggested that the rule in *Howe v Dartmouth* be repealed—above p 473.

[88] [1993] 1 WLR 1260.

[89] These criteria are not new. They first appeared in the Trustee Investments Act 1961, s 6(1).

[90] Trustee Act 2000, s 4(3).　　[91] Trustee Act 2000, s 4(1).

[92] See further *Gregson v HAE Trustees Ltd* [2008] EWHC 1006 (Ch), at [83] per Deputy Judge Robert Miles, QC.

When looking at the suitability of investments, the Trustee Act 2000 envisages a two-stage process. The trustees must both consider the suitability for the trust of a particular kind of investment. For instance, should the trust invest in purchasing shares in a unit trust? The trustees must then consider the suitability of the particular investment proposed. For instance, having decided that investing in a unit trust would be suitable, which fund manager and which of that manager's investment funds should be selected?

(3) The need for advice

A further requirement of the Trustee Act 2000 is that trustees must normally take proper advice on investment decisions.[93] The Trustee Investments Act 1961 required trustees always to take advice before making all but a very limited range of investments. This requirement has been changed by the 2000 Act. Trustees can dispense with seeking advice if they reasonably conclude that in all the circumstances it is unnecessary or inappropriate to do so.[94] For instance, the trustees may consider the sums involved to be too small, or they may already have sufficient expertise available to them through fellow trustees or employees of the trust. However, for trustees to dispense with advice requires a conscious decision on the part of the trustees. It would be a breach of trust for trustees to fail to seek advice through oversight, even in a situation where advice was unnecessary, although it is hardly likely in such an instance that any action for breach of trust would be pursued.

'Proper advice' is defined by the Act as 'the advice of a person who is reasonably believed by the trustee to be qualified to give it by his ability in and practical experience of financial and other matters relating to the proposed investment'.[95] The trustees are not obliged to follow the advice which they are given. Their obligation is only to obtain and consider it. They would not be discharging their function if they followed the advice without applying their own minds to it,[96] but equally it would be unwise to disregard the advice without good reason.[97]

(4) Financial considerations

The object of investment is to produce a financial return from trust assets. The trustees are expected to adopt an investment strategy which has regard to the nature and purpose of the trust. This will affect whether the trustees should be maximizing income, maximizing capital growth, or balancing the two, and what balance there should be between risk and return. Where there are both income and capital beneficiaries, the

---

[93] Trustee Act 2000, s 5(1) (new investments) and s 5(2) (review of existing investments).

[94] Trustee Act 2000, s 5(3).

[95] Trustee Act 2000, s 5(4). A person acting as an investment adviser must be authorized under s 19 Financial Services and Markets Act 2000.

[96] See *Jones v AMP Perpetual Trustee Co NZ Ltd* [1994] 1 NZLR 690.

[97] See *Cowan v Scargill* [1985] Ch 270, at 289 (discussed below).

trustees must seek a balance between high income and capital growth. It has been said that in all but the smallest fund, this will require a high proportion of the trust assets to be invested in company shares.[98] Where an income beneficiary would not be liable to tax on certain kinds of investment, however, this also should be considered by the trustees and would legitimately influence their investment decisions.[99] Because trustees must consider how to achieve a fair and proper balance between all the different classes of beneficiary, they will not be in breach of trust simply because their investment policy has resulted in greater erosion of the real capital value of the trust fund than would have been the case with a different investment strategy. Trustees are not under an absolute obligation to ensure that the capital value of the fund is maintained.[100] For instance, in *Nestlé v National Westminster Bank plc*[101] the heiress to the chocolate family fortune complained that, had the trustees invested differently, she could have received an inheritance four times greater than was the case. The Court of Appeal held that, although there had been errors of judgement on the part of the trustees, including a misunderstanding of the width of their powers of investment, and a failure to review the investments sufficiently often, there had not been any breach of trust resulting in liability to the heiress. It was also said that even if trustees had acted for the wrong reasons, they would still not be liable if their decision could be justified objectively by other, valid, reasons.[102] The case illustrates the difficulty which the beneficiary faces in seeking to prove a breach of trust in relation to investment by trustees.[103]

(5) Ethical considerations[104]

The extent to which trustees may have regard to ethical considerations was explored by Megarry V-C in *Cowan v Scargill*.[105] The National Coal Board pension fund was controlled by both management-appointed and union-appointed trustees. The union-appointed trustees objected to a proposed annual investment plan unless it adopted the policy of withdrawing from overseas investment and from investment in industries in competition with coal. This led to a direct clash between the union-appointed trustees, led by Arthur Scargill—the National Union of Mineworkers General Secretary and a veteran of industrial disputes—and the other trustees, leading to the hearing in court. Eschewing the use of a barrister, Arthur Scargill chose to represent himself in court. Sir Robert Megarry held that the action of the union trustees was unreasonable. The duty of trustees was to optimize the benefits which

---

98 *Nestlé v National Westminster Bank plc* [1993] 1 WLR 1260.   99 Ibid.

100 See *Jones v AMP Perpetual Trustee Co NZ Ltd* [1994] 1 NZLR 690.

101 [1993] 1 WLR 1260.   102 See also *Cowan v Scargill* [1985] Ch 270 .

103 See also *Jones v AMP Perpetual Trustee Co NZ Ltd* [1994] 1 NZLR 690, where trustees were held not liable for retaining shares in a falling market.

104 See Lord Nicholls 'Trustees and Their Broader Community; Where Duty, Morality and Ethics Converge' (1995) 9 TLI 71; Luxton 'Ethical Investments in Hard Times' (1992) 55 MLR 587; Thornton 'Ethical Investments: A Case of Disjointed Thinking' (2008) CLJ 396.

105 [1985] Ch 270.

the beneficiaries would receive. In the vast majority of cases, financial considerations would prevail. There could be rare cases where this was not so.

Plainly the present case is not one of this rare type of case. Subject to such matters, under a trust for the provision of financial benefits, the paramount duty of the trustees is to provide the greatest financial benefits for the present and future beneficiaries.[106]

Trustees were not to be deflected from this duty to the beneficiaries merely because the policy of seeking the best financial returns conflicted with their personal opinions:

Trustees may have strongly held social or political views. They may be firmly opposed to any investment in South Africa[107] or other countries, or they may object to any form of investment in companies concerned with alcohol, tobacco, armaments or other controversial products. In the conduct of their own affairs, of course, they are free to abstain from making any such investments. Yet under a trust, if investments of this type would be more beneficial to the beneficiaries than other investments, the trustees must not refrain from making the investments by reason of the views that they hold.[108]

It was not enough that they were honest and sincere in their cause. The general standard of conduct required of trustees demanded more:

Honesty and sincerity are not the same as prudence and reasonableness. Some of the most sincere people are the most unreasonable; and Mr Scargill told me that he had met quite a few of them. Accordingly, although a trustee who takes advice on investments is not bound to accept and act on that advice, he is not entitled to reject it merely because he sincerely disagrees with it, unless in addition to being sincere he is acting as an ordinary prudent man would act.[109]

One of the cases which Megarry V-C thought might be exceptional and where ethical or moral considerations could legitimately sway the decision of the trustees was where all the beneficiaries were adults who shared the same moral values who 'might well consider that it was far better to receive less than to receive more money from what they consider to be evil and tainted sources'.[110]

Such a situation arose in *Harries v Church Comrs for England*,[111] which concerned the investment policy of the body controlling the investment funds of the Church of England. The revenue from these funds, together with contributions from parishes, was used to maintain churches and to meet the stipends of the clergy. The Church Commissioners operated an ethical investment policy, under which they chose not to invest in businesses which might be offensive to the Church, including armaments, gambling, tobacco, newspapers, and South Africa.[112] Sir Donald Nicholls V-C considered that these exclusions were appropriate and justified for a religious charity whose members were likely to support such a policy, but he rejected a call by the Bishop of Oxford for a much wider group of exclusions. Even though ethical considerations were legitimate for the Church Commissioners, provided that they left an adequate width of investment, where charity trustees held assets for investments, their principal duty was to seek the maximum return consistent with commercial prudence. If they did

---

[106] Ibid., at 288.   [107] This remark was made before the end of apartheid.
[108] [1985] Ch 270, at 287.   [109] Ibid., at 289.   [110] Ibid., at 288.
[111] [1993] 2 All ER 300. See Nobles 'Charities and Ethical Investment' [1992] Conv 115.
[112] A very similar list of exclusions to those given by Megarry V-C in the passage cited above.

not do this, they would not be discharging their duty of furthering the purposes of the trust. If the Church Commissioners used their funds otherwise than for investment, how in the long term could they ensure that the clergy were paid and the Church's buildings maintained?

The danger of blind adherence to a political policy without considering the interests of the beneficiaries is illustrated by *Martin v Edinburgh District Council*,[113] where Lord Murray held that trustees were in breach of trust for pursuing a policy of disinvestment in South Africa prior to the end of apartheid 'without considering expressly whether it was in the best interests of the beneficiaries and without obtaining professional advice'. Trustees would only be entitled to adopt a blind policy of this nature where it was expressly permitted or required by the instrument establishing the trust. The decision to exclude a sector of possible investments in a way which 'runs contrary to the best financial indicators available at the time'[114] on political or ethical grounds is what constitutes the breach of trust. It is not relevant that the ethical investments may actually turn out to produce a reasonable return; the decision to invest in them should only have been made if other non-ethical investments were considered and rejected on the basis that they would not yield a greater return. Nevertheless, as Thornton suggests, there may be a disconnection between this legal orthodoxy and the ability of the beneficiaries to prove that pursuing an ethical investment policy necessarily resulted in loss to the trust.[115] There is also an arguable case that ethically based investments have a lower risk profile than other investments, or that in some instances (such as with investments in 'green' technology) that they have greater growth potential, which could justify a decision by trustees.[116]

(6) Periodic review of investments

The duty of trustees in relation to investment is a continuing one. They do not discharge their duty merely by giving proper consideration to the appropriateness of an investment at the time it is made or the asset acquired. They must also consider periodically whether the balance of investment is correct, and whether individual investments are retained. This responsibility is specifically imposed by the Trustee Act 2000, s 4(2), but would in any event apply on general trust principles. In *Bartlett v Barclays Bank Trust Co Ltd (No 2)*[117] trustees held a controlling shareholding in a property investment company. It was held that they were in breach of trust in failing to review

---

[113]   1988 SLT 329.

[114]   Thornton 'Ethical investments: a case of disjointed thinking' (2008) CLJ 396.

[115]   Ibid., pp 415–417.

[116]   See McCormack 'Sexy But Not Sleazy: Trustee Investments and Ethical Considerations' (1998) 19 *Company Lawyer* 39, who argues that pursuing an ethical investment policy may not be a poor decision for trustees. This is in relation to ethically managed unit trusts and their relative performance on the stock market (FTSE).

[117]   [1980] 1 All ER 139.

the activities of the company and in permitting the directors to engage in a speculative and inadvisable development scheme.

Provided that the trustees have given proper consideration to whether an investment should be retained, they will not be liable because it can be seen, with the benefit of hindsight, that they made a mistake. In *Re Chapman*[118] the trustees had properly invested in mortgages of agricultural land. The value of the land fell, placing the security of the mortgages at risk. The trustees nevertheless decided to retain them, hoping that the market would improve. Instead, land values fell still further. The Court of Appeal refused to find the trustees liable.

There is no rule of law which compels the court to hold that an honest trustee is liable to make good loss sustained by retaining an authorized security in a falling market, if he did so honestly and prudently, in the belief that it was the best course to take in the interests of all parties. Trustees acting honesty, with ordinary prudence and within the limits of their trust, are not liable for mere errors of judgment.[119]

It is believed that this will continue to be the case, notwithstanding the omission by the Trustee Act 2000 of s 4 of the Trustee Act 1925, under which trustees were not to be held liable for breach of trust by reason only of continuing to hold an investment which has ceased to be authorized either by the trust instrument or by the general law.

(7) Special rules for particular investments

(a) Mortgages of land

In the nineteenth century, before building societies played the major role which they did in the first half of the twentieth century in financing the purchase of residential property, private mortgages were very common and a frequent type of investment for trustees. Modern conditions of inflation, and the ready availability of commercial funds from the building societies and banks make this form of investment much less popular for trustees, although it still occurs to a limited extent, and is envisaged by the Trustee Act 2000, s 3(3). Special rules used to be provided by the Trustee Act 1925, s 8 for trustees lending on mortgage. These rules protected trustees against liability for advancing too high a proportion of the value of the property if they lent no more than two-thirds of a valuation made by an independent surveyor or valuer. These rules have now been removed by the Trustee Act 2000 so that the question of whether a mortgage transaction was prudent and appropriate must be decided without recourse to any such guidelines.[120] It is not considered advisable for trustees to lend on the security of anything other than a first legal mortgage,[121] although it is possible that a loan on a properly registered second mortgage would not, in itself,

---

[118] [1896] 2 Ch 763.
[119] See also *Jones v AMP Perpetual Trustee Co NZ Ltd* [1994] 1 NZLR 690.
[120] See *Re Solomon* [1912] 1 Ch 261; *Re Dive* [1909] 1 Ch 328; *Shaw v Cates* [1909] 1 Ch 389.
[121] See *Chapman v Browne* [1902] 1 Ch 785, CA.

be a breach of trust. The trust instrument may, of course, permit a loan on a second mortgage, or even an unsecured loan.

(b) Controlling interest in a company

Trustees who have a shareholding which gives them a controlling interest in a company are expected to take more than a passive interest in the affairs of the company. They should either ensure that one of the trustees is a member of the board (if not an executive director) or, at the very least, they should keep a watching brief lest the company seeks to act in an improvident way.[122]

(8) Special considerations for charity investment

The Charities Act 1993, s 24 authorizes the court or the Charity Commissioners to approve schemes for the establishment of common investment funds where trustees wish to pool the investments of two or more charitable trusts.[123] There should normally be some connection between the participating charities. Section 25 of the Act contains provisions for the establishment of common deposit schemes for charities.

8 Delegation of investment decisions

(1) Authority to delegate investment management

Investment decisions and their execution are so complex that in many cases it will not be appropriate for trustees to manage the investment of trust funds themselves. This is more likely to be the case where large funds are under investment, or where the trustees do not themselves have investment experience. In such cases, the management of the investments might be delegated by the trustees. For instance, as the case of *Cowan v Scargill*[124] illustrated, the National Coal Board pension fund, one of the largest such funds, was not invested directly by the trustees. Instead, it was managed by professional financial advisers on behalf of the trustees, subject to the approval of an annual investment plan giving direction, which was prepared by the advisers for consideration by the board of trustees.

Prior to the Trustee Act 2000 it was not clear whether the delegation of investment management was permitted by general law, so that it was considered wise for a trust instrument expressly to authorize the delegation by trustees of investment management to professional portfolio managers.[125] The Pensions Act 1995 contains provisions

---

122 *Re Lucking's Will Trusts* [1967] 3 All ER 726.
123 For a common investment scheme approved under previous legislation see *Re University of London Charitable Trusts* [1964] Ch 282.
124 [1985] Ch 270.   125 See Hayton 'Investment Management Problems' (1990) 106 LQR 88.

enabling trustees to delegate certain of their functions concerning investment subject to a number of safeguards.[126] The Trustee Act 2000 has now extended to all trustees the explicit authority to delegate investment management.[127] This implements a proposal made by the Law Commission.[128] The change has been achieved by authorizing trustees to delegate any function relating to the trust, with certain exceptions.[129] Investment management is one of the functions which can be delegated.[130]

(2) Conditions

Where trustees do choose to delegate investment management, or *asset management,* to use the wider phrase used in the Trustee Act 2000, certain conditions must be satisfied. These conditions probably apply even in cases where this is done under an express power in the trust instrument rather than under the statutory power to delegate. First, the delegation to the agent must be in writing, or must be evidenced in writing.[131] Second, the trustees must produce a policy statement in writing, or evidenced in writing, which gives guidance as to how the asset management functions should be exercised.[132] This policy statement should, for instance, indicate what level of risk the trustees consider acceptable, what balance is being sought between income and capital growth, and whether there are any types of investment that should be avoided. Third, the contract with the agent must require the agent to comply with the current policy statement given by the trustees.[133] Finally, the trustees must exercise reasonable care in the selection of the agent, since the selection of agents is one of the functions to which the statutory duty of care applies.[134]

In addition, the Act specifically imposes on the agent the obligation to have regard to the standard investment criteria, described above.[135] However, the agent is dispensed from the need to obtain advice if the agent is the sort of person from whom it would have been proper to seek advice.[136] Thus, where, as will often be the case, the trustees delegate investment management to a professional fund manager (such as an investment bank), the agent does not have to seek advice from other professionals. Professional fund managers will sometimes insist on a limitation of liability, or permission to act where there may be a potential conflict of interest, and the trustees are authorized by the Act to agree to such terms if it is reasonably necessary to do so.[137] The appointment of an agent will be valid notwithstanding any failure by the trustees

---

[126] Pensions Act 1995, s 34.

[127] The powers granted in the Trustee Act 2000 do not, therefore, apply to pension trusts.

[128] Law Commission Report No 260 (1999), *Trustees Powers and Duties.* This proposal adopts a recommendation of the Trust Law Revision Committee.

[129] Trustee Act 2000, s 11.

[130] Investment functions are included in the list of functions which can be delegated by trustees of a charitable trust, and are not excluded from the general authority given to other trustees.

[131] Trustee Act 2000, s 15(1).   [132] Ibid., s 15(2)(a).   [133] Ibid., s 15(2)(b).

[134] Ibid., s 1 and Sch 1, para 3.   [135] Ibid., s 13(1).

[136] Ibid., s 13(2).   [137] Ibid., s 14(2) and (3).

to comply with the limits relating to the appointment,[138] but the trustees will thereby expose themselves to potential liability for breach of trust.

(3) Supervision and review

Just as the functions of trustees are not completed once they have made the initial investments of the trust fund, so their functions are not completed where they have appointed an agent. The trustees must keep the arrangement under review,[139] they must intervene if necessary by giving directions or terminating the agency,[140] and they must review and revise the investment policy statement.[141]

(4) Related functions

In addition to the delegation of investment management, trustees may also appoint nominees to act on their behalf, custodians to hold documents relating to trust assets or the trust assets themselves, and custodian trustees in whom the trust assets are vested. These arrangements are described in Chapter 21.

---

[138] Ibid., s 24.   [139] Ibid., s 22(1).
[140] Ibid., s 22(1) and (4).   [141] Ibid., s 22(2).

24

Collective assets and investments

This chapter considers collective investment vehicles. These are facilitated by the conceptual creation of equity, the fund, which enables a beneficiary's wealth to be considered to have an identity that is distinct from the assets in which that wealth may at any particular time be invested. The chapter considers a number of these collective asset schemes, with particular attention given to occupational pension trusts and unincorporated associations such as clubs and societies.

1 Introduction

The equitable conception of the fund can be used to enable a number of individuals to pool their assets, the advantage being that the combined assets of the investors can be used more effectively than the separate assets of the individuals. The group can take advantage of economies of scale, thereby reducing dealing and other management costs. It may also, because of the size of the combined fund, benefit from a wider spread of investments, both in order through diversification to reduce the risk of a narrower range of investment, and also through a balanced portfolio, to take greater risk with parts of the fund which would be unacceptable without the balance of another part which is being employed more conservatively.

The issues that arise from the establishment of groups for collective investment are similar to those that are raised by other forms of association. Not every association, whether for investment or other purposes, requires the assistance of equity. There are some forms of association that can enjoy the benefits of collective investment in other ways. These are considered briefly below. Most rely upon the association acquiring some form of independent legal status. The great advantage of equity's fund and trust concepts is that the members of the group can enjoy the benefits of scale which have been described above and yet retain the security of direct beneficial ownership of the investments.

Most collective investment vehicles are now subject to regulation under the Financial Services and Markets Act 2000. The provisions of this Act are intended to safeguard the public, and a detailed consideration of the rules set out by the Act falls outside the scope of this book.[1]

2 Incorporation of a company

(i) Incorporation

One way in which a group of like-minded individuals can form an association is to establish a company that is incorporated under the Companies Acts.[2] The company then has an independent legal status, but is owned by the subscribing shareholders who can control the company by using the votes that most shareholdings confer. They will participate in the annual profits which the company makes through a distribution of dividends, and can benefit in any capital appreciation of the company's assets either through special distributions, or through a winding-up, dissolution, and distribution of the company's assets, or, more commonly, through the sale of their shareholding to a willing purchaser. Equity plays no special role in such arrangements although, before the introduction of the modern company through legislation, lawyers used the trust concept as the basis for the creation of the joint stock company,[3] the predecessor of the modern limited liability company.

(ii) Duties of directors

Although the directors of the company are no longer to be considered to be trustees for the shareholders,[4] they are treated as being in a fiduciary position, and in this respect are subject to some of the obligations and liabilities that apply to trustees. Directors are now also under a series of statutory duties of care, introduced by the Companies Act 2006,[5] such as a duty to exercise 'reasonable care, skill and diligence'[6] in exercising any of their functions as directors. The existing case law on the fiduciary duties of directors remains relevant, as regard is to be had under s 171(4) to 'equitable principles in interpreting and applying the general duties'.[7]

(iii) Trading companies

Most companies are established for trading purposes. They enable a group of individuals to combine their assets for this purpose by subscribing for shareholdings in the company, and to share in the benefits that derive from the profits made by the

---

[1] See further Hudson, *The Law of Finance* (2009).   [2] Companies Act 2006.
[3] The Joint Stock Companies Act 1856 allowed joint stock companies to be established with limited liability.
[4] See *Saloman v A Saloman & Co Ltd* [1897] AC 22. Compare the earlier case of *Smith v Anderson* (1880) 15 Ch D 247, in which the directors of a joint stock company were considered to be in the position of trustees for the members of the company.
[5] Part 10, Chapter 2, ss 170–181.   [6] Companies Act 2006, s 174.
[7] Duties of company directors are considered further in Chapter 30.

trading operations. The shareholdings in most large companies are bought and sold on the stock exchange. It is therefore possible for investors who have little interest in the trading activities of the company to buy its shares in the hope of making profits through capital appreciation and the income derived from dividend payments (the annual or twice yearly distribution of profits to shareholders). The trading operations in which the company is involved may relate to the provision of financial services, so it is also possible for third parties to enter into contracts with the company to obtain these financial services. For instance, most banks and insurance companies are incorporated under the Companies Acts.

(iv) Bank deposits do not create a trust

A person putting money on deposit with a bank does not make the bank a trustee (even if the bank is called a trustee savings bank). The customer is in fact entering into a contract under which ownership of the money deposited is transferred to the bank and the depositor retains no proprietary interest in it. However, in return the bank contractually undertakes to repay a different but equivalent sum with interest. The law of trusts has no part to play in such a transaction, unless there is some special term in the contract that gives the depositor a proprietary interest.

3 Investment trusts

Despite the misleading nomenclature, these are not trusts at all, but companies quoted on the stock exchange whose purpose is not to trade directly, but instead to purchase shares in manufacturing or service companies. The word 'investment' is descriptive of the purpose of the corporation; the word 'trust' reflects the way in which joint stock companies were originally established, prior to modern company legislation permitting the statutory incorporation of companies.

The original investments of an investment trust are acquired through the sale of shares for which subscriptions are invited from the public. Further investments may be acquired through subsequent issues of shares, and from profits made from capital growth and the retention of dividends payable out of the company's own shareholdings, and which have not been fully distributed. The company may also be empowered to borrow, being able to use its shareholdings as security or collateral. Provided that the return from the investments made with the borrowings is greater than the cost of the loan, the investment trust company will increase its underlying asset value. The market capitalization of the company (ie the total value of the shares in the company) will normally tend to follow the underlying asset value of the company, but the market capitalization will sometimes exceed the value of the company (when its shares are said to trade at a premium), and will sometimes fall below it (when the shares are said to trade at a discount). A rise in the asset value of the company is not necessarily reflected directly in a rise in the value of the company's shares: their value is instead determined by how many investors wish to purchase them on the market, and how much they are prepared to pay.

4 Open-ended investment companies[8]

Investment trusts are closed-ended in that the company issues a fixed number of shares. If an investor who originally subscribed for those shares decides to realize his investment, he does so by selling his shareholding to a new investor. The company does not normally buy back the shareholding. Unless the company seeks exceptional power to buy back shares, or new shares are issued to raise additional capital, the number of shares issued remains unchanged.

Open-ended investment companies (or OEICs) operate differently. The only purpose of an OEIC is to provide a vehicle for collective investment. The company issues shares to prospective investors, and uses the funds so raised to make investments through the purchase of shares and other securities. These assets are held by a depositary (effectively a custodian trustee) on behalf of the OEIC.[9] If, after the initial launch of the company, new investors wish to join, then this is done by issuing additional shares. These shares are sold at the average asset value of the existing shares. The additional funds so raised are used to make additional investments. When an investor wants to realize his investment, this is done by cancelling the shares in return for payment to the investor of the average asset value per share. Of course, where the number of buyers and sellers is equal, the shares of one are in effect transferred to the other. In this respect the OEIC operates similarly to an investment trust company, but the difference is that where the number of buyers and sellers are not in balance, the number of issued shares changes. OEICs are thus quite similar in operation to unit trusts (see below), and are indeed marketed on that basis. Although only introduced in 1996, by 2000 OEICs accounted for approximately 20 per cent of investment through collective investment schemes, and that proportion was expected to rise.[10]

5 Mutual societies

English law does not automatically accord to clubs or societies a status of legal personality that is independent of the membership. Clubs, societies, or other unincorporated associations operate in a similar way to partnerships. Legal actions must be brought by

---

[8] See the Open-Ended Investment Companies Regulations 2001, SI 2001/1228, replacing the Open-Ended Investment Companies (Investment Companies with Variable Capital) Regulations 1996, SI 1996/2827. These Regulations have themselves been amended by the Open-Ended Investment Companies (Amendment) Regulations 2005.

[9] The Open-Ended Investment Companies Regulations 2001, SI 2001/1228, reg 5.

[10] HM Treasury consultation document preceding enactment of the Financial Services and Markets Act 2000 and associated regulations.

one member of the association on behalf of the others,[11] and legal actions are defended in a similar way.

This legal dogma produced difficulties for associations which wished to engage in commercial or quasi-commercial activities such as cooperative societies wishing to engage in retail trading, insurance companies which wished to provide insurance benefits for members,[12] credit unions which would take deposits from members and make short-term loans to depositing members at favourable rates of interest, and building societies which take longer-term deposits and loans. To overcome these difficulties, legislation was enacted which enabled these mutual associations, through a simple process of registration, to obtain limited independent legal personality, although they continued to be owned and governed by their members in accordance with their rules.[13] The legislation provided for a variety of different forms of association, for instance friendly societies set up to provide mutual insurance benefits;[14] and cooperative societies established to provide not-for-profit trading activities.[15] An example of the latter is the International Exhibition Co-operative Wine Society, which was set up in 1874 to supply good wines at fair prices to its members. Additional legislation covers specialist types of association, for instance credit unions,[16] building societies,[17] and housing associations.[18] Registration of an association as an industrial and provident society or as a friendly society was a convenient alternative to incorporation under the Companies' Acts for mutual groups, many of which remain in operation today.

Most industrial and provident or friendly societies (collectively called *mutual societies*, a phrase sometimes used in the society's name) were, in origin, local self-help organizations. In the early part of the twentieth century and onwards, however, some of them expanded considerably, as is particularly evident with building societies. They expanded their operations outside their local areas, often distanced themselves in practice from their original mutual ethos, with full-time, often self-perpetuating, professional management. By retaining rather than distributing some of each year's trading profit, the society would be able to build up substantial reserves, and through

[11] See eg *Verrall v Great Yarmouth Borough Council* [1981] QB 202, CA, where an action seeking specific performance of a contract for the hire of a conference hall for the National Front was brought by the association's secretary.

[12] Often on a very small scale: mutual insurance societies were frequently established to provide funeral benefits for members. Small premiums were collected weekly, often by a representative calling door-to-door, and in return for these, the policy would pay enough on the death of a policy-holder to meet the costs of a modest funeral.

[13] See, for example, Friendly Societies Act 1896, s 49(1), which states: 'All property belonging to a registered society, whether acquired before or after the society is registered, shall vest in the trustees for the time being of the society, for the use and benefit of the society and the members thereof, and of all persons claiming through the members according to the rules of the society.'

[14] Friendly Societies Act 1829, Friendly Societies Act 1896. The current legislation is the Friendly Societies Act 1974 and the Friendly Societies Act 1992.

[15] Industrial and Provident Societies Act 1852; Industrial and Provident Societies Act 1862. See now the Industrial and Provident Societies Acts 1965 (as amended by the Industrial and Provident Societies Act 2002) and 1978.

[16] Now governed by the Credit Unions Act 1979.

[17] Building Societies Act 1986, as amended by the Building Societies Act 1997.

[18] Housing Acts 1985, 1988, and 2004.

the acquisition of property could control assets of considerable value. In most practical respects, some mutual societies have become indistinguishable from companies incorporated under the Companies Acts. When the society is wound up, merged with another similar society, or taken over by a company incorporated under the Companies Acts, these assets are available for distribution between the members. There is a difference, however, in the way in which members can deal with their share in the society whilst it remains in being. In most companies, the shareholder is able to sell his interest upon leaving membership, and thereby gain a benefit from the surplus and capital appreciation of the asset base that has taken place during his membership. By comparison, the member of a mutual society loses all claim to the society's assets on leaving membership, normally without receiving any payment on ceasing to be a member. This can result in windfall gains accruing to those who happen to be members at the time that a society is wound up, privatized, or taken over, even though they may have been members for a very short period.

No doubt because they are endowed by statute with limited legal personality independent of the individual members, the only problems concerning the ownership or management of a mutual society's assets which have received recent judicial attention concern their dissolution, when such societies are treated in the same way as unincorporated associations.[19] Mutual societies receiving deposits or engaging in offering other financial services are subject to regulation under the Financial Services and Markets Act 2000.

The relevance of mutual societies in the present context—that of collective investment—is that many mutual societies have operated as vehicles for collective investment, albeit generally with some other social purpose. This is particularly evident with credit unions and building societies, both of which provided convenient vehicles for saving by small investors. It is also the case with many of the mutual insurance and tontine societies, which have increasingly developed a range of financial services that differ little from those offered by banks or incorporated insurance companies.

6 **Building societies**

Although they now operate in a very similar way to banks,[20] building societies were originally mutual organizations established for the purpose of enabling their members to build or acquire houses for residential use. The members would pool their savings. The fund thereby created would be used to make loans on mortgage to members for house purchase. Some building societies were set up for a limited period and were dissolved once the original membership had all acquired homes. Others were

---

[19] See below p 775 and Chapter 20.
[20] Northern Rock is a former building society that incorporated as a bank with public limited company status.

established on a permanent basis, and this was reflected in the name of the society, such as the Leeds Permanent Building Society.

Some early building societies took advantage of friendly society legislation, although they now have their own legislation.[21] Thus, they were able to obtain legal personality for the purpose of holding and managing property, for entering into contractual arrangements, and for bringing and defending legal actions. Nevertheless, as mutual organizations, they were—and in theory remain—controlled by their members (ie qualifying depositors and borrowers) without separate shareholders. The consequence of the controlling interest of the membership can be seen in what happens when it is proposed that a building society should merge with another, or be taken over by a public limited company. The members have to give their approval through a ballot to the proposed merger or takeover. Any payment made to the society will be distributed between the society's borrowers and depositors. The possibility of making a windfall gain was at one time so attractive that some investors were attracted to a society as 'carpetbaggers'. Some societies have taken measures to inhibit such activity by a variety of means, in some cases by requiring new depositors to agree to donate to charity any windfall gains they receive if the society converts to company status or is sold.

It has been argued that building societies have an unfair advantage over banks: although they are accountable to their members in a similar way to that in which banks are accountable to their shareholders, the building societies do not have to pay a rent on the capital which they employ, although the banks pay a dividend to their shareholders. Despite this advantage, it has been said, most building societies do not offer their members preferential rates on loans or deposits. Some building societies have met this objection by paying a bonus to their members. Many of the remaining building societies are therefore taking a more aggressive approach to protecting their mutual status.

7 Endowment policies

The purchase of an endowment policy represents an indirect way of investing in the stock market and other assets. In return for either a single lump sum premium, or periodical premium payments, an insurance company offers a combination of life insurance and investment. In return for the life insurance element, the insurance company guarantees a lump sum payment if the policy-holder dies during a specified period. If the policy-holder does not die during that period, then the insurance company instead makes a lump sum payment to the policy-holder at the end of the term. This could either be a predetermined fixed sum (normally the same as that guaranteed

---

[21] Building Societies Act 1986 (as amended by the Building Societies Act 1997 and the Financial Services and Markets Act 2000).

on death), or a variable sum ('with profits') depending on the success of the invest-ments made by the insurance company. With this latter form, each year the insurance company distributes a proportion of its profits between qualifying policy-holders. The policy-holders are not entitled to withdraw their allocated share of profits until their policy matures at the end of the specified period or earlier death. The allocated profits are therefore retained by the insurance company for this period and are available for it to lend at interest, to use for the purchase of property, or to invest on the stock mar-ket. These investments, in turn, will help to increase the insurance company's profits, which are again available for distribution between eligible policy-holders.

For many years, endowment policies were a popular way of repaying mortgages on residential property. When income tax relief was available on life insurance pre-miums, holders of endowment policies were also able to benefit from this tax relief. Endowment policies have now lost in popularity to unit trust arrangements.

8 Unit trusts

A unit trust is a complex form of equitable co-ownership.[22] An initial fund is estab-lished through subscriptions from investors. The fund thus established is used for the purchase of investments by the fund manager, the investments being held by a custo-dian trustee. The fund is valued, and on the basis of this valuation, notionally divided into units of equal value. Each investor is allocated a number of units proportionate to the amount that that investor originally subscribed. Although it is possible for a unit trust to contain no power of reinvestment,[23] most unit trusts permit the fund manager to alter the portfolio of investments, although often within special limits.

The fund would not normally be closed for further investment. Further subscrip-tions normally remain possible: for each new unit acquired the investor must pay a sum equivalent to the current unit value. The fund manager will, by means of such subscriptions, acquire further funds for investment. Equally, subscribers will nor-mally be able to withdraw from the fund without the whole fund being closed.[24] The investor wishing to realize his investment will either sell his units, via the fund man-ager, to someone else wishing to enter the fund, or the fund manager will realize suffi-cient of the collective pool of investments to meet the cost of repaying the investor the current unit value of the units which are being cashed in. Provision for such dealings will be made in the trust deed.

The fund manager covers the costs of operating the unit trust by fixing the price of units available for purchase at a higher level than the price that will be given to an investor surrendering units. This difference between the 'offer' price[25] and the 'bid'

---

22   See *Costa & Duppe Properties Ltd v Duppe* [1986] VR 90.
23   See *Re Municipal and General Securities Co Ltd's Trust* [1950] Ch 212.
24   See Financial Services and Markets Act 2000, s 243.
25   The price fixed for the purchase of units.

price[26] is known as the 'turn'. The fund manager and fund trustee also make an annual charge for the administration of the investment fund, usually by taking a percentage of the capital value. All of these matters are regulated by the trust deed governing the unit trust.

The rights of investors in a unit trust are a mix of contract and trust. The investment itself is made pursuant to a contract that defines the basis upon which units are bought and sold. It is common for the contract to state that the investor acquires no proprietary right in the underlying assets in which investments are made. The basis of the scheme, as its name suggests, is a trust, and this is confirmed by the Financial Services and Markets Act 2000.[27] The effect of the contractual term is that no individual participant in a unit trust can call for the vesting in him or her of the property held in the scheme. Although the matter is not free from doubt, it is likely that the effect of the trust on which the assets are held is that all of the participants, when combined together, command the whole beneficial interest in the fund. In theory they could therefore call for the termination of the fund and the vesting of ownership in themselves as beneficiaries under the principle in *Saunders v Vautier*.[28] More importantly, in the event of the insolvency of the fund manager, the assets of the fund should not be available to meet any general debts of the insolvent manager. Moreover, the fund manager is likely to be subject to all the obligations of a trustee in relation to the discharge of the manager's functions, including the obligation to comply with the duty of care in making investment decisions.[29]

9 Investment club

With this form of arrangement, a number of investors group into a syndicate. Each member of the syndicate subscribes an agreed amount each month or other agreed period. The members of the syndicate meet periodically and agree which investment will be acquired from the accumulated subscribed funds. The investment is purchased in the name of one or more of the syndicate who holds it upon trust for the others. The club rules provide what is to happen if the members of the syndicate fail to reach agreement, if they wish to wind the club up, or if one of them wishes to resign. An investment club is one type of unincorporated association, which will be considered later in this chapter. As described in Chapter 5, a syndicate purchasing tickets in the National Lottery works in a similar way. The organizer collects subscriptions from the members, and uses them to purchase tickets on behalf of the members. Any winnings will be held in trust for division between the members.

---

[26] The price for which units may be cashed in.   [27] S 237.

[28] (1841) 4 Beav 115. See also *Re AEG Unit Trust Managers Ltd's Deed* [1957] Ch 415.

[29] It is not possible for this liability to be excluded in the case of authorized unit trusts (ie unit trusts for which subscribers are solicited by means of advertisement): Financial Services and Markets Act 2000, s 253.

10 Pension funds[30] and provision for retirement

(1) Methods of providing for retirement

In addition to the retirement pensions that are offered by the state and funded out of taxation,[31] individuals may make their own arrangements. They may do this either individually or through an occupational pension scheme, or through a combination of both. A very simple way of making individual provision is to save until retirement, and either to draw income and capital from the accumulated fund after retirement, or to use it to purchase an annuity. This is an arrangement with an insurance company under which the insurance company, in return for a lump sum, agrees to make periodic or annual[32] payments at an agreed rate, either fixed or with provision for annual increases to allow for inflation, for the remainder of the annuitant's life. The arrangement is purely contractual. On the basis of actuarial information and advice, and a knowledge of current investment market conditions and returns, the insurance company can make a fairly accurate calculation of the cost of making the payments. In some cases, of course, the annuitant will live longer than expected, which will cost the insurance company more than the sum it received. If the insurance company has made its calculations correctly, however, these costs will be balanced by other cases in which the annuitant dies prematurely. The effect of an annuity is therefore to pass the risks of mortality on the erosion of the capital to the insurance company.

(2) Types of pension scheme

(a) Personal pensions

Instead of saving independently to raise the capital to purchase an annuity, most people planning to provide an income for retirement will do so through an arrangement with an insurance company. One reason for doing this is that very substantial tax relief is available for qualifying pension savings plans. The investor gains the benefit of this tax relief, but is obliged to use the savings made through the plan exclusively for the purpose of providing benefits on retirement. Part may be taken in the form of a capital sum, but the remainder must be used for the purchase of an annuity. Recent changes in legislation have made it possible for the person retiring to defer the purchase of an annuity for a short period, since low interest rates at the time an annuity is purchased significantly reduce the periodical payments which insurance companies are prepared to offer. The savings vehicles that are used in pension savings schemes are either endowment policies, or, increasingly frequently, unit trust

---

[30] See generally *Report of the Pension Law Review Committee*, Chairman Professor Roy Goode (1993 Cm 2342) (the Goode Report); Nobles, *Pensions, Employment and the Law* (1993); Inglis-Jones, *The Law of Occupational Pension Schemes* (1989); Ellison, *Pensions Law and Practice* (1987); Hayton 'Pension Trusts and Traditional Trust: Drastically Different Species of Trusts' [2005] Conv 229.

[31] Including National Insurance contributions.   [32] Hence the term 'annuity'.

schemes. Apart from the fact that the proceeds of the savings plan must be used to purchase retirement benefits, there is no material difference between an endowment or unit trust scheme used as a part of a pension plan and an endowment or unit trust used in any other way.

(b) Occupational pensions

Occupational pensions were first introduced in the late nineteenth century, but became very much more important over the course of the twentieth century. It has been calculated that in 1991, 10.7 million employees in the United Kingdom were active members of occupational pension schemes, representing 57 per cent of working men and 37 per cent of working women.[33] A variety of forms were used for the introduction of such schemes. Some were, and in the public sector remain, unfunded. The pensions are then payable out of the annual revenue of the enterprise. The overwhelming majority of private occupational pension schemes, however, are funded.

(c) Funded schemes

Under a funded occupational pension scheme the employee and the employer generally both make contributions to an investment fund. That fund is then used to finance the payment of the pensions when they fall due. Although other means of providing for pensions are possible, the overwhelming majority of private sector pension funds are held by trustees under irrevocable trusts. One substantial reason for this was that the tax privileges accorded to 'approved schemes' used to be available only to pension schemes established in this way.[34] This is no longer the case, and, since 6 April 2006, all pension schemes must be registered under the Finance Act 2004, Part 4 to obtain tax relief.[35] Funded schemes themselves divide into two main groups: money purchase schemes (otherwise known as defined contribution schemes) and defined benefit schemes.[36] There can in addition be special arrangements such as an 'executive pension plan' for a single employee.[37] Employers are now under a duty to enrol employees into a personal or occupational pension scheme, and must make contributions to it. This was introduced by the Pensions Act 2008,[38] and applies to low to moderately paid workers.[39]

---

[33] Goode Report, para 2.2.4.

[34] Income and Corporation Taxes Act 1988, s 592, re-enacting a provision first found in Finance Act 1921, repealed by Finance Act 2004.

[35] The tax reliefs applicable to registered pension schemes are listed in the Finance Act 2004, Part 4, Chapter 4.

[36] Goode Report, paras 2.2.11 2.2.23. Some hybrid schemes have features of both defined-benefit and money-purchase. More detailed definitions are provided in Finance Act 2004, s 152.

[37] As in *Brooks v Brooks* [1996] AC 375. In this case, the House of Lords considered that special features of this bespoke pension plan meant that it constituted a marriage settlement that could be varied on divorce.

[38] Pensions Act 2008, Part I, ss 1–33.

[39] The threshold was set under s 13(1) as a gross annual income of more than £5,035, but less than £33,540 for the first year of operation, the figures to be reviewed annually.

(i) Money purchase schemes

With a money purchase scheme, although the employee's and the employer's contributions are normally invested through a single investment fund, a separate individual account is kept for each member to record the value of that member's share of the total value of the fund. On an employee's retirement, the capital value of the employee's portion of the fund (i.e. the sum standing to his credit in the individual account) is used to provide pension benefits on his retirement. Part may be used to provide a lump sum, and the remainder is generally used to purchase an annuity from an insurance company. A money purchase scheme is therefore like an independently arranged pension savings plan used to purchase retirement benefits. The principal differences are, first, that the employer contributes at a rate which is agreed with the employee (or the employees generally) and, secondly, that (depending upon the size of the scheme) the collective investment fund may be maintained as a separate investment fund for the particular occupational scheme, rather than being pooled with funds from other sources and managed as a general fund by an insurance company (as would be the case with most personal pension schemes). It is because the rate contributed by the employer is fixed that money purchase schemes are sometimes called defined contribution schemes.

Money purchase schemes are on the whole less attractive to employees than defined benefit schemes, although money purchase schemes may be more advantageous to the early leaver: that is, the employee who leaves the scheme before having worked until retirement age. The original pension plan for university staff—the Federated Superannuation Scheme for Universities (FSSU)—was a money purchase plan in which participating employees were able to make choices themselves about the way in which their contributions would be invested. The scheme failed to make adequate provision for inflation, and was therefore superseded by a defined benefits scheme (USS) introduced in the early 1970s.

Changes to pensions rules made by the Pensions Act 1995 and the open-ended liability of employers to ensure that defined benefit schemes are fully funded mean that money purchase schemes are increasing in popularity. Unlike defined benefit schemes, there is no statutory obligation on an employer to increase contributions if investment returns prove to be lower than had been anticipated when contribution levels had previously been agreed. The significant decline in the value of shares in the period to 2002 and since the fourth quarter of 2008 has accelerated the move by employers to close defined benefit schemes and to move into defined contribution or money purchase schemes.

(ii) Defined benefit schemes

These used to represent the majority of managed occupational pension funds,[40] although increasingly employers are closing such schemes to new employees and even to existing employees because of the uncertain costs of funding such schemes and the

---

[40] Some 89 per cent of funded occupational schemes fell into this category, according to the National Association of Pension Funds Annual Survey of Pension Schemes 1993, Table 66.

uncertain financial market.[41] Most such schemes offer a pension that is related to the employee's salary in the last few years preceding leaving the scheme or retirement, and for this reason are called 'final salary' schemes. Pensions are usually paid at the rate of one-eightieth or one-sixtieth of final salary for each year of pensionable service. Such schemes are generally funded by means of each employee contributing a fixed percentage of salary, with the employer making up whatever sum an actuary calculates is necessary to ensure that the scheme has sufficient assets to meet its liabilities.[42] The liabilities of the fund will depend, amongst other variables, upon the number of employees, their likelihood of retiring at a salary higher than their current earnings, their life expectancy, the benefits offered to surviving spouses and other dependants, and the provision made by the scheme for increases in pensions to allow for inflation.[43] The assets needed to cover these liabilities will depend, amongst other variables, upon the assumptions that can be made about future returns from investment. Although actuaries can make estimates of these liabilities and necessary assets, the science is not an exact one, and it cannot be predicted accurately what contributions are required simply on the basis of current earnings. The calculations also make assumptions about future investment returns that may turn out to be too conservative or too optimistic. Actuarial reviews will therefore sometimes indicate that a pension fund is in deficit (ie that the liabilities exceed the available assets) and sometimes that it is in surplus (ie that the assets exceed the liabilities). In the former case, contributions will have to be increased if the fund is to continue to be able to meet its obligations. The Pensions Act 1995 contained detailed rules imposing an obligation on the trustees of defined benefit pension schemes to conduct regular actuarial reviews and on employers to make good any serious deficiencies which these reveal.[44] These rules have been replaced by a new framework established under Part 3 of the Pensions Act 2004,[45] which operates under the statutory funding objective that each scheme 'must have sufficient and appropriate assets to cover its technical provisions'.[46] This is a stricter set of rules that maintains the requirement for regular actuarial reviews,[47] but also requires the trustees to prepare and revise both a statement of funding principles[48] and a schedule of contributions for both employers and employees.[49] The scheme is overseen by the Pensions Regulator, to whom the actuary reports if there is any difficulty in meeting the statutory funding objective, and who has powers to intervene to make sure that any of the duties imposed on the trustees are carried out.[50] Where the actuarial reviews reveal that the fund has more assets than

---

[41] *HR Trustees Ltd v German* [2009] EWHC 2785 (Ch) provides an example. The 2007 annual report of the National Association of Pensions Funds noted that over 80 per cent of final salary defined benefit schemes were in deficit, and over 80 per cent of such schemes had been closed to new employees.

[42] Goode Report, para 2.2.13.   [43] The Pensions Act 1995, s 76 requires annual increases.

[44] Pensions Act 1995, ss 36–39; Occupational Pension Schemes (Minimum Funding Requirement and Actuarial Valuations) Regulations 1996, SI 1996/1536.

[45] Pensions Act 2004, ss 221–233.   [46] Ibid., s 222(1).

[47] Ibid., s 224.   [48] Ibid., s 223.   [49] Ibid., s 227.

[50] For example, if the pension fund is in trouble, the trustees and employer must agree a recovery plan, under s 226 and the Pensions Regulator has power to enforce any such agreement, such as by directing an increase in individual contributions (s.231(2)(c)).

are required to meet its liabilities, an issue may arise as to who should benefit from the superfluity of assets. It is in relation to this last issue that the legal debate concerning occupational pensions has been at its fiercest. We return to this question later. The 2004 Act contains detailed provisions for winding-up schemes in deficit.[50a]

(3) Trusts and pension schemes

(a) The use of trusts in pension schemes

The use of the trust as a means of providing for pensions enables the fund assets to be kept separate from the assets and liabilities of the employer. This offers some security in the event of the insolvency of the employer. The trust also means that where benefits are payable to someone other than the employee who is a member of the scheme, such as the employee's surviving spouse, the beneficiary has an enforceable claim which will not be barred by an absence of privity of contract. As explained above, it was previously a requirement for a scheme to qualify for tax benefits. Where the scheme is a defined benefit scheme, it might be wondered whether the trust vehicle is necessary at all. The benefits that the members will receive are defined by the rules of the scheme: the contributions that they make, and the benefits they will receive, are fixed. A simple contract could achieve the same. Similarly, the protection against the insolvency of the employer could equally be safeguarded by obtaining a guarantee from some third party, such as an insurance company or, indeed, by the contract for the provision of the pension being made directly by a third party such as an insurance company. It is now recognized that pension schemes, including occupational pension schemes, can operate without the use of a trust.   Where trusts are used in an occupational pension scheme, they have special features.[51] The size of pension funds can be very considerable.[52] Pension schemes are not established by way of the generosity of a settlor, but as the result of contractual contributions which both the employer and the employee are contractually obliged to make. The beneficiaries therefore help to finance their own benefits:

Even in a non-contributory scheme, the employer's payments are not bounty. They are part of the consideration for the services of the employee.[53]

The trustees are frequently interested in a pension fund as employers or employees,[54] rather than being wholly independent as they typically would be in a family trust. Under the Pensions Act 2004 at least one-third of the total number of trustees must be

---

50a See *Houldsworth v Bridge Trustees Ltd* [2010] EWCA Civ 179.

51 See generally Lord Browne-Wilkinson 'Equity and its Relevance to Superannuation Schemes Today' [1992] 6 *Trust Law International* 119.

52 Although there is very considerable variation. Less than 0.1 per cent of all pension schemes accounted for over 20 per cent of pension scheme members, while 75 per cent of the total number of schemes, with twelve members or fewer accounted for just 3 per cent of all scheme members: see Goode Report, para 2.2.6.

53 *McDonald v Horn* [1995] 1 All ER 961, at 973, per Hoffmann LJ.

54 There is no reason why the trustees should not also be beneficiaries of the scheme: *Edge v Pensions Ombudsman* [1998] 2 All ER 547.

trustees appointed by the members of the scheme (member-nominated trustees).[55] The membership is not fixed, but open-ended. There is generally a wide power to alter the terms of the trust[56] and it is not uncommon for the pension fund to be established by an interim trust deed that is then replaced by a subsequent definitive trust instrument. It has been held that such a definitive trust deed operates retrospectively from the date of the establishment of the scheme,[57] but this has been described as 'controversial', and not applicable to alter vested rights.[58]

The special features of pension schemes could be expected to produce differences in the way in which trust law applies, and this is evident in the special statutory rules[59] and in some of the emerging case law,[60] although there are judges who have said that the administration of pension trusts should not be treated differently from the administration of other trusts. Speaking of investment, for instance, Sir Robert Megarry said:

I can see no reason for holding that different principles apply to pension fund trusts from those which apply to other trusts. Of course, there are many provisions in pension schemes which are not to be found in private trusts, and to these the general law of trusts will be subordinated. But subject to that, I think that the trusts of pension funds are subject to the same rules as other trusts.[61]

Similarly, in *Re Trusts of Scientific Pension Plan* Ratee J, faced with a question as to the interpretation of a clause in a pension scheme, said:

I accept that, as was said in *Mettoy Pension Trustees Ltd v Evans*,[62] 'the court's approach to the construction of documents relating to a pension scheme should be practical and purposive,

---

[55] Pensions Act 2004, s 241. The Act makes it clear (in s 39) that such trustees are not affected by the ordinary rule that trustees cannot put themselves in a position where their duties and personal interest conflict merely because they may benefit as scheme members from the exercise of a power conferred on the trustees; see also *Edge v Pensions Ombudsman* [1998] 2 All ER 547 and *National Grid Co plc v Laws* [1997] PLR 157 (compare *Re Drexel Burnham Lambert UK Pension Plan* [1995] 1 WLR 32 on the position before the Act). See also Fitzsimons 'Managing Pension Scheme Trustee Conflicts of Interest' (2006) 20 TLI 211.

[56] Pensions Act 1995, s 67 limits the extent to which such powers can be exercised, as amended by the Pensions Act 2004, s 262, which added s 67A-I detailing the exercise of these powers. Sections 68 and 69 (as amended) provide for pension schemes to be modified to implement the requirements of the Pensions Acts.

[57] *Re Imperial Foods Ltd Pension Scheme* [1986] 2 All ER 802 Walton J, Pen Schemes 23: Feb 2000.

[58] *Trustee Corpn Ltd v Nadir* [2001] BPIR 541 (Lawrence Collins J).

[59] Including regulation by the Pensions Regulator established by the Pensions Act 2004, s 90. This corporate body replaces the Occupational Pensions Regulatory Authority (established under the Pensions Act 1995) and has wider powers to promote good practice (such as issuing Codes of Practice under ss 90–92), as well as reducing the risk of underfunding in pensions trusts., The Regulator can prohibit a person from acting as a trustee, impose financial penalties, and restrain the misuse of assets: ss 3–4 and ss 6–11 Pensions Act 1995, as amended by Pensions Act 2004, Part I. Pensions are also overseen by the Pensions Ombudsman, whose powers relate to maladministration of pensions trusts—Pensions Schemes Act 1993, as amended by the Pensions Acts 1995 and 2004. See further pp 774 et seq below.

[60] See, eg *Mihlenstedt v Barclays Bank plc* [1989] IRLR 522 and *Mettoy Pension Trustees Ltd v Evans* [1991] 2 All ER 513.

[61] *Cowan v Scargill* [1985] Ch 270, at 290. As we will see below, such is the nature of the regulatory scheme under the Pensions Act 1995 relating to investment, it would be difficult to assert that pension trust investment is now subject to the same basic principles as other trusts.

[62] [1991] 2 All ER 513, at 537.

rather than detached and literal', though I also accept that the ordinary principles of trust law apply to the terms of such a scheme once so construed.

The note, sounded in this statement, that a slightly different approach might be required from the ordinary for pension scheme deeds, was echoed in *Stevens v Bell*,[63] where Lady Justice Arden, giving the sole opinion of the Court of Appeal on a complex issue of interpretation of the Airways Pension Scheme, said:

A pension scheme should be construed so to give a reasonable and practical effect to the scheme. The administration of a pension fund is a complex matter and it seems to me that it would be crying for the moon to expect the draftsman to have legislated exhaustively for every eventuality.[64]

The Goode Committee, established to review the framework for occupational pension schemes in the wake of the Maxwell affair, favoured the retention of trust law as the basis for providing and regulating such pensions.[65] The committee observed that 'trust law is indeed of considerable antiquity, but it has shown a remarkable ability to adapt itself to modern commercial requirements'.[66] The value of trust law lay in segregating assets for the protection of the beneficiaries; in providing a mechanism for the collective representation and protection of members of a group of people linked by a common interest; and in the embodiment of highly developed concepts of fiduciary responsibility. The committee therefore concluded:

We therefore endorse the view expressed in the great weight of evidence submitted to us that trust law in itself is broadly satisfactory and should continue to provide the foundation for interests, rights and duties arising in relation to pension schemes. But, some of the principles of trust law require modification in their application to pensions.[67]

The committee recommended the introduction of a Pensions Act to place curbs on the permissible content of scheme rules, to secure the solvency of schemes, the monitoring of pension funds, and other matters of regulation. Some of the recommendations of the committee were implemented by the Pensions Act 1995, which has now been amended and supplemented by the provisions of the Pensions Act 2004, which introduces a new Pensions Regulator. The regulation of pensions funds under this new regime is discussed below.

(b) Special duty of pension fund trustees

Most occupational pension schemes confer a wide measure of discretion upon the trustees. In accordance with ordinary principles of trust law, any powers that are held by a trustee will prima facie be held by them in a fiduciary capacity.[68] The trustees must therefore consider the best interests of the beneficiaries and exercise the power impartially and in accordance with its purpose.[69] The power will not be validly

---

63 [2002] EWCA 672.   64 Ibid., at para 28.
65 Goode Report, para 4.1.14.   66 Ibid., para 4.1.9.
67 Ibid., para 4.1.14.   68 *Re Hay's Settlement Trusts* [1981] 3 All ER 786. See further Chapter 30.
69 See Chapter 27 for a consideration on the exercise of powers by trustees.

exercised if it has been exercised for an improper purpose, or as a result of illegitimate threats.[70] In *Re Courage Group's Pension Schemes* the Courage brewing group of companies had been taken over by Hanson Trust plc as part of the purchase of the Imperial Group. Hanson sought to be substituted as principal employer under the Courage Group scheme so that it could retain a surplus of approximately £70m on a sale of the Courage Group to Elders IXL Ltd, the brewers of Castlemaine XXXX. This surplus could then be used to fund pensions for other Hanson employees. Hanson sought to do this under a power in the pension trust deed that permitted variations that did not affect the **main purpose** of the fund. Millett J held that the power in the trust deed could be exercised only with the consent of the trustees,[71] and also that it would be improper for the trustees to give consent, since the exercise of the power in the present circumstances would be for a purpose inconsistent for that for which it was conferred.[72] The trustees were under an obligation to protect the interests of the employed members, pensioners, and deferred pensioners.[73] They would not be doing so if they permitted a variation in the trusts by the unilateral decision of a takeover raider. The employees, while having no legal right to any pension fund surpluses, were entitled to have them dealt with by consultation and negotiation.

The Pensions Act 2004 requires pension trustees to have high level of knowledge and understanding. Under s 247 they must be conversant with the trust deed and the rules of the scheme, any statement of investment principles maintained by the trust, the statement of funding principles prepared for the trust, and any other document recording policy for the time being adopted by the trustees relating to the administration of the scheme generally.[74] They are also required to have a knowledge and understanding of the law relating to pensions and trusts and the principles relating to the funding of occupational pension schemes and the investment of the assets of such schemes.[75] Corporate trustees of pension schemes are required to secure that each individual who exercises any function that the company has as a trustee of the scheme is conversant with these matters.[76]

(c) Duty to act in good faith

An attempt by Hanson Trust plc to capture a pension fund surplus again arose in *Imperial Group Pension Trust Ltd v Imperial Tobacco Ltd*.[77] The Imperial Group was taken over by Hanson plc. The Imperial Group pension scheme was very substantially

---

[70] *Hillsdown Holdings plc v Pensions Ombudsman* [1997] 1 All ER 862.

[71] See also *Stannard v Fisons Pension Trust Ltd* [1992] IRLR 27, where the Court of Appeal held that transfer payments made in respect of a group of employees transferring to another scheme could not be determined solely by the scheme actuary, but had to be approved as fair by the trustees. See also *Re Imperial Food Ltd's Pension Scheme* [1986] 1 WLR 717.

[72] See also *Lock v Westpac Banking Corpn* (1991) 25 NSWLR 593.

[73] Deferred pensioners are members of a pension scheme who leave it before retiring age, but are entitled under the rules of the scheme to receive a pension upon reaching normal retirement age. It is a requirement of legislation that retirement schemes should contain such a provision.

[74] S 247(3).   [75] Pensions Act 2004, s 247 (4).

[76] Ibid., s 248(3).   [77] [1991] 1 WLR 589.

in surplus. Hanson offered members the chance to transfer to a new pension scheme with enhanced guarantees against inflation, but under which the surplus could be transferred to Hanson instead of being used to augment pensions. Hanson did not appear to be prepared to consent to an amendment to the Imperial Group scheme to provide similar guarantees. Browne-Wilkinson V-C considered that it was a reasonable inference, although not a proven one, that Hanson was withholding its consent to the augmentation amendment under the Imperial scheme in order to seek control of the pension fund surplus by persuading members to transfer to the other scheme. In his view, if that were the case, Hanson would be withholding consent for a collateral purpose and would be acting unlawfully. Although in his view the power of the company to consent to variations in the scheme was not a fiduciary power, nor was it subject to an implied test of reasonableness, nevertheless pension schemes fell to be judged against the background of an employment relationship. As a matter of trust law:

> ... the pension trust deed and rules themselves are to be taken as being impliedly subject to the limitation that the rights and powers of the company can only be exercised in accordance with the implied obligation of good faith ... the company's right to give or withhold its consent to an amendment ... is subject to the implied obligation that the right shall not be exercised so as to destroy or seriously damage the relationship of confidence and trust between the company and its employees and former employees.[78]

There is a similar contractual obligation upon a company to act in good faith in regard to pension matters affecting employees and former employees.[79]

(d) Certain powers fiduciary

Browne-Wilkinson V-C held in the *Imperial Group* case that the power that the employer held was not fiduciary or subject to a test of reasonableness because such a limitation was not necessary to give business efficacy to the scheme. The question of implied limitations on powers held by employers must, however, be looked at in relation to each power individually. In *Mettoy Pension Trustees Ltd v Evans*[80] a provision in a pension trust provided that any surplus on dissolution 'may at the absolute discretion of the employer be applied to secure further benefits ... and any further balance thereafter remaining' shall be paid to the employer. The company went into compulsory winding-up on insolvency. Warner J held that the power just set out was a fiduciary power. If the power was a beneficial one that the company was free to exercise or not as it chose, then it was meaningless. If there had been no power, and the company had been the beneficial owner under the rules of any surplus, then it would still have been able to augment the benefits of members if it chose. The company had therefore to be under some obligation in relation to the power if the rule was to have any consequence. Secondly, the members of the pension scheme were contributories, not volunteers. The power to augment pensions out of any surplus was something which

---

78   Ibid., at 598.
79   *Mihlenstedt v Barclays Bank plc* [1989] IRLR 522; *National Grid plc v Mayes* [2001] 2 All ER 417, HL.
80   [1991] 2 All ER 513.

they had contracted for; it was also unrealistic to suggest that their contributions had not played at least some role in the generation of the surplus.

Having concluded that the power was fiduciary, Warner J held that it would not vest in a receiver under a debenture issued by the company, since it did not form part of the company's beneficial assets. Neither could it be exercised or released by the liquidator, whose duties were to have regard primarily to the interests of the creditors and contributories of the company, which would create a conflict of interest between those persons and the beneficiaries under the pension scheme to whom the person exercising the power was also to have regard. Nor could the power be exercised by the directors of the company, since they lost all their powers on the appointment of the liquidator. Warner J was therefore led to the conclusion that in the absence of any other person to exercise the fiduciary power, it was for the court to do so.[81]

It has been suggested by one commentator that the cases concerning the exercise by trustees and employers of powers relating to the application of a pension fund surplus are swayed not just by ordinary principles of trust law, but also by the deeper-lying consideration that such surpluses should not be left at the mercy of company creditors and takeover predators.[82] Where an employer becomes insolvent, the position of scheme members is strengthened by the requirement under the Pensions Act 1995 that an independent trustee be appointed[83] and only this trustee can exercise any fiduciary powers of the employer and any discretionary powers of the trustees under the scheme.[84]

(e) Investment of pension funds

The principles applicable to the investment of pension funds were considered in the previous chapter. Trustees of pensions funds benefit from two advantages: they have the same power to make investments as if they were beneficially entitled to the funds,[85] and they have no vicarious liability for the default of a qualified fund manager[86] to whom they delegate investment decisions.[87] In *Cowan v Scargill* Sir Robert Megarry V-C opined that the investment of pension funds was governed by the ordinary principles of trust law, although bearing in mind the size of some pension funds, he emphasized the need for diversification and expert advice. In his view, despite indications in an earlier case,[88] it would normally be improper for

---

[81] This was one of the options identified for the exercise of discretionary trusts by Lord Wilberforce in *McPhail v Doulton* [1970] 2 All ER 228, at 247. See Chapter 17.

[82] Gardner 'Fiduciary Powers in Toytown' (1991) 107 LQR 214.

[83] Pensions Act 1995, ss 22–24.

[84] Pensions Act 1995, s 25 (subject to amendment by the Pensions Act 2004).

[85] Pensions Act 1995, s 34(1).

[86] That is, a fund manager authorized to conduct investment business under the Financial Services Act 1986.

[87] Pensions Act 1995, s 34(2). Similar provisions now apply to the majority of trusts under the Trustee Act 2000. Where the trust's assets include investments, a fund manager must be appointed: Pensions Act 1995, s 47.

[88] *Evans v London Cooperative Society* reported in Ellison, *Private Occupational Pension Schemes* (1979), p 356.

trustees to invest in the employer's own business since it would not be fulfilling the duty of the trustees to have regard to the best financial interests of the beneficiaries. Only where a clause in the trust deed or rules permitted investment in the parent company on favourable terms would it be legitimate to show this kind of preference to the employer.[89]

(f) Information

Members of pension schemes, like the beneficiaries under any trust, have the right to be given information about the administration of the trust.[90] Statutory regulations give flesh to that obligation so far as accounts and other financial information is concerned.[91] David Hayton has argued that the common law should be developed, in recognition of the differences between pension trusts and conventional private trusts, so as to impose a duty on pension trustees to give beneficiaries reasons for their decisions.[92]

(g) Liability of trustees

It is common for the rules of pension schemes to confer exceptionally broad discretions on the trustees, and also to contain provisions exempting the trustees from liability for breaches of trust except those which have been committed knowingly or in bad faith. The Pensions Act 1995 now clarifies the position in relation to the delegation of investment decisions,[93] and prevents trustees from being exempt from liability for failure to take reasonable care. However, issues can easily arise concerning other functions of the trustees. The Goode Committee recommended that there should be a statutory statement of the responsibilities of pension trustees with an irreducible minimum core.[94] Even where discretions are conferred on trustees in the widest possible terms, the court will retain its jurisdiction to review the exercise of those discretions.[95]

(4) Pension fund surpluses

(a) Entitlement to a surplus while the scheme continues[96]

The question of entitlement to pension fund surpluses has arisen as an incidental issue in the cases that have just been described. The notional surplus in a pension fund is,

---

[89] Regulations under the Pension Schemes Act 1993 currently restrict self-investment by pension funds to 5 per cent of the fund's resources.

[90] *Re Londonderry's Settlement* [1965] Ch 918, CA discussed below, pp 834 *et seq.*

[91] Pensions Act 1995, s 41 (as amended by Pensions Act 2004, Schedules 12 and 13) and Occupational Pension Schemes (Disclosure of Information) Regulations 1996, SI 1996/1655.

[92] 'Pension Trusts and Traditional Trust: Drastically Different Species of Trusts' [2005] Conv 229. See below pp 842 *et seq* for an explanation of the current absence of any obligation on trustees to provide their beneficiaries with reasons for their decisions.

[93] Ss 33 (liability cannot be excluded or restricted by instrument or agreement) and 34(4) (liability for delegation to fund managers may be excluded provided trustees took all reasonable steps).

[94] Goode Report, paras 4.5.55–4.5.56.   [95] *See Boe v Alexander* (1987) 41 DLR (4th) 520.

[96] See Nobles 'Pensions as Property' (1994) 14 LS 345.

as has already been indicated, the amount by which the assets of the fund exceed the liabilities. While the fund continues, there is always the possibility that some of the assumptions made by the actuary were mistaken. The salaries of scheme members might rise faster than the actuary has allowed, or the return on the fund's investments may be poorer than projected. Even a small difference in the assumptions in these matters can turn an apparently large actuarial surplus into a significant actual deficit. This phenomenon was seen when returns from investments fell in the 1990s[97] and again in a global economic downturn in the late 2000s. In the case of one pension fund,[98] it was estimated that a reduction of 0.5 per cent in the assumed rate of future dividend growth would reduce the actuarial surplus from £460m to £293m, a reduction of more than 35 per cent. There has already been litigation that has involved the appropriate basis for calculating the solvency of a pension fund.[99] It is likely that there will be greater emphasis on this issue in future litigation.

The calculation of surplus is an imprecise matter. But if it is agreed that there is a surplus, who is entitled to it? The Inland Revenue requires that a surplus should be eliminated within a set period[100] but it imposes no requirement as to how the surplus should be reduced. That is a matter for the rules of the trust or for any approved amendment. The rules may permit augmentation of pension benefits, a suspension or reduction of the contributions payable by the employer and sometimes also of the employee, or a cash payment to the employer. In most instances, more than one of these options will be available, although in every case concerning the application of a surplus, the answer will depend upon the proper interpretation of the scheme rules.[101] For instance, in *British Coal Corpn v British Coal Staff Superannuation Scheme Trustees Ltd*[102] a question arose relating to a substantial actuarial surplus that had been built up within the coal industry pension scheme. Under the rules of the scheme, a surplus was to be applied, first, to provide full indexation for any pensions payable;[103] second, to reduce the contributions of the employer until the employer was reimbursed for any payments which had been made in respect of actuarial deficiencies in the fund; third, to meet any increase in pensions to reflect the cost of living in the next calendar year; and, finally, after retaining whatever reserve was considered desirable, to apply any remaining balance in equal parts for the benefit of members (by reducing contributions or increasing benefits) and for the benefit of the employer. The scheme contained a provision that permitted alterations to the rules, although a proviso prohibited any alteration 'making any of the moneys of the Scheme payable to any of the

---

[97] Goode Report, para 2.4.19.

[98] The LRT Pension Fund: see *London Regional Transport Pension Fund Trustee Co Ltd v Hatt* [1993] PLR 227.

[99] See *Stannard v Fisons Pension Trust Ltd* [1992] IRLR 27, CA.

[100] The period allowed for the elimination of the surplus depends upon the means used to reduce it. For an account of the rules and recommendations for change, see the Goode Report, paras 4.3.20–4.3.37.

[101] Subject to limits imposed by the Pensions Act 1995, s 37 (as amended by the Pensions Act 2004). These are mentioned below.

[102] [1995] 1 All ER 912.

[103] In other words, to increase pensions fully in line with any increase in the cost of living.

Employers'. As part of its plans to reduce its workforce, the Coal Corporation had entered into an agreement with the pension fund trustees to increase the benefits of employees made redundant by offering enhanced pensions. The Corporation agreed to fund these additional benefits by paying the additional costs to the pension fund trustees in instalments over a ten-year period. Before all the payments had been made, a revaluation of the fund showed that there was a surplus. The Corporation claimed to be able to set off the outstanding balance of the additional payments it had agreed to make against the part of the actuarial surplus that was to be applied to the employer. Vinelott J held that this was prohibited by the rules of the scheme. The Corporation had agreed to pay the trustees a lump sum. That could not be repaid to the Corporation under the rules. It made no difference that the sum was payable in instalments, since relieving the Corporation from liability in respect of an instalment would have the same effect as a repayment of an instalment already made.

An almost identical issue arose in *National Grid Co plc v Mayes*,[104] where the House of Lords was asked to rule whether the National Grid and International Power could use part of a pension fund surplus to meet the cost of supporting enhanced early retirement pensions which the companies had already agreed to pay by instalments, although they had not completed making those instalments. The House of Lords held that Vinelott J had come to the wrong conclusion in the *British Coal* case. The purpose of the prohibition on payments to the employers was to meet Inland Revenue restrictions that forbade the repayment of money contributed to the pension scheme, since those contributions had benefited from taxation privileges. That fiscal consideration did not apply to payments that, although agreed to be made, had not at that stage been paid. Moreover, it was not in dispute that the employer could take advantage of a surplus to reduce future contributions, if this was permitted by the rules of the scheme. There was no practical difference between reducing the standard rate of future contributions and cancelling instalment payments that had previously been agreed. Both actions had the same effect of reducing the total value of the fund. In the *National Grid* case, the House of Lords considered that, if it was necessary, the rules of the pension scheme could be amended to permit the payment of the surplus to the employers, since the rules conferred a power to make amendments, and did not forbid the use of the power to allocate the surplus in these circumstances.

We have already seen that the employer and trustees have at least a duty to act in good faith in relation to any such powers. But there is no principle that any surplus automatically belongs either to the employer or to the scheme members. Knott J in *London Regional Transport Pension Fund Trustee Co Ltd v Hatt*[105] has said that it is 'quite impossible, as well as simplistic, to try to identify the owner or owners of a surplus'.

The argument for the employees and pensioners is that an occupational pension represents deferred wages. An employee who was not in receipt of an occupational pension would expect higher pay if he was to be required to make his own provision for

---

104 [2001] WLR 864.   105 [1993] PLR 227.

retirement. An occupational pension is therefore an earned reward for employment.[106] The European Court of Justice has held that occupational pensions are to be regarded as deferred pay within the equal pay provisions of EU law.[107] Against this, it may be argued for the employers that the employees under a defined benefit scheme receive all to which they are entitled in return for their contributions if the defined benefits are paid. In most schemes, once the employee has made a fixed contribution, it is the employer who undertakes to meet the balance of the cost. If the employer bears the risk of having to increase contributions if the fund falls into deficit, then it is just that the employer should, by compensation, reap the benefit of any accrued surplus. An alternative but similar argument in a balance of cost scheme is that a surplus represents a mistaken overpayment by the employer that should be refunded.

The Pensions Act 1995, as amended, now imposes a duty on trustees[108] exercising any power under an ongoing scheme to exercise it only subject to strict conditions,[109] including that the trustees consider the payment to be 'in the best interests of the members' of the pension scheme[110] and notice of the proposal has been given to all scheme members.[111] These restrictions are designed to help prevent abuse, but do not provide a default rule as to the entitlement of employers or members to any surplus.

In every case but one, which will shortly be considered,[112] the courts have refused to fall sharply on one side of the divide or the other. For instance, in *Mettoy*, Warner J refused to allow the employer to claim beneficial ownership of the fund surplus, since this would be inconsistent with a power to augment pensions. But in the *Courage* case, Millett J emphasized that the members 'have no legal right to participate in the surpluses'. There is, in any event, the difficulty that since most pension schemes make provision for widows, widowers, and children or other dependants, some of the potential beneficiaries remain unidentifiable until the pension scheme has run its full course. The true position with pension schemes may therefore be that the search for an 'owner' of the fund, in the sense that is possible with fixed trusts, is illusory. Just as with discretionary trusts,[113] or with the administration of estates,[114] it may be that the real claim of both employers and members of a pension scheme is not to ownership, but to the due administration of the scheme and trust. In that context, it is likely that there will be further importation of principles from employment law and perhaps also of public and company law, where the courts have long sought to defend legitimate expectations and minority rights.

---

[106] See *Parry v Cleaver* [1970] AC 1, at 16, per Lord Reid; *McDonald v Horn* [1995] 1 All ER 961, at 973.

[107] *Barber v Guardian Royal Exchange Insurance Group* [1991] 1 QB 344, ECJ.

[108] If a power is conferred on any other person under a scheme, under s 37(2) Pensions Act 1995 (as amended) such power may only be validly exercised by the trustees.

[109] The nature of this conditions may be altered by regulations, as provided by Pensions Act 1995, s 37(4).

[110] Pensions Act 1995, s 37(3)(d).   [111] Pensions Act 1995, s 37(3)(g).

[112] *Davis v Richards and Wallington Industries Ltd* [1991] 2 All ER 563.

[113] See *McPhail v Doulton* [1971] AC 424, HL.

[114] *Stamp Duties Comr (Queensland) v Livingston* [1965] AC 694, PC.

(b) Entitlement to pension fund surplus on liquidation of employer

When an employer ceases business, any associated pension scheme is likely to be closed to new members unless it either formed part of an industry-wide or group-wide scheme, or the whole scheme is transferred to another continuing scheme. When a pension fund closes, it becomes much easier to quantify any surplus, since some of the variables affecting the calculation are eliminated.[115] A number of possibilities arise.[116] The scheme might be merged with another, transferring all assets and liabilities. Alternatively, the scheme could continue in existence until all pension entitlements are discharged in full. Or the trustees could use the assets of the fund to purchase cover from an insurance company for the pensions which have or may become payable. In the latter two cases, if the scheme is solvent, a surplus will arise for distribution. One possibility is that the surplus is property without an owner that should pass as bona vacantia to the Crown. The courts are generally reluctant to choose this as a solution.[117] The question then remains as to how the balance should be divided between the only two other groups of potential claimant, the employers and the scheme members. In *Davis v Richards and Wallington Industries Ltd*,[118] Scott J chose to adopt a resulting trust analysis in allocating the surplus of a pension scheme being wound up and where, on one of the assumptions which he had to consider, no express rule had provided for that eventuality. The pension fund had been created by contributions from both employers and employees. In the absence of some term in the trust deed or rules excluding a resulting trust,[119] any surplus should revert to them as contributors.[120] The employees had received all the benefits for which they had contracted, although that was not conclusive against retaining an interest under resulting trust. However, it was unlikely that funds deriving from the employees themselves would have been sufficient to finance the payment of the pensions. Their contributions, Scott J said, could therefore be seen as exhausted. The surplus had therefore been generated by contributions from the employer who, with hindsight, had contributed more than was necessary under the balance of cost provisions in the scheme. Moreover, it would probably be unworkable to seek to apportion a surplus fairly and equitably among the various classes of member, and, in any event, further payments

---

[115]   On the winding up of a pension scheme, the Pensions Act 1995 (as amended) requires that the assets must be applied to discharge any liabilities in a prescribed order, and provides mechanisms for doing so—see ss 73–75. Only when such liabilities are discharged, and there are surplus assets, do the common law rules apply (in the absence of express provision as to their allocation in the scheme).

[116]   The scheme may well provide that any surplus is to be paid to the employer, once augmentation of benefits has been made to all members. The same constraints do not apply as with ongoing pension funds, as there will be a defined fund.

[117]   *Jones v Williams* (15 March 1988, unreported) (Knox J), cited by Scott J in *Davis v Richard and Wallington Industries Ltd* [1991] 2 All ER 563; *Air Jamaica Ltd v Charlton* [1999] 1 WLR 1399.

[118]   [1991] 2 All ER 563. See also Chapter 20.

[119]   As in the decision of Foster J in *Re ABC Television Pension Scheme* [1989] PLR 21, to which he referred.

[120]   Compare *Re Gillingham Bus Disaster Fund* [1958] Ch 300 and *Re West Sussex Constabulary's Widows, Children and Benevolent (1930) Fund Trusts* [1971] Ch 1, discussed above.

to some members might exceed Inland Revenue limits. The whole of the surplus was therefore held upon trust for the employers.

The decision of Scott J in this case does not fit well with the tenor of most other decisions, which seek to draw a balance between the interests of employers and scheme members. It may also be based on a misunderstanding of the current approach to the allocation of funds on the winding up of benevolent funds.[121] The decision has been criticized by Lord Millett in *Air Jamaica Ltd v Charlton*, where the Privy Council took the view that a surplus resulted just as much from the contributions of the employees as it did from the contributions of the employer. In the *Air Jamaica* case the employees had not received all the benefits they anticipated because certain provisions of the pension trust were void for perpetuity.[122] This was therefore no bar to a resulting trust in their favour, nor was it a bar to a resulting trust that it might confer benefits on the employees that exceeded the limits allowed by tax law. So far as the employers were concerned, an express term in the pension deed that no moneys contributed by the company 'shall in any circumstances be repayable to the company' equally did not bar a resulting trust in favour of the employer, since the resulting trust arose outside or *dehors* the pension scheme. The Privy Council therefore held that the surplus was held on resulting trust for the employees and the employer in proportion to the ratio of contributions, which happened to be equal proportions.

(5) Enforcement of rights by members

Employees, former employees, and pensioners are all beneficiaries under the trust deed in a pension scheme and therefore have the rights of any beneficiary to bring actions for breach of trust or in relation to the administration of the trust. The costs of the litigation can be substantial,[123] with little direct benefit to an individual plaintiff. Plaintiffs might be assisted in bringing an action by a trade union, and there is also the possibility of the court ordering that the costs of a hearing should be borne out of the pension fund assets, whatever the outcome at trial.[124] Members of a pension scheme may also take complaints to the Pensions Ombudsman, who has statutory powers to deal with complaints concerning occupational and personal pension schemes.[125] The Pensions Ombudsman has substantial authority to resolve disputes, subject to appeal on points of law to the High Court.[126] Advice is also available through a non-departmental public body and independent non-profit organization, the Pensions Advisory

---

[121] See the subsequent decision on this matter of Warner J in *Re Bucks Constabulary Widows' and Orphans' Fund Friendly Society (No 2)* [1979] 1 WLR 936, discussed below in relation to unincorporated associations.

[122] The Pensions Schemes Act 1993, s 163 exempts qualifying approved occupational schemes from the rule against perpetuities. There was no such exemption for the pension scheme in the *Air Jamaica* case.

[123] Moffat, *Trusts Law Text and Materials* (3rd edn, 1999), p 535 provides examples.

[124] See *McDonald v Horn* [1995] 1 All ER 961.

[125] Pension Schemes Act 1993, ss 146–151; Pensions Act 1995, s 157.

[126] For an example of an appeal against a decision of the Pensions Ombudsman, see *Newham London Borough Council v Skingle* [2002] 3 All ER 287.

Service (TPAS). It should not be forgotten that in some cases a member of a pension scheme who has been given careless advice or has suffered in some other way by the negligence of a financial adviser might have a claim in negligence or other rights conferred by the Financial Services and Markets Act 2000.

(6) Regulation of pension funds

(a) The Pensions Regulator

The Pensions Act 2004 has created a new body to regulate pension funds, the Pensions Regulator.[127] The Pensions Regulator replaces the Occupational Pensions Regulatory Authority set up by the Pensions Act 1995. The key objectives of the Pensions Regulator are set out in section 5 and include the protection of the benefits of the members of personal and occupational pension schemes, reducing the risk that such pension schemes may be under-funded or misappropriated by fraud, and promoting and improving understanding of the good administration of work-based pension schemes. To this end the Pensions Regulator has the statutory power to prohibit a person from serving as a pension trustee if it is 'satisfied that he is not a fit and proper person to be a trustee of the scheme',[128] and may impose financial penalties on trustees who breach their statutory duties.[129] The Regulator can order a scheme to be wound up so as to protect the interests of the members,[130] and may issue a freezing order pending consideration of winding up if there is 'an immediate risk to the interests of members under the scheme or the assets of the scheme'.[131] The Regulator must also ensure that pension schemes are adequately funded so that they are able to meet their liabilities. Every scheme must meet the 'statutory funding objective', which requires the fund to have 'sufficient and appropriate assets to cover its technical provisions',[132] meaning 'the amount required on an actuarial calculation, to make provision for the scheme's liabilities'.[133] The trustees and managers of the fund must prepare, and from time to time review, a 'written statement of funding principles' which will state their policy for securing that the funding objective is met.[134] An actuarial valuation of the fund must be obtained at least annually,[135] and the actuary must certify whether the funding objective has been met.[136] If the funding objective has not been met, the trustees must prepare and implement a 'recovery plan' that sets out 'the steps to be taken to meet the statutory funding objective'.[137] If the trustees fail to prepare and implement a recovery plan the Regulator may require increased contributions to be made to the fund to ensure that the funding objective is met.[138] A scheme which cannot be rescued may be wound up by the Regulator.[139]

---

[127] Pensions Act 2004, s 1. [128] Ibid., s 33(1). [129] Pensions Act 1995, s 10.
[130] Ibid., s 11. [131] Pensions Act 2004, s 23. [132] Ibid., s 222(1).
[133] Ibid., s 222(2). [134] Ibid., s 223. [135] Ibid., s 224.
[136] Ibid., s 225. [137] Ibid., s 226. [138] Ibid., s 231.
[139] Ibid., s 154.

(b) The Pension Protection Fund

The Pensions Act 2004 also establishes a statutory Pension Protection Fund[140] to compensate the members of occupational pension schemes who suffer as a result of fraud,[141] or because the company to which they relate becomes insolvent and the assets of the pension fund are insufficient to meets its liabilities.[142] The Pension Protection Fund is funded by a risk-based protection levy imposed on defined benefit occupational pension scheme by the Pension Protection Fund Board.[143]

11 Clubs and societies

(1) Types of clubs and societies

English law, as has already been observed,[144] does not accord automatically an independent status to clubs, societies, or other unincorporated associations. The question that arises is how a society with no legal status as such can hold or manage property. Equity, as is so often the case in relation to the management of property, has sought to supply the answer. It is desirable first, however, to distinguish four different kinds of club or society.

(a) Proprietary clubs

A proprietary club is privately owned by an individual or company. The owner permits members to use the facilities in return for membership and other fees. A hotel with leisure facilities that permits members of the public to use the swimming pool and exercise rooms in return for an annual fee, describing those subscribing in terms such as members of the 'Park Hotel Health Club' would be a club of this kind. Since all the club assets belong to the owner, there are no special considerations for the involvement of equity.

(b) Incorporated clubs and societies

A variant of the proprietary club is where the proprietor that owns the club assets is a company and its shareholders are also the members of the club. In such a case, each member of the club may be required to acquire a share in the company owning the club assets at the time of being admitted as a member. On leaving membership, the member may then be required to surrender the share. In this way, only members of the club are shareholders and through their shareholdings, they own and control the club assets, although it is the company that will be treated as owner for such legal purposes as bringing and defending legal actions. On the dissolution of the club, any club assets will be distributed in accordance with company law.

---

[140] Ibid., s 107. [141] Ibid., s 182. [142] Ibid., ss 126, 127, and 131.
[143] Ibid., ss 173 and 174. [144] See above, p 752.

(c) Members' club

Another type of club is a members' club. The club assets are neither owned by a company nor an individual, whether associated with the membership or not. It is in this situation that the issue arises of who owns and controls the club assets. Clubs and societies belonging to this category are generally described as unincorporated associations. They are a group of individuals, bound together in some way by club rules, but without having acquired separate legal personality for the group by incorporation or in some other way such as registration as a friendly society.

(d) Societies that are not unincorporated associations

After we have considered the theory upon which unincorporated associations legally own and manage property, we shall see that there is, in fact, a further type of association or society which cannot fit within the ordinary principles created by equity, and a further set of extraordinary principles have had to be developed to cover this situation.

(2) The 'problem' of asset holding and management[145]

The absence of an independent legal personality for an unincorporated association creates only a theoretical problem of asset holding and management. Most clubs and societies get along perfectly well, raising funds by subscriptions from members and by fund-raising events such as cake sales, car boot sales, and other activities. They will find little difficulty in opening a bank or building society account. A problem arises only when someone leaves a legacy by will to an unincorporated association, and the next of kin or residuary beneficiary challenges the validity of the legacy; or when the association is being wound up and there is a dispute between the members; or in some similar situation.

The courts have been prevented by precedent and English legal tradition from saying that an unincorporated association, as such, is capable of owning property. Yet were the courts to say that the association is incapable of enjoying or managing property, they would be flying in the face of reality. The courts have therefore had to invent or construct[146] a solution to the 'problem' in order to justify the fact that in practice unincorporated associations can enjoy and manage, and receive by subscription or gift (sometimes substantial) funds and assets.

(3) The purpose trust theory

It has been seen in Chapter 13 that, except in the case of charities, English law does not permit the creation of a trust that has no beneficiaries, with the exception of a few narrowly defined categories. One such exception used to apply to gifts to

---

[145] See Warburton, *Unincorporated Associations: Law and Practice* (2nd edn, 1990), Ch 5.
[146] See Hackney, *Understanding Equity and Trusts* (1987), pp 75–82.

unincorporated associations[147] which were considered valid as gifts for the purposes of the association provided that the association was free to dispose of its assets at any time.[148] If the terms of the gift, or the rules of the association to which it was made, did not permit the association to be wound up and its assets disposed of within a period of lives in being, plus up to a further 21 years, then the disposition would be invalid for infringing the rule against perpetual trusts, otherwise known as the rule against inalienability.[149]

Judicial doubt has been expressed as to whether, even if the gift to an unincorporated association were limited to the perpetuity period, it could take effect as a gift for the purposes of the society. In *Leahy v A-G of New South Wales*,[150] Viscount Simonds expressed the firm opinion that a gift upon trust for the purposes of an unincorporated association would be invalid for want of beneficiaries. Viscount Simonds believed that the cases upholding gifts to unincorporated associations could be upheld on a different principle, namely that they were beneficial gifts to the members of the society. This analysis is considered below.

It has been suggested by Goff J in *Re Denley's Trust Deed*[151] that a gift for non-charitable purposes would not fall foul of the beneficiary principle if the purposes were directly or indirectly for the benefit of an individual or individuals. This may mean that, subject to the gift being confined to the perpetuity period, a gift for the purposes of an unincorporated association that benefits the members of that association can be valid notwithstanding Viscount Simonds' observations.

(4) Gift to members

The theory that Lord Simonds believed explained the unincorporated association cases was that the law treated a gift to an association as valid if the gift could be treated as to the present members rather than upon trust for the purposes of the society. The case before the Privy Council in *Leahy v A-G of New South Wales*[152] concerned a gift by will of a homestead and land upon trust to whatever order of Roman Catholic nuns or Christian Brothers his executors might select. The gift could not be treated as wholly charitable, because his executors were at liberty to select a purely contemplative order of nuns.[153] Could the gift be treated as a valid private trust in favour of a contemplative order of nuns if the executors wished to choose such a group? The Privy Council advised that it could not. The gift could not be valid as a gift for the purposes of such a group. It could therefore be upheld only if it were a gift to the members of the chosen order. In the opinion of the Privy Council, a gift to an unincorporated association was

---

[147] See *Re Endacott* [1960] Ch 232.

[148] *Re Drummond* [1914] 2 Ch 90; *Re Clarke* [1901] 2 Ch 110; *Re Taylor* [1940] Ch 481; *Re Price* [1943] Ch 422.

[149] *Carne v Long* (1860) 2 De GF & J 75; *Re Macaulay' Estate* [1943] Ch 435.

[150] [1959] AC 457.   [151] [1969] 1 Ch 373.   [152] [1959] AC 457.

[153] The necessary element of demonstrable public benefit for the advancement of religion was lacking see Chapter 19.

to be treated prima facie as a gift to the individual members of that association at the time of the gift so that they could together dispose of it as they thought fit. On that footing, a gift to an unincorporated association would be valid.

But that interpretation of the gift was not possible in this case, and the gift was invalid in so far as a contemplative order of nuns could be selected. The testator had not made a gift to the members of a selected order, but upon trust for the order itself; the order could be numerically very large and spread over the whole world, and although the homestead had twenty rooms and there were 730 acres of land, it was unrealistic to expect this to be shared beneficially by the members of a religious order. The Privy Council believed that:

> ...however little the testator understood the effect in law of a gift to an unincorporated body of persons by their society name, his intention was to create a trust not merely for the benefit of the existing members of the selected order but for its benefit as a continuing society and for the furtherance of its work.[154]

To give effect to this, the gift would have to include future as well as present members of the order. It would then fail for perpetuity. The statement by Viscount Simonds exposes one of the difficulties with the theory that he adopted. The court was obliged to frustrate the intentions of the testator because of the lack of an adequate theory to explain how a contemplative order of nuns could receive, hold, and manage assets. Yet there are contemplative orders with substantial property interests. The theory is clearly inadequate to explain this.

There are other problems. If a gift to a club or society is treated as a gift to the individual members beneficially, it enables them to deal with it collectively however they wish. But if they are tenants-in-common of the gift, each member could claim payment directly of his share, and if joint tenants, each member could do the same after an act of severance converting his interest into that of a tenant-in-common. Again, the theory does not explain how club or society assets should be dealt with when new members join or existing members resign.[155] An existing member with a share as tenant-in-common or joint tenant of property derived from gifts to which the *Leahy* analysis applies would continue to be entitled to it even after leaving membership of the club, unless there was an assignment of the share to the continuing members, which would require writing.[156]

---

[154] [1959] AC 457, at 486.

[155] In *Hanchett-Stamford v Attorney-General* [2009] Ch 173, Lewison J rejected any suggestion that members of unincorporated associations held under any specialized form of co-ownership: '*Megarry & Wade, The Law of Real Property*, 6th ed (2000), para 9–095 accuses the courts of having developed "a new form of property holding by unincorporated associations" in order to escape from technical difficulties of the classic models of joint tenancies and tenancies in common. I do not think that the courts have purported to do so...the "ownership" of assets by an unincorporated association must, somehow, fit into accepted structures of property ownership' (at 183 [31]).

[156] The assignment of any existing equitable interest requires a written disposition: Law of Property Act 1925, s 53(1)(c). See Chapter 7.

(5) Gift subject to the rules of the association

In *Neville Estates Ltd v Madden*,[157] Cross J put forward a refined version of the *Leahy* theory that goes some way to meet the objections. He said that a gift could be con strued as:

...a gift to the existing members not as joint tenants, but subject to their respective contractual rights and liabilities towards one another as members of the association. In such a case a member cannot sever his share. It will accrue to the other members on his death or resignation, even though such members include persons who became members after the gift took effect. If this is the effect of the gift, it will not now be open to objection on the ground of perpetuity or uncertainty unless there is something in its terms or circumstances or in the rules of the association which precludes the members at any given time from dividing the subject of the gift between them on the footing that they are solely entitled to it in equity.[158]

Cross J did not need to apply the analysis to the case before him, since he was concerned with a charitable association in relation to which it is clear that property may validly be held upon trust for the purposes of the association. The analysis was, however, adopted by Brightman J in *Re Recher's Will Trusts*,[159] the case with which this theory is most frequently associated. In that case, Brightman J held that a gift by will to the London and Provincial Anti-Vivisection Society would have been valid on this interpretation if the society had still been in existence at the date of the testatrix's death. Other cases subsequently have adopted the same analysis and it is now generally accepted as the proper way in which to explain how unincorporated associations receive gifts, hold their assets, and distribute them on the winding-up of the association.[160] As Walton J said in *Re Bucks Constabulary Fund (No 2)*:[161]

I can see no reason for thinking that this analysis is any different whether the purpose for which the members of the association associate are a social club, a sporting club, to establish a widows' and orphans' fund, to obtain a separate Parliament for Cornwall, or to further the advance of alchemy. It matters not. All the assets of the association are held in trust for its members (of course subject to the contractual claims of anybody having a valid contract with the association) save and except to the extent to which valid trusts have otherwise been declared of its property.

The theory allows the club or society to own assets by deeming them to be vested beneficially in the members, although legal title will normally be held by some trustee, such as the treasurer, who will hold the assets upon trust to deal with them in accordance with the instructions of the committee of management;[162] but it prevents members from withdrawing their share of the assets from the society by treating the rules of the society as paramount, which members have mutually agreed by contract to observe.[163]

---

[157] [1962] Ch 832.   [138] Ibid., at 849.   [159] [1972] Ch 526.
[160] See Chapter 20.   [161] [1979] 1 All ER 623.
[162] It is desirable that a gift by will to an unincorporated association should provide that the receipt of the treasurer or other officer is a sufficient discharge, for if this is not provided for by the rules of the society, the administrators of the estate should technically obtain the discharge by way of receipt from every member.
[163] As in *Clarke v Earl of Dunraven and Mount-Earl* [1897] AC 59.

In *Hanchett-Stamford v Attorney-General*,[164] Leahy J affirmed this analysis in dealing with the proprietary entitlements of the sole survivor of an unincorporated association established for the purpose of securing a ban on the use of performing animals in film. In holding that all property vested in the sole surviving member under the rules of survivorship of a joint tenancy, he held:

> It is true that this is not a joint tenancy according to the classical model; but since any collective ownership of property must be a species of joint tenancy or tenancy in common, this kind of collective ownership must, in my judgment, be a subspecies of joint tenancy, albeit taking effect subject to any contractual restrictions applicable as between members. In some cases...those contractual restrictions may be such as to exclude any possibility of a future claim. In others they may not. The cases are united in saying that on a dissolution the members of a dissolved association have a beneficial interest in its assets...I cannot see why the legal principle should be any different if the reason for the dissolution is the permanent cessation of the association's activities or the fall in its membership to below two. The same principle ought also to hold if the contractual restrictions are abrogated or varied by agreement of the members.[165]

(6) Limits to the mutual contract theory

The mutual contract theory explained in *Neville Estates Ltd v Madden* and *Re Recher's Will Trusts* can only apply, as Cross J explained, where there is nothing in the terms of the gift or in the rules of the society that will prevent the distribution of the association's assets. If there is, then even under this analysis, any gift will fail under the rule against perpetual trusts. In *Carne v Long*[166] a testator had made a gift of his house to the trustees of the Penzance Public Library, a subscription library. The rules of the library provided that it could not be broken up as long as ten members remained. The House of Lords held that, under the rules, the library was intended to be a perpetual institution, so that the gift could not be upheld. In the leading case of *Re Grant's Will Trusts*[167] a testator left property 'to the Labour Party Property Committee for the benefit of the Chertsey Headquarters of the Chertsey and Walton Constituency Labour Party'. Under the rules of the Constituency Labour Party, its constitution could not be altered without the consent of the National Labour Party, to which it was subordinate. Vinelott J held that the element of control by an outside body meant that the gift infringed the rule against perpetual trusts, since the Constituency Party was not at liberty to dissolve itself.[168] This reasoning was distinguished by Lawrence

---

[164] [2009] Ch 173.

[165] Ibid., at 188. See also *Re Horley Town Football Club* [2006] EWHC 2386 (Ch), in which Lawrence Collins J, in considering the entitlement of members to land settled on trust to provide a permanent ground for Horley FC, applied the contractual theory to find that property was settled on a bare trust for the full time members on a per capita basis, to the exclusion of associate and temporary members.

[166] (1860) 2 De G.F. & J. 75.   [167] [1980] 1 WLR 360.

[168] Compare *News Group Newspapers Ltd v Society of Graphical and Allied Trades 1982* [1986] ICR 716, CA, where, although the local branch of a trade union was subordinate to the national union, it was in theory possible for the local branch to secede from the union and dissolve itself. It may be that even where there is no provision under the rules of an association for amendment and dissolution, this would be permitted by

Collins J in *Re Horley Town Football Club*,[169] who held that the ability of a body, not itself the member of the unincorporated association, to vote at meetings of the Club was not sufficient to defeat the application of contract-holding theory. The case concerned identifying the nature of the members of Horley Town Football club's entitlement to property settled on trust for the purpose of securing a permanent football ground for the team. On the facts of the case, the relevant rules of the association had been altered in 2000, so that independently constituted clubs enjoying associate membership were to be entitled to attend the AGM and to cast one vote, and it was argued that this prevented the entitlement of any members after the rule change in the property, as the mutual contract-holding theory could not apply. The distinction Lawrence Collins J reached was a technical one. He contrasted the situation in the instant case with the seriousness of the voting rights in *Re Grants Will Trusts*, and therefore held that the members could hold the property on mutual contracts on a per capita basis:

> I do not consider that it matters that the Rules were changed in 2000 to confer a right to vote on a body which is not itself a member, namely the club of which Associate Members are members. This is far from the case of *Re Grant's Will Trusts*, where Vinelott J held that the influence of a body (not itself a member) on the rules and the destination of Club property was fatal to the argument that a gift should be analysed as one within [mutual contract theory]...[170]

The theory can only apply where there is an identifiable membership, who are capable (in theory) of being beneficial owners subject to the rules of membership. This presented a problem in *Conservative and Unionist Central Office v Burrell*.[171] The party was considered by the Court of Appeal to be a combination of a number of elements that could not be considered an unincorporated association because of the lack of a body of mutual rights and duties binding those elements together.

(7) Conditions attached to gifts to unincorporated associations

There may be something in the terms of a gift rather than in the rules of an association that makes the mutual contract theory inapplicable. The theory cannot apply if the terms of the gift exclude the possibility of the members of the association taking beneficially. This was considered by Oliver J in *Re Lipinski's Will Trusts*.[172] Harry Lipinski had left his residuary estate to an unincorporated association, the Hull Judeans (Maccabi) Association, 'in memory of my late wife to be used solely in the work of constructing new buildings for the association and/or improvements to the said buildings'. The next-of-kin disputed the validity of this gift. Their counsel

the unanimous agreement of the members: see *Universe Tankships Inc of Monrovia v International Transport Workers Federation* [1983] 1 AC 366, HL.

[169] [2006] EWHC 2386 (Ch).
[170] Ibid., at [117]. See further, in support, Luxton 'Gifts to Clubs: Contract-Holding Is Trumps' [2007] Conv 274.
[171] [1982] 1 WLR 522.   [172] [1976] Ch 235.

argued that the terms of the gift meant that the members of the association could not take beneficially, since the money had to be used for a particular purpose and because there was an intention to create a permanent endowment. Oliver J rejected the argument that the words of the gift showed an intention to create a permanent endowment: the whole of the money could be spent immediately. Nor did he think that the direction of Harry Lipinski as to how the money should be spent was binding on the association. The association was free within its rules to alter its constitution and to divide the whole of its assets between the members.[173] Oliver J therefore believed that there was nothing to prevent the application of the mutual contract theory. As an alternative, he considered that, even if the association was bound to apply the money for a particular purpose, on the authority of *Re Denley's Trust Deed* 'a trust which, though expressed as a purpose, was directly or indirectly for the benefit of an individual or individuals was valid provided that those individuals were ascertainable at any one time and the trust was not otherwise void for uncertainty'.[174]

The latter analysis might ensure that Harry Lipinski's bounty was used as he intended, although even in this case some of Oliver J's remarks suggest that the members of the association would be free as both trustees and beneficiaries of the gift to treat it as an absolute one.[175] In order to sustain the validity of Harry Lipinski's gift, Oliver J is thus permitting the association to disregard his directions. One wonders if Harry Lipinski would have turned in his grave at the suggestion that the members of the association would be free to divide the legacy among themselves, rather than building as he requested. If he intended an absolute gift to the members, why did he seek to impose a direction as to how it was to be used?

There might be situations in which the addition of a direction in a gift to an unincorporated association could not be overcome in one of the ways suggested by Oliver J in *Re Lipinski's Will Trusts*.[176] If a gift to an unincorporated association imposes in clear terms a trust to use that gift in a way which is neither directly nor indirectly for the benefit of the members, it would be rather more difficult to treat the gift as an absolute one to the members of the association subject to its rules, since the members would not also be beneficiaries. Even in this case, however, if the purposes of the trust were within the purposes of the society, it might be possible to take the view that the direction to hold upon trust was otiose and could therefore be disregarded. There is persuasive authority that in the case of benevolent associations

---

[173] He drew an analogy with *Re Bowes* [1896] 1 Ch 507, where it was held that a gift by will to be used for planting trees on the Wemmergill Estate could be used in any way which the landowner chose.

[174] This analysis of the gift appears to represent a return to the purpose trust theory that was rejected in *Leahy v A-G for New South Wales*. Some doubt about the decision in *Re Denley* was expressed by Lawrence Collins J in *Re Horley Town Football Club* [2006] EWHC 2386 (Ch), at [99] and [131] because 'there are difficulties with regard to termination of such a trust which make it an unsafe basis for decision'.

[175] By analogy with *Re Turkington* [1937] 4 All ER 501. This appears to be an application of the rule in *Saunders v Vautier* (1841) 10 LJ Ch 354.

[176] [1976] Ch 235.

established for altruistic purposes the mutual contract analysis is the one which prima facie applies to the assets of the association.[177]

(8) Associations without mutual contract status

Mention has already been made of *Conservative and Unionist Central Office v Burrell*,[178] a case that involved the tax status of the Conservative Party. If it was an unincorporated association, then the treasurer would have been liable to pay corporation tax on behalf of the association. The Court of Appeal held that the Conservative Party was not an unincorporated association because, although it was an association of individuals, it lacked a set of rules regulating its affairs and binding its members together by means of mutually enforceable rights and obligations.[179] Since the existence of such a body of rules is essential to the mutual contract analysis of property-holding by clubs and societies, the court felt obliged to offer a solution as to how the Conservative Party was legally entitled to manage its finances. In the High Court,[180] Vinelott J put forward the suggestion that a person making a donation to the party entered into a contract with the treasurer under which the latter would be in breach of contract if he failed to apply the sums received for the purposes of the party, and that the treasurer might also be under some special equitable obligation akin to that of an executor. Without commenting on these possibilities, Brightman LJ in the Court of Appeal put forward another possibility. He suggested that the contributor would confer an irrevocable mandate on the party treasurer[181] to add the donation or subscription to the general funds of the party. The contributor would have the right to prevent a misapplication of the general funds, or to have a misapplication remedied, until on ordinary accounting principles no part of the contributor's donation is represented in the general funds.

Brightman LJ acknowledged that the mandate theory could not easily support donations by will, since mandate and agency relationships can subsist only during the lifetime of the principal.[182] It would, however, be possible for a testator to authorize his personal representatives to enter into a mandate on his behalf.

The potential of the mandate theory to explain and justify gifts where there is no obvious beneficiary has yet to be fully explored or exploited. For instance, there is no

[177] *Re Bucks Constabulary Widows' and Orphans' Fund Friendly Society (No 2)* [1979] 1 All ER 623, where Walton J believed that nothing turned upon the status of the benevolent fund as a Friendly Society for the purpose of deciding how its property was held for the purpose of distribution on its dissolution.
[178] [1982] 1 WLR 522, CA.
[179] The Court of Appeal also suggested that an unincorporated association required a defined date upon which it had come into existence, and that members should be free to join or to leave at will. The necessity for these requirements may be doubted.
[180] [1980] 3 All ER 42.
[181] The effect of the mandate would be to make the treasurer the contributor's agent in relation to the funds transferred.
[182] See *Re Wilson* [1908] 1 Ch 839. There might also be difficulty where a new treasurer took office, since the relationship between principal and agent is essentially a personal one.

reason why mandate or agency theory could not equally apply to gifts to unincorporated associations with clear rules as it does to less formally constituted groups. The
mandate theory could also make a gift for purposes effective even without any ascertainable human beneficiaries.[183] The willingness of the court to put the theory forward
in the *Conservative Central Office* case, even though any such theory is unlikely to
have been in the mind of many Conservative Party members, is an indication of how
the courts will stretch legal theory to solve a problem which legal theory has itself
created.

[183] See Chapter 13.

25

Delegation by trustees

In consequence of his position, a trustee enjoys powers of control and management over the trust fund. In some situations, for example where property is subject to a discretionary trust, the trustee even enjoys the discretion to choose how the trust fund should be allocated amongst the beneficiaries. The precise duties and powers that a trustee will have depend upon the express terms of the trust deed creating the trust, or those that are implied by statute. In some circumstances it will be clear that the trustee is not the appropriate person to perform all the functions required of him as trustee, perhaps because he lacks the necessary expertise. He could obviously take advice and then carry out the function, but he may also wish to delegate the function to someone who can perform it properly for him. This chapter considers the authority, rights, and responsibilities involved in trustees delegating some or all of their trustee functions to third parties.

1 Introduction

Traditionally, equity has been reluctant to permit delegation by trustees of their powers in the absence of an express power provided in the trust instrument, but statutory powers of delegation have increasingly been available to trustees. The position for most trusts is now governed by the Trustee Act 2000, which has substantially changed the approach to delegation.

It should be noted that there are two forms of delegation. The trustees, acting together, may decide to delegate collectively a function to an agent. Alternatively, a single trustee may seek, for instance during a temporary period of absence, to assign his individual functions to a person to exercise on his behalf. This chapter looks first at collective delegation before considering individual delegation, although some elements of the discussion apply to both forms of delegation.

2 **Delegation at common law**

(1) **The general principle: no delegation of trustees' duties**

Traditionally, equity took the view that a trustee had no power to delegate his powers to an agent, either individually or collectively. As the Latin maxim expresses it: *delegatus non potest delegare*. This was emphasized by Lord Langdale MR in *Turner v Corney*,[1] which involved a trust where there was an express power of delegation. He stated that:

trustees who take on themselves the management of property for the benefit of others have no right to shift their duty on other persons; and if they employ an agent, they remain subject to responsibility toward their cestui que trust, for whom they have undertaken the duty.

The rationale for this restriction was that the settlor had placed his confidence in the trustees he had chosen to perform the trust obligations.[2] As Lord Westbury stated in *Robson v Flight*:

such trusts and powers are supposed to have been committed by the [settlor] to the trustees he appoints by reason of his personal confidence in their discretion, and it would be wrong to permit them to be exercised by [another].[3]

However, in consequence of the evolution of the law, this general principle must now be replaced by the more moderate position stated by Lord Radcliffe in *Pilkington v IRC*:[4] 'the law is not that trustees cannot delegate: it is that trustees cannot delegate unless they have authority to do so'. Thus, the central question is as to the circumstances in which trustees enjoy the authority to delegate their responsibilities.

(2) **A limited entitlement to delegate**

(a) Delegation in the ordinary course of business

During the eighteenth century the courts came to accept that, in some circumstances, delegation to an agent was required for reasons of commercial practicality. In *Learoyd v Whiteley*,[5] Lord Watson therefore stated a general principle permitting trustees to delegate their functions:

whilst trustees cannot delegate the execution of the trust, they may...avail themselves of the services of others wherever such employment is according to the usual course of business.[6]

(b) Scope of the right to delegate

The common law power of trustees to delegate within the ordinary course of business did not, however, entitle trustees to delegate all of their functions or duties. The right

---

[1] (1841) 5 Beav 515. See also *Robson v Flight* (1865) 4 De GJ & SM 608, at 613, per Lord Westbury LC; *Speight v Gaunt* (1883) 22 Ch D 727, at 756, per Lindley LJ.

[2] *Speight v Gaunt* (1883) 9 App Cas 1, at 29, per Lord Fitzgerald.

[3] (1865) 4 De GJ & SM 608, at 613.

[4] [1964] AC 612, HL. See also Jones 'Delegation by Trustees: A Reappraisal' [1959] MLR 381.

[5] (1887) 12 App Cas 727.   [6] Ibid., 734.

to delegate extended only in respect of their ministerial acts, in other words those that did not require an exercise of discretion on their part. Trustees were not permitted to delegate their discretions,[7] such as the selection of trust investments,[8] or the decision whether or not to sell[9] or lease[10] trust property. Thus, whilst trustees were able to delegate the implementation of their decisions and the routine administration of the trust, they were required to continue to take all the basic decisions themselves.

(3) Trustees' liability for the acts of their agent

The mere fact that trustees were entitled to appoint an agent, whether because such an appointment was within the ordinary course of business or for reasons of necessity, did not mean that they were free from personal liability for any loss caused by the acts of the agent. Trustees would be personally liable for breach of trust if the agent they appointed was not appropriate, or if they failed to exercise adequate supervision, on the grounds that they had acted other than as reasonably prudent men of business.

(a) Agent employed outside of the scope of his business

A trustee who had legitimately delegated to an agent was liable to the trust if he employed an agent to carry out functions that were outside of the scope of his ordinary business.[11] As Kay J said in *Fry v Tapson*:[12]

Speight v Gaunt did not lay down any new rule, but only illustrated a very old one, viz., that trustees acting according to the ordinary course of business, and employing agents as a prudent man of business would do on his own behalf are not liable for the default of an agent so employed. But an obvious limitation to that rule is that the agent must not be employed out of the ordinary scope of his business. If the trustee employs an agent to do that which is not the ordinary business of such an agent, and he performs that unusual task improperly, and loss is thereby occasioned, the trustee would not be exonerated.[13]

The trustees, who were considering investing trust funds on a mortgage, had delegated the task of selecting a valuer for the land concerned to their solicitors. The solicitors recommended a London surveyor, who did not have local knowledge of the area where the land was situated,[14] and who also had a pecuniary interest in the grant of the mortgage, as he would receive a commission of £75 if the mortgage was granted. He overvalued the property and the trustees lent £5,000, which was lost when the mortgagor became bankrupt. The trustees were held liable to replace this loss to the trust fund because it was out of the ordinary course of business of solicitors to appoint a valuer.

---

[7] *Speight v Gaunt* (1883) 9 App Cas 1. This limitation was restated in *Scott v National Trust* [1998] 2 All ER 705, at 717, per Robert Walker J.

[8] *Rowland v Witherden* (1851) 3 Mac & G 568.

[9] *Clarke v Royal Panopticon* (1857) 4 Drew 26; *Green v Whitehead* [1930] 1 Ch 38.

[10] *Robson v Flight* (1865) 4 De GJ & SM 608.

[11] See *Re Earl of Litchfield* (1737) 1 Atk 87; *Ghost v Waller* (1846) 9 Beav 497; *Rowland v Witherden* (1851) 3 Mac & G 568; *Re Gasquoine* [1894] 1 Ch 470.

[12] (1884) 28 Ch D 268.   [13] Ibid., at 280.

[14] See also *Budge v Gummow* (1872) 7 Ch App 719.

(b) Trustees' duty to supervise agents

Trustees who appointed an agent were under a duty properly to supervise his activities. The standard of care required was that of the ordinary prudence which a man uses in his own business affairs.[15] In *Rowland v Witherden*,[16] for example, trustees had committed the management of a trust fund completely to a solicitor, who had misapplied it. The Lord Chancellor held that the trustees were liable for their failure properly to supervise the solicitor's activities:

The short result of the case is, that the trustees, instead of themselves seeing to the investment of the trust fund, delegated that duty to their solicitor, who misapplied the money... The trustees were bound to satisfy themselves in some way other than by the mere assurances of their solicitor, and by payments made by him as for interest, that the money was really advanced on mortgage. But they did not even require a sight of the mortgage deed, but simply paid the money to their solicitor and implicitly relied on his integrity...[17]

Similarly, in *Fry v Tapson*[18] Kay J held that the trustees would be liable for their acceptance of the valuation 'without attempting to check it'.[19]

3 **Trustee Act 1925: A statutory right to delegate**

Prior to the Trustee Act 1925 trustees were only entitled to appoint an agent when this was reasonably necessary or was within the ordinary course of business. The Trustee Act 1925[20] considerably extended the powers of trustees to delegate functions to agents by dispensing with the requirement that the delegation be reasonably necessary or in the ordinary course of business. However, the powers were still relatively restrictive—for instance only ministerial functions could normally be delegated—and the provisions of the Act relating to the liability of trustees where they had delegated a function were obscure to the point of unintelligibility. The leading case on the liability of trustees who had delegated functions to an agent was *Re Vickery*,[21] but even though this was reported in 1931, questions remained about the interpretation both of the statutory provisions and of this case some 70 years later. Few doubted that the position under the Act was unsatisfactory, not least the students who were required to grapple in examinations with the problems created by the statutory provisions or practitioners giving advice on them.[22]

In 1982 the Law Reform Committee considered whether the scope for delegation should be widened to encompass the trustees' discretions as well as ministerial

---

[15] *Munch v Cockerell* (1840) 5 My & Cr 178; *Mendes v Guedalla* (1862) 2 John & H 259; *Speight v Gaunt* (1883) 22 Ch D 727.

[16] (1851) 3 Mac & G 568.   [17] Ibid., at 574.   [18] (1884) 28 Ch D 268.

[19] Ibid., at 282.   [20] Section 23 (now repealed).   [21] [1931]1 Ch 572.

[22] For a lively discussion and summary of the issues, see *Trustees' Powers and Duties* (1997) Law Comm Consultation Paper No 146, Part IV.

functions, but concluded that the distinction between the delegation of administrative and managerial functions and of their discretions should be maintained.[23] However, in its Consultation Paper, *Trustees' Powers and Duties*, the Law Commission suggested that the climate of opinion had changed and that trustees should be entitled to delegate the task of managing the trust property to a fund manager, who would be entitled to make investment decisions within the context of an investment policy determined by the trustees:

> We consider that there is no longer any continued justification for the existing restrictions on trustees' powers of collective delegation. The principal objection to the present law is that trustees' powers of investment and certain of their powers of management (such as the power to sell, lease or mortgage trust property) are regarded in all respects as fiduciary. As such they must be exercised by the trustees alone and are non-delegable. This position was the product of a time when the decisions which trustees had to take were both comparatively straightforward and infrequent. However, it is increasingly unrealistic, given that many of these tasks (particularly in relation to investment) now arise regularly and often require speedy professional advice and execution. We consider that the 'exigencies of business' now justify the delegation of these discretions because adherence to the present restrictions is likely to frustrate the trustees' paramount duty to act in the best interests of the trust.[24]

Judicial notice was also taken of the difficulty caused by the inability of the trustees to delegate their discretions. In *Scott v National Trust* Robert Walker J stated:

> trustees may not (except in so far as they are authorised to do so) delegate the exercise of their discretions, even to experts. This sometimes creates real difficulties, especially when lay trustees have to digest and assess expert advice on a highly technical matter (to take merely one instance, the disposal of actuarial surplus in a superannuation fund).[25]

4 The current statutory framework

The Trustee Act 2000 now provides the framework for delegation by trustees. It distinguishes between two principal situations: delegation by charity trustees, and delegation by other trustees. The position the Act takes is much more radical in the latter case than it is in the former. There is also special provision for pension scheme trustees and some other special situations. Although not so described in the Act, the power of delegation conferred on most trustees can conveniently be called the general power of delegation.

(1) General power of delegation

The approach adopted by the Trustee Act 2000 to most trustees is radically new. Instead of specifying when trustees may appoint agents, the Act confers a general power to

---

[23] Law Reform Committee, 23rd report (Cmnd 8733) para 4.3.
[24] Para 5.16.   [25] [1998] 2 All ER 705, at 717.

delegate any function other than certain non-delegable functions.[26] This is a complete reversal of the previous position.

The functions that *cannot* be delegated by trustees to an agent are:

(a) decisions concerning the distribution of the trust assets;[27]

(b) decisions as to whether costs or fees should be debited to capital or to income;[28]

(c) the appointment of new trustees;[29]

(d) any power to delegate trustee functions or to appoint a nominee or custodian.[30]

In addition, trustees of land who are obliged to consult the beneficiaries before exercising any of their powers may not delegate the obligation to carry out this consultation.[31] Should they delegate any function that involves a duty to consult, it must be on terms that enable the trustees to conduct that consultation and to give effect to the wishes of the beneficiaries.[32]

The connecting link between the matters that the trustees cannot delegate is that they are functions that lie at the heart of trusteeship and have a clear fiduciary content.[33] The functions that can be delegated include all ministerial acts (i.e. the implementation of decisions already taken), including the implementation of decisions relating to the distribution of trust funds. However, unlike the previous position, it is also possible for the trustees to delegate functions that may require the exercise of discretions or decisions. For instance, if Andrew and Brenda are appointed as trustees of a valuable collection of antiquarian books, some of which need rebinding, they could delegate to a librarian acquaintance the task of finding a craftsman with the appropriate skills. Similarly, they can delegate their investment functions, including the choice of which investments to make, although there are special rules applying to the delegation of asset management that were considered in Chapter 23.[34]

(2) Delegation by charity trustees

The Act maintains for charity trustees the position under the pre-existing law that the trustees can delegate only in prescribed situations.[35] The reason for limiting the powers of charity trustees to delegate is that there are some functions that are so

---

[26] Trustee Act 2000, s 11(1) and (2).   [27] Ibid., s 11(2)(a).

[28] Ibid., s 11(2)(b).   [29] Ibid., s 11(2)(c).   [30] Ibid., s 11(2)(d).

[31] Ibid., ss 13(3) (4) and (5).   [32] Ibid., s 13(4).

[33] See further Chapter 30 for a discussion of the fiduciary duties imposed on trustees.

[34] See pp 746 *et seq*. In essence, this requires that the trustees make the delegation in writing or evidenced in writing, and prepare a policy statement giving guidance as to how the agent must exercise their investment functions in the best interests of the trust. Liability arises if the trustees fail to keep the appointment of the agent under review, and/or fail to intervene if a problem arises, under the general duty of care in s 1 and Sch 1 of the Trustee Act 2000—see below pp 794 *et seq*.

[35] Trustee Act 2000, s 11(3).

central to the trust that it would not be appropriate for anyone other than the trustees to exercise them. For instance, the decision as to how to distribute funds by a charity established to make grants is something that should be under the immediate control of the trustees. The Explanatory Memorandum to the Act suggests that to have conferred a general authority on charity trustees to delegate, but to prohibit the delegation by charity trustees of distributive functions, or even of 'charitable functions', could unduly have narrowed the powers of charity trustees to appoint agents.

The delegable functions[36] of charity trustees are:

(a) carrying out a decision already made by the charity trustees;[37]

(b) investing the trust assets, or carrying out any function relating to investment;[38]

(c) carrying out any function relating to fund raising other than the raising of funds 'by means of profits of a trade which is an integral part of carrying out the trust's charitable purpose', the trade being something which is carried out as a primary purpose of the trust or is mainly carried out by the beneficiaries of the trust.[39]

This short list of delegable functions can be extended by delegated legislation made by the Secretary of State.[40]

The policy adopted by the Act is to allow the delegation of ministerial acts (executing decisions already taken). So far as discretions are concerned, the Act distinguishes between the functions of charity trustees relating to the generation of income to finance the charitable purposes (which can be delegated) and those relating to carrying out of the charitable purposes (which cannot be delegated). The proviso in s 13(3)(c) relating to trades which are conducted mainly by beneficiaries or which are a primary purpose of the trust is designed to prevent, say, the trustees of a school operating under a charitable trust from delegating their discretions relating to the running of the school. The trustees of a charitable housing association operating by way of trust would be in a similar position.

(3) Delegation by pension fund trustees and other special cases

The general power of delegation described above is restricted in its application to pension scheme trustees. Pension scheme trustees are not permitted to delegate investment functions under the general power,[41] or to appoint nominees or custodians,[42] although in other respects pension fund trustees may employ the general power of delegation. Another restriction on pension scheme trustees is that, in order to avoid

---

[36] Current guidance from the Charity Commission on the delegable functions by charity trustees can be found in OG86, 'Power to Employ Agents and Delegate Functions to them' (Charity Commission, 2001).

[37] Trustee Act 2000, s 11(3)(a).   [38] Ibid., s 11(3)(b).   [39] Ibid., s 11(3)(c) and s 11(4).

[40] Ibid., s 11(3)(d) and s 11(5).   [41] Ibid., s 36(5).   [42] Ibid., s 36(8).

potential conflicts of interest, they may not appoint as an agent an employer or a person who is connected with or an associate of an employer.[43]

The reason for excluding the power to delegate investment functions is that there are special provisions dealing with this in the Pensions Act 1995, which contains special safeguards to protect the rights of occupational pension scheme members. Section 34(2)(a) of the Pensions Act 1995 provides that the trustees of a pension trust scheme may delegate any decision about investments to a fund manager, who must be authorized to conduct investment business under the Financial Services and Markets Act 2000. Where such delegation occurs the trustees are required to prepare, maintain, and from time to time revise a written statement of the principles governing decisions about investments for the purpose of the scheme outlining their policy about the following matters: the kinds of investments to be held; the balance between different kinds of investments; risk; the expected return on investments; and the realization of investments.[44] Thus, the trustees are required to set the general policy that investment decisions should follow, but they can delegate the selection of specific investments to meet such a strategy to the fund manager. The trustees may also delegate decisions about investments to two or more of their number,[45] or to a fund manager operating outside the United Kingdom in respect of overseas investment business.[46]

The general power of delegation does not apply to trustees of authorized unit trusts[47] or to trustees of a common investment scheme or of a common deposit scheme made under the Charities Act 1993.[48]

(4) Who may be appointed agent

The trustees have a wide discretion as to whom they may appoint as an agent. They may even appoint one or more of the trustees as agent[49] (for instance four trustees might wish to delegate to one of their number the task of negotiating the terms of a lease for premises to be occupied by the trust), or a person who has already been appointed as a nominee or custodian.[50] The trustees may not authorize two different people to undertake the same function[51] unless they are appointed to exercise the function jointly. That is a matter of common sense. The trustees are also prohibited from appointing a beneficiary as an agent,[52] even if the beneficiary is also a trustee. This particular restriction does not apply to trusts of land, where under the Trusts of Land and Appointment of Trustees Act 1996, s 9 it is possible for trustees of land to delegate to a beneficiary of full age 'any of their functions as trustees which relate to the land'. This provision would enable trustees of land to delegate the functions relating to the management of the land to the beneficiary who is tenant for life for

---

[43] Ibid., s 36(7).   [44] Pensions Act 1995, s 35(1)–(3).   [45] Ibid., s 34(5)(a).
[46] Ibid., s 34(5)(b).   [47] Trustee Act 2000, s 37.   [48] Ibid., s 38.
[49] Ibid., s 12(1).   [50] Ibid., s 12(4).   [51] Ibid., s 12(2).
[52] Ibid., s 12(3).

the time being. It would not permit them to delegate to the beneficiary any function relating to the application of the proceeds from any dealings with the land.

(5) Terms of agency

The appointment of an agent by trustees does not have to be in writing, or evidenced in writing, except in the case of the delegation of asset management functions.[53] The terms of the appointment, including the remuneration of the agent, are at the discretion of the trustees[54] (although the amount of the remuneration must be reasonable),[55] with a number of significant caveats. The special restrictions applicable to the delegation of asset management functions are explained in Chapter 23.[56] Another limitation on the power of trustees to set their own terms is that where a function being delegated is subject to any specific duties or restrictions attached to that function, then those duties or restrictions apply to the agent as they would have done to the trustee,[57] although if that restriction relates to obtaining advice, there is no need for the agent to seek advice if he is the kind of person who could have given it to the trustees.[58] For instance, a trust might authorize the trustees to take out insurance on buildings belonging to the trust only after consulting a qualified surveyor or valuer. If the trustees delegate this function to a chartered surveyor, there is no need for that agent to consult another valuer.

There are certain terms relating to the appointment of agents which can be agreed by trustees only if 'it is reasonably necessary for them to do so'.[59] These are terms:

(a) allowing the agent to appoint a substitute;[60]

(b) exemption clauses limiting the liability of the agent;[61]

(c) terms permitting the agent to act in circumstances giving rise to a conflict of interest.[62]

No definition is given in the Act of what is meant by the words 'reasonably necessary'.[63] Trustees will therefore need to act cautiously and to be prepared to demonstrate the basis on which they considered the inclusion of one of these terms to be reasonably necessary. This might be that it was usual business practice for specialists operating in a particular field to require such a provision. The Explanatory Memorandum to the Act provides an example:

The appointment of a fund manager will often be essential to the efficient and effective management of the assets of the trust...As the standard terms of business of fund managers generally require limits on liability and the ability to act despite a conflict of interest, the

---

[53] Ibid., s 15, see above, Chapter 23   [54] Ibid., s 14.   [55] Ibid., s 32(2).
[56] See pp 746 *et seq.*   [57] Trustee Act 2000, s 13.
[58] Trustee Act 2000, s 13(2).   [59] Ibid., s 14(2).   [60] Ibid., s 14(3)(a).
[61] Ibid., s 14(3)(b).   [62] Ibid., s 14(3)(c).
[63] See Hanbury and Martin, *Modern Equity* (18th edn, 2009), p 608, where it is suggested that these amendments were introduced to permit delegation to fund managers on their standard terms of business.

ability to appoint a manager would amount to little in practice if trustees were unable to accept such terms.

(6) Liability of agent

It has already been noted that powers and functions delegated to agents are subject to the same conditions and restrictions as applied to that power or function in the hands of the trustees. The Act does not apply any special statutory duty upon agents, so their position is governed by the contractual principles of agency. In most situations these will impose a duty upon the agent to exercise due care and diligence in the exercise of the functions assigned to him. Because these duties arise in contract, the agent's principal liability is to the trustees who appointed him. An unresolved issue is whether there might be some circumstances in which the agent might be directly liable to the beneficiaries, whether under the Contracts (Rights of Third Parties) Act 1999 or under common law or equitable principles arising from interference with the rights of third parties.[64] An analogous situation is where a solicitor negligently draws up a will for a testator, with the result that a beneficiary fails to obtain the benefit intended by the testator. It is now well established that the solicitor owes a duty of care in tort to the beneficiary, which is directly enforceable, in addition to the contractual duty owed to the testator.[65] However, a difference in this situation is that the testator (or his estate), although having a cause of action, has suffered no loss, and it is only if the beneficiary can sue that the wrongdoing solicitor can be held to account. In the case of a trust, any action brought by the trustees against an agent will enlarge the trust assets and so normally benefit the beneficiaries, reducing or even eliminating one of the justifications for conceding a direct cause of action. In addition, if the beneficiaries have a direct cause of action against an agent, it could give rise to potential double jeopardy, a matter that was of concern to the Court of Appeal in *Carr-Glyn v Frearsons*[66] when dealing with an action by a beneficiary under a will. The court in that case was able to resolve the issue by holding that any action by the testatrix's estate could only be complementary to that by the beneficiary: each could sue for their own loss only.

(7) Liability of trustees

(a) Liability in deciding whether or not to delegate

The Trustee Act 2000 adopts the same approach to the liability of trustees as at common law. Essentially trustees are obliged to exercise care in both the appointment and in the supervision of agents. This is achieved by the imposition of the statutory duty of care. The Act says nothing, however, about the duty of trustees in deciding whether or

---

[64]   For a discussion of the liability of third parties who cause loss to a trust, see Chapter 31.

[65]   See *Ross v Caunters* [1980] Ch 297; *White v Jones* [1995] 2 AC 207; *Carr-Glyn v Frearsons* [1999] Ch 326.

[66]   [1999] Ch 326. See also *Worby v Rosser* [2000] PNLR 140.

not to delegate. Trustees are therefore under no *statutory* duty to exercise due care in deciding whether or not to delegate any of their functions, except in relation to decisions by trustees of land to delegate to a beneficiary.[67] They do not, for instance, need to demonstrate that it was reasonably necessary to delegate, nor that delegation was in the best interests of the beneficiaries. The fact that trustees can delegate even where there is no need to do so has been criticized, on the basis that it is unfair that the trustee should be able to delegate tasks to agents at the expense of the trust which he could easily and reasonably undertake himself. For this reason the Law Reform Committee recommended in their 23rd Report in 1982 that trustees should only be able to charge the trust for the expenses of delegation which were reasonably incurred.[68] There could also be the converse problem, where trustees unreasonably decide to undertake a specialist activity without appointing an agent. It remains to be seen whether the courts will impose a duty of care in such situations on the basis that the trustees are in breach of their general duty to act in the best interests of the beneficiaries.

(b) Duty of care in selection and appointment

Having made a decision to appoint an agent, the trustees are subject to the statutory duty to take reasonable care in selecting the agent, in determining the terms on which the agent is to act, and in preparing the investment policy statement where investment functions are delegated.[69] So, for instance, the trustees would be liable for appointing an agent to sell trust property who did not have the relevant expertise, if this is something that the trustees could reasonably have been expected to discover. Suppose that Stephanie is the trustee of a shop, which had been let to Rufus before Stephanie was appointed as a trustee. She needs to negotiate an increase in the rent under a rent review clause in the lease. Having no experience herself, she appoints a local estate agent to act on the trust's behalf. She fails to ask if he has any experience of dealing with commercial property, and his lack of experience causes a loss because the rent obtained on review is far below the level it should be. Stephanie will be liable for breach of trust.[70]

(c) Duty of care in supervision

The trustees are also under a statutory duty to keep an eye on the activities of the agent by keeping the arrangements for the delegation under review, monitoring the actions of the agent, considering whether to intervene, and taking appropriate action where necessary.[71] Imagine, for instance, that Veronica has employed an antiquarian book specialist to catalogue and value a collection of rare books that she holds on trust. Veronica allows the specialist free access to the collection for

---

[67] Trusts of Land and Appointment of Trustees Act 1996, s 9A (added by Trustee Act 2000, Sch 2).

[68] Law Reform Committee, 23rd report (Cmnd 8733), para 4.6. See Trustee Act 2000, ss 14 and 32, concerning the reasonable remuneration of agents.

[69] Trustee Act 2000, s 1 and Sch 1, para 3.

[70] The agent will be liable for breach of his contractual duty of care.

[71] Trustee Act 2000, ss 21, 22.

this purpose. When a scholar asks to see a book, it is discovered that this book and several others are missing. Veronica takes no action, and it later transpires that the specialist had yielded to temptation by stealing a number of the books, something which would not have happened if his access had been supervised. Veronica could be liable for breach of trust for failure to review the arrangements if it is considered that in the circumstances she failed to exercise reasonable care. The position in this respect is just as it was at common law. For instance, in *Re Lucking's Will Trusts*,[72] Mr Lucking was the sole trustee of a trust fund which consisted of a majority shareholding in a private company. He appointed a Lieutenant-Colonel Dewar to manage the company, who sent a blank cheque which Lucking signed. Dewar subsequently misappropriated some £16,000. Cross J held that Lucking was liable for his own breach of trust in failing to supervise the activities of Dewar after he became aware of reasons to doubt his honesty.[73] The standard of care applied was that of *Speight v Gaunt*,[74] namely that the trustee is 'bound to conduct the business of the trust in such a way as an ordinary prudent man of business would conduct a business of his own'.[75] The duty so expressed is effectively the same duty as the statutory duty of care.

(d) Liability for failure to observe restrictions

Where trustees have failed to comply with one of the restrictions on the appointment of agents, for instance where they have agreed to a clause limiting the liability of the agent where it was not reasonably necessary to do so, the trustees will be in breach of trust. There may also be limitations on the appointment of agents contained in the trust instrument that they are required to observe at pain of committing a breach of trust. The fact that the trustees have exceeded their powers in authorizing a person to act as their agent does not, however, invalidate the appointment.[76]

(e) Vicarious liability

Where the trustees have exercised due care in the appointment and supervision of an agent, however, they are not liable merely because the agent does something which causes a loss to the trust. Section 23 of the Trustee Act 2000 exempts trustees who are not personally in breach of the statutory duty of care from what may be called vicarious liability.[77] For instance, in the example above of the theft by a specialist of books from a valuable collection of which Veronica was the trustee, Veronica is not automatically liable because her agent was dishonest and stole the books. To hold her liable it

---

[72] [1968] 1 WLR 866. *Bartlett v Barclays Bank Trust Co Ltd (Nos 1 & 2)* [1980] Ch 515 provides another example.

[73] Cross J considered that the statutory protection for trustees then in force gave no indemnity to trustees who were themselves at fault.

[74] (1833) 22 Ch D 727.   [75] Ibid., at 874.   [76] Trustee Act 2000, s 24.

[77] The Law Commission in *Trustees' Powers and Duties* (1997) Law Com Consultation Paper No 146, paras 4.29–4.31 suggests that this description is not particularly helpful or accurate since there is no case in which a trustee has been held vicariously liable. However, the expression accurately conveys the concept of liability for the fault of others, even where there is no personal fault.

has to be shown that she did not exercise reasonable care in selecting the specialist (perhaps she should have taken up references from other clients) or that she did not take appropriate action in supervising him.

Section 23 may not be happily worded. It states that 'a trustee is not liable for any act or default of the agent' unless the trustee has failed to comply with the statutory duty 'when entering into the arrangements under which the person acts as agent' or 'when carrying out his duties' of keeping the appointment under review. On a literal interpretation, a trustee who fails to conduct a review at all, rather than carrying out a review badly, would not be liable. This interpretation, however, would undoubtedly be contrary to the policy of the Act, and it is likely that the courts will give the section a purposive interpretation to make trustees liable for unreasonable omissions as well as careless commissions.

(8) Liability of pension fund trustees

Trustees of a pension fund are not liable under the statutory duty of care imposed by the Trustee Act 2000 when delegating their investment functions, as they are not subject to the general powers of investment.[78] Instead, if the trustees of a pension fund exercise their right to delegate investment decisions to a fund manager their liability for the acts of their agent are specified by Pensions Act 1995, s 34(4):

The trustees are not responsible for the act or default of any fund manager in the exercise of any discretion delegated to him ... if they have taken all such steps as are reasonable to satisfy themselves or the person who made the delegation on their behalf has taken all such steps as are reasonable to satisfy himself—

(a) that the fund manager has the appropriate knowledge and experience for managing the investments in the scheme, and

(b) that he is carrying out his work competently and complying with section 36.[79]

These obligations are very similar to the statutory duty of care imposed on other trustees who have appointed an agent, although the language used is not identical. If the delegation is made to a fund manager who is not authorized to conduct investments under the Financial Services and Markets Act 2000, such a delegation is still effective to vest the powers in the manager, but the trustees will normally be liable for the defaults and acts of such a person.[80]

(9) Liability of trustees of land for the acts of their agents

Where trustees of land have delegated their functions to a beneficiary under the special power to do so in the Trusts of Land and Appointment of Trustees Act 1996[81] they

---

[78] Trustee Act 2000, s 36.

[79] See s 36 of the Pensions Act 1995, which requires the trustees to consider the need for diversification and to the suitability of investments.

[80] Pensions Act 1995, s 34(5).   [81] Trusts of Land and Appointment of Trustees Act 1996, s 9.

are subject to the statutory duty of care in respect of the decision to delegate and in the supervision of the arrangement.[82]

5 Individual delegation

In addition to the trustees acting together to appoint an agent, it is also possible for an individual trustee to delegate by appointing a substitute to exercise all or any of his powers. This was not something that was possible at common law, because of the principle *delegatus non potest delegare*. There is now statutory authority contained in Trustee Act 1925, s 25. As originally enacted, this section permitted delegation only during the absence of a trustee overseas. The section was substantially enlarged by the Powers of Attorney Act 1971 to confer a general authority to delegate trustee functions (including discretions), but only for a period not exceeding 12 months. The current provisions date from the Trustee Delegation Act 1999, which made further minor amendments. Section 25(l) of the Trustee Act 1925 (as amended) provides that:

Notwithstanding any rule of law or equity to the contrary, a trustee may, by power of attorney,[83] delegate the execution or exercise of all or any of the trusts, powers and discretions vested in him as trustee either alone or jointly with any other person or persons.

The delegation may not exceed twelve months,[84] must be by made by deed,[85] and notice must be given to the other trustees and to the person entitled to appoint new trustees.[86] The purpose of this last requirement is to enable the trustees to consider whether the trustee making the delegation should be replaced. Where a trustee delegates his functions under s 25(1), he remains strictly liable for any losses caused by the agent, as s 25(7) provides that the donor of the power of attorney 'shall be liable for the acts or defaults of the donee in the same manner as if they were the acts or defaults of the donor'. Appointment of an agent under this section is thus a far less satisfactory course of action for a trustee than appointment of an agent under the powers of collective delegation provided by the Trustee Act 2000.

A delegation by means of a power of attorney will, like all such appointments of an agent, lapse should the principal cease to have full mental capacity, but the Trustee Delegation Act 1999[87] permits the power to be executed as a lasting power, which remains valid despite the incapacity of the principal.

---

[82] Ibid., s 9A (inserted by Trustee Act 2000).   [83] See Chapter 5, p 112.

[84] Trustee Act 1925, s 25(2)(a) (as amended).

[85] This is a requirement of all powers of attorney.

[86] Trustee Act 1925, s 25(4) (as amended).

[87] Trustee Delegation Act 1999, ss 6 and 9. The Act repeals Enduring Powers of Attorney Act 1985, s 3(3), which previously permitted the delegation of trustee functions by enduring power of attorney. See now Mental Capacity Act 2005, Sch 4.

26

Appointment, removal, and retirement of trustees

Previous chapters have considered the powers of trustees. This chapter turns to consider the rules and restrictions applicable to the appointment, removal, and retirement of trustees. Together these rules demonstrate the importance attached to the office of trustee, and the ongoing nature of the rights and obligations they owe to the beneficiaries of a trust. The rules seek to ensure that proper persons are appointed as trustees, and that such persons may be removed or replaced if they are not carrying out their obligations. The way in which the duties imposed upon trustees and those dealing with trust property are enforced will be considered in the following chapters of this book.

1 The appointment of the original trustees of a trust fund

(1) Appointment by the settlor

(a) Express trusts[1]

When a trust of property is created, generally the settlor will appoint the initial trustees of the settlement. If he creates the trust inter vivos by declaring that he holds the property on trust for the beneficiaries, he will be the trustee. If he transfers the property to a third party subject to a trust, that person will become the trustee. Usually, the deed creating the trust will appoint the trustees. If the trust is testamentary, so that it is only created after his death, the testator will usually nominate the trustees in his will.

(b) Implied trusts[2]

A trust may also come into being without the express intention of the original legal owner of the property. In some instances the recipient of the legal title of property will

---

[1] See generally Chapter 7.   [2] See Chapters 9 and 10.

be deemed to hold it on trust for someone else. As has been seen, trusts which arise by implication from the circumstances or conduct of the parties are known as 'resulting' and 'constructive' trusts. The person who is deemed to hold property on either a constructive or resulting trust becomes a trustee, even though he may not be aware of the fact of the trust, provided he was aware of the circumstances affecting his conscience which gave rise to the trust.[3]

(c) Capacity to act as a trustee

Any legal person with legal capacity, whether an individual or corporation,[4] may act as a trustee. However, the Law of Property Act 1925, s 20 provides that: 'The appointment of an infant to be a trustee in relation to any settlement or trust shall be void...'. This restriction only applies in respect of express trusts, and if a minor receives property in circumstances that would create a resulting or constructive trust he will become a trustee of the property.[5] However, this will only be possible in the case of personal property, as s 1(6) of the Law of Property Act 1925 provides that an infant cannot hold a legal estate in land. If a minor is appointed trustee of an express trust there are mechanisms which will enable the minor to be removed from his position and replaced.[6] Special rules are applicable to the appointment of trustees in a charitable purpose trust. Certain persons are disqualified from acting as trustees, to try and prevent fraud and maladministration of such trusts.[7] Therefore, persons convicted of an 'offence involving dishonesty or deception',[8] 'adjudged bankrupt',[9] or that have previously been removed from the office of trustee for mismanagement may not be appointed.[10] A similar scheme operates in relation to pensions, under the Pensions Act 1993.[11]

---

[3] *Westdeutsche Landesbank Girozentrale v Islington London Borough Council* [1996] AC 669, at 705, per Lord Browne-Wilkinson. Although this judgment causes problems by suggesting that a person does not become a trustee of property until he is aware that he is intended to hold the property for the benefit of others, or of the factors which affect his conscience, it is probably better to regard Lord Browne-Wilkinson's comments as intimating that the trustee is not subject to the full fiduciary duties of trusteeship until he is aware of the existence of the trust. The trust exists irrespective of his knowledge in the sense that the property belongs in equity to the beneficiaries. However, the mere fact that there is a 'trust' in this sense does not mean that the trustee will be subject to personal liability for breach of trust if he acts in a manner inconsistent with the existence of the trust.

[4] See *A-G v St John's Hospital Bedford* (1865) 2 De GJ & Sm 621; *Re Thompson's Settlement Trust* [1905] 1 Ch 229; *Bankes v Salisbury Diocesan Council of Education Inc* [1960] Ch 631.

[5] See *Re Vinogradoff* [1935] WN 68.

[6] See, for example, Trustee Act 1925, s 36(1). See below, pp 805 *et seq.*

[7] This is enforced under s 73 of the Charities Act 2003, which makes it a criminal offence for a disqualified person to act as a trustee.

[8] Charities Act 1993, s 72(1)(a).   [9] Ibid., s 72(1)(b).

[10] Ibid., s 72(1)(d). There are three other classes of disqualified persons under s 72. It is worth noting that the Charity Commission may waive the disqualification of any person under s 72(4), except in certain matters relating to company directors detailed in the sub-section.

[11] Pensions Act 1993. Section 29 (disqualification from appointment); s 30 (criminal offence for a disqualified person to act as trustee).

(d) A trust will not fail for want of a trustee[12]

If a trust has been validly created by the transfer of the trust property to the trustees, or by the death of the testator who has specified trusts in his will, the trust will not fail if the nominated trustees disclaim the trust,[13] are incapable of acting as trustees,[14] or have predeceased the testator. Equity will not permit a trust to fail for want of a trustee and will seek to carry the settlor's intentions into effect as far as is possible. This principle operates in different ways, depending on whether the trust was created by an inter vivos or testamentary transfer.

(i) Inter vivos transfer of property to trustees upon trust

If the settlor effectively transferred the trust property to trustees by means of an inter vivos conveyance and the trustees disclaim, the trust property will revest in the settlor subject to the trusts. For example, in *Mallott v Wilson*[15] the settlor transferred land in 1866 to a trustee on trust. When the trustee executed a deed of disclaimer in 1867, it was held that the trust did not fail but that the property was automatically revested in the settlor by operation of law, and that he held the land subject to the trusts that had been validly created.[16] If the settlor has died since the trust was created, the property will revest in his personal representatives, who will again hold it subject to the trusts.

(ii) Testamentary transfers of property upon trust

If the trust was intended to be created by the testamentary transfer of the trust property to trustees and they predecease the testator, the deceased's personal representatives will hold the property on the terms of the trust that he had intended to create. For example, in *Re Willis*[17] a testatrix had left property on discretionary trusts for various charities. The trustee, who was to select how the property was to be allocated between the charities, had predeceased her. However, the court held that the trust did not fail but that the fund would vest in her executors and the court would select how the fund should be allocated.[18] Similarly, if the trustee survives the testator but then disclaims the trust, the property will also revest in the settlor's personal representatives, again subject to the trusts.

In either case the trust will not fail and the court has the power to appoint new trustees.[19] However, this principle is subject to the qualification that the trust will

---

[12] *Robson v Flight* (1865) 4 De GJ & Sm 608.

[13] A person appointed trustee can disclaim the trust at any time before he has accepted it. He may disclaim by deed, although that is not necessary and a disclaimer can be inferred from his conduct: *Stacey v Elph* (1833) 1 My & K 195; *White v Barton* (1854) 18 Beav 192; *Holder v Holder* [1968] Ch 353. Once the trust has been accepted, the trustee cannot disclaim: *Re Sharman's Will Trusts* [1942] Ch 311. A trustee cannot disclaim part of a trust, and therefore acceptance of part will amount to an acceptance of the whole: *Re Lord and Fullerton's Contract* [1896] 1 Ch 228; *Re Lister* [1926] Ch 149, CA.

[14] See *Re Armitage* [1972] Ch 438.   [15] [1903] 2 Ch 494.

[16] See also *Jones v Jones* [1874] WN 190.   [17] [1921] 1 Ch 44.

[18] See also *Moggridge v Thackwell* (1803) 7 Ves 36.

[19] *A-G v Stephens* (1834) 3 My & K 347; *Jones v Jones* (1874) 31 LT 535; *Mallott v Wilson* [1903] 2 Ch 494.

fail if the identity of the disclaiming trustee was essential to the trust. In *Re Lysaght (Decd)*[20] a testator left the residue of her estate to the Royal College of Surgeons to provide scholarships which were not to be awarded to Jews or Roman Catholics. In these circumstances the RCS, as trustee, refused to accept the trust. Buckley J held that the trust therefore failed, stating that:

If it is of the essence of a trust that the trustees selected by the settlor and no one else shall act as the trustees of it and those trustees cannot or will not undertake the office, the trust must fail.

In the circumstances, because the gift was charitable and had failed, it was applied cy-près.[21]

(e) Limitation on the number of trustees

Where the trust fund consists of personal property there is no limit on the number of trustees that the settlor may appoint when the trust is created. However, in the case of a trust of land, the property legislation of 1925 restricts the number of persons who may hold the legal title. This restriction was introduced with the objective of increasing conveyancing efficiency. The Trustee Act 1925, s 34(2)[22] provides that for settlements created after 1925:

(a) the number of trustees thereof shall not in any case exceed four, and where more than four persons are named as such trustees, the four first named (who are able and willing to act) shall alone be the trustees, and the other persons named shall not be trustees unless appointed on the occurrence of a vacancy.

(b) the number of trustees shall not be increased beyond four.[23]

It is to be noted that those who are named after the first four persons named as trustees do not automatically become trustees if a vacancy arises, and they will only become a trustee if they are properly appointed by whoever has the authority to appoint replacement trustees. In the context of land it is also worth noting that although it is possible to have a sole trustee, overreaching of equitable trust interests cannot take place unless there is a payment to two trustees of land.[24] This is the case even where there are two trustees, but one has appointed the other as his attorney so that the attorney is acting in two capacities—on his own behalf and on behalf of the trustee for whom he is attorney.[25]

---

[20] [1966] Ch 191: see also *Reeve v A-G* (1843) 3 Hare 191; *Re Lawton* [1936] 3 All ER 378.

[21] See Chapter 20.

[22] See also Law of Property Act 1925, s 34(2) (3).

[23] There are a number of very limited exceptions to the principle in s 34(3), primarily being land held on trust for 'charitable, ecclesiastical, or public purposes'.

[24] See Law of Property Act 1925, ss 2, 27. Overreaching is the process by which interests in the land are transferred to the proceeds of sale, so that, for example, a beneficial interest in land does not bind a purchaser, but is instead expressed as a proportion of the price paid to the vendor. See further Chapter 3, at pp 68 *et seq.*

[25] Trustee Delegation Act 1999, s 7. The same applies where the attorney acts for two or more trustees and is not acting with another trustee.

2 Retirement of trustees

(1) Voluntary retirement of trustees

Once a trustee has been appointed and has taken up his office, he may subsequently wish to retire from the trust. It is possible for the trust to contain an express power permitting retirement, but s 39 of the Trustee Act 1925 provides a general power which is usually adequate.

> Where a trustee is desirous of being discharged from the trust, and after his discharge there will be either a trust corporation or at least two individuals to act as trustees to perform the trust, then, if such trustee as aforesaid by deed declares that he is desirous of being discharged from the trust, and if his co-trustees and such other person, if any, as is empowered to appoint trustees, by deed consent to the discharge of the trustee, and to the vesting in the co-trustees alone of the trust property, the trustee desirous of being discharged shall be deemed to have retired from the trust, and shall, by the deed, be discharged therefrom under this Act, without any new trustee being appointed in his place.

This provision permits the retirement of a trustee without a replacement being appointed, but this will only be possible if at least two trustees, or a trust corporation remain. Where these conditions are not satisfied, a trustee may retire and be replaced under the power contained in s 36 of the Trustee Act 1925, which is considered below. Retirement will not protect a trustee from liability for breaches of trust that he committed whilst he was a trustee, and he will be liable for breaches of trust committed after his retirement if he retired to facilitate those breaches.[26]

(2) Compulsory retirement of trustees at the direction of the beneficiaries

Historically, trustees could not be forced to retire by the beneficiaries of a trust, no matter how much the beneficiaries may have wished to have them replaced, and they could only be forcibly removed on grounds of incapacity or maladministration. However, where the beneficiaries are of age and legally competent it has been seen that they can demand that the trust be brought to an end under the rule in *Saunders v Vautier*.[27] If they wish they could therefore effectively remove the trustees and replace them by settling the property on new trusts. This process may be both costly (including potential liability to additional tax) and inefficient, as it requires a transfer of the legal title to the trust property from the original trustees to the beneficiaries, and then from the beneficiaries to the new trustees. Consequently, the Trusts of Land and Appointment of Trustees Act 1996 introduced a new statutory power enabling the beneficiaries of a trust to require a trustee to retire in circumstances where they could have taken advantage of the rule in

---

[26] See Chapter 29, at p 879.   [27] (1841) 4 Beav 115.

Saunders v Vautier to achieve the same result. By s 19(2)(a) of the Act, the beneficiaries of a trust may give a written direction to a trustee or trustees to retire from the trust. This right is only exercisable if there is no person nominated for the purpose of appointing new trustees by the trust instrument,[28] and if the beneficiaries of the trust are of full age and capacity and, taken together, are absolutely entitled to the property subject to the trust.[29] This means that the right to direct retirement will not be available where there are infant beneficiaries of the trust, which will often be the case in respect of a discretionary trust. Where a trustee has been directed to retire by the beneficiaries, s 19(3) provides that he will be required to make a deed declaring his retirement and shall be deemed to have retired and be discharged from the trust. However, he will only be required to retire if three conditions are satisfied:

(i)   reasonable arrangements have been made for the protection of any rights he has in connection with the trust;[30]

(ii)   after he has retired there will be either a trust corporation or at least two persons to act as trustees to perform the trust;[31] and

(iii) either another person is to be appointed a new trustee on his retirement, or the continuing trustees consent by deed to his retirement.[32]

The power to compulsorily retire trustees under s 19 thus enables the beneficiaries to defeat the intentions of the settlor, who may have intended that a specific individual act as trustee. This ability to undermine the settlor's express intentions is the inevitable consequence of the rule in *Saunders v Vautier*. A settlor can, however, expressly exclude the right to compulsorily retire trustees under s 19,[33] and in reality a standard exclusion may be utilized in express trusts so that the statutory provision will only be applicable in respect of resulting and constructive trusts, especially of the family home.[34] Where trusts have come into existence before the commencement of the Act, the power to direct retirement can be excluded by the execution of a deed to that effect by the settlor, or surviving settlors, who created the trust.[35] If such a deed is executed, it is irrevocable in effect.[36]

---

[28] S 19(1)(a).

[29] Trusts of Land and Appointment of Trustees Act 1996, s 19(1)(b).

[30] S 19(3)(b). This would include, for example, unpaid fees and expenses.

[31] S 19(3)(c). This is consistent with s 39 of the Trustee Act 1925.

[32] S 19(3)(d). In the event that the co-trustees refuse to consent to the retirement directed by the beneficiaries, the only means of removal of the trustee will be by order of the court exercising its jurisdiction under s 41 of the Trustee Act 1925.

[33] S 21(5).

[34] Although, even here, the provision cannot be exercised if one of the beneficiaries (who may also be the trustee) does not agree.

[35] Trusts of Land and Appointment of Trustees Act 1996, s 21(6).

[36] S 21(7).

3 The appointment of replacement or additional trustees

(1) The need for new appointments

It is inevitable that in the lifetime of many trusts circumstances may arise where it is necessary to appoint new trustees.

(a) Appointment of additional trustees

It may be necessary or beneficial for the number of original trustees appointed by the settlor to be increased by the appointment of additional trustees. This may be because of the workload that the trustees are experiencing, or for simple reasons of convenience. In the case of land, if the settlor has created a trust for sale with a single trustee it may be necessary to appoint at least one additional trustee (or a trust corporation) so that, if the land is sold, the purchaser can gain the benefit of overreaching.[37]

(b) Appointment of replacement trustees

It may be necessary to appoint new trustees as replacements for those who are no longer able to act as such, for example because of death or mental incapacity, or who have retired from the trust.

(c) Removal of trustees

In some circumstances it may be necessary to remove a trustee from the trust against his will, for example if he proves to be incompetent or is frustrating the efficient exercise of the trust.

(2) Power to appoint new trustees

Having recognized that there may be a need in some circumstances to appoint new trustees, the central question is how such appointments can be made: ie who has the power to select and appoint new trustees, and in what circumstances can such powers be exercised?

(a) Express powers

In keeping with the fundamental philosophy that, as far as possible the settlor's intentions will be carried out, the trust deed may contain an express power authorizing the appointment of new trustees. Such a power will be strictly construed.[38] There is some question whether the donee of such a power can appoint

---

[37] The Trustee Delegation Act 1999, s 7 makes it clear that the 'two trustee' rule is not satisfied if all of the trustees are represented by a single person acting under a power of attorney, or where the same single person is both a trustee and acts under a power of attorney for the other trustees.

[38] *Stones v Rowton* (1853) 17 Beav 308; *Re Norris* (1884) 27 Ch D 333.

himself as trustee of the settlement. In *Re Skeats' Settlement*[39] a trust contained an express power granting certain persons the power to appoint 'any other person' to be trustee. They exercised the power to appoint themselves. Kay J held that this was invalid since the power was fiduciary in character and it would thus be 'extremely improper for a person who has a power to appoint or select new trustees to appoint or select himself . . .'.[40] This principle was followed by Kekewich J in *Re Newen*,[41] but was doubted by Buckley J in *Montefiore v Guedalla*,[42] where he stated that:

> On the cases, I am clearly of opinion that it has not been laid down that the appointors are outside the class who can be appointed, although it has been said, and it is a very salutary rule, than an appointor ought not, save in exceptional circumstances, to appoint himself.[43]

However, in *Re Sampson*[44] Kekewich J considered that the decision in *Montefiore v Guedalla*[45] might require future reconsideration.[46]

Today, express powers are of little significance because of the statutory powers that are available to provide for the appointment of new trustees. These statutory powers were themselves modelled on the express powers which had previously been included in trust deeds. If there is an express power providing for the removal of trustees from the trust, s 36(2) of the Trustee Act 1925 applies, which provides:

> Where a trustee has been removed under a power contained in the instrument creating the trust, a new trustee or trustees may be appointed in the place of the trustee who is removed, as if he were dead, or, in the case of a corporation, as if the corporation desired to be discharged from the trust, and the provisions of this section shall apply accordingly, but subject to the restriction imposed by this act on the number of trustees.

(b) Statutory powers

There are three important statutory provisions granting the power of appointment of new trustees.

(i) Trustee Act 1925, s 36

This section provides for the appointment of new trustees in a wide range of circumstances by persons either nominated in the trust deed by the settlor, or, in the absence of any such nomination, by the persons provided for by the section. The intervention of the court is not required for appointments made under the power contained in s 36.

(ii) Trustee Act 1925, s 41

This section grants the court a wide power to appoint new trustees either in addition to or in substitution for present trustees. The power is discretionary and may be exercised whenever the court considers it is expedient.

---

[39] (1889) 42 Ch D 522.　　[40] Ibid, at 527.　　[41] [1894] 2 Ch 297.
[42] [1903] 2 Ch 723.　　[43] Ibid., at 725.　　[44] [1906] 1 Ch 435.
[45] [1903] 2 Ch 723.
[46] *Re Sampson* concerned a statutory rather than an express power to appoint new trustees.

(iii) Trusts of Land and Appointment of Trustees Act 1996, ss 19 and 20

It has already been noted how the Trusts of Land and Appointment of Trustees Act 1996 has introduced a new statutory right enabling the beneficiaries of a trust to direct the compulsory retirement of a trustee. Section 19(2)(b) also grants the beneficiaries the right to direct the appointment of new trustees, and s 20 provides for the appointment of a replacement trustee where a trustee is mentally incapable of acting and there is no person willing and able to appoint a replacement under s 36(1) of the Trustee Act 1925.

4 Trustee Act 1925, s 36

(1) Appointing substitute trustees

(a) The power to appoint substitute trustees

The Trustee Act 1925, s 36(1) provides:

Where a trustee, either original or substituted, and whether appointed by a court or otherwise, is dead, or remains out of the United Kingdom for more than twelve months, or desires to be discharged from all or any of the trusts or powers reposed in or conferred on him, or refuses or is unfit to act therein, or is incapable of acting therein, or is an infant, then subject to the restrictions imposed by this Act on the number of trustees—

  (a) the person or persons nominated for the purpose of appointing new trustees by the instrument, if any, creating the trust; or

  (b) if there is no such person, or no such person able and willing to act, then the surviving or continuing trustees or trustee for the time being, or the personal representatives of the last surviving or continuing trustee;

may, by writing, appoint one or more other person (whether or not being the persons exercising the power) to be a trustee or trustees in the place of the trustee so deceased, remaining out of the United Kingdom, desiring to be discharged from the trust, and the provisions of this section shall apply accordingly, but subject to the restrictions imposed by this Act on the number of trustees.

(b) Circumstances in which the power may be exercised

Section 36 provides that the power to appoint new trustees may be exercised in seven well-defined circumstances, which cover many of the most likely situations in which new trustees would need to be appointed. It is to be noted that s 36 applies only to trustees and not to personal representatives.[47] An improper appointment not made in compliance with the statutory powers is invalid, so that

---

[47] See *Re Cockburn's Will Trust* [1957] Ch 438; *Re King's Will Trusts* [1964] Ch 542. However, the court has power to appoint substituted person representative under the Administration of Justice Act 1985, s 50.

no substitution takes place and the original trustees remain in office (or their personal representatives).[48]

(i) The trustee is dead

By s 36(8) the power of appointment under s 36(1) is also exercisable where a person who is nominated trustee in a will predeceases the testator. There is some authority[49] that the sections will also be operative in the unlikely event that the settlor attempts an inter vivos transfer to a trustee who is already dead. However, this will only be the case if the dead trustee was one of a number of others who were alive, since an attempt by the settlor to transfer property inter vivos to trustees who are all dead will not create a trust in the first place.

(ii) The trustee remains out of the United Kingdom for more than twelve months

The rationale for this provision was that the limited and slow means of communication and travel would prevent a trustee who was absent from the country from being able to properly carry out the trust business. It is possible under s 25 of the Trustee Act 1925 for a trustee to delegate his managerial functions and discretions by a power of attorney for up to twelve months, for instance, during absence abroad.[50] Today, with such instant means of communication as email, telephone and fax, and with the availability of rapid air transport, it is questionable whether the absence of a trustee abroad inevitably prevents him from conducting the business of the trust. The absence from the UK must be for a continuous period of twelve months. In *Re Walker*[51] Mr Walker was co-trustee of a settlement with Mrs Walker. He was out of the UK for more than a year from spring 1899, with the exception of one week in London in November 1899. In these circumstances Farwell J held that Mrs Walker could not exercise the power of appointment under what is now s 36(1).[52] The power enables a trustee to be removed against his will, as was held by Danckwerts J in *Re Stoneham's Settlement Trusts*.[53]

(iii) The trustee desires to be discharged from all or any of the trusts or powers reposed in or conferred on him

This provision means that a trustee can be discharged from only part of his trust responsibility, which prior to the Act was only possible through the court.[54]

(iv) The trustee refuses to act

This clearly covers the case where a trustee disclaims the trust.

---

[48] See *Jasmine Trustees Ltd v Wells & Hind (A Firm)* [2008] Ch 194, at 216 [52] per Mann J.
[49] See *Re Hadley* (1851) 5 De G & Sm 67.   [50] See Chapter 25.
[51] [1901] 1 Ch 259.   [52] Previously, Trustee Act 1893, s 10.
[53] [1953] Ch 59.
[54] See *Savile v Couper* (1887) 36 Ch D 520; *Re Moss's Trusts* (1888) 37 Ch D 513.

(v) The trustee is unfit or incapable

This refers to any personal incapacity that would prevent the trustee acting as such. It clearly includes mental incapacity, so in *Re East*[55] the court held that there was a valid exercise of a power to appoint new trustees where one of three co-trustees became of unsound mind.[56] Similarly, in *Re Lemann's Trust*[57] age and infirmity were considered sufficient 'incapacity'. A trustee will also be considered unfit to act if he is bankrupt, as was held in *Re Wheeler and De Rochow*.[58] It seems that a trustee is not unfit to act merely through absence abroad.[59] However, in *Mesnard v Welford*[60] a trustee who had been absent in New York for twenty years was held to be incapable of acting for the purposes of an express power of appointment.[61] The cases holding that a trustee resident overseas may be incapable of acting all date from the nineteenth century, and improvements in communications and in the speed of international travel cast their current reliability into doubt.[62] In the case of the dissolution of a corporate trustee, s 36(3) provides:

> Where a corporation being a trustee is or has been dissolved . . . then, for the purposes of this section . . . the corporation shall be deemed to be and to have been from the date of the dissolution incapable of acting in the trusts or powers reposed in or conferred on the corporation.

(vi) The trustee is an infant

Such an eventuality is only likely to arise in respect of a constructive or resulting trust of personal property, since in other cases the appointment of an infant as trustee is void.[63]

(vii) The trustee has been removed under an express power

If the trust instrument includes an express provision for the removal of trustees, any trustee who is so removed may be replaced under the powers of appointment of s 36 as if he were a trustee who had died.[64]

(c) Persons who may exercise the power to appoint new trustees

In addition to defining the circumstances in which new trustees may be appointed, s 36 of the Trustee Act also specifies who is to make any such appointments. The

---

[55] (1873) 8 Ch App 735.

[56] It is possible for a trustee to execute a lasting power of attorney before becoming of unsound mind that has the effect of delegating to an agent his functions as a trustee of land and which operates in the event of his incapacity: Trustee Delegation Act 1999, s 1. See generally Mental Capacity Act 2005, ss 9–14 for the distinction between enduring powers of attorney (which have been repealed) and lasting powers of attorney (which must be registered to be effective).

[57] (1883) 22 Ch D 633.

[58] [1896] 1 Ch 315. See also *Re Roche* (1842) 1 Con & Law 306; *Re Hopkins* (1881) 19 Ch D 61.

[59] See *Withington v Withington* (1848) 16 Sim 104; *O'Reilly v Alderson* (1849) 8 Hare 101; *Re Harrison's Trusts* (1852) 22 LJ Ch 69; *Re Bignold's Settlement Trusts* (1872) 7 Ch App 223.

[60] (1853) 1 Sm & G 426.

[61] See also *Re Lemann's Trusts* (1883) 22 Ch D 633, where Chitty J gave the residence of a trustee abroad as one instance of incapacity.

[62] See the remarks by Millett J in *Richard v Mackay* (1997) 11 *Trust Law International* 22.

[63] Law of Property Act 1925, s 20.   [64] S 36(2).

section adopts an order of priority as to who can exercise the power. It emphasizes the settlor's intentions by giving priority to any person nominated for the purpose in the trust instrument, but provides alternative mechanisms for appointment if there is no such person nominated.

(i) The person or persons nominated by the trust instrument

By s 36(1)(a), if the settlor has nominated a person or persons in the instrument creating the trust to exercise the power of appointment of new trustees, then it is they who can exercise the power to appoint under s 36(1). Such persons only fall within s 36(1) if they have a general power to make appointments[65] and not a power which is only granted in specific circumstances. In *Re Sichel's Settlements*[66] the nominated persons were given the power to appoint new trustees in the event of the present trustees becoming 'incapable to act'. Neville J held, following the decision of Kekewick J in *Re Wheeler and De Rochow*,[67] that they were not the appropriate persons to appoint a new trustee where one of the existing trustees was 'unfit' to act. Where several persons are jointly nominated, in the absence of a contrary intention[68] the survivor or survivors cannot exercise the power.[69] In that event, the power to appoint will be exercisable by those indicted in s 36(1). The same result will follow if the nominated persons are incapable of acting, for example because of disagreement.[70]

(ii) The surviving or continuing trustee or trustees

If there are no persons nominated in the trust instrument, or if such persons are unable or unwilling to act, s 36(1)(b) provides that it is the 'surviving or continuing trustee or trustees for the time being' who may appoint new trustees. It has been held that the last surviving or continuing trustee includes a sole trustee.[71] The central difficulty concerns the questions as to who are the 'continuing trustees' where it is intended to remove a trustee who is alive and capable, since it is a

---

65   *Re Walker and Hughes' Contract* (1883) 24 Ch D 698.
66   [1916] 1 Ch 358.
67   [1896] 1 Ch 315. However, he did express his disagreement with the decision.
68   *Re Harding* [1923] 1 Ch 182.
69   This is subject to the exceptions that the survivors can exercise the power if the property is vested in them (*Re Bacon* [1907] 1 Ch 475), they hold the power as trustees (Trustee Act 1925, s 18(1)), or the power was granted to a class of which two or more members survive (*Jefferys v Marshall* (1870) 19 WR 94).
70   *Re Sheppard's Settlement Trust* [1888] WN 234. Alternatively, because they cannot be found: *Cradock v Witham* [1895] WN 75.
71   *Re Shafto's Trusts* (1885) 29 Ch D 247. *Adam and Company International Trustees Ltd v Theodore Goddard (a firm)* [2000] WTLR 349; Barlow 'The Appointment of Trustees: A Disappointing Decision' [2003] Conv 15. See also *Jasmine Trustees Ltd v Wells & Hind (A Firm)* [2008] Ch 194, where it was held by Mann J that, in a trust subject to the older version of the wording of s 37(1)(c) existing before 1 January 1997, a company was not to be classed as a trustee, as it was not an 'individual' as required under the old wording of s 37(1)(c). The statutory provision now talks of 'persons' (following amendment by the Trust of Land and Appointment of Trustees Act 1996, Sch 3) and a company is a legal person.

basic principle that trustees must act with unanimity. It would prove impossible to remove a trustee against his will if he was to be regarded as a 'continuing trustee' and therefore had to be party to the decision to remove and replace him. The position is complicated by s 36(8), which provides that the continuing trustees include 'a refusing or retiring trustee, if willing to act in the execution of the provisions of this section'. This has the effect that a retiring sole trustee or retiring group of trustees are able to appoint their successors, although s 37(1)(c) means that two retiring trustees cannot be replaced by one, not being a trust corporation.[72] Whether a trustee should be regarded as 'refusing or retiring' was considered by Danckwerts J in *Re Stoneham's Settlement Trusts*.[73] He took the general view that a trustee who is being removed from the trust is not retiring and therefore does not fall within the scope of s 36(8):

> It seems to me, in the absence of any authority which binds me to decide otherwise, that a person who is compulsorily removed from a trust is not a person who retires and is not a retiring trustee.

Similarly, following *Re Coates to Parsons*,[74] he held that a trustee who has been abroad for more than twelve months was not a 'refusing or retiring trustee' within the meaning of s 38, and that therefore he was not a 'continuing trustee' and his concurrence was not needed for the appointment of a new trustee.

(iii) The personal representatives of the last surviving or continuing trustee

As a last resort, if there are no nominated persons who can make new appointments and there are no 'surviving or continuing' trustees, the statute pragmatically provides in s 36(1)(a) that the 'personal representatives of the last surviving or continuing trustee' have the power to appoint new trustees.

(d) No one is able to appoint a substitute trustee

In some extreme circumstances, even where there is a jurisdiction to appoint a substitute trustee under s 36 there will be no one who is capable of exercising it. Such a problem is especially likely where property is held by sole trustee who has become mentally incapable. Since a sole incapable trustee is a surviving trustee, he alone is entitled to exercise the power to appoint a substitute for himself, and yet is incapable of so doing. In such circumstances where the power to appoint under s 36 is moribund, the court may exercise its jurisdiction to appoint new trustees under s 41. The Trusts of Land and Appointment of Trustees Act 1996 has conferred upon the beneficiaries of the trust the right to direct the appointment of a substitute. This jurisdiction is examined later in this chapter.

---

[72] *Adam and Company International Trustees Ltd v Theodore Goddard (a firm)* [2000] WTLR 349; Barlow 'The Appointment of Trustees: A Disappointing Decision' [2003] Conv 15.
[73] [1953] Ch 59.   [74] (1886) 34 Ch D 370.

(2) **Appointing additional trustees**

(a) The power to appoint additional trustees

The Trustee Act 1925, s 36(6)[75] also provides for the appointment of additional trustees:

Where, in the case of any trust, there are not more than three trustees—

(a) the person or persons nominated for the purpose of appointing new trustees by the instrument, if any, creating the trust; or

(b) if there is no such person, or no such person able and willing to act, then the trustee or trustees for the time being;

may, by writing appoint another person or other persons to be an additional trustee or additional trustees, but it shall not be obligatory to appoint any additional trustees, unless the instrument, if any creating the trust, or any statutory enactment provides to the contrary, nor shall the number of trustees be increased beyond four by virtue of any such appointment.

(b) Circumstances in which the power may be exercised

Section 36(6) gives the trustee of a trust the option to increase the number of trustees to a maximum of four through the appointment of additional trustees. This power is subject to any express terms in the trust or by statute requiring the number of trustees to be increased.

(c) Persons who may appoint additional trustees

The mechanisms by which such appointments may be made are almost identical to those adopted under s 36(1).

(i) The person or persons nominated by the trust instrument

Priority is given to the settlor's express intention in the form of persons nominated for the purpose of appointing trustees in the trust instrument. Providing they are willing and able to act, they alone can exercise the power.

(ii) The trustee or trustees for the time being

In the absence of any nominated persons the other trustees, whether a sole trustee or co-trustees, may appoint additional trustees. Obviously, if there are no trustees remaining because of death, the provisions of s 36(1) will operate. A limited power is available to the donee of an unregistered enduring power of attorney[76] or a registered lasting[77] power of attorney to exercise the functions of the trustees to appoint a new trustee if to do so is necessary to ensure that there are two trustees to receive capital money arising from a disposition of land.[78]

---

[75] As amended by Trusts of Land and Appointment of Trustees Act 1996, Sch 3, para 3(11).

[76] It is no longer possible to create enduring powers of attorney, although existing unregistered powers may still be used, if registered—Mental Capacity Act 2005, Schedule 4, Part 1 para 1.

[77] Added by the Mental Capacity Act 2005.

[78] Trustee Act 1925, s 36(6A)–(6D), as inserted by the Trustee Delegation Act 1999.

(3) Making appointments under s 36

(a) Persons who may be appointed

In the case of substitute appointments, under s 36(1) the persons who may exercise the power can appoint whoever they desire as trustees and it is specifically provided that they may appoint themselves if they wish. However, due to a slight difference in drafting, persons who are nominated to appoint additional trustees are not specifically permitted to appoint themselves under s 36(6), and in *Re Power's Settlement*[79] it has been held that they cannot appoint themselves. Where there are already two trustees, it is not possible for them to retire and to be replaced by a single trustee, unless that trustee is a trust corporation recognized under English law.[80]

(b) Relevance of the beneficiaries' wishes

The person (or persons) entitled to appoint new trustees are under no obligation to consult the beneficiaries of the trust and ascertain their wishes as to who should be appointed. In *Re Brockbank*[81] Vaisey J held that the person entitled to appoint under s 36 could not be compelled to do what the beneficiaries wanted, as the right to appoint belonged solely to those whom it was given by the statute and the court was unwilling to interfere with its exercise.[82] The only means by which the beneficiaries could compel the appointment of the persons they wanted to be trustees would be to put an end to the trust[83] under the rule in *Saunders v Vautier* or to make a direction under the Trusts of Land and Appointment of Trustees Act 1996.[84] The power to make a direction under the 1996 Act does not apply if the person entitled to appoint new trustees was nominated by the trust instrument.

(c) Formalities of appointment

The appointment of new trustees, whether substitute trustees under s 36(1) or additional trustees under s 36(6), must be made in writing. However, an appointment made by deed will have the effect of vesting the trust property in the new trustees under s 40 of the Trustee Act 1925, subject to registration of the trustees as legal owners in the case of land and shares.

(d) Effect of appointment

Section 36(7) provides that:

Every new trustee appointed under this section as well before as after all the trust property becomes by law, or by assurance, or otherwise vested in him, shall have the same powers,

---

[79] [1951] Ch 1074, CA.
[80] See *Adam and Co International Trustees Ltd v Theodore Goddard* (2000) ITELR 634.
[81] [1948] Ch 206.
[82] See also *Re Gadd* (1883) 23 Ch D 134; *Re Higginbottom* [1892] 3 Ch 132.
[83] [1948] Ch 206, at 210.
[84] Section 19. This jurisdiction is discussed later in this chapter.

authorities and discretions, and may in all respects act as if he had been originally appointed a trustee by the instrument, if any, creating the trust.

This provision applies equally to the appointment of additional or substitute trustees.

5 Trustee Act 1925, s 41

(1) The power of the court to appoint new trustees

Section 41(1) of the Trustee Act 1925 provides:

The court may, whenever it is expedient to appoint a new trustee or new trustees, and if it is found inexpedient difficult or impracticable so to do without the assistance of the court, make an order appointing a new trustee or new trustees either in substitution for or in addition to any existing trustee or trustees, or although there is no existing trustee.

(2) Scope of the power under s 41

This provision gives the court a very wide discretion to appoint trustees, either in substitution for, or in addition to, existing trustees. However, a number of features should be noted.

(a) Relation to other powers of appointment of trustees

Appointments will generally only be made under the jurisdiction of s 41 where they cannot be made through the exercise of an express power within the trust instrument, nor under the statutory power granted by s 36 of the Trustee Act 1925.[85]

(b) 'Whenever it is expedient to appoint... and if it is found inexpedient difficult or impractical so to do without the assistance of the court'

This double-limbed test sets down the circumstances in which the court may exercise the power of appointment. It must be both expedient for a substitute or additional trustee to be appointed and in some sense, because of the circumstances, the assistance of the court must be necessary. Section 41(1) itself specifies some such circumstances where the jurisdiction may need to be exercised:

In particular... the court may make an order appointing a new trustee in substitution for a trustee who lacks capacity[86] to exercise his functions as a trustee or is a bankrupt, or is a corporation which is in liquidation or has been dissolved.

A number of illustrations can be given of other circumstances in which the power has been exercised. In *Re Smirthwaite's Trust*[87] the court exercised its statutory

---

[85] *Re Soulby's Trusts* (1873) 21 WR 256; *Re Gibbon's Trusts* (1882) 45 LT 756; *Re Sutton* [1885] WN 122.
[86] The words were substituted for the original wording of the statute by the Mental Capacity Act 2005.
[87] (1871) LR 11 Eq 251.

power[88] to appoint new trustees when all of the trustees named in the settlor's will had predeceased him. In *Re May's Will Trust*[89] one of three trustees of a will was in Belgium during the time of the German invasion and had not escaped. It was held that there was no evidence that she was 'incapable of acting' within the meaning of s 36(1) so that she could not be replaced by the continuing trustees, but the court appointed a new trustee under s 41. The court may also act where an express power or the power under s 36 is incapable of being exercised, for example if the donee of an express power is an infant.[90] In *Re Rendell's Trusts*[91] the court exercised its power to appoint a trustee where one of the surviving trustees was opposed to the appointment.

(c) Removal of trustees against their will

It is clear that s 41 permits the court to remove trustees from the trust against their will. In *Re Henderson* Bennet J stated:

I do not think that it is open to doubt that on the language of the sub-section the court has juris-diction to displace a trustee against his will and to appoint a new trustee in substitution for him. Take the case of a trustee who is a convicted felon or a bankrupt whom the beneficiaries desire to have replaced by a new trustee. On the language of the sub-section, in my judgement, the court has a discretion, which it can exercise, if it regards it as expedient so to do, by appointing a new trustee in place of the trustee who has been convicted of felony, or who is a bankrupt... I do not doubt that the section gives the court jurisdiction in a proper case to appoint new trustees in place of and against the will of an existing trustee. Before exercising that jurisdiction the court must be satisfied that it is expedient to make such an appointment.[92]

He held that a trustee who had refused to retire in place of the Public Trustee should be removed against her will because she had previously agreed to retire but had changed her mind for no reason of substance. This was followed by Roxburgh J in *Re Solicitor, A*[93] where a bankrupt solicitor was replaced by the court acting under s 41.

One limitation to the principle that the court can remove a trustee against his will under s 41 is that there must be no dispute as to the facts. This was emphasized by Cotton LJ in *Re Combs*[94] and accepted by Bennet J in *Re Henderson*.[95]

(3) Exercise of the court's discretion

The court's power to appoint under s 41 is discretionary, and it must be satisfied that any appointments are 'expedient'. The question whether an appointment was 'expedient' was raised in *Re Weston's Settlement*,[96] where there was an attempt to move a trust from England to Jersey for tax reasons, and to replace the English trustees with trustees in Jersey. Applications were made under the Variation of Trusts Act 1958[97] in favour of the infant beneficiaries of the trust and under s 41 for the appointment of

---

88 Under the Trustee Act 1850.   89 [1941] Ch 109.
90 *Re Parson's* [1940] Ch 973.   91 (1915) 139 LT Jo 249.
92 [1940] Ch 764, at 767.   93 [1952] Ch 328.   94 (1884) 51 LT 45.
95 [1940] Ch 764. See also *Popoff v Actus Management Ltd* [1985] 5 WWR 660.
96 [1969] 1 Ch 223.   97 See Chapter 18.

new trustees. The court refused to exercise its discretion under either of these provisions. As to s 41, Lord Denning MR said:

with the appointment of new trustees the Trustee Act 1925 gives no guide. It simply says that the court may appoint new trustees 'whenever it is expedient'. There being no guidance in the statute, it remains for the court to do the best it can.[98]

Several reasons for the refusal of the court to appoint appear from the judgment. First, the proposed move of the trust to Jersey was solely for reasons of tax avoidance. Second, there was a relatively slight connection between the beneficiaries and Jersey. They had lived there for only a short time, and there was a high probability that they would move after the trust had been transferred. As Harman LJ said, they 'cannot be said to have proved that they truly intend to make Jersey their home'.[99] Finally, the court referred to the inadequacy of the law in Jersey for dealing with trusts. In these circumstances the court refused to appoint trustees, and instead held that 'these are English settlements and they should . . . remain so unless some good reason connected with the trusts themselves can be put forward'.[100]

In contrast, it should be noted that in *Re Windeatt's Will Trusts*[101] the court was willing to approve a scheme for the variation of a trust, including the appointment of new trustees in Jersey, where the family had lived there for some nineteen years. In such circumstances it seems likely that the court would have equally found it 'expedient' to appoint new trustees under s 41 if that had been necessary. Given the significant improvement in communications, and the increased recognition of trusts overseas, it is quite possible that the courts would now be more willing to entertain the appointment of trustees overseas than they have in the past where there is some real overseas connection or other justification.[102] In *Richard v The Hon A.B. Mackay*,[103] Millett J suggested that where trustees were exercising their own discretion to appoint an overseas trustee and seek merely approval from the court, the court should only need to be satisfied that the decision was 'not so inappropriate that no reasonable trustee could entertain it'. He recognized that social conditions had moved on and that international families with international interests 'are as likely to make their home in one country as in another and as likely to choose one jurisdiction as another for the investment of their capital'. The court should not act in a way that frustrated this.

(4) Persons the court will appoint trustees

(a) General principles guiding the court's selection

In *Re Tempest*,[104] which concerned the appointment of new trustees under a predecessor to s 41,[105] the Court of Appeal laid down three criteria that the court will apply in exercising its discretion to appoint new trustees. These were set out by Turner LJ.

---

[98] [1969] 1 Ch 223, at 245.   [99] Ibid., at 248.   [100] Ibid., at 284.

[101] [1969] 1 WLR 692.

[102] See *Re Beatty's WT (No 2)* (1997) 11 *Trust Law International* 77; *Richard v Mackay* (1997) 11 *Trust Law International* 22 (decided 1987).

[103] (1997) 11 *Trust Law International* 22.   [104] (1866) 1 Ch App 485.   [105] Trustee Act 1850.

(i) Regard to the wishes of the settlor

First, the court will have regard to the wishes of the persons by whom the trust has been created, if expressed in the instrument creating the trust, or clearly to be collected from it.[106]

(ii) Regard to the interests of the beneficiaries

Another rule which may, I think, safely be laid down is this—that the court will not appoint a person to be a trustee with a view to the interest of some of the persons interested under the trust, in opposition either to the wishes of the testator or to the interests of the other cestuis que trust. I think so for this reason that it is of the essence of the duty of every trustee to hold an even hand between the parties interested under a trust.[107]

(iii) Regard to the effective execution of the trust

A third rule which, I think, may safely be laid down is this—that the court in appointing a trustee will have regard to the question, whether his appointment will promote or impede the execution of the trust, for the very purpose of the appointment is that the trust may be better carried into execution.[108]

(iv) Applying the principles

The Court of Appeal held that the proposed trustee, Mr Petre, should not be appointed. Although there could be no objection to him 'in point of character, position or ability', he fell foul of the rules proposed. First, he was the nominee of the beneficiary of the trust, Charles Tempest, and the testator's intentions had been to exclude him 'from all connection with his estate'. Second, the court considered that he had been:

proposed as a trustee . . . with a view to his acting in the trust in the interests of some only of the objects of it . . . and not with a view to his acting as an independent trustee for the benefit of all the objects of the trusts.

(b) Persons the court will not normally appoint trustees

There are some persons who, irrespective of their abilities, the court will not normally appoint as trustees because of their relationship to the trust and the likelihood of a conflict of interest. The court will not appoint, except in exceptional circumstances,[109] a beneficiary or a beneficiary's spouse as trustee,[110] nor the solicitor to the life tenant or the solicitor to an existing trustee.[111] Nor, according to a number of cases, will the court appoint a person living abroad unless the trust's

---

[106] (1866) 1 Ch App 485, at 487.   [107] Ibid.   [108] Ibid., at 488.

[109] For example, where no independent person can he found to take up the office: *ex p Clutton* (1853) 17 Jur 988; *Re Clissold's Settlement* (1864) 10 LT 642; *Re Burgess' Trusts* [1877] WN 87; *Re Parrott* (1881) 30 WR 97; *Re Lightbody's Trusts* (1884) 33 WR 452.

[110] *Ex p Clutton* (1853) 17 Jur 988; *ex p Conybeare's Settlement* (1853) 1 WR 458; *Re Orde* (1883) 24 Ch D 271; *Re Kemp's Settled Estate* (1883) 24 Ch D 485, CA; *Re Coode* (1913) 108 LT 94.

[111] *Re Kemp's Settled Estates* (1883) 24 Ch D 485 27; *Re Norris* (1884) 27 Ch D 333; *Re Earl of Stamford* [1896] 1 Ch 288; *Re Spencer's Settled Estates* [1903] 1 Ch 75.

property or the beneficiaries are also abroad,[112] although it may be that this attitude is changing.[113]

6 Trusts of Land and Appointment of Trustees Act 1996

(1) Appointment of trustees at the direction of the beneficiaries

It has been seen that ss 36 and 41 of the Trustee Act 1925 provide mechanisms for the appointment of new trustees, whether additional or replacement, in specified circumstances. However, in neither case do the beneficiaries of the trust have the right to require the appointment of a specific person as a trustee, as the right to appoint is vested in either other persons (the surviving or continuing trustees, or the personal representatives of the last surviving trustee) or the court. However, the Trusts of Land and Appointment of Trustees Act 1996, s 19 has granted the beneficiaries of a trust the right to direct the appointment of new trustees. Section 19(2)(b) provides that the beneficiaries can give:

a written direction to the trustees or trustee for the time being (or, if there are none, to the personal representative of the last person who was a trustee) to appoint by writing to be a trustee or trustees the person or persons specified in the direction.

As in the case of the power to direct the retirement of trustees, this right to direct appointment can only be exercised if the beneficiaries would otherwise be entitled to take advantage of the rule in *Saunders v Vautier*[114] because they are of age, legally competent, and collectively entitled to the trust property.[115] The right to direct appointments is also excluded if the trust instrument expressly nominates a person for the purpose of appointing new trustees,[116] or if the right has been expressly excluded.[117] The beneficiaries' right to direct the appointment of new trustees cannot be exercised so as to appoint more than the maximum number of trustees permitted under the Trustee Act 1925.[118]

Problems remain concerning the practical implementation of the beneficiaries' right to direct the appointment of new trustees. Whereas s 19(3) makes clear that a trustee who is directed to retire must do so, there is no equivalent provision requiring the trustees (or the personal representative of the last surviving trustee) to carry into effect a direction to appoint. If the trustees are required to make the directed appointment, it is unclear whether they would be liable if the person nominated by

---

[112] *Re Guibert's Trust Estate* (1852) 16 Jur 852; *Re Hill's Trusts* [1874] WN 228; *Re Drewe's Settlement Trusts* [1876] WN 168; *Re Freeman's Settlement Trusts* (1887) 37 Ch D 148; *Re Liddiard* (1880) 14 Ch D 310; *Re Whitehead's Will Trusts* [1971] 1 WLR 833.

[113] See *Re Beatty's WT (No 2)* (1997) 11 *Trust Law International* 77; *Richard v Mackay* (1997) 11 *Trust Law International* 22.

[114] (1841) 4 Beav 115.   [115] S 19(1)(b).   [116] S 19(1)(a).   [117] S 21(5)–(8).

[118] Trusts of Land and Appointment of Trustees Act 1996, s 19(5).

the beneficiaries was unsuitable and the trust suffered a loss in consequence of the appointment. Presumably, the appointing trustees would be exempt from any liability for breach of trust in such circumstances because the appointment would have been made at the unanimous instigation of the beneficiaries.

(2) Appointment of a substitute for a mentally incapable trustee

It has already been noted that, where a trustee has become mentally incapable, the right to appoint a substitute trustee may have become moribund. This may be because the persons enjoying the right to appoint, whether under an express power or under s 36 of the Trustee Act 1925, are unwilling to do so, or because there is no one entitled to appoint a substitute: for example, where there is a sole trustee who has become incapable and the trust instrument does not include an express power of appointment. In order to facilitate the appointment of a substitute without the need for the court to intervene, s 20(2) of the Trusts of Land and Appointment of Trustees Act 1996 (as amended by the Mental Capacity Act 2005) provides that the beneficiaries of the trust may give 'a written direction to appoint by writing the person or persons specified in the direction to be a trustee or trustees in place of the incapable trustee'. The right to give such a direction only arises where a trustee lacks capacity to exercise his functions as trustee,[119] and there is no person who is both entitled and willing and able to appoint a trustee in place of him under s 36(1) of the Trustee Act 1925.[120] The right to direct an appointment in such circumstances is only conferred upon the beneficiaries if they would otherwise be entitled to take advantage of the rule in *Saunders v Vautier*: ie they are of age, legally competent, and collectively entitled to the trust property.[121] The direction to appoint must be made to either a receiver of the incapable trustee,[122] or a person acting for him under an enduring or lasting power of attorney,[123] or a person with authority to act under the Court of Protection.[124] The beneficiaries' right to direct an appointment under s 20 may be expressly excluded in the trust instrument,[125] or, in the case of a trust created before the commencement of the Act, may be excluded by the execution of a deed to that effect by all the surviving settlors.[126]

7 Appointment of special trustees

A number of statutory provisions provide for the appointment of special trustees.

---

[119] S 20(1)(a). Capacity is defined under the Mental Capacity Act 2005, ss 1 and 2.
[120] S 20(1)(b).   [121] S 20(1)(c).   [122] S 20(2)(a).   [123] S 20(2)(b).
[124] S 20(2)(c) (as amended by the Mental Capacity Act 2005). For details of the Court of Protection, see Mental Capacity Act 2005.
[125] S 21(5).   [126] S 21(6).

(1) Judicial Trustees Act 1896

(a) Nature of a judicial trustee

A judicial trustee is a trustee appointed by the court under s 1 of the Judicial Trustees Act 1896. The person appointed a judicial trustee is an officer of the court, and is therefore subject to its control and supervision. The purpose of appointing a judicial trustee is to ensure the proper execution of the trust, but without incurring the full expense of having the trust administered by the court. This was explained by Jenkins J in *Re Ridsdel*:[127]

The object of the Judicial Trustees Act 1896...was to provide a middle course in cases where the administration of the estate by the ordinary trustees had broken down, and it was not desired to put the estate to the expense of a full administration of the estate...a solution was found in the appointment of a judicial trustee, who acts in close concert with the court and under conditions enabling the court to supervise his transactions.[128]

Although the judicial trustee may be given special directions by the court, and he may apply for the court's directions in his decisions, the purpose is not to 'reduce the administration of an estate by a judicial trustee to very much the same position as where an estate is being administered by the court and every step has to be taken in pursuance of the court's directions'.[129]

The appointment of a judicial trustee was particularly important prior to the enactment of s 50 of the Administration of Justice Act 1985, since it was the only way that a personal representative could be replaced. Although a judicial trustee is largely in the same position as any other trustee, for example he has the power to compromise claims,[130] he cannot appoint his successor under the provisions of s 36 of the Trustee Act 1925.

(b) Appointment of a judicial trustee

(i) The power to appoint

The Judicial Trustees Act 1896, s 1(1) provides that:

Where application is made to the court by or on behalf of the person creating or intending to create a trust, or by or on behalf of a trustee or beneficiary, the court may, in its discretion, appoint a person (in this Act called a judicial trustee) to be a trustee, either jointly with any other person or as sole trustee, and if sufficient cause is shown, in place of any existing trustees.

The power to appoint a judicial trustee is therefore purely discretionary. It is also clear that a trustee may be removed against his will and replaced by a judicial trustee. In *Thomas and Agnes Carvel Foundation v Carvel*,[131] Lewison J held that the survivor of two persons who had made mutual wills and his personal representative was a trustee for the purposes of this section:

As Clauson J made clear in *In re Hagger*[132] the survivor of two persons who make mutual wills is treated as a trustee, and as Lord Camden in *Dufour v Pereira*[133] said the trust binds those who

---

127 [1947] Ch 597.   128 Ibid., at 605.   129 *Re Ridsdel* [1947] Ch 597.
130 Ibid.   131 [2008] Ch 395.   132 [1930] 2 Ch 190, at 195.
133 (1769) 21 ER 332.

claim under him. Accordingly, in my judgment the survivor and his executor are trustees in the usual sense of that word. A person entitled to enforce the trust thus imposed by law is, in my judgment, a beneficiary. In my judgment, therefore, although a person claiming under the English doctrine of mutual wills is not entitled to make an application under section 50 of the 1985 Act, he is entitled to apply under section 1 of the 1896 Act.[134]

(ii) Persons who may be appointed

Section 1(3) provides that:

Any fit and proper person nominated for the purpose in the application may be appointed a judicial trustee, and, in the absence of such nomination, an official of the court may be appointed, and in any case a judicial trustee shall be subject to the control and supervision of the court as an officer thereof.

(iii) Remuneration of judicial trustees

Section 1(5) provides that the court may direct that the judicial trustee be remunerated for his services from the trust property.

(2) Public Trustee Act 1906

(a) Nature of the public trustee

The Public Trustee is a corporation sole which may act as an ordinary trustee, custodian trustee,[135] or judicial trustee.[136] He was established by the Public Trustee Act 1906, and one main function is to administer small estates. Once appointed, he has the same powers and duties, rights and liabilities as an ordinary trustee.

(b) Appointment of the public trustee

(i) Appointment as an ordinary trustee

Section 5(1) provides that the Public Trustee may be appointed trustee of any will or settlement:

either as an original or as a new trustee, or as an additional trustee, in the same cases, and in the same manner, and by the same persons or court, as if he were a private trustee, with this addition, that, though the trustees originally appointed were two or more, the public trustee may be appointed sole trustee.

This is subject to the limitations that he may decline to accept any trust, although not on the grounds of the small value of the trust fund,[137] that he may not act as the trustee of any trust under a deed of arrangement for the benefit of creditors or as administrator of an insolvent estate,[138] and that he shall not accept any trust exclusively for

---

[134] Ibid., at 404 [29].

[135] A custodian trustee holds the property of the trust fund and the documents relating to such property, but leaves the administration of the trust to the managing trustee. See Public Trustee Act 1906, s 4(2). See Chapter 21.

[136] Public Trustee Act 1906, s 2(1).   [137] S 2(3).

[138] S 2(4).

religious or charitable purposes.[139] The court may order the appointment of the Public Trustee even if the trust instrument prohibits his appointment.[140]

(ii) Appointment as a custodian trustee

Section 4(1) provides that:

Subject to rules under this Act the public trustee may, if he consents to act as such, and whether or not the number of trustees has been reduced below the original number, be appointed to be custodian trustee of any trust—

  (a) by order of the court made on the application of any person on whose application the court may order the appointment of a new trustee; or

  (b) by the testator, settlor or other creator of any trust; or

  (c) by the person having power to appoint new trustees.

(iii) Intestate estates

The Public Trustee holds the estate of a person who dies intestate, pending the appointment of an administrator.[141]

8 The court's inherent jurisdiction to remove trustees

In addition to the statutory power to remove trustees under s 41 of the Trustee Act 1925, the court possesses an inherent jurisdiction to remove trustees in an action begun by writ for the administration or execution of a trust.[142] Although there is little authority as to the exercise of this jurisdiction, the overriding consideration seems to be the welfare of the beneficiaries and the trust estate. Some guidance was provided by the Privy Council in *Letterstedt v Broers*,[143] where Lord Blackburn said:

The reason why there is so little to be found in the books on this subject is probably that suggested by Mr Davey in his argument. As soon as all questions of character are as far settled as the nature of the case admits, if it appears clear that the continuance of the trustee would be detrimental to the execution of the trusts, even if for no other reason than that human infirmity would prevent those beneficially interested, or those who act for them, from working in harmony with the trustee, and if there is no reason to the contrary from the intentions of the framer of the trust to give this trustee a benefit or otherwise, the trustee is always advised by his own counsel to resign, and does so. If, without any reasonable ground, he refused to do so, it seems to their Lordships that the court might think it proper to remove him . . .[144]

---

[139] S 2(5).   [140] S 5(3).
[141] Law of Property (Miscellaneous Provisions) Act 1994, s 14.
[142] *Re Wrightson* [1908] 1 Ch 789; *Re Henderson* [1940] Ch 764.
[143] (1884) 9 App Cas 371.   [144] Ibid., at 386.

Circumstances	Relevant power	Exercised by?
Initial appointment	Own choice	Settlor/testator Court (if original trustee disclaims the trust, or if the trust would otherwise fail for want of a trustee)
Appointment of additional trustee	Express power	Person nominated
	Trustee Act 1925, s 36(6)	Trustees for the time being
	TOLATA* 1996, s 19	Beneficiaries
Replacement of existing trustee	Express power	Person nominated
	Trustee Act 1925, s 36 (in specified circumstances)	'Surviving or continuing trustees' or personal representatives of last such
	TOLATA 1996, s 19	Beneficiaries
	TOLATA 1996, s 20 (mentally incapable trustee)	Beneficiaries
	Trustee Act 1925, s 41	Court
Retirement without replacement	Trustee Act 1925, s 39	Retiring trustee with consent of others
	TOLATA 1996, s 19	Beneficiaries with consent of remaining trustees
Removal of trustee	Trustee Act 1925, s 36	'Surviving or continuing trustees' or personal representatives of last such
	TOLATA 1996, s 19	Beneficiaries (with consent of remaining trustees if not being replaced)
	Trustee Act 1925, s 41	Court
	Inherent jurisdiction	Court

* Trusts of Land and Appointment of Trustees Act 1996.

Figure 26.1 Summary of powers to appoint and remove trustees

The court may act under its inherent jurisdiction even where the facts are in dispute.[145] The inherent jurisdiction was used to remove three trustees against their will in *Clarke v Heathfield (No 2)*.[146] The case concerned a trust fund of money belonging to the National Union of Mineworkers. The three trustees transferred the funds abroad to

---

[145] *Re Chetwynd's Settlement* [1902] 1 Ch 692; *Re Wrightson* [1908] 1 Ch 789; *Re Henderson* [1940] Ch 764.
[146] [1985] ICR 606.

prevent them being sequestrated as a result of the illegal industrial action by the union. Members of the NUM sought to have the trustees removed by the court. Mervyn Davies J held that the court should exercise its power to remove the trustees under its inherent jurisdiction. A number of factors influenced his decision to remove, including the trustees' refusal to obey orders of the court and that the transfer of the funds abroad rendered them unavailable for the purposes for which they were contributed by the membership of the union.[147]

9 Summary

Having considered the range of powers by which trustees may be appointed, it is possible to summarize how they may operate in practice. This is set out in Figure 26.1.

---

[147] The jurisdiction has also been used in *Bridge Trustees Ltd v Noel Penny Turbines* [2008] EWHC 2054 (Ch), to remove the donee of a fiduciary power against his will. The donee was not a trustee, and therefore fell outside the jurisdiction of the Trustee Act 1925, s 41.

27

Accountability of trustees

Throughout Part IV it has been seen that trustees, by virtue of their legal ownership, enjoy powers of management and control over the trust property. They are under a duty to act in the best interests of the beneficiaries of the trust, but inevitably their position opens to them tremendous possibilities for abuse. There are some basic equitable duties and liabilities imposed on trustees to make them accountable to the beneficiaries, which are explored in this chapter.

1 Introduction

Part V of this book considers the question of how the trustees of a trust are controlled and supervised, and in particular Chapter 28 details the general mechanisms by which such control is affected. It will be seen that the prime responsibility for supervising the activities of the trustees falls to the beneficiaries, who are able to complain to the court if they believe the trustees have committed, or are about to commit, a breach of trust. If the beneficiaries are able to apply to the court before the alleged breach has taken place they may obtain an injunction against the trustees to restrain them from committing the contemplated breach.[1] If the breach has already occurred, there are a number of other remedies which may be available to the beneficiaries.[2]

Trustees are also subject to a number of duties which enable the beneficiaries to keep a better check on their activities by entitling them to obtain information which will inform them of the trustees' actions and may enable the beneficiaries to detect breaches of trust. This chapter will consider those duties.

2 The duty to act unanimously

One safeguard to the proper conduct of a trust is the appointment of joint trustees. Where the trust property is held by a sole trustee, the opportunities for abuse will be greater, since a co-trustee cannot act alone without the collusion of his fellow trustees.

---

[1] See Chapter 6, at pp 129 *et seq.*   [2] See Chapters 29–32.

For this reason, in the context of land, overreaching, which defeats the interests of the beneficiaries of a trust of land, is only permitted by statute where the legal title to the land is held by more than two trustees.[3] The 'two-trustee' rule has been clarified and strengthened by the Trustee Delegation Act 1999 under which, if one of two trustees has delegated his powers relating to the sale of land to the other trustee, the sole trustee-cum-attorney cannot give a valid receipt without a second person being added as trustee.[4]

Except in the case of pension fund trusts[5] and charity trusts, co-trustees must generally act unanimously.[6] They cannot act on the basis of a majority decision.[7] The principle was stated by Jessel MR in *Luke v South Kensington Hotel Ltd*:

There is no law that I am acquainted with which enables the majority of trustees to bind the minority. The only power to bind is the act of [them all].[8]

Illustrations of the application of the requirement of unanimity can be drawn from a number of areas. If one of several co-trustees enters into a contract to sell trust property to a third party, the duty to act unanimously means that the contract cannot be enforced against the trust.[9] Similarly, the trustees must act unanimously in the exercise of their discretions. In *Tempest v Lord Camoys*[10] one of two trustees wished to exercise their discretion to purchase land with the trust property, but the other trustee refused to concur in the purchase. The Court of Appeal held that, as the refusing trustee had properly exercised his discretion, the court could not interfere and the purchase could not take place as the trustees were not unanimous. However, in *Messeena v Carr*[11] Lord Romilly MR held that there was no breach of trust where a discretion was exercised by one of two trustees and the other 'approved and sanctioned what was done'. A receipt which is given for money by only one of two trustees will be ineffective to discharge the payor unless this is done by way of an express term in the trust instrument. Therefore, in *Lee v Sankey*[12] a firm of solicitors was held not to have been discharged when it paid over the proceeds of a testator's real estate and was given a receipt by one of the two trustees of the will, who misappropriated the money and died insolvent.

In some exceptional circumstances it seems that the duty to act unanimously will not apply. In *Nicholson v Smith*,[13] for example, it was held that notice of the intention to renew a lease by one of two trustees was sufficient.

---

[3] Law of Property Act 1925, ss 2, 27. See also *State Bank of India v Sood* [1997] 1 All ER 169.

[4] Trustee Delegation Act 1999, s 7. The same is true where there are two or more trustees all of whom have delegated their powers to the same agent.

[5] S 32 Pensions Act 1995 provides that trustees of an occupational pension scheme may make decisions by a majority.

[6] The trust instrument may specify circumstances in which the trustees do not need to be unanimous.

[7] See *Leyton v Sneyd* (1818) 8 Taunt 532; *Tempest v Lord Camoys* (1882) 21 Ch D 571, CA; *Astbury v Astbury* [1898] 2 Ch 111; *Boardman v Phipps* [1967] 2 AC 46. HL.

[8] (1879) 11 Ch D 121, at 125.   [9] *Naylor v Goodall* (1877) 47 LJ Ch 53.

[10] (1882) 21 Ch D 571.   [11] (1870) LR 9 Eq 260.   [12] (1873) LR 15 Eq 204.

[13] (1882) 22 Ch D 640.

3 The duty to exercise discretions properly

(1) The duties of trustees relating to the exercise of discretion

Where trustees have discretion as to how the trust property should be managed or allocated, they must exercise their discretion properly. It is not for the courts to force the trustees to reach a particular conclusion in the exercise of their discretion, but they will intervene if the trustees exercise their discretion improperly or improperly fail to exercise it. In *Tempest v Lord Camoys*[14] Jessel MR said:

It is settled law that when a [settlor] has given a pure discretion to trustees as to the exercise of a power, the court does not enforce the exercise of the power against the wish of the trustees, but it does prevent them from exercising it improperly.[15]

(2) The trustees' duty to consider exercising a discretion

Trustees are under a duty to consider whether they should exercise any discretion that they hold with regard to the trust property, even though the court cannot compel how the discretion should be exercised. These principles were applied in *Tempest v Lord Camoys*. Mr Fleming, one of the trustees, had properly considered the exercise of his discretion and had refused to invest the trust property in land or to raise money by way of a mortgage. As Brett LJ said:

there was undoubtedly an absolute discretion in the trustees as to what land they should purchase. Mr Fleming has not refused to exercise the power at all, but has objected to purchase this particular property. It needs no authority to induce us to hold that if a discretion is given to trustees as to what property they should purchase the Court will not take it out of their hands.[16]

In *Turner v Turner*[17] the court set aside deeds of appointment which had been exercised by the trustees on the grounds that, although they appeared to be valid, the trustees had not even read them. In effect, there had been no real consideration whether or not the power should be exercised. In *Klug v Klug*,[18] a trustee had refused to concur in an advancement because the beneficiary (her daughter) had married without her consent. Neville J held that the court would intervene to direct the payment because the trustee 'has not exercised her discretion at all'.

(3) Relevance of the beneficiaries' wishes in the exercise of the trustees' discretion

Where the trustees of a trust hold discretionary powers it is they alone who must decide whether or not to exercise the discretion. Except in respect of a trust of land,[19]

---

[14] (1882) 21 Ch D 571.   [15] Ibid., at 578.   [16] Ibid.
[17] [1984] Ch 100.   [18] [1918] 2 Ch 67.
[19] Trusts of Land and Appointment of Trustees Act 1996, s 11. See Jackson, Stevens, and Pearce, *Land Law* (4th edn, 2008), p 416.

trustees are not subject to an obligation to consult their beneficiaries before they exercise their discretions, nor are they obliged to follow beneficiaries' wishes. In *Re Brockbank*[20] Vaisey J refused to compel a trustee to exercise his power to appoint new trustees under s 36 of the Trustee Act 1925[21] in the manner demanded by the beneficiaries and other trustees. He emphasized the discretionary nature of the power:

The power of nominating a new trustee is a discretionary power, and, in my opinion is no longer exercisable and, indeed, can no longer exist if it has become one of which the exercise can be dictated by others.

This statement no longer holds completely true following the Trusts of Land and Appointment of Trustees Act 1996, which gives beneficiaries a limited authority to direct the appointment of new trustees.[22] However, the proposition set out remains accurate in respect of other trustee discretions, even in situations where the beneficiaries can call for the appointment of new trustees or bring the trust to an end under the rule in *Saunders v Vautier*.[23] The beneficiaries cannot dictate how the trustees should exercise their discretion.

(4) Improper exercise of discretion

(a) General principles

Given that the courts will intervene if trustees exercise, or threaten to exercise, their discretion improperly, the question naturally arises as to the circumstances in which an exercise will be regarded as improper. The difficulty, similar to that faced in the judicial review of administrative decisions, is that the court does not act as the judge of whether trustees make the 'right' decision. The court will only interfere in limited circumstances. This was explained by Lord Truro LC in *Re Beloved Wilkes' Charity*:

it is to the discretion of the trustees that the execution of the trust is confided, that discretion being exercised with an entire absence of indirect motive, with honesty of intention, and with a fair consideration of the subject. The duty of supervision on the part of the court will thus be confined to the question of the honesty, integrity, and fairness with which the deliberation has been conducted, and will not be extended to the accuracy of the conclusion arrived at...[24]

However, it is clear that trustees do not enjoy an absolute discretion. The ability of the court to intervene and impugn an exercise of the trustees' discretion was recognized by the House of Lords in *Dundee General Hospital Board of Management v Walker*,[25] where Lord Reid stated:

If it can be shown that the trustees considered the wrong question, or that, although they purported to consider the right question they did not really apply their minds to it or perversely

[20] [1948] Ch 206.   [21] See Chapter 26, at pp 807 *et seq.*
[22] See Chapter 26. Trusts of Land and Appointment of Trustees Act 1996, ss 19–21 enable the beneficiaries of a trust to direct the trustees to make appointments, or compel retirements, if they would otherwise be able to bring the trust to an end under the rule in *Saunders v Vautier*.
[23] (1841) 4 Beav 115.   [24] (1851) 3 Mac & G 440.   [25] [1952] 1 All ER 896.

shut their eyes to the facts or that they did not act honestly or in good faith, then there was no true decision and the court will intervene.[26]

The principles under which the court will be willing to intervene to set aside an improper exercise of a discretion by a trustee have been undergoing continual development and are still not finally settled.[27]

Trustees, it will be seen, are not normally under an obligation to provide reasons for a decision. In consequence, it will not often be possible to demonstrate that they have ignored relevant considerations or taken into account irrelevant considerations. However, certain formulations of the circumstances in which the courts will intervene suggest that there will be occasions when the facts may speak for themselves. Thus, a court would be prepared to intervene if the trustees' decision 'can be said to be one that no reasonable body of trustees properly directing themselves could have reached'.[28] If the decision of the trustees is not so much at odds with any sensible expectation of the person creating the trust, the court will not intervene merely because it would have reached a different decision.[29]

(b) Fraudulent exercise

The court will clearly intervene if it can be shown that the discretion was exercised fraudulently.

(c) Improper motives

The court will intervene if the trustee exercises or refuses to exercise the power for irrelevant and extraneous motives. For example, in *Klug v Klug*[30] the court intervened where one of two trustees refused to exercise her discretionary power of advancement[31] in favour of her daughter because she had married without her consent. In the Irish case of *Tomkin v Tomkin*[32] a valuable house and land near Dublin had been left under a family trust. The trustee, who was also a beneficiary, had a power to postpone sale. TC Smyth J held that the trustee 'by deliberate inaction, was content to let matters lie so that at a future date he could more conveniently acquire the trust property without having explored or realized its development potential'. He also allowed members of his family to occupy the property without payment of rent.

---

[26] Ibid., at 905. This formulation was cited with approval by Robert Walker J in *Scott v National Trust* [1998] 2 All ER 705, at 717–718.

[27] See *Re Hastings-Bass* [1975] Ch 25; *Mettoy Pension Trustees Ltd v Evans* [1990] 1 WLR 1587; *Stannard v Fisons Pension Trust* [1992] IRLR 27; *Breadner v Granville-Grossman* [2000] 4 All 705; *Re Barr's Settlement Trusts* [2003] Ch 409; *Sieff v Fox* [2005] 1 WLR 3811.

[28] *Edge v Pensions Ombudsman* [1998] Ch 512, at 534 per Scott VC; an approach confirmed by the Court of Appeal [2000] Ch 602. The language used reflects the standard laid down for the review of decisions made by administrative bodies in *Associated Provincial Picture House v Wednesbury Corpn* [1948] 1 KB 223.

[29] See *Edge v Pensions Ombudsman* [1998] Ch 512 and *Breadner v Granville-Grossman* [2000] 4 All ER 705, at 732–733, where Park J refused to overturn the exercise of a power because, even if they were fully informed, 'it is at least possible that the trustees…would still have gone ahead'.

[30] [1918] 2 Ch 67.   [31] See Chapter 15.   [32] 1998/6924P (8 July 2003).

It was held that the trustee was in breach of trust for acting as if he were the sole owner and for disregarding the interests of the other beneficiaries. The judge indicated that the property should be sold.

(d) Failure to take account of relevant matters

Since the decision in *Re Hastings-Bass (decd)*,[33] it has been clear that the court can set aside an exercise of discretion by a trustee[33a] which was made improperly, either because the trustee took into account irrelevant considerations, or failed to take account of relevant considerations. As Robert Walker J stated in *Scott v National Trust*,[34] trustees are under a duty to take account of all relevant matters when they decide whether or not to exercise their discretion:

Trustees must act in good faith, responsibly and reasonably. They must inform themselves, before making a decision, of matters which are relevant to the decision. These matters may not be limited to simple matters of fact but will, on occasion (indeed quite often) include taking advice from appropriate experts, whether the experts are lawyers, accountants, actuaries, surveyors, scientists or whomsoever.[35]

However, the precise scope of what has become known as 'the *Hastings-Bass* principle' has been continually evolving, and has yet to be definitively clarified. The principle has been restated a number of times in different cases,[36] most significantly by Lloyd LJ, sitting as a judge of the Chancery Division, in *Sieff v Fox*.[37] He stated the principle as follows:

Where trustees act under a discretion given to them by the terms of the trust, in circumstances in which they are free to decide whether or not to exercise that discretion, but the effect of the exercise is different from that which they intended, the court will interfere with their action if it is clear that they would not have acted as they did had they not failed to take into account considerations which they ought to have taken into account, or taken into account considerations which they ought not to have taken into account.[38]

The most significant aspect of this formulation is the assertion that an exercise of discretion will only be set aside if it is clear that the trustees would have decided differently if they had considered appropriately.[39] Only in cases where the trustees were obliged to act would the lesser requirement that they 'might' have acted differently apply.[40] Lloyd LJ therefore held that the exercise of a discretionary power of appointment could be set aside because the trustees had failed to take into account the true consequences of the appointment as regards capital gains tax, because they had been wrongly advised, and they would not have acted as they did if they had known the correct position. In

---

[33] [1975] Ch 25.

[33a] Or certain other fiduciaries: *Pitt v Holt* [2010] EWHC 45 (Ch) at [39].

[34] [1998] 2 All ER 705.   [35] Ibid., at 717.

[36] *Mettoy Pension Trustees Ltd v Evans* [1990] 1 WLR 1587, at 1621; *Re Barr's Settlement Trusts* [2003] Ch 409.

[37] [2005] 1 WLR 3811; Mitchell 'Reining in the Rule in *Re Hastings-Bass*' (2006) 122 LQR 35; Nolan and Conglen (2006) '*Hastings-Bass* and Third Parties' 65 CLJ 499 499; Hayton 'A Review of Current Trusts Law Issues' (2008) 22 TLI 81, at 86.

[38] [2005] 1 WLR 3811, at 3847 [119].

[39] Contra to the formulation adopted by Lightman J in *Re Barr's Settlement Trusts* [2003] Ch 409.

[40] [2005] 1 WLR 3811, at 3847 [119].

Re Barr's Settlement Trusts[41] Lightman J held that the principle will only apply where the trustee[42] failed to consider what he was under a duty to consider, and not merely because he made a mistake or by reason of ignorance or mistake, did not take into account a relevant consideration.[43]

It has not yet been finally determined whether a discretion exercised without proper consideration of relevant matters is voidable or void. In *Re Barr's Settlement Trusts*, Lightman J held that the effect was to render the exercise voidable.[44] While attracted to this conclusion, Lloyd LJ did not have to decide whether an improper exercise was void or voidable in *Sieff v Fox*.[45] However, he opined that the proposition would require further consideration in the light of earlier authority. He stated what he considered to be the main ways at present open to the court to control the application of the principle:

(a) to insist on a stringent application of the tests as they have been laid down; (b) to take a reasonable and not over-exigent view of what it is that the trustees ought to have taken into account, and (c) to adopt a critical approach to contentions that the trustees would have acted differently if they had realized the true position, perhaps especially so in cases (unlike the present) where it is in the interests of all who are before the court that the appointment should be set aside.[46]

The rule in *Hastings-Bass* has been described as a 'blunt instrument'. In *Smithson v Hamilton*[47] a definitive pension scheme introduced to replace the interim pension scheme rules included (among many other matters) provision for early retirement. By mistake one of the rules allowing for early retirement did not include an actuarial reduction to reflect the cost of early payment. Sir Andrew Park declined to hold that this early retirement rule alone should be held invalid under the *Hastings-Bass* principle. On the facts he considered that the pension scheme trustees had not acted under a misapprehension: the mistake was on the part of the employers who had drafted the scheme, and in his view rectification was the only way in which such a mistake could be corrected. In his view, the *Hastings-Bass* principle only 'applies to things done by trustees as respects which they have a fiduciary duty or responsibility to the beneficiaries (who in the case of a pension trust, are the members of the pension scheme)'.[48] However, even if the conditions for applying the *Hastings-Bass* principle had been met, Sir Andrew Park considered that an order under the principle should

---

[41] [2003] Ch 409. See Conaglen 'Judicial Review of Trustees' Discretionary Decisions' [2004] 63 CLJ 283; Hilliard 'Limiting *Re Hastings-Bass*?' [2004] Conv 208. See also, in the context of charities, Dennis 'The Judicial Control of the Exercise of Discretionary Powers by Charitable Trustees' (2007) 9 *Charity Law and Practice Review* 1.

[42] See *Smith v Hamilton* [2008] 1 WLR 1453, where it was made clear that the exercise of discretion only applies to the acts of *trustees*. Thus, it could not be used to correct a mistake in the drafting of a pension trust, which was a mistake of the settlor.

[43] [2003] Ch 409, at 417 [23].

[44] Ibid., at 421. Norris J in *Futter v Futter* [2010] EWHC 449 (Ch) at [33] to [35] considered that the rule made transactions void.

[45] [2005] 1 WLR 3811.   [46] Ibid., at 3837 [82].   [47] [2007] EWHC 2900 Ch.

[48] Ibid., at [97]. Contrast *Ogden v Griffiths Trustees* [2008] EWHC 118 (Ch), where Lewison J applied the principle to set aside a voluntary settlement intended to avoid inheritance tax made by a man unaware that he was terminally ill. There was an alternative equitable basis for setting aside a voluntary transaction made by mistake which was not suggested to the judge: see *Gibbon v Mitchell* [1990] 1 WLR 1304.

not be made because its effect 'could not modify the [early retirement] rule but could only set it aside in its entirety'.[49] He was not prepared to allow the *Hastings-Bass* principle to be used as a back-door route to rectification where the requirements for rectification had not been met.

(e) Capriciousness

Re Manisty's Settlement[50] suggests that the court will intervene if trustees exercise a discretion capriciously. Templeman J stated that:

The court may also be persuaded to intervene if the trustees act 'capriciously', that is to say, act for reasons which I apprehend could be said to be irrational, perverse or irrelevant to any sensible expectation of the settlor; for example, if they chose a beneficiary by height or complexion or by the irrelevant fact that he was a resident of Greater London.

(f) Unreasonableness

The extent to which the courts will interfere with the exercise of a discretion by trustees merely on the grounds that it can be considered as unreasonable remains relatively uncertain. However, there appears to be a growing willingness on the part of the courts to intervene. Some of the older authorities suggested that a distinction could be drawn between discretions which were stated in the trust instrument to be 'uncontrollable' and those which contained no such provision. Where the discretion given to the trustees is expressly stated to be 'uncontrollable' by the trust instrument, there are authorities which suggest that the court cannot interfere unless the trustees have exercised their discretion mala fides.[51] In the absence of such an express declaration, some nineteenth-century cases suggested a wide jurisdiction to intervene, so for example in *Re Roper's Trust*[52] Fry J considered that the court could intervene if the trustees had 'not exercised a sound discretion'.[53] In contrast, cases in the mid-twentieth century favoured the view that the court would not intervene merely on the grounds that the exercise was unreasonable if it was made in good faith.[54] In the Scottish case of *Dundee General Hospitals v Walker*[55] the trustees had accepted that the test for the exercise of their discretion was whether it was reasonable, but the House of Lords doubted that this was appropriate. Lord Normand concluded:

I desire to reserve the question whether the trustee's decision . . . was . . . open to question on any other grounds save that it was dishonest, or that it involved a trespass beyond the limits of what was committed to them by the [settlor] . . . [I]t is one thing to say that the trustees must honestly discharge their trust and keep within the bounds of the powers and duties entrusted to them, and quite another to say that they must not fall into errors which other persons, including a court of law, might consider unreasonable.[56]

---

49 Ibid., at [76].   50 [1974] Ch 17.
51 See *Gisborne v Gisborne* (1877) 2 App Cas 300; *Tabor v Brooks* (1878) 10 Ch D 273.
52 (1879) 11 Ch D 272.
53 See also *Re Hodges* (1878) 7 Ch D 754; *Re Lofthouse* (1885) 29 Ch D 921, CA.
54 See *Re Steed's Will Trusts* [1960] Ch 407, at 418.
55 [1952] 1 All ER 896.   56 Ibid., at 901.

The House of Lords reiterated its unwillingness to question the trustees' exercise of their discretion on the grounds of unreasonableness in *Re Gulbenkian's Settlement Trusts*.[57] The trustees had a discretion whether or not to pay income from the trust fund to certain beneficiaries. Lord Reid said of their position:

They are given an absolute discretion. So if they decide in good faith at appropriate times to give none of the income to any of the beneficiaries the court cannot pronounce their reasons to be bad. And similarly if they decide to give some or all of the income to a particular beneficiary the court will not review their decision. That was decided by this House in *Gisborne v Gisborne*...[58]

In the twenty-first century there are indications that the courts might be willing to go a little further. This is reflected in the *Hastings-Bass* principle adopted by Park J in *Breadner v Granville-Grossman*[59] and which he described as having 'obvious affinities to the much more developed area of the principles which the courts will apply when judicially reviewing the exercises of statutory powers by public authorities'.[60] Similarly, in *Scott v National Trust*,[61] Robert Walker J described the public law concept of legitimate expectation as being potentially relevant in reviewing the decisions of trustees, and in *Edge v Pensions Ombudsman* Scott V-C, in speaking of the basis on which a court would review trustees' decisions, said:

The judge may disagree with the manner in which the trustees have exercised their discretion, but unless they can be seen to have taken into account irrelevant, improper or irrational factors, or unless their decision can be said to be one that no reasonable body of trustees properly directing themselves could have reached, the judge cannot intervene.[62]

The language used is the language of the *Wednesbury*[63] test of reasonableness then used in reviewing the decisions of public bodies. This importation of public law principles has been criticized as unnecessary and potentially misleading,[64] since it could result in the importation of principles such as the need to hear both sides before reaching a decision, a concept which has not so far formed part of the law of trusts. It remains to be seen how far the analogy will be pursued. Even in cases which have made the analogy with judicial review, limits are recognized. For instance, in *Edge v Pensions Ombudsman*,[65] Scott V-C reaffirmed that the court would not subject to an objective test of fairness an exercise by the trustees of a discretionary power to provide additional benefits to members of a pension scheme:

It was within their discretion to provide benefits to members in service to the exclusion of members no longer in service. They certainly had a duty to exercise their discretionary power honestly and for the purpose for which the power was given and not so as to accomplish any ulterior purposes. But they were the judges of whether or not their exercise of the power was

---

57 [1970] AC 508.   58 (1877) 2 App Cas 300.   59 [2000] 4 All ER 705.
60 Ibid., at 721 and 732.   61 [1998] 2 All ER 705.   62 [1998] Ch 512, at 534.
63 *Associated Provincial Picture Houses v Wednesbury Corpn* [1948] 1 KB 223, CA, per Lord Greene MR: 'It must be proved to be unreasonable in the sense that the court considers it to be a decision that no reasonable body could have come to. It is not what the court considers unreasonable, a different thing altogether.'
64 By Professor Hayton in *Hayton and Marshall: Cases and Commentary on the Law of Trusts and Equitable Remedies* (12th edn, 2005), pp 656–657.
65 [1998] 1998] Ch 512.

fair as between the benefited beneficiaries and other beneficiaries. Their exercise of the discretionary power cannot be set aside simply because a judge... thinks it was not fair.[66]

(g) Compelling action

According to Park J in *Breadner v Granville-Grossman*,[67] there is a substantial distinction 'between on the one hand, the courts declaring something which the trustees have done to be void, and, on the other hand, the courts holding that a trust takes effect as if the trustees had done something which they never did at all'. He considered that he had no jurisdiction to treat as effective the purported exercise of a power outside the time limits for its exercise where the trustees had made a mistake about the last date for its exercise. The power in that instance was a mere power, which in his view lapsed when the time limit expired. Fiduciary powers may be treated differently by the courts. It was recognized in *McPhail v Doulton*[68] that there were various ways in which the courts could secure the performance of discretionary trusts, and those methods may be equally applicable to fiduciary powers. They include directing the trustees to act in a particular way. For instance in *Klug v Klug*[69] the court ordered a payment to be made to a beneficiary despite the improper refusal of one trustee to concur in the decision; and in *Mettoy Pension Trustees Ltd v Evans*[70] Warner J was prepared to exercise a fiduciary power himself where there was no other person able to do so by reason of a conflict of interest. Also, in *Bridge Trustees Ltd v Noel Penny Turbines*[71] Purle, QC felt able to invoke the court's inherent jurisdiction to replace an ex-trustee[72] of a pension trust for failure to exercise a fiduciary power to distribute surplus assets vested in him under the terms of the pension scheme.

(5) **Are trustees' required to give reasons for their decisions?**

(a) No duty to give reasons

The basic rule was stated by Harman LJ in *Re Londonderry's Settlement*:[73]

trustees exercising a discretionary power are not bound to disclose to their beneficiaries the reasons actuating them in coming to a decision.

This statement accords with a long line of authorities establishing that trustees, who have decided either to exercise or not to exercise their discretion, are under no duty to provide the beneficiaries with reasons for their decision. This decision was reaffirmed by Scott V-C in *Edge v Pensions Ombudsman*.[74] The absence of a requirement to give reasons for a decision was applied in *Re Beloved Wilkes' Charity*.[75] The case

---

[66] Ibid., at 535.   [67] [2000] 4 All ER 705, at 723.   [68] [1971] AC 424
[69] [1918] 2 Ch 67.   [70] [1990] 1 WLR 1587.   [71] [2008] EWHC 2054 (Ch).
[72] If the donee had remained a trustee, the court would have been able to use the power to remove trustees under Trustee Act 1925, s 41.
[73] [1965] Ch 918, at 928.
[74] [1998] Ch 512, at 534. See also *Wilson v Law Debenture Trust Corpn* [1995] 2 All ER 337.
[75] (1851) 3 Mac & G 440.

concerned a trust to provide for the education of a boy from one of three named parishes, or, if there was no suitable candidate from those parishes, a boy from any parish. The trustees decided to use the funds to support a boy, Charles Joyce, who was outside of the parish. Their exercise of the discretion was challenged on the grounds that there was a suitable boy, William Gale, from within the parishes. Lord Truro LC held that the trustees were under no duty to disclose the 'particulars' of why they had exercised the discretion in that way, and that there was no ground for imputing bad motives to the trustees from the affidavits. This principle was confirmed by the Court of Appeal in *Re Gresham Life Assurance Society, ex p Penney*[76] in the context of the directors of a company who, under the deed of settlement, had the discretion whether to accept a proposed transferee of the company shares. The court held that they were not obliged to provide reasons for their decision to refuse to accept a transferee and that in the absence of contrary evidence the court would take it for granted that they had acted bona fide.

(b) Justification for the rule

In *Re Londonderry's Settlement*[77] Salmon LJ provided a number of justifications for the rule that trustees were not obliged to provide the beneficiaries with reasons for their decisions:

> So long as the trustees exercise [the power]... bona fide with no improper motive, their exercise of the power cannot be challenged in the courts—and their reasons for acting as they did are, accordingly, immaterial. This is one of the grounds for the rule that trustees are not obliged to disclose to beneficiaries their reasons for exercising a discretionary power. Another ground for this rule is that it would not be for the good of the beneficiaries as a whole, and yet another that it might make the lives of trustees intolerable should an obligation rest upon them... Nothing would be more likely to embitter family feelings and the relationship between the trustees and members of the family, were the trustees obliged to state their reasons for the exercise of the powers entrusted to them. It might indeed well be difficult to persuade any persons to act as trustees were a duty to disclose their reasons, with all the embarrassment, arguments and quarrels that might ensue, added to their present not inconsiderable burdens.[78]

(c) Trustees voluntarily provide reasons

Although there is no obligation on the trustees to give reasons for decisions regarding the exercise of their discretion, if they do choose to give reasons this may reveal grounds for the court to intervene. As Lord Truro LC said in *Re Beloved Wilkes' Charity*:

> If, however, as stated by Lord Ellenborough in *R v Archbishop of Canterbury*,[79] trustees think fit to state a reason and the reason is one which does not justify their conclusion, then the Court may say that they have acted by mistake and in error, and that it will correct their decision; but if, without entering into details, they simply state, as in many cases it would be most prudent and judicious for them to do, that they have met and considered and come to a conclusion, the Court has then no means of saying that they have failed in their duty, or to consider the accuracy of their conclusion.[80]

---

[76] (1872) 8 Ch App 446.
[77] [1965] Ch 918, CA.
[78] Ibid., at 936–937.
[79] (1812) 15 East 117.
[80] (1851) 3 Mac & G 440.

(d) Reasons required where trustees decide to deprive a beneficiary of a legitimate expectation?

While there has been no general relaxation of the rule that beneficiaries are not entitled to be informed by trustees of their reason for a decision, in *Scott v National Trust*[81] Robert Walker J suggested that where the beneficiaries of a trust enjoy a legitimate expectation that a discretion will be exercised in their favour, they may be entitled to be given the reasons for a change of policy. He stated:

> if (for instance) trustees (whether of a charity, or a pension fund, or a private family trust) have for the last ten years paid £1,000 per quarter to an elderly, impoverished beneficiary of the trust it seems at least arguable that no reasonable body of trustees would discontinue the payment, without any warning, and without giving the beneficiary the opportunity of trying to persuade the trustees to continue the payment, at least temporarily. The beneficiary has no legal or equitable right to continued payment, but he or she has an expectation. So I am inclined to think that legitimate expectation may have some part to play in trust law as well as in judicial review cases.[82]

It has yet to be seen how far such a principle may be taken in the context of private trusts. However, it might perhaps have led to a different result in *Wilson v Law Debenture Trust Corpn plc*,[83] where it was held that pension trustees were not required to disclose their reasons for reversing a policy that they had pursued in the preceding years concerning the transfer of a fund surplus.

(e) Access to trust documents

The beneficiaries of a trust are prima facie entitled to have access to inspect trust documents. This can raise a potential conflict of principles where the exercise of a right of access to trust documents would disclose the trustees' reasons for the exercise of their discretions to the beneficiaries.

(i) The right of beneficiaries to disclosure of trust documents

The beneficiaries of a trust were historically regarded as enjoying the entitlement to access to trust documents on the basis of their proprietary right in the trust property. In *O'Rourke v Darbishire*[84] Lord Parmoor stated that a beneficiary 'is generally entitled to the production for inspection of all documents relating to the affairs of the trust'.[85] The rationale for this entitlement was explained by Lord Wrenbury:

> The beneficiary is entitled to see all trust documents because they are trust documents and because he is a beneficiary. They are in this sense his own . . . The proprietary right is a right to access to documents which are your own.[86]

This rationale was reconsidered by the Privy Council in *Schmidt v Rosewood Trust Ltd*,[87] which concerned an appeal from the Isle of Man by the object of a power of appointment under a trust who sought access to the trust documents. The Privy

---

81 [1998] 2 All ER 705. 82 Ibid., at 718. 83 [1995] 2 All ER 337.
84 [1920] AC 581. 85 Ibid., at 619. 86 Ibid., at 626–627.
87 [2003] 2 AC 709; Davies 'Integrity of Trusteeship' (2004) 120 LQR 1. Hayton argues that the courts should take a lead from this decision and regard it as appropriate to insist on pension trustees providing

Council rejected the contention that an object of a power of appointment could not obtain disclosure of trusts documents because he did not have a proprietary interest under the trust, and preferred to regard the right to seek disclosure of trust documents as an aspect of the inherent jurisdiction of the court to supervise the administration of trusts. This relocation of the entitlement to disclosure of trust documents to the inherent jurisdiction of the court, rather than in the proprietary right of the beneficiaries, means that a beneficiary will not enjoy an absolute right to disclosure of trust documents, as the court may exercise its inherent jurisdiction so as to limit disclosure. Lord Walker stated:

no beneficiary (and least of all a discretionary object) has any entitlement as of right to disclosure of anything which can plausibly be described as a trust document. Especially when there are issues as to personal or commercial confidentiality, the court may have to balance the competing interests of different beneficiaries, the trustees' themselves and third parties. Disclosure may have to be limited and safeguards may have to be put in place. Evaluation of the claims of a beneficiary (and especially of a discretionary object) may be an important part of the balancing exercise which the court has to perform on the materials placed before it.[88]

The case did not require the Privy Council to decide whether the object of the power of appointment in question should be entitled to the disclosure sought, as this was remitted to the High Court of the Isle of Man for further consideration. The Privy Council did not provide comprehensive guidance as to the circumstances in which a request for disclosure might be denied. However, it did suggest that limits and safeguards may have to be put in place where there are issues of personal confidentiality and a need to balance the competing interests of different beneficiaries, the trustees, and third parties.[89]

(ii) The meaning of trust documents

It has proved difficult to provide any definition of trust documents. On one reckoning, they would be any documents that relate to the administration of the trust. This was not, however, the view taken in *Re Londonderry's Settlement*, where Salmon LJ observed that 'the category of trust documents has never been comprehensively defined'.[90] He went on to suggest some common characteristics of 'trust documents':

(1) they are documents in the possession of the trustees as trustees; (2) they contain information about the trust which the beneficiaries are entitled to know; (3) the beneficiaries have a proprietary interest in the documents and, accordingly, are entitled to see them.

The assignment of these characteristics to trust documents is circular. Salmon LJ appears to suggest that a document is trust document because the trustee is entitled to see it, but that he is entitled to see it because it is a trust document in which he has a

---

reasons for their decisions: 'Pension Trusts and Traditional Trusts: Drastically Different Species of Trusts' [2005] Conv 229.

[88] Ibid., at 734 [67].

[89] See also *Foreman v Kingstone* [2004] 1 NZLR 841 for further examination of the circumstances in which the court may refuse to limit disclosure of trust documents to beneficiaries.

[90] [1965] Ch 918, at 938.

proprietary right. In any event, in the light of *Schmidt v Rosewood Trust Ltd*[91] it is no longer the case that the entitlement to disclosure of trust documents is founded upon the proprietary right of the beneficiary. In *Hartigan Nominees Pty Ltd v Rydge*[92] it was held that the beneficiaries of a discretionary trust were not entitled to see the settlor's confidential memorandum of wishes stating how he wanted the trustees to exercise their discretion, as this was of no legal force.

It would be better to treat the obligation of disclosure by trustees as being based upon the nature of trusteeship and their fiduciary obligations than upon any artificial characterization of the documents held by trustees.[93] This would permit the policy issues relating to disclosure of information by trustees to be more openly addressed, and it is policy considerations that lie at the heart of the question of disclosure.

(iii) No disclosure of trust documents which would reveal the trustees' reasons for exercising their discretion

Despite the remaining uncertainties as to the definition of trust documents and the manner in which the court will exercise its inherent jurisdiction to order disclosure of trust documents, it seems clear that beneficiaries will not be entitled to disclosure of trust documents which would reveal the trustees' reasons for the exercise of their discretions. In *Re Londonderry's Settlement*,[94] which concerned the minutes of trustees meetings, Harman LJ concluded:

I would hold that even if documents of this type ought properly to be described as trust documents, they are protected for the special reason which protects the trustees' deliberations on a discretionary matter from disclosure. If necessary, I hold that this principle overrides the ordinary rule...[95]

The change in the understanding of the basis for the beneficiaries' entitlement to the disclosure of trust documents in *Schmidt v Rosewood Trust Ltd*[96] has not affected this principle, since the revelation of the reasons for the exercise of a discretion would be an issue of personal confidentiality which would cause the court to limit the right to disclosure. In the New Zealand case of *Foreman v Kingstone*,[97] Potter J expressly stated that the decision in *Schmidt v Rosewood Trust Ltd* would not affect the subordination of the right to disclosure of trust documents to the right of the trustees to confidentiality for their reasons:

Approached as a matter of principle, the entitlement of the beneficiaries to disclosure of trust documents pursuant to the trustees' fundamental obligation to be accountable to beneficiaries, must be measured against another fundamental principle that the autonomy of trustees in the exercise of their discretions under the trust must be ensured. Hence trustees are not obliged to disclose to beneficiaries their reasons for exercising their discretionary power.[98]

---

[91] [2003] 2 AC 709.   [92] (1992) 29 NSWLR 405

[93] See the discussion in *Hartigan Nominees Ltd v Rydge* (1992) 29 NSWLR 405. See also *Re Murphy's Settlements* [1998] 3 All ER 1.

[94] [1965] Ch 918.   [95] Ibid., at 933.   [96] [2003] 2 AC 709.

[97] [2004] 1 NZLR 841   [98] Ibid., at [89].

The decisions relating to disclosure by trustees of reasons for their decisions have traditionally shown a higher regard for the principle that the trustees should be able to keep these reasons confidential than for the interest of the beneficiaries in seeing that the discretions are properly exercised. In *Wilson v Law Debenture Trust Corpn plc*,[99] two members of a pension scheme asked the trustees to disclose all the trust documents in their possession, including the minutes of their meetings, which might indicate the reasons for their decision not to transfer the whole of a fund surplus, as had been done in preceding years. The trustees refused to disclose these documents on the basis that they were not required to disclose documents which would divulge their reasons for exercising their discretion. Rattee J held that he was required to give effect to settled principles of trust law, so that in the absence of any evidence of impropriety the court would not compel the trustees of a pension scheme to disclose their reasons for the exercise of a discretion.[100]

One important issue concerns whether beneficiaries are entitled to see a 'letter of wishes' as part of the trust documentation. This is a document which is intended to give non-binding guidance,[101] passed on by the settlor to the trustees as to how the settlor wishes the trustees to exercise any powers under the trust. This is very important to beneficiaries in understanding the intentions of the settlor and the purpose of the trust of which they are beneficiaries. Previously, there was no English law decision on this issue, but both Australian[102] and Jersey[103] decisions had held that if the settlor intended this expression of wishes to remain confidential from the beneficiaries, in the interests of family harmony, this confidentiality should be respected. This line of reasoning has been followed in English law by Biggs J in the case of *Breakspear v Ackland*.[104] The case concerned a discretionary family settlement, the trust property of which consisted of an area of farmland and buildings, shares, and cash. The claimant beneficiaries brought proceedings seeking the disclosure of a wish letter and oral statements as to his wishes sent or communicated to the then trustees by the settlor. Biggs J conducted an extensive overview of authorities (including the Australian and Jersey decisions) and academic commentary relating to the *Londonderry* principle, and concluded that a beneficiary was not normally entitled to see any statement of wishes from a settlor of family property on a discretionary trust. He felt there were good reasons in the due administration of family

---

[99] [1995] 2 All ER 337.

[100] Ibid., at 347. But see the comments of Robert Walker J in *Scott v National Trust* [1998] 2 All ER 705, at 718 that trustees can be compelled to disclose their reasons if challenged in legal proceedings, and his implicit criticism of the National Trust's failure to record any details of the long debate on the controversial decision to ban stag hunting.

[101] If a letter by a settlor is intended to be legally binding, then logically it should be subject to the same requirement of disclosure as the trust instrument.

[102] *Hartigan Nominees Ltd v Rydge* (1992) 29 NSWLR 405.

[103] *Re Rabaiotti's 1989 Settlement* [2001] WTLR 953.

[104] [2009] Ch 32. See Griffiths 'An Inevitable Tension? The Disclosure of Letters of Wishes' [2008] Conv 322; Fox 'Disclosure of a Settlor's Wish Letter in a Discretionary Trust' (2008) 67 CLJ 252.

trusts that made this appropriate to do with family harmony and to protect the trustees from suit:

Such confidentiality serves the due administration of family trusts both because it tends to reduce the scope for litigation about the rationality of the exercise by trustees of their discretions, and because it is likely to encourage suitable trustees to accept office, undeterred by a perception that their discretionary deliberations will be subjected to scrutiny by disappointed or hostile beneficiaries, and to potentially expensive litigation in the courts.[105]

Moreover, Biggs J held that because letters of wishes fell within the category of documents that enjoy immunity as they would reveal the reasons underlying the exercise of discretions by the trustees:

The defining characteristic of a wish letter is that it contains material which the settlor desires that the trustees should take into account when exercising their (usually dispositive) discretionary powers. It is therefore brought into existence for the sole purpose of serving and facilitating an inherently confidential process. It seems to me axiomatic that a document brought into existence for the sole or predominant purpose of being used in furtherance of an inherently confidential process is itself properly to be regarded as confidential, to substantially the same extent and effect as the process which it is intended to serve.[106]

(f) Reform required?

The rule that trustees are not obliged to provide reasons for their decisions may mean that it is almost impossible for the beneficiaries to challenge a decision because they do not have sufficient evidence to sustain a claim that the trustees acted dishonestly, took irrelevant matters into consideration, or failed to take account of all relevant factors. For example, in *Re Beloved Wilkes' Charity*[107] one suggestion was that the trustees had chosen Charles Joyce rather than William Gale because Joyce was the brother of a clergyman who had been in contact with one of the trustees, who was also a clergyman. Without a comprehensive statement of the trustees' deliberations and reasons it was impossible to demonstrate that the discretion had been improperly exercised. In the contrasting case of *Klug v Klug*,[108] a daughter was able to show that her mother had acted improperly because she had letters where she had made clear that she would not exercise the discretion because of her daughter marrying contrary to her wishes.

Thus, the present law creates an inherent inconsistency. While equity seeks to prevent trustees acting improperly, it also fails to provide the beneficiaries with the right to know how decisions were reached so as to enable them to be subjected to proper scrutiny. This inconsistency runs deeper than this. Where a beneficiary takes legal action to challenge the exercise of a discretion, it is likely that he will be able to force the trustees to disclose their reasons. As Robert Walker J observed in *Scott v National Trust*:

If a decision taken by trustees is directly attacked in legal proceedings, the trustees may be compelled either legally (through discovery or subpoena) or practically (in order to avoid adverse inferences being drawn) to disclose the substance of the reasons for their decision.[109]

---

[105] [2009] Ch 32, at 51 [54].   [106] Ibid., at 52 [58].
[107] (1851) 3 Mac & G 440.   [108] [1918] 2 Ch 67.
[109] [1998] 2 All ER 705, at 719.

However, it is submitted that the real need for reasons arises before any question relating to an exercise of discretion is brought to court. At present, the beneficiary is required to decide whether there are sufficient grounds to mount a legal challenge to an exercise of discretion—and to provide evidence to support this claim—while remaining in the dark as to the real reasons for it. In some circumstances the facts themselves may prima facie indicate that the discretion was wrongly exercised, but in many cases there may be no such external indications. In such circumstances the presumption that, in the absence of evidence to the contrary, a trustee has exercised his discretion properly, operates so as to present an insurmountable obstacle to effective scrutiny of the trustees' decision-making. The problems facing beneficiaries were well captured in a submission of counsel for the plaintiffs in *Wilson v Law Debenture Trust Corpn plc*,[110] where he argued that the trustee of a pension scheme was:

in fact bound to give reasons for the exercise of discretions conferred upon the trustee by the relevant trust instrument because...it would be unreasonable that members of the scheme who had bought their interests should not be able to see that the trustee has exercised its discretion properly—which they cannot see in the absence of reasons given for the trustee's actual exercise of its discretion.[111]

In contrast to the reluctance of equity to oblige trustees to provide reasons for their decisions the law relating to the scrutiny of decision-making by public bodies has developed rapidly over the past fifty years, including the emergence of a duty to give reasons for decisions.[112] There is clear evidence in the recent trusts cases that the principles under which administrative decisions may be judicially reviewed have cross-fertilized the equity principles determining the duty of trustees in the exercise of their duties. It remains to be seen how far these developments will be carried. One possibility is that the general principle that trustees are not required to give reasons for their decisions may be abandoned, irrespective of the type of trust concerned. Alternatively, the principle could be abandoned for certain types of trusts, including pension funds and other quasi-public trusts, where the argument that trustees required the safety of secrecy to enable them to perform their duties is less compelling than in respect of small family trusts. This is certainly inherent in the judgment of *Breakspear v Ackland*,[113] in which Biggs J deliberately left open the question of whether the principle of immunity applied outside the family trusts context.[114] Moreover, in that case, he indicated that while a trustee could not be compelled to surrender up non-binding letters of wishes to the beneficiaries, the trustees could give such letters to the beneficiaries if they felt it was in the best interests of the good administration of the trust so to do.[115] It is submitted

---

[110] [1995] 2 All ER 337.   [111] Ibid., at 348, summarized by Rattee J.
[112] See *Padfield v Minister of Agriculture, Fisheries and Food* [1968] AC 997; *R v Secretary of State for the Home Department, ex p Doody* [1994] 1 AC 531; *R v Secretary of State for the Home Department, ex p Fayed* [1997] 1 All ER 228.
[113] [2009] Ch 32.   [114] Ibid., at 52 [58].
[115] Ibid., at 54 [67]. This would only be true if such discretion was not removed by the terms of the trust, although Biggs J cast doubt on whether any fetter of the trustee's discretion in the trust instrument should be permitted.

that such an approach may provide a stepping stone for later decisions, so that equity is no longer bound by nineteenth-century cases which place the interests of the trustees above those of the beneficiaries, and that no discretion should be able to be exercised without proper scrutiny.

4 The duty to keep accounts and records

(1) Accounts and their availability to beneficiaries

Trustees are under a duty to keep accounts of the trusts and to allow the beneficiaries to inspect them as requested. This was so held in *Pearse v Green*,[116] where Plumer MR said that: 'It is the first duty of an accounting party, whether an agent, trustee, a receiver or executor... to be constantly ready with his accounts.'[117] The beneficiaries, who include for this purpose the potential beneficiaries of a discretionary trust,[118] are entitled to a copy of the accounts at their own expense.[119] If the trustee fails to deliver accounts he will be liable to pay the costs of any application to the court to enforce the performance of his duty.[120] The beneficiaries of a trust are entitled to be told who the trustees are and given their addresses, since otherwise the right to be informed of the state of the trust funds and how they have been distributed would be meaningless.[121]

(2) Audit

There is no general duty on trustees to have the trust accounts audited. However, a number of statutory provisions permit either the trustees or the beneficiaries to obtain an audit of the accounts. Audits may also be required by the trust instrument.

(a) The Trustee Act 1925, s 22(4)

This section enables the trustees in their absolute discretion to have the trust account audited once every three years:

Trustees may, in their absolute discretion, from time to time, but not more than once in every three years unless the nature of the trust or any special dealings with the trust property make a more frequent exercise of the right reasonable, cause the accounts of the trust property to be examined or audited by an independent accountant, and shall, for that purpose, produce such vouchers and give such information to him as he may require.

---

[116] (1819) 1 Jac & W 135.
[117] See also *Clarke v Lord Ormonde* (1821) Jac 108; *Springett v Dashwood* (1860) 2 Giff 521.
[118] *Chaine-Nickson v Bank of Ireland* [1976] IR 393.
[119] See *Ottley v Gilby* (1845) 8 Beav 602; *Kemp v Burn* (1863) 4 Giff 348; *Re Watson* (1904) 49 Sol Jo 54.
[120] *Re Skinner* [1904] 1 Ch 289.
[121] *Re Murphy's Settlements* [1998] 3 All ER 1, a case where the settlor was required to provide this information to the objects of a discretionary trust.

The costs of such an audit may be met from the capital and income of the trust property.

(b) The Public Trustee Act 1906, s 13(1)

This section enables the trustees or the beneficiaries to apply for an audit of the trust accounts:

Subject to rules under this Act and unless the court otherwise orders, the condition and accounts of any trust shall, on an application being made and notice thereof given in the prescribed manner by any trustee or beneficiary, be investigated and audited by such a solicitor or public accountant as may be agreed on by the applicant and the trustees or, in default of agreement, by the public trustee or some person appointed by him:

Provided that (except with the leave of the court) such an investigation or audit shall not be required within 12 months after any such previous investigation or audit, and that a trustee or beneficiary shall not be appointed under this section to make an investigation of audit.

This section has been described as an 'exceedingly drastic enactment'[122] as it establishes the right to an audit. However, if an improper application is made, the applicant may be ordered to bear the costs of the audit,[123] which, it is suggested, may deter legitimate applications.

(c) Pensions

The Pensions Act 2004 imposes special requirements for periodic actuarial valuations.[124]

(d) Charities

Charities are under special duties to provide audit information to the Charity Commission under the Charities Act 1993.[125] These are detailed in Chapter 28.

(3) Information regarding the trust property

Trustees are subject to a general duty to provide their beneficiaries with information concerning the trust property. In *Low v Bouverie*,[126] Lindley LJ said the trustees must: 'give all his cestui que trust, on demand, information with respect to the mode in which the trust fund has been dealt with, and where it is'. He went on to indicate that there was some information that the trustee was not obliged to provide to the beneficiary:

But it is no part of the duty of a trustee to tell his cestui que trust what incumbrances the latter has created, nor which of his incumbrancers have given notice of their respective charges.

---

[122] *Re Oddy* [1911] 1 Ch 532, per Parker J.
[123] *Re Oddy* [1911] 1 Ch 532; *Re Utley* (1912) 106 LT 858.
[124] S 224.   [125] Ss 42–44.   [126] [1891] 3 Ch 82, at 99.

However, s 137(8) of the Law of Property Act 1925 now provides that the beneficiaries can require the production of any notice concerning the dealing with the equitable interest which has been served upon them. Special provisions are applicable to pension funds under the Pensions Act 1995, s 41 and regulations made thereunder.

(4) Advice

The duty of the trustees is simply to provide the beneficiaries with information, not to provide them with advice. As Megarry V-C said in *Tito v Waddell (No 2)*:

trustees...are under a duty to answer inquiries by the beneficiaries about the trust property...But that is a far remove from saying that trustees have a duty to proffer information and advice to their beneficiaries; and I think the courts should be very slow to advance along the road of imposing such a duty. I say nothing about what may be kindly or helpful; I deal only with a duty for the breach of which the trustees may be held liable in equity. Short of the alter ego type of case I do not think that trustees can be said to be under any duty to proffer information to their beneficiary, or to see that he has proper advice, merely because they are trustees for him and know that he is entering into a transaction with his beneficial interest with some person or body connected in some way with the trustees, such as a company in which the trustees own some shares beneficially.[127]

---

[127] [1977] Ch 106, at 242–243.

PART V

CHECKS AND CONTROLS

28

Control of trusts and trustees

In Parts III and IV it has been seen how the mechanisms developed by equity, primarily the trust and the power, enable the separation of the management and the ownership of property. This chapter looks at the means by which trustees can be prevented from abusing their position.

1 The need for control

(1) The potential for abuse

It is obvious that whenever one person has the effective control of property but is required to act for the benefit of another there is a possibility that he will misuse the powers that he holds. For example, a trustee may be tempted to apply the trust property for his own benefit rather than for the benefit of the beneficiaries, or the donee of a special power of appointment may attempt to appoint to someone outside of the class. The exact limits that circumscribe the actions of a person enjoying the responsibility to manage and allocate property are determined by the nature of the relationship that has been created. He will have a range of rights and duties, some of which are imposed by the general principles of equity, and others of which may have been imposed expressly when the mechanism was created. The question arises as to how to ensure that the holder of the management responsibility carries out his duties properly.

(2) The reality of abuse

Human nature being what it is, the reports are littered with cases where trustees enjoying the responsibility to manage trust property have abused their position and failed to carry out their duties. For example, in *Lipkin Gorman v Karpnale Ltd*[1] a solicitor misappropriated money from his firm's client account to finance his gambling habit.

---

[1] [1987] 1 WLR 987.

Bishopsgate Investment Management Ltd v Maxwell (No 2)[2] concerned the infamous Maxwell pension fraud. Ian and Kevin Maxwell were directors of a company that held assets on trust for the pension schemes of companies owned by Robert Maxwell. To support other private companies that Robert Maxwell owned, property was misappropriated from the trust fund. Kevin and Ian, as directors, were responsible for signing transfer forms authorizing the misappropriations. This was a classic case where those who held the management power over the property by virtue of their position as directors and trustees abused their position and were able to apply the property for improper purposes, rather than for the benefit of the pensioners.

(3) Preventing abuse

It is often impossible to prevent those who are dishonest from taking advantage of the opportunities for abuse that their position brings, and the crucial question is generally whether an adequate remedy is available when an abuse has taken place. However, the legal system possesses some mechanisms by which to attempt to prevent abuses occurring.

(a) Supervision and regulation

The law could introduce methods requiring the ongoing supervision of trustees, by the court or by independent regulators, so that their dealings are closely scrutinized and the potential for abuse is greatly reduced. It might be possible to establish regulatory bodies with the responsibility of ensuring that trustees do their duty, although in practice this would prove impossible because of the number and range of trusts that exist. However, in the case of charitable trusts a sophisticated scheme of regulation is in place through the Charity Commission. Regulatory regimes have been introduced in specific contexts where trust relationships may play an important part, for example to oversee the financial services industry and especially pension fund managers. The Pensions Act 1995 introduced the Occupational Pensions Regulatory Authority with the object of reducing the opportunities for fraud.

Generally, abuse occurs because of the dishonesty of an individual trustee or trustees. The choice of trustee is therefore of the utmost importance. At present, there is no general provision disqualifying certain individuals from holding office as trustees, although the Charities Act 1993 does disqualify certain persons from serving as charity trustees. Following the recommendations of the Pension Law Review Committee, which sat under the chairmanship of Professor Roy Goode after the Maxwell scandal, s 29(1) of the Pensions Act 1995 provides that a person is disqualified from being a trustee of any pension trust scheme if he has been convicted of any offence involving dishonesty or deception, is an undischarged bankrupt, or is disqualified to act as a company director.[3] A company cannot serve as trustee of a pension fund if any of its directors are disqualified from acting as trustee under the section.

---

[2] [1994] 1 All ER 261.   [3] Under the Company Directors' Disqualification Act 1986.

Obviously, the greatest dangers of abuse arise where the trust property is held and managed by a sole trustee. Where there are multiple trustees the general rule that all decisions must be unanimous provides a measure of protection for the beneficiaries.

(b) Deterrence and remedies

Rather than supervising trustees so as to prevent abuse occurring, equity has put in place powerful remedies that are available when an abuse occurs, which therefore act to deter those who might consider abusing their position. If the remedies available to the beneficiaries of a trust operate to deprive a trustee of any gain made through abuse of his position, this will act as a disincentive to abuse in the first place. Some abuses, particularly the misappropriation of trust property, also constitute criminal offences, in which case the possibility of criminal conviction will also act as a deterrent.

2 The means of control

(1) Criminal sanctions

Some measure of control over the conduct of trustees is provided by the general criminal law. In particular, if a trustee misappropriates trust property he will be guilty of theft. The Theft Act 1968 defines theft in s 1(1):

A person is guilty of theft if he dishonestly appropriates property belonging to another with the intention of permanently depriving the other of it...

'Property belonging to another' is defined in s 5(2) to include property held on trust so that 'where property is subject to a trust, the persons to whom it belongs shall be regarded as including any person having a right to enforce the trust, and an intention to defeat the trust shall be regarded accordingly as an intention to deprive of the property any person having that right'. Thus, the trustee, or anyone else who misappropriates the trust property, will be guilty of theft.[4] However, although the prospect of a conviction for theft may serve as a deterrent to abuse, it does not restore the trust property to the beneficiaries, which is often their prime concern.

(2) Supervision by the court

Every trust is technically under the jurisdiction and the supervision of the court. However, in practice the court does not exercise a day-to-day function of supervising the activities of trustees, ensuring that they do not abuse their powers and that they carry out their duties properly. The court is dependent on the beneficiaries of the trust to bring complaints regarding the trustees' conduct to their attention. If

---

[4] See *Re A-G's Reference (No 1 of 1985)* [1986] QB 491; (1986) 102 LQR 486; (1986) 45 CLJ 367 (Gearty); (1986) 136 NLJ 913 (Smart); [1987] Conv 209 (Martin).

the beneficiaries approach the court before a trustee acts improperly, it will be able to issue an injunction to restrain the proposed breach of trust. Where a breach has already occurred, the beneficiaries will be awarded an appropriate remedy.

Even though it does not act as a day-to-day watchdog over trustees, the court serves the very important function of setting the standard of probity that trustees are required to observe in their dealings, by which their conduct will be tested if a claim is made against them by the beneficiaries. The higher the standard of care that is required, the greater the probability that the trustee will not be able to gain by abusing his position, and the greater the deterrent effect. Traditionally, the courts have set extremely high standards for the conduct of trustees, and the remedies available border on the draconian.

(a) The fiduciary position of the trustee

Trustees stand in a fiduciary position to the beneficiaries of the trust. This means that they are always expected to act in the interests of the beneficiaries, with the implication that they are not permitted to take advantage of their position for their own benefit. As such, they owe a duty of exclusive loyalty to the beneficiaries. Trustees are not the only persons deemed fiduciaries in equity. Those occupying positions of trust and responsibility for the affairs of others, such as company directors, agents, and partners, are also regarded as fiduciaries. Equity imposes a rigid rule that a fiduciary must not benefit by virtue of his position, which thus acts as a safeguard to ensure that there is no possibility that he is abusing it. A fiduciary will be forced to disgorge any profits that he may have made in breach of his fiduciary duty by making restitution of them to the persons to whom the duty was owed. The standard of probity expected of a fiduciary is extremely high, as was confirmed in *Boardman v Phipps*,[5] where the majority of the House of Lords held that a fiduciary was liable to make restitution of profits he had made if there had been a mere possibility of a conflict between his duty and his personal interests.

(b) The standard of care expected of trustees

Equity imposes an objective standard of care on the way that trustees carry out their duties. They are expected to act with the standard of care of an ordinary prudent man of business who is acting on behalf of someone else.[6] If the trustee fails to exercise the requisite standard of care, or fails to carry out his duties, or acts outside of his powers or the terms of the trust, he will have committed a breach of trust and will be liable to compensate the beneficiaries for any loss caused by his breach.

(3) Supervision by the beneficiaries

As the court cannot supervise the activities of every trustee, the prime responsibility for such supervision falls to the beneficiaries of the trust. They are expected to monitor

---

[5] [1967] 2 AC 46.
[6] *Speight v Gaunt* (1883) 9 App Cas 1, HL; *Bartlett v Barclay's Bank Trust Co Ltd* [1980] Ch 515.

the trustee's activities, and to complain to the court if there is any breach of fiduciary duty or breach of trust. It is entirely appropriate that this burden should fall to them, as they are the very people who are most interested in the proper performance of the trust. It is they who will be most anxious to ensure that the trustee carries out his duties properly, that trust property is not misapplied, and that the trustee does not use his position to his own advantage at their expense. A number of principles, which have been examined earlier in this book, confirm that the beneficiaries are the persons primarily responsible for the supervision of the trustees.

(a) Beneficiary principle

The beneficiary principle examined in Chapter 13 is predicated on the understanding that the beneficiaries are primarily responsible for supervising the trustees. The very reason equity requires a trust to have identifiable legal persons as beneficiaries is that in the absence of such a beneficiary no one possesses the necessary locus standi to apply to the court in the event of a breach by the trustees, and there is no one in whose favour the court can decree specific performance of the trust.[7] If the trust is created in favour of a pure purpose, who can enforce the trust? In the case of charitable trusts this problem has been overcome, as they are enforced by the Attorney-General, acting on behalf of the Crown, or by the Charity Commission. It is notable that the limited anomalous exceptions to the beneficiary principle give rise to valid but unenforceable trusts.

(b) Beneficiaries' entitlement to information

As was seen in Chapter 27, although the beneficiaries of a trust cannot require the trustees to provide reasons for the exercise, or non-exercise, of their discretions,[8] they are entitled to receive information detailing how the trust assets are held.[9] The fact that the beneficiaries are entitled to obtain such information enables them to supervise to some measure the activities of the trustees. The court will intervene if a trustee can be shown to have exercised his discretion wrongly.[10] The general effectiveness of the beneficiaries' supervision of the trustees' exercise of their discretion is limited by the fact that they are not entitled to reasons from the trustees for their decisions. This means that, although a beneficiary may suspect that a discretion has been exercised wrongly, he is unable to gain the evidence necessary to make out his case.

(c) Beneficiaries may approve breaches of trust

Whilst it might be expected that trustees are subject to an absolute obligation to carry out the terms of a trust as specified by the original settlor, this is not in fact the case. If the beneficiaries consent to the trustees acting otherwise than in accordance with

---

[7] *Morice v Bishop of Durham* (1804) 9 Ves 399; *Bowman v Secular Society Ltd* [1917] AC 406; *Re Astor's Settlement* [1952] Ch 534; *Re Shaw* [1957] 1 WLR 729.

[8] *Re Beloved Wilkes' Charity* (1851) 3 Mac & G 440; *Re Londonderry's Settlement* [1965] Ch 918, CA; *Wilson v Law Debenture Trust Corpn* [1995] 2 All ER 337.

[9] *Low v Bouverie* [1891] 3 Ch 82, at 99.   [10] *Klug v Klug* [1918] 2 Ch 67.

the terms of the trust, then they will not attract liability for their breach. Trustees may vary the terms of the trust with the consent of the beneficiaries, or even bring the trust to an end.[11] The courts have no jurisdiction to step in and prevent a breach of trust which is made with the full consent of all the beneficiaries, even if this defeats the intentions of the settlor.

(d) Beneficiaries entitled to seek remedies

Where a trustee has abused his powers or position the trustees may come to the court to seek a remedy. There are a variety of remedies that may be available to them, each of which will be examined in detail in the following chapters.

(i) Compensation for breach of trust

Where trustees have committed a breach of trust, the beneficiaries are prima facie entitled to recover compensation from them for any loss the trust has sustained as a result of the breach. The remedy of damages for breach of trust is purely personal against the trustee, and will therefore be ineffective if the trustee is insolvent. The nature and scope of the remedy for breach of trust is considered in Chapter 29.

(ii) Account of profits for breach of fiduciary duty

If the trustee has made an unauthorized profit for himself by allowing his duty and his personal interest to conflict, he will be in breach of his fiduciary duty and the beneficiaries will be able to recover from him any profit that he has made. The duty to account for profits made is a purely personal duty, although the beneficiaries may have a proprietary claim to any profits remaining in the hands of the trustee, or property that can be regarded as the proceeds of such profits.[12] The nature and scope of the equitable duty to account for profits received in breach of fiduciary duty is considered in Chapter 30.

(iii) Proprietary remedies

If the trustee who has committed a breach of trust or made an unauthorized profit is insolvent, any personal remedies of the beneficiaries will be rendered largely ineffective. They will merely rank amongst the trustee's general creditors. However, if they can show that the trustee has property amongst his assets which was trust property, or if he has assets which can be shown to be the product of trust property by application of the rules of tracing, the beneficiaries will be able to claim those assets as belonging to the trust. They will not fall to be considered as comprising part of his general assets, and in effect the trust will gain priority over the interests of the general creditors. The availability of proprietary remedies, and the rules used to identify trust property, are considered in Chapter 32.

[11]   *Saunders v Vautier* (1841) Cr & Ph 240; see also Chapter 18.
[12]   *A-G for Hong Kong v Reid* [1994] 1 All ER 1.

(iv) Remedies against strangers to the trust

Where a breach of trust involves third parties who are strangers to the trust, the beneficiaries may have both personal and proprietary remedies against them. If such a stranger has received and retained property that was misappropriated from the trust, the beneficiaries will be able to assert their equitable entitlement to it unless he had acquired it as a bona fide purchaser for value without notice of the existence of the trust. This is also the case if he can be shown to have property amongst his assets which is the product of trust property he received by the rules of tracing. If, however, he received property from the trust but has subsequently dissipated it, or its proceeds, he may yet be liable to account to the trust for the value of the property he received. The obligation to account for the value of such property is a restitutionary remedy and at present only in circumstances where the court would consider it unconscionable for a recipient to retain the value of the property, as for example where he acted dishonestly, will he be obliged to make restitution. There are increasing calls by academics for the adoption of a strict liability to make restitution against the recipients of trust property.

A stranger who has not himself received trust property, but who has assisted the trustees in a misappropriation of trust property, may also be liable to compensate the trust for the value of the misappropriated property. This liability is analogous to the tort of conversion. Such an assistor will only attract liability if he acted dishonestly. The remedies available to the beneficiaries against strangers to a trust are considered in Chapter 31.

(4) Evaluating the effectiveness of supervision by the beneficiaries

It is obvious that the beneficiaries of a trust have a strong vested interest in ensuring that it is properly carried out according to its terms, and that the trustees do not abuse their position. However, the effectiveness of their supervision depends upon the nature of the trust. In the case of a small family trust, where the trustees and the terms of the trust are well known to the beneficiaries, such scrutiny is likely to be close and effective. In the case of large modern trust funds, with many thousands of beneficiaries and millions of pounds of assets, the beneficiaries are not in a position to scrutinize the day-to-day conduct of the trustees, both because of the enormity of the task, and the complexity of the situations involved. In such circumstances it is not realistic to expect the beneficiaries effectively to supervise the trustees' performance of their duties. To take the Maxwell pension fraud as an example: could the employees entitled to pensions realistically be expected to scrutinize the dealings of the directors of the companies holding the assets on trust so as to prevent the wrongful transfer of trust assets to the Maxwell private companies? Another limitation is that the trustees' misconduct often only comes to light after the event, when it is too late to prevent it, and when the beneficiaries' remedies may be all but ineffective because of the trustees' insolvency and because the trust property has been dissipated. Both these problems demonstrate the limitation of the effectiveness of supervision by the beneficiaries, and emphasize the importance of appointing appropriate persons to act in that capacity.

3 Controlling and supervising charitable trusts

Just as the trustees of a private trust have the potential to breach their duty and act in their own interests rather than in the interests of their beneficiaries, the trustees of charitable trusts have the opportunity to defraud both the charity for which they act as trustee and the public at large who make donations. It is essential to protect against spurious charities, and to ensure that the funds of genuine charities are properly applied. In 1992, the Charity Commissioners reported two examples of fraud by charity trustees that illustrate the kind of abuse that the law seeks to prevent. In the case of the Hospital Fund, a registered charity, two trustees were investigated after the Commissioners learnt of their lifestyle. It was found that the charity was raising some £0.5m per annum by the sale of tickets for a prize draw, door to door in Kent, but that only some 20 per cent of the money raised was being applied to the hospitals. The trustees were arrested and convicted of false accounting. In the case of the National Hospital for Neurology and Neurosurgery Development Foundation, an employee, Miss Rosemary Aberdour, was in charge of fund raising and stole some £2.7m. Abuse may also take a less dramatic form. In 2009, the Charity Commission reported on an inquiry into Tariqa Burhaniya D'Suqiyya Shazuliyya (TBDS) (Registered Charity Number 1041647). The Commission found that TBDS had insufficient financial controls. Large sums of cash were regularly used in the charity's transactions for which there were insufficient records to accurately account for this expenditure. The inquiry found that the trustees operated a complex system of loans, and donations to its members, and that a number of the trustees had benefited personally from loans that were provided on advantageous terms and conditions and constituted a trustee benefit prohibited by the Charity's governing document. The Commission identified corrective action which needed to be taken by the Charity. Also in 2009, the Commission reported on the Children's Welfare Foundation, a registered charity which, following an investigation into concerns, was removed from the register of charities. CWF was set up in March 2006. Its only fundraising came from selling unwanted clothing and similar items acquired through door-to-door collections. Over two years it raised £36,519 but spent £35,303—or 97 per cent—on 'expenses' and the only welfare activity claimed (but never substantiated) was taking a boy in a wheelchair for a day out in Blackpool.[13] The Charity Commission may also investigate allegations that charities are not acting within the proper bounds of charity law. For example, in March 2009 the Charity Commission opened a statutory inquiry into the charity Green Crescent

---

[13] A holiday resort on the north-west coast of England.

Bangladesh UK following media reports about alleged terrorist activity in an orphanage and madrassa (Islamic school) said to be supported by the charity in Bangladesh. No report had been published one year later.

In the case of private trusts the primary task of supervising the trustees and ensuring that they do not abuse their position falls to the beneficiaries. Charitable trusts do not have beneficiaries as such since, by their very nature, they are purpose trusts[14] and an exception to the beneficiary principle,[15] although there may obviously be persons who are interested in seeing that assets held on trust for charity are properly applied, for example donors.[16] Historically, charities were supervised and controlled by the Attorney-General acting on behalf of the Crown. However, his function has largely been replaced by a regulatory system with a statutory footing. The law was revised by the Charities Act 1993 and is further revised by the Charities Act 2006.

(1) Features of the regulatory system

The main feature of the regulatory mechanism for charities is the role of the Charity Commission, which is now a body corporate following the enactment of the Charities Act 2006.[17, 18] The Charity Commission has the task of overseeing charities in general and investigating abuses. It is obliged to maintain a register of charities. The legislation provides that some persons (for instance undischarged bankrupts) are disqualified from holding office as trustees and requires charity trustees to maintain accounts and to submit an annual report of the charity's activities and an annual statement of accounts to the Commissioners. The report and accounting requirements enable the Commissioners to supervise the conduct of charities, and they are also open to public inspection. Some charities are under the jurisdiction of visitors, although the authority of visitors to universities has been significantly reduced by legislation and no longer applies to employment matters or to complaints by students. Disputes relating to the former fall within the jurisdiction of employment tribunals, and student complaints are now within the jurisdiction of the Independent Adjudicator for Higher Education, an office established by the Higher Education Act 2004.

The Charities Act 2006 further extended the role of the Charity Commission in the regulation of charities, conferring on it extended powers to suspend or remove trustees,[19] to give specific directions for the protection of charity,[20] and to direct the application of charity property.[21] The Commission is given the power, on issue of a

---

[14] See Chapter 19.   [15] See Chapter 13.

[16] See also Warburton 'Charities, Members, Accountability And Control' [1997] Conv 106.

[17] Charities Act 2006, s 6 and Sch 1, which introduced s 1A and Sch 1A into the Charities Act 1993.

[18] Charities Bill 2005, cl 6. While the functions of the Commission are to be exercised on behalf of the Crown, cl 6(4) states that it shall not be subject to control by a government department or any Minister of the Crown.

[19] Charities Act 1993, s 18A inserted by Charities Act 2006, s 19.

[20] Ibid., s 19A inserted by Charities Act 2006, s 20.

[21] Ibid., s 19B inserted by Charities Act 2006, s 21.

search warrant, to enter premises.[22] There is, however, an obligation on the Charity Commission to have regard to the principles of best regulatory practice, 'including the principles under which regulatory activities should be proportionate, accountable, consistent, transparent and targeted only at cases in which action is needed'.[23] The role of the Charity Commission is considered in detail below.

(2) The Crown

The Crown is *parens patriae* of charity,[24] and therefore protector of charity in general.[25] However, this function is exercised on behalf of the Crown by the Attorney-General.

(3) The Attorney-General

Historically, the main mechanism for the supervision and control of charitable trusts was the Attorney-General, acting on behalf of the Crown. As Hoffmann J stated in *Bradshaw v University College of Wales, Aberystwyth*: 'So far as the enforcement of the trust is a matter of public interest, the guardian of that interest is the Attorney-General.'[26]

Prior to the Charities Act 1993 the Attorney-General was generally a necessary party to charity proceedings[27] because he represented the beneficial interest,[28] in other words the charitable purposes of the trust. As Lord Simmonds observed in *National Anti-Vivisection Society v IRC*,[29] it is the right and duty of the Attorney-General to inform the courts if the trustees of a charity fall short of their duty,[30] and to help the court formulate schemes for the execution of charitable trusts.[31]

Prior to the 1993 Act, only the Attorney-General was entitled to bring an action to determine whether a trust was charitable. However, s 32 of the Charities Act 1993 grants the Charity Commission the same powers as the Attorney-General to take legal proceedings with reference to charities, or the property affairs of charities, and to compromise claims to avoid or end proceedings. This emphasizes that the primary responsibility for controlling and enforcing charitable trusts falls today to the Commission.

---

[22] Ibid., s 31A inserted by Charities Act 2006, s 26.

[23] Ibid., s 1D inserted by Charities Act 2006, s 7.

[24] *Wallis v Solicitor-General for New Zealand* [1903] AC 173, at 181–182.

[25] *A-G v Glegg* (1738) 1 Atk 356; *Moggridge v Thackwell* (1803) 7 Ves 36; *Incorporated Society v Richards* (1841) 1 Dr & War 258; *A-G v Compton* (1842) 1 Y & C Ch Cas 417; *National Anti-Vivisection Society v IRC* [1948] AC 31, HL; *Re Belling* [1967] Ch 425; *Hauxwell v Barton-upon-Humber UDC* [1974] Ch 432.

[26] [1987] 3 All ER 200, at 203.

[27] See *Wellbeloved v Jones* (1822) 1 Sim & St 40; *National Anti-Vivisection Society v IRC* [1948] AC 31, HL; *Hauxwell v Barton-upon-Humber UDC* [1974] Ch 432.

[28] *Ware v Cumberlege* (1855) 20 Beav 503; *Re King* [1917] 2 Ch 420.

[29] [1948] AC 31, at 62.

[30] *A-G v Brown* (1818) 1 Swan 265; *National Anti-Vivisection Society v IRC* [1948] AC 31.

[31] *National Anti-Vivisection Society v IRC* [1948] AC 31; *Re Harpur's Will Trusts* [1962] Ch 78, CA.

(4) The court

(a) The jurisdiction of the court

The court possesses a general inherent jurisdiction[32] over charitable trusts. It has the power to draw up schemes for the administration of a charity,[33] particularly where there is a need to administer a fund cy-près,[34] and it remedies breaches of trust by charity trustees. This jurisdiction derives from the court's general jurisdiction over trusts. If a gift has been made to charity in general, or simply to one of the heads of charity, for example the poor, the court has the jurisdiction to draw up a scheme for the application of the property if a trust was intended, but if no trust was intended the Crown applies the property under the sign manual.[35] The court has no jurisdiction in the case of a charity founded by Royal Charter[36] or over a charity completely regulated by statute.[37] However, the court does have jurisdiction to ensure that the terms of the charter or statute are properly kept. The court retains an inherent jurisdiction over corporate charities, even though, in the strict sense, a company required to apply its assets for charitable purposes does not hold those assets on trust.[38] The Court of Appeal has held that the court has no jurisdiction under the Charities Act 1993 in respect of charities established outside England and Wales under a foreign legal system.[39]

An example of the exercise of the court's supervisory jurisdiction over charitable trusts is provided by *Royal Society for the Prevention of Cruelty to Animals v A-G*.[40] The Society sought to exclude members and applicants for membership who had joined for the ulterior purpose of changing its anti-hunting policy. Members and applicants who fell within defined categories would be treated as conclusively proved deserving of exclusion, without the need to consider the merits of their individual cases. Lightman J held that whilst the policy of exclusion did not contravene the Human Rights Act, the Society should not operate its chosen method of implementing its membership policy. He considered that it was 'arbitrary and unattractive' and that it was not necessary to exclude from membership persons to whom no conceivable objection could be taken if the full facts were allowed to be taken into account. Given that emergency action was not required, the 'plight of the innocent' needed to be given greater weight.

---

[32] *Mills v Farmer* (1815) 1 Mer 55; *A-G v Sherborne Grammar Schools Governors* (1854) 18 Beav 256.

[33] See *A-G v Coopers' Co* (1812) 19 Ves 187; *A-G v St Olave's Grammar School* (1837) Coop Pr Cas 267; *A-G v Dedham School* (1857) 23 Beav 350.

[34] See Chapter 20.

[35] *Moggridge v Thackwell* (1803) 7 Ves 36; *Paice v Archbishop of Canterbury* (1807) 14 Ves 364; *Spiller v Maude* (1881) 32 Ch D 158n; *Re Slevin* [1891] 2 Ch 236, CA; *Re White* [1893] 2 Ch 41, CA; *Re Bennett* [1960] Ch 18.

[36] *A-G v Smart* (1748) 1 Ves Sen 72; *A-G v Middleton* (1751) 2 Ves Sen 327; *A-G v Governors of the Foundling Hospital* (1793) 2 Ves 42. If the charity was granted a Royal Charter subsequent to its foundation to provide an incorporated trustee, the court retains its inherent jurisdiction: *A-G v Dedham School* (1857) 23 Beav 350.

[37] *Re Shrewsbury Grammar School* (1849) 1 Mac & G 324.

[38] *Liverpool and District Hospital for Diseases of the Heart v A-G* [1981] 1 All ER 994.

[39] *Gaudiya Mission v Brahmachary* [1998] Ch 341.   [40] [2001] 3 All ER 530.

He also considered that the 'public image and reputation' of the Society had not been sufficiently taken into account in adopting such a draconian policy.

(b) Concurrent jurisdiction of the Charity Commission

The primacy of the role of the Charity Commission in the supervision and control of charitable trusts is also evident, in that the Commission enjoys concurrent jurisdiction alongside that of the court. It is thus able to exercise many of the functions formerly the exclusive preserve of the court. By s 16(1) of the Charities Act 1993, the Charity Commission enjoys the same jurisdiction and powers that are exercisable by the High Court in charity proceedings for the purposes of: (a) establishing a scheme for the administration of a charity; (b) appointing, discharging, or removing a charity trustee or trustee for a charity, or removing an officer or employee; (c) vesting or transferring property, or requiring or entitling any person to call for or make any transfer of property or any payment.

(c) Charity proceedings

The effectiveness of the supervision of charitable trusts by the court depends on those who might have some interest being able to start an action. Other than the Attorney-General and the Charity Commission, s 33(1) of the Charities Act 1993 provides that:

Charity proceedings may be taken with reference to a charity either by the charity, or by any of the charity trustees, or by any person interested in the charity, or by any two or more inhabitants of the area of the charity if it is a local charity, but not by any other person.

(i) Any person interested in the charity

The definition of this phrase has been considered in a number of cases. *Re Hampton Fuel Allotment Charity*[41] concerned a charity relieving hardship and distress amongst residents of Hampton. The charity sought to sell land that it owned to a supermarket for £8m. A minority of the trustees felt that the sale was at a gross undervalue, and that the real value was some £14m. They started an action seeking orders concerning the administration of the charity along with Richmond Council, which had the power to appoint three of the trustees and in whose borough the charity operated. At first instance the council was struck out as not being a person 'interested in the charity'. However, the Court of Appeal held that it did enjoy sufficient interest to maintain an action. It was unwilling to attempt a comprehensive definition of 'any person interested in the charity' but stated that:

If a person has an interest in securing the due administration of a trust materially greater than, or different from, that possessed by ordinary members of the public... that interest may, depending on the circumstances, qualify him as a 'person interested'...[42]

The council had an interest greater than that of the ordinary public because it had a functional role with regard to the charity, in that it appointed three of the eleven

---

[41] [1989] Ch 484.   [42] Ibid., at 494.

trustees, and it was the local authority of the area benefited by the carrying out of the purposes. The Court of Appeal referred to *Haslemere Estates Ltd v Baker*,[43] where Megarry V-C had held that enjoyment of an adverse interest against a charity did not necessarily equate with having a good reason for seeking to enforce the trust. Thus, he suggested that not even tenants of charity land, or those with easements, profits, mortgages, or restrictive covenants, or those who had contracted to repair or decorate charity houses or had agreed to buy or sell goods to the charity, would have sufficient interest. It seems that a donor to a charity may have sufficient interest,[44] but not the executors of a donor.[45]

Haslemere Estates Ltd v Baker, which concerned a claim by a property developer against the trustees of Dulwich College, was distinguished by Robert Walker J in *Scott v National Trust*[46] on the grounds that it concerned a wholly commercial dispute which had no real connection with the internal or functional administration of charitable trusts.[47] In contrast, he held that the hunts and tenant farmers which were affected by a decision of the National Trust not to allow the hunting of deer with hounds on its land in Devon and Somerset were sufficiently interested in the charity to bring proceedings. He pointed out that they had been hunting there since long before the land had belonged to the Trust, and that they had been partners with the National Trust in the management of its land.[48]

The ambit of s 33(1) was most recently considered in *Royal Society for the Prevention of Cruelty to Animals v A-G*.[49] The RSPCA sought to change its membership rules so as to exclude members who had been campaigning to persuade the Society to change its anti-hunting stance and prevent applicants becoming members who shared this objective. Lightman J held that an existing member of the Society did have sufficient interest in the charity to commence charity proceedings challenging the propriety of the Society's actions, but that a mere applicant for membership did not:

> But I do not think that a disappointed applicant for membership has any such sufficient interest. Any member of the public is free to apply for membership; the exercise of that liberty cannot elevate the status of a non-member into that of a person interested. To extend the right of suit to any such applicant would be to cast the net too wide.[50]

(ii) Consent of the Charity Commission

Section 33(2) provides that no proceedings shall be taken in any court without the authorization of the Charity Commission. The Commission is not to authorize proceedings if the case could be dealt with under their own powers.[51] The reason for these limitations is to prevent pointless actions which would simply waste the charity's money.

---

43 [1982] 1 WLR 1109.   44 *Brooks v Richardson* [1986] 1 WLR 385.
45 *Bradshaw v University College of Wales, Aberystwyth* [1988] 1 WLR 190.
46 [1998] 2 All ER 705.   47 Ibid., at 715.
48 [1998] 2 All ER 705.   49 [2001] 3 All ER 530.
50 Ibid., at [21].   51 S 33(3).

(5) **The Charity Commission**

The Charity Commissioners were first appointed under the Charitable Trusts Act 1853. Their position was modernized by the Charities Act 1960, which implemented the recommendations of the Nathan Committee Report.[52] It is now enshrined in the Charities Act 1993, which followed the Woodfield Report[53] and which is further amended by the Charities Act 2006. The 2006 Act makes the Charity Commission a body corporate with a membership and structure specified in a new schedule to the Charities Act 1993, and with newly specified objectives:[54]

1. to increase public trust and confidence in charities;
2. to promote awareness and understanding of the operation of the public benefit requirement;
3. to promote compliance by charity trustees with their legal obligations in exercising control and management of the administration of their charities;
4. to promote the effective use of charitable resources; and
5. to enhance the accountability of charities to donors, beneficiaries and the general public.

The functions of the Charity Commission underline the importance of the Charity Commission in applying charity law, regulating charities, disseminating information, and providing information and advice.

(a) Annual report

The Commission has the duty under s 2 of the Charities Act 1993 to make an annual report to the Secretary of State, which must be laid before Parliament. These reports provide a review of the administration of charities and bring attention to any particular problems. The Commission also provides precedents for purposes that it has registered as charitable, and any changes in their requirements.

(b) Power to institute inquiries

By s 8(1) the Commission has the power to 'institute inquiries with regard to charities, or a particular charity or class of charities'.[55] In connection with this power it has wide-ranging ancillary powers to obtain relevant information. It may order any person to furnish accounts and statements and to return answers in writing to any questions or inquiries,[56] to furnish copies of documents under his control[57] and to give

---

[52] The Committee on the Law and Practice relating to Charitable Trusts, Cmnd 8710 of 1952.

[53] Efficiency Scrutiny of the Supervision of Charities, 1987; National Audit Office Report, House of Commons Paper 380, 1986–87; Annual Report 1987.

[54] Charities Act 1993, Sch 1B inserted by Charities Act 2006, s 7.

[55] This power did not extend to exempt charities, but this has been modified by the Charities Act 2006, s 12, Sch 5, which now allows such an inquiry to be undertaken for exempt charities—see below.

[56] S 8(3)(a).   [57] S 8(3)(b).

evidence,[58] which may be taken under oath.[59] By s 11 of the Act it is a criminal offence knowingly or recklessly to provide the Commission with false or misleading information, or to wilfully alter, suppress, conceal, or destroy any document required to be produced to the Commission. As has been noted above, the Commission may obtain a warrant to search premises.

The Charity Commission is increasingly adopting a risk-based approach in order to concentrate its engagement with charities where it is most needed and which takes account of the risk involved to the charity and its beneficiaries, and the capacity of the charity to comply.[60] In 2001 the Charity Commissioners published 123 inquiry reports.[61] In the year ending March 2009, only twenty-one statutory inquiries were completed and reports published, which concerned the most serious cases.[62] The Commission completed 167 regulatory compliance cases that did not require the use of their statutory powers to resolve. This is symptomatic of a move towards resolving most compliance issues through guidance and supervision, on the basis that '[p]revention is invariably better than cure'.[63] The Commission also published its first ever 'compendium' of issues and lessons learned from its compliance work in *Charities Back on Track*, which demonstrated that in the year 2007–08, some £16m of charity assets were protected through the Commission's compliance work.[64]

(c) Power to act for the protection of charities

Section 18 grants the Commission wide-ranging powers to take action where it has instituted an inquiry under s 8 and is satisfied:

(a) that there is or has been any misconduct or mismanagement in the administration of the charity; or

(b) that it is necessary or desirable to act for the purpose of protecting the property of the charity or securing a proper application for the purposes of the charity of that property or of property coming to the charity.[65]

The action the Commission may take includes: the suspension of any trustee pending consideration of his removal;[66] appointing additional trustees;[67] vesting the property of the charity in the Official Custodian;[68] restraining persons who hold property on behalf of the charity from parting with it without their approval;[69] restricting the transactions and payments that may be entered or made without approval;[70] and appointing a receiver and manager.[71] In addition, where the Commission is satisfied that both criteria (a) and (b) above are met, it has the power to: (i) remove any trustee, charity trustee, officer, agent, or employee of the charity who has been responsible for or privy to the misconduct or mismanagement or has by his conduct contributed to it

---

[58] S 8(3)(c).   [59] S 8(4).   [60] Annual Report 2004–2005, p 5.
[61] Annual Report 2001, p 12.   [62] Annual Report 2008–2009, p 21.
[63] Ibid., p 2.
[64] (September 2008), at p 6. The publication includes a series of case studies, centred on key themes of regulation.
[65] S 18(1).   [66] S 8(1)(i).   [67] S 8(1)(ii).   [68] S 8(1)(iii).
[69] S 8(1)(iv).   [70] S 8(1)(vi).   [71] S 8(1)(vii).

or facilitated it; (ii) by order establish a scheme for the administration of the charity.[72] Additional powers were conferred on the Charity Commission by the Charities Act 2006, including the power to give specific directions for the protection of charity and to direct the application of charity property.[73]

(d) Duty to maintain a register of charities

Section 3 requires the Commissioners to maintain a register of all charities. The scope and purpose of this register is considered below.

(e) Duty to inform the Charity Commission of the desirability of bringing legal proceedings

Section 33(2) places the trustees under a duty to inform the Charity Commission if it is desirable to take legal proceedings with reference to any charity. The Charity Commission will inform the Attorney-General if it feels legal proceedings are desirable under s 33(7).

(f) Power to give advice to charity trustees

Section 29, as substituted by the s 24 of the Charities Act 2006, empowers the Commission to give its opinion or advice to a charity trustee on any matter affecting the performance of his duties as such or the proper administration of the trust. A charity trustee who acts in accordance with such advice is deemed 'to have acted in accordance with his trust', unless he knew or had reasonable cause to suspect that the advice had been given in ignorance of material facts.

(g) The Official Custodian

By s 2 of the Charities Act 1993 (as amended by the Charities Act 2006) the Charity Commission is required to designate a person to act as the Official Custodian for charitable trusts, so that charity trustees can vest charity property in him as custodian trustee, thereby obviating the need for property (and, in particular, land) to be transferred to the new trustees every time the trustees of a charity change.

(h) Cost

In 1999–2000 the Commission was allocated £21.8m.[74] In its Annual Report for 2008–09 the Commission reports that it spent a total £32.3m on operating activity and capital investment in the year ending in March 2009.[75]

(6) The Charities Register

A scheme of general registration of charities was first introduced by the Charities Act 1960. It is now the duty of the Commission to maintain such a register under

---

[72] S 18(2)(i)–(ii).
[73] Charities Act 2006, inserting ss 19A and 19B into the Charities Act 1993. See further Lloyd, *Charities— The New Law 2006: A Practical Guide To The Charities Acts* (2007), Ch 7.
[74] Annual Report 1999, para 6.3.9.   [75] Annual Report 2008–9, p 14.

s 3,[76] which by s 3(3) of the Charities Act 1993 Act shall contain the name of the charity and any other information the Commission thinks fit. Some charities are not required to register, namely: the 'exempt' charities;[77] charities which are exempted by order or regulations and which have a gross income of less than £100,000 per annum;[78] charities with a low income (less than £5,000 gross per annum).[79] All other charities are required to register and are required to provide a copy of their trusts when they apply for registration.[80] The register, including the copies of the charities' trust instruments, is open to public inspection at all reasonable times.[81] The register can be inspected online.

It was formerly the case that exempt charities were exempt not only from the requirement to register, but also from many of the regulatory provisions contained in the Charities Acts. This was because they were drawn from sectors which had alternative forms of regulation. The Charities Act 2006 significantly altered that position. It made some changes (by s 11) to the categories of institution with exempt charity status. It also requires a 'principal regulator' to be appointed for all exempt charities.[82] The principal regulator is charged with 'promoting compliance by the charity trustees with their legal obligations in exercising control and management of the administration of the charity'. By s 12, Sch 5, the Charities Act 2006 increased the degree of regulation of exempt charities, giving the Charity Commission, *inter alia*, the power to institute inquiries. This power to institute an inquiry can only be exercised at the request of the principal regulator.

Universities are exempt charities, and as such are not required to register with the Charity Commission. Universities were already subject to detailed scrutiny by the Higher Education Funding Councils in England and Wales, and in England (but not in Wales) the Funding Council is now the principal regulator for this group of exempt charities. Universities in Wales will be regulated directly by the Charity Commission in regard to charity matters.

(7) The First-Tier Tribunal (Charity)

The Charities Act 2006 established a new body, the Charity Tribunal.[83] From 1 September 2009, the Charity Tribunal has been abolished and its jurisdiction has been passed to First-Tier Tribunal (Charity), following the Transfer of Functions of the Charity Tribunal Order 2009/1834.[84] The First–Tier Tribunal (Charity) is administered by the unified Tribunals Service, an executive agency of the Ministry of Justice. Before the establishment of any Tribunal service for charity appeals, a person

---

[76] Section 9 of the Charities Act 2006 replaced s 3 of the Charities Act 1993 with ss 3, 3A, and 3B.

[77] S 3A(2)(a) and Sch 2.   [78] S 3A(2)(b)(c).

[79] S 3A(2)(d). The requirement that small charities must register if they hold land or have a permanent endowment has not been re-enacted by the Charities Act 2006.

[80] S 3B(2).   [81] S 3(7).   [82] S 13.

[83] Charities Act 2006, s 8, introducing ss 2A–2D and Sch 1C into the Charities Act 1993.

[84] This order amends and repeals various sub-sections of the Charities Act 1993. Full details can be found in Sch 1 of the order.

who was unhappy with a decision of the Charity Commission, for instance because of a refusal to register a body or a trust as a charity, could ask the Commission to review the decision using its own internal review processes and, if still unhappy, could appeal to the High Court. There is now in many cases a right of appeal to the First-Tier Tribunal (Charity) following a final decision, direction, or order of the Charity Commission.[85]

There is then a further right of appeal to Upper-Tier Tribunal and then the High Court, but only on points of law. The Upper-Tier Tribunal, established under the wholesale reform of the Tribunal system under the Tribunals, Courts and Enforcement Act 1997, is established as a court of superior record with the power to bind itself and the Lower-Tier Tribunals on matters within its remit.[86] The Attorney-General has the right to refer certain matters to the Tribunal,[87] and is given the power to intervene in proceedings before the Tribunal, to which he is not a party.[88]

The sorts of matter over which the First-Tier Tribunal (Charity) has jurisdiction are appeals against decisions to register or to refuse to register an institution as a charity, to institute an inquiry with regard to a particular institution or group of institutions, a decision to appoint or remove a charity trustee, and many other decisions listed in Sch 1C of the 2006 Act. It is anticipated that the flexible Tribunal procedure will allow matters of law to be 'fast-tracked' directly to the Upper-Tier Tribunal, and, if necessary, remitted to the First-Tier Tribunal. This would promote a particular saving in terms of cost to charities, but the new Tribunal structure is in its infancy and much remains unclear about the scope and nature of its operation. Such a procedure is certainly the wish of the then President[89] of the original Charity Tribunal.[90]

The changes to the Tribunal system should mean that the Tribunals will have a very important role to play in the future. Before the Charities Act 2006, many disputed decisions made by the Charity Commission did not get any further than the internal review process, due to the high expense of an appeal action in the High Court. The Tribunal system should offer a cheaper and speedier alternative, which should increase the number of Charity Commission decisions that are appealed. Despite the introduction of the original Charity Tribunal, there was still major criticism of the way in which the service operated. Namely, it was considered that the legal costs of accessing the Charity Tribunal were too high for most charities, the lack of formal rules led to lengthy procedural arguments, and a combination of an adversarial atmosphere and a feeling that it was an uneven playing field for the parties weakened

---

[85] S 2A(4)(a) and Sch 1C.

[86] Indeed, under s 25(2)(c) it has the same powers as the High Court for matters within its remit. See further McKenna 'Transforming Tribunals: The Reform of the Charity Tribunal by the Tribunals, Courts and Enforcement Act 1997' (2009) 11 *Charity Law and Practice Review* 1.

[87] S 2A(4)(b).   [88] S 2D.

[89] This person now serves as a judge of the First-Tier Tribunal and as a Deputy Judge of the Upper Tribunal—The Transfer of Functions of the Charity Tribunal Order 2009/1834, s 3.

[90] McKenna 'Transforming Tribunals: The Reform of the Charity Tribunal by the Tribunals, Courts and Enforcement Act 1997' (2009) 11 *Charity Law and Practice Review* 1, at p 10.

the effectiveness of the system.[91] It remains to be seen whether the introduction of the new Tribunal structure will deal with these 'teething problems' effectively, but it must surely only be a matter of time before such issues are addressed as practice develops, and the frequency of appeals increases. In particular, the powers and remit of the Upper-Tier Tribunal are likely to mean that, where a point of law is involved, fewer cases will be dealt with by the courts. The role of the Tribunals in the development and interpretation of charity law, and in particular the recognition of charitable purposes, is therefore likely to be considerable.

(8) Control of charity trustees

The legislative framework recognizes the importance of the role of the trustees of charities, and that they enjoy major opportunities for abuse. Some persons are disqualified from serving as charity trustees, whilst those who can occupy such positions are subject to onerous duties.

(a) Disqualification

The Charities Act 1993, s 72 disqualifies certain individuals from serving as charity trustees. The main circumstances in which a person will be so disqualified are:[92] (i) previous conviction of any offence involving dishonesty or deception; (ii) undischarged bankruptcy; (iii) previous removal from the office of a charity trustee by an order of the Commission; (iv) previous disqualification from serving as a company director under the Company Directors' Disqualification Act 1986. Any person who serves as a charity trustee while disqualified commits a criminal offence.[93] The Charity Commission now has a power, in limited circumstances, to waive the disqualification.[94]

(b) Duties of charity trustees

The trustees of most charities are under a duty to keep proper financial records and to provide an annual report to the Charity Commission. However, the trustees of exempt charities are merely under a duty to keep proper books of account that must be preserved for six years.[95] Where the charity is a company the trustees are exempt from the accounting requirements of the Charities Act 1993[96] but must comply with the company law provisions relating to accounts.[97] Under the Charities (Accounts and Reports) Regulations 1995[98] a new framework was introduced for charity accounting requiring charities to produce annual accounts and a trustee report, the Statement of Recommended Practice (SORP).[99] The presentation of this information is required to

---

[91] Third Sector 'Teething Problems for the Charity Tribunal' (23 June 2008).
[92] See s 72(1)(a)–(f).   [93] Charities Act 1993, s 73.
[94] Charities Act 1993, s 4A, inserted by the Charities Act 2006, s 35.
[95] S 46.   [96] Ss 41(5); s 42(7); s 43(9); s 45(5).
[97] Companies Act 2006, Pt 15.   [98] SI 1995 2724.
[99] The SORP has undergone many revisions since its inception. The most current detailed regulations are Charities (Accounts and Reports) Regulations 2008, SI 2008/629, and the SORP 2004, published by the

be uniform, thus allowing people to see more clearly how charities are spending their money and to compare different charities. A system of thresholds seeks to ensure that the heaviest burden falls to the larger charities, where a stricter regime of external scrutiny will apply. Smaller charities are subject to less demanding requirements. The annual report and charity accounts are open to public inspection.[100]

(i) Duty to apply for registration

Under s 3B(1)(a), the trustees of a charity which is not registered and is not exempted or excepted from the requirement to be registered are under a duty to apply for it to be registered.

(ii) Duty to keep accounts

Charity trustees are under a duty to keep accounting records that are sufficient to show and explain all the charity's transactions, and which must be retained for at least six years.[101]

(iii) Duty to prepare annual accounts

They are also under a duty to prepare an annual statement of accounts in accordance with the regulations made by the Secretary of State.[102]

(iv) Duty to have an annual audit

If the annual income of the charity exceeds a specified limit the accounts must be audited, but if it does not exceed that amount they can be examined by an independent examiner. If an audit is not carried out the Commission may order an audit at the expense of the charity or the charity trustees.[103]

(v) Duty to prepare an annual report

The trustees of a charity are under a duty to prepare an annual report for each financial year containing a report on the activities of the charity during the past year and other information, as may be prescribed by regulation. The annual report must be transmitted to the Charity Commission and have attached the statement of accounts[104] and, where appropriate, the auditor or independent examiner's report.[105] The annual report is to be kept open to public inspection by the Commission.[106]

(9) Local authorities and local charities

Although the Charity Commission operates a national scheme for the registration and supervision of charities, the Charities Act 1993 also makes provision for localized

Charity Commission. See further Pianca and Dawes *Charity Accounts: A Practitioner's Guide to the SORP* (4th edn, 2009).

[100] S 47.   [101] S 41.
[102] S 42. These statements must also be retained for the next six years.
[103] S 43.   [104] With the exception of charities which are companies: s 46(5).
[105] S 46.   [106] S 47.

schemes. Under s 76 county and district councils, London borough councils and the Common Council of the City of London may maintain an index of local charities, from which they may publish information, summaries, or extracts, and which is to be open to public inspection. They are entitled to receive from the Commission copies of entries on the register which are relevant for the index.

(10) Visitors

(a) Charities under the jurisdiction of visitors

Ecclesiastical and eleemosynary corporations are under the jurisdiction of visitors. Ecclesiastical corporations are those which exist for the furtherance of religion and the perpetuation of the rites of the Church.[107] The visitor is generally the Ordinary,[108] although in the case of Royal Foundations or free chapels, the visitor is the patron. Eleemosynary corporations are corporations constituted for the perpetual distribution of free alms or bounty of the founder to such persons as he has directed. They are generally hospitals[109] or colleges. They include the majority of the older universities, which were created by Royal Charter. The visitor for such corporations may be appointed by the founder, or if no such appointment was made, the founder and his heirs are the visitor.[110] Where the visitor is the Crown, the powers are exercised by the Lord Chancellor.

(b) Extent of the jurisdiction of the visitor

The jurisdiction of the visitor extends only to the internal affairs of the charity, and has no application to relations between the members of corporations and those outside.[111] In the case of universities created by Royal Charter, the visitor formerly had jurisdiction over matters between the university and students who are members of the university,[112] although the visitor's jurisdiction to consider complaints from students has now been transferred by the Higher Education Act 2004 to the Independent Adjudicator for Higher Education. The visitor's jurisdiction, in those instances where it remains, is sole and exclusive,[113] although he must act within his jurisdiction and

---

[107] 1 Bl Com (16th edn), p 470; *A-G v St Cross Hospital* (1853) 17 Beav 435.

[108] 1 Bl Comm (16th edn), p 479; *Re Dean of York* (1841) 2 QB 1; *R v Dean of Rochester* (1851) 17 QB 1; *Revised Canons Ecclesiastical*, Canon C18, para 4.

[109] See *Dilworth v Stamps Comrs* [1899] AC 99; *Moses v Marsland* [1901] 1 KB 668.

[110] *Phillips v Bury* (1694) Skin 447.

[111] This includes the undergraduates at the majority of Colleges of Oxford and Cambridge, where only the master, fellows, and exhibitioners are members of the college. See also *R v Industrial Disputes Tribunal, ex p Queen Mary College, University of London* [1957] 2 QB 483; *Herring v Templeman* [1973] 3 All ER 569, CA; *Casson v University of Aston in Birmingham* [1983] 1 All ER 88; *Thomas v University of Bradford* [1987] 1 All ER 834, HL.

[112] *Patel v Bradford University Senate* [1978] 1 WLR 1488; *Oakes v Sidney Sussex College, Cambridge* [1988] 1 WLR 431; *R v HM the Queen in Council, ex p Vijayatunga* [1990] 2 QB 444.

[113] *A-G v Harrow School Governors* (1754) 2 Ves Sen 551; *A-G v Magdalen College, Oxford* (1847) 10 Beav 402; *Thomson v University of London* (1864) 33 LJ Ch 625; *Thorne v University of London* [1966] 2 QB 237, CA; *Patel v Bradford University Senate* [1978] 1 WLR 1488.

the rules of natural justice.[114] The visitor is subject to control by the courts through judicial review.

(c) Statutory limitation of the visitor's jurisdiction

In the case of universities the jurisdiction of the visitor has been greatly curtailed by the Education Reform Act 1988. Section 206 provides that the visitor has no jurisdiction in respect of any dispute relating to a member of the academic staff that concerns his appointment or employment or the termination of his appointment or employment.[115] The visitor's former jurisdiction over student complaints has also been removed by statute.

(11) Judicial review of decisions taken by charities

In *Scott v National Trust*,[116] Robert Walker J considered the question whether a decision of the National Trust to ban deer hunting with hounds on its land was amenable to judicial review. He noted that charitable trusts involved a public element and that the charity enjoyed powers and discretions which might affect different sections of the public directly or indirectly. Whilst he was unwilling to consider whether any charity, or even any charity specially established by statute is subject to judicial review, he stated his opinion that the National Trust would be susceptible:

> the National Trust is a charity of exceptional importance to the nation, regulated by its own special Acts of Parliament. Its purposes and functions are of high public importance, as is reflected by the special statutory provisions (in the fields of taxation and compulsory acquisition) to which I have already referred. It seems to me to have all the characteristics of a public body which is, prima facie, amenable to judicial review, and to have been exercising its statutory public functions in making the decision which is challenged.[117]

However, he held that the availability of judicial monitoring through charity proceedings in the Chancery Division meant that judicial review would not be appropriate in all but the most exceptional cases, which he suggested might include where a local authority held land on charitable trusts and questions about its dealings with that land were caught up with other questions about its dealings with land which it owned beneficially.[118]

In contrast, in *Royal Society for the Prevention of Cruelty to Animals v A-G*[119] Lightman J held that disappointed applicants for membership of the Society were not entitled to seek judicial review. He held that, whilst the Society was a very important charity and its activities were of great value to society, it could be distinguished from

---

[114] *R v Lord President of the Privy Council, ex p Page* [1993] AC 682.

[115] See Pettit 'Academic Tenure and the Education Reform Act 1988' (1991) 54 MLR 137; *Thomas v University of Bradford* [1987] 1 All ER 834; *Pearce v University of Aston in Birmingham* [1991] 2 All ER 461 and *(No 2)* [1991] 2 All ER 469; *Hines v Birkbeck College (No 2)* [1992] Ch 33, CA.

[116] [1998] 2 All ER 705.   [117] Ibid., at 716.

[118] Ibid., at 717–718.   [119] [2001] 3 All ER 530.

the National Trust on the grounds that it had no statutory or public law role. Thus, although it is the largest non-governmental law enforcement agency in England and Wales, in carrying out these activities it is in no different position from that of any citizen or other organization.

Recently, the Court of Appeal in *R (Weaver) v London and Quadrant Housing*[120] held that a registered social landlord was a 'public body' for the purposes of judicial review in carrying out allocation or management of housing stock. The claimant, an assured tenant, contended that the trust was in breach of a legitimate expectation in failing to pursue all reasonable alternatives before resorting to a mandatory ground for possession and that the decision was in breach of, inter alia, art 8 of the European Convention on Human Rights, guaranteeing respect for home life. Although the claim was dismissed, Richards LJ held that the functions a social landlord carried out were of a public nature. The nature and level of public subsidy and state control of such bodies were essential factors in finding that a social landlord was a public authority. The fact that eviction may be considered a private act was not sufficient to withdraw the public character of the action.

This has since been applied in *R (McIntyre) v Gentoo Group Ltd.*[121] Judicial review was not approved on the facts, as the tenants had other options open to them, where it was confirmed that the decision in *R v London and Quadrant Housing* extended beyond acts relating to termination of a tenancy, and would allow for review of other management functions of a social landlord in relation to stock—the case concerned a mutual exchange of tenancies.

The impact of the decision in *R v London and Quadrant Housing* for other charities has yet to be felt, but it suggests that a restrictive approach is no longer tenable.

(12) Human Rights Act

Those charities which are public authorities are subject to the provisions of the Human Rights Act 1998. The Charity Commission is a public authority, and thus subject to the provisions of the Act. Most charities, however, as *RSPCA v A-G*[122] shows, will not be considered to be public authorities. It is now clear that registered social landlords in discharging at least some of their functions will be classified as 'public authorities' for the purposes of s 6(3)(b) of the Human Rights Act 1998, and decisions relating to management and allocation of stock must adhere to human rights principles or can be challenged in court. This is likely to be a fertile source of litigation over the coming years.

---

[120] [2009] EWCA Civ 507.   [121] [2010] EWHC 5.
[122] Ibid. See immediately above.

29

Remedies against the trustee for breach of trust

The duties and obligations imposed on trustees are enforceable by the beneficiaries against the trustees. The nature of such liability for breach of trust is, as we shall see, personal, so that trustees are liable to make good any losses to the trust property from their own pockets. In addition to the remedies against a trustee for breach of trust, trustees are also subject to fiduciary duties that limit their ability to act in conflict with the trust (considered in the next chapter). There are also situations in which personal remedies will be available against third parties who have assisted a breach of trust or come into contact with trust property (considered in Chapter 31) and proprietary remedies against both trustees and third parties to reclaim the trust property itself (explored in Chapter 32).

1 Meaning of breach of trust

(1) General definition

It is difficult to provide a simple definition of a breach of trust. Sir Robert Megarry V-C was unwilling to attempt any 'comprehensive definition of a breach of trust' in *Tito v Waddell (No 2)*,[1] but referred to two American definitions that had found approval in the courts. First, *Pomeroy's Equity Jurisprudence*[2] states that 'every omission or violation by a trustee of a duty which equity lays on him...is a breach of trust'. Second, Professor Scott states that a trustee 'commits a breach of trust if he violates any duty which he owes as trustee to the beneficiaries'.[3] These two definitions demonstrate that the essence of a breach of trust is the failure of the trustees properly to carry out the duties expected of them. Their duties may either be expressly required of them by the

---

[1] [1977] 3 All ER 129. He regarded such an attempt as a 'perilous task' (at 247).
[2] As adopted by Corpus Juris Secundum (1955) vol 90, pp 225, 228, para 247.
[3] *Scott on Trusts* (3rd edn 1967), vol 3, p 1605, para 201.

trust deed creating the trust, or imposed by the general principles of equity. Trustees can be liable for breach of trust for both their acts and their omissions.

(a) Acts of trustees in breach of trust

If trustees act in a manner inconsistent with the terms of the trust they will have committed a breach of trust.[4] For example, if the trustees of a discretionary trust allocate the trust property to a person outside the class of potential beneficiaries, they will be acting in breach of trust.[5] Similarly, if a trustee exceeds any powers that he has been granted by the trust he will be liable.[6] So, for example, if a trust deed contains an express power of investment which excludes the general power of investment granted under s 3 of the Trustee Act 2000,[7] the trustee will commit a breach of trust if he invests the trust fund in investments other than those which are authorized by the trust deed.

(b) Omissions of trustees in breach of trust

If trustees fail to fulfil their duties to the trust through neglect or omission, they will also commit a breach of trust.[8] Historically, the standard of care required of trustees was the objective standard of the 'ordinary prudent man of business'. As Brightman J said in *Bartlett v Barclays Bank Trust Co Ltd*:[9]

The cases establish that it is the duty of a trustee to conduct the business of the trust with the same care as an ordinary prudent man of business would extend towards his own affairs.[10]

A higher standard of care was demanded of professional trustees, such as trust corporations. This is entirely appropriate since such corporations, which carry on a specialized business of trust management, hold themselves out as having a level of expertise beyond that of the 'ordinary prudent man of business'. They will be held liable 'if loss is caused to the trust fund because it neglects to exercise the special care and skill which it professes to have'.[11]

---

[4] *Pye v Gorges* (1710) Prec Ch 308; *Mansell v Mansell* (1732) 2 P Wms 678; *Charitable Corpn v Sutton* (1742) 9 Mod Rep 349; *Clough v Bond* (1838) 3 My & Cr 490; *Harrison v Randall* (1851) 9 Hare 397; *Reid v Thompson and M'Namara* (1851) 2 I Ch R 26; *Dance v Goldingham* (1873) 8 Ch App 902.

[5] See Chapter 17.

[6] *Adair v Shaw* (1803) 1 Sch & Lef 243; *Collier v M'Bean* (1865) 34 Beav 426.

[7] Trustee Act 2000, s 6(1). See Chapter 23.

[8] *Charitable Corpn v Sutton* (1742) 9 Mod Rep 349; *Lord Montfort v Lord Cadogan* (1810) 17 Ves 485; *Moyle v Moyle* (1831) 2 Russ & M 710; *Taylor v Tabrum* (1833) 6 Sim 281; *Clough v Bond* (1838) 3 My & Cr 490; *Fenwick v Greenwell* (1847) 10 Beav 412; *Dix v Burford* (1854) 19 Beav 409; *Stone v Stone* (1869) 5 Ch App 74; *Jefferys v Marshall* (1870) 19 WR 94; *Re Brogden* (1888) 38 Ch D 546, CA; *Evans v London Co-operative Society* (1976) The Times, 6 July; *Bartlett v Barclays Bank Trust Co Ltd* [1980] Ch 515.

[9] [1980] Ch 515, at 531.

[10] *Re Speight* (1883) 22 Ch D 727; affd sum nom *Speight v Gaunt* (1883) 9 App Cas 1; *Learoyd v Whiteley* (1887) 12 App Cas 727, HL; *Re Godfrey* (1883) 23 Ch D 483; *Re Chapman* [1896] 2 Ch 763, CA; *Re Lucking's Will Trusts* [1967] 3 All ER 726, [1968] 1 WLR 866.

[11] [1980] Ch 515, at 531, per Brightman J. See also *Re Waterman's Will Trusts* [1952] 2 All ER 1054; *Nestlé v National Westminster Bank plc* (29 June 1988, unreported).

The duty of care demanded of trustees in respect of the performance of some of their duties has now been placed on a statutory footing. Section 1(1) of the Trustee Act 2000 provides that:

Whenever the duty under this subsection applies to a trustee, he must exercise such care and skill as is reasonable in the circumstances, having regard in particular—

(a) to any special knowledge or experience that he has or holds himself out as having, and

(b) if he acts as trustee in the course of a business or profession, to any special knowledge or experience that it is reasonable to expect of a person acting in the course of that kind of business or profession.[12]

This statutory duty of care applies to certain specific situations which are outlined in Sch 1 to the Trustee Act 2000. These include the exercise of the power of investment, review of the trust investments, obtaining advice about trust investments, the exercise of powers in relation to land (including the power to acquire land), and the appointment of agents, custodians, or nominees.

If a trustee has failed to exercise the required standard of care, and loss is caused to the trust, he will be liable for breach of trust. For example, in *Re Lucking's Will Trusts*[13] a trustee was held liable for his failure adequately to supervise the management of a company in which the trust held a controlling interest. Similarly, in *Bartlett v Barclays Bank Trust Co Ltd (No 2)*[14] a bank was held liable for its failure to supervise two land development projects undertaken by a company of which the bank held 99.8 per cent of the shares as trustee for the Bartlett Trust.[15] The investment subsequently proved to have been imprudent and hazardous and wholly unsuitable for a trust. It may not always be easy to determine whether a trustee's breach was one of commission or omission, as was seen in *Bishopsgate Investment Management Ltd v Maxwell (No 2)*,[16] but the distinction may be important, especially as to the issue of causation.[17]

(c) Exemption clauses

While trustees are subject to the general duty to act with the prudence of an ordinary man of business, the trust instrument may specifically exclude their liability for conduct that was not dishonest.[18] Even the new statutory duty of care introduced by s 1

---

[12] Detailed statutory duties have also been imposed on company directors under Part 2, Chapter 10 of the Companies Act 2006, including a duty to exercise due care, skill, and diligence under s 174, which are of relevance where the directors act as trustees. This largely replicates the same duty as that applicable to trustees, with the realization that higher standards may be required of trustee directors than lay trustees. Hence, s 174(2)(a) holds that the duty is one of a reasonably diligent person with the 'the general knowledge, skill and experience that may reasonably be expected of a person carrying out the functions carried out by the director in relation to the company'. See further, in relation to fiduciary duties of directors, Chapter 30.

[13] [1967] 3 All ER 726, [1968] 1 WLR 866.   [14] [1980] Ch 515.

[15] See also *Armitage v Nurse* [1997] 2 All ER 705, at 716.

[16] [1994] 1 All ER 261.   [17] See below, p 880.

[18] Some groups of trustees, such as pension trustees, may not exclude their liability for a breach of trust in this way—Pensions Act 1995, s 33. This includes trustees of unit trusts (Financial Services and Markets Act 2000, s 253) and trustees of debenture trusts (Companies Act 2006, s 750).

of the Trustee Act 2000 may be expressly excluded by the trust instrument.[19] Where such a clause is included in the trust deed it is intended to have the practical effect of lowering the standard of care required of the trustees in the conduct of their business. In *Armitage v Nurse*[20] the Court of Appeal considered the efficacy of a term of a trust instrument which provided that:

No trustee shall be liable for any loss or damage which may happen to Paula's fund or any part thereof or the income thereof at any time or from any cause whatsoever unless such loss or damage shall be caused by his own actual fraud

Millett LJ rejected the submission that a trustee exemption clause which purports to exclude all liability except for actual fraud is void, either because it is repugnant or contrary to public policy. While he accepted that there was an irreducible core of obligations owed by trustees to the beneficiaries of a trust, he held that these did not include the obligation to act without negligence:

But I do not accept the further submission that these core obligations include the duties of skill and care, prudence and diligence. The duty of the trustee to perform the trusts honestly and in good faith for the benefit of the beneficiaries is the minimum necessary to give substance to the trusts, but in my opinion it is sufficient.[21]

He therefore held that the clause was effective to exclude the trustees from liability for loss or damage to the trust property no matter how indolent, imprudent, lacking in diligence, negligent, or wilful he may have been, so long as he has not acted dishonestly.[22] However, he did express his opinion that such exemption clauses had gone too far,[23] with the result that professional trustees charging for their services were able to exclude liability for gross negligence when they would not dream of excluding liability for ordinary professional negligence, but thought that it was for Parliament to deny them effect.[24]

The operation of exemption clauses was further elucidated by the Court of Appeal in *Walker v Stones*.[25] The central issue concerned the application of an exclusion clause which purported to protect trustees from liability arising other than through 'wilful fraud or dishonesty'. At first instance Rattee J, relying on *Armitage v Nurse*, had held that this clause would protect a trustee who had knowingly acted in breach of trust, providing that he had acted in a genuine (even if misguided) belief that what he was doing was for the benefit of the beneficiaries, on the grounds that this would not amount to dishonesty. The Court of Appeal rejected this approach, holding that the test for dishonesty could not be limited to an inquiry into the subjective state of mind

---

[19] Sch 1, para 7.

[20] [1998] Ch 241; Pollard and Walsh 'Exclusion Clause in Trust Deed Validly Excludes Liability for Gross Negligence' (1997) 11 TLI 52; McBride 'Trustee Exemption Clauses' [1998] CLJ 33.

[21] [1998] Ch 421, at 253–4.   [22] Ibid., at 251.

[23] Ibid., at 256.

[24] See Hayton, 'The Irreducible Core Content of Trusteeship' in Oakley, *Trends in Contemporary Trust Law* (1996); McCormack 'The Liability of Trustees for Gross Negligence' [1998] Conv 100.

[25] [2001] QB 902.

of the trustee, but included an irreducible objective standard.[26] Giving the judgment of the court, Sir Christopher Slade held that the exclusion clause must be interpreted so as to 'take account of the case where the trustee's so-called "honest belief", though actually held, is so unreasonable that, by any objective standard, no reasonable solicitor trustee could have thought that what he did or agreed to was for the benefit of the beneficiaries'.[27] He considered that such clauses should be construed 'no more widely than their language on a fair reading suggests' and concluded:

That clause in my judgement would not exempt the trustees from liability for breaches of trust, even if committed in the genuine belief that the course taken was in the best interests of the beneficiaries, if such belief was so unreasonable that no reasonable solicitor-trustee could have held that belief.[28]

Sir Christopher Slade expressly confined his construal of the exclusion clause to the case of a solicitor-trustee, noting that the test of honesty may vary from case to case, depending upon the role and calling of the trustee.[29]

Subsequent cases have added little to an understanding of how such clauses will be construed.[30] In *Re Clapham (decd)*,[31] for example, Behrens J held that a trustee who had not known of the wrongfulness of her actions in making unauthorized payments of the trust fund was entitled to rely on an exclusion clause exempting her from any liability. While the trustee had been grossly negligent, this was covered under the exemption clause and permissible under the principles laid down in *Armitage v Nurse*. This was a case involving a family trust. Behrens J did note, however, that this was an area of law 'ripe for reform'.[32] In *Breadner v Granville-Grossman (Costs)*,[33] however, it was held that a solicitor-trustee was not entitled to rely on an exclusion clause to set aside personal liability for the costs of litigation arising from mis-exercise of powers under a discretionary trust. The case law therefore does little more than follow the principles set out in the existing cases.

The Law Commission conducted a review of the operation of trustee exemption clauses[34] and has now issued a final report.[35] The Law Commission found that it was relatively common to find express provision for exclusion of liability in modern trust instruments and that professional trustees have come to rely on them as a means of affording protection from liability for breach of trusts. Thus, it rejected an absolute prohibition on all trustee exemption clauses on the grounds that denying settlers all

---

[26] Applying the test of dishonesty adopted by the House of Lords in *Royal Brunei Airlines Sdn Bhd v Tan* [1995] 3 All ER 97 and by the Court of Appeal in *Twinsectra Ltd v Yardley* [1999] Lloyd's Rep Bank 438.

[27] [2001] QB 902, at 939.   [28] Ibid., at 941.   [29] Ibid., at 939.

[30] Much of the debate has been over what is required for a dishonesty (see, for example, *Newgate Stud Company v Penfold* [2004] EWHC 2993 (Ch)), something which has also plagued the law in the related area of the test of dishonesty to make a third party liable as an accessory to a breach of trust—see Chapter 31. It is suggested that the definition of dishonesty in relation to trustees should follow the objective standard applicable to third parties.

[31] [2005] EWHC 3387 (Ch).   [32] Ibid., at [89].

[33] [2006] W.T.L.R. 411; arising from [2001] Ch 523.

[34] *Trustee Exemption Clauses*, Law Commission Consultation Paper No 171 (2003).

[35] *Trustee Exemption Clauses*, Law Commission No 301 (2006).

power to modify or restrict the extent of the obligations and liabilities of trustees would undermine the flexibility and adaptability of the trust relationship. However, while many professional trustees considered such clauses to be a necessary component of modern trust practice, and the inclusion of an exclusion clause is likely to lead to lower liability insurance premiums, the Law Commission had originally considered that there was a very strong case for some regulation of trustee exemption clauses. More particularly, it proposed that professional trustees should not be able to rely on clauses which exclude their liability for breach of trust arising from negligence, and that in so far as professional trustees may not exclude liability for breach of trust, that they should not be permitted to claim indemnity from the trust fund. There was little support for this approach in the consultation exercise, and the Law Commission has now abandoned legislative intervention. Instead, it is proposed that trustee exemption clauses should be regulated by rules of good practice agreed by the professional and regulatory bodies,[36] and that, where an exemption clause seeks to limit liability for negligence for paid trustees, such steps must be taken as are reasonable to inform the settlor of the meaning and effect of the clause.[37] Breach of any of the rules would not lead to damages for breach of trust, but breach of discipline. This change of approach, and in particular the abandonment of any legislative intervention, has met with criticism, not least that it does nothing to prevent a professional, paid trustee escaping liability through such clauses in the absence of dishonesty.[38] It remains to be seen whether regulation by code of practice will raise awareness of the effect of such clauses on settlors or provide adequate protection for beneficiaries from negligence by paid trustees.[39]

(d) Breach of trust in the context of constructive and resulting trusts

Whereas the trustees of an express trust are liable for breach of trust, the position of a trustee of a resulting or constructive trust is more complex. The essential difference relates to the nature of the duties of such trustees, since in many cases they will not be expected to perform the ordinary functions of express trustee such as the investment of the trust fund. As Millet LJ observed in *Lonrho plc v Al-Fayed (No 2)*:

It is a mistake to suppose that in every situation in which a constructive trust arises the legal owner is necessarily subject to all the fiduciary obligations and disabilities of an express trustee.[40]

---

[36] Ibid., at para 7.2.   [37] Ibid., at para 6.65.

[38] See Kenny 'Conveyancer's Notebook: The Good, the Bad and the Law Commission' [2007] Conv 103, at pp 103–108. See also Delaney 'Trustee Exemption Clauses—Proposals for Regulation in Ireland' (2009) Tru LI 89, at 99, where she concluded that there 'is a strong case for some form of statutory regulation, and the Law Commission's earlier assertion that the current legal position is too deferential to professional trustees in particular is one that has commanded support from both academics and members of the judiciary'.

[39] It appears other legislative enactments regulating the use of exemption clauses are inapplicable in the trust context—see *Baker v J E Clark Co (Transport) UK Ltd* [2006] EWCA Civ 464, at [21], where Tuckey LJ held that the Unfair Contract Terms Act 1977 did not apply to trustee exemption clauses.

[40] [1992] 1 WLR 1, at 12.

The primary duty of a constructive trustee is often simply to preserve the trust property for the benefit of the beneficiaries, and to ensure that it is not dissipated. If the trust property is dissipated by the trustee he may be liable to compensate the beneficiaries for their loss, ie the value of the trust property. However, it appears that a constructive trustee will only be personally liable in this way if, at the time that the property was dissipated, he was consciously aware of his obligations as a trustee, so that he had acted contrary to them. In *Westdeutsche Landesbank Girozentrale v Islington London Borough Council*, Lord Browne-Wilkinson stated:

Since the equitable jurisdiction to enforce trusts depends upon the conscience of the holder of the legal interest being affected, he cannot be a trustee of the property if and so long as he is ignorant of the facts alleged to affect his conscience, i.e. until he is aware that he is intended to hold the property for the benefit of others in the case of an express trust, or, in the case of a constructive trust, of the factors which are alleged to affect his conscience.[41]

While the precise import of this analysis is somewhat obscure, the best interpretation is probably that a person who receives property as a trustee cannot be held liable for any breach of trust, or breach of fiduciary duty, if he was unaware of the fact that he was such a trustee, or of the circumstances making him a trustee. Thus, a third party recipient of trust property who is not a bona fide purchaser thereby becomes a constructive trustee of it, and the beneficial interest of the beneficiaries is preserved. However, the fact that he is a trustee does not mean that he will attract personal liability for breach of trust if he dissipates the property in circumstances where he was unaware of the constructive trust. In *Bristol and West Building Society v Mothew*, Millett LJ adopted this analysis as a summary of the practical outworking of Lord Browne-Wilkinson's comments:

In *Westdeutsche Landesbank Girozentrale v Islington London Borough Council* Lord Browne-Wilkinson expressly rejected the possibility that a recipient of trust money could be personally liable, regardless of fault, for any subsequent payment away of the moneys to third parties even though, at the date of such payment, he was ignorant of the existence of any trust.[42]

(2) Nature of liability for breach of trust

(a) A compensatory remedy

The remedy for breach of trust is essentially compensatory. When a breach has been committed the trustee responsible is liable to compensate the trust for all the loss flowing directly or indirectly from the breach.[43]

---

[41] [1996] AC 669.

[42] [1996] 4 All ER 698, at 716. See also *Statek Corp v Alford* [2008] EWHC 32, discussed in Chapter 30, at p 959.

[43] *Bateman v Davis* (1818) 3 Madd 98; *Lander v Weston* (1855) 3 Drew 389; *Knott v Cottee* (1852) 16 Beav 77; *Re Miller's Deed Trusts* [1978] LS Gaz R 454; *Bartlett v Barclays Trust Co Ltd* [1980] Ch 515.

(b) A personal remedy

The liability of a trustee who has committed a breach to compensate the trust is entirely personal. It is only available against him as an individual and it is not a proprietary remedy against specific assets in his hands. If the trustee retains trust property in his hands due to his breach of trust, or has made a profit because of such a breach and still holds the profit in his hands, the beneficiaries may seek proprietary remedies. These are considered in Chapters 31 and 32, and will be particularly important if the trustee in breach is bankrupt, since the beneficiaries' claim to compensation for breach of trust will only rank alongside the claims of his other general creditors. If the trustee in breach has died, the liability continues against his estate.[44]

(c) Election between compensatory and restitutionary remedies

Whereas a trustee who commits a breach of trust will be liable to compensate the trust for any loss sustained, a trustee who receives an unauthorized profit in breach of his fiduciary duty will be liable to make restitution of the profit received, which constitutes an unjust enrichment. Difficulties arise where a trustee's conduct constitutes both a breach of trust and a breach of fiduciary duty. In such circumstances it is essential to determine whether the potential remedies for breach of trust and breach of fiduciary duty are cumulative—in which case the beneficiaries will be entitled to recover both compensation (for the loss they have suffered) and restitution (of the profit received by the trustee)—or alternative—in which case the beneficiaries must elect between them. In *Tung Man Sit (Decd) v Capacious Investments Ltd*[45] the Privy Council held that the remedies of compensation for breach of trust and restitution where a trustee has breached his fiduciary duty are alternative, and that the beneficiaries must elect between them to prevent double recovery. The case concerned a planned joint venture for the development of land. The defendant provided land for the development, which was funded by the plaintiff company. It was agreed that the defendant would assign legal title to sixteen of the houses built to the plaintiffs. From the time of this agreement the defendant held the house on trust for the plaintiffs, and in breach of trust the title was never assigned. Over a period of years he let the houses to tenants and received a profit of some HK$2m in the form of rent. The plaintiffs claimed that they were entitled to an equitable account of these profits on the grounds that they were unauthorized remuneration received by the defendant trustee in breach of its fiduciary duty, and also damages for breach of trust for the rent that they could have obtained from the houses if they had been assigned at the appropriate time, a sum which was assessed at HK£17m. The defendant had paid HK$1.8m to the plaintiffs by way of account of the profit received, and the plaintiffs subsequently sought the damages due. The defendant argued that by accepting the account of profits the plaintiffs had made an irrevocable election between the restitutionary and compensatory remedies. The

---

[44] See *Fry v Fry* (1859) 27 Beav 144.

[45] [1996] AC 514. See Stevens 'Election between Alternative Remedies' [1996] RLR 117; Birks 'Inconsistency between Compensation and Restitution' (1996) 112 LQR 375.

Privy Council held that in the circumstances no election had been made, so that the plaintiffs were entitled to recover full damages, less the KH$1.8m they had already received. The Privy Council clearly stated that where a defendant's conduct can be characterized both as a breach of trust and a breach of fiduciary duty the respective remedies are alternative and the plaintiff must choose between them:

Faced with alternative and inconsistent remedies a plaintiff must choose, or elect, between them. He cannot have both to some extent at least the remedies claimed by the plaintiff included two alternative and inconsistent remedies. An account of the profits Mr Tang had made from the lettings is an alternative remedy to damages for the loss of use of the houses.[46]

(3) Scope of a trustee's liability for breach of trust

(a) Trustees are liable only for their own breaches of trust

Trustees are only liable for their own breaches of trust and not for the breaches of their co-trustees.[47] However, where several trustees are liable for a breach of trust they are jointly and severally liable. Thus, in *Bishopsgate Investment Management Ltd v Maxwell (No 2)*[48] Kevin and Ian Maxwell, who had both signed transfers misappropriating assets held on trust for the pensions of the employees of Maxwell-owned companies, were jointly and severally liable for their breaches. Joint and several liability means that the beneficiary can recover the entire loss to the trust from any one of the trustees alone.[49] Even where the beneficiary has obtained a judgment against all the trustees he may choose to execute it against any one.[50] As Leach MR stated in *Wilson v Moore*:[51] 'all parties to a breach of trust are equally liable; there is between them no primary liability'.

Although the beneficiaries may be able to recover the entire loss suffered by the trust from just one of the trustees in breach, that trustee may be able to recover a contribution to the damages he has had to pay from his fellow trustees who are in breach under the Civil Liability (Contribution) Act 1978.[52]

(b) Trustees are generally not liable for breaches committed before they were appointed

A trustee is not liable for breaches of trust which were committed before his appointment.[53] On appointment he is obliged to make reasonable inquiries to ensure that the trust affairs are in order,[54] but, except in so far as a discrepancy appears, he 'is entitled to assume that everything has been duly attended to up to the time of his

46   [1996] 1 All ER 193, at 197 and 201, per Lord Nicholls.
47   *Townley v Sherborn* (1634) J Bridg 35.   48   [1994] 1 All ER 261, CA.
49   *Walker v Symonds* (1818) 3 Swan 1; *Re Harrison* [1891] 2 Ch 349; *McCheane v Gyles (No 2)* [1902] 1 Ch 911.
50   *A-G v Wilson* (1840) Cr & Ph 1; *Fletcher v Green* (1864) 33 Beav 426.
51   (1833) 1 My & K 126, at 146.   52   See below.
53   *Re Strahan* (1856) 8 De GM & G 291.
54   *Harvey v Oliver* (1887) 57 LT 239; *Re Lucking's Will Trusts* [1968] 1 WLR 866.

becoming trustee'.[55] However, if he does discover such a breach he should take proceedings against the former trustees responsible.

(c) Trustees' continuing liability after they have retired from the trust

Retirement does not save a trustee from liability for breaches of trust committed while he was a trustee. He will also be liable if he retired to enable a breach of trust to take place. The principle was stated by Kekewich J in *Head v Gould*:

in order to make a retiring trustee liable for a breach of trust committed by his successor you must show, and show clearly, that the breach of trust which was in fact committed was not merely the outcome of the retirement and new appointment, but was contemplated by the further trustee when such retirement and appointment took place.[56]

The key factor which renders a retired trustee liable is the fact that he was fully aware of, and connived in, the subsequent breach of trust.

(d) Trustees generally not vicariously liable for the acts of others

Until recently the liability of trustees for the actions of his fellow trustees or properly appointed agents was limited by s 30(1) of the Trustee Act 1925, which provided that:

A trustee...shall be answerable and accountable only for his own acts, receipts, neglects, or defaults, and not for those of any other trustee, nor for any banker, broker, or other person with whom any trust money or securities may be deposited, nor for the insufficiency or deficiency of any securities, nor for any other loss, unless the same happens through his own wilful default.

However, this provision was repealed by Trustee Act 2000, with the effect that trustees will be liable when they have failed to act in accordance with their duty of care.

2 The remedy for breach of trust

(1) General principles

(a) Compensation for loss[57]

A trustee who acts in breach of trust will be liable to compensate the trust for any loss suffered as a result of his breach.[58] As Street J said in *Re Dawson*:

the trustee is liable to place the trust estate in the same position it would have been in if no breach had been committed.[59]

---

[55] *Re Strahan* (1856) 8 De GM & G 291, at 309, per Turner LJ.

[56] [1898] 2 Ch 250, at 273–274.

[57] See Oakley, 'The Liberalising Nature of Remedies for Breach of Trust' in Oakley, *Trends in Contemporary Trust Law* (1996), pp 219–230; Capper 'Compensation for Breach of Trust' [1997] Conv 14; Sealy 'Mortgagees and Receivers—A Duty of Care Resurrected and Extended' (2000) 59 CLJ 31; P Birks and F Rose (eds), *Restitution and Equity, Vol 1: Resulting Trusts and Equitable Compensation.*

[58] See also Baxter 'Trustees' Personal Liability and the Role of Liability Insurance' [1996] Conv 186.

[59] [1966] 2 NSWLR 211, at 215.

In some cases, for example *Target Holdings Ltd v Redferns*[60] this compensation has been described as 'restitution' of the trust estate.[61] However, this usage is not strictly accurate, and is liable to be confused with the recently recognized law of restitution. As a legal term of art, restitution is the response which consists in a defendant giving up to the plaintiff any unjust gain, known as an enrichment, which he has received at his expense without legal justification.[62] A trustee may not have received any personal gain from his breach, in which case it is impossible to regard him as 'enriched'. While the compensatory remedy does in effect restore the trust fund, it is not a restitutionary remedy. The trustee is required to compensate the trust for the loss it has sustained in consequence of his conduct, not to return an enrichment he has received. As Lord Browne-Wilkinson observed in *Target Holdings Ltd v Redferns*:

> in the case of a breach of such a trust involving the wrongful paying away of trust assets, the liability of the trustee is to restore to the trust fund, often called the trust estate, what ought to have been there.[63]

(b) Causation

A trustee who has acted in breach is only liable to compensate the trust for loss which was caused by his breach. If there is no causal link between the breach and the loss, the trustee will not be liable. This is clear from the decision of the Court of Appeal in *Bishopsgate Investment Management Ltd v Maxwell (No 2)*.[64] This case arose out of the Maxwell pension fraud. Ian Maxwell was the director of the plaintiff company, which acted as trustee of a number of pension schemes for the employees of companies owned by Robert Maxwell. Assets held by the company had been misappropriated and applied to the benefit of Robert Maxwell's private companies. Ian Maxwell, as a director, had signed transfers beneath the signature of his brother, Kevin, and had also signed blank transfers. He had made no inquiry about the transactions and had signed the transfers because his brother had done so. The plaintiff obtained summary judgment against him, and an order for an interim payment of £500,000 while damages were assessed. He appealed on the basis that the plaintiff had not shown that his inactivity had caused the loss. The Court of Appeal made it clear that where a fiduciary has committed a breach of duty by omission, the plaintiff claiming damages must prove that the omission caused the loss, in the sense that compliance would have prevented the damage.[65] However, the court held that this was not a case where the breach was in the nature of an omission, but that the breach was simply the improper transfer of the shares to Robert Maxwell Group plc. Causation was thus clearly established and the summary judgment was upheld.

---

[60] [1996] 1 AC 421.
[61] Ibid., at 434, per Lord Browne-Wilkinson. See also Hanbury and Martin, *Modern Equity* (18th edn, 2009), which describes the liability as 'restitutionary' (at p 685).
[62] Birks, *Introduction to the Law of Restitution* (1985), pp 9–27.
[63] [1996] 1 AC 421, at 434.   [64] [1994] 1 All ER 261.
[65] Ibid., at 264, per Hoffmann LJ.

The requirement of causation was considered at length by the House of Lords in *Target Holdings Ltd v Redferns*.[66] The case concerned the purchase of properties in Birmingham by a company, Crowngate Developments Ltd, which was owned by Mr Kohli and Mr Musafir. The vendor was Mirage Properties Ltd, and the purchase was made through two companies registered in Jersey, Panther Ltd and Kholi & Co, also owned by Kohli and Musafir. Redferns was a firm of solicitors acting for the purchasers. Crowngate applied for a loan of £1.7m to purchase the properties from Target, which was granted on the basis of a £2m valuation of the properties made by a firm of estate agents. In fact, Mirage had agreed to sell the properties to Crowngate for £775,000 but Target were not aware of this. The loan was paid into Redferns' client account on 28 June 1989, without any express instructions as to the release of the funds. On 29 June £1.25m was transferred to the account of Panther in Jersey, although at this stage the contract for the purchase of the properties had not yet been entered, and it was not until July that the contracts and mortgages in favour of Target were executed. Subsequently, the value of the properties dropped sharply and Target sought to recover their loss.

Any action against the estate agents, who had carried out the valuation, was of little value because they were in liquidation. Target therefore sought to recover its loss (less anything they would realize from the sale of the property) from Redferns, on the grounds that the transfer of funds before the contracts for sale and the mortgages had been entered had constituted a breach of trust. There was no doubt that this payment was made in breach of trust, and the central question was whether the solicitors should be liable for all the loss suffered by Target on the loans when the most immediate cause was the drop in property prices. At first instance, Warner J gave Redferns leave to defend the claim upon condition that they make an interim payment of £1m to Target. Target appealed to the Court of Appeal, claiming that it should have been given final judgment. The majority of the Court of Appeal held that Warner J should have granted final judgment in their favour. They held that Target was entitled to recover the whole of its loss from Redferns, since the payment of the trust money to a stranger in breach of trust had caused its loss. Peter Gibson LJ[67] concluded:

The cause of action is constituted simply by the payment away of Target's moneys in breach of trust and the loss is quantified in the amount of those moneys, subject to Target giving credit for the realisation of the security it received. It was for Redferns to justify their action or otherwise show why Target was not entitled to compensation in the sum claimed.[68]

He approved a number of authorities which upheld the view that the principles of remoteness of damage as applied in the context of damages for breach of contract or

---

[66] [1996] 1 AC 421: (1996) 112 LQR 27 (Rickett); [1996] LMCLQ 161 (Nolan); [1997] Conv 14 (Capper); (1995) 9 TLI 86 (Ulph). See also (1998) 114 LQR 214 (Sir Peter Millett).

[67] With whom Hirst LJ agreed.

[68] [1994] 2 All ER 337, at 353.

tort have no application to breach of trust.[69] In particular he referred to the judgment of Street J in *Re Dawson*, who explained the operation of the rule:

> The principles...do not appear to involve any inquiry as to whether the loss was caused by or flowed from the breach. Rather the inquiry in each instance would appear to be whether the loss would have happened if there had been no breach...The cases...demonstrate that the obligation to make restitution, which the courts of equity have from very early times imposed on defaulting trustees and other fiduciaries is of a more absolute nature than the common law obligation to pay damages for tort or breach of contract.[70]

However, Ralph Gibson LJ delivered a powerful dissenting judgment, in which he held that Warner J had been correct to refuse to give Target final judgment. He did not dissent on the issue of remoteness, but took the view that there was an arguable defence that the breach had not caused the loss. Although he felt that Target was likely to succeed, he held that it was arguable that it would have gone ahead with the transaction in any event, relying on the valuation of the properties by the estate agents, and that in such circumstances the breach of trust by Redferns would not have been the cause of the loss:

> If it appears just to the court, having regard to [the fiduciary relationship between the parties] and its purpose, and the obligations of the parties within it, and to the way in which the parties would have behaved, for the court to regard the breach as having caused no loss to the plaintiff, because the loss would have happened if there had been no breach, then the court can and must so hold.[71]

As Redferns had made out an arguable defence, he felt that Warner J had correctly granted them conditional leave to defend.

Redferns appealed to the House of Lords, which held that Target was not entitled to final judgment. Lord Browne-Wilkinson stated the underlying principle as follows:

> there does have to be some causal connection between the breach of trust and the loss to the trust estate for which compensation is recoverable, viz the fact that the loss would not have occurred but for the breach.[72]

He went on to conclude that, on the assumption that the transaction would have gone ahead irrespective of the breach of trust, the breach had not been the cause of the loss suffered:

> Target has not demonstrated that it is entitled to any compensation for breach of trust. Assuming that moneys would have been forthcoming from some other source to complete the purchase from Mirage if the moneys had not been wrongly provided by Redferns in breach of trust, Target obtained exactly what it would have obtained had no breach occurred, ie a valid security for the sum advanced.[73]

---

[69]   *Clough v Bond* (1838) 3 My & Cr 490; *Re Dawson* [1966] 2 NSWLR 211; *Alliance and Leicester Building Society v Edgestop Ltd* [1994] 2 All ER 38; *Bishopsgate Investment Management Ltd v Maxwell (No 2)* [1994] 1 All ER 261, CA.

[70]   [1966] 2 NSWLR 211, at 215–216.   [71]   [1994] 2 All ER 337, at 347.

[72]   [1996] 1 AC 421, at 434. See also *Re Miller's Deed Trusts* [1978] LS Gaz 454; *Nestlé v National Westminster Bank plc* [1994] 1 All ER 118.

[73]   [1996] 1 AC 421, at 440.

In the course of his judgment he rejected Target's argument that Redferns were under an immediate duty to restore the trust fund, holding that in a commercial conveyancing context a client has no right to have the solicitor's client account reconstituted after the transaction is completed.[74] He also rejected the argument that the quantum of compensation was to be fixed at the date that the alleged breach occurred. Instead he held:

> The quantum is fixed at the date of judgment, at which date, according to the circumstances then pertaining, the compensation is assessed as the figure then necessary to put the trust estate or the beneficiary back into the position it would have been in had there been no breach.[75]

Despite concluding that Target had not proved causation, the House of Lords was doubtful whether Redferns would ultimately be able to show that their breach had not caused the loss. Lord Browne-Wilkinson summarized:

> There must be a high probability that, at trial, it will emerge that the use of Target's money to pay for the purchase from Mirage and the other intermediate transactions was a vital feature of this transaction ... If the moneys made available by Redfern's breach of trust were essential to enable the transaction to go through, but for Redfern's breach of trust Target would not have advanced any money. In that case the loss suffered by Target by reason of the breach of trust will be the total sum advanced to Crowngate less the proceeds of the security.[76]

For this reason, although Redferns were granted leave to defend the action, the order requiring them to pay £1m into court was not set aside.

In conclusion, the decision of the House of Lords in *Target Holdings Ltd v Redferns* requires a claimant seeking compensation when trust property has been transferred contrary to the terms of the trust (or in the case of a bare trust, contrary to the instructions of the beneficiary) to demonstrate that, but for the alleged breach of trust, he would not have suffered the loss sustained. Conversely, the defendant can escape liability by demonstrating that the loss would have been sustained even if the breach had not occurred, and the transaction would have been entered irrespectively.

By way of qualification to this general proposition, in *Bristol and West Building Society v May, May & Merrimans (No 1)*[77] it was held that a mortgagee claiming compensation from a solicitor who paid over money advanced on completion—where the money had been received in response to a request based upon a warranty or misrepresentation which the solicitor knew[78] to be misleading—need not demonstrate that the transaction would not have gone ahead but for the misrepresentation. Chadwick J held that there was no need for the claimant to answer the 'what if' question:

> It would, as it seems to me, be a strange principle of equity which allowed a solicitor who, in breach of the duty of good faith owed to his client, had given a warranty which he knew to be false with the intention that the client should act upon it, to say, in answer to a claim for

---

[74] Ibid., at 436.   [75] Ibid., at 437.   [76] Ibid., at 440–441.
[77] [1996] 2 All ER 801; Alcock 'Limiting Contractual and Tortious Damages' [1997] LMCLQ 26.
[78] Or must be taken to have known.

compensation in respect of loss which had resulted from the client relying on the warranty and acting as he intended, that the client must establish that he would not have so acted if he had been told the true facts. After all, a common reason for giving a warranty which the warrantor knows to be false is the fear that, without the false warranty, the lender will refuse to proceed. If it were not for that fear the warrantor would have no reason to withhold the truth... [W]here a fiduciary has failed to disclose material facts, he cannot be heard to say, in answer to a claim for equitable compensation, that disclosure would not have altered the decision to proceed with the transaction.[79]

He held that this approach was supported by the earlier decision of the Privy Council in *Brickenden v London Loan & Savings Co*,[80] which he considered had not been overruled by the House of Lords in *Target Holdings Ltd v Redferns*. In *Swindle v Harrison*[81] the Court of Appeal held that the mere fact that a fiduciary had failed to disclose material facts did not establish liability if the transaction would have proceeded irrespective, unless the fiduciary had acted fraudulently.

(c) Remoteness and foreseeability of loss

Although *Target Holdings Ltd v Redferns (a firm)*[82] demonstrates a need to establish causation in order to render a trustee liable to compensate for breach of trust, the further question arises whether, where such causation is established, a trustee is liable for all the loss which flows from his breach, directly or indirectly, or whether some principle of remoteness operates to limit his liability to such losses as were reasonably foreseeable as a result of the breach. Traditionally it has been held that the trustee's liability is not mitigated by such principles as remoteness of damage.[83] Indeed, in *Target Holdings Ltd v Redferns* itself,[84] the House of Lords held that the common law principle of remoteness of damage has no application to liability where trust property was wrongly transferred by the trustee in breach of the terms of the trust. Lord Browne-Wilkinson stated:

If specific restitution of the trust property is not possible, then the liability of the trustee is to pay sufficient compensation to the trust estate to put it back to what it would have been had the breach not been committed. Even if the immediate cause of the loss is the dishonesty or failure of a third party the trustee is liable to make good that loss to the trust estate if, but for the breach, such loss would not have occurred. Thus the common law rules of remoteness of damage and causation do not apply.[85]

However, where a trustee has acted without due care, thus causing a loss to the trust, it is possible that the principles of remoteness may apply. In *Bristol and West Building*

---

[79] [1996] 2 All ER 801, at 825–826.   [80] [1934] 3 DLR 465.

[81] [1997] 4 All ER 705; Elliott 'Restitutionary Compensatory Damages for Breach of Fiduciary Duty?' [1998] RLR 135.

[82] [1996] AC 421.

[83] Underhill and Hayton, *Law Relating to Trusts and Trustees* (16th edn, 2003), p 855.

[84] [1996] 1 AC 421.

[85] Ibid., at 434. For criticism of this position, see: *Bank of New Zealand v New Zealand Guardian Trust Co Ltd* [1999] 1 NZLR 213; aff'd [1999] 1 NZLR 664; *Collins v Brebner* [2000] Lloyd's Rep PN 587; Elliott 'Remoteness Criteria in Equity' (2002) 65 MLR 588.

Society v Mothew[86] the Court of Appeal considered the nature of the equitable liability of a fiduciary in breach of his duty to act with due skill and care. Millett LJ stated:

Although the remedy which equity makes available for breach of the equitable duty of skill and care is equitable compensation rather than damages, this is merely the product of history and in this context is in my opinion a distinction without a difference. Equitable compensation for breach of the duty of skill and care resembles common law damages in that it is awarded by way of compensation to the plaintiff of his loss. There is no reason in principle why the common law rules of causation, remoteness of damage and measure of damages should not be applied by analogy in such a case.[87]

(d) Accounting for tax liability

The rule that tax liability is to be taken into account when calculating damages for personal injury in tort[88] is not applied, and in *Re Bell's Indenture*[89] it was held that a trustee should restore the value of misappropriated property to the trust without allowance for the tax that would have had to be paid on it by the trust if it had not been misappropriated.

(2) Investment[90]

Some settled principles have developed for calculating the loss to the trust where the breach of trust relates to improper investment. It is worth noting that the much wider powers of investment now given to trustees means that it is much less likely that a trustee will have invested in an unauthorized form of investment, but liability can still arise where trustees have not satisfied their duties of care relating to investment.

(a) Trustee purchases unauthorized investments

Where the trustee has purchased unauthorized investments he will be liable for any loss resulting from the purchase. In *Knott v Cottee*[91] an executor who had an express power to invest in British Government Stocks or land invested in foreign stock and Exchequer bills, which were subsequently sold by order of the court at a loss. It was held that the trustee was liable to compensate for the loss caused by the unauthorized investment, even though had they been retained they would have produced a profit for the trust because of a subsequent rise in value following the order of the court to sell.

(b) Trustee retains unauthorized investments

If the trustee retains unauthorized investments he will be liable to the beneficiaries for any loss that the trust suffers as a result. The measure of loss will be the amount that the investments could have realized if they had been sold at the proper time, less the value that they actually realized. In *Fry v Fry*[92] trustees received the Longford

[86] [1998] Ch 1.   [87] Ibid., at 17.
[88] *British Transport Commission v Gourley* [1956] AC 185, HL.
[89] [1980] 1 WLR 1217.   [90] See Chapter 23.   [91] (1852) 16 Beav 77.
[92] (1859) 27 Beav 144.

Inn on trust in 1834. The testator's will stated that they were to sell it 'as soon as convenient after his decease...'. In 1836 they refused an offer of £900. By 1859 the inn remained unsold, and had dramatically fallen in value because of the opening of a railway, depriving it of much of its business. Romilly MR held that the estates of the now dead trustees were liable for any loss to the trust, which would be the difference between the £900 offer they had refused and the price eventually obtained.[93]

(c) Trustee retains authorized investments

Under s 5 of the Trustee Act 2000 a trustee is under duty to review the investments of the trust and to obtain and consider proper advice about whether they should be varied. If he fails to fulfil this duty, or fails to exercise the requisite duty of care, he will be liable to compensate the trust for the resulting loss.

(d) Trustee improperly sells authorized investments

If the trustee improperly sells an authorized investment he will be liable to the trust for any loss. In *Re Massingberd's Settlement*[94] the trustees had power to invest in government stock. In 1875 they sold Consols, which were authorized investments, and reinvested in unauthorized mortgages. In proceedings, begun in 1887, the Court of Appeal held that although the whole of the money invested on the mortgages was recovered, the trustees must replace the Consols which had been sold, even though they now stood at a higher price.

(e) Mortgages

Where a trustee has invested in mortgages he will be liable to the trust if the security subsequently proves insufficient. However, the trustee may enjoy some protection under ss 8 and 9 of the Trustee Act 1925. Section 9 provides that if the trustee makes an investment on a mortgage which is unauthorized merely because of the amount that has been advanced, the security shall be deemed an authorized investment for the sum that could properly have been advanced, and the trustee 'shall only be liable to make good the sum advanced in excess thereof with interest'. If the trustee has chosen to follow the procedure of s 8,[95] and obtained a valuation and advanced a loan of not more than two-thirds of the amount of the valuation on the advice of the valuer, he 'shall not be chargeable with breach of trust by reason only of the proportion borne by the amount of the loan to the value of the property at the time when the loan was made'.

(3) Assessing compensation

In *Target Holdings Ltd v Redferns*[96] it was held that the quantum of equitable compensation payable in respect of a breach of trust is to be assessed not at the date that the breach occurred, but at the date of judgment. The House of Lords overruled the

---

[93] See *Jaffray v Marshall* [1994] 1 All ER 143.
[94] (1890) 63 LT 296.
[95] A trustee is not obliged to follow this procedure.
[96] [1996] 1 AC 401.

decision in *Jaffray v Marshall*,[97] where it had been held that a trustee who committed an ongoing breach of trust by failing to restore trust property to the trust fund was required to compensate the beneficiaries to the level of the best possible price that he could have obtained for the property during the period when it was not restored. A settlement had been created in favour of Lady Jaffray for life, remainder to her children. In 1979 Lady Jaffray wished to purchase a new house for £75,000 but did not have sufficient funds. The trustees provided some £35,000 toward the purchase from the trust and it was agreed that the house should be shared between Lady Jaffray and the trust as tenants-in-common in shares of eight fifteenths and seven fifteenths. At the same time as the purchase was completed, the purchasers executed a mortgage in favour of Coutts & Co. This was admitted to be in breach of trust. The question at issue concerned the appropriate measure of compensation for the breach. If the compensation was to be assessed at the date the writ was issued in 1989 the value of the house would have been £160,000. However, due to a fall in property prices by the date of the judgment it was only worth £117,000. Nicholas Stewart, QC, sitting as a deputy judge of the High Court, held that the compensation was to be assessed on the basis that the trustees could have sold the property at the date of the writ, and that the trust had only failed to realize the increased value of the property because of their continuing breach of trust in not selling.[98] However, Lord Browne-Wilkinson in *Target Holdings* held that the case had been decided by an application of the wrong principle:

the principles applicable in an action for an account of profits were, to my mind, wrongly applied to a claim for compensation for breach of trust. In my judgment [*Jaffray v Marshall*] was wrongly decided not only because the wrong principle was applied but also because the judge awarded compensation by assessing the quantum on an assumption (viz that the house in question would have been sold at a particular date) when he found as a fact that such sale would not have taken place even if there had been no breach of trust.[99]

(4) Offsetting losses and gains

(a) The general rule

It is a basic principle that each breach of trust is to be treated independently of the trustee's other activities. A loss suffered by the trust as a result of a breach in one transaction cannot be offset against a gain achieved for the trust in another. The trustee remains liable for the loss caused by his breach, irrespective of the gain. This principle was accepted in *Bartlett v Barclays Bank Trust Co Ltd (No 2)*,[100] where Brightman J stated:

The general rule...is that where a trustee is liable in respect of distinct breaches of trust, one of which resulted in a loss and the other in a gain, he is not entitled to set the gain against the loss, unless they arise in the same transaction.[101]

---

[97] [1994] 1 All ER 143.   [98] Ibid., at 154.   [99] [1996] 1 AC 401, at 440.
[100] [1980] Ch 515; [1980] Conv 155 (Shindler); [1983] Conv 127 (Pearce and Samuels).
[101] [1980] Ch 515, at 538. See also *Adye v Feuilleteau* (1783) 3 Swan 84n; *Robinson v Robinson* (1848) 11 Beav 371; *Wiles v Gresham* (1854) 2 Drew 258.

This rule was applied in *Dimes v Scott*,[102] where the trustees of a settlement created on the death of Captain Piercey in 1802 failed to sell an investment in the East India Company which they had been directed to convert into money by the Captain's will. The trustees paid the full income received (10 per cent per annum) to the life beneficiary. Under the rule in *Howe v Dartmouth*[103] the life tenant was only entitled to a 4 per cent return on the value of the investment as income.[104] When the unauthorized investment was realized in 1813 the proceeds were used to purchase Consuls. As the price of the Consuls had fallen since the date of the testator's death, they were able to purchase more than they would have been able to at that time. It was held that the gain to the beneficiaries of the extra Consuls could not be offset against the trustees' liability for excessive payments made to the life tenant while the unauthorized investment was retained.

(b) Distinct breaches of trust

The rule preventing any set-off between losses and gains only applies if there are distinct, independent breaches of trust. If the breaches occur in the course of one indivisible transaction then any gain will be taken into account. This provides an adequate explanation for *Fletcher v Green*.[105] Here the trustee of a settlement committed a breach of trust by lending money on a mortgage which proved insufficient security. When the security was realized the money was invested in Consuls, which rose in value, producing a gain of £251. The court held that this gain must be set off against the trustee's liability for the failure of the security.

(c) Set-off in exceptional circumstances

In *Bartlett v Barclays Bank Trust Co Ltd (No 2)*[106] the general principle that there should be no set-off between gains and losses flowing from a breach of trust was reaffirmed. However, on the specific facts Brightman J did permit the defendant bank to set off the gain that had been made in one investment in breach of trust against a loss made in another. A company owned by the trust made two investments in property development schemes which were wholly inappropriate, and the bank was liable for having failed adequately to supervise the operations of the company. On one project, the 'Old Bailey Project', the company lost £580,000 capital and a great deal of income. On another project, the 'Guildford Development', which was entered under exactly the same policy of investment, the company made a profit of some £271,000. Brightman J held that this profit could be offset against the liability of the bank for the loss incurred by the 'Old Bailey Project'. However he failed to provide an adequate explanation of why the set-off was permitted. Having stated the general principle, he continued:

the relevant cases are ... not altogether easy to reconcile. All are centenarians and none is quite like the present. The Guildford development stemmed from exactly the same policy and (to a lesser degree because it proceeded less far) exemplified the same folly as the Old Bailey project. Part of the profit was in fact used to finance the Old Bailey disaster. By sheer luck the gamble paid off handsomely, on capital account. I think it would be unjust to deprive the bank of this

---

[102] (1828) 4 Russ 195.　　[103] (1802) 7 Ves 137.　　[104] See Chapter 13.
[105] (1864) 33 Beav 426.　　[106] [1980] Ch 515.

element of salvage in the course of assessing the cost of the shipwreck. My order will therefore reflect the bank's right to an appropriate set-off.[107]

Despite the fact that the developments took place under the same policy, it cannot be said that they were effectively part of the same transaction so as not to be 'distinct' breaches of trust. A more satisfactory interpretation is that the judge recognized a residuary power to grant a set-off on the basis of the balance of justice between the parties in the particular circumstances.

(5) Interest

(a) General principle

Where a trustee is liable to compensate the trust for loss caused by his misapplication of trust property, the trust is also entitled to recover interest on the sum misapplied. The rationale for this was explained by Buckley LJ in *Wallersteiner v Moir (No 2)*:

It is well established in equity that a trustee who in breach of trust misapplies trust funds will be liable not only to replace the misapplied principal fund but to do so with interest from the date of the misapplication. This is on the notional ground that the money so applied was in fact the trustee's own money and that he has retained the misapplied trust money in his own hands and used it for his own purposes.[108]

The court assumes that the trustee has retained the misapplied property and has therefore had the opportunity to earn interest on it.

(b) Rate of interest

Historically, the rate of interest awarded was 4 per cent per annum,[109] with an increase to 5 per cent if the trustee was guilty of fraud[110] or had used the money to pursue his own trade.[111] If the trustee had in fact received a higher rate of interest than that, he had to pay the beneficiary whatever he had received.[112] However, in times of high inflation such a low rate fails to reflect the conditions of the lending market. As Brightman LJ observed in *Bartlett v Barclays Bank Trust Co Ltd (No 2)*:

In these days of huge and constantly changing interest rates[113] (the movement being usually upwards so far) I think it would be unrealistic for a court of equity to abide by the modest rate of interest which was current in the stable times of our forefathers.[114]

---

[107] Ibid., at 538.   [108] [1975] QB 373, at 397.

[109] *Hall v Hallet* (1784) 1 Cox Eq Cas 134; *Jones v Foxall* (1852) 15 Beav 388; *A-G v Alford* (1855) 4 De GM & G 843; *Fletcher v Green* (1864) 33 Beav 426; *Imperial Mercantile Credit Association (liquidators) v Coleman* (1873) LR 6 HL 189; *Re Beech* [1920] 1 Ch 40.

[110] *A-G v Alford* (1855) 4 De GM & G 843.

[111] If the trustee has made a profit, the beneficiaries have the option of claiming the profit instead. See *Vyse v Foster* (1872) 8 Ch App 309; *Re Davis* [1902] 2 Ch 314; *Gordon v Gonda* [1955] 2 All ER 762.

[112] *Jones v Foxall* (1852) 15 Beav 388. See also *Mathew v TM Sutton Ltd* [1994] 4 All ER 793.

[113] He noted how in the years 1963–80 the bank rate of minimum lending had changed 80 times, varying between 4 per cent and 17 per cent, and the bank deposit rate had changed 70 times, varying between 2 per cent and 15 per cent.

[114] [1980] Ch 515, at 547.

He therefore concluded that the proper rate of interest ought to be that allowed from time to time on the court's short-term investment account, established under s 6(1) of the Administration of Justice Act 1965. Other cases have held that the rate should be 1 per cent above bank base rate.[115] In *Guardian Ocean Cargoes Ltd v Banco do Brasil (No 3),*[116] Hirst J awarded interest at 1 per cent above the New York prime rate. Ultimately, the determination of the appropriate rate of interest is a matter for the discretion of the court. In *Jaffray v Marshall*[117] Nicholas Stewart, QC, sitting as a deputy High Court judge, took judicial notice that 'the period since 1989 has not been a period of the very high level of inflation that has been seen at times in fairly recent years. Accordingly, the rate of return needed to preserve capital is not as high.'[118] He held that compensation should be paid with interest at the special account rate. In *Re Evans (decd),*[119] Richard McCombe, QC awarded interest of 8 per cent to satisfy equity in a case involving the non-professional administrator of a small estate in time of gentle inflation, where interest rates had varied between 8 per cent and 14.5 per cent during the relevant period.

(c) Simple or compound interest?

Whereas the common law only enjoys the jurisdiction to award simple interest on damages awarded, in equity the court may award compound interest.[120] Whether compound or simple interest should be paid on the equitable compensation due to the trust is also a matter for the court's discretion. Historically, compound interest was usually awarded because of the trustee's fraud, or his having used misapplied property in his trade.[121] In *Wallersteiner v Moir (No 2)*[122] where a company director misused company funds for his own purposes, Lord Denning MR rejected the view that interest was awarded 'by way of a punishment'.[123] Instead, he held that compound interest should be awarded where this represents what the trustee should reasonably have obtained with the trust property if it has been misapplied:

[S]hould it be simple interest or compound interest? On general principles I think it should be presumed that the company (had it not been deprived of the money) would have made the most beneficial use open to it: cf *Armory v Delamirie*[124] ... it may be that the company would

---

[115] *Wallersteiner v Moir (No 2)* [1975] QB 373, 508n; *Belmont Finance Corpn Ltd v Williams Furniture Ltd (No 2)* [1980] 1 All ER 393, CA; *O'Sullivan v Management Agency and Music Ltd* [1985] QB 428, CA.

[116] [1992] 2 Lloyd's Rep 193.   [117] [1994] 1 All ER 143.

[118] Ibid., at 154.   [119] [1999] 2 All ER 777.

[120] See *Westdeutsche Landesbank Girozentrale v Islington London Borough Council* [1996] AC 669, where the House of Lords held that the court did not possess the jurisdiction to award compound interest on a common law claim to restitution. See now, revisiting this decision—*Sempra Metals Ltd v IRC* [2008] 1 AC 561, where the majority held that compound interest was awardable in appropriate circumstances in a common law restitution case. See further Nicholl 'Compound Interest for Late Payment of an Insurance Claim' (2008) 124 LQR 199; Mitchell 'Recovery of Compound Interest as Restitution or Damages' (2008) 71 MLR 290.

[121] *Piety v Stace* (1799) 4 Ves 620; *Heathcote v Hulme* (1819) 1 Jac & W 122; *Brown v Sansome* (1825) M'Cle & Yo 427; *Jones v Foxall* (1852) 15 Beav 388; *Penny v Avison* (1856) 3 Jur NS 62; *Re Davis* [1902] 2 Ch 314.

[122] [1975] QB 373.

[123] See *Jones v Foxall* (1852) 15 Beav 388; *Gordon v Gonda* [1955] 2 All ER 762, CA.

[124] (1722) 1 Stra 505.

have used it in its own trading operation; or that it would have used it to help its subsidiaries. Alternatively it should be presumed that the wrongdoer made the most beneficial use of it. But, whichever it is, in order to give adequate compensation, the money should be replaced at interest with yearly rests, ie, compound interest.[125]

Since it will almost always be the case that either the trust or the wrongdoer would have made 'most beneficial use' of the property by obtaining compound interest, there is a virtual presumption in favour of awarding compound interest. Although the Law Commission has made proposals for the reforms of the statutory jurisdiction to award compound interest on debts and damages, it has not proposed any change to the inherent equitable jurisdiction, which will continue to operate alongside the statutory jurisdiction.[126]

3 Defences to liability for breach of trust

Even if a trustee has committed a breach of trust which has caused loss to the trust, it is not inevitable that he will be required to pay equitable compensation to the trust. A number of defences are available to trustees which may wholly or partially protect them from liability.

(1) Beneficiaries' consent or concurrence

(a) General principles

A beneficiary cannot complain of a breach of trust by a trustee to which he consented, or in which he actively concurred or passively acquiesced.[127] As Wilmer LJ stated in the context of an advance of trust property made by a trustee bank to the beneficiaries in breach of trust in *Re Pauling's Settlement Trusts*:

if the bank can establish a valid request or consent by the advanced beneficiary to the advance in question, that is a good defence on the part of the bank to the beneficiary's claim, even though it can be plain that the advance was made in breach of trust.[128]

The case concerned a marriage settlement created in 1919 on the marriage of Violet Pauling and Commander Younghusband. The trustees were the bank Coutts & Co. By an express provision of the trust deed the trustees had the power to advance up to one-half of the beneficiaries' presumptive share under the trust for their advancement or absolute use. The family consistently lived beyond its means, and Violet's current account with the trustees was often overdrawn. Between 1948 and 1954 a number of

---

[125] [1975] QB 373, at 388.
[126] Law Com No 287 (2004), Pre-Judgment Interest on Debts and Damages, para 5.50.
[127] *Walker v Symonds* (1818) 3 Swan 1; *Stafford v Stafford* (1857) 1 De G & J 193; *Ghillingworth v Chambers* [1896] 1 Ch 685, CA.
[128] [1964] Ch 303, at 335.

advancements were made to the children of the marriage, Francis, George, Anne, and Anthony, who were all of age by 1951, ostensibly for such purposes as improvements to their homes and the purchase of furniture. The money advanced was generally paid into Violet's overdrawn current account. The children subsequently complained that the bank had acted in breach of trust in making these advancements.

In respect of an advance of £2,000 to George and Francis in 1949, stated to be for improvements to a house in the Isle of Man, and of advances of some £5,350 to Francis, George, and Ann between September 1953 and June 1954, the Court of Appeal held that the bank was not liable because the beneficiaries had validly consented to the advances being made, with full knowledge that the money would be applied to reduce their mother's overdraft.

If a trustee wishes to avoid liability completely he must have gained the consent of all the beneficiaries of the trust. If only some had consented, the remainder will retain the right to maintain an action against him for his breach.

(b) Requirements for relief from liability

(i) The beneficiary must be of age

A beneficiary's consent to a breach of trust will only be effective to protect the trustee from liability if he had reached the age of majority. The consent of a minor is ineffective.[129] However, a minor who fraudulently misrepresents his age to persuade trustees to pay trust money over to him will not be permitted to deny that his consent was effective because of his age.[130]

(ii) The beneficiary must not have consented while under any other incapacity

If the beneficiary is under any incapacity that would invalidate his consent a trustee remains liable.[131] Therefore, a beneficiary who is of age but under a mental incapacity cannot give an effective consent to a breach of trust. In *Re Pauling's Settlement Trusts*[132] one son, Francis, was a schizophrenic, but it was held that his mental condition was not sufficiently serious to render his consent invalid.[133]

(iii) The beneficiary must have freely given consent

Only the freely given consent of a beneficiary will be sufficient to protect a trustee from liability. In *Re Pauling's Settlement Trusts*[134] it was held that the trustees could not rely

---

[129] *Adye v Feuilleteau* (1783) 3 Swan 84n; *Lord Montfort v Lord Cadogan* (1816) 19 Ves 635; *Wilkinson v Parry* (1828) 4 Russ 272; *March v Russell* (1837) 3 My & Cr 31.

[130] *Overton v Banister* (1844) 3 Hare 503; *Wright v Snowe* (1848) 2 De G & Sm 321.

[131] *Crosby v Church* (1841) 3 Beav 485; *Mara v Manning* (1845) 2 Jo & Lat 311; *Fletcher v Green* (1864) 33 Beav 426.

[132] [1961] 3 All ER 713, at 731–732; on appeal [1964] Ch 303, at 347–348.

[133] See now Mental Capacity Act 2005, which provides a presumption of capacity in relation to a transaction, unless it can be proved otherwise.

[134] [1964] Ch 303.

on the beneficiaries' consent where it was given while the children were acting under the undue influence of their parents. It was only when they were 'emancipated' from parental control that their consent was effective. However, in such circumstances a trustee will only be liable 'if he knew, or ought to have known that the beneficiary was acting under the undue influence of another'.[135]

(iv) The beneficiary must have given an informed consent

A trustee will only be protected if the beneficiary's consent to the breach of trust was an informed consent.[136] The principle was stated by Wilberforce J, at first instance, in *Re Pauling's Settlement Trusts*:

the court has to consider all the circumstances in which the concurrence of the cestui que trust was given with a view to seeing whether it is fair and equitable that, having given his concurrence, he should afterwards turn round and sue the trustees: that subject to this, it is not necessary that he should know that what he is concurring in is a breach of trust, provided that he fully understands what he is concurring in...[137]

This principle was also adopted by Harman J in *Holder v Holder*[138] and Goff LJ in *Re Freeston's Charity*.[139]

(v) The beneficiary need not have benefited from the breach of trust

In *Fletcher v Collis*[140] it was held that a trustee will be protected from liability where a beneficiary has consented to the breach even if he did not obtain any personal benefit from that breach.[141]

(2) Breach subsequently condoned by the beneficiaries

A trustee is similarly protected from liability if, after a breach has been committed, the beneficiaries condone it, release him from liability, or indemnify him. This principle is subject to the same qualifications as apply to the rule that a trustee is not liable to a beneficiary who has consented to a breach of trust: ie the condoning or releasing beneficiary must be of age;[142] the condoning or releasing beneficiary must not be under any other incapacity; the beneficiary must freely condone the breach or release the trustee from liability;[143] the beneficiary must have known what he was condoning or from what he was releasing the trustee. Condonation obtained

---

[135] Ibid., at 338, per Willmer LJ.

[136] There must be a full and frank disclosure by the trustee. See *Phipps v Boardman* [1964] 2 All ER 187.

[137] [1961] 3 All ER 713, at 730.   [138] [1968] Ch 353.

[139] [1979] 1 All ER 51.   [140] [1905] 2 Ch 24.

[141] See also *Re Pauling's Settlement Trusts* [1961] 3 All ER 713, at 730; *Allen v Rea Brothers Trustees Ltd* [2002] WTLR 625.

[142] *Wade v Cox* (1835) 4 LJ Ch 105; *Parker v Bloxam* (1855) 20 Beav 295.

[143] Westbury LC stated in *Farrant v Blanchford* that a trustee must be able to show that the beneficiary 'gave the release freely and without pressure or undue influence or any description'. See also *Lloyd v Attwood* (1859) 3 De G & J 614; *Reade v Reade* (1881) 9 LR Ir 409.

through undue influence will be of no effect. As Westbury LC stated in *Farrant v Blanchford*:[144]

Where a breach of trust has been committed from which a trustee alleges that he has been released, it is incumbent on him to show that such release was given by the cestui que trust deliberately and advisedly, with full knowledge of all the circumstances, and of his own rights and claims against the trustee…[145]

(3) **The discretion of the court to grant relief from liability**

(a) Trustee Act 1925, s 61[146]

Section 61 confers upon the court a general discretion to grant a trustee relief from liability for breach of trust. The section provides:

If it appears to the court that a trustee, whether appointed by the court or otherwise, is or may be personally liable for any breach of trust…but has acted honestly and reasonably, and ought fairly to be excused for the breach of trust and for omitting to obtain the direction of the court in the matter in which he committed such breach, then the court may relieve him either wholly or in part from personal liability for the same.

This section clearly grants a wide discretion to the court, both as to whether a trustee should be relieved at all and, if so, the extent to which he should be relieved. This enables the court to take account of the circumstances in which the breach occurred and to assess the culpability of the trustee in the light of them. However, the starting point of the law is that a trustee is prima facie liable even for honest technical breaches of trust, and the burden falls to the trustee to demonstrate that he should be granted relief.[147]

(b) Preconditions for the grant of relief under s 61

The courts have emphasized that the discretion conferred by s 61 is not to be exercised on the basis of strict and narrow interpretations. As Bryne J observed in *Re Turner*:[148]

It would be impossible to lay down any general rules or principles to be acted on in carrying out the provisions of the section, and I think that each case must depend on its own circumstances.[149]

However, for the court even to consider relief the trustee must show that he had acted 'honestly and reasonably', and that he 'ought fairly to be excused'. Although there is little authority, some consideration has been given to the meaning of these requirements.

---

144 (1863) 1 De GJ & Sm 107, at 119.

145 See also *Ramsden v Hylton* (1751) 2 Ves Sen 304; *Hore v Becher* (1842) 12 Sim 465; *Pritt v Clay* (1843) 6 Beav 503; *Thomson v Eastwood* (1877) 2 App Cas 215, HL; *Re Garnett* (1885) 31 Ch D 1, CA.

146 Trustee Act 1925, s 61 re-enacts s 3 of the Judicial Trustees Act 1896, and many of the cases below consider the effect of s 3.

147 *Re Stuart* [1897] 2 Ch 583.   148 [1897] 1 Ch 536, at 542.

149 See also *Re Pauling's Settlement Trusts* [1964] Ch 303, at 359, per Upjohn LJ: 's 61 is purely discretionary, and its application necessarily depends on the particular facts of each case'.

(i) 'Honesty'

It is clear that a trustee cannot be granted relief from liability if he has acted dishonestly. However, as Kekewich J observed in *Perrins v Bellamy*,[150] in a large majority of cases where a breach of trust has been committed the trustee will not have acted dishonestly and the real question will concern whether the trustee had acted 'reasonably':

> The legislature has made the absence of all dishonesty a condition precedent to the relief of the trustee from all liability. But that is not the grit of the section. The grit is in the words 'reasonably, and ought fairly to be excused for the breach of trust' . . . [151]

(ii) 'Reasonably'

A trustee will only be granted relief from liability if he had acted reasonably. As Kekewich J pointed out in *Perrins v Bellamy*[152] this means that the trustees must have 'acted reasonably in their breach of trust'. It will therefore be very hard for a trustee to gain relief if the very basis of his breach of trust was that he had failed to observe the appropriate standard of care expected of a trustee.[153] For example, in *Bartlett v Barclays Bank Trust Co Ltd (No 2)*[154] the bank was liable because they had failed adequately to supervise the management of the company owned by the trust. Since the very grounds of their liability was their negligence they could not be said to be entitled to relief under s 61 as they had not acted 'reasonably'.

Even where trustees have committed a breach of trust by exceeding their powers, for example by misappropriation of trust property or unauthorized investment, relief can only be granted if they acted reasonably.[155] In *Re Turner*[156] Byrne J was not prepared to find that a trustee who had invested trust money upon an equitable mortgage, which was not an authorized investment, had acted 'reasonably'. He had not acted as he would have done if it had been a transaction of his own. He had relied on his co-trustee, who was a solicitor. In *Re Stuart*[157] a trustee who had invested money on a mortgage where the security had proved insufficient was held not to have acted reasonably because the mortgage had been granted outside the terms of what is now s 8 of the Trustee Act 1925.[158] No proper valuation had been obtained and the amount lent was greater than two-thirds of the amount stated in the valuation. Although Stirling J held that this 'was not necessarily fatal' to the application of s 61, the legislature had laid down a standard by which the trustee was to be judged. He concluded that, if the trustee had been dealing with his own money, he would not have advanced

---

[150] [1898] 2 Ch 521. See, however, *Re Clapham* [2005] EWHC 3387 (Ch), where, in the case of a wrongful payment out of the trust funds by the trustee, it was confirmed that the section does not apply where the mistaken actions of the trustee have been grossly negligent.

[151] Ibid., at 527–528.   [152] Ibid., at 529.

[153] The appropriate standard of care will either be the new statutory duty of care under s 1 of the Trustee Act 2000 or, if this does not apply, the common law standard of the 'ordinary prudent man of business'.

[154] [1980] Ch 515.

[155] See *Re Turner* [1897] 1 Ch 536; *Re Stuart* [1897] 2 Ch 583; *Re Dive* [1909] 1 Ch 328; *Shaw v Cates* [1909] 1 Ch 389; *Re Mackay* [1911] 1 Ch 300.

[156] [1897] 1 Ch 536.   [157] [1897] 2 Ch 583.

[158] Then s 4 of the Trustee Act 1888 and s 8 of the Trustee Act 1893.

the mortgage without further inquiry.[159] In *Ward-Smith v Jebb*[160] a trustee had paid trust money to a person he assumed was a beneficiary because of the effect of the Adoption of Children Act 1949, when in fact the Act had no application to the person. Buckley J applied the test of reasonableness of an ordinary man of business acting on his own behalf and said that 'a prudent man, whose affairs were affected by a statute would either satisfy himself that he fully understood its effect or would seek legal advice'. There were therefore no grounds for the court to grant relief under s 61. In contrast, relief was granted in the recent case of *Re Evans*.[161] The defendant had administered her mother's small estate by distributing it to herself on the assumption that her brother, from whom she had not heard for thirty years, was no longer alive. Prior to the distribution she had sought legal advice and purchased a missing-beneficiary policy to cover the value of approximately half of the capital value of the assets. Richard McCombe, QC held that while the mere fact that a trustee has acted on legal advice does not automatically entitle relief under s 61,[162] the defendant had acted reasonably. The estate was relatively small, she was a lay person who was at all times willing to abide by the advice of her solicitors, and some provision had been made for her brother's potential claims.

It is clear that s 61 applies to professional as well as non-professional trustees.[163] However, in the case of a 'professional trustee', the courts have held that a higher standard of care is expected,[164] and they are more reluctant to grant relief under s 61. As the Court of Appeal said in *Re Pauling's Settlement Trusts*:

Where a banker undertakes to act as a paid trustee of a settlement created by a customer, and so deliberately places itself in a position where its duty as trustee conflicts with its interest as a banker, we think that the court should be very slow to relieve such a trustee under [s 61].[165]

(iii) 'Ought fairly to be excused'

The difficulty with this requirement is to identify precisely what it adds over and above the requirement that the trustee must have acted 'reasonably'. As Kekewich J observed in *Perrins v Bellamy*:

I venture ... to think that, in general and in the absence of special circumstances, a trustee who has acted 'reasonably' ought to be relieved, and that it is not incumbent on the Court to consider whether he ought 'fairly' to be excused, unless there is evidence of a special character showing that the provisions of the section ought not to be applied in his favour.[166]

---

[159] [1897] 2 Ch 583, at 591–592.   [160] (1964) 108 Sol Jo 919.

[161] [1999] 2 All ER 777.

[162] *Marsden v Regan* [1954] 1 All ER 475, at 482, per Evershed MR.

[163] In *Re Pauling's Settlement Trusts* [1964] Ch 303, at 338 the Court of Appeal said that 'it would be a misconstruction of the section to say that it does not apply to professional trustees'; and (at 356) Wilmer LJ said that 'all of us are agreed that in the very special circumstances of this case the bank should be accorded some relief notwithstanding the fact that they were professional trustees paid for their services'.

[164] *National Trustees Co of Australia Ltd v General Finance Co of Australasia Ltd* [1905] AC 373; *Bartlett v Barclays Bank Trust Co Ltd* [1980] Ch 515.

[165] [1964] Ch 303, at 339.   [166] [1898] 2 Ch 521, at 529.

However, he seemed to contradict himself in *Davis v Hutchings*,[167] where he held that a trustee who had acted both honesty and reasonably ought not to be relieved from liability. The trustees had distributed a share of the trust fund to their solicitor, who claimed that he was the assignee of the share. They failed to investigate his title, which would have revealed that the assignment was subject to the plaintiff's charge over the share. He held that it would be impossible for them to be excused 'without departing from well-established rules'[168] and there was no justification for the trustees being 'let off'.[169] However, the case can perhaps be better explained on the grounds that the trustees' conduct was unreasonable. Surely a prudent man of business acting on his own behalf would not fail to investigate the assignee's alleged title in such circumstances, particularly when that would be the well-established rule. Ultimately, the inclusion of the expression 'ought fairly to be excused' emphasizes the wide discretion given to the court as to whether, in all the circumstances, the trustee should be granted relief. The preconditions are that he acted honestly and reasonably, but it is then a matter for the court. As Evershed MR said in *Marsden v Regan*, having found that the trustee had acted honestly and reasonably:

There still remains the question: Ought she fairly to be excused? That is the most difficult point of all. But it is essentially a matter within the discretion of the judge...[170]

In *Re Wightwick's Will Trusts*[171] trustees had paid over money to the National Anti-Vivisection Society on the basis of the generally held view that the gift was a valid charitable gift, even though the gift was in fact invalid. Wynn-Parry J held that because the trustees had acted bona fides throughout it was 'proper to declare under s 61 Trustee Act 1925, that they acted honestly and reasonably and ought fairly to be excused for any breach of trust which they might have committed'.[172]

(c) The extent of relief

If the court finds that the conditions for granting relief are met, the extent to which the trustee may be relieved is a matter for the discretion of the court. Section 61 provides that the trustee may be relieved 'wholly or in part'. In *Re Pauling's Settlement Trusts*[173] one breach of trust by the bank involved the advance of £2,600 to Francis and George to pay off a debt owed by their mother secured on her life interest, known as the 'Hodson Loan'. In return, the mother assigned to them life policies with a surrender value of £650, on which she promised to continue to pay the premiums, and which would pay £3,000 on her death. There was a division between the members of the Court of Appeal as to the extent to which the bank should be relieved of liability in respect of this transaction. The majority found that, in the circumstances, the bank had acted honestly and reasonably, but that it should only be relieved to the extent of

---

[167] [1907] 1 Ch 356. But see *Re Allsop* [1914] 1 Ch 1, where the Court of Appeal, while accepting that *Davis v Hutchings* may have been right on its facts, rejected the wider dicta of Kekewich J.

[168] [1907] 1 Ch 356, at 364.　　[169] Ibid., at 365.

[170] [1954] 1 WLR 423, at 435.　　[171] [1950] Ch 260.

[172] Ibid., at 266.　　[173] [1964] Ch 303.

the surrender value of the policies which had been assigned to them. Willmer J, dissenting, held that they should be relieved from all liability:

whereas my brethren think that the bank should be relieved only in part, I take the view that if relief is to be accorded to all, it should be accorded in full. I can see no logical reason for stopping short of relief in full.[174]

In *Re Evans (decd)*[175] Richard McCombe, QC held that the defendant was entitled to relief from liability to pay interest to her brother on the sum that had not been distributed to him on the administration of their mother's estate, but only to the extent that his claim would not be able to be satisfied out of the proceeds of the sale of a house which had derived from the estate and was still at her disposal.

(4) Limitation[176]

(a) General principle

Section 21(3) of the Limitation Act 1980 provides:

Subject to the preceding provisions of this section, an action by a beneficiary to recover trust property or in respect of any breach of trust, not being an action for which a period of limitation is prescribed by any other provision of this Act shall not be brought after the expiration of six years from the date on which the right of action accrued.

This has the effect that a beneficiary cannot bring an action for a breach of trust which occurred more than six years ago. Some details of the provision require further examination.

(i) 'Trustees'

Section 21 concerns remedies available against 'trustees' who commit breaches of trust. By s 38(1), 'trustee' is given the same definition as in the Trustee Act 1925, and therefore includes express trustees, personal representatives, and trustees holding property on implied or constructive trusts.[177]

(ii) 'Breach of trust'

The period of limitation applies only to breaches of trust. In *Tito v Waddell (No 2)*[178] Megarry V-C held that it did not apply to claims made against trustees who had acted in breach of fiduciary duty by purchasing property from the trust in contravention of the self-dealing rule, or by purchasing the beneficiaries' beneficial interest

---

[174] Ibid., at 356.   [175] [1999] 2 All ER 777.

[176] See Birks and Pretto (eds), *Breach of Trust* (2002), Chs 11 and 12.

[177] Trustee Act 1925, s 68(17). It has also been held to include fiduciary agents: *Burdick v Garrick* (1870) 5 Ch App 233; company directors: *Re Lands Allotment Co* [1894] 1 Ch 616, CA; a mortgagee in respect of the proceeds of sale: *Thorne v Heard* [1895] AC 495; but not a trustee in bankruptcy: *Re Cornish* [1896] 1 QB 99; nor the liquidator of a company in voluntary liquidation: *Re Windsor Steam Coal Co (1901) Ltd* [1928] Ch 609.

[178] [1977] Ch 106, at 249.

in contravention of the fair-dealing rule.[179] In such cases, the doctrine of laches may operate to protect a trustee from unduly tardy proceedings.[180]

(iii) 'The date on which the right of action accrued'

Section 21(3) provides that 'for the purposes of this subsection, the right of action shall not be treated as having accrued to any beneficiary entitled to a future interest in the trust property until the interest fell into possession'. This means that time does not begin to run against a remainderman, or beneficiary with a reversionary interest, until his interest has fallen into possession.

(b) Exceptions

In some circumstances the Limitation Act 1980 provides for a period of limitation other than the standard six years applicable to claims for breach of trust.

(i) Trustee was party to fraud

Section 21(1)(a) provides that there is no limitation period to an action by the beneficiary 'in respect of any fraud or fraudulent breach of trust to which the trustee was a party or privy'.[181] The meaning of fraud was considered in *Re Sale Hotel and Botanical Gardens Co*,[182] where it was held that a promoter of a company who himself received £250 from the sale was not entitled to protection under the section.[183] Wright J stated:

> It would be impossible to hold that moral fraud . . . is required for the purposes of that section. That section seems to me directed to the relief of trustees from what may be called innocent or negligent breaches of trust, and not breaches of trust in which, for their own personal gain, the trustees have committed knowingly acts from the nature of which the law imputes to them knowledge that they are doing wrong.[184]

However, in *Armitage v Nurse*[185] Millett LJ stated that the section was only applicable in cases involving dishonesty. The exception will only apply if the fraud was committed by the trustee himself. In *Thorne v Heard*[186] the trustees allowed a solicitor who was acting for them to retain the proceeds of sale of trust property, which he then fraudulently applied to his own use. The Court of Appeal held that the plaintiff's action was barred by the Statute of Limitations and that the case did not fall within the exception because the fraud was the fraud of the solicitor and not of the trustees, who were therefore neither party nor privy to the fraud.

---

[179] See Chapter 30.   [180] See below, p 902.
[181] This subsection enacts the rule of permanent liability which was applied by equity to express trustees. See *North American Land and Timber Co Ltd v Watkins* [1904] 1 Ch 242; affd [1904] 2 Ch 233, CA.
[182] (1897) 77 LT 681. See also *Vane v Vane* (1873) 8 Ch App 383; *North American Land and Timber Co Ltd v Watkins* [1904] 2 Ch 233, CA.
[183] Then the Trustee Act 1888, s 8.
[184] See *Collings v Wade* [1896] 1 IR 340, where it was held that fraud must amount to dishonesty.
[185] [1998] Ch 241.   [186] [1894] 1 Ch 599.

(ii) Trustee who retains trust property in his hands

Section 21(1)(b) provides that there is no limitation period to an action by the beneficiary 'to recover from the trustee trust property or the proceeds of trust property in
the possession of the trustee, or previously received by the trustee and converted to
his use'. There is no requirement here that the trustee be guilty of fraud. The action
lies due to the mere fact that the trustee still holds trust property, or its proceeds, in
his hands. The exception was applied in *Re Howlett*,[187] where a trustee occupied trust
property without paying any occupational rents to the beneficiary. Dankwerts J held
that the beneficiary could recover such rent from the trustee even after the limitation period had expired because the situation fell within the exception. The trustee
should have obtained a rent from the property, and since he had not done so he 'must
be considered as having it in his own pocket at the material date'.[188] If the trust property has been dissipated by the trustee, for example if it has been lost,[189] spent on the
maintenance of an infant beneficiary,[190] or applied in the discharge of a debt,[191] the
exception will not apply.

(iii) Claims to the personal estate of a deceased person

Section 22(1)(a) provides that:

No action in respect of any claim to the personal estate of a deceased person or to any share or
interest in any such estate (whether under a will or on intestacy) shall be brought after the expiration of twelve years from the date on which the right to receive the share or interest accrued.

Since a personal representative may also be a trustee, the question has arisen whether
in such circumstances the six-year limitation period in s 21(3), or the twelve-year
period in s 22(1)(a), should apply. Under the preceding legislation,[192] it was essential to
determine whether the personal representative had become a trustee. If he had, then
the six-year period would displace the twelve-year period.[193] The better view seems
to be that under the Limitation Act 1980 the period of twelve years will apply to all
actions concerning the personal estate of a deceased person, whether or not the personal representative became a trustee.[194]

(iv) Actions to account

Section 23 prescribes the time limit for actions for an account:

An action for an account shall not be brought after the expiration of any time limit under this
Act which is applicable to the claim which is the basis of the duty to account.

---

[187] [1949] Ch 767. See also *James v Williams* [2000] Ch 1.
[188] [1949] Ch 767, at 778.   [189] *Re Tufnell* (1902) 18 TLR 705; *Re Fountaine* [1909] 2 Ch 382.
[190] *Re Page* [1893] 1 Ch 304; *Re Timmis* [1902] 1 Ch 176.
[191] Even when the trustee was a partner in the bank to which the debt was owed. See *Re Gurney* [1893] 1
Ch 590.
[192] Real Property Limitation Act 1874, s 8; Trustee Act 1888, s 8.
[193] See *Re Swain* [1891] 3 Ch 233; *Re Timmis* [1902] 1 Ch 176; *Re Richardson* [1920] 1 Ch 423, CA; *Re Oliver*
[1927] 2 Ch 323; *Re Diplock* [1948] Ch 465, CA; affd sub nom *Ministry of Health v Simpson* [1951] AC 251, HL.
[194] See, in support of this view, *Re Loftus* [2007] 1 WLR 591; Preston and Newsom, *Limitation of Actions*
(4th edn, 1989), p 51.

Until recently it was thought that this provision had the effect that no statutory limitation period operated in respect of an action for an account of unauthorized profits from a fiduciary.[195] However, in *Coulthard v Disco Mix Club Ltd*[196] it was held that an action for an account against a fiduciary was subject to the same limitation period as a common law action for damages. Thus an action for account for breach of fiduciary duty will be subject to a six-year limitation period unless it involved a genuine misappropriation of trust property by the fiduciary, in which circumstances s 21(1)(a) will apply and there will be no limitation period.[197] Where there is no limitation period the equitable doctrine of laches may apply to protect fiduciaries from unduly delayed proceedings.[198] This is discussed more fully in the following chapter.

(v) Postponement of limitation period

Section 32(1) provides that the date from which the Limitation Act shall run may be postponed to a date later than the date of the cause of action:

where in the case of any action for which a period of limitation is prescribed by this Act, either—

(a) the action is based upon the fraud of the defendant; or

(b) any fact relevant to the plaintiff's right of action has been deliberately concealed from him by the defendant; or

(c) the action is for relief from the consequences of a mistake;

the period of limitation shall not begin to run until the plaintiff has discovered the fraud, concealment or mistake (as the case may be) or could with reasonable diligence have discovered it.

It has been held that this section applies to actions against trustees.[199]

(c) Reform of limitation

The Law Commission has recommended sweeping reform of the limitation period applicable to claims for a remedy for a wrong in its Report *Limitation of Actions*,[200] which, if implemented, would simplify and radically alter the limitation period applicable to actions for breach of trust. The Law Commission proposes the introduction of a single core limitation regime applicable to all claims. This would consist of a primary limitation period of three years starting from the date on which the claimant knows, or ought reasonably to know (a) the facts which give rise to the cause of action; (b) the identity of the defendant; and (c) if the claimant has suffered injury, loss, or damage or the defendant has received a benefit, that the injury, loss, damage, or benefit was significant. This primary limitation period would be supplemented by a long-stop limitation

---

[195] *A-G v Cocke* [1988] Ch 414; *Nelson v Rye* [1996] 2 All ER 186; Stevens 'Too Late to Face the Music? Limitation and Laches as Defences to an Action for Breach of Fiduciary Duty' [1997] Conv 225.

[196] [2000] 1 WLR 707.   [197] *Paragon Finance v DB Thakerar & Co* [1999] 1 All ER 400.

[198] See below p 902.

[199] *Beaman v ARTS Ltd* [1949] 1 KB 550, CA; *Kitchen v Royal Air Forces Association* [1958] 1 WLR 563; *Phillips-Higgins v Harper* [1954] 1 QB 411; *Bartlett v Barclays Bank Trust Co Ltd* [1980] Ch 515.

[200] Law Com No 270 (2001).

period of ten years, starting from the date of the accrual of the cause of action, or from the date of the act or omission which gives rise to the cause of action. It is proposed that this core regime should apply to all claims for breach of trust and claims to recover trust property,[201] and to claims for breach of fiduciary duty.[202] No distinction would be made between fraudulent and non-fraudulent breaches of trust,[203] nor would a special limitation period operate where the claimant was bringing a claim to recover property against his or her trustee.[204] A special rule would operate in the case of a claim for the recovery of property held on a bare trust so that the cause of action shall not accrue unless and until the trustee acts in breach of trust.[205]

(5) Laches[206]

If a claimant delays bringing his action, the court may consider it inequitable for him to succeed, and the defendant will be protected from any liability. The doctrine was explained by the Privy Council in *Lindsay Petroleum Co v Hurd*:

the doctrine of laches in courts of equity is not an arbitrary or a technical doctrine. Where it would be practically unjust to give a remedy, either because the party has, by his conduct, done that which might fairly be regarded as equivalent to waiver of it, or where by his conduct and neglect he has, though perhaps not waiving that remedy, yet put the other party in a situation in which it would not be reasonable to place him if the remedy were afterwards to be asserted, in either of these cases, lapse of time and delay are most material.[207]

In *Nelson v Rye*[208] Laddie J rejected a submission that delay per se is insufficient to raise the defence unless the defendant shows that he had suffered substantial prejudice or detriment. He stated that there were no defined hurdles over each of which a litigant must struggle before the defence is made out,[209] and instead identified a number of main factors which should be taken in to account by the court:

The courts have indicated over the years some of the factors which must be taken into consideration in deciding whether the defence runs. Those factors include the period of the delay, the extent to which the defendant's position has been prejudiced by the delay, and the extent to which the prejudice was caused by the actions of the plaintiff.[210]

In some circumstances, the defence of laches may even operate so as to prevent a beneficiary from asserting their equitable interest in the trust property because it would be unconscionable for them to do so.[211] In *Patel v Shah*[212] commercial properties had been purchased in the late 1980s in circumstances which gave rise to a resulting trust in favour of the claimants. However, following the property slump in the early 1990s, when the properties were in negative equity and the rental income was insufficient to

---

[201] Ibid., para 4.94.   [202] Ibid., para 4.95.   [203] Ibid., paras 4.97–4.101.
[204] Ibid., paras 4.102–4.106.   [205] Ibid., para 4.105.
[206] To the bemusement of students, this is pronounced as 'lay cheese'.
[207] (1874) LR 5 PC 221, at 239–240.
[208] [1996] 2 All ER 186; Stevens 'Too Late to Face the Music? Limitation and Laches as Defences to an Action for Breach of Fiduciary Duty' [1997] Conv 225.
[209] [1996] 2 All ER 186, at 200.   [210] Ibid., at 201.
[211] See *Frawley v Neill* [2000] CP Reports 20.   [212] [2005] EWCA Civ 157.

meet the mortgage instalments, the claimants left the defendants to deal with every-thing relating to the properties, and the defendants took on the whole burden of keep-ing the properties afloat. The claimants only sought to assert their beneficial interest in the properties in 2002, when market prices had recovered and the properties were producing income and capital gains. The Court of Appeal held that in these circum-stances the claimants were barred from asserting their equitable interest by the defence of laches. They had acted unconscionably by leaving the defendants to deal with the properties, and had departed from their commercial arrangements by ceasing to bear any risk or expense. In effect the venture between the defendants and the claimants had ceased to be joint.

(a) Relation to statutory limitation periods

There is some debate whether the doctrine of laches has any application where a statu-tory period of limitation applies. In *Re Pauling's Settlement Trusts*[213] Wilberforce J held that there was no room for the operation of the equitable doctrine of laches because there was an express statutory provision.[214] In *Gwembe Valley Development Co Ltd v Koshy*,[215] the Court of Appeal affirmed this view, but this has since been doubted in *Re Loftus*,[216] where it was suggested that the equitable doctrine was not excluded under cases coming within s 21(1) of the Limitation Act 1980. This case concerned fiduciary duties, and is explored in Chapter 30.

It is beyond doubt that laches will continue to apply to those situations where there is no statutory limitation period, particularly those falling within the scope of s 21(3).

(b) Knowledge of the right of action

It seems that the doctrine of laches will only apply if the claimant had knowledge of the rights he failed to pursue. In *Lindsay Petroleum Co v Hurd*[217] the Privy Council stated that 'in order that the remedy should be lost by laches or delay, it is…necessary that there should be sufficient knowledge of the facts constituting the title to relief'.

(c) Length of delay

There is no set length of time that will cause the court to apply the doctrine of laches. Instead the court must determine whether, given the circumstances, it would be inequitable to allow the claim to succeed. Very short periods, if not accompanied by acts of acquiescence by the claimant, will not be sufficient. In *Lindsay Petroleum Co v Hurd*[218] the Privy Council held that a delay of fifteen months was insufficient, as was a delay of two-and-a-quarter years in *Re Sharpe*.[219] In *Weld v Petre*,[220] in the context of

---

[213] [1961] 3 All ER 713.   [214] Ibid., at 735. Affirmed by the Court of Appeal [1964] Ch 303.
[215] [2004] WTLR 97, at [140].   [216] [2007] 1 WLR 591, at [41], per Chadwick LJ.
[217] (1874) LR 5 PC 221, at 241.   [218] (1874) LR 5 PC 221.
[219] [1892] 1 Ch 154. In *Bunn v BBC* [1998] 3 All ER 552; Lightman J refused to grant an injunction prevent-ing a television broadcast because it had been delayed until the last minute. This would not, however, have affected any remedy in damages for the alleged breach of confidence.
[220] [1929] 1 Ch 33, at 54–55.

the redemption of a mortgage, the Court of Appeal suggested a period of twenty years, therefore holding that a delay of eighteen years and four months was 'not of itself sufficient to disentitle the plaintiffs to relief'.[221]

(d) Prejudice to the defendant

The doctrine of laches operates very closely with the principle of acquiescence. As the Privy Council noted in *Lindsay Petroleum Co v Hurd*,[222] equity will grant relief where to allow the claimant his remedy would be practically unjust because he has 'by his conduct, done that which might fairly be regarded as equivalent to a waiver'.

While the authorities recognize that the defence may apply where the only action (or rather, inaction) on the part of the claimant has been a prolonged period of silence or inactivity,[223] the mere fact of a delay in commencing proceedings is not usually sufficient to give rise to the defence of laches. As Laddie J observed in *Nelson v Rye*:

I accept that mere delay alone will almost never suffice, but the court has to look at all the circumstances... and then decide whether the balance of justice or injustice is in favour of granting the remedy or withholding it. If substantial prejudice will be suffered by the defendant, it is not necessary to prove that it was caused by the delay. On the other hand, the plaintiff's knowledge that the delay will cause such prejudice is a factor to be taken into account.[224]

He held that, in the circumstances, Nelson had caused an unreasonable delay by ignoring Rye's advice that they should get around the table to see how the figures worked out, but that he had done this because he did not want to hear Rye's warnings that he was living beyond his means. He further held that Rye would be prejudiced by the proceedings because he had not retained documents relating to the receipt of earnings for the entire period of the claim, having cleared them out to make space after a six-year period. He would be incapable of remembering the details of the accounts, especially relating to any expenses incurred that he would be entitled to set off against the gross earnings received.

In *Fisher v Brooker*[225] (in which one of the composers of Procol Harum's *A Whiter Shade of Pale* sought to enforce his authorship after a delay of over thirty years), Lord Neuberger said:

Although I would not suggest that it is an immutable requirement, some sort of detrimental reliance is usually an essential ingredient of laches, in my opinion.[226]

The House of Lords in that case did not think that the delay, in itself, was a bar to equitable relief. There were no evidential problems and any prejudice on the part of the defendants was balanced by the fact that they had not had to account for royalties to the composer until he indicated that he intended to enforce his rights.

---

[221] Ibid., at 55, per Lawrence LJ.   [222] (1874) LR 5 PC 221, at 239–240.
[223] *Lindsay Petroleum Co v Hurd* (1874) LR 5 PC 221; *Erlanger v New Sombrero Phosphate Co* (1878) 3 App Cas 1218; *Brooks v Muckleston* [1909] 2 Ch 519.
[224] [1996] 2 All ER 186, at 201.   [225] [2009] 1 WLR 1764.
[226] Ibid., at [64].

4 Contribution and indemnity where a trustee is liable

Although a trustee may be liable to the beneficiaries for breach of trust without any defence, in some circumstances he may be entitled to a contribution or indemnity from his co-trustees, or from the beneficiaries of the trust, which will have the practical effect of partially or completely alleviating his obligation to provide equitable compensation.

(1) Indemnity from co-trustees

As was noted above, trustees who together commit a breach of trust are jointly and severally liable for that breach. However, in some circumstances a trustee may be entitled to receive a full indemnity from liability for his breach from his fellow trustees.

(a) Co-trustee acted fraudulently

Where one of several trustees acts fraudulently, the others are entitled to a complete indemnity from liability. In *Re Smith*[227] two trustees invested in debentures. One, who was also the tenant for life of the settlement, invested because he believed that this would increase his income from the trust, while the other invested because he had received a bribe to do so. Kekewich J held that, because of his dishonesty, the bribed trustee alone was liable.

(b) Co-trustee is a professional

A trustee may be entitled to an indemnity if his co-trustee was a professional whose advice he could reasonably be expected to rely on. This has most often been the case where a co-trustee was a solicitor.[228] In *Re Partington*[229] the two trustees of a settlement invested in a mortgage which was an improper investment for the trust. Stirling J held that Mr Allen, who was a solicitor, was liable to indemnify his co-trustee, Mrs Partington, because she had 'been misled by her co-trustee by reason of his not giving her full information as to the nature of the investments which he was asking her to advance the money upon'. For an indemnity the trustee must have acted purely on the basis of the solicitor trustee. In *Head v Gould*[230] Kekewich J said that there was no right to an indemnity merely because a co-trustee is a solicitor when the trustee 'was an active participator in the breach of trust complained of, and is not proved to have participated merely in consequence of the advice and control of the solicitor'.[231]

(c) Co-trustee has personally benefited from the breach of trust

The general principle was considered by the Court of Appeal in *Bahin v Hughes*.[232] Cotton LJ said that a trustee is entitled to an indemnity from his co-trustee either

---

[227] [1896] 1 Ch 71.
[228] See *Lockhart v Reilly* (1856) 25 LJ Ch 697; *Bahin v Hughes* (1886) 31 Ch D 390, CA.
[229] (1887) 57 LT 654.   [230] [1898] 2 Ch 250.   [231] Ibid., at 265.
[232] (1886) 31 Ch D 390.

when they are both liable to the beneficiary because the co-trustee got trust money into his own hands and made use of it,[233] or 'against a trustee who has himself got the benefit of the breach of trust'.[234] Where the trustee is also a beneficiary, and has benefited by the breach of trust, he is liable to indemnify his co-trustees to the extent of his beneficial interest. The principle was stated by Kay J in *Chillingworth v Chambers*:

> the weight of authority is in favour of the holding that a trustee who, being also a [beneficiary], has received, as between himself and his co-trustee, an exclusive benefit by the breach of trust, must indemnify his co-trustee to the extent of his interest in the trust fund, and not merely to the extent of the benefit which he has received.[235]

The trustees of a will invested in mortgages which proved to provide insufficient security. Chillingworth had also become a beneficiary, and the purposes of the investment had been to produce a higher rate of interest from the trust property, which was for his benefit. The court held that the deficit of £1,580 was to be made good from Chillingworth's beneficial interest, and that Chambers was indemnified from liability. If the trustee-beneficiary's interest is insufficient to cover the total loss, the trustees will be equally liable for the remaining loss.

(2) Contribution from co-trustees

(a) Position pre-1979

Prior to the enactment of the Civil Liability (Contribution) Act 1978 trustees who were jointly and severally liable for a breach of trust were equally liable, irrespective of the degree of blame warranted by their conduct. A trustee who had been held liable to the beneficiaries could recover equal contributions from his co-trustees. The effect of this rule was seen in *Bahin v Hughes*,[236] where an unauthorized investment was made by two of the three trustees of a settlement, with the third trustee, Mr Edwards, taking no active part. He claimed that he was not liable to contribute, but the Court of Appeal held that the trustees were equally liable and there was no ground for an indemnity. As Cotton LJ concluded:

> in my opinion it would be laying down a wrong rule to hold that where one trustee acts honestly, though erroneously, the other trustee is to be held entitled to an indemnity who by doing nothing neglects his duty more than the acting trustee.[237]

(b) Civil Liability (Contribution) Act 1978[238]

The Civil Liability (Contribution) Act 1978 gives the court a wide discretion to apportion liability between trustees who are jointly and severally liable for breach of trust.[239] Section 1(1) states the general principle of contribution:

---

[233] See *Thompson v Finch* (1856) 25 LJ Ch 681.   [234] (1886) 31 Ch D 390, at 396.
[235] [1896] 1 Ch 685, at 707.   [236] (1886) 31 Ch D 390.   [237] Ibid., at 396.
[238] For the comparable position in Australia see: *Alexander v Perpetual Trustees WA Ltd* [2003] 216 CLR 109; Vann 'Breach of Trust and Statutory Contribution (2005) 122 LQR 563.
[239] S 6(1) makes clear that the statute applies to damage caused by breach of trust. *Friends' Provident Life Office v Hillier Parker May & Rowden (a firm)* [1997] QB 85; *Dubai Aluminium Co Ltd v Salaam* [2003] 2 AC 366; *Charter plc v City Index Ltd* [2008] Ch 313; Virgo 'Contribution Revisited' (2008) 67 CLJ 254.

any person liable in respect of any damage suffered by another person may recover contribution from any other person liable in respect of the same damage (whether jointly with him or otherwise).

The general discretion of the court is found in s 2(1):

in any proceedings for contribution under s 1...the amount of the contribution recoverable from any person shall be such as may be found by the court to be just and equitable having regard to the extent of that person's responsibility for the damage in question.

The court can therefore reflect the respective blameworthiness of co-trustees in the extent to which they permit contribution. Under s 2(2) the court has the power to find that a trustee is exempt from making contributions to his co-trustee, or that a trustee is entitled to a complete indemnity from his co-trustee.

(3) Indemnity from a beneficiary

As has already been noted, a trustee will not incur any liability for a breach of trust to a beneficiary who consented to it, or subsequently concurred in it.[240] The trustee remains liable to any beneficiaries who did not so consent or concur. However, the trustee may be entitled to be indemnified from the beneficial interest of any trustee who requested, or consented to the breach.

(a) The court's inherent jurisdiction

If a trustee commits a breach of trust at the instigation or the request of a beneficiary the court has the power, under its inherent jurisdiction, to impound the beneficiary's beneficial interest to indemnify the trustee for any liability he might incur.[241] There is no need for the request or instigation to be made in writing.[242] However, the trustee will not be entitled to an indemnity unless the beneficiary knew the facts of what was happening. Where the beneficiary has not requested or instigated the breach of trust but merely consented to it, the trustee may still be entitled to an indemnity from his beneficial interest. This will only be the case if the consent was given in writing and the beneficiary gained a personal benefit from the breach.[243] The indemnity will only extend to the amount of that benefit.[244]

(b) Trustee Act 1925, s 62

This section grants the court a wide discretion to impound the beneficial interest of a beneficiary who has instigated, requested, or consented to a breach of trust, to indemnify the trustee. Section 62(1) provides:

Where a trustee commits a breach of trust at the instigation or request or with the consent in writing of a beneficiary, the court may, if it thinks fit, make such orders as the court thinks just,

---

[240] See above, p 891.

[241] *Booth v Booth* (1838) 1 Beav 125; *Lincoln v Wright* (1841) 4 Beav 427; *Raby v Ridehalgh* (1855) 7 De GM & G 104; *Bentley v Robinson* (1859) 9 I Ch R 479; *Sawyer v Sawyer* (1885) 28 Ch D 595, CA; *Ricketts v Ricketts* (1891) 64 LT 263; *Chillingworth v Chambers* [1896] 1 Ch 685.

[242] *Griffiths v Hughes* [1892] 3 Ch 105; *Mara v Browne* [1895] 2 Ch 69.

[243] *Booth v Booth* (1838) 1 Beav 125; *Chillingworth v Chambers* [1896] 1 Ch 685.

[244] *Raby v Ridehaigh* (1855) 7 De GM & G 104.

for impounding all or any part of the interest of the beneficiary in the trust estate by way of indemnity to the trustee or persons claiming through him.

In *Re Pauling's Settlement Trusts (No 2)*[245] Wilberforce J stated that the purpose of the section was to extend the courts' inherent jurisdiction, and in *Bolton v Curre*[246] Romer J said that the forerunner to s 62[247] 'was intended to enlarge the power of the court as to indemnifying trustees, and to give greater relief to trustees, and was not intended and did not operate to curtail the previously existing rights and remedies of trustees, or to alter the law except by giving greater power to the court'. It has been held that the requirement of writing applies only to a beneficiary's consent,[248] and the court may impound the beneficiary's interest under s 62 where there has been instigation or a request irrespective of the absence of writing. The court will only impound the beneficiary's interest if he had sufficient knowledge. In *Re Somerset* Smith LJ stated:

upon the true reading of this section, a trustee in order to obtain the benefit conferred thereby, must establish that the beneficiary knew the facts which rendered what he was instigating, requesting or consenting to in writing a breach of trust.[249]

It is not necessary that he actually know that those facts amount to a breach of trust. In *Re Pauling's Settlement Trusts (No 2)*[250] Wilberforce J held that the protection of the section was not only available to existing trustees of the trust, but also to former trustees who had since retired from the trust or been replaced. The only requirement is that the person seeking the indemnity was a trustee at the time of the breach.

---

245 [1963] Ch 576.   246 [1895] 1 Ch 544, at 549.
247 Trustee Act 1888, s 6; repeated by the Trustee Act 1893, s 45.
248 *Griffiths v Hughes* [1892] 3 Ch 105; *Re Somerset* [1894] 1 Ch 231.
249 [1894] 1 Ch 231.   250 [1963] Ch 576.

30

Fiduciary position of trustees

In the previous chapter it was seen that a trustee will be liable to pay equitable compensation for any loss suffered in consequence of a breach of trust. Such a breach will occur if he acts in a manner inconsistent with the express terms of the trust, or if he fails to act as required with insufficient care. However, the duties of a trustee are not confined solely to his obligation not to act in breach of trust. A further essential aspect of the multifaceted nature of trusteeship is that a trustee stands in a fiduciary relationship to the beneficiaries of the trust. This means that he must not allow any conflict between his own interests and the interests of the beneficiary, and that he must not make any unauthorized profit for himself from his position as trustee. Other parties acting alongside the trust, such as solicitor advisors, may also owe fiduciary duties to the beneficiaries of the trust. The nature and extent of fiduciary duties are explored in this chapter.

1 Fiduciary relationships[1]

(1) The trustee as a fiduciary

The fiduciary position of a trustee[2] subjects him to onerous negative obligations in equity, which are designed to prevent him from abusing his position by acting in his own interests at the expense of the interests of his beneficiaries. It has already been seen how the division between legal and equitable ownership under a trust separates the control and management of property from the entitlement to its ultimate enjoyment. Although this separation provides great flexibility, it also equally provides opportunity for abuse. The trustee who controls the property can thereby use it for his own advantage, for example by selling himself the trust property at an undervalue. To prevent the trustee gaining personal advantages at the expense of the beneficiaries'

---

[1] See Glover, *Commercial Equity: Fiduciary Relationships* (1995); Goff and Jones, *The Law of Restitution* (7th edn, 2006), Ch 33; Oakley, *Constructive Trusts* (3rd edn, 1997), Ch 3; Finn, *Fiduciary Obligations* (1977); Jones 'Unjust Enrichment and the Fiduciary's Duty of Loyalty' (1968) 84 LQR 472; Shepherd 'Towards a Unified Concept of Fiduciary Relationships' (1981) 97 LQR 51.

[2] *Keech v Sandford* (1726) Sel Cas Ch 61; *Price v Blakemore* (1843) 6 Beav 507.

equity characterizes the relationship as a 'fiduciary', which entitles the beneficiaries to a remedy if the trustee makes unauthorized personal gains by virtue of his position. A trustee in breach of his fiduciary duty will be required to make restitution to the beneficiaries of any unauthorized profits he has received through the abuse of his position.

(2) Fiduciary relationships

(a) Types of fiduciary relationship

The fiduciary relationship has been described as 'one of the most ill-defined, if not altogether misleading terms in our law'.[3] It has also been said that 'there are few legal concepts more frequently invoked but less conceptually certain than that of the fiduciary relationship'.[4] As Frankfurter J said in the American case *SEC v Chenery Corpn*:[5]

To say that a man is a fiduciary only begins analysis; it gives direction to further inquiry. To whom is he a fiduciary? What obligations does he owe as a fiduciary? In what respect has he failed to discharge these obligations? And what are the consequences of his deviation from duty?[6]

It is important to recognize that a fiduciary relationship may arise in a number of ways. In *LAC Minerals Ltd v International Corona Resources Ltd*,[7] a decision of the Canadian Supreme Court, Wilson J distinguished between relationships which in their very nature are fiduciary, and those which take on a fiduciary character because of the particular relationship between the parties:

It is . . . my view of the law that there are certain relationships which are almost per se fiduciary, such as trustee and beneficiary, guardian and ward, principal and agent, and that where such relationships subsist they give rise to fiduciary duties. On the other hand, there are relationships which are not in their essence fiduciary, such as the relationship brought into being by the parties in the present case by virtue of their arm's length negotiations towards a joint venture agreement, but this does not preclude a fiduciary duty from arising out of specific conduct engaged in them or either of them within the confines of the relationship.[8]

(b) Relationships fiduciary per se

English law has never provided a comprehensive definition of fiduciary relationships. Instead, certain relationships, because of their very nature, have come to be regarded as fiduciary. This obviously allows for flexibility as circumstances and commercial practice change. As Finn has stated, a fiduciary 'is, simply, someone who undertakes to act for or on behalf of another in some particular matter or matters'.[9] In the unusual case

---

[3] Finn, *Fiduciary Obligations* (1977), p 1.
[4] *LAC Minerals Ltd v International Corona Resources Ltd* (1989) 61 DLR (4th) 14, at 26, per La Forest J.
[5] 518 US 80 (1943), at 85–86.
[6] Cited by the Privy Council in *Re Goldcorp Exchanges Ltd* [1994] 2 All ER 806.
[7] (1989) 61 DLR (4th) 14.   [8] Ibid., at 16.
[9] Finn, *Fiduciary Obligations* (1977), p 201.

of *Reading v A-G*[10] the House of Lords held that an army sergeant who had used his uniform to enable lorries smuggling spirits and drugs to pass through army checkpoints was a fiduciary, and therefore he was obliged to account to the Crown for the money he had received from the smugglers for his services. In the Court of Appeal Asquith LJ had attempted a summary of the characteristics of a fiduciary relationship:

a fiduciary relationship exists (a) whenever the plaintiff entrusts to the defendant property... and relies on the defendant to deal with such property for the benefit of the plaintiff or purposes authorised by him, and not otherwise, and (b) whenever the plaintiff entrusts to the defendant a job to be performed... and relies on the defendant to procure for the plaintiff the best terms available...[11]

The relationship of trustee and beneficiary is not the only one that is characterized as fiduciary by equity. Other recognized fiduciary relationships include: mortgagee and mortgagor;[12] principal and agent;[13] solicitor and client;[14] partners and co-partners;[15] company directors and the company;[16] senior management and their employer company;[17] confidential employees and their employers;[18] government employees and the Crown;[19] and pawnbroker and pawnor.[20] The essence of all these relationships is that one person occupies a position in which he has a duty to act on behalf

---

[10] [1951] AC 507.   [11] [1949] 2 KB 232, at 236.

[12] *Farrars v Farrars Ltd* (1888) 40 Ch D 395, CA.

[13] *De Bussche v Alt* (1878) 8 Ch D 286; *Kirkham v Peel* (1880) 43 LT 171; *Lamb v Evans* [1893] 1 Ch 218, CA; *New Zealand Netherlands Society Oranje Inc v Kuys* [1973] 1 WLR 1126, PC; *Imageview Management Ltd v Jack* [2009] EWCA Civ 63; *Korkontzilas v Soulos* (1997) 146 DLR (4th) 214.

[14] *Re Hallet's Estate* (1880) 13 Ch D 696, CA; *McMaster v Bryne* [1952] 1 All ER 1362; *Brown v IRC* [1965] AC 244, HL; *Oswald Hickson Collier Co v Carter-Ruck* [1984] AC 720n; *Swindle v Harrison* [1997] 4 All ER 705; *Logstaff v Birtles* [2002] 1 WLR 470. In *Conway v Ratiu* [2006] 1 All ER 571, the Court of Appeal said, contra Lord Millett in *Prince Jefri Bolkiah v KPMG (a firm)* [1999] 2 AC 222, that the fiduciary relationship of a solicitor to his client is distinct from the contractual obligations arising under his retainer. As such the fiduciary duty is not necessarily to be found or confined to the terms of the contractual retainer, so that the fiduciary relationship may outlive the contractual solicitor/client relationship. See also *Hilton v Barker Booth and Eastwood (a firm)* [2005] 1 All ER 651, at [28]–[29], per Lord Walker; *Cobbetts LLP v Hodge* [2009] EWHC 786.

[15] *Bentley v Craven* (1853) 18 Beav 75; *Aas v Benham* [1891] 2 Ch 244; *Thompson's Trustee in Bankruptcy v Heaton* [1974] 1 WLR 605. See also *Holiday Inns Inc v Yorkstone Properties (Harlington)* (1974) 232 Estates Gazette 951.

[16] *Sinclair v Brougham* [1914] AC 398; *Regal (Hastings) v Gulliver* [1967] 2 AC 134n; *Selangor United Rubber Estates Ltd v Craddock (No 3)* [1968] 1 WLR 1555; *Industrial Development Consultants Ltd v Cooley* [1972] 1 WLR 443; *Cowan de Groot Properties Ltd v Eagle Trust plc* [1992] 4 All ER 700; *Item Software (UK) Ltd v Fassihi* [2004] EWCA 1244. See Berg 'Fiduciary Duties: A Director's Duty to Disclose His Own Misconduct' (2005) 121 LQR 213; (2003) MLR 852 (Scott) and 894 (Koh). See also Koh, 'Once a Director, Always a Fiduciary?' [2003] 62 CLJ 403 for a consideration whether a director continue to be a fiduciary even after he ceases to be a director of the company.

[17] *Sybron Corpn v Rochem Ltd* [1984] Ch 112; *Canadian Aero-Services v O'Malley* (1973) 40 DLR (3d) 371; *Agip (Africa) Ltd v Jackson* [1990] Ch 265.

[18] *Triplex Safety Glass Co Ltd v Scorah* [1938] Ch 211; *British Celanese Ltd v Montcrieff* [1948] Ch 564; *British Syphon Co v Homewood* [1956] 1 WLR 1190; *A-G v Guardian Newspapers Ltd (No 2)* [1990] 1 AC 109, HL; *A-G v Blake* [1998] 1 All ER 833.

[19] *Reading v A-G* [1951] AC 507; *A-G v Guardian Newspapers Ltd (No 2)* [1990] 1 AC 109; *A-G for Hong Kong v Reid* [1994] 1 All ER 1, PC; *A-G v Blake* [1998] 1 All ER 833.

[20] *Mathew v TM Sutton Ltd* [1994] 4 All ER 793.

of another, thereby enjoying the potential to abuse his position by acting for his own interests. They are relationships in which there is an inherent element of 'trust and confidence'[21] between the parties. The duties of directors have been codified in the Companies Act 2006.

In Canada it has been held that the relationship between doctor and patient[22] and between child-abuser and victim[23] are also fiduciary, and it has been suggested that the relationship between priest and parishioner should likewise be fiduciary.[24] English law has not yet adopted these relationships as fiduciary per se, although individual relationships of this type could be found to be fiduciary if the circumstances suggested that there was a sufficient degree of reliance between the parties.

(c) Fiduciary duties arising within relationships not fiduciary per se[25]

The majority of commercial relationships cannot be characterized as fiduciary per se, as the parties simply bargain with each other at arm's length. However, the specific nature of a particular relationship may bring about a fiduciary relationship between the parties. This was the case in *LAC Minerals Ltd v International Corona Resources Ltd*,[26] where two companies were negotiating at arm's length about the possibility of a joint venture of exploit minerals from land over which the plaintiff company (LAC) owned mining rights. In the course of these negotiations it was clear to the defendants from results of the plaintiffs' drilling that adjacent land was also likely to include mineral deposits. The defendants then purchased the adjacent land, defeating a competing bid from the plaintiffs, and developed a mine alone. Although the relationship between the defendants and the plaintiffs was not fiduciary per se, the Supreme Court held that fiduciary duties were owed because the defendants had received confidential information from the plaintiffs in the course of the negotiations. In *A-G v Blake*[27] Lord Woolf MR similarly suggested that a fiduciary relationship arises whenever information is imparted by one person to another in confidence,[28] although he noted that in the majority of cases such information will be imparted in the context of a relationship which is already fiduciary, for example where the recipient of the information was an employee.

In contrast, in *Re Goldcorp Exchange Ltd (in receivership)*[29] the Privy Council held that a relationship had remained exclusively commercial so that it had not become fiduciary. The case concerned a company in New Zealand that dealt in gold bullion and other precious metals. Customers purchased what was described as 'non-allocated metal' that would be held for them by the company free of charge. They were entitled to

---

[21] [2006] 1 All ER 571, at [71] per Auld LJ.

[22] *Norberg v Wynrib* (1992) 92 DLR (4th) 449.

[23] *M (K) v M (H)* (1992) 96 DLR (4th) 289.

[24] Frankel, *Equity, Fiduciaries and Trusts*, ed Waters (1993).

[25] See Oakley, 'The Liberalising Nature of Remedies for Breach of Trust' in Oakley, *Trends in Contemporary Trust Law* (1996), pp 230–233.

[26] (1989) 61 DLR (4th) 14.   [27] [1998] 1 All ER 833.   [28] Ibid., at 842.

[29] [1994] 2 All ER 806. See also *Khodai v Tamimi* [2009] EWCA Civ 1109 (relationship between lender and borrower).

take physical delivery of the metal by giving seven days' notice, at which point it would be appropriated from the metal that the company held in bulk. It was argued that the company stood in a fiduciary relationship to the customers, but the Privy Council held that their relationship was purely contractual. As Lord Mustill explained:

No doubt the fact that one person is placed in a particular position vis-à-vis another through the medium of a contract does not necessarily mean that he does not also owe fiduciary duties to that other by virtue of being in that position. But the essence of a fiduciary relationship is that it creates obligations of a different character from those deriving from the contract itself. Their Lordships have not heard in argument any submission which went beyond suggesting that by virtue of being a fiduciary the company was obliged honestly and conscientiously to do what it had by contract promised to do…It is possible, without misuse of language to say that the customers put faith in the company, and that their trust has not been repaid. But the vocabulary is misleading; high expectations do not necessarily lead to equitable remedies.[30]

The case of *Sinclair Investments Holdings SA v Versailles Trade Finance Ltd*[31] provides an example of a commercial relationship giving rise to a fiduciary status, and of the core content of a fiduciary relationship. The facts as alleged were that Mr Cushnie was a director and had a substantial interest in companies within the Versailles Group. The Versailles Group inflated its turnover through dishonest dealings, and as a result Mr Cushnie was able to sell his shareholding at a profit, repay a mortgage on a property he owned, and sell it for £8.6 million. One of the Group's victims was Sinclair, which was seeking to recover from Mr Cushnie the money that had been misappropriated. It was argued that he stood in a fiduciary position in relation to the claimants. A company director is not normally a fiduciary for people dealing with the company, even where he makes personal representations,[32] but the Court of Appeal held that the pleadings in the case contained an arguable case that Mr Cushnie had undertaken a duty of loyalty to Sinclair so as to make him a fiduciary. According to Arden LJ:

if it is alleged that a person who does not fall within the usual categories of a fiduciary relationship, such as trustee and director, made manifest his intention to enter into a fiduciary relationship—that is, to undertake to the other a duty of loyalty—there would be a sufficient pleading of fiduciary relationship.[33]

The fiduciary did not need to receive the claimant's property, but in her view:

In a case such as this, it seems to me to be necessary that the fiduciary relationship should be with respect to an item of property, and that requirement explains why a fiduciary relationship may be specific and govern only part of a party's relationship with another.[34]

That condition would have been satisfied in this case because there was an express term that Sinclair's funds were to be held on trust if they were not used for trading.

---

[30] Ibid., at 821–822.

[31] [2005] EWCA Civ 722. See Panesar 'The Nature of Fiduciary Liability in English Law' [2007] Conv 2, pp. 11–12.

[32] See *Hageman v Holmes* [2009] EWHC 50 (Ch), where a fiduciary obligation was not imposed on a director in relation to a deed of covenant, on the basis that the rights between the relevant parties were contractual only.

[33] [2005] EWCA Civ 722, at [20].   [34] Ibid, at [21].

(3) The function of fiduciary relationships in English law[35]

It has been seen that it is difficult to define fiduciary relationships with comprehensive accuracy. This difficulty is compounded by the varied functions that they perform in English law at present. They operate so as to impose duties that restrict the fiduciary's ability to act in his own interests, and also as a trigger that may lead to the creation of an equitable trust interest in property by way of a constructive trust.

(a) Fiduciary duties[36]

A person who stands in a fiduciary relationship may owe a range of duties to his principal. Not all of these duties can properly be characterized as fiduciary in nature. For example a trustee, who is by definition also a fiduciary, will owe duties of care regarding his conduct of the trust business to the beneficiaries alongside his fiduciaries duties. In *Bristol and West Building Society v Mothew*[37] Millett LJ commented:

The expression fiduciary duty is properly confined to those duties which are peculiar to fiduciaries and the breach of which attracts legal consequences differing from those consequent upon the breach of other duties. Unless the expression is so limited it is lacking in practical utility. In this sense it is obvious that not every breach of duty by a fiduciary is a breach of fiduciary duty.[38]

He therefore held that it was inappropriate to apply the expression fiduciary to the obligation of a trustee to use proper skill and care in the discharge of his duties. In *A-G v Blake*[39] the Court of Appeal similarly held that an employee in the security services who had published an unauthorized autobiography had acted in breach of contract but not in breach of fiduciary duty. In *Swindle v Harrison*[40] the Court of Appeal considered that the duties imposed by equity upon a fiduciary go beyond the common law duties of skill and care.[41]

Given that not every duty owed by a fiduciary to his principal can be characterized as fiduciary in nature, the question arises as to the content of his specifically fiduciary duties. In *Bristol and West Building Society v Mothew*[42] Millett LJ identified the core content of the fiduciary duty:

A fiduciary is someone who has undertaken to act for or on behalf of another in a particular matter in circumstances which give rise to a relationship of trust and confidence. The distinguishing obligation of a fiduciary is the obligation of loyalty. The principal is entitled to the single-minded loyalty of his fiduciary. This core liability has several facets: a fiduciary must act in good faith; he must not make a profit out of his trust; he must not place himself in a position where his duty and his interest may conflict; he may not act for his own benefit or the benefit

[35] See Conaglen 'The Nature and Function of Fiduciary Loyalty' (2005) 121 LQR 452; Hilliard 'The Flexibility of Fiduciary Doctrine in Trust Law: How Far Does It Stretch in Practice?' (2009) TLI 119.
[36] See Austin, 'Moulding the Content of Fiduciary Duties' in Oakley, *Trends in Contemporary Trust Law* (1996).
[37] [1996] 4 All ER 698; Nolan 'Multiple Duties and Multiple Employment' [1997] CLJ 39.
[38] Ibid., at 710.   [39] [1998] 1 All ER 833.   [40] [1997] 4 All ER 705.
[41] Ibid., at 716, per Evans LJ.   [42] [1998] Ch 1.

of a third person without the informed consent of his principal. This is not intended to be an exhaustive list, but it is sufficient to indicate the nature of fiduciary obligations.[43]

While the core content of a fiduciary duty can be identified as an obligation of exclusive loyalty, the precise content of specific fiduciary relationships will vary. As Lord Browne-Wilkinson observed in *Henderson v Merrett Syndicates Ltd*,[44] the phrase 'fiduciary duties' is a dangerous one, giving rise to a mistaken assumption that all fiduciaries owe the same duties in all circumstances. In *A-G v Blake* Lord Woolf MR stated:

There is more than one category of fiduciary relationship, and the different categories possess different characteristics and attract different kinds of fiduciary obligations.[45]

The duration of the core fiduciary duty of loyalty is also determined by the context of the relationship in which the fiduciary duty arose. The mere fact that a person once occupied a fiduciary position does not necessarily mean that they will be subject to a lifelong duty of loyalty. *A-G v Blake* concerned the nature of the fiduciary duties of a former secret service agent. George Blake had served as a member of the security services from 1944 until 1960. In 1951 he had become an agent for the Soviet Union. He was arrested and imprisoned, but escaped to live in Moscow. He subsequently wrote an autobiography entitled *No Other Choice*, which was published in England. The Crown sought to recover the profits derived from the book on the grounds that the publication was in breach of fiduciary duty. The Court of Appeal held that, although Blake's employment had rendered him subject to a fiduciary duty, his fiduciary duties did not endure beyond the termination of his employment. Lord Woolf MR explained:

We do not recognise the concept of a fiduciary obligation which continues notwithstanding the determination of the particular relationship which gives rise to it. Equity does not demand a duty of undivided loyalty from a former employee to his former employer...A former employee owes no duty of loyalty to his former employer. It is trite law that an employer who wishes to prevent his employee from damaging his legitimate commercial interests after he has left his employment must obtain contractual undertakings from his employee to this effect. He cannot achieve his object by invoking the fiduciary relationship which formerly subsisted between them.[46]

Whether Blake was a fiduciary or not was not an issue that arose in the subsequent appeal to the House of Lords.[47] However, Lord Nicholls[48] and Lord Steyn[49] were both at pains to stress that the position he occupied was at least very closely akin to a fiduciary relationship, suggesting that this might have been a fruitful avenue for appeal.

(b) Remedies for breach of fiduciary duties

Where a fiduciary acts in breach of his duty he will have committed an equitable wrong against his principal. As such, his principal will be able to recover either equitable compensation or restitution from his fiduciary.

---

[43] Ibid., at 18. See also *A-G v Blake* [1998] 1 All ER 833, at 842, per Lord Woolf MR.
[44] [1995] 2 AC 145, at 206.   [45] [1998] 1 All ER 833, at 842.
[46] Ibid., at 841–842.   [47] [2000] 4 All ER 385.
[48] Ibid., at 400.   [49] Ibid., at 404.

(i) Equitable compensation for loss sustained[50]

If a fiduciary commits a breach of duty his principal will be entitled to recover equitable damages to compensate him for any loss he has suffered. Where the fiduciary was a trustee his breach will probably have constituted a breach of trust, entitling the beneficiaries to receive compensation. A right to receive equitable compensation for breach of fiduciary duty will arise where the fiduciary was not also a trustee. The principal will be entitled to recover such compensation as would put him in the position he would have been in if the wrong had not been committed. To establish the right to compensation, the principal must demonstrate that the alleged breach of fiduciary duty caused the loss sustained. In *Swindle v Harrison*[51] Mrs Harrison mortgaged her house in order to enable her son to purchase and restore a hotel. Further finance was required to complete the transaction that it was expected would be provided by way of a loan from a brewery. At the date of completion the loan had not been forthcoming and the plaintiff solicitors therefore offered her a bridging loan to complete the hotel purchase. She wished to go ahead with the transaction because she felt the purchase would be advantageous to her and her son. However, the solicitors failed to disclose to her that they would be making a profit for themselves from the bridging loan, and that her son's bank was unlikely to provide him with the references needed to obtain the brewery loan. The hotel business was unsuccessful and the solicitors sought possession. Mrs Harrison counterclaimed that she was entitled to receive equitable compensation for the equity she had lost in her home on the grounds that the solicitors has committed a breach of their fiduciary duty. The Court of Appeal held that the solicitors had breached their duty by failing to make full disclosure of the circumstances and that they were therefore liable to compensate her for any loss suffered. However, the essential issue was whether her loss had been caused by the breach. Mrs Harrison submitted that she was not required to prove that she would not have completed the purchase in any event,[52] and that she should be compensated merely because the bridging loan had enabled her to complete the purchase. The Court of Appeal rejected this submission and held that, unless the breach could properly be regarded as the equivalent of fraud,[53] she was required to demonstrate causation. In the circumstances it concluded that she would have completed the transaction anyway. Evans LJ explained that she had failed to establish causation:

The failure to disclose cannot be said to have led to the making of the loan, even on a but for basis, precisely because disclosure of the true facts would not have affected her decision to accept it. Since she would have accepted the loan and completed the purchase, even if full disclosure had been made to her, she would have lost the value of the equity in her home in any event. She cannot recover damages or compensation for that loss, in my judgement, except on

[50]　See Conaglen, 'Equitable Compensation for Breach of Fiduciary Dealing Rules' (2003) 119 LQR 246.

[51]　[1997] 4 All ER 705; Tjio and Yeo 'Limited Liability for Breach of Fiduciary Duty' (1998) 114 LQR 181; Elliott 'Restitutionary Compensatory Damages for Breach of Fiduciary Duty?' [1998] RLR 135. See also Sir Peter Millett 'Equity's Place in the Law of Commerce' (1998) 114 LQR 214.

[52]　Cf *Target Holdings v Redferns* [1996] AC 421. See above pp 881 *et seq*.

[53]　[1997] 4 All ER 705, at 717, per Evans LJ.

proof *either* that the plaintiffs acted fraudulently or in a manner equivalent to fraud *or* that she would not have completed the purchase if full disclosure had been made, i.e. if the breach of duty had not occurred.[54]

The obligation to pay equitable compensation for breach of fiduciary duty is a purely personal remedy.

(ii) Restitution of the unauthorized profit

Where a fiduciary breaches his duty of exclusive loyalty and receives an unauthorized profit he will be liable to make restitution[55] to his principal by way of an equitable duty to account for the profit received. He is obliged to pay over to his principal a sum of money equivalent to the amount of profit received, though not necessarily the actual money (or its proceeds) which comprised the profit. It is sometimes said that the fiduciary is required to disgorge his unauthorized profit. The obligation to account operates as a personal remedy.

(iii) Constructive trust of the unauthorized profit

The fact that a fiduciary is under a personal obligation in equity to account for the profit received may also give rise to a constructive trust of the specific property comprising the profit. The ability to establish such a constructive trust will prove especially significant if the fiduciary is insolvent, since otherwise the principal will merely rank as a general creditor of the fiduciary, in which case the personal duty to account is unlikely to provide an adequate remedy. If the actual profit, or its proceeds,[56] can be identified in the fiduciary's hands, his principal will be entitled to it in equity, and will be able to claim priority ahead of any other general creditors. A constructive trust of an unauthorized profit obtained in breach of fiduciary duty was held to have arisen in *A-G of Hong Kong v Reid*.[57] Reid, the acting Director of Public Prosecutions for Hong Kong, had accepted bribes in the course of his duties. The Privy Council held that three houses that Reid had purchased in New Zealand with the bribe money were held on trust for the Crown (see Figure 30.1). However, in *Paragon Finance v DB Thakerar & Co*[58] Millett LJ held that no constructive trust would arise if the fiduciary was an agent who received payments on behalf of his principal which he was entitled to pay into his own account and mix with his own money. Such an agent would not have been subject to a duty to keep the receipts separate from his own and to apply them exclusively to the benefit of his principal. Thus a manager of a musician who had received royalty payments on behalf of his client, which had been paid into his

---

[54] Ibid., at 718.

[55] See Goff and Jones, *The Law of Restitution* (6th edn, 2002), pp 707–739; Birks, *Introduction to the Law of Restitution* (1985), pp 313–357; Burrows, *The Law of Restitution* (2nd edn, 2002), pp 493–508; (1989) CLJ 302 (Jackman). See also: R C Nolan, 'Conflicts of Interest, Unjust Enrichment and Wrongdoing', Ch 7, in Cornish, Nolan, O'Sullivan, and Virgo (eds) *Restitution Past, Present and Future* (1998).

[56] Whether the fiduciary retain in his hands any property that is or represents the profit received will depend on the laws of tracing. See Chapter 32.

[57] [1994] 1 All ER 1.   [58] [1999] 1 All ER 400.

Figure 30.1 Proprietary claims to profits: *A-G of Hong Kong v Reid*

own account, mixed with his own money, and from which his commission had been deducted, would be liable to account to his client for any underpayments, but no constructive trust would arise.[59]

(c) Fiduciary relationships and equitable property rights

It is thus clear that a fiduciary relationship is capable of generating equitable interests in property by way of a constructive trust. If a fiduciary receives property (whether money or not) as an unauthorized profit, he will hold it on constructive trust for his principal, even though it was not previously subject to any trust. Thus, the money received by the DPP in *A-G of Hong Kong v Reid* was not previously subject to any trust relationship, but was the absolute property of the briber. The Crown enjoyed no prior interest in it and only derived an entitlement because the DPP stood in a fiduciary relationship. Alongside this principle that any unauthorized profit received by a fiduciary is subjected to a constructive trust, it seems that property which is misappropriated by a fiduciary from his principal will also be subject to a constructive trust, irrespective of whether the property was received by the fiduciary or a third party. For example, in

---

[59] Thus rejecting the earlier decision of Laddie J in *Nelson v Rye* [[1996] 2 All ER 186.

Agip (Africa) Ltd v Jackson[60] a company was defrauded by its chief accountant, Zdiri, who altered the name of the payees of genuine payment orders so that they were payable to dummy companies he had created. Millett J held that as the accountant was a fiduciary of the company by virtue of his senior position and responsibility, the misappropriated money was held on constructive trust by the recipient dummy companies and Agip was enabled to trace it. The money paid to such companies was not previously subject to a trust but had been the absolute property of the company. Similarly, in *Brinks Ltd v Abu-Saleh (No 3)*[61] Rimmer J held that gold bullion that had been stolen was subject to a constructive trust in favour of its corporate owners because the robbery had been carried out with the assistance of a security guard who stood in a fiduciary relationship.

While it is clear that an unauthorized profit received by a fiduciary, and property misappropriated from a principal by (or with the assistance) of a fiduciary, will be held subject to a constructive trust in favour of the principal, some cases have held that the mere fact that a transaction was subject to a vitiating factor entitling the transferor to restitution from the transferee will establish a fiduciary relationship between them, so that the transferee holds the property received subject to a constructive trust in favour of the transferor. In *Chase Manhattan Bank NA v Israel-British Bank (London) Ltd*[62] the plaintiff bank paid $1m to the defendant bank by mistake, having forgotten that they had previously made an identical payment. Goulding J held that as a consequence of the mistaken payment the defendant bank had become a fiduciary of the plaintiff bank, so that the $1m was held on constructive trust for them. By means of this reasoning, the plaintiff could maintain a proprietary claim to $1m in the assets of the defendant, which was insolvent, thus negating the value of any personal right to restitution at common law on the grounds of mistake. However, it is far from clear that this approach is correct. In *Westdeutsche Landesbank Girozentrale v Islington London Borough Council*[63] Lord Browne-Wilkinson considered that, while the decision in *Chase-Manhattan* could be regarded as rightly decided, the reasoning of Goulding J was erroneous. He considered that a constructive trust was constituted not by the mere receipt of the mistaken payment, but by the fact that the bank to whom the payment had been made knew of the mistake within two days of their receipt of the money:

Although the mere receipt of the moneys, in ignorance of the mistake, gives rise to no trust, the retention of the moneys after the recipient bank learned of the mistake may well have given rise to a constructive trust.[64]

However, it is submitted that even this reasoning does not adequately explain the creation of an equitable proprietary interest in the money mistakenly paid. The central

---

[60] [1990] Ch 265, [1992] 4 All ER 385; (1989) 105 LQR 528 (Birks); (1991) 107 LQR 71 (Sir Peter Millett); [1991] Ch 547, [1992] 4 All ER 451; (1991) 50 CLJ 409 (Harpum); [1992] Conv 367 (Goulding); All ER Rev 1992, 258–265 (Swadling).

[61] (1995) The Times, 23 October; Stevens 'Delimiting the Scope of Accessory Liability' [1996] Conv 447.

[62] [1981] Ch 105.   [63] [1996] AC 669.   [64] Ibid., at 715.

question should focus rather on the proprietary effects of the mistaken payment. If the mistake was sufficient to prevent property in the money passing to the payee, then the payee will hold it subject to an immediate constructive trust from the moment that it was received. He may not become a fiduciary for the payor until he becomes aware that the mistake had been made and he was conscious of the circumstances giving rise to the constructive trust. The mere fact that he becomes aware of a mistake rendering him subject to a personal obligation to make restitution should neither make him a fiduciary of the payor nor subject the money in his hands to a constructive trust.

(d) The artificial use of fiduciary relationships

The power of a fiduciary relationship to generate proprietary rights and remedies has provided a major incentive for the encroachment of such relationships into the commercial arena. For example, increasingly, the employment relationship has come to be characterized as fiduciary and not merely contractual. The lack of a clear definition has enabled the courts to manipulate fiduciary relationships as a means of achieving remedial justice, so that the use of the term 'fiduciary' has often seemed artificial. It has already been argued that the finding of a fiduciary relationship in *Chase Manhattan Bank NA v Israel-British Bank (London) Ltd*[65] was artificial, and the reason for it was to ensure that the mistaken payor bank was entitled to a proprietary remedy so as to gain priority over the payee's general creditors. This artificiality was recognized by the Supreme Court of Canada in *LAC Minerals Ltd v International Corona Resources Ltd*,[66] where La Forest J said that there was a third category of the usage of 'fiduciary':

[the] third usage of 'fiduciary' stems, it seems, from a perception of remedial inflexibility in equity. Courts have resorted to fiduciary language because of the view that certain remedies, deemed appropriate in the circumstances, would not be available unless a fiduciary relationship was present. In this sense, the label fiduciary imposes no obligations, but is rather merely instrumental or facilitative in achieving what appears to be the appropriate result.

He regarded the use of 'fiduciary' in *Chase-Manhattan* as an example of this 'third usage'. It was not that the relationship between the banks was genuinely 'fiduciary', as they were simply businesses operating at arm's length. Rather, the characterization of the relationship as fiduciary was an essential prerequisite to the availability of tracing in equity, and the relationship was so characterized merely to facilitate the availability of such tracing as the foundation of a proprietary claim. The requirement of a fiduciary relationship with regard to tracing will be fully discussed in Chapter 32.

(e) Directors of trustee companies and 'dog's leg' claims

The directors of corporate trustees will not be liable to beneficiaries for a breach of trust or breach of directors' duty of care owed to the trustee company. Such claims, referred to as 'dog's leg claims', arise where the trustee company has no assets to meet a claim, but the directors do, and a beneficiary of a trust seeks to make the directors

---

[65] [1981] Ch 105.   [66] (1989) 61 DLR (4th) 14.

liable for breach of a duty of care owed to the company, which as it comprises trust property, makes them liable to the beneficiary. This arose in *Gregson v HAE Trustees Ltd*,[67] where Ms Gregson argued that the trust company, HAE Trustees Ltd, was in breach of the duty to diversify investments of the trust settlement. The trust investments had become worthless and the trust company had no other assets. Mrs Gregson therefore sued the directors. She argued that the duties of the directors were directed to avoid losses to the trust, and, by analogy to advisers such as solicitors, claims against the directors formed part of the trust property itself. In rejecting Ms Gregson's claim, Deputy Judge Robert Miles, QC held that the fiduciary duties owed by directors were owed to the company, not to the beneficiaries.[68] Moreover, he held that to allow such a claim 'would for all practical purposes, circumvent the clear and established principle that no direct duty is owed by the directors to the beneficiaries'.[69] However, as *Sinclair Investments Holdings SA v Versailles Trade Finance Ltd*[70] shows, a direct duty can arise in the very rare situation where a director represents directly to a beneficiary that he is undertaking a personal duty of loyalty to that beneficiary.

(4) Abuse of position

(a) Fiduciaries owe a duty of exclusive loyalty to their principals

As Millett LJ indicated in *Bristol and West Building Society v Mothew*,[71] a fiduciary owes a duty of exclusive loyalty to his principal. This duty of loyalty applies to prevent the fiduciary abusing his position. It operates to deter fiduciaries from acting in breach and to provide restitution for the principal if a breach is committed. Where the fiduciary is a trustee the potential for abuse of position arises because the trustee may use his powers of management over the trust property for his own benefit rather than in the best interest of the beneficiaries. This danger was recognized in early cases. In *Keech v Sandford*[72] a trustee held the lease of a market on trust for an infant. When the lease came to an end the lessor refused to renew it to the trust and the trustee took it personally. King LC held that the trustee could not take the lease for himself and noted the danger of the trustee abusing his position at the expense of the interests of the beneficiary:

I very well see, if a trustee, on the refusal to renew, might have a lease for himself, few trust estates would be renewed to the [beneficiary].

---

[67] [2008] EWHC 1006 (Ch); Court, '*Gregson v HAE Trustees Ltd*: It's a Dog's Life' [2008] PCB 298; Nolan 'Shopping for Defendants: Worthless Trust Companies and Their Directors' (2008) 67 CLJ 472.

[68] [2008] EWHC 1006 (Ch), at [58]. The fiduciary duties of directors have been codified under the Companies Act 2006, and operate according to existing legal principles—s 170(3). The statutory duty on directors to exercise reasonable care, skill, and diligence is found in s 174.

[69] [2008] EWHC 1006 (Ch), at [46].

[70] [2005] EWCA Civ 722. See Panesar 'The Nature of Fiduciary Liability in English Law' [2007] Conv 2, pp. 11–12.

[71] [1998] Ch 1.   [72] (1726) Sel Cas Ch 61.

Similarly, if the trustee wishes to sell part of the trust property he may be tempted to sell it to himself at an undervalue. In his capacity as trustee his duty would be to gain the best possible price for the beneficiaries, but as an individual he would obviously wish to obtain the lowest price to enjoy the best bargain for himself. As trustee he would be both the purchaser, who offers a price, and the seller, who agrees to the price. It would be easy for him to abuse his position so that he benefits at the expense of the beneficiaries by selling to himself at an undervalue.[73]

In *Item Software (UK) Ltd v Fassihi*[74] the Court of Appeal held that a fiduciary was under a duty to disclose his own misconduct to his principal, even though he had not obtained any unauthorized profit. However, this decision has been criticized,[75] and it remains unclear whether such an extension of the fiduciary duty is consistent with earlier authorities.[76]

(b) The difficulty of weighing motives

If a trustee does act in circumstances where it could be suggested that he had abused his position to gain a personal benefit, it may be impossible to weigh his true motives: i.e. whether he was in fact allowing his own interests to prevail over those of the beneficiaries. As Lord Eldon LC observed in *Ex p James*,[77] 'no court is equal to the examination and ascertainment' of these facts. Indeed, because of the practical impossibility of discovering a fiduciary's true motives, equity has taken the very strict view that a fiduciary is liable to account for any profits he makes whenever there was an objective possibility of a conflict between his interests and his duty.[78] There is no need to demonstrate that the fiduciary acted with the subjective intention of benefiting himself at the expense of the beneficiaries. This is a blunt instrument applied in the beneficiaries' favour. As Lord Herschell stated in *Bray v Ford*:

It is an inflexible rule of a Court of Equity that a person in a fiduciary position...is not, unless otherwise expressly provided, entitled to make a profit; he is not allowed to put himself in a position where his interest and duty conflict.[79]

The duty of exclusive loyalty imposed by a fiduciary duty is not absolute. The fiduciary is not prevented from ever acting in his own interests and receiving a benefit by virtue of his position. He is only prevented from retaining unauthorized profits for himself. A fiduciary will not be liable to make restitution if he breaches his duty with the full informed consent of his principal.

---

[73] See *Holder v Holder* [1968] Ch 353; *Re Thompson's Settlement* [1986] Ch 99; *O'Donnell v Shanahan* [2009] EWCA Civ 751.

[74] [2004] EWCA 1244; Conaglen 'Directorial Disclosure' [2005] 64 CLJ 48.

[75] See Berg 'Fiduciary Duties: A Director's Duty to Disclose His Own Misconduct' (2005) 121 LQR 213.

[76] See *Horcal Ltd v Gartland* [1984] BCLC 549, at 554, per Robert Goff LJ.

[77] (1803) 8 Ves 337, at 345.

[78] See *Regal (Hastings) Ltd v Gulliver* [1967] 2 AC 134n, [1942] 1 All ER 378, HL; *Boardman v Phipps* [1967] 2 AC 46, HL.

[79] [1896] AC 44.

2 Unauthorized remuneration

(1) General principle[80]

As a general rule a trustee is not entitled to receive remuneration for his work unless authorized by the trust deed appointing him, or by statute.[81] The rationale for this principle was stated by Lord Normand in *Dale v IRC*:

It is not that reward for services is repugnant to the fiduciary duty, but that he who has the duty shall not take any secret remuneration or any financial benefit not authorised by the law...or by the trust deed under which he acts...[82]

This statement makes clear that the bar on remuneration is not absolute, so that properly authorized remuneration may be retained by the trustee. In the modern commercial world, where the majority of trusts are administered by professional trustees, the general principle still stands, but it has been recognized that there are other competing objectives. As Fox LJ observed in *Re Duke of Norfolk's Settlement Trusts*:

the court has to balance two influences which are to some extent in conflict. The first is that the office of trustee is, as such, gratuitous; the court will accordingly be careful to protect the interests of the beneficiaries against claims by the trustees. The second is that it is of great importance to the trust that the trust should be well administered.[83]

To balance these objectives the courts have a wide inherent jurisdiction to permit trustees to receive remuneration.

(2) Reimbursement of trustee's expenses

Although a trustee is not prima facie entitled to receive remuneration, he is entitled to the reimbursement of any expenses incurred by him in the work of the trust.[84] Section 31(1)(a) of the Trustee Act 2000 provides that a trustee is entitled to be reimbursed from the trust funds for 'expenses properly incurred by him when acting on behalf of the trust'.

(3) Authorized remuneration

A trustee is perfectly entitled to retain remuneration that he was authorized to receive, and he is therefore not liable to make restitution of it to the trust.

---

[80] Bishop and Prentice 'Some Legal and Economic Aspects of Fiduciary Remuneration' (1983) 46 MLR 289.

[81] *How v Godfrey and White* (1678) Cas temp Finch 361; *Bonithon v Hockmore* (1685) 1 Vern 316; *Robinson v Pett* (1734) 3 P Wms 249; *Re Ormsby* (1809) 1 Ball & B 189; *Taylor v Taylor* (1843) 4 Dr & War 124; *Re Barber* (1886) 34 Ch D 77; *Re Bedingfield* (1887) 57 LT 332; *Barrett v Hartley* (1866) LR 2 Eq 789; *Re Accles Ltd* [1902] WN 164.

[82] [1954] AC 11, at 27.   [83] [1982] Ch 61, at 79.

[84] *Stott v Milne* (1884) 25 Ch D 710; *Re Chapman* (1894) 72 LT 66, CA; *Hardoon v Belilios* [1901] AC 118; *Holding and Management Ltd v Property Holding and Investment Trust plc* [1990] 1 All ER 938, CA; see also *Boardman v Phipps* [1967] 2 AC 46, HL, where the fiduciary received payment 'on a liberal scale' for his work and skill in obtaining a profit for himself and the trust.

(a) Trust instrument

A trustee is not accountable for remuneration he is entitled to receive under the trust instrument.[85] Such provisions are extremely common, and professional trustees will only act if the trust deed contains such a provision. Section 28 of the Trustee Act 2000 provides that a trustee who is acting in a professional capacity is entitled to receive payment for his services on behalf of the trust even if those services are capable of being provided by a lay trustee.

(b) Statute

Section 29 of the Trustee Act 2000 provides that, in the absence of an express entitlement in the trust instrument, a trust corporation, or a professional trustee who is not a sole trustee,[86] is entitled to receive reasonable remuneration for any services provided on behalf of the trust. Such a professional trustee will only be entitled to reasonable remuneration if 'each other trustee has agreed in writing that he may be remunerated for the services'. It should be noted that different rules apply to the remuneration of the trustees of a charitable trust.[87]

Other statutory provisions govern the remuneration of certain specialized trustees. The Public Trustee may charge fees fixed by the Treasury,[88] as may anybody appointed a custodian trustee.[89] The court may grant remuneration to a person appointed a judicial trustee.[90] If the court appoints a corporation to be a trustee, then it may authorize the corporation to receive remuneration for its services.[91]

(c) Court's inherent jurisdiction

The court enjoys an inherent jurisdiction to authorize a trustee to receive remuneration, both in respect of work already done and for future work.[92] However, as Lord Goff recognized in *Guinness plc v Saunders*,[93] this jurisdiction is irreconcilable with the rule that a trustee is not entitled to remuneration for services rendered by him to the trust except as expressly provided in the trust deed. He therefore held that the exercise of the jurisdiction should be 'restricted to those cases where it cannot have the effect of encouraging the trustees in any way to put themselves in a position where their interests conflict with their duties as trustees'.

---

[85] *Webb v Earl of Shaftesbury* (1802) 7 Ves 480; *Willis v Kibble* (1839) 1 Beav 559; *Public Trustee v IRC* [1960] AC 398, HL; *Space Investments Ltd v Canadian Imperial Bank of Commerce Trust Co (Bahamas) Ltd* [1986] 1 WLR 1072, PC.

[86] S 29(1),(2).   [87] Ss 28(3), 29(1), 29(2), and 30 of the Trustee Act 2000.

[88] *Re Masters* [1953] 1 WLR 81.

[89] Public Trustee Act 1906, s 9, as amended by the Public Trustee (Fees) Act 1957 and subsequent orders.

[90] Ibid., s 4(3).   [91] Judicial Trustees Act 1896, s 1(5).

[92] *Brown v Litton* (1711) 1 P Wms 140; *Re Masters* [1953] 1 All ER 19; *Re Worthington* [1954] 1 WLR 526; *Re Jarvis* [1958] 2 All ER 336; *Boardman v Phipps* [1967] 2 AC 46, HL; *Re Duke of Norfolk's Settlement Trusts* [1982] Ch 61, CA; *O'Sullivan v Management Agency and Music Ltd* [1985] QB 428, CA.

[93] [1990] 1 All ER 652, at 667.

The scope of the inherent jurisdiction was examined in *Re Duke of Norfolk's Settlement Trusts*.[94] The Court of Appeal accepted 'without doubt' that the court possesses an inherent jurisdiction to authorize the payment of remuneration to trustees, both in the case of prospective trustees for future services and in the case of an unpaid trustee who has already accepted office and has embarked on his fiduciary duties on a voluntary basis. It also held that the court had the jurisdiction to increase the level of remuneration to which a trustee was entitled under the trust instrument. Fox LJ indicated the factors that the court should take into account in exercising this jurisdiction:

If therefore the court concludes, having regard to the nature of the trust, the experience and skill of a particular trustee and to the amounts which he seeks to charge when compared with what other trustees might require to be paid for their services and to all the other circumstances of the case, that it would be in the interests of the beneficiaries to increase the remuneration, then the court may properly do so.[95]

(d) Solicitor-trustees

A solicitor-trustee who acts in legal proceedings on behalf of the trust, himself, and his co-trustees, or himself and his beneficiaries, is entitled to receive the usual costs under the rule in *Cradock v Piper*.[96] In *Re Worthington*,[97] Upjohn J said that this rule was 'exceptional, anomalous and not to be extended'.[98]

3 Purchase of trust property by trustees

The court is keen to ensure that fiduciaries do not gain any advantage by exploiting their position at the expense of those for whose benefit they are supposed to be acting. One of the most obvious dangers is that the trustee, who has control over the trust property, will sell it to himself at an undervalue. A similar difficulty is that the trustee may use the advantages of his position to purchase the beneficial interest from the beneficiaries at an undervalue. Equity has applied two rules, or presumptions, which are designed to prevent the trustee abusing his position. They were summarized by Megarry V-C in *Tito v Waddell (No 2)*:

there are two separate rules. The self-dealing rule is that if a trustee sells the trust property to himself the sale is voidable by any beneficiary ex debito justitiae, however fair the transaction. The fair-dealing rule is that if a trustee purchases the beneficial interest of any of his beneficiaries, the transaction is not voidable ex debito justitiae, but can be set aside by the beneficiary

---

[94] [1982] Ch 61; (1981) 40 CLJ 243 (Oakleton); (1982) 45 MLR 211 (Green); (1982) 98 LQR 181 (P V B); [1982] Conv 231 (Hodkinson); (1982) 126 Sol Jo 195 (Fox).

[95] [1982] Ch 61, at 79.

[96] (1850) 1 Mac & G 664; *Lincoln v Windsor* (1851) 9 Hare 158; *Broughton v Broughton* (1855) 5 De GM & G 160; *Whitney v Smith* (1869) 4 Ch App 513; *Pince v Beattie* (1863) 9 Jur NS 1119; *Re Corsellis* (1887) 34 Ch D 675; *Re Worthington* [1954] 1 All ER 677.

[97] [1954] 1 WLR 526.   [98] Ibid., at 529.

unless the trustee can show that he has taken no advantage of his position and has made full disclosure to the beneficiary, and that the transaction is fair and honest.[99]

These two rules therefore differ in their sphere of operation and standard of liability.

(1) The self-dealing rule[100]

(a) Application of the self-dealing rule

The self-dealing rule applies when a trustee[101] purchases property from the trust. As Arden MR stated in *Campbell v Walker*:

Any trustee purchasing the trust property is liable to have the purchase set aside, if in any reasonable time the [beneficiary] trust chooses to say, he is not satisfied with it.[102]

The self-dealing rule also applies against a trustee who has retired from the trust with the object of buying trust property[103] and a trustee who has recently retired.[104] However, in *Re Boles and British Land Co's Contract*[105] it was held that it did not apply where a trustee had retired for twelve years. It will have no application against trustees with no active duties to perform[106] or who have disclaimed the trust.[107] The rule will not catch a transaction completed by a trustee if the contract was entered before he became a fiduciary.[108]

The leading authority concerning the application of the self-dealing rule is *Holder v Holder*.[109] Frank Holder died, leaving an estate that included two farms. He appointed as his executors his wife, one of his daughters, and one of his sons, Victor. Victor was the tenant of one of the two farms, 'Lower Farm'. He renounced his executorship to enable him to buy the farm, although beforehand he had performed some minor acts in the administration of the estate, including signing a few cheques for trivial sums and endorsing a few insurance policies. He subsequently purchased the farm at public auction. His brother sought to have the sale set aside on the basis that he had, as executor, purchased trust property. The Court of Appeal held that although the purported renunciation of his executorship was technically ineffective he had never assumed the duties of an executor and had not interfered in any way with the administration of the estate. He had not therefore been in the position of both vendor and purchaser of the farm and the sale was not set aside.[110]

---

99 [1977] Ch 106.
100 See McPherson J, 'Self-dealing Trustees' in Oakley, *Trends in Contemporary Trust Law* (1996).
101 The rule cannot apply in the absence of a trust relationship over the property concerned—see *Hollis v Rolfe* [2008] EWHC 1747 (Ch), where it was held there was no breach of the rule against self-dealing by a trustee joining with her co-trustees in transferring the property to her ex-husband, who had no relationship either with the trustee or the trust property.
102 (1800) 5 Ves 678, at 680.
103 *Spring v Pride* (1864) 4 De GJ & Sm 395; *Re Mulholland's Will Trusts* [1949] 1 All ER 460.
104 *Wright v Morgan* [1926] AC 788.   105 [1902] 1 Ch 244.
106 *Parkes v White* (1805) 11 Ves 209.   107 *Stacey v Elph* (1833) 1 My & K 195.
108 *Vyse v Foster* [1874] LR 7 HL 318; *Re Mulholland's Will Trusts* [1949] 1 All ER 460.
109 [1968] Ch 353.
110 This explanation of the case was preferred by Vinelott J in *Re Thompson's Settlement* [1986] Ch 99; see below, p 790. See also *In Plus Group Ltd v Pyke* [2002] 2 BCLC 201; [2003] 62 CLJ 42 (Koh), where the Court

The self-dealing rule was also applied in *Kane v Radley-Kane*.[111] The defendant was the administrator of her husband's estate and stepmother to his three sons. He had died intestate, leaving amongst his assets shares in a software company that were valued at £50,000 at the date of his death. Since the entire estate was worth only £93,000, and the defendant was entitled by statute to a legacy of £125,000, she transferred the shares into her own name. Some three years later she sold them for £1,131,438. The plaintiff, one of her stepsons, sought a declaration that the transaction by which the defendant had appropriated the shares to herself was rendered void by the self-dealing rule. Sir Richard Scott V-C held that the self-dealing rule applied to the transaction. He explained that it had involved a conflict of interest:

> It was her duty as a personal representative owed to the other beneficiaries in the intestate estate, that is to say, to the three sons, to realise the assets of the estate as advantageously as she properly could, and not to apply a greater part of those assets towards payment or discharge of any liability or charge payable out of the estate than was necessary for that purpose. If she had been a creditor of the estate and, as I understand it, she may well be, and had purported to take some asset of the estate in satisfaction of her debt, that would have been a transaction in which her duty and interest would have conflicted. Similarly, in taking the Shiredean shares in satisfaction of her £125,000 statutory legacy she was entering into a transaction in which her duty and interest conflicted.[112]

As the transaction was not expressly or impliedly authorized by statute, and the beneficiaries had not consented to it, it was held to be void. The proceeds of sale were therefore to be treated as part of the assets of the state and the defendant entitled merely to the legacy of £125,000.

(b) Standard required by the self-dealing rule

From the earliest cases the self-dealing rule has been applied strictly, and the courts have been unwilling to enter into any consideration of whether the trustee in fact abused his position. An affected transaction is liable to be set aside whenever a trustee has purchased trust property, no matter whether the purchase was to all intents and purposes fair. As Lord Eldon LC stated in *Ex p James*:

> This doctrine as to purchase by trustees, assignees, and persons having a confidential character, stands more upon general principle than upon the circumstances of any individual case. It rests upon this: that the purchase is not permitted in any case, however honest the circumstances; the general interests of justice requiring it to be destroyed in every instance.[113]

The law has adopted a strict objective approach that whenever a trustee is both vendor and purchaser the transaction may be set aside. Thus, even a purchase by a trustee at public auction can be set aside by the beneficiaries.[114] In *Wright v Morgan*[115] the Privy

---

of Appeal held that a company director was not in breach of his fiduciary duties by competing with the company in circumstances where he had been wholly excluded from the management of the company such that his position was entirely nominal.

[111] [1999] Ch 274.   [112] [1998] 3 All ER 753, at 757.
[113] (1803) 8 Ves 337, at 344.
[114] *Whichcote v Lawrence* (1798) 3 Ves 740; *Campbell v Walker* (1800) 5 Ves 678; *Dyson v Lum* (1866) 14 LT 588.
[115] [1926] AC 788.

Council held that a sale of land to the trustee at a price fixed by independent valuers must be set aside.

Some doubt was cast upon this strict application of the self-dealing rule by the Court of Appeal in *Holder v Holder*.[116] Sachs LJ took the view that there was no longer any need for the court to be shackled by a rigid rule of an irrebuttable presumption 'which stems from the alleged inability of a court to ascertain the state of mind of a trustee',[117] and that it should be treated merely as a rule of practice. Danckwerts LJ seemed, similarly, to take the view that the rule was a matter for the discretion of the judge. However, in *Re Thompson's Settlement*[118] Vinelott J seemed to prefer to view the decision in *Holder v Holder* as turning on the fact that the brother had never acted as executor in a way which could be taken to amount to acceptance of a duty to act in the interests of the beneficiaries under the will. He affirmed the more traditional approach:

The principle is applied stringently in cases where a trustee concurs in a transaction which cannot be carried into effect without his concurrence and who also has an interest or owes a fiduciary duty to another in relation to the same transaction. The transaction cannot stand if challenged by a beneficiary because in the absence of an express provision in the trust instrument the beneficiaries are entitled to require that the trustees act unanimously and that each brings to bear a mind unclouded by any contrary interest or duty in deciding whether it is in the interests of the beneficiaries that the trustees concur in it.[119]

The application of a strict approach was also supported by Sir Richard Scott V-C in *Kane v Radley-Kane*, where he stated that it was 'a general and highly salutary principle of law that a trustee cannot validly contract with himself and cannot exercise his trust powers to his own advantage'.[120]

(c) Exceptions to the self-dealing rule

The self-dealing rule will not apply if the trust instrument authorizes the trustee to purchase trust property.[121] Similarly, if the beneficiaries consent[122] to the purchase, they cannot subsequently have it set aside. The court also possesses the discretion to permit a purchase.[123] Where land is subject to a strict settlement,[124] s 68 of the Settled Land Act 1925 provides that the tenant for life of settled land may purchase the property.

(d) Remedies of the beneficiary

Where trust property has been acquired by a trustee in contravention of the self-dealing rule, the transaction is voidable at the option of the beneficiaries. If the trustee has resold the property, he will be required to make restitution to the trust of any

---

[116] [1968] Ch 353.   [117] Ibid., at 402.   [118] [1986] Ch 99.
[119] Ibid., at 115.   [120] [1998] 3 All ER 753, at 757.
[121] *Sargeant v National Westminster Bank plc* (1990) 61 P & CR 518.
[122] See below, p 956.   [123] *Farmer v Dean* (1863) 32 Beav 327.
[124] Following the introduction of the trust of land in the Trusts of Land and Appointment of Trustees Act 1996, no new strict settlements can be created, but existing settlements will continue.

profits he made.[125] If he has retained the property, the beneficiary may insist that it is re-conveyed to the trust, or a new sale may be ordered.

(2) The fair-dealing rule

The fair-dealing rule applies where a trustee purchases the beneficial interest from one or more of the beneficiaries. Since such a transaction is the result of negotiation between the trustee and the beneficiary, there is less risk that the trustee will exploit his position. Equity therefore adopts a less strict approach than under the self-dealing rule. Transactions entered in violation of the fair-dealing rule are voidable by the beneficiary unless the trustee can show that he has not taken any advantage by virtue of his position.[126] The rule was stated by Lord Eldon in *Coles v Trecothick*:

> a trustee may buy from the [beneficiary], provided that there is a distinct and clear contract, ascertained to be such after a jealous and scrupulous examination of all the circumstances, proving that the [beneficiary of the] trust intended the trustee should buy; there is no fraud, no concealment, no advantage taken, by the trustee of information acquired by him in the character of trustee.[127]

In *Thomson v Eastwood*[128] Lord Cairns stated that a court of equity would examine such a transaction and 'ascertain that value paid by the trustee, and will throw upon the trustee the onus of proving that he gave full value, and that all information was laid before the [beneficiary] when it was sold'.

4 Incidental profits

As a trustee stands in a fiduciary relationship to the beneficiaries of the trust, he will not be permitted to retain unauthorized profits that he receives as a result of holding his position.[129] He must not permit his interests and his duties to conflict. The rationale for this rule was clearly expressed by Lord Herschell in *Bray v Ford*:

> It is an inflexible rule of a court of equity that a person in a fiduciary position, such as the respondent, is not, unless otherwise expressly provided, entitled to make a profit; he is not allowed to put himself in a position where his interest and his duty conflict. It does not appear to me that this rule is as has been said, founded upon principles of morality. I regard it rather as based on the consideration that, human nature being what it is, there is danger, in such circumstances, of the person holding a fiduciary position being swayed by interest rather than

---

[125] *Hall v Hallet* (1784) 1 Cox Eq Cas 134; *ex p James* (1803) 8 Ves 337.

[126] *Clarke v Swaile* (1762) 2 Eden 134; *Coles v Trecothick* (1804) 9 Ves 234; *Randall v Errington* (1805) 10 Ves 423; *Morse v Royal* (1806) 12 Ves 355; *Sanderson v Walker* (1807) 13 Ves 601; *Dover v Buck* (1865) 5 Giff 57.

[127] (1804) 9 Ves 234.   [128] (1877) 2 App Cas 215.

[129] A vendor of land who holds the property on constructive trust for the purchaser as a result of the specifically enforceable contract for sale is not required to account for benefits received from the trust property in the absence of agreement to the contrary: *Engelwood Properties v Patel* [2005] 3 All ER 307.

by duty, and thus prejudicing those whom he was bound to protect. It has, therefore, been deemed expedient to lay down this positive rule.[130]

The concept of conflict of interest, which the rule aims to prevent, was explained by Lord Cranworth LC in *Aberdeen Rly Bros v Blaikie*:[131]

And it is a rule of universal application, that no one, having such duties to discharge, shall be allowed to enter into engagements in which he has, or can have, a personal interest conflicting, or which possibly may conflict, with the interests of those whom he is bound to protect.[132]

It is necessary to consider first the circumstances in which the courts have held trustees liable to account for incidental profits which they have made as a result of their conflict of interest, and, second the standard of liability required by the rule.

(1) Renewal of a lease

A trustee who renews for himself a lease which was previously held on trust for the beneficiaries will hold the lease on trust for them. This rule was applied in *Keech v Sandford*.[133] The trustee held the profits of Romford market on trust for a minor. When the lease expired, the landlord refused to renew the lease to the trust. Instead, he renewed the lease to the trustee personally. King LC held that the lease should be assigned by the trustee to the infant and that he should account for the profits he had made. He recognized that it 'may seem hard that the trustee is the only person of all mankind who might not have the lease', but justified the result in the light of general policy considerations:

it is very proper that the rule should be strictly pursued, and not in the least relaxed; for it is very obvious what would be the consequences of letting trustees have the lease, on refusal to renew to [the beneficiary].[134]

The principle of *Keech v Sandford* applies only where a lease owned by a trust is renewed to a fiduciary. In *Re Biss*[135] a man rented premises for his business. When he died his widow, who was the administratrix of his estate, continued the business with the help of their adult son. The landlord refused to renew the lease to the widow but granted it to the adult son. It was held that the son did not hold the lease on trust for the estate because he did not stand in a fiduciary relationship with the estate. He was therefore under no personal incapacity to take the benefit, the renewal was not an accretion to the original term, and it had not been renewed to him until there had been an absolute refusal by the landlord to renew to the administratrix for the estate.

In *Don King Productions Inc v Warren*[136] the principle of *Keech v Sandford* was applied by analogy to the renewal of a contract held on trust for a partnership to one

---

[130] [1896] AC 44, at 51.   [131] (1854) 2 Eq Rep 1281.

[132] See also *Richardson v Chapman* (1760) 7 Bro Parl Cas 318, HL; *Phayre v Peree* (1815) 3 Dow 116, HL; *Shallcross v Oldham* (1862) 2 John & H 609; *Bennett v Gas Light and Coke Co* (1882) 52 LJ Ch 98; *Lagunas Nitrate Co v Lagunas Syndicate* [1899] 2 Ch 392; *Costa Rica Rly Co v Forwood* [1901] 1 Ch 746; *Re Thomson* [1930] 1 Ch 203.

[133] (1726) Sel Cas Ch 61.   [134] Ibid., at 62.   [135] [1903] 2 Ch 40.

[136] [2000] Ch 291.

of the partners in a personal capacity. The case concerned a partnership established between boxing promoters Don King and Frank Warren in 1994. The partnership was subsequently dissolved in 1997. On the basis that partners stand in a fiduciary relationship, the Court of Appeal held that the entire benefit of any management or promotion agreements concluded by a partner after the date of the dissolution but before the conclusion of the winding up of the partnership affairs with a boxer with whom he already has such an agreement would be held on trust for the partnership.

(2) Purchase of a freehold reversion

The principle of *Keech v Sandford* has been extended to include the purchase by a trustee of the freehold reversion of land leased to the trust. Until recently there were doubts whether the rule operated in the same absolute manner. In *Protheroe v Protheroe*[137] the rule was applied strictly to a husband who purchased the freehold reversion of a house he held on trust jointly with his wife, but earlier cases suggested that the rule would only apply if the lease was renewable to the trust by law or custom.[138] However, it was applied without any such qualification in *Thompson's Trustee in Bankruptcy v Heaton*,[139] where a partner had purchased the freehold reversion of a farm that was a partnership asset. Following *Protheroe v Protheroe*,[140] Pennycuick V-C held that:

it is also well established that where someone holding a leasehold interest in a fiduciary capacity acquires the freehold reversion, he must hold that reversion as part of the trust estate.[141]

Thompson's Trustee in Bankruptcy v Heaton was cited with approval by the Court of Appeal in *Don King Productions Inc v Warren*,[142] suggesting that the rule will be applied equally strictly where a trustee acquires the freehold reversion.

(3) Remuneration received as a director

Where the trust assets include company shares, the trustees control the associated voting rights at company meetings. If the trustees exploit this power to appoint themselves as directors of the company they will be liable to account for any remuneration they thereby receive. The position was considered in *Re Macadam*,[143] where the trustees of a will were granted the power to appoint two directors of a company. They duly appointed themselves and received remuneration for their services. Cohen J held that

---

[137] [1968] 1 WLR 519; (1968) 32 Conv 220 (Crane); (1968) 31 MLR 707 (Jackson); (1968) 84 LQR 309 (Megarry).

[138] *Re Lord Ranelagh's Will* (1884) 26 Ch D 590; *Phillips v Phillips* (1885) 29 Ch D 673, CA; *Longton v Wilsby* (1897) 76 LT 770; *Bevan v Webb* [1905] 1 Ch 620; *Phipps v Boardman* [1964] 1 WLR 993, at 1009; (1969) Conv (NS) 161 (Cretney).

[139] [1974] 1 WLR 605.   [140] [1968] 1 WLR 519.   [141] Ibid., at 521.

[142] [2000] Ch 291, at 340.

[143] [1946] Ch 73. See also *Re Francis* (1905) 74 LJ Ch 198; *Re Orwell's Will Trusts* [1982] 1 WLR 1337.

they were accountable to the trust for the remuneration they had received, and stated the general principles that apply:

I think the root of the matter really is: did [the trustee] acquire the position in respect of which he drew the remuneration by virtue of his position as trustee? In the present case there can be no doubt that the only way in which the plaintiffs became directors was by the exercise of the powers vested in the trustees of the will although the remuneration was remuneration for services as director of the company, the opportunity to receive that remuneration was gained as a result of the exercise of a discretion vested in the trustees, and they had put themselves in a position where their interest and duty conflicted.[144]

It follows from this that a trustee will not be accountable for any remuneration he received from a directorship if he did not in fact use his position to obtain it.[145] Thus, in *Re Dover Coalfield Extension Ltd*[146] it was held that a trustee would be able to retain remuneration received from a directorship to which he had been appointed before becoming a trustee, as it would not have been obtained by use of his position. In *Re Gee*[147] it was held that a trustee who is elected to a directorship would be entitled to retain any remuneration he received if he would still have been elected a director even if the trust shares he controlled had been voted against him, since he would not then have obtained his position through the use of the trust share. However, he would not be protected from liability merely because he abstained from using the trust shares.

Trustees will not be liable to make restitution if the trust instrument permits them to appoint themselves directors and receive remuneration.[148] The court also possesses an inherent jurisdiction to permit trustees to retain remuneration they receive as directors on a similar basis to the inherent jurisdiction accepted in *Re Duke of Norfolk's Settlement Trusts*.[149] Goulding J considered that the court would permit a trustee 'to retain reasonable remuneration for effort and skill applied by him in performing the duties of the directorship over and above the effort and skill ordinarily required of a director appointed to represent the interests of a substantial shareholder'.[150]

(4) Commission earned

A trustee who receives a commission for introducing trust business will be liable to account for the commission he has received as unauthorized profit. In *Williams v Barton*[151] a trustee was employed as a clerk at a firm of stock brokers. The firm was employed to value the trust securities and the trustee received a commission for introducing the business. Russell J held that the commission received was to be treated as part of the trust estate.

---

144   [1946] Ch 73, at 82.   145   *Re Lewis* (1910) 103 LT 495.   146   [1907] 2 Ch 76.
147   [1948] Ch 284.   148   *Re Llewellin's Will Trusts* [1949] Ch 225.   149   [1979] Ch 37.
150   Ibid., at 162–163.   151   [1927] 2 Ch 9.

(5) **Competition**

If the trust assets include a business the trustee must not set up in competition. In *Re Thomson*[152] Clauson J held that it would be a breach of fiduciary duty for a trustee of a yacht broking business to set up independently as a yacht broker because he would have been 'entering into an engagement in which he would have a personal interest conflicting or which possibly might conflict with the interests of those he was bound to protect'.[153] The rationale for this decision may be the relatively specialized nature of the yacht broking business, where it was inevitable that brokers would be in competition with each other. In *Aas v Benham*[154] it was held that there was no breach of fiduciary duty where a member of a partnership of shipbrokers formed a company to build ships. The two operations would not be in competition. In *In Plus Group Ltd v Pyke*[155] Sedley LJ considered that a director of a company could not simply become involved with a competing third party without the consent of the company because of his fiduciary duty,[156] although on the facts of the case he held that the fiduciary duty had not been breached.

(6) **Bribes**

A trustee or other fiduciary who receives a bribe by virtue of his position will not be entitled to retain it. He will be required to make restitution to the trust, or his principal, by way of an equitable liability to account. His liability to make personal restitution in this way is uncontroversial. However, in *A-G of Hong Kong v Reid*[157] the Privy Council held that a fiduciary also holds such a bribe on constructive trust for the principal. This important decision will be discussed more fully below.

(7) **Opportunities**

A fiduciary is liable to make restitution to his principal if he obtains a profit by exploiting an opportunity that rightfully belonged to his principal. A fiduciary who exploits such an opportunity for his own benefit without the authorization of his principal will be liable to account even where the principal could not have taken advantage of the opportunity himself.[158]

---

[152] [1930] 1 Ch 203.   [153] Ibid., at 216.

[154] [1891] 2 Ch 244; *Moore v M'Glynn* [1894] 1 IR 74.

[155] [2002] 2 BCLC 201; Grantham 'Can Directors Compete with the Company?' (2003) 66 MLR 109.

[156] Rejecting dicta to the opposite effect in *London and Marshonaland Exploration Co Ltd v New Marshonaland Exploration Co Ltd* [1891] WN 165.

[157] [1994] 1 All ER 1. See Pearce 'Personal and. Proprietary Claims Against Bribees' [1994] LMCLQ 189.

[158] See *Regal (Hastings) Ltd v Gullier* [1967] 2 AC 134n, [1942] 1 All ER 378; *Industrial Development Consultants Ltd v Cooley* [1972] 1 WLR 443; *Boardman v Phipps* [1967] 2 AC 46, HL; *O'Donnell v Shanahan* [2009] EWCA Civ 751.

(a) Company directors

One of the most common situations in which fiduciaries exploit opportunities belonging to their principals is that of company directors who take up opportunities properly belonging to their company, to which they stand in a fiduciary relationship. In *Cook v Deeks*[159] three of the four directors of a company who were negotiating for a contract to construct a railway took the contract for themselves in their private capacity so as to exclude the fourth director. The Privy Council held that this amounted to a breach of their fiduciary duty, and that they were liable to account to the company for the profits they made from the transaction. In the leading case, *Regal (Hastings) Ltd v Gulliver*,[160] a company that owned cinemas, wanted to acquire two other cinemas in Hastings. To enable the company to achieve this objective it formed a subsidiary with 5,000 shares. The company was financially only able to take up 2,000 of the shares in the subsidiary. Since the owner of the cinemas refused to sell them unless the share capital was completely taken up, the directors of the company purchased the remaining 3,000 shares and the deal went ahead. The company was subsequently sold and the directors made a profit of £2 16s 1d on each of the shares they had taken up. The House of Lords held that the directors were accountable to the purchasers of the company for the profit they had made on the shares because they had obtained it by reason of their fiduciary position. As Lord Russell of Killowen concluded:

The directors standing in a fiduciary relationship to Regal . . . and having obtained these shares by reason and only by reason of the fact that they were directors of Regal and in the course of the execution of that office, are accountable for the profits which they have made out of them.[161]

It made no difference that the company could not have taken up the opportunity itself for lack of finance, nor that the directors had acted bona fides without fraud.[162]

In *Industrial Development Consultants Ltd v Cooley*[163] Neville Cooley was the managing director of Industrial Development Consultants Ltd, a company that provided construction consultancy services. He entered into negotiations on behalf of the company with the Eastern Gas Board for a contract to build new depots. The Board refused to enter into a contract with the company because of their policy of not employing development companies, but they offered a contract to Cooley in his personal capacity, which he accepted. He then gained release from his position as managing director by representing that he was suffering from a serious illness. Roskill J held that Cooley was liable to account for the profit he had gained from the contract because in entering it he had allowed his duty and his interests to conflict.

---

[159]   [1916] 1 AC 554.   [160]   [1967] 2 AC 134n, [1942] 1 All ER 378.
[161]   [1942] 1 All ER 378, at 389.
[162]   See below, p 939. For a review of the authorities in this area, see *Ultraframe (UK) Ltd v Fielding* [2005] EWHC 1638 (Ch), where Lewison J preferred the dissenting opinion of Lord Upjohn in *Boardman v Phipps* [1967] 2 AC 46, at 124 that there must be a realistic possibility of conflict of duty and interest for the duty to be breached.
[163]   [1972] 1 WLR 443.

Although directors are prima facie liable to make restitution of any profit they receive by appropriating an opportunity belonging to their company, they will be protected from liability if they were authorized to take up the opportunity. This seems to be the correct analysis of the decision of the Privy Council in *Queensland Mines Ltd v Hudson*.[164] Hudson was the managing director of Queensland Mines, a company that was investigating the possibility of mining iron ore in Tasmania. Two licences were obtained from the Tasmanian government, but the company was not able to start mining operations because of lack of finance. Instead, Hudson resigned as managing director and exploited the licences himself, eventually selling them to an American company from which he received royalties on the ore mined. The company argued that he should account for the profits he had made, but the Privy Council held that he was not liable. As Lord Scarman observed, the difficulty of the case lay 'not in the formulation of the law but in the analysis of the facts'.[165] On the facts the Privy Council concluded that by 1962 the board of directors, 'fully informed as to all the relevant facts, had reached a firm decision to renounce all interest in the exploitation of the licence and had assented to Mr Hudson taking over the venture for his own account'. The basis of the decision thus seems to be that the directors had decided that the company would not take up the opportunity, and that Hudson was therefore free to take it up himself. Although this reasoning is attractive, it is open to the objection that the board of directors is not the appropriate organ of the company to reject such an opportunity and permit a director to take it up for himself. The only organ of the company competent to grant such authorization is the shareholders' meeting.[166]

The equitable duties of directors have been codified in the Companies Act 2006.[167] Hence, by s 175(1):

A director of a company must avoid a situation in which he has, or can have, a direct or indirect conflict of interest that conflicts, or possibly may conflict, with the interests of the company.

The director must also not exploit any property, information, or opportunity, and it is immaterial whether the company could take advantage of it.[168] In distinction to the authorities explored above relating to the strict nature of liability, it is clear that the duty is not infringed if the situation complained of cannot reasonably be regarded as likely to give rise to a conflict of interest.[169] The Act also codifies that there will be

---

[164] (1978) 18 ALR 1; Sullivan 'Going it Alone—*Queensland Mines v Hudson*' (1979) 42 MLR 711. See also *Island Export Finance Ltd v Umunna* [1986] BCLC 460; *In Plus Group Lyd v Pyke* [2002] 2 BCLC 201.

[165] (1978) 18 ALR 1, at 3.

[166] Sullivan 'Going it Alone—*Queensland Mines v Hudson*' (1979) MLR 711. See also *Prudential Assurance Co v Newman Industries (No 2)* [1980] 2 All ER 841, at 862; *Shaker v Al-Bedrawi* [2002] 4 All ER 835.

[167] This followed from recommendation of the Law Commission in *Company Directors: Regulating Conflicts of Interest and Formulating a Statement of Duties* Law Com No 261.

[168] Companies Act 2006, s 175(2).

[169] Ibid, s 175(4)(a). See further Mayson, French, and Ryan, *Company Law* (25th edn, 2009), Ch 16, pp 480–486.

no conflict of duty and interest if the matter in question has been authorized by the directors.[170]

(b) Trustees

Since a trustee is a fiduciary vis-à-vis the beneficiaries of the trust he will similarly act in breach of duty if he takes personal advantage of opportunities that properly belong to the trust. For example, if a trust includes shares amongst its assets, and a rights issue is proposed, the trustees cannot purchase the shares offered under the rights issue for themselves unless authorized to do so by the beneficiaries. If they do purchase the shares without authorization they will be held on constructive trust for the beneficiaries.

(c) Other fiduciaries

Fiduciaries other than company directors and trustees will also be held liable to account for any unauthorized profits they receive through exploiting an opportunity belonging to their principal. This can be seen from the leading case of *Boardman v Phipps*.[171] A trust had been established by Charles Phipps on behalf of his wife for life, and after her death for his four children. The trustees were his widow, daughter, and a professional trustee. One asset of the trust was a 27 per cent holding in a private company, Lester & Harris Ltd. Thomas Boardman was the solicitor to the trust and the Phipps family. Boardman and one of the beneficiaries, Thomas Phipps, were unhappy with the way that the company was being run and decided that the only way to protect the trust asset was to acquire a controlling interest in the company. Boardman suggested this to the managing trustee, who made it clear that he was against the trustees buying such a controlling interest and that, without applying to the court, they had no power to do so. Boardman and Phipps, having informed two of the trustees but not the third, who was the testator's elderly widow, subsequently purchased a controlling interest in the company. They then capitalized some of the company's assets, making a profit of some £47,000 for the trust and £75,000 for themselves. One of the other beneficiaries, John Phipps, claimed that they should account for this profit to the trust. By a bare majority the House of Lords held that Boardman was liable to account. He had stood in a fiduciary relationship to the trust and, although he had acted honestly throughout, in exploiting the opportunity there had been a possibility of a conflict between his duty and his interest.

(8) Use of confidential information[172]

A fiduciary who makes use of confidential information belonging to his principal will be liable for any profit that he makes.[173] In *A-G v Guardian Newspapers Ltd (No 2)*[174]

---

170 Ibid., s 175(4)(b). The conditions for the exercise of effective authorization are contained in ss 175(5) and (6), and s 180.

171 [1967] 2 AC 46, HL.

172 See Glover 'Is Breach of Confidence a Fiduciary Wrong?' (2001) 21 LS 595.

173 *York and North Midland Rly Co v Hudson* (1853) 16 Beav 485; *Kirkham v Peel* (1881) 44 LT 195.

174 [1990] 1 AC 109.

the House of Lords held that the Sunday Times was liable to account for the profits made by its publication of extracts of *Spycatcher*, a book written by a former member of the British security services, who stood in a fiduciary relationship to the Crown, and which contained confidential information.[175] In *Peter Pan Manufacturing Corpn v Corsets Silhouette Ltd*[176] the defendant company's designer was shown a sample copy of the design of a new brassiere in confidence by the plaintiff company. When the defendants subsequently manufactured it Pennycuick J ordered that they account for their profits. Liability on the basis of the exploitation of confidential information was also established in the Canadian case of *LAC Minerals Ltd v International Corona Resources Ltd*.[177] LAC received confidential information from Corona during the course of negotiations with a view to establishing a joint venture to exploit minerals from land owned by Corona, which indicated that adjacent land was also likely to contain mineral deposits. LAC subsequently purchased the adjacent land in their own right, and exploited the minerals themselves. The Supreme Court held that there was a fiduciary relationship between the parties, and that LAC should hold the land on constructive trust for Corona because of their breach of confidence.[178]

The exploitation of confidential information provides a further possible explanation for the decision in *Boardman v Phipps*.[179] In the course of negotiations for the purchase of the majority shareholding in the company Boardman, while purporting to act as the trust solicitor on the business of the trust, received essential information about the value of the company's assets and the prices at which shares had recently changed hands. This information enabled him to put forward his offer for the majority shareholding. Lord Hodson and Lord Guest held that Boardman was accountable for the profit he made because he had acquired the shares using this confidential information, which they considered to be trust property. However, Lord Cohen took the view that the information that had been obtained was not 'property in the strict sense'[180] and decided the case on the basis of the rule in *Regal (Hastings) Ltd v Gulliver*,[181] and Lord Upjohn rejected the argument that the information was to be regarded as part of the trust assets.[182]

However, it is clear that the duty not to profit from confidential information only subsists for so long as the information received retains its confidential status. Once it has entered the public sphere, the obligation of confidentiality no longer subsists. Thus, in *A-G v Blake*[183] the Court of Appeal held that a former spy was not in breach of any

---

[175] See Jones 'Breach of Confidence after *Spycatcher*' [1989] CLP 49.
[176] [1964] 1 WLR 96.   [177] (1989) 61 DLR (4th) 14.
[178] Tang argues that there was no justification for a constructive trust in *LAC Minerals v International Corona Resources*: 'Confidence and the Constructive Trust' (2003) 23 LS 135.
[179] [1967] 2 AC 46, HL.
[180] [1967] 2 AC 46, at 103. Note that in *Crown Dilmun plc v Sutton* [2004] 1 BCLC 468 it was accepted that confidential information was not property. However, it may have a market value, and can, indeed, be sold on the market—see *Douglas v Hello! Ltd* (No 3) [2008] AC 1. The potential development of the concept of the law of privacy is considered in Chapter 6.
[181] [1967] 2 AC 134n, [1942] 1 All ER 378.   [182] [1967] 2 AC 46, at 127–128.
[183] [1998] 1 All ER 833, at 842.

fiduciary duty when he had published an autobiography that contained information concerning his work which had entered the public sphere prior to publication. Lord Woolf MR commented:

The duty to respect confidence is also a fiduciary duty, but it subsists only as long as the information remains confidential.[184]

This was subsequently confirmed by the House of Lords.[185] It has also been held that a third party who receives confidential information disclosed by a fiduciary in breach of his duty is not automatically liable to account for any profits resulting from his exploitation of that information. In *Satnam Ltd v Dunlop Heywood & Co Ltd*[186] a development company owned an option to purchase a site that was determinable by the site owners if it went into receivership. The company of surveyors acting for the development company subsequently told a rival developer that their client had been placed into receivership and that the local authority was favourable towards development. On the basis of this information the rival developers purchased the site. While the surveyors had clearly breached their fiduciary duty in revealing this confidential information, the Court of Appeal held that the rival developers did not hold the land acquired on constructive trust for the original developers, nor were they liable to account for their profits. Nourse LJ, giving the judgment of the Court, explained that mere knowledge of a breach of fiduciary duty was insufficient to render a person who was not himself a fiduciary a constructive trustee. He held that the third party would only have been liable to make an account of profits if it had acted dishonestly.

5 Liability for breach of fiduciary duty

Having examined the circumstances in which a fiduciary will be held to have acted in breach of his duty, it is possible to extrapolate from the cases the standard of liability required to trigger a remedy. It appears that the courts have adopted a strict test of liability that does not require the principal to demonstrate that the fiduciary in fact permitted his duty and his interest to conflict. Instead, a fiduciary will be liable to account if there was a mere possibility that his duty and his interests would conflict.[187] The adoption of such a strict approach has attracted criticism. While in the majority of cases a fiduciary who has profited from his position will have acted dishonestly and without regard for the interest of his principle, in some cases a fiduciary who received a profit may have been entirely innocent of any wrongdoing or fraudulent conduct, especially if he exploited an opportunity which his principal could not have exploited, or where the danger of a conflict of interest had been so remote that there was no realistic possibility that such a conflict had occurred. In such cases it may

---

184   Ibid., at 842.   185   [2000] 4 All ER 385.
186   [1999] 3 All ER 652.
187   The duties of directors, where they differ, are detailed above, at pp 934 *et seq.*

seem questionable whether the fiduciary should be liable to make restitution of his profits. Such difficulties were evident in *Boardman v Phipps*,[188] the facts of which were discussed above.[189] The House of Lords consistently emphasized that Boardman and his colleague had been entirely innocent of any misconduct. Lord Cohen, for example, said that their integrity was 'not in doubt' and that they had acted 'with complete honesty throughout'.[190] However, it nevertheless held that Boardman was required to make restitution of the profits he had received by way of an equitable account. Given the success of the defendants' venture, which it must be remembered also resulted in a considerable profit for the trust, the plaintiff was, as Lord Cohen observed, a 'fortunate man in that the rigour of equity enables him to participate in the profits'.[191]

(1) Strict liability

Despite the potential for unfairness in some cases, English law has adopted a strict principle that a fiduciary is liable to account for any unauthorized profits obtained in circumstances where there was a mere possibility that his duty and his interest had conflicted. In *Bray v Ford*[192] Lord Herschell described this as 'an inflexible rule of equity'. In *Regal (Hastings) Ltd v Gulliver*[193] Lord Russell of Killowen stressed that the fiduciary was required to give up the profit he had made irrespective of his honesty:

> The rule of equity, which insists on those, who by use of a fiduciary position make a profit, being liable to account for that profit, in no way depends on fraud, or absence of bona fides; or upon such questions or considerations as whether the profit would or should otherwise have gone to the plaintiff, or whether the profiteer was under a duty to obtain the source of the profit for the plaintiff, or whether he took a risk or acted as he did for the benefit of the plaintiff, or whether the plaintiff has in fact been damaged or benefited by his action. The liability arises from the mere fact of a profit having, in the stated circumstances, been made. The profiteer, however honest and well intentioned, cannot escape the risk of being called upon to account.[194]

In reaching this conclusion he drew upon the language of Lord King LC in *Keech v Sandford*,[195] and of Lord Eldon LC in *Ex p James*,[196] who had said that the self-dealing rule 'rests upon this: that the purchase is not permitted in any case however honest the circumstances'. In *Guinness plc v Saunders*[197] the House of Lords held that a company director who had received an unauthorized payment of £5.2m was liable to account to his company because he had allowed his duty and his interest to conflict, even though he had acted in complete good faith throughout.[198]

A divergence of views was apparent in the House of Lord in *Boardman v Phipps*[199] as to the degree of likelihood of a real conflict of interest required to render a fiduciary liability to account. It was alleged that Boardman had allowed his duty and his interest to conflict by purchasing a controlling interest in a company partially owned by the trust while there was a possibility that, as the trust solicitor, he could be called upon by

---

[188] [1967] 2 AC 46.
[189] See p 937.
[190] Ibid., at 104.
[191] Ibid., at 104.
[192] [1896] AC 44, at 51.
[193] [1942] 1 All ER 378.
[194] Ibid., at 386.
[195] (1726) Sel Cas Ch 61.
[196] (1803) 8 Ves 337.
[197] [1990] 2 AC 663.
[198] Ibid., at 710, per Lord Goff.
[199] [1967] 2 AC 46.

the trustees to advise whether it would be wise for them to seek to acquire the power to pursue a similar investment. Lord Upjohn, dissenting, took the view that a fiduciary should only be required to disgorge his profits where there had been a 'real sensible possibility' of a conflict of interest. In the circumstances, he considered that the possibility of a conflict was simply too remote to render Boardman liable:

The relevant rule for the decision of this case is the fundamental rule of equity that a person in a fiduciary capacity must not make a profit out of his trust which is a part of the wider rule that a trustee must not place himself in a position where his duty and his interest may conflict. It is perhaps most highly against trustees or directors in the celebrated speech of Lord Cranworth LC in *Aberdeen Rly Bros v Blaikie Bros*, where he said: 'And it is a rule of universal application, that no one, having such duties to discharge, shall be allowed to enter into engagements in which he has, or can have, a personal interest conflicting, or which possibly may conflict, with the interests of those whom he is bound to protect.' The phrase 'possibly may conflict' requires consideration. In my view it means that the reasonable man looking at the relevant facts and circumstances of the particular case would think that there was a real sensible possibility of conflict; not that you could imagine some situation arising which might, in some conceivable possibility in events not contemplated as real sensible possibilities by any reasonable person, result in a conflict.[200]

He therefore concluded that Boardman had not acted in breach of his duty because there had been no 'real sensible possibility' of a conflict of interest, and that he should not be required to disgorge his profits.

In contrast, the majority of the House of Lords held that the remoteness of the possibility of a genuine conflict of interest was irrelevant to the liability of a fiduciary. Lord Cohen,[201] Lord Hodson, and Lord Guest cited with approval the statement of principle of Lord Russell in *Regal (Hastings) Ltd v Gulliver*.[202] As Lord Hodson observed:

No doubt it was but a remote possibility that Mr Boardman would ever be asked by the trustees to advise on the desirability of an application to the court in order that the trustees might avail themselves of the information obtained. Nevertheless, even if the possibility of conflict is present between personal interest and the fiduciary position the rule of equity must be applied.[203]

In consequence of the decision of the majority in *Boardman v Phipps*, English law imposes a very strict liability for breach of fiduciary duty so that a fiduciary is liable to account for profits he has received whenever there was a mere possibility, no matter how remote, that his duty and his interest might conflict.

A number of arguments can be put forward in defence of the strict liability of fiduciaries. First, it should be remembered that a fiduciary is only required to make restitution of unauthorized profits. He is able to protect himself from liability by full disclosure of his proposed activities to his principal, which in the case of a trust will mean the beneficiaries. If the principal consents or acquiesces in the conduct disclosed the fiduciary will not be held accountable for any profits he receives thereby. However,

---

[200] Ibid., at 124.

[201] Who had read the speeches to be delivered by Lord Hodson and Lord Guest and agreed in substance with them.

[202] [1967] 2 AC 134n, [1942] 1 All ER 378.   [203] [1967] 2 AC 46, at 111.

where a fiduciary fails to fully disclose his intended course of action to his principal it is not unfair to presume that he was acting in a manner that he did not expect would be condoned. Second, it has already been noted that it is impossible to conduct an inquiry into the subjective motives that influenced a fiduciary's conduct to determine whether a genuine conflict of interest occurred.[204] The court can only look to the objective reality of external appearances, and the mere possibility of such a conflict triggers a remedial response in favour of the principal. This ensures that a situation can never arise where the fiduciary does in fact profit from a breach of his duty. Third, it has to be remembered that the rule has implications beyond any immediate case in point. It operates to deter fiduciaries who may consider abusing their position. This has been described as the prophylactic function of the rule: equity does not wait to see whether the principal has suffered any detriment as a result of the fiduciaries, conduct but imposes a duty which will hold the fiduciary accountable if he might have been tempted to sacrifice the interests of the beneficiary.[205] This prophylactic approach appeared to be to the fore in the reasoning of the House of Lords in *Guinness plc v Saunders*,[206] where Lord Goff emphasized that the court must not act in a manner that would provide any encouragement to trustees to put themselves in a position where their duty would conflict with their personal interests.

(2) Amelioration of the consequences of strict liability

While the adoption of a strict liability to make restitution of unauthorized profits may sometimes be perceived to operate unfairly against an honest fiduciary, such unfairness may partially be alleviated at the remedial stage. Whereas, prima facie, a fiduciary in breach will be required to disgorge the entirety of the profit he received, in some circumstances the courts have held that a fiduciary may be permitted to retain a proportion thereof for himself.[207] The exercise of such relief is akin to the inherent jurisdiction to authorize a trustee to retain past remuneration, and to recoup his expenses from the trust. For example, in *Boardman v Phipps*[208] the majority of the House of Lords held that although Boardman was liable to account for the profits he had received, he should enjoy an allowance to represent his work and skill, which had contributed substantially to the making of the profit. This allowance was to be calculated 'on a liberal scale'.

---

[204] *Ex p James* (1803) 8 Ves 337.

[205] P Birks, *Introduction to the Law of Restitution* (1985), pp 332–333, 339–343.

[206] [1990] 2 AC 663.

[207] In *Warman International v Dwyer* (1995) 128 ALR 201, the High Court suggested that where a fiduciary had acted in breach of his duty in the context of a business rather than through the receipt of a specific asset it may well be inappropriate and inequitable to compel the errant fiduciary to account for the whole of the profit of his conduct of the business or exploitation of the principal's goodwill over an indefinite period of time. In such a case it might therefore be appropriate to allow the fiduciary a proportion of the profits, depending upon the particular circumstances.

[208] [1967] 2 AC 46.

It remains unclear, however, whether the allowance granted in *Boardman v Phipps* included any share of the profits made, or whether it was intended solely to reflect the expenses he had incurred. In *O'Sullivan v Management Agency and Music Ltd*[209] the court expressly permitted a fiduciary to retain a share of the profit it had received. An exclusive management contract between a musician and a management company was set aside on the grounds of undue influence. The Court of Appeal held that while the company was required to account for the profits that it had received under contract, it should be permitted to retain an allowance of reasonable remuneration for their skill and labour. This allowance explicitly included a small share of the profits made. The principle was stated by Fox LJ:

> Once it is accepted that the court can make an appropriate allowance to a fiduciary for his skill and labour I do not see why, in principle, it should not be able to give him some part of the profit of the venture if it was thought that justice as between the parties demanded that.[210]

The allowance is therefore entirely within the court's discretion, and on the facts it was held that a profit element should be included to recognize the contribution that the company had made to the singer's success, but that this would be less than the profit they might have made if the contract had been properly negotiated in the first place to reflect disapprobation of their conduct in obtaining the contract through undue influence.[211]

The stated objective was to 'achieve substantial justice between the parties'.[212] It might be thought that this would provide a way of adjusting the harsh consequences of the strict approach taken in *Boardman v Phipps*.[213] However, *Guinness plc v Saunders*[214] suggests that the courts will be unlikely to award a share of the profits to directors or trustees who allow their duty and their interests to conflict. The case concerned a director, Mr Ward, who received £5.2m under a contract he had entered to provide his services to help with a take-over bid. He was held liable to account for this money because he had acted in breach of fiduciary duty and had not disclosed his interest to the company board. The question arose whether he should receive any allowance for the services he had performed. The House of Lords held that he should not. Lord Goff analysed the rationale for the award of an allowance on a liberal scale in *Boardman v Phipps*[215] and concluded:

> The decision has to be reconciled with the fundamental principle that a trustee is not entitled to remuneration for services rendered by him to the trust except as expressly provided in the trust deed. Strictly speaking, it is irreconcilable with the rule so stated. It seems to me therefore that it can only be reconciled with it to the extent that the exercise of the equitable jurisdiction does not conflict with the policy underlying the rule. As I see it, such a conflict will only be avoided if the exercise of the jurisdiction is restricted to those cases where it cannot have the effect of

---

[209] [1985] QB 428.   [210] Ibid., at 468.

[211] Ibid., at 469, per Fox LJ: 'the defendants must suffer...because of the circumstances in which the contracts were procured'.

[212] [1985] QB 428, at 469, per Fox LJ.   [213] [1967] 2 AC 46.

[214] [1990] 2 AC 663, HL.   [215] [1967] 2 AC 46.

encouraging trustees in any way to put themselves in a position where their interests conflict with their duties as trustees.[216]

The allowance in *Boardman v Phipps* was therefore justified because of the 'equity underlying Mr Boardman's claim', and as such it would not provide any encouragement to trustees to put themselves in a position where their duties as trustees conflicted with their interests. In the case of Mr Ward, remuneration would be inappropriate because he had agreed to provide his services in return for a substantial fee and 'was most plainly putting himself in a position in which his interests were in stark contrast with his duty as a director'.[217]

(3) A higher threshold before a fiduciary is liable for breach of duty?

Some Commonwealth jurisdictions have not adopted the strict penal approach exemplified in England by *Regal (Hastings) Ltd v Gulliver*[218] and *Boardman v Phipps*.[219] They have been more willing to examine whether a conflict of interest had arisen so as to prejudice the principal. In the Canadian case *Peso Silver Mines v Cropper*[220] a less strict approach was taken towards the fiduciary duty of company directors. Cropper was a member of the Board of Peso, a mining company that was offered 126 prospecting claims near their own mines. The company board decided bona fides not to purchase the claims and Cropper then joined a syndicate that formed a company and purchased them. Peso claimed that Cropper was liable to account for the profit he had made. The British Columbia Court of Appeal[221] held that he was not accountable, and rejected the approach adopted in *Regal (Hastings) v Gulliver*. It considered that the strict rules of equity had been carried far enough and were not appropriate for a modern country in a modern era. The Supreme Court of Canada[222] subsequently also held that Cropper was not accountable, but on the narrower ground that the facts fell outside the rule in *Regal (Hastings) v Gulliver* because the board had bona fides come to the conclusion that the investment was not one the company should make, and that the director could not therefore be treated as having made the investment on behalf of the company.[223]

In Australia the High Court has adopted the approach taken by Lord Upjohn in *Boardman v Phipps*. Thus, in *Consul Development Pty Ltd v DPC Estates Pty Ltd*[224] Gibbs J specifically cited Lord Upjohn's suggestion that the words 'possibly may conflict' require consideration.[225] In *Chan (Kak Loui) v Zacharia*[226] Deane J suggested that it might still be arguable in the High Court that 'the liability to account for a personal benefit or gain obtained or received by use or by reason of fiduciary position,

---

[216] [1990] 2 AC 663, at 701.   [217] Ibid., at 702.
[218] [1967] 2 AC 134n, [1942] 1 All ER 378.   [219] [1967] 2 AC 46.
[220] (1966) 58 DLR (2d) 1; (1967) 30 MLR 450 (Prentice); (1971) 49 Can B Rev 80 (Beck); (1975) 53 Can B Rev 771 (Beck).
[221] (1966) 56 DLR (2d) 117.   [222] (1966) 58 DLR (2d) 1.
[223] Citing Lord Greene MR in the Court of Appeal, which was referred to by Lord Russell in the House of Lords.
[224] (1975) 5 ALR 231.   [225] Ibid., at 249.   [226] (1983) 154 CLR 178.

opportunity or knowledge will not arise in circumstances where it would be unconscientious to assert it or in which, for example, there is no possible conflict between personal interest and fiduciary duty...'.[227]

There are now indications that the English courts wish to move away from the strict liability advocated in *Boardman v Phipps*,[228] but are unable to do so, given the strength of authority.[229] In *Murad v Al-Saraji*,[230] for example, Clarke, Arden, and Jonathan Parker LJJ all expressed a desire to soften the position of the law on fiduciary liability where a fiduciary had acted without concealment, but felt unable to do so.[231] Academic opinion remains divided on the subject, with some commentators welcoming a potential relaxation of strict liability,[232] while others feel that the strictness of the rules serves a useful purpose.[233]

(4) Conclusion

It might be thought that in practice there is very little difference between the two standards of liability propounded by the House of Lords in *Boardman v Phipps*.[234] Lord Upjohn's 'real sensible possibility' of a conflict of interest test will exclude only those cases where it seems there is absolutely no danger of the beneficiaries in fact being prejudiced by the fiduciary's conduct. It is an objective test and therefore there is still no need to inquire into actual motives, and it is sufficiently harsh to serve as an adequate deterrent to trustees who might contemplate abusing their position. However, although Lord Upjohn's test has much to commend it, and it has found

---

[227] Ibid., at 204–205. See also *Warman International v Dwyer* (1995) 128 ALR 201, discussed by Oakley, 'The Liberalising Nature of Remedies for Breach of Trust' in Oakley, *Trends in Contemporary Trust Law* (1996), pp 236–239.

[228] [1967] 2 AC 46.

[229] *Guinness v Saunders* [1990] 2 AC 663. Note, however, the dicta of Sedley LJ in *In Plus Group Ltd v Pyke* [2002] 2 BCLC 201 that a company director would not commit a breach of fiduciary duty by serving a competing company without consent if he had been treated unfairly. Grantham argues that this is inconsistent with the strict duty imposed on fiduciaries: (2003) 66 MLR 109.

[230] [2005] EWCA Civ 959, CA; McInnes 'Account of Profits for Breach of Fiduciary Duty' (2006) LQR 11; *Ultraframe (UK) Ltd v Fielding* [2005] EWHC 1638 (Ch) (where Lewison J expressed his support for an approach based on a realistic possibility of conflict of interest, in preference to the strict approach).

[231] See also the dicta of Sedley LJ in *In Plus Group Ltd v Pyke* [2002] 2 BCLC 201 that a company director would not commit a breach of fiduciary duty by serving a competing company without consent if he had been treated unfairly. Grantham argues that this is inconsistent with the strict duty imposed on fiduciaries: (2003) 66 MLR 109.

[232] See, for example, Panesar 'The Nature of Fiduciary Liability in English Law' [2007] Conv 2, pp. 11–19: 'whilst the strict liability rule was justified in the context of some of the nineteenth century cases where evidential issues prevented the court from ascertaining the intention of the fiduciary, in modern cases it is questionable whether such an approach is justified. There is much to be said for recent judicial calls for recognition that it is not appropriate to apply laws decided in a wholly different context to a different kind of situation.'

[233] See, for example, Samet 'Guarding the Fiduciary's Conscience—A Justification of a Stringent Profit-Stripping Rule' (2008) OJLS 763, arguing that allowing the fiduciary to argue that he acted as an honest person would therefore be more than a mere decrease in its overall deterrent effect. The strict no-profit rule prevents manipulation.

[234] [1967] 2 AC 46.

favour with academic commentators,[235] the strict approach that a fiduciary will be liable to account whenever there was a mere possibility of a conflict of interest, no matter how remote or unlikely the circumstances, represents the present position of English law. The only way that the fiduciary can avoid liability, no matter how honest he may have been, is by ensuring that his profit-making activities are authorized by his principal following full disclosure.

6 Remedies where a fiduciary makes an unauthorized profit

A fiduciary who has made an unauthorized profit will be required to make restitution thereof to his principal. Such restitution or disgorgement can be effected either by a personal or a proprietary remedy. It has often proved difficult to determine whether a personal or proprietary remedy is available, and in many cases the courts have not clearly identified the remedy awarded. The problem was stated clearly in the Australian High Court by Gibbs J in *Consul Development Pty Ltd v DPC Estates Pty Ltd*:

The question whether the remedy which the person to whom the duty is owed may obtain against the person who has violated the duty is proprietary or personal may sometimes be one of some difficulty. In some cases the fiduciary has been declared a trustee of the property which he has gained by his breach; in others he has been called upon to account for his profits and sometimes the distinction between the two remedies has not...been kept clearly in mind.[236]

In many cases it will not be necessary to determine whether the principal is entitled to a proprietary remedy, as a personal remedy will suffice. However, the availability of a proprietary remedy will be of crucial importance if the fiduciary is insolvent,[237] or if he has invested the profit received in assets that have appreciated in value. In the case of insolvency a principal will gain priority over the general creditors of the fiduciary if he can demonstrate a proprietary entitlement to any assets that represent the profit received. In the case of asset appreciation the principal will only be able to claim entitlement to the increased value by means of a proprietary right.

It should be noted that if a trustee has received a profit in breach of fiduciary duty his conduct may also constitute a breach of trust. If so, his obligations to make restitution of his profit gained in breach of fiduciary duty and to compensate the trust for any loss suffered in consequence of his breach are alternative remedies. The beneficiaries are required to elect between them and cannot recover both, otherwise they would gain

---

[235] Jones 'Unjust Enrichment and the Fiduciary's Duty of Loyalty' (1968) 84 LQR 472; Goff and Jones, *The Law of Restitution* (6th edn, 2002), pp 730–731; Finn, *Fiduciary Obligations* (1997), pp 130–168. It is also arguably the basis of the rule relating to directors duties in s 175(4)(a) of the Companies Act 2006.

[236] (1975) 5 ALR 231, at 249.

[237] See Oakley 'Proprietary Claims and their Priority in Insolvency' [1995] CLJ 377.

double recovery. The need to elect was identified by the Privy Council in *Tang Man Sit (Decd) v Capacious Investments*,[238] which was discussed in detail in Chapter 29.[239]

(1) Personal remedies

Whenever a fiduciary receives an unauthorized profit in breach of his fiduciary duty he is subject to a personal obligation to make restitution of the amount of the profit received to his principal. This personal restitutionary obligation is effected through the equitable duty to account. The personal remedy of account will be adequate to effect restitution where the fiduciary remains solvent and able to pay his principal an amount of money equivalent to the profit he received. Such a personal remedy appears to have been awarded in *Boardman v Phipps*.[240] In many cases where an equitable account of profits was ordered there was no need to determine whether a proprietary remedy by way of a constructive trust was also available because the personal remedy provided adequate satisfaction of the principal's right to receive restitution. As Professor Birks notes,[241] 'the vital fact is that [Boardman] was not insolvent. It was not necessary, therefore, for the plaintiff to claim any right in rem.'[242] A personal remedy will also be preferred to a proprietary claim if the fiduciary is solvent but the assets remaining in his hands representing the profit he received have fallen in value. As Lord Tempelman stated in *A-G of Hong Kong v Reid*:

If the property representing the [profit[243]] decreases in value the fiduciary must pay the difference between that value and the initial amount of the [profit]...[244]

The relevant date for the assessment of the quantum of the personal remedy is the date that the profit was received. The principal will only be entitled to recover the actual or net profit that was received by the fiduciary.[245]

(2) Proprietary remedies

(a) A constructive trust of unauthorized profits

It has always been clear that in some circumstances a proprietary constructive trust is imposed when a fiduciary receives an unauthorized profit in breach of his duty. This is evident in *Keech v Sandford*,[246] where the court held that a lease that had been renewed to a trustee in his personal capacity, rather than on behalf of the trust, should be assigned to the infant beneficiary. This suggests that the infant enjoyed an equitable

---

[238] [1996] AC 514. See Stevens 'Election between Alternative Remedies' [1995] RLR 117; Birks 'Inconsistency between Compensation and Restitution' (1996) 112 LQR 375.

[239] See p 877, above.　　[240] [1967] 2 AC 46.

[241] Birks, *An Introduction to the Law of Restitution* (Oxford, 1985).

[242] Ibid., p 388.

[243] In fact, Lord Templeman used the term 'bribe', since this was what the fiduciary had in fact received, but the principle remains the same irrespective of the source of the profit received.

[244] [1994] 1 All ER 1.　　[245] *Patel v London Borough of Brent* [2003] EWHC 3081.

[246] (1726) Sel Cas Ch 61.

entitlement to the lease from the moment that the trustee had acquired it. The trustee was also obliged to account for the profits he had received in the meantime. This account of profits is also explicable on the basis that the lease was always the property of the trust. In *Cook v Deeks*[247] the Privy Council similarly held that a contract entered by directors personally, in breach of their fiduciary duty, was held 'on behalf of the company',[248] such that 'it belonged in equity to the company and ought to have been dealt with as an asset of the company'.[249] In *Williams v Barton*[250] the court held that a commission received by a trustee in breach of fiduciary duty was to be treated as part of the estate of which he was executor, as he held it on constructive trust. In *Boardman v Phipps*[251] the House of Lords seems to have come to the conclusion that the majority shareholding that had been acquired in breach of fiduciary duty was held on constructive trust for the beneficiaries of the trust.[252] Likewise, in *Guinness plc v Saunders*[253] the House of Lords held that a £5.2m fee received by a director in breach of fiduciary duty was held on constructive trust for the company. He was therefore required to 'restore that money'[254] to the company.[255]

Although these cases established that a fiduciary may sometimes hold any unauthorized profits he has received on constructive trust, it remained unclear whether such a trust would arise in all such circumstances. In particular, there was a long established authority that a fiduciary who had received a bribe would not hold it on constructive trust for his principal. The resulting inconsistency was only resolved by the decision of the Privy Council in *A-G of Hong Kong v Reid*.[256]

(b) Constructive trust of a bribe received by a fiduciary

Whereas a proprietary remedy by way of a constructive trust has always been available in some instances where a fiduciary has received an unauthorized profit, in the case of bribes it was historically held that no such proprietary remedy was available to a principal. A bribed fiduciary did not hold the bribe received on constructive trust, and the principal was confined to a personal remedy of account.[257] In *Lister & Co v Stubbs*[258] Stubbs, the foreman dyer of Lister & Co, received £5,500 in bribes from another company with whom he placed business while acting as agent for Lister. The Court of Appeal held that the money he received was not held on constructive trust, and that Lister & Co therefore had had no proprietary claim to it. Stubbs was under a

---

[247] [1916] 1 AC 554.   [248] Ibid., at 563.   [249] Ibid., at 564.
[250] [1927] 2 Ch 9.   [251] [1967] 2 AC 46.

[252] Ibid., at 117, per Lord Guest: 'I have no hesitation in coming to the conclusion that the appellants hold the Lester & Harris shares as constructive trustees...' This understanding of the claim in *Boardman v Phipps* was also expressed by the Privy Council in *A-G for Hong Kong v Reid* [1994] 1 All ER 1, at 11. See, however, *Ultraframe (UK) Ltd v Fielding* [2005] EWHC 1638 (Ch), where it was suggested by Lewison J that the remedy was not proprietary.

[253] [1990] 2 AC 663.   [254] Ibid., at 702, per Lord Goff.

[255] See also *Neptune (Vehicle Washing Equipment) Ltd v Fitzgerald* [1996] Ch 274; *CMS Dolphin Ltd v Simonet* [2001] BCLC 704.

[256] [1994] 1 All ER 1.   [257] *Metropolitan Bank v Heiron* (1880) 5 Ex D 319, CA.
[258] (1890) 45 Ch D 1.

personal duty to account for the money he had received, and the relationship between Stubbs and the company was simply one of debtor and creditor.

Lister & Co v Stubbs was followed in *A-G's Reference (No 1 of 1985).*[259] A pub landlord was contractually obliged to sell only goods supplied by a brewery. He moved barrels of his own beer into the pub at night. He was charged under s 25(1) of the Theft Act 1968 with going equipped for theft. The trial judge ruled that there was no case to answer, and it was referred to the Court of Appeal by the Attorney General. The central issue was whether the landlord would have been a constructive trustee of any money paid to him by customers for beer sold in breach of his contract. The Court of Appeal held that this did not fall within the ambit of s 5 of the Theft Act because 'a person in a fiduciary position who uses that position to make a secret profit...is not a trustee'.[260] Lord Lane CJ concluded that:

A trustee is not permitted to make a profit from his trust. Therefore if he uses trust property to make a profit from the trust, he is accountable for that profit. If and when such a profit is identified as a separate piece of property, he may be a constructive trustee of it. However, until the profit is identifiable as a separate piece of property, it is not trust property and his obligation is to account only.[261]

However, it is contended that little weight should be placed upon this decision. It is clearly correct that a proprietary remedy cannot subsist when specific property cannot be identified as representing the profit received, but it does not follow that no such proprietary entitlement exists at the moment that such a profit is received. The property is specifically identifiable when the customer pays over the price of the beer, although if mixed with other money it may then prove impossible to identify it subsequently in the assets of the recipient.

Although the rule in *Lister & Co v Stubbs*[262] was supported by some academic commentators,[263] it was subjected to heavy criticism by others.[264] In *A-G of Hong Kong v Reid*[265] the Privy Council considered that it should no longer be followed. Reid received bribes exceeding NZ$2.5m in the course of his work as a public prosecutor in

---

[259] [1986] QB 491; (1986) 102 LQR 486; (1986) 45 CLJ (Gearty); (1986) 136 NLJ 913 (Smart); [1987] Conv 209 (Martin). See also *Powell and Thomas v Evans Jones & Co* [1905] 1 KB 11, CA; *A-G's Reference (No 1 of 1985)* [1986] QB 491; *Logicrose Ltd v Southend United Football Club Ltd* [1988] 1 WLR 1256; *A-G for Hong Kong v Reid* [1992] 2 NZLR 385. For those who supported the decision in *Lister v Stubbs*, see Birks, *An Introduction to the Law of Restitution* (1985), p 388; (1987) 103 LQR 433 (Goode).

[260] [1986] QB 491, at 503, citing *Reading v A-G* [1951] AC 507, HL; *In Re Sharpe* [1980] 1 WLR 219; *R v Governor of Pentonville Prison, ex p Tarling* (1978) 70 Cr App Rep 77; *Lister & Co v Stubbs* (1890) 45 Ch D 1.

[261] [1986] QB 491, at 506.   [262] (1890) 45 Ch D 1.

[263] Goode 'Ownership and Obligation in Commercial Transactions' (1987) 103 LQR 433.

[264] Underhill and Hayton, *Law Relating to Trust and Trustees* (15th edn, 1995), p 877; Oakley, *Constructive Trusts* (2nd edn, 1997), p 56; Goff and Jones, *The Law of Restitution* (6th edn, 2002), pp 740–742; Pettit, *Equity and the Law of Trusts* (9th edn, 2001), p 143; Meagher, Gummow, and Lehane, *Equity Doctrines and Remedies* (3rd edn, 1992), para 1323; Sir Anthony Mason, *Essays in Equity* (1985), p 246; Finn, *Fiduciary Obligations* (1977), para 513; Jacobs, *Law of Trusts in Australia* (5th edn), p 297; (1979) 95 LQR 536 (Needham); [1980] Conv 200 (Braithwaite); [1993] RLR 7 (Sir Peter Millett).

[265] [1994] 1 All ER 1; Allen 'Bribes and Constructive Trusts: A-G of Hong Kong v Reid' (1995) 58 MLR 87.

Hong Kong. Part of this money was used to purchase three freehold properties in New Zealand. The Privy Council considered that, since Reid had acted in breach of his fiduciary duty, he held the money he received on constructive trust for the Crown. Since the houses were the traceable proceeds of the bribes received, they were also held on trust for the Crown. Lord Templeman, delivering the advice of the Board, explained the rationale for the decision:

> The decision in *Lister & Co v Stubbs* is not consistent with the principles that a fiduciary must not be allowed to benefit from his own breach of duty, that the fiduciary should account for the bribe as soon as he receives it and that equity regards as done that which ought to be done. From these principles it would appear to follow that the bribe and the property from time to time representing the bribe are held on a constructive trust for the person injured.[266]

The rejection of *Lister & Co v Stubbs* eliminated an anomaly in the law. As can be seen from *Boardman v Phipps*,[267] an 'honest' fiduciary will be held to be a constructive trustee of any unauthorized profit received if there was the mere possibility of a conflict between his interest and his duty. It was unacceptable that a proprietary remedy was available against an honest fiduciary but not against a 'dishonest' fiduciary who had accepted a bribe.[268]

The exact status of the decision in *A-G of Hong Kong v Reid* has continued to be debated, since it is a Privy Council decision, and some cases have suggested that *Lister & Co v Stubbs* continues to be binding on English courts.[269] However, in *Daraydan Holdings Ltd v Solland International Ltd*,[270] which concerned a defendant who had received a secret commission of £1.8m from the claimants on contracts for the luxurious refurbishment of properties in London and Qatar, Lawrence Collins J held that *A-G of Hong Kong v Reid* ought to be applied:

> The system of precedent would be shown in a most unfavourable light if a litigant in such a case were forced by the doctrine of binding precedent to go to the House of Lords in order to have the decision of the Privy Council affirmed. That would be particularly so where the decision of the Privy Council is recent, where it was a decision on the English common law, where the Board consisted mainly of serving Law Lords, and where the decision had been made after full argument on the correctness of the earlier decision.[271]

Strictly speaking these comments were themselves obiter, since the case was distinguishable from *A-G of Hong Kong v Reid* because the bribe involved had been derived directly from the claimant's property because the price paid by the claimant had been increased by the amount of the bribe, but they reflect a strong judicial sentiment that *Lister v Stubbs* has been overruled in practice.

---

266 [1994] 1 All ER 1, at 9. See also *Sumitomo Bank Ltd v Kartika Ratna Thahir* (1993) 1 SLR 735.

267 [1967] 2 AC 46, HL.   268 See below.

269 *A-G v Blake* [1997] Ch 84; *Halifax Building Society v Thomas* [1996] Ch 217. See, however, *Ocular Sciences Ltd v Aspect Vision Care Ltd* [1997] RPC 289 and *Fyffes Group Ltd v Tempelman* [2000] Lloyd's Rep 643, where *A-G for Hong Kong v Reid* was applied and *Hurstanger v Wilson* [2007] 1 WLR 2351.

270 [2005] 4 All ER 73.

271 Ibid., at [85]–[86].

(c) Constructive trust of unauthorized profits in all circumstances

It is hard to overestimate the significance of *A-G for Hong Kong v Reid*.[272] The rejection of *Lister & Co v Stubbs* and the reasoning of Lord Templeman suggest that in all situations in which a fiduciary receives an unauthorized profit a constructive trust will be imposed in favour of his principal. The constructive trust arises as an inexorable consequence of the equitable duty to account. As Lord Templeman explained:

> As soon as the bribe was received it should have been paid or transferred instanter to the person who suffered from the breach of duty. Equity considers as done that which ought to be have been done. As soon as the bribe was received, whether in cash or in kind, the false fiduciary held the bribe on a constructive trust for the person injured.[273]

The imposition of the constructive trust is therefore analogous to the trust that arises when a specifically enforceable contract for the creation or transfer of an equitable interest is entered. For example, a contract for the sale of land creates an immediate constructive trust in favour of the purchaser, and a contract for the grant of a legal lease will create an equitable lease.[274] If this analysis is correct, a constructive trust would certainly have been available as a remedy in *Boardman v Phipps*.[275] Boardman had received an unauthorized profit in breach of his fiduciary duty, and he was therefore subject to an equitable duty to account to his principal. Since equity would treat as done that which ought to be done, namely payment over of the profit received, he would hold the profit on constructive trust. It is also difficult to see how the decision of the Court of Appeal in *A-G's Reference (No 1 of 1985)*[276] can survive as good authority in the light of *A-G of Hong Kong v Reid*.[277] The publican would have held any profit derived from the sale of his own beer in breach of the exclusive supply contract on constructive trust, as he was admittedly subject to a personal duty to account.

(d) Agent not required to apply money exclusively for principal's benefit

In spite of the fact that *A-G for Hong Kong v Reid* seems to suggest that a fiduciary will always hold any unauthorized profits he has received on constructive trust for his principal, this has been questioned in relation to an agent. More particularly, the issue is whether such a constructive trust will arise where an agent has failed to account to his principal for money received on his behalf if he was not subject to a duty to keep the money received separate from his own, and to apply it exclusively for the benefit of his principal. In *Nelson v Rye*[278] the manager of a musician had agreed to receive all the income arising from his client's activities, and to account annually to him for the income received, less his agreed commission and expenses. Laddie J held that in these

[272] [1994] 1 All ER 1.
[273] Ibid., at 5. See also *MacIntosh v Fortex Group Ltd* [1997] 1 NZLR 711. See Worthington, *Proprietary Interests in Commercial Transactions* (1996), pp 192–194.
[274] *Walsh v Lonsdale* (1882) 21 Ch D 9; see also *Job v Job* (1877) 6 Ch D 562; *Lowe v Dixon* (1885) 16 QBD 455.
[275] [1967] 2 AC 46.   [276] [1986] QB 491.
[277] See Smith '*Lister v Stubbs* and the Criminal Law' (1994) 110 LQR 180.
[278] [1996] 2 All ER 186.

circumstances the manager was a constructive trustee of any income he had failed to pay to his client in accordance with their agreement, citing with approval an academic article authored by Sir Peter Millett.[279] Somewhat ironically, in *Paragon Finance plc v Thakerar & Co*[280] Millett LJ suggested that *Nelson v Rye* had been wrongly decided, and that the income wrongly retained could not have been held on constructive trust for the client. Millett LJ explained that, in his opinion, the nature of the agency agreement had rendered it impossible to establish a constructive trust:

Unless I have misunderstood the facts or they were very unusual it would appear that the defendant was entitled to pay receipts into his own account, mix them with his own money, use them for his own cash flow, deduct his own commission, and account for the balance to the plaintiff only at the end of the year. It is fundamental to the existence of a trust that the trustee is bound to keep the trust property separate from his own and apply it exclusively for the benefit of the beneficiary. Any right on the part of the defendant to mix the money which he received with his own and use it for his own cash flow would be inconsistent with the existence of a trust.[281]

The limitation suggested in *Paragon Finance plc v Thakerar & Co*, which was followed by Jules Sher, QC in *Coulthard v Disco Mix Club Ltd*,[282] will only apply in a very narrow range of circumstances. In the vast majority of cases where a fiduciary has received an unauthorized profit he will be subject to an immediate duty to account to his principal, thus generating a constructive trust.

(e) Identifying assets subject to a constructive trust

A proprietary right can only subsist in respect of specific property. A principal will therefore only be able to assert his equitable ownership against assets in the hands of his fiduciary (or a third party) which he can identify as representing the profit received, or the proceeds of the profit received. Whether such identification is possible will be determined by the equitable rules of tracing. In some cases it will be relatively straightforward to identify assets representing the profit received, as for example in *A-G of Hong Kong v Reid*,[283] where the houses claimed could be shown to have been purchased with the bribe received. If it is not possible to identify any traceable proceeds of the profit received, the principal will be confined to seeking a personal remedy by way of an equitable account. The rules of tracing will be examined in Chapter 32.

(3) Criticism of the present remedial structure

It now seems clear that in English law, in consequence of the decision in *A-G of Hong Kong v Reid*, a constructive trust will arise whenever a fiduciary receives an unauthorized profit. However, this general availability of a proprietary remedy has been subjected to criticism, on both theoretical and practical grounds, and alternative approaches have been advocated.

---

[279] 'Bribes and Secret Commissions' [1993] RLR 7.   [280] [1999] 1 All ER 400.
[281] Ibid., at 416.   [282] [2000] 1 WLR 707.   [283] [1994] 1 All ER 1.

(a) Criticism of *A-G of Hong Kong v Reid*[284]

It is somewhat ironic that, whereas *Lister & Co v Stubbs*[285] had been subjected to strong criticism before it was set aside by the Privy Council, *A-G of Hong Kong v Reid*[286] has since become the subject of equally vociferous criticism. The imposition of a constructive trust in *Reid* was clearly motivated by policy considerations. As Lord Templeman observed:

Bribery is an evil practice which threatens the foundation of any civilised society. In particular, bribery of policemen and prosecutors brings the administration of justice into disrepute. Where bribes are accepted by a trustee, servant, agent or other fiduciary, loss and damage are caused to the beneficiaries, master or principal whose interests have been betrayed. The amount of loss or damage resulting from the acceptance of a bribe may or may not be quantifiable.[287]

It therefore seemed morally unacceptable that an honest fiduciary might hold an unauthorized profit on constructive trust but a blatantly dishonest fiduciary who had accepted a bribe would not. Surely the morally more repugnant conduct demands the more powerful remedy. While *Lister & Co v Stubbs* was largely criticized by property lawyers on grounds of inconsistency, *A-G of Hong Kong v Reid* has largely been criticized by restitution lawyers on the grounds of proprietary overkill.[288] The main criticism concerns the perceived danger of unfairness to other creditors of the fiduciary if he is insolvent and assets representing the bribe received are subject to a constructive trust, thus gaining the principal priority. This danger did not in fact arise in *Reid* because he was not insolvent. Lord Templeman considered that the right of the principal should prevail over the entitlements of other general creditors:

it is said that if the false fiduciary holds property representing the bribe in trust for the person injured, and if the false fiduciary is or becomes insolvent, the unsecured creditors of the false fiduciary will be deprived of their right to share in the proceeds of that property. But the unsecured creditors cannot be in a better position than their debtor. The authorities show that property acquired by a trustee innocently but in breach of trust and the property from time to time representing the same belong in equity to the cestui que trust and not to the trustee personally, whether he is solvent or insolvent. Property acquired by a trustee as a result of a criminal breach of trust and the property from time to time representing the same must also belong in equity to the cestui que trust and not to the trustee whether he is solvent or insolvent.[289]

Central to the criticism of the constructive trust analysis adopted in *Reid* is the perception that there was insufficient nexus between the principal and the bribe received by the fiduciary to justify the imposition of a proprietary right, irrespective of the fact that the relationship between the fiduciary and his principal justifies a personal obligation to make restitution. If the automatic constructive trust founded upon the

---

[284]   See (1994) 53 CLJ 31 (Oakley); [1994] RLR 57 (Crilley); (1995) 54 CLJ 60 (Gardner). See also R Goode, 'Proprietary Restitutionary Claims', Ch 5 in Cornish, Nolan, O'Sullivan, and Virgo (eds) *Restitution Past, Present and Future* (1998).

[285]   (1890) 45 ChD 1.   [286]   [1994] 1 All ER 1.   [287]   Ibid., at 4.

[288]   See Crilley 'A Case of Proprietary Overkill' [1994] RLR 57; Rotherham 'The Recovery of the Profits of Wrongdoing and Insolvency: When Is Proprietary Relief Justified?' [1997] CFILR 43; Burrows, *The Law of Restitution* (2nd edn, 2002), pp 72 and 499–500.

[289]   [1994] 1 All ER 1, at 5.

equitable duty to account is to be rejected, an alternative analysis is needed by which to differentiate the circumstances in which a constructive trust will be imposed over profits received in breach of fiduciary duty, and situations where the principal will be confined to a personal remedy.

(b) Constructive trust should require a proprietary base?

Some academics have suggested that an unauthorized profit received by a fiduciary should only be subject to a constructive trust if the profit was obtained through a misuse of the principal's property. Professor Birks has argued that a proprietary remedy should only be available where there was a sufficient 'proprietary base' connecting the profit and the principal.[290] Hanbury and Martin[291] argued that a constructive trust should only arise where a profit has been made by the fiduciary's use of trust property, and that in all other circumstances there should only be a personal duty to account. If a proprietary nexus were to be required between the profit and the principal the proceeds of a bribe could not be subject to a constructive trust as the principal had no prior connection with the property constituting the bribe, nor was it received by the fiduciary as a product of property belonging to the principal.[292] If this analysis were to be applied to the earlier case of *Boardman v Phipps*[293] a proprietary constructive trust would only have been justified if the confidential information exploited to generate the profit was characterized as trust property.

While this approach would certainly restrict the scope of proprietary claims, it is predicated upon a distinction between abuse of property and abuse of position. Where a fiduciary had received a profit through abuse of his principal's property the principal would be entitled either to a proprietary claim by way of constructive trust or a personal restitutionary remedy. If the fiduciary had merely exploited his position, but not the principal's property, the principal would be confined to a personal right to receive restitution. In *A-G of Hong Kong v Reid*[294] the Privy Council was unwilling to draw such a distinction, so that any abuse by a fiduciary, whether of property or position, will give rise to a constructive trust. The constructive trust arises from the mandatory nature of the equitable duty to account.

(c) A remedial constructive trust

Under the approach adopted in *Reid,* the court possesses no discretion to determine whether a principal should be entitled to a proprietary claim if his fiduciary received an unauthorized profit. The constructive trust arises automatically, without the intervention of the court, at the moment that the profit was received. The constructive trust operates in what has been described as an institutional manner. However, other jurisdictions, and especially Canada, have adopted a more flexible form of constructive trust, termed the remedial constructive trust. The remedial constructive trust has

---

[290] *An Introduction to the Law of Restitution* (1985), pp 378–393.
[291] *Modern Equity* (14th edn, 1993), p 598. See now (18th edn, 2009), pp 656–659.
[292] See also Tang, 'Confidence and the Constructive Trust' (2003) 23 LS 135.
[293] [1967] 2 AC 46.   [294] [1994] 1 All ER 1.

two significant characteristics. First, it is a trust imposed to reverse unjust enrichment. Second, where unjust enrichment is identified it is for the court to determine whether a constructive trust would be an appropriate remedy to effect restitution. Thus, if a fiduciary has received an unauthorized profit in breach of duty he will have been unjustly enriched thereby, and the court will enjoy the discretion to decide whether the principle should be entitled to a proprietary remedy. No trust arises at the moment that the profit was received, but only when the court determines that a constructive trust should be imposed. In this way the interests of third parties, for example other general creditors of an insolvent fiduciary, can be taken into account. In *LAC Minerals Ltd v International Corona Resources Ltd*[295] the defendant had acted in breach of fiduciary duty by misusing confidential information to purchase land that contained substantial mineral deposits. A majority of the Supreme Court of Canada held that a constructive trust should be imposed. A remedial constructive trust was also utilized in *Korkontzilas v Soulos*,[296] where a gratuitous agent acting for the potential purchaser of land had failed to deliver her offer to the vendor and arranged to sell the property to his own wife instead. The majority of the Supreme Court held that a constructive trust should be imposed. The discretionary nature of the remedy was stressed, so that a constructive trust would not be imposed if it would be unjust, for example if the interests of intervening creditors would be affected. The operation of such a remedial constructive trust is so different from the present English approach that *A-G of Hong v Reid* was not even cited.

While the remedial constructive trust offers the attraction of flexibility, this is gained at the expense of certainty. For this reason English law has so far refused to adopt the remedial constructive trust. In *Westdeutsche Landesbank Girozentrale v Islington London Borough Council*[297] Lord Browne-Wilkinson tentatively suggested that it may conceivably be introduced when an appropriate case arises for decision.[298] However, in *Re Polly Peck (No 2)*[299] the Court of Appeal strongly indicated that the remedial constructive trust should not be introduced into English law without the intervention of Parliament. If in the future the remedial constructive trust is adopted, the present orthodoxy found in *A-G of Hong Kong v Reid* will have to be revised. The nature and operation of the remedial constructive trust has been discussed in detail in Chapter 10 above.

(d) Redefining the fiduciary relationship

While much debate has concerned the nature of the remedies available to a principal whose fiduciary has received an unauthorized profit, many of the difficulties in this area have been caused by the extension of the concept of the 'fiduciary relationship'

[295] (1989) 61 DLR (4th) 14.   [296] (1997) 146 DLR (4th) 214.   [297] [1996] AC 669.

[298] Lord Scott has suggested in the context of the family home, that a remedial constructive trust exists and has existed for many years to allow the acquisition of an interest by a non-legal owning cohabitant (see, for example, *Yeoman's Row Management Ltd v Cobbe* [2008] UKHL 55). Lord Scott appears to be alone in this view, and his comments have since been doubted by the House of Lords—see *Thorner v Major* [2009] UKHL 18, at [67], per Lord Walker. This is discussed further in Chapter 11, at p 396.

[299] [1998] 3 All ER 812.

into commercial relationships. The proprietary remedies triggered by a fiduciary relationship may be justified in the context of a trust but are less clearly applicable where the fiduciary is an employee who has committed a breach of contract that has generated a profit. In such circumstances it may be difficult to determine whether the employee's breach caused any loss to his employer, or to assess the quantum of such loss. It is much simpler to identify the extent of the gain received by the employee. If an employee were liable to make restitution to his employer of any profit earned by his breach of contract, this would provide the employer with adequate remedial satisfaction while eliminating the need to demonstrate a fiduciary relationship. Historically, such an alternative analysis was impossible because it had been held that a defendant in breach of contract was not subject to an obligation to make restitution of his profit.[300] If the breach enabled the defendant to enter a more profitable contract with someone else,[301] the availability of restitution would have the effect of undermining the incentive to commit efficient breach. However, in *A-G v Blake*[302] the House of Lords held that in exceptional circumstances a contract breaker could be required to account for the profits he had derived from his breach. Lord Nicholls examined the relevant authorities and concluded:

> My conclusion is that there seems to be no reason, *in principle,* why the court must in all circumstances rule out an account of profits as a remedy for breach of contract... When, exceptionally, a just response to a breach of contract so requires, the court should be able to grant the discretionary remedy of requiring a defendant to account to the plaintiff for the benefits he has received from his breach of contract.[303]

The case concerned a traitorous former member of the security services who had published an autobiography without the consent of his former employers, in contravention of an express term of his contract. In the Court of Appeal Lord Woolf MR had suggested that restitution of profits obtained by a breach of contract should only be required where a defendant had done the very thing he contracted not to do, or had saved himself expenditure by skimping on the performance required under his contract.[304] However, the House of Lords was unwilling to adopt any specific guidelines as to when the remedy of account should be awarded, other than that the usual remedies of damages, specific performance, and injunction must be 'inadequate'. Lord Nicholls stated:

> It will only be in exceptional cases, where those remedies are inadequate, that any question of accounting for profits will arise. No fixed rules can be prescribed. The court will have regard to all the circumstances, including the subject matter of the contract, the purpose of the contractual provision which has been breached, the circumstances in which the breach occurred, the consequences of the breach and the circumstances in which relief is being sought. A useful guide, although not exhaustive, is whether the plaintiff had a legitimate interest in preventing

---

[300] *Surrey County Council v Bredero Homes Ltd* [1993] 1 WLR 1361.

[301] *Teacher v Calder* [1899] AC 451.

[302] [2000] 4 All ER 385. See also *Experience Hendrix LLC v PXX Enterprises Inc* [2003] 1 All ER (Comm) 830; Lee 'Responses to a Breach of Contract' [2003] LMCLQ 301. Note the criticisms of *A-G v Blake* in Campbell 'The Treatment of *Teacher v Calder* in *AG v Blake*' (2002) 65 MLR 256, and Campbell and Harris 'In Defence of Breach: A Critique of Restitution and the Performance Interest' (2002) 22 LS 208.

[303] [2000] 4 All ER 385, at 396.

[304] [1998] 1 All ER 833, at 846. See Virgo 'Clarifying Restitution for Wrongs' [1998] RLR 118.

the defendant's profit-making activity and, hence, in depriving him of his profit. It would be difficult, and unwise, to attempt to be more specific.[305]

The adoption of a restitution remedy to recover profits obtained by a breach of contract may allow for a contraction of the scope of relationships that need to be characterized as fiduciary in nature, especially in the context of employment relationships. In such cases the duty of exclusive loyalty will be replaced by specific contractual obligations of loyalty. An employee such as Reid could thus be required to make restitution of unauthorized profits received in breach of contract, which would certainly include a bribe, without inevitably requiring the imposition of a constructive trust. The remedy would be personal and the principal would stand alongside other general creditors in the event of insolvency.

(4) Conclusion

Despite criticism and alternatives, the overwhelming weight of English principle and authority favours the view that a fiduciary who receives an unauthorized profit will hold it on constructive trust for his principal. His principal will therefore enjoy an immediate equitable proprietary interest in the profit received, which may be maintained against any assets which can be identified as its product by the rules of tracing. In the event that the fiduciary is insolvent, he will be able to obtain priority over other general creditors. Similarly, his proprietary rights enable him to claim any appreciation in the value of property representing the profit. However, in the majority of cases the fiduciary will be solvent, so there will be little advantage in asserting a proprietary claim. The fiduciary will be subject to a personal obligation to account for the profit received. The appropriateness of the imposition of a constructive trust where a fiduciary has received an unauthorized profit was defended by Lawrence Collins J in *Daraydan Holdings Ltd v Solland International Ltd*:

> There are powerful policy reasons for ensuring that a fiduciary does not retain gains acquired in violation of fiduciary duty, and I do not consider that it should make any difference whether the fiduciary is insolvent. There is no injustice to the creditors in their not sharing in an asset for which the fiduciary has not given value, and which the fiduciary should not have had.[306]

7 Defences to an action for breach of fiduciary duty

(1) Conduct authorized by principal

A fiduciary is not subject to an absolute duty of self-denial preventing him from retaining any benefits for himself. He will only be required to make restitution of

---

305 [2000] 4 All ER 385, at 398.

306 [2004] EWHC 622, at [86]. See also Goff and Jones, *The Law of Restitution* (6th edn, 2002), who argue at p 739 that *A-G for Hong Kong v Reid* should be followed.

unauthorized profits that were obtained without the consent or acquiescence of his principal. He will only be entitled to rely on such consent or acquiescence if he made full disclosure of the course he intended to pursue. In *Boardman v Phipps*[307] the House of Lords accepted that if Boardman had acted with the consent of the trustees and beneficiaries he would not have been in breach of fiduciary duty and would not therefore have been liable to account for the profits he had received.[308] However, he had failed to obtain the consent of one of the trustees,[309] and had not sought the approval of the plaintiff beneficiary. By contrast, in *Queensland Mines Ltd v Hudson*[310] a company director who had taken up an opportunity initially offered to the company was not held liable to account for his profits because he had acted after full disclosure to the other directors.

(2) Limitation

The defence of limitation in regard to an action for compensation for breach of trust was examined in the previous chapter.[311] It has proved more difficult to apply the provisions of the Limitation Act 1980 to actions against fiduciaries who have received an unauthorized profit, because the legislation does not make any express provision for such claims. Instead, provisions designed primarily with express trusts in mind have had to be interpreted so as to provide a limitation period for actions for breach of fiduciary duty and the concomitant constructive trusts of unauthorized profits which arise from them. The relevant principles have been considered and clarified by a number of decisions.[312]

It had been thought that no limitation period was applicable to an action for an account, as s 23 of the Limitation Act 1980 was thought not to apply to such a claim.[313] However, in *Coulthard v Disco Mix Club Ltd*[314] it was held that an action for an account against a dishonest fiduciary should be subject to the same limitation period as a common law action for damages, namely six years. The case concerned an agency agreement between a disc-jockey and a manager for the commercial exploitation of his beat-mixed recordings. It was alleged that the defendant manager had dishonestly failed to pay the plaintiff everything he was entitled to receive under the agreement. The central question was whether the claim was time-barred by the limitation period.

---

[307] [1967] 2 AC 46.   [308] Ibid., at 93, per Viscount Dilhorne.

[309] Who was, incidentally, suffering from senile dementia.

[310] (1978) 18 ALR 1; Sullivan 'Going it Alone—*Queensland Mines v Hudson*' (1979) 42 MLR 711.

[311] See above p 898.

[312] *Bristol and West Building Society v Mothew* [1998] Ch 1; *Paragon Finance plc v DB Thackerar* [1999] 1 All ER 400; *Cia De Seguros Imperio v Heath (REBX) Ltd* [2001] 1 WLR 112; *JJ Harrison v Harrison* [2002] BCLC 162; *Gwembe Valley Development Company Ltd (in receivership) v Koshy* 2004] WTLR 97; *Re Loftus* [2007] 1 WLR 591.

[313] *A-G v Cocke* [1988] Ch 414; *Nelson v Rye* [1996] 2 All ER 186; Stevens 'Too Late to Face the Music? Limitation and Laches as Defences to an Action for Breach of Fiduciary Duty' [1997] Conv 225. See above, p 900.

[314] [2000] 1 WLR 707.

Jules Sher, QC held that, applying s 36 of the Limitation Act 1980,[315] the claim founded on breach of fiduciary duty was subject to the six-year limitation period because it was an equitable jurisdiction equivalent to a common law claim of fraud. He explained as follows:

Now, in my judgement, the true breaches of fiduciary duty, i.e. the allegations of deliberate and dishonest under accounting, are based on the same factual allegations as the common law claims of fraud. The breaches of fiduciary duty are thus no more than the equitable counterparts of the claims at common law. The court of equity, in granting relief for such breaches would be exercising a concurrent jurisdiction with that of the common law. I have little doubt but that to such a claim the statute would have applied.... I am happy to come to what seems to be the sensible conclusion that no distinction in point of limitation can be made between an action for damages for fraud at common law and its counterpart in equity based on the same facts.[316]

Coulthard v Disco Mix Club Ltd concerned an action for an account but did not involve trust property because the defendant had not been obliged to keep the money in question separate from his own. Different principles apply where a fiduciary has held an unauthorized profit on constructive trust for his principal. In such cases the claim against the fiduciary may be regarded as analogous to an action by a beneficiary for breach of trust and so fall within the scope of s 21 of the Limitation Act 1980. In *Bristol and West Building Society v Mothew*[317] and *Paragon Finance plc v Thackerar & Co*[318] Millett LJ held that for the purposes of limitation it was necessary to distinguish between a fiduciary who had enjoyed a pre-existing relationship with the principal under which he had assumed the duties of a trustee, even though he had not been expressly appointed as such, and a situation in which a constructive trust of an unauthorized profit was only the response of equity in supplying a remedial formula for dealing with the consequences of a fraud. Where a constructive trust of an unauthorized profit arose in the context of such a pre-existing duty the limitation provisions of s 21 would apply, so that the action would be subject to a six-year limitation period, unless the fiduciary had acted fraudulently or dishonestly,[319] or retained the profit or its traceable proceeds in his possession,[320] in which case there would be no applicable limitation period. Where there was no such pre-existing duty the action would be subject to a six-year limitation period since s 21 would not apply. These principles were adopted and affirmed by the Court of Appeal in the more recent case of *Gwembe Valley Development Company Ltd v Koshy*, where Mummery LJ stated:

In the light of those cases, in our view, it is possible to simplify the court's task when considering the application of the 1980 Act to claims against fiduciaries. The starting assumption should

---

[315] While in *Nelson v Rye* [1996] 2 All ER 186 Laddie J, relying on the authority of *A-G v Cocke* [1988] Ch 414, had held that an action for breach of fiduciary duty was not subject to a period of limitation, Jules Sher, QC considered that the case was 'unsafe' because the possible application of s 36 of the Limitation Act 1980 had not been argued.

[316] [2000] 1 WLR 707, at 730.   [317] [1998] Ch 1.

[318] [1999] 1 All ER 400.   [319] S 21(1)(a).   [320] S 21(1)(b).

be that a six-year limitation period will apply—under one or other provision of the Act, applied directly or by analogy—unless it is specifically excluded by the Act or established case-law. Personal claims against fiduciaries will normally be subject to limits by analogy with claims in tort or contract... By contrast, claims for breach of fiduciary duty, in the special sense explained in Mothew, will normally be covered by section 21. The six-year time limit under section 21(3) will apply, directly or by analogy, unless excluded by subsection 21(1)(a) (fraud) or (b).[321]

The case concerned a company director who had received undisclosed profits from a contract with the company. The court held that his position meant that he had had 'trustee-like responsibilities' in the exercise of his powers of management of the property of the company and in dealing with the application of its property, and that therefore the claim for an account was within the scope of s 21. Since he had acted dishonestly in breaching his fiduciary duty, s 21(1)(a) applied to exclude the six-year limitation period and he was not entitled to any defence of limitation. Nevertheless, in *Statek Corp v Alford*,[322] Evans-Lombe J suggested that s 21(1)(a) could be relied upon against a dishonest assistant to a breach of trust, even though such person was not recognized as being a trustee by Millet LJ in *Paragon Finance* for the purposes of limitation. The case concerned a de facto director of a company, so that the observation was strictly *obiter*:

if I had not already concluded that a defence of limitation was not available to Mr Alford because he was a category 1 fiduciary but was to be treated as an accessory to the fraudulent breaches of trust of [the trustees]...I...would have concluded that no limitation period applied to Statek's claim against him as an accessory to that fraudulent breach of trust.[323]

This aspect of the decision has drawn criticism,[324] on the basis that it is against authority and principle.

The equitable doctrine of laches will be available where a claim to an account is not subject to a statutory limitation period, in which case it may protect a fiduciary from unduly delayed proceedings if it would be inequitable to allow them to proceed, for example because he would suffer substantial prejudice or detriment. However, there is debate as to whether the defence of laches will be available where s 21(1) of the Limitation Act 1980 applies. In *Gwembe Valley Development Co Ltd v Koshy* the Court of Appeal held that the defence of laches was not available as a defence to the action for dishonest breach of fiduciary duty, as the defence of laches was not available where s 21(1) applies.[325] This has since been doubted in *Re Loftus*,[326] where it was suggested that the equitable doctrine was not excluded under cases coming within s 21(1) of the Limitation Act 1980. Chadwick LJ, on reprising earlier authorities, concluded:

If the court were saying, in the Gwembe Valley case, that there is no scope for a defence of laches or acquiescence in a case where the 1980 Act prescribes no period of limitation, I would

321 [2004] WTLR 97, at [111]. See also *Cattley v Pollard* [2007[Ch 353.
322 [2008] EWHC 32.   323 Ibid., at [126].
324 Mitchell 'Dishonest Assistance, Knowing Receipt, and the Law of Limitation' [2008] Conv 226.
325 Ibid., at [140].   326 [2007] 1 WLR 591, at [41], per Chadwick LJ.

respectfully disagree; although, of course, if that proposition were binding upon me I would have no choice but to apply it. But the court did not say that in terms; and, because I think the proposition obviously wrong, I am not persuaded that the court intended to be understood as endorsing it.[327]

It would appear that Chadwick LJ's position is the better view.[328] The operation of the doctrine of laches was examined in detail in Chapter 29[329] in the context of actions for breach of trust.

---

[327] Ibid., at [40].
[328] It is cited with approval, for example, in Hanbury and Martin, *Modern Equity* (18th edn, 2009), at 708.
[329] See above, p 902.

31

Remedies against strangers to the trust

In some circumstances beneficiaries will be able to bring claims not only against the trustees, but also against third parties who have assisted in the breach of a trust, who have received trust property in breach of trust, or who have assumed the mantle of trusteeship by acting as a trustee in relation to the trust property. This is a complex and challenging area. Such problems occur because of the highly complex factual situations in which an action against a third party may be sought, and the difficulty of defining an appropriate legal test for liability so as to balance the rights of beneficiaries and third parties.

This chapter seeks to explain the nature of the remedies against third parties in context, demonstrating how they fit with remedies against the trustees explored in previous chapters and the proprietary process of tracing (explored in Chapter 32). The practical and legal difficulties of finding an assistant or a recipient liable to the beneficiaries of a trust will be explored separately to enhance understanding. Alternative remedies through the law of restitution will be considered, and this chapter ends by suggesting a structure to help navigate through the difficult issues presented by application of the equitable principles.

1 Introduction

This is an area that causes considerable difficulties in practice and for students. Third parties are liable, not because they are trustees of the trust, but because they have come into contact with the trust property, either through dealing with it or receiving it outright, or because they have been instrumental in contributing to a loss suffered by the trust. The factual circumstances are often highly complex instances of commercial fraud. The concepts of liability can be complex, and are not aided by a lack of clarity and confusion over the tests to be applied in the case law.

(1) Relationship to remedies against trustees

The previous two chapters have examined the remedies that beneficiaries may pursue against a trustee who acts in breach of trust, or in breach of his fiduciary duty.

However, if a trustee commits a breach of trust which involves a third party who was a stranger to the trust, either as a participant in the breach or as the recipient of trust property transferred to him in breach of trust, the beneficiaries of the trust may be entitled to pursue remedies against the stranger. The third party is termed a 'stranger to the trust' because he was not a trustee and therefore was not subject to any obligations prior to his involvement in the breach. It includes those parties who have normal business transactions with trusts, such as banks, and accountants.

Remedies against third parties may prove more attractive to the beneficiaries than their remedies against the trustee in breach. The availability of remedies against a stranger to the trust will be especially important if the trustee is insolvent, thus rendering direct remedies against him ineffective. While a stranger to a trust may be liable at common law in tort, for example if he provides the trustee with negligent advice,[1] beneficiaries may enjoy equitable remedies against a stranger who has wrongfully received trust property or wrongfully involved himself in the administration of the trust.

(2) Personal and proprietary remedies against strangers to the trust

Where a stranger is liable in equity to the beneficiaries of a trust, the beneficiaries may enjoy either personal or proprietary remedies. It is important to distinguish between them, as proprietary remedies relate to the property itself in the hands of the stranger and cannot survive the dissipation of the property, whereas personal remedies are against the stranger personally for their participation in receiving trust property or becoming involved in the administration of the trust (see Figure 31.1).

(a) Proprietary remedies

It is a basic axiom of the law of property that a third party who receives property subject to a subsisting equitable interest cannot take free from that interest unless he is a bona fide purchaser for value without prior notice of the interest. Since the beneficiaries of a trust enjoy the equitable ownership of the trust property,[2] it follows that, if the trustee transfers trust property to a stranger in breach of trust, the stranger will acquire the legal title subject to the beneficiaries' equitable pre-existing interests, unless he was a bona fide purchaser for value without notice thereof.[3] The beneficiaries' equitable interests in the trust property will be preserved and they will be able to claim the property in the stranger's hands as their own in equity. If the stranger has subsequently dealt with the trust property he received, for example by exchanging it for different property or mixing it with other property (whether his own or also

---

[1] See *Royal Brunei Airlines v Tan* [1995] 3 All ER 97, at 108.

[2] See Chapter 3.

[3] In the context of the equitable doctrine of notice, 'valuable consideration' means money or money's worth, and includes marriage consideration. The consideration need not be adequate and may be nominal. See *Midland Bank Trust Co Ltd v Green* [1981] AC 513, HL, where sale of land at a gross undervalue nevertheless would have been valuable consideration.

belonging to a third party), the beneficiaries will be entitled to assert their equitable interest against any assets in his hands which can be shown to represent the trust property originally received. Equity has developed a complex set of rules to enable it to determine whether any such property can be identified in the hands of the stranger, known as the rules of tracing. These rules and their application are examined in detail in Chapter 32,[4] but an example can be provided. In *Re Diplock*[5] the executors of Caleb Diplock had wrongfully distributed his residuary estate among various charities.[6] Since the charities were innocent volunteers, who had not provided valuable consideration, they received the money subject to the pre-existing equitable interests of the beneficiaries to whom it should have been allocated. His next of kin were therefore able to claim from the charities any assets that could be shown to represent the trust property by the rules of tracing.

If the stranger who receives trust property in breach of trust has disposed of it, so that no assets remain in his hands that can be said to represent the trust property, the property is said to have been dissipated. Once the trust property has been dissipated it is no longer possible for the beneficiaries to maintain any proprietary claim against the stranger who had received it. However, the stranger may still be subject to a personal liability to make restitution of the value of the property he had received in breach of trust.

(b) Personal remedies

Where a stranger has participated in the commission of a breach of trust, but has not received any trust property into his hands, it will not be possible for the beneficiaries to seek a proprietary remedy against him. Similarly, if a stranger did receive trust property, but it has been dissipated so that no traceable proceeds remain in his hands, the beneficiaries cannot enjoy any proprietary remedy. They will be confined to a personal action for restitution. If the stranger has only partially dissipated the trust property he received, or it is traceable into assets that have fallen in value, a personal action may also be preferred, as the stranger will be liable to restore the value of the trust property. The personal liability of the stranger who has assisted in the commission of a breach of trust or who has received trust property is by way of an equitable action of account. He is often said to be 'liable to account as a constructive trustee'. In effect, the stranger is held liable to account to the trust just as if he had been a properly appointed trustee, even though in fact he was not. In *Polly Peck International plc v Nadir (Asil) (No 2)*[7] Scott LJ described this remedy as 'the *in personam* constructive trust claim'. The personal nature of the claim can also be seen from cases such as *Re Montagu*[8] and *Lipkin Gorman v Karpnale Ltd*,[9] which are considered below. The equitable liability to

---

4 Together, in some circumstances, with the common law.   5 [1948] Ch 465, CA.

6 The executors acted under the mistaken belief that their power under the will to distribute the residuary estate amongst 'such charitable institutions or other charitable or benevolent object or objects in England' was valid. The court held that it was void, as it was not exclusively charitable.

7 [1992] 4 All ER 769, at 781.   8 [1987] Ch 264, [1992] 4 All ER 308.

9 [1992] 4 All ER 331, [1987] 1 WLR 987.

(i) The personal duty to account

(ii) Holding the property on constructive trust

Figure 31.1 The contrast between personal and proprietary claims

account as a constructive trustee is essentially fault-based, so that a stranger will only be required to account if he acted with the requisite degree of fault.

(3) Circumstances in which a stranger will be liable as a constructive trustee

The circumstances in which a stranger may be held liable as a 'constructive trustee' were identified by Lord Selbourne LC in *Barnes v Addy*:

those who create a trust clothe the trustee with a legal power and control over the trust property, imposing on him a corresponding responsibility. That responsibility may no doubt be extended in equity to others who are not properly trustees, if they are found either making themselves trustees de son tort, or actually participating in any fraudulent conduct of the trustee to the injury of the [beneficiary]. But, on the other hand, strangers are not to be made constructive trustees merely because they act as agents of trustees in transactions within their legal powers, transactions, perhaps of which the Court of Equity may disapprove, unless those agents receive and become chargeable with some part of the trust property, or unless they assist with knowledge in a dishonest and fraudulent design on the part of the trustees...[10]

More modern terminology is now used to describe the three circumstances in which a stranger will be held liable.

(a) Trustee de son tort

Where a stranger who had not been appointed as a trustee takes it upon himself to act as a trustee, and deals with the trust property accordingly, he will be held liable for any breach of trust that was committed just as if he were in fact a properly appointed trustee.

(b) Dishonest assistance in a breach of trust

Where a stranger dishonestly participates in a breach of trust committed by the trustees he will be liable to account personally as a constructive trustee for any loss suffered by the trust.

(c) Knowing receipt of trust property

Where a stranger receives trust property, knowing that it is trust property, he will be liable to account as a constructive trustee to the trust for the value of the property received.

(4) Implications of making a stranger to a trust liable

Lord Selbourne LC, in outlining the situations when a stranger would be liable as a constructive trustee in *Barnes v Addy*,[11] was principally concerned to stress the practical importance of setting limits to the scope of the remedies. The category of strangers is so wide that it would be inappropriate to impose liability without some element of fault on the stranger's part. Solicitors or bankers may temporarily be in possession of trust property as part of the normal process of trust management and delegation, but this does not necessarily mean that if their conduct is inconsistent with the terms of the trust they should be liable as constructive trustees, as where they honestly follow instructions from the trustees. Similarly, commercial companies may come into contact with trustees and trust funds as part of everyday commerce. They may make attractive defendants to beneficiaries in a breach of trust action, as they have deep pockets from which to meet a personal liability to account as a constructive trustee. If

---

[10] (1874) 9 Ch App 244, at 251–252.   [11] (1874) 9 Ch App 244.

all of these parties were liable for breaches of trust irrespective of knowledge or fault, they would be overexposed to liability, which could deter them from dealing with trust funds and inhibit the normal operations of trade or business. The protection of beneficiaries needs to be balanced by safeguards that do not hinder ordinary business transactions.

(5) The nomenclature of personal remedies

While the liability of a stranger to a trust has historically been termed 'liability to account as a constructive trustee' the language of constructive trusteeship has been subjected to criticism on the grounds of artificiality. In *Paragon Finance plc v Thakerar & Co* Millett LJ considered that it had been unfortunate that such liability was described in this way:

In such a case the expressions 'constructive trust' and 'constructive trustee' are misleading, for there is no trust and usually no possibility of a proprietary remedy; they are 'nothing more than a formula for equitable relief': *Selangor United Rubber Estates Ltd v Craddock (No 3)*[12] per Ungoed Thomas J.[13]

While this is certainly true in respect of the liability of a stranger who has dishonestly assisted in a breach of trust, it is questionable whether the criticism applies equally forcefully to the liability of strangers who have dealt with the trust property as a trustee de son tort, or who have knowingly received and misapplied trust property. In such cases the stranger is liable to account because of his conscious misdealing with the trust property. It is not artificial to regard him as a 'constructive trustee', and the language of constructive trusteeship is not operating as a mere formula for equitable relief.[14] Nevertheless, caution needs to be exercised when encountering the phrase 'constructive trustee'. In *Dubai Aluminium Co Ltd v Salaam*[15] Lord Millett suggested that the terminology 'accountable in equity' should replace the terminology 'accountable as a constructive trustee'.[16]

(6) A multiplicity of remedies

One of the difficulties in approaching stranger liability is placing the actions in context with the other remedies available to beneficiaries where there has been a breach of trust and trust property has been misapplied. The key to understanding is to recognize that this is not an action against the trustee for their breach of trust in dealing with the trust property improperly (which was discussed in Chapter 29), but an action which seeks to make a person liable who is not the trustee, but who nonetheless has come into contact with and misapplied the trust property. Similarly, beneficiaries may have an action against the trust property itself, to have the property or its substitute value

---

[12] [1999] 1 All ER 400, at 409.   [13] [1968] 2 All ER 1073, at 1097.
[14] See Martin 'Recipient Liability after *Westdeutsche*' [1998] Conv 13.
[15] [2003] 2 AC 366.   [16] Ibid., at 404 [142].

returned. This involves the process of tracing the property into the hands of someone other than the trustee (explored in Chapter 32). Any remedy as a result of the tracing process is directed against the property itself, rather than the person who currently holds it. This might be useful where the property is of unique value, such as an original Picasso painting, so that a remedy against either the trustee for breach of trust or against a stranger would not provide adequate compensation.

2 Stranger who takes it upon himself to act as a trustee

(1) Definition

A person who has not been appointed a trustee but intermeddles in the administration of a trust by taking it upon himself to act as if he were a trustee, will be held liable as if he were in fact a properly appointed trustee. He is known as a trustee de son tort. The principle was explained by Smith LJ in *Mara v Browne*:

> if one, not being a trustee and not having authority from a trustee, takes upon himself to intermeddle with trust matters or to do acts characteristic of the office of trustee, he may thereby make himself what is called in law a trustee of his own wrong—i.e. a trustee de son tort, or, as it is also termed a constructive trustee.[17]

The same essential characteristics were identified by Ungoed-Thomas J in the later case of *Selangor United Rubber Estates Ltd v Cradock (No 3)*:

> Those who, though not appointed trustees, take on themselves to act as such and to possess and administer trust property for the beneficiaries, become trustees de son tort. Distinguishing features...are (a) they do not claim to act in their own right but for the beneficiaries, and (b) their assumption to act is not itself a ground of liability...and so their status as trustees precedes the occurrence which may be the subject of a claim against them.[18]

The principle that an intermeddling stranger may become a trustee de son tort is an application to the law of trusts of the principle that anyone who takes it upon himself to act in a fiduciary capacity will be treated and held accountable as if he in fact held the fiduciary position he assumed. Thus, a person who takes it upon himself to act as an agent for another will be held liable to account to his principal just as if he had been properly appointed.[19] The principle was applied in *Blyth v Fladgate*,[20] where a firm of solicitors, Fladgates, held Exchequer bills that were assets of a marriage settlement. After all three trustees of the settlement had died, the moneys were advanced by the firm on a mortgage at the instigation of the husband. The securities proved to be insufficient and it was held that the partners of the firm were liable to make good the shortfall. The rationale for this was that when the Exchequer bills were sold, the

---

[17] [1896] 1 Ch 199, at 209.   [18] [1968] 2 All ER 1073, at 1095.

[19] See *Lyell v Kennedy* (1889) 14 App Cas 437, HL; *English v Dedham Vale Properties Ltd* [1978] 1 WLR 93.

[20] [1891] 1 Ch 337.

firm (meaning each and every partner) became a constructive trustee of the money. They could not possibly be seen as acting as the agents of the trustees[21] because at that stage there were no trustees. By their actions they had assumed upon themselves the position of trustees and it was their duty to see that the moneys were properly applied. They were therefore liable.[22]

One limitation to the principle seems to be that a person will only be held liable as a trustee de son tort if he had the trust property vested in him or had the right to call for its transfer. This was made clear in *Re Barney*,[23] where Kekewich J held that it was essential to the character of a trustee that 'he should have trust property actually vested in him, or so far under his control that he has nothing to do but require that...it should be vested in him', and that 'if that is true of a trustee properly appointed, why is it not also true of a trustee de son tort'.[24] However, it should be noted that he may be using the concept of a trustee de son tort in the wider sense of a constructive trustee, rather than the more limited modern usage of an intermeddling stranger.

(2) Remedies

In *Soar v Ashwell* Lord Esher MR took the view that an intermeddling stranger must be treated, and therefore held liable, as if he were a properly appointed trustee:

Where a person has assumed, either with or without consent, to act as a trustee of money or other property...a Court of Equity will impose upon him all the liabilities of an express trustee...[25]

The prime liability of the express trustee is not to act in breach of trust, and the trustee de son tort will likewise be held personally liable to account for any such breach. In particular, if he has wrongfully transferred or dissipated trust property he will have to account for it to the trust. As already illustrated in *Blyth v Fladgate*,[26] the partners of a firm of solicitors who had become trustees de son tort were held liable to the trust for the loss caused by an investment in a mortgage. If the trustee de son tort has trust property, or property which can be shown to represent the original trust property,[27] in his hands the trust will be able to claim that property as its own. This will be particularly important if the trustee de son tort is insolvent.

---

[21] A person who receives and deals with trust property as an agent of the trustees will not be held liable as a trustee de son tort when he deals with the property. In *Williams-Ashman v Price and Williams* [1942] Ch 219, Bennett J held that *Mara v Browne* [1896] 1 Ch 199, CA, was authority that 'an agent in possession of money which he knows to be trust money, so long as he acts honestly, is not accountable to the beneficiaries interested in the trust money unless he intermeddles in the trust by doing acts characteristic of a trustee and outside the duties of an agent'. Any liability will be governed by the principles concerning delegation: see Chapter 25.

[22] Following the explanation of the case by Vinelott J in *Re Bell's Indenture* [1980] 3 All ER 425, at 433–435.

[23] [1892] 2 Ch 265.   [24] Ibid., at 272–273.   [25] [1893] 2 QB 390, at 394.

[26] [1891] 1 Ch 337.   [27] See Chapter 32, where the equitable rules of tracing are examined.

3 Strangers who assist a breach of trust[28]

(1) Definition

Where a trustee commits a breach of trust he will be personally liable to compensate the trust for any loss suffered in consequence of his breach. His liability is a primary liability, as he was subject to the trust obligations. However, equity will also hold liable a stranger who participates in a breach of trust by assisting a trustee in action that constitutes a breach. The liability of such an assisting stranger is a secondary liability. The stranger is liable as an accessory to the breach of trust. Such accessory liability may provide the only effective remedy for the beneficiaries if the trustee is insolvent. Equity will hold a stranger who assisted a breach of trust liable to account as a constructive trustee. This was recognized in *Barnes v Addy*,[29] where Lord Selbourne stated that the responsibilities and liabilities of a trustee may be 'extended to those who are not properly trustees, if they are found... actually participating in any fraudulent conduct of the trustees to the injury of the [beneficiary] trust'. The rationale for the imposition of accessory liability against strangers to a trust was examined by the Privy Council in *Royal Brunei Airlines Sdn Bhd v Tan*,[30] where Lord Nicholls stated:

Beneficiaries are entitled to expect that those who become trustees will fulfil their obligations. They are also entitled to expect, and this is only a short step further, that those who become trustees will be permitted to fulfil their obligations without deliberate intervention from third parties. They are entitled to expect that third parties will refrain from intentionally intruding in the trustee–beneficiary relationship and thereby hindering a beneficiary from receiving his entitlement in accordance with the terms of the trust instrument. There is here a close analogy with breach of contract. A person who knowingly procures a breach of contract, or knowingly interferes with the due performance of a contract, is liable to the innocent party. The underlying rationale [of accessory liability] is the same.[31]

The accessory liability may prove particularly important if a misappropriation of trust property was perpetrated by a trustee in breach of trust and a financial institution, such as a bank, was involved in the transaction. For example in *Lipkin Gorman v Karpnale Ltd*[32] Cass, a partner in a firm of solicitors, had used money from the firm's client account to finance his gambling habit. As well as seeking a remedy against the club in which the money had been spent[33] the firm claimed that the bank at which the client account was held was liable as an accessory to the partner's breach of trust. The manager of the bank, which also held Cass's personal account, had been aware that

---

[28] See (1996) 112 LQR 56 (Gardner); A J Oakley, 'The Liberalising Nature of Remedies for Breach of Trust' in Oakley, *Trends in Contemporary Trust Law* (1996), pp 239–247; Elliott and Mitchell 'Remedies for Dishonest Assistance' (2004) 67 MLR 16.

[29] (1874) 9 Ch App 244, at 251–252.

[30] [1995] 2 AC 378, [1995] 3 All ER 97; (1995) 111 LQR 545 (Harpum); [1995] Conv 339 (Halliwell); (1995) 54 CLJ 505 (Nolan); [1995] RLR 105 (Stevens); [1996] LMCLQ 1 (Birks); (1996) 112 LQR 56 (Gardner); (1997) 60 MLR 443 (Berg).

[31] [1995] 3 All ER 97, at 103–104.   [32] [1992] 4 All ER 331, [1987] 1 WLR 987.

[33] See below, p 1004.

Cass had been cashing cheques at the casino and had warned him that his gambling was not controlled. At first instance it was held that the bank had sufficient knowledge of Cass's misuse of funds to render them liable to account for the money that had been misappropriated. The claim against the bank was, however, subsequently dismissed by the Court of Appeal[34] on the grounds that the bank had not been sufficiently aware that a breach of trust was being committed. Thus, there is a clear element of fault required on the part of the third party before constructive trusteeship is imposed, and it is in determining the degree of fault required that most of the difficulties have arisen in the case law.

(2) A personal remedy

A stranger who acts as an accessory to a breach of trust will generally only be subject to a personal liability to account to the trust for the loss suffered in consequence of the breach. Ordinarily he will not have received any trust property, and consequently the beneficiaries will be unable to identify any assets in his hands that could be the subject of a proprietary claim.[35] As has been noted above, it is highly artificial to describe the liability of a stranger who has assisted a breach of trust as 'liability to account as a constructive trustee'. Nor can his liability be characterized as genuinely restitutionary. Since he did not receive any trust property he was not enriched at the expense of the beneficiaries by his assistance. By definition, restitution is only available to reverse an unjust enrichment. This was recognized by the Privy Council in *Royal Brunei Airlines Sdn Bhd v Tan*:

> Liability as an accessory is not dependent upon receipt of trust property, It arises even though no trust property has reached the hands of the accessory. It is a form of secondary liability in the sense that it only arises where there has been a breach of trust.[36]

The extent of liability of the accessory is considered to be joint and several with that of the trustee for any loss caused to the trust.[37] However, where a profit has arisen from the breach, the stranger is only liable for his own share of the profit, not that of the trustee.[38]

(3) Requirements of accessory liability

A stranger will only be held liable as an accessory to a breach of trust if four requirements are satisfied. These requirements were identified by Peter Gibson J in *Baden*

---

[34] [1992] 4 All ER 409: on the grounds that the bank could not be liable to account as a constructive trustee unless it was also liable for breach of contract to its customer and that there had been wholly inadequate material on which to base a finding of fraud or dishonesty on the part of the bank manager.

[35] However, many of the cases concern banks or other financial organizations where the trust property has passed through their hands. See *Baden Delvaux and Lecuit v Société Générale pour Favoriser le Développement du Commerce et de l'Industrie en France SA* [1983] BCLC 325; *Lipkin Gorman v Karpnale Ltd* [1987] 1 WLR 987; *Agip (Africa) Ltd v Jackson* [1990] Ch 265.

[36] [1995] 3 All ER 97, at 99–100. This is considered further below under knowing receipt.

[37] *Ultraframe (UK) Ltd v Fielding* [2007] WTLR 835.

[38] See Ridge 'Justifying the Remedies for Dishonest Assistance' (2008) 124 LQR 445.

Delvaux v Société Générale[39] and subjected to significant revision by the Privy Council in *Royal Brunei Airlines Sdn Bhd v Tan*.

(a) The existence of a trust

A stranger can only be held liable as an accessory to a breach of trust if there was in fact a trust in existence. This requirement is generally uncontroversial, although some cases have extended the principle to other fiduciary relationships. *Royal Brunei Airlines v Tan* is a case involving a trust. The plaintiffs were an airline that employed a firm to act as their agents for the sale of tickets. Under the contract between the parties, the firm agreed to hold any money received from the sale of tickets on trust for the airline until it was paid over. The defendant was the founder and principal shareholder of the firm. In breach of the terms of the contract the firm, authorized by the defendant, used money received from ticket sales for its own purposes. On the insolvency of the firm the airline claimed that the defendant was liable to account as an accessory to the breach of trust that had been committed by the firm. In these circumstances there was clearly an express trust, thus opening the possibility of accessory liability. Cases which have extended accessory liability to other fiduciary relationships include *Selangor United Rubber Estates v Craddock (No 3)*.[40] The directors of the company were treated as having sufficient control of the company's property for an action as an accessory to be run against them. There may even be no need for there to be property. In *JD Wetherspoon Plc v Van de Berg & Co Ltd*[41] an action was brought in respect of allegations of breach of fiduciary duty by a company engaged to find new pubs for the Wetherspoon chain. The claims included allegations of accessory liability. Peter Smith J stated:[42]

> In my view in a case for accessory liability there is no requirement for there to be trust property. Such a requirement wrongly associates accessory liability with trust concepts...Accessory liability does not involve a trust. It involves providing dishonest assistance to somebody else who in a fiduciary capacity has committed a breach of his fiduciary duties.

In the event that he was wrong about this point, he was willing to find that confidential information could be treated as property for the purpose of the claim.

(b) A breach of trust

A stranger will almost certainly[43] only be liable as an accessory if a breach of trust was committed by a trustee or the fiduciary has broken his fiduciary duties. In *Baden Delvaux v Société Générale*,[44] Peter Gibson J had held that a stranger would only be

---

[39] *Baden, Delvaux and Lecuit v Société Générale pour Favoriser le Développement du Commerce et de l'Industrie en France SA* [1983] BCLC 325.

[40] [1968] 2 All ER 1073, see also *Adnan Shubaan v City Express Bank Lagos* [2006] 1 All ER 247.

[41] [2009] EWHC 639.   [42] Ibid., at 518.

[43] The cases so far indicate that there must be a breach of trust but, by analogy with the tort of interference with contract, there is no reason why a dishonest assistor could not be liable even if a trustee is protected by a valid trust provision excluding liability.

[44] *Baden, Delvaux and Lecuit v Société Générale pour Favoriser le Développement du Commerce et de l'Industrie en France SA* [1983] BCLC 325.

liable if the trustee had assisted in a dishonest and fraudulent design of the trustees.[45] In *Royal Brunei Airlines v Tan*[46] the defendant therefore claimed that he should not be liable as an accessory because the firm, which had misused money held on trust, had not acted fraudulently or dishonestly.[47] As was seen in Chapter 29, a trustee may commit a breach of trust innocently or negligently. The Privy Council rejected the defendant's argument and held that there was no need to demonstrate that the trustee had acted dishonestly or fraudulently.[48] All that was required was a breach of trust, irrespective of whether it had been committed honestly or dishonestly. A stranger will therefore be liable as an accessory if he acted with a sufficient degree of personal fault, irrespective of the degree of fault of the trustee in breach:

> what matters is the state of mind of the third party sought to be made liable, not the state of mind of the trustee. The trustee will be liable in any event for the breach of trust, even if he acted innocently, unless excused by an exemption clause in the trust instrument or relieved by the court. But *his* state of mind is essentially irrelevant to the question whether the *third party* should be made liable to the beneficiaries for the breach of trust. If the liability of the third party is fault-based, what matters is the nature of his fault, not that of the trustee. In this regard dishonesty on the part of the third party would seem to be a sufficient basis for his liability, irrespective of the state of mind of the trustee who is in breach. It is difficult to see why, if the third party dishonestly assisted in a breach, there should be a further prerequisite to his liability, namely that the trustee also must have been acting dishonestly. The alternative view would mean that a dishonest third party is liable if the trustee is dishonest, but if the trustee did not act dishonestly that of itself would excuse a dishonest third party from liability. That would make no sense.[49]

There is no need for the defendant to have known of the existence of the trust or to be aware what the concept of a trust in English law means.[50]

(c) Assistance in the breach of trust

A stranger will only be liable as an accessory if he in fact assisted the commission of a breach of trust or breach of fiduciary duty. Peter Smith J in *JD Wetherspoon plc v Van de Berg & Co Ltd*[51] observed that 'in most cases the breach can only occur as a result of the activities of the assistor'. In *Royal Brunei Airlines Sdn Bhd v Tan*[52] the defendant had authorized the use of trust money by the firm for its ordinary business purposes, including the paying of salaries and expenses and keeping its bank overdraft down. He had clearly assisted in the commission of the breach. However, where it cannot be

---

[45] This position was also supported in *Barnes v Addy* (1874) 9 Ch App 244 and *Belmont Finance Corpn Ltd v Williams Furniture Ltd* [1979] Ch 250.

[46] [1995] 3 All ER 97.

[47] The Privy Council held that, in fact, the company had acted dishonestly since the state of mind of the defendant could be imputed to it: [1995] 3 All ER 97, at 109.

[48] The Privy Council relied on earlier authorities to reach this conclusion: *Fyler v Fyler* (1841) 3 Beav 550; *A-G v Leicester Corpn* (1844) 7 Beav 176; *Eaves v Hickson* (1861) 30 Beav 136. In Canada it has been held that a fraudulent and dishonest breach must have been committed by the trustee: *Air Canada v M & C Travel Ltd* (1993) 108 DLR (4th) 592; *Gold v Rosenberg* (1995) 25 OR (3d) 601.

[49] [1995] 3 All ER 97, at 102.   [50] See *Barlow Clowes v Eurotrust* [2006] 1 All ER 333.

[51] [2009] EWHC 639, at [518].   [52] [1995] 3 All ER 97.

shown that the stranger has assisted the breach of trust, there will be no grounds for any accessory liability. In *Brinks Ltd v Abu-Saleh (No 3)*[53] the defendant's husband had couriered some of the proceeds of the Brinks-Matt gold robbery to Switzerland. It was claimed that the defendant had knowingly assisted in a breach of trust by accompanying her husband on his trips so as to give the impression that they were enjoying a family holiday, thus cloaking the illegal nature of his activities and making it easier for him to cross borders. Rimer J held that she had not in fact assisted the breach of trust, and that she was not therefore liable to account for the £3m her husband had couriered. He held that she had not participated in the breach because she was not party to the couriering agreements entered into by her husband, and he had carried out all elements of the couriering exercise. Her only role had been to provide him with company on the long and tiring drives. In essence, Rimer J seems to have held that a stranger will only be liable as an accessory if he participates in the breach by performing positive acts of assistance. Mere passive acquiescence in the activity alleged to constitute a breach of trust will accordingly be insufficient to establish liability. It is submitted that this reasoning is unduly narrow, and that a person should be liable as an accessory whenever his or her conduct passively encourages the commission of a breach of trust, provided that it was dishonest.

(d) Dishonesty

We have already seen that the equitable liability of a stranger as an accessory to a breach of trust is fault-based.[54] It operates as a species of equitable wrong, similar to a common law tort. Much of the debate over the years has concerned the degree of fault that must be demonstrated before an assistor will be held liable as an accessory. Prior to *Royal Brunei Airlines Sdn Bhd v Tan*,[55] this debate was couched in the language of 'knowledge'. In some cases it had been held that a stranger would be liable as a knowing assistor if he had participated in a breach of trust without any actual knowledge but in circumstances where he had been negligent in not realizing, or discovering, that he was assisting a breach of trust.[56] However, increasingly it came to be held that a higher standard of fault than mere negligence was required to establish accessory liability. In *Agip (Africa) Ltd v Jackson*[57] Millett J held a firm of accountants liable to account to the plaintiff company because they had knowingly

---

[53] (1995) The Times, 23 October; Stevens 'Delimiting the Scope of Accessory Liability' [1996] Conv 447; Oakley 'Is Knowledge Still a Prerequisite of the Imposition of "Accessory Liability"'? (1996) 10 TLI 53.

[54] *Twinsectra v Yardley* [2002] 2 All ER 377, at [107], per Lord Millett.

[55] [1995] 3 All ER 97.

[56] *Selangor United Rubber Estates Ltd v Cradock (No 3)* [1968] 1 WLR 1555; *Karak Rubber Co Ltd v Burden (No 2)* [1972] 1 WLR 602, *Rowlandson v National Westminster Bank Ltd* [1978] 1 WLR 798; *Baden, Delvaux and Lecuit v Société Générale pour Favoriser le Développement du Commerce et de l'Industrie en France SA* [1983] BCLC 325.

[57] [1990] Ch 265, [1992] 4 All ER 385; Sir Peter Millett 'Tracing the Proceeds of Fraud' (1991) 107 LQR 71; affd [1991] Ch 547, [1992] 4 All ER 451; Harpum 'Equitable Liability for Money Laundering' (1991) 50 CLJ 40; Goulding 'Equity and the Money Launderers' [1992] Conv 367; Nolan 'Knowing Assistance—A Plea for Help' (1992) 12 LS 332.

participated in the laundering of money defrauded by its chief accountant.[58] He warned against over-refinement of the shades of knowledge required to establish accessory liability and suggested instead that the assistor must have acted with 'dishonesty'.[59] This higher threshold for liability was adopted by the Court of Appeal in *Lipkin Gorman v Karpnale Ltd*[60] and *Polly Peck International plc v Nadir (Asil) (No 2)*.[61] In *Royal Brunei Airlines Sdn Bhd v Tan*[62] the Privy Council held that accessory liability was founded upon the dishonesty of the assistor.[63] Lord Nicholls explained why the requirement of dishonesty was to be preferred to that of knowledge:

> To inquire...whether a person dishonestly assisted in what is later held to be a breach of trust is to ask a meaningful question, which is capable of being given a meaningful answer. That is not always so if the question is posed in terms of knowingly assisted. Framing the question in the latter form all too often leads one into tortious convolutions about the sort of knowledge required, when the truth is that knowingly is inapt as a criterion when applied to the gradually darkening spectrum where the differences are of degree and not kind.[64]

In *Twinsectra Ltd v Yardley*[65] the House of Lords confirmed that dishonesty was the necessary condition for the imposition of accessory liability, thus affirming the decision in *Royal Brunei Airlines Sdn Bhd v Tan*.

(4) The test for 'dishonesty'

While it is easy to specify that the dishonesty of the assistor is the requisite degree of fault to establish accessory liability, it is more difficult to identify precisely what conduct will be characterized as dishonest, and whether the test is objective or subjective. In *Royal Brunei Airlines Sdn Bhd v Tan* the Privy Council gave some indications as to how the concept should be applied. The courts have struggled with this concept ever since, and the applicable test has been thoroughly examined by the House of Lords in *Twinsectra Ltd v Yardley,* re-examined by the Privy Council in *Barlow Clowes International Ltd (in liquidation) v Eurotrust*[66]and considered at length at first instance in *Attorney General of Zambia v Meer Care & Desai*.[67]

---

[58] While the Court of Appeal held that the lower negligence threshold was applicable, subsequent cases demonstrate that the approach of Millett J has prevailed. See also *Eagle Trust plc v SBC Securities Ltd* [1992] 4 All ER 488; *Cowan de Groot Properties Ltd v Eagle Trust plc* [1992] 4 All ER 700, at 754.

[59] Birks 'Misdirected funds again' (1989) 105 LQR 528.

[60] [1992] 4 All ER 409, [1989] 1 WLR 1340.   [61] [1992] 4 All ER 769, at 777, per Scott LJ.

[62] [1995] 3 All ER 97.

[63] *Royal Brunei Airlines v Tan* was followed by the Court of Appeal in *Satnam Ltd v Dunlop Hetwood Ltd* [1999] 3 All ER 652 and applied in *Cigna Life Insurance New Zealand Ltd v Westpac Securities Ltd* [1996] 1 NZLR 80.

[64] [1995] 3 All ER 97, at 107.

[65] [2002] 2 AC 164; [2002] 10 RLR 112 (Rickett); [2002] Con 303 (Kenny) and 387 (Thompson); (2002) 16 TLI 165 (Penner); [2003] Con 398 (Andrews); (2004) 120 LQR 208 (Yeo). See also *Barlow Clowes v Eurotrust* [2006] 1 All ER 333.

[66] [2006] 1 All ER 333.   [67] [2007] EWHC 92 (Ch).

(a) Dishonesty an objective criterion for liability

There has been much debate in the years since the decision in *Royal Brunei Airlines Sdn Bhd v Tan* as to the precise meaning of dishonesty, and especially whether it is objective or subjective in nature, and therefore whether the defendant must have been consciously aware that he was acting wrongly. In *Royal Brunei Airlines v Tan* Lord Nicholls was at pains to explain that dishonesty provided an objective criterion for assessment of the defendant's conduct:

Whatever may be the position in some criminal or other contexts   in the context of the accessory liability principle acting dishonestly, or with a lack of probity, which is synonymous, means simply not acting as an honest person would in the circumstances. This is an objective standard. At first sight this might seem surprising. Honesty has a connotation of subjectivity, as distinct from the objectivity of negligence. Honesty, indeed, does have a strong subjective element in that it is a description of a type of conduct assessed in the light of what a person actually knew at the time, as distinct from what a reasonable person would have known or appreciated. Further, honesty and its counterpart dishonesty are mostly concerned with adverting conduct, not inadvertent conduct. Carelessness is not dishonesty. Thus for the most part dishonesty is to be equated with conscious impropriety.[68]

He held that these inherently subjective characteristics of dishonesty did not mean that individuals were free to set their own standards. Honesty is not an optional scale, with higher and lower values according to the moral standards of each individual. Therefore, a person who knowingly appropriates a person's property will not escape a finding of dishonesty simply because he sees nothing wrong in such behaviour.[69] He considered that in the majority of circumstances there would be little difficulty identifying how an honest person would behave. For example, he stated:

Unless there is a very good and compelling reason, an honest person does not participate in a transaction if he knows it involves a misapplication of trust assets to the detriment of the beneficiaries. Nor does an honest person in such a case deliberately close his eyes and ears, or deliberately not ask questions, lest he learn something he would rather not know, and then proceed regardless.[70]

He also indicated that any assessment of dishonesty would have to be contextual, taking account of the circumstances of the transaction which constituted a breach of trust and the personal attributes of the assistor, including his experience and intelligence,[71] and that strangers should not generally be liable as assistors if they had acted negligently.[72] Strangers who owe a duty of care to the trust (for example, advisers, consultants, bankers, and agents) are liable in tort if they fail to exercise reasonable skill and care, and there is no compelling reason to impose any additional liability in equity.

(b) Dishonesty a subjective criterion for liability?

In *Twinsectra Ltd v Yardley*, the House of Lords subjected the comments of Lord Nicholls to careful scrutiny in order to identify the essential elements of dishonesty,

---

[68] [1995] 3 All ER 97, at 106.   [69] Ibid.   [70] Ibid., at 106.
[71] Ibid., at 107.   [72] Ibid., at 108.

and made comments that appeared to require a subjective awareness of wrongdoing on the part of the defendant. Lord Hutton identified three ways in which the standard of dishonesty may be applied, varying by whether the concept is viewed subjectively or objectively. First, dishonesty may operate as a purely subjective standard, 'whereby a person is only dishonest if he transgresses his own standard of honesty, even if that standard is contrary to that of reasonable and honest people'.[73] This purely subjective standard has been rejected by the courts; for example; in *Walker v Stones*, Sir Christopher Slade LJ considered that a solicitor-trustee would have acted dishonestly even though he held an 'honest belief' that his actions were in the best interests of his beneficiaries if his belief was 'so unreasonable that, by any objective standard, no reasonable solicitor-trustee could have thought that what he did or agreed to do was for the benefit of the beneficiaries'.[74] Second, dishonesty may operate as a purely objective standard, 'whereby a person acts dishonestly if his conduct is dishonest by the ordinary standards of reasonable and honest people'.[75] Finally, dishonesty may operate in a manner that combines elements of objectivity and subjectivity. Lord Hutton explained:

> Thirdly, there is a standard which combines an objective and a subjective test, and which requires that before there can be a finding of dishonesty it must be established that the defendant's conduct was dishonest by the standards of reasonable and honest people and that he himself realised that by those standards his conduct was dishonest. I will term this 'the combined test'.[76]

A similar approach had previously been adopted by Nourse LJ in *Heinl v Jyske Bank*,[77] where it was suggested that the defendant actually had to appreciate that funds probably had been procured in breach of trust, not whether he ought to have appreciated that they had been so procured. The majority of the House of Lords held that the combined test explained by Lord Hutton should be adopted as the standard of dishonesty necessary for the imposition of accessory liability. Lord Millett dissented in favour of the adoption of a purely objective test which does not require the defendant to have realized that he was acting dishonestly. In Lord Millett's view, the only subjective elements were findings of fact as to the defendant's experience, intelligence, and actual state of knowledge of the breach of trust. The subjective parts of the test were thus an evidential aid to deciding objectively whether a defendant had been dishonest.

(c) Understanding the difficulties of the subjective criterion

It is clear from Lord Hutton's speech that the impact of a finding that a professional person had acted dishonestly weighed heavily in reaching his decision, and his Lordship drew assistance from the test used to determine the *mens rea* of theft in *R v Ghosh*[78]

---

[73] [2002] 2 AC 164, at [27].
[74] [2001] QB 902, at 939. See Hunter 'The Honest Truth about Dishonesty' (2002) PCB 390.
[75] [2002] 2 AC 164, at [27].   [76] Ibid.
[77] [1999] Lloyd's Rep Bank 511.   [78] [1982] QB 901.

in formulating a subjective conception of dishonesty which required the defendant to appreciate that what he was doing would be regarded as dishonest by honest people:

Notwithstanding that the issue arises in equity law and not in a criminal context. I think that it would be less than just for the law to permit a finding that a defendant had been 'dishonest' in assisting in a breach of trust where he knew of facts which created the trust and its breach but had not been aware that what he was doing would be regarded by honest men as being dishonest...[79]

Lord Hutton was thus equating civil liability with a need for guilt, which it is suggested is too high a standard on which to make the stranger liable.[80] If Lord Millett's dissenting view of the test had been applied, then it would 'not be necessary that the defendant realized that his conduct was dishonest; it should be sufficient that it constituted intentional wrongdoing'.[81]

(d) The meaning of dishonesty clarified as a primarily objective criterion for liability

The test adopted by the majority in *Twinsectra Ltd v Yardley* was thus ambiguous, and open to a possible interpretation whereby a defendant would not be regarded as dishonest if he had acted dishonestly according to the objective standards of honest men, but had personally set himself a different standard of honesty such that he was not consciously aware that his conduct would be regarded as dishonest by ordinary standards.[82] In the light of this ambiguity and uncertainty the exact meaning and application of the test of dishonesty propounded by the House of Lords in *Twinsectra Ltd v Yardley* was clarified by the Privy Council in *Barlow Clowes International Ltd v Eurotrust International Ltd*.[83] The central issue in this case was whether liability on the basis of dishonesty required the court to conduct an inquiry into the defendant's views as to what the ordinary standards of honesty would be, so as to then determine whether he had consciously reflected that he was transgressing them. Lord Hoffmann stated that, although some of the comments made in *Twinsectra Ltd v Yardley* might have contained an 'element of ambiguity', they had not intended to be different from the principles stated in *Royal Brunei Airlines Sdn Bhd v Tan*.[84] Lord Hoffmann therefore explained that Lord Hutton, who had stated in *Twinsectra v Yardley* that a defendant should not escape liability 'because he sets his own standards of honesty and does

---

[79] [2002] 2 AC 164, at [35].

[80] See Thompson 'Criminal Law and Property Law: An Unhappy Combination' [2002] Con 387. See also Lord Millett in *Twinsectra v Yardley* [2002] 2 AC 164, who said that: 'Consciousness of wrongdoing is an aspect of mens rea and an appropriate condition of criminal liability; it is not an appropriate condition of civil liability' (at [127]).

[81] [2002] 2 AC 164, at [127]. Lord Millett's reasoning is explored below, at p 982.

[82] The Court of Appeal of New Zealand expressed obiter reservations about the subjective element of the combined test in *US International Marketing Ltd v National Bank of New Zealand Ltd*, 28 October 2003; Yeo '*Twinsectra*: New Zealand's "Reasonable Banker" Response' (2004) 120 LQR 208. Note, however, that in *Harvey v The Law Society* [2003] EWHC 535, Patton J, while purporting to apply the majority test in *Twinsectra*, instead seemed to apply a more objective version of the test by asking whether an honest person in the defendant's position would act as he did, knowing what the defendant knew.

[83] [2006] 1 All ER 333.   [84] [1995] 2 AC 378.

not regard as dishonest what he knows would offend the normally accepted standards of honest conduct',[85] had not intended to impose a requirement that the defendant must have had reflections about what the normally accepted standards were. He further indicated that his own comments in *Twinsectra Ltd v Yardley* that a dishonest state of mind meant 'consciousness that one is transgressing ordinary standards of honest behaviour'[86] were only intended 'to require consciousness of those elements of the transaction which make participation transgress ordinary standards of honest behaviour'.[87] They did not, therefore, 'also require him to have thought about what those standards were'.[88] The Privy Council therefore accepted the following statement of the trial judge as a correct statement of the law:

> liability for dishonest assistance requires a dishonest state of mind on the part of the person who assists in a breach of trust. Such a state of mind may consist in knowledge that the transaction is one in which he cannot honestly participate (for example, a misappropriation of other people's money), or it may consist in suspicion combined with a conscious decision not to make inquiries which might result in knowledge[89] ... Although a dishonest state of mind is a subjective mental state, the standard by which the law determines whether it is dishonest is objective. If by ordinary standards a defendant's mental state would be characterized as dishonest, it is irrelevant that the defendant judges by different standards.[90]

Their Lordships made no mention of Lord Millett's dissenting opinion in *Twinsectra*, though it is submitted that it is difficult to see any real variance other than in language between Lord Millett's statement of an objective test of dishonesty and that adopted by the Privy Council.

(e) The application of the criterion of dishonesty

In *Barlow Clowes v Eurotrust*[91] the defendant, Mr Henwood, had been one of the principal directors of an Isle of Man company providing offshore financial services, which paid away money that had been misappropriated from investors by Peter Clowes and one of his associates, a Mr Cramer. The Privy Council held that there was sufficient evidence to conclude that Mr Henwood had acted dishonestly. The evidence indicated that he had been made fully aware of the Barlow Clowes business, such that it must have come home to him that there was a real possibility that the large amount of money being put through the company could well be the investors' money. He also knew of previous dishonesty by Mr Cramer, and told lies in evidence, denying that he had any knowledge of the Barlow Clowes business and the money laundering transactions which passed through the company. In contrast, in *Twinsectra Ltd v Yardley* the defendant solicitor was held not to have acted dishonestly. The claimant lenders had advanced £1m to a firm of solicitors subject to an undertaking that the money would be retained until it was applied in the acquisition of property by the borrower,

---

85 [2002] 2 AC 164, at [36].   86 Ibid., at [20].
87 [2006] 1 All ER 339, at [16].   88 Ibid.
89 Citing *Manifest Shipping Co Ltd v Uni-Polaris Insurance Co Ltd* [2001] 1 All ER 743; [2003] 1 AC 469.
90 [2006] 1 All ER 333, at [10].
91 [2006] 1 All ER 33; Ryan '*Royal Brunei* Dishonesty: Clarity at Last?' [2006] Conv 188.

Yardley. In breach of this undertaking the firm of solicitors subsequently paid the money to Leach, another solicitor who was acting for Yardley in respect of the transaction. Leach then failed to ensure that the money was utilized solely for the acquisition of property in accordance with the undertaking, and Yardley used £358,000 for other purposes. At first instance Carnwath J held that the money had not been held on trust, and that Leach had not acted dishonestly, although he had been 'misguided'. While he had been aware of all the facts he had 'simply shut his eyes to the problems' and had considered it a matter for the other solicitors whether he could release the money to his client. The Court of Appeal reversed these findings, holding that Leach had acted dishonestly because he had shut his eyes to the rights of *Twinsectra*. The House of Lords held by a majority that Leach had not acted dishonestly. Lords Hutton and Hoffmann considered it unfortunate that Carnwath J had referred to Leach as having shut his eyes to the obvious, but considered that this alone did not render him dishonest. Instead, the crucial question was whether 'Leach realized that his action was dishonest by the standards of responsible and honest solicitors'.[92] The majority held that Carnwath J had not applied an incorrect test, and there was no justification for taking the exceptional step of reversing a finding by the trial judge on a question of fact, as he had had the advantage of seeing the party give evidence in the witness box. In *Barlow Clowes v Eurotrust*[93] the Privy Council affirmed the decision in *Twinsectra Ltd v Yardley*, but seemed to do so for very different reasons from those that had been given in the judgments. Lord Hoffmann explained:

> On the facts of the *Twinsectra* case, neither the judge who acquitted Mr Leach of dishonesty nor the House undertook any inquiry into the views of the defendant solicitor Mr Leach about ordinary standards of honest behaviour. He had received on behalf of his client a payment from another solicitor who he knew had given an undertaking to pay it to Mr Leach's client only for a particular use. But the other solicitor had paid the money to Mr Leach without requiring any undertaking. The judge found that he was not dishonest because he honestly believed that the undertaking did not, so to speak, run with the money and that, as between him and his client, he held it for his client unconditionally. He was therefore bound to pay it upon his client's instructions without restriction on its use. The majority of the House of Lords considered that a solicitor who held this view of the law, even though he knew all the facts, was not by normal standards dishonest.[94]

It is hard to avoid the conclusion that this is a re-rationalization of the decision.[95] The Privy Council appears to claim that the House of Lords held that Leach was honest because his conduct would not have been regarded as dishonest by the objective criteria of 'normal standards' for solicitors. In fact, the House of Lords repeatedly stressed that he was not dishonest because he had not subjectively realized that his conduct was dishonest by normal standards. Indeed, applying the test as stated by the Privy Council

---

[92] [2002] 2 AC 164, at [49] per Lord Hutton. See also at [20] per Lord Hoffmann.
[93] [2006] 1 All ER 333.   [94] Ibid., at [17].
[95] This has not gone unremarked—see, for example, Conaglen and Goymour 'Dishonesty in the Context of Assistance—Again' (2006) 65 CLJ 18, who suggest this is judicial 'sleight of hand'. See also Yeo 'Dishonest Assistance: Restatement from the Privy Council' [2006] LQR 171; Ryan '*Royal Brunei* Dishonesty: Clarity at Last?' [2006] Con 188.

to the facts of *Twinsectra*, it is hard to escape the conclusion that Mr Leach would have been held dishonest.[96] Since the rationale given for the decision in *Twinsectra* is dubious, it appears that the Privy Council in *Barlow Clowes v Eurotrust* has changed the test for dishonesty without admitting that the House of Lords had been mistaken in the earlier case.

(f) Further developments

The *Barlow Clowes* decision does not represent the final word. The courts have continued to grapple with the test for dishonesty. The reinterpretation of the dishonesty standard by the Privy Council in *Barlow Clowes* was applied in *Abou-Rahmah v Abacha*,[97] in which Arden LJ confirmed that all that was required to impose liability was the defendant's knowledge of facts and that he acted contrary to normal standards of honest conduct.[98] This case concerned money laundering. The appellants were victims of a fraud, having unwittingly transferred some US $1.375 million through an account at HSBC Bank in London to the City Express Bank in Nigeria on the instructions of fraudsters. These payments were made for the benefit of 'Trust International' (TI), which the City Express Bank thought was the beneficiary of a customer of the bank with an account at its local branch. Persons associated with officers of TI had led the appellants to make the payments by fraudulent misrepresentations and they disappeared with the money. One issue before the court was whether the bank could be liable for dishonest assistance. The local bank manager had been suspicious that the fraudsters might be involved in money laundering, as the method used was a common form of money laundering. However, there was nothing in the particular transactions concerned that was unduly suspicious. At first instance, the court found that the bank was not liable, as the manager had not acted dishonestly, despite his general suspicions about the fraudsters. This decision was upheld in the Court of Appeal. Lady Justice Arden, in considering the apparent contradiction between the *Twinsectra* and *Barlow Clowes* approaches to dishonesty, noted that in fact:

the *Barlow Clowes* case gives guidance as to the proper interpretation to be placed on it as a matter of English law. It shows how the *Royal Brunei* case and the *Twinsectra* case can be read together to form a consistent corpus of law.[99]

The test for dishonesty was comprehensively reviewed by Peter Smith J in *AG of Zambia v Meer Care & Desai*,[100] a case concerning a complex international fraud involving the corrupt spending of huge sums by the former President of Zambia and the actions of a solicitor in handling various tainted transactions through his client account. The judge thought that the issue was not as complicated as it had been made to appear:

---

[96] Mr Leach would also have been unlikely to escape liability under the old formulation of the test preceding *Royal Brunei v Tan*, as he clearly had actual knowledge of the terms of the undertaking.

[97] [2006] EWCA Civ 1492. See Lee 'Dishonesty and Bad Faith after *Barlow Clowes*: *Abou-Rahmah v Abacha*' [2007] JBL 209; Ruan 'Royal Brunei Dishonesty: A Clear Welcome for *Barlow Clowes*' [2007] Conv 168.

[98] See also *Statek Corporation v Alford* [2008] EWHC 32(Ch).

[99] [2006] EWCA Civ 1492, at [68].   [100] [2007] EWHC 952.

In my view when the cases are analysed the question of subjective/objective test is an over elaboration. All of the cases when analysed in my view actually determine that the test for dishonesty is essentially a question of fact whereby the state of mind of the Defendant had to be judged in the light of his subjective knowledge but by reference to an objective standard of honesty.[101]

Having considered the authorities, the judge concluded, following a formulation by Lord Clarke MR, writing extra-judicially:[102]

the test for dishonest assistance is 'an objective one, but an objective one which takes account of the individuals in questions characteristics. It is a test which requires the Court to assess the individual's conduct according to an objective standard of dishonesty. In doing so the Court has to take into account as to what the individual knew; his experience, intelligence and reasons for acting as he did. Whether the individual was aware that his conduct fell below the objective standard is not part of the test.[103]

It is worth noting, however, that on appeal, while the legal test applied by Peter Smith J was conceded by the appellant to be correct, the judge's application of the test to the facts was considered by the Court of Appeal to have been inadequate.[104] Much was made in the Court of Appeal of the familiar concerns over finding a professional person 'dishonest', and the impact that would have on their reputation and business. On the facts, the court was not convinced that the actions of the solicitor should be considered dishonest; they could simply have been explained as poor judgement. Thus, it is suggested there may yet be factual difficulties in the application of the test in determining the objective standard required for liability to be imposed.[105]

(g) The current test for dishonesty

While the matter cannot be considered to be entirely free from doubt,[106] the test for dishonesty now appears to be reasonably well settled. Using the facts of the *Desai* case, where money had been misappropriated, and it was alleged that Mr Meer had acted as an accessory, he would be liable if he:

either knew that the instructions which he carried out involved, in effect, handling stolen money, or he had a clear suspicion that this was the case which he chose to ignore...If either aspect of the test is satisfied on the facts, Mr Meer would be correctly characterised as dishonest. Plainly that would be so if he actually knew that his client had no right to require the relevant funds in the firm's client account to be paid out to the particular person or for the particular purpose for which he instructed Mr Meer to apply the money. Equally, if Mr Meer had a clear suspicion that this was the case and he deliberately decided not to enquire in order

---

[101] Ibid., at [334].

[102] 'Claims Against Professionals: Negligence, Dishonesty and Fraud' [2006] 22 *Professional Negligence* 70/85.

[103] [2007] EWHC 952, at [357].   [104] [2008] EWCA Civ 1007.

[105] See Halliwell and Proschaska 'Assistance and Dishonesty: Ring-a-Ring O'Roses' [2006] Conv 465, where it is argued that changing tests are unhelpful, as a determination of dishonesty can really only be made on a 'forensic examination' of the facts.

[106] For instance, counsel in the *Desai* case initially argued that Peter Smith J had applied the wrong test: [2008] EWCA Civ 1007 at [20].

to avoid having confirmation that it was so, that is properly characterised as dishonesty, of the kind often called blind-eye, or Nelsonian.[107]

A defendant will be held liable if he had clear reasons to be suspicious about a transaction, and consciously ignored these suspicions, even though he was not consciously aware that by so doing he was transgressing ordinary standards.

(5) **Alternatives to dishonesty as the criteria for accessory liability**[108]

While dishonesty has been firmly established as the touchstone for accessory liability in English law, other approaches have been advocated.

(a) Unconscionability

In *Royal Brunei Airlines Sdn Bhd v Tan*[109] the Privy Council considered the viability of unconscionability as a touchstone for liability but felt that it was either synonymous with dishonesty, or if not, that it was too vague:

unconscionable is not a word in everyday use by non-lawyers. If it is to be used in this context, and if it is to be the touchstone for liability as an accessory, it is essential to be clear on what, *in this context*, unconscionable *means*. If unconscionable means no more than dishonesty, then dishonesty is the preferable label. If unconscionable means something different, it must be said that it is not clear what that something different is. Either way, therefore, the term is better avoided in this context.[110]

(b) Knowing assistance

Lord Millett delivered a dissenting opinion in *Twinsectra Ltd v Yardley*,[111] rejecting the 'combined test' for dishonesty adopted by the majority in favour of a purely objective test. He gave three reasons for preferring such an objective approach:

(1) consciousness of wrongdoing is an aspect of mens rea and an appropriate condition of criminal liability: it is not an appropriate condition of civil liability. This generally results from negligent or intentional conduct. For the purpose of civil liability, it should not be necessary that the defendant realised that his conduct was dishonest; it should be sufficient that it constituted intentional wrongdoing. (2) The objective test is in accordance with Lord Selbourne LC's statement in *Barnes v Addy* and traditional doctrine. This taught that a person who knowingly participates in the misdirection of money is liable to compensate the injured party. While negligence is not sufficient condition of liability, intentional wrongdoing is. Such conduct is culpable and falls below the standards of honesty adopted by ordinary people. (3) The claim for 'knowing assistance' is the equitable counterpart of the economic torts. They are intentional torts; negligence is not sufficient and dishonesty is not necessary. Liability depends on knowledge. A requirement of subjective dishonesty introduces an unnecessary and unjustified distinction between the elements of the equitable claim and those of the tort of wrongful interference with the performance of a contract.[112]

---

[107] [2008] EWCA Civ 1007, at [20]–[21].
[108] See also Andrews 'The Redundancy of Dishonest Assistance' [2003] Con 398.
[109] [1995] 3 All ER 97.   [110] Ibid., at 108.
[111] [2002] 2 AC 164.   [112] Ibid., at [127].

In his opinion the adoption of such an objective standard for liability should lead to a return to the traditional nomenclature of the equitable claim as liability for 'knowing assistance':

For my own part, I have no difficulty in equating the knowing mishandling of money with dishonest conduct. But the introduction of dishonesty is an unnecessary distraction, and conducive to error. Many judges would be reluctant to brand a professional man as dishonest where he was unaware that honest people would consider his conduct to be so. If the condition of liability is intentional wrongdoing and not conscious dishonesty as understood in the criminal courts, I think we should return to the traditional description of this head of equitable liability as arising from 'knowing assistance'.[113]

It seems somewhat ironic that Lord Millett, who had begun the task of cutting the Gordian knot of 'knowledge' and replacing it with 'dishonesty' in *Agip (Africa) Ltd v Jackson*,[114] should now seek a return to the earlier terminology. It also appears to be self-contradictory to advocate abandonment of the language of dishonesty to avoiding slurring the reputations of professionals who have committed intentional wrongdoing, while at the same time stating that such intentional wrongdoing is 'culpable and falls below the objective standards of honesty adopted by ordinary people'. It is perhaps explicable on the wider impact of holding a person 'dishonest', which could have an influence on their general business beyond their dealings on a particular set of facts. It is also clear that this aspect of his Lordship's reasoning has not been followed in any of the subsequent cases.

4 Proprietary remedies for receipt in breach of trust

The prime obligation of trustees is to allocate the trust property to those entitled to it under the terms of the trust. If they misappropriate the trust property and transfer it to third party strangers to the trust they will clearly have acted in breach. However, if the trustees are insolvent, any remedy that the beneficiaries might be able to maintain against them for breach of trust will be useless as a means of restoring the trust fund. In such circumstances the beneficiaries may instead seek a remedy against the stranger who received the trust property. A stranger who has received trust property may be liable as a constructive trustee, and the beneficiaries may be able to pursue either proprietary or personal remedies against him. This section briefly considers the proprietary remedies available to recover the property in the recipient's hands. The ability of beneficiaries to trace trust funds into the hands of third parties is explored in Chapter 32.

(1) Proprietary remedies against a stranger who has received trust property

Where property is subject to a pre-existing trust, the beneficiaries are already entitled to the equitable ownership of the trust property. They enjoy a proprietary interest in

---

[113] Ibid., at [134].   [114] [1990] Ch 265.

the trust fund that is capable of enduring through changes in the legal ownership thereof. While the trustees are able to transfer the legal title to the trust property, mere transfer of the legal title does not defeat the interests of the beneficiaries. Thus, if trust property is transferred by trustees to a stranger in breach of trust, the beneficiaries may be able to assert a proprietary interest in such of the property (or its traceable proceeds[115]) as remains in the hands of the stranger. If the stranger is insolvent, any assets identifiable in his hands as representing the trust property will continue to belong to the trust in equity, and they will not therefore be available to satisfy the claims of his creditors.

(2) Applying the proprietary remedies

A stranger who receives trust property transferred in breach of trust will not gain priority over the equitable interests of the beneficiaries unless he was a bona fide purchaser for value without notice. The interests of the beneficiaries will therefore be preserved if the stranger was a volunteer who had provided no consideration in return for receipt of the trust property, irrespective of whether he was aware of the existence of the trust or not. If the stranger had provided valuable consideration, the interests of the beneficiaries will only be preserved if he purchased the property with notice that it was subject to a trust. In essence, the burden falls to the recipient of trust property to demonstrate that his conscience was not affected so as to require him to observe the trust. He will only be able to do this if he can satisfy all the elements of the equitable doctrine of notice.

(a) Stranger was a volunteer

A stranger who receives trust property as an innocent volunteer will hold it subject to the beneficiaries' pre-existing equitable interest, irrespective of whether he had knowledge that it was trust property. The beneficiaries will be able to demand that he returns it or its traceable proceeds. As Lord Browne-Wilkinson observed in *Westdeutsche Landesbank Girozentrale Bank v Islington London Borough Council*:

Even if the [third party recipient] is not aware that what he has received is trust property [the beneficiary] is entitled to assert his title in that property.[116]

The preservation of the beneficiaries' proprietary rights to the trust property is not therefore determined by the fault of the recipient, and it provides extremely important protection of their interests. In *Re Diplock*[117] the executors of a will transferred a testator's residuary estate to charities in the belief that valid charitable bequests had been made. As the recipient charities were innocent volunteers, who had provided no consideration in return for the gifts received, the Court of Appeal held that beneficiaries under the will were entitled to recover any trust property, or its traceable proceeds, remaining in their hands. Where the recipient of trust property was an

---

[115] See Chapter 32.   [116] [1996] AC 669, at 707.   [117] [1948] Ch 465, CA.

innocent volunteer, the beneficiaries' proprietary interests therein will be preserved in any asset identifiable in his hands by the rules of tracing, but he will not be subject to a personal liability to account as a constructive trustee. As Megarry V-C explained in *Re Montagu's Settlement Trusts*:

Suppose...a trustee transfers trust property to a person who takes it in all innocence, believing that he is entitled to it as a beneficiary...He cannot claim to be a purchaser for value without notice, for he is a mere volunteer. If when the truth emerges he still has the property he must restore it, whereas if he no longer has either the property or its traceable proceeds, he is under no liability, unless he has become a constructive trustee.[118]

As will be seen below, liability as a constructive trustee is imposed only if the stranger had received the trust property with the requisite degree of fault. The position of an innocent volunteer who has received trust property without fault therefore clearly highlights the dichotomy between the proprietary and personal remedies which may be available against a stranger who receives trust property.[119]

(b) Stranger provided valuable consideration

A stranger who acquires trust property for valuable consideration will still hold it subject to the pre-existing equitable interest of the beneficiaries if, at the time he acquired it, he had sufficient knowledge that it was trust property to affect his conscience. He is not protected by the equitable doctrine of notice and must yield priority to the beneficiaries. If he still possesses the property received (or its traceable proceeds[120]) he will hold it on constructive trust for the beneficiaries. The beneficiaries' equitable interests will be preserved if the purchaser acquired the trust property with actual, implied, or constructive notice of the existence of the trust. Such constructive notice includes notice of everything that he would have known about the property if he had made all the inspections and investigations expected of a reasonably prudent man of business.[121] As Millett J stated in *Macmillan Inc v Bishopsgate Investment Trust plc*:

In English law notice...includes not only actual notice (including wilful blindness or contrived ignorance, where the purchaser deliberately abstains from an inquiry in order to avoid learning the truth) but also constructive notice, that is to say notice of such facts as he would have discovered if he had taken proper measures to investigate them.[122]

This amounts to a negligence standard, so that a purchaser will be affixed with constructive notice if he negligently failed to realize that the property was trust property. It is important to note that, while this negligence standard of constructive notice is sufficient to prevent a purchaser acquiring trust property free from the equitable interest of the beneficiaries, it seems that it is insufficient to fix the purchaser with a liability

---

[118] [1987] Ch 264, at 271.

[119] See Birks, *Introduction to the law of Restitution* (1985), pp 411–412 and 439–447.

[120] See Chapter 32.

[121] See types (iv) and (v) of knowledge categorized by Peter Gibson J in *Baden Delvaux and Lecuit v Société Générale pour Favoriser le Développement du Commerce et de l'Industrie en France SA* [1983] BCLC 325. See also *Northern Bank Ltd v Henry* [1981] IR 1.

[122] [1995] 3 All ER 747, at 769.

to account as a constructive trustee for the property he received. As Megarry V-C observed in *Re Montagu's Settlement Trusts*:

one has to be very careful to distinguish the notice that is relevant in the doctrine of purchase without notice from the knowledge that suffices for the imposition of a constructive trust.[123]

Although the doctrine of constructive notice might seem to place a very heavy burden upon a purchaser of property to satisfy himself that it was not subject to a trust, in reality the extent of inquiries necessary to discharge that burden will vary with the nature of the property concerned and the circumstances of the transaction. While a purchaser of land is required to make comprehensive investigations into the title of the vendor, there has been a reluctance to carry a similarly onerous requirement into commercial transactions, where the speed of transfer does not permit such extensive pre-acquisition inquiries.[124] In *Macmillan Inc v Bishopsgate Investment Trust plc*[125] Millett J was reluctant to impose an onerous duty to investigate title to shares offered for sale when commercial custom and practice did not require close investigation of the transferor's title. He therefore held that banks which had acquired shares which were held on trust for the plaintiff, having been wrongly transferred as part of the attempt to support the ailing Maxwell business empire, were not affixed with constructive notice because they had not acted with actual knowledge or suspicion that the transferee was not the beneficial owner.[126] In *El Ajou v Dollar Land Holdings plc (No 1)*[127] he had cautioned that a commercial party was not expected to be unduly suspicious.[128]

(c) Stranger was a bona fide purchaser

Where trust property is received by a stranger to the trust who was a bona fide purchaser for value without knowledge of the existence of the trust (whether actual or constructive), the stranger will acquire the property free from any interests of the beneficiaries. They will no longer be able to maintain any proprietary claim to the erstwhile trust property (or its proceeds) in the stranger's hands, as equitable title has validly passed to the purchaser free from their interest. This does not affect the possibility of pursuing personal remedies.

5 Personal remedies for receipt in breach of trust

(1) Accounting as a constructive trustee for receipt in breach of trust

If a stranger receives trust property in breach of trust and subsequently dissipates it so that there are no traceable proceeds in his hands, the beneficiaries of the trust

---

[123] [1987] Ch 264, [1992] 4 All ER 308, at 324–325, citing the Court of Appeal in *Re Diplock* [1948] Ch 465, at 478–479.
[124] See *Manchester Trust v Furness* [1895] 2 QB 539; *Greer v Downs Supply Co* [1927] 2 KB 28.
[125] [1995] 3 All ER 747.
[126] [1995] 3 All ER 747, at 780–781. See: N Gegal, 'Cross-Border Security Enforcement, Restitution and Priorities', Ch 7 in Rose (ed), *Restitution and Banking Law* (1998), pp 112–119.
[127] [1993] 3 All ER 717.   [128] Ibid., at 739.

will not be able to pursue a proprietary claim against him. They may, however, be entitled to seek a personal remedy requiring him to return to the trust the value of the property he received. This remedy is restitutionary, in that it requires him to restore the enrichment he received at the expense of the beneficiaries, who were entitled to the property under the trust.[129] The stranger who received the trust property in breach of trust was thereby unjustly enriched, and is required to make restitution to the trust of the value of his enrichment, ie the value of the trust property he received.

If the trust property has been partially dissipated the beneficiaries may likewise seek a personal remedy in respect of the value of the property that has been dissipated. The remedy by which such restitution is effected is the imposition of an equitable duty to account as a constructive trustee. Equity requires a stranger who has received trust property to restore equivalent value to the trust fund if he has wrongfully dissipated it. His liability is fault-based and rooted in equitable notions of conscience. Unless the stranger was aware that the property he received was subject to a trust, he was entitled to treat it as his own, for example by disposing of it, consuming it on services which leave no traceable end product, or transferring it to others. His conscience will only be affected if he knew that the property was subject to a trust, in which case he will have become subject to an obligation to preserve it for the beneficiaries. As Lord Browne-Wilkinson stated in *Westdeutsche Landesbank Girozentrale v Islington London Borough Council*:

> Since the equitable jurisdiction to enforce trusts depends upon the conscience of the holder of the legal interest being affected, he cannot be a trustee of the property if and so long as he is ignorant of the facts alleged to affect his conscience, i.e. until he is aware that he is intended to hold the property for the benefit of others in the case of an express or implied trust, or, in the case of a constructive trust, of the factors which are alleged to affect his conscience.[130]

This seems to mean that a recipient of trust property will not be subject to a duty to preserve the trust fund unless and until he knew that it was subject to a trust. If he dissipates the property after becoming aware that it was trust property he acts in breach of his duty to preserve the trust fund, which is imposed by equity because he is a constructive trustee. He will therefore be liable to account to the beneficiaries. As was noted above, the language of liability to account as a constructive trustee has been criticized on the grounds of artificiality. While this criticism is admittedly accurate in the case of the liability of strangers who have assisted in a breach of trust, it is less justified in the case of the liability of strangers who receive trust property. Their liability derives from the fact that they held the property on trust for the beneficiaries and failed to carry out their duties as trustee.

---

[129] This was made clear by Megarry V-C in *Re Montagu's Settlement Trusts*, where he described the imposition of liability to account as a constructive trustee as imposing 'a personal obligation on a man' in contrast to the equitable doctrine of notice, which determines 'the burdens on property': [1987] Ch 264, at 272–273.

[130] [1996] AC 669, at 705.

(2) **Factual requirement of receipt**

It goes almost without saying that liability for knowing receipt requires the person charged to have in fact received the trust property, unlike the liability of a dishonest accessory, where receipt of property is not a requirement. What constitutes receipt in this context is not entirely clear. Some situations will be clear-cut. Where a casino owed money for a gambling debt is paid money which the gambler has embezzled from a trust fund, it would undoubtedly be considered a recipient for the purposes of liability if the other conditions are met. A 'fence' engaged in a money laundering activity by paying misappropriated cheques through his bank account would similarly be considered a recipient.[131] It would also be a sufficient basis for liability (if the other conditions are met) if the property could have been traced to the hands of the stranger if they had retained it.[132] A vesting of legal or equitable title in the recipient is not necessary, since having control over the property appears to be sufficient.[133]

In some of the case law, it is suggested that property must be retained by the recipient for his own use and benefit, so that an agent would not be liable under recipient liability.[134] Indeed, Millett J (as he then was) in *Agip v Jackson* suggested that a bank would normally not be liable under receipt, as they would be acting de facto as the agents of their customers.[135] The application of *Agip v Jackson* was doubted by Lord Justice Moore-Bick in *Uzinterimpex JSC v Standard Bank plc*,[136] but on the facts there was sufficient receipt, as the account in question the bank had set up was a transaction account to allow the recipient bank to claim fees and expenses, and was clearly for the benefit of the bank, not a customer. If receipt as an agent cannot give rise to liability, but receipt on one's own account can, there would be a difference between an auctioneer selling antique furniture held on trust and a second-hand dealer who buys and resells. The exoneration of agents from liability may unduly limit the operation of personal liability for knowing receipt, but in many cases there will be an alternative claim for knowing assistance.

The receipt of trust property does not have to arise from a breach of trust, as with liability as a dishonest assistor. The circumstances in which the action may arise were summarized by Brightman J in *Karak Rubber Co Ltd v Burden (No 2)* as follows:

cases where a person:

(1) knowingly receives trust property in breach of trust, or

(2) receives trust property without notice of the trust, and subsequently deal with it in a manner inconsistent with trust of which she has become aware, or

---

[131] See *Statek Corporation v McNeill Alford & Anor* [2008] EWHC 32.

[132] *El Ajou v Dollar Land Holdings plc (No.2)* [1995] 2 All ER 213.

[133] See, for example, *Karak Rubber Co Ltd v Burden (No 2)* [1972] 1 WLR 602.

[134] See *Williams-Ashman v Price & Williams* [1942] 1 Ch. 219, and, in support, *Twinsectra v Yardley* [2002] 2 AC 164, at [105] *per* Lord Millett.

[135] [1990] Ch 265. In fact, Millett J suggested that it was only where a bank reduced an overdraft that this was seen as them acting for their own benefit so that they could be liable for receipt.

[136] [2008] EWCA Civ 819, at [39–40].

(3) receives trust property knowing it to be such but without breach of trust, and subsequently deals with it in a manner inconsistent with the trusts.[137]

(3) Examples

The operation of the personal liability to account can be illustrated by four important cases. In *Re Montagu's Settlement Trusts*[138] the beneficiaries of a trust sought to render a stranger liable to account for the value of trust property he had received and subsequently dissipated. In 1923 the tenth Duke of Manchester promised to create a trust of the chattels to which he would become entitled on the death of the ninth Duke. The trustees were supposed to draw up an inventory of such chattels, but failed to do so. After the death of the ninth Duke in 1947 they released all the chattels to the tenth Duke, who disposed of a number of them during his lifetime. On the death of the tenth Duke in 1977, the eleventh Duke claimed that his estate was liable to account for the value of the items that had been sold. As the tenth Duke had received the chattels as a volunteer, he had received them subject to the trust because he was not a bona fide purchaser. His estate was therefore required to return any remaining chattels or their traceable proceeds. However, his estate was only liable to account for the value of the chattels that had been sold if the tenth Duke had sold them with knowledge that they were subject to the 1923 settlement. Megarry V-C held that, in the circumstances, the Duke had not known that the chattels were subject to the trust when he had disposed of them. In *Lipkin Gorman v Karpnale Ltd*,[139] Norman Cass was a partner in a firm of solicitors who used some £223,000 from the firm's client account to finance his gambling at the Playboy Club. The firm subsequently sought to recover the money that had been paid to the club. It alleged that the club was liable to account as a constructive trustee for the money received, which was no longer identifiable by the rules of tracing because it had become mixed with its other receipts. It was held that the club had not received the money with sufficient knowledge that it was subject to a trust to render it liable to account as a constructive trustee. In *Eagle Trust plc v SBC Securities Ltd*[140] the defendants had received some £13.5m from the plaintiff company through the fraud of its chief executive as part of the underwriting of a rights issue or cash alternative in the course of a takeover. It claimed that the defendants were liable to account for what they had received in equity because they had received it knowing that it had been misappropriated. It was held that the defendants had not received the property with sufficient knowledge to render them liable as constructive trustees. In *BCCI (Overseas) Ltd v Akindele*[141] the liquidators of BCCI claimed that an investor was liable to account as a constructive trustee for over $16 million, which he had received in performance of an investment agreement he had entered with a company controlled by the BCCI group, purportedly to buy and sell shares in BCCI, which was alleged to have been a sham. Although the agreement was not found to have been a sham, the payments were

137 [1972] 1 W.L.R. 602, at 632.   138 [1987] Ch 264.
139 [1992] 4 All ER 331, [1987] 1 WLR 987.   140 [1992] 4 All ER 488.
141 [2001] Ch 437.

held to have been procured in consequence of a fraudulent breach of fiduciary duty by directors of BCCI, and they were therefore impressed with a constructive trust. As such the investor had received trust property. The Court of Appeal held, however, that he was not personally liable to account for the trust money he had received because he had not acted 'unconscionably'. He had not been aware of the internal arrangements within BCCI that had rendered the payment a breach of fiduciary duty. These four cases clearly illustrate that the duty to account as a constructive trustee is a personal remedy, available against a person who has received property that he knew was trust property, with which he has subsequently dealt in a manner inconsistent with his duty to observe the trust.

(4) Fault required to render a recipient of trust property liable to account

There is currently a great deal of debate, which engenders inevitable uncertainty, regarding the requirements which must be satisfied before a recipient of trust property will be held personally liable to account for the value of what he received. In his dissenting opinion in *Twinsectra Ltd v Yardley*, Lord Millett asserted that the personal liability of a recipient was not founded upon fault:

Liability for 'knowing receipt' is receipt-based. It does not depend on fault. The cause of action is restitutionary and is available only where the defendant received or applied the money in breach of trust for his own use and benefit. There is no basis for requiring actual knowledge of the breach of trust, let alone dishonesty, as a condition of liability. Constructive notice is sufficient, and may not even be necessary. There is powerful academic support for the proposition that the liability of the recipient is the same as in other cases of restitution, that is to say strict but subject to a change of position defence.[142]

If this view were correct, then in order to avoid injustice, a narrow view would have to be taken of the circumstances in which a person is considered to be a recipient. However, these obiter comments are inconsistent with the tenor of the leading judgments of the House of Lords and Court of Appeal, which have consistently held that the equitable obligation to account as a constructive trustee for the value of property received in breach of trust is founded upon the fault of the recipient, and in only one exceptional situation have the courts found that liability should be strict.[143] As Lord Browne-Wilkinson stated in *Westdeutsche Landesbank Girozentrale v Islington London Borough Council*:

unless [the recipient of trust property] has the requisite degree of knowledge he is not personally liable to account as trustee.[144]

---

[142] [2002] 2 AC 164, at [105].

[143] Lord Millett has argued extra-judicially that recipient liability should be strict—see, for example, his comments in a book review 'Landmark Cases in the Law of Restitution' (2007) 123 LQR 159, at 164–5.

[144] [1996] AC 669, at 707. In support of this proposition he cited *Re Diplock* [1948] Ch 465 and *Re Montagu's Settlement Trusts* [1987] Ch 264.

In the four cases discussed above, this crucial element was found to be lacking, demonstrating how difficult it can be to establish entitlement to a personal remedy.

The most controversial issue in relation to the personal liability to account has concerned the degree of fault required to establish liability. It is clear that the level of fault sufficient to found a personal liability to account as a constructive trustee is not synonymous with the element of notice that will determine whether a recipient of property acquired it free from pre-existing equitable rights. As Megarry V-C observed in *Re Montagu's Settlement Trusts*:

> It should be remembered that the doctrine of purchaser without notice and constructive trust are concerned with matters which differ in important respects. The former is concerned with the question whether a person takes property subject to or free from some equity. The latter is concerned with whether or not a person is to have imposed upon him the personal burdens and obligations of trusteeship.[145]

A stranger may therefore receive property subject to a trust because he is affixed with notice thereof, yet not attract any personal liability if he dissipates the trust property.

(a) Degrees of knowledge

While some cases have indicated that liability can be founded upon the mere negligence of the recipient, or in very narrow circumstances that liability may even be strict, the majority of more recent cases have required a higher threshold of fault, which is consistent with the developments in the context of accessory liability examined above, where the Privy Council has stated that an assisting stranger will only be liable if he acted dishonestly. Many cases have addressed the requirement of fault in terms of the knowledge of the stranger who received trust property, and this terminology was utilized by Lord Browne-Wilkinson in *Westdeutsche Landesbank Girozentrale v Islington London Borough Council*.[146] A scale of the knowledge that a recipient might have possessed was provided by Peter Gibson J in *Baden Delvaux v Société Général*.[147] Having considered all the previous decisions, and drawing heavily from the doctrine of notice operating in the context of land conveyancing, including the definition of constructive notice provided in s 199 of the Law of Property Act 1925, he identified five classes of knowledge:[148] (i) actual knowledge; (ii) wilfully shutting one's eyes to the obvious; (iii) wilfully and recklessly failing to make such inquiries as an honest and reasonable man would make; (iv) knowledge of circumstances which would indicate the facts to an honest and reasonable man; (v) knowledge of circumstances which would put an honest and reasonable man on inquiry.

Although there is some correlation between knowledge and fault, equating the two is both confusing and misleading. Peter Gibson J's analysis shows that the concept of knowledge for these purposes includes not only facts that the recipient of trust property

---

[145] [1987] Ch 264, at 272–273, [1994] 4 All ER 308, at 320.
[146] [1996] AC 669, at 707.
[147] *Baden, Delvaux and Lecuit v Société Général pour Favoriser le Développement du Commerce et de l'Industrie en France SA* [1983] BCLC 325.
[148] [1983] BCLC 325, at 407, considered, at 408–421.

actually knew, but also facts that he could and should have known. In other words, someone would have knowledge if they failed to make such inquiries as an honest and reasonable person would make. Subsequent cases have sought to distinguish between knowledge of types (i)–(iii) and knowledge of types (iv) and (v). Whereas knowledge of types (i)–(iii) are rooted in some degree of conscious moral culpability on the part of the recipient, knowledge of types (iv) and (v) derive from his negligence or inadvertence. The question then becomes one of the degree of culpability required, rather than the extent of knowledge, although the link between the two remains. The majority of recent cases suggest that mere negligence on the part of the recipient should not be sufficient to give rise to liability to account as a constructive trustee, and that deliberate wrongdoing is needed. Putting this in the language of knowledge, the recipient will not be liable because of facts about which he ought to have made inquiries, but only for what he knows, pretends not to know, or refuses to know. Each of the degrees of fault that have been proposed as the touchstone for liability will be examined.

(b) Strict liability

It was noted above that there was one exceptional case in which strict liability was applied as the basis for recipient liability. In *Re Diplock*[149] the Court of Appeal held that charities which had mistakenly received money from an estate, because the executors had erroneously believed that a valid charitable bequest had been made, were personally liable to account to the estate for the property they had received, irrespective of the fact that they had acted entirely innocently. Liability of the charities was affirmed by the House of Lords.[150] The decision amounts to the imposition of a strict liability to account as a constructive trustee, and it has not found favour in subsequent decisions. Such strict liability has been confined to claims involving the administration of estates, or analogous circumstances. In *Ministry of Health v Simpson*,[151] Lord Simonds was careful to limit the principle to the administration of an estate. He started his judgment with a warning that it was 'important in the discussion of this question to remember that the particular branch of the jurisdiction of the Court of Chancery with which we are concerned relates to the administration of assets of a deceased person'.[152] He based his judgment on the principle stated by Lord Davey in *Harrison v Kirk*:

The Court of Chancery in order to do justice and to avoid the evil of allowing one man to retain what is really and legally applicable to the payment of another man devised a remedy by which where the estate had been distributed without regard to the rights of a creditor, it has allowed the creditor to recover back what has been paid to the beneficiaries or the next of kin who derive title from the deceased testator or intestate.[153]

He then extended this principle to the facts of *Re Diplock*:[154]

It would be strange if a court of equity, whose self-sought duty it was to see that the assets of a deceased person were duly administered and came into the right hands and not into the wrong

---

149 [1948] Ch 465.
150 *Ministry of Health v Simpson* [1951] AC 251.
151 [1951] AC 251.
152 [1951] AC 251, at 265.
153 [1904] AC 1.
154 [1948] Ch 465.

hands, devised a remedy for the protection of the unpaid creditor but left the unpaid legatee or next of kin unprotected.[155]

Subsequent cases have extended the personal liability imposed in *Re Diplock*[156] to circumstances analogous to the administration of estates.[157] In *Butler v Broadhead*[158] and *Re J Leslie Engineers Co Ltd (in liquidation)*[159] it was held that there was sufficient analogy between the position of the executor of an estate and the liquidator of a company to entitle a creditor to recover from overpaid contributories in a winding-up. However, the claim did not succeed in either case,[160] and there has been no general extension of the principle to all trust situations.

The strict liability of the recipients in *Re Diplock* was also ameliorated by a requirement that the claimants first exhaust their personal remedies against the executors who had wrongly paid the charities. The Court of Appeal stated:

Since the original wrong payment was attributable to the blunder of the personal representatives, the right of the unpaid beneficiary is in the first instance against the wrongdoing executor or administrator; and the beneficiary's direct claim in equity against those overpaid or wrongly paid should be limited to the amount which he cannot recover from the party responsible.[161]

As the court observed, this may mean that in some circumstances the whole amount will have to be recovered from the innocent volunteers, for example if the executors are insolvent, have acted under a court order, or are protected by s 27 of the Trustee Act 1925.[162] The strict liability imposed in *Re Diplock* has left the law in a state of confusion. The scope of the liability appears extremely limited if other remedies against the blundering executor must be exhausted first. It is submitted that the imposition of a strict liability to account as a constructive trustee is inconsistent with the equitable nature of the remedy. In *Westdeutsche Landesbank Girozentrale v Islington London Borough Council* Lord Browne-Wilkinson stressed that equity operates on the conscience of the owner of the legal interest,[163] but in *Re Diplock* the entirely innocent recipients of property, who had committed no wrong by disposing of it because they honestly believed that they were entitled to it, were required to account.

In reality the award of an equitable account in *Re Diplock* was a consequence of an inadequacy in the availability of common law restitution at the time that the case was decided. Until the decision of the House of Lords in *Kleinwort Benson Ltd v Lincoln City Council*[164] a plaintiff was only entitled to recover restitution from the payee of money paid under a mistake of fact,[165] but not of money paid under

---

[155] [1951] AC 251, at 266.   [156] [1948] Ch 465.

[157] See also Smith 'Unjust Enrichment, Property and the Structure of Trusts' (2000) 116 LQR 412.

[158] [1975] Ch 97.   [159] [1976] 1 WLR 292.

[160] In *Butler v Broadhead* the claim was barred by the Companies Act, and in *Re J Leslie Engineers Co Ltd* the creditors exhausted their claim against the liquidators.

[161] [1948] Ch 465, at 503.

[162] Trustee Act 1925, s 23 provides that the personal representatives may gain protection where they advertise their intention to distribute in the Gazette and a newspaper.

[163] [1996] AC 669, at 705.   [164] [1999] 2 AC 349, [1998] 4 All ER 513.

[165] See *Barclays Bank v W J Simms* [1980] QB 677; *Rover International Ltd v Cannon Film Sales Ltd (No 3)* [1989] 1 WLR 912, CA; *Lipkin Gorman v Karpnale Ltd* [1991] 2 AC 548, HL.

a mistake of law.[166] The executors in *Re Diplock* had paid money to persons they believed were legally entitled to receive because of their misconstruction of the relevant law, and would not therefore have been entitled to recover restitution on the grounds of mistake. However, now that the barrier preventing recovery of money paid under a mistake of law has been removed,[167] such beneficiaries would be entitled to receive restitution from the wrongly paid charities, but the charities would also be entitled to claim the defence of change of position.[168] Provided that the charities had acted in good faith, it is unlikely that they would have to make restitution of the money they had dissipated, since such dissipation would constitute a change of position. They would therefore only be liable to make restitution in full if they had not acted in good faith, which is tantamount to the introduction of a species of fault-based liability.

While the general attitude of the courts towards *Re Diplock* has been hostile,[169] so that it has been characterized as exceptional and its scope has not been extended, some academics have suggested that it should provide the paradigm for the availability of personal restitutionary remedies against a stranger who received trust property. Although this proposal has not yet been adopted, it is discussed at the end of this chapter.

(c) Negligence of the recipient

Some English cases[170] have held that a stranger should be liable to account as a constructive trustee if he received trust property with knowledge of any of the five types identified in *Baden Delvaux*,[171] including mere negligence. In *El Ajou v Dollar Land Holdings plc*[172] Millett J suggested, albeit obiter, that liability could be founded upon something less than dishonesty:

I am content to assume, without deciding, that dishonesty or want of probity involving actual knowledge (whether proved or inferred) is not a precondition of liability; but that a recipient is not expected to be unduly suspicious and is not to be held liable unless he went ahead without further inquiry in circumstances in which an honest and reasonable man would have realised that the money was probably trust money and was being misapplied.[173]

---

[166] See *Bilbie v Lumley* (1802) 2 East 469; *Brisbane v Dacres* (1813) 5 Taunt 143; *William Whiteley v R* (1909) 101 LT 741; *Sawyer and Vincent v Window Brace Ltd* [1943] 1 KB 32; *Avon County Council v Howlett* [1983] 1 All ER 1073, CA; *R v Tower Hamlets London Borough Council, ex p Chetnik Developments Ltd* [1988] AC 858; *Woolwich Building Society v IRC* [1993] AC 70, CA.

[167] The decision of the House of Lords to abrogate the distinction between mistakes of fact and law in *Kleinwort Benson v Lincoln City Council* [1999] 2 AC 349, [1998] 4 All ER 513 had been presaged in other jurisdictions. See: Judicature Amendment Act 1958, s 2 (New Zealand); *Air Canada v British Columbia* (1989) 59 DLR (4th) 161 (Canada); *David Securities Pty Ltd v Commonwealth Bank of Australia* (1992) 109 ALR 57 (Australia); *Morgan Guaranty Trust Co of New York v Lothian Regional Council* 1995 SLT 299 (Scotland).

[168] *Lipkin Gorman v Karpnale Ltd* [1991] 2 AC 548.

[169] See the comments of Nourse LJ in *BCCI Ltd v Akindele* [2000] 4 All ER 221, at 236.

[170] *Selangor United Rubber Estates v Cradock (No 3)* [1968] 1 WLR 1555; *Karak Rubber Co Ltd v Burden (No 2)* [1972] 1 All ER 1210; *Rowlandson v National Westminster Bank Ltd* [1978] 3 All ER 370; *Belmont Finance Corpn v Williams Furniture Ltd* [1979] 1 All ER 118, CA.

[171] [1983] BCLC 325.   [172] [1993] 3 All ER 717.

[173] Ibid., at 739.

In New Zealand the courts have held that knowledge of all five types identified in *Baden Delvaux*, therefore including negligence, are sufficient to give rise to liability.[174] Until the judgment of the Court of Appeal in *BCCI (Overseas) Ltd v Akindele*[175] it was generally thought that the criteria of negligence had been rejected in favour of a requirement of conscious wrongdoing. However, Nourse LJ, while rejecting the formulation of a test of liability in terms of 'knowledge' in favour of a generalized requirement of 'unconscionability', held that dishonesty was not a 'necessary ingredient of liability in knowing receipt'.[176] He approved those English and New Zealand authorities favouring liability on the basis of the lower threshold of 'constructive knowledge', which thus favours the adoption of a negligence standard.

It would almost certainly be wrong to interpret these English cases as accepting that 'mere' negligence will be sufficient to ground liability. The language of Millett J in *El Ajou* falls short of accepting that mere negligence would be sufficient. At the least he would have required that the recipient *ought* because of the circumstances to have been made suspicious. Similarly, it is submitted that, despite the suggestions in more recent cases, Nourse LJ in *BCCI (Overseas) v Akindele* did not suggest that mere negligence should be enough for liability; he cited with approval the statements of Megarry VC in *Re Montagu's Settlement Trusts* requiring conscious impropriety and did consider that an element of fault was necessary. Indeed, on the facts it was held that the decision of an investor to enter into an agreement with a commercial bank was to be treated as an 'arm's length business transaction'. The investor was not therefore put on notice that some fraud or breach of trust was being perpetrated merely because the agreement was artificial in nature and offered a high rate of interest.[177] Moreover, this view is consistent with other authorities in which negligence was held to be insufficient, which have not been overruled.[178] This accords with the view that commercial parties in particular should not be burdened by the imposition of personal liability for receipt of trust property unless they are at fault. Indeed, in *Cowan de Groot Properties v Eagle Trust*[179] Knox J pointed out that the duty of the directors of a purchasing company is to buy as cheaply as they can.[180] This, after all, fits the philosophy of profit: buy cheap and sell dear. In the view of Knox J, it would be unduly onerous to impose upon directors of a company a positive duty to inquire into the reasons for a sale to them at a bargain price. His view is supported by *Eagle Trust plc v SBC Securities Ltd*,[181] where Vinelott J emphasized that the doctrines of constructive notice had developed 'in the field of property transactions' and that the courts had been particularly reluctant to extend the doctrine of constructive notice

---

[174] *Westpac Banking Corpn v Savin* [1985] 2 NZLR 41; *Powell v Thompson* [1991] 1 NZLR 597; *Equiticorp Industries Group v Hawkins* [1991] 3 NZLR 700; *Lankshear v ANZ Banking Group* [1993] 1 NZLR 481; *Nimmo v Westpac Banking Corpn* [1993] 3 NZLR 218; *Springfield Acres (in liquidation) v Abacus (Hong Kong)* [1994] 3 NZLR 502.

[175] [2000] 4 All ER 221.   [176] Ibid., at 231.   [177] [2000] 4 All ER 221, at 237.

[178] See the cases under headings (d)–(e) in the treatment above.

[179] [1992] 4 All ER 700, at 761.   [180] Ibid.   [181] [1992] 4 All ER 488.

to cases where moneys are paid in the ordinary course of business to the defendant in discharge of a liability.[182]

There is therefore no real authority if favour of the proposition that 'mere negligence' is sufficient for liability. The lowest test suggested is that the circumstances should have been such that a reasonable and honest recipient would have made further enquiries.

(d) Conscious wrongdoing

The requisite degree of fault for the imposition of liability to account as a constructive trustee was examined by Megarry V-C in *Re Montagu's Settlement Trusts*,[183] the facts of which were considered above.[184] He held that the tenth Duke of Manchester should only be held liable to account for the value of the chattels sold in breach of trust if he had acted with 'want of probity'.[185] He considered that knowledge stemming from negligence would not establish sufficient fault to justify liability:

> knowledge is not confined to actual knowledge, but includes at least knowledge of types (ii) and (iii) in the *Baden* case... for in such cases there is a want of probity which justifies imposing a constructive trust... Whether knowledge of the *Baden* types (iv) and (v) suffices for this purpose is at best doubtful; in my view it does not, for I cannot see that the carelessness involved will normally amount to a want of probity.[186]

He referred to authorities decided prior to *Baden Delvaux*, where it had been held that negligence was insufficient to give rise to a constructive trust,[187] and emphasized that the requirement of 'knowledge' was essentially different from the concept of 'notice' used to determine whether equitable property rights had been defeated. Subsequent cases followed the approach of Megarry V-C. In *Lipkin Gorman v Karpnale Ltd*[188] Alliott J held that 'want of probity is the key aspect in the approach the court should take'.[189] This was affirmed by the Court of Appeal.[190] In *Eagle Trust plc v SBC Securities Ltd*[191] Vinelott J reiterated that in the context of a commercial transaction:

> to make a defendant liable as a constructive trustee, it must be shown that he knew, in one of the senses set out in categories (i) (ii) and (iii) of Peter Gibson J's analysis in *Baden*, that the moneys were misapplied.[192]

---

[182] Ibid., at 507.

[183] [1987] Ch 264, [1992] 4 All ER 308; (1986) 102 LQR 267 and (1987) 50 MLR 217 (C Harpum); [1987] CLJ 385 (Hayton).

[184] See above, p 989.

[185] This picks up the language of Sachs LJ in *Carl-Zeiss-Stifung v Herbert Smith & Co (No 2)* [1969] 2 All ER 367, at 379 that there must be an 'element... of dishonesty or of consciously acting improperly, as opposed to an innocent failure to make what a court may later decide to have been proper enquiry', and Edmund Davies LJ, who spoke of 'want of probity'.

[186] [1987] Ch 264, at 285. For a description of the types of knowledge identified in *Baden* see above.

[187] *Carl-Zeiss-Stifung v Herbert Smith & Co (No 2)* [1969] 2 Ch 276; *Competitive Insurance Co Ltd v Davies Investments Ltd* [1975] 1 WLR 1240.

[188] [1992] 4 All ER 331, [1987] 1 WLR 987.   [189] [1992] 4 All ER 331, at 349.

[190] [1992] 4 All ER 409, at 420, per May LJ; Jones 'The Gambling Fiduciary, the Casino and the Bank' [1990] CLJ 17.

[191] [1992] 4 All ER 488, [1991] BCLC 438.

[192] [1991] BCLC 438, at 509.

In *Cowan de Groot Properties v Eagle Trust*[193] Knox J similarly held that it was essential for a plaintiff to demonstrate that the recipient of trust property had knowledge within categories (i), (ii), and (iii).[194] *Re Montagu* was also endorsed by Lord Browne-Wilkinson in *Westdeutsche Landesbank Girozentrale v Islington London Borough Council*[195] and by Knox J in *Hillsdown Holdings plc v Pensions Ombudsman.*[196]

(e) Dishonesty

While *Re Montagu* held that liability to account as a constructive trustee would only be imposed against a conscious wrongdoer, the standard of liability could also be expressed as a requirement of dishonesty. In *Agip (Africa) Ltd v Jackson*[197] Millett J warned against an 'over refinement or a too ready assumption that categories (iv) and (v) are necessarily cases of constructive notice only' and suggested that the 'true distinction is between honesty and dishonesty', which is essentially a jury question.[198] As was discussed above, in the context of liability of a stranger as an accessory to a breach of trust, the Privy Council has adopted dishonesty as the touchstone of liability in preference to knowledge.[199] In the context of the liability of a recipient of trust property, it is arguable that dishonesty is synonymous with the want of probity identified in *Re Montagu*. Both terms were used by the Court of Appeal in *Carl-Zeiss-Stifung v Herbert Smith & Co (No 2)*.[200] More recently, the requirement of dishonesty was applied by the Court of Appeal in *Twinsectra Ltd v Yardley*.[201] As was noted above, the requirement of dishonesty was rejected by the Court of Appeal in *BCCI (Overseas) v Akindele* in favour of a requirement of 'unconscionability' which might encompass elements of constructive notice. Although Nourse LJ rejected the language of dishonesty, he did accept that at least some degree of fault would be required to render it unconscionable for the defendant to retain the benefit he had received, and it is very difficult to determine where this line is to be drawn. At all events, it is clear that no personal liability to account can be maintained against an innocent recipient who has received trust property, except in the anomalous situations where *Re Diplock* may still apply.

(f) Unconscionability

The determination of an appropriate standard of personal liability applicable to a stranger who has received trust property has been bedevilled by terminological debates. In *BCCI (Overseas) v Akindele*[202] the Court of Appeal sought to cut through

---

[193] [1992] 4 All ER 700.

[194] Ibid., at 760. He also held that if it was necessary to have regard to knowledge of types (iv) and (v) that there still was no knowledge on the facts.

[195] [1996] AC 669, at 707. See also *Hillsdown Holdings plc v Pensions Ombudsman* [1997] 1 All ER 862.

[196] [1997] 1 All ER 862, at 902.–903.   [197] [1990] Ch 265, [1992] 4 All ER 305, at 405.

[198] See also *Metall und Rohstoff AG v Donaldson Lufkin & Jenrette Inc* [1990] 1 QB 391, at 474; *Polly Peck International plc v Nadir (No 2)* [1992] 4 All ER 769, at 781–782.

[199] *Royal Brunei Airlines v Tan* [1995] 3 All ER 97; *Barlow Clowes v Eurotrust* [2006] 1 All ER 333.

[200] [1969] 2 All ER 367.   [201] [1999] Lloyd's Rep Bank 438; (2000) 59 CLJ 444 (D. Fox).

[202] [2000] 4 All ER 221; Stevens 'No New Landmark—An Unconscionable Mess in Knowing Receipt' [2001] RLR 99.

this Gordian knot by means of the introduction of a new test of 'unconscionability'.[203] Nourse LJ rejected previous attempts to provide a categorization of different types of knowledge or notice and proposed a new generalized test of liability:

I have come to the view that, just as there is now a single test of dishonesty for knowing assistance, so ought there to be a single test of knowledge for knowing receipt. The recipient's state of knowledge must be such as to make it unconscionable for him to retain the benefit of the receipt.[204]

However, it must be questioned whether this new approach provides a more comprehensible means of determining liability. The use of the test of unconscionability has been eschewed in other areas because of its vague and uncertain meaning. It fails to resolve the significant question whether 'conscious wrongdoing', as understood by Megarry VC in *Re Montagu's Settlement Trusts*,[205] is required for a successful action, or whether some species of negligence is sufficient to found a claim. The adoption of unconscionability as the test indeed reopens the possibility that something akin to negligence on behalf of the recipient may well be sufficient to impose liability. To put it in other language, there may be times when it is unconscionable for the recipient to receive the trust property, not because of what he knew or ought to have known, but because of what could have been discovered had the transaction been conducted differently and a different range of information had been disclosed. The test could even conceivably make liability appropriate in other circumstances where there is no kind of knowledge whatsoever, but where the recipient can be considered, for instance, to have been unfairly enriched.

Nourse LJ himself noted that the test of unconscionability would not avoid 'difficulties of application', although he felt that it would 'avoid those difficulties of definition and allocation to which the previous categorizations have led'.[206] While Nourse LJ appears to acknowledge the difficulties associated with the adoption of 'knowledge' as a criterion for liability, he reintroduces them by requiring the court to determine if the recipient's 'state of knowledge' would render it unconscionable to retain the benefit. Moreover, it is difficult to see how the test of unconscionability differs from that of dishonesty in practice, particularly as Nourse LJ found on the facts that the investor had not acted 'unconscionably' on the basis that he had not acted dishonestly.[207] If it is different in a substantive sense, as Nourse LJ clearly intended by dismissing dishonesty as an essential ingredient of recipient liability as we have seen above in the discussion of negligence, Nourse LJ gives no guidance as to what that difference is. This gives considerable weight to Lord Nicholls' assertion in *Royal Brunei Airlines v Tan* that 'if unconscionable means something different, it must be said that it is not clear what that something different is'.[208] At best, what this seems to create is a value judgment for the court, based upon individual facts, because the vague concept of 'unconscionability' is so malleable. If it involves concepts of dishonesty, it is submitted it would be better

---

[203] See, Barkehall '"Goodbye" Knowing Receipt. "Hello" Unconscientious Receipt' (2001) 21(2) OJLS 239.
[204] [2000] 4 All ER 221, at 235.   [205] [1987] Ch 264.   [206] [2000] 4 All ER 221, at 236.
[207] Ibid., at 238.   [208] [1995] 3 All ER 97, at 108.

to use a test of dishonesty and have a single measure of liability for both categories of the personal liability of strangers to the trust. There would also be clear limits, understandable by both the courts and recipients, as to when personal liability may be imposed for improper receipt of trust property.

Nevertheless, the application of 'unconscionability' to provide the requisite fault for imposing liability has been followed (even if only because the court is compelled to follow the decision of a higher court). In *City Index Ltd v Gawler*, Carnwarth LJ and Mummery LJ were of the view that:

In this court also it is accepted that *Akindele* represents the present law. Accordingly liability for 'knowing receipt' depends on the defendant having sufficient knowledge of the circumstances of the payment to make it 'unconscionable' for him to retain the benefit or pay it away for his own purposes.[209]

Since the recipient in this case, City Index Ltd, was on the assumed facts aware that that the monies it received had been procured in breach of trust or fiduciary duty by an employee of the claimant, there was no need for the limits of the test to be explored.

In *Independent Trustee Services Ltd v GP Noble Trustees Ltd & Ors*,[210] a freezing order had been made to protect pension funds which had been improperly invested, a contributing factor being the alleged dishonesty of two directors. Lewison J had to deal with an application to vary the order on the application of a defendant company that had received some of the funds and wanted a relaxation to enable it to pay for its legal defence. Without stating what the test was, Lewison J expressed his view that there was an arguable case that the defendant had been dishonest, but added that 'It is also clear from *BCCI v Akindele* that a lower threshold than dishonesty will suffice to impose liability for knowing receipt'.[211] He considered that the recipient could well be liable for failing to make further enquiries on the constraints on the investment powers, as that 'may well amount to notice'.[212] The recipient should also have been alerted to issues over the terms of the bonds which made them questionable investments, and should not have relied solely on the assertions of the trustee. It was suggested that such manifestly bad investments 'may themselves amount to notice of a breach of trust'.[213] This is an interesting application of the requirements of fault, and does suggest that negligence will be sufficient to impose liability on the recipient. It is also noteworthy that the language used throughout the judgment of Lewison J is couched in terms of 'notice'; a return to the language used in the cases before *Re Montagu's Settlement Trusts*. It is not clear how this adds to any suggestion of how unconscionability works as a separate concept of liability.

(g) Personal attributes

In *Re Clasper Group Services Ltd*[214] it was held that in determining whether a defendant had the requisite knowledge to justify the imposition of liability to account as

---

[209] [2008] Ch 313 (CA). Mummery LJ did not give a separate opinion, but agreed with Carnwarth LJ. Arden LJ seemed to consider the case to be one of unjust enrichment.
[210] [2009] EWHC 161 (Ch).   [211] Ibid., at [16].   [212] Ibid.   [213] Ibid., at [17].
[214] [1989] BCLC 143.

a constructive trustee the court must take his personal 'attributes'[215] into account. Whereas a mature and experienced person might be held to have had sufficient knowledge, an innocent and inexperienced person might not. The case concerned a boy employed by his father's company who was given a cheque for £2,000 by his father a month before the company went into voluntary liquidation. He paid it into his bank account and then lent £3,000 from the account to another company that his father had acquired. Warner J held that, bearing in mind the youth of the boy,[216] the fact that his only experience was his work in a lowly position for a group of companies owned by his father, and the fact that he was not particularly intelligent, he did not have sufficient knowledge affecting his conscience to justify the imposition of a constructive trust. In *Royal Brunei Airlines Sdn Bhd v Tan*[217] the Privy Council likewise held that in determining whether a person had acted dishonestly the court should have regard to the personal attributes of the person concerned, including his experience and intelligence.

(h) Commercial transactions

In *Eagle Trust plc v SBC Securities Ltd*,[218] Vinelott J held that the level of enquiry that purchasers of land are expected to make should not be transposed to other types of business deal. He applied instead the criterion of whether there was commercially unacceptable conduct in the particular context involved, an approach approved in *Royal Brunei Airlines v Tan*.[219]

(i) Time of knowledge or fault

A recipient of trust property will only be held liable to account as a constructive trustee if he had the requisite level of knowledge or fault when he received it or disposed of it. A recipient of trust property will not therefore be liable to account if he had been aware of the existence of the trust before he received the property, but had honestly forgotten that it was subject to a trust at the time that it was received. Thus, in *Re Montagu's Settlement Trusts*[220] Megarry V-C held that the tenth Duke of Manchester was not liable to account for the value of the trust chattels he had received because he had not been aware of the existence of the trust at the date that he had received them. He explained:

> If a person once has clear and distinct knowledge of some fact, is he treated as knowing that fact for the rest of his life, even after he has genuinely forgotten all about it? ... it seems to me that a person should not be said to have knowledge of a fact that he once knew if at the time in question he has genuinely forgotten all about it, so that it could not be said to operate on his mind any longer.[221]

He suggested a cautious approach, stating that the court should be slow to conclude that what was once known had been forgotten. Conversely, a stranger who received property without any awareness that it was subject to the trust, but without having given value for it, will still be held liable to account as a constructive trustee if he

---

215 Following Lawson J in *International Sales and Agencies Ltd v Marcus* [1982] 3 All ER 551, at 558.
216 Who was 17.   217 [1995] 3 All ER 97, at 107.   218 [1992] 4 All ER 488.
219 [1995] 3 All ER 97, at 107.   220 [1987] Ch 264.   221 [1987] Ch 264, at 284.

subsequently disposed of it after having become aware that it was trust property.[222] This follows from the comment of Lord Browne-Wilkinson in *Westdeutsche Landesbank Girozentrale v Islington London Borough Council*[223] that a person is liable as a trustee from such time as he becomes aware that it was intended to be held on trust.[224] He will not be liable to account for any part of such property dissipated before he became aware of the trust, as his conduct would not, to that extent, have been dishonest. Nor will he be liable, despite subsequent knowledge if, at the time of acquiring the property, he was a bona fide purchaser for value without notice.[225]

(j) Conclusion

It cannot be said that the test for liability for 'knowing receipt' is clear. There remains much confusion between knowledge, notice, and fault, none of which is resolved by the use of the inherently vague notion of unconscionability. There does appear to be a need for some level of fault, which at the very least is a failure to enquire further when the circumstances reasonably give cause to be suspicious. There may even be a need for conscious wrongdoing. The courts have, however, been hampered by two considerations: a desire not to hinder trade or business by setting too low a threshold of what should make a recipient suspicious; and a desire not to taint professionals with the badge of having acted fraudulently. These two considerations point in opposite directions and the courts have as yet been unable to find a way of expressing intelligibly where the middle ground is to be found. The task is complicated further by an occasional difficulty in determining the boundaries between knowing receipt, dishonest assistance, and restitutionary claims.[226]

(5) Restitution:[227] an alternative approach to recipients of trust property

(a) Restitution and the receipt of trust property

Restitution is a technical term describing the remedy by which a defendant is required to return to a plaintiff the amount of an enrichment he received at the plaintiff's

---

[222] See *Karak Rubber Co Ltd v Burden (No 2)* [1972] 1 WLR 602, at 632, per Brightman J.

[223] [1996] AC 669, at 705.

[224] See *Sheridan v Joyce* (1844) 1 Jo & Lat 401, where a trustee loaned trust money in breach of trust. The recipient, Fair, did not initially know that the money was trust money, but later discovered. The Court of Chancery of Ireland held that he had become a constructive trustee of the money as soon as he had become aware of the facts.

[225] See above.

[226] See *Criterion Properties plc v Stratford UK Properties LLC* [2004] 1 WLR 1846; [2004] LMCLQ 421, where it was held that the Court of Appeal had fallen into error by considering 'knowing receipt' in a claim to recover benefits conferred under a contract which is set aside since this does not involve any trust property, and hence is a matter for the common law of restitution, where the personal liability is strict, subject to the defence of change of position.

[227] Birks, *An Introduction to the Law of Restitution* (1985), pp 140–146, 445–446; Burrows, *The Law of Restitution* (2nd edn, 2005); Goff & Jones, *The Law of Restitution* (7th edn, 2009); Virgo, *The Principles of the Law of Restitution* (2nd edn, 2006); Gerard McMeel, *The Modern Law of Restitution* (2000), pp 384–396. See also Payne 'Unjust Enrichment Trusts and Recipient Liability for Unlawful Dividends' (2003)

expense. Unlike a compensatory remedy, the quantum of recovery is not assessed by reference to any loss suffered by the plaintiff, but is determined by the gain received by the defendant. Where a defendant receives value at the expense of the plaintiff he may be required to make restitution of equivalent value to him. Restitution is only available where the enrichment of the defendant was unjust, in the sense that the law regards it as inappropriate that he should be entitled to retain it. Thus, the unjust enrichment of a defendant is the cause of action which leads to the award of restitution. Until recently, English law did not recognize an autonomous cause of action in unjust enrichment. However, in *Lipkin Gorman v Karpnale Ltd*[228] the House of Lords affirmed that unjust enrichment is an independent cause of action alongside breach of contract, tort, or breach of trust.

Although the precise scope of unjust enrichment has yet to be determined, there are many areas where it is clear that restitution is available, for example where a plaintiff has paid money to a defendant by mistake. Prior to the recognition of unjust enrichment, English law did award restitutionary remedies, both at common law (by means of the action for money had and received) and in equity. In consequence of the legitimization of unjust enrichment as an autonomous cause of action it has been argued that all such restitutionary remedies should be re-analysed under the single rubric of unjust enrichment, irrespective of their historical pedigree. Inevitably, integration into such a unitary principle would require harmonization of the ingredients necessary for a claim to succeed, which may involve the abandonment of traditional precedents and doctrines. This process has ramifications in respect of strangers who have received trust property because the personal liability to account as a constructive trustee is a species of restitutionary remedy. The stranger who is liable to account is required to make restitution of the value he received from the trust (ie the value of the trust property he received) at the expense of the beneficiaries. As has been seen above, this equitable obligation to make restitution is currently only imposed if the recipient was at fault. In contrast, at common law an unjustly enriched defendant is required to make restitution irrespective of whether he was at fault. Liability is strict. Some academic writers have therefore suggested that a stranger who receives trust property in breach of trust, and is thereby unjustly enriched, should be strictly liable to make restitution, subject to defences intended to prevent injustice.

In New Zealand[229] the equitable liability of a stranger receiving trust property to account as a constructive trustee has been analysed as a right to restitution on the grounds of unjust enrichment. The courts have held that knowledge of all five categories identified in *Baden* will be sufficient to give rise to a constructive trust. In *Powell v*

---

119 LQR 583, who argues for a restitutionary rather than trusts approach to unlawfully paid dividends. These views are criticized by Tham 'Unjust Enrichment and Unlawful Dividends: A Step Too Far?' [2005] 64 CLJ 177.

[228]   [1991] 2 AC 548.

[229]   See *Westpac Banking Corpn v Savin* [1985] 2 NZLR 41; *Elders Pastoral Ltd v Bank of New Zealand* [1989] 2 NZLR 180; *Powell v Thompson* [1991] 1 NZLR 597; *Equiticorp Industries Group Ltd v Hawkins* [1991] 3 NZLR 700.

Thompson[230] Thomas J considered that the observations of Sir Robert Megarry V-C in *Re Montagu's Settlement Trusts*[231] did not accurately reflect the present law. In *Equiticorp Industries Group Ltd v Hawkins*[232] Wylie J held that all five types of knowledge apply to cases of knowing receipt. The courts have held that the underlying basis of the liability to account as a constructive trustee for knowing receipt of trust property is 'the unjust enrichment of the defendant at the expense of the plaintiff'.[233] Since the basis of the remedy is unjust enrichment, the court must conduct a general inquiry whether in the circumstances it would be inequitable not to require the defendant to account to the plaintiff. This analysis clearly affects the issue of the knowledge required, as Thomas J explained in *Powell v Thompson*:

in certain circumstances a Court of Equity could be persuaded to examine the equities of the competing claims where the defendant was not aware that he or she was receiving or dealing with the property in a way which was inconsistent with a trust. Because liability in this class of case stems from equity's unwillingness to accept the enrichment of the third party at the expense of the beneficiary, and not any particular conduct or misconduct on the part of either the trustee or the third party, such knowledge may not be necessary in order to activate equity's jurisdiction with the objective of ensuring a result which is consonant with good conscience.[234]

In consequence, the New Zealand position differs greatly from that currently taken by the English courts. However, the New Zealand courts have also taken a completely different approach to the development of constructive trusts. As Thomas J had observed in *Elders Pastoral Ltd v Bank of New Zealand*:[235]

Unquestionably, in New Zealand the constructive trust has become a broad equitable remedy for reversing that which is inequitable or unconscionable. With this approach it is unlikely that the courts of New Zealand will be encouraged to adopt the more restricted approach evident in Great Britain.[236]

(b) Restitution at common law: strict liability subject to defences

As has been noted, at common law the obligation to make restitution is imposed against a defendant irrespective of whether he was at fault. If a defendant receives money from a payor who was acting under a mistake, it is irrelevant whether he was aware that the payor was mistaken. He is obliged to make restitution merely because he has been enriched in circumstances where the enrichment was unjust because the payor's consent to the payment was vitiated by the mistake. Similarly, where a contract is set aside a defendant who has received benefits under the contract will be strictly liable to make restitution subject to the defence of change of position.[237] The factor requiring restitution (termed the unjust factor) is intrinsically one-sided, in the sense that it is the payor's lack of true consent to the transaction which rendered the enrichment unjust. Provided that the defendant can be demonstrated to have been enriched, his liability to

---

[230] [1991] 1 NZLR 597.   [231] [1987] Ch 264.
[232] [1991] 3 NZLR 700.   [233] *Powell v Thompson* [1991] 1 NZLR 597, at 607, per Thomas J.
[234] [1991] 1 NZLR 597, at 608.   [235] [1989] 2 NZLR 180.
[236] [1991] 1 NZLR 597, at 615.
[237] *Criterion Properties plc v Stratford UK Properties LCC* [2004] 1 WLR 1846.

make restitution is strict. While such liability might appear unduly harsh, the enriched defendant is protected from an unjust outcome by the availability of the defence of change of position.[238] This defence is available only in response to restitutionary claims, and it allows the court to hold that a defendant should not be required to make full restitution of the entire enrichment he received. This defence was also recognized by the House of Lords in *Lipkin Gorman v Karpnale Ltd*.[239] The rationale for the defence was outlined by Lord Goff: 'where an innocent defendant's position is so changed that he will suffer an injustice if called upon to repay or to repay in full, the injustice of requiring him so to repay outweighs the injustice of denying the plaintiff restitution'.[240] Although he did not provide a comprehensive analysis of how the defence would apply in all situations, he went on to formulate a broad general principle:

> At present I do not wish to state the principle any less broadly than this: that the defence is available to a person whose position has so changed that it would be inequitable in all the circumstances to require him to make restitution or alternatively to make restitution in full. I wish to stress however that the mere fact that the defendant has spent the money, in whole or in part, does not of itself render it inequitable that he should be called upon to repay, because the expenditure might in any event have been incurred by him in the ordinary course of things. I fear that the mistaken assumption that mere expenditure of money may be regarded as amounting to a change of position for present purposes has led in the past to opposition by some to recognition of a defence which in fact is likely to be available only on comparatively rare occasions.[241]

He provided examples of circumstances in which he thought that the defence of change of position would apply, including a defendant who makes a donation to charity in good faith having received a payment of money from a plaintiff acting under a mistake of fact, and a third party who similarly gives money to a charity which he had received from a thief.

(c) Distinguishing restitution at common law from restitution in equity

The history of the litigation in *Lipkin Gorman Ltd v Karpnale* provides a useful illustration of the differences between the strict liability of the common law restitutionary claim and the fault-based liability in equity. It will be remembered that the case concerned a solicitor (Cass) who had stolen money from his firm's client account to finance his gambling at the Playboy Club. The firm initially claimed that the club was liable to account in equity as a constructive trustee for the money it had received. This claim was rejected at first instance because the club had not lacked probity in its receipt of the money. In essence, the club was not at fault in receiving the money. In contrast, the House of Lords held that the club was liable at common law to make restitution of the stolen money it had received. The money received had belonged at common law to the firm and the club had not provided good consideration when it was received in return for gambling chips.[242] Although no traceable proceeds of the money were identifiable

---

[238] See Goff and Jones, *The Law of Restitution* (6th edn, 2002), pp 821–837; Burrows, *The Law of Restitution* (2nd edn, 2002), pp 510–529; Mitchell 'Change of Position: The Developing Law' [2005] 1 LMCLQ 168.

[239] [1991] 2 AC 548.   [240] Ibid., at 579.   [241] Ibid., at 580.

[242] [1991] 2 AC 548, at 575. Lord Goff explained: 'when Cass placed a bet, he received nothing in return which constituted valuable consideration. The contract of gaming was void; in other words, it was binding in

among the club's assets, it had been unjustly enriched by the receipt thereof and was therefore strictly liable to make restitution. However, the House of Lords went on to hold that the club's liability to make restitution should be ameliorated by application of the defence of change of position. Lord Goff held that it would be inequitable to require the club to repay the money it had received in full without making allowance for the winnings that it had paid on some of the bets placed by Cass. Thus, although the club had received £222,909, they were required to make restitution of only £150,960.

(d) Identifying an unjust factor requiring the recipient of trust property to make restitution

While it is clear that the liability of a defendant to make restitution at common law is strict, it is less easy to identify the unjust factor which requires a third party receiving trust property to make restitution. When a trustee transfers the trust property to a stranger in breach of trust, the stranger receives good legal title irrespective of the breach. The trustee is able to transfer the trust property by virtue of his legal ownership and the powers of management attendant thereon. As Lord Browne-Wilkinson explained in *Hammersmith and Fulham London Borough Council v Monk*, 'the fact that a trustee acts in breach of trust does not mean that he has no capacity to do the act he wrongly did'.[243] Restitution theorists have therefore sought to identify an unjust factor that would justify the award of restitution where a stranger has received trust property. While there is general agreement that the mere receipt of trust property should give rise to a right to restitution, there is disagreement as to the identification of an appropriate unjust factor. Some academics have favoured the adoption of 'ignorance' as an unjust factor, by which it is meant that the property was misdirected to the defendant without the consent or knowledge of the owner.[244] Such misdirection may be perpetrated with dishonesty, for example where a thief steals the plaintiff's money and passes it to the defendant, or it may occur through an honest mistake, for example where a trustee misunderstands his duty and pays money to the defendant which ought to go to the plaintiff. Others have rejected ignorance in favour of restitution to vindicate a property right.[245] In either case, the right to receive restitution arises irrespective of any fault on the part of the recipient. Although liability is strict, the recipient will be protected from injustice by the defence of change of position.

(e) Ignorance as an unjust factor at common law

No case has yet adopted the language of ignorance to justify the imposition of an obligation to make restitution.[246] While the recipient club in *Lipkin Gorman v Karpnale*

---

honour only... Even when a winning bet is has been paid, the gambler does not receive valuable consideration for his money. All he receives is, in law, a gift from the club.'

[243] [1992] 1 AC 478, 493.

[244] Birks 'Misdirected funds: restitution from the recipient' [1989] LMCLQ 296.

[245] See, for example, Virgo, *The Principles of the Law of Restitution* (1999) pp 128–129, 666–672.

[246] See McKendrick 'Restitution, Misdirected Funds and Change of Position' (1992) 55 MLR 377; Swadling 'A Claim in Restitution?' [1996] LMCLQ 63; Grantham and Rickett 'Restitution, Property and

Ltd[247] was required to make restitution, the precise factor making its enrichment unjust was left unclear. Lord Goff seemed to indicate that the right to restitution arose simply because the club had received legal title to the firm's money without having provided valuable consideration:

> here the money had been paid to the respondents by a third party, Cass; and in such a case the [plaintiff] has to establish a basis on which he is entitled to the money. This (at least as a general rule) he does by showing that the money is his legal property...If he can do so, he may be entitled to succeed in a claim against a third party for money had and received to his use, though not if the third party has received the money in good faith and for a valuable consideration.[248]

In the earlier case of *Banque Belge pour l'Etranger v Hambrouck*,[249] a mistress was held liable to make restitution at common law of money she had received from her lover, who had stolen it from his employer. The plaintiffs claimed restitution of £315 remaining in her bank account, which was traceable as their money. Although they sought a personal action for money had and received, they only claimed the amount that remained and not the amount that she had received. In principle, they would have been entitled to receive restitution of all the money that she had received, subject to a defence of change of position.

It should be noted that the availability of restitution at common law is severely limited, not merely by the defence of change of position, but also by the restrictive common law rules of tracing by which it can be demonstrated that the defendant received the plaintiff's money. As Lord Goff indicated in *Lipkin Gorman v Karpnale Ltd*,[250] the fact that at common law property in money is lost as such when it is mixed with other money has made the number of successful claims to restitution founded on mere receipt of the plaintiff's property very rare.[251]

(f) Criticisms of the proposed adoption of strict liability restitution in equity

The central question is thus whether the current fault-based personal liability of a recipient of trust property should be re-explained as a strict liability to make restitution of the value of the property received, subject to the availability of a defence of change of position. This would entirely eliminate the need to demonstrate fault, whether characterized as knowledge, dishonesty, or unconscionability, as a prerequisite of liability. Although such a radical departure from the traditional analysis of equity was initially greeted with hostility by equity lawyers,[252] some have come to advocate it.[253] In effect, it would amount to the adoption of the strict personal liability of the charities in *Re Diplock* in every situation in which a stranger receives trust property, subject to the modification that they would be entitled to the defence of change of

Ignorance—A Reply to Mr Swadling' [1996] LMCLQ 463; Bant '"Ignorance" as a Ground of Restitution—Can It Survive?' [1998] LMCLQ 18.

247 [1991] 2 AC 548.   248 Ibid., at 572.   249 [1921] 1 KB 321.
250 [1991] 2 AC 548.   251 Ibid., at 572.
252 Harpum 'The Stranger as Constructive Trustee: Part 1' (1986) 102 LQR 114.
253 Harpum, 'The Basis of Equitable Liability' in Birks (ed), *The Frontiers of Liability* (1994); Oakley, 'The Liberalising Nature of Remedies for Breach of Trust' in Oakley, *Trends in Contemporary Trust Law* (1996), pp 247–251; Martin 'Recipient Liability after *Westdeutsche*' [1998] Conv 13.

position.[254] Such a development has been advocated by Lord Nicholls, speaking extra-judicially.[255] Despite the unsubstantiated assertion of Lord Millett in *Twinsectra Ltd v Yardley* that liability for 'knowing receipt' is receipt-based and does not depend upon fault,[256] at present English law has not adopted such a strict liability right to restitution against a stranger who has received trust property in place of the equitable liability to account as a constructive trustee, and the leading authorities strongly support the current approach. In *Westdeutsche Landesbank Girozentrale v Islington London Borough Council*[257] Lord Browne-Wilkinson reiterated the fault-based approach of *Re Montagu*. In *BCCI (Overseas) Ltd v Akindele*, Nourse LJ openly doubted the prevailing academic orthodoxy that the adoption of strict liability coupled with a change of position defence would be preferable to the current fault-based liability.[258]

The advantages of a strict liability claim in restitution, whether based on ignorance or the vindication of property rights, are said to be the harmonization of the equitable and common law rules, the elimination of unhelpful terminology (such as liability to account as a constructive trustee), and the prevention of injustice. In particular, the debate has focused on the position of an innocent donee who has dissipated the property he received. Following the common law approach, such a person would be strictly liable to make restitution, subject to the defence of change of position. In equity, he would attract no personal liability at all. However, it is not obvious that in reality the position in equity is less adequate than that at common law. Where trust property has been received by an innocent donee, but not dissipated by him, the beneficiaries will be able to recover it from him. As a volunteer, he will not enjoy the protection of the doctrine of notice and the beneficiaries' equitable interest will have been preserved. Where the property has been dissipated, leaving no traceable proceeds, the innocent donee will not be liable to make restitution under the current law.[259] At common law the act of dissipation may itself give rise to a defence of change of position. The only circumstances in which the common law and equitable approaches would produce different results are therefore where an innocent donee had dissipated the property he received in circumstances in which he would not be entitled to the benefit of the defence of change of position, for example where it had been utilized to cover his ordinary living expenses. The scope of the defence of change of position is thus the crucial element that will determine the availability of restitution in practice. In equity, an innocent donee is not required to account as a constructive trustee, even if the specific money received has been dissipated

---

[254] See also Smith 'Unjust Enrichment, Property and the Structure of Trusts' (2000) 116 LQR 412, who argues that the strict liability principle adopted in *Re Diplock* might properly be confined to situations involving the administration of an estate.

[255] Lord Nicholls, 'Knowing Receipt: The Need for a New Landmark', Ch 17 in Cornish, Nolan, O'Sullivan, and Virgo, *Restitution Past, Present and Future* (1998).

[256] [2002] 2 AC 164, at [105].   [257] [1996] AC 669, at 705.   [258] [2000] 4 All ER 221.

[259] It should also be remembered that, where property subject to a trust has been received by a stranger the trustees, or a person owing a fiduciary relationship, will have acted in breach of trust, whether innocently or dishonestly, and will therefore be liable to restore the misdirected trust fund. However, it does not seem that the beneficiaries are required to exhaust their remedies against the misdirecting trustee first: *Omar v Omar* (29 November 1996, unreported), Blackburne J; [1997] RLR 139 (Swadling).

by ordinary expenditure. In *Lipkin Gorman v Karpnale Ltd*[260] Lord Goff seemed to suggest that the dissipation of property received through ordinary expenditure would not operate as a defence. Only exceptional expenditure which could be related to the receipt of the enrichment would suffice. In *Scottish Equitable plc v Derby*[261] the Court of Appeal held that the defence was not limited to specific items of expenditure, and that it may be right for the court not to apply too demanding a standard of proof when an honest defendant says that he has spent an overpayment by improving his lifestyle but cannot produce any detailed accounting. However, it held that the defence did not apply to an overpayment made to reduce a mortgage, as it was not a detriment to pay off a debt which would have to be paid sooner or later.

At the heart of the debate is a desire to harmonize the rules of equity and the common law. Although this might seem superficially attractive, it is questionable whether the philosophy underlying equity and the common law are truly compatible.[262] It is easy to assume that a restitutionary right founded on the receipt of property should operate identically, irrespective of whether the property received was legal or equitable. In reality, legal and equitable ownership differ in nature. Equitable ownership is a product of the historic bifurcation of English law that led to the evolution of a concept of double-ownership through the trust. Unlike legal ownership, equitable ownership only arises because the conscience of the legal owner is affected in such a way as to require him to observe the interests of the beneficiaries. The idea of fault is inherent in the creation, or imposition, of trusts, and is clearly operative through the equitable doctrine of notice that determines when equitable ownership rights are defeated. The remedy requiring a stranger to account as a constructive trustee is similarly rooted in the concept of conscience, and the overriding presumption is that a recipient of the legal title of property is entitled to enjoy security of receipt until such time as he becomes aware that it was subject to a trust, and that he should therefore be entitled to treat it as if it was his own. From the perspective of equity he is not unjustly enriched by the mere receipt of trust property. His enrichment only becomes unjust from such time as he was aware that he had received trust property and was therefore subject to an obligation to preserve it for the beneficiaries. The philosophies of equity and the common law in this respect are different. The common law right to restitution has developed so that liability is strict but defences are broad. It should be noted that this does not eliminate entirely the need to assess fault. It merely changes the stage of the process at which fault must be considered. The defence of change of position only operates if the defendant acted bona fides. A dishonest defendant would not be able to take advantage of the defence, for example if he gave money to charity knowing that it had been paid to him by mistake. In contrast, equity regards the element of fault as crucial to liability itself. The charge that such notions as dishonesty are uncertain and difficult to apply can be met with the equally valid criticism that the defence of change of position is vague, underdeveloped,

---

[260] [1991] 2 AC 548.   [261] [2001] 3 All ER 818.
[262] See, for example, Jaffey, *The Nature and Scope of Restitution* (2000), pp 327–346, who argues that the nature of equitable property rights does not demand the imposition of strict liability.

and arbitrary. The adoption of strict liability in place of the current fault-based liability would also effect a change in the allocation of the burden of proof where a claim is made against a recipient of trust property. Currently, the burden of proof falls to the claimant, who must establish that the recipient dishonestly received trust property. If strict liability were to be adopted instead, the claimant would merely have to demonstrate that the property had been received, passing the burden to the recipient to establish a defence by way of change of position.

In the light of such criticisms Nourse LJ expressed his opinion that the current fault-based liability should not be superseded by strict liability restitution in *BCCI (Overseas) Ltd v Akindele*. Although his remarks were strictly obiter they are a significant counter-voice advocating the maintenance of the current position:

> While in general it may be possible to sympathize with a tendency to subsume a further part of our law under the principle of unjust enrichment, I beg leave to doubt whether strict liability coupled with a change of position defence would be preferable to fault-based liability in many commercial transactions, for example where, as here, the receipt is of a company's funds which have been misapplied by its directors. Without having heard argument it is unwise to be dogmatic, but in such a case it would appear to be commercially unworkable and contrary to the spirit of the rule in *Royal British Bank v Turquand*,[263] that, simply on proof of an internal misapplication of the company's funds, the burden should shift to the recipient to defend the receipt either by a change of position or perhaps in some other way.[264]

In the light of these arguments, the contention of Professor Birks that 'there is no rational argument for depriving the equitable owner of the claim in unjust enrichment based on strict liability'[265] is clearly overstated and cannot be accepted as anything other than a polemical assertion.

(g) Wider implications of the adoption of strict liability restitution in equity

If equity is forced to abandon its present commitment to fault as the basis of liability to make personal restitution, the implications may be yet further reaching. It is presently alleged to be inconsistent that an innocent donee of trust property is under no obligation to make restitution. Might it not equally be argued that it would be inconsistent if an innocent donee were entitled to enjoy a defence of change of position to a strict liability to make restitution if he had dissipated trust property, but that if he had retained it the beneficiaries could recover it as their property, even though he might have changed his position in good faith on the basis that he thought he had received a valid gift? For example, imagine that a person owned 1,000 shares in a public company and then received a further 1,000 shares in the same company which were subject to a trust. He was entirely innocent and, in the light of his windfall, he gave his original block of shares to charity. Since he was not a bona fide purchaser, the beneficiaries would be able to claim the 1,000 shares remaining in his hands as subject to the

---

[263]   (1856) 6 E & B 327.
[264]   [2000] 4 All ER 221,, at 236, Goff and Jones do not share his doubt: *The Law of Restitution* (6th edn, 2002), p 744.
[265]   Birks and Pretto (eds), *Breach of Trust*, p 239.

trust, and it would be no defence to their proprietary claim that he had changed his position.[266] It would then, no doubt, be argued that the defence of change of position should be utilized to entitle the court to re-apportion equitable proprietary interests, and the entire concept of the equitable ownership of property would be reduced to a subset of a rampant law of unjust enrichment. The law of unjust enrichment should rather be seen as subordinate to the law of property and parasitic upon it. A recipient is only unjustly enriched because he receives property belonging to another. Where that property is equitable in character, it should be for the principles of equity to determine the circumstances in which the recipient was enriched. Given that the very nature of equitable property is founded upon notions of conscience, it is perfectly logical to find that a recipient is not unjustly enriched until he dishonestly dissipates such property. The mere fact that this result is inconsistent with a common law approach does not render it unacceptable. Inconsistency is only illogical where there is a real similarity between the things which are allegedly inconsistent. Legal title and equitable title are different, and therefore there is no reason to expect them to adopt identical rules regarding the circumstances in which a recipient of property will be unjustly enriched so as to oblige him to make restitution. It is quite clear that equity and the common law have different rules concerning the circumstances in which a third party will acquire property free from pre-existing property rights. In equity, a bona fide purchaser of trust property is not unjustly enriched because the pre-existing equitable property right of the beneficiaries is brought to an end by the process of the acquisition. In contrast, legal ownership is generally not destroyed by bona fide purchase and the *nemo dat* rule operates, subject to limited exceptions. As the decision of the majority of the House of Lords in *Westdeutsche Landesbank Girozentrale v Islington London Borough Council*[267] demonstrates, differences between common law rights and remedies and equitable rights and remedies cannot be ignored merely by the invocation of the language of restitution and unjust enrichment.

In *El Ajou v Dollar Land Holdings plc (No 1)*[268] Millett J stated that a personal remedy based on knowing receipt was the counterpart in equity of the common law claim for money had and received. He noted that the common law action was a receipt-based claim to restitution and concluded: 'So, in my judgment, is the [personal remedy based on knowing receipt], unless arbitrary and anomalous distinctions between the common law and equitable claims are to be insisted upon.'[269] However, it is submitted that the present distinctions are not arbitrary and anomalous but reflect the intrinsic difference in the character of legal and equitable proprietary rights. It is entirely appropriate for equity, which reflects conscience, to retain a fault-based liability to make restitution, and this is the present position in English law.

---

[266] Unless the defence of change of position extends to proprietary interests. See *Re Diplock* [1948] Ch 465; (1991) 107 LQR 71 (Millett LJ); Birks, 'Change of Position and Surviving Enrichment', in Swadling (ed), *The Limits of Restitutionary Claims* (1997).

[267] [1996] AC 669,, at 705.   [268] [1993] 3 All ER 717.

[269] Ibid., at 738.

6 Mapping a way through personal stranger claims

What follows is a tabular synopsis of how to apply the tests for personal liability for dishonest assistors and knowing recipients of trust property. It is intended as an aid only, and the relevant law has already been discussed in the rest of this chapter in detail.

(1) Stranger who assists in a breach of trust

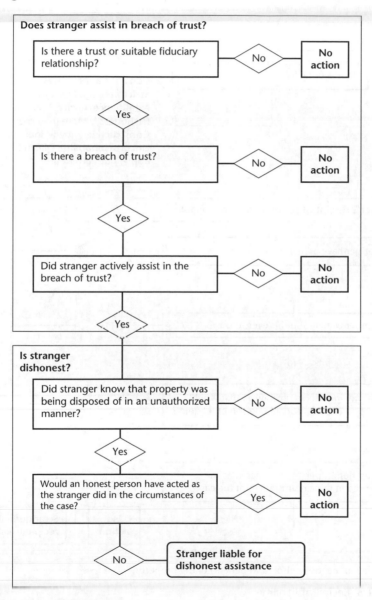

Figure 31.2 Dishonest assistance

(2) **Stranger who receives trust property in breach of trust**

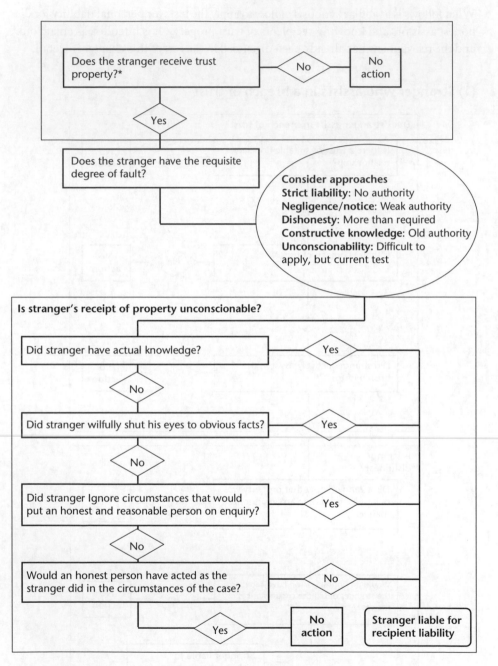

*Receipt needs control (and benefit) of the property.

Figure 31.3 Recipient liability

32

Tracing

The previous chapters have considered the remedies available against trustees and other fiduciaries for breach of their duties, and remedies against third parties who become involved with the trust property (strangers to the trust). This chapter considers the process of tracing, which identifies the property or its substitute value, and allows a claim to be brought to recover the property or to extend the range of recipients against whom a claim can be made. Tracing therefore has two elements—the tracing process and the tracing claim.

1 What is tracing?[1]

(1) Tracing is a process by which property is identified

Tracing describes the process by which the law allows the original owner of property to identify assets in the hands of a third party which represent it because they are its exchange product or proceeds. For example, if a car is stolen and the thief sells it for cash that he uses to purchase shares in a company, the car owner will be entitled to identify the shares as the product of his original property. In *Foskett v McKeown*, one of the leading modern cases on tracing, Lord Millett distinguished between 'following' and 'tracing' as follows:

Following is the process of following the same asset as it moves from hand to hand. Tracing is the process of identifying a new asset as the substitute for the old.[2]

For convenience, the word 'tracing' is often used in this chapter to describe both following and tracing. If tracing is the process by which the proceeds of property can be identified, the rules of tracing provide the framework of principles that determine

---

[1] For extensive considerations of tracing see: Birks (ed), *Laundering and Tracing* (1995); Smith, *The Law of Tracing* (1997).

[2] [2001] 1 AC 102, at 127; Stevens 'Vindicating the Proprietary Nature of Tracing' [2001] Conv 94; Grantham and Rickett 'Tracing and Property Rights: The Categorical Truth' [2000] 63 MLR 905; Berg 'Permitting A Trustee To Retain A Profit' (2001) 117 LQR 366; Sir Robert Walker 'Tracing after *Foskett v McKeown*' [2000] RLR 573; Jaffey 'Tracing, Property and Unjust Enrichment' (2000) 14 Tru LI 194.

whether such identification is possible. In some cases, for example where there was a clean substitution of one type of property for another, the identification of assets representing the original property is relatively easy. In the example given above, the car was swapped for money, which was in turn swapped for the shares. Thus the shares can be identified as representing the car. However, in most cases the transactions that have occurred will have been far more complex, especially where the property sought to be traced was money. There may have been numerous exchanges, and at various stages in the chain of exchange the property may have become mixed with other property. Where such mixing occurs, the process of identification becomes much more difficult. If, for example, the car was stolen and then sold for cash, which was paid into a bank account of the thief that already contained a substantial balance, and shares were then purchased using money from the bank account, it is much less easy to demonstrate that the shares are the proceeds of the car. The shares could equally have been purchased using the money that was already in the account, rather than using the proceeds of the sale of the car. The rules of tracing have evolved to try to determine the circumstances in which property can be traced through these more complicated exchanges and mixed funds.

(2) Tracing at common law and in equity

A variety of rules and presumptions have been developed to enable the identification of specific property, and to determine whether it has continued to be identifiable as such through transfers, substitutions, and mixing. The distinction between legal and equitable ownership is fundamental to English property law. This historic bifurcation has led to the development of two separate bodies of rules for tracing property, one operative for tracing ownership at common law, and the other for tracing the equitable beneficial ownership that arises under a trust. While the common law rules have little application beyond the most simple of dealings with property, the equitable rules are considerably more generous and facilitate tracing through more complex transactions. The rules in equity have developed particularly to trace property through mixed funds. The equitable rules also have a moral dimension, operating more harshly against a wrongdoer who misappropriates property than an innocent party. While many have argued that the common law rules of tracing are unduly restrictive, and that the rules should be harmonized for both legal and equitable ownership, it has traditionally been the case that it is not possible to utilize the equitable rules to trace property unless it is held on trust (although there are some indications that this may be changing).

(3) Tracing and claiming

Tracing is merely a process that enables an owner of property to identify assets as representing his original property. As such, the process of tracing does not itself determine the rights that the original owner may assert in any assets identified by the rules of tracing. Tracing is not therefore a remedy but a mechanism. However, tracing as a process is pursued with the object of providing a foundation for the assertion of a right or a remedy. The original owner may seek to assert a proprietary right to any assets identified by the rules of tracing, with the consequence that they are his property and they do not belong to the holder. Alternatively, he may seek a purely personal remedy requiring that the holder of the identified assets make restitution of the value of the property he had received. The assertion of an appropriate remedy in respect of assets identified by the rules of tracing has been termed 'claiming'.[3] This purpose and nature of tracing was explained by Lord Millett in *Foskett v McKeown*:

Tracing is thus neither a claim nor a remedy. It is merely the process by which a claimant demonstrates what has happened to his property, identifies its proceeds and the persons who have handled or received them, and justifies his claim that the proceeds can properly be regarded as representing his property.[4]

Whether an original owner will be able to assert a proprietary claim to any assets identified by the tracing process as representing his property will depend upon a number of factors, including the nature of his interest in the original asset, and whether any intervening defences negate his ability to claim. Where he can assert such a proprietary claim his right of ownership is, in effect, preserved into the exchange product of his original property. The claiming of specific assets will be especially significant in two circumstances. First, the person presently holding the identified assets may be insolvent.[5] If the identified assets are subject to a proprietary claim they will not fall to be distributed among his general creditors, and as such a claiming owner will enjoy a priority which could not be achieved through a personal claim. Second, the identified assets may be more valuable than the original property that has been traced into them. If so, a proprietary claim will enable the original owner to take the benefit of the appreciation that has occurred.[6]

Given the distinction between tracing and claiming, this chapter will examine in turn the rules of tracing at common law and in equity, and then the ensuing claiming rights of an original owner who has been able to identify assets which represent his original property.

(4) The nature of the tracing process[7]

(a) Tracing and restitution

There has been a great deal of debate in recent years as to the conceptual nature of the tracing process. Traditionally, tracing was understood to form part of the law of

---

[3] See Smith, *The Law of Tracing* (1997), pp 284–369.   [4] [2001] 1 AC 102, at 128.
[5] See Oakley 'Propriety Claims and Their Priority in Insolvency' [1995] CLJ 377.
[6] Re *Tilley's Will Trust* [1967] Ch 1179; *Jones (FC) & Sons v Jones* [1996] 4 All ER 721; *Foskett v McKeown* [2001] 1 AC 102.
[7] See Birks 'Mixing and Tracing: Property and Restitution' (1992) 45 CLP 69; Moriarty, 'Tracing, Mixing and Laundering' in Birks (ed), *Laundering and Tracing* (1995), pp 73–94; Smith, *The Law of Tracing* (1997); Birks 'On Taking Seriously the Difference Between Tracing and Claiming' (1997) 11 TLI 2; Smith 'Unjust

property, and to operate by preserving title to property through substitutions and mixtures. However, some academics have argued that the tracing process should be understood rather as part of the law of restitution.

Restitution is the response which consists of a defendant giving up to a claimant an unjust enrichment that he has received at the claimant's expense. Generally, restitution will be effected by means of a personal remedy, so that the defendant will be ordered to pay to the claimant a sum of money equivalent to the enrichment he has received. In his seminal work *Introduction to the Law of Restitution*, Professor Birks classified this remedy as 'restitution in the first measure', and the measure of the restitution is the 'value received', ie the extent to which the defendant was unjustly enriched. However, he has argued that restitution will sometimes be effected by means of a proprietary remedy, so that the defendant is forced to give up to the claimant any property in his hands which represents the enrichment he received. This is termed 'restitution in the second measure', and the measure of restitution is the 'value surviving' in the defendant's hands.[8] Tracing is regarded merely as a process by which 'value surviving' is identified. This is not a matter of mere semantics as this analysis has important consequences for the understanding of the nature of the tracing process.

This restitutionary analysis cuts to the very heart of the nature of tracing. Traditionally, tracing has been understood to operate by descent of title, or 'vested interest'. A claimant is entitled to trace because he initially had title to property, which title he is able to follow into mixtures and exchange products because it was never lost. This analysis is rejected because of the perceived danger of a 'geometric multiplication'[9] in the claimant's wealth as he gains interests in all the exchange products for his property as well. For example, if a trustee takes £5,000 from the trust and purchases a diamond ring, which he sells for £10,000 and then purchases a car with the money, the beneficiary could have equitable title to the ring, the car, and the £10,000 in the hands of the seller of the car, all at the same time. As an alternative to this 'vested interest' approach, Professor Birks has argued that the original owner of property has only a 'power in rem which he can bring down on assets that by the rules of tracing are identified as the surviving enrichment'.[10] The original owner has no proprietary rights to any mixed fund or to assets purchased out of a mixed fund, but only a 'power to crystallise such a right'.[11]

In later work Professor Burrows has argued that tracing operates not as a proprietary process but to prevent unjust enrichment. He asserts that the tracing of rights into substitute assets cannot be explained on a proprietary basis:

Enrichment, Property and the Structure of Trusts' (2000) 116 LQR 412; Burrows 'Proprietary Restitution: Unmasking Unjust Enrichment' (2001) 117 LQR 412.

[8] Birks, *Introduction to the Law of Restitution* (1985), pp 75–98 and 358–401.

[9] Ibid., p 394. See also Burrows, *The Law of Restitution* (2nd edn, 2002), p 92.

[10] See Birks 'Mixing and Tracing: Property and Restitution' (1992) 45(2) CLP 69, at 89–95.

[11] Birks, *Introduction to the Law of Restitution* (1985), p 393. See also *Re J Leslie Engineers Co Ltd* [1976] 1 WLR 292.

Ownership of a pig can explain ownership of the piglets but does not explain why P can be said to own the horse that D has obtained in substitution for the pig stolen from P. To reason from one to the other is to apply a very tempting but, in truth, fictional notion of property.[12]

In his view, where a substitution occurs the owner of the original property is given a new title to reverse the unjust enrichment of the third party who has substituted it. Unmasking the underlying principle of unjust enrichment thus opens the door to consideration whether the act of substitution should automatically entitle an original owner to obtain title to the new asset. However, it can be countered that it is well established in English law that an original owner has an automatic right to claim entitlement to assets which are substituted for his property. Given that both 'unjust enrichment' and 'property' are both essentially rhetorical constructs it is perfectly legitimate for a legal system to characterize such an automatic entitlement as an aspect of property. The ownership of piglets produced by a pig is equally determined by long-established conventions which are characterized as property, and is no more or less fictitious that the conventions which dictate entitlements to substitute property.

In his final work before his untimely death, Professor Birks reiterated his long-held view that tracing is merely a power on the part of an owner to vest a currently traceable substitute in himself, not a right, although he acknowledged that this view is not uncontroversial.[13]

(b) Tracing as a proprietary process

Whilst the use of tracing as a means of identifying the receipt of enrichment is unquestioned, it is submitted that the relegation of tracing to a mere process without proprietary implications is unduly reductionist and at odds with both authority and principle. While tracing may functionally operate to demonstrate receipt, and thus as the foundation for a personal claim to restitution at common law or in equity, the process of tracing is intrinsically proprietary in nature. Value cannot exist in the abstract but only in the form of specific assets or property. The leading cases concerning the right to trace at common law and in equity support the view that tracing operates by 'descent of title', so that a claimant can trace his property through mixtures and substitutions.[14] At every stage of the chain of events he continues to be the owner, whether at law or in equity, of the assets identified by the rules of tracing. If at any point he ceases to be the owner, his right to trace comes to an automatic end, as when trust property is acquired by a bona fide purchaser.

---

[12] 'Proprietary Restitution: Unmasking Unjust Enrichment' (2002) 117 LQR 412, at 418. See also Craig Rotherham 'The Metaphysics of Tracing: Substituted Title and Property Rhetoric' (1996) 34 Osgoode Hall LJ 321.

[13] Birks, *Unjust Enrichment* (2nd edn, 2005), p 198. See also Hedley and Halliwell (eds), *The Law of Restitution* (2002) p 58.

[14] Except for the judgment of Robert Walker J in *El Ajou v Dollar Land Holdings plc (No 2)* [1995] 2 All ER 213, who suggested (at 223) that: 'tracing claims depend not on equitable ownership as such but on the concept of an equitable charge'.

In *Lipkin Gorman v Karpnale Ltd*, the leading case concerning common law tracing, Lord Goff held that the implication of tracing money from a solicitor's client account by the beneficiaries was that it remained 'their property at common law'.[15] He therefore understood the tracing claim to operate on a proprietary basis. In *Jones (FC) & Sons (a firm) v Jones*[16] the Court of Appeal similarly held that money was traceable at common law because the recipient had not obtained title to it. In *Foskett v McKeown*, which concerned the tracing of trust property in equity, the House of Lords clearly stated that the tracing process was to be viewed as part of the law of property, rather than restitution. Lord Millett explained:

The transmission of a claimant's property rights from one asset to its traceable proceeds is part of our law of property, not of the law of unjust enrichment. There is no 'unjust factor' to justify restitution (unless 'want of title' be one, which makes the point). The claimant succeeds if at all by virtue of his own title, not to reverse unjust enrichment. Property rights are to be determined by fixed rules and settled principles, they are not discretionary. They do not depend upon ideas of what is 'fair, just or reasonable'. Such concepts, which in reality mask decisions of legal policy, have no place in the law of property. A beneficiary of a trust is entitled to a continuing beneficial interest not merely in the trust property but in its traceable proceeds also, and his interest binds every one who takes the property or its traceable proceeds except a bona fide purchaser for value without notice.[17]

Professor Burrows[18] considers this affirmation of the proprietary nature of tracing to have been unfortunate. He argues that it is a fiction to say that a claimant is given ownership of traced property because his or her ownership of the original property continues through the substitute property, and he argues that the truth is that the claimant may be given a new title to the traced property to reverse the defendant's unjust enrichment at the claimant's expense.[19] However, the rules of tracing, which will be examined below, have evolved specifically to identify property. Their one object is to identify specific assets in which the claimant has a continuing proprietary interest. This is evident from rules such as the 'lowest intermediate balance', which prevents tracing into money added later to an account which has been depleted, because that additional money is not in equity the property of the claimant. Similarly, the limitation that property will not be traced into the hands of a bona fide purchaser for value without notice demonstrates that the basis is descent of title. Tracing is impossible in such circumstances, because the proprietary chain is broken at the point where the equitable interest is defeated. The right of a claimant to take advantage of any increase

---

[15] [1992] 4 All ER 512, at 529.   [16] [1997] Ch 159.

[17] [2001] 1 AC 102, at 127. Similar sentiments were also expressed by Lord Browne-Wilkinson, at 109. Earlier cases supporting the proprietary nature of tracing in equity include: *Sinclair v Brougham* [1914] AC 398; *Re Diplock* [1948] Ch 465; *Chase Manhattan Bank NA v Israeli-British Bank (London) Ltd* [1981] Ch 105; *Agip v Jackson* [1992] 4 All ER 451. For criticism of such a proprietary understanding of the tracing process see Burrows 'Proprietary Restitution: Unmasking Unjust Enrichment' (2001) 117 LQR 412.

[18] Burrows, *The Law of Restitution* (2nd edn, 2002), p 81. See also Burrows 'Proprietary Restitution: Unmasking Unjust Enrichment' (2001) 117 LQR 412 and Birks 'Property, Unjust Enrichment, And Tracing' (2001) 54 CLP 231.

[19] See also Rotherham 'Tracing Misconceptions in *Foskett v McKeown*' [2003] RLR 57.

in value of assets identified by the rules of tracing also points to the proprietary nature of the tracing process.[20]

It is questionable whether the supposed fear of 'geometric multiplication' of the claimant's property is justified in practice. The danger is only apparent at common law in consequence of the principle *nemo dat quod non habet*.[21] The well-established limitation that the common law cannot trace into a mixed fund itself prevents such 'geometric progression'. In equity, 'geometric multiplication' is curtailed by the principle that the right to trace is lost as against a bona fide purchaser for value. Geometric multiplication is also inhibited by the principle that a claimant cannot recover twice for the same loss. Geometric multiplication provides a claimant with a choice of trails of ownership, from among which he can choose. It is therefore no more of a problem than other situations in which a claimant has a choice of remedies, as for example where the purchaser of a defective product can choose to sue either the manufacturer or the retailer.

While restitution theorists have helpfully clarified the distinction between 'tracing' and 'claiming', so that tracing is seen as a process and not a remedy in itself, it is submitted that the tracing process is inherently proprietary in nature. What is traced is not abstract value but property in specific assets.[22] When specific assets are identified as representing the claimant's original property, the claimant is able to assert a proprietary entitlement to them and claim them as belonging to himself. If assets are identified by the equitable rules of tracing, the present legal owner will be treated as holding them on a constructive trust for the claimant, or, alternatively, the claimant may be entitled to vindicate his proprietary right by means of an equitable charge.[23] Similarly, where specific assets are identified by the common law rules of tracing, the claimant will be entitled to claim them as his property.[24] In many cases the claimant will be forced to resort to a personal claim to restitution because the specific assets have been dissipated in whole or in part. In such circumstances, the restitutionary claim is parasitic upon the proprietary tracing process, which operates to demonstrate that the defendant was enriched at the expense of the claimant.[25]

---

[20] See also the arguments of Grantham and Rickett, 'Property Rights as a Legally Significant Event' (2003) 62 CLJ 717.

[21] On a literal translation, 'no one gives what he does not have', this is interpreted to mean that no person may give a better title to property than he enjoys himself.

[22] See also *Westdeutsche Landesbank Girozentrale v Islington London Borough Council* [1996] AC 669 at 709, where Lord Browne-Wilkinson stated in respect of Professor Birk's argument that unjust enrichment would give rise to an automatic resulting trust: 'First, the argument elides rights in property (which is the only proper subject matter of a trust) into rights in "the value transferred". A trust can only arise where there is defined property: it is therefore not consistent with trust principles to say that a person is a trustee of property which cannot be defined. The same argument applies to the right to trace in equity. It can only subsist in respect of identified property which is held on trust for the person tracing and not in respect of some abstract concept of value.'

[23] *Boscawen v Bajwa* [1995] 4 All ER 769: *Foskett v McKeown* [2001] 1 AC 102.

[24] *Jones (FC) & Sons v Jones* [1997] Ch 159.

[25] Detailed treatment of claims in restitution, and the defence of change of position to such claims, is therefore outside the scope of this book, but see further below at pp 1030–1031.

2 Tracing and claiming at common law[26]

(1) Common law tracing through clean substitutions

The common law rules of tracing are clearly capable of following the ownership of property through a clean substitution, in other words through an exchange which did not involve any mixing of the original property being traced with other property. This was established in the leading early case, *Taylor v Plumer*.[27] Sir Thomas Plumer had entrusted a stockbroker, Walsh, with money for investment in Exchequer bills. Walsh instead misappropriated the money and used it to purchase bullion and American bonds. He was apprehended and surrendered the property. The central issue was whether the bullion and bonds were rightly the property of Sir Thomas or of Walsh's trustee in bankruptcy. Lord Ellenborough held that the money which Sir Thomas had given to Walsh could be traced into the bullion and securities, and that they were properly the property of Sir Thomas. He stated the principle:

It makes no difference in reason or law into what other form, different from the original, the change may have been made . . . for the product or the substitute for the original thing still follows the nature of the thing itself . . .

(2) Common law tracing of tangible property into a mixed bulk

Alongside tracing property through clean substitutions, the common law is also able to trace tangible property which is mixed with identical property so as to create a bulk. Where such mixing occurs the owners of the goods which have been mixed become tenants in common of the whole in the proportions which they have contributed to it.[28] In *Indian Oil Corpn Ltd v Greenstone Shipping Co SA (Panama) (The Ypatianna)*[29] an owner's crude oil was mixed with other crude oil belonging to a shipowner, which was already on board a vessel. Staughton J held that the owner was entitled to trace his oil into the bulk. In *Glencore International AG v Metro Trading International Inc (No 2)*,[30] Moore-Bick J extended this principle to a situation where oil was blended with oil of a different grade or specification, with the result that a new product was produced. The original owner was held able to trace his oil into the mixture, identifying a proportion in the new blend which takes account of both the quantity and the value of the oil contributed to the new bulk. However, the right to trace will be

---

[26] See Worthington, *Proprietary Interests in Commercial Transactions* (1996), pp 133–144; Smith, *The Law of Tracing* (1997), pp 162–174; Matthews, 'The Legal and Moral Limits of Common Law Tracing', in Birks (ed), *Laundering and Tracing* (1995), pp 23–72; Burrows, *The Law of Restitution* (2nd edn, 2002), pp 83–93; (1966) 7 WALR 463 (Scott); (1976) 92 LQR 360 (Goode); (1976) 40 Conv (NS) 277 (Pearce); (1979) 95 LQR 78 (Khurshid and Matthews); [1997] LMCLQ 65 (Band).

[27] (1815) 3 M & S 562. It has been argued that this case has been fundamentally misinterpreted: see below, p 1026.

[28] *Spence v Union Marine Insurance Co* (1868) LR 3 CP 427.

[29] [1988] QB 345.　　　[30] [2001] 1 Lloyd's Rep 284.

lost where tangible property is not merely mixed to form a bulk but is consumed in the manufacture of an entirely new product so as to lose its identity altogether. Thus, in *Borden (UK) Ltd v Scottish Timber Products Ltd*[31] it was not possible to trace resin which was mixed with other materials so as to manufacture chipboard. Where tangible property is mixed so as to form a bulk, the rights of the original owner will vary depending upon whether the mixing was wrongful or innocent, and whether the property can be divided between the parties.

(3) Common law tracing of money through mixed funds

While *Taylor v Plumer*[32] demonstrates that the common law can trace property through clean substitutions, it also established the limitation that the common law is incapable of tracing money through a mixed fund. Lord Ellenborough stated that it was only possible to follow assets where they are able to be 'ascertained' to represent the original property, and that such ascertainment becomes impossible 'when the subject is turned into money, and mixed and confounded in a general mass of the same description'.

Subsequent cases have thus held that the common law cannot trace money through a mixed fund.[33] Say, for example, that an agent holds shares on behalf of his principal. If the agent sells the shares and uses the proceeds to purchase a diamond ring, the common law can trace his property into the ring. However, if the agent sells the shares and then mixes the proceeds with money of his own to create a mixed fund, and then uses money from the fund to purchase the ring, the common law can no longer trace because of the mixing which had taken place. The rationale for this limitation was said by Lord Ellenborough to be a difficulty of fact, not law. Money has no earmark and therefore cannot be distinguished within a mixed fund, whereas 'money in a bag, or otherwise kept apart from other money' is ear-marked and so outside of the limitation.

The limitation was accepted by the Court of Appeal in *Banque Belge Pour l'Etranger v Hambrouck*.[34] The case concerned a man who obtained cheques by fraud from his employers, which were paid into his bank account. He then passed the money to his mistress, Mlle Spanoghe, who paid it into her bank account. The Court of Appeal held that it was possible to trace the money at common law into Mlle Spanoghe's account. Previously it had been thought that the common law would not trace money into a bank account at all, but the court held that, following the equity case *Re Hallet's Estate*,[35] there was nothing to prevent the court examining the details of a bank account.[36] The

---

[31] [1981] Ch 25.   [32] (1815) 3 M & S 562.

[33] See *Re Diplock* [1948] Ch 465, at 519–520; *Agip (Africa) Ltd v Jackson* [1990] Ch 265; *El Ajou v Dollar Land Holdings plc* [1993] BCLC 735; *Bank Tejarat v Hong Kong and Shanghai Banking Corpn* [1995] 1 Lloyd's Rep 239; *Jones (FC) & Sons v Jones* [1997] Ch 159.

[34] [1921] 1 KB 321.   [35] (1880) 13 Ch D 696.

[36] See *Jones (FC) & Sons v Jones* [1997] Ch 159, where money was traced at common law into a bank account.

mere fact that the money had been paid into a bank account did not itself cause a failure of the means of ascertainment.[37] However, in granting the claim, the court stressed that there had been no mixing of the money in the bank accounts concerned. If there had been mixing, then it seems that common law tracing, unlike equitable tracing, would not have been available.[38] Similarly, in *Lipkin Gorman v Karpnale Ltd*[39] common law tracing was only possible because the defendants had conceded that there had been no mixing of the misappropriated money.

It is important to note that while the common law is incapable of tracing money *through* a mixed fund, it is capable of tracing money *into* a mixed fund so as to establish that the recipient was enriched by the receipt of that property.

(4) Common law tracing of money through the banking system[40]

While the common law is prima facie capable of tracing money through a bank account, provided that it remains unmixed, later cases have found that tracing is not possible at common law where money has been transferred between bank accounts and the means of exchange has inevitably involved some element of mixing. In *Agip (Africa) Ltd v Jackson*[41] the claimant firm was defrauded by its chief accountant, Zdiri. He altered the names of the payee on genuine payment orders in favour of dummy companies he had created. One payment of $518,000 was made to a dummy company, Baker Oil Services Ltd, who held an account at a branch of Lloyds Bank in London. On receiving the payment order Agip's bankers telegraphed instructions to Lloyds Bank Overseas Division to credit the account of Baker Oil at their London Branch with a corresponding amount. At the same time, their correspondent bank in New York debited their account and credited Lloyds Bank's correspondent bank in New York. The next day the money was transferred from the Baker Oil account to the account of the defendants, who were a firm of accountants in the Isle of Man. All but $45,000 was then paid out. There had been no mixing of the money in the Baker Oil account. At first instance Millett J held that Agip could not trace the money at common law. One reason for this denial focused on the nature of the transfer. He held that:

The money was transmitted by telegraphic transfer. There was no cheque or any equivalent. The payment order was not a cheque or its equivalent...Nothing passed between Tunisia and London but a stream of electrons. It is not possible to treat the money as received by Lloyds Bank of London, or its correspondent bank in New York, as representing the proceeds of the payment order or of any other physical asset previously in its hands...[42]

---

[37] As Atkin LJ graphically said: 'But if in 1815 the common law halted outside the banker's door, by 1879 equity had the courage to lift the latch, walk in and examine the books...I see no reason why the means of ascertainment so provided should not now be available both for common law and equity proceedings.'

[38] [1921] 1 KB 321, at 336, per Atkin LJ; at 330, per Scrutton LJ.

[39] [1991] 2 AC 548.   [40] See Smith, *The Law of Tracing* (1997), pp 249–262.

[41] [1990] Ch 265, [1992] 4 All ER 385; Birks 'Misdirected Funds Again' (1989) 105 LQR 528; Sir Peter Millett 'Tracing the Proceeds of Fraud' (1991) 107 LQR 71; [1991] Ch 547, [1992] 4 All ER 451; Harpum 'Equitable Liability For Money Laundering' (1991) 50 CLJ 409; Goulding 'Equity and the Money Launderers' [1992] Conv 367; Swadling 'The Law of Restitution' All ER Rev 1992, pp 258–265.

[42] [1990] Ch 265, at 399.

This argument was rejected by the Court of Appeal, where Fox LJ took the view that it did not matter that the transfer had been by order rather than cheque.[43] More significantly, however, Millett J had held that the claimants were not entitled to trace at common law because the money must have been mixed with other money when the transfer took place through the New York clearing system between Agip and Lloyds' correspondent banks. This reasoning was supported by the Court of Appeal,[44] and tracing at common law was thus prevented.

Similar reasoning was employed in *Bank Tejarat v Hong Kong and Shanghai Banking Corpn (CI) Ltd*,[45] where the claimant had paid the defendants DM3.4m via the Frankfurt clearing system. Tuckey J applied the principle identified in *Agip (Africa) Ltd v Jackson* and held that, as the claimant's money would inevitably have become mixed with other money through the Frankfurt deutschmark clearing system, it was impossible to trace the money at common law into the hands of the defendants.[46] The claimant's claim to personal restitution at common law by way of an action for money had and received therefore failed.

In both cases the inadequacy of the common law rules of tracing required the claimants to turn instead to equity, asserting that the misappropriated money was subject to a trust and that the respective defendants were liable on the grounds of knowing assistance.[47] It is submitted that the refusal to allow common law tracing on the grounds of inevitable mixing during the process of transfer of funds involves an unduly literalistic analysis of the tracing process. Whenever transfers occur between banks, whether by virtue of an electronic transfer or a cheque which is presented through the clearing system, it is not as if the specific money held in the account from which the funds are drawn is transferred to the bank holding the account into which it is to be paid. Where money is held in a bank account, the nature of the relationship between the bank and its customer is one of debtor and creditor, so that there is no real connection between the balance in an account and any specific money as such. Where money is debited from one account and credited to another, there should simply be an evidential presumption that the money represented thereby has passed from one account to the other. The means of transfer operative between the banks holding the accounts should not prevent that inference.

Unless such an inference is operative there is no reason why the common law should ever be able to trace into or through a bank account. The mere transfer of money between accounts held at different domestic banks is effected through the clearing system and yet this does not seem to have prevented common law tracing. In *Jones (FC) & Sons (a firm) v Jones*[48] the partner of the claimant firm drew cheques totalling £11,700 on a joint account at the Midland Bank, which were paid

---

[43] [1992] 4 All ER 451, at 465.   [44] Ibid., per Fox LJ.

[45] [1995] 1 Lloyd's Rep 239; Birks 'Tracing Misused *Bank Tejarat v Hong Kong and Shanghai Banking Corp*' (1995) 9 TLI 91 and 'Persistent Problems in Misdirected Money' [1996] LMCLQ 1.

[46] [1995] 1 Lloyd's Rep 239, at 245.

[47] Now dishonest assistance. *Royal Brunei Airlines v Tan* [1995] 2 AC 378.

[48] [1997] Ch 159.

into an account opened in the name of his wife with a firm of commodity brokers. She then received cheques for £50,760 from the commodity brokers, which she paid into a deposit account. The Court of Appeal held that the firm's trustee in bankruptcy should be entitled to trace at common law and that it was not necessary to take account of the reality of the clearing system which lay behind the transaction. Millett LJ stated that:

Accordingly, the trustee can follow the money in the joint account at Midland Bank, which had been vested by statute in him, into the proceeds of the three cheques which Mrs Jones received from her husband. The trustee does not need to follow money from one recipient to another or follow it through the clearing system; he can follow the cheques as they pass from hand to hand. It is sufficient for him to be able to trace the money into the cheques and the cheques into their proceeds.[49]

If this reasoning is correct (and it is suggested that it is, since it reflects the reality of banking practice), there is equally no reason why the court should have been concerned with the means of transfer through the clearing system in *Agip (Africa) Ltd v Jackson* and *Bank Tejarat v Hong Kong and Shanghai Banking Corpn (CI) Ltd*. Surely it is enough to identify a debit from one account echoed by a corresponding receipt by another. This is as much a swap of one chose in action for another as if a cheque had physically changed hands. Millett LJ seems to lay great stress upon the presence of a physical cheque, which would suggest a return to his argument in *Agip (Africa) Ltd v Jackson*[50] that the common law cannot trace through an electronic transfer, which was rejected by the Court of Appeal.[51]

The nature of a bank account is also a cause for difficulty in relation to common law tracing. As has been noted, the relationship between banker and customer is one of debtor and creditor. In *R v Preddy*,[52] a criminal case concerning mortgage fraud, the House of Lords held that where money was debited from one account and paid into another account, the second account holder had not obtained the property of the first account holder so as to render him liable to conviction for theft under s 15(1) of the Theft Act 1968.[53] Lord Goff explained:

The question remains...whether the debiting of the lending institution's bank account, and the corresponding crediting of the bank account of the defendant or his solicitor, constitutes obtaining of that property. The difficulty in the way of that conclusion is simply that, when the bank account of the defendant (or his solicitor) is credited, he does not obtain the lending institution's chose in action. On the contrary that chose in action is extinguished or reduced pro tanto, and a chose in action is brought into existence representing a debt in an equivalent sum owed by a different bank to the defendant or his solicitor. In these circumstances it is difficult to see how the defendant thereby obtained *property belonging to another*, ie to the lending institution.

Professor Sir John Smith has suggested that 'Effectively, the victim's property has been changed into another form and now belongs to the defendant. There is the gain and equivalent

---

[49] Ibid., at 169.   [50] [1990] Ch 265, [1992] 4 All ER 385.

[51] In *SmithKline Beecham v Apotex Europe Ltd* [2007] Ch 71, Jacobs LJ considered that the *Jones* case was a clear example of constructive trusteeship, and therefore equitable tracing would have been available. If true, this would, of course, solve the issue, as will be demonstrated below at pp 1032–1041.

[52] [1996] AC 815; Fox 'Property Rights and Electronic Funds Transfers' [1996] LMCLQ 456.

[53] Obtaining property by deception.

loss which is characteristic of, and perhaps the substance of, obtaining'.[54] But even if this were right, I do not for myself see how this can properly be described as obtaining property belonging to another. In truth the property which the defendant has obtained is the new chose in action constituted by the debt now owed to him by his bank, and represented by the credit entry in his own bank account. This did not come into existence until the debt so created was owed to him by his bank, and so never belonged to anyone else. True, it corresponded to the debit entered in the lending institution's bank account; but it does not follow that the property which the defendant acquired can be identified with the property which the lending institution lost when its account was debited.[55]

If this analysis is correct, it appears to remove any ability of the common law to trace money through bank accounts. If the increased balance in the credited account cannot be identified with the corresponding reduction in the balance of the debited account, then it is untraceable into that account. This is fundamentally inconsistent with the decision of the Court of Appeal in *Jones (FC) & Sons (a firm) v Jones*,[56] where it was held that the money credited to Mrs Jones's account belonged at law to the firm from whose account it had been debited. It is equally inconsistent with *Banque Belge Pour l'Etranger v Hambrouck*.[57] Even though the claimants were seeking a personal remedy, their right to restitution was dependent upon establishing that the defendant had received their money into her bank account. It is also submitted that it is inconsistent with the judgment of the House of Lords in *Lipkin Gorman v Karpnale Ltd*,[58] where Lord Goff held that the claimant firm of solicitors was entitled to trace money misappropriated from their client account:

There is in my opinion no reason why the solicitors should not be able to trace their property at common law in that chose in action, or in any part of it, into its products, ie cash drawn by Cass from their client account at the bank. Such a claim is consistent with their assertion that the money so obtained by Cass was their property at common law.[59]

It would be utterly illogical if the firm were permitted to trace if Cass withdrew cash from their client account, and presumably also if he subsequently paid the cash into his own bank account, but not if he arranged for a direct transfer of money from their client account to his own bank account. Yet this would seem to be the implication of the decision in *R v Preddy*.[60] The ramifications of this case for the ability to trace through bank accounts at common law have yet to be fully considered by the courts.[61] However, the decision prompted statutory reform of the law of theft to ensure that defendants who received mortgage funds by fraud would be guilty of an offence.[62]

(5) Criticism of the common law rules of tracing

While the authorities have consistently held that the common law is incapable of tracing property through a mixed fund, this limitation has been subject to much criticism.

---

[54] [1995] Crim LR 564, 565–566.   [55] [1996] AC 815, at 834.
[56] [1997] AC 159.   [57] [1921] 1 KB 321.   [58] [1991] 2 AC 548.
[59] Ibid., at 574.   [60] [1996] AC 815.
[61] For comment on the implications of *R v Preddy* in the context of tracing, see Fox 'Property Rights and Electronic Funds Transfers' [1996] LMCLQ 456.
[62] Theft (Amendment) Act 1996.

The very origins of this limitation have been challenged by Lionel Smith, who has argued that in *Taylor v Plumer*[63] the common law court was in fact considering the equitable rules of tracing, with the implication that there was therefore no reason for the common law to consider itself limited in subsequent cases.[64] While this misunderstanding was acknowledged by Millett LJ in *Jones (FC) & Sons (a firm) v Jones*,[65] he made clear that this alone did not permit the overthrow of the settled common law, principle which had emerged despite the misunderstanding.[66]

Given that the limitation cannot be eliminated merely because of historical misunderstanding of *Taylor v Plumer*,[67] it is open to objections on its own terms. It appears to be rooted in the perception that the common law cannot identify property in a mixed fund but, as commentators have pointed out,[68] there is no reason why the common law cannot recognize joint title to a mixed fund through a tenancy-in-common. This possibility was recognized in *Spence v Union Marine Insurance Co Ltd*,[69] where bales of wool were mixed and it was not possible to identify their owners because the identifying marks had been lost in a shipwreck. The court held that there was a tenancy-in-common.

Although in principle the recognition of a tenancy in common at law should enable the common law to trace into mixtures, the cases have not adopted this analysis. The inability of the common law to trace into mixed funds has had the effect of obliging claimants to seek relief in equity, since the equitable rules permit tracing through a mixed fund. While this might achieve practical justice, equitable tracing is dependent upon the existence of a trust relationship. The desire to trace in equity has therefore tended to lead to an expansion of the circumstances in which misappropriated property will be treated as subject to a constructive trust, usually through the medium of a fiduciary relationship. It is questionable whether the expansion of equitable rights and interests in the commercial field is appropriate, and this view seems to have been reflected in a number of cases.[70] The common law rules of tracing have also restricted the availability of common law restitution through the action for money had and received, since it cannot be demonstrated that a defendant was enriched by the receipt of the claimant's property where it has passed through a mixed fund. Thus, in *Bank Tejarat v Hong Kong and Shanghai Banking Corpn (CI) Ltd*[71] the claimant's claim for common law restitution on the grounds of mistake failed because it was not able to trace its money into the hands of the defendants because it had become mixed in the Frankfurt clearing system. At present it is impossible to utilize the equitable rules of tracing to found a common law claim to restitution.[72]

---

63   (1815) 3 M & S 562.

64   Smith 'Tracing in *Taylor v Plumer*: Equity in the Court of King's Bench' (1995) LMCLQ 240.

65   [1997] AC 159.   66   Ibid., at 169.   67   (1815) 3 M & S 562.

68   Pearce 'A Tracing Paper' (1976) Conv (NS) 277.   69   (1868) LR 3 CP 427.

70   Eg: *Re Goldcorp Exchange* [1995] 1 AC 74; *Westdeutsche Landesbank Girozentrale v Islington London Borough Council* [1996] AC 669.

71   [1995] 1 Lloyd's Rep 239; (1995) 9 TLI 91 (Birks).

72   See *Jones (FC) & Sons v Jones* [1997] AC 159, at 169–9–170, per Millett LJ.

It is therefore submitted that there is no basis in principle, or in practice, for the emasculated common law rules that do not permit tracing through a mixed fund. If the common law rules were to develop so as to enable such tracing, there would be less need for an expansion of equity, trusts, and fiduciary relationships into the commercial sphere as adequate restitutionary remedies would be available to a claimant whose property had been misappropriated or misdirected. In *Jones (FC) & Sons (a firm) v Jones*[73] Millett LJ expressed dissatisfaction with the present position:

There is no merit in having distinct and different tracing rules at law and in equity, given that tracing is neither a right nor a remedy but merely the process by which the plaintiff establishes what has happened to his property and makes good his claim that the assets which he claims can properly be regarded as representing his property. The fact that there are different tracing rules at law and in equity is unfortunate through probably inevitable, but unnecessary differences should not be created where they are not required by the different nature of legal and equitable doctrines and remedies. There is, in my view, even less merit in the present rule which precludes the invocation of the equitable tracing rules to support a common law claim; until that rule is swept away unnecessary obstacles to the development of a rational and coherent law of restitution will remain.[74]

In *Foskett v McKeown* he reiterated his dissatisfaction with the current position in the House of Lords, and stated:

Given its nature, there is nothing inherently legal or equitable about the tracing exercise. There is thus no sense in maintaining different rules for tracing at law and in equity. One set of tracing rules is enough…There is certainly no logical justification for allowing any distinctions between them to produce capricious results in cases of mixed substitutions by insisting on the existence of a fiduciary relationship as a precondition for applying equity's tracing rules. The existence of such a relationship may be relevant to the nature of the claim which the plaintiff can maintain, whether personal or proprietary, but that is a different matter.[75]

However, given that the case involved a straightforward situation where a trustee had misappropriated trust property, and that the equitable tracing rules were therefore undoubtedly available, he concluded that it was not the occasion to explore the relationship between equitable and common law tracing rules further. His comments are therefore strictly obiter, and the traditional dichotomy between the rules of tracing in equity and at common law remains intact, albeit on notice of impending demise.[76]

(6) Claiming at common law

It has been seen that the common law enables legal owners to trace their property though clean substitutions, and to trace tangible property into a mixed bulk. Once the tracing process has identified assets which represent the original property, the original owner may be able to assert a claim thereto. The original owner may be entitled

---

[73] [1997] Ch 159.   [74] [1997] Ch 159, at 169–170.   [75] [2001] 1 AC 102, at 128.

[76] See, however, *Shalson v Russo* [2005] Ch 281 at 314[104], where Rimer J opined that the distinction between common law and equitable tracing remained, despite obiter comments to the contrary by Lord Millet in *Foskett v McKeown* [2001] 1 AC 102 (at 129).

to assert a proprietary right, or he may be entitled to claim restitution, which is a personal remedy.

(a) Claiming assets which are the product of a clean substitution

Common law tracing through clean substitutions operates on the basis of the preservation of the claimant's title to the property being traced. The claimant had legal title before any clean substitutions took place, and such substitutions are not able to deprive him of his title. Except in the case of currency (banknotes and coins), to which special rules apply,[77] even a bona fide purchaser will not take free from the claimant's original title because his legal title is good against the world and cannot be defeated. This seems to have been the rationale of *Taylor v Plumer*,[78] where Lord Ellenborough said that Sir Thomas had simply 'repossessed himself of that, of which ... he had never ceased to be the lawful proprietor'. In *Lipkin Gorman v Karpnale Ltd*, where a solicitor had taken money for gambling from the client account of his firm, Lord Goff held that the firm could trace at common law:

There is in my opinion no reason why the solicitors should not be able to trace their property at common law in that chose in action [the client account], in any part of it, into its product, ie cash drawn by Cass from their client account at the bank. Such a claim is consistent with their assertion that the money so obtained by Cass was their property at common law.[79]

Historically, the common law did not possess adequate remedies to enable the claimant to vindicate his proprietary entitlement to assets identified as representing his original property. While the common law developed real actions to enable a claimant to recover land, there were no equivalent actions to enable an owner to recover a specific chattel. As Professor Goode[80] has pointed out, the common law was only ever able to offer a personal remedy in damages for detinue or conversion. By statute, the court enjoyed the discretion to award specific recovery in an action in detinue.[81] Section 3 of the Torts (Interference with Goods) Act 1977 entitles the court to order the delivery of goods. However, in some older cases the owner was able to recover his property[82] and more recent cases have now established beyond doubt that an original owner may claim legal title to any assets identified by the rules of tracing.[83]

It is now clear that where a legal owner can identify assets in the hands of a third party as representing his original property, he will be entitled to claim them as his own. In *Lipkin Gorman v Karpnale Ltd*,[84] Lord Goff stated that the legal owner of property was entitled to trace or follow his property into its product. This principle

---

[77] See Fox 'Bona Fide Purchase and the Currency of Money' [1996] CLJ 547; Fox 'The Transfer of Legal Title to Money' [1996] RLR 60.

[78] (1815) 3 M & S 562.

[79] [1991] 2 AC 548, at 529, [1992] 4 All ER 512; (1991) Lloyd's MCLQ 473 (Birks); (1991) 107 LQR 521 (Watts); [1992] Conv 124 (Halliwell); (1992) 55 MLR 377 (McKendrick); (1992) 45(2) CLP 69 (Birks).

[80] Goode 'The Right to Trace and its Impact in Commercial Transactions' (1976) LQR 360.

[81] Common Law Procedure Act 1854, s 78. Detinue was abolished by s 2 of the Torts (Interference with Goods) Act 1977.

[82] As in *Taylor v Plumer* (1815) 3 M & S 562.   [83] See *Jones (FC) & Sons v Jones* [1997] AC 159.

[84] [1991] 2 AC 548, at 573.

was applied by the Court of Appeal in *Jones (FC) & Sons (a firm) v Jones*,[85] where the defendant had received money drawn from the bank account of a firm which had committed an act of bankruptcy before it had been adjudicated bankrupt. The money was invested in an account held by a firm of commodity brokers which dealt in potato futures. The investment was highly successful and the account contained almost five times as much money as had been initially invested. The Court of Appeal held that, as the firm could trace the money at common law into the account with the brokers, its trustee in bankruptcy was entitled to the money in the account (which had been paid into court). Beldam LJ stated:

> There is now ample authority for the proposition that a person who can trace his property into its product, provided the product is identifiable as the product of his property, he may lay legal claim to that property.[86]

Where an owner is entitled to claim specific assets at common law he will be entitled to take advantage of any appreciation in value which they have experienced.

(b) Claiming assets where tangible property has been mixed to form a bulk

The common law permits the tracing of tangible property into a mixed bulk. Where a mixed bulk has been created, the rights of an original owner will vary depending upon whether the bulk is able to be separated into proportionate shares representing the assets of the contributors.

(i) Claiming where the bulk can be divided into proportionate shares

Where the bulk is capable of division, a contributor will be entitled to claim the proportionate share which represents his original property, and of which he is a tenant in common. Such division will usually be possible if the property is fungible in nature, such as when it consists of grain, oil, or wine.[87] The principle was stated by Staughton J in *Indian Oil Corpn Ltd v Greenstone Shipping Co SA (Panama) (The Ypatianna)*:

> where B wrongfully mixes the goods of A with goods of his own, which are substantially of the same nature and quality, and they cannot in practice be separated, the mixture is held in common and A is entitled to receive out of it a quantity equal to that of his goods which went into the mixture, any doubt as to that quantity being resolved in favour of A.[88]

(ii) Claiming where the bulk cannot be divided into proportionate shares

In contrast, where property was wrongfully mixed to form a bulk that cannot be divided into the proportionate shares of the contributors, the original owner will be entitled to claim the entire bulk. The right to claim the entire bulk in such circumstances was recognized by the House of Lords in *Foskett v McKeown*,[89] on the grounds that a pro rata division of the property is the best that the wrongdoer can hope for.

---

[85] [1997] AC 159; Andrews and Beatson 'Common Law Tracing: Springboard or Swan Song?'; Fox 'Common Law Claims to Substituted Assets' [1997] CLJ 30. See also Davern 'Common Law Tracing, Profits and the Doctrine of Relation Back' [1997] RLR 92–96.

[86] [1997] AC 159, at 171   [87] *Foskett v McKeown* [2001] 1 AC 102, at 133, per Lord Millett.

[88] [1988] QB 345, 371.   [89] [2001] 1 AC 102.

Such circumstances are admittedly likely to be rare, but Lord Millet referred to the Canadian case of *Jones v De Marchant*[90] by way of example. In that case, a husband had wrongfully used eighteen beaver skins belonging to his wife, together with fours skins of his own, to have a fur coat made up, which he gave to his mistress. Since the skins were no longer able to be separated it was held that the wife was entitled to ownership of the entire coat.

(c) Claiming personal restitution at common law

The process of tracing may also provide a foundation for a personal claim to restitution. Where property is misappropriated or misdirected, a recipient will be treated as having been unjustly enriched. The extent of his enrichment is the value of the property that he had received. If nothing remains in his hands which can be said to represent the property he received then a proprietary claim will not be available because the property has been dissipated. A proprietary claim can only subsist in relation to some specific identifiable asset. As Lord Lane CJ observed in *A-G's Reference (No 1 of 1985)*,[91] there can be no proprietary remedy unless there is an asset which can be 'identified as a separate piece of property'. The original owners may, however, be entitled to claim personal restitution from the recipient. In the context of such a claim, tracing is operating as a process by which it can be demonstrated that a defendant was in fact enriched at the expense of the original owner by receipt of his property. A personal restitutionary claim may also be more advantageous to an original owner than a proprietary claim, even where the property has not been dissipated if the assets which represent his property have subsequently fallen in value, since the measure of restitution will be determined by the value of the property at the point of receipt. However, such a personal remedy will only be more advantageous in practice if the recipient is solvent and able to discharge the obligation to make restitution.

The liability of a person who has received property belonging to another to make restitution at common law is strict, subject to the availability of the defence of change of position. The role of common law tracing as a foundation for a personal liability to make restitution is evident in *Lipkin Gorman v Karpnale Ltd*,[92] where a solicitor had misappropriated money from his firm's client account in order to finance his gambling at the Playboy Club. His firm sought to recover restitution from the club of the misappropriated money it had received. The firm could not make a proprietary claim to any assets in the club's hands as none could be identified which were the product of the money received. The common law rules would not permit tracing once the money had become mixed with other money of the club. However, the rules of common law tracing did establish that the club had received money which belonged to the firm, and thus entitled the firm to maintain the common law action for money had and received. As Lord Goff explained:

It is well established that a legal owner is entitled to trace his property into its product, provided that the latter is indeed identifiable as the product of his property . . . Before Cass drew

[90] (1916) 28 DLR 561.   [91] [1986] QB 491, at 506.   [92] [1991] 2 AC 548.

upon the solicitor's client account at the bank, there was of course no question of the solicitor's having any legal property in any cash lying at the bank. The relationship of the bank with the solicitors was essentially that of debtor and creditor; and since the client account was at all material times in credit, the bank was the debtor and the solicitors were its creditors. Such a debt constitutes a chose in action, which is a species of property; and since the debt was enforceable at common law, the chose in action was legal property belonging to the solicitors at common law. There is in my opinion no reason why the solicitors should not be able to trace their property at common law in that chose in action, or in any part of it, into its product, ie cash drawn by Cass from their client account at the bank. Such a claim is consistent with their assertion that the money obtained by Cass was their property at common law...it further follows, from the concession made by the respondents,[93] that the solicitors can follow their property into the hands of the respondents when it was paid to them at the club.[94]

Thus, the firm's ability to trace the money drawn from the client account into the hands of the club, via the activities of the misappropriating solicitor, was vital to the establishment of their entitlement to restitution by way of an action for money had and received. Lord Goff stressed that the firm's claim was not proprietary, although it was founded upon the receipt of property:

the solicitors seek to show that the money in question was their property at common law. But their claim in the present case for money had and received is nevertheless a personal claim; it is not a proprietary claim, advanced on the basis that money remaining in the hands of the respondents is their property.[95]

3 Tracing and claiming in equity[96]

(1) The scope of equitable tracing

Whereas the common law rules of tracing have remained restrictive, equity developed rules which are much more flexible. There is no barrier preventing the tracing of equitable proprietary interests through a mixed fund. The rules, which originated in the context of the misappropriation of property subject to an express trust, are derived from evidential presumptions which enable the court to determine whether property has survived through mixing, and whether any assets purchased with money from a mixed fund can be said to represent property contributed to the mixture. The equitable rules are particularly designed to deal with mixing of funds in a bank account. By necessity they are rough and ready and not overly sophisticated. The presumptions on which they are founded also take account of the moral blameworthiness of the parties

---

[93] The respondents had conceded that if it could be shown that the firm enjoyed legal title to the money from the client account in the hands of the solicitor, then that title was not defeated by mixing of that money with other money in his hands.

[94] [1991] 2 AC 548, at 572–573.   [95] Ibid., at 572.

[96] Hayton, 'Equity's Identification Rules', in Birks (ed), *Laundering and Tracing* (1995), pp 1–22; Worthington, *Proprietary Interests in Commercial Transactions* (1996), pp 173–186; Burrows, *The Law of Restitution* (2nd edn, 2002), pp 93–104.

whose funds have been mixed. If a mixed fund consists of misappropriated trust property and the property of the wrongdoing trustee, the rules operate harshly against the wrongdoer. In contrast, if the mixture is comprised of misappropriated trust property and that of an innocent volunteer, they seek to achieve a fair balance between the two innocent parties.

(2) The right to trace in equity

Equitable tracing is not available in every situation in which property has been misappropriated or misapplied. Historically, equity has taken the view that tracing is only possible where there was an initial fiduciary relationship. While the language of a fiduciary relationship is somewhat imprecise and opaque,[97] what is really required is that the property sought to be traced was subject to a trust and thus belonged to the claimant in equity. This follows from the fact that the equitable rules of tracing seek to identify trust property. The question whether tracing in equity is possible is therefore closely connected to the question whether the original property was subject to a trust. Many of the early cases concerning equitable tracing concerned the misappropriation of property held under an express trust, as for example in *Re Hallet's Estate*[98] and *Re Oatway*.[99] Problems have occurred where claimants have sought to trace property in equity which was not subject to a pre-existing trust and where the very circumstances of misappropriation or transfer are alleged to have given rise to a constructive trust, thus entitling the claimant to trace. In many commercial contexts the inadequacy of the common law rules of tracing has forced claimants to turn to equity, which has tended to exert pressure on the court to find a trust relationship through the artificial use of fiduciary relationships.

(a) The requirement of a fiduciary relationship

The present position of the English cases is that an initial fiduciary relationship is a prerequisite of the right to trace in equity. This was reaffirmed in *Westdeutsche Landesbank Girozentrale v Islington London Borough Council*.[100] While the House of Lords overruled the earlier decision of *Sinclair v Brougham*,[101] Lord Browne-Wilkinson was at pains to stress that this did not amount to a rejection of the requirement of a fiduciary relationship, since the House of Lords was not wishing to cast any doubt on the principles of tracing established in the later case of *Re Diplock*.

In *Re Diplock*[102] charities had wrongly received payments of £203,000 under a will. The next of kin were held entitled to trace the money in equity into the charities' hands, because the executors clearly stood in a fiduciary relationship to the estate. The Court of Appeal had examined the judgments of the House of Lords in *Sinclair v*

---

[97] See Chapter 30.   [98] (1880) 13 Ch D 696.   [99] [1903] 2 Ch 356.

[100] [1996] AC 669. In *Dublin Corpn v Building and Allied Trade Union* [1996] 1 IR 468 the Irish Supreme Court doubted that *Sinclair v Brougham* was authority for the proposition that a fiduciary relationship was a prerequisite of equitable tracing.

[101] [1914] AC 398.   [102] [1948] Ch 465.

Brougham[103] and concluded that a fiduciary relationship was a prerequisite to tracing in equity. Lord Greene MR stated:

Lord Parker and Lord Haldane both predicate the existence of a right of property recognised by equity which depends upon there having existed at some stage a fiduciary relationship of some kind (though not necessarily a positive duty of trusteeship) sufficient to give rise to the equitable right to trace property. Exactly what relationships are sufficient to bring such an equitable right into existence for the purposes of the rule which we are considering is a matter which has not been precisely laid down. Certain relationships are clearly included; eg trustee (actual or constructive) and cestui que trust; and 'fiduciary' relationships such as that of principal and agent...[104]

In *Sinclair v Brougham* a building society had operated an ultra vires banking business. The case concerned the rights of the depositors who had invested their money with the bank when the building society had become insolvent. The House of Lords held that they were not entitled to claim restitution at common law through the action for money had and received, which would have meant that they would have stood as creditors in the insolvency and they would have ranked pari passu with the other general creditors of the society. At that time the right to restitution was said to be founded upon an implied contract to repay money had and received. The House of Lords held that, since the building society had acted ultra vires in conducting the banking business, any contract to repay the depositors would also have been ultra vires and was therefore void and unenforceable. Since this would have the consequence that the depositors would have no entitlement to claim as creditors in the insolvency, the House of Lords held that the building society had received their deposits as a fiduciary and that they were entitled to trace their money in equity into its remaining assets. In subsequent cases, the implied contract theory was rejected as artificial, and the right to restitution is now available through the autonomous cause of action in unjust enrichment. In *Westdeutsche Landesbank Girozentrale v Islington London Borough Council*[105] the House of Lords therefore held that, if the same facts had arisen for decision today, the depositors would have been entitled to personal restitution on the grounds that the building society had been unjustly enriched by the receipt of their deposits when there had been a total failure of consideration because their promise to repay was ultra vires and void. There would therefore be no need to trace in equity and, in as far as the House of Lords had found that the deposits were held on trust for the depositors by the building society so as to be traceable in equity, it was overruled.

Other cases also support the view that a fiduciary relationship is an essential prerequisite for equitable tracing. In *Agip (Africa) Ltd v Jackson*,[106] Fox LJ observed:

Equity...will follow money into a mixed fund and charge the fund. There is, in the present case, no difficulty about the mechanics of tracing in equity. The money can be traced through the various bank accounts to Baker Oil and onwards. It is, however, a prerequisite to the operation

---

103 [1914] AC 398.   104 [1948] Ch 465, at 540.
105 [1996] AC 669.   106 [1992] 4 All ER 451.

of the remedy in equity that there must be a fiduciary relationship which calls the equitable jurisdiction into being...[107]

On the facts this presented no difficulty, because it was held that the claimant's fraudulent accountant stood in a fiduciary relationship to them. A fiduciary relationship was also held to be a prerequisite of the right to trace in equity by the Court of Appeal in *Boscawen v Bajwa*.[108] In *Jones (FC) & Sons (a firm) v Jones*[109] the misappropriated money was traced at common law rather than in equity because Mrs Jones had not received it in a fiduciary capacity, so that it was not subject to a constructive trust. While in *Foskett v McKeown*[110] Lord Millett considered that there was no logical justification for insisting upon the existence of a fiduciary relationship as a precondition for applying equity's tracing rules, the requirement was not overruled because the case concerned a straightforward case of the misappropriation of trust money.

Where trust property has been misappropriated or misdirected, the essential requirement of a fiduciary relationship will be satisfied. The trustee stood in a fiduciary relationship vis-à-vis the beneficiary who is seeking to trace in equity. However, it is also clear that the fiduciary relationship need not have existed prior to the misappropriation or misdirection of the property concerned, since the circumstances of the misappropriation or misdirection may themselves give rise to a fiduciary relationship entitling the original owner to trace in equity. In *Chase Manhattan Bank NA v Israeli-British Bank (London) Ltd*[111] Chase Manhattan paid the Israeli-British Bank $1m. Due to a clerical error the same amount was paid again later the same day. The Israeli-British bank became insolvent and Chase Manhattan sought to trace the second mistaken payment money into its assets. Although they would clearly have had a personal action for restitution of the sum paid by mistake, it was essential that they could maintain a proprietary claim, because they would otherwise merely rank among the general creditors. However, the banks were two commercial organizations, dealing with each other at arm's length, and as such they did not stand in a fiduciary relationship, nor was the money paid subject to a pre-existing trust. Despite this, Goulding J held that the very fact that the payment had been made by mistake brought about a fiduciary relationship that entitled Chase Manhattan to trace. He stated his rationale:

a person who pays money to another under a factual mistake retains an equitable property in it and the conscience of that other is subjected to a fiduciary duty to respect his proprietary right.[112]

However, this decision was subjected to criticism by the House of Lords in *Westdeutsche Landesbank Girozentrale v Islington London Borough Council*,[113] where Lord Browne-Wilkinson stated that he could not agree that the mere fact that the payment had been made by mistake meant that the payor retained the equitable interest

---

[107] Ibid., at 466.
[108] [1995] 4 All ER 769, at 777, per Millett LJ.
[109] [1997] Ch 159.
[110] [2001] 1 AC 102, at 128–129.
[111] [1981] Ch 105.
[112] Ibid., at 119.
[113] [1996] AC 669.

in the money paid when it had not previously been subject to a trust.[114] Although the judge's reasoning was doubted, Lord Browne-Wilkinson felt that the case may have been rightly decided:

The defendant bank knew of the mistake made by the paying bank within two days of the receipt of the moneys. The judge treated this fact as irrelevant but in my judgement it may well provide a proper foundation for the decision. Although the mere receipt of the moneys, in ignorance of the mistake, gives rise to no trust, the retention of the moneys after the recipient bank learned of the mistake may well have given rise to a constructive trust.[115]

It is submitted, however, that this reasoning is spurious. If the mistaken payment effected a transfer of the ownership of the money to the payee when it was received, there is no reason why a trust should have been imposed when the bank discovered that a mistake had occurred. The bank was clearly subject to an obligation to make restitution at common law, but the mere fact that it should have to make restitution does not generate a constructive trust. While the equitable obligation to account has been held to give rise to a constructive trust because of the operation of the maxim that equity treats as done that which ought to be done, there is no equivalent principle at common law. It is submitted that the crucial question should focus on the proprietary consequences of the mistaken payment at the moment it was made, in other words, whether the mistake prevented title in the money passing to the payee. Lord Goff indicated that a fundamental mistake might prevent the beneficial interest in property passing to a payee.[116]

The requirement of an initial fiduciary relationship has been subject to heavy criticism, both on the grounds that it is not supported in authority and that it is not justified in principle.[117] The major criticism is that the requirement is artificial, the courts being willing to find, or 'discover',[118] a fiduciary relationship whenever they feel that tracing is justified, as in *Chase Manhattan Bank NA v Israeli-British Bank (London) Ltd*.[119] For this reason, Goff and Jones suggested in an earlier edition of their seminal text that whether tracing (which they call a 'restitutionary proprietary claim') should be available should 'depend on whether it is just, in the particular circumstances of the case, to impose a constructive trust on, or an equitable lien over, particular assets...'.[120] However, this proposal is equally unsuitable because of its arbitrary nature and it has not been maintained in subsequent editions, where it is regretted that the courts have not taken opportunities which have been presented to overrule the requirement.[121]

---

[114] Ibid., at 714.   [115] Ibid., at 715.   [116] Ibid., at 690.

[117] See Goff and Jones, *The Law of Restitution* (6th edn, 2002), pp 104–106; Birks, *Introduction to the Law of Restitution* (1985), pp 377–385; Pearce 'A Tracing Paper' (1976) 40 Conv 277. It is argued that *Sinclair v Brougham* [1914] AC 398 did not require an initial fiduciary relationship and that the case was misunderstood by the Court of Appeal in *Re Diplock* [1948] Ch 465.

[118] Goff and Jones, *The Law of Restitution* (6th edn, 2002), p 105.

[119] [1981] Ch 105.

[120] Goff and Jones, *The Law of Restitution* (3rd edn, 1987), p 79.

[121] Goff and Jones, *The Law of Restitution* (6th edn, 2002), pp 104–106. In this edition, Goff and Jones argue that the comments of the House of Lords in *Foskett v McKeown* [2001] 1 AC 102 that 'there is no sense

In practice, it seems that the requirement of a 'fiduciary relationship' is less of a limitation than some critics have suggested. In any case, involving property that was held upon trust there will be no difficulty and equitable tracing will always be available. It is the commercial situations which have generated difficulty. However, even in the commercial context the requirement is easily circumvented. As Millett J observed in *Agip (Africa) Ltd v Jackson*[122] it is 'readily satisfied in most cases of commercial fraud, since the embezzlement of a company's funds almost invariably involves a breach of fiduciary duty on the part of one of the company's employees or agents'.[123] Although he noted the criticism, he felt that it was not for a court of first instance to reconsider the requirement, and as has been seen the Court of Appeal merely reasserted it.[124]

(b) Equitable ownership of the property traced

While it is true that the requirement of a fiduciary relationship has not prevented tracing in practice, the language is confusing because it conceals the true basis of equitable tracing. Equity is not concerned with the presence of a fiduciary relationship per se, but rather with the identification of a trust. A person will only be entitled to trace property in equity of which he was the equitable owner. Where trust property was misappropriated or misdirected, the beneficiaries are entitled to trace the trust property which belongs to them in equity. Where the property of an absolute owner is misappropriated or misdirected, he will only be entitled to trace if the circumstances of the misappropriation or misdirection gave rise to a trust in his favour.[125] An alternative analysis of tracing was propounded by Pearce, who argued that equitable tracing should be available whenever there is a 'continuing right of property recognised in equity', which would recognize the possibility of using equity to trace beneficial ownership.[126] If the circumstances do not disclose a transfer of equitable beneficial ownership, the recipient should be obliged to give effect to the owner's continuing proprietary interest. Professor Birks has adopted the argument that equitable tracing should be available whenever there is a sufficient 'proprietary base'. By this he means that:

the circumstances of the original receipt by the defendant must be such that, either at law or in equity, the plaintiff retained or obtained the property in the matter received by the defendant, and then continued to retain it until the moment at which the substitution or intermixture took place.[127]

The trust analysis of the right to trace in equity was supported by the Privy Council in *Re Goldcorp Exchange Ltd (in receivership)*.[128] The customers who had purchased 'non-allocated metal' were not entitled to trace their purchase money into the bulk

---

in maintaining different rules for tracing at law and in equity' lead to the conclusion that the courts should no longer insist on a fiduciary relationship before a claimant can trace in equity.

[122] [1992] 4 All ER 385.   [123] Ibid., at 402.   [124] [1992] 4 All ER 451.
[125] See *Westdeutsche Landesbank Girozentrale v Islington London Borough Council* [1996] AC 669, at 706, per Lord Browne-Wilkinson.
[126] (1976) 40 Conv 275.   [127] Birks, *Introduction to the Law of Restitution* (1985), p 378.
[128] [1994] 2 All ER 806.

of metal held by the company because they could not be shown to have any equitable proprietary interest in it arising through the contract of sale.[129]

It is submitted that there is a strong argument for permitting equitable tracing to be employed wherever property has changed hands in circumstances where there has been no transfer of the equitable beneficial interest. However, such a development would not lead to any significant practical change in the operation of equitable tracing, since there is such a close connection between equitable ownership and a fiduciary relationship that the two terms could almost be seen to be synonymous. This much is admitted by Birks.

the requirement of a fiduciary relationship is, in this context one and the same as the requirement of an undestroyed proprietary base . . . a plaintiff who wants to assert an equitable proprietary interest in the surviving enrichment must show facts such that the property in the original receipt did not pass at law and in equity to the recipient. If he can show such facts, so that, at least in equity, he retained the property in the res, he will, after identifying the surviving enrichment, be able to raise an equitable proprietary interest in those different assets. Where such facts are shown, the relationship between him and the recipient can, rightly, be described as 'fiduciary' in that it will resemble the relationship between cestui que trust and trustee.[130]

While the continuing proprietary interest analysis may be little more than an alternative label for the present search for a 'fiduciary relationship', it has the definite merit of de-mythologizing the process because it is a more accurate and precise description of what the court is looking for. That said, the mere fact that a different label is used does not answer the difficult questions as to the circumstances in which a trust will arise so as to justify tracing in equity.

(c) Circumstances in which it will be possible to trace in equity

(i) Misappropriation of trust property by a trustee

Equitable tracing will always be available against a trustee who has wrongfully misappropriated trust property, because the beneficiary retains his equitable title to the trust property. Thus equitable tracing was permitted in *Foskett v McKeown*,[131] where a trustee had wrongfully used trust money to pay the premiums due under his insurance policy.

(ii) Receipt of trust property by a stranger to a trust

Where property subject to a trust is transferred to a stranger in breach of trust, the beneficiary will be entitled to trace the trust property into the hands of the stranger unless he was a bona fide purchaser for value without notice, in which case the beneficiary's equitable title will be defeated.

---

[129] See Birks 'Establishing a Proprietary Base' [1995] RLR 83). Compare *El Ajou v Dollar Land Holdings plc (No 2)* [1995] 2 All ER 213, where Robert Walker J suggested that tracing depends on the concept of an equitable charge and not equitable ownership.

[130] Birks, *Introduction to the Law of Restitution* (1985), p 381.

[131] [2001] 1 AC 102.

(iii) Profits received by a fiduciary in breach of duty

As unauthorized profits received by a fiduciary are held on constructive trust for his principal, the principal will be entitled to trace them in equity. Thus, in *A-G of Hong Kong v Reid*[132] the Crown was able to trace the bribes that had been received by a fiduciary into the houses he had purchased with them.

(iv) Stolen or misappropriated property

In *Lipkin Gorman v Karpnale Ltd*[133] Lord Templeman approved Australian authorities, which hold that a thief does not gain title to his property, but holds it on trust. He cited with approval O'Connor J in *Black v S Freedman & Co*:

> Where money has been stolen, it is trust money in the hands of the thief and he cannot divest it of that character. If he pays it over to another person, then it may be followed into that person's hands. If, of course, that other person shows that it has come to him bona fides for valuable consideration, and without notice, it then may lose its character as trust money and cannot be recovered…[134]

In *Westdeutsche Landesbank Girozentrale v Islington London Borough Council*[135] Lord Browne-Wilkinson also held that theft would generate a constructive trust sufficient to give rise to the right to trace in equity. He considered whether a resulting trust would arise when a thief stole a bag of coins:

> I agree that the stolen moneys are traceable in equity. But the proprietary interest which equity is enforcing in such circumstances arises under a constructive, not a resulting, trust. Although it is difficult to find clear authority for the proposition, when property is obtained by fraud equity imposes a constructive trust on the fraudulent recipient; the property is recoverable and traceable in equity…Money stolen from a bank account can be traced in equity.[136]

This principle is sufficient to justify tracing in equity in *Agip (Africa) Ltd v Jackson*[137] without having to find that the accountant, Zdiri, was a fiduciary. He was simply a thief who never gained title to the money he misappropriated, so it was possible to follow it into Baker Oil's account and beyond. The principle that a constructive trust arises from the fraudulent receipt of property was applied to establish a right to trace by Lawrence Collins J in *Commerzbank Aktiengesellschaft v IMB Morgan plc*,[138] where a stockbroker in Nigeria had received money into its accounts which had been obtained as a result of fraud.

It may be noted that, although the authorities now support the view that the thief holds on trust, it is an unusual kind of trust since, so far as the property originally

---

[132] [1994] 1 All ER 1.   [133] [1991] 2 AC 548, [1992] 4 All ER 512.
[134] (1910) 12 CLR 105.   [135] [1996] AC 669.
[136] Ibid., at 716. The following cases were cited in favour of this proposition: *Stocks v Wilson* [1913] 2 KB 235; *R Leslie Ltd v Sheill* [1914] 3 KB 607; *Bankers Trust Co v Shapira* [1980] 1 WLR 1274; *McCormick v Grogan* (1869) LR 4 HL 82. The proposition has been doubted in a number of subsequent authorities, including *Halifax Building Society v Thomas* [1996] Ch 217; *Paragon Finance v DB Thakerar* [1999] 1 All ER 400; and *Shalson v Russo* [2003] WTLR 1165. In *Sinclair Investment Holding SA v Versailles Trade Finance Ltd* [2005] EWCA Civ 722 the Court of Appeal expressed reservations about the principle but refused to strike out a claim founded upon it on the grounds that there was at least an arguable cause of action based on a constructive trust of property obtained by fraud or theft.
[137] [1990] Ch 265; affd [1992] 4 All ER 451.   [138] [2004] EWHC 2771.

stolen is concerned, the thief does not normally have legal title. This is always the case where tangible property is stolen, and may even be the case in relation to certain intangible property, such as money.[139] Because of this unusual characteristic, there is much to be said for the view that the right to trace exists because of the continuing equitable proprietary rights of the true owner, rather than because of the existence of a trust in the conventional sense.[140]

(v) Payments made under a void contract[141]

A recent area of controversy has concerned the question whether a payment made under a contract void ab initio is traceable in equity. It had been argued that such a payment would give rise to a resulting trust in favour of the payor, thus entitling him to trace the payment into the assets of the payee. However, this analysis was comprehensively rejected by the House of Lords in *Westdeutsche Landesbank Girozentrale v Islington London Borough Council*,[142] where it was held that money paid under a void interest rate swap agreement was not subject to a resulting trust. Lord Goff stated:

> there is no general rule that the property in money paid under a void contract does not pass to the payee; and it is difficult to escape the conclusion that, as a general rule, the beneficial interest in the money likewise passes to the payee.[143]

The House of Lords reversed the decision of the Court of Appeal[144] that a resulting trust had arisen, and overruled *Sinclair v Brougham*.[145] It therefore seems that it will generally be impossible to trace money paid under a void contract in equity and that the payor will be confined to seeking restitution at common law. However, Lord Browne-Wilkinson did seem to suggest that a trust would be imposed if the recipient of the payment was aware of the invalidity of the contract so as to affect his conscience and justify the imposition of a constructive trust, and that such a trust could arise even after receipt if the payee became aware of the invalidity while the payment was still identifiable in his hands.

(vi) Payments made under a voidable contract[146]

In *El Ajou v Dollar Land Holdings plc (No 1)*[147] Millett J held that a resulting trust arose when a payment had been made under a voidable contract. The case concerned a

---

[139] Where intangible property is obtained by fraud, legal title may pass to the thief, as for instance if shares or registered land are registered in his name.

[140] See above, p 1036.

[141] See Worthington, *Proprietary Interests in Commercial Transactions* (1996), pp 148–161.

[142] [1996] AC 669.   [143] Ibid., at 690.

[144] [1994] 1 WLR 938; [1994] RLR 73 (Swadling). Dillon LJ had adopted the following conclusion: 'Since, contrary to the expectation of the parties, the swap transaction and contract are, and were from the outset, ultra vires and void, the purpose for which the £2.5 million was paid by the bank to the council has wholly failed, and the £2.5 million has, from the time the council received it, been held on a resulting trust for the bank.'

[145] [1914] AC 398.

[146] See Worthington, *Proprietary Interests in Commercial Transactions* (1996), pp 161–168.

[147] [1993] BCLC 735; revsd [1994] BCLC 464, CA. See also: *Daly v Sydney Stock Exchange* (1986) 160 CLR 371; *Lonrho plc v Fayed (No 2)* [1992] 1 WLR 1; *Halifax Building Society v Thomas* [1996] Ch 217.

fraudulent share-selling scheme operated by three Canadians. The claimants' money was invested in the scheme after their agent was bribed to invest in it. The proceeds were eventually invested in a property development project carried on with the defendants, Dollar Land Holdings. The claimants sought to recover their money from the defendants. Millett J held that although they could not trace at common law, because the money had been mixed, they could trace in equity because there was a fiduciary relationship between them and their agent, who was bribed. However, Millett J went on to consider the position of other victims of the fraud who had not invested through a fiduciary and concluded that they too would be entitled to trace:

> Other victims, however, were less fortunate. They employed no fiduciary. They were simply swindled. No breach of any fiduciary obligation was involved. It would, of course, be an intolerable reproach to our system of jurisprudence if the plaintiff were the only victim who could trace and recover his money. Neither party before me suggested that this is the case; and I agree with them. But if the other victims of the fraud can trace their money in equity it must be because, having been induced to purchase the shares by false and fraudulent misrepresentations, they are entitled to rescind the transaction and revest the equitable title to the purchase money in themselves, at least to the extent necessary to support an equitable tracing claim...[148]

While this neatly emphasizes that the essence of the right to trace is not a fiduciary relationship per se but the need to demonstrate an equitable proprietary interest, the judgment of the Privy Council in *Re Goldcorp Exchange Ltd (in receivership)*[149] casts doubt upon the proposition. The purchasers of 'non-allocated metal' argued that they were entitled to rescind the contract on the grounds of misrepresentation. Although they had not in fact rescinded their contracts, the Privy Council suggested that even if they had they would not have been entitled to an equitable proprietary right. As Lord Mustill explained:

> even if this fatal objection could be overcome, the argument would, in their Lordships' opinion, be bound to fail. While it is convenient to speak of the customers 'getting their money back' this expression is misleading. Upon payment by the customers the purchase moneys became, and rescission or no rescission remained, the unencumbered property of the company. What the customers would recover on rescission would not be 'their' money, but an equivalent sum...[150]

In the light of *Westdeutsche Landesbank Girozentrale v Islington London Borough Council*,[151] it seems that the mere fact that a contract is avoided will not give rise to a trust entitling a payor to trace in equity.[152]

(vii) Payments made by mistake

As has already been seen in *Chase Manhattan Bank NA v Israeli-British Bank (London) Ltd*,[153] it was held that a payor was entitled to trace in equity a payment caused by his mistake of fact. However, it remains unclear why equitable tracing was permitted. In

---

[148] [1993] BCLC 735, at 753.   [149] [1994] 2 All ER 806.
[150] Ibid., at 825–826.   [151] [1996] AC 669.
[152] See also *Criterion Properties plc v Stratford UK Properties LLC* [2004] 1 WLR 1846.
[153] [1981] Ch 105.

Westdeutsche Landesbank Girozentrale v Islington London Borough Council[154] Lord Browne-Wilkinson doubted that the payor could be said to have retained the equitable title to his money when it was not subject to a trust prior to the payment, and the payee had not known at the moment that the payment was made that the payor was acting under a mistake. He seemed to suggest that a trust only arose because the payee became aware of the mistake two days later, thus affecting his conscience and leading to the imposition of a trust. This analysis has been subject to criticism[155] and, as was noted above, the true question should be whether the payee received good title to the money paid at the moment that it was transferred to him. If so, no trust arises and, while the recipient may be required to make restitution of the amount of the payment, the payor should not be entitled to trace. Tracing should only be possible if the money was paid under a mistake of fact so fundamental as to prevent property passing. The real difficulty is in identifying mistakes sufficiently fundamental to prevent property passing. As Robert Goff J said in *Barclays Bank Ltd v W J Simms*[156] in the majority of cases property will pass in payments made under a mistake of fact.[157] In *Re Goldcorp Exchange Ltd*[158] the Privy Council emphasized that the mistake in *Chase Manhattan* was a mistake whereby one party mistakenly made the same payment twice.[159] In *Westdeutsche* Lord Goff suggested that only a fundamental mistake of fact might prevent the equitable interest in money passing to a payee.[160]

(3) Equitable tracing through clean substitutions

Where trust property has been exchanged for other property, the beneficiaries are entitled to trace into the exchange product. Thus, if a trustee uses trust money to purchase a diamond ring, the beneficiaries will be able to trace their equitable ownership into the ring.

(4) Equitable tracing of tangible property into a mixed bulk

If the trust property consists of tangible property, for example if it is a quantity of crude oil, it is possible that the trustee may wrongfully allow the trust property to be mixed with other property so as to form a bulk. In such circumstances, the beneficiaries would be entitled to trace the trust property into the bulk, and they would be entitled to a share of the equitable ownership proportionate to their contribution.[161]

(5) Equitable tracing of money through a mixed fund

More difficult problems present themselves if misappropriated trust property is mixed with other property so that it can no longer be identified as such. Assets purchased

---

[154] [1996] AC 669.
[155] Birks 'Trusts Raised to Avoid Unjust Enrichment: The *Westdeutche* Case' [1996] RLR 3, pp 21–23.
[156] [1980] QB 677.   [157] See Swadling 'Restitution for No Consideration' [1994] RLR 73.
[158] [1994] 2 All ER 806.   [159] Ibid., at 826.   [160] [1996] AC 669, at 690.
[161] *Foskett v McKeown* [2001] 1 AC 102, at 141.

from the mixed fund cannot then be regarded as solely the product of the trust property. Unlike the rules of tracing at common law, the equitable rules of tracing permit the trust property to be traced through a mixed fund of money and into assets acquired from it. *Foskett v McKeown*[162] involved just such a situation. The case concerned a Mr Murphy, who in 1986 had taken out a unit-linked life insurance policy, which provided for the payment of a death benefit of £1million. The initial annual premiums due under this policy were paid by Mr Murphy using his own money. However, the premiums due in 1989 and 1990 were paid using money from a bank account which he held on trust for the customers of a company he controlled which had contracted to buy land on their behalf in Portugal. The proceeds of the life insurance policy were written in trust for the benefit of his children. In 1991 Mr Murphy committed suicide, and the death benefit was paid. The question at issue was whether the beneficiaries were entitled to trace their misappropriated money into the proceeds of the policy. The House of Lords held, by a bare majority, that the beneficiaries were entitled to a share of the proceeds proportionate to the contribution of the trust money to the payment of the premiums. Lord Millett explained that the beneficiaries were able to trace their trust money into the insurance policy itself, and thence into the proceeds of the policy:

> It is, however, of critical importance in the present case to appreciate that the purchasers do not trace the premiums directly into the insurance money. They trace them first into the policy and thence into the proceeds of the policy. It is essential not to elide the two steps. In this context, of course, the word 'policy' does not mean the contract of insurance. You do not trace the payment of a premium into the insurance contract any more than you trace a payment into a bank account in to the banking contract. The word 'policy' is here used to describe the bundle of rights to which the policyholder is entitled in return for the premiums. These rights, which may be very complex, together constitute a chose in action, viz the right to payment of a debt payable on a future event and contingent upon the continued payment of further premiums until the happening of the event. That chose in action represents the traceable proceeds of the premiums; its current value fluctuates from time to time. When the property matures, the insurance money represents the traceable proceeds of the policy and hence indirectly of the premiums. It follows that, if a claimant can show that premiums were paid with his money, he can claim a proportionate share of the policy.[163]

Foskett v McKeown involved a somewhat unusual mixture of funds in the form of the payment of premiums of an insurance policy. More commonly, misappropriated funds will become mixed in a bank account. Equity has developed special rules to determine whether trust property can be traced through a mixture of funds in a bank account.

(6) Equitable tracing of money through the banking system

While equity is capable of tracing property through a mixed fund, the process of identification can be extremely complex where money has become mixed with funds in a bank account. Where trust property was paid into a bank account, it may be essential to determine whether the remaining balance, or assets purchased from it,

---

[162] [2001] 1 AC 102.   [163] Ibid., at 134.

can be seen as representing the original trust property. Of necessity, this inquiry is often conducted ex post facto, only after the misappropriation of the trust property has been discovered and the transactions have taken place. The rules that have evolved are simply rough and ready presumptions which operate to determine whether any remaining balance, or property purchased, can be identified as the product of the trust money. They operate differently depending upon whether the mixture consisted of trust money and the money of the wrongdoing trustee, or the money of the trust and of another innocent party, for example money misappropriated from another trust. The rules emerged in the last century, and they are only really appropriate for simple bank accounts.

(a) Mixture in a bank account consisting of the trust property and the trustee's own property

Where a wrongdoing trustee has mixed trust property with his own property in a bank account, the rules operate harshly against him. If the mixed fund has been partially dissipated, any remaining balance, or assets acquired from the account, are presumed to belong to the trust. The burden is on the wrongdoer to show that the asset or balance represents his own money.[164] Where the account balance has been reduced by withdrawals which have been dissipated, the court will presume that the remaining balance represents the trust property and that the wrongdoer's own money has been dissipated. The wrongdoer will not be permitted to assert that it represents his own money and that the money he has spent and dissipated was the trust money. As Millett LJ stated in *Boscawen v Bajwa*:

A trustee will not be allowed to defeat the claim of his beneficiaries by saying that he has resorted to trust money when he could have made use of his own.[165]

This presumption was applied in *Re Hallet's Estate*. A solicitor, who was a trustee of his own marriage settlement, was entrusted with money by a client for investment. He paid money from the trust and his client's money into his bank account, which also contained some of his own money. He made various payments out, which had been dissipated. On his death, the account contained enough money to satisfy the claims of the trust and the client, but not his other creditors. The central question was whether the money in the account could be said to be the property of the trust and client, in which case they would gain priority over the general creditors. The Court of Appeal held that the trustee must be presumed to have spent his own money first, and to have preserved the trust monies (see Figure 32.1). Jessel MR stated the principle applying to a trustee who has blended trust moneys with his own:

it seems to me perfectly plain that he cannot be heard to say that he took away the trust money when he had a right to take away his own money...His money was there, and he had a right to draw it out, and why should the natural act of simply drawing out the money be attributed to anything except to his ownership of money which was at the bankers.[166]

---

[164] *Lupton v White* (1808) 15 Ves 432. [165] [1995] 4 All ER 769, at 778.
[166] (1880) 13 Ch D 696, at 727–728.

Figure 32.1 Preference for trust beneficiaries: *Re Hallet's Estate*

If the presumption adopted in *Re Hallet's Estate* were absolute, it would produce an anomalous result if the wrongdoing trustee purchased assets from the account and then dissipated the remaining balance. The trustee would be able to claim that the assets had been acquired with his own money, since he was deemed to spend this first. In consequence, the presumption that the trustee withdraws and spends his own money first is not absolute but a specific application of the general maxim that 'everything is presumed against a wrongdoer'. Whatever the circumstances and the order of events, the wrongdoer is presumed to have acted so as to preserve the trust money. Thus, assets acquired before the remaining balance of the account was dissipated may be claimed to represent the trust property. As Millett LJ stated in *Boscawen v Bajwa*:

if the beneficiary asserts that the trustee has made use of the trust money there is no reason why he should not be allowed to prove it.[167]

Hence in *Re Oatway*,[168] where application of the presumption in *Re Hallet's Estate* would have worked an injustice, exactly the opposite presumption was applied, namely that the trustee had spent the trust money first (see Figure 32.2). Lewis Oatway was a solicitor and the trustee of a will. He misappropriated £3,000 from the trust and paid this into a bank account where it was mixed with his own money. He purchased Oceana shares for £2,137 using money from the account. At the time that he purchased them there would have been enough of his own money in the account to purchase the shares. After the purchase, he dissipated the balance of the account and died insolvent, leaving the shares, now valued at £2,474. If the rule in *Re Hallet* were applied, the shares would have been purchased with his money, and therefore form part of his general assets. However, Joyce J held that the shares were to be regarded as the product of the trust money. Having examined the rule in *Re Hallet's Estate* he concluded:

---

167 [1995] 4 All ER 769, at 778.   168 [1903] 2 Ch 356.

Figure 32.2 Tracing by substitution: *Re Oatway*

It is, in my opinion, equally clear that when any of the money drawn out has been invested, and that investment remains in the name or under the control of the trustee, the rest of the balance having been afterwards dissipated by him, he cannot maintain that the investment which remains represents his own money alone, and that what has been spent and can no longer be traced and recovered was the money belonging to the trust.[169]

The contrasting decisions in *Re Hallet's Estate*[170] and *Re Oatway*[171] are not in conflict with each other, but can be seen as applications of a general principle that the trustee is estopped from asserting that he has dissipated trust money before his own. This principle will operate differently depending on the individual facts of each situation. This rule works to the advantage of the beneficiaries of the trust, but it must be remembered that it acts to the detriment of the general creditors, who will inevitably receive a lower dividend from the insolvency. It is questionable whether this priority is always just.

There seems little authority as to the position if a trustee wrongfully mixes trust property with his own in a bank account, from which assets are purchased, and either those assets or the balance remaining in the account are sufficient to cover the money taken from the trust. This would be of particular significance if the asset purchased has increased in value, because if the beneficiaries can show that the property was purchased with their money they would be entitled to claim the increase in value. In *Re Tilley's Will Trusts*[172] it seems to have been accepted that if the beneficiaries could show that the asset had been purchased with trust money, or partially with trust money, they could claim the increase in value proportionately. However, the difficulty is that it is impossible to show whose money was used. In such circumstances Professor Birks suggests that the principles operating in the case of funds consisting of the mixed money of innocent volunteers should apply, so that the trust would share any gain with the wrongdoer pari passu[173] unless the account was a current account, in which case the rule in *Clayton's case* would apply: ie 'first in, first out'. However, there is now

[169] Ibid., at 360.   [170] (1880) 13 Ch D 696.   [171] [1903] 2 Ch 356.
[172] [1967] Ch 1179.   [173] Birks, *Introduction to the Law of Restitution* (1985), p 370.

direct authority on this issue, albeit at first instance. In *Turner v Jacob*,[174] Mrs Turner put money to which her daughter (Mrs Jacob) was entitled into a deposit account. A number of withdrawals were made which reduced the balance to around £10,000. The balance in the account never subsequently fell below this level, but there were a significant number of deposits and withdrawals, including withdrawals to support the purchase of two houses. Patten J considered that Mrs Jacob could not claim that the money to which she had a claim had been used to purchase either of the houses:

> It seems to me that in a case (such as the present) where the trustee maintains in the account an amount equal to the remaining trust fund, the beneficiary's right to trace is limited to that fund. It is not open to the beneficiary to assert a lien against an investment made using monies out of the mixed account unless the sum expended is of such a size that it must have included trust monies or the balance remaining in the account after the investment is then expended so as to become untraceable.[175]

(b) Property of trust and innocent volunteer mixed in a bank account

The harsh presumptions which operate against a wrongdoer who has mixed trust property with his own are not applied where trust property has been mixed with that of other innocent volunteers. In such a case, the rules reflect the moral blamelessness of the parties whose money has been mixed, and they aim to do substantive justice between them. However, a distinction is made between different types of account. Where the money of innocent parties has been mixed in a current account, the rule in *Clayton's case*[176] will prima facie apply.[177] *Clayton's case* presumes that money is paid out of a current account in the same order in which it had been paid in. In other words, that the first money to be spent from the account represents the first money that was paid in, hence the rule is known as 'first in, first out' (see Figure 32.3). This is a rough and ready rule which originally developed in the banker and client context. It reflects the fact that current accounts are often extremely active.

However, the presumption is not absolute, and it will not be applied if the result would be unjust. Starting with the decision in *Barlow Clowes International Ltd (in liquidation) v Vaughan*,[178] the trend of recent cases has been to consider that application of the rule would be unjust in almost all circumstances where the money of innocent volunteers has been mixed in a bank account, such that the 'rule' will only apply in the most exceptional circumstances. In *Barlow Clowes International Ltd v Vaughan*, the Court of Appeal was faced with the consequences of the collapse of the Barlow Clowes investment company in Gibraltar. Depositors had paid into investment plans,

---

[174] [2006] EWHC 1317 (Ch).

[175] Ibid., at [102]. Mrs Jacob was the residuary beneficiary under her mother's will. A personal claim by Mrs Jacob against her mother would have reduced the value of the residuary estate, which also included the proceeds of selling the first house to be purchased. Mrs Jacob claimed to be entitled to a proportion of the value of the second house to be purchased, which her mother had left in her will to her husband.

[176] (1816) 1 Mer 572.

[177] See *Re Hallett's Estate* (1879) 13 Ch D 696 (Fry J); *Hancock v Smith* (1889) 41 Ch D 456; *Re Stenning* [1895] 2 Ch 433; *Mutton v Peat* [1899] 2 Ch 556; *Re Diplock* [1948] Ch 465, CA.

[178] [1992] 4 All ER 22. See Fox 'Legal Title as a Ground of Restitutionary Liability' [2000] RLT 465.

Figure 32.3 The rule in *Clayton's case*: 'first in, first out'

but the money had been misapplied and the company was left owing some £115m to investors, with assets far less than that amount. Some investors argued that the rule in *Clayton's case* should be applied, with the consequence that the late investors would recover virtually all their money, leaving the early investors with nothing. After a wide-ranging examination of the authorities, the court held that the rule was well established and that it was not open to them to overrule it. As Dillon LJ observed:

the decisions of this court…establish and recognise a general rule of practice that *Clayton's case* is to be applied when several beneficiaries' moneys have been blended in one bank account and there is a deficiency. It is not…for this court to reject that long established general practice.[179]

However, the court felt free to depart from the rule in the circumstances of the case, because it would work injustice. The principle governing the application of the rule was stated by Woolf LJ:

The rule need only be applied when it is convenient to do so and when its application can be said to do broad justice having regard to the nature of the competing claims…It is not applied if this is the intention or presumed intention of the beneficiaries. The rule is sensibly not applied when the cost of applying it is likely to exhaust the fund available for the beneficiaries.[180]

On the facts, it was held that the rule would not be applied because the investment fund was regarded by the investors as a common pool, and that they should share pari passu in what remained because they had experienced a common misfortune (see Figure 32.4). It would have been wholly inequitable to apply the rule in *Clayton's case*, which would have meant some investors recovering everything to the exclusion of the rest, who would recover nothing. The court also considered an alternative and more sophisticated version of the rule. The 'North American' approach would treat each withdrawal from the account as a withdrawal in the same proportions as the

---

[179] [1992] 4 All ER 22, at 33.   [180] Ibid., at 39.

Figure 32.4 Sharing losses pari passu

different interests in the account at the moment of withdrawal. Woolf LJ accepted that this solution could have advantages over a distribution pari passu, but the complications made it impracticable to apply in these circumstances.[181] Subsequent cases have continued to reject the application of the rule.[182] In *Russell-Cooke Trust Co v Prentis*, Lindsay J went so far as to suggest that the fact that the first-in first-out principle will not usually be applied where beneficiaries have shared a common misfortune means that it might be 'more accurate to refer to the exception that is, rather than the rule in *Clayton's case*'.[183] Lawrence Collins J also refused to apply the rule in *Commerbank Aktiengesellschaft v IMB Morgan plc*,[184] where money obtained by fraud had been paid into the account of a firm of stockbrokers, where it had become mixed so that it was not possible to identify any part of the funds as belonging to a particular client. He held that the rule would be 'impracticable and unjust' to apply, and held that the balance in the account should be divided in proportion among the clients. The rule in *Clayton's case* has no application to mixtures of tangible property, where any abatement in the mixture must be shared pari passu (see Figure 32.4).[185]

Where the mixing of the trust property and the property of an innocent volunteer takes place in a bank account other than a current account, the rule in *Clayton's case* will not apply. In *Sinclair v Brougham*[186] and *Re Diplock*[187] it was held that the parties will share pari passu in any assets that have been purchased from the mixed fund and any balance remaining in the account. They will also bear any increase or loss in value in proportion to their contributions.

---

[181]   See also *Re Eastern Capital Futures Ltd* [1989] BCLC 371.
[182]   See also the discussion of the rule in *Re French Caledonia Travel* (2004) 22 ACLC 498; [2003] NSWSC 1008; Conaglen 'Contests between Rival Beneficiaries' [2005] 64 CLJ 45.
[183]   [2003] 2 All ER 478, Conaglen 'Contests between Rival Beneficiaries' [2005] 64 CLJ 45.
[184]   [2004] EWHC 2771.
[185]   *Re Goldcorp Exchange Ltd* [1995] 1 AC 74, HC New Zealand (Thorp J).
[186]   [1914] AC 398.   [187]   [1948] Ch 465, CA.

Figure 32.5 Lowest intermediate balance: *Roscoe v Winder*

(c) The lowest intermediate balance

Whether a fund consists of a mixture of trust money with the wrongdoer's own, or the money of an innocent volunteer, if money has been dissipated from the account and then further money is paid into the account, the trust has no claim to any of that other money. The trust is limited to what is known as the lowest intermediate balance, because it is impossible that anything in the account above that figure represents trust property. The operation of this rule is seen in *Roscoe v Winder* (see Figure 32.5).[188] A wrongdoer misappropriated some £455, which he paid into his own bank account. After a few days the balance was reduced to £25, though by his death it had risen to £358. It was held that a charge could only extend over the £25. Sargant J explained this on the basis that the principle of *Re Hallet's Estate*[189] only applied to such an amount of the balance ultimately standing to the credit of the trustee as did not exceed the lowest balance of the account during the intervening period. If the subsequent payments in had been specifically intended to replenish the trust funds, then the trust would be entitled to a charge over them because this would be expressly imposing upon the later payment a trust equivalent to the trust which rested on the previous balance.[190] The rule preventing tracing beyond the lowest intermediate balance was reaffirmed by the Court of Appeal in *Bishopsgate Investment Management v Homan*.[191]

---

[188] [1915] 1 Ch 62.   [189] (1880) 13 Ch D 696.

[190] Sargant J took the view that if the account was a separate trust account then, the mere fact of a payment in would be sufficient indication of an intention to substitute the additional moneys (see eg *Re Hughes* [1970] IR 237), but there was no such intention in the case of a payment into a general trading account.

[191] [1995] 1 All ER 347; Smith 'Tracing, "Swollen Assets" and the Lowest Intermediate Balance: *Bishopsgate Investment Management Ltd v Homan*' (1994) 8 TLI 102. See also *British Columbia v National Bank of Canada* (1994) 119 DLR (4th) 669.

(d) Bank trustee depositing trust money with itself

The above situations have all involved cases where a trustee has mixed trust money with either his own or that of innocent volunteers in bank accounts. However, given that banks may themselves act as trustees, they may deposit trust money with themselves. If they then become insolvent, the question may arise as to whether the beneficiaries can trace the money in the hands of the bank. This issue was considered by the Privy Council in *Space Investments Ltd v Canadian Imperial Bank of Commerce Trust Co (Bahamas) Ltd*.[192] The case concerned a bank, the Mercantile Bank Trust Co Ltd, which was the trustee of various settlements. The trust instruments contained clauses permitting the trustee to open and maintain savings accounts with any bank, including itself. The bank deposited trust money with itself, and then became insolvent. The question was whether the beneficiaries were entitled to trace the trust money into the bank accounts and therefore gain priority over the other unsecured creditors of the bank. The Privy Council held that they were not entitled to do so because the deposit was entirely lawful and not in breach of trust. The beneficiaries were to be treated like all the other depositors of the bank, who were restricted to proving in the liquidation as unsecured creditors for the amount that ought to have been credited to their accounts at the date of liquidation. However, the Privy Council considered that the position would have been different if the bank trustee had misappropriated the trust money and had acted in breach of trust by depositing the trust property with itself. In such circumstances the beneficiaries would be entitled to an equitable charge over all the assets of the bank. Lord Templeman explained the Board's reasoning:

A bank in fact uses all deposit moneys for the general purposes of the bank... in these circumstances it is impossible for the beneficiaries interested in trust money misappropriated from their trust to trace their money to any particular asset belonging to the trustee bank. But equity allows the beneficiaries, or a new trustee appointed in place of an insolvent bank trustee to protect the interests of the beneficiaries, to trace the trust money to all the assets of the bank and to recover the trust money by the exercise of an equitable charge over all the assets of the bank.[193]

This accorded the beneficiaries priority over all the unsecured creditors of the bank. This was justified by the Board on the grounds that the settlor and beneficiaries of the trust had never accepted the risks involved in the possible insolvency of the bank, whereas the unsecured other creditors had voluntarily accepted that risk. In conclusion, the distinction between the beneficiaries' position where the deposit was authorized and where it was not was justified on the basis that:

Equity... protects beneficiaries against breaches of trust. But equity does not protect beneficiaries against the consequences of the exercise in good faith of powers conferred by the trust instrument.[194]

This decision has been criticized, since in effect it enables the beneficiaries to maintain a security interest over assets that could not possibly be the product of the trust

---

[192] [1986] 1 WLR 1072.   [193] Ibid., at 1974.   [194] Ibid.

property.[195] In *Re Goldcorp Exchange Ltd*[196] the Privy Council referred to *Space Investments* and the criticisms which had been levelled at the judgment, but concluded that:

In the present case it is not necessary or appropriate to consider the scope and ambit of the observations in *Space Investments* or their application to trustees other than bank trustees...

The exact scope and application of the principle therefore awaits further judicial clarification.

(7) Tracing into assets acquired prior to receiving misappropriated trust property[197]

The question has arisen whether misappropriated money can be traced in equity into an asset acquired before the trust property was received. Such a process has been described as 'backward tracing'. In *Bishopsgate Investment Management v Homan*[198] Dillon LJ was willing to accept that in some circumstances trust money could be traced into a pre-acquired asset. The first instance judge had suggested that tracing would be possible if property had been acquired with borrowed money, either by way of loan or overdraft, and there was an inference that when the borrowing was incurred it was the intention that it should be repaid[199] with the misappropriated money. He considered that the beneficiary would be entitled to a charge over the asset acquired provided that the connection between the misappropriation and the asset was sufficiently proved. In contrast, Leggatt LJ entirely dismissed the possibility of such backward tracing:

there can be no equitable remedy against an asset acquired *before* misappropriation of money takes place, since ex hypothesi it cannot be followed into something which existed and so had been acquired before the money was received and therefore without its aid.[200]

In *Foskett v McKeown*[201] in the Court of Appeal, Scott V-C expressed the opinion that it should be possible to trace into assets acquired with borrowed money if the trust money was used to repay the borrowing and it had always been the intention that the trust money would be used to acquire the asset.

(8) The limits of equitable tracing

While the right to trace in equity is not lost merely because the property becomes mixed with other property, there are circumstances in which it will no longer be possible to identify assets as representing the original property.

---

[195] Goode 'Ownership and Obligation in Commercial Transactions' (1987) 103 LQR 433.

[196] [1994] 2 All ER 806.

[197] Sir Peter Millett 'Law of Restitution (Publication Review)' (1995) 111 LQR 517; Oliver 'The Extent of Equitable Tracing' (1995) 9 TLI 78; Oakley 'Propriety Claims and Their Priority in Insolvency' (1995) 54 CLJ 377.

[198] [1995] 1 All ER 347.   [199] Ibid., at 351.

[200] Ibid., at 355.   [201] [1997] 3 All ER 392, at 409.

(a) Bona fide purchaser

It is not possible to trace trust property into the hands of a bona fide purchaser for value without notice. In such circumstances the equitable ownership of the property is entirely defeated and the purchaser receives the absolute ownership thereof. The beneficiaries may, however, be able to trace into the consideration provided by the purchaser, since this will represent the proceeds of the property.

(b) Dissipation

Once property and its proceeds have been dissipated, or used up, tracing is impossible because there is clearly no asset that represents the original property. The principle was stated by the Court of Appeal in *Re Diplock*:

The equitable remedies presuppose the continued existence of the money either as a separate fund or as part of a mixed fund or as latent in property acquired by means of such a fund. If, on the facts of any individual case, such continued existence is not established, equity is as helpless as the common law itself.[202]

Therefore, beneficiaries would be unable to trace if a trustee used trust property to pay for a meal which he consumed, or a foreign holiday which he has taken, as no asset would remain. Similarly, if the property has been used to discharge a debt, nothing would be left that could be said to represent the trust property.[203] A debt is a chose in action and once it has been paid it ceases to exist. There is no longer a relationship of debtor and creditor. In *Re Diplock*,[204] the Court of Appeal held that it was not possible to trace trust money wrongfully transferred to two charities which had used it to discharge debts. In *Re Tilley's Will Trusts*[205] it was held that it was not possible to trace money paid into an overdrawn bank account, because such payment only goes to reduce the amount of the overdraft, which is simply a debt owed by the customer to the bank. The inability to trace money paid into an overdrawn account was also accepted by the Court of Appeal in *Bishopsgate Investment Management Ltd v Homan*[206] and by the Privy Council in *Re Goldcorp Exchange*.[207] This was also the position in *Moriarty v Atkinson*.[208] A yacht brokering company received client funds to finance the purchase of new boats. Some of these funds were paid into the client account and were found to be held subject to a trust. Most, however, was paid into the company's current account that was always in debit. The Court of Appeal held that there was no trust in respect of these sums as the purchase money 'was effectively used to reduce the company's liability with the bank and it effectively disappeared

---

[202] [1948] Ch 465, at 521.

[203] For an alternative view, see Smith 'Tracing into the Payment of a Debt' [1995] 54 CLJ 290.

[204] [1948] Ch 465.   [205] [1967] Ch 1179.

[206] [1995] Ch 211; Gullifer 'Recovery of Misappropriated Assets: Orthodoxy Re-established?' [1995] LMCLQ 446.

[207] [1995] 1 AC 74. See also *Boscawen v Bajwa* [1995] 4 All ER 769, at 775; *PMPA v PMPS* (27 June 1994, unreported) [1995] RLR 217, HC of Ireland.

[208] [2008] EWCA Civ 1604.

so that there was never any fund on which a proprietary claim could operate'.[209] The court did not accept that the undertaking of the company to pay the money into the client account was sufficient to impose a trust on a different account from the one into which the money had been paid.[210]

Nevertheless, where a beneficiary's money is used in breach of trust to discharge a secured debt the beneficiary will be entitled to be subrogated to the position of the secured creditor and therefore able to recover the amount of the discharged loan from the debtor. This was considered in *Boscawen v Bajwa*.[211] Money was held on trust by a solicitor for the Abbey National, which had advanced it intending that it be used to complete the purchase of a house owned by Mr Bajwa which was subject to a charge in favour of the Halifax. In breach of trust, the money was used to redeem the charge but the purchase fell through. The Court of Appeal held that the Abbey National's money could be traced into the discharge of the debt and that they should be subrogated to the position of the Halifax, which had been the creditor of the legal charge. Millett LJ explained that the Abbey National was entitled to subrogation because they had intended to retain the beneficial interest in its money unless and until that interest was replaced by a first legal mortgage on the property[212] and that in the circumstances Mr Bajwa could not claim that the charge had been redeemed for his benefit as this would be unconscionable.[213] While subrogation may provide some answer to the problem of dissipation where money has been used to discharge a debt, it will only operate to the claimant's advantage if the debt was secured. Despite these authorities supporting the view that it is impossible to trace into an overdrawn bank account, in *Foskett v McKeown*[214] Scott V-C considered that it remained an open question whether it was possible to trace into assets acquired from an overdrawn bank account:

The availability of equitable remedies ought, in my view, to depend upon the substance of the transaction in question and not upon the strict order in which associated events happen... I would wish, for my part, to make it clear that I regard the point as still open and, in particular, that I do not regard the fact that an asset is paid for out of borrowed money with the borrowing subsequently repaid out of trust money as being necessarily fatal to an equitable tracing claim by the trust beneficiaries. If, in such a case, it can be shown that it was always the intention to use the trust money to acquire the asset, I do not see why the order in which the events happen should be regarded as critical to the claim.[215]

In *Re Diplock*[216] the Court of Appeal suggested that the use of trust property to improve a house where the improvement added no value to the house, or even caused a loss in value, would amount to a dissipation preventing tracing. In such circumstances there

---

[209] Ibid., at [15], per Lord Neuberger.   [210] Ibid., at [16]–[21].
[211] [1995] 4 All ER 769; Birks 'Tracing, Subrogation and Change of Position' (1995) 9 TLI 124; Mitchell 'Subrogation, Tracing and the *Quistclose* Principle' [1995] LMCLQ 451; Andrews 'Tracing and Subrogation' (1996) 55 CLJ 199; Oakley 'The Availability of Proprietary Remedies' [1997] Conv 1.
[212] [1995] 4 All ER 769, at 782.   [213] Ibid., at 784.
[214] [1997] 3 All ER 392.
[215] Ibid., at 409. In support of this proposition he cited *Agricultural Credit Corpn of Saskatchewan v Pettyjohn* (1991) 79 DLR (4th) 22 and Smith 'Tracing into the Payment of a Debt' (1995) 54 CLJ 290.
[216] [1948] Ch 465, at 547.

is nothing to trace, because 'the money will have disappeared leaving no monetary trace behind'. If the property has been dissipated, the only possible remedy will be a personal remedy against the trustee for breach of trust, or if it was received by a stranger who is liable to account for its value as a constructive trustee because he acted dishonestly.

(c) Unascertained goods

It seems that it is not possible to trace in equity into unascertained goods, because the purchaser does not gain title to those goods under the contract of sale until they have been separated from the bulk. This was so held in *Re London Wine Co (Shippers) Ltd*[217] and by the Privy Council in *Re Goldcorp Exchange Ltd*.[218] In the latter case, a company dealing in precious metals sold customers 'non-allocated metal' which the company stored as a bulk on their behalf. The customers were entitled to physical delivery of the metal on seven days' notice. The company became insolvent and, after the payment of the secured creditors, there would be nothing left for the customers who had bought 'non-allocated metal'. The customers sought to claim a proprietary right to the gold that was held by the company by way of equitable tracing, but the Privy Council held that they had no proprietary rights. One reason was that the customers had purchased unascertained goods and that title, including equitable title, would not pass until the goods were ascertained by the seller from the bulk. Clearly, there could be a declaration of trust on behalf of the purchaser of unascertained goods by the seller, but on the facts the Privy Council held that was not the intention of the company:

The company cannot have intended to create an interest in its general stock of gold which would have inhibited any dealings with it otherwise than for the purpose of delivery under the non-allocated sale contracts.[219]

It follows that if trust property is used to purchase unascertained goods, there will be no possibility of tracing into the bulk unless the relationship is such that it can be shown that there was a trust in favour of the purchaser.[220]

(d) Inequitable to trace

In *Re Diplock*[221] the Court of Appeal considered that there should be no tracing if an innocent volunteer has used trust property to improve land. To impose a charge over the land for the increase in value in such circumstances would not, in the court's view, produce an equitable result.[222] The reason for this is that a charge is enforceable by sale, and the result is that the innocent volunteer could be compelled to sell his house. This limitation may perhaps be seen as an example of the general defence of

---

[217] (1975) 126 NLJ 977.   [218] [1994] 2 All ER 806.   [219] Ibid., at 815.
[220] See *Hunter v Moss* [1994] 3 All ER 215.   [221] [1948] Ch 465.
[222] [1948] Ch 465, at 546–548. The inability to trace where money has been expended on maintaining or improving land was accepted by Lord Browne-Wilkinson in *Foskett v McKeown* [2001] 1 AC 102, at 109. Where property is used for such purposes, he considered that it would 'at most' give rise to a proprietary lien to recover the money expended.

change of position, which was recognized by the House of Lords in *Lipkin Gorman Ltd v Karpnale*.[223] Whether it will be inequitable to trace will depend on the circumstances of each case. *Re Diplock*[224] concerned charities who were innocent volunteers. As Goff and Jones suggest,[225] the result might have been different if the innocent volunteer had been a rich banker who had used trust money wisely to increase the value of his country house, and he has ample liquid assets to discharge any charge over the house without having to sell it. It may now be the case that the Trusts of Land and Appointment of Trustees Act 1996 contains sufficient safeguards to protect the innocent volunteer against the unfair pursuit of a claim to an interest in land through the rules of tracing.

(9) Claiming in equity

Once the equitable tracing process has identified assets which represent the original trust property, the beneficiaries may be able to assert a claim thereto. The potential claims available to beneficiaries in equity are wider than at common law. Depending upon the precise circumstances, the beneficiaries may either be able to assert a proprietary claim to the assets identified, an equitable lien to restore the trust fund, or a personal claim to restitution.

(a) Claiming assets identified as representing the original trust property

Where assets have been identified as representing the original trust property, the beneficiaries may wish to claim a proprietary entitlement to them by asserting their equitable ownership. The ability to make such a claim will be especially important if the person who possesses the assets is insolvent, since this will gain the beneficiaries priority over their other creditors. Beneficiaries may also wish to assert a proprietary claim in order to take advantage of any rise in value of the assets identified.[226] A proprietary claim may therefore enable them to gain a windfall benefit. In *Foskett v McKeown*[227] Lord Millet considered that if A misappropriates B's money and uses it to buy a winning ticket in the lottery, B is entitled to claim the winnings. In the same case, the House of Lords clarified the entitlement of beneficiaries to claim assets that are identified by the equitable tracing process as representing their original trust property, thus eliminating previous uncertainty as to the rights of beneficiaries.

---

[223] [1991] 2 AC 548.   [224] [1948] Ch 465.

[225] Goff and Jones, *The Law of Restitution* (6th edn, 2002), p 111.

[226] Some earlier cases, such as the decision of the House of Lords in *Sinclair v Brougham* [1914] AC 398, suggested that a beneficiary was not able to assert a proprietary claim so as to take advantage of an increase in the value of the property. However, this was questioned in *Re Tilley's Will Trusts* [1967] 1 Ch 1179, and in *Foskett v McKeown* [2001] 1 AC 102 the House of Lords finally held definitively that beneficiaries are entitled to gain the advantage of an increase in value of assets acquired from the trust property.

[227] [2001] 1 AC 102.

(i) Claiming assets that were cleanly substituted for the trust property

It has long been established that where trust property has been misappropriated the beneficiaries will be entitled to claim any assets which can be identified as the product of a clean substitution.[228] Lord Millett explained as follows:

> The simplest case is where a trustee wrongfully misappropriates trust property and uses it exclusively to acquire other property for his benefit. In such a case the beneficiary is entitled *at his option* either to assert his beneficial ownership of the proceeds or to bring a personal claim against the trustees for breach of trust and enforce an equitable lien or charge on the proceeds to secure restoration of the trust fund. He will normally be able to exercise the option in the way most advantageous to himself.[229]

(ii) Claiming assets that were acquired from a mixed fund

Prior to *Foskett v McKeown* a distinction appears to have been drawn between the rights of beneficiaries where assets identified as representing the original trust property were acquired from a mixed fund consisting of the trust property and the property of another innocent party, and where they had been acquired from a mixed fund consisting of the trust property and the property of the wrongdoing trustee. Where the mixed fund had consisted of the trust property and the property of another innocent party, for example another trust or an innocent volunteer, the assets acquired would be shared *pari passu* and the beneficiaries would be entitled to claim a share of the equitable ownership proportionate to their contribution. However, where the mixed fund consisted of the misappropriated trust property and the property of the wrongdoing trustee it was thought that the beneficiaries were not able to claim a proportionate share of any assets acquired. Instead, they were limited to claiming an equitable lien over the property to secure the restoration of the trust fund. This distinction originated with the judgment of Jessel MR in *Re Hallet's Estate*,[230] and was applied by Scott V-C in the Court of Appeal in *Foskett v McKeown*.[231] However, in the House of Lords, Lord Millett held that no such distinction was to be drawn between the right of beneficiaries to claim a proportionate share of assets acquired from a mixed fund:

> In my view the time has come to state unequivocally that English law has no such rule. It conflicts with the rule that a trustee must not benefit from his trust. I agree with Burrows that the beneficiary's right to elect to have a proportionate share of a mixed substitution necessarily follows once one accepts, as English law does (i) that a claimant can trace in equity into a mixed fund and (ii) that he can trace unmixed money into its proceeds and assert ownership of the proceeds.
>
> Accordingly, I would state the basic rule as follows. Where a trustee wrongfully uses trust money to provide part of the cost of acquiring an asset, the beneficiary is entitled at his option either to claim a proportionate share of the asset or to enforce a lien upon it to secure his personal claim against the trustee for the amount of the misapplied money.[232]

---

[228] *Re Hallett's Estate* (1880) 13 Ch D 696.   [229] [2001] 1 AC 102, at 130.
[230] (1880) 13 Ch D 696.   [231] [1998] Ch 265.
[232] [2001] 1 AC 102, at 131.

(iii) Claiming assets where tangible property has been mixed to form a bulk

If the trust property consists of tangible property that has been mixed so as to form a physical bulk, the beneficiary will be entitled to claim a share of the equitable ownership of the bulk proportionate to his contribution. In the event that pro rata division is impossible, the beneficiary will be entitled to take the whole bulk.[233] However, given the greater ability of equity to facilitate the co-ownership of property through the medium of a trust, it is much less likely that such a situation will arise than at common law.

(b) Enforcing an equitable lien to secure a personal claim to restore the trust fund

Beneficiaries are able to claim a proportionate share of assets acquired from a mixed fund that included the trust property. In many cases, this proprietary claim will prove most advantageous to the beneficiaries, since it will enable them to gain priority over other general creditors in the event of an insolvency, or to take advantage of any increase in value of the assets. Such a proprietary claim will not, however, be advantageous if the assets acquired from the mixed fund have fallen in value, since a proprietary claim will force the beneficiaries to bear a rateable share of the loss. In order to protect the beneficiaries in such circumstances, they are entitled to choose to claim to enforce an equitable lien against the mixed fund to secure their personal claim against the trustee to have the trust fund restored. The availability of such a lien was recognized in *Re Hallet's Estate*.[234] In *Foskett v McKeown*, the House of Lords asserted a general rule that a beneficiary has the right to elect between claiming a proportionate share of an asset acquired from a mixed fund and enforcing an equitable lien. However, Lord Millett explained that a lien will only be available where the mixed fund consisted of the trust property and the wrongdoing trustee's own property, and not where the mixed fund consisted of the property of equally innocent parties:

> Innocent contributors, however, must be treated equally inter se. Where the beneficiary's claim is in competition with the claims of other innocent contributors, there is no basis upon which any of the claims can be subordinated to any of the others. Where the fund is deficient, the beneficiary is not entitled to enforce a lien for his contribution; all must share rateably in the fund. The primary rule in regard to a mixed fund, therefore, is that gains and losses are borne by the contributors rateably. The beneficiary's right to elect instead to enforce a lien to obtain repayment is an exception to the primary rule, exercisable where the fund is deficient and the claim is made against the wrongdoer and those claiming through him.[235]

Thus if a trustee misappropriates £5,000 from a trust fund and mixes it with £5,000 of his own money and purchases shares for £10,000, the beneficiaries will either be able to claim half of the equitable interest in the shares or enforce a lien for £5,000 against the shares. If the shares have risen in value to £12,000 the assertion of a proportionate proprietary interest will be more advantageous. If they have fallen

---

[233] *Foskett v McKeown* [2001] 1 AC 102, at 132, per Lord Millett.
[234] (1880) 13 Ch D 696.   [235] [2001] 1 AC 102, at 132.

in value to £8,000 the enforcement of a lien will ensure that the trust fund is fully restored, and that the beneficiaries do not have to bear the consequences of the wrongdoer's poor investment.

(c) Claiming personal restitution in equity

Where trust property has been misapplied and dissipated so that there are no longer any assets remaining which can be identified as its traceable proceeds, the beneficiaries will not be able to assert a proprietary claim. However, they may be able to claim personal restitution from a stranger who received the trust property. In this context the rules of tracing operate as a process by which it can be established that a stranger had in fact received trust property. This was recognized by Millett LJ in *Boscawen v Bajwa*:

Tracing properly so-called . . . is neither a claim nor a remedy but a process. Moreover, it is not confined to the case where the plaintiff seeks a proprietary remedy; it is equally necessary where he seeks a personal remedy against the knowing recipient or knowing assistant.[236]

The personal liability of a stranger who has received trust property to make restitution was considered in the previous chapter. As was seen, unlike at common law the mere fact of receipt alone is presently insufficient to generate a personal liability to make restitution in equity. The equitable liability to account as a knowing recipient of trust property requires that the recipient has such a state of knowledge that it would be 'unconscionable' for the benefit of receipt to be retained. If the present position is abandoned in favour of a strict liability to make restitution subject to the defence of change of position, the rules of equitable tracing will still serve the same purpose of demonstrating receipt.

---

[236] [1995] 4 All ER 769, at 776.

Index